CITE AS

Wright & Graham,
Federal Practice and Procedure:
Evidence § ___

FEDERAL PRACTICE

AND

PROCEDURE®

By
CHARLES ALAN WRIGHT
Charles Alan Wright Chair in Federal Courts
The University of Texas

and

KENNETH W. GRAHAM, JR.
Professor of Law, University of California, Los Angeles

Federal Rules of Evidence

Confrontation and Hearsay

Sections 6355 to 6374

Volume 30A

ST. PAUL, MN.
WEST GROUP
2000

 TEXT IS PRINTED ON 10% POST
CONSUMER RECYCLED PAPER

To
Jim and Ann

*who exemplify so many
traditional values.*

*

ACKNOWLEDGMENTS

The Authors wish to express our appreciation to the members of the secretarial and clerical staff of the UCLA Law School, particularly Diane LeCover who provided invaluable assistance on this volume.

*

PREFACE

It is sometimes said that the Confrontation Clause has no history. Readers who have seen such statements may be startled to see hundreds of pages devoted to this supposedly non-existent subject. Hence we must defend ourselves against charges of needless display of erudition—or worse.

If, in the spirit of confrontation, we were to cross-examine Clio, the muse of history, she might point out how unlikely it is that an idea that some judges have thought originated with Magna Carta, or even earlier, should be without any intervening history. And, were Clio a feminist, she might add: "a history of being ignored is still a history."

Some of those who find no history of confrontation are looking for what historians call, not always with a sneer, "lawyer's history;" that is, history contained in writings that lawyers are accustomed to using—statutes, judicial decisions, treatises, or legal documents. The "lawyer's history" of confrontation is, indeed, slight—though not so slight as will appear if confrontation is viewed holistically; that is, as part of an adversary system of trial with the jury at its core.

But even viewed more broadly, the history of confrontation is a history of ignorance. To oversimplify to the point of parody, judges, elite lawyers, and legal scholars ignored, or downplayed, adversary rights like confrontation because they thought the nation was too fragile to endure the empowering of those they saw as its enemies— "The Other" as we shall sometimes call them. Unless we can see how those in power saw frontier people, Jacksonians, abolitionists, populists, anarchists, labor unions, Communists, and feminists, we shall not understand the fear that drove them to denigrate the adversary system in practice while exalting it in theory.

Since our history of confrontation is largely the history of fear, disorder, and actual or attempted repression, it is not a pretty story. For those accustomed to the celebratory nature of what sometimes passes for "constitutional history," our darker picture may seem excessively gloomy. But unless we can appreciate how much disorder and the fear of disorder dominated the thinking of powerholders for a century-and-a-half, it is too easy to dismiss such fears as episodic interruptions of otherwise routinized lives. But the interpretation of the right of confrontation was never routine—it was sporadic and often occurred during times of crisis.

The story is, of course, not quite so tidy. We have tried to tell it in all its messiness, partly in the hope that readers may see other patterns that elude us. Bulky as our account may first appear, it is far from comprehensive. For example, we have only hinted at the influence of popular culture on judicial attitudes about confrontation when a book might be written on this subject. We have also skimped in the telling of related stories that have been well-told elsewhere; e.g., the incorporation debate and the influence of the civil-rights movement on the interpretation of the Bill of Rights.

Readers sophisticated in historiography may be concerned about our sources. We have relied on history books for facts and ideas; the inferences and interpretations are mostly our own. Hence, we have taken historians as they came to hand, without regard to the "school" to which they belong. (Though, in retrospect, we see that ideologically our sources are quite varied.) For the same reason, we have not troubled to cite every account we have found of an incident nor searched for the most recent study. Newer books may offer a different interpretation of what Teddy Roosevelt meant, but they will seldom change what he said. It is usually the latter for which we look to historians.

Finally a word about Babe Ruth. We have occasionally, and particularly in our recounting of the 20th Century, mentioned facts with slight relation to the right of confrontation. We have two reasons for this, beyond the desire to amuse. It is easy to suppose that because people in the past used the same words that we do, that they must have thought about them as we do. Noting that these words were uttered in the year that Yale won the national championship in football is a useful reminder of how remote we are from the utterance. In addition, reminding the reader of technological or cultural milestones will underscore those parts of history whose relation to confrontation we have been forced to slight.

Readers may find our account unsatisfying. We know we do. It is easy to say that legal doctrine is not autonomous; it is far more difficult to say just how it was influenced by extralegal ideas and events. We wish we had found better models for the kind of intellectual history we have tried to write—or that we might have provided a model for others. But given the paucity of articles and monographs that explore the intellectual history of the adversary system, the best we can hope for is that we have provided that "something" that is reputedly better than "nothing."

CHARLES ALAN WRIGHT
KENNETH GRAHAM, JR.

October, 1999

*

SHORT FORM CITATIONS FOR LEGISLATIVE HISTORY

The following short form citations are used for recurring items of legislative history. For further explanation, see volume 21 § 5023.

"House Report"...................	H.R.Rep. No. 93–650, 93d Cong. 1st Sess.
"Senate Report"..................	S. Rep. No. 93–1227, 93d Cong. 2d Sess.
"Conference Report"..........	H.R. Rep. No. 93–1597, 93d Cong. 2d Sess.
"1 House Hearings"............	Hearings on Proposed Rules of Evidence Before the Special Subcommittee on the Reform of the Federal Criminal Laws of the House Comm. on the Judiciary, 93d Cong., 1st Sess., ser. 2, 1973.
"2 House Hearings"............	Hearings on Proposed Rules of Evidence Before the Subcommittee on Criminal Justice of the House, Comm. on the Judiciary (Supp.), 93d Cong., 1st Sess., ser. 2, 1973.
"Senate Hearings"..............	Hearings on H.R. 5463 Before Senate Comm. on Judiciary, 93d Cong., 2d Sess., 1974.
"EV"..................................	Congressional Information Service, Records of The U.S. Judicial Conference, Committees on Rules of Practice and Procedure—Committee on Evidence (microfiche), 1991.

*

CONTENTS

Volume 21

Volume 22

Volume 23

Volume 24

Volume 25

Volume 26

Volume 26A

Volume 27

Volume 28

CONTENTS

Volume 29

Volume 30

Volume 30A

SECTION ANALYSIS

Volume 30A

CHAPTER 9. HEARSAY

[IN VOLUME 30]

A. HEARSAY POLICY

B. CONFRONTATION AND HEARSAY

[IN VOLUME 30A]

SECTION ANALYSIS

FEDERAL PRACTICE AND PROCEDURE

EVIDENCE
CONFRONTATION AND HEARSAY

VOLUME 30A

CHAPTER 9

HEARSAY—Continued

Analysis

[In Volume 30]

[In Volume 30]

A. HEARSAY POLICY

B. CONFRONTATION AND HEARSAY—Continued

---

§ 6355. Construing Confrontation; The Ante–Bellum Years*

Nearly a century passed from the time the Confrontation Clause was drafted to the time it was first construed by the

Supreme Court.[1] Similarly, with a single exception, none of the state confrontation clauses was the subject of judicial interpretation while its drafters were still alive.[2] Accounting for this absence of contemporaneous construction will be one of our tasks in this section.[3] We shall also examine the earliest state confrontation decisions.[4]

On the federal side, the Confrontation Clause did not stand alone in absence of construction; the meaning of the Constitution was not frequently litigated during the generation following its adoption and almost none of the few decisions involved the Bill of Rights.[5] We should not be surprised by this because none of the techniques for raising and arguing constitutional questions that we now take for granted were to be found in the law books of the time; the first generation of judges and lawyers had to invent the process of constitutional adjudication.[6]

Other developments more specific to criminal cases help explain the absence of early confrontation claims.[7] Criminal prosecu-

1. Nearly a Century

The period is even longer if one begins it with George Mason's initial drafting of the right of confrontation in 1776. See § 6346, text at notecall 110. The earliest reported Supreme Court decision is Reynolds v. U.S., 1878, 98 U.S. (8 Otto) 145, 25 L.Ed. 244, discussed in § 6356.

2. Single exception

State v. Atkins, 1807, 1 Tenn. (1 Overton) 229.

3. Accounting for absence

Though this section is not a history of confrontation like §§ 6341–6348, we must of necessity say something about history in our explanation for the absence of confrontation cases.

4. Earliest state

There were about 20 such decisions prior to the Civil War.

5. Almost none

Friedman, Crime and Punishment in American History, 1992, pp. 72–73 (few decisions on Bill of Rights in 19th Century); 1 Goebel, History of the Supreme Court of the United States: Antecedents and Beginnings to 1801, 1971, p. 116 (constitutional adjudication in the first generation); 1 Warren, the Supreme Court in United States History, 1947 ed., p. 454 (from 1800–1816 only six constitutional adjudications).

6. Had to invent

Pound, The Formative Era of American Law, 1938, p. 97. Or to put it in more mundane terms, nothing in the experience or training of lawyers prepared them to think of the Constitution as an adversary tool.

7. Help explain

We do not think that this and the preceding paragraph provide a complete explanation. For example, why were lower court opinions, which were beginning to be published in this era, devoid of confrontation issues?

tions were not a significant part of the federal trial docket in those days;[8] for the first fifty years, federal and state courts had concurrent jurisdiction over some federal crimes.[9] Moreover, the Supreme Court's appellate jurisdiction in criminal cases was all but nonexistent for much of the 19th Century.[10] If there was any Supreme Court supervision of federal criminal cases, it must have come through the actions of the individual justices sitting on circuit.[11] Finally, in one of the few early Supreme Court decisions on the Bill of Rights, the Court held that it did not apply to the states——thus cutting off that potential source of confrontation cases.[12]

The Judiciary Act of 1789

The absence of judicial decisions does not mean that we are completely ignorant of the attitudes of Americans toward confrontation as they launched "the great experiment" in self-government.[13] For example, the Judiciary Act of 1789 was being debated at the same time Congress was drafting the Bill of Rights and it is apparent that the same motives that favored a right of confrontation had an impact on the statutory framework for the federal judiciary.[14] The members of Congress were suspicious of anything that smelled of "civil law" trials of the sort that had given admiralty a bad name.[15] A provision giving federal courts the power to

8. Criminal not significant

Henderson, Courts For A New Nation, 1971, pp. 70, 115. Of course, some of those cases were politically significant; e.g., prosecutions arising out of the Whiskey Rebellion and the Alien and Sedition Acts.

From 1800–1814, the Attorney General was something of an "absent" cabinet officer; William Wirt was the first to treat it as a full-time professional role. Cummings & McFarland, Federal Justice, 1937, p. 78.

9. Concurrent jurisdiction

Warren, Federal Criminal Laws and The State Courts, 1925, 38 Harv.L.Rev. 545.

10. Nonexistent jurisdiction

Frankfurter & Landis, The Business of the Supreme Court, 1927, pp. 79, 109.

11. On circuit

The Golden Age of American Law, Haar ed. 1969, p. 100.

12. Not to states

Barron v. Mayor of Baltimore, 1833, 32 U.S. (7 Peters) 243, 8 L.Ed. 672.

13. "Great experiment"

Miller, The Federalist Era, paper 1963, p. 1.

14. Same motives

Warren, New Light on The History of The Federal Judiciary Act of 1789, 1923, 37 Harv.L.Rev. 49, 54.

15. "Civil law"

Id. at p. 99. For more on contemporary attitudes toward admiralty courts, see 1 Goebel, History of The Supreme Court of the United States: Antecedents and Beginnings to 1801, 1971, p. 153.

compel production of books and papers was denounced as "inquisitorial."[16] An attempt to give federal judges some of the inquisitorial powers of English justices of the peace was rejected.[17] Congress was so anxious to dispel Anti–Federalist suspicions about jury trial that a statutory guarantee was added to that in Article III, and the Senate even wanted to extend jury trial to suits in equity.[18]

However, the debates on the Judiciary Act most relevant to the right of confrontation were those over the use of depositions in civil cases.[19] State law and practice varied widely,[20] but Congress determined that the mode of proof in civil actions was to be the same as that required in criminal cases by the Confrontation Clause; that is, viva voce testimony in open court.[21] Samuel Chase tried to salvage the traditional mode of equity proof by arguing that the popular objection to depositions was a result of their secrecy and being taken ex parte without opportunity for viva voce cross-examination.[22] By rejecting Chase's more limited reform in favor of a total ban on the traditional mode of proof in equity and admiralty,[23] Congress cast doubt on the argument that the Sixth Amendment was intended only to continue the common law and not to alter it.[24]

The French Revolution and The Whiskey Rebellion

American hostility to "civil law" procedures probably grew as the French Revolution, first seen as a flattering imitation of our own, turned increasingly bloody.[25] Although the trial of Louis XVI

16. "Inquisitorial"

Id. at p. 95.

17. Justices of peace

1 Goebel, History of The Supreme Court of the United States: Antecedents and Beginnings to 1801, 1971, p. 501.

18. Jury in equity

Warren, New Light on the History of The Federal Judiciary Act of 1789, 1923, 37 Harv.L.Rev. 49, 75, 99.

19. Use of depositions

1 Goebel, History of The Supreme Court of the United States: Antecedents and Beginnings to 1801, 1971, pp. 497–498.

Though he liked the idea of juries to try impeachments, Jefferson doubted the arguments that the Sixth Amendment required this. 2 The Republic of Letters, Smith ed. 1945, p. 1025.

20. State practice varied

Id. at p. 485 n. 83.

21. Viva voce

Id. at p. 484.

22. Secrecy and ex parte

Id. at p. 493 n. 103.

23. Ban traditional mode

Warren, New Light on The History of The Federal Judiciary Act of 1789, 1923, 37 Harv.L.Rev. 49, 100.

24. Alter

See vol. 30, § 6348, text at notecall 43.

25. Turned bloody

Encyclopedia of American History, Morris ed. 1976, p. 150. See also, Ellis, Passionate Sage, 1993, p. 93 (John Adams' opposition to radical change).

in 1792 was not, strictly speaking, a true civil-law proceeding but a political process devised for the occasion by the Convention, it did have inquisitorial features of the sort that were anathema to most Americans.[26] For example, the deposed King only confronted his accusers on two occasions; once on the reading of the accusation and a second time on the day he presented his defense.[27] This limited confrontation was ironic because one of the charges against Louis Capet accused him of "two-faced" conduct toward his people.[28] American supporters of confrontation might also have found confirmation for their preferences in the opinions of many observers that attitudes toward Louis softened greatly as a result of the way he conducted himself during his confrontation with the Convention.[29]

The trial of Louis XVI departed most strikingly from the adversarial ideal in combining the functions of accuser and jury in the same tribunal—the Convention itself.[30] This was apparently too much even for civilian sensibilities; the King's advocates made this irregularity a prominent feature of the defense.[31] As one of them told the Convention,

> Citizens, I will speak to you here with the frankness of a free man. I search among you for judges, and I see only accusers. * * * You want to pronounce on Louis's fate, and it is you yourselves who accuse him.[32]

Thomas Paine, the propagandist of the American Revolution who had been elected to the Convention, probably spoke for many

26. Inquisitorial

Jordan, The King's Trial, 1992, p. 65. Even so, the trial compares favorably to the one the English revolutionaries provided Charles I.

27. Presented defense

Id. at p. xvi.

28. "Two-faced" conduct

That is, the King appeared in public to be sympathetic to the demands of the Revolution while privately seeking to destroy it. Id. at pp. 72–73.

29. Conducted himself

Id. at p. 141. It was widely believed at the time that the jury could determine the defendant's character and through it, the likelihood of guilt, by observing the defendant's conduct when facing the accusers. See below, text at note-call 416.

30. Combining functions

Id. at p. 61. One of the latent functions of the right of confrontation as part of the adversarial system is to separate the role of judge from the role of accuser.

31. Feature of defense

Id. at p. 146 (arguing that the Convention had assumed to itself the functions "of grand jury, of jury, of legislators determining the form of judgment, and of judge").

32. "You who accuse"

Id. at p. 131.

Americans when he warned his colleagues about the importance of a fair procedure: "He that would make his own liberty secure must guard even his enemy from oppression; for if he violates this duty he establishes a precedent that will reach to himself."[33]

Paine's forebodings proved prophetic.[34] Shortly after the execution of the King in 1793, the Jacobins began the "Reign of Terror" in which more than 20,000 "enemies of the people", including many revolutionaries were executed.[35] On June 10, 1794, Robespierre and his compatriots promulgated the "Prairial Law" that sparked an acceleration of the Terror by, among other things, denying the right of those brought before the revolutionary tribunal to cross-examine witnesses "if material or moral proofs exist independently of witness' evidence."[36] This was certainly as hypocritical as anything that Louis Capet had done; Robespierre himself, when attacked by the Girondins in the Convention two years before, had demanded that his accusers come forth and confront him, a dramatic gesture memorialized by the poet Wordsworth, who happened to be in the gallery that day.[37]

Given events in France, it is not surprising that when word of backcountry resistance to Alexander Hamilton's excise tax on whis-

---

33. "Reach himself"

Keane, Tom Paine: A Political Life, 1995, p. 362.

34. Forebodings

Paine had also warned of the dangers of unsupported accusations: "If every individual is to indulge his private malignancy or his private ambition, to denounce at random and without any kind of proof, all confidence will be undermined and all authority be destroyed." Id. at p. 378. One of the functions of confrontation is to expose such "private malignancy" and to bolster the legitimacy of the courts.

35. Revolutionaries executed

Slaughter, The Whiskey Rebellion, 1986, p. 155.

36. "Proofs exist"

Starobinski, Rousseau in the Revolution, N.Y.Rev.Bks., April 12, 1990, pp. 47, 50.

37. Memorialized by poet

Wordsworth, "The Prelude" (written in 1799–1805):

"When Robespierre, not ignorant for what mark
Some words of indirect reproof had been
Intended, rose in hardihood, and dared
The man who had an ill surmise of him
To bring his charge in openness; whereat
When a dead pause ensued, and no one stirred,
In silence of all present, from his seat
Louvet walked single through the avenue,
And took his station in the Tribune, saying
'I, Robespierre, accuse thee!' "

For a less poetic description of this encounter, see Jordan, The King's Trial, 1992, p. 53.

key reached the seaboard, the right wing of the Federalist party heard tumbrels rolling through the streets of Philadelphia.[38] To the rebels and their Anti–Federalist supporters, the tax was viewed as a confirmation of the class warfare they had predicted the aristocrats would launch if the Constitution were adopted.[39] Even historians agree that the tax threatened the economic survival of small farmers on the frontier who brewed for themselves and their neighbors, and that it was supported by large Eastern distillers who could afford the tax and its attendant record-keeping requirements with greater ease.[40] For our purposes, the most notable grievance was the provision for trials for violations of the excise in the federal court in Philadelphia.[41] The notion that westerners were being denied a trial by the jury of the vicinage was heightened when the U.S. Attorney refused to stipulate that violators could use depositions in their defense rather than go to the expense of dragging their witnesses clear across the Alleghenies to testify.[42]

Prosecution of the "Whiskey Rebellion" was "political" in almost every sense of the word.[43] Despite the fact that resistance to the tax was widespread on the frontier in every state, Secretary of Treasury Hamilton chose to focus federal enforcement on the Pennsylvania backcountry where President Washington, as one of the largest absentee landlords in that part of the nation, stood to

38. Heard tumbrels

Slaughter, The Whiskey Rebellion, 1986, pp. 59, 133–135. For Hamilton's use of anti-Bonapartist rhetoric against the Jeffersonians, see 2 The Republic of Letters, Smith ed. 1995, p. 1138.

39. Class warfare

Id. at pp. 130–132. One Philadelphia newspaper wrote: "[a]s violent means appear the desire of high toned government men, it is to be hoped that those who derive the most benefit from our revenue laws will be the foremost to march against the western insurgents. Let stockholders, bank directors, speculators, and revenue officers arrange themselves immediately under the banner of the treasury, and try their prowess at arms as they have done in calculation." Id. at p. 195.

Jefferson wrote Washington that Hamilton wanted "to prepare the way for a change, from the present republican form of government, to that of a monarchy, of which the English constitution is to be the model." 2 The Republic of Letters, Smith ed. 1995, p. 728 n. 36.

40. Large distillers support

Id. at pp. 147–148.

41. Trials in Philadelphia

Elkins & McKitrick, The Age of Federalism, 1993, p. 463.

42. Refused to stipulate

Slaughter, The Whiskey Rebellion, 1986, p. 170.

43. "Whiskey rebellion"

For an excellent short account, see Miller, The Federalist Era, paper 1963, pp. 155–159.

(and in fact did) profit from the vindication of federal authority.[44] Hamilton wanted to prosecute peaceful petitioners against the excise on the grounds that they had "incited" the unlawful resistance of extremists but met resistance from Attorney General Randolph.[45] Hamilton had apparently anticipated J. Edgar Hoover by more than a century in planting federal spies within the frontier organizations seeking a nonviolent resolution of grievances.[46] When the President tried to negotiate an end to the resistance with frontier moderates, Hamilton took to the newspapers to denounce them (anonymously) as "anarchists" who were plotting an overthrow of the government.[47] The rebels, on the other hand, saw themselves as walking in the footsteps of those who had resisted the Stamp Tax and mounted the Boston Tea Party.[48]

This heroic self-portrait was vindicated for the frontiersmen when the U.S. Attorney summoned sixty western farmers to appear in Philadelphia to answer charges of violation of the excise.[49] Their outrage over the denial of the right to confront their accusers before a jury of their neighbors from the vicinage was not weakened by the discovery that the summons were technically invalid because the court was not scheduled to sit at the appointed time.[50] When federal officers attempting to serve summons were violently repelled, a military force dubbed "The Watermelon Army" by westerners was dispatched to quash the rebellion.[51] By the time the military reached the frontier, the genuinely guilty had fled into the

44. Focus on Pennsylvania

Slaughter, The Whiskey Rebellion, 1986, pp. 118, 151 (resistance to tax in other states), 82 (Washington owned over 63,000 acres in backcountry), 224 (value of Washington's land jumped by nearly 50% following suppression of the rebellion). It was also widely thought that Hamilton wished to relive past military glory, which would be more difficult to do if the President were to choose to attack the rebellion in South Carolina instead. Miller, The Federalist Era, paper 1963, p. 158.

45. Resistance from Randolph

Id. at pp. 121–124.

46. Planting spies

Id. at p. 164. On Hoover's conduct, see vol. 26, § 5663, text at notecall 462.

47. "Anarchists" plotting

Id. at p. 198.

48. Boston Tea Party

Id. at pp. 124, 128. On the role of the Tea Party in the history of confrontation, see vol. 30, § 6345, text at notecall 792.

49. Summoned sixty

Id. at pp. 177–178.

50. Summons invalid

Id. at p. 182.

51. "Watermelon Army"

Id. at p. 205. The name refers to a supposed penchant of the soldiers for commandeering produce rather than capturing rebels.

Ohio country, and the best the soldiers could do was to round up a score of camp-followers and frontier trash and march them back east for trial.[52] Six persons charged with treason against the state were all acquitted.[53] Of the 20 federal prisoners, all but two were acquitted—and those two convictions were tainted by the conduct of the trial judge.[54] Washington pardoned the two, but this was hardly seen as a magnanimous gesture in light of the widespread belief that both of them were either feeble-minded or even insane.[55] Perhaps the most enduring consequence of the affair for our purposes is the role it played in reopening the rift between "Tories" and "Whigs" within the Federalist faction that had been papered over during the struggle to ratify the Constitution.[56]

Attitudes toward Hearsay

At about the same time the Whiskey Rebellion collapsed, Tom Paine began publishing "The Age of Reason"——a Deist attack upon traditional religion.[57] In it, Paine trashed the Christian doctrine of "revelation" as mere "story telling" by pseudo-historians who piled "hearsay on hearsay."[58] Perhaps a better indication of the Founders' attitudes toward hearsay was the first American practice manual, also published in 1794, that purports to tell us "what is, and what is not legal evidence to a jury."[59] After explaining that evidence falls into two categories, viva voce and written, it says that the law rejects as incompetent the testimony of those with

52. March back east

Miller, The Federalist Era, paper 1963, p. 159.

53. Treason against state

Slaughter, The Whiskey Rebellion, 1986, p. 211.

54. Convictions tainted

Id. at p. 219, 226.

55. Two pardoned

Miller, The Federalist Era, paper 1963, p. 159.

56. Reopened rift

Slaughter, The Whiskey Rebellion, 1986, p. 227. On the split between "Whigs" and "Tories", see vol. 30, §6346, text at notecalls 562, 593. The Whiskey Rebellion and fears of pro-French sentiment among the populace set the stage for the Alien and Sedition Acts,

whose implications for the right of confrontation are discussed below, text at notecall 74.

See also, Ellis, Passionate Sage, 1993, pp. 62, 73, 227–231.

57. Deist attack

On the influence of Deism on American thought, see Nye, The Cultural Life of The New Nation, paper 1963, pp. 63–64. On the impact of Paine's book on politics, see Miller, The Federalist Era, paper 1963, p. 265.

58. "Hearsay on hearsay"

Keane, Tom Paine: A Political Life, 1995, p. 393.

59. "Legal evidence"

Wyche, A Treatise on The Practice of The Supreme Court of Judicature of The State of New York, 1794, p. 158.

motives to lie.[60] It continues: "[o]n this idea of possible deception, the law rejects hearsay evidence, always requiring the best proof of which the nature of the case is capable."[61] Hearsay is not defined, but the author apparently only recognizes two exceptions, reputation evidence and party admissions, "but [otherwise] such evidence will not, in general, be received of any distinct facts."[62] Apparently writings were not seen as hearsay; without citing that rule, the author tells us "[a]n affidavit cannot, in general, be read in evidence before a jury" though it can be used to impeach.[63] If this treatise is any indication, the hearsay rule was far more rudimentary when the Confrontation Clause was adopted than Wigmore and his followers have supposed.[64]

The Alien and Sedition Acts

The fracturing of the Federalist faction that we saw in connection with the Whiskey Rebellion fissured even further when a crisis in relations with France produced an epistemological crisis that had been simmering at least since the debates over the Constitution.[65] With the nation engaged in a "quasi-war" with France, the Federalists saw those who opposed their desire for open warfare as "Jacobins" already sharpening the guillotine.[66] Since under the

60. Motives to lie

Ibid.

61. "Best proof"

Id. at p. 160. For more on this "best evidence" theory of hearsay, see § 6329.

62. "Distinct facts"

Id. at p. 161.

63. "Read in evidence"

Id. at p. 162.

64. Hearsay rudimentary

See 5 Wigmore, Evidence, Chadbourn rev. 1974, § 1364, p. 27 (claiming hearsay was established a century earlier).

65. Epistemological crisis

Wood, The Radicalism of the American Revolution, 1992, p. 362.

66. "Jacobins" sharpening

Miller, The Federalist Era, paper 1963, p. 234.

Henry Adams, an astute judge of the Federalist mentality, wrote:

" . . . the mark of a wise and good man was that he abhorred the French Revolution, and believed democracy to be its cause. * * * The answer to every democratic suggestion ran in a set phrase, 'Look at France!' This idea became a monomania * * * until it degenerated into a morbid illusion." Adams, History of the United States of America during The Administrations of Jefferson and Madison, Samuels abrdg. 1967, p. 63.

Abigail Adams denounced as "traitors to their country" those "whom the French boast of as their Partisans," 2 The Republic of Letters, Smith ed. 1995, p. 1003. A letter to Adams listed as the "grandest of all grand Villains that traitor to his country—that infernal scoundrel Jefferson." Id. at 1005.

Hamiltonian theory of the Constitution the function of the federal government was to suppress faction, no one should have been surprised that the Federalists showed little allegiance to revolutionary rhetoric or the First Amendment.[67] But even the Republican faction was not above using governmental power to suppress its enemies.[68]

In 1798, the Anti–Federalist argument that even a democratic government needed a bill of rights was vindicated with a vengeance.[69] William Cobbett, perhaps the most notorious Federalist propagandist of the time, was charged by Republican authorities in Pennsylvania with being a "common libeller" after he attacked Jefferson and his faction as Jacobins, atheists, and stooges of the French government.[70] When the authorities attempted to enforce a bond he had given for his "good behavior" after he continued such attacks, Cobbett, an English subject, sought to remove the case to federal court under a provision of the Judiciary Act of 1789 authorizing this.[71] In passing on Cobbett's petition, the Republican Chief Justice of Pennsylvania, Thomas McKean, wrote:

> Can the Legislature of the United States be supposed to have intended * * * that an alien, residing three or four hundred miles from where the circuit court is held * * * should, after a breach of his recognizance and a prosecution for it commenced, be enabled to remove the prosecution before a court at such a distance * * * to be tried by a jury, who know neither the persons, nor characters, of the witnesses, and consequently are unqualified to try their credit; and to oblige the prosecutor and witnesses to incur such an expense of time and money * * *?[72]

This use of vicinage as a tool to aid the prosecutor certainly twists the Constitution as much as it was contorted by the Federalists, but it also shows that more than a decade after confrontation had first been constitutionalized, judges still have a very weak grip on the "blank pad rule."[73]

67. Hamiltonian theory

Elkins & McKitrick, The Age of Federalism, 1993, p. 103.

68. Suppress enemies

Wood, Politics Without Party, N.Y.Rev. Bks. Oct. 11, 1984, p. 20.

69. Vindicated

See vol. 30, § 6347, text at notecall 388.

70. Cobbett attacked

Powell, Languages of Power, 1991, p. 121.

71. Sought to remove

Ibid.

72. "Incur such expense"

Respublica v. Cobbett, 1798, 3 Dallas (3 U.S.) 467, 1 L.Ed. 683, quoted id. at p. 123.

73. "Blank pad rule"

As we shall see, the notion that the jury could rely on their own knowledge of the facts persisted well into the 19th Century.

In the summer of 1798, in a fervor of nativism and Anglophilia, Congress passed a quartet of statutes that have come down to us as "The Alien and Sedition Acts."[74] Though they are better known as part of the history of the First Amendment, these statutes have implications for the right of confrontation as well.[75] The Alien Act gave the President the power to imprison or deport aliens "he shall judge dangerous to the peace and safety of the United States."[76] In a set of resolutions drafted for the South Carolina legislature, Thomas Jefferson argued that the Alien Act "is contrary to the Constitution" because it violated the Sixth Amendment when it authorized

> the President to remove a person out of the United States, who is under the protection of the law, on his own suspicion, without accusation, without jury, without public trial, without confrontation of the witnesses against him, without hearing witnesses in his favor, without defense, without counsel * * *.[77]

When the Jefferson draft was adopted in modified form by the Kentucky legislature in November of 1798, it was hoped that other Republican state legislatures would also enact the "Kentucky Resolutions" but this did not happen.[78] Virginia did adopt resolutions

---

74. "Alien and Sedition"

Miller, The Federalist Era, paper 1963, pp. 229–231. On the intent to use the common-law crime of sedition against Jeffersonians, see 2 The Republic of Letters, Smith ed. 1995, pp. 1064–1065.

75. History of First

This is due, in part, to the fact that the Sedition Act was the only statute that was ever enforced. Id. at pp. 230, 235.

76. "Judge dangerous"

1 Stat. 570, June 25, 1798, quoted in Powell, Languages of Power, 1991, pp. 127–128.

77. "Without confrontation"

Jefferson, Writings, Peterson ed. 1984, pp. 145–452.

Jefferson's draft of the Kentucky Resolutions of 1798 argued that the Alien Act violated the Sixth Amendment by "undertaking to authorize the President to remove a person out of the U.S. * * * on his own suspicion, without accusation, without jury, without public trial, without confrontation of the witnesses against him, without hearing witnesses in his favor, without defense, without counsel" and so is "utterly void, and of no force." 2 Republic of Letters, Smith ed. 1995, p. 1082.

Later the draft argued that the Act violated the separation of functions presupposed by the adversary system by giving power to the President or his delegate "who may himself by the accuser, counsel, judge and jury, whose suspicions may be the evidence, his order the sentence, his officer the executioner, and his breast the sole record of the transaction; * * *." Id. at p. 1083.

78. Did not happen

Article 6 of The Kentucky Resolutions is substantially identical to the Jefferson draft quoted in the text. See Powell, Languages of Power, 1991, pp. 131–132.

drafted by Madison but these were less explicit about which provisions of the Constitution were thought to invalidate the Alien and Sedition Acts.[79]

The Federalists denied that the punishment of seditious speech violated the First Amendment.[80] On the floor of the House of Representatives, Harrison Gray Otis of Massachusetts argued that the First Amendment was intended to adopt the English common law, which "provided for the punishment of defamatory and seditious libels."[81] In reply, Madison drafted a report for the Virginia legislature defending their view of the Constitution and flatly rejecting the appeal to English law by distinguishing the governments of the two nations:

> In the United States, the case is altogether different. The people, not the government, possess absolute sovereignty. The legislature, no less than the executive, is under limitations of power. Encroachments are regarded as possible from the one as well as the other. * * * The state of the press, therefore, under the common law, cannot, in this point of view, be the standard of its freedom in the United States.[82]

This is significant because it would be later argued by some courts that the Confrontation Clause was intended to do no more than adopt the English common law.[83]

The Supreme Court never addressed the constitutionality of the Alien and Sedition laws, though some individual justices on circuit expressed the view that they were valid.[84] Other federal

79. Less explicit

The Virginia Resolutions were most explicit about the First Amendment. See id. at pp. 133–134.

80. Denied violated

Miller, The Federalist Era, paper 1963, p. 232.

81. "Provided punishment"

Powell, Languages of Power, 1991, p. 127.

82. "Common law cannot"

Id. at p. 143.

83. Intended to adopt

Madison made another argument relevant to confrontation when he pointed out that freedom of the press was coupled with freedom of religion and even the Federalists could not claim that religious freedom was intended to be limited to what was allowed under English law. Id. at p. 144. Similarly, the Sixth Amendment includes rights, such as the right to counsel and a right to see the indictment, that were nonexistent in the English common law.

84. Valid

1 Warren, The Supreme Court in United States History, 1947 ed., p. 159. In his first State of the Union Message, Jefferson planned to call the Sedition Act a "palpable and unqualified contradiction to the constitution" and "a nullity" but Madison and others convinced him to omit this. 2 Republic of Letters, Smith ed. 1995, p. 1203.

judges adopted the spirit of the Sedition Act when they demanded that the U.S. Attorney prosecute the author of an attack on the judiciary.[85] Indeed, the Federalist view was to prevail among American judges and lawyers long after the demise of the Federalist party.[86] And on the other side, Jacksonian opponents of the Federalist constitutional theory tied it to the Hamiltonian excesses;[87] at his famous Fourth of July Oration at Scituate, Robert Rantoul, Jr. said: "The alien and sedition laws, the muzzling of the press, the unrelenting proscription for opinion's sake, made that period emphatically the reign of terror."[88]

Beneath these partisan political posturings lurked a genuine difference in epistemological outlook.[89] While the Federalists clung to the traditional assumption that truth was constant and universal and capable of being discovered by enlightened and reasonable men, their Republican opponents argued that opinions about government and rulers were many and diverse and the truth of such opinions could not be determined simply by judges and members of juries, no matter how educated and reasonable such men might be.[90] The implications of this for the adversary system and confrontation are suggested by the Federalist judge who said that "[t]ruth has but one side and listening to error and falsehood is indeed a strange way to discover truth."[91] The Federalist view that the rich and the well-born were more capable of knowing the truth than ordinary people was to play a significant role over the course of the 19th Century in the diminution of the power of the jury and the constriction of the right of confrontation.[92]

85. Prosecute author

Id. at p. 195.

86. Long after demise

See, e.g., The Legal Mind in America, Miller ed. 1969, pp. 72–73 (address of Mr. Justice Story to the Suffolk Bar, 1821).

87. Tied to Hamiltonian

Memoirs, Speeches, and Writings of Robert Rantoul, Jr., Hamilton ed. 1854, p. 255.

88. "Reign of terror"

Id. at p. 256.

89. Epistemological outlook

This difference predated the crisis of 1798 and it continues today, albeit in a much more sophisticated form; see,

for example, the debate in 1996 between practitioners of "post-modernism" and adherents of traditional science. See Weinberg, Sokal's Hoax, N.Y.Rev.Bks., August 8, 1996, p. 11.

90. "Not determined simply"

Wood, The Radicalism of The American Revolution, 1992, p. 362.

91. "Strange way"

Id. at p. 363.

92. Constriction of right

See below, text at notecall 799.

However, the Federalist epistemology suffered another blow when the turn of the century brought the Second Great Awakening.[93] Though partly a reaction to Paine and the Deists who made up much of the leadership of both parties, the Second Great Awakening has been characterized as an effort to "republicanize" Christianity.[94] As one Baptist preacher proclaimed in 1809, Christians must be "wholly free to examine for ourselves what is truth, without being bound to a catechism, creed, confession of faith, discipline or any rule excepting the scriptures."[95] Challenging of established institutions appealed to the younger generation that had missed the Revolutionary fervor, and there is reason to believe that the Second Great Awakening served a psychological role in the rise of Jacksonianism analogous to that which the Revolution had played in the rise of the Anti–Federalist wing of the Jeffersonian party.[96] Given the Biblical roots and dissenting patrimony of confrontation, that right could only be strengthened with the rise in power of the Methodists and Baptists.[97] Moreover, the ritualistic and nonrational elements of the revivalists could have given a boost to the nonrational elements of the Sixth Amendment.[98] As the Presbyterian Timothy Dwight wryly observed, the Calvinists understood what the Deists did not; that "no heart was ever won by reason's power alone."[99]

Early American Evidence Books

The turn of the century brought another development of some significance for our understanding of the confrontation clause; the American publication of a number of books on evidence.[100] It would

---

93. Second Awakening

Nye, The Cultural Life of The New Nation, paper 1963, p. 219. For the impact of the First Great Awakening on confrontation, see § 6344, text at notecall 260. John Adams distrusted such popular movements, seeing religious fanaticism and its secular counterparts as likely to produce bloody repression of opponents. Ellis, Passionate Sage, 1993, p. 123.

94. "Republicanize" Christianity

Wood, The Radicalism of the American Revolution, 1992, p. 332.

95. "Excepting scriptures"

Ibid.

96. Appealed to younger

Cross, The Burned–Over District, paper 1965, p. 6.

97. Methodists and Baptists

Nye, The Cultural Life of the New Nation, paper 1963, p. 219. On the Biblical roots of confrontation, see vol. 30, § 6342, text at notecall 350.

98. Non-rational

Id. at pp. 217–218.

99. "Reason's power alone"

Id. at p. 211.

100. Books on evidence

Lawyers were still relying on Baron Gilbert's book until well into the 19th Century. See Blume, Civil Procedure

help us determine how the Founders saw the relationship between confrontation and the hearsay rule if we knew what courts were doing in the late colonial and early national period—but we don't.[101] Hence, some scholars want to infer American evidentiary practices from English law and practice.[102] This desperate expedient founders on the fact that English legal historians concede that the records on that side of the Atlantic do not suffice to determine when and how the hearsay rule and the right of confrontation were first applied there.[103] Hence, one finds English historians attempting to fill the gap by relying on Wigmore's history[104]—the very source whose inadequacy drives American scholars to look at English sources.

Even if we had a better idea of how English courts were handling hearsay, from what we know about the class-biased English practice of the time there is good reason for supposing that the Sixth Amendment was meant to repudiate, not to emulate it.[105] Down to the end of the 18th Century, aristocratic English justices of the peace were still conducting preliminary examinations with the inquisitorial procedures laid down by the Tudor monarchs.[106] Lawyers did not appear in significant numbers in English criminal trials until the 19th Century, so it was left to the untutored defendants to assert the privilege against self-incrimination.[107] When the case came to trial, the "prosecutor" was a private person, often the victim of the crime, so the judge examined the witnesses.[108] English defendants, without counsel, were expected to

---

on the American Frontier, 1957, 56 Mich.L.Rev. 161, 167 n. 32. For what light Gilbert sheds on the development of hearsay, see § 6344, text at notecall 477.

101. We don't know

Friedman, Crime and Punishment in American History, 1992, p. 236.

102. Infer from English

Since it would be invidious to single out others, we invite readers to examine our own attempts to draw such inferences. See vol. 30, § 6343, text at notecall 304.

103. Records do not suffice

See, e.g., Beattie, Crime and the Courts in England, 1660–1880, 1986, p. 363.

104. Relying on Wigmore's

Id. at pp. 273, 364.

105. Not emulate

Id. at pp. 316–317. On American opposition to aristocratic pretensions, see vol. 30, § 6346, text at notecall 395.

106. Tudor monarchs

Id. at p. 270. For discussion of these statutes, see vol. 30, § 6342, text at notecall 286.

107. Untutored defendants

Id. at p. 276.

108. Judge examined

Id. at pp. 343–344.

The only exceptions to this rudimentary hearsay rule appear to be dying declarations and, pursuant to the English statutes, testimony of an unavailable witness given at the preliminary examination; even former testimony is not admissible, except to impeach.[127] This book suggests that, at least for the author, there was no conflict between confrontation and hearsay because neither had developed

of confrontation and hearsay, but it also illustrates with maddening clarity how far from modern were 18th Century evidentiary concepts. The 46th Chapter of the edition of Hawkins most contemporaneous with the drafting of the Sixth Amendment begins: "[a]s to the nature of evidence, so far as it more particularly concerns criminal cases, having premised that it is the settled rule, That in cases of life no evidence is to be given against a prisoner but in his presence * * *." 2 Hawkins, A Treatise of The Pleas of The Crown, 1787, p. 602. This is supported by a citation to the State Trials, the same source upon which Wigmore's history is largely based.

After wandering off on another point, Hawkins explains the organization of the chapter: "First, How many witnesses are required in criminal cases. Secondly, what is to be allowed as evidence. Thirdly, Who may be witnesses. Fourthly, in what manner the witnesses for the defendant are to give their evidence. Fifthly, Whether a defendant have right to process to bring in his witnesses. Sixthly, What evidence maintains an indictment, & . Seventhly, What may be given in evidence on the part of the defendant. Eighthly, In what cases witnesses may be allowed their expences." Ibid.

Hawkins divides the second point in this manner: "First, Where the confession of the defendant or the depositions of others out of court may be allowed as evidence. Secondly, How far hearsay is evidence. Thirdly, Whether similitude of hands be any evidence in criminal cases." Id. at p. 603. Three of the less than four pages Hawkins devotes to

the second point are taken up with the use of depositions——a tangled analysis impossible to summarize.

Only a single paragraph is required to dispose of the hearsay question: "It seems agreed, That what a stranger has been heard to say is in strictness no manner of evidence either for or against a prisoner, not only because it is not upon oath, but also because the other side hath no opportunity of a cross examination; and therefore it seems a settled rule, That it shall never be made use of but only by way of inducement or illustration of what is properly evidence. Yet it seems that what the prisoner had been heard to say another time, may be given in evidence for him, as well as against him, and also what a witness hath been heard to say at another time, may be given in evidence in order either to invalidate or confirm the testimony which he gives in court." Id. at pp. 606–607.

Hawkins apparently saw no connection between hearsay and the requirement that evidence be given in the presence of the accused and did not consider depositions or other writings to be "hearsay."

127. Exceptions

Id. at pp. 153–154. Since the writer does not define "hearsay," it is not clear whether these are truly "exceptions" or matters beyond the scope of the rule. The author goes on to say that though hearsay cannot be used "as direct evidence," it can be used "to invalidate or confirm the testimony" given by the declarant in court. Id. at p. 154.

to the point where conflict could occur.[128]

In 1804, a Philadelphia publisher pirated an 1802 book on the rules of evidence in criminal cases by an Irish barrister, Leonard MacNally.[129] Perhaps because of his ethnicity, the author has some harsh words to say about the conduct of judges in the State Trials, including Raleigh's trial.[130] However, despite invoking that icon of confrontation and despite the fact that by this time——according to Wigmore——the right of confrontation was well-established at common law, MacNally never uses the word "confrontation."[131] He does say, citing Hawkins, that "it is a well settled rule of law, that no evidence is to be given against a prisoner but in his presence."[132] As a corollary to this rule, MacNally says that "depositions of a witness taken ex parte at a preliminary hearing before a magistrate are not admissible in misdemeanors and only pursuant to statute in felonies."[133] Later, though again without using the word, MacNally states something like the modern notion of "confrontation":

> The most common and ordinary species of legal evidence, consists in the deposition of witnesses taken on oath, before the jury in the face of the court, in the presence of the prisoner, and received under all the advantages which examination and cross-examination can give.[134]

MacNally seems to recognize only two exceptions; dying declarations and depositions taken at a preliminary hearing pursuant to statute, but says that the latter is admissible only if the deponent is dead.[135]

When he comes to hearsay, MacNally again paraphrases Hawkins, but with an addition that shows how hearsay and confrontation were intertwined:

128. Neither developed

This assumes that the requirement that evidence must be given in the defendant's "presence" is intended to state the English common law right of confrontation.

129. Pirated MacNally

MacNally, The Rules of Evidence on Pleas of the Crown, 1804.

130. Raleigh's trial

Id. at pp. 7, 26.

131. Never uses word

As we shall see, this is not an isolated instance. Nor does the word appear in modern English evidence scholarship that we have seen.

132. "But in his presence"

Id. at p. 14.

133. "Depositions taken ex parte"

Id. at p. 15. See also, id. at p. 282.

134. "Advantages can give"

Id. at p. 298.

135. Only two exceptions

Ibid.

No evidence can be received against a prisoner but in his presence; and therefore it is agreed, that what a stranger has been heard to say, is in strictness, no manner of evidence, either for or against the prisoner. * * * The reasons assigned as the grounds for this rule are, because such evidence is not upon oath; and also because the party, who would be affected by such evidence, had no opportunity of cross-examination.[136]

If this is a reflection of the English right of confrontation, notice that it differs from the American version in giving the right to the prosecution as well as the defense.[137] MacNally recognizes different "exceptions" to the hearsay rule than he did to the requirement of "presence;" the defendant's confession, prior consistent and inconsistent statements, and dying declarations.[138] He also allows official records to be admitted, but it is not clear whether this is by virtue of an "exception" or because he does not regard writings as "hearsay."[139]

In 1810, Justice Zephaniah Swift of the Connecticut Supreme Court published the first American treatise on evidence.[140] Swift makes no mention of confrontation, though he does express a preference for viva voce testimony over depositions.[141] This would

136. "No cross-examination"

Id. at p. 360.

137. Right to prosecution

In another passage relevant to cross-examination, MacNally repeats Coke's claim that "[o]ne who can only witness by hearsay what he has heard a good witness say, is not a lawful accuser" under the English statutes that require two lawful witnesses as accusers for certain crimes. Id. at pp. 23–25.

138. Different exceptions

Id. at pp. 361, 378, 381, 383. The major difference is that no mention is made here of testimony of unavailable witnesses at the preliminary examination. One might infer that this was not regarded as hearsay, either because it would normally be presented in the form of a writing or because the witness had been under oath and subject to cross. However, in a note on p. 360, MacNally says he intended to deal with written as well as verbal hearsay and on page 390 he tells us

that "[w]hat has been sworn against a defendant on the trial of another person ought not to be given in evidence against him on his own trial."

139. Official records

Id. at p. 475. This is part of MacNally's treatment of written evidence. But see note 138 above.

140. First American treatise

Swift, A Digest of the Law of Evidence in Civil and Criminal Cases and a Treatise on Bills of Exchange and Promissory Notes, 1810.

141. Preference for viva voce

"There can be no question, but that the practice of taking depositions is of great accommodation to the parties * * * but it must be acknowledged to be a mode, by no means so well calculated to discover truth as viva voce examination in open Court. Much depends on the manner in which a witness testifies, and in complex cases,

not be surprising if this were a Connecticut treatise, since that state had no right of confrontation; but Swift claims to be writing an American treatise, not one on local law.[142] He does write:

> Hearsay evidence, generally speaking, is not admissible, for the law requires that witnesses should appear in Court, so as to be sworn, and examined; but the mere hearsay of persons not under the sanction of an oath, and not examined in Court, can have little weight, and is of too uncertain a nature to be relied on. The law has, therefore, very wisely rejected all such evidence, excepting where it is impossible, in the nature of things, to obtain any other; and where this is sufficient to establish the matter in question.[143]

As examples of such exceptions, Swift speaks of family history and the use of hearsay to corroborate or impeach,[144] but then adds:

> In criminal cases, it is a very important principle, that no evidence shall be received against a prisoner, but in his presence; and that hearsay evidence is not admissible, for it is not on oath, and the party to be affected by it, has no opportunity of cross examination; but to this rule there is a very important exception.[145]

That exception is dying declarations.[146] Swift cites MacNally as his authority for this proposition, but as we have just seen, MacNally recognized several other exceptions.[147] Swift goes on to say that former testimony of a now-deceased witness is admissible, but it is not clear that he limits this to civil cases.[148] He has earlier told us that depositions are not admissible at common law[149] and in dis-

---

many questions will arise upon a cross-examination, which could not be thought of in taking a deposition, and which could wholly change the complexion of the case; and it is much easier to shape a deposition, so as to meet the views of a designing party, than a public testimony." Id. at p. 115.

142. Claims American

"Though sundry valuable Treatises have been written upon Evidence in England, yet they contain many things of little use here, and are not well adapted to our Country. On this subject no work has been published in America; and a Digest comprising all the principles of Evidence, in civil and criminal cases, adapted to the practice of our Courts, and to the local circumstances of our Country, has justly been deemed a desideratum in American jurisprudence." Id. at p. x.

143. "Sufficient to establish"

Id. at p. 121.

144. Or impeach

Id. at pp. 121–123.

145. "Important exception"

Id. at p. 124.

146. Dying declarations

Ibid.

147. Other exceptions

See text at notecall 138, above.

148. Former testimony

Id. at p. 125.

149. Depositions not

Id. at p. 112.

cussing a case in which testimony of a deceased witness at the preliminary hearing was held inadmissible, he begins "[i]n England, it has been decided * * * '', perhaps implying that the law in America is different.[150]

It is worth noting that the Connecticut cases do not always support Justice Swift's description of American law.[151] For example, there are several cases that admit hearsay statements of an agent against the principle.[152] More significant is Rex v. Barber, in which witnesses were allowed to testify what one White had testified at the preliminary hearing and before the grand jury after the prosecutor introduced evidence that White's absence at trial had been procured by a friend of the defendant.[153] However, this was a 1775 case, so Swift may have regarded it as having been decided under English rather than American law and thus not inconsistent with his more restrictive view of what was admissible in criminal cases.[154]

The year after Swift's treatise, an English jury enthusiast, Sir Richard Phillips, published a work that he hoped would encourage jurors to ignore the "false learning" of lawyers and judges in order to maintain the authority of the jury.[155] This book, by a layman, was surprisingly popular with American lawyers.[156] The best-evidence principle leads off Phillips' chapter on evidence and is immediately followed by this:[157]

150. "In England"

Id. at p. 125.

151. Not always support

Some cases do; see, e.g., Porter v. Warner, 1793, 2 Conn. (Root) 22 (reputation re boundary admissible).

152. Hearsay of agent

Perkins v. Burnet, 1793, 2 Conn. (Root) 30; Mather v. Phelps, 1794, id. at 150.

153. Absence procured

Rex v. Barber, 1775, 1 Conn. (Root) 76.

154. American law

Compare McDonald v. Hobby, 1790, 1 Conn. (Root) 154 (in bastardy proceeding, ex parte deposition of the now deceased mother of the bastard inadmissible).

155. "False learning"

Phillips, On the Powers and Duties of Juries, 1811, p. vi.

156. Popular

Brown, Frontier Justice: Wayne County, 1796–1836, 1972, 16 Am.J.Leg.Hist. 126, 146.

157. Best-evidence principle

"The best evidence the nature of the case will admit must be produced, for if it appear that better evidence might have been brought forward, the circumstance of its being withheld affords a strong suspicion that it would have prejudiced the party who withholds it." Phillips, On The Powers and Duties of Juries, 1811, p. 150.

> The law never gives credit to the bare assertion of any one,
> however high his rank, or pure his morals, but always requires the
> sanction of an oath; it further requires his personal attendance in
> Court, that he may be examined and cross-examined by the
> different parties.[158]

Phillips then discusses the admissibility of dying declarations,[159]
without connecting it with this rule or with his discussion of
hearsay:

> what another has been heard to say is no evidence, because the
> assertion was not on oath; also because the party who is affected
> thereby, had not an opportunity of cross-examining; * * *[160]

After discussing use of hearsay to impeach or corroborate or to
prove "pedigree, prescription, or custom", Phillips continues:

> What a party has himself been heard to say, does not fall within
> the objection to hearsay evidence. Anything, therefore, which he
> has admitted, or which another has asserted in his presence, and
> which he did not contradict, is received as evidence against his
> claim; * * *[161]

Like the other writers, Phillips does not use the word "confrontation" though much of what he says is consistent with the way the
Founders seem to have understood that term.[162]

In 1812, Josiah Randall published an American edition of
Thomas Peake's text on evidence.[163] Like its predecessors, this
work does not mention the word "confrontation" at the places one
might expect to find it discussed, either in the English text or in the

---

158. "May be examined"

Ibid.

159. Dying declarations

Id. at p. 153.

160. "Opportunity of cross"

Id. at p. 156.

161. "Did not contradict"

Id. at p. 157.

162. Founders understood

He makes two other statements that
resonate with the beliefs of the Revolutionary generation. "All the features
of the English Jury System are essential to its perfection." Id. at p. 11.

This is consistent with the demands to
have all of the incidents of trial by
jury specified in the Constitution. See
§ 6347. "Lawyers in general are constant friends to power and prerogative, and consequently not attached to
popular interference in the jurisdiction of their courts." Id. at p. 17. This
is followed by a prophecy of the various ways that American courts would
attempt to restrict the power of the
jury during the 19th Century. Id. at
pp. 19–28.

163. Peake's text

Peake, Compendium of The Law of Evidence, Randall ed. 1812. The work
was first published in England in
1801.

American annotations.[164] However, under the heading of "Hearsay," Peake writes:

> The Law never gives credit to the bare assertion of any one, however high his rank or pure his morals. It further requires his personal attendance in Court, that he may be examined and cross-examined by the different parties; and, therefore, in cases depending on parole evidence, the testimony of persons who are themselves conusant of the facts they relate, must in general be produced; for the relation of one who has no other knowledge of the subject than the information which he has received from others, is not a relation upon oath; and moreover, the party against whom such evidence would be permitted would be precluded from the benefit of cross-examination. The few instances in which this general rule has been departed from, and in which hearsay evidence has been admitted, will be found, on examination, to be such as were, in their very nature, incapable of positive and direct proof.[165]

Among the "few instances" Peake lists are family or local history, the shopbook role, dying declarations, and admissions.[166] Depositions and former testimony are treated under the heading "Of Public Writings not being Records" and Peake asserts that former testimony "is not allowed in a criminal prosecution."[167]

Several points may be gleaned from these early treatises.[168] First, if there was a right of "confrontation" at common law, as Wigmore was to later claim, it certainly traveled in a heavy disguise.[169] Second, the writers support the notion that by the beginning of the 19th Century there was a "hearsay rule," but they

164. Expect to find

That is, where the author discusses the examination of witnesses or the admissibility of depositions. Id. at pp. 62–66, 186.

165. "Incapable of direct proof"

Id. at pp. 15–16.

166. Shopbook and admissions

Id. at pp. 15–29.

167. "Not allowed in criminal"

Id. at p. 62. In discussing the statute making depositions at a preliminary hearing admissible, Peake adds "but if the prisoner be not present at the time of the examination, it cannot be read as a deposition taken on oath" though it might come in as a dying declaration. Id. at p. 63.

168. Early treatises

The preceding pages do not claim to be an exhaustive compilation of writings on evidence at the beginning of the 19th Century, though they include all of those that seem to have been popular with American lawyers. Later treatises are discussed below, text at notecall 783.

169. Heavy disguise

Wigmore's attempts to get around the right of confrontation are discussed in § 6358.

paint a very mixed picture on exactly what it was and, more importantly, what were the exceptions that might be operative in criminal cases.[170] Third, the hearsay rule was not as important then as it was to become later in the century; we have quoted most of what each writer has had to say about hearsay, but these paragraphs are dwarfed by the hundreds of pages devoted to other rules of evidence.[171] Finally, these writers rarely invoke the cases relied upon by Wigmore; instead, they cite earlier writers and each other.[172] Moreover, given his popularity with the Revolutionary generation and his relevance to hearsay and confrontation, the absence of so much as a single citation to Blackstone is startling.[173]

Reception of the Common Law

We have previously seen that the right of confrontation was sometimes linked with the "common law."[174] We shall soon see how a subsequent generation of judges were to claim that the Sixth Amendment and state confrontation provisions were intended to adopt the "English common law."[175] Hence, we must inquire into the Founders' attitudes toward that law.[176]

We begin by noting the imprecision of the term "common law."[177] It had no precise meaning at the time the Constitution was

170. What exceptions

This is important because the next generation of judges was to claim that the state confrontation clauses were not intended to alter the common law rules of evidence that then existed. See below, text at notecall 799.

171. Dwarfed

MacNally, for example, who dealt only with evidence in criminal cases, has nearly 700 pages but fewer than 30 of these deal with hearsay.

172. Each other

For example, it is apparent that Phillips copied most of his discussion of hearsay from Peake's work. See text, above, at notecalls 158 and 165.

173. Blackstone

See vol. 30, § 6345, text at notecall 641.

174. Linked with "common law"

See vol. 30, § 6346, text at notecall 138. But see, 2 The Republic of Letters, Smith ed. 1995, p. 1195 (Jefferson again denouncing English courts of admiralty in 1801).

175. Intended to adopt "English"

See below, text at notecall 799.

176. Founders' attitudes

As the text implies, there is no direct evidence that the Sixth Amendment was or was not intended to adopt the English law of confrontation, whatever that might have been at the time. See § 6347.

177. Imprecision of term

Though we are concerned with usage in the 19th Century, the imprecision continues today. We make no claims that we have been precise in our prior usage of the term.

drafted and ratified.[178] Sometimes the phrase "common law" was used to distinguish judge-made law from legislation or codification, a usage of little direct relevance to our inquiry.[179] Of greater interest is the use of "common law" to mean "customary law" or "natural law" as distinguished from artificial or "positive law."[180] For example, in 1798, Jesse Root, who was to become the Chief Justice of the Connecticut Superior Court, defined "common law" as "the perfection of reason, arising from the nature of God, of man, and of things, and from their relations, dependencies, and connections: It is universal and extends to all men * * * ";[181] Root regarded it as superior to "positive laws" in the same sense that we regard the Constitution as superior to legislation and judge-made law.[182] This usage was quite common in the Revolutionary generation, though it is not always easy to distinguish it from similar but distinct usages.[183]

A more specific definition of "common law" that is closely allied to the last one is the use of the phrase to distinguish between Anglo–American law and the law that is derived from the Roman law, the so-called "civil law."[184] This usage is directly relevant to our inquiry because the demand for confrontation was frequently phrased in terms of an adversary system of justice, associated with the "common law" and in opposition to an inquisitorial system derived from the civil law and Roman law.[185] This explains an

178. No precise meaning

1 Goebel, History of the Supreme Court of the United States, 1971, p. 655.

179. Judge-made law

This is the sense in which the term is used later in the 19th Century during the debates over codification. See, e.g., Robert Rantoul, Oration at Scituate, 1836, in Memoirs, Speeches, and Writings, Hamilton ed. 1854, pp. 254, 298.

180. "Natural law"

See, e.g., Horwitz, The Transformation of American Law, 1780–1860, 1977, p. 7 ("natural law"); The Legal Mind in America, Miller, ed. 1969, p. 37 ("customary law").

181. "Perfection of reason"

The Legal Mind in America, Miller ed. 1969, p. 34. The problem of different referents may explain Robert Rantoul's response to this definition:

"The common law is the perfection of human reason,——just as alcohol is the perfection of sugar." Rantoul, Memoirs, Speeches, and Writings, Hamilton ed. 1854, p. 279.

182. Superior to "positive laws"

Id. at p. 35.

183. Common in Revolutionary

Mullett, Fundamental Law and The American Revolution, 1966 ed., p. 44.

184. From "civil law"

The Legal Mind in America, Miller ed. 1969, p. 299.

185. "Inquisitorial"

See vol. 30, § 6347, text at notecall 587.

adjacent usage, but one of lesser relevance; the use of "common law" to refer to those English courts that employed the adversary system as distinguished from courts of equity and admiralty that employed procedures derived from the Roman law.[186]

Finally, and most confusingly, "common law" was sometimes used to mean "English law."[187] For example, David Dudley Field defined "common law" as "the customary law of England, as it existed before the coronation of Richard I" and subsequent statutory amendments.[188] This usage is often difficult to distinguish from common law as natural law or as Anglo–American law, but it is the only usage that would unequivocally support the later judicial view that the Confrontation Clause was intended to adopt 18th Century English law.[189] We shall use the expression "English common law" when we refer to this definition.[190]

It would help us understand the Founders' attitudes toward the "English common law" if we knew what they thought of the "American common law"——but there was no such thing; all they had was the law of the various states and that was highly uncertain when confrontation clauses were being drafted.[191] Our knowledge of colonial law is very skimpy, yet it is probably not simply legal historian's hyperbole to say that we know more about it than did the Revolutionary generation.[192] We summarize what is now known without any pretense that the Founders knew this.[193]

186. Equity and admiralty

Wolfram, The Constitutional History of the Seventh Amendment, 1973, 57 Minn.L.Rev. 639, 715.

187. "English law"

The Legal Mind in America, Miller ed. 1969, pp. 34 (criticizing this usage) 101–111.

188. Field defined

Id. at pp. 287–288.

189. Only one

If confrontation is a "natural law" or "adversary" right, English law would not be irrelevant as to its scope, but it would not be controlling as the 19th Century judges assumed.

190. "English common law"

Even this term is not as unambiguous as it is sometimes supposed to be. 1 Goe-bel, History of the Supreme Court of the United States, 1971, p. 655.

191. Highly uncertain

This may have been why Madison expected that Congress would adopt a code of federal law to be applied in federal courts. 1 Goebel, History of the Supreme Court of the United States, 1971, p. 229.

192. We know more

The Legal Mind in America, Miller ed. 1969, p. 17.

193. Founders knew

The state of legal knowledge in 1789 is discussed below, text at notecall 284.

Even in the colonies that were settled by the English and claimed to follow the "common law," adherence to English law was neither slavish nor perfect.[194] Some colonies departed quite markedly and in early Massachusetts Bay the English common law figured very little in jurisprudential thought.[195] As we have previously seen,[196] the Puritans used a number of inquisitorial procedures in their desire to enforce religious orthodoxy.[197] Even when the English common law was used, it was not necessarily seen as an authoritative source of law; some jurists saw it as simply illustrative of "natural law," which was the true "authority" in their eyes.[198]

Turning to the substantive criminal law, the various colonies differed markedly among themselves in the degree to which they purported to follow the English criminal law and adherence was often by virtue of a colonial statute rather than by direct application of English decisional law.[199] There was a far greater conformity with the English common law and uniformity among the colonies with respect to the institutions of criminal law enforcement, particularly trial by jury and the use of viva voce testimony.[200] However, even here American practices departed from the English in ways significant for the right of confrontation; e.g., the greater and earlier use of public prosecutors.[201]

The degree to which the colonies could or must follow the English common law was a matter of sometimes bitter controversy

194.　Neither slavish nor perfect

Reinsch, The English Common Law in the Early American Colonies, in 1 Select Essays in Anglo–American Legal History, 1907, pp. 367, 369.

195.　Massachusetts

Id. at p. 371.

196.　Previously seen

See vol. 30, § 6344, text at notecall 669.

197.　Puritan inquisitorial

Friedman, Crime and Punishment in American History, 1993, pp. 24–25, 32.

198.　Illustrative of "natural"

Reinsch, The English Common Law in the Early American Colonies, in 1 Select Essays in Anglo–American Legal History, 1907, p. 377.

199.　English criminal law

Smith & Barnes, The English Legal System: Carryover to the Colonies, 1975, p. 41.

200.　Trial by jury

Reinsch, The English Common Law in the Early American Colonies, in 1 Select Essays in Anglo–American Legal History, 1907, p. 378; Friedman, Crime and Punishment in American History, 1993, p. 20.

201.　Public prosecutors

Friedman, Crime and Punishment in American History, 1993, p. 29.

during the colonial period.[202] But as we have seen, as the Revolution approached, the demands for the "common law" grew more insistent and more uniform in the different colonies.[203] But as one historian of the colonial period wrote,

> when we * * * find expressions of admiration for or adherence to the common law, such as are very common in the succeeding century, and especially at the beginning of the Revolutionary War, they refer rather to the general principles of personal liberty than to the vast body of rules regulating the rights of contract and property and the ordinary proceedings in court.[204]

Hence, after Independence more was required of the states than simply striking the King's name from criminal pleadings; they had to consider anew just what were the sources of the law to be applied in their courts.[205]

Between 1776 and 1784, 11 of the 13 original states attempted to deal with this uncertainty by adopting what have come to be known, somewhat misleadingly, as "reception statutes;" legislative authorization for courts to draw on the English common law.[206] By 1824, "High Federalists" were using these statutes to claim that "all the original states * * * adopted the English Common Law."[207] This overstates in more than numbers; only one of the reception statutes could be read as a wholesale adoption of the English common law—and that in a state that very quickly began a rather wholesale legislative alteration of that law.[208] Most of the statutes

202. Bitter controversy

Smith & Barnes, The English Legal System: Carryover to the Colonies, 1975, p. 17.

203. Demands for "common law"

Id. at p. 21. See also, vol. 30, § 6345, text at notecall 497.

204. "General principles"

Reinsch, The English Common Law in the Early American Colonies, in 1 Select Essays in Anglo–American Legal History, 1907, p. 384.

205. Striking King's name

Friedman, Crime and Punishment in American History, 1993, p. 20.

206. "Reception statutes"

Horwitz, The Transformation of American Law, 1977, p. 4. For Madison's comments on the Virginia statute, see 2 The Republic of Letters, Smith ed. 1995, pp. 1125–11–26.

For Randolph's proposal for a federal statute adopting the common law for federal courts, see Cummings & McFarland, Federal Justice, 1933, p . 21.

207. "All adopted"

The Legal Mind in America, Miller ed. 1969, p. 139.

208. Legislative alteration

The state was Virginia. 1 Goebel, History of the Supreme Court of the United States, 1971, pp. 110 n. 53, 230.

qualified the adoption of the English common law by specifying only as that law was used during the colonial period or only as it was used prior to a certain date.[209] These qualifications recognized that in many cases colonial courts and legislatures had rejected the English common law as unsuitable for American conditions.[210] The original draft of the Rules of Decision Act shows that those who drafted the Confrontation Clause were well aware that the common law of the states had diverged from the English common law.[211] Moreover, the Second Congress rejected a proposal to adopt English common-law practice.[212] But for our purposes the most significant feature of the reception statutes is that they all barred the use of common-law rules that were inconsistent with state constitutions or bills of rights.[213]

Even without reception statutes, the English common law provided something like a fall-back authority that could be used when there was no American law available; certainly this was how it was used by the federal courts.[214] The use of English precedents in early cases was less a result of the reception statutes than of the absence of any printed sources of colonial judicial decisions; with the publication of reports of American judicial opinions, the citation of English cases declined.[215] When the United States Supreme Court appointed a Reporter to arrange for publication of their opinions, an editorial writer for the National Intelligencer applaud-

209. Used prior to certain date

1 Goebel, History of the Supreme Court of the United States, 1971, p. 110 n. 53.

210. Rejected as unsuitable

The Legal Mind in America, Miller ed. 1969, p. 301.

211. States had diverged.

The draft would have required federal courts to follow state statutes "and their unwritten or common law now in use, whether by adoption from the common law of England" or from English statutes or of local origin. 1 Goebel, History of the Supreme Court of the United States, 1971, p. 502.

212. Rejected common law

Henderson, Courts For A New Nation, 1971, p. 41. The closest thing to a reception statute the Confederation Congress ever adopted was the Northwest Ordinance, which gave the territorial courts common law jurisdiction and required proceedings "according to the course of the common law." Blume, Civil Procedure on The American Frontier, 1957, 56 Mich.L.Rev. 161, 168. However, the draft of the statute makes it clear that "common law" was being used in contradistinction to "chancery." Id. at 169.

213. Bills of rights

1 Goebel, History of the Supreme Court of the United States, 1971, p. 110.

214. Fall-back authority

Id. at p. 618.

215. Citation declined

Brown, British Statutes in American Law, 1776–1846, 1964, p. 41.

ed this as a step that would produce an American common law "independent of that servile recourse to the decisions of foreign Judicatures to which, since our revolution, we have been too much accustomed."[216] The "foreign Judicatures" alludes to the fact that some American courts had been quite eclectic in fashioning their own common law, borrowing from the French as well as the British authorities.[217]

This eclecticism was driven by a number of socio-political forces opposing wholesale adoption of English law.[218] Perhaps the most powerful of these was the rise of the notion of American exceptionalism.[219] Even as sober a person as Chancellor James Kent of New York believed that Americans were "distinguished from all other people on the face of the globe" and were destined to "change the conditions of humanity."[220] Americans, or so they thought, were a forward-looking and progressive lot without a decadent past.[221] They were not bound to the feudal institutions that had shaped the English common law;[222] as one poet wrote:

Where happy millions their own fields possess,

No tyrant awes them, and no lords oppress.[223]

216. "Too much accustomed"

1 Warren, The Supreme Court in United States History, 1947 ed. p. 288 n. 1.

217. Eclectic

Aumann, The Influence of English and Civil Law Principles Upon The American Legal System During The Critical Post–Revolutionary Period, 1938, 12 U.Cinci.L.Rev. 289; Stein, The Attraction of The Civil Law in Post–Revolutionary America, 1966, 52 Va.L.Rev. 403, 407.

218. Forces opposing

Many of these intellectual currents flowed from the Revolution. See, e.g., vol. 30, § 6345, text at notecall 256.

219. American exceptionalism

Nye, The Cultural Life of The New Nation, paper 1963, p. 45. Readers unfamiliar with the connotations of this term need only recall the way in which our television networks presented the 1996 Olympic games.

220. "Change humanity"

Id. at p. 47. For more on Kent, see below, text at notecall 569.

221. Progressive lot

Welter, The Mind of America, 1820–1836, 1975, p. 11.

222. Feudal past

"[T]he spirit of liberty and reform is making its way in every corner of the globe, and sooner or later, will consign to one common ruin, all those despotic institutions, which are the time-work relics of a feudal age." Ibid. (quoting Kenneth Rayner of North Carolina). The Legal Mind in America, Miller ed. 1969, p. 137 (common law shaped by feudalism).

223. "No lords oppress"

Nye, The Cultural Life of the New Nation, paper 1963, p. 46.

The United States, if not a classless society, was not class-obsessed like the English judges who shaped the common law.[224] The physical environment of the New World supposedly provided an environment conducive to the evolution of a New People; as one popular song went

> The fruits of our country, our flocks and our fleeces,
>
> The treasures immersed in our mountains that lie,
>
> While discord is tearing old Europe to pieces,
>
> Shall amply the wants of our people supply.[225]

Like the editor of the National Intelligencer, many Americans thought that reliance upon British sources compromised our independence.[226] Even Noah Webster, no Anglophobe, thought that "America must be as independent in literature as she is in politics."[227] A people who wanted their children to speak "an American tongue" did not look kindly on judicial opinions written in the diction of the English common law.[228]

By the end of the 18th Century, Americans of English descent were a dwindling but still powerful minority.[229] Envy often came disguised as a strong anti-British prejudice.[230] We have previously seen how the Federalists were attacked as seeking to re-impose English institutions, such as the monarchy and an aristocracy, on the country.[231] The Alien Act did little to endear them or the English to Americans from other lands.[232] The War of 1812 solidi-

224. Class-obsessed

Welter, The Mind of America, 1820–1836, 1975, p. 7.

225. "Wants supply"

Nye, The Cultural Life of the New Nation, paper 1963, p. 45.

226. Compromised independence

The Legal Mind in America, Miller ed. 1969, p. 114.

227. Must be independent

Nye, The Cultural Life of the New Nation, paper 1963, 239.

228. "American tongue"

Id. at p. 243.

229. Powerful minority

Nye, The Cultural Life of the New Nation, paper 1963, p. 121.

230. Anti–British prejudice

Welter, The Mind of America, 1820–1860, 1975, p. 32.

231. Seeking monarchy

See vol. 30, § 6346, text at notecall 438. Even John Adams wondered "that some persons among us are so eager to rush into the arms of Great Britain, but it is unaccountable that there should be so many." Ellis, Passionate Sage, 1993, p. 108.

232. Seeking monarchy

Elkins & McKitrick, The Age of Federalism, 1993, pp. 694–700.

fied anti-British sentiments.[233] A British precedent for any policy was enough to condemn it in the eyes of many and the Republicans of Jefferson were as eager to exploit such feelings as their post-Civil War namesakes were to "wave the bloody flag."[234] Naturally this antipathy rubbed off on the English common law.[235]

Popular hatred of the common law persisted well into the 19th Century.[236] Many leaders of the legal profession had been Tories during the Revolution.[237] Many prominent judges and lawyers in the new nation favored High Federalism;[238] even Jared Ingersoll, himself the son of a loyalist, thought "American lawyers and judges adhere with professional tenacity to the laws of the mother country."[239] Chancellor James Kent wrote that "the influence of the Common Law was strongly felt and widely diffused by our American ancestors, from the time of their emigration from Europe and settlement on this side of the Atlantic."[240] The aristocratic attitudes of High Federalist judges and lawyers bred a resentment of them and the law they stood for.[241] One labor leader, in a Fourth of July oration, declaimed:

> [t]he judiciary * * * is the headquarters of the aristocracy and every plan to humble and subdue the people originates there. One of the most enormous usurpations of the judiciary is the claim * * * of common law jurisdiction. Common law, although con-

233. War of 1812

Welter, The Mind of America, 1820–1860, 1975, p. 32.

234. Eager to exploit

Ibid.

235. Rubbed off

Horton, James Kent: A Study in Conservatism, 1939, p. 141.

236. Hatred persisted

The Legal Mind in America, Miller ed. 1969, p. 41.

237. Been Tories

Aumann, The Influence of English and Civil Law Principles Upon The American Legal System During the Critical Post–Revolutionary Period, 1938, 12 U.Cinci.L.Rev. 289, 296.

238. Favored Federalism

Id. at p. 300.

239. "Adhere with tenacity"

The Legal Mind in America, Miller ed. 1969, pp. 76, 78.

240. "Influence of Common Law"

Kent's Introductory Lecture, 1903, 3 Col.L.Rev. 330, 332. For more on Kent, see below, text at notecall 569.

241. Bred resentment

Aumann, The Influence of English and Civil Law Principles Upon The American Legal System During the Critical Post–Revolutionary Period, 1938, 12 U.Cinci.L.Rev. 289, 301.

For Attorney General Rodney's complaint about how quickly new judges caught "the leprosy of the Bench," see Cummings & McFarland, Federal Justice, 1937, p. 70.

tained in ten thousand books, is said to be unwritten law, deposited only in the head of the judge, so that what he says is common law, must be common law.[242]

Little wonder that newspapers proclaimed the use of the common law a step toward monarchy and even lawyers thought the profession should shed its attachment to the English common law.[243]

The common law seemed to many to be inconsistent with a republican form of government.[244] A newspaper editorial said "the English common law [is not] exactly calculated for a free nation and a virtuous people."[245] Attorney General Richard Rush argued that this was particularly true of the common law of crimes.

> I do not think that a Federal Republic, like ours, resting upon, as its only pillars, the limited political concessions of distinct and independent sovereign States, drew to itself, by any just implication, at the moment of its circumscribed structure, the whole common law of England, with all or any portion of its dark catalogue of crimes and punishments; * * * a code which, among the vast variety of actions that, in a complicated community, human frailty may be betrayed into, denounces, upon scarcely less than two hundred, capital infliction, thereby, as the melancholy fruits of such a system * * * imprinting more of human blood upon the gibbet than is known to the same extent of population in any other portion of Europe.[246]

William Sampson feared the influence of the common law upon students of the law.

> The Commentaries of Sir William Blackstone are still the only clue where by to tread the mazy labyrinth through which they have to pass; and the fascinating eloquence of that author, conceals a thousand sophistries dangerous to the principles which every

242. "What he says must be"

Dunne, Justice Joseph Story and The Rise of The Supreme Court, 1970, p. 316.

243. Should shed common law

1 Warren, The Supreme Court in United States History, 1947 ed. 163; The Legal Mind in America, Miller ed. 1069, p. 17.

244. Republican form

Aumann, The Influence of English and Civil Law Principles Upon The Ameri-

can Legal System During The Critical Post–Revolutionary Period, 1938, 12 U.Cinci.L.Rev. 289, 305.

245. "Free and virtuous"

1 Warren, The Supreme Court in United States History, 1947 ed., p. 310.

246. "More human blood"

Id. at p. 439.

citizen of our free republic ought, and every professor of our laws is sworn, to maintain.[247]

Others found the fictions and formalities of the English common law alien to the values of clear-sighted and plain-speaking Americans.[248]

The cry that the English common law was undemocratic rested on a number of concrete objections.[249] In the wake of the Revolution, English creditors relied on the common law to collect debts that some Americans thought they ought not to, or at least would not have to, pay.[250] With the fragmentation of the Federalist consensus into proto-party factions, the common law of seditious libel was a handy weapon against political opponents.[251] The English common law was relied upon for and became associated with the hated Alien and Sedition laws.[252] As capitalists increasingly relied on repressive common law to beat back the attempts of labor to improve wages and working conditions, it was seen as "the enemy of the people" and the tool of judicial "aristocrats" out of step with ordinary people.[253] Finally, since the English common law did not recognize slavery, it could not be used by slaveholders to bolster their increasingly tenuous moral position, and its failure to provide any limits on what masters could do to slaves neutralized any appeal it might have had to incipient abolitionists.[254]

Behind the anti-common law rhetoric lurked genuine jurisprudential issues.[255] Federalist distaste for "faction" and controversy led to a desire to substitute law for politics.[256] Common law,

247. "Thousand sophistries"

The Legal Mind in America, Miller ed. 1969, p. 122.

248. Fictions and formalities

Horton, James Kent: A Study in Conservatism, 1939, p. 142.

249. Undemocratic

Horton, James Kent: A Study in Conservatism, 1939, p. 144.

250. Collect debts

Ibid.

251. Handy weapon

Id. at p. 145.

252. Alien and Sedition

1 Warren, The Supreme Court in United States History, 1947 ed. pp. 159–163.

253. "Enemy of people"

Levy, The Law of the Commonwealth and Chief Justice Shaw, 1957, 197.

254. Slavery

Rose, What We Didn't Know About Slavery, N.Y.Rev.Bks., Oct. 17, 1974, p. 29.

255. Genuine issues

Issues that are by no means resolved today, even though they no longer play so prominent a role in partisan politics.

256. Law for politics

Welter, The Mind of America, 1820–1860, pp. 187–188.

whether English or American, was and is a device for judicial policymaking.[257] But policymaking by judges ran counter to the Republican desire for popular control of government.[258] Moreover, it revived Revolutionary concerns and rhetoric over official discretion.[259] Judges, it was said "by boundless construction of common law assume the most dangerous power."[260] "Judicial legislation" was troublesome because it seemed to operate free of the constitutional restraints on legislative bodies.[261] Since it only became certain after the courts decided a specific case, it looked like a kind of "ex post facto law."[262] Finally, since the common law could not be known by ordinary people, it left them at the mercy of the "aristocrats" of the bench and the legal profession, thus depriving them of the autonomy that the Revolution had seemed to promise.[263]

However, these deeper questions got short shrift when with the hardening of the two Federalist factions into political parties, the English common law became something of a political football.[264] The majority of the Philadelphia Convention rejected the idea that the common law should be made a part of the constitution as had been proposed by some states.[265] However, the states themselves soon turned against the English common law; a prominent Michigan judge denied that the common law had ever been part of territorial or state law despite a provision in the Northwest Ordinance that might be read as contemplating such incorporation.[266] Some states attempted to prohibit the citation of English authori-

257. Judicial policymaking

Foner, Get A Lawyer!, N.Y.Rev.Bks., April 14, 1977, p. 37.

258. Popular control

See vol. 30, § 6346, text at notecall 593.

259. Discretion

Horwitz, The Transformation of American Law, 1977, p. 12.

260. "Boundless power"

1 Warren, The Supreme Court in United States History, 1947 ed., p. 205.

261. "Judicial legislation"

Rantoul, Memoirs, Speeches, and Writings, Hamilton ed. 1854, p. 278.

262. "Ex post facto"

Ibid.

263. Depriving of autonomy

The Legal Mind in America, Miller ed. 1969, p. 223.

264. Political parties.

Nye, The Cultural Life of the New Nation, paper 1963, p. 110.

265. Majority rejected

1 Goebel, History of the Supreme Court of the United States, 1971, pp. 229–230.

266. Michigan judge denied

Blume, Civil Procedure on the American Frontier, 1957, 56 Mich.L.Rev. 161, 168.

ties in their courts.[267] Perhaps in reaction to the use of English common law to justify the Alien and Sedition Acts,[268] Edmund Pendleton of the Virginia Court of Appeals proposed an amendment to the U.S. Constitution "[t]o declare that the Common Law of England, or of any other foreign country, in criminal cases, shall not be considered as a law of the United States."[269] Those who wanted to see the English common law play a more prominent role in American law were hindered in the early years of the Republic by the scarcity of English lawbooks on this side of the Atlantic.[270] One lawyer, apparently wishing it had stayed that way, told Emerson that it ought to be a crime to bring English lawbooks into the country.[271]

As the leader of the party associated most strongly with opposition to the English common law and as a drafter of a confrontation clause proposed for the Virginia Constitution, the views of Thomas Jefferson are significant.[272] As a political leader, Jefferson expressed doubts about John Adams as President because of "his bias to an English constitution"—an ironic judgment since this is precisely what Adams disliked in the Hamiltonian wing of his own party.[273] Jefferson saw the English common law as part of the "Norman yoke" that the Conqueror had imposed upon a supposedly more

267. Prohibit citation

Brown, British Statutes in American Law, 1776–1836, 1964 p. 41 (New Jersey, Kentucky, and Pennsylvania); Aumann, The Influence of English and Civil Law Principles Upon the American Legal System During the Critical Post–Revolutionary Period, 1938, 12 U.Cinci.L.Rev. 289, 293.

268. Justify Sedition Acts

Pendleton also thought that the Treason Clause of the Constitution should be literally construed "so as not to be extended further, by law, or construction, or by using terms such as sedition." Powell, Languages of Power, 1991, p. 152. On the use of English common law to justify the Sedition Act, see id. at p. 127.

269. "Not law of United States"

Ibid.

270. Scarcity of lawbooks

Horton, James Kent: A Study in Conservatism, 1939, p. 140.

271. Crime to bring lawbooks

Aumann, The Influence of English and Civil Law Principles Upon The American Legal System During the Critical Post–Revolutionary Period, 1938, 12 U.Cinci.L.Rev. 289, 293.

272. Jefferson

On Jefferson's confrontation proposal, see vol. 30, § 6346, text at notecall 133. For his proposal for the election of jurors, see 2 The Republic of Letters, Smith ed. 1995, p. 1076.

273. "Bias to English"

Elkins & McKitrick, The Age of Federalism, 1993, pp. 540 (Jefferson on Adams), p. 736 (Adams on the "British faction" of Federalists).

democratic indigenous law.[274] Jefferson thought that the English common law could be made part of American law only by specific legislative authorization.[275]

Other members of the Founding Generation also opposed the common law; for example, James Monroe thought judges who cited the English common law should be impeached.[276] On the Federalist side, John Marshall, who had been a member of the Virginia Convention, thought the notion that the Federal judiciary was embarked on a campaign to incorporate the English common law into federal jurisprudence was a "strange & absurd doctrine" concocted "by some frothy newspaper."[277] Writing to St. George Tucker, a prominent Republican jurist and professor of law at William and Mary who had sent him a copy of a pamphlet he had written refuting the claim that the Constitution adopted the English common law, Marshall said:

> I do not believe that one man can be found who maintains the affirmative of this proposition. Neither in public nor in private have I ever heard it advocated, & I am as entirely confident as I can be at anything of the sort, that it has never been advocated.[278]

Marshall was not the only Justice of the Supreme Court who rejected the idea; Samuel Chase, later to be impeached by the Jeffersonians, ruled from the bench that the common law of England was not part of federal law.[279] Even James Kent, who was later to play such a prominent role in the reception of English common law into American state law, conceded in his law lectures at Columbia

---

274. "Norman yoke"

Waterman, Thomas Jefferson and Blackstone's Commentaries, 1933, 27 Ill. L.Rev. 629, 640-641. For the origins of the "Norman yoke" theory, see vol. 30, § 6342, text at notecall 71.

275. Specific authorization

Nye, The Cultural Life of the New Nation, paper 1963, p. 238.

276. Impeached

1 Warren, The Supreme Court in United States History, 1947 ed., p. 229.

277. "Frothy newspaper"

Powell, Languages of Power, 1991, pp. 175–176.

278. "Never been advocated"

Id. at p. 175. A cynic might say that Marshall had little need for the common law because as a judge he seldom cited precedents but simply made up the law as he went along. However, even as a lawyer he had followed a practice of reasoning from supposedly basic principles rather than peppering his briefs with authorities. Elkins & McKitrick, The Age of Federalism, 1993, p. 559.

279. Not federal law

Id. at p. 119.

that many of the fundamental doctrines of [English] Government, and Axioms of their Jurisprudence, are utterly subversive of an Equality of Rights, and totally incompatible with the liberal spirit of our American Establishments.[280]

Similar sentiments were expressed by Kent's contemporaries.[281] Hence, it is little wonder that when the issue reached it, the Supreme Court rejected the notion that federal courts had been given common law criminal powers by the Constitution.[282]

Even lawyers who appreciated the uncertainty created by the rejection of the common law were in a poor position to defend it.[283] As to the English common law, the lack of law books made it impossible for lawyers in many parts of the new nation to know just what it was.[284] The absence of reliable records of the colonial courts made it difficult to construct an "American" or even a "Virginian" common law.[285] But perhaps the greatest source of vulnerability was what one lawyer has called "the sorry state" of the profession.[286] Many leading lawyers had fled and their Loyalist sentiments tarred those who remained.[287] Moreover, hostility to the English common law could easily extend to lawyers who defended it, adding yet another count to the indictment of the profession.[288]

The Judiciary and The Chase Impeachment

Nor was the judiciary in a particularly strong position at the turn of the Century.[289] The notion that the law could provide a substitute for politics took a beating in the episode of the so-called "midnight judges"; as they were about to turn over power to the

280. "Utterly subversive"

Id. at p. 91.

281. Similar sentiments

The Legal Mind in America, Miller ed. 1969, pp. 20, 29, 34.

282. Supreme Court rejected

1 Warren, The Supreme Court in United States History, 1947 ed., p. 785.

283. Uncertainty created

Miller, The Legal Mind in America, 1969, p. 17.

284. Lack of law books

Ibid.

285. Colonial records

Ibid.

286. "Sorry state"

Ibid.

287. Loyalist lawyers

Ibid.

288. Hostility

Ibid.

289. Position of judiciary

Federalist partisans continued to trumpet this vulnerability long after it had ceased to exist, partly as a justification for their domination of this branch of government long after they had been repudiated at the polls. See, e.g., id. at p. 73.

Republicans, the Federalists in Congress created a number of additional judicial positions and President Adams filled many of them on the very eve of his departure from office.[290] As a result, throughout the Jeffersonian era there was not a single Republican on the federal bench.[291] Indeed, the Federalists continued to dominate the federal judiciary long after they had ceased to be a viable electoral force.[292]

The Jeffersonians, still steaming over the role of the federal judges in the political prosecutions of a number of Republican stalwarts, launched a counterattack that included the impeachment of Federalist judges for their conduct of these trials.[293] Justice Chase of the Supreme Court was an attractive target because he rather noisily blamed all the social evils of the time on the Republican values of liberty and equality.[294] Indeed, one of the charges in the articles of Chase's impeachment involved a political harangue to a grand jury in Baltimore that included the following line:

> The change of the State constitution, by allowing universal suffrage, will in my opinion, certainly and rapidly destroy all protection to property and all security to personal liberty; and our republican constitution will sink into a mobocracy, the worst of all possible governments.[295]

Given the scant relevance of these sentiments to the duties of the grand jury, it is not surprising that Chase became the first——and the last——Supreme Court Justice to be impeached.[296]

The trial of Justice Chase reveals much of the conceptual apparatus in which the right of confrontation was embedded.[297] For

---

290. "Midnight judges"

Encyclopedia of American History, Morris ed. 1976, p. 157. See also, Frankfurter & Landis, The Business of the Supreme Court, 1928 p. 25 (the Midnight Judges Act "combined thoughtful concern for the federal judiciary with selfish concern for the Federalist Party").

291. Not a Republican

1 Warren, The Supreme Court in United States History, 1947 ed., p. 190.

292. Continued to dominate

Bartlett, Daniel Webster, 1978, p. 75.

293. Republicans steaming

Miller, The Federalist Era, paper 1963, p. 236.

294. Blamed evils on equality

1 Warren, The Supreme Court in United States History, 1947 ed., p. 277.

295. "Mobocracy"

14 Annals of Congress, 8th Cong., 2d.Sess., 1804, p. 146.

296. Chase impeached

Encyclopedia of American History, Morris ed. 1976, p. 160.

297. Right embedded

As we have previously seen, "trial by jury" was often a synonym for an

example, one of the grounds of impeachment was that while sitting on circuit at the trial of a Republican publicist charged with violating the Sedition Act, Chase refused to allow counsel to argue the law to the jury.[298] Apparently counsel wished to argue that the Alien and Sedition Acts were unconstitutional.[299] Denying the jury the power to decide law as well as fact was claimed to be a denial of trial by jury.[300] Except for Luther Martin,[301] no one seems to have thought that the jury did not have the power to decide law as well as fact or that the denial of a single incident of jury trial violated the right to trial by jury.[302] Chase admitted that he refused to allow counsel to cite English treason cases, defending this on the ground that English law did not apply in America, but showed that he had told the jury that they had the power to decide the law.[303] To this, one of the Republican managers replied that he had never before heard anyone argue that the jury had the power, but not the right, to decide the law.[304] Edmund Randolph emphatically denied that the jury was bound by the judge's exposition of the law and tried to tar the defense with allusions to Popery and the hint that Justice Chase's conduct of the trial resembled the hated inquisitorial tribunals.[305]

In some cases, Republican complaints of Chase's inquisitorial behavior were tied explicitly to the Sixth Amendment; e.g., when his refusal to grant a continuance until defense witnesses arrived was cast as a denial of the right of compulsory process.[306] The

accusatorial system of justice rather than a narrow right to have twelve men in the box. See vol. 30, § 6347, text at notecall 314.

298. Argue law

14 Annals of Congress, 8th Cong., 2d. Sess., 1804, p. 85.

299. Unconstitutional

Id. at p. 202.

300. Denial of jury trial

Id. at p. 610.

301. Luther Martin

Id. at p. 501. Martin had been a delegate to the Constitutional Convention, but this gave him no special insight into the meaning of the Sixth Amendment because "the framers of the Constitution" that Martin invoked were not

the people who had drafted the Bill of Rights.

302. No one thought did not

Id. at 155. The notion that the jury had the power to determine the law was dominant for much of the 19th Century. See Howe, Juries as Judges of Criminal Law, 1939, 52 Harv.L.Rev. 582.

303. Chase told jury

Id. at pp. 110, 115.

304. Never heard

Id. at p. 580 (Mr. Nicholson).

305. Allusions to Popery

Id. at pp. 155, 655.

306. Compulsory process

Id. at pp. 210, 326.

connections to confrontation values were more subtle.[307] When Chase required defense counsel to submit questions to be put to witnesses in writing for his approval,[308] this smacked of the questioning by interrogatories that was the characteristic of vice-admiralty procedure.[309] Moreover, Chase was charged with blurring the separation of functions that confrontation serves to foster by his "indecent solicitude * * * for the conviction of the accused, unbecoming even a public prosecutor, but highly disgraceful to the character of a judge, as it was subversive of justice."[310]

This violation of separation of functions is seen more clearly in the explanation of the seventh article of impeachment, in which it was alleged that "the said Samuel Chase, disregarding the duties of his office, did descend from the dignity of a judge, and stoop to the level of an informer * * *."[311] This charge was based on Chase's alleged refusal to discharge a grand jury that had refused to return any indictments under the Sedition Act, complaining to the jurors about an unnamed "most seditious printer" of whom he had personal knowledge, and ordering the prosecutor to procure a file of seditious printings for the grand jury's perusal.[312] This charge was expanded upon by one of the managers:

> But Judge Chase, disregarding these principles [of judicial impartiality], always held sacred in a land of laws, converts himself into a hunter after accusations. He who, in the humane language of the laws, should be counsel for the accused, becomes himself an accuser. He, whose duty it is impartially to decide between the

307. Connections subtle

For example, Luther Martin in defense of Chase had been harshly critical of the lack of evidence in support of the charges, but then made clear that he did not mean to excoriate the House: "In saying this, I do not mean in the slightest to censure that honorable body, they were acting as the grand inquest of the nation; they only had, and they only could have, before them, ex parte evidence." Id. at p. 501. In other words, it might be all right for the House, functioning in the inquisitorial role of the grand jury, to rely on unconfronted testimony, but the Senate as the "jurors" in the case could see how confrontation had melted away the probative force of the accusers.

308. Reduced to writing

Id. at p. 86.

309. Vice-admiralty

See vol. 30, § 6345, text at notecall 388.

310. "Subversive of justice"

14 Annals of Congress, 8th Cong., 2d Sess. 1804, p. 86. On the relationship between confrontation and the separation of functions, see vol. 30, § 6341, text at notecall 22.

311. "Level of informer"

Id. at p. 87.

312. "Seditious printer"

Id. at p. 327.

prosecutor and the prosecuted, becomes himself the procurer of prosecutions.[313]

This picture of an inquisitorial judge would be distressingly familiar to those who had read of the conduct of the judges of the court of High Commission or Star Chamber in Foxe's Book of Martyrs.[314] The tendency of judges to assume the inquisitorial role was also advanced as a reason for giving the jury the right to determine the law; "it is the glory of the laws of this country, that the offence of the accused should be left exclusively to the judgment of those least liable to be swayed by the weight of the accusing influence."[315]

As the belief that the jury has the right to determine the law suggests, the Founders' notion of just where the functions of judge, jury, and witness were to be separated was not the same as ours.[316] A better illustration of the differing notions is the belief expressed more than once at the Chase trial that jurors were to decide the case on their own knowledge, not solely on the testimony of witnesses; indeed, one speaker claimed that a juror who had witnessed the commission of a crime was not disqualified from serving in a prosecution for its commission.[317]

The Chase trial provides one tantalizing bit of evidence about how the relationship between hearsay and confrontation was perceived.[318] When a witness testified to a hearsay description of the conduct of Justice Chase, his counsel rose and said:

> Mr. President, surely it is improper that the witness should repeat what Mr. Lewis told him, not in court, nor when the judge was present.[319]

The witness, who was a lawyer, responded:

> Sir, I know the rules of evidence, and I mean to conform to them.
> * * * If, Mr. President, the counsel's patience had lasted for a

313. "Becomes procurer"

Ibid.

314. Book of Martyrs

See vol. 30, § 6342, text at notecall 443.

315. "Accusing influence"

14 Annals of Congress, 8th Cong., 2d Sess., 1804, p. 314.

316. Not the same as ours

See the remarks cited in notes 298–304 above.

317. Juror witnessed crime

14 Annals of Congress, 8th Cong., 2d Sess., 1804, p. 457.

318. Hearsay perceived

It is noteworthy that neither of the speakers uttered the word hearsay. Id. at pp. 173–174. This seems to support the idea that hearsay was still not a well-developed part of the trial lawyer's conceptual armory.

319. "Judge was present"

Id. at p. 173.

minute, he would have heard that I repeated Mr. Lewis's communication to the court and that it was not contradicted.[320]

This seems to have satisfied the objector.[321] Both he and the witness seem to have assumed that the defect in this bit of hearsay was that the accused had not been confronted with it and that once the accused had had an opportunity to respond to the statement, it became admissible under "the rules of evidence."[322]

In view of what courts were to hold with respect to the meaning of the right of confrontation, it is worth adding yet another bit of evidence regarding the Founders' attitude toward English law.[323] One of the managers, Mr. Nicholson, in explaining why he disdained to cite English precedents regarding impeachable offenses, said:

> I feel no disposition to resort to foreign precedents. In my judgment, the Constitution of the United States ought to be expounded upon its own principles, and that foreign aid ought never to be called in. Our Constitution was fashioned after none other in the known world, and if we understand the language in which it is written, we require no assistance in giving it a true exposition.[324]

Similar statements were made by other speakers.[325]

Confrontation and Dueling

Judicial confrontation in the early years of the republic drew psychological sustenance from the political confrontations that erupted with the fissuring of the Federalist consensus and the growth of political parties.[326] No confrontation was more dramatic

320. Not contradicted

Id. at p. 374.

321. Satisfied objector

Ibid.

322. Became admissible

In modern parlance, this might be seen as an "adoptive admission"—but we have seen no evidence that this concept then existed.

323. Founders' attitude

See text at note 236, above.

324. "Require no assistance"

Id. at p. 562.

325. Similar statements

See, e.g., id. at p. 619 ("The text of our Constitution is sufficiently plain without any British glossary.").

326. Political confrontations

One of the most salacious involved the Secretary of the Treasury, Alexander Hamilton. Two men under indictment for fraud and suborning perjury tried to blackmail Hamilton into using his influence on their behalf and when he refused, one of them tried to suggest to Hamilton's political enemies that Hamilton had been involved in improper speculation. When two Congressmen and Senator James Monroe decided to confront Hamilton with these insinuations, Hamilton read let-

than the one between Alexander Hamilton, the Federalist elitist who cared little for ordinary people whom he viewed as hostile to his nationalist ambitions, and Aaron Burr, the Republican politician who was regarded even by Jefferson as the epitome of the corrupt power seeker the Constitution was designed to restrain.[327] On July 11, 1804, the two men met in a duel in Weehawken, New Jersey where Burr killed Hamilton.[328] The public outrage renewed anti-dueling sentiments.[329]

Despite the fact that dueling was illegal in most states,[330] the public then was as ambivalent about these fatal confrontations as modern editorialists are about judicial confrontations.[331] The resemblances between the two ran deep.[332] Like the excesses that fuel modern complaints about the adversary system, the Burr–Hamilton duel was atypical; most duels did not end in death.[333] Like cross-examination, most duels were highly ritualistic; a book on the etiquette of dueling first published in 1838, ran through several editions over the next twenty years.[334] One student of its history has described "the great evil" at which dueling was aimed in terms

ters to them which documented his real connection to the two crooks; he had been making whoopee with a woman who was married to both of the culprits. Elkins & McKitrick, The Age of Federalism, 1993, pp. 293–294.

327. Corrupt power seeker

On Hamilton's elitism, see Miller, The Federalist Era, paper 1963, p. 39. Burr, whose correspondence was unique among the statesmen of the Revolutionary era in having little to say about government or political philosophy, but was filled with wheeling and dealing in speculative political ventures, was said by his contemporaries to be "unsettled in his politics" and to have "no fixed principles, no consistency of character"—the Bill Clinton of his time. Wood, The Revenge of Aaron Burr, N.Y.Rev.Bks., February 2, 1984, pp. 23, 25. See also, note 419, below.

For John Marshall's analysis of confrontation as the trial judge in the Burr conspiracy trial, see § 6356, text at notecall 748.

328. Burr killed Hamilton

Friedman, Crime and Punishment in American History, 1993, p. 177.

329. Anti-dueling sentiments

Boorstin, The Americans: The National Experience, paper 1965, p. 207.

330. Illegal in most states

Ibid.

331. Ambivalent

Friedman, Crime and Punishment in American History, 1993, pp. 177–179.

332. Resemblances

In both, the willingness to stand up to one's adversary was symbolic of one's rectitude. Both involved the use of intermediaries to arrange them—lawyers and "seconds."

333. Did not end in death

Id. at p. 178.

334. Book on etiquette

Boorstin, The Americans: The National Experience, paper 1965, p. 209.

that display its resemblance to judicial confrontation: "[t]he slanderous tongue of the calumniator, who, by secret whisper or artful innuendo, has sapped and undermined [the challenger's] reputation."[335] Andrew Jackson, himself a frequent dueler, thought that "the slanderer [is] worse than the murderer."[336] As the historian wrote "[t]he duel was a ritual in which a gentleman submitted himself to the community's good opinion."[337] Those who opposed dueling might well have seen judicial confrontation as a more rational and less violent alternative to the duels of gentlemen and the tavern brawls by which the great unwashed vindicated their own claims to "honor."[338]

The year 1807 marked the first reported construction of a state confrontation clause.[339] In a case of petit larceny, the principal witness against the defendant——called in the report of the case "the prosecutor"——had died and the attorney-general offered in evidence his testimony at a former trial of the same offense.[340] The

---

335. "Secret whisper"

Id. at p. 210 (quoting book on dueling).

336. "Slanderer worse"

Ibid.

337. "Duel was a ritual"

Id. at pp. 210–211.

338. Claims to "honor"

Id. at p. 210. While dueling died out in the original colonies after the Civil War, it continued on the frontier in the form that retains cinematic vitality down to the present day——the "walkdown" at "High Noon," in which the hero invites the villain to "step outside and say that." Furnas, The Americans: A Social History of The United States, 1969, pp. 528–531. See also, Woodward, The Primal Code, N.Y.Rev.Bks., Nov. 18, 1982, pp. 26, 27 ("Duels, like other rituals of virility and violence, were not assertions of individualism but responses to the demands of community opinion * * *.")

339. First construction

Or at least the first one we have been able to find using conventional research methods.

In a very early case, a North Carolina court rejected a prosecution attempt to use a South Carolina deposition, saying "it is a rule of the common law, founded on natural justice, that no man shall be prejudiced by evidence which he had not the liberty to cross examine." State v. Webb, 1794, 2 N.C. (1 Hayw.) 103. One writer apparently thinks this case supports the view that the right of confrontation is a right to cross examine. Jonankait, The Origins of The Confrontation Clause: An Alternative History, 1995, 27 Rutgers L.J. 77, 122. However, the case does not cite or mention the North Carolina confrontation clause, which gave the accused the right "to confront the accusers and witnesses with other testimony." See vol. 30, § 6346, text at notecall 212.

340. Former trial

State v. Atkins, 1807, 1 Tenn. (Overton) 229. At the time misdemeanors were apparently tried in the County Court and the defendant could appeal through a trial de novo in the District Court. Hence, though technically on appeal, the decision was by a trial court excluding the evidence.

defense "objected, and relied upon the Constitution, which provided that the witnesses should be confronted with the accused."[341] The opinion of the District Court was brief:

> The testimony cannot be received. In England, in criminal cases other than informations it could not. No case in point is recollected in the books. The principal reason is trials in Nisi Prius where, agreeably to Magna Charta, witnesses are confronted are not generally reported. Though no cases in point have been produced, we understand that evidence could not be received agreeable to Magna Charta.[342]

The court is mistaken here; Magna Carta has nothing on the right of confrontation[343] and the testimony of deceased witnesses given at the preliminary hearing was admissible.[344] After explaining that in Tennessee cases are first tried in the county courts with an appeal de novo to the district court, the report continues:

> * * * frequent deaths may take place between the trial there and here, and it seems to us that it would be dangerous to liberty to admit such evidence. It would go a great length in overthrowing this wise provision of the Constitution.[345]

As we shall see, except for its resort to English law, this opinion has little in common with and takes a more expansive view of the right of confrontation than the next batch of confrontation cases.[346]

Yazoo and The War of 1812

The Tennessee court says nothing about the hearsay rule but some insight into contemporary view of hearsay emerged at about the same time in connection with the infamous Yazoo land scandal.[347] In 1810, the Supreme Court heard arguments concerning the validity of an attempt by the Georgia legislature to repeal a land grant that had allegedly been procured by Northern speculators

341. "Should be confronted"
Ibid.

342. "Agreeable to Magna Charta"
Ibid.

343. Has nothing
See vol. 30, § 6342, text at notecall 108.

344. At preliminary hearing
Id., text at notecall 286.

345. "Wise provision"
State v. Atkins, 1807, 1 Tenn. (Overton) 229.

346. More expansive
See Anthony v. State, 1838, 19 Tenn. 265, 277–278 (admission of dying declarations not a denial of right of confrontation).

347. Yazoo land scandal
See generally, Magrath, Yazoo: Law and Politics in the New Republic, 1966.

bribing virtually the entire membership of the previous legislature.[348] Robert Goodloe Harper, a South Carolina Federalist who was both a shareholder in the land company and its lawyer, published a pamphlet defending the grant.[349] In attacking the affidavits submitted to the legislature to prove the bribes, Harper points out that from the imperfections of human testimony "has resulted a rule which is invariably observed in all our courts; that testimony is never admitted, unless both parties have had an opportunity of joining in the examination."[350] After charging the legislative committee that took the affidavits with having refused to take down exculpatory testimony, Harper continues:

> But the evidence itself, if properly taken, is liable to many strong objections. * * * It depends in a great degree on hearsay, which the best known rules of law, and the dictates of common justice, concur in rejecting.[351]

It seems clear from the context that Harper is not asserting that the affidavits are hearsay but rather that the affiants are reporting "confessions of members [of the legislature] made, not to the legislature, or the committee, but to the witnesses, about the impropriety of their own conduct."[352]

But if the affidavits are not themselves hearsay, they are nonetheless objectionable because

> they were ex parte, taken in private, before a committee of the house of representatives; the witnesses not confronted with those persons against whom their testimony was to operate; not subjected to cross-examination. The admission of testimony taken in this manner is no less contradictory to practice of every court known to the American constitutions, than to the plain principles of natural justice.[353]

348.   **Speculators bribing**

2 Haskins & Johnson, History of the Supreme Court of the United States, 1981, pp. 336–353. Joseph Story, who two years later was to join the court, had lobbied for the land speculators and argued for them in the Supreme Court. See Newmyer, Supreme Court Justice Joseph Story, 1985, p. 66. The Supreme Court held the repeal invalid in Fletcher v. Peck, 1810, 6 Cranch (10 U.S.) 87, 3 L.Ed. 162.

349.   **Published pamphlet**

Magrath, Yazoo: Law and Politics in the New Republic, 1966, p. 20.

350.   **"Both had opportunity"**

Id. at p. 146.

351.   **"Dictates of common justice"**

Ibid.

352.   **"But to the witnesses"**

Ibid.

353.   **"Natural justice"**

Id. at pl. 145.

Harper did not specifically invoke the constitutional right of confrontation, perhaps because the proceeding was not criminal or because the Georgia constitution had no bill of rights.[354] Nonetheless, his use of a denial of confrontation to discredit the legislative fact-finding suggests that he felt that confrontation still had the political appeal it enjoyed during the Revolutionary era.[355]

The War of 1812 influenced the fate of confrontation in complex but important ways.[356] On the one hand, the "Second Revolutionary War" strengthened the Anglophobia that fed hostility to the English common law as a source of American law, including evidence and confrontation.[357] Moreover, threats of treason prosecutions of Federalist opponents of the war revived elite fears of political prosecutions of the sort that had characterized much of the history of the rights of the accused in general and confrontation in particular.[358] Ironically, however, the political parties had switched sides, the Federalists now becoming potential victims of government oppression and some Jeffersonian Republicans advocating the very sort of sedition laws they had opposed during the Adams administration.[359] On the other hand, the way in which this switch played out over the course of the War would ultimately lead the governing classes to conclude that they had little to fear from their opponents' use of the common law and could thus unloose it on ordinary criminal defendants.[360]

These conflicting strands are woven into the Supreme Court's decision in United States v. Hudson and Goodwin.[361] The defendants were charged with criminal libel of the President and Congress by charging that Jefferson had given Napoleon a $2 million

354. Georgia had no

See vol. 30, § 6346, text at notecall 216.

355. Political appeal

See vol. 30, § 6345, text at notecall 507.

356. War of 1812

Newmyer, Supreme Court Justice Joseph Story, 1985, p. 83.

357. Anglophobia

Hickey, The War of 1812, 1989, pp. 47, 56.

358. Threats of treason

Id. at p. 55.

359. Sedition laws

Id. at p. 70.

360. Little to fear

Or to put it somewhat differently, having had a taste of power the elites of both parties were now aware of the utility of inquisitorial procedures for achieving political goals and became more tolerant of institutions they condemned when the British had used them against Americans.

361. Hudson and Goodwin

1812, 7 Cranch (11 U.S.) 32, 3 L.Ed. 259.

bribe to procure a treaty with Spain.[362] Since Congress had not created a statutory crime, the case was one of a number of political prosecutions of Federalists purportedly based on English common law.[363] Though Jefferson had ordered such prosecutions dismissed, somehow this one survived to reach the Supreme Court.[364] The issue presented was whether federal courts had the power to punish common-law crimes.[365]

This did not seem a promising issue for defendants because federal judges had all but unanimously answered in the affirmative.[366] Indeed, with the ironic exception of Chief Justice Chase, most of the members of the Supreme Court had embraced this view.[367] This may be why the lawyers for the defendants declined to argue the case.[368] On the other side, given the dismissal of other similar prosecutions, Attorney–General William Pinckney refused to defend the decision below.[369] Nonetheless, with war drums sounding and even ardent Federalists eager to disprove Republican charges of pro-English leanings, the Supreme Court was not about to pass up the chance to demonstrate its patriotism.[370] In a short opinion that hardly satisfied those of the contrary view, Justice Johnson pronounced the issue one that had long been "settled in public opinion * * *.[A]nd the general acquiescence of legal men shews the prevalence of opinion in favor of the negative of the proposition."[371] The Court's political decision was, perhaps, the

362. Given bribe

Dunne, Justice Joseph Story and The Rise of The Supreme Court, 1970, p. 85.

363. Based on English law

2 Haskins & Johnson, History of the Supreme Court of the United States, 1981, pp. 354–355.

364. Ordered dismissed

Id. at p. 355.

365. Common law crimes

Powell, Languages of Power, 1991, p. 265.

366. Answered affirmative

1 Warren, The Supreme Court in United States History, 1947 ed., p. 433.

367. Supreme Court embraced

2 Haskins & Johnson, History of the Supreme Court of the United States, 1981, p. 354.

368. Declined to argue

Id. at p. 355.

369. Refused to defend

Ibid.

370. Patriotism

Hickey, The War of 1812, 1989, p. 33.

371. "Favor of negative"

U.S. v. Hudson and Goodwin, 1812, 7 Cranch (11 U.S.) 32, 3 L.Ed. 259. Justice Johnson was a Jefferson appointee and one of the few federal judges to have expressed this view on circuit. 2 Haskins & Johnson, History of the Supreme Court of the United States, 1981, p. 354.

high water mark of the post-Revolutionary tide against the English common law.[372] Though some lawyers thought that had the case been fully argued the Supreme Court might have come to a different conclusion,[373] similar views were expressed by state court judges.[374]

However, since Congress had adopted few federal criminal statutes, the decision in Hudson and Goodwin left the federal government without criminal sanctions to enforce war measures, such as a prohibition on trading with the enemy.[375] These American versions of the hated English "Navigation Acts" revived the Yankee talent for smuggling as opposition to the war grew in New England.[376] Justice Story, adopting a strategy similar to that of his English predecessors, tried to evade Hudson and Goodwin by invoking federal admiralty jurisdiction.[377] When the Supreme Court invalidated this ploy,[378] Story then tried to get Congress to adopt a statute giving federal courts common-law criminal jurisdiction.[379] When this failed, Story gnashed his teeth in frustration: "The Courts are crippled; offenders, conspirators, and traitors are enabled to carry on their purposes almost without check."[380] While he never won this particular point, in the long run Story played a significant role in limiting the provisions in the Bill of Rights that were designed to make it difficult for the government to punish its opponents as "offenders, conspirators, and traitors."[381]

372. Against common law

Horwitz, The Transformation of American Law, 1977, pp. 9–11.

373. Different conclusion

Miller, The Legal Mind in America, 1969, p. 45.

374. State court judges

Horwitz, The Transformation of American Law, 1977, p. 14.

375. Without sanctions

2 Haskins & Johnson, History of The Supreme Court of the United States, 1981, p. 355.

376. Yankee smuggling

Newmyer, Supreme Court Justice Joseph Story, 1985, p. 89.

377. Invoking admiralty

2 Haskins & Johnson, History of the Supreme Court of the United States, 1981, p. 356. See also, Cummings &

McFarland, Federal Justice, 1937, p. 71.

378. Invalidated ploy

U.S. v. Coolidge, 1916, 1 Wheat. (14 U.S.) 415, 4 L.Ed. 124.

379. Tried to get statute

Dunne, Justice Joseph Story and The Rise of the Supreme Court, 1970, p. 105.

380. "Almost without check"

Ibid.

381. Role in limiting

Id. at p. 99; see also text below at note-call 767.

The War of 1812 severely tested the commitment of the new nation to confrontation.[382] Anticipating the reaction of later generations of Americans to unpopular wars, members of the militia in some sections refused to report for duty or submit to military discipline.[383] Congress responded by enacting a law giving military courts jurisdiction over recalcitrant militiamen which, while serving confrontation by providing power to compel the attendance and testimony of witnesses, seemed to violate it by authorizing delinquents to be tried in absentia.[384] However, when it was proposed to extend this authority to civilians suspected of spying for the enemy, Congress reacted with indignation; one Federalist member called the proposal "monstrous" because it would "subvert every principle of civil liberty."[385]

In addition to war, 1812 brought the publication of another treatise that sheds light on the early views of hearsay and confrontation. Daniel McKinnon's "The Philosophy of Evidence" attempts to apply Locke's psychology to the emerging law of evidence.[386] In the three pages devoted to "hearsay evidence," McKinnon begins:

> This species of testimony is excluded, not solely because the original witness of the fact may be sworn and cross-examined, which is sometimes impossible, but because his bare assertion, however positive, does not import a probability of sufficient strength to command our belief, or to be received as satisfactory proof of the truth. This will sufficiently appear, if we reflect on the inconsiderate habits of speaking, and the numerous instances of misapprehension and inadvertence, not to say wilful deceit, which may be discovered in the common declarations of mankind.[387]

McKinnon recognizes several exceptions; dying declarations, state of mind, family history, and reputation.[388]

In discussing the examination of witnesses, McKinnon writes:

382. Severely tested

This was the first time since the Revolutionary War that the national government had to deal with civil liberties in a crisis. For the failures of the earlier crisis, see vol. 30, § 6346, text at note 26.

383. Refused to submit

Hickey, The War of 1812, 1989, p. 164.

384. Tried in absentia

Id. at p. 165.

385. "Monstrous"

Ibid.

386. Apply Locke

McKinnon, The Philosophy of Evidence, 1812, pp. 2–27.

387. "Declarations of mankind"

Id. at p. 65.

388. Exceptions

Id. at pp. 65–68.

His testimony must be delivered viva voce, and in the absence of all other witnesses in the same cause, who are generally ordered out of court at the same time, a mode of examination to which Blackstone gives a decided preference, as most conducive to truth, on comparison with the practice of taking written depositions.[389]

After quoting Blackstone's encomium, McKinnon continues:

But if the attendance of a witness cannot be procured at the trial, as where, having been subpoenaed, he has fallen sick by the way, or after diligent search, is not found, a previous examination may be sometimes introduced in proof of facts which, if present, he might be able to attest.[390]

But, he says, this exception has a "considerable qualification;" namely, "that a previous opportunity of cross-examination has been afforded the adverse party."[391] McKinnon points out that former testimony meets this requirement in a civil case "although it would not be allowed in a criminal prosecution."[392] But he points out that by English statute, testimony at a preliminary examination is admissible against the accused.[393]

The Jacksonian Era; Hearsay

The quarter century following the War of 1812 was crucial in the development of American institutions and ideas—including those that would shape the interpretation of the right of confrontation.[394] It was a period of rapid economic growth that saw much of the economy transformed from an agrarian, subsistence basis to production or manufacture for sale.[395] The ease and speed of transportation of people and goods increased markedly.[396] Five new states were added to the union.[397] The post-war period was one of Republican dominance of government that quickly led to the frac-

389. "Decided preference"

Id. at pp. 102–103.

390. "Able to attest"

Id. at pp. 103–104.

391. "Afforded adverse party"

Id. at p. 104.

392. "Not allowed in criminal"

Ibid.

393. English preliminary

Id. at pp. 104–105.

394. Crucial era

Sellers, The Market Revolution: Jacksonian America, 1815–1846, 1991, p. 4.

395. Rapid economic growth

Id. at p. 20.

396. Transportation

Id. at p. 41. The impact of these developments on crime and law enforcement will be discussed below.

397. New states

Id. at p. 131.

turing of the Jeffersonian party into factions.[398] This political conflict grew out of differing opinions about the future of the nation.[399] Hence, our examination of this period must include not only events but intellectual currents and historical forces that cannot be pinned down to specific dates.[400]

In 1815, Congress, contrary to the myth of "no standing army," authorized a substantial peacetime military establishment.[401] One of the targets of this force was the indigenous population, rapidly becoming extinct in most of the older states but still capable of raising resistance to encroachment on their lands in what was then called "the West."[402] In 1818, in what may or may not have been a government-sanctioned effort to seize Florida from nominal rule by the Spanish, Andrew Jackson marched a contingent of militia and regulars across the border in what was called "The First Seminole War."[403] The ostensible targets of this raid were runaway slaves and fugitive Creeks who reportedly had engaged in depredations on the American side of the border.[404]

During the campaign, Jackson's forces captured two British traders, Alexander Arbuthnot and Robert Armbrister, who were more sympathetic to Creek and Cherokee grievances than Jackson thought tolerable.[405] Announcing that "the laws of war did not apply to conflicts with savages," Jackson convened a drumhead court martial to convict the two civilians of inciting the Creeks and Seminoles to war and spying for them.[406] Arbuthnot managed to get

398. Republican dominance

Id. at p. 37.

399. Future of nation

Id. at p. 4.

400. Events and forces

These broader currents will be analyzed in connection with the events that seem to us to reflect or symbolize these gradual developments.

401. Peacetime military

Encyclopedia of American History, Morris ed. 1976, p. 184.

402. Indigenous targets

On the extinction of Native Americans in the older states, see Sellers, The Market Revolution: Jacksonian America, 1915–1846, 1991, p. 7. On the

continuing conflict on the frontier, see Hurt, The Ohio Frontier, 1996.

403. "Seminole War"

Encyclopedia of American History, Morris ed. 1976, p. 187.

404. Slaves and Creeks

The Creeks had more than ample provocation for murdering and torturing someone, though not necessarily the unfortunate settlers who fell into their hands. The disgraceful treatment of our onetime Creek allies is set forth in painful detail in Heidler & Heidler, Old Hickory's War, 1996, pp. 1–54.

405. Captured traders

Id. at p. 152.

406. "Laws did not apply"

Id. at p. 153.

his hands on some law books and learned enough during his brief captivity to object that all of the evidence against him was inadmissible hearsay—as it apparently was.[407] The court overruled the objection, found Arbuthnot guilty, and he was hanged forthwith.[408] All in all, not a very exemplary incident in a nation that had so recently proclaimed a right for an accused to be confronted with the witnesses against him.[409]

Though Arbuthnot's court martial did not recognize it, this was an era in which the hearsay rule began to take on its modern shape.[410] The law of evidence of the 19th Century focussed on witnesses rather than the substance of their testimony, on the liar rather than the lie; large categories of witnesses were per se incompetent to testify on grounds of interest in the outcome of the case, the infamy of a prior conviction, idolatry to some despised religion, insanity or infancy.[411] At times the hearsay rule wanted to be a rule that regulated witnesses; "a mere hearsay is no evidence," the last word then bearing the meaning of "witness."[412] Judges seem to have sensed that the elaborate rules of competence could be evaded if a competent witness could relate from the stand the out-of-court "testimony" of possibly incompetent declarants.[413]

The history of the law of evidence in the 19th Century is in large measure a tale of the decline of the common-law rules of competence.[414] The change in focus from the witness to the particulars of the testimony reflected a number of intellectual forces.[415]

407. Inadmissible hearsay

Dangerfield, The Era of Good Feelings, paper 1989, p. 134.

408. Hanged forthwith

Id. at p. 135.

409. Right to be confronted

The incident might be cited in support of the view that the right of confrontation was not intended to bar the use of hearsay, but it is also possible that the military court did not think the Sixth Amendment applied to it. In any event, there is nothing in the historical record to suggest that anyone thought about confrontation—precisely our point in the text.

410. Modern shape

Nelson, Americanization of the Common Law, 1975, p. 25.

411. Large categories

Id. at p. 24.

412. Meaning "witness"

See vol. 30, § 6344, text at notecall 477.

413. Incompetent declarants

Nelson, Americanization of The Common Law, 1975, p. 25.

414. Decline of competence

See vol. 21, § 5001; vol. 27, § 6001, p. 10.

415. Number of forces

We limit our attention to those that also bore on hearsay and confrontation.

For example, the concept of "character" underwent a subtle change of meaning. In Washington's time it had a public meaning that was virtually synonymous with "reputation."[416] Under the influence of faculty psychology, which held that the mind was a mental muscle shaped by exercise, "character" began to take on its modern connotation as a semi-private quality akin to "personality."[417] Increasing mobility sapped the value of "character-as-reputation" and the growing commercial culture had many Americans exercising their moral muscles in a way that produced what many saw as a decline in "character" as an internal mental quality.[418] The crude categories of incompetence were inadequate to deal with characters like Aaron Burr.[419] Hence, cross-examination became far more important than in the days in which jurors could decide the case on their own knowledge and that knowledge included the reputation of most people in the community.[420] The rise of cross-examination was eventually to shift the justification for and the understanding of the hearsay rule.[421]

Changes in Legal Culture

The development of the hearsay rule was fostered by developments in legal institutions and culture. Legalization of the judiciary—the takeover of the judicial office by legal professionals—proceeded at a rapid rate.[422] The requirement of written opinions fueled a rapid growth in American legal literature;[423] by 1830 nearly all the states were publishing reports of judicial decisions, the first legal periodicals appeared, and several significant legal

416. Synonymous with "reputation"

Elkins & McKitrick, The Age of Federalism, 1993, p. 37.

417. Faculty psychology

Nye, The Cultural Life of The New Nation, paper 1963, p. 184.

418. Decline in "character"

Sellers, The Market Revolution, 1991, p. 230.

419. Aaron Burr

Burr, very much the prototype of the "American on the make" that so repelled Continental visitors like Mrs. Trollope, was said by his own countrymen to have "no fixed principle, no

consistency of character." Wood, The Revenge of Aaron Burr, N.Y.Rev.Bks., February 2, 1984, pp. 23, 25. See also, note 327, above.

420. Decide on own knowledge

Friedman, Crime and Punishment in American History, 1993, p. 27.

421. Shift justification

See vol. 30, § 6325.

422. Legalization

Sellers, The Market Revolution: Jacksonian America 1815–1846, 1991, p. 48.

423. Growth in literature

Id. at p. 50.

treatises had been published.[424] For example, in 1823 Nathan Dane published his eight volume "General Abridgment and Digest of American law."[425] Judges embarked on their crusade to seize power from juries.[426] An important weapon in this campaign was erosion of the power of jurors to rely on their own knowledge.[427]

Legalization of the judiciary went hand in hand with its politicization.[428] The political repercussions of the Marshall Court's constitutional coup d'etat are well known but similar controversy erupted at the state level.[429] For example, Andrew Jackson was outraged that the Tennessee courts were packed with judges who favored land speculators over settlers.[430] In his argument in the Dartmouth College case, Daniel Webster praised the judiciary as an anti-democratic force.[431] And so it might have appeared; by 1825 ten states had had laws declared unconstitutional.[432] This produced the Jacksonian backlash—an attempt to democratize the judiciary by making judicial office elective or otherwise subject to the popular will.[433]

The connection between law and politics requires us to note the demise of the Federalist party.[434] The original appeal of the

424. Treatises published

Nelson, Americanization of the Common Law, 1975, p. 2.

425. Dane "Abridgment"

Boorstin, The Americans: The National Experience, paper 1965, p. 37. The money from Dane's work was later to support Joseph Story's installation of Federalist jurisprudence at Harvard.

426. Seize power

Sellers, The Market Revolution: Jacksonian America, 1815–1846, 1991, p. 49.

427. Rely on own knowledge

Id. at p. 50.

428. Politicization

Legalization gave the judges the ability to cloak their own ideological predilections in rules of law, which may have increased their ambitions but does not seem to have fooled many people.

429. State level

Id. at p. 64.

430. Courts packed

Id. at p. 173.

431. Anti-democratic force

The Legal Mind in America, Miller ed. 1969, p. 61.

432. Unconstitutional

Sellers, The Market Revolution: Jacksonian America, 1815–1846, 1991, p. 146.

433. Popular will

Id. at p. 64. Conflict with the judiciary at the federal level goes back to the Jeffersonian attempt to overcome the "Midnight Judges;" during the Chase impeachment one of the speakers thought the concept of judicial independence had turned the judges into "spoiled children." 14 Annals of Congress, 8th Cong., 2d Sess., 1804–1805, p. 587.

434. Federalist party

As we shall see, the demise of the party did not mean the end of Federalist ideology. Indeed, those values are alive and well among lawyers and judges who are associated with today's "Federalist Society." Ironically, John

Federalists lay in the belief that they had saved the nation from chaos in 1787–1788, that they represented the forces of law and order against "levelling" demagogues of the Shaysite persuasion, and that they were the best safeguards of the national honor and private property.[435] However, by the time of economic upheavals following the War of 1812, they had squandered their political capital with their insistence on the primacy of property rights over human rights and their treasonable attempts to sever the union during time of war.[436] Epistemologically, they thought that elites were more intelligent than ordinary people.[437] This contrasted markedly with the Jeffersonian belief that every human had an innate sense of justice.[438] Even Federalists like Chancellor Kent conceded that "wisdom is as much an offspring of the heart as the head."[439] But the heart of most Federalists was filled with contempt for ordinary people[440]——a view that was to play a large role in legal thought in general and the decline of confrontation in particular.[441] The Jeffersonian ideal became an important part of American

Adams, the last Federalist President, associated "ideology" with the ideals of Jefferson and The French Revolution, ideas he said that were "taught in the school of folly." Ellis, Passionate Sage, 1993, p. 96.

435. Honor and property

Miller, The Federalist Era, paper 1963, p. 122.

436. Sever union

Id. at p. 117; Dangerfield, The Era of Good Feelings, paper 1989, pp. 88, 98.

437. Elites more intelligent

Miller, The Federalist Era, paper 1963, p. 39.

"Equality is one of those equivocal words which the philosophy of the 19th Century has made fraudulent. In the last twenty-five years it has cheated millions out of their lives and tens of millions out of their property." Ellis, Passionate Sage, 1993, p. 90 (quoting John Adams).

438. Innate sense

Miller, The Federalist Era, paper 1963, p. 71.

439. "Heart as head"

The Legal Mind in America, Miller ed. 1969, p. 97.

440. Contempt

For an equation of Demos with The Mob, see Miller, The Federalist Era, paper 1963, p. 112 ("the discontented and factious at the head of the poor. * * * The jealousy of the rich is a passion in the poor which can always be appealed with success on every question, and * * * the engine by which a giddy populous can most easily wrought on to do mischief."). Readers of the Wall Street Journal will know this as "the politics of envy." See also, Ellis, Passionate Sage, 1993, pp. 128–129 (in his exchanges with Jefferson, John Adams denied the existence of "the People.").

441. Decline

Those who see the jury as a mob bent on plundering the rich at the behest of some demagogue will find the adversary system less appealing than those who take the Jeffersonian point of view.

romanticism, but it was to have far less impact on the development of legal thought in the 19th Century.[442]

To the Federalists, this Romantic mush was contrary to their "science of human nature."[443] This "science" required that "[h]onest men must submit to the force that is necessary to govern rogues. * * * To make a nation free, the crafty must be kept in awe, and the violent in restraint."[444] It is in this Calvinistic sense that the Federalists could argue that "the Common Law * * * is the law of freedom."[445] The common law, they thought, "is a science, and, like all the other sciences, progressive."[446] This view of law as a "science" was shared by one of the founders of American legal education, David Hoffman.[447] In his introductory lecture in a series delivered in 1823, he asked: "What are the rules of evidence, but metaphysical and ethical modes of investigating truth on the one hand, and limiting our deductions by a regard to human rights and feelings, and to our moral constitution, on the other?"[448] This "scientific" evidence could not help but notice the decline in the perceived efficacy of the oath as a guarantor of truth, and what could be more "progressive" than to substitute cross-examination for the panoply of confrontation values.[449] Jurors have less need of "scientific" judges to tell them to disregard hearsay than they do for someone to justify and grant them permission to use such

442. Romanticism

Among the elements of Romanticism described by one historian are:

"An emphasis on the emotional and imaginative aspects of life * * * over the reason as a source of aesthetic and moral truth.

"A recognition of the importance of individual and subjective values * * *.

"A belief * * * in the dignity and worth of the common man, his freedom from restraints, and his capacity for improvement."

Nye, The Cultural Life of The New Nation, paper 1965, p. 248.

443. "Human nature"

Miller, The Federalist Era, paper 1963, p. 110.

John Adams: "Ambition springs from the desire for esteem and from emulation, not from property." Ellis, Passionate Sage, 1993, p. 91. See also, id. at pp. 166–168.

444. "In restraint"

Id. at p. 111.

445. "Law of freedom"

The Legal Mind in America, Miller ed. 1969, p. 140.

446. "Progressive"

Id. at p. 169.

447. Hoffman "science"

Id. at p. 84.

448. "Moral constitution"

Id. at p. 90.

449. Decline in oath

Friedman, Crime and Punishment in American History, 1993, p. 114.

unconfronted "testimony."[450]

Far more important to the future of confrontation than Hoffman was another law teacher, Joseph Story.[451] In 1829, on the occasion of his inauguration as the Dane Professor of Law at Harvard, Story embraced the notion that "law is a science."[452]

> In truth, the Common Law, as a science, must be for ever in progress; and no limits can be assigned to its principles or improvements. In this respect, it resembles the natural sciences, where new discoveries continually lead the way to new, and sometimes to astonishing, results.[453]

As we shall see, Story applied his "science" to the Constitution as well with "astonishing results" for the right of confrontation. But for other Harvard men, like the one who delivered the address at the dedication of the Dane College of Law, the common law was one of the tools of "a thorough professional training, such as would eliminate the unfit and the unable, a training which the profession had gallantly maintained against the strong press of egalitarianism."[454] The common law was also the weapon of choice against Jacksonian codifiers who wanted law reduced to a form that any educated person could read and understand.[455] And by the end of the Jacksonian era, another lawyer illustrated the way of the fate of his profession and the law of evidence were intertwined.

> The learning and ingenuity of skillful and practiced men are absolutely necessary to explain and apply the technicalities of the law in regard to evidence. For if all evidence is to be indiscriminately admitted, then the most perjured villain has the most spotless character, completely under his control.[456]

As we shall see, this man's view that "[e]very avenue of escape for the prisoner should be kept open" was not the one that would drive interpretation of the confrontation clauses of state constitutions.[457]

450. Justify unconfronted

Id. at p. 248.

451. Story important

See below, text at notecall 704.

452. "Law is science"

The Legal Mind in America, Miller ed. 1969, p. 182.

453. "Astonishing results"

Id. at p. 184. In this same address, Story told the audience that "[o]ne of the glorious, and not infrequently perilous

duties of the Bar is the protection of property; * * *." Id. at p. 181.

454. "Against egalitarianism"

Id. at p. 202.

455. Against codifiers

Id. at pp. 141, 153, 202.

456. "Under his control"

Id. at p. 281.

457. "Kept open"

Ibid.

The Panic of 1819: Politico–Economic Change

The post-war period had been one of rapid economic growth.[458] The Panic of 1819 ended complacency about economic change and political control of the economy, awakening many Americans to the social costs of a market economy.[459] Long before anyone had ever heard of Karl Marx, Americans learned that the growth of capitalism brought an increase in economic inequality.[460] This fell hardest on the generation of the 1820s, who saw the share of the national wealth held by the top 10% increase from 50% to 73% and that of the richest 1% more than double from 13% to 29%.[461] In New York City, 40% of the wealth was owned by fewer than 1% of the populace.[462] The rise in inequality necessitated an increase in the mechanisms of repression of the lower classes, largely but not entirely through the criminal law.[463] Mobs took their cue from legitimate institutions, attacking Irish immigrants and their churches as scapegoats for their own misery.[464]

Adherents of "the politics of envy" notwithstanding, the major objection to economic inequality was its effect on democratic institutions.[465] Though true corruption was not unknown, as a historian of the period has written

> [m]ajority rule is frustrated not by the venality of politicians but by the political advantages of elites——wealth, influence, intellectual resources, control of public media, and sleepless involvement—— to which office seekers learn to accommodate.[466]

So, one critic argued, "[c]apital and the companies of capitalists have filled your halls of legislation, and have given to the owner of property an individuality of possession, which places property entirely above the claims of humanity."[467] For many, the Bank of the

458. Economic growth

Sellers, The Market Revolution: Jacksonian America, 1815–1846, p. 20.

459. Social costs

Id. at pp. 137, 161.

460. Increase inequality

Id. at p. 340.

461. More than double

Id. at p. 238.

462. Fewer than 1%

Ibid.

463. Increase in repression

Id. at p. 257.

464. Irish scapegoats

Id. at p. 389.

465. Effect on democratic

Id. at p. 166.

466. "Accommodate"

Ibid.

467. "Claims of humanity"

Welter, The Mind of America, 1820–1860, 1975, p. 96.

"Every man is equally entitled to protection by law; but when the laws undertake to add to these natural and just advantages artificial distinctions, to

United States came to symbolize this corruption of democracy by capitalist elites.[468]

Rivaling the Bank in Jacksonian demonology was the Supreme Court, which in a series of decisions from 1816 to 1819, seemed to embrace the political economy of capitalist development.[469] Lawyers, then as now, had been trained by the adversary system to practice and preach the ethic of the market—that the unbridled pursuit of personal advantage is the path to public good.[470] The Jacksonians, on the other hand, saw the creation of the market infrastructure by state and national government as producing a system of laws in which some were able to benefit from the labor of others, to extract wealth from the pockets of others by legal means.[471] Legislative creation of corporations was the prime example.[472] At a time when ordinary Americans were still being imprisoned for debt and denied the relief of bankruptcy and foreclosure moratoria, limited liability for capitalists seemed like the epitome of aristocratic privilege.[473] Judicial extension of constitutional rights to corporations served both to discredit the notion of constitutional protection and to increase demands for political control of the judiciary.[474]

grant titles, gratuities and exclusive privilege, to make the rich richer and the potent more powerful, the humble members of society—the farmers, mechanics, and laborers—who have neither the time nor the means of securing favors to themselves, have a right to complain of the injustice of their government." Cummings & McFarland, Federal Justice, 1937, p . 102 (quoting Andrew Jackson).

468. Bank came to symbolize

Sellers, The Market Revolution: Jacksonian America, 1815–1846, 1991, p. 332. The Bank's major lawyer was elected to Congress with Bank support where he used loans and bribes disguised as legal fees to garner support from his colleagues. Daniel Webster, who did legal work for the Bank, also received clandestine payments for his support in the Senate, payments he euphemistically referred to as a "retainer." The Bank also made loans and payments to newspapers for fa-vorable coverage and endorsement of favorable candidates.

See also, Ellis, Passionate Sage, 1993, pp. 136, 161, 164 (John Adams opposed banking, calling it "an infinity of successive felonious larcenies").

469. Embrace political economy

Id. at p. 84.

470. Path to public good

Id. at p. 47.

471. By legal means

Welter, The Mind of America, 1820–1860, 1975, p. 78.

472. Corporations

Id. at p. 79.

473. Aristocratic privilege

Id. at p. 80.

474. Control of judiciary

Id. at p. 237.

Since the left-wing Jacksonians were the losers, the views of the emerging Whigs are more relevant to the future of confrontation.[475] The Whigs learned from the failure of the Federalists how to wrap business interests in a democratic rhetoric.[476] In the vision of the Whigs, the purpose of elections was to bring "the best men" into government so that these Platonic guardians could reason together to advance the public interest.[477] Allowing the voters to "instruct" their elected representatives how to vote on key issues only allowed local interest to prevail over the public interest.[478] The Whigs preached a democracy of deference in which "[t]he largest amount of liberty consists in the most extensive obedience to good laws."[479]

The Whig view of the judiciary revived the Federalist strategy of constitutionalism as an obstacle to democracy.[480] While the Whigs opposed the Jacksonian call for an elective judiciary, they thought that the method of selection of judges was less crucial than defining their role.[481] To them, the ideal judge was autonomous and immune from popular pressures.[482] The acme of this perfection was the apolitical, even antipolitical judge, described by Chancellor Kent.[483] To modern lawyers, this all seems quite unremarkable

475. Emerging Whigs

This is not to say that the Jacksonian views lacked all significance, if for no other reason than that they stimulated the formulation of the elite lawyers' defense of the profession and the Court. Moreover, as we shall see, the Jacksonians had some short term impact on the development of confrontation.

476. Wrap in rhetoric

Sellers, The Market Revolution: Jacksonian America, 1815–1846, 1991, p. 350.

477. Elect Platonic guardians

Welter, The Mind of America, 1820–1860, 1975, p. 190.

478. Local interest

Id. at p. 196.

479. "Obedience to laws"

Id. at p. 207.

480. Obstacle to democracy

Id. at pp. 205, 213, 218.

481. Defining role

Id. at p. 215.

482. Immune from popular

Id. at p. 212.

483. Described by Kent

"The just and vigorous investigation and punishment of every species of fraud and violence, and the exercise of the power of compelling every man to the punctual performance of his contracts, are grave duties, not of the most popular character, though the faithful discharge of them will certainly command the calm approbation of the judicious observer. The fittest men would probably have too much reservedness of manners, and severity of morals, to secure an election resting on universal suffrage." Id. at pp. 212–213.

because the Whig judicial ideology was to become the dominant discourse of legal writers and law schools.[484]

Goodenow and Instrumentalism

These developments received an impetus from an influential work published in the year of The Panic.[485] John Milton Goodenow's "Historical Sketches of The Principles and Maxims of American Jurisprudence in Contrast With The Doctrines of The English Common Law on The Subject of Crimes and Punishments" sought to replace the Revolutionary doctrines of natural law with the Austinian theory that was more conducive to capitalist political economy;[486] " . . . all human laws for the punishment of crimes, are merely matters of social policy" not dependent on natural reason.[487] Goodenow's popularity stemmed in part from an epistemological switch from Locke to Rousseau.[488] The individualistic notion of natural rights was unsuitable for an era of social engineering.[489]

The 1820s saw the beginning of an intense period of social legislation by the states.[490] The number, size, and influence of business corporations increased rapidly.[491] This was accompanied by a decline in communal norms regarding use of land and the rise of capitalistic notions of property.[492] At a time when Baptists and Methodists relied on communal efforts toward repentance and

484. Dominant discourse

See, e.g., any contemporary text on constitutional law or any Law Day speech on behalf of "the Missouri plan" or other scheme for removing the judiciary from popular control.

485. Influential work

Horwitz, The Transformation of American Law, 1780–1860, 1977, p. 15.

486. Austinian

John Austin was an English legal philosopher who defined "law" as "the command of a sovereign."

487. "Merely social policy"

Goodenow, History Sketches of The Principles and Maxims of American Jurisprudence, 1819, p. 6.

488. Locke to Rousseau

Smith, Roger B. Taney: Jacksonian Jurist, 1936, p. 26. That is, from the notion that human nature was immut-

able to the notion that it was infinitely malleable through education and coercion.

489. Rights unsuitable

Ibid.

490. Social legislation

Id. at p. 121.

491. Corporations increased

Swisher, Roger B. Taney, 1935, p. 390. The reader will recall that in this era, incorporation was not a legal form available to anyone but a grant of state power that required legislation and some showing of a public purpose.

492. Rise of property

Sellers, The Market Revolution: Jacksonian America, 1815–1846, 1991, p. 10.

reformation of offenders,[493] Jacksonian judges such as Taney supported the police power of the state.[494] The Jacksonian trust in the power of democracy to do good resonated in ways they failed to appreciate with the older Federalist view that there was no need for constitutional rights in a republican government.[495] In retrospect, one can see in the Jacksonian belief in a hierarchy based on equality of opportunity a betrayal of Revolutionary egalitarianism that is still felt in our own time.[496]

Goodenow's embrace of amoral Austinianism was, ironically, part of an attempt to liberate Americans from the harshness of the English common law.[497] Goodenow was particularly critical of common law procedure, in large part because of its denial of rights found in the Sixth Amendment and similar state constitutional provisions.[498] He attacked the ancient common law because it allowed accusations to be founded on hearsay.[499] He noted that in the Elizabethan era, quoting Hume, "[t]he practice, also, of not confronting the witnesses with the prisoner gave the crown lawyers all imaginable advantage against him".[500] Goodenow also objected to combining the roles of "accusors, indictors and triers" in the same body.[501]

But at the same time that Goodenow embraced confrontation values, he rejected the natural law that had been a principle support for their development, wishing to see it "disregarded [to] lie for ages buried beneath the rubbish of human invention."[502] The notion that the criminal law was simply a tool for social engineering that required no moral basis was to lead to an expansion of the criminal sanction and its rooting in "the will of the people" that

493. Communal efforts
Id. at p. 160.

494. Supported police power
Smith, Roger B. Taney: Jacksonian Jurist, 1936, p. 177.

495. Trust in democracy
Id. at p. 211.

496. Jacksonian betrayal
Welter, The Mind of America, 1820–1860, p. 122.

497. Liberate from common law
Goodenow, Historical Sketches of The Principles and Maxims of American Jurisprudence, 1819, p. iv.

498. Denial of rights
Id. at p . 18.

499. Founded on hearsay
Id. at p. 110.

500. "Advantage against him"
Id. at p. 140.

501. "Accusors and triers"
Id. at p. 112.

502. "Beneath rubbish"
Id. at p. 33.

cast the Bill of Rights in the role of villain in the Story of Progress.[503] Was there any reason to offer constitutional support to the defendant who resisted efforts by the state, not to hang, draw, and quarter him, but to reform him and return him to a productive role in society?[504] The answer was clear to Jacksonians who thought the major danger was not government oppression but the undermining of the will of the majority by the privileged classes.[505] Moreover, far from freeing Americans from the English common law, Goodenow cleared the ground for its reconstruction by Kent and Story with contract rather than God as its moral basis.[506]

Slavery, Instrumentalism, and Confrontation

The Jacksonian era brought change in and a hardening of attitudes toward an institution whose impact on constitutional rights is difficult to underestimate—slavery.[507] The Constitution that was celebrated as a "bulwark of liberty" legitimated the total lack of freedom of most African–Americans.[508] We have previously seen how the Supreme Court manipulated the law of hearsay to further the interests of slaveholders.[509] Worse yet, in most states even free African–Americans were barred from testifying against whites[510]—a law that left them vulnerable to the depredations of racist mobs.[511] Nonetheless, even Founders from the Southern states were willing to contemplate the abolition of slavery.[512] By the

503. Bill of Rights

Horwitz, The Transformation of American Law, 1780–1860, 1977, p. 15.

504. Reform him

Friedman, Crime and Punishment in American History, 1993, p. 79.

505. Major danger

Smith, Roger B. Taney: Jacksonian Jurist, 1936, pp. 65, 202.

506. Contract as God

Newmyer, Supreme Court Justice Joseph Story, 1985, p. 232. This touched on confrontation in two ways. First, the Constitution itself came to be seen as a special kind of contract, the only quarrel being whether the parties were the states or the citizens thereof. Smith, Roger B. Taney: Jacksonian Jurist, 1936, p. 82. Second, the Bill of Rights itself was part of a "deal"— ratification in return for a Bill of Rights. See vol. 30, § 6347, text at note 749.

507. Slavery attitudes

Sellers, The Market Revolution: Jacksonian America, 1815–1846, 1991, p. 4.

508. "Bulwark of liberty"

Newmyer, Supreme Court Justice Joseph Story, 1985, p. 344.

509. Hearsay for slaveholders

Id. at p. 346. For our discussion, see vol. 30, § 6321, p. 18.

510. Barred from testifying

Sellers, The Market Revolution: Jacksonian America, 1815–1846, 1991, p. 127.

511. Racist mobs

Id. at p. 388.

512. Contemplate abolition

Id. at p. 275.

end of the Jacksonian era, that attitude was anathema in the South and among the Northern elite.[513]

In 1819, Congress provided a bounty for informers against those who engaged in the slave trade[514]——a move probably motivated as much by a desire to increase the value of slaves as by more lofty ideals. Though informers were the major villains of the vice-admiralty courts that did so much to further the Founders' appreciation of confrontation, only a few were prepared to denounce the revival of this once abhorrent practice.[515] Despite efforts to end the importation of slaves, their number grew from 700,000 at the time of the Constitution to 2-1/2 million by the end of the Jacksonian era.[516] Worse yet, the territorial expansion of slavery threatened to make it the dominant national form of economic organization.[517]

If outnumbered Southerners feared revolt by slaves, they positively detested abolitionists.[518] Not only did abolitionism become an increasingly organized movement during the Jacksonian era, the number of those in the movement swelled.[519] Whereas early abolitionists had been moved as much by practical as moral considerations, the new abolitionism was religiously based.[520] This uncompromising moral opposition to slavery was a threat to politicians who hoped to find some way of continuing the Constitutional compromise on this issue.[521] We may speculate that one reason that Goodenow's Austinian instrumentalism caught on so quickly is that

---

513. Attitude anathema

Id. at p. 276.

514. Informers' bounty

Encyclopedia of American History, Morris ed. 1976, p. 191.

515. Few denounce

Swisher, Roger B. Taney, 1935, p. 567.

516. Grew to 2-1/2 million

Newmyer, Supreme Court Justice Joseph Story, 1985, p. 366.

517. Dominant form

Ibid. As every schoolchild knows, conflict over the territorial expansion of slavery was the locus of the earliest resistance to the "peculiar institution"——as it used to be euphemistically called. Encyclopedia of American

History, Morris ed. 1976, p. 190 (Missouri Compromise of 1820).

518. Detested abolitionists

Id. at p. 209 (abolitionist literature seized from mails and burned, abolitionists expelled from the South, proposed to make advocacy of abolition punishable by death without benefit of clergy).

519. Movement swelled

Id. at p. 757. See also, Bartlett, Daniel Webster, 1978, pp. 258–259.

520. Religiously based

Sellers, The Market Revolution: Jacksonian America, 1815–1846, 1991, p. 235.

521. Continuing compromise

Bartlett, Daniel Webster, 1978, p. 258.

it provided an antidote to the moral attacks on the legitimacy of a Constitution that supported slavery.[522]

In 1822, the worst fears of Southerners were realized when an informer revealed a supposed insurrectionist plot led by a free African–American, Denmark Vesey, and urban slave artisans.[523] Since slaves vastly outnumbered whites in the South Carolina low country, the discovery provoked hysteria and a frenzy of repression.[524] After closed trials, 35 of the supposed conspirators were executed.[525] While his countrymen were acquiring a new fondness for informers, Supreme Court Justice William Johnson wrote Thomas Jefferson in defense of the values of the Revolution:

> I have lived to see what I really never believed possible I should see——courts held with closed doors and men dying by scores who had never seen the faces nor heard the voices of their accusers.[526]

Alas, Justice Johnson was indeed part of a dying breed.[527] In 1831 following Nat Turner's rebellion in Virginia, slave codes in that state and others were made even more repressive.[528] These repressive attitudes were not congenial to a liberal construction of state confrontation clauses.[529]

Abolitionists were not only anathematized in the South; they were also excoriated by accommodationists in the North——those

---

522. Antidote to moral

Nelson, The Impact of The Anti-slavery Movement Upon Styles of Judicial Reasoning in Nineteenth Century America, 1974, 87 Harv.L.Rev. 513, 543.

523. Vesey plot

Encyclopedia of American History, Morris ed. 1976, p. 757.

524. Hysteria and repression

Sellers, The Market Revolution: Jacksonian America, 1815–1846, 1991, pp. 143, 274, 400.

525. Conspirators executed

Id. at p. 274. Another 37 were banished from the state.

526. "Never seen accusers"

Wiggins, Freedom or Secrecy, 1964, pp. 25–26.

527. Dying breed

In 1823, sitting on circuit, Justice Johnson struck down a South Carolina statute authorizing the imprisonment of free African–American sailors disembarking in Charleston. Newmyer, Supreme Court Justice Joseph Story, 1985, p. 366. The state refused to abide by the ruling in one of the earliest instances of the application of the doctrine of nullification. Sellers, The Market Revolution: Jacksonian America, 1815–1846, 1991, p. 276. Justice Johnson was himself a South Carolinian appointed by Jefferson; he died in 1834. Dictionary of American Biography, 1995, p. 379.

528. Turner's rebellion

Encyclopedia of American History, Morris ed. 1976, p. 757.

529. Not congenial

See below, text at note 684.

who for economic or political reasons wished to preserve the Constitution's compromise with slavery.[530] Given its dominant role in evidentiary scholarship, it is worth noting that the Harvard Law School was a hotbed of pro-Southern accommodationist thought.[531] A student there in the early 1850s wrote that

> [a] Southern slave holder, or his son at Harvard, was more welcome in society than any guest except a foreigner * * *. The deference to rich Southern planters was marked.[532]

Similarly, Daniel Webster thought that abolitionists who obstructed the return of escaped slaves were guilty of treason.[533]

If we may jump ahead of our chronology for a moment, we can see more directly the effects of slavery on confrontation.[534] The Fugitive Slave Law of 1850, one of the monuments of accommodationist jurisprudence, denied the accused slave trial by jury.[535] Worse yet, it made slaveowner hearsay not only admissible but sufficient to prove servile status and made contrary testimony by the accused slave inadmissible.[536] This was too much for some state courts; they held the Act unconstitutional[537]—a move frustrated by the Supreme Court.[538] The Fugitive Slave Laws were extremely unpopular in the North—except in Boston; there they were greeted with a 100 gun salute.[539]

530. Abolitionists excoriated

Newmyer, Supreme Court Justice Joseph Story, 1985, p. 366.

531. Harvard hotbed

On the Harvard dominance in evidence scholarship, see vol. 21, pp. 20–21.

532. "Slave holder welcome"

Levy, The Law of The Commonwealth and Chief Justice Shaw, 1957, p. 86.

533. Webster thought treason

Id. at p. 89.

534. Effects of Slavery

On the earlier impact of slavery, see vol. 30, § 6347, pp. 741–742.

535. Denied jury

Dalzell, Daniel Webster and The Trial of American Nationalism, 1843–1852, 1975 p. 218.

536. Hearsay admissible

Bartlett, Daniel Webster, 1978, p. 258; Levy, The Law of The Commonwealth and Chief Justice Shaw, 1957, p. 94.

537. Unconstitutional

Nelson, The Impact of The Antislavery Movement Upon Styles of Judicial Reasoning in Nineteenth Century America, 1974, 87 Harv.L.Rev. 513, 542.

538. Frustrated by Court

Newmyer, Supreme Court Justice Joseph Story, 1985, p. 352.

539. A 100 gun salute

Levy, The Law of the Commonwealth and Chief Justice Shaw, 1957, p. 86.

In the South, racism and slavery muffled class distinctions by providing that "Other" needed to engender fear and popular support for repressive measures.[540] In the North, the bogeyman for repression, at least among the still Federalist-minded elite, was the "unruly, dangerous, radically minded white mob, which haunted Europe and strengthened its need for hierarchy."[541] Daniel Webster's wife referred to a Jacksonian gathering as "tag rag & scanderbag," observing that there "were only three or four gentlemen belonging to our class."[542] Such snobbery was not the only feature of Federalism that survived the death of the party.[543] In 1820, Webster and Story led the opposition to democratic changes at the Massachusetts constitutional convention, arguing this would "give too much power to poor people and threaten protection of property."[544] In shaking down a wealthy businessman for money to support Webster, one of his supporters wrote that the "present political contest [is] nothing less than a war of numbers against property * * * carried on in the proscriptive and remorseless spirit of the French Revolution."[545] If that were not a sufficiently powerful metaphor, the writer added that Webster "has all his life fought the battles of property, order and law" against the "side of the Levellers."[546] Such expressions were not friendly to the Leveller-inspired right of confrontation.[547] Little wonder that John Calhoun found it plausible to imagine that southern planters might agree with Northern businessmen that if the latter would agree not to interfere with slavery, the former would assist them in putting down labor agitation.[548]

Historians agree that the period 1820–1850 saw the rise of an instrumental conception of law.[549] This came to mean a preference

---

540. Engender fear

Plumb, How Freedom Took Root in Slavery, N.Y.Rev.Bks., Nov. 17, 1975, p. 3.

541. "White mob"

Ibid.

542. "Our class"

Bartlett, Daniel Webster, 1978, p. 89.

543. Survived death

Id. at p. 90.

544. "Threaten property"

Id. at p. 82.

545. "French Revolution"

Id. at p. 145.

546. "Levellers"

Id. at p. 146.

547. Inspired confrontation

See vol. 30, § 6343, p. 272.

548. Labor agitation

Dangerfield, The Era of Good Feelings, 1989, p. 412.

549. Rise of instrumental

Nelson, The Impact of the Antislavery Movement Upon Styles of Judicial Reasoning in Nineteenth Century America, 1974, 87 Harv.L.Rev. 513, 514.

for policy results over doctrinal purity, most often the "practical economic results" of judicial decisions.[550] In the case of constitutional interpretation this meant constructions that broadened governmental powers to assist the capitalist political economy.[551] John Calhoun, who fancied himself "no advocate for refined arguments on the Constitution," declared that it "was not intended as a thesis for the logician to exercise his ingenuity on. It ought to be construed with plain, good sense."[552] Most significant for the right of confrontation, the rise of instrumentalism saw the decline of Blackstone's legal universe, the one in which the adversary jury trial with its confrontation of witnesses was the brightest star.[553]

Instrumentalism colored the second of the early interpretations of state confrontation clauses, Johnston v. State, decided in 1821.[554] In a prosecution for horse-stealing, the prosecution was allowed to read into evidence an affidavit of a deceased witness taken by the magistrate in a preliminary examination in another county.[555] The defendant claimed this was a violation of § 9 of the Tennessee constitution, which provided that "the accused has a right to meet the witnesses face to face."[556] Ignoring Tennessee precedent supporting the defense,[557] the Tennessee Supreme Court turned instead to the law of North Carolina, arguing first that since the English common-law practice had been included in a revision of the laws of that state, it must not have been thought to have been a violation of that state's confrontation clause.[558] The Tennessee court believed that the difference in the language of the North

550. "Practical economic"

Newmyer, Supreme Court Justice Joseph Story, 1985, p. 231.

551. Assist capitalist

Sellers, The Market Revolution: Jacksonian America, 1815–1846, 1991, p. 77.

552. "Plain, good sense"

Ibid.

553. Decline of Blackstone

Newmyer, Supreme Court Justice Joseph Story, 1985, p. 218.

554. Second interpretation

1821, 10 Tenn. (2 Yer.) 58. For the first interpretation, see above, text at note 339.

555. Affidavit used

The court calls this a "deposition," but in modern parlance it would be called an "affidavit" or a "signed statement" as it did not purport to be a verbatim account of testimony and cross-examination.

556. "Face to face"

Id. at p. 59.

557. Tennessee precedent

State v. Atkins, 1807, 1 Tenn. 229 (confrontation bars use of former testimony of deceased witness).

558. Not thought violation

10 Tenn. at 59.

Carolina clause made no difference.[559] The court glossed over a North Carolina decision rejecting the use of such evidence on common-law foundations of "natural justice."[560] Perhaps sensing the weakness of its authority, the Court sought to clinch its holding with an instrumental argument: holding that the hearsay of a deceased witness could not be used against the defendant would provide an incentive for killing the witness.[561] Thus, less than a generation after the constitutionalization of confrontation, the Tennessee court had adopted the position of the English court that condemned Raleigh to death: to wit, "many horse-stealers would escape if they may not be condemned without witnesses."[562]

Adams, Kent, and The End of The Revolutionary Generation

The so-called "Era of Good Feelings" and the "Virginia Dynasty" of Presidents both ended in 1824, when John Quincy Adams, despite having fewer electoral and popular votes than Andrew Jackson, was named to the presidency by what many Jacksonians regarded as a corrupted House of Representatives.[563] Adams had once told his father that he held "some very heretical opinions upon the merits of the common law, so idolized by all English lawyers and by all who parrot their words in America."[564] So perhaps it was not mere coincidence that the same year Willam Sampson, an expatriate Irishman, delivered an attack on the common law that signaled a new enthusiasm for codification.[565] Sampson and other advocates of codification made the English common law their bugbear, but they also embraced some of the same values as the English dissenters who did so much to advance the right of confrontation.[566] For example, Robert Rantoul, one of the leading

559. Made no difference

Ibid. The North Carolina constitution says "every man hath a right to confront the accusers and witnesses with other testimony." On the uniqueness of this formulation, see vol. 30, § 6346, pp. 592, 611–612.

560. "Natural justice"

State v. Webb, 1794, 2 N.C. (1 Hayw.) 139. The case might have been distinguished on the ground that in that case there was no showing the witness was dead.

561. Incentive for killing

10 Tenn. at 60.

562. "Horse-stealers escape"

See vol. 30, § 6342, p. 264.

563. Adams named

Encyclopedia of American History, Morris ed. 1976, pp. 195–196.

564. "Parrot their words"

Sellers, The Market Revolution: Jacksonian America, 1815–1846, 1991, p. 58.

565. Sampson attack

The Legal Mind in America, Miller ed. 1969, p. 119.

566. Embraced values

For these values, see vol. 30, § 6343.

Jacksonian lawyers, praised the intelligence of ordinary people and decried the ex post facto making of rules by judges who were out of touch with everyday life and popular influence.[567] Codification would make the law intelligible to all without the need for professional mediaries.[568]

However at the very time that Sampson spoke, the nemesis of the codification movement was a work on a treatise that reconstructed the common law in ways that made it more acceptable to a capitalist political economy.[569] Chancellor James Kent, forced to retire from the New York chancery bench in 1923, delivered a defense of the common law in 1824.[570] Two years later the first of the four volumes of his "Commentaries on American Law" was published.[571] This work went through five editions during Kent's lifetime and eight more over the balance of the 19th Century.[572] Only Story rivaled Kent in influence on the future of American law.

Kent's fondness for things English is not surprising; his family were Tories, his father was suspected of being a Loyalist, and Kent himself played no part in the Revolution.[573] Kent opposed codification and despised the Jacksonians; in a critique of Livingston's Code, he wrote "I have imbibed from * * * the French Revolution * * * an aversion to innovation."[574] He admired Lord Mansfield, the English judge who wanted to hang American Revolutionary leaders.[575] Kent attributed opposition to the common law to pseudo-patriotism and ignorance.[576] Ironically, Kent himself was ignorant

567. Judge out of touch

Meyers, The Jacksonian Persuasion: Politics and Belief, paper 1960, p. 229.

568. Without mediaries

Ibid. Compare vol. 30, § 6343, pp. 291–295.

569. Reconstructed

Friedman, A History of American Law, 1973, p. 288.

570. Kent defense

The Legal Mind in America, Miller ed. 1969, p. 93.

571. "Commentaries"

Sellers, The Market Revolution: Jacksonian America, 1815–1846, 1991, p. 50.

572. More editions

The Legal Mind in America, Miller ed. 1969, p. 92.

573. Played no part

Horton, James Kent: A Study in Conservatism, 1939, pp. 15, 56.

574. "Aversion to innovation"

Id. at p. 271 n. 25. See also, The Legal Mind in America, Miller ed. 1969, pp. 93–94.

575. Admired Mansfield

Id. at p. 47.

576. Patriotism and ignorance

Aumann, The Influence of English and Civil Law Principles Upon The American Legal System during the Critical

of the changes made in the English common law by American judges during the 150 years prior to the Revolution.[577] Kent admired the civil law, whose inquisitorial procedure the Sixth Amendment rejected.[578] However, critics have suggested that his knowledge of the civil law was shallow and that the citations to the civilians in his work was little more than name-dropping designed to impress readers with his erudition.[579] Be that as it may, Kent found the civil law a useful weapon against the codifiers, arguing that experience in civilian jurisdictions did not bear out the claims of the supposed advantages of codification.[580] He also made it part of the eclectic mix of authority to support his avoidance of common law precedents not suitable to the interests of an emerging capitalist economy.[581]

Since he spent most of his career in the court of equity, Kent had little experience with criminal prosecutions—though this did not hinder him from opining that Livingston's Code was too lenient on criminals.[582] Moreover, he once upheld a conviction for blasphemy, exemplifying his belief that Christianity was part of the common law.[583] Kent is best known for toughening the commercial bias of the common law so his impact on confrontation rights was indirect.[584] Nonetheless, it was profound. He popularized the notion of judges as lawmakers, even "legislators"[585]—a view that made it easier to judges to reduce confrontation from a constitutional right to a mere common law rule of preference. In this respect, he has

Post–Revolutionary Period, 1938, 12 U.Cinci.L.Rev. 289, 296.

577. Ignorant of changes

Horton, James Kent: A Study in Conservatism, 1939, p. 140.

578. Admired civil law

The Legal Mind in America, Miller ed. 1969, p. 101.

579. Name-dropping

Id. at pp. 101, 105.

580. Did not bear out

Id. at p. 113.

581. Support avoidance

Stein, The Attraction of the Civil Law in Post–Revolutionary America, 1966, 52 Va.L.Rev. 403, 409.

582. Too lenient

Horton, James Kent: A Study in Conservatism, 1939, 271.

583. Christianity part

Id. at p. 188.

584. Commercial bias

Sellers, The Market Revolution: Jacksonian America, 1915–1846, 1991, p. 50.

585. "Legislators"

Ibid.

been said to have "stood Blackstone on his head."[586]

Kent was also responsible for the attitude toward politics that permeates American legal education to this day.[587] He believed in aristocracy and thought the major function of government was to protect private property.[588] This flowed from his notion that private property was essential to personal liberty——a view that cynics might think has been confirmed by legal developments in the 20th Century.[589] Ironically, Kent did not foresee how property could be used to contain politics, so he was opposed to anything that smacked of democracy; e.g., universal suffrage.[590] He spoke of the "evil genius of democracy," "this great moral pestilence" that meant "inflammatory appeals to the worst passions of the worst men in society" so as to produce "fierce and vindictive majorities" that would plunder the rich.[591] He opposed education for ordinary Americans on the grounds that it would

586. "Stood on head"

Ibid.

587. Attitude to politics

He condemned the provision in state constitutions that allowed voters to "instruct" their representatives how to vote on the ground that this would lead to interest group politics rather than the Federalist notion that elections were occasions for the ordinary people to determine which members of the elite would meet to determine their common welfare. Welter, The Mind of America, 1820–1860, 1975, p. 196.

588. Aristocracy and property

Horton, James Kent: A Study in Conservatism, 1939, p. 55.

589. Property and liberty

Welter, The Mind of America, 1820–1860, 1975, p. 169. The allusion in the text to modern developments encompasses everything from the O.J. Simpson trial to Supreme Court holdings that money not only talks but has First Amendment rights.

Daniel Webster, by contrast, shared the Revolutionary belief that republican government required a relative equality of wealth and deluded himself that the colonies had no aristocracy and "a condition of comparative equality in regard to wealth"——a condition he thought the common law had preserved. Bartlett, Daniel Webster, 1978, p. 169. Kent, on the other hand, believed that "[a] state of equality as to property is impossible to be maintained for it is against the laws of our nature * * *." Horton, James Kent: A Study in Conservatism, 1939, p. 278.

590. Opposed suffrage

Welter, The Mind of America, 1820–1860, 1975, p. 14. In the New York constitutional convention of 1821, Kent was still defending property qualifications for voting. Aumann, The Influence of English and Civil Law Principles Upon the American Legal System During The Critical Post–Revolutionary Period, 1938, 12 U.Cinci.L.Rev. 289, 302.

591. Plunder the rich

Sellers, The Market Revolution: Jacksonian America, 1815–1846, 1991, p. 113.

only enlarge their capacity for mischief and add a fresh stimulus to delinquencies and novelties, to change and revolution, and contempt for the ordinary restraints of law, morality and religion.[592]

This is a rather far cry from those Founders who thought of government in general and jury trial in particular as serving an educative function and who believed that ordinary people were better suited to determining the truth of testimony than judges.[593]

In 1825, another loyalist "draft dodger," William Rawle, published the first edition of "A View of The Constitution," which became a popular textbook.[594] In his discussion of the Sixth Amendment, this is all Rawle has to say about the right of confrontation:

> It seems monstrous that in any country the testimony on which a person might be convicted should be taken in his absence. Yet it is certain, that in some places, the testimony on which a person might be convicted of the greatest crimes was often taken without his being present, sometimes even without his knowing who the witnesses were. The evidence thus collected was embodied in the accusation, and he was required to defend himself against invisible enemies.[595]

This impoverished version of confrontation and reluctance to identify the "places" in which has it been denied is what we might expect from one who spent the Revolution hiding out in the Inns of Court.[596]

On July 4, 1826, Americans celebrated the semicentennial of Independence.[597] In written remarks on the occasion, the author of the Declaration of Independence rejoiced that people everywhere were coming to recognize the essence of the Declaration——"the palpable truth, that the mass of mankind has not been born with saddles on their backs, nor a favored few, booted and spurred,

---

592. "Contempt for restraints"

Horton, James Kent: A Study in Conservatism, 1939, p. 321.

593. Educative function

See vol. 30, § 6346, pp. 643–644.

594. Popular textbook

Dictionary of American Biography, Bowman ed. 1995, p. 599.

595. "Invisible enemies"

Rawle, A View of the Constitution, 2d ed. 1829, pp. 128–129.

596. Impoverished

Rawle does mention cross-examination, but only as a reason for the importance of the right to counsel. Id. at p. 129.

597. Celebrated semicentennial

Ellis, Passionate Sage, 1993, p. 205; Sellers, The Market Revolution: Jacksonian America, 1815–1846, 1991, p. 237.

ready to ride them, by the grace of God."[598] John Adams took a gloomier view, one that Jefferson seems to have shared when a decade earlier he wrote that the younger generation seemed to have "nothing in them of the feelings of principles of '76," giving their approval to a "single and splendid government of an aristocracy, founded on banking institutions, and moneyed incorporations," which he predicted would soon be "riding and ruling over the plundered ploughman and beggared yeomanry."[599] As the semicentennial celebrated their achievements, it also symbolized the demise of the Revolutionary generation.[600] As every schoolchild knows, the second and third Presidents died within a few hours of each other on that July 4th.[601]

Not only did the Revolutionists die without giving us a definitive reading of the Confrontation Clause, but over the next two decades their successors began to rewrite the state constitutions in the name of Progress.[602] In the Michigan convention of 1850, a delegate seeking to abolish the grand jury argued that if "institutions were venerable and useful for reason of their antiquity, there was no object in the American revolution."[603] The implications of this attitude for the right of confrontation are unclear.[604] But the demise of the Revolutionary ideology made it possible for the Whigs to invoke the Constitution as an obstacle to democracy.[605] The view that constitutionalism is the essence of democratic government gave rise to a veneration of the judiciary that was ultimately to expand the power of judges at the expense of those the Founders hoped to empower through the Sixth amendment.[606] Kent's view

598. "Grace of God"

Id. at p. 269.

599. "Beggared yeomanry"

Id. at p. 106.

600. Symbolized demise

Id. at p. 158.

601. Adams and Jefferson

Encyclopedia of American History, Morris ed. 1976, p. 197.

602. Rewrite constitutions

Welter, The Mind of America, 1820–1860, p. 11.

603. "Reason of antiquity"

Id. at pp. 11–12.

604. Implications unclear

If one thinks of confrontation as an ancient common law right, as the courts came to see it, then the spirit of "Progress" might suggest it should be improved out of existence. If, on the other hand, the Founders are seen as creating the right, then the argument from modernity loses its force.

605. Obstacle to democracy

Id. at p. 205. See also, above text at note 480.

606. Veneration of judiciary

Id. at pp. 212–213. In 1847, citizens were urged to "[r]evere and support the Judiciary" on the grounds it was "the civilized and christian institution." Id. at p. 218.

that liberty lies in property seems benign when contrasted with the Whig view that "liberty=obedience."[607] Even Big Brother could tolerate a right of confrontation if those who were to invoke or interpret it were of the view that the "largest amount of liberty consists in the most extensive obedience to good laws."[608] This slave mentality is hardly conducive to a vigorous adversary system.[609]

Bentham and Confrontation

In 1827, Jeremy Bentham's "Rationale of Judicial Evidence" was published.[610] In chapter nineteen, Bentham analyzed "confrontation under the Roman law" and criticized the German version because the civil law's "imperfect modification of cross-examination" was there "left in express terms to the arbitrary will and pleasure of the judge" whereas "[i]n English law * * * cross-examination is in principle regarded as the indefeasible right of each party [and] the examination of a witness is never regarded as complete without it."[611] As the language quoted suggests, Bentham was skeptical of the claim that the English right of cross-examination originated in the Roman law.[612] He argued that the lack of any word for cross-examination in other European languages supported his view that it was uniquely English.[613]

Later, in his "recapitulation" of the English and Roman law regarding the "collection of evidence," he opined that

> the mode of collecting evidence by means of its delivery viva voce, and subsequent though immediate consignment to writing, is essentially preferable to the mode which operates by the delivery of the testimony in writing in the first instance.[614]

Bentham criticized the English law for too extensively allowing the use of depositions and affidavits where there was no need for the

---

607. "Liberty=obedience"

Id. at p. 206.

608. "Obedience to laws"

Id. at p. 207. Big Brother's version was "Freedom is slavery." Orwell, Nineteen Eighty–Four, 1949, pt. 1, ch.1.

609. Vigorous adversary

On the right of confrontation as an element of the adversary system, see vol. 30, § 6348, p. 780.

610. Bentham's "Rationale"

See vol. 21, § 5005, p. 64.

611. "Never without it"

2 Bentham, Rationale of Judicial Evidence, 1827, p. 423.

612. Skeptical of claim

Id. at p. 430.

613. Uniquely English

Id. at p. 433.

614. "Essentially preferable"

Id. at pp. 425–426.

use of written evidence.[615]

Since Bentham was the godfather of the American codification movement, his views of confrontation were undoubtedly influential with them.[616] However, Bentham's support for confrontation would have made the right somewhat suspect in the eyes of devotees of the English common law.[617] Moreover, it seems plausible that Bentham's linking of cross-examination with Roman confrontation, despite his reservations about that relationship, played a role in a similar equation by judges and legal scholars in America.[618] In addition, Bentham abetted American reductionists when he attacked Blackstone's view, shared by the Founders, that confrontation was an aspect of trial by jury and an essential element of an adversary system of procedure.[619]

In 1827, a Virginia court decided a case that Wigmore thinks became a misguided precedent on the meaning of the right of confrontation.[620] Finn v. Commonwealth was a counterfeiting prosecution that arose in what is now part of West Virginia.[621] After calling a witness to testify that the defendant had told him that what one Candler had said during testimony in an earlier proceeding "was strictly true, as far as it went" but was incomplete, the prosecution called witnesses to testify to Candler's incriminating testimony.[622] Candler was still alive but beyond the jurisdiction.[623]

615. Criticizing use

Id. at p. 426.

616. Bentham influential

See vol. 21, § 5005, pp. 64–65.

617. Suspect

Twining, Theories of Evidence: Bentham & Wigmore, 1985, p. 3.

618. Similar equation

See below, text at note 833.

619. Attacked Blackstone

2 Bentham, Rationale of Judicial Evidence, 1827, p. 431. Bentham claimed that the connection between cross-examination and jury trial was "altogether accident" —betraying a somewhat stunted view of historical causation. Bentham correctly notes that cross-examination can be used as well in court trials as jury trials, but this ignores the fact that since the judge can question witnesses, he has less need for cross by the parties.

Ironically, in the Frenchman Dumont's condensation of "The Rationale," which was published in an English translation just two years earlier, the author in discussing the "different modes of examination" has Bentham saying: "1. Oral examination, conducted publicly, in the presence of the judge, between the parties. This is the mode in trial by jury."

620. Misguided precedent

5 Wigmore. Evidence, Chadbourn rev. 1974, § 1398, pp. 185–186.

621. Finn case

1827, 26 Va. (5 Rand.) 701.

622. Testify to testimony

Id. at pp. 701–703.

To modern eyes, this looks like an attempt to prove an adoptive admission by the defendant, but it is not clear from the opinion what the objection was or what was the theory of admissibility.[624] Two things are clear.[625] First, the court held that former testimony was not admissible in a criminal case.[626] Second, this decision was not based on the right of confrontation, which is never mentioned, but on English precedents.[627] While this case might be cited as evidence of the still rudimentary understanding of the hearsay rule, Wigmore is clearly correct in saying it is no precedent for the constitutional right of confrontation.[628]

Jacksonian Politico–Legal Culture and Confrontation

Since the 1830s were to provide the first significant batch of confrontation precedents, we must pause to describe the socio-political intellectual climate in which those decisions were made.[629] In 1828, Andrew Jackson became the first American President who was not born into an elite family.[630] Jackson's election owed much to the rise of democratic suffrage; only two states did not choose their presidential electors by popular vote.[631] However, we should

623. Beyond jurisdiction

Id. at p. 702.

624. Objection not clear

The reporter says the objection was that the testimony was "irrelevant and impertinent." Id. at p. 703.

625. Two things clear

The court says that the supposed "confession" of the defendant was not an adequate "foundation" for admission of the former testimony. The court's reasoning might be characterized as holding that defendant's remarks were not an adoption of the testimony because far from manifesting a belief in the truth of the testimony, the defendant claimed it was misleadingly incomplete. But the court does not say this.

626. Not in criminal

Id. at p. 708.

627. English precedents

The court relies on Peake's treatise, quoted above at note 167. Ibid. However, Peake is not dealing with the

right of confrontation and Wigmore claims that the case Peake relies upon in fact holds to the contrary. 5 Wigmore, Evidence, Chadbourn rev. 1974, § 1398, p. 186.

628. No precedent

5 Wigmore, Evidence, Chadbourn rev. 1974, § 1398, p. 186.

629. First batch

Wigmore thought that the most significant decisions were not to come until the period 1840–1860. 5 Wigmore, Evidence, Chadbourn rev. 1974, § 1398, p. 185.

630. Jackson not elite

Sellers, The Market Revolution: Jacksonian America, 1815–1846, 1991, p. 174.

631. Choose electors

Encyclopedia of American History, Morris ed. 1976, p. 198.

not overstate the extent of democracy; only about one-quarter of white males were eligible to vote and, as we have seen, there was still much opposition to the abolition of property qualifications for voters.[632] While the Jacksonians continued to press for democratic controls on the capitalist political economy,[633] the rise of democracy may well have diluted support for the right of confrontation. Some Jacksonians seemed to see suffrage as the ordinary person's "bill of rights"[634]—an unwitting revival of the Federalist view that in a republican government there was no need for a bill of rights.[635]

The Jacksonian era saw a revival of Revolutionary demands for equality.[636] The Jacksonians claimed to be the only true heirs of the Founders, using the Alien and Sedition Acts and the Hartford Convention to tar the Whigs as part of the eternal conspiracy against liberty.[637] The Masonic Order provided a handy symbol in what was called a "struggle of republican equality against an odious aristocracy."[638] Equality became such a powerful political totem that even the Whigs seized upon it to advance their program of government aid for the emerging capitalist order.[639] However, the Whig version paled by comparison with the lurid novel "Quaker City," the most widely read piece of fiction prior to "Uncle Tom's Cabin."[640] The author depicted a conspiracy of rich Philadelphians seeking to enslave poor men while debauching their women in a luxurious dungeon.[641]

632. Only one-quarter

Sellers, The Market Revolution: Jacksonian America, 1815–1846, 1991, p. 200. On the opposition to democratic suffrage, see above, text at note 590. See also, Welter, The Mind of America, 1820–1860, 1975, p. 14.

633. Democratic controls

Id. at p. 108.

634. Ordinary person's "bill"

Welter, The Mind of America, 1820–1860, 1975, pp. 182–183.

635. Federalist view

See vol. 30, § 6347, p. 681.

636. Revolutionary equality

Sellers, The Market Revolution: Jacksonian America, 1815–1846, 1991, p. 281. For the Federalist view of equality, see Ellis, Passionate Sage, 1993, pp. 90, 132.

637. Against liberty

Welter, The Mind of America, 1820–1860, 1975, pp. 27–28.

638. "Odious aristocracy"

Sellers, The Market Revolution: Jacksonian America, 1815–1846, 1991, p. 282.

639. Even Whigs

Id. at p. 282 (Whig use of anti-Masonic imagery).

640. "Quaker City"

Id. at p. 385.

641. Debauching women

The author, George Lippard, devoted his royalties and much of his life in political efforts to resist the "degradation of the Workers of America." Ibid. See also Dictionary of American Biography, Bowman ed. 1995, p. 444.

For purposes of confrontation, the most significant effect of the new egalitarianism was the revival of the Leveller epistemology of the Revolutionary era.[642] Even as judicious a thinker as the historian George Bancroft spoke of "an internal sense, which places us in connexion with the world of intelligence and the decrees of God"— a "sentiment of truth, justice, love, and beauty [that] exists in every one" not just "the privileged few."[643] The belief that "the common judgment in taste, politics, and religion, is the highest authority on earth, and the nearest possible approach to an infallible decision" underlays both trial by jury and confrontation as a basis for judging "truth."[644] The consensus historians overlooked the levelling tendency of Jacksonian radicals because they made no demand for economic equality, but recent scholarship has shown that these Jacksonians thought that equality of result would be the inevitable result of a true equality of opportunity.[645]

Another strain of the Jacksonian persuasion relevant to the interpretation of confrontation is a strong anti-English bias.[646] It has been suggested that the existence of a British precedent for some policy measure was sufficient to condemn it in the eyes of Jacksonians.[647] To the extent that this was a preference for indigenous ideas as against those associated with the colonialist oppressors, it undoubtedly weakened in response to changes in English foreign policy following the so-called "Second War of Independence."[648] But the image of England as a class-driven antithesis to democratic equality retained its power down to comparatively re-

642. Leveller epistemology

See vol. 30, § 6345, pp. 456–457.

643. "Privileged few"

Sellers, The Market Revolution: Jacksonian America, 1815–1846, 1991, p. 341.

644. "Infallible decision"

Ibid.

645. Overlooked levelling

Ashworth, The Jacksonian as Leveller, 1980, 14 J.Am.Stud. 407.

646. Anti–English bias

Welter, The Mind of America, 1820–1846, 1975, pp. 7–8.

647. Sufficient to condemn

Id. at p. 32. Hence, to the extent that people believed it, the judicial view that confrontation was a product of the English common law served to undermine popular support for the right.

648. "Second war"

Sellers, The Market Revolution: Jacksonian America, 1915–1846, 1991, p. 93. On the changes in British attitudes and policies following the War of 1812, see generally, Dangerfield, The Era of Good Feelings, 1989. As an exemplar of this species of anti-British sentiment, see Robert Rantoul, Memoirs, Speeches, and Writings, Hamilton ed. 1854, p. 277.

cent times.[649]

Anti-English idioms figured prominently in the Jacksonian struggle against the common law and the power of the judiciary to impose its will to restrain democracy.[650] Lawyers and judges were portrayed as a new "aristocracy" bringing in the "despotic consequences" found "in the provisions of the common Law."[651] In keeping with Leveller epistemology, the Jacksonians claimed that

> the whole contrivance of courts of judicature is a fraud upon the community * * * [because] there is no question of right or wrong which a savage is not as competent to decide as the ablest judge in the land.[652]

The view of an independent judiciary as a relic of monarchy provoked a furious counterattack from the Whigs, whose vision of an apolitical judiciary triumphed over Jacksonian legal realism.[653] We shall see how Story was able to impose his view of the common law as a restraint on democracy upon American legal thought, with serious side-effects on the right of confrontation.[654] The victory of Federalist legal thought owed something to the ambivalence of the

649. England class-driven

Welter, The Mind of America, 1820–1860. p. 7.

650. Against judiciary

Id. at p. 171. See also, above, text at note 469.

651. "Despotic consequences"

Id. at p. 82.

652. "Savage as competent"

Ibid. It was also argued that under the Revolutionary constitutions "the legislature represents the will of the people, the executive their power, and the judiciary their reason or justice * * * [so] they have no power or authority whatever beyond what is given by the people in express terms, set forth in the people's constitutions." Id. at p. 221. The implication is that no constitution gives the judge the express power to act legislatively.

In 1834, an assembly of labor unionists was told: "We want no part of our government independent of the peo-

ple. Those, who are responsible to nobody, ought to be entrusted by nobody. But to whom are the judges responsible? The aristocracy always centre around power placed beyond the reach of the people * * *." Id. at p. 235. For similar sentiments directed to the Federal judiciary, see id. at p. 237.

653. Whig counterattack

After noting the Jacksonian attacks on unelected judges, one Whig editorialist wrote "There is scarcely any dangerously radical opinion, any specious, delusive theory, on social, political, or moral points, which does not * * * find its peculiar aliment and growth among the elements of that party." Id. at p. 15. On the Whig vision of an apolitical judiciary, see id. at pp. 212–213. See also, above, text at note 475.

654. Story view

Newmyer, Supreme Court Justice Joseph Story, 1985, p. 272.

Jacksonians regarding popular control of the judiciary.[655] Not only did they fail in their attempt to substitute the ballot for the bill of rights, they also lost much of the bill of rights in the process.[656]

Though opposition continued for some time, by the 1830s the common law had triumphed over the Revolutionary ideology.[657] This initiated a gradual but inexorable shift of power from the jury to the judge, a shift that produced subtle but profound changes in the adversary system which supported and was supported by the right of confrontation.[658] One indicia of this shift was the growing importance and sophistication of the rules of evidence.[659] We can see this if we compare the evidence treatises then extant with the arguments of Robert Rantoul, a prominent Jacksonian lawyer, in opposition to a bill in the Massachusetts legislature that would have continued the common-law incompetence of infidels—that is, those professing non-Christian religions or atheistic beliefs.[660] In addition to invoking the Inquisition as an exemplar of the consequences of applying religious dogma to governmental institutions, Rantoul pointed out the unreliability of hearsay evidence of a person's state of mind and of the value of character evidence for credibility.[661] Moreover, he seems to have been one of the first persons to suggest that persons rendered incompetent to testify can

---

655. Ambivalence of Jacksonians

Welter, The Mind of America, 1820–1860, 1975, pp. 176, 187.

656. Ballot for bill

See text at note 634, above. Notice that the demand for popular control of the judiciary seems to concede legislative power to the judiciary.

657. Common law triumphed

The Legal Mind in America, Miller ed. 1969, p. 119.

658. Shift of power

Friedman, Crime and Punishment in American History, 1993, p. 245. One of the most bitterly contested of these changes was the denial of the power of the jury to decide law as well as fact, a change that in some states was not completed until the middle of the 20th Century. Levy, The Law of The Commonwealth and Chief Justice Shaw, 1957, p. 290 (after court held jurors lacked this power, popular outcry forced the legislature to pass a statute restoring this power). See also, Nelson, Americanization of the Common Law, 1975, p. 3 (detailing powers of 18th Century juries). One consequence of this was to enhance the importance of the fact-finding role of the jury, with significant impact on the right of confrontation.

659. Rules of evidence

Id. at p. 248.

660. Rantoul argument

Rantoul, Memoirs, Speeches, and Writings, Hamilton ed. 1854, p. 343. The extent evidence treatises are discussed above, text at note 123. For more on the incompetence of infidels, see vol. 27, § 6005, p. 63.

661. Hearsay and character

Id. at pp. 346, 347.

become a target population for unscrupulous predators——a point that is sometimes overlooked even today.[662]

The 1830s also made more visible a series of changes in the institutions of criminal justice that altered the environment in which the right of confrontation was to be exercised.[663] For example, a century-long shift from private to institutional "accusers" reached fruition; that is, police and prosecutors rather than victims decided when criminal charges should be brought.[664] This accompanied a growing politicization of the police force as police departments were incorporated into the local "spoils system" so that the officer's job depended on pleasing powerful elites.[665] A cause or consequence of these changes was a decline in the inquisitorial preliminary examination in which justices of the peace questioned witnesses in private and harangued uncounseled defendants to confess.[666] Somewhat paradoxically, this led to a decline in adversariness as guilty pleas came to supplant jury trial as the major mode of disposition of criminal charges.[667]

As youth moved West to seek their fortune, America saw the

662. Target population

Id. at p. 349.

663. Altered environment

For example, in an era of private prosecution of crime, the "accusers" and the "witnesses against" were to a great degree overlapping categories; once prosecution becomes a public function, the "accuser" may never be a "witness against" the accused. This is significant because some state confrontation clauses seem to distinguish the two.

664. Institutional "accusers"

Friedman, Crime and Punishment in American History, 1992, p. 70.

665. Politicization of police

Id. at p. 149.

666. Inquisitorial prelim

In Dumont's abridgment of Bentham's "Treatise on Judicial Evidence," in discussing "the different modes of examination" of witnesses, it is said: "Oral examination, conducted by the judge, in the absence of the parties, but publicly. Such is, in England, the procedure of the justices of the peace in taking preliminary examinations." Bentham, Treatise on Judicial Evidence, Dumont ed. 1825, p. 92. The American departure from English practice is described in Nelson, The Americanization of The Common Law, 1975, p. 100. To the extent that the preliminary hearing becomes truly adversarial, this deprives the confrontation argument against use of the prelim testimony against the defendant of much of its force.

667. Growth in guilty pleas

Friedman, Crime and Punishment in American History, 1993, p. 251. The paradox may be more apparent than real. An adversary preliminary examination gives both attorney and client a more realistic appraisal of the evidence and of the likely outcome of the trial. Moreover, it gives the defendant a chance to confront his accusers and "have his say"——an opportunity that once could only be exercised at trial.

rise of "crimes of mobility."[668] In the urban areas from which they had fled, increasing economic inequality and the comparative anonymity among neighbors went hand in hand with the growth of what we now think of as "urban crime"——stranger assaults and robberies.[669] Although this was an era that traditionalists saw as one of declining morality, it was also an era of declining morals prosecutions.[670] One reason for this can be found in the response of Robert Rantoul to a proposal in the town meeting to choose a committee to prosecute sumptuary offenses:

> What more inquisitorial or arbitrary measure can be conceived, than the appointment of a committee for the avowed purpose of getting up prosecutions and plunging their fellow-citizens into vexatious and ruinous lawsuits? * * * If they should search the annals of despotism back to the bloody laws of Draco, they could find nothing more arbitrary and despotic. They would see nothing in all the dark details more abominable than the sending of spies and agents to draw their chosen victims before judicial tribunals.[671]

On only has to contrast this with the accepted functions of modern police departments to see how far confrontation values have lost their hold on the popular mind.[672]

The decline in the prosecution of morals offenses accompanied a rise in the prosecution of property crimes.[673] In part this may have reflected an increase in the incidence of property crimes that accompanied the rise of a "stranger" society with vast disparities in wealth, but it also reflected an increase in the moral significance of private property.[674] Some historians have seen this as part of a broader trend to adapt the law to the needs of an emerging

668. "Crimes of mobility"

Id. at p. 193. See also, Sellers, The Market Revolution: Jacksonian America, 1815–1846, 1991, p. 239 (fracturing of family ties by movement of young for economic reasons).

669. "Urban crime"

Id. at pp. 68–69 (mobs and riots).

670. Decline in morals

Nelson, Americanization of the Common Law, 1975, p. 110 (decline in prosecutions); Sellers, The Market Revolution: Jacksonian America, 1815–1846, 1991, pp. 9, 48 (declining morality).

671. "Sending spies"

Rantoul, Memoirs, Speeches, and Writings, Hamilton ed. 1854, p. 341.

672. Confrontation values

See vol. 30, § 6343, pp. 341–342 (confrontation and informers).

673. Rise in property

Sellers, The Market Revolution: Jacksonian America, 1815–1846, 1991, p. 47.

674. Moral significance

Nelson, Americanization of the Common Law, 1975, pp. 117–118.

capitalist political economy.[675] One indicia of this was the use by courts of conspiracy prosecutions against workers who attempted to organize labor unions.[676] Indeed, John Calhoun began predicting class warfare when Karl Marx was still a boy.[677]

The rise in guilty pleas and the decline in the instances of public punishments for crimes (such as whipping, branding, or standing in stocks) made the administration of justice less populist than it had been in early times.[678] People ignorant of the operations of the courts or impatient with constraints on punishment, such as the right of confrontation, began to turn again to extra-legal forms of punishment.[679] Though the legitimacy of the mob as an instrument of social control had diminished following the Revolution, the lack of legitimacy was not a deterrent to mob action.[680] Some mob activities, such as the burning of a Catholic convent in Massachusetts in 1834, did little to burnish the legitimacy of extra-legal action.[681] Nonetheless, vigilantes and vigilantism continued to flourish against the despised; abolitionists were the frequent target of mobs and vigilantes.[682] But extra-legal tribunals continued to be

675. Needs of capitalist

"[T]he law came to be a tool by which those interest groups that had emerged victorious in the competition for control of law-making institutions could seize most of society's wealth for themselves and enforce their seizure upon the losers." Id. at p. 174.

676. Against unions

Boorstin, The Americans: The National Experience, paper 1965, p. 47 (12 such prosecutions between 1805–1842).

677. Class warfare

"[T]he contest will be between the capitalists and operatives; for into these two classes it [the inequality of property] must, ultimately, divide society. The issue of the struggle here must be the same as it has been in Europe. Under the operation of the system, wages must sink more rapidly than the necessaries of life, till the operatives will be reduced to the lowest point,—when the portion of the products of their labor left to them, will be barely sufficient to preserve exis-

tence." Dangerfield, The Era of Good Feelings, 1989, p. 412.

678. Decline in public

Friedman, Crime and Punishment in American History, 1993, pp. 74–75. As modern adherents of capital punishment argue, locking up persons out of sight in a penitentiary makes their punishment less visible and, arguably, less of a deterrent.

679. Extra-legal forms

Id. at p. 174.

680. Legitimacy

Ibid. Those who doubt the legitimacy of extra-legal action should revisit their study of the Boston Tea Party. See vol. 30, § 6345, p. 550.

681. Burning convent

Nelson, Americanization of the Common Law, 1975, p. 115.

682. Abolitionists

Friedman, Crime and Punishment in American History, 1993, p. 179.

used for tasks the courts could not or would not perform; e.g., punishing persons or banishing them for exhibiting a general bad character.[683]

Jacksonian Confrontation Cases

Against this faintly repressive backdrop, in the mid–1830s three different state courts interpreted their confrontation clauses.[684] Commonwealth v. Richards was a perjury prosecution in which the state was allowed to introduce oral testimony stating what the now-deceased victim of the original crime had testified in the preliminary examination in the present case.[685] The defense objected that this was inadmissible hearsay, that the defense had had no opportunity for cross-examination at the preliminary hearing, and that it violated the provision in the Massachusetts Declaration of Rights giving the Defendant the right to "meet the witnesses against him face to face."[686] The defense argued that the declarant "was the accuser; for it was his name that was alleged to have been forged" in the prosecution in which the perjured testimony was given.[687]

The Massachusetts court rejected the confrontation argument:

We do not think the case falls within the constitutional objection. That provision was made to exclude any evidence by deposition, which could be given orally in the presence of the accused, but was not intended to affect the question as to what was or was not competent evidence to be given face to face according to the settled rules of the common law.[688]

683. Bad character

Id. at p. 184.

684. Three interpreted

For the earliest decisions, see above, text at notes 339, 554, and 620.

685. Richards case

1836, 35 Mass. (18 Pick) 434.

686. "Face to face"

The defense argued that "[t]he objects of this provision are: 1, to prevent any mistake as to the identity of the person accused; 2, to deter the witness from testifying falsely, by the presence of the accused; and 3, to give the jurors an opportunity to see the effect of the meeting of the accused and the witness. It is not sufficient that such a meeting takes place at a preliminary examination of the accused before a magistrate, but they must meet face to face before the court and jury." Id. at p. 435. The defense cited the Atkins case, above, text at note 339, in support of the last proposition. Notice that the argument says nothing about cross-examination, though the lack of cross-examination at the preliminary examination was made the basis of another objection. Ibid.

687. "Was the accuser"

Id. at p. 436.

688. "Settled rules"

Id. at p. 437.

The court cited no authority for this proposition.[689] Instead, it cited English authority for the proposition that dying declarations were admissible because "[t]hey are not considered as hearsay evidence * * *," adding "and were not intended to be excluded or touched by the provision cited from the bill of rights."[690]

Dying declarations were directly at issue in Woodsides v. State, a murder prosecution.[691] The defense conceded that the evidence satisfied the common law rules of evidence, but argued that admission violated the section of the Mississippi bill of rights giving the defendant a right "to be confronted by the witnesses against him."[692] The court responded:

> The bill of rights, in respect to the right of the accused of being confronted by the witness for the prosecution, is but an affirmation of a long cherished principle of the common law. By the bill of rights the accused is secured in the right of oral examination of the opposing witnesses and of the advantages of cross-examination. The same right belongs to the subjects of England, but there they have no constitutional provision guarantying its perpetuity.[693]

The court cited no authority for this proposition.[694]

The court goes on to point out that the "argument proceeded upon the supposition that the deceased party was the witness" and since he could not be "confronted or cross-examined by the prisoner, it was a violation of the prisoner's rights."[695] But, the court pointed out, dying declarations are only admissible when the declarant is not available as a witness.[696] Hence, "it is the individual who swears to the statements of the deceased that is the witness, not

689. No authority

Nor did the court attempt to distinguish the authority cited by the defense.

690. "Not intended"

Id. at p. 437. The court cited Peake's treatise, see above, text at note 165, and an English case. Ironically, the court went on to reverse the trial court because the witnesses did not purport to give a full or verbatim account of the testimony at the preliminary examination. Id. at p. 439.

691. Woodsides case

1837, 2 How. (3 Miss.) 655.

692. "Be confronted"

Id. at pp. 664–665. This is the same language as the Sixth Amendment.

693. "Guarantying perpetuity"

Id. at p. 665.

694. Cited no authority

Nor did it offer any evidence to support its historical claims.

695. "Deceased was witness"

Ibid.

696. Not available

Ibid.

the deceased."[697] Again, the court cited no authority for its conceptual argument that a hearsay declarant was not a "witness against" the accused within the meaning of the confrontation clause.[698]

Dying declarations were also at issue in Anthony v. State, an 1838 Tennessee murder prosecution.[699] The court accepted the prosecution's demeaning characterization of the Tennessee confrontation clause.[700]

> The provision in the bill of rights was intended only to ascertain and perpetuate a principle in favor of the liberty and safety of the citizen, which, although fully acknowledged and acted upon before and at the time of our revolution, had been yielded to the liberal or popular party in Great Britain after a long contest * * *. The object of the bill of rights was not to introduce a new principle, but to keep ground already gained, and to preserve and perpetuate the fruits of a political and judicial victory, achieved with difficulty, after a violent and protected contest.[701]

The court cites no authority, but apparently recognizing that its questionable history may not be enough, it adds:

> That our view of this question is correct, is made manifest by the fact, that after more than forty years from the adoption of our first constitution, this argument against the admissibility of dying declarations, on the ground of the bill of rights, is for the first time made * * *.[702]

697. "Not the deceased"

Ibid.

698. Not "witness against"

This argument, as we shall see, was popular in the Nineteenth Century. It has the advantage of neatly resolving the conflict between the right of confrontation and the hearsay rule, albeit at the expense of the right.

699. Anthony case

1838, 19 Tenn. 265.

700. Demeaning clause

"[T]he right of a party accused of a crime to meet the witnesses against him face to face, and the admissibility of dying declarations * * * were principles of the common law of like antiquity and authority; that because the former had been questioned and de-

nied in the relentless state prosecutions engendered in England by party animosity, it was thought by the framers of our constitution to be a rule of fundamental importance, and to be worth of recognition in that instrument. But it was not to be supposed, that because a particular rule of law had, from adventitious circumstances, become invested with the character of a political principle, therefore it annulled a correlative rule, introduced by the same authority, common usage, and founded upon reasons equally cogent." Id. at p. 275. No authority or evidence is cited for this claim.

701. "Preserve the fruits"

Id. at pp. 277–278.

702. "First time made"

Id. at p. 278.

The court never mentions the two previous Tennessee decisions that had reached conflicting results on the effect of the state's confrontation clause but its argument is still technically correct because neither of those cases involved a dying declaration.[703]

Story and Confrontation

This may be an appropriate place to depart from our chronology to consider the person who arguably had the most influence on judicial construction of confrontation ——Joseph Story.[704] Born in 1779, Story lacked first-hand knowledge of the colonial and revolutionary eras.[705] He had family and personal ties to the emerging capitalist political economy; in his youth he represented land speculators who sought to enforce fraudulently procured land grants and later in life he was a close friend of Francis Biddle and a loyal judicial supporter of the Bank of the United States.[706] Although in his youth he was thought to be something of a Jeffersonian, Jefferson himself characterized Story as "unquestionably a Tory."[707] Whatever his youthful beliefs, later in life he recanted his opposition to the hated Alien and Sedition Acts, suggesting that they were constitutional.[708] Something of a snob, he stooped to attacking Jefferson because of his manner of dress.[709] But his incipient High Federalist loyalties must not have been apparent in 1812, when Madison appointed him to the Supreme Court.[710]

703. Two previous decisions

See above, text at notes 339, 554.

704. Story influence

See below, text at note 757.

705. Lacked knowledge

Dunne, Justice Joseph Story and The Rise of The Supreme Court, 1970, p. 90. On the significance of this for confrontation, see vol. 30, §§ 6344–6346.

706. Ties to capitalist

Newmyer, Supreme Court Justice Joseph Story, 1985, p. 117; Swisher, Roger B. Taney, 1935, p. 202. On Story's defense of the Yazoo Land Frauds, see above, note 348.

707. "Unquestionably Tory"

1 Warren, The Supreme Court in United States History, 1947 ed. p. 506.

708. Constitutional

Newmyer, Supreme Court Justice Joseph Story, 1985, p. 164.

709. Manner of dress

Dunne, Joseph Story and The Rise of The Supreme Court, 1970, p. 50.

710. Madison appointed

Newmyer, Supreme Court Justice Joseph Story, 1985, p. 71 (Story was Madison's fourth choice for the nomination).

A familiar story traces his conversion to the Jeffersonian embargo that cost his commercial friends dearly. The Legal Mind in America, Miller ed. 1969, p. 64.

Nathan Dane, Federalist politician and author of one of the leading works on American law, apparently saw what Madison did not.[711] He gave the Harvard Law School money for a professorship bearing his name——a gift contingent on Story being named as the first holder of the chair.[712] Harvard, founded on a bequest from a Loyalist lawyer who fled to England during the Revolution, found Story's pedagogic principles easy to accept:[713]

> [i]f anything can retard * * * the jacobinical torrent which is sweeping past and undermining the foundations of * * * our institutions, the barrier of sound law and conservative influences which the Harvard Law School is building up will do it.[714]

As we shall see, Story was something of a 19th Century Henry Kissinger.[715] Ironically, John Chipman Gray, the first holder of the Story professorship at Harvard, was not as dazzled by Story's reputation as some modern writers.[716] Gray wrote that Story "was a man of great learning, and of a reputation for learning greater even than the learning itself * * * he was fond of glittering generalities; and he was possessed by a restless vanity."[717]

More than a jurist and a scholar, Story was a political activist in ways that would be unthinkable under modern notions of judicial ethics.[718] His most recent biographer casts him as the leader of the conservative counterrevolution mounted by the remnants of the old Federalist party in the quarter century after the War of 1812.[719]

711. Nathan Dane

Dictionary of American Biography, Bowman ed. 1995, p. 173.

712. Story named

Newmyer, Supreme Court Justice Joseph Story, 1985, p. 240.

713. Loyalist lawyer

Graham, "There'll Always Be An England": The Instrumental Ideology of Evidence, 1987, 85 Mich.L.Rev. 1204.

714. "Harvard will do it"

Dunne, Justice Joseph Story and The Rise of The Supreme Court, 1970, p. 426.

715. Something of a Kissinger

One could never glean this from his entry in the Dictionary of American Biography, Bowman ed. 1995, p. 704 (giving more space to Story's son, a poet and sculptor). For a capsule biography, see 2 Parrington, Main Currents in American Thought, 1954, pp. 291–195.

Like Kissinger, Story was an admirer of Metternich. Newmyer, Supreme Court Justice Joseph Story, 1985, p. 356.

716. First holder

Newmyer, Supreme Court Justice Joseph Story, 1985, p. 385.

717. "Restless vanity"

Id. at p. 336, quoting Gray, The Nature and Sources of the Law, 1909, p. 253.

718. Unthinkable

Id. at p. 172.

719. Leader of counterrevolution

Id. at pp. 155–156.

Andrew Jackson described Story and Kent as "dangerous men." Miller, The

Story revived the supposedly defunct New England Federalism as an ideological counterweight to Jacksonian egalitarianism.[720] In 1820, he took leave of his judicial duties to serve as a delegate to the Massachusetts constitutional convention.[721] Frightened by what he saw as the social disorder of democracy, Story favored property qualifications for voters.[722] In a similar vein, he opposed reapportionment as well as disestablishment of the Congregational churches.[723]

As Dane had hoped, Story used his classroom at Harvard as a forum to advance so-called "creative conservatism."[724] Much of the curriculum that he developed still shapes American legal education today.[725] Story foresaw how lawyers and judges could serve as a conservative counterweight to Jacksonian ideology and he thought his professorial role was as a producer of a cadre of conservative lawyer-statesmen—a model that is still sometimes visible in remarks to entering law students at the end of the 20th Century.[726] Of course, modern libertarians might find it somewhat hypocritical for Story to extol the virtues of capitalism while seeking governmental subsidies for Harvard.[727] Similarly, his denunciations of the Jacksonian "spoils system" are hard to square with his private lobbying for government jobs for his students and political allies.[728]

Even more troubling for modern sensibilities are Story's rather loose constructions of the limitations of the judicial role.[729] He gave Daniel Webster, his ideological compatriot, advice on legal strategy—even suggesting arguments Webster could make to the Supreme Court.[730] Story also saw nothing unethical in sitting in cases

Legal Mind in America, paper 1969, p. 63.

720. Ideological counterweight
Id. at p. 162.

721. Serve as delegate
Id. at p. 164.

722. Fear and property
Id. at pp. 365, 168.

723. Disestablishment
Id. at p. 167.

724. Dane hoped
Id. at p. 241.

725. Harvard curriculum
Id. at p. 165.

726. Conservative cadre
Id. at pp. 178, 269. See also, The Legal Mind in America, Miller ed. 1969, pp. 176–177.

727. Seeking subsidies
Id. at p. 167.

728. Lobbying
Id. at pp. 173–175.

729. Loose constructions
Id. at p. 172.

730. Suggesting arguments
Id. at p. 361; Dunne, Justice Joseph Story and The Rise of the Supreme Court, 1970, p. 301; Swisher, Roger B. Taney, 1935, p. 202.

in which he and his friends had a financial stake in the outcome.[731] For confrontation purposes, perhaps the most significant acts of Story's brand of "judicial activism" was his participation in the drafting of the Fugitive Slave Laws whose constitutionality was then being questioned, in part because they denied the defendant any right to confront those who asserted her servile status.[732]

To understand Story's rather formidable contributions to American conservatism, we must take a closer look at his ideology.[733] Like many of the Founders, Story was opposed to "democracy;" he and other members of the Court opposed Andrew Jackson's candidacy for President and when Jackson won, Story proclaimed his administration as "the reign of King Mob."[734] For Story, the function of law was to provide a model of social decision-making to rival politics.[735] In this view, law was a kind of "anti-politics" in the sense of "anti-matter."[736] In this view, the function of the Supreme Court was to defeat the will of the majority.[737] Story thought the Court "will perpetually thwart the wishes and views of demagogues;" hence, "[i]ts only support is the wise and good and the elevated in society"—a minority consisting of Story and his friends.[738] Judges who disagreed with Story's views were constantly accused of "playing politics."[739] In popularizing the view that the Supreme Court is above politics, Story can claim to be the inventor of modern constitutional law—at least as it is practiced in the academy.[740]

731. Financial stake

Newmyer, Supreme Court Justice Joseph Story, 1985, p. 226.

732. Slave Laws

Id. at p. 377. See also above, text at note 535.

733. His contributions

Newmyer, Supreme Court Justice Joseph Story, 1985, p. 390.

734. "King Mob"

Dunne, Joseph Story and The Rise of the Supreme Court, 1970, p. 282. Chief Justice Marshall went so far as to vote for the first time in 20 years. Id. at p. 281.

735. Rival politics

Newmyer, Supreme Court Justice Joseph Story, 1985, p. 248.

736. "Anti-politics"

Id. at p. 114.

737. Defeat majority

Id. at p. 197.

738. "The wise and good"

Dunne, Joseph Story and The Rise of The Supreme Court, 1970, p. 214. It is clear that to Story "the demagogues" meant the Jacksonians. Id. at p. 235.

739. "Playing politics"

Newmyer, Supreme Court Justice Joseph Story, 1985, p. 197.

740. Court above politics

Id. at p. 191.

Somehow, Story's "anti-politics" always seemed to turn out to be "pro-capitalist."[741] This policy fueled much of the Marshall Court's constitutional nationalism.[742] Capitalism and its needs provided the underpinning of many of the Court's best-known constitutional decisions.[743] Story himself never missed a chance to praise businessmen—a key portion of "the wise and good."[744] The Court allowed governmental powers to be devolved on private groups—what today is called "privatization."[745] As a result, business corporations began to have more powers than municipal corporations and even the states that created them.[746] Story claimed to "rejoice, that the Supreme Court has at last come to the conclusion, that a corporation is a citizen"—albeit a citizen with little need for a right of confrontation.[747] But as the Court was endowing corporations with legal humanity, that status was denied slaves.[748]

For Story, constitutional law was not the only restraint on the democratic impulses; it shared this function with the far more active principles of the common law.[749] Story worshipped the Tory Lord Mansfield who was busily reshaping the common law to make it more congenial to capitalism.[750] For this reason, Story made the most extravagant claims for the common-law powers of federal judges.[751] Similarly, the common law was his curriculum at Harvard Law School.[752] Story thought that the inquisitorial civil law of evidence was more favorable to capitalists.[753] Nonetheless, he wanted to codify the common law of evidence in his native state.[754] More

---

741. "Pro-capitalist"

Id. at pp. 116–117.

742. Fueled nationalism

Ibid.

743. Underpinning

Id. at pp. 126–127.

744. Praise businessmen

Id. at p. 118.

745. "Privatization"

Id. at p. 128.

746. Business more powers

Id. at p. 132.

747. "Rejoice, citizen"

Dunne, Joseph Story and The Rise of the Supreme Court, 1970, p. 392.

748. Denied slaves

Id. at p. 393.

749. Active common law

Newmyer, Supreme Court Justice Joseph Story, 1985, p. 292.

750. Worshipped Mansfield

Id. at p. 246. On Mansfield's retrograde views of confrontation values, see vol. 30, § 6345, p. 547.

751. Powers of judges

Id. at pp. 98–99.

752. His curriculum

Id. at pp. 243–245.

753. Inquisitorial

Id. at p. 292.

754. Codify evidence

Id. at pp. 278–279.

significantly for our purposes, Story viewed the common law as a significant source for the interpretation of the Constitution.[755] For this purpose, "common law" often meant "English law."[756]

With this background, we may now consider Story's "Commentaries on The Constitution of The United States," begun in 1829 and finished in 1833.[757] The historian Vernon Parrington described this work as the "triumph of the lawyer" over "the historian and political philosopher" and marking "the beginning of the lawyer's custodianship of the fundamental law."[758] It was filled with "crabbed and narrow legalism" disguising a "new-modeled Federalism".[759] One of Story's biographers remarks on the number of anti-Jacksonian diatribes in the treatise, and another describes it as "ammunition for [the] shock troops of conservatism."[760] The "Commentaries" became the text for the teaching of constitutional law at Harvard.[761] This gave it a nationwide influence because over half of Story's students were from outside New England.[762] In addition, Story prepared simplified versions to be used as high school and college texts.[763]

In the history that fills the first volume, Story came to the conclusion that the common law

> has become the guardian of our political and civil rights; it has protected our infant liberties, watched over our maturer growth, it has expanded with our wants, it has nurtured that spirit of independence which has checked the first approaches of arbitrary power, it has enabled us to triumph in the midst of difficulties and dangers threatening our political existence; and, by the goodness

755. Interpretation

Id. at p. 104.

756. "English law"

Id. at p. 124.

757. "Commentaries"

Id. at p. 181.

758. "Custodianship"

2 Parrington, Main Currents in American Thought, paper 1954, p. 295.

759. "Crabbed legalism"

Ibid.

760. "Ammunition for troops"

Dunne, Justice Joseph Story and The Rise of The Supreme Court, 1970, p. 310 (diatribes); Newmyer, Supreme Court Justice Joseph Story, 1985, p. 182 ("ammunition"). See also, Sellers, The Market Revolution: Jacksonian America, 1915–1946, 1991, p. 50 ("commercial bias").

761. Harvard text

Newmyer, Supreme Court Justice Joseph Story, 1985, p. 194.

762. Students from outside

Id. at p. 264.

763. Simplified versions

Dunne, Justice Joseph Story and The Rise of The Supreme Court, 1970, p. 339.

> of God, we are now enjoying under its bold and manly principles,
> the blessings of a free, independent, and united government.[764]

This makes modern television advertising look positively factual by comparison.[765] If we substitute for "the common law," which is an abstraction, the more concrete expression "judicial rule," Story's rhetoric stands as ludicrous.[766]

Not surprisingly then, in the sole paragraph devoted to the Sixth Amendment, Story claims that the rights there enumerated, including the right "to be confronted with the witnesses against him, does but follow out the established course of the common law in all trials for crimes."[767] But Story's common-law trial is a faded version of the Blackstonian version that animated the Founders.[768] Confrontation means no more than that "the witnesses * * * give in their testimony (at least in capital cases) in the presence of the accused."[769] However, in a surprisingly prescient aside, Story adds

> there seems to have been an undue solicitude to introduce into the
> constitution some of the general guards and proceedings of the
> common law trials * * * without sufficiently adverting to the
> consideration, that unless the whole system is incorporated, and
> especially the law of evidence, a corrupt legislature, or a debated
> and servile people, may render the whole little more than a solemn
> pageantry.[770]

As it turns out, it was not the legislature or the people, but a frightened judiciary that did most to reduce confrontation to mere "pageantry."

764. "Manly principles"

Newmyer, Supreme Court Justice Joseph Story, 1985, p. 186. Story once told students at Harvard that "Christianity is a part of the Common Law." The Legal Mind in America, Miller ed. 1969, p. 178.

765. Look factual

Story thought the Constitution emerged from the colonial common law. Id. at p. 189. Perhaps it did, but the records of the colonial period are too skimpy to allow us to make any judgments. See vol. 30, § 6344, p. 378.

766. Ludicrous

As we have seen, the American law of confrontation emerged, like its English predecessor, out of struggles with, not as a gift of, the judiciary. See vol. 30, §§ 6342–6343, 6345–6346.

767. "Follow common law"

3 Story, Commentaries on The Constitution of The United States, 1970, § 1785, p. 662. To support this, Story cites Blackstone and Hawkins. See also, 5 The Founders' Constitution, Kurland & Lerner eds. 1987, p. 296.

768. Blackstonian version

See vol. 30, § 6344, p. 432.

769. "Presence of accused"

3 Story, Commentaries on The Constitution of the United States, 1970, § 1785, p. 296.

770. "Solemn pageantry"

Ibid.

The Dorr War and Greenleaf

Judicial anxieties ratcheted up a bit as a result of the so-called "Dorr War."[771] Rhode Island had never adopted a modern constitution but continued the royal charter of 1663 that disenfranchised all but a small minority of the population.[772] When that minority understandably rejected all suggestions for constitutional change, the majority determined to emulate the Founders and called a convention in 1841 that adopted a so-called "People's Constitution" (which restricted the suffrage to white males).[773] After the constitution was approved by a majority of the voters, Thomas Dorr was elected governor, but his government was suppressed by the state militia backed by federal troops and Dorr was convicted of treason.[774]

Democrats thought that the Rhode Island rebellion was sanctified by American constitutional practice.[775] Conservatives, such as Daniel Webster, thought that they could distinguish the actions of the Dorrites from those of the Founders.[776] For our purposes, the most significant feature of the whole affair was the way in which both federal and state judges jumped in on the side of the aristocratic minority government.[777] Federal judges thought it a condemnation to label the Dorrites "revolutionaries."[778] In a charge to the grand jury that was widely circulated in the propaganda of the charter government, Justice Story opined that the Dorrites were guilty of treason—despite the language of the Constitution and an earlier opinion by Chief Justice Marshall that suggested other-

771. "Dorr War"

Or as modern scholars prefer to call it, the "Dorr Rebellion." In truth, it was not very much of either.

772. Small minority

Encyclopedia of American History, Morris ed. 1976, p. 222.

773. Adopted "People's"

Newmyer, Supreme Court Justice Joseph Story, 1985, p. 359.

774. Dorr convicted

Encyclopedia of American History, Morris ed. 1976, p. 222.

775. Sanctified

Welter, The Mind of America, 1820–1860, 1975, p. 224. Public opinion apparently was on the side of the rebels.

Dunne, Justice Joseph Story and The Rise of the Supreme Court, 1970, p. 425.

776. Distinguish

Dalzell, Daniel Webster and The Trial of American Nationalism, 1843–1852, paper 1975, pp. 9–10. Ironically, Webster's effort came in a speech at the dedication of the Bunker Hill Monument.

777. Side of minority

Schuchuman, The Political Background of the Political Question Doctrine: The Judges and the Dorr War, 1972, 16 Am.J.Leg.Hist. 111, 113.

778. "Revolutionaries"

Id. at p. 114.

wise.[779] Story also thought that the government should make it a crime for any group of citizens to assemble to frame a constitution—a statute that would have made felons of Madison, Hamilton, et al.[780] At Dorr's treason trial, the court refused to admit any evidence of the popular government or the constitution that Dorr claimed legitimated his opposition to the charter government.[781] In a speech to Harvard alumni, Story claimed that "the predominant danger of our day" was "the tendency to ultraism of all sorts" and used the Dorrites to tar those who wanted to alter the political economy erected by the Marshall court.[782]

In 1842, as the Dorr War was playing out and the Oregon Trail was opened, Simon Greenleaf published his treatise on evidence—a book that Roscoe Pound listed as one of the most influential of the antebellum American lawbooks.[783] Greenleaf was the reporter for the Maine Supreme Court when he met Joseph Story.[784] After failing in an effort to get Greenleaf the job of reporter for the U.S. Supreme Court, Story arranged for him to be appointed Royall Professor at the Harvard Law School in 1834.[785] Greenleaf was a better teacher than Story and did most of the work of running the law school.[786] When Greenleaf was proffered an appointment to the Supreme Judicial Court of Massachusetts, Story talked him into declining the post.[787] Nonetheless, Greenleaf dedicated his treatise to Story.[788]

779. Suggested otherwise

Id. at p. 119.

780. Felons of Madison

Id. at p. 118.

781. Refused to admit

Id. at p. 122.

782. "Ultraism"

Newmyer, Supreme Court Justice Joseph Story, 1985, p. 356.

783. Most influential

Pound, The Formative Era of American Law, 1938, p. 140.

784. Met Story

Newmyer, Supreme Court Justice Joseph Story, 1985, p. 260.

785. Royall Professor

Id. at p. 259. We have found little of Greenleaf's politics so it is difficult to know whether he was comfortable in a chair named after a Loyalist who had fled the country for good at the time of the Revolution.

786. Running law school

Id. at pp. 261–262. Greenleaf may have been the originator of the Harvard "Southern strategy" in which the law school added to its coffers by inviting planters to send their sons to Boston to "sow their wild oats" under the guise of getting an education. Dunne, Justice Joseph Story and The Rise of The Supreme Court, 1970, p. 429.

787. Declining post

Id. at p. 260.

788. Dedicated to Story

By modern standards, the dedication is quite extravagant. 1 Greenleaf, A Treatise on the Law of Evidence, 9th ed. 1858, p. iii.

Greenleaf's treatise says nothing about the right of confrontation, though his discussion of the policy of the hearsay rule hints at it:

> The principal of this rule is, that such evidence requires credit to be given to a statement, made by a person who is not subjected to the ordinary tests, enjoined by the law, for ascertaining the correctness and completeness of testimony; namely, that oral testimony should be delivered in the presence of the Court or a magistrate, under the moral and intellectual character, the motives and deportment of the witness can be examined, and his capacity and opportunities for observation, and his memory can be tested by cross-examination.[789]

Though elsewhere, Greenleaf seems less modern in his approach to hearsay,[790] his treatise demonstrates how far the law of evidence had developed since the adoption of the right of confrontation in American constitutions.[791] Indeed, Greenleaf himself says that "[t]he rule excluding hearsay is not of great antiquity."[792]

Though Greenleaf's treatise was well-received, its impact on interpretation of the Confrontation Clause was at best faint and indirect.[793] However, it did have a significant impact on the law of evidence; by making the decisional law more accessible, it undermined one of the arguments for codification.[794] This may have been unintentional as Story was one of those who favored codification of the common law rules of evidence.[795] If Greenleaf was opposed to codification, he was certainly not as vociferous as some of his contemporaries.[796] Moreover, to the extent that codification was

---

789. "Memory tested"

Id. at p. 185.

790. Less modern

Elsewhere he repeats, without criticism, the older notions that hearsay is a particularly weak form of evidence and is not the best evidence. Id. at pp. 138–139. Moreover, his definition of "hearsay" is far from the modern view. Id. at pp. 147 (conduct is hearsay), 153 (same as "verbal acts"), 184 (statements of state of mind, pedigree, or as part of res gestae not hearsay).

791. How far developed

Whereas the earlier treatises, see text at notes 100–173 above, had devoted very few pages, Greenleaf has over a hundred pages on the topic. Id. at pp. 98–235.

792. "Great antiquity"

Id. at p. 185 n. 2.

793. Well-received

The Golden Age of American Law, Haar ed. 1969, p. 77.

794. Undermined

Id. at p. 79.

795. Story favored

Id. at p. 250.

796. Contemporaries

The Legal Mind in America, Miller ed. 1969, p. 107.

part of the search by the young nation for its own identity apart from Great Britain, Greenleaf's treatise may have provided an alternative route.[797] Prior to his treatise, law students had been forced to rely on English evidence books; now they could study an American view of the subject.[798]

The Rise of Wigmorean Confrontation

In 1845, in a Virginia murder trial, the defense argued that admission of a dying declaration violated the Virginia confrontation clause.[799] In rejecting this argument, the Virginia court first said that if the argument was correct, "for nearly 70 years past, the courts of this Commonwealth have been in the constant practice of violating the bill of rights in a most important particular."[800] Recognizing that the argument from desuetude was not dispositive, the Court then turned to the defense argument that the common-law basis of the exception did not legitimize it because the right of confrontation did not exist at common law.[801]

> In this respect, we think learned counsel is in error. Magna Charta provides that a subject accused of crime should be tried by his peers; and according to the principles of the common law; and it is a well established principle of the common law, that an accused should be tried by a jury of the vicinage; that the trial should be public; and the witnesses against him examined in his presence. This was no new principle. It was familiar to Virginia in her colonial condition.[802]

Notice how this passage evades, while seeming to endorse, the proposition that the confrontation clause was intended to adopt the common law.[803] Similarly, the claim that the right of confrontation

797. Search for identity

The Golden Age of American Law, Haar ed. 1969, p. 424.

798. Relied on English

Newmyer, Supreme Court Justice Joseph Story, 1985, p. 255.

799. Virginia confrontation

The Virginia clause reads "to be confronted with the accusers and witnesses."

800. "Practice of violating"

Hill v. Commonwealth, 1845, 2 Va. (Gratt.) 594, 607.

801. Did not exist

"One of the learned counsel for the prisoner maintained, in the argument, that the provision in the bill of rights, that the accused had a right to be confronted with the witnesses against him, was a new principle; the offspring of American liberty; and that it had no existence in the great charter of English liberty." Ibid.

802. "Colonial condition"

Ibid.

803. Intended to adopt

This was the position of Story and others. See above, text at notes 691, 767.

was "familiar" to the colonists does not say that confrontation was practiced in the colonial era.[804] Moreover, the insinuation that the right of confrontation arose from Magna Carta has little historical validity.[805] Notice, however, that the Court correctly sees confrontation as an aspect of trial by jury and one that is linked to the vicinage and public trial guarantees.[806]

The Court goes on to say that dying declarations were admissible in England long before 1776, and no one supposed that this was a violation of Magna Carta.[807] Apparently sensing that the historical argument is suspect, the Court concludes with a conceptual argument; that is, that the hearsay declarant is not a "witness against" the defendant.[808] Hence, the confrontation clause is satisfied if the defendant is able to confront the witness who relates the hearsay statement.[809] Though there is precedent for this proposition, the opinion of the Court does not cite it——or any other authority, for that matter.[810]

While Story and other conservatives trembled at the prospect of anarchy, thousands of Americans existed in a "state of nature" far different from the one imagined by Hobbes.[811] The opening of the Oregon Trail and the Gold Rush to California required overland emigrants to spend months traversing parts of the continent that

804. Colonial era

On confrontation in the colonial era, see vol. 30, § 6344, p. 419.

805. Little validity

See vol. 30, § 6342, p. 209.

806. Linked to vicinage

See vol. 30, § 6347, p. 742.

807. Long admissible

Hill v. Commonwealth, 1845, 2 Gratt. (43 Va.) 594, 608.

808. Not "witness"

Ibid.

809. Witness who relates

Ibid. The court ignores the fact that the Virginia provision applies not only to witnesses, but also to "accusers." See note 799, above. Notice that the court also refers to "the bill of rights" when the Virginia Constitution calls it the "Declaration of Rights." One might infer from this that the court did not take textual analysis very seriously.

810. Precedent

See above, text at note 691.

811. Anarchy and Hobbes

Philosophically, anarchism is simply the belief that society would be better off without organized government. See generally, Woodcock, Anarchism, paper, 1962. However, partly because of the propaganda of statists and partly because adherents of anarchism have sometimes resorted to violence to achieve their goals, "anarchy" in popular parlance has come to connote chaos and violence. In short, as Hobbes said of those in a "state of nature" without organized government found only "continual fear and danger of violent death; and the life of man, solitary, poor, nasty, brutish, and short." Hobbes, Leviathan, 1651, pt. I, ch. 13.

lacked organized government.[812] It quickly became customary for wagon trains and other groupings of emigrants to draft their own "constitutions" for their governance on the trail.[813] Not surprisingly, these documents sounded very much like the state and federal constitutions—even proscribing trial by jury for those accused of criminal offenses.[814] When they arrived at their destination, the Forty-Niners often found the existing government unwilling or unable to adequately govern the mining camps or other settlements so they formed "claim clubs" or other quasi-governmental associations better equipped to resolve disputes.[815] Similarly, when corruption or incompetence of existing law-enforcement agencies made them insufficient to the perceived needs of urban communities, they formed "vigilance communities" to enforce the law, relying on Jeffersonian "natural law" to justify their actions.[816] While some of these vigilante groups resembled the lynch mobs with which they are often confused in popular culture, many of them were made up of the most respected members of the community and insisted on trials before punishment could be imposed.[817] Far from criminalizing these extra-legal agencies, as Story had proposed for the Dorrites, both state and federal government took steps to legitimate the rulings of these popular tribunals.[818] Even where this was not done, we may suppose that the existence of these "parallel" tribunals exerted some influence, for good or bad, on the way in which courts went about their business; for example, it is possible that worry about citizens "taking the law into their own hands" may have made judges as impatient with the more demanding requirements of the Sixth Amendment as lynch mobs claimed to be about the normal judicial processes.[819]

812. Oregon and California

Sellers, The Market Revolution: Jacksonian America, 1815–1846, p. 411 (Oregon): Encyclopedia of American History, Morris ed. 1976, p. 228 (California).

813. "Constitutions"

Boorstin, The Americans: The National Experience, paper 1965, p. 66.

814. Trial by jury

Id. at p. 67.

815. "Claim clubs"

Id. at pp. 74–76.

816. "Natural law"

The Golden Age of American Law, Haar ed. 1969, p. 427.

817. Insisted on trials

Ibid. See also, Boorstin, The Americans: The National Experience, paper 1965, pp. 81–90. For a darker view, see Friedman, Crime and Punishment in American History, 1992, pp. 179–187.

818. Legitimate rulings

Boorstin, The Americans: The National Experience, paper 1965, pp. 78–79.

819. Judges impatient

Friedman, Crime and Punishment in American History, 1992, p. 192.

The decade from 1850–1860 produced a veritable flood of state confrontation cases that doubled the number of precedents produced in the three-quarters of a century that had elapsed since the first confrontation clause took effect.[820] The reader can be spared a tedious recapitulation of these cases; they add very little to the handful of earlier cases.[821] Almost all of them find that two hearsay exceptions previously considered do not offend the confrontation clause: dying declarations[822] and former testimony.[823] However, they offer two different justifications for these holdings.[824] Some say that the confrontation clause was simply intended to constitutionalize the common law; hence, hearsay exceptions recognized at common law do not violate the defendant's right of confrontation.[825] Others rely on a conceptual argument; that is, that a hearsay declarant is not a "witness against" the accused, so confrontation is

820. Doubled number

For discussion of the earliest cases, see above, text at notes 339, 554, 620., 685, 691, 800.

821. Earlier cases

Indeed very few of the cases even consider the prior precedents. For two that do, see State v. Nash, 1858, 7 Iowa 347; Summons v. State, 1856, 5 Ohio St. 325.

822. Dying declarations

State v. Nash, 1858, 7 Iowa 347; Robbins v. State, 1857, 8 Ohio St. 131, 163; State v Oliver, 1863, 2 Houst. (7 Del.) 585, 589; Walston v. Commonwealth, 1855, 16 B.Monr. (55 Ky.) 15, 36; Commonwealth v. Carey, 1853, 12 Cush. (6 Mass.) 246, 249 (that did not meet common law requirements); Campbell v. State, 1852, 11 Ga. 353, 375; Lambeth v. State, 1852, 23 Miss. 322, 356; State v. Price, 1851, 6 La. Ann. 691, 693; State v. Tilghman, 1850, 11 Ired. (33 N.C.) 513, 554.

823. Former testimony

Pope v. State, 1860, 22 Ark. 372, 373 (from former trial; defense evidence); State v. Houser, 1858, 26 Mo. 431, 437 (testimony from preliminary examina-

tion); State v. McO'Blenis, 1857, 24 Mo. 402, 417 (same; strong dissent); Summons v. State, 1856, 5 Ohio St. 293, 341, 345 (former trial); Williams v. State, 1856, 19 Ga. 402, 403 (testimony from preliminary examination).

824. Different justifications

Cases offering novel analyses will be considered below.

825. Common law

State v. Houser, 1858, 26 Mo. 431, 434–435; State v. McO'Blenis, 1857, 24 Mo. 402, 415, 416 ("The purpose of the people was not * * * to introduce any new principle into the law of criminal procedure, but to secure those that already existed as part of the law of the land from future change by elevating them into constitutional law."); Campbell v. State, 1852, 11 Ga. 353, 368, 374; Lambeth v. State, 1852, 23 Miss. 322, 357.

Interestingly, none of the opinions we have found seems to have invoked the authority of Story's Commentaries for this proposition; see above, text at note 767. This cannot be because treatises were not regarded as authoritative because the opinions cite both English and American treatises, in-

satisfied if the defendant is allowed the opportunity to confront the person who testifies to the hearsay statement.[826]

The conceptual argument was forcefully rejected by the Missouri Supreme Court:

> To say that the witness who must meet the accused "face to face" is he who repeats what the dying man said, is a mere evasion; and if the constitution admits of this evasive interpretation in relation to dying declarations, it is just as easy to apply the same rule of construction to the deposition of a dead witness. * * * It is the dying man who is speaking through him, whose evidence is to have the weight and efficacy to take away the prisoner's life. The living witness is but a conduit pipe——a mere organ, through whom this evidence is conveyed to the court and jury.[827]

This seems to have convinced other judges; in the subsequent decisions, the conceptual argument slowly disappears.[828] But rejecting one definition of "witness against" does not relieve courts of finding some alternative meaning for the phrase; assuming that the hearsay declarant is always a "witness against" the defendant is what brought the modern Supreme Court to grief.[829]

The common-law incorporation argument is equally problematic.[830] In most cases, courts simply assert that this was the intent of

cluding Greenleaf, for other propositions.

826. Not "witness against"

"The person who testifies to the dying declarations is the witness against the accused * * *. The Constitution does not alter the rules of evidence, or determine what shall be admissible testimony against the prisoner, but it only secures to him the right to confront the witnesses who may be introduced to prove such matters as, according to the settled principles of law, are evidence against him." Walston v. Commonwealth, 1855, 16 B.Mon. (55 Ky.) 15, 35.

See also, Robbins v. State, 1857, 8 Ohio St. 131, 163; Summons v. State, 1856, 5 Ohio St. 325, 341–342; Campbell v. State, 1852, 11 Ga. 353, 374; Lambeth v. State, 1852, 23 Miss. 322, 358; State v. Price, 1851, 6 La. Ann. 691, 694; State v. Tilghman, 1850, 11 Ired. (33 N.C.) 513, 554.

827. "A conduit pipe"

State v. Houser, 1858, 26 Mo. 431, 437–438.

828. Slowly disappears

See § 6356.

829. Brought to grief

Though it has been a quarter-century since this was pointed out, modern courts continue to assume themselves into problems. See Graham, The Right of Confrontation and the Hearsay Rule: Sir Walter Raleigh Loses Another One, 1972, 8 Crim.L.Bull. 99, 107, 125–134. For a rare exception, see White v. Illinois, 1992, 112 S.Ct. 736, 744, 502 U.S. 346, 359, 116 L.Ed.2d 848 (Thomas, J. concurring).

830. Problematic

One is defining the term "common law." Most courts assume the English common law, but seldom explain why the

the drafters without offering any historical evidence of this intent.[831] The courts that do support the Founders' intent with history often suppose that history can be established by mere ipse dixit; hence, their account of history does not mesh very well with the historical evidence.[832] Only one court has suggested a purpose for the right of confrontation that matches our reading of history; that is, that the purpose was to preserve the common-law adversary system as against the hated inquisitorial system of the civil law.[833] Other plausible, though we think less convincing, purposes advanced for the right of confrontation are to bar the use of depositions as evidence, or at least those that are procured ex parte and in secret.[834]

In only three of the cases did the courts find that the right of confrontation was a bar to prosecutorial use of hearsay.[835] In one of these the court applied a standard of "unavailability" that was severe even by Nineteenth Century standards and would not be applied today.[836] In the second, the Wisconsin Supreme Court held the Fugitive Slave Law unconstitutional.[837] Although the Wisconsin

colonists who were then in armed revolt against the English government would want to bind themselves to the decisions of English courts. Moreover, some decisions invoke the "common law" for rules that were established in England by statute rather than judicial decision; for example, the admissibility of testimony at a preliminary hearing. See vol. 30, § 6342, p. 229. Indeed, the right of confrontation in England was initially conferred by statute. Id. at p. 227.

831. Without evidence

See, e.g., State v. Price, 1851, 6 La.Ann. 691, 694 ("it has always been [so] regarded").

832. Does not mesh

See, e.g., State v. Houser, 1858, 26 Mo. 431, 433–435 (taking colonists invocation of common law against English government as proof that at the time first clauses were drafted "loyalty to Great Britain was professed and honestly entertained").

833. Adversary system

State v. McO'Blenis, 1857, 24 Mo. 402, 412–416 (but offering very slim evidence in support of this reading).

834. In secret

Williams v. State, 1856, 19 Ga. 402, 403 ("secret examinations, so much abused during the reign of the Stuarts"; no authority for this reading); Summons v. State, 1856, 5 Ohio St. 325, 341 ("exclude testimony by depositions"; no authority cited).

835. Bar prosecutorial

In Pope v. State, 1860, 22 Ark. 372, the court held that confrontation did not bar defense use of former testimony of a now deceased witness.

836. Standard severe

State v. Houser, 1858, 26 Mo. 431, 439 (death is only ground upon which preliminary hearing testimony is admissible; mere absence of witness beyond jurisdiction does not suffice).

837. Unconstitutional

The decision was subsequently overturned by the U.S. Supreme Court.

court accepted the federal view that slaves were not "persons," it condemned the process by which that status was to be determined:[838]

> testimony is taken, and this record is made, in the absence of the person to be affected by the proceeding. He has no opportunity to cross examine the witnesses who depose to the facts which are thus conclusively proved; but without his knowledge, evidence is manufactured, which, by virtue of this act, proves beyond question that he is a slave and that he has escaped from servitude.[839]

The court finessed the question of whether the Fugitive Slave Law was a "criminal case" by relying on the Due Process Clause rather than the Confrontation Clause.[840]

The third case is one that his biographer thinks is one of the great opinions by Chief Justice Lemuel Shaw of Massachusetts.[841] In a proceeding involving the forfeiture of liquor under a regulatory scheme, the court held that a forfeiture proceeding was a criminal proceeding subject to the state's Declaration of Rights.[842] Turning to the procedure authorized by the statute, the court pointed out that in

> the course of proceeding under this statute, the first step required is the complaint of three persons ex parte; and no provision is made that in any stage of the proceeding these complainants are to be again examined, nor that the party whose property is taken shall have opportunity to meet them face to face; yet as we shall see, their oath to their belief of a certain fact is the only evidence, upon which the property may be adjudged forfeited.[843]

To the claim that defendant could call the witnesses and question them if he so chose, the court replied that the presumption of

838. Condemned process

"Here the status or condition of the person is instantly changed in his absence, without process, without notice, without opportunity, to meet or examine the witnesses against him, or rebut their testimony." In re Booth, 1854, 3 Wis. 1, 48 (statement of judge whose ruling is under review).

839. "Escaped servitude"

Id. at 70.

840. Due Process

Ibid. The Sixth Amendment only applies in "criminal cases."

841. Great opinions

Levy, The Law of the Commonwealth and Chief Justice Shaw, 1957, p. 283.

842. Forfeiture criminal

Fisher v. McGirr, 1854, 67 Mass. (1 Grey) 1, 27.

843. "Adjudged forfeited"

Id. at 33.

innocence precluded putting the burden on the defendant to disprove the prosecution case.[844] If the affidavits of the complainants were regarded as evidence to support the prosecution's case, then this constituted a denial of the right of confrontation.[845]

The Rise of Formalism

The diminution of the doctrine of confrontation drew upon Story's fear of the masses as a source of social disorder.[846] The increasing growth in the numbers and political influence of the unpropertied represented a threat to what Story liked to call "the sacred rights of property"——a right he thought prior to all other rights, even protections of personal security such as the right of confrontation.[847] The primary institution for popular intervention in judicial control of property rights was the jury; hence, in order to support the public subsidies for capitalist development, such as the leasing of the power of eminent domain to railroad corporations, it became necessary to eliminate jury trial for the opponents of such takings.[848] The major ideological weapon used to control the jury was "instrumentalism"——the notion that legal rules and institutions have no intrinsic value other than the consequences of their actions.[849] As we shall see, the substitution of "reliability" for "morality" as the criterion for judging the adversary system was to have devastating impact on the value accorded the right of confrontation.[850]

The contempt that Story and other aging Federalists had for ordinary people was reflected in the notion that they would be quiescent were it not for the influence of "outside agitators."

> Our danger lies in the facility with which, under the popular cast of our institutions, honest but visionary legislators, and artful

844. Burden on defendant

Id. at 36–37.

845. Denial of confrontation

Id. at 38–39.

846. Fear of masses

Newmyer, Supreme Court Justice Joseph Story, 1985, p. 365.

847. "Sacred property"

The Legal Mind in America, Miller ed. 1969, pp. 177, 181. The reader will recall that the Communist Manifesto and the events in Europe that led to its publication had already occurred

when the confrontation decisions just discussed were written.

848. Eliminate jury

Horwitz, The Transformation of American Law, 1780–1860, pp. 84–85.

849. "Instrumentalism" and jury

Id. at p. 28.

850. "Reliability" for "morality"

Of course, the "reliability" of verdicts has a moral component, but that morality is pushed off-stage by instrumental reasoning and seldom examined.

leaders may approach to sap the foundations of our government [to] expose us to the opposite inconvenience of too little regard for what is established, and too warm a zeal for untried theories.[851]

A useful example of the artful sappers so feared by Story and his contemporaries is Robert Rantoul, whose name, at least, is familiar to those who have ridden "the train they call 'The City of New Orleans.' "[852] Rantoul was a lawyer, a Harvard graduate, and a Jacksonian—to the horror of those like Story who counted on Harvard educated lawyers to carry on the ideology of High Federalism.[853] He favored codification, public schools, and labor unions.[854] He represented not only the Dorr rebels but also fugitive slaves and abolitionists.[855] During Story's declining years, the anti-slavery movement was the premier example of social unrest that threatened the "sacred rights of property" in other human beings.[856] Like other abolitionist lawyers, Rantoul opposed the Fugitive Slave Laws on the ground, inter alia, that they denied the accused fugitive the right of confrontation.[857] Even more troublesome for the conserva-

851. "Untried theories"

The Legal Mind in America, Miller ed. 1969, p. 72. Notice that this passage anticipates the flight from principles discussed in the next paragraph in the text; i.e., the principles that Story disapproves become "untried theories."

852. "City of New Orleans"

"The City of New Orleans" was a passenger train celebrated in a song of the same name by Arlo Guthrie. It ran on the Illinois Central Railroad (one of Abraham Lincoln's clients) from Chicago to New Orleans passing by the town in Illinois that bears Rantoul's name, probably not for his antislavery and prolabor advocacy but because he was lawyer for and chief promoter of the Illinois Central.

853. Rantoul horror

The Legal Mind in America, Miller ed. 1969, pp. 220–221; Meyers, The Jacksonian Persuasion: Politics and Belief, 1960, pp. 206–207. As Story said upon his inauguration as Dane Professor at Harvard, "[o]ne of the glorious, and not unfrequently perilous duties of the Bar is the protection of property;

* * *." The Legal Mind in America, Miller ed. 1969, p. 181.

854. Favored labor unions

Id. at p. 221.

855. Represented fugitives

Meyers, The Jacksonian Persuasion: Politics and Belief, 1960, p. 207.

856. Unrest threatened

During Rantoul's argument in the Sims case in 1852, the courthouse in Boston was chained shut and surrounded by a cordon of armed state and federal officers. Rantoul, Memoirs, Speeches, and Writings, Hamilton ed. 1854, p. 49.

857. Denied confrontation

Rantoul argued that the transcript of testimony taken before a magistrate in Georgia, which was made conclusive evidence of servitude by the statute, was "incompetent; the captive was not represented at the taking thereof, and had no opportunity for cross-examination." Id. at p. 50. See also, Dunne, Justice Joseph Story and The Rise of The Supreme Court, 1970, pp. 398–399 (Fugitive Slave Law attacked for denying confrontation).

tives was Rantoul's artful use of Story's own dictum as part of his attack upon the denial of confrontation.[858]

The antislavery movement confronted proslavery instrumentalism with principled, moralistic arguments.[859] The result was to discredit instrumentalism and, to a lesser extent, even constitutionalism.[860] As one abolitionist said of Story's opinion upholding the Fugitive Slave Law: "[i]t is not law * * * [i]t is to be spit upon, hooted at, trampled in the dust resolutely and openly."[861] Even one of Story's former students said of his mentor's position on slavery: "No oath of office, no obligation to the Constitution of the United States can excuse an outrage on humanity."[862] And after the Dred Scott decision, the man who would be Lincoln's Vice President said on the floor of the Senate that "[o]f all despotisms upon earth, the despotism of a judiciary is the worst."[863] This was hardly an intellectual or political climate conducive to bold interpretations of the right of confrontation.[864]

Since constitutionalism was too important to the power of the judiciary to be abandoned, it was easier for judges to downplay instrumentalism now that it had served its purpose in converting the English common law to accommodate the capitalist political economy.[865] This left an argumentative void that was soon filled by formalism, a rhetoric more suited to making the pro-business rulings of the courts appear apolitical.[866] The effort to make the law

858. Story's dictum

Rantoul's fourth argument was that the Georgia record was incompetent "because taken in an ex parte proceeding, and in the absence of the defendant. This point he argued on general principles of law and reason, and cited a passage of indignant eloquence from Judge Story's decision in Bradstreet v. Neptune Insurance Company, 3 Sumner, 608, on the admission of ex parte evidence." Rantoul, Memoirs, Speeches, and Writings, Hamilton ed. 1854, pp. 54–55.

859. Moralistic arguments

Nelson, The Impact of The Antislavery Movement Upon Styles of Judicial Reasoning in Nineteenth Century America, 1974, 87 Harv.L.Rev. 513, 543.

860. Discredit instrumentalism

Id. at 548.

861. "Spit upon, hooted at"

Dunne, Justice Joseph Story and The Rise of the Supreme Court, 1970, p. 401.

862. "Outrage on humanity"

Id. at p. 402.

863. "Judiciary the worst"

Welter, The Mind of America, 1820–1860, 1975, p. 358.

864. Conducive to bold

But see, § 6356, text at notecall 43.

865. Judges downplay

Horwitz, The Transformation of American Law, 1780–1860, p. 254.

866. Appear apolitical

Id. at pp. 256. See also, Nelson, The Impact of The Antislavery Movement Upon Styles of Judicial Reasoning in

appear "scientific" now invoked the analogy of biology and the other natural sciences where the vogue for reductionism was accompanied by an emphasis on classification.[867] The job of placing jurisprudential specimens into the proper categories fell to the treatise writers, who were to enjoy an influence in the next 100 years that is the envy of those who write in this genre today.[868]

The judicial flight from principles and morality in the face of the anti-slavery onslaught was ultimately to produce pragmatism—what one historian has called "an American substitute for philosophy."[869] We need not ponder whether or not pragmatism was merely instrumentalism with its principles in disguise but at its worst, it degenerated into a practice of ad hoc responses to individual cases whose limitations would be amply exposed in the next century of confrontation jurisprudence.[870]

§ 6356. ___; The Gilded Age*

During the roughly 100 years between the bloodiest war and the most unpopular war the United States ever fought, the Supreme Court finally began to construe the Confrontation Clause of the Sixth Amendment.[1] These early federal decisions resembled the state decisions of the ante-bellum era in their use of spurious history to evade the challenges to the construction of the modern capitalist state posed by the Revolutionary attitudes toward the criminal sanction.[2] Indeed, these decisions are so undistinguished that they are not even mentioned in the Supreme Court's semi-

---

Nineteenth Century America, 1974, 87 Harv.L.Rev. 513, 548.

867. Classification

Id. at 560.

868. Treatise writers

Horwitz, The Transformation of American Law, 1780–1860, 1977, p. 257–258.

869. "Substitute for philosophy"

Boorstin, The Americans: The National Experience, 1965, pp. 41–42.

870. Limitations exposed

Indeed, at this writing the Supreme Court is still searching for some coher-

ent theory of the Confrontation Clause and the Sixth Amendment. See § 6360, below.

§ 6356

* This is a long section; a listing of topics within notecall 5 below may help the reader to the subject of interest.

1. Began to construe

For a description of the obstacles to Supreme Court review of confrontation decisions in the previous century, see § 6355, text at notecalls 1–12.

2. Ante-bellum state decisions

See § 6355, text at notecalls 339, 684, 799.

official history.[3] Accounting for the desultory treatment of confrontation between 1865 and 1965 will require a more complete account of the socio-political context of these decisions than some readers may think necessary.[4] The outline in the note below will permit the hurried reader to go directly to the desired discussion.[5]

Our periodization of this history is for convenience only; some of the causes of the post-war constructions of confrontation come from the antebellum period.[6] For example, the split in the Democratic party over the issues of slavery and secession weakened the Jacksonian resistance to the conservative effort to impose the English common law on American governments.[7] Moreover, abolitionist revulsion over the Dred Scott decision discredited the authority of the Supreme Court.[8] Faced with this threat to its legitimacy, the Court understandably sought a powerful constituency, choosing to ally itself with capitalists rather than civil libertarians.[9]

3. Not even mentioned

See the Table of Cases in The Oliver Wendell Homes Devise History of the Supreme Court, vols. 7–8: Fairman, Reconstruction and Reunion, 1864–1888 Part II, 1987; Fiss, Troubled Beginnings of the Modern State, 1888–1910, 1993.

4. Context of decisions

Given what we have said about the judicial use of history, we owe it to any judicial readers to provide a more complete history than is customary in some treatments of constitutional law.

5. Outline

The numbers indicate the notecall at which the topic begins.

1   **Introduction**
11   **The Civil War and Confrontation**
155   **State Confrontation Clauses**
176   **Reconstruction and Radicalism**
223   **Communism and Confrontation**
237   **Cooley's Confrontation**
254   **The Grangers**
274   **Racism and Repression**
290   **Anglophilia and Elitism**
318   **The Ku Klux Klan and Confrontation**

373   **Langdell and Legal Culture**
414   **Capitalism and Confrontation**
445   **Natural Law and Due Process**
463   **Depression and Reaction**
473   **Socio-economics and Confrontation**
562   **Procedure and Proof**
597   **Molly Maguires and Mother Jones**
658   **"The Great Strike"**
691   **Darwin and Democracy**
749   **U.S. v. Reynolds**
793   **The A.B.A. and Elite Ideology**
830   **Railroad Rights and Human Rights**
904   **"The Great Upheaval"**

6. Ante-bellum period

See § 6355.

7. Weakened resistance

Jacobs, Law Writers and The Courts, 1954, p. 13.

8. Discredited Court

Welter, The Mind of America, 1820–1860, 1975, p. 377.

9. Constituency

Since under our conception of the judiciary judges ought not to enter the

Hence, it was not till this alliance with business interests came under attack in the New Deal that the Court first attempted, ultimately unsuccessfully, to carve out a moral rather than an economic constituency.[10]

Confrontation and The Civil War

In 1860, with threats of secession in the air, the Republican party platform embraced the Declaration of Independence, and at least implicitly the confrontation values that document evoked.[11] When Lincoln was elected with less than a majority of the popular vote, South Carolina—the state that had been most vociferous in the Constitutional Convention in opposing a Bill of Rights because of its supposed inconsistency with slavery—became the first state to secede.[12] That same year, John Appleton, a justice of the Supreme Judicial Court of Maine, published the most thorough-going Benthamite American book on the law of evidence.[13]

Appleton's The Rules of Evidence offers some evidence of how ill-formed the hearsay rule was nearly a century after the Confrontation Clause was adopted.[14] Far from embracing the Wigmorean orthodoxy—that is, that preserving the right to cross-examination is the sole justification for the hearsay rule—Appleton embraces nearly all of those justifications that Wigmore called "spurious;"[15]

political arena to create popular support for their governance, judges have to rely on others to do this for them; the group that the Court expects to support its decisions is what we mean by its "constituency." This does not imply that every decision will favor some member of the constituency, but it does mean that the Court's opinion will attempt to justify its decision by invoking values it thinks will appeal to that constituency; for example, a decision that goes against business interests is going to be justified by "stability" rather than by some appeal to Marxist or Populist values.

10. Moral constituency

That is, when the Warren Court began to defend minorities other than the rich, it did not justify those decisions by "efficiency," but rather it appealed to non-marketplace values such as "fairness."

11. Embraced Declaration

Encyclopedia of American History, Morris ed. 1976, p. 270. The confrontation values in the Declaration are described in vol. 30, § 6345, p. 557.

12. First state to secede

Encyclopedia of American History, Morris ed. 1976, p. 271. Ironically, the secession was also justified by a document resembling the Declaration of Independence. On South Carolina's position on a bill of rights, see vol. 30, § 6347, pp. 741–742.

13. Benthamite book

See vol. 21, § 5001, pp. 21–22.

14. Ill-formed hearsay

For discussion of earlier evidence books, see § 6355, text at notecalls 100, 783.

15. "Spurious"

See vol. 30, §§ 6326–6331.

e.g., that hearsay is an "inferior species of evidence,"[16] that it is barred by the best-evidence rule,[17] that among the dangers to be guarded against is misreporting by the witness who testifies,[18] and, finally, that multiple hearsay is worse than ordinary hearsay because of the "hand-me-down" problem.[19] However, Appleton also prefigures Wigmore's Benthamite reforming impulse, demolishing Starkie's defense of the hearsay rule,[20] pointing out how the rule has been shaped by the dominant interests in society, such as the slaveholder interest,[21] and even making the Progressive argument that hearsay is relied upon "without scruple in the ordinary affairs of life."[22]

Although Appleton does not discuss confrontation as such, he does embrace it as one of the principle attributes of trial by jury—just as many of the founders saw it.[23] Moreover, he demonstrates

16. "Inferior evidence"

"Hearsay being an inferior species of evidence should never be received, except in those cases, when from death or other sufficient cause, better proof is unattainable." Appleton, The Rules of Evidence, 1860, p. 189.

17. Best evidence rule

Id. at p. 190.

18. Misreporting

"In hearsay, the narrating is avowedly not the percipient witness; he speaks or purports to speak from the narration of others and those others are the efficient witnesses. There may have been no such relators, whose alleged conversations the testifying witness reports; or being such, their relations may have been partially or entirely false, either from simple incorrectness, incompleteness, temerity or design; or being true, they may have been misunderstood, misrecollected or misreported." Id. at p. 189. For the conventional response to this argument, see vol. 30, § 6330.

19. "Hand-me-down"

"One thing is certain, that the more media through which any fact has been transmitted, the greater the dangers of deception. In this cases, who or what was the original witness, when he lived, to whom he first narrated his extrajudicial testimony, through how many media it has passed to the narrating witness—the character, quality, trustworthiness of the original source and of each intervening narrating witness, their means of knowledge, their integrity—all that it is desirable to know, in relation to it, is enveloped in darkness * * *." Id. at p . 215.

20. Demolishing Starkie

Id. at pp. 192–197.

21. Slaveholder interest

"Hearsay to aid the master is received——for the protection of the alleged slave refused." Id. at p. 208. For a similar criticism of the relevant Supreme Court decision, see vol. 30, § 6321, p. 18 (pointing out that such critiques have been rare).

22. "Ordinary affairs"

Id. at p. 191.

23. Confrontation and jury trial

Id. at p. 220, quoted in full in volume 30, § 6327, p. 61 at notecall 43. On the Founders' views, see vol. 30, § 6347, pp. 695–705.

that opposition to the inquisitorial civilian mode of procedure used by the Vice–Admiralty courts was still as strong a century later as it was at the time of the Revolution.[24] Finally, Appleton takes the view, rejected by some state constructions of the right of confrontation, that in a hearsay situation the "witness against" the defendant is the hearsay declarant, not the witness on the stand.[25]

In early 1861, seven more states joined South Carolina in secession and on February 4, representatives of these states assembled in Montgomery, Alabama, to draft the Confederate Constitution.[26] Though that document departed from the U.S. Constitution in a number of respects, particularly regarding slavery, it was generally similar.[27] Indeed, though some of the states of the Confederacy had no confrontation clause in their state constitutions, the Confederate Constitution was identical to the Sixth Amendment in its phrasing of the right of confrontation.[28] However, we are unaware of any cases in which the Confederate right of confrontation was applied.[29]

As is usual in wartime, one of the first casualties of the Civil

24. Opposition strong

"In opposition to, and in direct contrast with this best and most effective, is the worst and most defective mode of proof * * *. Affidavits cautiously and deliberately prepared, carefully worded, vague when particularity is desirable, particular and specific when unimportant, evasive when certainty is demanded, certain as to the immaterials, suggesting or implying falsehood, not uttering it, concealing the truth, giving special and peculiar prominence to all facts important to the affiant, withholding all adverse or injurious, without cross-examination, with no opportunity for contradiction, present evidence in the most deceptitious and untrustworthy form * * *." Id. at p. 221.

25. Declarant is "witness"

See note 18, above. For cases suggesting that confrontation is satisfied by facing the witness rather than the declarant, see § 6355, text at notes 695, 826.

26. Draft constitution

Encyclopedia of American History, Morris ed. 1976, p. 272.

27. Generally similar

See generally, Lee, The Confederate Constitutions, 1963.

28. Identical phrasing

Id. at pp. 163, 184. However, most of the Bill of rights was incorporated into the body of the Confederate Constitution rather than placed in a separate document. Id. at p. 102. Of the original 13 states, Georgia and South Carolina had no confrontation clause in their constitutions. See vol. 30, § 6346, pp. 611–612.

29. Cases applied

The Confederate Constitution also deleted jurisdiction of Confederate courts "in law and equity" but this does not seem to have been a result of any opposition to inquisitorial tribunals. Lee, The Confederate Constitutions, 1963, p. 107.

War was civil liberties.[30] In May, 1861, military authorities thumbed their noses at no less a figure than Chief Justice Taney when he issued a writ of habeas corpus for a prisoner being held in military custody.[31] So far had the prestige of the Court sunk and so widespread was the feeling that it was proslavery that the federal courts in general and the Supreme Court in particular were able to do little when newspapers were shut down and suspected Confederate sympathizers were locked up or banished without trial.[32] For example, in Saint Louis a minister was arrested and banished without trial by military authorities, then allowed to remain so long as he refrained from preaching.[33] Futile invocation of the Bill of Rights as against a claim of military necessity probably played some part in weakening public allegiance to constitutional rights and thus permitted the postwar weakening of the right of confrontation.[34]

Given the role of treason in the development of the right of confrontation, it is worth noting how that crime was employed in the War Between The States.[35] Given the Virginia conviction for treason of abolitionist martyr John Brown, one might have expected secessionists to be treated as traitors.[36] And, in 1861, a group of Confederate privateers were convicted of treason in federal court in Philadelphia.[37] However, the defendants were not executed but treated instead as prisoners of war.[38] Thereafter, though both state and federal grand juries indicted many Confederate sympathizers for treason, few of these cases ever came to trial, much less

---

30. Civil liberties

Swisher, History of the Supreme Court of The United States: The Taney Period, 1836–1864, p. 901. This was apparently true in the South as well, but such Confederate delinquencies would hardly provide precedents for the federal courts.

31. Thumbed noses at Taney

Id. at pp. 843, 915, 947.

32. Courts do little

Id. at pp. 902, 912, 918, 920, 936.

33. Minister banished

Id. at p. 908.

34. Futile invocation

Id. at p . 905.

35. Treason and confrontation

See vol. 30, § 6346, p. 564–566; § 6347, pp. 664–667.

36. John Brown

Encyclopedia of American History, Morris, ed. 1976, p. 328.

37. Confederate privateers

Swisher, History of The Supreme Court of the United States: The Taney Period, 1836–1864, 1974, pp. 874.

38. Prisoners of war

Id. at p. 876. It seems likely that fear of Confederate retaliation against captured Union troops played a significant role in the decision not to treat secessionists as traitors.

proceeded to the ultimate punishment.[39] Thereafter, threats to prosecute the rebels and their sympathizers for treason for the most part remained just that.[40] This did not prevent rhetorical use of the label "traitor" against Confederates by both Republicans and Freedmen.[41] However, so far as we can tell, all this talk of treason did little to revive public interest in constitutional guarantees that represented the English response to the brutality of the Tudor treason trials.[42]

The wartime federal case with the most significance for the right of confrontation was an 1862 admiralty case for the forfeiture of goods supposedly shipped to the enemy by Confederate sympathizers in violation of the embargo on such shipments.[43] Relying on a hearsay report that a Confederate agent had come to Baltimore for the purpose of buying drugs, federal officers gave carte blanche to detectives to take whatever steps were necessary to prevent this shipment.[44] One of the detectives, posing as a Confederate officer, attempted to enlist the aid of the uncle of the reputed smuggler, but that man rebuffed the detective's offers.[45]

Thereafter, according to the opinion of Chief Justice Taney sitting as Circuit Justice, the detective "insinuated himself into [the suspect's] house and into acquaintance with his children and family * * * made presents to the children, who became very fond

39. Few came to trial

Id. at pp. 925–929, 951–957.

40. Remained threats

Id. at p . 925.

41. Rhetorical use

Foner, Reconstruction: America's Unfinished Revolution, 1863–1877, 1988, pp. 43, 111.

42. Revive public

It is possible that the disuse of treason prosecutions in the Civil War convinced political elites that they had little to fear from that quarter and thus decreased any empathy they might have had for those charged with lesser crimes.

43. Forfeiture of goods

Swisher, History of the Supreme Court of The United States: The Taney Years, 1836–1864, 1974, p. 956.

44. Prevent shipment

This, and subsequent statements of fact, are taken from the opinion of Chief Justice Taney, reprinted in Tyler, Memoir of Roger Brook Taney, 1972, p. 436. The opinion appears not to have been published in the reports of the Circuit Court, but is treated as genuine by Professor Swisher.

45. Rebuffed offers

Id. at p. 437. The uncle told the detective that his nephew probably had meant him to enlist the aid of a former employee of the uncle, a Virginian who had gone to Philadelphia and who was later inveigled into participating in the scheme.

of him; and otherwise sought to work himself into the family's confidence."[46] When further importunings failed, the detective, still posing as a friend of the nephew, then claimed that he was intimate with many prominent southerners, showing letters from these persons, whom he claimed had enabled him to bribe U.S. officials to give him a pass, a certificate of loyalty, and a customs' clearance that made the proposed smuggling virtually foolproof.[47] Only then was the detective able to convince one person to assist him in the smuggling scheme and other members of the family to provide him with money to pay for the goods and their passage.[48] The trap was eventually sprung, the entrapped goods and money seized, and the dupes arrested.[49]

In an opinion reversing the forfeiture, restoring the money and goods to the defendants, and finding that the federal officers lacked probable cause for arrest (thus making them liable for damages and costs), the Chief Justice found that the parties had "been seduced and betrayed" by federal officers and condemned the "deceptions practiced," especially those practiced on the family and children.[50] He spoke of "the great evil that would arise from a court countenancing such behavior"; it would "encourage officers to betray the weak and imprudent into all sorts of violation of law."[51] The Chief Justice's opinion reminds one of the attitude of the Founders toward the use of informers by the Vice–Admiralty courts in the years prior to the Revolution——an attitude that is more consonant with confrontation values than the opinions of modern courts when faced with similar entrapments by government officials.[52]

A decade later, Taney's biographer wrote:

46. "Became fond of him"

Ibid.

47. Displayed documents

Id. at pp. 438–439. Since these had been provided him by his superiors, it seems quite likely that they knew what the detective was up to.

48. Pay for goods

Ibid. The goods were not contraband of war but ordinary trade goods whose value had increased in the South because of wartime scarcity,

49. Dupes arrested

Id. at pp. 439–440.

50. "Deceptions practiced"

Id. at p. 441. The Chief Justice claimed to be surprised by the conduct of the officers and said he "could recall no similar case in the jurisprudence of either this country or England." Id. at pp. 440–441.

51. "Encourage violation"

Id. at p. 441. Modern courts would characterize this as "entrapment."

52. Attitude of Founders

See vol. 30, § 6345, pp. 535–541. Today the informer is the one sort of "accuser" the defendant is least likely to be able to confront. See vol. 26A. § 5702.

The vile practices disclosed in this case that were authorized by the Government during the war, and the disregard of the Constitution and the law, have chiefly contributed to demoralize the public sense, and bring about in our country the stupendous official corruption of the present time.[53]

Lincoln, on the other hand, said he could not believe the repressive measure during the war posed any danger that "the people would lose for all time the right of public discussion, the liberty of speech and press, the law of evidence, the right to trial by jury and the writ of habeas corpus" comparing this to the belief "that a man could contract so strong an appetite for emetics during temporary illness, as to persist in feeding upon them during the remainder of his healthful life."[54] The reader may judge for herself which of these views is most supported by the historical record.[55]

In 1862, Congress repealed the Fugitive Slave Law,[56] fulfilling a pledge of the Republican party that the President had once sought to repudiate.[57] Though the 1850 statute was unpopular as a symbol of slaveholder power, it was also despised as a violation of traditional adversary procedures, including confrontation.[58] Indeed, the Republican fallback position in case repeal was unattainable was to seek "such modification of it as shall secure the right of habeas corpus and trial by jury" in state rather than federal courts.[59] Even Lincoln favored changes that would make the Fugitive Slave Law no "more likely to carry a free man into slavery,

53. "Bring about corruption"

Tyler, Memoir of Roger Brook Taney, 1872, p. 443. The corruption alluded to is discussed below, text at notecall 414.

54. "Healthful life"

Swisher, History of The Supreme Court of the United States, The Taney Years, 1836–1864, 1974, p. 928.

55. Supported by record

As we shall see, there were many other influences besides the example of wartime repression that might have led courts to favor a more repressive regime of social control.

56. Fugitive slave repeal

Kyvig, Explicit and Authentic Acts, 1996, p. 157.

57. Repudiate pledge

The Lincoln–Douglas Debates, Holzer ed. 1993, pp. 93–113.

58. Adversary procedures

The statute not only denied trial by jury, but also made slaveholder hearsay admissible and sufficient to prove servile status while making testimony of the accused slave inadmissible. See § 6349, text at notecall 535.

59. "Trial by jury"

The Lincoln–Douglas Debates, Holzer ed. 1993, p. 120.

than our ordinary criminal laws are to hang an innocent one."[60]

At the same time Congress launched a more direct attack on slavery—the institution that had done so much to undermine confrontation values in American law.[61] First, it repealed slavery in the District of Columbia, but in keeping with the moderate Republican position provided for compensation for loyal slaveholders.[62] But a few months later the Radical Republican position came to the fore in the Second Confiscation Act, which provided that slaves who escaped to Union lines or were seized by Union forces from persons engaged in rebellion should be "deemed captives of war, and shall forever be free of their servitude, and not again held as slaves."[63] Though the Act opened the possibility of forfeiture of all Confederate property, the public response may have encouraged Lincoln to issue the Emancipation Proclamation the following year.[64]

Ironically, the abolition of slavery also had an adverse effect on the right of confrontation.[65] The Second Confiscation Act was seen by some even in time of war as an unconstitutional deprivation of property and some conservatives later saw abolition of slavery as a massive destruction of the rights of private property.[66] The fear that this presaged a redistribution of property did much to fuel the Supreme Court's subsequent preoccupation with property rights at the expense of civil liberties, such as the right of confrontation.[67]

60. "Hang an innocent one"

Id. at p. 62.

61. Undermine confrontation

See § 6349, text at footnote 507.

62. Provided compensation

Kyvig, Explicit and Authentic Acts, 1996, p. 157; The Lincoln–Douglas Debates, Holzer ed. 1993, p. 93.

63. Second Confiscation Act

Kyvig, Explicit and Authentic Acts, 1996, p. 157.

64. All Confederate property

Foner, Reconstruction: America's Unfinished Revolution, 1863–1877, 1988, p. 51.

65. Adverse effect

As we shall see, the attempt to substitute peonage for slavery in the South and Northern attempts to protect

freedmen both generated repressive mechanisms that would have previously been unthinkable.

66. Destruction of rights

Swisher, History of the Supreme Court of the United States: The Taney Period, 1974, p. 932.

67. Property rights

Of course, to many conservatives property rights are the ultimate civil liberty. John W. Davis, the Democratic Presidential candidate in 1824, once wrote: "human rights and rights of property are not different or antagonistic but parts of one and the same thing going to make up the bundle of rights which constitute American liberty. History furnishes no instance where the right of man to acquire and hold property has been taken away without the complete destruction of liberty in all its

Conservatives were neither paranoid nor alone in seeing abolition as an opening wedge for more radical attacks on property rights.[68] For example, the Radical Republican George Julian, an avowed enemy of "land monopoly" and Chairman of the House Committee on Public Lands wanted to confiscate plantations and turn them over to the newly freed slaves lest they fall into "a system of wage slavery * * * more galling than slavery itself."[69] That this was no mere utopian dream can be seen in an order of General Sherman in 1865 that provided 40 acres of confiscated land and the loan of mules for Freedmen and their families.[70] Two years later at a political gathering of Freedmen in Savannah, they were urged to seek the division of the plantations of "rich whites" among newly freed black families.[71] When this call for redistribution of the wealth of the South was taken up by upcountry whites as well, even those in the North had cause to worry.[72] Any illusions that "wage slavery" was reserved for Southern poor would have been dispelled when in 1867, the powerful Republican Ben Wade told a Kansas audience: "[p]roperty is not equally divided, and a more equal distribution of capital must be wrought out."[73] By the end of Reconstruction, Northern labor reformers began urging the Republican party to take the side of the poor in the class war that was coming to open conflict.[74]

Preoccupation with property was heightened by another 1862

forms." Harbaugh, Lawyer's Lawyer: The Life of John W. Davis, 1973, p. xiii.

68. Radical attacks

In one sense, conservatives were hoist on their own petard. If ownership of property was the ultimate human right, see note 67, above, then it was easy to argue that the ex-slaves would not be truly free until they enjoyed some of the fruits of their years in bondage.

69. "Wage slavery"

Foner, Reconstruction: America's Unfinished Revolution, 1988, p. 68. This was to turn against the slaveholders one of their arguments against the abolitionists; i.e., that slaveholder felt more concern for their own "property" than Northern capitalists did for their "wage slaves"—an argument

that resembled the Wall Street Journal argument of the late 20th Century that the dependent Japanese labor force was better off than the unionized American work force.

70. Forty acres and mules

Id. at p. 70. See also, id. at p. 69 (Freedman's Bureau authorized to rent or sell 40 acre tracts of confiscated land).

71. "Rich whites"

Id. at p . 290.

72. Upcountry whites

Id. at p. 302.

73. "More equal distribution"

Id. at p. 309.

74. Take sides

Id. at p . 484.

statute——the Homestead Act.[75] On the idealistic level, the justification for the Act supported the view of the Radical Republicans that the freedmen would never be truly emancipated without land to support them and their families.[76] At a pragmatic level, the Homestead Act created another group besides Southern slaveholders whose moral claims to their property was suspect and who might have been the targets of any scheme to redistribute the wealth.[77] Mythology to the contrary, even with the Homestead Act very little of the public domain came into the hands of settlers and almost none went to the needy.[78] Instead, speculators gobbled up the choice acreage either by fraud or violence.[79]

In 1863, the year of the Emancipation Proclamation, Congress passed the First Conscription Act, which made military service mandatory——except for the rich who could buy their way out by a payment of $300 or hiring a substitute.[80] A similar Confederate provision the year before had been denounced as "class legislation" because it exempted owners of 20 slaves as well as those who could afford substitutes.[81] In New York those subject to the draft responded by rioting, originally targeting symbols of authority, much like the riots of the Revolutionary era, but then turning into a slaughter of uncounted black men, women, and children.[82] Troops were diverted from Gettysburg to suppress the riot.[83] A similar use of the troops to quell strikes set the stage for the use of force to suppress workers in the "Second Civil War" that followed Appo-

75. Homestead Act

Encyclopedia of American History, Morris ed. 1976, p. 285.

76. Without land to support

Recall, also, the view of the Founders that democracy required a relatively equal distribution of property. See vol. 30, § 6345, p. 513,

77. Redistribute

See text at notecall 71, above.

78. None to needy

Garraty, The New Commonwealth, 1877–1890, 1968 pp. 9, 23.

79. Fraud or violence

Id. at pp. 12, 23. See also, New York Public Library, American History Desk Reference, 1997, p. 264.

80. First Conscription Act

Encyclopedia of American History, Morris ed. 1976, p. 284.

81. "Class legislation"

Foner, Reconstruction: America's Unfinished Revolution, 1863–1877, 1988, p. 15.

82. New York riots

Encyclopedia of American History, Morris ed. 1976, p. 284. See also, Foner, Reconstruction: America's Unfinished Revolution, 1863–1877, 1988, p. 32; Zinn, A People's History of The United States, 1980, p. 187.

83. Troops from Gettysburg

Foner, Reconstruction: America's Unfinished Revolution, 1863–1877, 1988, p. 33.

mattox.[84] Similarly, civilian repressive mechanisms were beefed up in response to elite fear of the "dangerous classes."[85] Ironically, by viewing lawbreakers as "The Other," rather than as a fellow humans reacting as we might in their stead, the upper classes responded much as had the rioters.[86] Denying the humanity of those who transgress does nothing to further support for adversary values such as confrontation.[87] Nor were such sentiments congenial to the hopes recalled that same year at Gettysburg——"government of the people, by the people, and for the people."[88]

In 1864 one might glimpse a "new birth of freedom" when military courts allowed blacks to testify against whites.[89] In 1865, Missouri made this a constitutional right and the Civil Rights Act of the following year specified the right to testify as one of the indicia of citizenship to be federally protected.[90] Gradually, in order to get rid of courts operated by the Freedman's Bureau, Southern states moved to eliminate racial disqualifications of witnesses.[91] The sight of testimony of blacks being treated with respect by Republican judges and jurors did much to cement the Freedman's loyalty to the G.O.P. and made some slight inroads in the ideology

84. "Second Civil War"

Id. at p. 31; Zinn, A People's History of the United States, 1980, p. 206.

85. "Dangerous Classes"

Foner, Reconstruction: America's Unfinished Revolution, 1963–1877, 1988, p. 33.

86. Responded to rioters

Even historians a century later exhibited a similar mechanism. See Encyclopedia of American History, Morris ed. 1976, p. 284 (Columbia historians blame riots on the Irish). There is no evidence, so far as we know, that the Irish were more racist than other Americans and appeals to racism were a prominent part of political speech by politicians of all stripes. For a melancholy example, see The Lincoln–Douglas Debates, Holzer ed. 1993, pp. 54–55, 61, 79, 110–111, 142–143, 151.

87. Confrontation

For a political illustration of this one might invoke the challenge in 1854, four years prior to his famous debates with Lincoln, of Stephen Douglas to engage in an "ebony and ivory" face-to-face debate with Frederich Douglas—which the Senator refused. The challenger later charged that "no man of his time has done more [than the Senator] to intensify hatred of the negro."

88. "For the people"

Wills, Lincoln At Gettysburg, 1992, p. 263.

89. "New birth"

Ibid. Foner, Reconstruction: America's Unfinished Revolution, 1863–1877, 1988, p. 8 (pointing out this was unheard of in the South and in many Northern states prior to the war).

90. Missouri and Civil Rights

Id. at pp. 42, 471.

91. Moved to eliminate

Id. at p. 149.

of racism.[92] Nonetheless, there were many like the Georgian who thought it an outrage when blacks could have "white men arrested and carried to the Freedman's court * * * where their testimony is taken as equal to a white man's."[93] As late as 1872, Kentucky still barred black testimony against whites.[94] Nonetheless, the expansion of the competence of witnesses increased the importance of confrontation by lessening the need to use hearsay and increasing the importance of cross-examination as a check on the reliability of evidence.

In 1865 as the Confederacy was crumbling, its government began repressive measures to stamp out growing disunion, imitating some of the same steps taken by the Union in the early days of the war.[95] The end of the war did not put an end to this bypassing of the Bill of Rights; the commander of the notorious Andersonville prison camp and those charged with having conspired in the assassination of the President were all tried in military rather than civilian courts.[96]

But if the Civil War accustomed governments to repression by means of dubious constitutionality, it had a radicalizing effect on many citizens.[97] As was the case in the English Civil War, military service gave many soldiers a taste of ideology and activism that were to have profound effects on the history of confrontation over the next century.[98] Black soldiers, in particular, became "apostles of equality" who carried home radical sentiments along with their discharge papers.[99] This radicalism, symbolized by the admission of the first black lawyer to the Supreme Court bar, had roots in abolitionist agitation.[100] A good illustration was the Louisiana con-

92. Slight inroads

Id. at p. 363.

93. "Equal to white"

Id. at p. 151.

94. Kentucky barred

Id. at p. 421.

95. Imitating Union

Encyclopedia of American History, Morris ed. 1976, p. 291 (suspension of habeas corpus, expansive use of conspiracy law).

96. Tried in military courts

Id. at p. 292.

97. Radicalizing

Foner, Reconstruction: America's Unfinished Revolution, 1863–1877, 1988, p. 9.

98. Military service

See vol. 30, § 6343, p. 272 (spread of Leveller sentiments by New Model Army).

99. "Apostles of equality"

Foner, Reconstruction: America's Unfinished Revolution, 1863–1877, 1988, p. 80.

100. Abolitionist

Id. at pp. 28, 67.

stitution of 1865 that abolished slavery, provided for progressive income taxation, opened the public schools to children of all races between the ages of 6 and 16, and established a nine-hour work-day.[101]

Perhaps this radicalizing influence played a part in Howser v. Commonwealth, decided the same year the Civil War ended.[102] In a murder prosecution, the trial judge allowed a juror to step out of the jury box and testify against the accused. Defense counsel quoted the Sixth Amendment and a similar provision in the Pennsylvania Constitution, then argued:

> These provisions imply that jurors and witnesses should be dis-tinct persons. If one juror can be a witness so may the whole number; and if the whole twelve are the prisoner's accusers and triers, where is the just distinction between the "impartial jury" by whom the prisoner is to be tried and the witnesses with whom he is "to be confronted" and whom he has a right to "meet face to face"?[103]

This sophisticated appreciation of the connection between the sepa-ration of functions, confrontation, and the right to an impartial jury is quite uncommon in the prior confrontation literature.[104]

The Pennsylvania Supreme Court understood the argument, but in rejecting it the Court also rejected Wigmorean history:

> When the common law of England was transported to these colonies, it gave a person charged with a capital crime no compul-sory process to obtain witnesses, and entitled him to no examina-tion by himself or his counsel of witnesses brought against him. * * * To remedy this state of the law our constitutions all de-clared, what statutes had then provided in England, that the accused should have an impartial trial by jury, should have process for witnesses, and be entitled to counsel to examine them, and to cross-examine those for the prosecution in the presence of (con-fronting) the accused.[105]

Though the opinion adopts the Wigmorean view of the scope of the right, it goes on in a dictum to suggest that it bars the use of

101. Nine-hour workday

Brodie, Thaddeus Stevens: Scourge of the South, 1959, p. 211.

102. Howser case

1865, 51 Pa. 332.

103. "Just distinction"

Id. at 334–335.

104. Separation of functions

See vol. 30, § 6342, pp. 217–218; § 6343, p. 330.

105. "To remedy this state"

Howser v. Commonwealth, 1865, 51 Pa. 332, 337–338.

unconfronted hearsay. Referring to a prior case in which the preliminary-hearing testimony of a witness who had fled was sought to be used against the accused under the Tudor statute, the Court reports that

> it was finally decided that, notwithstanding the above-named statute had been extended to Pennsylvania, it was displaced by our constitution, and that no ex parte testimony could be given against the prisoner in a capital case.[106]

However, neither the judges nor the lawyers seems to have thought that the state confrontation clause, so construed, barred testimony of a witness about her own hearsay statements.[107]

The Pennsylvania court's objection to "ex parte evidence" was echoed in Congress the following year.[108] Congress was debating a bill to increase immunity against liability for soldiers and other government officers for "any search, seizure, arrest or imprisonment made, or acts done or omitted to be done" under federal authority during the war.[109] In addition to allowing the removal of cases from state to federal courts, the statute would have relaxed the rules of evidence to make it easier to prove authority for the acts as against objections to authentication or under the best evidence rule.[110] Opponents objected that "[e]very provision * * * is manifestly framed in the interest of the defendant, to the utter exclusion of the rights of the plaintiff."[111] Although it was argued that the statute would "overthrow the bulwarks of truth and justice, and invite the barbarians of former days to thunder at the gates of American liberty," no one seems to have invoked confrontation values against the proposed relaxation of the hearsay rule.[112]

106. "No ex parte testimony"

Id. at 338.

107. Own hearsay statements

The opinion holds that these were either within the res gestae or harmless error. Id. at 340–341.

108. "Ex parte evidence"

Fairman, History of the Supreme Court of the United States: Reconstruction and Reunion, Part II, 1864–1888, 1987, p. 378.

109. "Done or omitted"

Id. at p. 377.

110. Best evidence rule

The statute allowed certified copies of original orders to be used, permitted the use of secondary evidence if the original could not be found, and made a telegram purporting to be from a higher authority self-authenticating. Ibid.

111. "Exclusion of rights"

Id. at p. 378.

112. "Overthrow truth"

Id. at p. 379. On the relationship between authentication, the best evidence rule, and hearsay, see vol. 30, § 6337, pp. 158–162.

Reconstruction and Constitutionalism

The passage of the Thirteenth Amendment outlawing slavery presented the former slaveholders with a problem they euphemistically referred to as the "question of the control of labor;" that is, how to appropriate the labor of the former slave in what was ostensibly a "free labor" system.[113] The Southern states immediately begin to enact so-called "Black Codes" in an effort to substitute peonage for slavery.[114] Mississippi's was the model for other states.[115] It made it a crime for any black not to have a written contract of employment or to leave work before the contract had expired and punished whites who offered jobs to blacks who were already under contract.[116] As one historian has put it, the effect was "to put the state much in the place of the former master."[117]

The criminal law was used broadly to force blacks into peonage.[118] The hunting, fishing, foraging, and ranging of livestock that poor whites had used to eke out a living were now criminalized.[119] Vagrancy laws were enacted to prevent blacks from moving in search of higher wages.[120] In some cases, vagrancy laws punished those who misspent what they earned, preached the Gospel without a license, rented land, or used insulting gestures or words; Florida made "disrespect" of one's employer a crime.[121] Finally, most

113. "Control of labor"

Foner, Reconstruction: America's Unfinished Revolution, 1863–1877, 1988, p. 198.

114. Peonage for slavery

Friedman, Crime and Punishment in American History, 1992, p. 94.

115. Mississippi model

Ibid. See also, Foner, Reconstruction: America's Unfinished Revelation, 1863–1877, 1988, p. 199.

116. Under contract

Ibid.

117. "State in place of master"

Foner, Reconstruction: America's Unfinished Revolution, 1863–1877, 1988, p. 198.

118. Force into peonage

In addition, many states enacted "apprenticeship" laws that forced black orphans or minors whose parents were deemed unable to support them into working for their former masters who were allowed to "chastize" them with whips. Id. at p. 201.

119. Hunting and fishing

Id. at p. 403. For a more comprehensive discussion, see Foner, Nothing But Freedom: Emancipation and Its Legacy, 1983, pp. 61–67.

120. Vagrancy laws

Friedman, Crime and Punishment in American History, 1992, p. 94.

121. "Disrespect" a crime

Foner, Reconstruction: America's Unfinished Revolution, 1863–1877, 1988, p. 200.

Southern states increased the penalties for property crimes.[122] The effect of thus criminalizing freedom was to make the state literally "the master;" Southern prisons and jails were filled with blacks who were then leased out, often to their former masters, in what was "legalized slavery" in all but name.[123]

Northern capitalists, particularly those in the textile industry, and bankers who worried about the ability of the former slaveholders to repay prewar debts applauded the Black Codes.[124] Indeed, later in the struggle against labor, some features of the Black Codes, such as vagrancy laws, would be emulated in Northern states.[125] But in 1866, business leaders were more fearful of any federal action that would "disrupt the cheap Southern labor force."[126] When President Johnson vetoed the Freedman's Bureau Bill that, among other things, would provide a federal alternative to the racialized system of justice that enforced the Black Codes, a mass meeting of leading bankers and businessmen at New York's Cooper Union disparaged the Bureau for interfering with the plantation discipline essential for a revival of cotton production.[127]

Most Northerners, on the other hand, were outraged by the transparent attempt to impose peonage as a violation of the ideology of "free labor."[128] The result was the prolongation of military rule in the former Confederacy and the beginning of "Radical Reconstruction," the most ambitious attempt at social engineering prior to the New Deal.[129] More significantly for the Confrontation

---

122. Property crimes

Id. at p. 202.

123. "Legalized slavery"

Id. at p. 205; Friedman, Crime and Punishment in American History, 1992, p. 94.

124. Bankers applauded

Id. at p. 220.

125. Vagrancy laws emulated

Id. at p. 519.

126. "Cheap labor"

Id. at p. 234.

127. Disparaged Bureau

Id. at p. 249. On the Bureau's role in opposing racialized Southern justice, see id. at pp. 150, 166, 206.

128. "Free labor"

Id. at p. 208. One New Yorker wrote about the capitalist support of the Black Codes: "[t]here is a great clamor to coerce black men to work ,but I hear none to make those who have heretofore lived upon the black man's labor do likewise." Id. at p. 249.

129. Social engineering

The military commanders had barred enforcement of the Black Codes in some instances. Id. at pp. 208–209.

Clause, the Black Codes were a significant impetus for what has been called "the Second American Revolution"——the series of Constitutional amendments that was ultimately to overturn much ante-bellum constitutionalism.[130]

Between 1790 and the outbreak of the Civil War, more than 1000 amendments to the Constitution had been proposed in Congress, 57 in the session of 1860–1861 alone, but only two had been adopted.[131] Traditional constitutionalism had been stretched by government action during the Civil War, particularly by Emancipation.[132] Beginning in 1865 with the Thirteenth Amendment, Congress set out to constitutionalize the wartime expansion of federal power and, in so doing, set the stage for developments over the next century.[133] For purposes of the Confrontation Clause, the most significant of the postwar amendments was the Fourteenth.[134]

One historian has suggested that "[t]he Fourteenth Amendment must be understood as the Republican party's plan for securing the fruits both of the war and of the three decades of antislavery agitation preceding it."[135] However, many attempts to discern the "original intent" of the drafters have suffered from reliance on quotations taken out of the historical context of Republican ideology and its evolution during the Civil War.[136] Senator Jacob Howard of Michigan, who guided the amendment to passage in the Senate, made clear at the time that the states could no longer infringe "the personal rights guaranteed and secured by the first eight amendments"——including, of course, the Confrontation Clause of the Sixth Amendment.[137] Representative Bingham said much the same

130. "Second Revolution"

Kyvig, Explicit and Authentic Acts, 1996, p. 155.

131. Only two adopted

Id. at pp. 118–146.

132. Stretched by action

Id. at p. 154.

133. Thirteenth Amendment

Id. at pp. 161–162.

134. Most significant

As we shall see, this was held a century later to make the Confrontation Clause binding on the states. See Pointer v. Texas, 1965, 85 S.Ct. 1065, 380 U.S. 400, 13 L.Ed.2d 923.

135. "Securing fruits"

Kyvig, Explicit and Authentic Acts, 1996, p . 167.

136. Out of historical context

Kaczorowski, Searching For The Intent of The Framers of the Fourteenth Amendment, 1973, 5 Conn.L.Rev. 368.

137. "First eight amendments"

Foner, Reconstruction: America's Unfinished Revolution, 1863–1877, 1988, p. 258.

in the House, and in an 1871 speech on the floor repeated the claim that he had drafted the language explicitly to reverse John Marshall's holding that the Bill of Rights did not bind the states.[138] One historian finds it "abundantly clear that Republicans wished to give constitutional sanction to * * * trial by impartial jury" as spelled out in the Sixth Amendment.[139] As we have seen, one of the incidents of trial by jury is the right of confrontation.[140]

The revolutionary attempt by the Radical Republicans to exploit the crisis to reformulate the purposes of government is best captured by the remarks of Thaddeus Stevens just before the passage of the Fourteenth Amendment by the House.[141]

> In my youth, in my manhood, in my old age, I had fondly dreamed that when any fortunate chance should have broken up for awhile the foundation of our institutions, and released us from obligations the most tyrannical that ever man imposed in the name of freedom, the intelligent, pure and just men of this Republic * * * would have so remodeled all our institutions as freed them from every vestige of human oppression, of inequality of rights, of the recognized degradation of the poor, and the superior caste of the rich.[142]

Stevens conceded that the Fourteenth Amendment alone did not accomplish his dream but was mere "patching up the worst portions of the ancient edifice."[143] By the time the Supreme Court got around to construing the Amendment, the Radical Republicans had lost the ideological war and their idealistic version of the Amendment was to lie dormant for decades.[144]

These revolutionary purposes were not lost on conservative politicians who had no desire to see the abolitionist roots of the Republican party enshrined in the Constitution where they would

138. Reverse holding

Ibid; Kyvig, Explicit and Authentic Acts, 1996, p. 168, See also, § 6355, text at notecall 12 (Marshall holding).

139. "Abundantly clear"

Foner, Reconstruction: America's Unfinished Revolution, 1863–1877, 1988, p. 258.

140. Incident of jury trial

See vol. 30, § 6347, pp. 695–697.

141. Reformulate purposes

Kyvig, Explicit and Authentic Acts, 1996, p. 179.

142. "Caste of rich"

Foner, Reconstruction: America's Unfinished Revolution, 1863–1877, 1988, p. 254.

143. "Patching up worst"

Ibid.

144. Lie dormant

Kyvig, Explicit and Authentic Acts, 1996, p. 156.

be beyond political conquest.[145] President Johnson claimed that the Amendment had been invalidly adopted because of the absence of the Southern states from Congress.[146] The legislatures of the slave-holding border and southern states rejected the Amendment, but the Northern state legislatures dominated by Republicans quickly ratified.[147] However, to get the required number of ratifications the Radical Republicans had to pass the Military Reconstruction Act under which new Southern legislatures freed from Confederate domination joined with the North to ratify the Amendment.[148] If the Amendment had the modest purposes the Supreme Court was later to give it, it is difficult to explain the depth of opposition to it.[149]

The postwar era brought a veritable orgy of constitution-making and constitutional revision.[150] During Reconstruction, Republican governments in some Southern states adopted radically egalitarian constitutions.[151] With the end of Reconstruction, the slaveholder aristocracy not only repudiated these Republican constitutions but adopted new ones designed to restore as many vestiges of slavery as the Supreme Court would tolerate.[152] Meanwhile, in the North new states were adopting constitutions for the first time and almost all of the older states revised their constitutions, often to reflect the popular suspicion of capitalists engendered by railroad ripoffs of municipalities and state governments and by the antilabor violence of private police forces and paramili-

145. Beyond political

Id. at p. 179.

146. Invalidly adopted

Id. at pp. 170.

147. Quickly ratified

Id. at pp. 171–172.

148. Joined to ratify

Id. at pp. 173–174. Ratification was complicated because several Northern states in which the Republicans lost power tried to revoke ratifications.

149. Modest purposes

Id. at pp. 184. One historian has said that during the balance of the Nineteenth Century "the Court acted in ways that minimized the Impact of the Civil War amendments but satisfied the dominant conservative and racist political-legal community." Our analysis of these developments as they affected the right of confrontation appears below, text at notecalls 366. 830.

150. Orgy of constitutions

Friedman, A History of American Law, 1973, p. 302.

151. Radically egalitarian

Ibid. See also, Brodie, Thaddeus Stevens: Scourge of the South, 1959, p. 211; Foner, Reconstruction: America's Unfinished Revolution, 1863–1877, 1988.

152. Restore vestiges of slavery

Id. at p . 308.

tary legions organized by businessmen.[153] Thus, this may be an appropriate place to pause to tell as much of the story of state confrontation clauses during the Nineteenth Century as is known to us.[154]

When we left the state constitutional conventions in 1790, five states—Connecticut, Maine, New Jersey, New York, and South Carolina—had no confrontation clauses in their constitutions.[155] Over the course of the 19th Century, all of these states, except New York, adopted confrontation clauses.[156] However, three new states in the Far West joined the Union without any confrontation guarantee in their constitutions—California, Idaho, and Nevada.[157] Hence, by the end of the Nineteenth Century there were still four states without any constitutional right of confrontation.[158]

Of the eight states with confrontation clauses in 1790, three—Delaware, North Carolina, and Virginia—gave the defendant the right to confront both "accusers" and "witnesses."[159] These all proved to be constitutional dead ends; that is, no other state ever used "accuser" in its confrontation clause.[160]

The remaining states were divided between what we shall call "the Maryland model" and "the Massachusetts model." The Mary-

153. Suspicion of capitalists

Id. at pp. 305–307. Insofar as relevant to the history of confrontation, the clash of capital with state governments and labor unions will be discussed below.

154. Known to us

We have found no history of state constitutional conventions during this period comparable to those available for the Revolutionary state conventions. See vol. 30, § 6346. Given the comparatively little payoff from our research in these earlier histories, we declined to write the history of Nineteenth or Twentieth Century state constitutions ourselves.

155. Had no clauses

See vol. 30, § 6346.

156. All except New York

1 Thorne, The Federal and State Constitutions, 1909, p. 538 (Connecticut); 3 id. at p. 1647 (Maine); 5 id. at pp. 2600 (New Jersey), 2647, 2654, 2684 (New York); 6 id. at pp. 3282, 3308 (South Carolina).

157. Three Far West

1 id. at pp. 391, 414 (California); 2 id. at p. 920 (Idaho); 4 id. at p. 2402 (Nevada).

158. Four without

Some of these states may have had statutory confrontation clauses. See, e.g., Comment, Cal.Evid.Code § 711.

159. "Accusers" and "witnesses"

See vol. 30, § 6346, pp. 611–612.

160. Dead ends

However, the Virginia and North Carolina provisions remained in effect for the balance of the Nineteenth Century. See 5 Thorne, The State and Federal Constitutions, 1909, pp. 2801, 2823 (North Carolina); 6 id. at pp. 3820, 3830, 3842, 3874, 3905 (Virginia).

land confrontation provision was identical with the Sixth Amendment: "to be confronted with the witnesses against him."[161] Pennsylvania and Vermont deleted the last two words—"against him"—but were otherwise identical.[162] The Massachusetts model, also adopted in New Hampshire gave the accused the right "to meet the witnesses against him face to face."[163]

Over the course of the Nineteenth Century, a total of 21 states chose to follow the Maryland model, more or less. Thirteen of those states followed the Sixth Amendment verbatim: Arkansas, Florida, Iowa, Louisiana, Michigan, Minnesota, Mississippi, Nebraska, New Jersey, Rhode Island, South Carolina and Wyoming.[164] Four states—Alabama, Connecticut, Maine, and Utah—provided that the accused was to be confronted "by" rather than "with"[165] and Kansas said "by the witness or witnesses."[166] Three states—Oklahoma, Texas, and West Virginia—substituted "shall be" for "to be" in the Maryland model.[167] Georgia had an idiosyncratic version: "shall be confronted with the witnesses testifying against him."[168]

On the other hand, 20 states chose to follow the Massachusetts model, but only eight of them did so verbatim—Colorado, Florida, Missouri, Montana, Nebraska, South Carolina, South Dakota and Washington.[169] Ten states deleted "against him" so the clause read

161. Maryland

See vol. 30, § 6346, p. 612.

162. Identical

Ibid.

163. "Face to face"

Ibid.

164. Verbatim

1 Thorne, The Federal and State Constitutions, 1909, p. 335 (Arkansas); 2 id. at pp. 665, 686 (Florida), 1124, 1138 (Iowa); 3 id. at p. 1472 (Louisiana); 4 id. at pp. 1931, 1956 (Michigan), 1992 (Minnesota); 2033, 2049, 2069, 2092 (Mississippi); 5 id. at pp. 2349 (Nebraska), 2600 (New Jersey); 6 id. at pp. 3223 (Rhode Island), 3308 (South Carolina); 7 id. at 4118 (Wyoming).

165. "By" rather than "with"

1 id. at pp. 97, 116, 133, 154, 183 (Alabama), 538 (Connecticut); 3 id. at p. 1647 (Maine); 6 id. at p. 3703 (Utah).

166. Kansas

2 id. at p . 1216. We should add that there is some question as to whether this constitution was ever in effect. See Encyclopedia of American History, Morris ed. 1976, pp. 264–265.

167. "Shall be"

5 Thorne, The Federal and State Constitutions, 1909, p. 4274 (Oklahoma); 6 id. at pp. 3542, 3548, 3570, 3592, 3622 (Texas); 7 id. at pp. 4015, 4037, 4239 (West Virginia).

168. Georgia

2 id. at pp. 810, 823, 842.

169. Only eight

1 id. at p. 477 (Colorado); 2 id. at p. 733 (Florida); 4 id. at pp. 2163, 2193, 2232 (Missouri), 2303 (Montana), 2632 (Nebraska); 7 id. at pp. 3278, 3282 (South Carolina), 3370 (South Dakota); 7 id. at p. 3975 (Washington).

"to meet the witnesses face to face"——Arkansas, Illinois, Indiana, Kansas, Kentucky, Ohio, Oregon, Pennsylvania, Tennessee and Wisconsin.[170] Louisiana changed "to meet" to "of meeting" and Delaware provided a right "to meet the witnesses in their examination face to face."[171]

Readers who have done the math will discover that we have more confrontation clauses than there were states in the union. But careful readers who have noted the same state appearing more than once will have the explanation.[172] Eight states——Arkansas, Delaware, Florida, Kansas, Louisiana, Nebraska, Pennsylvania, and South Carolina——switched from one confrontation clause to another.[173]

170. Deleted "against"

1 id. at pp. 270, 290 (Arkansas); 2 id. at pp. 982, 1008, 1014 (Illinois), 1059, 1074 (Indiana), 1180, 1223, 1242 (Kansas); 3 id. at pp. 1275, 1289, 1313, 1317 (Kentucky); 4 id. at pp. 2910, 1914 (Ohio), 2999 (Oregon); 5 id. at pp. 3100, 3113, 3122 (Pennsylvania); 6 id. at pp. 3422, 3427, 3450 (Tennessee); 7 id. at p. 4077 (Wisconsin).

171. Louisiana and Delaware

1 id. at pp. 569, 583, 601 (Delaware); 3 id. at pp. 1389, 1104, 1422, 1449 (Louisiana).

172. Explanation

This actually understates the amount of switching; some states went from having a confrontation clause to not having one, and vice versa.

173. States switched

Arkansas went from the Massachusetts model, to having no confrontation clause in its Reconstruction, to the Maryland model. 1 Thorne, The Federal and State Constitutions, 1909, pp. 270, 290, 307, 335.

Delaware originally had "to be confronted with the accusers or witnesses," then changed to "to meet the witnesses in their examination face to face." Id. at pp. 569, 583, 601.

Florida first adopted the Maryland model, dropped it during Reconstruction, then in 1885 adopted the Massachusetts model. 2 id. at pp. 665, 686, 705, 733.

Kansas adopted the Massachusetts model, then the Lecompton Constitution went with Maryland, but all subsequent constitutions stayed with Massachusetts. Id. at pp. 1180, 1216, 1223, 1242.

Louisiana holds the record for the most versions of the right of confrontation. In 1812 it read "of meeting the witnesses face to face." In 1845 this was changed to "[h]e shall have the right, unless he shall have fled from justice, of meeting the witnesses face to face." Just seven years later the "unless" clause was deleted and this was kept through the next two constitutions. Then in 1879 the Maryland model was adopted, but this was subsequently amended to insert "[t]he accused in every instance shall have the right" to Maryland confrontation. 3 id. at pp. 1389, 1404, 1422, 1442, 1449, 1472, 1523.

Nebraska started out with the Maryland model, then switched to Massachusetts. 4 id. at pp. 2349, 2362.

Pennsylvania started with Maryland but switched to Massachusetts. 5 id. at pp. 3083, 3100, 3113, 3122.

South Carolina had no confrontation clause in its first three constitutions,

The varying versions of state confrontation clauses might support different versions of the right that was intended to be granted.[174] But we have found no evidence that this was the intent of the drafters and state courts have rarely used the language of the local confrontation provision as a reason for departing from the interpretations of the right given by courts in other states.[175]

Reconstruction and Radicalism

We return to our chronology in 1867, a year that saw the death of the last Revolutionary War veteran, the publication of "Capital" by Karl Marx, and the beginning of "Radical," or less pejoratively, "Congressional Reconstruction."[176] The convergence of these events was doubtless fortuitous, but they were to combine with significant impact on the right of confrontation.

Northern outrage over the Black Codes and the use of violence to reimpose the plantation economy provided the political force that allowed Congress to prevail over President Johnson and those who favored a prompt return to the status quo, but the vision behind Radical Reconstruction was a Revolutionary utopianism.[177] The Radical Republicans wanted a nation whose citizens enjoyed an equality of civil and political rights secured by a powerful federal government.[178] Some Republicans wanted to make the Declaration

but adopted the Massachusetts version during Reconstruction, then switched to the Maryland model in 1895. 6 id. at pp. 3278, 3282, 3308.

174. Different versions

For example, the Delaware version quoted at notecall 171 in the text above might be said to have adopted the pure Wigmorean model, but on second reading it is unclear whether it gives a right to cross-examination or only a right to be present during whatever examination occurs.

175. No evidence

Should such evidence turn up, it will appear under this note in the annual supplement.

176. "Capital", "Reconstruction"

Foner, Reconstruction: America's Unfinished Revolution, 1988, pp. 228 (Radical Reconstruction), 278 (last Revolutionary veteran), 309 (Capital). See also Fairman, History of the Supreme

Court of the United States: Reconstruction and Reunion, Part I, 1971, p. 253 ("Congressional Reconstruction").

177. Utopianism

Understandably, Fairman, History of the Supreme Court of the United States: Reconstruction and Reunion, Part I, 1971, pp. 254–257, emphasizes the fear that the Fourteenth Amendment was not going to be ratified and focuses on political maneuvering in Congress rather than public opinion and the ideological vision of the actors; the Supreme Court was to treat the ideology of the framers as largely irrelevant.

178. Equality secured

Foner, Reconstruction: America's Unfinished Revolution, 1988, pp. 230–231.

of Independence a coequal part of fundamental law, claiming that its declaration of human equality gave meaning to the constitutional provision guaranteeing the states a republican form of government.[179]

This vision derived its Marxian tint from the republican belief that political equality required a comparatively equal distribution of property.[180] The Black Codes had made it clear that if the newly freed slaves were not to be forced into a new form of servitude, they would have to have a measure of economic equality to defend their political equality, if not Sherman's "forty acres and a mule," at least something like it.[181] Hence, the most radical of the Republicans wanted to overturn the plantation system and replace it with a system of self-sufficient small producers—turning the Freedmen into something like Jeffersonian "yeoman."[182] Indeed, Thaddeus Stevens had calculated that confiscation of rebel property would pay not only for farms for the slaves but the costs of the war as well.[183]

The Freedman embraced similar values. One convention of blacks declared

> [w]e simply desire that we shall be recognized as men; that we have no obstructions placed in our way; that the same laws which govern white men shall direct colored men; that we have the right of trial by a jury of our peers * * *.[184]

The intersection between the right to testify, the right of confrontation, and the right to trial by jury and the concept of equal citizenship that we have previously noted was familiar because even before Reconstruction, black churches had been hotbeds of confrontation values.[185] Moreover, the message of all those Fourth of July

179. Republican form

Id. at p. 232.

180. Equal property

For the sources of this in early republicanism, see vol. 30, § 6346, p. 616. This idea was carried forward in the Republican ideology of "Free Labor." See Foner, The Story of American Freedom, 1998, pp. 65–68.

181. "Forty acres and mule"

See above, text at notecall 70. See also Refousse, The Radical Republicans: Lincoln's Vanguard for Racial Justice, 1969, p. 369.

182. Freedman "yeoman"

Foner, Reconstruction: America's Unfinished Revolution, 1988, p. 235–237.

183. Pay for costs

Brodie, Thaddeus Stevens: Scourge of the South, 1959, pp. 207, 232.

184. "Trial by jury"

Williams, The Great South Carolina Ku Klux Klan Trials, 1871–1872, 1996, p. 5.

185. Black churches

Foner, Reconstruction: America's Unfinished Revolution, 1863–1877, pp. 92–94.

celebrations had not been lost on the slaves; the Freedmen repeatedly invoked the Declaration of Independence to support their demands for equality.[186] Without ever having read Marx, the Freedmen espoused the labor theory of value, arguing that since their ancestors had worked without pay to produce the wealth of the South, they were now entitled to a share of that wealth.[187] In some states, governments of Radical Republican Freedmen and Northerners tried to use the taxing power as an instrument for redistribution of the wealth.[188]

As the previous quotation from Stevens predicts, Radical Reconstruction would fall far short of such utopian (or dysutopian) goals.[189] The Act of March 2, 1867, simply required that the former Confederate states would be readmitted to the Union only if, inter alia, they approved the 14th Amendment and adopted constitutions guaranteeing male suffrage.[190] As we shall see, what this seems to have accomplished is to add a political motivation to the economic motives that led Southern elites to seek some new form of dependent status for the Freedman.[191]

In terms of benefiting Freedmen, one might say that the Radical Republicans' "bark was worse than their bite"; but their woofing was to have long-term impacts far worse than mere ineffectiveness.[192] For example, at an impromptu speech in Lawrence,

186. Invoked Declaration

Id. at pp. 110, 114, 288, 320. The power of this icon can be seen by the attempts of Stephen Douglas in his debates with Lincoln to deny that the Founders meant what they had said in the Declaration.

187. Entitled to share

Williams, The Great South Carolina Ku Klux Klan Trials, 1871–1872, 1996, p 4; Foner, Reconstruction: America's Unfinished Revolution, 1863–1877, 1988, pp. 102–110.

188. Redistribution

Williams, The Great South Carolina Ku Klux Klan Trials, 1871–1872, 1996, pp. 12–13; Foner, Reconstruction: America's Unfinished Revolution, 1863–1877, 1988, p. 375.

189. Stevens predicts

See above, text at notecalls 142–143.

190. Male suffrage

Williams, The Great South Carolina Ku Klux Klan Trials, 1871–1872, 1996, p. 7; Fairman, History of The Supreme Court of the United States: Reconstruction and Reunion, Part One, 1971, p . 292.

191. Political motivation

That is, the Freedman could not be reduced to serfs until they had first been stripped of citizenship.

192. Far worse

The Radical Republican rhetoric proved to be far more short-lived than that of other ideologies favorable to redistribution of wealth, but what gave it a greater significance was that it was enunciated by those who had achieved power through the ballot box rather than the bomb and who had actually used that power to deprive property

Kansas, the Radical President pro tem of the Senate Ben Wade suggested that once Reconstruction in the South was completed, the Republicans could move on to the pressing problems of the North such as the maldistribution of property, the class war being waged by capital on labor, and the denial of the vote to women.[193] Having already lost the support of those commercial interests that favored doing business with the former slaveholders over providing freedom to the former slaves, such attacks on capitalism cost the Radicals the support of Republican moderates needed to carry out Reconstruction.[194]

The impact of Radical Republican rhetoric on the right of confrontation was more subtle and indirect.[195] When Ben Wade spoke of an economic system "which degrades the poor man and elevates the rich, which makes the rich richer and the poor poorer, which drags the very soul out of a poor man for a pitiful existence,"[196] he and others may have characterized this as simply an example of the Republican "Free Labor" ideology. Even so, it could hardly have consoled the privileged, many of whom are in constant fear that those who are less favored than they are endlessly plotting to take away their privileges. Wade's language supported what otherwise might have seemed like paranoia. Marx now provided the privileged with a vocabulary to attack their enemies, real or imagined. Hence, when the Patrons of Husbandry, an agrarian organization better known as "The Grange," sought legislation to revive the common-law doctrine of "the just price" and apply it to the quasi-monopoly enjoyed by railroads, the editor of the Chicago Tribune

owners of what they regarded as theirs——their slaves.

193. Vote to women

Trefousse, The Radical Republicans: Lincoln's Vanguard for Radical Justice, 1969, p. 362. For a quotation from that speech, see above text at notecall 73.

194. Support of moderates

For example, it has been thought that one reason for opposition to the impeachment of President Johnson was that Wade would take his place. Ibid. Similarly, Grant supposedly removed an Attorney General who was vigorously prosecuting the Ku Klux Klan because he was thought to share the Radical view of equality. Williams, The Great South Carolina Ku Klux Klan Trials, 1871–1872, 1996, p. 101 (describing effects of this on further prosecutions).

195. Subtle and indirect

We shall subsequently see how it combined with other beliefs that were hostile to the rights of criminal defendants.

196. "Pitiful existence"

Trefousse, The Radical Republicans: Lincoln's Vanguard for Racial Justice, 1969, p. 396.

attacked this as "a communistic war upon vested rights and property."[197]

Grousing of editorialists, corporate executives, or even corporate lawyers would have some impact on judges, but this rhetoric soon entered courtrooms.[198] When the Granger legislation came before the U.S. Supreme Court, one of the railroad lawyers wrote in his brief: "It is quite true that the theory of the Statute is distinct from the doctrine of the Communists. The latter divides property ratably between the plundered and the plunderers, while the former takes all for the Grangers."[199] Another lawyer, more modestly, claimed only that it "is the beginning of the operations of the commune in the legislation of this country."[200] Another urged the justices to follow their predecessors who had "held in check all the efforts of radical politicians and crazy communists" to overthrow business interests.[201] The majority of the Court was unimpressed by this rhetoric—and so became its target. In a petition for rehearing, one of the railroad lawyers claimed that the Court's opinion "has pushed aside the obstructions which stood in the way of communism * * * against which the prohibitions were directed."[202] To Professor John Norton Pomeroy, the Court's reasoning "invokes the very essence of the destructive theories maintained by the socialists and communists."[203] Rufus Peckham, a future Supreme Court Justice then on the New York Court of Appeals was more

197. "Communistic war"

Foner, Reconstruction: America's Unfinished Revolution, 1863–1877, 1988, p. 518.

198. Entered courtrooms

We did not begin our research seeking this rhetoric and did not begin to collect it until its significance became clear; when we did, we soon began to tire of it. We shall not impose all of it on the reader but simply note for those who think the Communist bogeyman began with Joe McCarthy that there is a lot more where this came from.

199. "Former takes all"

Fairman, History of the Supreme Court of the United States: Reconstruction and Reunion, Part II, 1987, p. 350. Not having read Marx, we cannot vouch for the accuracy of counsel's characterization of his doctrine; however, it does not seem to reflect the practice of those who claimed to be the followers of Marx.

The brief was filed in Peik v. Chicago & N.W. Ry. Co., 1876, 4 Otto (94 U.S.) 164, 24 L.Ed. 97.

200. "Beginning of commune"

Id. at p. 349.

201. "Crazy communists"

Id. at p. 357.

202. "Way of communism"

Id. at p. 366.

203. "Maintained by socialists"

Magrath, Morrison R. Waite: The Triumph of Character, 1963, p. 220.

turgid when refusing to follow the Court's decision——he called it "communistic."[204]

Invoking the Communist bogeyman remained a common political ploy for well over a century——and not only among those that judges could easily dismiss.[205] For example, when a constitutional amendment was proposed that would give Congress the power to prohibit child labor, the American Bar Association denounced it as "a communist effort to nationalize children."[206] A President of the A.B.A. regarded the "New Deal as a long step toward socialism"[207] Nor was Pomeroy the only law professor to resort to red-bashing.[208] C.G. Tiedeman, author of a leading treatise on constitutional law opined that "socialism, communism, and anarchism are rampant throughout the civilized world."[209]

The label "communist" was applied to an astounding range of ideas, institutions and individuals over the next century. In addition to the proposal to ban child labor, Marx was blamed for everything from a statute authorizing cities to loan money to capitalists to build factories to the United Nations Declaration of Human Rights, from Legal Realism to spendthrift trusts.[210] Among

204. "Communistic"

Paul, Conservative Crisis and The Rule of Law: Attitudes of Bar and Bench, 1887–1895, 1960, p. 73.

205. Easily dismiss

See, e.g., Swisher, Steven J. Field: Craftsman of the Law, 1969, 246 (railroad executive despairs that only Supreme Court can save nation from communism); Twiss, Lawyers and The Constitution: How Laissez Faire Came to The Supreme Court, 1942, p. 197 (writer in Harvard Law Review).

206. "Nationalize children"

Kyvig, Explicit and authentic Acts, 1996, p. 309.

207. "Long step toward"

Id. at p. 399.

208. Law professor

Paul, Conservative Crisis and The Rule of Law: Attitudes of Bar and Bench, 1887–1895, 1960, p. 17.

209. "Rampant throughout"

Twiss, Lawyers and The Constitution: How Laissez Faire Came to The Supreme Court, 1942, p. 122.

210. Ideas

John Chipman Gray thought "paternalism" was "the fundamental essence alike of spendthrift trusts and "socialism;" Friedman, A History of American Law, 1973, p. 369; Kyvig, Explicit and Authentic Acts, 1996, p. 259 (Child Labor Amendment "a highly socialistic measure); id. at p . 340 (U.N. Declaration of Rights would turn country "into a completely socialistic state"); Jacobs, Law Writers and the Courts, 1954, p. 132 (Chief Justice Appleton, author of evidence treatise, on statute allowing cities to loan money to manufacturers: "It is communism incipient, if not perfected."); Wigdor, Roscoe Pound, 1974, p. 264 (Pound identified Legal Realism as "Marxist").

the groups supposed to be riddled with reds were the United States Senate, the Ladies Garment Workers Union, the Democratic Party of 1880, the Columbia Law School faculty, the New Deal, teachers of commercial law who did not participate in the drafting of the Uniform Commercial Code, and the U.C.L.A. Daily Bruin.[211] People supposed to be tainted by socialism included Franklin D. Roosevelt, Roscoe, Pound, Felix Frankfurter, Louis Brandeis, and Shirley Temple.[212]

How all this "Red Scare" influenced judges cannot be determined easily; expression of such fears was inconsistent with the more formal style of judicial reasoning then coming into vogue.[213] Occasionally judges expressed similar sentiments when charging grand juries on circuit; e.g., Justice Bradley reportedly used one

211. Institutions

Kyvig, Explicit and Authentic Acts, 1996, p. 339 (New Deal); Magrath, Morrison R. Waite: The Triumph of Character, 1963, p. 241 (President-elect Garfield: Democrats "rapidly drifting, in the wake of the Greenback party, toward Communism."); Auerbach, Enmity and Amity: Law Teachers and Practitioners, 1900–1922, 1971, 5 Perspectives in American History 549, 571 (Columbia law faculty); Mason, William Howard Taft: Chief Justice, 1965, P. 93 (Taft called Senate "a Bolshevik body"); Mitgang, The Man Who Rode The Tiger: The Life and Times of Judge Samuel Seabury, 1963, p. 139 (New York Times calls I.L.G.W.U. "Bolshevist"); Twining, Karl Llewellyn and The Realist Movement, 1973, p. 292 (A.L.I. bigwig brags that none of the law professors involved in drafting U.C.C. were "radicals, Communists, or anarchists or revolutionaries of any kind"); Wigdor, Roscoe Pound, 1974, p. 278 (during his sojourn at U.C.L.A., Pound regularly referred to the student newspaper as "The Daily Communist;" in fairness to Pound who by then was not as mentally acute as he once was, it should be noted that at that time the Los Angeles Times liked to call U.C.L.A. "the Big Red Schoolhouse" and the then-Dean of the Law School tried to bar faculty from joining the Faculty Club because he believed that revolution was being hatched over lunches there).

212. Individuals

Schlegel, American Legal Realism and Empirical Social Science: From The Yale Experience, 1979, 28 Buff.L.Rev. 459, 480 n. 100 (Chief Justice Taft: Frankfurter seems to be "closely in touch with every Bolshevistic communist movement in this country")' Cray, "It was Lies, All Lies," California Bar J., Sept. 1983, pp. 42, 92 (during 1938 gubernatorial election, Republican candidate called Shirley Temple a "Communist front"); Todd, Justice on Trial: The Case of Louis D. Brandeis, 1964, P. 78 (Chief Justice Taft calls Brandeis "a socialist, a muckraker, and a hypocrite"); Wigdor, Roscoe Pound, 1974, pp. 202, 274 (Pound was thought by lawyers to be a socialist because of his work with sociologists; after Roosevelt vetoed an A.B.A. bill to curb the power of administrative tribunals, Pound said this was "thoroughly in keeping with the Marxian idea of the disappearance of law").

213. Formal style

Friedman, A History of American Law, 1973, p. 540.

such occasion to give "a forcible denunciation of anarchy and communism."[214] Similar thoughts were sometimes uttered in public addresses; Justice Miller delivered a commencement address at the University of Iowa on "The Conflict in This Country Between Socialism and Organized Society" which, according to an official historian, "became an alarming discourse wherein anarchists, nihilists, socialists, and communists were banded together for indiscriminate condemnation."[215] In the Slaughterhouse Cases, a former Justice argued to the Court that rights under the Fourteenth Amendment might be invaded "under the names of socialism, communism, and other specious pretenses."[216]

A few Supreme Court Justices railed against Marxism in private correspondence and conversations.[217] A good example is Stephen Field, whose fear of communism is attributed by his biographer to Field's presence in Paris at the time of The Commune.[218] When Democrats in California failed to respond with sufficient enthusiasm to Field's Presidential ambitions, he said that the majority of the party was committed "to the lawlessness of confiscation and the chaos of communism."[219] He wrote another correspondent that he was "against the appointment of any men who entertain communistic or agrarian views, thinking only those should hold office who believe in order and law and property."[220] Justice David Brewer, Field's son-in-law, carried on the family tradition in a speech to the New York State Bar Association in 1893 attacking those who under "the black flag of anarchism, flaunting destruction of property" or "the red flag of socialism, inviting a redistribution of property" wanted "to transfer to themselves through political power the wealth they lacked the ability or pa-

214. Bradley

Fairman, History of the Supreme Court of the United States: Reconstruction and Reunion, Part Two, 1864–1888, 1987, p. 780.

215. Miller

Ibid.

216. "Specious pretenses"

Twiss, Lawyers and The Constitution: How Laissez Faire Came To The Supreme Court, 1942, p. 52 (ex-Justice Campbell, an unreconstructed Confederate).

217. In private

Whether similar views were expressed during judicial conferences cannot be determined.

218. Field and Commune

Swisher, Stephen J. Field: Craftsman of the Law, 1969, p. xv.

219. "Chaos of communism"

Id. at p. 314.

220. "Law and property"

Id. at p. 315.

tience to earn in the ordinary pursuit of their business."[221] Early in this century the torch was taken up by Chief Justice Taft, who called the Senate "a Bolshevik body" (apparently unaware that "bolshevik" means "the majority" in Russian), denounced Justice Brandeis as a "muck-raker, a socialist, and a hypocrite," and insisted that Supreme Court nominees should be sworn to protect the Constitution against "radicals, progressives, bolshevists, and socialists."[222]

To assess its impact on the right of confrontation, it would be helpful to know what "communism" meant to those who heard or uttered the word. The matter previously quoted suggests it was seen as a threat to property, or more specifically, to the distribution of property characteristic of the latter half of the Nineteenth Century. Another fear is captured by references to Marxists as "un-American."[223] The head of the West Virginia Bar Association developed this in his reference to "secret conclaves of socialism, agrarianism, and anarchism conspiring for the subversion of our American institutions."[224] In Justice Miller's commencement speech, he warned the "virtuous population of the Northwest against foreign agitators who meet at night and in secluded places" to plot the overthrow of private property.[225] In short, at this elemental level, "communism" was "foreign" in both the nativist sense of the word and in the sense of being alien to the American values of openness embodied in the Confrontation Clause.[226] Moreover, since they threatened "American institutions" by their conspiratorial activities, they did not deserve openness in return and they, like the Confederates, were best met with force rather than reason.[227]

221. "Lacked ability"

Mason, William Howard Taft: Chief Justice, 1965, p. 42.

222. Taft

Id. at pp. 93, 164; Todd, Justice on Trial: The Case of Louis D. Brandeis, 1964, p. 78.

223. "Un–American"

David, The History of The Haymarket Affair, 1963, p. 34.

224. "Conspiring for subversion"

Paul, Conservative Crisis and The Rule of Law: Attitudes of Bar and Bench. 1887–1895, p. 21.

225. "Secluded places"

Fairman, History of the Supreme Court of the United States: Reconstruction and Reunion, Part Two, 1864–1888, 1987, p. 780.

226. Being alien

We shall show below how nativism fostered the view of the criminal defendant as "The Other" to encourage a stingy attitude toward constitutional rights.

227. Met by force

No one will be surprised that even back then, those opposed to "communism" thought that the best way to conquer it was to emulate its supposed worst

This attitude would have been detrimental to the right of confrontation even had it been limited to foreign-born Marxists who were guilty of conspiring to violently overthrow the government——but it was seldom so limited. An organization of employers equated Marxism with any form of radicalism, swearing not to employ "any communist, anarchist, nihilist, or socialist, or any other person denying the right of private property or recommending destruction or bloodshed as remedies for existing evils"[228]——a locution that might include some of the abolitionists who founded the Republican party. Similarly, when the Haymarket anarchists argued that their jury was biased because it included persons who were prejudiced against anarchists, socialists, and communists, the Illinois Supreme Court brushed off the argument by equating a prejudice against Marxists with a prejudice against crime.[229] The constitutional scholar C.J. Tiedeman thought it was socialism when "the state is called on to protect the weak against the shrewdness of the stronger."[230] A writer from the Harvard Law School opined that "the worst forms of socialism will breed under the superstition so rampant that legislation is a sovereign cure-all for social ills."[231] Modern thinkers who fancy that they originated the idea that meliorist government was bad might applaud this had the author not added: "Public policy is the deadly weapon of Socialism and Communism."[232]

Communism was seen as opposed to property rights; not until late Stalinism did people begin to equate Marxism with the denial of civil liberties and the right to fair and open trials of the sort guaranteed by the Confrontation Clause.[233] Down to the end of World War II, many shared Boss Hague's view that "real Americans" do not talk about constitutional rights, only Communists do.[234] After World War II, the President of the American Bar

features——spying, conspiracy, and violence.

228. "Existing evils"

David, The History of The Haymarket Affair, 1963, p. 183.

229. Prejudice against crime

Id. at p. 309.

230. "Protect the weak"

Twiss, Lawyers and The Constitution: How Laissez Faire Came To The Supreme Court, 1942, p. 122.

231. "Cure-all"

Id. at p. 198.

232. "Public policy"

Id. at p. 197. "Public Policy" is the name of the house journal of an organization opposed to government regulation and meliorism.

233. Denial of civil liberties

Kyvig, Explicit and Authentic Acts, 1996, p. 373.

234. "Real Americans"

Vanderbilt, Changing Law: A Biography of Arthur T. Vanderbilt, 1977, p. 97.

Association could argue that if implemented here, the United Nations Declaration of Human Rights would transform the United States "into a completely socialistic state."[235] Even a Supreme Court Justice could adopt this view; after the Court had held that the Fourth Amendment did not bar wiretapping, over the dissent of Brandeis, Holmes, and Stone, Justice Willis Van Devanter predicted:

> Every communist in the country and every sympathizer with communism naturally will be against the decision [of the majority], and so will those who call themselves reformers but in truth are infected with communism.[236]

In short, until quite recently, opposition to communism was not conducive to liberal interpretations of the right of confrontation.

Cooley, Color, and Confrontation

When Grant was elected President in 1868, the anticommunist rhetoric had yet to begin; it was a good year for the Reds——The Cincinnati professional baseball team, the world's first, was founded. Also Andrew Johnson became the first American President to be impeached, George Westinghouse invented the air brake, Louisa May Alcott published "Little Women," and the Fourteenth Amendment was declared ratified.[237] There was another turning point in constitutional law that year with the publication of Cooley's "Constitutional Limitations."[238]

Thomas McIntyre Cooley had studied law under Justice Strong of the Supreme Court and in 1864, just 40 years old, he was elected to the Michigan Supreme Court where he served for more than 20 years.[239] In 1885, Cooley was defeated for reelection after the Detroit News, which had lost a libel case at Cooley's hands, published a chart showing that in the previous five years Cooley had written 30 opinions favoring corporations, nineteen favoring railroads, and only two in which business interests lost——a percentage

---

235. "Completely socialistic"

Kyvig, Explicit and Authentic Acts, 1996, p. 340.

236. "Infected with communism"

Mason, William Howard Taft: Chief Justice, 1965, p. 228.

237. Declared ratified

The Encyclopedia of American Facts and Dates, 9th ed. 1993, pp. 296–301.

238. Turning point

Twiss, Lawyers and The Constitution: How Laissez Faire Came To The Supreme Court, 1942, p. 18.

239. More than 20 years

Dictionary of American Biography, Bowman ed. 1995, p. 151. As we shall see, Cooley's career intersected with a number of other important strands in the history of confrontation; hence, the details in the text.

of probusiness rulings that was far above the average even for the Republican-dominated Michigan tribunal.[240] After his defeat, Cooley went to work for the railroads until President Cleveland appointed him as the first Chairman of the Interstate Commerce Commission, where he continued to favor railroads.[241]

Cooley, then, was clearly no liberal. In 1894 he called Coxey's march of poor people on Washington "an incipient revolution" and in his Presidential address to the American Bar Association he denounced Debs and the Pullman strike.[242] He sought to erect constitutional protection for property interests and he has been credited by some as the person who turned the Due Process Clause from a procedural to a substantive guarantee.[243] He was not, of course, thinking of the Fourteenth Amendment, which only went into effect the year his treatise was published; he was concerned with state constitutional limitations.[244] He tried to make the English common law the test for American constitutional provisions.[245]

What Cooley had to say about the right of confrontation doubtless influenced some courts:

> The testimony for the people in criminal cases can only be given, as a general rule, by witnesses who are present in court. The defendant is entitled to be confronted with the witnesses against him; and if any of them be absent from the Commonwealth, so that their attendance cannot be compelled, or be dead, or have become incapable of being sworn, there is no mode by which their statements against the prisoner can be used for his conviction. The exceptions to this rule are of cases which are excluded from its reasons from their peculiar circumstances; but they are far from numerous.[246]

240. Above average

Edward, Why Justice Cooley Left The Bench: A Missing Piece of Legal History, 1964, 10 Wayne L.Rev. 490, 496.

241. Favor railroads

Kolko, Railroads and Regulation, 1877–1916, 1965, pp. 47–48.

242. Denounced Debs

Paul, Conservative Crisis and The Rule of Law: Attitudes of Bar and Bench, 1887–1895, 1960, pp. 129, 142.

243. Turned substantive

Twiss, Lawyers and The Constitution: How Laissez Faire Came To The Supreme Court, 1942, pp. 15, 26.

244. State limitations

Id. at p. 32.

245. Common law test

Id. at p. 25.

246. "Far from numerous"

Cooley, Constitutional Limitations, 1868, p. 318.

Indeed. Cooley lists only two exceptions: testimony before an examining magistrate or coroner or at a former trial, if the witness was sworn and the accused had an opportunity to cross-examine him, and dying declarations.[247] Cooley, unlike some state courts, clearly believes that a hearsay declarant is a "witness against" the defendant; that is, the right of confrontation bars hearsay.[248] Nor, despite Cooley's admiration of the common law or his reliance on Greenleaf for authority, is there any suggestion that cross-examination is the essence of confrontation——as Wigmore and some modern courts have supposed.[249]

Cooley's view was confirmed that same year. In State v. Reidel, the defendant was charged with fraud.[250] The prosecution sought to prove that the defendant did not have money on deposit in a bank in an adjacent state by use of a certificate of protest of a notary public of that state. After citing statutory provisions that would have made the evidence admissible in a civil case, the court held "the deposition of the notary could not be used against the defendant in a criminal prosecution; the Constitution forbids it."[251] The court said:

> Under the Constitution, he has the right to see the witnesses against him, face to face. Hence, the state could not prove the nonexistence of funds in the bank at St. Paul, by the deposition of any officer of the bank, nor could it prove this fact by showing the

247. Two exceptions

"If the witness was sworn before the examining magistrate, and the accused had an opportunity then to cross-examine him, or before a coroner, or if there was a former trial on which he was sworn, it seems allowable to make use of his deposition or the minutes of his examination, if the witness has since deceased, or is out of the jurisdiction, or cannot be found after diligent search, or is insane, or sick and unable to testify, or has been summoned, but appears to have been kept away by the opposite party. So also if a party is on trial for homicide, the declarations of the party whom he is charged with having killed, if made under the solemnity of a conviction that he was at the point of death, and relating to matters of fact concerning the homicide, which passed under his

own observation, may be given in evidence against him,——the condition of the party who made them being such that every motive to falsehood must be supposed to be silenced, and the mind to be induced by the most powerful considerations to speak the truth." Ibid., citing Greenleaf, §§ 163, 166.

248. Bars hearsay

See § 6355, text at notecall 826.

249. Court supposed

See § 6357.

250. Reidel case

1868, 26 Iowa 430.

251. "Constitution forbids"

Id. at p. 437.

declarations of those officers.[252]

This is more in keeping with the views of the Founders than those modern courts that hold that any sort of business or official record is admissible against the defendant—even though it was far more inconvenient to bring the witnesses from St. Paul to Iowa in those days than it is today.[253]

About the time Cooley's book came off the press, the specter that haunted its author came to life with the founding of the Patrons of Husbandry—better known as "the Grange."[254] The Grange was an agrarian response to the growth of monopoly power associated with railroad corporations.[255] Some saw that growth as a product of the federal power over corporations, spawned by the use of legal fictions that were used to provide very real protection from state regulation.[256] The Grange opposed those intermediaries between farmers and consumers who were seen as using monopoly power to extract unjustified profits—e.g., railroads, warehouses, and grain elevators.[257] What made the Grange frightening to conservatives was its desire to use the activist state that grew out of the Civil War to control corporations condemned as parasitic intermediaries between producers and consumers, much as the Confrontation Clause condemned intermediaries between the jury and the hearsay declarant.[258]

The American Law Review denounced the Grange as "rank communism."[259] We have seen how Granger legislation had been

252. "Declarations of officers"

Ibid.

253. More inconvenient

For a particularly egregious modern case, see U.S. v. Knox, C.A.9th, 1973, 474 F.2d 1253 (prosecution can prove defendant guilty of refusal to submit to induction by introducing no more than defendant's Selective Service file). On the Founders' objections to proof by deposition, see vol. 30, § 6345, pp. 524–527.

254. "The Grange"

Encyclopedia of American History, Morris ed. 1976, p. 295. See also, Garraty, The New Commonwealth, 1877–1890, 1968, p. 52.

255. Response to power

Twiss, Lawyers and The Constitution: How Laissez Faire Came To The Supreme Court, 1942, p. 63.

256. Fiction and regulation

Id. at pp. 64, 68.

257. Grain elevators

Friedman, A History of American Law, 1973, p. 391.

258. Activist state

Foner, Reconstruction: America's Unfinished Revolution, 1863–1877, 1988, p. 474. On confrontation and monopoly, see vol. 30, § 6343, p. 287.

259. "Rank communism"

2 Warren, The Supreme Court in United States History, 1836–1918, 1947, p. 578.

tarred with the brush of Marxism,[260] It was also called "a wanton assault on property."[261] Justice Doe of the New Hampshire Supreme Court, Wigmore's hero, saw the Grange as a "Western conspiracy to rob Eastern people of their property invested in Western railroads."[262] He said that property rights were being "openly and directly attacked for the first time in this state since their safety was assured by the establishment of constitutional government at the close of the Revolutionary War."[263] Doe's notion that property rights were in greater danger than civil rights, such as the right of confrontation, did not augur well for the future of the rights of criminal defendants, coupled as it was with a claim that a conspiracy against property rights was afoot.

When elite lawyers and judges ganged up on the Grangers, fear for the rights of property was not their sole concern.[264] The Grangers had been able to defeat the reelection of judges who had held their legislative program unconstitutional[265] This not only strengthened the motives of elite judges and lawyers to join together in bar associations and to favor removing judges from the electoral process,[266] but it also increased their dependence on federal courts to save them from what they viewed as the excesses of democracy.

Defeat of such expectations does much to explain the overwrought reaction to The Granger Cases.[267] In those cases, lawyers for the railroads had argued that profits were property that could only be taken in accordance with the common law; otherwise, regulation that "took" profits constituted a denial of "due process of law" guaranteed by the Fourteenth Amendment.[268] The Court

---

260. Tarred with Marxism

See text at notecall 199, above.

261. "Wanton assault"

Twiss, Lawyers and The Constitution: How Laissez Faire Came To The Supreme Court, 1942, p. 70.

262. "Conspiracy to rob"

Reid, Chief Justice: The Judicial World of Charles Doe, 1967, p. 263.

263. "Revolutionary War"

Id. at p. 256.

264. Ganged up on Grangers

Twiss, Lawyers and The Constitution: How Laissez Faire Came to The Supreme Court, 1942, pp. 79–80. The rise of bar associations and their asso-

ciation with antidemocratic sentiments will be discussed below.

265. Defeat judges

Id. at p. 66.

266. Electoral politics

Friedman, A History of American Law, 1973, pp. 323–326.

267. Granger Cases

Id. at p. 392. See Munn v. Illinois, 1877, 4 Otto (94 U.S.) 113, 24 L.Ed. 77.

268. Profits and Due Process

Twiss, Lawyers and The Constitution: How Laissez Faire Came To The Supreme Court, 1942, p. 83; Magrath, Morrison R. Waite: The Triumph of Character, 1963, p. 181.

rejected this argument on the facts of the case, but in a dictum left open the possibility that on another state of facts the argument might prevail.[269] John Norton Pomeroy fumed that the Court's decision encouraged more "communistic legislation."[270] Whether or not it did, it was an early harbinger of the Court's coming view that the Fourteenth Amendment was designed to protect property rights rather than civil liberties.

The Granger Cases had another subtle effect on confrontation. The railroads had argued that legislators lacked the expertise to set rates, that this could only be done by experts—presumably the railroad executives.[271] However, fearing that rates were going to continue to be political footballs in a game that the Grangers had shown they could play, railroad lawyers sought refuge in supposedly apolitical tribunals.[272] Indeed, some historians have argued that it was the railroads rather than Grangers who were responsible for the formation of the Interstate Commerce Commission.[273] Be that as it may, the growth of administrative tribunals over the next century, with their freedom from the judicial rules of evidence, was to place increasing strain of the right of confrontation and, ultimately, to lead to it being read back into the Due Process Clause.

As the Grange responded to corporate power, southern elites began to respond to the rise of black power, part of a cycle of repression and resistance in which every effort of Republicans to empower the Freedmen was met with violence and intimidation.[274] Southern resistance was rooted in a racist ideology that had implications for confrontation. Despite ante-bellum claims that Southerners knew their slaves better than Northerners, (presumably because of their face to face meetings with them), whites who before the War had been amazed that the slaves did not often rise and murder their masters were, paradoxically, surprised after Emancipation by how little loyalty the Freedmen had to the indi-

---

269. Might prevail

94 U.S. at 135.

270. "Communistic"

2 Warren, The Supreme Court in United States History, 1836–1918, 1947, p. 583.

271. Done by experts

Twiss, Lawyers and The Constitution: How Laissez Faire Came To The Supreme Court, 1942, p. 69.

272. Apolitical tribunals

Kolko, Railroads and Regulation, 1877–1916, 1965, p. 16.

273. Railroads responsible

Id. at p. 21.

274. Met with violence

Williams, The Great South Carolina Ku Klux Klan Trials, 1871–1872, 1996, p. 1.

viduals and institutions that held them in bondage.[275] Hence, when blacks were finally able to testify, white southerners resorted to crude, racist concepts of competence rather than to the sophisticated inquiry into individual credibility posited by confrontation, refusing to credit testimony accusing southern "gentlemen" who had "put their white sheets on again" of raping the wives of black political activists.[276]

Since racism was linked to an antidemocratic constitutionalism that impacted the right of confrontation,[277] we must consider how both played out in the North. Pervasive racism in American society requires no documentation; evidence of its power in the North can be found in Stephen Douglas' resort to it in his famous debates with Abraham Lincoln.[278] What does require emphasis is that racism was no disease of the Great Unwashed from which educated elites were immune.[279] President Eliott of Harvard, who encouraged the Langdellian reform of legal education, was a believer in "racial purity."[280] Black students were excluded from white dormitories at Harvard, and black graduates were not welcome at meetings of the Harvard alumni clubs.[281] A black Harvard graduate who was an Assistant U.S. Attorney was expelled from the American Bar Association when his race was discovered and steps were taken to insure that no persons of color were admitted to membership in the future.[282]

Racism was not limited to nonwhites. Under the tenets of "scientific racism," there was an "Irish race" and a "Jewish race,"

275. Little loyalty

Id. at p. 3; Woodward, Not So Freed Men, N.Y.Rev.Bks., Aug. 16, 1979, p. 8.

276. Refusing to credit

Williams, The Great South Carolina Ku Klux Klan trials, 1871–1872, 1996, p. 89.

277. Anti-democratic

As the former governor of South Carolina put it, "[i]t is a maxim founded in truth that virtue and intelligence alone can sustain a republican form of government." As similar quotations collected in id. at p. 9 make clear, only the "educated and propertied classes" could meet this test.

278. Douglas debates

The Lincoln–Douglas Debates, Holzer ed. 1993, pp. 142–143.

279. Elites immune

Todd, Justice on Trial: The Case of Louis D. Brandeis, 1964, p. 217.

280. "Racial purity"

Hixson, Moorfield Story and The Abolitionist Tradition, 1972, p. 115.

281. Harvard alumni

Id. at p. 119.

282. Expelled from A.B.A.

Id. at pp. 117–118. Though the ban was rescinded at the national level, it continued in local organs until well into the 1960s.

each with stereotypical and supposedly genetically determined mental and physical characteristics.[283] Scientific racism, then, was more than a sociological rationalization for Jim Crow; it was a cover as well for religious and ethnic bigotry.[284] Under this ideology, the "Master Race" was the "Anglo–Saxon."[285] For example, one lawyer, in the controversy over his appointment to the Supreme Court, said this of Louis Brandeis:

> He has no power of feeling or understanding the position of an opponent, and none of the spirit of playing the game with courtesy and good-nature which is part of the standard of the Anglo–Saxon. He fights to win, and fights up to the limits of his rights with a stern and even cruel exultation in the defeat of his adversary.[286]

Another wrote:

> In the main his ideas of right and wrong are those of the rest of us but he is a Hebrew and, therefore, of Oriental race and his mind is an Oriental mind, and I think it very probable that some of his ideas of what were fair might not be the same as those of a man possessing an Anglo–Saxon mind.[287]

These were defenders of Brandeis. One shudders to think what his opponents, who denied any racial animus, were thinking.[288] If only Anglo–Saxons could properly execute the adversary system and if adversary excess was a genetic predisposition, the implications for adversary rights such as confrontation are profound. This is particularly true when the "races" predisposed to excess were also those with a genetic affinity for communism.[289]

Though the post-War era saw the rise of national law and a decline in the use of English common-law precedents,[290] it also saw

283. "Scientific racism"

Id. at p. 108. Of course, in this hierarchy of races, people of color were at the bottom. Id. at p._12.

284. "Ethnic bigotry"

Kenny, Making Sense of The Molly Maguires, 1998, pp. 74, 79.

285. "Anglo–Saxon"

No surprise to those who recall the WASPS—"white, Anglo–Saxon Protestants."

286. "Cruel exultation"

Todd, Justice on Trial: The Case of Louis D. Brandeis, 1964, p. 87.

287. "Anglo–Saxon mind"

Id. at p. 130.

288. Denied animus

Ibid.

289. Affinity for communism

It is easy to see cross-examination as being "abused" and hence subject to limitation when the person doing it is both a member of a despised ethnic group and in the defense of one who is predisposed to overthrow Anglo–Saxon institutions.

290. Use of English

Twining, Karl Llewellyn and The Realist Movement, 1973, p. 6; Kales, A Further Word on The Next Step in The Evolution of The Casebook, 1909, 4 Ill.L.Rev. 11, 13–14.

a rise in Anglophilia—in many ways the flip side of racism.[291]
Supreme Court Justice Brown, who liked to brag about his Anglo–
Saxon ancestors, filled his letters with racial and ethnic slurs.[292]
Other judges who flaunted their Anglo–Saxon heritage went on to
prove it by spending their annual "holidays" in the British Isles[293]
—nobody's idea of a gastronomic or climactic paradise. Anglophilia
shaped law school classes,[294] producing the uncritical worship of
things English that still characterizes some academic work. Part of
the appeal of England was that it provided a model for an antidemocratic judiciary to counter the power of the Grangers and other
alien political forces.[295] Chief Justice Taft held up the English
barrister as a model of adversary behavior and sought out English
practice as a blueprint for American procedural reform.[296] Many
lawyers and academics used the English as a model for judicial
reform, including evidentiary reform.[297] However, with rare exceptions, what American Anglophiles worshipped was not the real
England of brutal industrialism, class conflict, and social disintegra-
tion portrayed by Dickens, but some romanticized Arthurian
past.[298] Anglophilia served in many instances as an excuse for a
truly "unAmerican" elitism.[299]

291. Flip side

This is not a peculiarly English problem;
elevating any group, whether it be
Poles or Polynesians, is most easily
done by invidious comparison with
some supposed inferior groups.

292. Ethnic slurs

Glennon, Justice Henry Billings Brown:
Values in Tension, 1973, 44 Colo.
L.Rev. 553, 600.

293. Spending "holidays"

Mitgang, The Man Who Rode The Tiger:
The Life and Times of Judge Samuel
Seabury, 1963, pp. 7, 17.

294. Shaped classes

Sayre, The Life of Roscoe Pound, 1948,
p. 183; Wigdor, Roscoe Pound, 1974,
p. 36.

295. Anti-democratic model

Strong, Landmarks of A Lawyer's Lifetime, 1914, p. 149.

296. English blueprint

Mason, William Howard Taft: Chief Justice, 1965, pp. 63, 119.

297. Model for reform

Vanderbilt, Changing Law: A Biography
of Arthur T. Vanderbilt, 1977, p. 91;
Thayer, Observations On The Law of
Evidence, 1915, 13 Mich.L.Rev. 355,
363. By this time, the right of confrontation had largely disappeared from
English evidentiary lore.

298. Romanticized past

Foner, Reconstruction: America's Unfinished Revolution, 1863–1877, 1988, p.
492.

299. Excuse for elitism

At a dinner hailing the "rapprochement
of the Anglo–Saxon nations," this
poem was read:

"Our Anglo–Saxon name and fame,
Our Anglo–Saxon speech,
Received their mission straight from

Renewing monarchical paternalism and anticipating Marxist vanguardism, a future president of the American Bar Association proclaimed at his graduation from Harvard: "The educated men should form the crown of the state, its leaders, whose object should be to raise the weaker and more ignorant members of the community to a higher plane."[300] This was fitting; bar associations carried the shotgun at the wedding of elitism and exclusion.[301] The way to raise the quality of the bar was to exclude "those people" from it.[302] When this was criticized as contrary to the American ethos of upward mobility, Roscoe Pound enunciated the elite lawyer's contempt for democracy: "The wail of the unfit is very apt to be made in the name of Demos."[303] Pound was later to equate the recall of judges to lynching.[304] One of the political uses of elitism was to convince the privileged that economic inequality was inevitable; the Chicago Tribune editorialized:

> The great law which nature seems to have prescribed for the government of the world, and the only law of human society which we are able to extract from history, is that the more intelligent and thoughtful of the race shall inherit the earth and have the best time, and that all others shall find life on the whole dull and unprofitable.[305]

Like the Marxists they detested, elite lawyers sought to disguise their prejudices as "science."[306]

This produced what was soon to be called "The Cult of the Expert."[307] One of the functions of expertise was to depoliticize

Heaven
To civilize and teach."
Furnas, The Americans: A Social History of The United States, 1587–1914, 1969, p. 610.

300. "Higher plane"
Hixson, Moorfield Story and The Abolitionist Tradition, 1972, p. 5.

301. Elitism and exclusion
Wigdor, Roscoe Pound, 1974, p. 82.

302. Exclude "people"
Id. at pp. 198–199.

303. "Wail of unfit"
Id. at pp. 198–199.

304. Lynching
Id. at p. 222.

305. "Dull and unprofitable"
Kirkland, Dream and Thought in The Business Community, 1860–1900, 1964, pp. 20–21.

306. "Science"
Note, The Democratic Faith of Felix Frankfurter, 1973, 25 Stan.L.Rev. 430, 433.

307. "Cult of Expert"
One symptom of this was the growth in the demand for books and magazines with expert opinions; e.g., books on how to diet or die by people who have never done either. Hofstadter, The Age of Reform: From Bryan to F.D.R. 1956, p. 155.

politics for the benefit of those who wanted to exercise power
without democratic accountability.[308] Thus, judges, lawyers, and
legal academics sought to portray themselves as beyond the criticism of those who lacked their supposed expertise.[309] A good illustration of this is Arthur Vanderbilt who never ran for office, while
deriding those who did as "backslappers," yet sought to and did
make significant changes in the judiciary of his state.[310] The Progressives sought to enhance and exalt executive power while dis-
missing any suspicion of such power as an outmoded relic of the
fear of royal power.[311]

The most familiar product of this elitism is judicial rulemaking,[312] but it had other consequences relevant to confrontation. It
downplayed trials as political events; e.g., Karl Llewellyn's belief
that the problem with the trial of Sacco and Vanzetti was "a
technical one, and that only technicians are equipped to handle
it."[313] Expertise was antithetical to trial by jury and those who
embraced the expert were usually contemptuous of jurors—and by
implication, of the value of confrontation.[314] Thurman Arnold exemplified the anti-adversary attitudes of the legal elite when he wrote:
"A man of gentlemanly instincts and cultural background often
finds himself seriously handicapped in competition with persons of
inferior character and greater aggressiveness."[315] One is tempted to
paraphrase Pound—"the wail of the unfit is very apt to be made
in the name of good breeding."

308. Without accountability

Hixson, Moorfield Storey and The Abolitionist Tradition, 1972, p. 203. This
may account for the sportswriter's epistemology, so prevalent today, that
cannot distinguish between kibitzing
and playing the game. It is a common
failing of law professors.

309. Beyond criticism

Wigdor, Roscoe Pound, 1974, p. 222.

310. "Backslappers"

Vanderbilt, Changing Law: A Biography
of Arthur T. Vanderbilt, 1977, pp. 62–
63.

311. Outmoded relic

Hofstadter, The Age of Reform: From
Bryan to F.D.R., 1972, p. 263.

312. Rulemaking

Ayer, In Quest of Efficiency: The Ideo-
logical Journey of Thurman Arnold in
The Interwar Period, 1971, 23 Stan.
L.Rev. 1049, 1060–1061.

313. "Only technicians"

Twining, Karl Llewellyn and The Realist
Movement, 1973, p. 347.

314. Contemptuous

Wigdor, Roscoe Pound, 1974, p. 99.

315. "Gentlemanly instincts"

Ayer, In Quest of Efficiency: The Ideological Journey of Thurman Arnold in
the Interwar Period, 1971, 23 Stan.
L.Rev. 1049, 1063.

Fur purposes of confrontation, perhaps the most challenging product of the culture of elitism is Walter Lippman's antidemocratic epistemology.[316] Lippman seems to honor confrontation values when he argues that democracy assumes that people are politically concerned with those matters whose cause and effect are within the personal knowledge of the members of the community. Democracy, Lippman continues, falters when it must address matters that citizens can only know by hearsay, whose cause or effects take place beyond the community of knowledge with the power to decide; e.g., Boston and Bosnia. Today one might argue that the way to deal with this problem is to equip citizens with some method that would substitute for cross-examination of the hearsay declarants. For Lippman, on the other hand, public affairs in a modern, global economy "can be managed only by a specialized class whose personal interests reach beyond the locality."[317] In other words, someone like Lippman. The drafters of the confrontation clauses had a better idea.

Confrontation and the Ku Klux Klan

In 1869, the Black Friday Panic demonstrated that Wall Street was not the habitat of the "Anglo–Saxon gentleman" and the ratification of the Fifteenth Amendment by four Southern states opened the door to political power to those who were the bete noir of "Southern gentlemen."[318] In anticipation of increased violence against Freedmen who exercised the franchise, the Judiciary Act of 1869 created circuit judges with all the power of a Supreme Court justice on circuit.[319] Congress hoped that the circuit judges would add a national perspective to balance the parochialism of the local district judges.[320]

316. Walter Lippman

Cover, The Left, The Right, and The First Amendment: 1918–1928, 1981, 40 Md. L.Rev. 349, 368.

317. "Specialized class"

Ibid., quoting Lippman, Public Opinion, 1922, p. 195.

318. "Gentlemen"

Morris, Encyclopedia of American History, Morris ed. 1976, p. 298; Encyclopedia of American Facts and Dates, 9th ed. 1993, p. 302. The Black Friday Panic was triggered by an attempt to corner the market in gold by Jay Gould and James Fisk that rested on the false claim that President Grant would not release gold from the federal stockpile to break the corner. Gould and Fisk evaded responsibility for their shenanigans by bribing judges, including the father of Benjamin Cardozo, with the help of such leaders of the corporate bar as David Dudley Field, the demon codifier.

319. Judiciary Act

Willliams, The Great South Carolina Ku Klux Klan Trials, 1871–1872, 1996, pp. 49–50.

320. Parochialism

Id. at p. 50.

One of the most pressing problems for the federal judiciary in the South was the use of violence against newly freed slaves.[321] Such violence began as soon as the war ended, but initially was sporadic—the rage of whites against blacks who failed to show the appropriate deference to their former masters.[322] But if mindless, such violence was not trivial; in 1866, 24 men, women, and children were lynched in a single incident in Pine Bluff, Arkansas.[323] Soon, however, violence became a political tool to force blacks back into peonage, attacking institutions of black empowerment like schools and churches.[324] When Freedmen got the vote, violence was used to prevent them from voting—particularly in states such as South Carolina where blacks were 60% of the population.[325] While Republicans, both black and white, suffered at the hands of Southern thugs, blacks bore the brunt of the attacks and suffered the worst abuses; one study found that at least 10% of the black delegates to Reconstruction constitutional conventions were subsequently murdered by whites.[326] By 1871, the Republican party was in ruins in many Southern communities.[327]

Emblematic of this political violence was the Ku Klux Klan, founded in Tennessee in 1866, but rapidly spreading into nearly every Southern state.[328] The Klan was rooted in the antebellum "patrol" system, an extralegal force fed by fears of a slave insurrection, that attempted to use terror to make such rebellion unthinkable.[329] In most areas, the leaders of the Klan were planters and professionals who lost power during Reconstruction and sought the aid of the still deferential white underclass to keep blacks "in their

321. Use of violence

Foner, Reconstruction: America's Unfinished Revolution, 1863–1877, 1988, p. 119.

322. Show deference

Id. at p. 120.

323. Children lynched

Id. at p. 119.

324. Schools and churches

Id. at p. 428–429. See also, Williams, The Great South Carolina Ku Klux Klan Trials, 1871–1872, 1996, p. 3.

325. Prevent voting

Id. at p. 342. See also, Williams, The Great South Carolina Ku Klux Klan Trials, 1871–1872, p. 7.

326. Delegates murdered

Id. at p. 426.

327. Party in ruins

Id. at p. 442.

328. Klan spreading

Id. at p. 342.

329. "Patrol" system

Williams, The Great South Carolina Ku Klux Klan Trials, 1871–1872, 1996, p. 27.

place."[330] From 1868 to 1871, the Klan launched a counterrevolutionary reign of terror throughout the South.[331] Some of the worst abuses were in upcountry South Carolina, where 38 blacks were murdered by the Klan in less than a year.[332] Like most guerilla terrorists, the Klan had the support of white South Carolinians who, according to the newly appointed circuit judge, "preferred to live amongst this outrageous Klan than under the government of law."[333] Southerners might have justified their reliance on a system of extragovernmental force by pointing to the private police forces that were then being organized by railroads and other corporations in the North, but those forces had at least a veneer of legality conferred by statutory authority.[334]

State governments were powerless against the Klan, even where there was a will to repress; white jurors were unwilling to believe black witnesses or to convict other whites of crimes against blacks.[335] This may have undone the faith the Freedman had earlier shown in trial by jury and its trappings, such as the right of confrontation.[336] Moreover, Southern sympathy for those who met in secrecy, rode out in masks, and killed under cover of darkness undermined the virtue of openness that is one of the underpinnings of confrontation.[337] Moreover, by producing real Americans who were willing to conspire against established authority, the Ku Klux Klan complemented the Communists in feeding the paranoia of those who feared their property was endangered by forces that a democratic government was powerless to stop.[338]

330. "In their place"

Id. at pp. 16, 28; Foner, Reconstruction: America's Unfinished Revolution, 1863–1877, 1988, p. 30.

331. Reign of terror

Foner, Reconstruction: America's Unfinished Revolution, 1863–1877, 1988, p. 425.

332. Murdered by Klan

Williams, The Great Ku Klux Klan Trials, 1871–1872, 1996, pp. 16, 29.

333. "Outrageous Klan"

Id. at p. 31.

334. Private police

Friedman, A History of American Law, 1973, p. 507.

335. Unwilling to convict

Williams, The Great South Carolina Ku Klux Klan Trials, 1871–1872, 1996, p. 37.

336. Faith of Freedman

See above, text at notecall 139.

337. Openness

The codes of dueling suggest that Southerners may have felt that only "gentlemen" were entitled to such fair play. If so, then toleration of the Klan helped cement the notion that constitutional rights were not to be extended to "The Other."

338. Complemented Communists

As we shall see, it was not long before labor unions were being compared unfavorably to the Klan.

Be that as it may, the Radical Republicans were not going to stand by and watch Reconstruction and their party be undone by a mob of cowardly thugs. In 1870, Congress adopted the First Enforcement Act and created the Department of Justice.[339] This was followed by the Ku Klux Klan Act of 1871.[340] Meanwhile, the President authorized the use of troops to quell the Klan.[341] The military arrested and jailed suspected Klan members. In Texas, where martial law was declared, three Klansmen were executed following trials in military courts.[342] Acting under the Ku Klux Klan Act, the President suspended the writ of habeas corpus in nine upcountry counties in South Carolina, thus allowing the arrest and detention of suspected Klan members without the normal processes of law.[343] The military authorities used undercover spies and informers paid by the Department of Justice to ferret out Klansmen.[344] However effective these tactics were, they left the government open to charges that it was emulating the Klan in its efforts to eradicate it.[345] The government's plea of necessity was to prove to be one difficult to limit to government agencies.[346]

Legal measures against the Klan had more immediate impact on the right of confrontation.[347] In a series of trials of Klansmen in

339. Department of Justice

Williams, The Great South Carolina Ku Klux Klan Trials, 1871–1872, 1996, pp. 41, 43.

340. Klan Act

Id. at p. 42; Foner, Reconstruction: America's Unfinished Revolution, 1863–1877, 1988, p. 454.

341. Troops to quell

Id. at pp. 41, 49.

342. Three executed

Foner, Reconstruction: America's Unfinished Revolution, 1863–1877, 1988, p. 440.

343. Suspended habeas

Williams, The Great South Carolina Ku Klux Klan Trials, 1871–1872, 1996, p. 39.

344. Spies and informers

Id. at p. 45.

345. Emulating Klan

In the sense that both were using extralegal measures to obtain their goals. For an assessment that in other states the government's use of the military succeeded in quashing the Klan, see Foner, Reconstruction: America's Unfinished Revolution, 1863–1877, 1988, p. 440.

346. Difficult to limit

It also tends to vindicate those who argued that suspension of civil liberties in the North during the Civil War was to set a dangerous precedent.

347. Impact on confrontation

The trials offer some insight into the legal culture of the time. The defendants were not allowed to testify because their incompetence was not removed in federal courts until 1878. Williams, The Great South Carolina Ku Klux Klan Trials, 1871–1872, 1996, pp. 92–93. This may be why the defense was allowed to use a good deal

South Carolina, the prosecutors had three political goals.[348] First, they wanted to publicize the truth about Klan atrocities.[349] Second, they wanted to break the power of the Klan by showing the government's determination to punish their acts.[350] Third, they wanted to validate the claim that the Fourteenth Amendment had nationalized the Bill of Rights.[351] Only the latter of these requires explanation.[352] The provision of the Ku Klux Klan Act used in one count of the indictments punished those who conspired to deprive others of federal constitutional rights.[353] In addition to the right to vote under the Fifteenth Amendment, the prosecution wanted to treat the Klan's breaking into homes and seizing weapons with which the blacks had armed themselves as deprivations of rights under the Second and Fourth Amendments.[354] This argument rested on the assumption that the Fourteenth Amendment had made those amendments applicable to the states.[355] If this assumption was correct, then the Confrontation Clause of the Sixth Amendment would also be applicable in state prosecutions.[356]

of hearsay whose admissibility is not clear from accounts we have seen. Id. at p. 79. Anticipating what was to become a common feature of prosecutions of labor leaders and radicals over the rest of the century, the prosecution was allowed to use the Klan's organizational documents to prove the existence of a conspiracy. Id. at p. 77. Finally, when the judge ruled that counsel could not use the attorney-client privilege to shield what the client had told him about his plans to flee, the lawyer denounced the judge for trying to make him an "informer" against his client. Id. at p . 98.

348. Political goals

That is, in addition to seeing the defendants punished for the crimes. It appears that the new circuit judge, as Congress had expected, shared some of the prosecution's political goals, but the district judge, as Congress had feared, was more sympathetic to local views of the defendants. Id. at pp. 50, 52.

349. Publicize Klan

Id. at p. 87.

350. Showing determination

Id. at p. 122.

351. Nationalized

Id. at pp. 62–63.

352. Explanation

We simplify to make clear the impact on confrontation, passing over some complicating questions of constitutional and statutory jurisdiction.

353. Deprive of rights

Id. at p. 42.

354. Second and Fourth

Id. at p. 64.

355. Made applicable

Id. at p. 62.

356. Also applicable

Technically, the claim would be that a denial of the right in a state court would be remediable in federal courts, but as a practical matter the result would be as stated in the text.

The government was more successful in its penal than in its political goals; jurors typically took little time convicting the accused Klansmen.[357] By the standards of the time, the government's conviction rate was remarkable.[358] In the short term, this seemed to partially fulfill one of the political goals. In the view of one historian, this broke the back of the Klan and led to an immediate decline in violence against blacks in South Carolina.[359] However, in the long term the trials were a failure. The Grant administration lost interest in protecting the Freedmen, Congress refused to appropriate money to continue the prosecutions, and judges concerned about their dockets began to dismiss cases.[360] Most of those arrested by the military were never convicted.[361] Hence, when the "Redeemers" sought to regain control of South Carolina politics, they were able to use violence with impunity to coerce blacks and other Republicans not to vote.[362]

As subsequent romantic portrayals suggest, the trials did not do a very good job of discrediting the Klan, at least in the long run. Northerners probably did not need trial to confirm what the military had reported and Southerners were in a state of denial.[363] The local newspapers claimed that the government had only been able to obtain convictions because it had "packed" the jury and called "witnesses willing to swear to anything."[364] If Southern whites were not prepared to believe black witnesses against the Klan in state courts, they were unlikely to credit them in federal courts that were being roundly condemned in southern newspapers as worse than Star Chamber.[365]

At the outset, the government seemed to have a good shot at nationalizing the Bill of Rights; one federal court had already held that the Fourteenth Amendment had made the first ten amend-

357. Little time

Id. at p . 83.

358. Remarkable

Id. at p. 85.

359. Decline in violence

Id. at pp. 458–459.

360. Dismiss cases

Id. at pp. 111, 113, 124.

361. Never convicted

Id. at p. 122–123.

362. Redeemers

Id. at pp. 128–129.

363. Denial

Id. at p. 106.

364. "Swear to anything"

Ibid. The claim of jury packing may refer to the provision of the Ku Klux Klan Act that required jurors to take an oath that they had never participated in Klan activities. Id. at p. 42.

365. Star Chamber

Ibid.

ments applicable to the states.[366] However, after hearing a week of argument prior to trial, the circuit court ruled against the government.[367] However, the court certified the issue to the Supreme Court.[368] But, Grant's Attorney General, mired in his own corrupt acts, botched the first appeal, so the Supreme Court was able to duck the issue.[369] After the Supreme Court in the Slaughterhouse cases seemed to reject the prosecution argument, the Attorney General went into the tank on a later appeal[370] Thus, the South Carolina cases had long since lapsed when the Supreme Court finally issued a definitive ruling against nationalization of the Bill of Rights.[371] It was to be another century before the Radical Republican view of the Fourteenth Amendment was to prevail.[372]

Langdell and The Homogenization of Legal Culture

In 1870, Christopher Columbus Langdell took over the Harvard Law School—with significant consequences for confrontation.[373] Although Langdell was not the first to use it, he appropriated the casebook method.[374] We need not tell the tale of the triumph of this pedagogy over older methods of legal education.[375] Suffice it to say that Langdell was opposed not only by lawyers but by students.[376] But despite the fact that as a student at Harvard he had hated the casebook and used legal texts instead, when Roscoe Pound became Dean of the University of Nebraska Law School, he

366. Already held

U.S. v. Hall, Cir.Ct.Ala.1871, 26 Fed. Cas. 79.

367. Ruled against

Williams, The Great South Carolina Ku Klux Klan Trials, 1871–1872, 1996, pp. 73–76.

368. Certified issue

Id. at p. 74.

369. Able to duck

Id. at p. 101–102. The court dismissed the appeal for lack of jurisdiction. U.S. v. Avery, 1872, 13 Wall. (80 U.S.) 251, 20 L.Ed. 610.

370. Went into tank

Id. at pp. 132, 137. The government conceded defeat in the Supreme Court.

371. Definitive ruling

U.S. v. Cruikshank, 1876, 2 Otto (92 U.S.) 542, 23 L.Ed. 588.

372. Republican view

See above, text at notecall 135.

373. Langdell

Friedman, A History of American Law, 1973, p. 530.

374. Appropriated

Id. at p. 531 n. 19.

375. Tale

Those who need more can find it in Stevens, Law School, 1980.

376. Opposed

See, e.g., Strong, Landmarks of A Lawyer's Lifetime, 1914, p. 252.

imposed Langdell's system on the hapless Huskers.[377]

The Harvardization of American legal education is not a pretty story.[378] Langdell raised standards to gentrify the student body, then with so much "good stock" available, Harvard began inbreeding.[379] The triumph of Langdell's system owed as much to politics as it did to educational merit, and not a very gentlemanly politics at that; Theodore Dwight, who for years had been at the Columbia Law School, was forced out of that institution because of his opposition to Langdellianism.[380] So successful were the Harvardians at colonizing other law schools that by 1927, almost a quarter of A.A.L.S. law professors were Harvard graduates.[381] Whether or not homogenization of American law schools was good for the country, it certainly makes it easier for those who are trying to discern what lawyers may have been thinking about things that affected their views of confrontation.

Contrary to what its Ivy League rivals sometime supposed, elitism and conformity were not Harvard's most important products.[382] Langdell was a hopeless Anglophile and at the very time that American courts were declaring their independence of English precedents, Langdell made those precedents the centerpiece of legal education.[383] Fifty years later, at a time when other law schools were in a ferment of proposed innovation, Roscoe Pound and the

377. Pound imposed

Wigdor, Roscoe Pound, 1974, p. 36.

378. Not pretty

And a touchy one. Most American law schools regard themselves as, if not unique, at least peculiar. In fact, no Stalin could ever hope to impose the level of uniformity that exists across law schools with different histories and set in different sociolegal cultures.

379. Inbreeding

Friedman, A History of American Law, 1973, pp. 530–531. When Roscoe Pound joined the Harvard faculty in 1910, most of the faculty were from the New York–Boston corridor. Sayre, The Life of Roscoe Pound, 1948, p. 233.

380. Forced out

Strong, Landmarks of Lawyer's Life, 1914, p. 258. For more on Harvard's strong-arm tactics, see Stevens, Two

Cheers for 1870: The American Law School, in Law in American History, Fleming & Bailyn eds. 1971, pp. 405, 438 n. 56.

381. Almost a quarter

Of the 605 teachers listed by the Association of American Law Schools, 143 were Harvard graduates. Sayre, The Life of Roscoe Pound, 1948, p. 211.

382. Elitism and conformity

Twining, Karl Llewellyn and The Realist Movement, 1973, p. 67, 143.

383. Centerpiece

Friedman, A History of American Law, 1973, p. 532.

deans of two Harvard clones banded together to preserve the historic mission of law schools as they saw it: "to teach the technique of the common law and ability to handle common-law materials."[384] Though Harvard was historically weak in procedure generally, it dominated evidentiary scholarship for the better part of a century and was ideally situated to propagate a crabbed interpretation of the Confrontation Clause.[385]

Langdell claimed his method would make law more scientific, but his view of science was Euclidian, not Darwinian.[386] Hence, Harvard did much to foment formalism in legal thinking—with consequences to be discussed shortly.[387] Pound and others developed a more biological version of Langdellianism that allowed for evolutionary change in the law, but still made the scholar's job largely one of collecting and categorizing precedents.[388] No one should be fooled by this scientism into supposing that legal thought became depoliticized; in fact, Harvard's influence over legal education made it an attractive investment for those anxious to preserve the status quo.[389] For example, the House of Morgan paid one Harvard law professor an annual retainer of $10,000 to give lectures that favored railroad interests.[390]

Courts, too, tried to affect an apolitical stance. The period after the Civil War saw a rise in the elective judiciary.[391] After seeing what happened to Cooley, judges could not admit that they made law and so were subject to the same criticisms and sanctions as bad legislators.[392] Caught between predatory capitalists and rebellious masses, judges adopted "the formal style"——described by one historian as "bombastic and repetitious; case reports were filled with

---

384. "Common-law"

Wigdor, Roscoe Pound, 1974, p. 253.

385. Dominated

See vol. 21, § 5001, pp. 20–21. On the weakness of procedural scholarship at Harvard, see Twining, Karl Llewellyn and The Realist Movement, 1973, p. 67.

386. Euclidian

Friedman, A History of American Law, 1973, p. 535.

387. Formalism

Ibid.

388. Categorizing

Wigdor, Roscoe Pound, 1974, p. 207.

389. Investment

Id. at p. 249.

390. Favored railroad

Todd, Justice on Trial: The Case of Louis D. Brandeis, 1964, pp. 60–61.

391. Elective judiciary

Friedman, A History of American Law, 1973, p. 333.

392. Same sanctions

Twining, Karl Llewellyn and The Realist Movement, 1973, p. 32.

strings of useless citations; barren logic and bad English abounded."[393] As we have seen in the passage from Cooley, this style infected treatises as well.[394] As Roscoe Pound, one of the leaders in "the revolt against formalism" that marked the turn of the century, wrote:

> Jurisprudence is the last in the march of sciences away from the method of deduction from predetermined conceptions. The sociological movement in jurisprudence, the movement for pragmatism as a philosophy of law, the movement for adjustment of principles and doctrine to the human conditions they are to govern rather than to assumed first principles, the movement for putting the human factor in the central place and relegating logic to its true position as an instrument, has scarcely shown itself as yet in America.[395]

By the time it did, it was too late to help the right of confrontation.[396]

Some lawyers saw the decline of the judiciary after the Civil War as caused by the mass of precedents and legislation judges had to deal with.[397] Perhaps. But it was also a product of the isolation of judges from ordinary people. Judges lived in the world of the wealthy and were incapable of seeing that this might infect their judicial behavior.[398] Justice Field found it difficult to understand why anyone would be upset that he attended a dinner thrown by Leland Stanford for him while a case involving Stanford's railroad was awaiting decision before the Supreme Court.[399] Chief Justice Waite rode around the country in private cars on passes provided him by the railroads and once on circuit, while trying a case in which the defendant was charged with violence against Freedmen, he went to dinner with the defendant's lawyer——himself the perpe-

---

393. "Bad English"

Friedman, A History of American Law, 1973, pp. 334, 540.

394. Infected treatise

Id. at p. 543.

395. "Scarcely shown"

Twining, Karl Llewellyn and The Realist Movement, 1973, 1973, pp. 22–23.

396. Too late

The notion that "confrontation equals cross-examination" and "witnesses against means only those who testify at trial" are much more suited to the formal style than is the more sophisticated picture of that right that emerges from history.

397. Mass of precedents

Dos Passos, The American Lawyer, 1907, pp. 13–14, 31.

398. Infect behavior

Magrath, Morrison R. Waite: The Triumph of Character, 1963, p. 206.

399. Stanford's party

Id. at p. 221.

trator of similar atrocities.[400] In the face of such behavior, their idea that wearing robes would restore confidence in the judiciary shows how out of touch some judges had become.[401]

The founding of the Association of the Bar of The City of New York in 1870 highlights another development that undercut confrontation values; the bureaucratization of the bar.[402] Increasingly over the last half of the century, those lawyers with most influence upon and most likely to become judges were dealing with paper not people.[403] Roscoe Pound is a good example of those who Learned Hand described as "hardly lawyers at all."[404] He preferred to stay in the office drafting pleadings and appellate briefs, while practicing "petty trickery" on younger lawyers to get them to argue his cases for him.[405] Older lawyers admired those who could practice law without books and sneered at the new breed as "precedent lawyers."[406] As the criminal law became identified with the dangerous "Other" they never saw, elite lawyers and judges could hardly empathize with the confrontation values that empowered "the criminal classes" and lawyers who could not get into Harvard.

The year before the Great Chicago Fire, the Illinois Supreme Court torched that state's confrontation clause.[407] In a murder trial, the state was allowed to prove the testimony of a deceased witness given at a preliminary hearing before a justice of the peace through the recollection of witnesses who had heard him testify rather than by some record of the testimony. The court held that the inability

---

400. Ku Klux dinner

Id. at pp. 160, 206.

401. Wearing robes

"[J]udges should be clothed in robes, not only that those who witness the administration of justice should be properly advised that the function performed is different from, and higher than, that which a man discharges as a citizen in the ordinary walks of life; but also, in order to impress the judge himself with the constant consciousness that he is a high-priest in the temple of justice and is surrounded with obligations of a sacred character that he cannot escape and that require his utmost care, attention and self-suppression." Mason, William Howard Taft: Chief Justice, 1965, p. 58.

402. Bureaucratization

Friedman, A History of American Law, 1973, p. 561.

403. Paper not people

Id. at pp. 549, 555.

404. "Hardly lawyers"

Harbaugh, Lawyer's Lawyer: The Life of John W. Davis, 1973, p. 251.

405. "Petty trickery"

Sayre, The Life of Roscoe Pound, 1948, pp. 138–139.

406. "Precedent lawyers"

Strong, Landmarks of A Lawyer's Lifetime, 1914, pp. 422–423.

407. Torched

Barnett v. People, 1870, 54 Ill. 325.

of the witnesses to recall the precise words gave rise to no "constitutional objection * * * as the witness was confronted with the accused, and he was afforded an opportunity of cross-examination in the examining court."[408] The only authority cited was a federal case in which no objection was made to the testimony.[409]

The following year, the Iowa Supreme Court took the contrary position on similar facts.[410] In a prosecution for assault with intent to commit murder, the state offered what purported to be "the substance of the testimony" of a witness at the preliminary hearing as taken down by the justice of the peace.[411] The court held this was error; after quoting the state confrontation clause and emphasizing that it was a "right" of the defendant, the court continued:

> This right to have them brought into court, where he can see them, while they give evidence against him is secured by this constitutional provision. Their testimony can only be given only upon the trial of the cause, and face to face with the accused; * * *[412]

Since in the court's view legislation could not authorize the use of depositions, a fortiori the state could not use evidence that did "not rise even to the dignity of a deposition."[413]

Credit Mobilier, Outlaw Capitalism, and Confrontation

In 1872, the major railroads began kickbacks to the Rockefeller interests and Herbert Spencer, whose writings would be used to defend "outlaw capitalism," was first published in the United States.[414] The following year the Credit Mobilier scandal broke, demonstrating for all who cared to see that American political and economic leaders had little to fear from the criminal sanction no matter how far beyond the law they went.[415] Hence, for the balance of the century, American elites could maintain an attitude of

408. "Afforded opportunity"
Id. at p. 330.

409. Federal case
U.S. v. Wood, 1866, 3 Wash. C.C.R. 440.

410. Contrary position
State v. Collins, 1871, 32 Iowa 36.

411. "Substance"
Id. at 39.

412. "Only upon trial"
Id. at 40.

413. "Rise to dignity"
Id. at 41.

414. Spencer and kickbacks
Encyclopedia of American Facts and Dates, 9th ed. 1993, pp. 308, 309.

415. Credit Mobilier
Encyclopedia of American History, Morris ed. 1976, p. 299.

indifference, or worse, toward constitutional limitations on the prosecution of criminal cases.[416]

Corporations had long been instruments of public policy, chartered by the state for particular purposes, but in the Jacksonian era the nature of incorporation changed, making it a fitter instrument for the peculiarly American version of state socialism.[417] The immediate antecedents of Credit Mobilier lie just before the Civil War, when the government began using the public domain to subsidize the building of railroads; for example, when the Illinois Central in 1850 was granted two-and-a-half million acres of land, most of that land served to enrich speculators rather than finance construction.[418] At about the same time, a few foresighted individuals discovered that it was possible to create wealth without producing anything—a prospect that troubled members of the Supreme Court who clung to traditional values.[419] Sometimes investors discovered that stock, like milk, could be watered to their detriment.[420] Nonetheless, the new kind of corporation touched off a speculative mania that was eventually to make Wall Street one of the best known avenues in America.[421]

The Civil War not only increased the federal interest in expansion of the existing system of railroads, it also provided rapacious capitalists with further opportunities to defraud.[422] Hence, while those who could not buy their way out of the draft were dying, some of the leading names in the history of American enterprise were honing their predatory skills by exploiting the needs of the

416. Indifferent

This parallels the decline in the risk of treason prosecution of unsuccessful politicians discussed in § 6355, text at note 356 and symbolized by the dismissal of such charges against leaders of the Confederacy.

417. Corporations changed

Furnas, The Americans: A Social History of The United States, 1587–1914, 1969, p. 651.

418. Enrich speculators

Josephson, The Robber Barons, 1962, pp. 23–24.

419. Troubled members

Furnas, The Americans: A Social History of the United States, 1587–1914, 1969, p. 650. Justice Miller, no radical, wrote that financiers "engage in no commerce, no trade, no manufacturing * * * [t]hey produce nothing." Wiebe, The Search For Order, 1877–1920, 1967, p. 98.

420. Stock watered

Id. at p. 651.

421. Mania

Id. at p. 652.

422. Opportunities to defraud

Josephson, The Robber Barons, 1962, p. 51.

troops.[423] The first indication that such predations were, so far as the criminal law was concerned, comparatively risk free came when Gould and Fisk were able to loot the Erie Railroad but only their underlings suffered any sanctions.[424]

In 1862 and 1864, Congress sought to speed the development of transcontinental railroads by giving the Union Pacific and Central Pacific 22 million acres of land and $75 million in government loans.[425] The owners of the two railroads had organized Credit Mobilier, a holding company, and members of Congress were either given, or allowed to purchase at discount prices, shares of stock in this company. The railroads immediately mortgaged the land they had been granted plus the other corporate assets to pay Credit Mobilier to construct the railroad tracks at prices three times above the prevailing cost for such construction, leaving the railroads broke and those who held shares in Credit Mobilier rich.[426] When the scandal broke in 1873, it was discovered that fifteen members of Congress, and perhaps more, had obtained stock to encourage them to vote for the subsidy or to cover up the corrupt methods used to secure it.[427] While the Congressmen, and the popular branch of the government they represented, were discredited, the railroad barons emerged unscathed.[428]

The Credit Mobilier promoters were not unique in their methods; other railroads received immense public subsidies and used

---

423. Honing skills

Josephson, The Robber Barons, 1962, pp. 50, 59, 61.

The irony did not go unremarked; in a debate on the Legal Tender Bill in 1862, Congressman Kellogg of Illinois said "Yes, sir, they will vote six hundred thousand of the flower of American youth for the Army to be sacrificed without a blush; but the great interests of capital, of currency, must not be touched. We have summoned the youth; they have come. I would summon the capital and if it does not come voluntarily * * * I would take every cent * * *." Id. p. 56 n. 3.

424. Loot Erie

Friedman, A History of American Law, 1973, p. 448.

425. Government loans

Brodie, Thaddeus Stevens: Scourge of the South, 1959, p. 183.

426. Railroads broke

Id. at p. 184.

427. Corrupt methods

Id. at pp. 183, 185. In addition, the sitting and future Vice Presidents were also implicated. Encyclopedia of American History, Morris ed. 1976, p. 299.

428. Unscathed

Ordinary people could well believe Vanderbilt's boast: "What do I care about the law? Ain't I got the power?" Josephson, The Robber Barons, 1962, p. 15.

separate construction firms to loot the corporate treasury.[429] Nor was the federal government the only source of funds; states, counties, and municipalities succumbed to the railroads' threats and blandishments.[430] Indeed, it has been estimated that governments paid 60% of the costs of construction of American railroads, some of which had to be rebuilt in less than fifteen years because of shoddy construction by Credit Mobilier clones.[431] Some might find a contemporary parallel for this mania for "privatization" in the states of the former Soviet Union, but a more apt comparison is the way governments had been induced to tax citizens for the benefit of owners of sports franchises.[432] At least the consequences were similar; America ended up with more railroads and more major-league baseball teams than it needed.[433]

Legislators were not the only government officials corrupted by the railroads nor was bribery a necessary means, as the case of Justice Field suggests.[434] Nor were taxpayers and shareholders

429. Other railroads

See id., pp. 77 n. 2, 78–79, 85; Lewis, The Big Four, 1966, p. 31.; Swisher, Stephen J. Field: Craftsman of The Law, 1969, p. 242.

430. Succumbed

Cities and counties were led to bid against each other by railroad promoters with promises of economic and political power thought to accumulate to those with access to the railroad; to this day in the Midwest one can find towns that were once the county seat but lost that designation to communities favored by railroad promoters. At one time, every county in California was in debt because of bonds issued to lure railroads. Id. at pp. 85, 249. The Missouri Pacific received more than $25 million in subsidies from the state of Missouri; after the promoters got through with the company, Jay Gould was able to buy it for $3.8 million. Id. at p. 202.

431. Shoddy construction

Id. at pp. 77, 225.

432. "Privatization" mania

Id. at pp. 77, 79 n. 3. For an explanation for the rise of predatory capitalism

that bears comparison with newspaper accounts of the "free market" in the former Soviet Union, see Wiebe, The Search for Order, 1877–1920, 1967, pp. 37–38.

433. More than needed

Id. at p. 292. No amount of documentation will satisfy those who think that what is played in those taxpayer-funded stadia that have not yet been abandoned is "major league baseball." Ironically, unhappy taxpayers in some cities have been dusting off constitutional provisions passed in the aftermath of the railroad mania that purport to bar municipalities from issuing bonds to aid private corporations.

434. Justice Field

Field was exceedingly close to Leland Stanford and other California railroad capitalists, but the exact nature of the relationship has escaped historians because after a tantalizing glimpse during a lawsuit following a falling out among them, Field's papers were expurgated to remove the body of all his letters to his railroad patrons. Swisher, Stephen J. Field: Craftsman of the Law, 1969, pp. 240, 243–244, 245 n. 8

their only victims; the railroads imported Chinese laborers to work for half the wages of American laborers, skimming off some of the difference in separate companies that brought in the laborers.[435] As we shall see, when railroads could not get what they wanted by fraud or bribery, they could resort to violence.[436]

Railroad men went to great lengths to cultivate a culture and a public image favorable to them with a not insignificant impact on public opinion.[437] Their activities ranged from denouncing those who could not be bribed as "Communists" to seeing that critical opinions were not uttered from the pulpit to offering prizes for the best anti-Socialist poetry.[438] In some cases, the railroads were able to suppress news of their misdeeds.[439] These efforts were aided by the strain of anarchism cum predation that runs through American culture; examples of the "romantic outlaw" abound, from Huck Finn to Dillinger to John Rambo.[440] Even critics of those who have come to be called "the Robber Barons" cannot but help exhibit a grudging respect for their effrontery and their success.[441]

(destruction of letters), 248 n. 15 (portions of letters read into evidence at trial). Whatever their hold over him, the railroad magnates felt comfortable ordering Field around until Field fired back an indignant response when they sent an underling to tell him what to do in a pending case. Id. at p. 265. Field's biographer could find no case in which Field had ever ruled against one of the California railroads. Id. at p. 263.

435. Chinese laborers

Josephson, The Robber Barons, 1962, p. 86; Lewis, The Big Four, 1966, p. 51. This is not the cause of the racial animosity that runs through California politics for the next century, but it does offer a partial explanation of how hatred was able to become a political platform.

436. Violence

Josephson, The Robber Barons, 1962, pp. 224; Lewis, The Big Four, 1966, pp. 282–286.

437. Public opinion

Josephson, The Robber Barons, 1962, pp. 322, 324–325.

438. Anti-Socialist poetry.

Lewis, The Big Four, 1966, pp. 146, 174, 252. Id. at p. 222.

439. Suppress news

Lewis, The Big Four, 1966, p. 286.

440. "Romantic outlaw"

The antigovernment strain might seem to support granting constitutional rights for criminal defendants. Perhaps, but one must weigh against this the fact that real crime is seldom as "romantic" as it appears in literature.

441. Grudging respect

The capitalists themselves seemed to share this admiration. When a railroad attorney who had aided their schemes was caught stealing $50,000 from them, the magnates had the charges dismissed because the lawyer was thought to be too valuable to be lost. Lewis, The Big Four, 1966, p . 80.

Given the dominant role of railroads in American political and economic life it is quite probable that their activities had a significant impact on the confrontation right even if these are difficult to trace.[442] The lawlessness of the railroads made it difficult to condemn the extralegal violence of vigilantes, Ku Klux Klan members, strikers, or impoverished farmers.[443] It was easy to justify resistance to legitimate government power when many Americans came to believe that "ruthless men had usurped the government and were now wielding it for their private benefit."[444] And as the cycle of violence appeared to increase, the apparent inability of government to suppress lawlessness by constitutional means had ominous implications for constitutional rights that might further hinder the urge to punish.

Natural law and Slaughterhouse Jive

Roscoe Pound once wrote: "While lawyers affect to despise philosophy in law, much of their legal thought is dominated by an obsolete philosophy."[445] He was speaking of natural law, which enjoyed something of a revival during the latter half of the Nineteenth Century.[446] Natural law holds that human beings have inherent notions of justice, that by virtue of our humanity we share common notions of equality, desert, status, and liberty.[447] To the true believer, natural law is a "higher law" that transcends mere human law; the best known example is the Declaration of Independence with its "self-evident" truths that justified rejection of monarchical law.[448] Natural law is antithetical to Austinian jurisprudence—the notion that law is the command of the sovereign that requires no moral content to command obedience.[449] The main

442. Impact

We shall have more to say about this when we examine the effect the railroads had on federal courts, both in the shaping of constitutional doctrine and in making them instruments for the suppression of political forces opposing the railroads.

443. Difficult to condemn

Particularly when the lawlessness was directed against the government itself. Josephson, The Robber Barons, 1962, p. 224. And when it was coupled with contempt for the law and lawyers. Id. at p. 299.

444. "Usurped government"

Wiebe, The Search for Order, 1877–1920, 1967, p. 6.

445. "Obsolete philosophy"

Wigdor, Roscoe Pound, 1974, p. 166.

446. Natural law

Id. at p. 167.

447. Status and liberty

Twining, Karl Llewellyn and The Realist Movement, 1973, p. 185.

448. Declaration of Independence

Wills, Inventing America, 1978, p. 60.

449. Austinian jurisprudence

Twining, Karl Llewellyn and The Realist Movement, 1973, p. 29.

rivals to natural law were positivism, utilitarianism, and Darwinism.[450]

An early proponent of natural law was Professor C.J. Tiedeman, who showed how it could be manipulated as a tool of judicial conservatism and as an antidote to the positivism of Austin and Bentham, which was far more favorable to legislation as the law-making instrument.[451] Tiedeman argued that natural rights were incorporated in the Bill of Rights, which required him to fast step around most of the antebellum judicial precedents.[452] John Dillon, a federal judge and legal scholar, explained that the purpose of the Bill of Rights was to restrain the unjust exercise of legislative power, the justness of legislation to be determined by judges on the basis of their inherent understanding of natural law.[453] Stephen Field, one of the major exponents of natural law thinking on the Supreme Court, indicated his intuitions of justice when he proclaimed that property rights were as worthy of protection as human rights.[454]

But by its own tenets, natural law was not the exclusive province of judges or law professors; anyone could express his or her own version of this higher law. Thus, Andrew Carnegie blended natural law with Darwinism to argue that legislation to redistribute wealth or provide equality was futile: "Our governors, all over the world, are at Sisyphus's work——ever rolling the stone uphill to see it roll back to its proper bed at the bottom."[455] The Haymarket anarchists agreed: "A statute is always used to oppose some natural law or sustain some other equally viscious statute."[456] Albert Parsons, who was to be executed for these views, wrote:

450. Darwinism

Hixson, Moorfield Storey and The Abolitionist Tradition, 1972, p. 34.

451. Antidote to Austin

Paul, Conservative Crisis and The Rule of Law: Attitudes of Bar and Bench, 1887–1895, 1960, p. 24.

452. Antebellum precedents

These, as we have seen, traced the Bill of Rights to the English common law. Id. at p. 25.

453. Determined by judges

Id. at p. 26.

454. Property and human rights

Id. at p. 64. The view is a durable one. See Lynch v. Household Finance Corp., 1972, 92 S.Ct. 1113, 405 U.S. 538, 552, 31 L.Ed.2d 424.

455. "Bed at the bottom"

Kirkland, Dream and Thought in the Business Community, 1860–1900, 1964, p. 122.

456. "Viscious statute"

David, The History of The Haymarket Affair, 1963, p. 107.

Anarchists would * * * abolish statute law and all law manufacturers and thus permit the laws of nature to have full sway. That would be in accordance with natural law which is only another phrase for natural necessity. This would remove the barriers which make and keep the producer poor.[457]

This does not seem to be quite what Tiedeman had in mind.

Natural law made an early appearance in Fourteenth Amendment jurisprudence in the Slaughter–House Cases, one of the first cases to raise the question of whether the Amendment had nationalized the Bill of Rights.[458] In these well-known 1873 cases, the argument was made by white butchers who were the victims of a monopoly created by a corrupt Louisiana legislature.[459] The opponents argued there was no support in the legislative history for this view, claiming that the sole purpose of the Amendment had been to assure equal citizenship for the newly freed slaves.[460] Justice Miller, for the majority of the court, accepted this argument, partly on the ground that the argument of the butchers was too revolutionary.[461] Justice Field, in dissent, argued that the Fourteenth Amendment "was intended to give practical effect to the declaration of 1776 of inalienable rights, rights which are the gift of the Creator, which the law does not confer, but only recognizes."[462] Since something like Field's view was later to prevail, it is a shame we do not know whether confrontation is one of the rights the Creator bestowed.

457. "Keep producer poor"

Id. at pp. 107–108.

458. Slaughterhouse cases

1873, 16 Wall. (83 U.S.) 36, 21 L.Ed. 394.

459. Victims of monopoly

Fairman, History of the Supreme Court of the United States: Reconstruction and Reunion, 1864–1888, Part II, 1971, pp. 1322, 1344. See also, Beth, The Development of The American Constitution, 1877–1917, 1971, p. 172 (how corporations turned case to their benefit); Fairman, Mr. Justice Miller and The Supreme Court, 1862–1890, 1939, p. 61 (same); Friedman, A History of American Law, 1973, p. 300 (case foreshadows use of Due Process Clause to strike down state regulation); Jacobs, Law Writers and The Courts, 1954, p. 39 (prior to case proponents of laissez faire had more success in state courts than in Supreme Court); Twiss, Lawyers and The Constitution: How Laissez Faire Came To The Supreme Court, 1942, pp. 42–48 (description of argument); Williams, the Great South Carolina Ku Klux Klan Trials, 1871–1872, 1996, pp. 132–134 (decision cut ground out from under prosecutions of Ku Klux Klan).

460. Newly freed slaves

Fairman, History of the Supreme Court of the United States: Reconstruction and Reunion, 1864–88, Part 2, 1987, p. 1347.

461. Too revolutionary

Id. at pp. 1351–1352.

462. "Only recognizes"

Id. at p. 1359.

Depression and Reaction

The Civil War had been a boom time in the board rooms as well as on the battlefield.[463] But the collapse of Jay Cooke's banking house triggered the Panic of 1873, bringing retribution for the era of speculation and overexpansion in business and finance.[464] The winter of 1873–1874 saw privation, starvation, and rebellion that was suppressed in some cities with extreme brutality.[465] The Panic brought on a five year period of economic contraction——the longest such period up to that time in American history.[466] More than 10,000 businesses failed.[467] Railroads controlling half of the nation's trackage went bankrupt.[468] Railroad promotions collapsed leaving states, counties, and cities that had issued bonds to support the railroads with unfinished tracks and heavy debt to English and Eastern bondholders.[469] Worse yet, the Panic ushered in a downturn that, with only occasional rebounds, was to last the rest of the century.[470] Some writers have found it paradoxical that an era of rapid industrialization——railroad trackage increased nearly tenfold during the period——could produce such overproduction and unem-

463. Boom time

Kenny, Making Sense of the Molly Maguires, 1998, p. 83.

464. Panic in 1873

Encyclopedia of American History, Morris ed. 1986, p. 300; Brecher, Strike!, 1972, pp. xiii-xvi (in 1873 alone 5,000 businesses worth more than $200 million failed); Swisher, Stephen J. Field: Craftsman of The Law, 1969, p. 197.

465. Extreme brutality

Josephson, The Robber Barons, 1962, p. 172.

466. Longest such period

Foner, Reconstruction: America's Unfinished Revolution, 1863–1877, 1988, pp. 512–513.

467. Businesses failed

Encyclopedia of American Facts and Dates, 9th ed. 1993, p. 310.

468. Railroads bankrupt

Swisher, Stephen Field: Craftsman of the Law, 1969, p. 370.

469. Heavy debt

Weibe, The Search for Order, 1877–1920, 1967, p. 7. For the role of federal courts as collection agents for the bondholders, see Fairman, History of the Supreme Court of the United States: Reconstruction and Reunion, 1864–1878, Part One, 1971, pp. 918–1116. Justice Miller remarked about these cases: "It is the most painful matter connected with my judicial life that I am compelled to take part in decisions whose result is invariably the same, namely to give more to those who have already, and to take away from those who have too little, the little that they have." Fairman, Mr. Justice Miller and The Supreme Court, 1862–1890, 1939, p. 231.

470. Rest of century

Kirkland, Dream and Thought in The Business Community, 1860–1900, 1964 p. 7 (two of the depressions rivaled 1929 as the worst in American history; fourteen of the twenty-five years between 1873 and 1897 were ones of recession or depression).

ployment.[471]Although agrarian discontent and urban unrest declined with the return of relative prosperity in 1877, the proximity of the Paris Commune made it difficult for the upper classes to relax.[472]

This is a convenient place to depart from chronology and sketch the socioeconomic forces operating when the Supreme Court first decided the meaning of the Confrontation Clause. By 1874, the outlines of the modern nation had emerged——big industry, big inequalities of wealth, and domination of the economy by a small group of men.[473] Despite increasing urbanization, this was still a nation of small-towns, big business, and a polyglot workforce.[474] Lacking any national center of authority and information comparable to modern media that could give citizens a sense of order, most Americans retained a small-town outlook that led them to direct their anger over change at the local agents of the national economy——the banker, the merchant, the lawyer.[475] "National policy" was a delusion because the power of national officials was still locally based.[476] Perhaps the only exception to this parochial vision was the Supreme Court, which saw an important part of its role as protecting private economic power from local control.[477] Hence, power tended to flow to large corporations that, along with the military, were the only institutions with national interests, national sources of information, and a national system of agents.[478] When the federal government's efforts at monetary policy failed, corporations tried to create something like a "command economy" through contracts and consolidations.[479]

471. Unemployment

Id. at p. 4; Weibe, The Search for Order, 1877–1920, 1967, pp. 22–23.

472. Difficult to relax

Magrath, Morrison R. Waite: The Triumph of Character, 1963, p. 191.

473. Outlines emerged

Id. at p. 109. Perhaps these are clearer to us than they were to those then living.

474. Polyglot workforce

Wiebe, The Search for Order, 1877–1920, 1967, p. 9.

475. Local agents

Id. at pp. 12, 17.

476. Locally based

Id. at pp. 32–33.

477. Protecting economic power

Jacobs, Law Writers and The Courts, 1954, p. 96.

478. National agents

Wiebe, The Search for Order, 1877–1920, 1967, p. 33.

479. Create "command"

Encyclopedia of American History, Morris ed. 1976, p. 300; Kenny, Making Sense of The Molly Maguires, 1998, p. 150 (first effort at nationwide price fixing was with coal in 1871).

Combination and consolidation in business came from causes other than "ruinous competition."[480] Changes in managerial philosophy contributed; before the Civil War it was thought that the optimum size of a railroad was 100 miles and a half-billion dollars, but inspired by Grant's massing of military power, capitalists were soon forming industrial armies of much larger scope.[481] Moreover, the traditional American hostility to monopoly—symbolized by the Boston Tea Party—was crumbling as more and more people sought to shield themselves from the rigors of the marketplace by occupational-licensing and other exclusionary state laws; lawyers were not the only group that feared competition.[482] Finally, combination was fostered by a contract ideology that pictured society as a set of interlocking agreements.[483]

Since the problem was overproduction and falling prices, corporations sought to control output and fix prices.[484] One way to do this was by agreement with other entities.[485] By 1880, the railroads all had pooling agreements with their rivals.[486] This was followed by similar arrangements with competing modes of transportation, principally canals and steamships.[487] The practice soon spread to other industries as well.[488] Capitalists saw no irony in labeling as "communists" those who opposed their conspiracies to escape the free market.[489] Price fixing often failed; since the agreements were not judicially enforceable, cheating was rampant. One Congression-

480. Causes

Garraty, The New Commonwealth, 1887–1890, 1968, p. 110 (describing rate wars and falling rate during depressions).

481. Industrial armies

Kirkland, Dream and Thought in the Business Community, 1860–1900, 1964, p. 5.

482. Feared competition

Friedman, A History of American Law, 1973, p. 397.

483. Contract ideology

Id. at p. 464.

484. Output and prices

Josephson, The Robber Barons, 1962, p. 115.

485. Other entities

Another way would have a been by government regulation, but the example of the railroads would hardly have inspired other industries to follow this path and consumers had little interest in setting minimum rates.

486. Pooling agreements

Id. at p. 189.

487. Steamships

Lewis, The Big Four, 1966, pp. 263–264.

488. Other industries

Josephson, The Robber Barons, 1962, pp. 281, 383.

489. "Communists"

Id. at p. 252.

al investigation found over 6,000 secret rebate agreements between railroads and shippers.[490]

Contract being found inadequate, capitalists turned to consolidation; corporations simply bought out their rivals, taking advantage of depression to acquire stock at fire-sale prices.[491] If the rivals did not wish to be bought out, capitalists used either federal courts or raw economic power to induce capitulation.[492] As fear of megacorporations threatened political interference, corporations turned to other forms of consolidation such as trusts or holding companies.[493]

The economic effect of these arrangements was strongest where they resulted in quasi-monopoly such as that enjoyed for a time by railroads in California.[494] From 1870 to 1910, the profits of every business and industry on the coast were at the mercy of the railroad barons, who were able to extort access to the books of some shippers and adjust rates according to the profitability of the enterprise.[495] Despite economies of scale, the Big Four railroads had the highest freight and passenger rates in the country.[496] As a result, it was cheaper for East Coast shippers to send goods by sea to Liverpool, then around the Horn to California ports.[497] In an effort to thwart this ploy, the Big Four got compliant federal courts to declare the practice illegal and confiscate the goods so shipped.[498] Even so, it was still cheaper for most shippers east of the Mississippi to ship goods around the Horn rather than directly by rail to California.[499] When they were unable to stop this practice, the Big

490. Secret rebate

Id. at p. 251.

491. Fire sale prices

Brooks, Walter Clark, Fighting Judge, 1944, p. 87 (Morgan interests and London bankers consolidate railroads in South Carolina).

492. Courts or power

Id. at p. 90 (South Carolina legislature petitions Congress to prohibit federal judges, who were receiving passes and private cars from them, from using receiverships to further railroad consolidation); Josephson, The Robber Barons, 1962, pp. 258–259 (Carnegie's brutal consolidation of steel).

493. Holding companies

Josephson, The Robber Barons, 1962, pp. 258–259, 443.

494. California

Id. at p. 226.

495. Adjust rates accordingly

Lewis, The Big Four, 1966, p. 264.

496. Highest in country

Josephson, The Robber Barons, 1962, p. 217.

497. Ship to Liverpool

Lewis, The Big Four, 1966, p. 288.

498. Confiscate goods

Ibid.

499. Cheaper around Horn

Id. at p. 289.

Four made drastic cuts in rates—except for fruits and other perishable products that could not be shipped by sea.[500] Elsewhere economic combination seldom worked this well or for this long.[501]

Capitalists did a much better job of converting economic to political power.[502] They were able to defeat or co-opt every attempt at regulation[503] In California every person elected to the office of governor was a railroad candidate.[504] When a commission was established to control rates, two-thirds of its members were railroad people.[505] The prescient Tocqueville had observed that "the manufacturing aristocracy which is growing up under our eyes is one of the harshest that ever existed in the world."[506] He may have envisioned John D. Rockefeller's ruthless conquest of the oil business.[507] When he was indicted in Pennsylvania for conspiring to restrain trade, Rockefeller escaped by lying on the stand in a fashion that did little to enhance the value of confrontation in the eyes of the public.[508]

The influence of big business during the latter half of the Nineteenth Century reached heights it would not again reach until our time.[509] This was not entirely the unintended consequence of their boldness and success. As the names "Johns Hopkins" and "Stanford" suggest, this period saw an unprecedented increase in capitalist investment in colleges and universities.[510] Unlike earlier

500. Could not be shipped

Id. at p. 290.

501. Seldom worked

Indeed, sometimes discombination worked better, as when the breakup of the Northern Securities combination under the antitrust law led to windfall profits. Josephson, The Robber Barons, 1962, p. 450.

502. Political power

Id. at p. 227.

503. Defeat regulation

Lewis, The Big Four, 1966, p. 291.

504. Railroad candidate

Josephson, The Robber Barons, 1962, p. 228.

505. Railroad people

Ibid.

506. "Harshest"

2 Tocqueville, Democracy in America, paper 1966, p. 171.

507. Conquest of oil

Josephson, The Robber Barons, 1962, p. 273.

508. Lying on stand

He testified he had never heard of "Southern Improvement Company" though he had been a director of "South Improvement Company"—a refiner's pool that was the obvious target of the question. Id. at p. 275.

509. Influence of business

Wiebe, The Search For Order, 1877–1920, p. 41.

510. Investment in colleges

Kirkland, Dream and Thought in the Business Community, 1860–1900, 1964, p. 83.

philanthropists, donors of the Gilded Age controlled how their money was spent; the founder of the Wharton School of Finance and Economy not only specified what courses would be offered but dictated that only procapitalist ideas should be taught.[511] Even at nominally public institutions, business-dominated boards such as the Regents of the University of California were able to make them submit to the "demands of practical men" that they turn out "successful business men" and keep "them at their career."[512] It was not surprising, then, when the leaders of the next generation believed that bigness was not only inevitable but more efficient—— at least if not too "predatory."[513]

The long-term consequence of the trend to combination was that by the turn of the century 100 men commanded the bulk of the economy.[514] The use of the corporate form meant that much power over productive property passed into the hands of managers who had little real accountability to its nominal owners and whose interests were often at odds with those of the productive workers that made the enterprise work.[515] Concentrated power in the hands of a few men who could use that power to control politics was suspect to many Americans of the time.[516] In discussing the "manufacturing aristocracy" that was just then emerging, Tocqueville wrote that "if ever a permanent inequality of conditions and aristocracy again penetrates into the world, it may be predicted that this is the gate by which they will enter."[517] Though the United States had never had the sort of equality that the Founders thought essential to a republic, in earlier days the wealthy had not devoted their riches to ostentation like their European counterparts.[518] However, after the Civil War, the rich embraced the "if you got it, flaunt it" attitude and yachts replaced clipper ships in

511. Only pro-capitalist
Id. at p. 97.

512. "Successful business men"
Id. at p. 99.

513. Not too "predatory"
Hofstadter, The Age of Reform: From Bryan to F.D.R., 1956, pp. 244–246.

514. Commanded bulk
Id. at p. 230.

515. Made enterprise work
Id. at p. 218.

516. Suspect
Id. at pp. 222, 227.

517. "Gate they will enter"
2 Tocqueville, Democracy in America, paper 1966, p. 171.

518. Like European
Furnas, The Americans: A Social History of The United States, 1587–1914, 1969, pp. 647–648.

American harbors.[519] The capitalist class had much to flaunt; when Vanderbilt died in 1877, he left a fortune of $90 million.[520] James Fisk epitomized what would later be called "conspicuous consumption," dressing his retainers in comic opera uniforms and casting alms to create an image of a modern-day "Robin Hood."[521] Though Fisk and his ilk may have given to the poor, they did not rob from the rich but from the admiring public.[522] As Howells wrote, "[i]n any average assembly of Americans, the great millionaire would take the eyes of all from the greatest statesman, the greatest poet, or the greatest soldier."[523]

Not everyone was bemused by the spectacle of great wealth.[524] A justice of the North Carolina Supreme Court wrote:

> Our people are being robbed by wholesale. They do not receive the just rewards of their labor. They are being pauperized and kept in want, while a few men by trick and combination are gathering to themselves the earnings of a continent.[525]

Rutherford Hayes, no Marxist, warned that "[f]ree government cannot long endure if property is largely in a few hands and large masses of people are unable to earn homes, education, and support in old age"——a quotation not often displayed at his party's conventions at the end of the next century.[526] Even Andrew Carnegie conceded that "[t]he problem of our age is the proper administra-

519. Yachts

Id. at p. 648.

520. Vanderbilt

Wiebe, The Search For Order, 1877–1920, 1967, p. 8. As the institution that bears his name attests, today it takes more than just money to buy a football team.

521. Fisk

Furnas, The Americans: A Social History of the United States, 1587–1914, 1969, pp. 649–650.

522. Admiring public

Hofstadter, The Age of Reform: From Bryan to F.D.R., 1956, p. 54 (describing looting of the public domain).

523. "Greatest soldier"

Quoted in Furnas, The Americans: A Social History of the United States, 1587–1914, 1969, p. 647.

524. Not bemused

When he was considering joining the Cravath firm, John W. Davis described them as "counsel for the predatory rich, railroads, Trust Co.s, combines and such." Harbaugh, Lawyer's Lawyer: The Life of John W. Davis, 1973, p. 122.

525. "Earnings of continent"

Brooks, Walter Clark, Fighting Judge, 1944, p. 99.

526. "Support in old age"

Wiebe, The Search For Order, 1877–1910, p. 45.

tion of wealth, so that the ties of brotherhood may still bind together the rich and poor in harmonious relationship.''[527] But while Carnegie was in a philanthropic mood, most of his peers harbored little more than anxieties; wealthy Americans, an English visitor wrote in 1877, are

> pervaded by an uneasy feeling that they were living over a mine of social and industrial discontent with which the power of the government, under American institutions, was wholly inadequate to deal; and that some day this mine would explode and blow society into the air.[528]

The right of confrontation was a part, though perhaps a minor one, of those "inadequate" American governmental institutions.

The anxieties of the rich owed less to Republican ideology than to the growth of other combinations in response to corporate power; the postwar period saw the rapid growth of what are now called "nongovernmental organizations" on a national scale.[529] The most feared of these were labor unions, which had already begun to organize strikes during the Jacksonian era.[530] For example, in 1858 a violent strike in the Pennsylvania coal mines was broken with the use of military force and the union leaders were sent to prison.[531] Then, as we have seen, during the Civil War draft riots and strikes had to be suppressed by the Union army.[532] These strikes stimulated all sorts of wild conspiracy theories among capitalists and their sympathizers.[533]

In 1874, bitter labor disputes broke out among the railroads and in the Western mines.[534] These were followed by the bloody "Long Strike" in the Pennsylvania coal fields in 1875.[535] Then in

527. "Bind rich and poor"
Kirkland, Dream and Thought in the Business Community, 1860–1900, 1964, p. 147.

528. "Explode into air"
Brecher, Strike!, 1972, p. xiv.

529. National scale
Garraty, The New Commonwealth, 1877–1890, 1968, pp. 107–108.

530. Jacksonian era
Kenny, Making Sense of The Molly Maguires, 1998, p. 67.

531. Sent to prison
Id. at p. 68.

532. Draft riots and strikes
Id. at p. 81.

533. Wild theories
Id. at pp. 94–95.

534. Western mines
Foner, Reconstruction: America's Unfinished Revolution, 1863–1877, 1988, p. 515.

535. "Long Strike"
Kenny, Making Sense of The Molly Maguires, 1998, p. 157.

1876, peaceful strikes broke out in the rice plantations of South Carolina—products of the rhetoric of emancipation and Free Labor rather than organized labor unions.[536] There were many other spontaneous strikes in 1873–1874, the worst years of the Panic, that served as preludes to the "Great Upheaval" of 1877.[537]

Economic issues dominated these strikes, which were often triggered by attempts of employers to shift the burden of economic downturn to workers rather than shareholders or financiers.[538] But wages are not the only features of working-class life that were abominable by modern standards. Working conditions were barbaric, particularly in the coal mines, where greed combined with primitive technology to produce frequent cave-ins.[539] In one five-year period in a single county in Pennsylvania 556 workers died in the mines and 1700 were injured.[540] Similarly, every year 16,000 to 17,000 railroad workers were killed or injured.[541] Boys as well as men were the victims of unsafe working conditions; it was common for children as young as eight to work ten-hour days in the coal industry.[542]

If these strikes were precedents for the industrial conflict that was known in some quarters as "The Second Civil War," this was true of management as well as labor.[543] Unions were crushed by a combination of naked force on the part of the military, the police, or paramilitary forces organized by employers, along with the repressive instruments of the criminal law.[544] This era also saw the

536. Rice strikes
Foner, Nothing But Freedom: Emancipation and Its Legacy, 1983, p. 74.

537. Served as preludes
Brecher, Strike!, 1972, p. 4.

538. Shift burden
Kenny, Making Sense of The Molly Maguires, 1998, p. 170.

539. Cave-ins
Id. at p. 126.

540. Workers died
Id. at p. 128 (from 1870–1875).

541. Railroad workers
Hofstader, The Age of Reform: From Bryan to F.D.R., 1956, p. 240.

542. Child labor
Kenny, Making Sense of The Molly Maguires, 1998, p. 60.

543. "Second Civil"
We will examine this conflict in greater detail as our chronology precedes because courts rapidly became embroiled in it in ways that did not further faith in adversary procedures such as confrontation.

544. Criminal law
Id. at pp. 67, 101.

beginning of the use of informants, labor spies, and provocateurs to attempt to control organizing in the work force.[545]

Repression and depression decimated the first large industrial unions; union membership is estimated to have declined from 300,000 to less than 50,000.[546] Unions may have declined but neither the grievances of the workers nor the fears of the well-off were ameliorated.[547] Fear of "The Other" made many Americans willing to accept antidemocratic and anticonfrontation techniques to secure their safety.[548] Such fears gained credence when some frustrated Irish workers took the sneaky violence that had become customary in their homeland against English occupiers and their allies and turned it against American employers and their agents.[549]

Repression crushed not only unions but also the "free labor" ideology of the Radical Republicans, a theory presupposing small-scale businesses with an apparent harmony of interests between masters and servants——a view that had been shared by some of the now-decimated unions.[550] Traditionalists tried to save the doctrine, as Justice Miller had, by distinguishing between productive and nonproductive capital with the latter blamed for putting owners and workers at odds.[551] While the ideological consequences emerged only gradually, by the end of the century reformers began to look like reactionaries or utopians who wished to return to small government, an economy of small producers, and the supposed virtues of small-town life.[552] The Republican party opted for modernity, abandoning the free-labor ideology in favor of a strategic alliance with the corporadoes.[553] They could even make a virtue out of the failings of capitalism by relying on economists who said "everybody

545. Provocateurs

The name Alan Pinkerson first surfaces here. Id. at pp. 3, 153, 154, 281.

546. Membership declined

Brecher, Strike!, 1972, p. 9.

547. Ameliorated

Even pro-corporate newspapers sometimes conceded that wages were "too low." Kenny, Making Sense of the Molly Maguires, 1998, p. 170.

548. Willing to accept

Friedman, A History of American Law, 1973, p. 297.

549. Employers and agents

Kenny, Making Sense of the Molly Maguires, 1998, p. 185.

550. Shared by unions

Id. at pp. 75, 120.

551. Non-productive capital

Id. at pp. 151–152.

552. Reformers reactionaries

Wiebe, The Search for Order, 1877–1920, 1967, p. 4.

553. Strategic alliance

Kenny, Making Sense of The Molly Maguires, 1998, pp. 151–152.

but an idiot knows that the lower classes must be kept poor or they will never be industrious."[554] That attitude greatly stressed institutions like the criminal courts and procedures like confrontation that presupposed some commonality of social perception.[555]

It was probably too early for these influences to have had much effect on the decision of the Pennsylvania Supreme Court in 1873 construing that state's confrontation clause in a murder case that arose in the heart of the coal fields that were about to erupt in labor-management violence.[556] In that case, defense counsel had taken notes of a now-deceased witness's testimony before the justice of the peace. At trial, the prosecution was allowed to introduce defense counsel's notes into evidence over the defense objection that this violated the right of confrontation. The Supreme Court affirmed on the basis of the Richards opinion and similar decisions in other states, without much attention to the language or history of the right.[557] However, in connection with a similar objection to the admission of the dying declarations of the wife of the victim, the court opined that the confrontation clause had no application because the hearsay declarant was not a "witness"—a rationale that would be equally applicable to the notes of the former testimony.[558]

Two years later the Alabama Supreme Court also faced the question of the admissibility of preliminary-hearing testimony of a now-deceased witness.[559] The defense argued on appeal:

> * * * it is the right of the accused to have the witness when the jury can see the manner of testifying to judge of the truth and

554. "Never industrious"

Foner, Nothing But Freedom: Emancipation and Its Legacy, 1983, p. 15.

555. Commonality

Nor were they consistent with the Biblical roots of confrontation, Christianity having originated and produced its founding documents as the religion of the dispossessed and the marginal folk of the Roman Empire.

556. Murder in coal fields

Brown v. Commonwealth, 1874, 73 Pa. 321. The case arose in Schuylkill County in Pottsville, the center of the Molly Maguire assassinations and the site of the trials of the assassins. See

Kenny, Making Sense of The Molly Maguires, 1998, pp. 53, 165 (map on following page). There is nothing to suggest that the murder was related to any labor dispute.

557. Affirmed on Richards

Id. at pp. 325–327. The Richards case from Massachusetts is discussed in § 6355, text at notecall 685. The Court never mentions its own decision in Howser just eight years before. See above, text at notecall 102.

558. Declarant not "witness"

Id. at p. 328.

559. Alabama Court

Horton v. State, 1875, 53 Ala. 488.

weight to which the evidence of the witness is entitled. It is a clear constitutional right of the defendant to be "confronted" at his trial, by all the witnesses against him * * *.[560]

The Alabama Court resolved this argument by ignoring it and deciding the case as if the common law and the Tudor statutes as enacted in Alabama were the last word.[561]

Procedure, Ritual, and Proof

In 1875, Congress gave the federal courts their full Article III powers.[562] This prompted a federal judge to write in his treatise on the removal jurisdiction that wartime and postwar amendments to the Judiciary Act "have tended uniformly in one direction, namely, an enlargement of [federal court] jurisdiction * * * [so that] the small tide of litigation that formerly flowed in federal channels has swollen to a mighty stream."[563] Supreme Court decisions also expanded jurisdiction; e.g., holdings that federally chartered corporations, principally railroads, were within federal-question jurisdiction.[564]

Jurisdictional imperialism had its limits. When Congress passed a statute in 1875 that would have given the Supreme Court writ-of-error jurisdiction over criminal appeals, the Justices of the Supreme Court successfully lobbied President Grant to veto the bill.[565] Hence, the "mighty stream" produced only a trickle of cases raising the meaning of the Confrontation Clause. Not that this was a propitious time for the issue to reach the Court. Though the Court was soon to rebound from the Dred Scott fiasco to reach what some historians have regarded as the pinnacle of its prestige, this prestige was based on the way in which the Court reflected the values and ideology of the upper classes.[566] In its first 81 years, the Court had found only four Acts of Congress to be unconstitutional;

560. "Clear right"

Id. at p. 490.

561. Last word

Id. at p. 495.

562. Full powers

Magrath, Morrison R. Waite: The Triumph of Character, 1963, p. 266.

563. "Mighty stream"

Fairman, History of the Supreme Court of the United States: Reconstruction and Reunion, 1864–1888, Part II, 1987, p. 374.

564. Chartered corporation

Magrath, Morrison R. Waite: The Triumph of Character, 1963, p. 266.

565. Lobbied to veto

Fairman, History of the Supreme Court of the United States: Reconstruction and Reunion, 1864–1888, Part II, 1987, pp. 4309–431.

566. Reflected ideology

Friedman, A History of American Law, 1973, p. 329.

in the years 1870–1873, it struck down six.[567] The Court's views of the direction the nation should take was apparently not that of the Radical Republicans.

The ambivalence of the upper classes to confrontation values was exemplified by the 1875 trial of the Beecher–Tilton scandal— what was called "the greatest national spectacle" of the decade.[568] When the jury inexplicably hung on the question of whether the Rev. Henry Ward Beecher, a prominent divine, had seduced the wife of Theodore Tilton, a reform editor, the opinion-makers of the day turned on the publisher who had broken the story. Her sin was exposing the hypocrisy of a minister who reviled from the pulpit what he was practicing in private. Ironically, at the very time that the confrontation value of openness was being repudiated back East, out on the frontier it was the heyday of the cowboy—who in a romanticized version would become an icon of confrontation in the 20th Century.[569]

But during an era when it was attending to the constituency that seemed to provide it legitimacy,[570] the Supreme Court was neglecting another tool of legitimacy—procedure. It has long been argued that in a democracy, procedure is a substitute for elections

567. Stuck down six

2 Warren, The Supreme Court in United States History, 1836–1918, 1947, p. 53.

568. "Greatest spectacle"

Foner, Reconstruction: America's Unfinished Revolution, 1863–1877, 1988, p. 520.

The Beecher–Tilton scandal was brought to light by Victoria Woodhull, a feminist, Communist, and advocate of "free love" who was pilloried for exposing the sins of Henry Ward Beecher, a feminist fellow-traveler and wildly popular preacher. Beecher was not the first (or the last) man to see feminism as an opportunity for sexual adventure, and his sexual appetites, if not open, were notorious; men joked that Beecher preached to 20 of his mistresses each Sunday. Woodhull sympathized with many of Beecher's views of the relationship of the sexes, especially his opinion that "marriage was the grave of love," but she criticized him for his unwillingness to express those views publicly. Woodhull told reporters that her "judges preach against 'free love' openly and practice it secretly." Bell, Victoria's Secrets, N.Y.Rev.Bks., May 14, 1998, pp. 29, 30. Even those who might otherwise have embraced the confrontation value of openness and publicity thought Woodhull carried them beyond the limits. Compare the late 20th Century debate over "outing," the practice of exposing the sexual orientation of people who prefer to conceal their sexual inclinations.

569. Icon of confrontation

Furnas, The Americans: A Social History of The United States, 1587–1914, 1969, 683.

570. Attending constituency

Hixson, Moorfield Storey and The Abolitionist Tradition, 1972, p. 28.

in conveying authority to judges.[571] Yet at the very time it was pushing its authority to the limits, the Supreme Court seemed to be almost as united against notions of procedural fairness as it was against democratic control of the economy.[572] Late in the century, a Court that was soon to rule that employers had a due-process right to work children in coal mines announced that the right to a grand-jury indictment and a unanimous verdict in a criminal case were "not fundamental in their nature, but * * * merely a method of procedure."[573] A few years later a prominent evidence teacher was to echo that view, pronouncing the rules of evidence "only procedure" that judges should have discretion to disregard.[574] It was an era in which personnel rather than procedure were to protect against abuses; what was needed was "good judges," not restrictions on judicial power.[575]

The traditional view was expressed by Justice Field, when he wrote that the test oaths imposed on ex-Confederates "subvert the presumptions of evidence, and alter the rules of evidence, which heretofore, under the universally recognized principles of the common law have been supposed to be fundamental and unchangeable."[576] The modern view, expressed by Field's colleague, Justice Miller, was that the common law of evidence was "a very artificial system, and probably more restrictive in the rules which admitted testimony than any civilized code of Laws."[577] Those who thought, like Miller, that the privilege against self-incrimination was "a mighty strange rule of law" were hardly likely to be sympathetic to the adjacent right of confrontation.[578]

571. Conveying authority

Id. at p. 187; Fiss, History of the Supreme Court of the United States: Troubled Beginnings of the Modern State, 1888–1910, 1993, p. 18.

572. Against procedural fairness

Fiss, History of The Supreme Court of the United States: Troubled Beginnings of the Modern State, 1888–1910, 1993, p. 296.

573. "Merely procedure"

Thayer, Observations on The Law of Evidence, 1915, 13 Mich.L.Rev. 355, 362.

574. "Only procedure"

Thayer, Observations on The Law of Evidence, 1915, 13 Mich.L.Rev. 355, 362.

575. "Good judges"

Hofstadter, The Age of Reform: From Bryan to F.D.R., 1956, p. 202.

576. "Unchangeable"

Swisher, Stephen J. Field: Craftsman of The Law, 1969, p. 149.

577. "Very artificial"

Fairman, Mr. Justice Miller and The Supreme Court, 1962–1890, 1939, p. 410.

578. "Mighty strange"

Id. at p. 419.

Lawyers and judges, at least in some parts of the country, were still taking their evidence rules from English treatises and the work of Greenleaf.[579] Judge Doe, to whom Wigmore was to dedicate his treatise, was already ignoring the common-law rules when it seemed convenient.[580] Moreover, at the very time that legislation was removing the principal common-law guardian of truth-telling—the disqualification of witnesses with a motive to lie—Doe and other judges of his ilk launched a campaign to restrict cross-examination, the supposed substitute for incompetency and, according to some, the essence of the right of confrontation.[581] Doe also complained that lawyers before him made too many objections, at least in comparison with what he supposed was the practice in English courts.[582] A scholar who wanted to abolish the privilege against self-incrimination bemoaned "the hardship suffered by the state through our extravagant protection of the accused."[583] However, those who thought the common-law rules of evidence were unsuited to the conditions of modern life wanted very much to see those rules applied to regulatory tribunals erected to restrain the excesses of capitalism.[584]

It was not until law-enforcement excesses in the Roaring Twenties that elite interest in procedural protections revived.[585] Thurman Arnold then began to question the

> unexamined assumption that courts are business institutions which engaged in some sort of production (presumably the production of justice measured in statistical terms by the production of convictions).[586]

579. English and Greenleaf

Poldervaart, Black–Robed Justice, 1948, p. 65.

580. Ignoring

Reid, Chief Justice: The Judicial World of Charles Doe, 1967, p. 87.

581. Restrict cross

Id. at p . 83.

582. Too many objections

Reid, Brandy in His Water: Correspondence Between Doe, Holmes, and Wigmore, 1962, 57 Nw.U.L.Rev. 522, 528.

583. "Suffered by state"

Thayer, Observations on The Law of Evidence, 1915, 13 Mich.L.Rev. 355, 359.

584. Applied to tribunals

Sayre, The Life of Roscoe Pound, 1948, p. 319.

585. Interest revived

Hixson, Moorfield Storey and The Abolitionist Tradition, 1972, p. 151.

586. "Measured by convictions"

Ayer, In Quest of Efficiency: The Ideological Journey of Thurman Arnold in the Interwar Period, 1971, 23 Stan. L.Rev. 1049, 1070.

Arnold analogized courts not to corporations but to the theatre:

> The operation of our judicial institutions may be likened to the presentation of a play. The judges are actors on the stage moving the audience with great lines, impressively delivered.[587]

He saw judicial theatrics, which could include confrontation, as "exercising a stabilizing influence on the manners and customs of the community."[588] Perhaps—though the Beecher–Tilton "spectacle" seems to have undermined confrontation values.[589]

Ironically, during the time that it was devaluing the confrontation ritual, the Supreme Court was taking the lead in ritualizing the role of judges and lawyers.[590] Justice Taft, with his fondness for robes and abhorrence of unbuttoned jackets exemplifies this trend.[591] Given how frequently the adoption of robes by judges is mentioned in memoirs and biographies, it may have had more than symbolic significance.[592] For those accustomed to supposing that robes and the ritual obeisance that accompanies their entrance upon the judicial stage are an American tradition, it is worth pointing out that lower-federal-court judges went unrobed in many parts of the country until Roscoe Pound's day and some state courts did not adopt robes until well into the 20th Century.[593] These new judicial rituals may not have the same meaning to all observers as they did for the judges who enforced them; e.g., the practice in federal courts in the South of opening sessions with the singing of "Dixie."[594]

Molly Maguires and Mother Jones

The year 1876 saw the founding of the National League, the Centennial of the Declaration of Independence, and a new burst of

587. "Impressively delivered"

Id. at p. 1071.

588. "Stabilizing influence"

Ibid.

589. Undermined

As did the Supreme Court justice who wanted to prove to lynch mobs that courts could deliver speedy justice by abolishing appeals in criminal cases. Fiss, History of the Supreme Court of the United States: Troubled Beginnings of the Modern State, 1888–1910, 1993, p. 296 n. 1.

590. Ritualizing role

Strong, Landmarks of a Lawyer's Life, 1914, p. 171.

591. Abhorrence of unbuttoned

Mason, William Howard Taft: Chief Justice, 1965, pp. 58, 267.

592. More than symbolic

Strong, Landmarks of a Lawyer's Life, 1914, pp. 39, 97, 122.

593. Did not adopt

Wigdor, Roscoe Pound, 1974, p. 72 (adoption by circuit judges); Vanderbilt, Changing Law: A Biography of Arthur T. Vanderbilt, 1977, p. 193 (rule requiring in New Jersey).

594. Singing "Dixie"

Id. at p. 197.

revolutionary fervor that few were celebrating.[595] As the rest of the nation was commemorating the Centennial in Philadelphia, to the west in the Pennsylvania coal fields a group of workers of Irish ancestry were on trial for their lives.[596] They were charged with having been members of an oath-bound secret society that assassinated corporate officials, sabotaged mining property, and intimidated other workers—the so-called "Molly Maguires."[597]

The Molly Maguires embodied all the anxieties of the comfortable classes. They were regularly compared to the Ku Klux Klan with whom they shared certain anticonfrontation characteristics, such as secrecy and cowardice, but, unlike the Klan, they had "foreign" roots that made their brand of terror "un-American" in an added sense.[598] Indeed, the Molly Maguires were regularly conflated with the Ancient Order of Hibernians—a pathetic attempt by those of Irish ancestry to mimic the Elks, Moose, and Masons.[599]

Though the crimes attributed to them are clear enough, whether or not the Molly Maguires existed as an organization remains murky.[600] Even if they were not created by the mineowners and their Pinkerton spies,[601] the Molly Maguires were certainly a conve-

---

595. Few celebrating

Furnas, The Americans: A Social History of the United States, 1587–1914, 1969, p. 656. Furnas sees baseball as deriving its popularity from the same values that led many Americans to admire the Robber Barons: "[f]ew other team sports so openly assume that any player in his right mind will consistently take all possible unfair advantage and break any rule when there is a chance for impunity." Id. at p. 658. This says more about Furnas' ignorance of other sports than it does about the supposed exceptionalism of baseball. Progressives were later to claim that baseball and similar pastimes were in fact the re-creation of the (to them) vices of the adversary system rather than of capitalism.

On the less-celebratory versions of Revolutionary romanticism, see Foner, Reconstruction: America's Unfinished Revolution, 1863–1877, 1988, p. 564

(e.g., a labor newspaper: "capital has now the same control over us that the aristocracy of England had at the time of the Revolution.").

596. On trial for lives

Kenny, Making Sense of The Molly Maguires, 1998, p. 243.

597. "Molly Maguires"

Id. at p. 3.

598. Compared to Klan

Id. at pp. 20–21, 167.

599. Hibernians

Id. at pp. 234–235.

600. Remains murky

Id. at p. 13.

601. Created by Pinkertons

The major Pinkerton operative was an Ulsterman named James McParlan

nient weapon with which to attack any organization that opposed the interests of the mineowners—particularly the nascent labor unions. And so they were used by newspapers, other capitalists, and some members of the judiciary.[602] One judge even condoned lynch law:

> [T]he Miners' Union is a criminal organization guilty of having frequently incited its members to murder, arson, and other crimes, and deserving of rigorous punishment, before it has even been notified that it has been accused.[603]

The union leadership, despite their frequent denunciations of violence and explicit repudiation of the Molly Maguires, were still referred to by the business press as "The Grand Council of conspirators" and an outside "class of agitators."[604] In anticipation of the "happy blacks" of Massive Resistance a century later, workers were said to be a contented lot when not intimidated by a "small, conspiratorial band of radicals."[605] The Molly Maguires were soon to join Communists in the demonology of those who wished to shift public anxieties about their own conspiracies on to combinations of workers and others.[606]

Enter Alan Pinkerton, who would make a career for himself catering to the anxieties of the upper classes. Pinkerton, who had been hired by General McClellan to do spying for the Union Army during the Civil War and was sacked along with McClellan, returned to and expanded a detective agency that specialized in labor spying.[607] Pinkerton romanticized anti-confrontation values, writing that "secrecy is the prime condition of success" because it "frequently becomes necessary for the detective, when brought in contact with criminals, to pretend to be a criminal."[608] In short, the Pinkertons were idolized for embracing the same values for which the Molly Maguires were condemned.[609]

who even before the investigation began had prepared a report that traced the supposed secret organization to Catholic organizations in Ireland. Id. at p. 14.

602. So used

Id. at pp. 119, 158, 172.

603. "Before accused"

Id. at p. 119.

604. "Class of agitators"

Id. at pp. 143, 183.

605. "Band of radicals"

Id. at p . 145.

606. Shift anxieties

See above, text at notecalls 198, 529.

607. Specialized in spying

Kenny, Making Sense of The Molly Maguires, 1998, p. 153.

608. "A criminal"

Id. at p. 154.

609. Same values

Id. at p. 161.

Pinkerton operatives were so successful with such tactics that during the Great Strike, some of the union officers in the coalfields were Pinkerton men.[610] Pinkertons, as they were called, became the chief source of evidence of supposed union violence.[611] However, when it came to the Molly Maguires, the Pinkertons produced much of the evidence for the existence of the organization but the state had to turn to the assassins themselves for evidence of the killings.[612] The state granted immunity to some killers in return for their testimony against other supposed Molly Maguires.[613] Some of the immunized killers later went to work for Pinkerton.[614]

Union men and Irish–Americans accused the Pinkertons of being agents provocateur for the employers.[615] One Irish–American newspaper referred to the Pinkertons as a group "whose main occupation runs about midway between pimp and blackmailer."[616] During the Molly Maguire trial it became apparent that Pinkertons had participated in the planning of some of the killings and had knowledge of other plans but in either case did nothing to warn the eventual victims.[617] Such tidbits, coupled with the secrecy which Pinkerton so highly valued, enabled workers to become as paranoid about Pinkertons as their employers were about workers—a result Pinkerton no doubt saw as part of the effectiveness of his organization.

Proponents of privatization would have loved the trials of the Molly Maguires; as one historian observed

> The Molly Maguire investigation and trials marked one of the most astounding surrenders of sovereignty in American history. A private corporation initiated the investigation through a private detective agency, a private police force arrested the supposed offenders, and the coal company attorneys prosecuted——the state provided only the courtroom and hangman.[618]

610. Officers were Pinkerton
Id. at p. 171.

611. Source of evidence
Id. at p. 173.

612. Turn to assassins
Id. at pp. 222, 231.

613. Granted immunity
Id. at p. 216.

614. Work for Pinkerton
Id. at p. 220.

615. Agents provocateur
Id. at p. 232.

616. "Pimp and blackmailer"
Id. at p. 266.

617. Nothing to warn
Id. at p. 200.

618. "Courtroom and hangman"
Id. at p. 213.

As this passage suggests, the judge was all but invisible. The company lawyer who prosecuted the case was allowed to try the case while dressed in a Union Army uniform.[619] No persons of Irish descent were allowed to serve on the juries.[620] Introduction of questionable hearsay was permitted; for example, the supposed declaration of a coconspirator suggesting that the then-Governor of Pennsylvania—a political opponent of the trial judge—had promised to pardon the assassins.[621]

Except for an early case where the prosecution case collapsed when the defense was able to show the inauthenticity of a key bit of evidence, the verdicts were predictable.[622] And quick; some juries took at little as 15 minutes to determine guilt.[623] This was not surprising given the hostile atmosphere generated by the business press.[624] As one defense attorney said: "[w]hen men are to be tried before courts and juries by public opinion instead of the law and evidence, then has the right of trial by jury fallen indeed."[625] Given the crabbed interpretation of the confrontation clause of the state constitution, the attorney can be pardoned for not seeing that trial by newspaper was a violation of the blank-pad rule that is part of the right of confrontation.[626]

The extraordinary procedure was justified by legal periodicals, such as the American Law Review, as part of a war by "civilized society" against The Other.[627] A different version of this message was conveyed by the way the executions were carried out; behind prison walls with an invited audience of the well-to-do while the ordinary members of the public were kept at bay by armed soldiers and policemen, public and private.[628] There is some evidence that the Molly Maguire prosecutions tended to delegitimate courts, not only among workers, but also among the respectable portions of the

619. In uniform
Id. at p. 214.

620. No Irish
Id. at p. 223.

621. Promised to pardon
Id. at p. 236.

622. Verdicts predictable
Id. at p. 166.

623. And quick
Id. at p. 224.

624. Hostile atmosphere
Id. at p. 213.

625. "Trial by jury fallen"
Id. at p. 220.

626. Blank-pad rule
See vol. 30A.

627. "Civilized society"
Kenny, Making Sense of the Molly Maguires, 1998, pp. 239, 258–259.

628. Public kept at bay
Id. at p. 244.

Irish–American community.[629] Be that as it may, a century later the Governor of Pennsylvania, calling the Molly Maguires "martyred men of labor" issued pardons, and a plaque was erected at the site of the executions noting the judgement of history "that the trials and executions were part of a repression directed against the fledgling mineworkers' union."[630] This was too late for the victims—and for the right of confrontation.

One small countertrend to these anti-confrontation developments was the move to make the Bible a source of law.[631] In response to a proposed constitutional amendment to make the First Amendment applicable to the states, Christians resisting secularization proposed an amendment that would recognize "the Bible [as] the formation of law and supreme rule for the conduct of nations."[632] Given the Biblical foundations of confrontation,[633] adoption of the proposed amendment might have offset developments in the criminal law that were devaluing the right.

During the latter half of the Nineteenth Century, the rate of violent crime in America seems to have been declining.[634] During the same period there was a decline in the use of capital and corporal punishment—steps that might have made confrontation seem less crucial since the consequences of erroneous verdicts were not as severe as in Tudor England.[635] But the decline in the crime rate was accompanied by increased demands for what today is called "law and order;" as a result, there was an increase in prosecutions for misdemeanors—mostly for sumptuary offenses such as drunkenness.[636]

One source of change in the criminal law enforcement was the increased tendency to view the criminal not as a wayward sinner but as The Other; paupers, blacks, and other capitalist misfits were

629. Respectable portions
Id. at p. 264.

630. "Part of a repression"
Id. at p. 284.

631. Bible source of law
As had earlier been suggested by the Puritans in Massachusetts. See vol. 30, § 6344, pp. 368–69.

632. "Supreme rule"
Kyvig, Explicit and Authentic Acts, 1996, p. 189.

633. Biblical foundations
See vol. 30, § 6342, pp. 236–247.

634. Crime declining
Friedman, A History of American Law, 1973, p. 513.

635. Capital punishment
Id. at p. 517.

636. Drunkenness
Id. at p. 514.

viewed as outgroups with no right to compassion.[637] The view that criminals were not capable of being saved but were, instead, inherently depraved and evil, led over the balance of the century, to the view that there was some genetic basis for this depravity—what came to be called "the criminal personality."[638] As we shall see shortly, this was partly a result of so-called "Social Darwinism."

Racism was a more powerful force than science in the development of the criminal as The Other.[639] Roscoe Pound, one of the leading reformers of the criminal law in the early 20th Century epitomizes this strand. Pound not only enjoyed telling racist jokes, but once pronounced "the nigger a great curse."[640] He denounced regulation of business by administrative tribunals as "Oriental despotism."[641] Not only did he oppose the appointment of Jews to the Harvard Law School Faculty, he was an early admirer of Hitler and thought France needed fascist leadership to quell its quibbling parliamentarians.[642]

Blacks and other racial and ethnic groups were frequently used as the excuse for measures whose true targets were the increasingly immigrant working class.[643] More privileged Americans feared that the republic was in danger from "swarms of sexually potent immigrants."[644] A good illustration is the frequent comparison of the Molly Maguires to the "Thugs of India."[645] The Thugs were supposed to be a religious organization in India whose adherents claimed to murder in the name of the goddess Kali.[646] In attempting to place the Irish-born defendants beyond the pale of respectable society, the prosecutor called on the jury to help him "exterminate this hellborn organization, and send it back to the Prince of

637. No compassion

Id. at p. 521.

638. Inherently depraved

Ibid. See also, Kenny, Making Sense of the Molly Maguires, 1998, p. 239.

639. Racism

Glennon, Justice Henry Billings Brown: Values in Tension, 1973, 44 Colo. L.Rev. 553, 599.

640. "Great curse"

Sayre, The Life of Roscoe Pound, 1948, pp. 196, 305.

641. "Oriental despotism"

Wigmore, Roscoe Pound, 1974, p. 220.

642. Admirer of Hitler

Id. at pp. 250, 251.

643. Used as excuse

Wiebe, The Search for Order, 1967, p. 109.

644. "Sexually potent"

Id. at p . 52.

645. "Thugs of India"

Kenny, Making Sense of the Molly Maguires, 1998, p. 257.

646. Goddess Kali

Id. at p. 262.

Darkness whence it came."[647] Similar rhetoric was employed by editorialists in the business press.[648]

This attitude began to spread even to respectable legal journals. A decade later, the Albany Law Journal unleashed this blast at those who had placed

> a great city at the mercy of a few long-haired, wild-eyed, bad smelling, atheistic, reckless foreign wretches, who never did an honest hour's work in their lives * * *. There ought to be some law * * * to enable society to crush such snakes when they raise their heads before they had the time to bite.[649]

A few employers anticipated modern economists in viewing working people as "human capital" with no greater claim on society than machines.[650] Similar attitudes soon began to emerge among the judiciary.[651]

The notion that respectable society was at war with a "criminal class" when coupled with the fear that traditional judicial procedures were failing made a deadly brew.[652] As during the War, it gave rise to a sort of lawless law enforcement whose object was social control, not justice.[653] As we shall see, the job of law enforcement agencies came to include beating and shooting and otherwise using force to disperse dissidents rather than helping to funnel them into the criminal justice system.[654] Indeed, eventually Justice Brown of the Supreme Court, who had praised Jefferson Davis as a "Southern gentleman of the finest type" but who had little sympathy for other rebels, excoriated the traditional system of criminal

647. "Exterminate"

Id. at pp. 239, 257.

648. Similar rhetoric

Id. at p. 259 (quoting other similar examples).

649. "Snakes"

David, The History of The Haymarket Affair, paper 1967, p. 188. Later, after the verdict, the Journal called on the community to "wake up to a realization of what a volcano they have been sleeping on; what a viper this free and hospitable land has taken to its hearth." Id. at p. 318.

650. Machines

"I regard my employees as I do a machine, to be used to my advantage, and when they are old and of no fur-

ther use I cast them in the street." Id. at p. 24.

651. Judiciary

Brooks, Walter Clark, Fighting Judge, 1944, p. 62.

652. "Criminal class"

Hixson, Moorfield Storey and The Abolitionist Tradition, 1972, p. 29.

653. Social control

Weibe, The Search for Order, 1877–1920, 1967, p. 39.

654. Force to disperse

Ibid.

justice as "deplorably weak and inefficient" and justified lynching as a popular substitute.[655]

In the summer of 1877, these developments were still in the future. Despite some improvement in the economy, wages were still only about half what they had been in 1870.[656] Then the major railroads imposed a further cut of 20% while increasing the workload of train crews.[657] This triggered "The Great Strike of 1877," which one historian has described as "one of the bitterest explosions of class warfare in American history"[658] and another thought "brought the country about as close to a real revolution as it has ever been."[659] Even the staid New York Tribune reported that "public opinion almost everywhere is in sympathy with the insurrection."[660]

Because the uprising was spontaneous and not organized by the still-infant railway unions, Pinkertons and other forms of control proved useless.[661] Local police and the railroads' private armies were insufficient and local police and militia were reluctant to shoot their friends and neighbors.[662] Hence, governors called for federal troops and President Hayes complied.[663] It was left to the outgoing President Grant to note the irony: during his administration both parties—except the Radical Republicans—found it "horrible [to employ federal troops] to protect the lives of negroes. Now, however, there is no hesitation about exhausting the whole power of the government to suppress a strike on the slightest

655. "Deplorably weak"

Glennon, Justice Henry Billings Brown: Values in Tension, 1973, 44 Colo. L.Rev. 553, 598.

656. Wages still half

Kenny, Making Sense of The Molly Maguires, 1998, p. 180.

657. Further cut of 20%

Josephson, The Robber Barons, 1962, p. 272.

658. "Bitterest explosions"

Foner, Reconstruction: America's Unfinished Revolution, 1988, p. 583.

659. "Real revolution"

Furnas, The Americans: A Social History of The United States, 1587–1914, 1969, p. 716.

660. "In sympathy"

Foner, Reconstruction: America's Unfinished Revolution, 1863–1877, 1988, p. 584.

661. Proved useless

Garraty, The New Commonwealth, 1877–1890, 1960, p. 158.

662. Reluctant to shoot

Brecher, Strike!, 1972, pp. 2–3.

663. Hayes complied

Id. at p. 3 (quoting letter of request).

intimation that danger threatens."[664] As the ex-President suggests, though the Army was supposed to simply restore the peace, it ended up using troops as strikebreakers.[665] Historical causation being what it is, it is difficult to say whether this use of force did more to further inflame the insurrection than it did to suppress it.[666] Given its lack of organization, it is possible that the uprising collapsed of its own weight——though not before violence on both sides that destroyed property and took 100 lives.[667] Whatever the historical truth, it is clear that those in positions of power thought that force was the determinative cause in saving the republic.[668]

Following so close on the triumphalism of the Centennial, the Great Strike provided the privileged classes with a close enough look at real revolution to sunder any romantic attachment they may have had to the Revolutionary ideas embedded in the confrontation clauses and similar constitutional provisions.[669] The New York Tribune warned that communism was abroad in the land and only the "substantial, property owning" classes could save "civilized society."[670] The New York Times chimed in: "We cannot too soon face the unwelcome fact that we have dangerous social elements to contend with, and they are rendered all the more dangerous by the peculiarities of our political system."[671] Once again, the uprising was blamed on The Other and their communist agitators; "all the 'Unsettled Humors' of society * * * the hard customers, the bummers and tramps, the Mollie Maguires and the Communists, the hoodlums, the pick-pockets."[672] Confirmation of these

664. "To suppress strike"

Foner, Reconstruction: America's Unfinished Revolution, 1863–1877, 1988, p. 586.

665. Strikebreakers

Id. at p. 584.

666. Suppress it

Garraty, The New Commonwealth, 1877–1890, 1968, p. 159.

667. Took 100 lives

Brecher, Strike!, 1972, p. 21.

668. Force determinative

This seems apparent by the actions taken immediately after the strike and the measures employed in subsequent labor disputes over the balance of the century.

669. Sunder attachments

Wiebe, The Search For Order, 1877–1920, 1967, p. 10.

670. "Civilized society"

Foner, Reconstruction: America's Unfinished Revolution, 1863–1877, 1988, p. 585.

671. "Peculiarities"

Ibid.

672. "Pickpockets"

Kenny, Making Sense of The Molly Maguires, 1998, p. 261.

fears could be found in some of the rhetoric that emerged from The Great Strike.[673]

Among the proposed remedies was to label strikes as "unAmerican" and pass statutes that would make them illegal.[674] Indeed, over the balance of the century the courts came close to doing just that through an exercise of their common law powers. However, the only immediate step taken was to strengthen and modernize the National Guard and to erect fortresses or "armories" from which it could march forth to put down any further insurrections.[675] In fact, the National Guard was to intervene in more than 100 strikes by the end of the century.[676]

As the fires cooled, some publicists sought to convince the public that the Great Strike was an aberration.[677] Nonetheless, it did little to calm the anxieties of the "respectable" people.[678] Scholars and journalists found a ready audience for tracts denouncing trade unions and other working class organizations.[679] Gradually, this anti-working class animus even spread into fiction.[680] William Dean Howells portrayed union leaders as "irresponsible tyrant[s] * * * employed in poisoning the mind of the workingman against his real interests and friends," a task he thought "perfectly easy" because the workers were too dull to appreciate that capitalists were their "real friends."[681] With

673. Confirmation in rhetoric

"All you have to do, gentlemen, for you have the numbers, is to unite on one idea——that the workingmen shall rule the country. What man makes, belongs to him, and the workingmen made this country." Brecher, Strike!, 1972, pp. 17–18.

"There was a time in the history of France when the poor found themselves oppressed to such an extent that forbearance ceased to be a virtue, and hundreds of heads tumbled into a basket. That time may have arrived with us." Id. at p. 19.

674. Make illegal

Garraty, The New Commonwealth, 1877–1890, 1960, p. 160.

675. National Guard

Ibid.

676. More than 100 strikes

Foner, Reconstruction: America's Unfinished Revolution, 1863–1877, 1988, p. 586.

677. Aberration

Wiebe, The Search For Order, 1877–1920, 1967, p. 10.

678. Anxieties of "respectable"

Id. at p. 51.

679. Tracts denouncing

Furnas, The Americans: A Social History of the United States, 1587–1914, 1969, p. 712.

680. Spread to fiction

Id. at p. 717.

681. "Real friends"

Id. at p. 718.

"friends" like these, workers needed no enemies.

Though the hysterical views of the elite may have affected interpretation of the Confrontation Clause, we must not suppose they had any relation to reality.[682] Sympathy for the strikers was probably fueled as much by animosity toward railroads as it was by any acceptance of unionism.[683] This was still largely an agricultural nation where immigrants of modest means could fulfill ambitions to become kulaks rather than serfs, and refugees from European feudal industrialism could become shopkeepers or artisans, where legislative and electoral calendars reflected the rhythms of agricultural life, where most people were citizens rather than customers, where there were enough people free from the tyranny of the timeclock that they could flock to hear Lincoln and Douglas debate, and where the indigenous radical tradition was sufficiently strong that those of a rebellious mind did not have to turn to imported ideologies to rationalize revolt.[684]

The fact that newer immigrants already familiar with the collectivist impulses of capitalism rejected the Republican free labor ideology did not prevent most Americans from subscribing to it long after elites had abandoned it.[685] But invocation of European socialist rhetoric allowed capitalists to appeal to nativist feeling to condemn it and its adherents as foreign.[686] The myth of American exceptionalism that had its roots in the efforts of the Federalists to disclaim any relationship between the American and French Revolutions was still strong enough that many Americans could believe

682. Relation to reality

We shall see paranoia again influence confrontation jurisprudence when we look at the McCarthy era.

683. Animosity toward railroads

Farmers and small-town merchants had personal experience with the predatory practices of railroads but little knowledge of factory life or mining death.

684. Did not need

Since industrial capitalism was the wave of the future and the target of discontent, it is easy to exaggerate its real significance in American life. As late as post World War II, it was still possible in many parts of the Midwest for one to practice subsistence agriculture with 40 acres and a few cows and pigs. However primitive this may have seemed to urban Americans, it was still a step up for refugees from European industrialism like the junior author's maternal grandfather, who was probably not atypical of such persons in his loathing of labor unions and his embrace of extreme laissez-faire economics—even while the government was supporting the price he was paid for his milk.

685. Rejected free labor

Furnas, The Americans: A Social History of the United States, 1587–1914, 1969, p. 711.

686. Radicalism and nativism

Id. at p. 710.

that democratic government could be used to restrain the excesses of industrializing capitalism despite the failure of the Grangers and the open acknowledgment of the Harvard School of constitutional interpretation that the purpose of the Supreme Court was to block the "radical experimentation of social reformers."[687] It would take a long period of antidemocratic activism by state and federal courts for significant numbers of Americans to understand what the Founders had to say about the relationship between economic and political power.[688]

Darwin and The Descent of Democracy

Americans insecure in their own success could turn to science for succor.[689]

> Charles Darwin's new theory of the evolution of species, with its stress on struggle and the destruction of the weak, offered, when applied to human society, an additional temptation for successful individuals to believe that their own achievements were both inevitable and socially desirable, and to harden their hearts against the "unfit" who failed to "survive" in the Darwinian world of tooth and claw.[690]

Since Darwin himself admitted to being influenced by political thinkers like Thomas Malthus, it is hardly surprising that his theory of evolution is expressed in the metaphors of laissez faire capitalism.[691] Hence it took no great imagination for Herbert

687. "Radical experimentation"

Jacobs, Law Writers and The Courts, 1954, p. 60.

688. Economic and political

For more on the submergence of the indigenous radical tradition in American historiography, see Woodward, Home Grown Radicals, N.Y.Rev.Bks., April 5, 1979, p. 3.

689. Science for succor

Or as businessmen seem to have seen it, as "science for suckers." Capitalists could use Social Darwinism, like any ideology, when it suited their needs and ignore it when it did not. Kirkland, Dream & Thought in The Business Community, 1860–1900, 1964, pp. 13–14. For example, John D. Rockefeller told a Sunday School class: "The growth of a large business is merely a survival of the fittest.... The American Beauty Rose can be produced in the splendor and fragrance which bring cheer to its beholder only by sacrificing the early buds which grow up around it. This is not an evil tendency in business. It is merely working-out of a law of nature and a law of God." Hofstadter, Social Darwinism in American Thought, 1955, p. 45. Standard Oil had little "splendor and fragrance" and the means by which it grew would hardly commend themselves to other Sunday School teachers. See also, Kolko, Railroads and Regulation, 1877–1916, 1965, p. 4.

690. "Tooth and claw"

Garraty, The New Commonwealth, 1877–1890, 1968, p. 17.

691. Metaphors of capitalism

Lewontin, Facts and the Factitious in Natural Sciences, 1991, 18 Crit.Inq. 140, 153 n. 14.

Spencer and William Graham Sumner to find in evolutionary biology a political ideology which could be dressed up in scientific disguise and used to support the emerging capitalist order.[692] "Social Darwinism," as this pseudoscience came to be known, was another form of the biological determinism that is as old as Aristotle and has been reincarnated in our time as "The Bell Curve."[693] Social Darwinism in the 1870s joined National Guard armories as "monuments to middle class fears of social revolution".[694]

Americans who rejected the economic determinism of Marx saw no irony in embracing the biological determinism of Spencer and Sumner. However, like many political ideologies, Social Darwinism was sufficiently protean to support different political agendas. For the complacent, it provided a handy excuse for political passivity.[695] However, it could also be wedded to traditional conservative values, such as noblesse oblige, to convince some social reformers that they had evolved to alleviate the errors in the existing political order.[696] For those dissatisfied with the descent of democratic politics, it provided scientific support for campaigns to disenfranchise the "unfit."

Given the way in which Social Darwinism reflected the ideology of the adversary system, lawyers fell for it with ridiculous ease. J.H. Choate, one of the leaders of the bar, argued that people like him had been selected for prominence "by a process of natural selection, for merit and fitness, from the whole Body of the Bar."[697] Langdell, it will be recalled, drew his inspiration for the Harvard method of legal education from biology.[698] The common law could be described as a kind of intellectual Darwinism in which the unfit precedents or

692. Spencer and Sumner

See, generally, Hofstadter, Social Darwinism in American Thought, 1955.

693. Old as Aristotle

In Poetica, Aristotle wrote: "From the hour of birth, some human beings are marked for subjection, others for rule." For an exploration and explosion of the scientific claims of "biological determinism," see Lewontin, Biology as Ideology, 1991.

694. "Monuments"

Garraty, The New Commonwealth, 1877–1890, 1968, p. 160. See also,

Russett, Darwin in America: The Intellectual Response, 1865–1912, 1976.

695. Political passivity

Hixson, Moorfield Storey and The Abolitionist Tradition, 1972, p. 33.

696. Evolved to alleviate

Id. at p . 29.

697. "Whole body of Bar"

Twiss, Lawyers and The Constitution: How Laissez Faire Came to the Supreme Court, 1942, p._115.

698. Harvard method

See above, text at note 373.

rules were culled out by the hidden hand of the judicial process.[699] Roscoe Pound, himself a biologist by training, developed the "organicist" theory of law reflected in Evidence Rule 102.[700]

The operation of Social Darwinism in the law may be glimpsed in the anticodification rhetoric of James C. Carter. He condemned Field's proposed codification of the common law as "unscientific in theory."[701] Legislators, not being naturally selected, were necessarily ignorant of "the science of lawmaking."[702] The common law, on the other hand, follows "the dictates of science" and reflects "the natural order."[703] In the hands of other elite lawyers, Social Darwinism evolved into "scientific racism" that could be deployed to preserve the dominance of the "Anglo–Saxon race;" e.g., George Templeton Strong's delight that Columbia was going to use tests to "keep out the little scrubs (German Jew boys mostly) whom the School now promotes from the grocery counters ... to be 'gentlemen of the Bar.' "[704]

Social Darwinism gathered converts on the bench.[705] The most notorious of these was Supreme Court Justice David Brewer, who frequently proclaimed the views of the Social Darwinist Herbert Spencer and his American disciple William Graham Sumner.[706] The antilabor views of these pundits resonated with Brewer's own political and judicial views.[707] The direct use of Social Darwinism in judicial opinions does not reflect its influence on judicial thought, though one can find instances of such use.[708] One historian has

699. Unfit culled out

Twining, Karl Llewellyn and The Realist Movement, 1973, pp. 31, 33, 42.

700. "Organicist"

Wigdor, Roscoe Pound, 1974, p. 85; vol 21, § 5025, p. 143.

701. "Unscientific theory"

Carter, The Proposed Codification of Our Common Law, 1884, p. 24.

702. "Science of lawmaking"

Id. at p. 89.

703. "Natural order"

Id. at p. 42.

704. "German Jew boys"

Friedman, A History of American Law, 1973, p. 553. For a depressing collection of similar racist and nativist statements by leaders of the bar, see

Auerbach, Unequal Justice, 1976, pp. 100–129.

705. Converts on bench

Friedman, A History of American Law, 1973, p. 298.

706. Brewer and Sumner

Mason, William Howard Taft: Chief Justice, 1965, p. 42.

707. Anti-labor views

David, The History of The Haymarket Affair, 1963, p. 48.

708. Instances of use

Twiss, Lawyers and The Constitution: How Laissez Faire Came To The Supreme Court, 1942, p. 106.

argued that during the latter half of the 19th Century, the Supreme Court switched from traditional conservatism to a Social Darwinist approach to the law.[709] Be that as it may, the impact of Social Darwinism on the right of confrontation could only have been indirect, perhaps adding a scientific gloss to the existing tendency to treat criminal defendants as "The Other"——an animalistic underclass of polyglot ancestry not deserving of the protection that evolved for the nobility of the Anglo–Saxons.

By the mid–1870s a pessimist might have predicted the incipient collapse of the Founders' version of republican government.[710] The Union had fallen apart and was only restored by force and the disregard of constitutional liberties.[711] The authority of state courts was rivaled and sometimes eclipsed by private centers of power, legal and extralegal, so that citizens were at the mercy of corporate armies or Ku Klux Klan hoodlums.[712] Both federal and state governments were riddled with corruption;[713] the president of the Union Pacific Railroad divided United States Senators into three groups: the "clean" (who would do what he wanted without asking for favors), the "commercial" (who would do the right thing only if paid for it), and the "communists" (who resisted both his logic and his money).[714] The economy seemed beyond repair by either private or public means.[715]

Political anxieties were projected onto Reconstruction governments of the former Confederacy, who at least were trying to do something about socioeconomic problems.[716] The New York Tribune in 1873 sent one of its racist reporters south for a series of reports on the failings of Reconstruction; not surprisingly he found "a mass of black barbarism ... the most ignorant democracy that mankind ever saw."[717] When the articles were published as a book, they

709. Supreme Court switched

Paul, Conservative Crisis and The Rule of Law: Attitudes of Bar and Bench, 1887–1895, 1960, p. 5.

710. Incipient collapse

Garraty, The New Commonwealth, 1877–1890, 1968, p. 225.

711. Disregard

See above, text at note 36.

712. Armies and hoodlums

See above, text at note 328.

713. Corruption

See above, text at note 422.

714. Three groups

Garraty, The New Commonwealth, 1877–1890, 1968, p. 231.

715. Beyond repair

See above, text at note 463.

716. Reconstruction governments

See above, text at note 187.

717. "Ignorant democracy"

Foner, Reconstruction: America's Unfinished Revolution, 1863–1877, 1988, p. 525.

elicited symptoms of what has recently been called "compassion fatigue;" those who might have been inclined to point out that the government of New York compared favorably to the worst of the reported corruption in Dixie were too preoccupied with their own problems to care. Others were quick to seize on the Reconstruction governments as an object lesson in the excesses of Jacksonian democracy; Charles Frances Adams, grandson of the Founder, wrote:

> [u]niversal suffrage can only mean in plain English the govern-ment of ignorance and vice:——it means a European, and especially Celtic, proletariat on the Atlantic coast, and African proletariat on the shores of the Gulf; and a Chinese proletariat on the Pacific.[718]

Adams symptomized the racism that was coming to the fore in the party of Lincoln. By the middle of the decade, the New York Times was calling for an end to the "era of moral politics" launched by the abolitionist and Radical Republicans.[719]

That era ended with the election of 1874——one of the more remarkable electoral turnabouts in American electoral history.[720] The Grand Old Party went from a 100 vote majority in the House to being down 60 votes to the Democrats——who had seemed dead in the water only a few years earlier.[721] Whether or not the economic depression caused this reversal of fortune, as historians seem to think, it launched a twenty year period of electoral instabil-ity and stalemate that ended only with the turn of the century.[722] During this decline in the fortunes of the political branches, the door was open to the one institution in the national government that had a clear agenda and no voters to satisfy. The rise in the power of the Supreme Court had significant impact on its constitu-tional jurisprudence——and thus on the Confrontation Clause.

The election of 1874 provided what little excuse the business wing of the Republican party needed to follow those like Thurlow Weed who advocated more "moderate" treatment of the former

---

718. "Chinese proletariat"

Id. at p. 497.

719. "Moral politics"

Id. at p. 527.

720. Electoral turnabout

Foner, Reconstruction: America's Unfin-ished Revolution, 1863–1877, 1988, p. 523.

721. Down 60 votes

The Encyclopedia of American Facts and Dates, Carruth ed., 9th ed. 1993, p. 314.

722. Stalemate

Foner, Reconstruction: America's Unfin-ished Revolution, 1863–1877, 1988, p. 523.

Confederates.[723] As one historian put it: "When it became clear that the price to be paid for Negro equality included continuing military rule and a certain amount of violence——at the cost of business profits——there could be but one outcome."[724] In 1876, the Republicans nominated Rutherford Hayes for President, a graduate of the Harvard Law School who Henry Adams called "a third-rate nonentity."[725] The Democratic nominee, Samuel Tilden, was also acceptable to Wall Street and, apparently, to the voters; he won in both the popular vote and carried enough states to win in the Electoral College as well.[726] However, Republican officials in three Southern states disqualified enough Tilden voters to make Hayes the winner in those states and leave the Democrat one vote short of an Electoral College victory.[727]

Since the Constitution did not specify how the disputed electoral votes were to be counted by Congress and the House and Senate were divided between the two parties, this produced a constitutional crisis.[728] To break the deadlock, Congress established a so-called "Electoral Commission" consisting of five members from each house, who were equally divided between the two parties, and five members of the Supreme Court.[729] The Commission, voting on straight party lines, decided not to go behind the returns and awarded all the disputed votes to Hayes.[730] Justice Bradley, who had originally favored Tilden, was accused of changing his vote under pressure from Republican politicians.[731] Whether or not this

723. Follow Weed

Brodie, Thaddeus Stevens: Scourge of the South, 1959, p. 311.

724. "But one outcome"

Magrath, Morrison R. Waite: The Triumph of Character, 1963, p. 115.

725. "Third-rate nonentity"

Foner, Reconstruction: America's Unfinished Revolution, 1863–1877, 1988, p. 567.

726. Tilden wins

Encyclopedia of American History, Morris ed. 1976, p. 301.

727. One vote short

Ibid. See also, Magrath, Morrison R. Waite: The Triumph of Character, 1963, pp. 137–138.

728. Constitutional crisis

Foner, Reconstruction: America's Unfinished Revolution, 1863–1877, 1988, pp. 575–582.

729. "Electoral Commission"

The Encyclopedia of American Facts and Dates, 9th ed. 1993, p. 320.

730. Awarded to Hayes

For a detailed study of the work of the Commission, see Fairman, History of the Supreme Court of the United States: Five Justices and the Electoral Commission of 1877, 1988.

731. Changing vote

The charge is subject to a detailed refutation in id., pp. 159–196. For an example of the charge——written before Fairman's work——see Encyclopedia of American History, Morris ed. 1976, p. 301.

was true, the participation of the Justices in the work of the Electoral Commission did little to enhance the prestige of the Court but it did symbolize the power of the judiciary in an era of political stalemate.[732]

However, in order to attain the approval of Southern Democrats to the results of the Electoral Commission, Republicans struck a deal with them that came to be called "The Compromise of 1877."[733] The precise terms of the compromise remain a subject of historical dispute, but its major thrust was clear enough; in return for allowing Hayes to take office, the Republicans agreed to end Reconstruction in the South.[734] One historian has argued that the effect, if not one of the terms, of the compromise was an expansion of the Fourteenth Amendment to protect business interests while leaving civil rights to the states.[735] This probably reads too much into the fact that Bradley, whose vote on the Electoral Commission made Hayes President, was also the author of the opinion declaring the Civil Rights Act of 1875 unconstitutional.[736] Nor is it clear such a deal would have made much difference; state and federal courts had equally dismal records on civil rights.[737] But it is clear that the Compromise of 1877 marked the abandonment of the Radical Republican ideal of a powerful national government protecting the civil liberties of all citizens.[738]

The end of Reconstruction meant the takeover of Southern government by the so-called "Redeemers" who over the next two decades dismantled the achievements of Republican government and reinstalled a new system of racial and class politics.[739] Blacks

---

732. Enhance prestige

Garraty, The New Commonwealth, 1877–1890, 1968, p. 260.

733. "Compromise of 1877"

Magrath, Morrison R. Waite: The Triumph of Character, 1963, p. 137.

734. End Reconstruction

Foner, Reconstruction: America's Unfinished Revolution, 1863–1877, 1988, p. 581.

735. Leaving to states

Beth, The Development of the American Constitution, 1877–1917, 1971, p. 191.

736. Unconstitutional

Civil Rights Cases, 1883, 3 S.Ct. 18, 109 U.S. 3, 27 L.Ed. 835.

Foner, Reconstruction: America's Unfinished Revolution, 1963–1877, 1988, p. 587.

737. Dismal records

Beth, The Development of the American Constitution, 1877–1917, p. 230.

738. Protecting liberties

Foner, Reconstruction: America's Unfinished Revolution, 1863–1877, 1988, p. 582.

739. "Redeemers"

Id. at p. 587.

were denied the right to serve on juries, which enhanced the power of the police, vigilante groups, and local militias to use violence to curb labor unrest and force many of the former slaves into a system of peonage——when they were not in prison and leased out to labor for their former masters.[740] The Redeemer governments quickly shifted tax burdens to the working class and institutionalized poverty as a method of social control.[741] Even before the end of 1877, one Northern business journal reported that "labor is under control for the first season since the war."[742] However, this class-based repression set the stage for a series of agrarian revolts that were to prove as troublesome for business interests and as significant for the history of confrontation as the industrial strikes in the North.[743]

The failure of Reconstruction had significant psychological impact far beyond the reach of the Redeemers.[744] For abolitionists and war veterans, the return to power of the former slaveholders represented a betrayal of the cause for which they had fought. Even those who did not care much about the fate of Southerners saw the end of Reconstruction as a confession of the inability of even a powerful national government with a strong military arm to control a violent minority. This loss of faith in the power of government played its part in the denigration of the right of confrontation.

Reynolds rapped

In 1878, the year in which criminal defendants were first given the right to testify in federal courts, the United States Supreme Court decided Reynolds v. United States——its first case raising the meaning of the Confrontation Clause of the Sixth Amendment.[745] In

740. Labor for masters

Id. at pp. 588, 595.

741. Social control

Foner, Nothing But Freedom: Emancipation and Its Legacy, 1983, pp. 60, 70–72.

742. "Labor under control"

Foner, Reconstruction: America's Unfinished Revolution, 1863–1877, 1988, p. 596.

743. Agrarian revolts

Brooks, Walter Clark, Fighting Judge, 1944, p. 69.

744. Psychological

This paragraph is drawn from Wiebe, The Search for Order, 1877–1920, 1967, p. 205 . .

745. First case

1878, 3 Otto (98 U.S.) 145, 25 L.Ed. 244.

Kirkpatrick, Confrontation and Hearsay: Exemptions From the Constitutional Unavailability Requirement, 1986, 70 Minn.L.Rev. 665, 671; Ross, Confrontation and Residual Hearsay: A Critical Examination and A Proposal for Military Courts, 1987, 118 Mil.L.Rev. 31, 38. On the right of defendants to testify, see vol. 21, § 5001, pp. 24–25.

the century since the right of confrontation was first established in the constitution, members of the Court had sometimes encountered confrontation issues while riding circuit, sometimes discussed it in private, and occasionally touched upon it tangentially in reported opinions, but had not been called on collectively to interpret the Sixth Amendment.[746] The Court came to the task with a constitutional crisis barely passed, the economy in disarray, and the privileged classes anxious over the power of the government to protect them, but with its own power and prestige on the rise from the low point of the Dred Scott decision.[747]

But before turning to the Court's decision, it may be useful to describe the Court's prior encounters with confrontation so the reader can appreciate why the Court chose to ignore them. The most important decision on confrontation by a Supreme Court justice on circuit is John Marshall's opinion in the Burr conspiracy trial.[748] Marshall was not only the most prestigious expounder of the Constitution, but he was also a Founder——having sat in the Virginia ratifying convention where the most extensive recorded debate over the Bill of Rights took place.[749] Marshall could not only claim to have some personal knowledge of the intent of the drafters but he was called upon to express those views in precisely the kind of political trial that had figured prominently in the development of the right of confrontation.[750]

The precise issue before Marshall in Burr's trial was the admissibility of the statements of an alleged coconspirator, one Herman Blennerhasset. Since the reporter notes that the "argument on the admissibility of the testimony lasted several days," Marshall's ruling must have been carefully considered.[751] He begins his opinion by invoking the confrontation right, though it is not the ground for his ruling.

> The rule of evidence which rejects mere hearsay testimony, which excludes from the trials of a criminal or civil nature the declara-

746. Collectively interpret

For one private comment, see § 6355, text at note 526.

747. From low point

Kyvig, Explicit and Authentic Acts, 1996, p. 127.

748. Burr conspiracy trial

U.S. v. Burr, C.C.Va.1807, 25 Fed.Cas. 187.

749. Sat in convention

See vol. 30, § 6347, p. 745.

750. Political trial

See, e.g., Malone, Jefferson The President: Second Term 1805–1809, 1974, p. 292 and following.

751. "Lasted several days"

U.S. v. Burr, C.C.Va.1807, 25 Fed.Cas. 187, 193.

tions of any other individual than of him against whom the proceedings are instituted, has been generally deemed all essential to the correct administration of justice. I know not why a declaration in court should be unavailing, unless made upon oath, if a declaration out of court was to criminate others than him who made it; nor why a man should have a constitutional claim to be confronted with the witnesses against him, if mere verbal declarations, made in his absence, may be evidence against him.[752]

Since confrontation is a "principle in the preservation of which all are ... concerned," it is therefore "incumbent on courts to be watchful of every inroad of a principle so truly important."[753] Marshall does just that, holding that the declaration of a co-conspirator is admissible only if conspiracy is charged in the indictment and excluding the testimony on that ground.[754] Marshall does not say that confrontation itself bars the use of hearsay so he has no need of the evasions state courts were forced to in order to explain the coexistence of the Confrontation Clause and the hearsay rule.[755]

Chief Justice Taney's opinion in United States v. Reid contains the most significant prior dicta on the Confrontation Clause.[756] The issue in that case was what law governed the competence of witnesses in federal criminal trials.[757] In explaining why the Judiciary Act of 1789, enacted by the same Congress that drafted the Bill of Rights, could not have been intended to require federal courts to follow the English common law, Taney conceded that

> [t]he colonists who established the English colonies in this country, undoubtedly brought with them the common ... laws of England.... And among the most cherished and familiar principles of the common law was the trial by jury in civil, and still more especially in criminal cases.[758]

752. "May be evidence"

Ibid.

753. "Every inroad"

Ibid.

754. Excluding testimony

Id. at 195. This makes the co-conspirators "exception" really a case of "legally operative conduct;" that is, the words are admitted not testimonially but as words by which the crime was committed. See discussion in this Treatise of Evidence Rule 801(d)(2)(E).

755. Evasions of state courts

See § 6355, text at note 820.

756. Reid dicta

1851, 12 How. (53 U.S.) 361, 13 L.Ed. 1023.

757. Competence of witnesses

See vol. 21, § 5003, p. 45.

758. "Cherished and familiar"

12 How. (53 U.S.) at 363. The Chief Justice adds that "the trial by jury in all of [the colonies] of English origin

But, the Chief Justice continued, "the value of this right was much impaired by the mode of proceeding in criminal cases" because the defendant had no right to call witnesses or to the assistance of counsel.[759] Of course, "[t]his oppressive mode of proceeding had been abolished in the colonies ... by different statutes before the declaration of independence."[760]

> But the memory of the abuses that had been practiced under [the common law] had not passed away. And the thirteen Colonies who united in the declaration of independence, as soon as they became States, placed in their respective constitutions or fundamental laws, safeguards against the restoration of proceedings which were so oppressive and odious while they remained in force. It was the people of these thirteen States which formed the Constitution of the United States, and engrafted on it the provision which secures the trial by jury, and abolishes the old common-law proceeding which had so often been used for the purposes of oppression.[761]

Taney recognizes that the Constitution as originally drafted failed to secure the reformed mode of procedure required by the state constitutions, though it did require trial by jury in criminal cases.

> But as soon as public attention was called to the fact, that the securities for a fair and impartial trial by jury in criminal cases had not been inserted among the cardinal principles of the new government, they hastened to amend it, and to secure to a party accused of an offense against the United States, the same mode of trial, and the same mode of proceeding, that had been previously established and practiced in the courts of the several states. It was for this purpose that the 5th and 6th amendments were added to the Constitution.[762]

The Chief Justice then paraphrased the provisions of the Sixth Amendment, capping his analysis of the intent of the Framers—an intent that is documented in the prior volume of this Treatise.[763]

was regarded as a right of inestimable value, and the best and only security for life, liberty, and property." Id. at 364.

759. "Impaired by mode"
Ibid.

760. "Abolished before"
Ibid.

761. "Used for oppression"
Ibid.

762. "For this purpose"
Ibid.

763. Intent documented
See vol. 30, § 6347, p. 697 and following. See also, Jonankait, The Origins of The Confrontation Clause: An Alternate History, 1995, 27 Rutgers L.J. 77, 121.

In the same year, in an admiralty case, the Court in an opinion by Justice Grier also took notice of the Judiciary Act of 1879; particularly the provision that allowed "ex parte depositions without notice to be taken."[764] In 1789, the Court opined, "such a provision may have been necessary" because of the difficulty of travel in those days.[765] However, with modern modes of transportation

> [t]here is now seldom any necessity for having recourse to this mode of taking testimony. Besides it is contrary to the course of the common law; and ... testimony thus taken is liable to great abuse. At best, it is calculated to elicit only such partial statement of the truth as may have the effect of entire falsehood.[766]

This reminds us of the complaints of the Founders about the similar procedure of the colonial Vice–Admiralty courts.[767] Justice Grier, after pointing out the motives of the crew members to elide the truth in collision cases, continued

> [i]n such cases, the oral examination of witnesses before the court, with a stringent cross-examination by skillful counsel is almost the only method of eliciting truth from such sources.[768]

The opinion concludes with the admonition that the provision for ex parte depositions "should never be resorted to unless in circumstances of absolute necessity."[769]

After this flurry of fine dicta, the opinion of Chief Justice Waite in Reynolds v. United States comes as something of a disappointment.[770] Reynolds was a prosecution for bigamy, which one does not normally think of as political prosecution, but the case was one of "celestial marriage" that arose in the Utah Territory.[771] When we

764. "Ex parte depositions"

Walsh v. Rogers, 1851, 13 How. (54 U.S.) 283, 286, 14 L.Ed. 147.

765. "Been necessary"

Id. at 287.

766. "Entire falsehood"

Ibid. The opinion continues: "The person who prepares the witness and examines him can generally have just so much or so little of the truth, or such a version of it, as will suit his case. In closely contested cases of fact, testimony thus obtained must always be unsatisfactory and liable to suspicion...." This analysis is equally applicable to hearsay elicited by police interrogation.

767. Vice Admiralty

See vol. 30, § 6345, p. 482 and following.

768. "The only method"

13 How. (54 U.S.) at 284.

769. "Never be resorted"

Id. at 287.

770. Reynolds case

1878, 8 Otto (98 U.S.) 145, 25 L.Ed. 244.

771. Arose in Utah

Ibid.

see the prominent role played by Mormons today in our political and economic life, it is difficult to recall the time when they represented "The Other" as much as Ku Klux Klanners and Communists.[772] But the persecutions of the Mormons by legal means and the use of mob violence to force them to flee from community to community lacks only racial or ethnic animosity to make it rival other acts of group repression in American history. The statute under which the prosecution took place was a product of anti-Mormon hysteria and the defendant, George Reynolds, had been secretary to Brigham Young and sought prosecution to test the constitutionality of the statute.[773]

The confrontation question, then, was not the most prominent issue in the case.[774] It arose from the prosecution's use of the testimony from an earlier trial of the case of the alleged bigamous wife.[775] The government sought to subpoena her for the second trial, but the process server was stonewalled by the defendant and other members of the household.[776] On the claim that it was error to have admitted her testimony from the prior trial, the Chief Justice wrote:

> The Constitution gives the accused the right to a trial, at which he should be confronted with the witnesses against him; but if a witness is absent by his own wrongful procurement, he cannot complain if competent evidence is admitted to supply the place of that which he has kept away. The Constitution does not guaranty an accused person against the legitimate consequences of his own wrongful acts. It grants him the *privilege* of being confronted with the witnesses against him; but if he voluntarily keeps the witnesses away, he cannot insist on his privilege. If, therefore, when absent by his procurement, their evidence is supplied by in some lawful way, he is in no condition to assert that his constitutional rights have been violated.[777]

772. "The Other"

That is, as persons not deserving of constitutional protection.

773. To test statute

Arrington & Bitton, the Mormon Experience, 1979, p. 180.

774. Not prominent

It was only one of six issues raised by the defense. Id. at 153, 25 L.Ed. at 245.

775. Earlier trial

Id. at 150, 25 L.Ed. 247.

776. Stonewalled

Reynolds v. U.S., 1878, 8 Otto. (98 U.S.) 145, 158, 25 L.Ed. 244, 248.

777. "No condition to assert"

Id. at 158, 25 L.Ed. at 247 (emphasis in original).

One might infer from the degree of repetition in this passage that the Court was not as certain as it would like to appear.

There are several things to be noted about Reynolds. First, the opinion seems to assume that, absent forfeiture by the accused, the Confrontation Clause would bar the use of former testimony and, by parity of reasoning, other hearsay.[778] Second, the Court does not suggest that confrontation was satisfied by the opportunity to cross-examine the witness at the first trial or that the "witness against" the defendant was the person who related the former testimony—ploys that can be found in the prior state jurisprudence.[779] Third, the Chief Justice does not find it necessary to resort to the history of the Confrontation Clause,, to look at the state decisions about the right of confrontation, or to consult the writers on constitutional law like Story or Cooley.[780] Instead, the court relies on quotations from the State Trials and citations from English decisions and American evidence writers to support its view.[781] One might infer that the Chief Justice thinks, as some state courts had held, that the Confrontation Clause incorporates common law, but the opinion does not say this.[782] Fourth, though it is clearly not intended to demean the constitutional guarantee, the opinion does not explain the distinction between a "right" and a "privilege" of confrontation.[783] Finally, the Court's treatment of the forfeiture proof does not meet modern standards; indeed, the court seems to acknowledge the weakness of the evidence that the defendant had engaged in "wrongful procurement" of the absence of the witness when it shifts the burden of proof to him to prove that he was not responsible for her absence.[784]

Meanwhile, state courts continued construing away confrontation in an equally ahistorical fashion and with little regard to the opinions of federal judges. The year before Reynolds the Supreme

778. Other hearsay

The opinion cites English common-law cases but never supposes that the issue at hand is one of hearsay.

779. Prior jurisprudence

See § 6355, text at notecall 820.

780. Storey or Cooley

See § 6355, text at notecall 704; above, text at notecall 237.

781. Evidence writers

Id. at 158-159, 25 L.Ed. at 247.

782. Incorporates common law

See, e.g., § 6355, text at notecall 691.

783. "Right" and "privilege"

See Amar, The Bill of Rights, 1998, pp. 181, 192 (other instances of this usage).

784. Shifts burden

Id. at 160, 25 L.Ed. at 248.

Court of Wisconsin assumed that the right of confrontation simply carried forward the common law, holding that because dying declarations were admissible at common law it was no violation of confrontation to expand the common-law rule beyond cases of homicide.[785] That same year the Nevada Supreme Court held that the use of the former testimony of a deceased witness satisfied the right of confrontation because at the former trial the accused "had the opportunity ... of cross-examination" and that was "all the law requires."[786]

A year earlier the Texas Court of Appeals displayed the contempt for the right of confrontation that characterized many of the state-court opinions.[787] At issue was the admission of testimony of witness A to the former testimony of a now-deceased witness relating the dying declaration of the victim; in other words, the question was the application of the right of confrontation to multiple hearsay.[788] Ignoring the fact this was a case of first impression and the eloquent arguments of counsel,[789] the Texas Court merely repeated the same tired arguments we have seen in earlier state

785. Expand common law

State v. Dickinson, 1877, 41 Wis. 299, 308 (confrontation clause does not bar use of dying declaration in abortion case "because when the constitution was adopted it was well settled that they were admissible in cases of homicide").

786. "All the law requires"

State v. Johnson, 1877, 12 Nev. 121, 123.

787. Texas contempt

Black v. State, 1876, 1 Tex.App. 368.

788. Multiple hearsay

Id. at 370.

789. Arguments of counsel

So far as we have been able to determine, counsel was correct in claiming that there was no prior case "which ever permitted testimony ... that was 'hearsay' three removes from the only lips ever capable of positively asserting its truth." Id. at p. 371. Counsel argued against committing the admissibility of evidence against the accused to the mercy of the common law because "the enlightened framers of our state Constitution had already guaranteed the 'defendant' the right to be confronted by his accusers." Counsel continued: "[w]hen the unqualified and emphatic language of the provision of our state Constitution ... is fairly considered" expanding the admission of hearsay "will be to make that a convenience which has heretofore ... been merely tolerated as rule from necessity." Id. at 373. Counsel also pointed out that the witness on the stand cannot be the "witness against" the defendant under the confrontation clause because she cannot be cross-examined about the basis of hearsay statements twice removed. Id. at 375. However, if counsel had read the prior state cases, perhaps he would not have supposed that the Texas court's holding "may well startle the understanding of him who has hitherto regarded" the right of confrontation as "a settled rule of organic ... law." Id. at 370.

cases, pyramiding them on the apparent theory that one questionable justification deserves another.

> The Constitution does not alter the common-law rule of evidence, but leaves it to the law to determine what a witness, when confronted, shall be allowed to state as evidence.[790]

In other words, the only person the accused has the right to confront is the person the state chooses to call; if the law of evidence does not require the proof of former testimony by some means other than the imperfect recollection of a witness, the inability of the defense to cross-examine (or to elicit former cross-examination of) the former witness or the person whose hearsay she relates raises no problems of the right of confrontation. One is left to wonder why the antifederalists became so exercised about such an easily permeable right.

Bureaucratization, Vigilantism, and the A.B.A.

We have previously touched upon the changes in the legal system following the Civil War; the increase in the number of statutes and judicial decisions that filled law libraries, the growth in legal transactions that transcended the law of a single jurisdiction, and the emergence of the professional legal scholar.[791] One might have expected the teaching profession to take over the function of the traditional treatise writers in providing the profession with a coherent view of the changing fabric of the law.[792] But Langdell's view of the lawyer as a narrow technician beyond redemption by scholarship in the grand manner and the scientistic reductionism of the law review article were both hostile to the kind of synthesis found in the best of the treatise writers.[793]

Bureaucratization of scholarship was matched by what may have been its model; i.e., the increasingly bureaucratized corporate law firm.[794] The new breed of Wall Street Lawyer wanted certainty, uniformity, predictability——not the messy contingency of the traditional law practice where the lawyer had to be ready to handle

---

790. "Does not alter"

Id. at 384.

791. Professional scholar

Crystal, Codification and The Rise of The Restatement Movement, 1979, 54 Wash.L.Rev. 239, 248–252.

792. Coherent view

Id. at p. 251.

793. Langdell hostile

Twining, Karl Llewellyn and The Realist Movement, 1973, p. 139.

794. Corporate law firm

Crystal, Codification and The Rise of The Restatement Movement, 1979, 54 Wash.L.Rev. 239, 254.

whatever case came through the door.[795] Since their corporate clients, for all their social Darwinist bluster, wanted to be shielded from the hazards of the market, a convergence of ideologies seems all but inevitable. Traditional lawyers groused that "many of the best-equipped lawyers of the present day are to all intents and purposes owned by the great corporate and individual interests they represent."[796] Bureaucratization was, in the eyes of such critics, the cause for a perceived decline in the public reputation of the profession.[797]

The separation of Big Time Lawyers from ordinary litigants had technological as well as ideological roots.[798] Where once documents were copied by law students, clerks, or professional copyists, using goose quill, then steel-tipped pens, the typewriter led to the replacement of these men by less expensive female stenographers and typists. Some lawyers thought this led to an increase in the amount of legal papers produced and to the rising prolixity of legal documents, thus increasing the cost of litigation and commercial transactions. Moreover, the presence of women made law offices more genteel and luxurious——a far cry from the barroom ambience of Lincoln's day. Moreover, the invention of the elevator allowed corporate lawyers to move into space closer to their clients and removed them geographically as well as socially from lives of ordinary lawyers and litigants. Finally, their earlier use of rubber bands to replace the traditional red tape for bundling documents allowed lawyers to apply "red tape" as a metaphor for government bureaucracy while ignoring their own bureaucratic practices.

These changes in the profession were well underway by 1878, when, at the invitation of a conservative Connecticut lawyer, "seventy five gentlemen" representing the "decent part" of the profession met at the spa at Saratoga, New York to enjoy the waters and form the American Bar Association.[799] The stated purpose of the A.B.A. was to

795. Wanted certainty

Id. at 255.

796. "Owned by interests"

Strong, Landmarks of A Lawyer's Lifetime, 1914, p. 354.

797. Cause for decline

Id. at p. 377.

798. Technological roots

These are described with great insight in id. at pp. 385–403, from which the conclusions in this paragraph are drawn.

799. "Decent part met"

Friedman, A History of American Law, 1973, p. 563.

advance the science of jurisprudence, promote the administration of justice and uniformity of legislation . . . uphold the honor of the profession . . . and encourage cordial intercourse among the members of the American Bar.[800]

The number of those entitled to cordiality seems to have been small; by 1902 the A.B.A. still only counted 1700 members.[801] However, what the A.B.A. lacked in numbers was outweighed by the clout those few carried within the profession.

The significance of the A.B.A. for the history of confrontation is that it allows us to see the thinking of the leaders of the profession, lawyers who appeared before and hobnobbed with members of the Supreme Court and whose thoughts may resemble those that the justices held but which appear only indistinctly, if at all, in their judicial opinions. For example, we have already seen how the racism of the privileged classes was reflected in the actions of the A.B.A. in barring blacks from membership.[802] Indeed as late as 1940, the A.B.A. application required an indication of the race of the applicant so that on the eve of Pearl Harbor the A.B.A. leadership had to convene a committee of notables to rebut charges that this information was being used to deny membership to lawyers of color.[803]

As part of its mandate to "advance the science of jurisprudence," the A.B.A. launched a propaganda campaign to convince the public that judges did not make law.[804] The President of the A.B.A. proclaimed that American constitutional law was above and beyond politics.[805] In pursuit of the vision of the law being brought down from Mount Sinai by some judicial Moses, the A.B.A. launched scathing attacks on judges and others who favored democratization of the judiciary.[806] Speeches at the A.B.A. convention

---

800. "Cordial intercourse"

Ibid.

801. Only 1700

Ibid.

802. Barring blacks

Hixson, Moorfield Story and The Abolitionist Tradition, 1972, p. 118.

803. Information used

Mitgang, The Man Who Rode The Tiger: The Life and Times of Judge Samuel Seabury, 1963, p. 352.

804. Did not make law

Twiss, Lawyers and The Constitution: How Laissez Faire Came To The Supreme Court, 1942, p. 146.

805. Above politics

Id. at 199.

806. Democratization of judiciary

Brooks, Walter Clark, Fighting Judge, 1944, p. 192.

regularly debunked democracy as a threat to the purity of the law.[807] Federal courts benefited the most from the A.B.A.'s defense of jurisprudence as a "science" beyond the comprehension of the masses.[808]

The A.B.A.'s ideal of promoting the "administration of justice" was to see to it that the law reflected the ideology of laissez-faire capitalism.[809] At a time when business combinations were under attack by the Populists, a paper read at the A.B.A. convention defended "the trusts" as a bulwark against communism.[810] The A.B.A. led the conservative attack against the New Deal and its President urged corporations to engage in civil disobedience against its unconstitutional incursions on the rights of property.[811] However, the best evidence of the reactionary nature of the A.B.A. membership is the response to Roscoe Pound's famous St. Paul address calling for procedural reform, a conservative speech that incorporated most of the tenets of the Progressive Procedural paradigm that has dominated legal thought ever since.[812] Pound was denounced as a radical.[813]

To "uphold the honor of the profession," the A.B.A. barred blacks and the foreign-born from membership.[814] Apparently the reason for the latter exclusion was the propensity of despised ethnicities for radical politics; Cooley told one convention of the A.B.A. that the duty of lawyers was not to defend anarchists but to take a leading role in the repression of anarchism.[815] Similar

807. Debunked democracy

Paul, Conservative Crisis and The Rule of Law: Attitudes of Bench and Bar, 1877–1895, p. 76.

808. Federal courts benefit

Mason, William Howard Taft: Chief Justice, 1965, p. 129.

809. Ideology of capitalism

Magrath, Morrison R. Waite: The Triumph of Character, 1963, p. 225.

810. Defended "trusts"

Twiss, Lawyers and The Constitution: How Laissez Faire Came To The Supreme Court, 1942, p. 155.

811. Attack on New Deal

Harbaugh, Lawyer's Lawyer: The Life of John W. Davis, 1973, pp. 348–349.

812. St. Paul address

See § 6358, text at notecall 318.

813. Pound denounced

Wigdor, Roscoe Pound, 1974, p. 128.

814. Foreign-born

Auerbach, Enmity and Amity: Law Teachers and Practitioners, 1900–1922, 1971, 5 Perspectives in American History 549, 585.

815. Repression of anarchism

Twiss, Lawyers and The Constitution: How Laissez Faire Came To The Supreme Court, 1942, p. 165.

nativist sentiments led a group of A.B.A. Presidents to sign a letter denouncing Louis Brandeis as "unfit" for a position on the Supreme Court.[816] In addition, the organization mailed an "anti-Brandeis brief" to opinion-makers throughout the country as part of the campaign to keep the High Court unpolluted by liberalism.[817] No such brief was ever filed supporting the right of confrontation.

Ironically, one example of "anarchy" that not only involved confrontation but might also have enjoyed the approbation of the A.B.A. was the vigilante movement.[818] Though vigilantes are usually associated with the frontier in general and San Francisco in particular, in fact vigilantism originated much earlier, lasted long after the Gold rush, and was more widespread than myth suggests.[819] The year after the A.B.A. was formed, an editor in Golden, Colorado, reported that "the popular verdict seemed to be that the [vigilante] hanging was not only well merited, but a positive gain for the county, saving at least five or six thousand dollars."[820] This anticipates by several decades the Progressive call for a more "efficient" law enforcement.[821] Some 729 persons are believed to have enjoyed this privatized system of criminal justice prior to suffering capital punishment via free enterprise.[822]

Given that vigilantes often included leading members of the community and generally were approved by journalists and historians, it would be surprising if there were not a few members of the A.B.A. who partook of this community based law enforcement, particularly in the South where, under the name of "lynching," vigilante action was more frequent and more fatal than in other sections.[823] However, once started by the local elites, vigilantism was hard for them to contain. It was difficult to justify the local

---

816. Brandeis unfit

Todd, Justice on Trial: The Case of Louis D. Brandeis, 1964, p. 132.

817. Keep Court unpolluted

Id. at p. 201.

818. Vigilante movement

See generally, Friedman, Crime and Punishment in American History, 1993, pp. 179–192.

819. More widespread

Friedman finds examples as early as 1820. Id. at p. 180. He has examples as late as 1898 in Alaska and in states, such as Indiana, not generally thought of as "frontier" at the time their vigilantes were active. Id. at pp. 185–186.

820. "Positive gain"

Friedman, A History of American Law, 1973, p. 506.

821. More "efficient"

Vol. 21, § 5003, p. 50.

822. Enjoyed privatized

Friedman, A History of American Law, 1973, p. 506.

823. Elite "lynching"

Friedman, Crime and Punishment in American History, 1993, pp. 184–186.

vigilance committee while condemning the Molly Maguires and the Ku Klux Klan, both of which relied on a similar justification for their murders.[824] Eventually such groups gave vigilante action a bad name, but it was still practiced as late as World War II in some parts of the nation.[825]

Vigilantes both embraced and perverted confrontation values. Vigilantes were certainly "adversary" and their victims were "confronted" with their accusers; indeed, sometimes "trials" with some of the trappings of judicial procedure were held.[826] But because they lacked separation of functions—the accusers were also jurors and executioners—and the accused lacked many of the other Sixth Amendment rights such as counsel and an impartial jury, vigilante "trials" mocked the real thing. Worse yet, vigilantes came to be used as an excuse for weakening the constitutional protections in the regular court systems; Progressive scholars argued that the only way to end lynch mobs was to make judicial trials more speedy.[827] Sadly, some of this argument is reminiscent of the sheriff in Western movies begging the mob "to give him a fair trial before we hang him."

Railroads and Rights

If "democracy" is defined as voting, then it peaked in the 19th Century United States around 1880; voting declined from over 80% of the electorate to around 65% by the end of the century.[828] One historian has described the nation at the turn of the century as a combination of intense partisanship and massive indifference[829] The decline was not accidental; the massive disenfranchisement of vot-

---

On the wide approval of vigilantes, see id. at p. 182.

824. Similar justifications

Kenny, Making Sense of the Molly Maguires, 1998, p. 20; Williams, The Great South Carolina Ku Klux Klan Trials, 1871–1872, 1996, pp. 13–14.

825. Practiced late

Friedman, Crime and Punishment in American History, 1993, pp. 191–192. Or later, depending on how one defines the term; does the murder of civil-rights workers by law-enforcement officers in Mississippi in the 1960s fall into the category?

826. "Trials"

Id. at p. 186.

827. Make trials more speedy

Vigilantes, themselves, justified their actions by the real or supposed inadequacies of official law enforcement agencies, including courts and juries. Id. at p. 185.

828. Peaked and declined

Beth, The Development of the American Constitution, 1877–1917, 1971, pp. 114 n. 15, 128.

829. Massive indifference

Wiebe, The Search for Order, 1967, p. 22.

ers in the South in order to maintain the power of the Bourbon elite is legendary.[830] But what was less recognized before the Supreme Court's "one-man, one vote" decisions in the mid–20th Century was the extent to which the parties in other parts of the nation had altered election laws to dilute the votes of nonrural voters and to keep parties that might appeal to those disenchanted by the Republicrats off the ballot.[831]

After the near collapse of democracy in 1876, the Presidential contest of 1880 could easily be seen as pivotal——which may explain why both parties selected candidates acceptable to the corporate elite.[832] No group had a greater stake in the election than railroad executives. The railroads had thrown their best lawyers into the attack on the Granger laws and had lost.[833] The Supreme Court, in fact, was deciding the case at the same time that several members of the Court were serving on the Electoral Commission.[834] If further state regulation was to be defeated by constitutional veto, something had to be done to turn the Court around.

It is difficult to find a contemporary analogy for the power and importance of railroads in the 1880s.[835] Railroads were the prototypical national business institutions, with political and economic interests in every state.[836] Railroads, not some international treaty, were the instruments by which rural economies were brought into and buffeted by the national economy.[837] Railroad employees, because their employers were the beneficiaries of so much governmental largesse, had an interest in national politics that was more immediate than that of most other ordinary voters.[838] Nonetheless,

830. Maintain Bourbon elite

Beth, The Development of the American Constitution, 1877, 1971, p . 114.

831. Keep off ballot

Id. at p. 134.

832. Both acceptable

Encyclopedia of American History, Morris ed. 1976, p. 305.

833. Railroads lost

Magrath, Morrison R. Waite: The Triumph of Character, 1963, p. 178.

834. At same time

Id. at p. 181.

835. Contemporary analogy

The only example that even comes close are media conglomerates, but they lack economic power to rival their political power; if one looks at government subsidies alone, the aerospace industry is somewhat comparable.

836. Economic interests

See above, text at note 442.

837. National economy

Wiebe, The Search for Order, 1877–1920, 1967, p. 47.

838. Governmental largesse

Jacobs, Law Writers and The Courts, 1954, p. 129.

the national power of railroads was not always able to control state governments——as the Granger cases so dramatically showed, the Supreme Court was the only national institution capable of freeing railroads from state regulation.[839]

Although financiers and corporate leaders had little to fear from the Democratic candidate, Winfield Scott Hancock, a division in the Republican party provided an opportunity to exert their influence.[840] James Garfield, who was in trouble with the Conkling machine in New York, entered into negotiations to secure the support of Jay Gould and other prominent financiers.[841] One of Gould's agents made clear to Garfield what the price of his support would be.

> The next President will almost certainly have the appointment of three new Judges.... All monied men, and especially all corporations, regarded the course of the Supreme Court in the Granger cases and in the Pacific R.R. case as bad law and bad faith. I believe that you sympathize with the general view of the law taken by Judge Field and his associates in the minority.... [Gould and other capitalists] hesitate because they say they are unwilling to elect a President unless they are sure that he disapproves of what they call the revolutionary course of the majority of the court.[842]

Garfield supplied the necessary assurances.

> I have stated to you, fully, my well considered views of the constitution in reference to the sanctity of Contracts and of vested rights——Under no circumstances would I entrust the high functions of a Justice of the Supreme Court to any person whom I did not believe to be entirely sound on these questions. I should insist upon evidence which would be satisfactory to you as well as to me.[843]

Garfield won Gould's support and, not incidentally, the election.[844] But, alas, Gould was never able to call in the "marker" Garfield

---

839. Only institution

The Court had to expand the scope of the commerce power to enable national regulation to preempt state regulation. Kolko, Railroads and Regulation, 1877–1916, 1965, p.14.

840. Republican division

Magrath, Morrison R. Waite: The Triumph of Character, 1963, p. 238.

841. Entered negotiations

Id. at pp. 238–239.

842. "Revolutionary majority"

Id. at pp. 239–240.

843. "Satisfactory to you"

Id. at p. 242.

844. Garfield won

Encyclopedia of American History, Morris ed. 1976, p. 305.

had given him because Garfield was assassinated shortly after taking office.[845] But the incident illustrates the sort of influence railroads and other corporations were able to bring to bear on the Supreme Court; that influence does much to explain the Court's preoccupation with property interests at the expense of human rights, including the right of confrontation.

Railroad influence on the Court was no secret. In 1875, Justice Miller wrote:

> It is vain to contest with judges who have been at the bar the advocates for forty years of railroad companies, and all associated forms of capital, when they are called upon to decide cases where such interests are in contest. All their training, all their feelings are from the start in favor of those who need no such influence.[846]

Similarly, the Chief Justice of the North Carolina Supreme Court thought the influence of big business interests kept the federal courts at all levels stacked with conservative lawyers whose political views were compatible with the interests of the capitalist class.[847] For example, the appointment of Louis Brandeis was opposed by business leaders and their allies in the Republican party; the Wall Street Journal editorialized against Brandeis, Wall Street lawyers and the Harvard establishment organized opposition to the appointment with the assistance of employees of United States Steel Corporation who were dispatched to serve them.[848]

This does not mean that every "railroad judge" behaved as such once he had achieved lifetime tenure on the federal bench.[849] But such tenure was no assurance of independence; Judge Dillon of the Eighth Circuit, who wrote a treatise on federal courts and many opinions favoring railroad interests, left the bench for a lucrative career as a railroad lawyer.[850] Supreme Court Justice Brown regaled an A.B.A. convention with a speech regarding property rights that mixed laissez faire and social Darwinism, in which he praised

---

845. Assassinated

Id. at p. 306.

846. "Need no influence"

Fairman, Mr. Justice Miller and The Supreme Court, 1862–1890, 1939, p. 374.

847. Federal courts stacked

Brooks, Walter Clark, Fighting Judge, 1944, p. 198.

848. Opposition to Brandeis

Todd, Justice on Trial: The Case of Louis D. Brandeis, 1964, pp. 73, 82, 89, 106.

849. Behaved as such

Kolko, Railroads and Regulation, 1877–1916, 1965, p. 80.

850. Lucrative career

Jacobs, Law Writers and The Courts, 1954, p. 112.

wealthy capitalists and opined that only lazy workers did not own their own homes; "the desire to earn money," he argued, "lies at the bottom of the greater efforts of genius."[851] Chief Justice Taft bragged that while serving on the lower federal courts he "issued injunctions against labor unions, almost by the bushel."[852] This could be expected of a judge who thought that the greatest threat to the nation was from "those who do manual labor for a living" and who railed against the "tyranny [of] coal mining and railroad unions."[853]

The conventional wisdom among historians is that federal courts favored railroads over all other litigants during the latter half of the Nineteenth Century,[854] though some Marxist historians have argued that federal courts were naive about the real interests of railroads so that some rulings that they thought favored railroads were in fact hostile to their true interests.[855] Public outrage over the antisocial conduct of some railroads fueled popular demands for everything from public ownership to rate regulation.[856] The railroads wanted protection against political interference with their business. Federal courts, they thought, were ideally suited to provide this because they were insulated from democratic influence.[857] Railroads were able to use the federal courts to place themselves beyond state regulation of their rates and then to defeat any serious efforts by the Interstate Commerce Commission to provide federal regulation.[858]

Rate regulation was important to railroads but it was not the

851. "Efforts of genius"

Glennon, Justice Henry Billings Brown: Values in Tension, 1973, 44 Colo. L.Rev. 553–561–564.

852. "By the bushel"

Mason, William Howard Taft: Chief Justice, 1965, p . 36.

853. "Tyranny of unions"

Id. at pp. 45, 140.

854. Favored railroads

Fairman, Mr. Justice Miller and The Supreme Court, 1862–1890, 1939, p. 235.

855. Hostile in fact

Kolko, Railroads and Regulation, 1877–1916, 1965, pp. 80–81.

856. Public demands

Josephson, The Robber Barons, 1962, p. 305.

857. Insulated from influence

Magrath, Morrison R. Waite: The Triumph of Character, 1963, p. 176. One industry publication wrote that "the interest of the railroads are safe in the hands of the [federal] courts." Kolko, Railroads and Regulation, 1877–1916, 1965, p.125.

858. Defeat federal regulation

Id. at p. 166; Josephson, The Robber Barons, 1962, p. 306.

only interest they sought to further in federal courts.[859] For example, state and local governments frequently sought to escape their obligations on bonds issued to finance railroad construction on the ground that they had been defrauded by railroad promoters; in one 30-year period after the Civil War, the Supreme Court alone had more than 300 such municipal-bond cases, more than on any other subject, and usually favored the bondholders over the taxpayers.[860] A favorite device of railroad lawyers was the federal receivership.[861] Receiverships were used for everything from escaping local taxation to defeating labor unions.[862] The number of such receiverships increased dramatically after the Civil War.[863]

In defense of the Supreme Court's tilt toward corporate interests, the New York Times wrote that the "Supreme Court, by its very nature, must be a conservative body."[864] Perhaps. But "conservative" inadequately describes the general ideology of the Supreme Court in this period and, in any event, does little to explain the Court's response to the right of confrontation and other human rights. More particularly, it was said that the Court equated "liberty to a demand for limited government," seeing the state as the natural enemy of freedom rather than as a tool by which conflicting demands for "liberty" could be resolved in democratic fashion.[865] Even more relevant to the Court's attitude toward confrontation, Chief Justice Taft argued that while the Constitution had been originally drafted to protect the poor from the powerful, Jacksonian democracy had shifted so much power to ordinary Americans that it was now necessary to convert the Constitution to a device to

859. Not only interest

They also sought protection from injured consumers and workers through the removal of state personal-injury actions, as well a repression of labor unions. See § 6357, text at notecall 314.

860. Municipal bonds

2 Warren, The Supreme Court in United States History: 1836–1918, 1947, p. 532.

861. Receivership

For an example of the sort of shenanigans federal courts permitted, under the guise of receivership, see Brooks, Walter Clark, Fighting Judge, 1944, pp. 142–145.

862. Defeating unions

Fairman, Mr. Justice Miller and The Supreme Court, 1862–1890, 1939, p. 242.

863. Increased dramatically

Id. at p. 237.

864. "Must be conservative"

Todd, Justice on Trial: The Case of Louis D. Brandeis, 1964, p. 242.

865. "Limited government"

Fiss, History of the Supreme Court of The United States: Troubled Beginnings of the Modern State, 1888–1910, 1993, p. 389.

protect the rich against the leveling, what he would have called "the Bolshevik" tendencies of "the mob."[866] Finally, though we would not expect the Court to acknowledge it, this notion of "flexible constitutionalism" took a good deal from the selfish individualism of capitalists, and their enemies, that viewed the law as something to be evaded or nullified.[867]

The doctrinal basis for the Court's defense of laissez-faire capitalism is well-known, at least to constitutional law-scholars, but the numbers are revealing. Down to 1860, the Supreme Court had decided only 20 cases dealing with the Commerce Clause; but 30 years later, as that doctrine began to be used to invalidate state regulation, the number had grown to 148.[868] A study of 216 Commerce Clause cases found that in 46 of them state statutes were held unconstitutional.[869] The Due Process Clauses rose even more rapidly; in the first fifteen years after the Fourteenth Amendment went into effect, the Court decided 70 cases applying it.[870] By the end of World War I, the number had increased 1000% to nearly 800.[871]

For purposes of the right of confrontation, the feature of this due-process jurisprudence to be noted is the way in which the Court used the Fourteenth Amendment to constitutionalize common-law protections of vested interests as a means of limiting the police power of the states.[872] One of the leading constitutional-law scholars of the era argued that this was necessary because prior to the Civil War legislatures had generally followed laissez-faire principles, but that once the full impact of Jacksonian democracy had hit, only courts could protect the free-market economy.[873] This task fell to federal courts because states had increased the power of juries and

866. "Bolshevik mob"

Mason, William Howard Taft: Chief Justice, 1965, p. 46.

867. Evaded or nullified

Adams, The Theory of Social Revolutions, 1913, pp. 212, 214.

868. Grown to 148

2 Warren, The Supreme Court in United States History: 1836–1918, 1947, p. 625.

869. Held unconstitutional

Id. at p. 742.

870. Due Process

Id. at p. 599.

871. Increased 1000%

Id. at p. 741. See also, id. at p. 599.

872. Limiting police power

Jacobs, Law Writers and The Courts, 1954, p. 21.

873. Only courts protect

Paul, Conservative Crisis and The Rule of Law: Attitudes of Bar and Bench, 1887–1895, 1960, p. 25.

restricted the common law powers of their judges.[874] Hence, it was argued in the Granger Cases that the "right" to engage in business could only be limited by common law, not by statutory means.[875]

The notion that the security of property rested on common-law principles was popular with lawyers because it suggested that legislators were not competent to deal with the problems of the emerging industrial order so these should be left to lawyers and judges to resolve.[876] Indeed, James Carter, a prominent lawyer of the day, tried to construct a system of jurisprudence out of the common law that would limit the federal as well as state governments.[877] As we shall see, this renaissance of the common law made it quite natural for the Supreme Court and state courts to read the Confrontation Clause as simply incorporating the common law.[878] But this use of the common law as a check on popular government also revived the hostility to the common law that had characterized the early years of the Republic.[879] For example, Wendell Phillips wrote: "I do not believe in an English freedom, that trusts the welfare of the dependent class to the good will and moral sense of the upper class."[880] He could have been thinking of the railroad magnate who wrote:

> The rights and interests of the laboring man will be protected and cared for by the Christian men to whom God has given control of the property rights of the country.[881]

This attitude did note bode well for constitutional protection of human rights.

The Supreme Court's favoritism toward property interests is conceded in the quasi-official history of the Court.[882] Indeed, even

874. Restricted judges

Mason, William Howard Taft: Chief Justice, 1965, p. 48.

875. Only by common law

Twiss, Lawyers and The Constitution: How Laissez Faire Came To The Supreme Court, 1942, p. 83.

876. Left to judges

Id. at p. 80.

877. Carter construct

Id. at p. 182.

878. Read confrontation

See § 6357.

879. Early years

See § 6355, text at note 174.

880. "Trusts upper class"

Foner, Reconstruction: America's Unfinished Revolution, 1863–1877, 1988, p. 67.

881. "God given control"

Josephson, The Robber Barons, 1962, p. 374.

882. Favoritism conceded

Fiss, History of the Supreme Court of the United States: Troubled Beginnings of the Modern State, 1888–1910, 1993, p. 593.

the attempts by corporate lawyers to rebut claims of such bias tend to confirm it.[883] Labor unions were the private organizations most often at the butt-end of the Court's procapitalist jurisprudence; e.g., the use of a supposed "liberty of contract" to invalidate state legislation attempting to restore some balance to the employer-employee relationship.[884] The Knights of Labor bitterly resented this.

> The facts are, the great conservative masses, together with the wage earners of the country, are not represented at court; their rights, in a majority of instances, owing to the persuasive blandishments of wealth, are compromised, and it seldom happens that they are fought and contended for ... unless it should chance to be that the principles involved in the security and protection of these rights are immediately and intimately connected with issues developed in some big legal fight between two huge corporations.... [885]

Unions would become even more vituperative when, in the famous Danbury Hatters case, federal courts entered a judgment for $250,-000 for an employer against a union and the federal marshals executed judgment against the homes of employees.[886]

Not that the state courts, despite their supposed Jacksonian leanings, were that much better in striking the balance between capital and labor; for example, state courts in West Virginia were notorious for their defense of the Rockefeller mining interests until well into the 20th Century.[887] Indeed, when Learned Hand ran on the Progressive ticket for the New York Court of Appeals, his co-candidate told the press:

> The reactionary decisions of the court of appeals judges are the natural results of their mental attitude and the class bias which unconsciously dominates them.... The court of appeals declared the Workmen's Compensation Law invalid, not because it offended

883. Attempts to rebut

Burdick, Is Law The Expression of Class Selfishness?, 1912, 25 Harv.L.Rev. 349.

884. "Liberty of contract"

Jacobs, Law Writers and The Courts, 1954, p. 64.

885. "Big legal fight"

David, The History of The Haymarket Affair, 1963, p. 55.

886. Against the homes

Todd, Justice on Trial: The Case of Louis D. Brandeis, 1964, pp. 10, 36.

887. West Virginia

Harbaugh, Lawyer's Lawyer: The Life of John W. Davis, 1973, p. 46.

any provision of the Constitution, but because they disapproved of the policy of such legislation.[888]

Perhaps if the attention devoted by historians to the Supreme Court had been equally lavished on state courts, we might see that they, too, preferred an economic to a moral constituency.[889]

For many, the Supreme Court's devotion to its economic constituency is exemplified by the manner in which it accepted the argument of elite lawyers, like David Dudley Field, that the Fourteenth Amendment was designed to protect the economic freedom of corporations, not the political freedom of the Freedmen.[890] It was rare for elite lawyers to advocate civil liberties, as the career of Moorfield Storey demonstrates.[891] Justice Brown of the Supreme Court, who objected to a subpoena for corporate documents as an illegal search and seizure, had no use for the civil rights of human beings, especially those who were foreign born.[892] Chief Justice Taft thought that property rights were preferred freedoms, but dismissed the rights of criminal defendants as "mere fetish."[893] This hostility to the rights of ordinary persons spread to the lower courts; when a North Carolina newspaper editor dared to criticize the rulings of a federal judge, he was cited for contempt, thrown in jail, and denied the right to seek review of his imprisonment.[894]

Though some historians carelessly attribute judicial hostility to human rights to political conservatism, it has been said with some justification that one of the major failings of the 19th Century liberalism was a preoccupation with political oppression and disregard of social and economic oppression.[895] For examples, liberals as

888. "They disapproved"

Mitgang, The Man Who Rode The Tiger: The Life and Times of Judge Samuel Seabury, 1963, p. 106. Though Judge Hand was not delighted by this platform at the time, he later conceded that this may have been a mistake on his part. Ibid.

889. Moral constituency

That is, the court saw its task as serving the economic interests of the nation rather than as exemplifying its political morality.

890. Not Freedmen

Magrath, Morrison R. Waite: The Triumph of Character, 1963, p. 129.

891. Storey demonstrates

Hixson, Moorfield Storey and The Abolitionist Tradition, 1972, p. 39.

892. Justice Brown

Glennon, Justice Henry Billings Brown: Values in Tension, 1973, 44 Colo. L.Rev. 553, 593.

893. Chief Justice Taft

Mason, William Howard Taft: Chief Justice, 1965, p. 48.

894. Editor jailed

Brooks, Walter Clark, Fighting Judge, 1944, p. 146.

895. Failings of liberalism

Hixson, Moorfield Storey and The Abolitionist Tradition, 1972, p. 200.

well as conservatives denounced statutes limiting the workday to eight hours as "class legislation."[896] A good illustration of the liberal bind is Justice Brandeis, who early in his career argued that too many lawyers were deployed to protect property rights.[897] Yet early in the 20th Century he thought it was news that the Supreme Court favored property rights over human rights.[898] When Brandeis was firmly ensconced on the Supreme Court and in a position to do something about this imbalance, he claimed to be trapped by the morality of role, writing:

> It may be morally wrong to use legal processes, great financial resources, and a high intelligence to lower miners' standards of living; but so long as the law sanctions it, economic force may not be repelled by physical force.[899]

From enforcement of the Fugitive Slave Laws to the demand in the 1950s for "neutral constitutional principles," a cramped and generally unexamined notion of the judicial role has been the excuse of those trapped between class loyalty and the demands of justice.[900]

The last word on this topic belongs to Brooks Adams:

> I should not suppose that any man could calmly turn over the pages of the recent volumes of the reports of the Supreme Court of the United States and not rise from the perusal convinced that the rich and the poor, the strong and the weak, do not receive a common measure of justice before that judgment seat.[901]

By the time that was written, the Supreme Court had already begun to defang the Confrontation Clause.

The Great Upheaval

In 1883, in The Civil Rights Cases, the Supreme Court displayed the influence of Social Darwinism on American legal

896. "Class legislation"

David, The History of The Haymarket Affair, 1963, p. 152.

897. Too many lawyers

Todd, Justice on Trial: The Case of Louis D. Brandeis, 1964, p. 68.

898. Thought it news

Levy & Murphy, Preserving The Progressive Spirit in a Conservative Time: The Joint Reform Efforts of Justice Brandeis and Professor Frankfurter, 1916–1933, 1980, 78 Mich. L.Rev. 1252, 1285.

899. "May not be repelled"

Cover, The Left, The Right and The First Amendment: 1918–19218, 1981, 40 Md.L.Rev. 349.

900. Judicial role

For a more sophisticated analysis, see Cover, Justice Accused: Antislavery and the Judicial Process, 1975.

901. "Rich and the poor"

Adams, The Theory of Social Revolutions, 1913, p. 107.

thought.[902] At about the same time, Fredrick Taylor was holding a stopwatch on a worker in a series of experiments to see how far human beings could be made to resemble machines.[903] Whether or not men could be merged with machines, the biological and mechanical theories of society could—with profound significance for the right of confrontation.

Had workers been aware of Taylor's attempts to see how much bosses could wring out of them, their conditions would have seemed even worse than it was.[904] Despite some improvement in wages since the postwar depression, the average worker did not earn enough to maintain a family at much above a subsistence level.[905] Spied upon by Pinkertons and rousted by the police after the strikes of 1877 were crushed, workers were in no mood to endure another tightening of the economic screws.[906] When the Panic of 1884 brought another round of ruinous competition that threatened profits, management again shifted the costs of the economic downturn from shareholders to workers with a set of drastic pay cuts.[907]

Workers struck back in a series of walkouts that quickly spread to the mines and other industries, setting off a two year period of labor strife that historians call "The Great Upheaval."[908] Though these strikes were largely spontaneous responses of non-unionized workers, union membership soared.[909] Public opinion initially fa-

902. Civil Rights Cases

Horan, Political and Sociological Theory As Influences Upon Judicial Policy-making: The Civil Rights Cases of 1883, 1972, 16 Am.J.Leg.Hist. 71, 82.

903. Taylor stopwatch

Garaty, The New Commonwealth, 1877–1890, 1968, pp. 128–129.

904. Worker's conditions

Friedman, A History of American Law, 1973, pp. 484–485.

905. Did not earn enough

Garraty, The New Commonwealth, 1877–1890, 1968, p. 129. The Massachusetts Bureau of Labor Statistics reported: "[a] family of workers can always live well, but the man with a family of small children to support, unless his wife works also, has a small chance of living properly." Id. at pp. 129–130.

906. No mood to endure

Friedman, A History of American Law, 1973, p. 486.

907. Panic of 1884

Josephson, The Robber Barons, 1962, p. 293; Brecher, Strike!, 1972, p. 26; Kolko, Railroads and Regulation, 1877–1916, 1965, p. 30.

908. "Great Upheaval"

Garraty, The New Commonwealth, 1877–1890, 1968, p. 164; David, The History of The Haymarket Affair, 1963, p. 21. Brecher uses this phrase to refer to the strikes of 1877. Brecher, Strike!, 1972, 1.

909. Membership soared

Brecher, Strike!, 1972, pp. 16, 28; Garaty, The New Commonwealth, 1877–1890, 1968, p. 165.

vored the workers——so much so that several Midwestern governors sided with labor.[910] As a result, as powerful a figure as Jay Gould was forced for a time to back off.[911] However, such modest successes as the strikers could claim were outweighed by a distressing lack of solidarity among the dispossessed that, in turn, led desperate men to resort to violence that quickly dissolved the temporary support of the public.[912]

By the portentous year of 1886, the Great Upheaval had grown from less than 450 strikes to more than 1400.[913] Using techniques honed since the labor unrest of 1877, employers quashed most of these strikes with a combination of legal action in the courts and extralegal violence by the police and private armies.[914] Chicago police fired on a group of strikers, killing three of them.[915] Local anarchists called for a mass meeting, which produced a heavy police presence but only about 3,000 demonstrators. As the crowd was dispersing peacefully after listening to radical harangues against the police and employers, the police marched in with clubs swinging; someone threw a bomb that killed one officer and wounded several others——and effectively put an end to the Great Upheaval.[916]

The so-called "Haymarket bombing" combined three forces much feared by the better off——radicals, foreigners, and workers.[917] The seismograph of middle-class anxiety went off the chart, shifting public opinion from sympathy to repression.[918] Though the identity of the bomber remains a mystery, several prominent anarchists were charged with being accessories to the bombing; after a controversial trial before a jury that had been packed by a hostile bailiff

---

910. Sided with labor

Garraty, The New Commonwealth, 1877–1890, pp. 164–165.

911. Gould back off

Id. at p. 164.

912. Violence dissolved

Id. at p. 165.

913. More than 1400

Brecher, Strike!, 1972, p. 31; Paul, Conservative Crisis and the Rule of Law: Attitudes of Bench and Bar, 1877–1895, 1960, p. 19.

914. Employers quashed

Brecher, Strike!, 1972, pp. 34–35.

915. Chicago police

Furnas, The Americans: A Social History of the United States, 1587–1914, 1969, p. 715.

916. Threw a bomb

Ibid.

917. Three forces

Wiebe, The Search for Order: 1917–1920, 1967, p. 78–79.

918. Shifted public opinion

David, The History of The Haymarket Affair, 1963, p. 180.

and an equally biased judge, several were hung and the rest sentenced to life imprisonment.[919] The trial allowed the press to tar labor unions and other radicals with the image of violent anarchism and, for purposes of the confrontation clause, further blackened the reputation of trial by jury.[920] The Great Upheaval began a period of social tension that lasted to the eve of the Supreme Court's most important confrontation decision.[921]

Capitalists were alarmed, but they were able to use the continuing crisis to accomplish two goals.[922] First, labor unions were discredited by a propaganda campaign that linked them to Haymarket——though unions had little to do with it and labor leaders denounced it.[923] Second, the railroads made great strides, with the assistance of the federal government, in regulating and cartelizing their industry to protect it from the uncertainties of the market.[924] The middle class found little succor for their anxieties; many feared the country was on the brink of a violent revolution of anarchists or communists.[925] Such hopes as they had focused on the President because he controlled the military and appointed the members of the Supreme Court.[926] Legal writers peddled judicial power as a panacea for their anxieties, one writing that "the efforts of the courts ... is our only means of defense against the inordinate demands of socialism" and another that they were "the only breakwater against the haste and passion of the people."[927] Thus was the stage set for the Panic of 1893, the Pullman and Home-

---

919. Biased judge and jury

Id. at pp. 10–11, 204, 292.

920. Image of violent anarchy

Paul, Conservative Crisis and The Rule of Law: Attitudes of Bench and Bar, 1877–1895, 1960, p. 20.

921. Period of social tension

Id. at p. 1; Hixson, Moorfield Storey and The Abolitionist Tradition, 1972, p. 46.

922. Capitalists alarmed

Garraty, The New Commonwealth, 1877–1890, 1968, p. 166.

923. Leaders denounced

Id. at p. 167; Furnas, The Americans: A Social History of the United States, 1587–1914, 1969, p._716.

924. Protect from uncertainties

Kolko, Railroads and Regulation: 1877–1916, 1965, p. 30.

925. Brink of revolution

Wiebe, The Search for Order: 1877–1920, 1967, p. 72.

926. Focused on President

Id. at p. 80.

927. "Only breakwater"

Wigdor, Roscoe Pound, 1974, p. 73.

stead strikes, and the Supreme Court's response to these and the Confrontation Clause.[928]

Meanwhile, sympathy for rights like confrontation waned as fear generated enthusiasm for the repressive power of the state. Rather than raise wages, corporate leaders donated money to help build up the National Guard.[929] Police resorted to a sort of "officialized vigilantism," using the night stick and the sap rather than the courts to enforce order.[930] Even legal academics wanted to scrap the First Amendment if that was what was necessary to stamp out dangerous thought.[931]

Judges, too, were afraid and did not understand the grievances that produced class conflict.[932] They became intolerant of lawyers who represented members of the underclass, throwing them in jail for contempt to discourage a too vigorous use of the adversary system and rights like confrontation.[933] The public supposed that dangerous criminals escaped punishment by resorting to "legal technicalities."[934] Even Chief Justice Taft denounced "loopholes" in criminal law and procedure.[935] Attitudes like these soon produced a one-sided use of supposedly neutral criminal law to punish workers while ignoring similar transgressions by employers.[936] Liberalization of labor laws ceased in many states.[937] Such evidence that judges favored business interests over those of workers and ordi-

---

928. Panic and Homestead

Fiss, History of the Supreme Court of the United States: Troubled Beginnings of the Modern State, 1888–1910, 1993, p. 57.

929. Build up National Guard

Kolko, Railroads and Regulation: 1877–1916, 1965, p. 13.

930. Using sap to enforce

Vanderbilt, Changing Law: A Biography of Arthur T. Vanderbilt, 1977, p. 49.

931. Stamp out thought

Wigdor, Roscoe Pound, 1974, p. 91.

932. Did not understand

Friedman, A History of American Law, 1973, p. 399.

933. Throwing in jail

Vanderbilt, Changing Law: A Biography of Arthur T. Vanderbilt, 1977, p. 51.

934. "Technicalities"

Wigdor, Roscoe Pound, 1974, p. 150.

935. "Loopholes"

Mason, William Howard Taft: Chief Justice, 1965, p. 49.

936. One-sided use

For example, workers who struck or boycotted were prosecuted for conspiracy, but employers who combined to "blacklist" union members were seldom punished for conspiracy, even though the law would have permitted this in most states. David, The History of The Haymarket Affair, 1963, p. 38.

937. Liberalization ceased

Id. at pp. 52, 54.

nary citizens did little to discourage the sentiment for revolution, or at least radical change.[938]

But Haymarket seemed to show that domestic radicalism had little appeal to alienated workers.[939] Indeed, the Haymarket trials may have blurred the distinction between "import" and "domestic" radicalism—at least for the general public.[940] Certainly historians have devoted far more attention to import radicalism, perhaps as a result of the peculiar inferiority complex that leads many intellectuals to prefer German cars, French wine, and English universities regardless of the evidence suggesting that their superiority is, if not nonexistent, at least overrated.[941] This is difficult to explain because even the Haymarket anarchists appreciated the appeal of our domestic tradition of radicalism, invoking the Declaration of Independence to justify their opposition to capitalism.[942]

Domestic radicalism, not surprisingly, shared some of the same values as capitalism. As Emerson observed, some Americans were "fanatics in freedom; they hated tolls, taxes, turnpikes, banks, hierarchies, governors, yea almost laws."[943] Domestic radicalism was rural rather than urban, rooted in some of the same Protestant values that supported confrontation, and was found mostly among old stock whites. Redneck radicals in Oklahoma and Texas provided many of the footsoldiers for the Populist movement, though they were strongly anarchistic. However, they persevered beyond the demise of Populism; a survey of Oklahoma prisoners early in the next century found they supported the socialist candidate, Eugene Debs, over either the Republican or Democratic candidates. The repression of redneck radicalism by government and vigilante repression has been thought by some historians to explain why Oklahoma once led the nation in the number of bank robberies.

938. Favored business

Id. at p. 55.

939. Little appeal

David, The History of The Haymarket Affair, 1963, p. 76.

940. Blurred distinction

Paul, Conservative Crisis and The Rule of Law: Attitudes of Bar and Bench, 1887–1895, 1960, p. 20.

941. More attention

Woodward, Home-grown Radicals, N.Y.Rev.Bks., April 5, 1979, p. 3.

942. Invoking Declaration

David, The History of The Haymarket Affair, 1963, p. 93.

943. "Almost laws"

This quotation is taken from, and this paragraph is based upon, Woodward, Home-grown Radicals, N.Y.Rev.Bks., April 5, 1979, p. 3.

Import radicalism, particularly when Marxist in nature, tended to be fatalistic, if not deterministic. During this period import anarchism romanticized what was called "propaganda by the deed"——a euphemism for terrorism and assassination of prominent individuals.[944] Though the anarchist faith in ritualistic acts of revolution might have some remote relation to the ritual of confrontation, anonymous bombthrowing ran very much against confrontation values.[945]

Radical thought had little to do with the future of confrontation. "Taylorism"——or "scientific management" as he preferred to call it——carried more influence.[946] Taylorism, which could claim to be "scientific" because of its roots in engineering, gave rise to the notion of "management"——a concept that downplayed the property interest of employers in favor of a social definition of their function that bore only a slight relationship to the "stewardship" theory of Christianity or the "trusteeship" principle of corporate law.[947] This quasi-governmental vision of capitalism played into the decisions of judges in strengthening the hand of "management" at the expense of workers, hardened the existing anti-union animus of the courts, and served to legitimate many of the self-help devices corporate lawyers had devised to aid in the subjugation of workers.[948]

On the other hand, it soon became apparent that Taylorism might enable engineers and economists to supplant lawyers as the principal apologists for capitalism.[949] Legal thinkers like Roscoe Pound moved to head off this threat by co-opting it with a reconceptualization of lawyers as "social engineers." Felix Frankfurter nicely expressed this legal version of Taylorism when he wrote:

> The public can be represented only by the dedication of the services of the social scientist.... [W]e must see these industrial

944. "Propaganda by deed"

Furnas, The Americans: A Social History of the United States, 1587–1914, 1969, p. 714.

945. Faith in ritualistic

David, The History of the Haymarket Affair, 1963, p. 68.

946. "Scientific management"

Taylor, The Principles of Scientific Management, 1911.

947. Corporate law

Heilbroner, Getting Down To Business, N.Y.Rev.Bks., February 9, 1978, p. 36.

948. Subjugation of workers

Friedman, A History of American Law, 1973, pp. 488 (anti-union animus), 489; David, The History of The Haymarket Affair, 1963, pp. 49–51 (self-help devices).

949. Supplant lawyers

Wigdor, Roscoe Pound, 1974, p. 210.

difficulties as a challenge to social engineering, to be grappled with as the medical and physical sciences meet their problems.[950]

In terms of confrontation, legal Taylorism not only elevated the judge at the expense of the jury, but also gave rise to the belief that the law was a system of social control that must be freed of moral underpinnings if it was to be scientific.[951] The reformism inherent in social engineering appealed to the anxieties of the middle class and their desire to see society as orderly, functioning in accordance with rational laws, but it was antithetical to the traditional values embodied in confrontation.[952]

At the time of the Great Upheaval, the threat of Taylorism remained incipient; at the moment legal ideologues had their hands full with such quasi-populist responses as the Michigan statute of 1885 that made it a crime for employers to "take advantage of the poverty of misfortune of any employee or one seeking employment."[953] One response to efforts to level the playing field between capital and labor was to denounce them as a biased expression of "class interest."[954] Another was to heap praise on judges who conspicuously sided with capital in the struggle.[955] The Great Upheaval had made antiworker bias respectable; even a staid publication like the Albany Law Journal could claim that strikes were analogous to lynching.[956] Legal scholars, including Wigmore, supported the criminalization of boycotts by unions——though not by employers.[957] Eventually popular unrest, such as the Great Upheaval, would provide an excuse for judicial "reform" and procedural "change"——changes such as increasing the admissibility of hearsay that threatened the right of confrontation.[958]

950. "Social engineering"

Note, The Democratic Faith of Felix Frankfurter, 1973, 25 Stan.L.Rev. 430, 434–435.

951. System of social control

Twining, Karl Llewellyn and The Realist Movement, 1973, p. 50.

952. Society as orderly

Wiebe, The Search For Order: 1877–1920, 1967, p. 62.

953. "Take advantage of"

David, The History of The Haymarket Affair, 1963, p. 42.

954. "Class interest"

Wigdor, Roscoe Pound, 1974, p. 217.

955. Praise judges

Id. at p. 219.

956. Strikes as lynching

David, The History of The Haymarket Affair, 1963, p. 49.

957. Wigmore supported

Id. at p. 54.

958. "Reform" and "change"

Mason, William Howard Taft: Chief Justice, 1965, p. 53.

At the moment, talk of "reform" sent shivers up the spines of conservatives already nervous from the symbolic attacks on property launched by anarchists like those involved in Haymarket.[959] Of course, stability of property rights had been a concern as far back as the Revolutionary era.[960] But the notion of an absolute right of property free from governmental regulation that was pushed by corporate lawyers after the Civil War was quite revolutionary.[961] The notion that there was no conflict between property rights and the public interest had taken a beating during the conflict over Emancipation.[962] One Congressman declared during debate:

> I could not lie down on my bed at night with a clear conscience if I had been guilty of being engaged as a participant in robbing a portion of the people of this country of millions of dollars invested under the Constitution in property in negroes.[963]

Proposals to confiscate rebel property were similarly described as "robbery."[964] Even Republicans unwilling to view Emancipation with shame vowed to oppose any further changes in rights of property.[965]

But at the same time the Freedmen had raised a profound threat to property by their claims that their uncompensated contributions to the Southern economy entitled them to their share of Southern property.[966] Lawyers saw at once the revolutionary implications of what they denounced as "mere nonsense."[967] As one of them said "as well may the Irish laborer claim New York city because by his labor all the stores and residences there were constructed. Or claim our railroads because they labored on them with their shovels and wheelbarrows."[968]

959. Symbolic attacks

David, The History of The Haymarket Affair, 1963, p. 68.

960. Stability of property

Wigdor, Roscoe Pound, 1974, p. 8.

961. Revolutionary

White, From Sociological Jurisprudence to Realism: Jurisprudence and Social Change in Early Twentieth Century America, 1972, 58 Va.L.Rev. 999, 1002.

962. No conflict

Wigdor, Roscoe Pound, 1974, p. 92.

963. "Robbing people"

Brodie, Thaddeus Stevens: Scourge of the South, 1959, p. 243.

964. "Robbery"

Id. at p. 304.

965. Oppose further change

Id. at p. 249.

966. Entitled to share

Foner, Nothing But Freedom: Emancipation and Its Legacy, 1983, p. 54.

967. "Mere nonsense"

Id. at p. 56.

968. "Claim New York"

Id. at p. 57.

The Freedmen's claim ran counter to the insistence that "labour's product ... be seen as something totally distinct, the property of landowner or employer."[969] Worse than this attack on what Marx had called the "appropriation of labor" was the ability of some Freedmen to turn the anti-Emancipationist claim on its head; that is, if confiscation was "robbery," then robbery was a sort of self-help confiscation—a reclaiming of what one was entitled to under the Freedmen's indigenous version of the "labor theory of value."[970] Hence, it was a necessary to strengthen the criminal law against such attempts at "emancipation" of the employer's property.[971] Confrontation stood as an obstacle to the use of criminal law as the last bulwark of property rights. Little wonder then that attitudes toward property came to be something of a litmus test for Supreme Court nominees. As one capitalist said, "[t]here are so many jack-asses about now days who think property has no rights, that the filling of Supreme Court vacancies is the most important function of the Presidential office."[972] Hence, those who wanted to dismantle traditional procedural protections, such as confrontation, had to reassure capitalists that they understood that law must "provide assured constancy of the conditions under which property is held and business is carried on."[973]

§ 6357. ___; The Tumultuous Nineties*

By the last quarter of the Nineteenth Century, long before the United States Supreme Court issued its first definitive ruling on

969. "Totally distinct"

Id. at p. 57.

970. Self-help confiscation

Id. at p. 58.

971. Strengthen criminal law

Ibid.

972. "So many jack asses"

Kirkland, Dream and Thought in The Business Community: 1860–1900, 1964, p. 135.

973. "Assured constancy"

Wigdor, Roscoe Pound, 1974, p. 263.

§ 6357

* This is a long section. For the convenience of readers looking for a specific topic, this outline may help; the numbers indicate the notecall at which the topic begins.

the Sixth Amendment right of confrontation, state courts interpreting state confrontation clauses had developed an extensive but not entirely consistent body of confrontation jurisprudence.[1] During the period from the end of Reconstruction to the end of the Century, state courts decided more cases than in the previous 100 years.[2] However, with few exceptions, these cases added little to the prior caselaw and can safely be discussed as a whole rather than individually.[3] We shall look first to what these cases say about the theory of confrontation, then turn to specific holdings on the admissibility of different forms of hearsay.

State courts remained split over the source of the right of confrontation.[4] Some courts insisted that confrontation is "no American invention" but was brought over on the Mayflower; hence, it "is the right as it existed at common law that was * * * secured" by state confrontation clauses.[5] This questionable history was sometimes attributed to Cooley.[6] Courts adopted this view because it avoided questions about the relationship between the hearsay rule and the right of confrontation.[7]

Other courts correctly rejected an English origin for the right of confrontation, noting that "our theory of government is constructed upon a basis fundamentally at variance with the principles

1. Body of jurisprudence

See § 6355, text at notecalls 339, 684, 799; § 6356, text at notecalls 11, 155, 237, 318, 473.

2. More cases

By our count, 31 cases in the earlier period and 35 down to the end of the century. Reasonable persons could differ as to our characterization of some of these cases.

3. Added little

One novel line of authority consists of cases addressing the applicability of the Sixth Amendment to the states. As we saw in § 6356, the Radical Republicans thought the Fourteenth Amendment extended the protection of the Bill of Rights to state courts. State courts generally rejected this notion. See People v. Fish, 1891, 26 N.E. 319, 125 N.Y. 136; Ryan v. People, 1895, 40 Pac. 775, 21 Col. 119.

4. Source of confrontation

For our views on this question, see vol. 30, § 6345, p. 562.

5. "Right at common law"

Jackson v. State, 1892, 51 N.W. 89, 91, 81 Wis. 127.

6. Attributed to Cooley

State v. Saunders, 1886, 12 Pac. 441, 14 Or. 300. On Cooley's views, see § 6356, text at notecall 237.

7. Confrontation and hearsay

On the primitive state of the hearsay rule at the time the right of confrontation was adopted, see § 6355, text at notecall 100.

of the British government."[8] As a Texas court observed, the confrontation clauses were adopted when the colonies had recently broken their ties to England:

> Not satisfied with the Magna Charta of English liberty and rights, the American people ordained and instituted a Magna Charta of their own rights and liberties * * *. They did not subordinate themselves to laws of the country from which they had so recently forcibly separated themselves.[9]

When faced with a claim that English practice allowed the use of depositions in criminal cases, the Michigan Supreme Court dismissed the argument on the ground that there was no right of confrontation in England, except by statute in treason cases.[10]

During the last quarter of the Nineteenth Century some courts began to adopt the interpretation of the confrontation that came to be associated with Wigmore; that is, the right of confrontation simply gives the defendant the right to cross-examine such witnesses as the prosecution chooses to call.[11] But other courts flatly rejected this interpretation in favor of the holistic view of the Bill of Rights favored by the Founders.[12] After collecting and quoting from other state cases, the Utah Supreme Court held it was "well established" that "one accused of a felony cannot be convicted

8. "At variance with the British"

Cline v. State, 1896, 36 S.W. 1099, 1105, 36 Tex.Crim. 320.

9. "Did not subordinate"

Id. at 1106. The court correctly notes that the state constitutions created "rights, some of which were unknown to the law 'as it existed at that time' of their adoption." Ibid.

10. No right in England

Sligh v. People, 1882, 11 N.W. 782, 783, 48 Mich. 54, 57.

11. Right to cross

Wray v. State, 1908, 45 So. 697, 698, 154 Ala. 36 (collecting earlier cases adopting this view); State v. Kindle, Ohio 1890, 24 N.E. 485, 486, 47 Ohio St. 358.

12. Holistic view

"The constitutional right to be confronted by witnesses against him, and to defend in person, would be of little avail to the accused if he could be compelled to remain away during his trial, out of sight and hearing of the witnesses against him. The right to defend in person would be a meaningless term if the accused is required to remain so far away from the witnesses that he cannot hear the testimony, and therefore cannot cross-examine them. The right of having counsel in his defense would amount to but little if the accused is required to remain so far away from him that he cannot confer with him concerning the testimony that is being given against him. The jury had a right to know whether the witness herself knew the facts stated by her from her own knowledge and recollection * * *." State v. Mannion, 1899, 57 Pac. 542, 544, 19 Utah 505.

except on the testimony of witnesses whom * * * he has had the opportunity of meeting face to face and openly examining and cross-examining in the presence of the parties and the jury."[13] This view did not, as we shall see, prevail.[14]

Some of the courts embracing the Wigmorean position coupled it with the older notion that a hearsay declarant was not a "witness against" the accused within the meaning of the confrontation clauses.[15] For example, in holding that a dying declaration was admissible, the New York Court of Appeals wrote that the Founders

> doubtless intended to confer upon the defendant in a criminal action the right to be confronted with any living witness against him. * * * It is invariably held that the deceased is not a witness within the meaning of such a provision of the bill of rights, and that it is sufficient if the defendant is confronted with the witness who testifies to the declaration.[16]

This rationale was not limited to dying declarations or to courts that took the Wigmorean view.[17]

Another argument that acquired greater force with the passage of time was the argument from desuetude; that is, since the confrontation clause had never been used before to bar the admission of hearsay, this proves that no one ever thought this was a permissible reading.[18] For example, the New York Court of Appeals wrote that in providing a right of confrontation,

> [w]e do not think the legislature intended to abolish the rule governing the admission of dying declarations. We are not aware that this question has ever been raised before in this state * * *.
> The right of the accused to be confronted with the witness against

---

13. "In presence of jury"

Id. at pp. 543, 544. The dissent advanced the Wigmorean view. Id. at p. 545.

14. Did not prevail

The court held that confrontation did not allow a child witness to testify out of the presence of the accused.

15. Not "witness against"

"It follows from this that the person making [the hearsay statement] is not, but the person by whom they are proven is, the witness. Hence, the witness by whom the accused has the right to be confronted, is the one used

to lay the foundation for the proof of the declaration, and by whom the making of the declaration is established." State v. Kindle, Ohio 1890, 24 N.E. 485, 486, 47 Ohio St. 358.

16. "Witness who testifies"

People v. Corey, N.Y. 1898, 51 N.E. 1024, 1029, 157 N.Y. 332.

17. Not limited

See § 6356, text at notecalls 556, 559.

18. No one ever thought

State v. Baldwin, 1896, 45 Pac. 650, 651, 15 Wash. 15.

him has always been a part of the bill of rights, and yet dying declarations have been received in evidence for time out of mind.[19]

In a similar vein, the Oregon Supreme Court wrote:

> This character of testimony has been regarded as competent for a very long time——long before the adoption of the constitutional guaranty * * * and has been universally admitted since,——and we could not determine that the bill of rights contained in the constitution of this state had changed the rule without admitting great arrogance upon our part.[20]

The argument from desuetude might have seemed less persuasive if the courts had realized that it was itself somewhat bewhiskered.[21]

Turning to the state confrontation clauses and hearsay, the one kind of hearsay that courts have found barred by the right of confrontation is the deposition of a witness.[22] However, some state constitutions expressly authorized the use of depositions.[23] The apparent unanimity of the caselaw, however, is deceiving. In the first place, many of the cases involve dicta——often in a case where it is the defendant who seeks to use a deposition.[24] In the second place, it is not always clear from the opinions what the court means by "deposition." In only one of the cases was the "deposition" one taken on interrogatories in the absence of the defendant of the sort that so upset the Founders in the Vice–Admiralty courts.[25] None-

19. "Time out of mind"

People v. Corey, 1898, 51 N.E. 1024, 1029, 157 N.Y. 332.

20. "Great arrogance"

State v. Saunders, 1886, 12 Pac. 441, 442, 14 Or. 300.

21. Bewhiskered

The argument had been made from the earliest confrontation decisions. See § 6355, text at note 800.

22. Deposition barred

For an earlier holding, see Summons v. State, 1856, 5 Ohio St. 325, 341.

23. Constitutions authorized

Ryan v. People, 1895, 40 Pac. 775, 21 Col. 119.

24. Defendant who seeks

Watkins v. U.S., 1897, 50 Pac. 88, 89, 5 Okla. 729 (depositions taken in land

office proceeding); Woodruff v. State, 1895, 32 S.W. 102, 105, 61 Ark. 157 (deposition taken by state in civil action); Anderson v. State, 1890, 7 So. 429, 89 Ala. 12 (deposition of aged and infirm witness taken on interrogatories by defendant; barred when offered by state); Tucker v. People, 1887, 13 N.E. 809, 122 Ill. 583 (pure dictum); Kaelin v. Commonwealth, 1886, 1 S.W. 594, 599, 84 Ky. 354 (not error to refuse continuance to take depositions of witness abroad for defendant).

25. Upset Founders

State v. Tomblin, 1897, 48 Pac. 144, 57 Kan. 841 (deposition taken on interrogatories of witness in another state by defendant; error to allow state to use). On the views of Founders, see vol. 30, § 6345, pp. 514–529.

theless, some of the holdings are quite strong; e.g., the state cannot use a deposition even though it was one taken by the defendant.[26] However, one court held, correctly it would seem, that where the defendant is charged with perjury, the confrontation clause does not prevent the stenographer from reading his notes of the perjured testimony to the jury.[27]

At the other extreme, courts all agreed that the confrontation clauses did not bar the admission of dying declarations.[28] However, confrontation values may have led some courts to insist that the hearsay exception be narrowly construed.[29] Courts differed, however, in their justifications for permitting the use of dying declarations. For some, such declarations were not within the terms of the confrontation clause; that is, the deceased person was not a "witness against" the accused.[30] Other courts treated dying declarations as an "exception" to the right of confrontation.[31] This was sometimes supported by the argument that since the exception was recognized in common law, the Founders must have intended to maintain the exception when they adopted the supposed "common law right" of confrontation.[32] Others justified the exception under the doctrine of desuetude;[33] as one court put it, the exception has been so often applied after the adoption of confrontation clauses, admissibility is "well settled" and no longer an open question.[34]

State courts generally approved the admissibility of former testimony in the face of a confrontation challenge.[35] This was

26. Taken by defendant

Ibid.; Anderson v. State, 1890, 7 So. 429, 89 Ala. 12.

27. Perjured testimony

Cutter v. Territory, 1899, 56 Pac. 861, 8 Okla. 101.

28. Dying declarations

For earlier cases, see § 6355, text at notecalls 800, 822; § 6356, text at notecalls 556, 787.

29. Narrowly construed

State v. Vansant, 1883, 80 Mo. 67.

30. Not "witness"

State v. Kindle, 1890, 24 N.E. 485, 486, 47 Ohio St. 358.

31. Exception

Government v. Hering, 1893, 9 Haw. 181.

32. "Common law right"

Jackson v. State, 1892, 51 N.W. 89, 81 Wis. 127.

33. Exception and desuetude

People v. Corey, 1898, 51 N.E. 1024, 1029, 157 N.Y. 332; State v. Saunders, 1886, 12 Pac. 441, 14 Or. 300.

34. "Well settled"

State v. Baldwin, 1896, 45 Pac. 650, 651, 15 Wash. 15.

35. Former testimony

For earlier cases, see § 6355, text at notecall 823; § 6356, text at notecalls 787, 789.

sometimes justified as an exception to the right of confrontation that had been sanctioned by the common law, at least in cases in which the declarant was now dead.[36] However, a few courts held that the confrontation clause was satisfied by the defendant's presence and opportunity to cross-examine at the first trial.[37] Courts taking this position were able to justify the use of former testimony on a less stringent showing of unavailability of the declarant; e.g., where the declarant was not dead but merely beyond the court's subpoena power.[38]

Perhaps because of its inquisitorial origins and practices, courts did not agree on the application of the confrontation clause to testimony given at a preliminary examination before a justice of the peace.[39] Despite its lack of common-law roots, courts were willing to find confrontation was satisfied—at least where the defendant had actually cross-examined and the declarant was dead at the time of the trial.[40] Other courts found it sufficient that the declarant failed to appear at trial.[41] One court held that where the witness did appear at trial but was reluctant to testify as the prosecution desired, the prosecution could go through his testimony at the previous hearing, item by item and ask whether he had so testified—a tactic condemned by the modern Supreme Court.[42]

Despite significant differences between the preliminary hearing and the trial, many courts held that confrontation at the preliminary hearing satisfied the confrontation requirement; in some the witness was now dead and the defendant had actually cross-examined him at the preliminary hearing.[43] But other courts held opportunity to cross-examine at the preliminary hearing satisfied

---

36. Declarant dead

Jackson v. State, 51 N.W. 89, 81 Wis. 127; Sligh v. People, 1882, 11 N.W. 782, 48 Mich. 54.

37. Confrontation satisfied

Gillespie v. People, 1898, 52 N.E. 250, 176 Ill. 238.

38. Beyond power

Commonwealth v. Cleary, 1892, 23 Atl. 1110, 1112, 148 Pa. 26.

39. Preliminary examination

For earlier cases, see § 6356, text at notes 556, 559.

40. Dead at time

State v. Byers, 1895, 41 Pac. 708, 16 Mont. 565.

41. Failed to appear

People v. Fish, 1891, 26 N.E. 319, 125 N.Y. 136 (dictum).

42. Tactic condemned

People v. Case, 1895, 62 N.W. 1017, 105 Mich. 92. Compare Douglas v. Alabama, 1965, 85 S.Ct. 1074, 380 U.S. 415, 13 L.Ed.2d 934.

43. Actually cross-examined

State v. Byers, 1895, 41 Pac. 708, 16 Mont. 565.

the confrontation clause, whether the witness was dead or merely absent[44]—even in one case where the witness had been allowed to depart the state after the preliminary examination.[45] One court even extended this view of confrontation to a coroner's hearing where the defendant was unrepresented by counsel.[46]

Among the courts taking a contrary position was one of the few federal courts to be heard on the question. The court wrote:

> I have found no case where the testimony of a witness, absent but living, given at a former trial, has been allowed to be proved at a subsequent trial. * * * And I think the law must be held to be that when the witness is living he must be produced or his testimony cannot be received in criminal cases, even if he be beyond the jurisdiction of the court or the United States. * * * Nor can it fairly be maintained that, if the witness has once been confronted with the accused, before the committing magistrate, that the requirements or guarantees of the constitution are answered.[47]

A minority of state courts took a similar position, in one case even where the declarant was dead.[48] However, state courts soon found the federal precedents trending in the opposite direction as federal courts took an increasing role in repressing the rebellious elements in society.[49]

Courts were also divided on the application of the confrontation clause to the use of official records. One court held that it was not a denial of the right of confrontation to prove the fact of a bigamous marriage through the use of public records.[50] And another court, in a dictum, opined that confrontation was no bar to the use of reports of the sale of intoxicating liquors that pharmacists

44. Merely absent

Territory v. Evans, 23 Pac. 232, 2 Idaho 627 (absent); State v. Fitzgerald, 1884, 19 N.W. 202, 63 Iowa 268.

45. Allowed to depart

State v. Banks, 1903, 35 So. 370, 111 La. 22.

46. Unrepresented

State v. McNamara, 1895, 30 S.W. 762, 60 Ark. 400.

47. "Requirements are answered"

U.S. v. Angell, C.C. N.H., 1881, 11 Fed. 34, 43.

48. Minority of state

Cline v. State, 1896, 36 S.W. 1099, 36 Tex.Crim. 320 (witness dead); State v. Lee, 1893, 33 Pac. 690, 13 Mont. 248.

49. Found federal trending

State v. Byers, 1895, 41 Pac. 708, 16 Mont. 565.

50. Bigamous marriage

Tucker v. People, 1887, 13 N.E. 809, 122 Ill. 583.

were required to file.[51] But another court held it was a denial of confrontation to impeach alibi witnesses by the use of records of the weather without calling persons who made the observation of the rain gauge and made the entry in the record.[52]

Although it takes us somewhat ahead of our story, it is appropriate to add here that it was not until after the Supreme Court made this a major function of the Confrontation Clause did state courts address the application of the right of confrontation to affidavits.[53] In accordance with the Supreme Court's dicta it was held that a clerk's affidavit could not be used to prove the absence of an official record.[54] A fortiori, a stenographic record of a codefendant's confession was barred from admission by the right of confrontation.[55] Finally, a federal court held that the prosecution could not get an affidavit of a witness in evidence under the guise of refreshing his recollection without violating the defendant's confrontation rights.[56] However, the significance of these rulings was minimal, given that the common law of most states barred the use of affidavits as evidence.[57]

Although state courts had by the end of the Nineteenth Century not addressed all the issues involving the relationship between the hearsay rule and the right of confrontation, they had decided far more than the federal courts.[58] They had also met issues concerning the scope of the right of confrontation; e.g., that there was no right to confrontation before a grand jury.[59] Moreover, they were beginning to address ancillary applications of the right of

51. Liquor reports

State v. Smith, 1888, 38 N.W. 492, 74 Iowa 580.

52. Weather records

People v. Dow, 1887, 31 N.W. 597, 64 Mich. 717.

53. Affidavits

Mattox v. U.S., 1895, 15 S.Ct. 337, 156 U.S. 237, 39 L.Ed. 409, discussed below, text at notecall 492.

54. Absence of record

People v. Goodrode, 1903, 94 N.W. 14, 132 Mich. 542.

55. Record of confession

Commonwealth v. Zorambo, 1903, 54 Atl. 716, 205 Pa. 109.

56. Guise of refreshing

Morris v. U.S., C.C.A.5th, 1906, 149 Fed. 123.

57. Common law barred

Wilburn v. State, Tex. Crim. 1903, 77 S.W. 3.

58. Federal courts

For the only earlier Supreme Court opinion, see § 6356, text at notecall 770.

59. Grand jury

State v. Smith, 1888, 38 N.W. 492, 74 Iowa 580.

confrontation, such as the defendant's right to be present and the blank-pad rule.[60] For example, almost a century before the Supreme Court would first address the issue, a state court held that a sex-abuse victim's unease at confronting the defendant did not justify removal of the defendant from a confronting position.[61] Similarly, it was held a denial of confrontation to allow the trial to proceed while a defendant suffering from dysentery was languishing in the restroom.[62] Finally, it was held that a deaf defendant had a right to have the proceedings interpreted, albeit not at state expense.[63]

Some state courts emphasized the importance of the right of confrontation; the Alabama Supreme Court wrote:

> The right of everyone accused of crime to be confronted by the witnesses against him is deeply imbedded in English jurisprudence, and dates back to Magna Charta, if not beyond it. It is classed as one of the bulwarks of liberty, whenever common-law principles obtain.[64]

Although the court's history is flawed, the notion of a common-law right led some courts to suggest that the only forms of hearsay admissible under the confrontation clauses were dying declarations and the former testimony of deceased witnesses.[65] However, most state courts, pressured by the need to suppress popular resistance to government, gave the right of confrontation a narrow reading, reducing it to a right to cross-examine witnesses called by the prosecution or still living.[66]

The Populist Threat

Judicial interpretations of the confrontation clauses took place against a backdrop of social, political, and economic unrest sketched

---

60. Blank-pad rule

For a federal decision that touches upon, but does not explicitly consider the blank-pad rule, see Morris v. U.S., C.C.A.5th, 1906, 149 Fed. 123 (violation of the right to deny defense counsel access to affidavit used by witness to refresh recollection while testifying).

61. Removal of defendant

State v. Mannion, 1899, 57 Pac. 542, 19 Utah 505.

62. In the restroom

Bennett v. State, 1896, 36 S.W. 947, 62 Ark. 516.

63. Interpreted

Ralph v. State, 1905, 52 S.E. 298, 124 Ga. 81.

64. "Bulwarks of liberty"

Anderson v. State, 1890, 7 So. 429, 89 Ala. 12.

65. Dying and former

Wray v. State, 1908, 45 So. 697, 154 Ala. 36.

66. Still living

People v. Corey, 1898, 51 N.E. 1024, 157 N.Y. 332.

in the previous section. Here we must introduce a new ingredient to the mix of social forces influencing confrontation jurisprudence——Populism. Since "populism" has been so perverted by journalists, some history is needed to explain why it was, and is, so frightening to the dominant economic powerholders. As used here, "Populism" refers to the last effort through mainstream politics to alter the economic structure of capitalism.[67] The People's Party tried to use traditional political means to switch control of the monetary system from bankers to a popularly controlled government.[68]

Agrarian discontent with the emerging capitalist order predated the Populists. We have already seen how the Granger Movement tried to use politics to revive common-law controls on the economy such as notions of "just price" and anti-monopoly regulation and how courts frustrated those efforts.[69] Former Grangers led many of the precursors to the People's Party, notably the Farmer's Alliance.[70] These precursors arose as early as 1877;[71] a decade later the number of members of the Farmer's Alliance dwarfed the number remaining loyal to the Grange.[72]

Populism rose as a result of a major change in the two political parties after the Civil War.[73] In place of the Jacksonian divisions, the Civil War substituted sectional, racial, and religious loyalties for economic interest as a determinant of party allegiance. Except for the urban working class, "voting as they shot" was the norm for most Americans down to the end of the Nineteenth Century.[74] This meant that business interests dominated both of the two major parties.[75] The People's Party emerged in the 1890's to threaten business hegemony with a vision of economic democracy that had

67. Alter economic structure
Goodwyn, The Populist Moment, 1978, p. 264.

68. Switch control
Id. at p. 93.

69. Granger Movement
See § 6356, text at notecall 254.

70. Grangers led
Hicks, The Populist Revolt, 1961, p. 97.

71. Arose early
Goodwyn, The Populist Moment, 1978, p. 25.

72. Dwarfed number
Id. at p. 53 (9,000 versus more than 200,000).

73. Major change
Id. at pp. 4–5.

74. "Voting as they shot"
Ibid.

75. Business dominated
Id. at pp. 7–8.

broad appeal.[76] The story of how this idea was driven from the mainstream political agenda shall be a large part of our chronological analysis, which now resumes.[77]

The changes in the major political parties emerged clearly in the presidential campaign of 1884, the first since the Civil War to elect a Democratic President and also one of the most scurrilous in history——this was the campaign in which a GOP worthy characterized the Democrats as the party of "Rum, Romanism, and Rebellion."[78] Over the balance of the century, the Republicans, repudiating their anti-slavery roots, became increasingly nativist and anti-foreign.[79] The next year, 1885, mobs attacked Chinese residents of Seattle, forcing hundreds to flee to San Francisco——not exactly a haven for those from the Orient.[80] Anti–Chinese sentiment had long been a staple of California politics.[81]

Nativism and racism bred a peculiar species of Social Darwinism known as "scientific racism."[82] Social Darwinism had been fostered by wealthy capitalists anxious to find some scientific defense for attacks on their domination of the economy.[83] Popularized by a Harvard biologist, scientific racism became increasingly virulent over the next half century.[84] Contrary to the journalistic notion that nativism was a product of competition among the dispossessed for jobs and status, scientific racism and nativism were eagerly embraced by the upper classes.[85] For older readers, the Daughters

76. People's Party

Youngdale, Populism: A Psychohistorical Perspective, 1975, p. 16.

77. Driven from agenda

Goodwyn, The Populist Moment, 1978, p. 284.

78. "Romanism and Rebellion"

Encyclopedia of American History, Morris ed. 1976, pp. 307–308.

79. Increasingly nativist

Goodwyn, The Populist Moment, 1978, p. 283.

80. From the Orient

The leaders of the Seattle mobs were promptly acquitted. Garraty, The New Commonwealth, 1977–1890, 1968, p. 7.

81. Staple of California

Furnas, The Americans: A Social History of the United States, 1587–1914, 1969, pp. 699–701.

82. "Scientific racism"

Garraty, The New Commonwealth, 1877–1890, 1968, p. 21 (tracing emergence to 1870s).

83. Defense for attacks

Encyclopedia of American History, Morris ed. 1976, p. 307.

84. Increasingly virulent

Garraty, The New Commonwealth, 1877–1890, 1968, p. 21.

85. Upper classes

Hays, The Response to Industrialism, 1885–1914, 1957, p. 42.

of the American Revolution typify the elite attachment to nativism.[86]

The year 1886 produced a wave of strikes that in terms of the number of firms and workers involved exceeded anything seen in the previous five years.[87] Much of this activity was part of the May Day agitation for an eight hour day that culminated in the Haymarket Affair.[88] However, other strikes were undertaken against the better judgement of union leaders, such as the "Great Southwest Strike" against the railroads.[89] This strike was supported by the nascent Populist Movement, some of whose leaders tried to organize a boycott to assist the unions.[90] Such support seems natural because the railroad was the common enemy that united Populists in all parts of the country.[91]

Populist antipathy to railroads rested in large part on the key role that railroads played in maintaining the South and West in a colonial subservience to the economic power of the Northeast.[92] Thanks to federal policies that allowed corporations and others to despoil the natural wealth of the public domain, the economies of the South and West were largely extractive—agriculture, mining, timber, and ranching.[93] The profits of the corporate sector of this economy increasingly rested on exploiting cheap labor in these sections.[94] Local elites seldom acquired sufficient capital to develop indigenous industry; for the most part, they were colonial agents who shipped profits back East.[95]

These local elites enabled the railroads, frequently a single railroad, to dominate state politics through a variety of corrupt

86. D.A.R. typify

Id. at p. 103.

87. Wave of strikes

Brecher, Strike!, 1972, p. 31 (numbers tripled the averages of the previous five years).

88. Haymarket

Id., at p. 38. For the significance of this Affair for confrontation, see § 6356, text at notecall 917.

89. "Southwest Strike"

Goodwyn, the Populist Moment, 1978, p. 35.

90. Boycott to support

Id. at pp. 36, 174.

91. Common enemy

Hicks, The Populist Revolt, 1961, p. 74.

92. Colonial subservience

Hays, The Response to Industrialism, 1885–1914, pp. 116, 128.

93. Largely extractive

Id. at pp. 117, 126.

94. Cheap labor

Id. at p. 124.

95. Profits back East

Id. at p. 129.

means; free passes, bribes disguised as retainers, and the like.[96] As a result, railroads evaded the tax burdens of local citizens.[97] This was particularly galling because many municipalities were heavily indebted through bonds issued to support the building of the railroads; in Kansas, for example, 80% of all municipal debt was in railroad bonds that Supreme Court decisions required to be paid even when there was fraud in their issuance or the railroad was never built.[98] At the same time, the monopoly position of the railroad and the resulting rate discrimination in favor of large shippers meant that a farmer paid more to ship his grain from the Dakotas to Minneapolis than the forerunners of Archer–Daniels–Midland paid to ship it to England.[99] Given all the governmental assistance devoted to the railroads, farmers grew increasingly impatient with the free-market platitudes that were mouthed to justify the denial of government intervention in the economy to benefit farmers.[100] Why, they asked, should farmers not be entitled to debt relief in hard times when the railroads could take shelter from their creditors in federal bankruptcy?[101]

Labor unions seemed natural allies of the farmers and it is clear that agrarian leaders sought some sort of coalition.[102] Both the Farmer's Alliance and the People's Party drafted platform planks that appealed to industrial workers.[103] Indeed, at the local level

96. Corrupt means

Hicks, The Populist Revolt, 1961, pp. 69–70.

97. Evaded tax burdens

Or in the current argot, they received "tax subsidies." Id. at p. 86; Hays, The Response to Industrialism, 1885–1914, 1957, p. 109.

98. Railroad bonds

Hicks, The Populist Revolt, 1961, pp. 28, 69.

99. More to Minneapolis

Goodwyn, The Populist Moment, 1978, p. 70.

100. Free market platitudes

Again in the current argot, "socialism for the rich." Hicks, The Populist Revolt, 1961, p. 3; Hays, The Response to Industrialism, 1885–1914, 1957, p. 18.

101. Take shelter

Hicks, The Populist Revolt, 1961, p. 84.

102. Sought coalition

Pollack, The Populist Response to Industrial America, 1962, p. 61.

103. Platform planks

"The urban workmen are denied the right of organization for self-protection; imported pauperized labor beats down their wages; a hireling standing army, unrecognized by our laws is established to shoot them down, and they are rapidly degenerating to European conditions. The fruits of the toil of millions are boldly stolen to build up colossal fortunes, unprecedented in the history of the world, while their possessors despise the republic and endanger liberty." Hicks, The Populist Revolt, 1961, p. 436. See also, Id. at p. 440; Goodwyn, The Populist Moment, 1978, pp. 42, 47.

there was much cooperation between the two groups, particularly in the Midwest in later times.[104] Nonetheless, the Populists never attracted the anticipated level of support from industrial workers and their own constituency never showed much enthusiasm for the union cause. Some historians have argued labor was to blame for the lack of unity; conservative union leaders, it was said, found the demands of the Populists too radical.[105] On the other hand, while farmers were sympathetic to the plight of the urban proletariat, they were turned off by accounts in the business press of union violence and, ironically, they were appalled by the real or imagined socialism of unions.[106]

However, one can find other explanations for the divide between workers and farmers that bear directly on the attitudes of the two groups toward the right of confrontation. Despite brave talk about cooperation, farmers were (and are) committed to an ethos of individuality that was very much at odds with the need for solidarity necessary for unions whose members, if they had not already resigned themselves to wage slavery, were well aware of the precarious position of the individual in urban society.[107] Populist rhetoric seems ill-suited both to agrarian individualism and as an appeal to like-minded union members. Populists argued that workers had been turned into a commodity (thus seeming to deny workers any agency) and that the power of employers stemmed from a surplus of labor (thus seeming to blame the victims).[108] Populist leaders should have known this was a "hard sell" because their attempts to convince farmers that they, too, were workers, not "hardy yeomen", never had much success.[109] Nonetheless, the resemblance of the Populist call for "industrial democracy" to the platform of the British Labor Party suggests that their efforts at coalition may have been premature.[110] Workers in late Nineteenth

104. Later times

Goodwyn, The Populist Moment, 1978, p. 40; Youngdale, Populism: A Psychohistorical Perspective, 1975, p. 35.

105. Conservative union

Pollack, The Populist Response to Industrial America, 1962, p. 64.

106. Socialism of unions

Hicks, The Populist Revolt, 1961, pp. 324–325.

107. Precarious position

Hays, The Response to Industrialism, 1885–1914, 1957, p. 44.

108. Blame victims

Pollack, The Populist Response to Industrial America, 1962, pp. 28, 30.

109. "Not hardy yeoman"

Goodwyn, The Populist Moment, 1978, p. 39.

110. Premature

Id. at p. 297; Pollack, The Populist Response to Industrial America, 1962, p.

Century America lived a daily vulnerability to the power of capitalism that was somewhat more remote for the typical farmer and, unlike the enthusiastic Populists, they had seen too many mass movements broken by that power to have the faith of the farmers in democratic politics.[111]

The events of 1887 played a key role in establishing the intellectual climate of the Supreme Court's first major confrontation decision. The prior years had seen capital flowing from the Northeast to the South and the West in search of the higher interest rates that desperation commands.[112] The flow was rooted in government fiscal policy; the withdrawal of the greenbacks issued during the war and a return to specie—what was called with no sense of irony, "hard money."[113] The Civil War, it was said "was fought with 50¢ dollars but paid for with the real thing."[114] The rise in the value of the dollar meant that each year farmers had to raise more wheat to meet the payments on their debt.[115] The system of commerce based on the gold standard and dominated by the House of Morgan favored bankers at the expense of debtors and taxpayers.[116] Farmers fell in both the latter classes. Hence, the rise of the Greenback party.[117]

In 1887, a drought triggered economic collapse and a rise in rural radicalism.[118] A simultaneous rapid drop in commodity prices set off an agricultural decline that lasted the rest of the century.[119] For example, in Kansas over the next few years more than 11,000 mortgages were foreclosed; in some counties more than 90% of the

28; Youngdale, Populism: A Psychohistorical Perspective, 1975, p. 136.

111. Movements broken

Goodwyn, The Populist Moment, 1978, p. 297.

112. Desperation commands

Hicks, The Populist Revolt, 1961, pp. 30, 32.

113. "Hard money"

Goodwyn, The Populist Moment, 1978, p. 10.

114. "Fought with 50¢ dollars"

Id. at p. 11.

115. More wheat for debt

Hicks, The Populist Revolt, 1961, pp. 88–89.

116. Favored bankers

Goodwyn, The Populist Moment, 1978, pp. 12, 69–70.

117. Greenback party

Id. at p. 13.

118. Drought triggered

Hicks, The Populist Revolt, 1961, p. 32; Youngdale, Populism: A Psychohistorical Perspective, 1975, p. 87.

119. Drop in prices

Hicks, The Populist Revolt, 1961, p. 56; Goodwyn, The Populist Moment, 1978, pp. 64–70.

land fell into the hands of Eastern capitalists.[120] Things were even worse in the rural South where the "crop lien" system left small farmers in a state of virtual peonage to bankers and merchants.[121] Even among farmers who did not lose their land, there grew an increased sense of the precariousness of their economic existence, a sense nicely captured in a folksong of the time:[122]

> We worked through spring and winter, through
>> summer and the fall,
> But the mortgage worked the hardest and the
>> steadiest of all,
> It worked on nights and Sundays, it worked each
>> holiday,
> It settled down among us and never went away . . .
> Worm or beetle, drought or tempest on a farmer's
>> land may fall,
> But for first class ruination, trust a mortgage
>> 'gainst them all.

Economic uncertainty set off a rapid growth in the membership of the Farmer's Alliance.[123]

The grievance of the farmers can be glimpsed in this passage from a North Carolina farm journal in the spring of 1887:

> There is something radically wrong in our industrial system. * * * The railroads have never been so prosperous, and yet agriculture languishes. The banks have never done a better or more profitable business, and yet agriculture languishes. Manufacturing enterprises never made more money or were in a more flourishing condition, yet agriculture languishes. * * * Salaries and fees were never so temptingly high and desirable, yet agriculture languishes.[124]

Add the elevator monopoly of the rural Midwest and one can see why farmers felt they were the victims of rules that benefited the

---

120. More than 90% fell

Id. at p. 84.

121. "Crop lien" system

Goodwyn, The Populist Moment, 1978, p. 21.

122. Precariousness

Youngdale, Populism: A Psychohistorical Perspective, 1975, p. 86.

123. Rapid growth

Hicks, the Populist Revolt, 1961, pp. 102–103.

124. "Agriculture languishes"

Id. at p. 54. See also, Id. at pp. 81–82:

"There are ninety and nine who live and die,
In want, and hunger, and cold,
That one may live in luxury,
And be wrapped in silken fold,
The ninety and nine in hovels bare,
The one in a palace with riches rare
* * *
And the one who owns cities, and houses and lands,

rich.[125] But the individualism with which farmers were imbued led them to personalize the Marxist critique: the problem was not the economic logic of capitalism but the greed of individual capitalists.[126]

Ironically, just as they were passing from the scene, 1887 saw one of the goals of the Grangers achieved with the creation of the Interstate Commerce Commission.[127] But while the agricultural crisis raged, the two major political parties were engaged in a battle over the return of captured Confederate flags.[128] Similarly, the victory of the Knights of Labor in the previous year was wiped out by the hysteria over Haymarket.[129] Corporations and governments, state and federal, began a rapid buildup of military force in anticipation of the next mass uprising.[130] Little noticed at the time was the launching of the Harvard Law Review, which would over the next few years provide the intellectual instruments for repression.[131]

With the Populists mobilizing, the election of 1888 was fought over the tariff issues.[132] The year that saw Yale crowned the first national college football champions was also the year that many Americans sought refuge from politics in fantasy.[133] Edward Bellamy's utopian tract "Looking Backward" set in the year 2000, was published and sold over a million copies in the next few years.[134]

And the ninety and nine have empty hands."

125. Rules benefited rich

Id. at p. 76; Goodwyn, The Populist Moment, 1978, p. 12.

126. Not capitalism but greed

Hays, The Response to Industrialism, 1885–1914, 1957, p. 29.

127. Creation of the I.C.C.

Encyclopedia of American History, Morris ed. 1976, p. 309.

128. Return of flags

Id. at p. 310.

129. Haymarket hysteria

David, The History of the Haymarket Affair, 1963, p. 180; Paul, Conservative Crisis and the Rule of Law: Attitudes of Bar and Bench, 1887–1895, p. 19.

130. Military force

Wiebe, the Search for Order, 1877–1920, 1967, pp. 78–79.

131. Harvard repression

See § 6356, text at notecall 373.

132. Tariff fight

Encyclopedia of American History, Morris ed. 1976, p. 311.

133. Refuge in fantasy

Encyclopedia of American Facts and Dates, Carruth ed. 1993, pp. 346–347.

134. "Looking Backward"

Wiebe, The Search for Order, 1877–1920, 1967, p. 69.

The novel, if that's what it was, depicted a society that functioned without money, bankers, politicians, and——tellingly——lawyers.[135] Bellamy's utopian vision rested in large part on the peculiar American faith in technology; the root of contemporary malaise, it supposed, rested on the lack of abundance of material goods that could be cured by machines and a few structural political changes.[136]

As a result of Bellamy's book, Nationalist Clubs, devoted to the nationalization of industry and the redistribution of the wealth, sprung up everywhere.[137] The clubs attracted mostly "middle class" professionals who shunned interest group politics in general and labor unions in particular——though they did cooperate for a time with the Populists.[138] This 19th Century version of the "tenured radicals" provided some of the inspiration and a few of the recruits for Progressivism in the next century. In the meantime, they avidly read the 38 or so utopian novels imitating Bellamy that were published over the next seven years.[139]

Meanwhile, the Populist movement was building; it's first mass meetings were held in 1888.[140] In May of that year, a convention in Waco, Texas, adopted a six-point platform calling for the abolition of the national banking system, the replacement of national-bank notes with legal-tender treasury notes, prohibition of alien land ownership, and "government ownership or control of the means of transportation and communication."[141] Later, when the Populists began to run candidates on similar platforms, Wall Street, the railroads, and insurance companies created massive war chests to insure the defeat of Populist candidates, saying of one candidate that he was "a sworn enemy of capital, and that his defeat was a

135. Without lawyers

Id. at p. 70. Those who suppose that the Sixth Amendment's right to counsel can be dispensed with are not likely to be favorably inclined toward other rights found in that Amendment.

136. Cured by machines

Hays, The Response to Industrialism, 1885–1914, 1957, p. 41.

137. Nationalist Clubs

Encyclopedia of American History, Morris ed. 1976, p. 861; Wiebe, The Search for Order, 1877–1920, 1967, p. 71.

138. Cooperate with Populists

Hays, The Response to Industrialism, 1885–1914, 1957, p. 42.

139. Utopian novels

Id. at p. 41.

140. Mass meetings

Goodwyn, The Populist Moment, 1978, p. 78.

141. "Government ownership"

Id. at p. 85.

matter of importance to every investor in the country."[142]

The Populists developed a number of effective propagandists and candidates of whom the most colorful was "Sockless" Jerry Simpson, a follower of Henry George, who was the party's candidate for Congress from Kansas.[143] Many of these leaders were lawyers, including James Otis, of Kansas, an abolitionist graduate of the Harvard Law School, and James B. Weaver, a graduate of the Cincinnati Law School, who won a seat in Congress from Iowa and was the Greenback Party's presidential nominee.[144] Remarkably, women played key roles in Populism despite the fact that in most places they could not yet vote or run for office.[145] The best known of these is Mary Ellen Lease, a mother of four who studied law and was admitted to the Kansas bar in 1885.[146] She reputedly exhorted farmers to "raise less corn and more hell".[147] It is a shame, therefore, that history books have made Tom Watson of Georgia the epitome of Populism, largely because he later became one of the most virulently racist demagogues in a long line of such politicians.[148]

Populist leaders helped the movement negotiate a paradigm shift whose force was misunderstood and underestimated by the elite hierarchs at the time.[149] Given the sectional loyalties emerging from the Civil War that were exploited by the major parties, Populists were forced by economic circumstances to undergo something like a "conversion experience" in order to leave the dominant local party in favor of a new national movement.[150] The laissez-faire

142. "Every investor"

Id. at p. 189.

143. "Sockless" Jerry

Hicks, The Populist Revolt, 1961, pp. 161–162.

144. Otis and Weaver

Id. at p. 164; Goodwyn, the Populist Moment, 1978, p. 136.

145. Key roles

Hicks, The Populist Revolt, 1961, pp. 164–166.

146. Mary Ellen Lease

Id. at p. 159.

147. "Raise more hell"

Id. at p. 160. A better documented saying and one more relevant to our pur-

poses is her statement: "[o]ur laws are the outpost of a system which clothes rascals in robes and honesty in rags." Ibid.

148. Watson

Id. at p. 176; Youngdale, Populism: A Psychohistorical Perspective, 1975, pp. 22–23.

149. Elite hierarchs

Goodwyn, The Populist Moment, 1978, p. 155.

150. "Conversion experience"

Id. at p. 94; Youngdale, Populism: A Psychohistorical Perspective, 1975, pp. 22–23.

paradigm had a powerful appeal, resting as it did on popular American values of individualism, carried out of Calvinism by the transcendentalist currents.[151] These values provided the intellectual support for confrontation so in order to understand the Populist impact on that right, we shall have to see how they went about deconstructing the "cowboy myth."[152] This is no easy matter since we remain in the grip of that same "democratic complacency"— the notion that maintaining democracy requires no more than regularly casting a ballot—that led political leaders of the time to mistake the challenge that Populism posed to their intellectual empire.[153] Reading the Populist calls for nationalization of the means of transportation and communication, the Marxist label leaps to the lips.[154] Yet if we look at the party platforms, we find something more complex.[155] In some of these, the nationalization of the railroads and the reclaiming of their holdings of land appears as a measure of last resort—to be employed only if the regulatory means proved incapable of freeing people from "The Octopus."[156] Similarly, Populist demands for restrictions on alien landholding can be seen as exemplifying the racism that was to prove the party's undoing—a sort of precursor of California's infamous

151. Laissez-faire paradigm

Id. at p. 27.

152. "Cowboy myth"

That is, the notion that economic life in the Midwest and West was a simple matter of exploiting the natural wealth of the public domain. Youngdale, Populism: A Psychohistorical Perspective, 1975, p. 31.

153. "Democratic complacency"

Goodwyn, The Populist Moment, 1978, p. 98. Anyone who has ever moaned about attending another faculty meeting will understand how unsettling was the Populist notion that democracy had to be made part of the daily struggle.

154. Calls for nationalization

Pollack, the Populist Response to Industrial America, 1962, p. 137.

155. Party platforms

"We demand that the means of communication and transportation shall be owned by and operated in the decent interest of the people as is the United States postal system." Hicks, The Populist Revolt, 1961, p. 428 (quoting St. Louis Demands of the Southern Alliance and Knights of Labor).

156. Proved incapable

"We demand the most rigid, honest, and just state and national government control and supervision of the means of public communication and transportation, and if this control and supervision does not remove the abuse now existing, we demand the government ownership of such means of communication and transportation." Id. at p. 434 (quoting the Ocala Demands of 1890). See also, Id. at pp. 434, 438, 443.

"The Octopus", a novel by Frank Norris, described the railroad domination of California government.

"Alien Land Laws"—until we recall that much of the public domain that had been distributed to the railroads was now being held for speculative purposes by English investors.[157] Moreover, Populist attacks on monopoly and their victory over the "Jute Trust" suggests some kind of Jacksonian nostalgia for a time of hardy yeomen, local merchants, and small producers.[158]

The true nature of Populism emerges in their local practices. The Farmer's Alliance began as an effort to form cooperatives to store and market crops.[159] When these were fought tooth and nail by local bankers and merchants using their economic power, the farmers then tried to develop their own system of currency and credit.[160] This culminated in the imaginative but ill-fated "subtreasury plan."[161] None of these proposals seem Marxist in inspiration—at least as Marxism is understood by most Americans. One would expect that Marxism would lead one to call for nationalization of all corporations, but the Populists wanted to convert them into partnerships.[162] More significant for our purposes is the action of local Populist organizations—despite the key role lawyers played in the movement—of barring lawyers, as well as merchants and bankers, from membership in their organizations.[163] A hint of

157. Alien landholding

"We demand the passage of laws prohibiting alien ownership of land, and that Congress take prompt action to devise some plan to obtain all lands now owned by alien and foreign syndicates, and that all land held by railroads and other corporations in excess of such as is actually used and needed by them be reclaimed by the government, and held for actual settlers only." Id. at p. 433 (quoting the Cincinnati Platform of 1891). On English ownership and speculation in land, see Goodwyn, The Populist Moment, 1978, p. 134.

158. Attacks on monopoly

"We hold therefore that to restore and preserve these rights under a republican form of government, private monopoly of public necessities for speculative purposes, whether of the means of production, distribution or exchange should be prohibited, and whenever any such public necessity or utility becomes a monopoly in private hands, the people of the municipality, state or nation, as the case may be, shall appropriate the same by right of eminent domain, paying a just value therefor, and operate them for, and in the interest of, the whole people." Goodwyn, The Populist Moment, 1978, p. 252 (quoting Farmer's Alliance platform of 1896). On the victory over the Jute Trust, see id. at pp. 87–88.

159. Form cooperatives

Id. at p. 73.

160. Currency and credit

Id. at pp. 80–81.

161. "Subtreasury plan"

Id. at p. 91.

162. Convert to partnerships

Youngdale, Populism: A Psychohistorical Perspective, 1975, p. 126.

163. Barring lawyers

Hicks, The Populist Revolt, 1961, p. 112.

what was afoot may be seen in the reluctance of those who opposed fusion with the Bryanists to follow the "lead of men known as corporation lawyers."[164]

The attitude towards corporation lawyers was part of the Populist contempt for those who the Social Darwinists had proclaimed "the fittest"; the "shallow-pated, sordid, unintellectual [who] stand there grabbing and grinning, while their brethren march past them to destruction."[165] Under the goad of economic hardship, the Populists developed a growing indigenous class consciousness to replace the individualist paradigms of the laissez-faire propagandists.[166] Viewed from this perspective, we "see arrayed on the one side the great magnates of the country, and the Wall Street brokers, and the plutocratic power; and on the other you will see the people."[167] The Populists "believe that the men who created our wonderful industrial system have the right to enjoy the institution which they have created."[168] As the St. Louis platform declared:

> Wealth belongs to him who creates it. Every dollar taken from industry without an equivalent is robbery. If any one will not work, neither shall he eat. The interests of rural and urban labor are the same, their enemies identical.[169]

This inversion of the capitalist ethic also mocked the claims for the efficiency of markets: "we have an overproduction of poverty, barefooted women, political thieves and many liars. There is no difference between legalized robbery and highway robbery."[170] The growth of class-conscious publications propagandizing for the Populists raised the elite fears of socialism, but the Populists invoked indigenous rhetoric more than that of Marx.[171] Echoing the Radical

---

164. "Corporation lawyers"

Pollack, The Populist Response to Industrial America, 1962, p. 133.

165. "Grabbing and grinning"

Id. at p. 21.

166. Populists developed

For a description of the grass-roots ferment of the time, see Hicks, The Populist Revolt, 1961, p. 132.

167. "Plutocratic power"

Goodwyn, The Populist Moment, 1978, p. 134.

168. "Right to enjoy"

Pollack, The Populist Response to Industrial America, 1962, p. 15.

169. "Enemies identical"

Hicks, The Populist Revolt, 1961, p. 437. For another similar plank, see id. at p. 442.

170. "Legalized robbery"

Goodwyn, The Populist Moment, 1978, pp. 45–46.

171. More than Marx

For a sample of the rhetoric of these class-conscious publications, see id. at p. 62.

Republicans, Populists invoked the precedent of the emancipation of slaves as support for confiscation of speculative landholdings.[172] Free-labor metaphors haunted those who had come to power via that ideology; "railroad corporations are penetrating almost every locality with their iron rails, they are binding the people in iron chains."[173] Another attack on corporate power even used a paraphrase of the Dred Scott decision.[174]

But the Populist impact on confrontation went farther than simply generating a repressive mood among American elites, an impact that requires us to look beyond programs and rhetoric to their underlying philosophy. The Populist Utopia was to be a "cooperative commonwealth."[175] As John Otis, the Harvard Law School abolitionist turned Populist wrote:

> When the American people shall introduce cooperation into the field of production as well as into the field of distribution, and shall organize for "work" as we organize for "war"! then shall we behold prosperity * * *. We are emerging from an age of intense individualism, supreme selfishness, and ungodly greed to a period of cooperative effort.[176]

While some Populists defined "politics" as the ability to control the distribution of wealth, and many Populist programs would have effected a redistribution of wealth,[177] their philosophy was not the usual American conception of Marxism. Indeed, one historian has seen their program as an attempt to revive the mercantilist economic system that had been destroyed during the Jacksonian era.[178]

172. Emancipation precedent

Youngdale, Populism: A Psychohistorical Perspective, 1975, p. 126.

173. "Iron chains"

Goodwyn, The Populist Moment, 1978, pp. 114–115.

174. Dred Scott

"Labor has no right that capital or its allies are bound to respect." Pollack, The Populist Response to Industrial America, 1962, p. 55. In his opinion, Justice Taney had described the status of slaves as "so far inferior, that they had no rights which the white man was bound to respect * * *." Dred Scott v. Sandford, 1857, 19 How. (60 U.S.) 393, 407, 15 L.Ed. 691. On the impact of Taney's phrase, see Fehrenbacher, The Dred Scott Case: Its Significance in American Law and Politics, 1978, pp. 347–348.

175. "Cooperative commonwealth"

Goodwyn, The Populist Moment, 1978, p. 90.

176. "Cooperative effort"

Id. at p. 136.

177. Redistribution

Id. at p. 302. On the definition of "politics", see Pollack, The Populist Response to Industrial America, 1962, p. 16.

178. Mercantilist

Youngdale, Populism: A Psychohistorical Perspective, 1975, p. 24.

Be that as it may, their ideas had a significant influence on the Progressive Paradigm that continues to shape (or plague) confrontation jurisprudence down to the present day.[179]

The Populists sought to redefine the relationship between the individual and society—a relationship that lies at the core of confrontation.[180] The Populists did not think they were out to destroy "individualism"; rather, they argued that true "individualism" required cooperation, not competition of the sort that underlies the adversary system.[181] To them, "freedom" required that society encourage the fullest possible development of human potentiality.[182] They did not think they were denigrating human rights by distinguishing them from property rights or when they argued that human rights were a sham unless predicated on an equitable distribution of wealth.[183] But given their attacks on lawyers and the existing legal system, the potential for devaluing rights such as confrontation was there. The ominous possibilities may be glimpsed in one of the earliest Populist programs, the St. Louis demands of 1889:

> we demand that Congress shall pass such laws as shall effectually prevent the dealing in futures of all agricultural and mechanical productions, preserving a stringent system of procedure in trials as shall secure the prompt conviction, and imposing such penalties as shall secure the most perfect compliance with the law.[184]

The Populists never achieved the power that would permit the construction of a "stringent system of procedure" but the desire for a "prompt conviction" and "perfect compliance with the law" sit uneasily with rights such as confrontation.

However, in the summer and fall of 1889 the Populist movement gathered momentum.[185] Six states in the West and Northwest were then being formed and in their constitutional conventions the Populists members played a key role in writing some agrarian demands into the fundamental law of these states, none of them

---

179. Influence on Progressive
Id. at p. 37.

180. Redefine relationship
Pollack, The Populist Response to Industrial America, 1962, p. 23.

181. "Individualism"
Id. at p. 19.

182. "Freedom"
Id. at p. 13.

183. Human rights sham
Id. at p. 14.

184. "Perfect compliance"
Hicks, The Populist Revolt, 1961, pp. 427–428.

185. Gathered momentum
Goodwyn, The Populist Moment, 1978, p. 87.

apparently dealing with criminal procedure.[186] An alternative federal constitution proposed the next year by a Missouri lawyer and newspaper editor suggests that dissatisfaction with the right of confrontation was not strong at the time; the alternative constitution copied the Sixth Amendment Confrontation Clause verbatim.[187] One historian has turned up at least ten such proposals since the adoption of the original Constitution.[188] Two earlier proposals—an "Imperial Constitution" in 1861 and a feminist draft in 1870—had no confrontation provisions.[189] Three subsequent alternative federal constitutions followed the 1890 proposal in having confrontation clauses identical to the Sixth Amendment and a fourth had a "face-to-face" version resembling those that had been a model for the Sixth.[190] Only when the influence of the Progressives had had time to mature did drafters of alternative constitutions see fit to meddle with the Sixth Amendment.[191] Even the most radical of these did not go as far as the modern Supreme Court in watering down the right of confrontation; this 1938 proposal gave the accused the right "to be confronted with the witnesses or sworn statements of dead witnesses against him."[192] The drafter explained the latter clause as designed to prevent the accused from killing off the witnesses against him, apparently assuming that confrontation otherwise barred the use of hearsay against an accused.[193]

Meanwhile, back in 1889 one of the major barriers to Supreme Court consideration of the right of confrontation dropped when the

186. Six new states

Hicks, The Populist Revolt, 1961, p. 149.

187. Copied verbatim

Boyd, Alternative Constitutions for the United States: A Documentary History, 1992, pp. 2, 89.

188. Ten proposals

Id. at p. 1.

189. No provisions

See Id. at pp. 22–41, 42–67. No implications regarding the right of confrontation should be drawn from these as neither had anything resembling a bill of rights.

190. "Face-to-face"

See id. at pp. 121 ("face-to-face"), 147, 198, 242 (all identical to Sixth).

191. Meddle with the Sixth

A 1974 proposal by Rexford Tugwell, a former New Dealer, said "accused persons" along with other Sixth Amendment rights "shall be allowed to confront witnesses or to call others * * *." Id. at p. 251. This could be read as shifting the onus for providing confrontation from the state to the accused, but nothing indicates that this was what was intended though the author was by this time disenchanted with the Warren Court's reading of the Constitution.

192. "Sworn statements"

Id. at pp. 159–160.

193. Killing off witnesses

Id. at p. 160, note 9.

Court finally got appellate jurisdiction in federal criminal cases.[194] Prior to this time, criminal cases could reach the Supreme Court only when the judges below certified to a division of opinion.[195] The Supreme Court did not lust after this extension of its power; indeed, in 1875 the Justices had prevailed upon the President to veto a bill bestowing criminal appellate jurisdiction on the court.[196] This reticence was atypical; in all other ways this was a period of much judicial muscle-flexing. For example, from 1885 to 1896 more than seventy state statutes were declared unconstitutional in Minnesota alone.[197] Judicial power was generally exercised in favor of the rich and powerful.[198] Eventually the Supreme Court became the lightning rod for accumulated Populist resentment at such judicial behavior.[199]

Accumulation of judicial power mirrored the growth of power in other institutions. New Jersey, also in 1889, enacted a statute that made it easier for capitalists to consolidate their power through holding companies.[200] This was also the period that saw the growth of corporate law firms and the rise of law schools, both developments that tended to cause the profession to lose touch with ordinary citizens.[201] The rise of the specialist and the decline of the lawyer as generalist decreased the power of sole practitioners, but even corporate lawyers were losing their independence and becoming corporate bureaucrats.[202] Unable to join the Populists, dissatisfied lawyers were the backbone of many Nationalist Clubs.[203] Some

194. Got jurisdiction

Fairman, History of the Supreme Court of the United States: Reconstruction and Reunion, 1864–1888, Part II, p. 97.

195. Certified to division

Id. at p. 730. As a result, the Court saw very few criminal cases.

196. Veto bill

Id. at p. 431.

197. Minnesota alone

Friedman, A History of American Law, 1973, p. 311.

198. Rich and powerful

Id. at p. 317.

199. Populist resentment

Magrath, Morrison R. Waite: The Triumph of Character, 1963, p. 201.

200. Holding companies

Hays, The Response to Industrialism, 1885–1914, 1957, p. 50.

201. Lose touch

Friedman, A History of American Law, 1973, pp. 525–527.

202. Becoming bureaucrats

Hays, The Response to Industrialism, 1885–1914, 1957, p. 52. On the decline of the generalist ideal, see Pollack, the Populist Response to Industrial America, 1962, p. 71.

203. Nationalist Clubs

Id. at p. 42.

thought centralization and bureaucratization were an inevitable product of technological change.[204] Only a few could see their own fate as part of the capitalist reorganization of the economy into dominants and subordinates.[205]

By 1890 the South and West felt the full effect of the deflation of real estate values following the collapse of speculation in agricultural land.[206] One law firm in Kansas foreclosed more than 1800 mortgages.[207] As a Populist commentator noted with irony, while coal miners were starving, farmers were burning corn for fuel.[208] Populist organizing needed no further fuel to take off.[209] Political insurgency of all sorts was on the rise, including the "free silver" fantasy that would ultimately sink Populism.[210] Nonetheless, the early 1890s saw the growth of a radical politics that brought into question the most fundamental tenets of the capitalist legal and social order.[211] Even a federal judge in Indiana flirted with Populism.[212] Moreover, mainstream economists expressed discontents with unbridled capitalism that have a surprisingly contemporary ring to them.[213]

This may explain another event of 1890 that some historians have found mysterious——the passage of the Sherman Antitrust

204. Technological change

Id. at p. 49.

205. Subordinates

Id. at p. 12.

206. Collapse of speculation

Hicks, The Populist Revolt, 1961, p. 153.

207. Foreclosed 1800

Goodwyn, The Populist Moment, 1978, p. 129.

208. Corn for fuel

Ibid.

209. Take off

Id. at pp. 117–118.

210. "Free silver"

Garraty, The New Commonwealth, 1877–1890, 1968, pp. 56–57.

211. Capitalist order

Fiss, History of the Supreme Court of the United States: Troubled Begin-

nings of the Modern State, 1888–1910, 1993, p. 37.

212. Federal judge flirted

Hicks, The Populist Revolt, 1961, p. 233.

213. Contemporary ring

E.g., this response to a 1889 tract on "Recent Economic Changes": "It seems to me that what we call civilization is to degrade and incapacitate the mass of men and women. * * * [It is] a preposterous fraud. It does not give us leisure; it does not enable us to be clean except at monstrous cost; it affects us with horrible diseases * * * poisoning our water and the air we breathe; it fosters the vicious classes * * * and it compels mankind to a strife for bread, which makes us all meaner than God intended us to be." Garraty, The New Commonwealth, 1877–1890, 1968, p. 334.

Act.[214] For our purposes it is sufficient to note that the Act conferred massive and undefined common-law powers on the federal courts.[215] The Supreme Court used those powers, not to restrain capitalists, but to repress union organizing——with consequences for confrontation as we shall see shortly.[216] Despite the Act, the end of the century was marked by an unprecedented merger mania that saw the rise in the number of trusts from 12 to 305 and a growth in their aggregate capital from less than $1 billion to more than $7 billion; these firms controlled nearly 40% of manufacturing capital and six railroad systems controlled 95% of the trackage.[217] The growth of finance capitalism and the House of Morgan also saw the formation of business organizations like the National Association of Manufacturers that were devoted to fighting unions and government regulation.[218]

The failure of the Sherman Act increased the despair Populists felt over the futility of legal safeguards; after the use of the Act to defeat the Pullman strike, one Populist paper remarked that "[w]e had supposed the courts were for the protection of the citizens, but now the citizen has to be protected from the courts."[219] The Populist critique of the legal system went from top to bottom. One paper saw an "immense, secret, cunning, unscrupulous" conspiracy by "railroad kings and millionaire bankers of the east" which was "packing the Supreme Court * * * to secure the undoing of * * * the power of the state to regulate its own internal affairs."[220] More significant in the day to day lives of the Populist constituency was the use by local law enforcement officials, who depended on convictions for fees, of vagrancy statutes originally intended to keep the Freedman in a state of peonage as tools to repress agrarian discontent.[221] When this proved ineffectual, local elites did not hesitate to use extralegal methods; in Mississippi when the Populists seemed poised to win an election, Ku Klux Klan-style nightriders burned a

214. Sherman Act

Id. at p. 124.

215. Common law powers

Id. at p. 125.

216. Repress organizing

Encyclopedia of American History, Morris ed. 1976, p. 212.

217. Merger mania

Hays, The Response to Industrialism, 1885–1914, 1957, pp. 50–51.

218. Fighting regulation

Id. at p. 53.

219. "Protected from courts"

Pollack, The Populist Response to Industrial America, 1962, p. 57.

220. "Packing court"

Id. at p. 80.

221. Vagrancy statutes

Id. at p. 38.

Populist press and destroyed voting records to prevent agrarian malcontents from voting.[222] Little wonder that one Populist editor wrote:

> Put a corporation on one side and a poor man upon the other and the courts will see to it that there is sufficient latitude to the law to satisfy the utmost demand of the corporation.[223]

Hence, the same Populist platform that called for "a stringent system of procedure" also demanded "the reform of unjust systems and the repeal of laws that bear unequally on the people."[224] More specific and more radical calls for legal change would soon follow.

Victories by Alliance-supported candidates in the election of 1890 came to little in terms of legislative action.[225] In some states pressure from business interests derailed Alliance reforms, but in others backsliding or outright bungling by supposedly agrarian legislators contributed.[226] But the election and its aftermath did expose control of the two major parties by corporate interests.[227] Or as a Populist Labor Day speaker who was to become Chief Justice of the Kansas Supreme Court put it, the election revealed

> the fatal inability in both Democratic and Republican parties to comprehend the new and strange conditions in our modern industrial and social life, an utter inability to cope with the new and vexing problems which have arisen * * *.[228]

But the election also exposed the organizational and strategic strengths and weakness of the Alliance.[229] Hence, in 1891 many leaders of the Alliance moved to form the People's Party.[230]

We shall not appreciate the fear that Populist successes, electoral and otherwise, raised among established power holders (such as federal judges), until we take account of the forces arrayed in

---

222. Nightriders burned

Goodwyn, The Populist Moment, 1978, p. 162.

223. "Satisfy corporation"

Pollack, The Populist Response to Industrial America, 1962, p. 55.

224. "Bear unequally"

Hicks, The Populist Revolt, 1961, pp. 427–428, 430.

225. Came to little

Id. at p. 181.

226. Outright bungling

Goodwyn, The Populist Moment, 1978, p. 152.

227. Expose control

Id. at p. 159.

228. "Utter inability"

Id. at p. 212.

229. Weakness of Alliance

Id. at p. 161.

230. Form People's Party

Hicks, The Populist Revolt, 1961, p. 210.

opposition to them. From the outset, local merchants and bankers had used their political and economic power to thwart Alliance institutions; e.g., getting legislators to impose discriminatory taxes on farmer cooperatives.[231] In many communities, bankers shut off credit to dissident farm groups.[232] But banker opposition only served to encourage Alliance members to find alternative sources of credit.[233] This produced the subtreasury plan—a proposal that upped the ante and raised the level of opposition from local to national.[234]

An historian of the Populists has concluded that the cooperative movement was eventually opposed by every major business group in the country.[235] These business interests funded massive war chests to fight Populist candidates.[236] This business opposition makes the Populist electoral strength quite remarkable, but the Populists were under no illusions about the ultimate outcome. As one of them put it: "In no event, will the workingmen and farmers be allowed, not matter what their majority, to take control of the government."[237] Referring to the National Guard armories then under construction in towns across the nation, one Populist paper wrote:

> The companies and regiments organized to occupy these city bastilles and equipped with the latest improved instruments of death constitute a private army directly under the command of the capitalists of these cities and ready, at their instance, to suppress any uprising of the common herd.[238]

We shall soon see whether or not these words are prophetic. But for the moment, words, not bullets, were the weapons of choice against the Populist insurgency.

With the growth of Populist publications, the business press was no longer the sole source of political and economic information and ideas—a fact that raised the anxiety of already troubled elites

231. Discriminatory taxes

Goodwyn, The Populist Moment, 1978, p. 73.

232. Shut off credit

Id. at p. 77.

233. Alternative sources

Id. at p. 142.

234. Upped the ante

Id. at p. 110.

235. Every business group

Id. at p. 305.

236. Funded war chests

Id. at p. 189.

237. "Take control"

Pollack, The Populist Response to Industrial America, 1962, p. 41.

238. "Suppress uprising"

Id. at p. 42.

more than a little.[239] The business press opposed the Farmer's Alliance from the outset; early on the movement was accused of being "dominated by the spirit of class legislation, class aggrandizement, class exclusiveness, and class proscription."[240] As this attack suggests, the very existence of an agrarian insurgency embarrassed the attempt of the business press to portray the United States as a nation of happy, striving, and often successful individuals—a classless society where merit, not birth determined one's place.[241] (Those who recall the earliest response of the business press to the 20th Century Civil Rights movement will find it a helpful analogy.)

As the Populist movement grew, so did the stridency of the business press. Defamatory attacks on Populist candidates were remarkable, even by the journalistic standards of the time.[242] Here is William Allen White on the Populist candidate previously quoted:

> We have another shabby, wild-eyed, rattle-brained fanatic who has openly said in a dozen speeches that "the rights of the user are paramount to the rights of the owner." We are running him for Chief Justice, so that capital will come tumbling over itself to get into the State.[243]

At least White got the program right. Elsewhere Populists were accused—what else?—of embracing "anarchy and communism."[244] Because the party opposed lynching, its candidates were accused of favoring the rape of white women.[245] Attacks on specific Populist proposals were seldom more analytical; the New York Times characterized the subtreasury plan as "one of the wildest and fantastic projects ever seriously proposed by sober man."[246] So serious was the Populist threat to the established order that a century later Populists were still being smeared by so-called "consensus historians."[247]

239. Raised anxiety

Goodwyn, The Populist Moment, 1978, p. 153.

240. "Class proscription"

Id. at p. 50.

241. Classless society

Id. at p. 97.

242. Defamatory attacks

Id. at p. 137.

243. "Tumbling over itself"

Hicks, The Populist Revolt, 1961, p. 374.

244. "Anarchy and communism"

Goodwyn, The Populist Moment, 1978, p. 189.

245. Favoring rape

Id. at p. 221.

246. "Wildest and fantastic"

Id. at p. 173.

247. "Consensus historians"

Youngdale, Populism: A Psychohistorical Perspective, 1975, p. 9.

In 1892 the desire of businessmen to defeat both the codification movement and the vagaries of local regulation led to the formation, under the aegis of the American Bar Association, of the National Conference of Commissioners on Uniform State Laws.[248] Among the products of NCCUSL were the Uniform Rules of Evidence, whose provisions would have to be tested by the Confrontation Clause later in the next century. In 1892, however, it was Congress that was providing new evidence rules; specifically, a provision in the anti-Chinese immigration statute that required those of Chinese ancestry to prove their right to remain in this country by the testimony of "credible white witnesses."[249] A decade later in passing on similar anti-Chinese laws, the Supreme Court would denigrate confrontation values; the Court found no Due Process violation in deportation hearings conducted entirely in English with no interpretation because the inability of the deportee to comprehend the proceedings was merely her own "misfortune."[250]

The jangled nerves of the business elite suffered two more jolts in 1892. In January of that year, in an effort to provoke a conflict that would allow it to destroy a union, the Carnegie Steel Corporation cut wages by 18% at its Homestead plant near Pittsburgh.[251] In anticipation of a strike, the company had assembled a private army of Pinkertons.[252] When during the strike-lockout the workers occupied the plant, the Pinkertons attempted an amphibious assault on the plant; in the ensuing conflagration, nine unionists and seven Pinkertons were killed and scores on both sides were injured.[253] At this point the state intervened with official military force, crushing the strike and destroying the union.[254]

248. Formation of the NCCUSL

Twining, Karl Llewellyn and the Realist Movement, 1973, p. 272; Friedman, A History of American Law, 1973, p. 355.

249. "Credible white"

Fiss, History of the Supreme Court of the United States: Troubled Beginnings of the Modern State, 1888–1910, 1993, p. 304.

250. Merely "misfortune"

Id. at p. 314, quoting Yamataya v. Fisher, 1903, 23 S.Ct. 611, 614–615, 189 U.S. 86, 101–102, 47 L.Ed. 721.

251. Cut Homestead wages

Brecher, Strike!, 1972, p. 54.

252. Army of Pinkertons

Id. at p. 55.

253. Killed and injured

Id. at p. 58.

254. Crushing strike

Id. at p. 62; Furnas, The Americans: A Social History of the United States, 1587–1914, 1969, p. 717.

Despite strike costs of more than $2 million, the corporation still came out more than $4 million to the good, a return to shareholders of 16% on their investment.[255] Carnegie was lauded by Rockefeller and other capitalists for his stand against "anarchy" and the plant manager was turned into a press hero.[256] But not everything came up roses for capitalists. The strikers were charged with murder, acquitted, then charged with treason, and also acquitted.[257] Moreover, some members of Congress criticized the corporation for its use of private military force.[258] Apparently the lessons of Homestead were to avoid state officials and juries——or so one might deduce from the tactics adopted two years later in the Pullman strike. For Populists, Homestead provided a vivid illustration of the drive of capitalism to atomize producers and destroy cooperative efforts to better their lot.[259]

The Presidential election of 1892 delivered another blow to corporate complacency. The People's Party ran James B. Weaver of Iowa on a platform of free silver, greenbacks, nationalization of railroads and other means of communication, a graduated income tax, a postal-savings system, direct election of Senators, the Australian ballot, initiative and referendum, a shorter working day, and restrictions on immigration and alien ownership of land.[260] To the horror of the elite, Weaver garnered more than a million votes (nearly 10% of those cast) and 22 electoral votes.[261] It seems likely that Weaver's candidacy played a major role in throwing the election to a Democrat, Grover Cleveland. However, a look at the

255. Return of 16%

Josephson, The Robber Barons, 1962, p. 371.

256. Press hero

Id. at p. 372. Ironically, in view of Rockefeller's comment, the plant manager was later shot by a real anarchist in retaliation for his role in the strike. Furnas, the Americans: A Social History of the United States, 1587–1914, 1969, p. 717.

257. Twice acquitted

Brecher, Strike!, 1972, p. 60.

258. Corporation criticized

Furnas, The Americans: A Social History of the United States: 1587–1914, 1969, p. 717.

259. Atomize producers

Pollack, The Populist Response to Industrial America, 1962, pp. 46–47.

260. Populist platform

Encyclopedia of American History, Morris ed. 1976, p. 313. For the full text of the platform, see Hicks, The Populist Revolt, 1961, pp. 439–444.

261. 22 electoral votes

Id. at p. 314; Wiebe. The Search for Order, 1877–1920, 1967, p. 261.

distribution of the Populist vote was even more unnerving; the Party received 66% of the vote in Nevada, 54% in Idaho, 57% in Colorado, 48% in North Dakota and Kansas, and 36% of the vote in Alabama.[262] The Party was weakest in the industrialized states of the Midwest and Northeast, a fact of little comfort to those aware of the Party's efforts to ally with urbanized workers in these areas. But a Party leader proclaimed:

> The time has arrived for the great West, the great South, and the great Northwest, to link their hands and hearts together and march to the ballot box and take possession of the government, restore it to the principles of our fathers, and run it in the interest of the people.[263]

Little did he know that the "Great South" had already shown how the Party could be defeated.

The election of 1892 strengthened the antidemocratic sentiments of hard-liners in the American Bar Association.[264] Southern lawyers did not need the A.B.A. to point the way. They resorted to the same tactics they had learned during Reconstruction to defeat popular majorities. The appearances of Populist candidates on the hustings were disrupted by thugs throwing eggs and rocks and the blasting of brass bands.[265] Potential voters were deterred by Ku Klux Klan-style intimidation.[266] If this were not enough, election fraud of the sort that marred the 1876 election was used; one Populist candidate for Congress was surprised to discover that his opponent had received more votes than there were registered voters.[267] As historians have noted, the Populists might have done as well in the South as they did in the West but for Democratic use of "intimidation, bribery, ballot-box stuffing, and manipulation of the count."[268]

262. Distribution of vote

Hicks, The Populist Revolt, 1961, p. 263.

263. "Interest of people"

Goodwyn, The Populist Moment, 1978, p. 167.

264. Anti-democratic hard-liners

Paul, Conservative Crisis and The Rule of Law: Attitudes of Bar and Bench, 1887–1895, 1960, p. 76.

265. Rocks and bands

Hicks, The Populist Revolt, 1961, p. 244.

266. Ku Klux intimidation

Goodwyn, The Populist Moment, 1978, p. 190.

267. More than voters

Hicks, The Populist Revolt, 1961, p. 253.

268. "Manipulation of the count"

Goodwyn, The Populist Moment, 1978, p. 190. Or as another one put it, "terror, fraud, corruption, and trickery." Ibid.

The Populists recognized from the outset the two major hindrances to their organizing were the white supremacist ideology in the South and ethnic and religious intolerance in the North.[269] The Populists worked to overcome racism but only in Louisiana were they able to achieve any significant interracial cooperation.[270] Elsewhere their efforts were hindered by their own racism and the distrust of Freedmen who had learned during Reconstruction they would bear the burden of the backlash against the radicalism of would-be white saviors.[271] Sexism also burdened the Populist effort; when Mary Ellen Lease made a swing through the South on behalf of the Populist ticket, one local paper sniffed that

> the sight of a woman traveling around the country making political speeches is simply disgusting * * * . Southern manhood revolts at the idea of degrading womanhood to the level of politics.[272]

That level can be judged by the way Southern Democrats used "the race card" against Populist candidates.[273] Even some Populists were disturbed when it appeared that in some places in the South the votes of African–Americans gave them the balance of power between Democrats and Populists.[274] Populism thus played some part in the efforts to disenfranchise African–American voters.[275] We may suppose that those who did wish to confront African–Americans at the polls were not terribly enthusiastic about confronting them from the witness stand where they might be shown not to be "credible white witnesses."

The Populist momentum, though it may not have been apparent at the time, seems to have crested in 1893. Populist agitation in that year forced the Nebraska legislature to pass a bill lowering railroad freight rates by an average of 30%.[276] However, five years later the U.S. Supreme Court struck down the statute as a denial of due process.[277] Other Populist achievements were less ephemeral.

269. Ideology and intolerance
Id. at p. 100.

270. Interracial cooperation
Id. at p. 194.

271. White saviors
Id. at p. 120.

272. "Degrading womanhood"
Hicks, The Populist Revolt, 1961, p. 244.

273. "Race card"
Id. at p. 393.

274. Balance of power
Id. at p. 392.

275. Disenfranchise
Id. at p. 412.

276. Lowered rates
Id. at p. 283.

277. Denial of due process
Id. at p. 284.

The movement launched a series of class-conscious publications. As one of these announced:

> This journal will aim to publish such matter as will tend to the education of the laboring classes, the farmers and the producer, and in every struggle it will endeavor to take the side of the oppressed as against the oppressor * * *.[278]

The Populists had more than a thousand such journals, some of which lasted into the next century, keeping Populist ideas alive to be picked up and picked over by the Progressives.[279]

Populism was ambivalent in its movement from individualism to cooperation.[280] As the passage just quoted suggests, Populist cooperation coexisted with a confrontational attitude towards capitalism. Perhaps this is because there are several ideological strains at war within Populism.[281] Determining which of these strains would come to the fore when Populists considered the right of confrontation may be quite difficult. Certainly cooperation lay at the root of Populist institutions. As a predecessor declared, "[b]y cooperation we will become a nation of employers—the employers of our own labor. The wealth of the land will pass into the hands of those who produce it."[282] Despite business opposition that drove many Alliance cooperatives under, enough of them survived to become the nucleus from which the agricultural cooperatives of the 20th Century arose.[283]

The Panic of 1893 and Coxey's Army

Corporate America received two more shocks in 1893. First, Governor Altgeld of Illinois pardoned those anarchists convicted of the Haymarket bombing who had not already been executed; the Gov-

---

278. "Against the oppressor"

Goodwyn, The Populist Moment, 1978, p. 62.

279. A thousand journals

Id. at p. 206.

280. Ambivalent

Youngdale, Populism: A Psychohistorical Perspective, 1975, p. 7.

281. Several strains

Id. at p. 13. The confrontational attitude seems to come from the streak of socialism that runs through Populist rhetoric.

282. "Those who produce"

Hays, The Response to Industrialism, 1885–1914, 1957, p. 33.

283. Cooperatives of 20th Century

Id. at p. 30. Though readers today may only be aware of large marketing cooperatives, such as Sunkist, when the junior author used to hitchhike through Michigan, Indiana, and Illinois at midcentury one could find in every small town some sort of cooperative, usually the local elevator, but often feed mills, gas stations, and even grocery stores.

ernor's reasons for this act——that the trial had been a "travesty of justice" conducted by Judge Gary with "malicious ferocity"——so incensed the law-and-order crowd that it insured Altgeld's political demise.[284] Second, the so-called "Panic of 1893", brought about by business over-expansion and fears of the future of the gold standard, plunged the nation into a depression comparable to the Great Depression of the 1930's.[285] When the full effects were felt the following year, more than 2 million workers lost their jobs and the unemployment rate in manufacturing and construction reached as high as 50% of the prior workforce.[286] The depression played particular havoc with railroads.[287] Nearly 40% of the nation's trackage fell into receivership——hastening the consolidation of smaller roads into the dominant carriers.[288] But while others were plunged into privation, bankers, led by the House of Morgan, profited handsomely from government efforts to prop up the economy.[289]

The year of the Panic also saw the initiation of a series of cases that brought the "labor injunction" into national prominence.[290] This procapitalist device grew out of the common law and, as we have previously remarked, the common-law powers of federal courts were substantially enhanced by the Sherman Act.[291] Federal courts were not reluctant to use the criminal law on behalf of employers; indeed, while serving on the Circuit Court Chief Justice Taft was happy to label a railroad union a "criminal conspiracy."[292]

284. Haymarket pardon

Lindsey, The Pullman Strike, 1971, p. 9.

285. "Panic of 1893"

Hicks, The Populist Revolt, 1961, pp. 308–309; Encyclopedia of American History, Morris ed. 1976, p. 315.

286. As high as 50%

Fiss, History of the Supreme Court of the United States: Troubled Beginnings of the Modern State, 1888–1910, 1993, p. 57: Paul, Conservative Crisis and the Rule of Law: Attitudes of Bar and Bench, 1887–1895, 1960, pp. 82, 128.

287. Havoc with railroads

Kolko, Railroads & Regulation, 1877–1916, 1965, p. 64.

288. Hastening consolidation

Wiebe, The Search for Order, 1877–1920, 1967, pp. 26, 46.

289. House of Morgan

Goodwyn, The Populist Moment, 1978, p. 208.

290. "Labor injunction"

Paul, Conservative Crisis and the Rule of Law: Attitudes of Bar and Bench, 1887–1895, 1960, p. 107.

291. Sherman Act enhanced

Id. at pp. 104, 107.

292. "Criminal conspiracy"

Id. at p. 113.

But the labor injunction was more "efficient" than the criminal law because it allowed the court to bypass the right to jury trial and other Sixth Amendment rights.[293] However, the use of the labor injunction presented a propaganda problem because of the way it closeted the federal judge and the U.S. Attorney with the employer—"in bed together" unionists might say.[294] This perception was furthered by cases like the one where a federal judge ordered workers to perform their jobs or suffer the penalties of contempt— an act so contrary to the "Free labor" ideology and the spirit of the Thirteenth Amendment that a Congressional committee called it a "gross abuse of judicial authority."[295] While the American Bar Association applauded this addition to the employer's arsenal, it is reasonable to suppose that workers and their sympathizers might have seen this as another illustration of the evils of the common law and the uselessness of Sixth Amendment guarantees like confrontation.[296]

The year before the Supreme Court's most important confrontation decision—1894—saw the country mired in the depths of depression; as many as three million workers were idled, 642 banks failed, and, thanks to Wall Street's loss of faith in railroads, lines with over 22,000 miles of trackage were in federal court receivership.[297] Those workers who were still employed, found their wages slashed dramatically.[298] While this was simply one more step in the widening gap between rich and poor, events about to follow made it hard for any but the extremely obtuse to maintain the myth that America was a classless society.[299] Since the major corporations had economic and political resources that dwarfed those of all but the largest state governments, desperate men looked to the federal government to come to the aid of the poor just as they came to the aid of beleaguered capitalists.[300]

293. Bypass Jury

Id. at p. 105.

294. "In bed together"

Id. at p. 109. This will be illustrated in our account of the Pullman strike, below, text at notecall 398.

295. "Gross abuse"

Id. at p. 117.

296. A.B.A. applauded

Id. at p. 122.

297. In receivership

Lindsey, The Pullman Strike, 1971, pp. 1, 12; Hays, The Response to Industrialism, 1885–1914, 1957, p. 8.

298. Wages slashed

Lindsey, The Pullman Strike, 1971, p. 98.

299. Maintain myth

Hays, The Response to Industrialism, 1957, p. 37.

300. Looked to federal

Id. at p. 85.

Early in 1894, the Populist Jacob Coxey of Massillon, Ohio, called on the unemployed to march on Washington to present their grievances to Congress and the President.[301] Thousands of men from the North and West answered Coxey's call for a "petition in boots."[302] Because of the distance from the West, marchers called on railroads in receivership to transport them and when they were refused, they "borrowed" idled trains.[303] Despite the ridicule heaped on the marchers by the business press, they frightened the "respectable" citizens who formed armed vigilantes to meet the marchers as they passed through their communities.[304] While some members of the elite thought it was time to provide some form of economic redress, many others called for violent repression of any expression of discontent.[305] One prominent businessman spoke for this element when he said: "[g]ive the workingmen and strikers gun bullet food for a few days and you will observe how they take that sort of bread."[306]

The federal government heeded these calls. Since many of the lines were in federal receivership, federal judges enjoined the Coxieites from any use of railroad property.[307] However, since much of the citizenry and more than a few federal marshals were sympathetic to the strikers, federal courts found it difficult to get their injunctions enforced.[308] Moreover, given the Populist strength in these western states, state officials were unwilling to call on the federal government to send troops to stop the marchers. However, the Attorney General devised a legal stratagem to get around this requirement; under the guise that they were simply enforcing the orders of federal courts or, in the case of railroads not in receivership, were preventing the obstruction of the mails, federal troops

301. March on Washington

Paul, Conservative Crisis and the Rule of Law: Attitudes of Bar and Bench, 1887–1895, 1960, p. 128.

302. "Petition in boots"

Wiebe, The Search for Order, 1877–1920, 1967, p. 91.

303. "Borrowed" trains

Goodwyn, The Populist Moment, 1978, p. 208.

304. Armed vigilantes

Wiebe, The Search for Order, 1877–1920, 1967, p. 91.

305. Violent repression

Hays, The Response to Industrialism, 1885–1914, 1957, p. 24.

306. "Gun bullet food"

Id. at p. 40.

307. Federal judges enjoined

Lindsey, The Pullman Strike, 1971, p. 13.

308. Difficult to get enforced

Ibid.

were dispatched to 14 western states.[309]

In the face of this show of official and unofficial force, only about 400 of "Coxey's army" ever reached Washington.[310] When they attempted to present their petition to Congress, the leaders were arrested for trespassing on the Capitol grounds.[311] Congress met the pleas of the marchers and their supporters with complete indifference.[312] But though the march on Washington produced nothing for the destitute, it did provide the federal government with something like a "dry run" for an even larger crisis that was about to explode.[313]

The Pullman Strike

The Pullman strike epitomized the turmoil of the 1890s that sharpened and intensified public reaction to the new industrial order.[314] One historian has characterized it as marking the first phase of the "conservative crisis" that produced the Mattox case— the first important Supreme Court decision on the meaning of the Confrontation Clause.[315] The strike showed how wealth had mobilized to defend its privileges and how far courts were willing to go in converting the common law into a weapon to defeat the organization of workers.[316]

George Pullman was lionized by the business press, feared by his competitors, and hated by his employees. The Pullman Palace Car Co. built railroad passenger cars; by the use of harassing patent litigation against competitors it had captured 75% of the market.[317]

309. Troops dispatched
Id. at p. 14.

310. Only about 400
Encyclopedia of American History, Morris ed. 1976, p. 318.

311. Leaders arrested
Ibid.

312. Complete indifference
Lindsey, The Pullman Strike, 1971, p. 12.

313. "Dry run"
Id. at p. 14. "Dry run" because the Coxeyites were few in number and did not respond in kind to shows of force.

314. New industrial order
Hays, The Response to Industrialism, 1885–1914, 1957, p. 43.

315. "Conservative crisis"
Paul, Conservative Crisis and the Rule of Law: Attitudes of Bar and Bench, 1887–1895, 1960, p. 131.

316. Weapon to defeat
Wiebe, The Search for Order, 1877–1920, 1967, p. 92; Hays, The Response to Industrialism, 1885–1914, 1957, p. 67.

317. Captured 75%
Lindsey, The Pullman Strike, 1971, p. 23. Indeed, so dominant was the company that sleeper cars were known generically as "pullmans" regardless of their source—much like the word "xerox" is used today for copiers.

The company leased its cars under leases that allowed it to fix ticket prices and capture most of the profits.[318] The Interstate Commerce Commission refused to regulate Pullman on the ground that it lacked the power to do so because Pullman did not operate the trains that pulled its cars.[319] Senator John Sherman called the company one of the two "most outrageous monopolies of the day."[320]

Pullman ran a company town with the powers of Big Brother—even controlling the priest and ministers in the local churches.[321] Speakers with union sympathies were barred from the town.[322] The company manipulated local elections, evaded state laws on the payment of wages, used company doctors to discourage filing of claims for industrial accidents, and blacklisted employees who spurned the owner's "benevolence."[323] The prominent economist Richard T. Ely did a study of the town that concluded

> that the idea of Pullman is un-American. It is a nearer approach than the writer has seen to what appears to be the ideal of the Great German Chancellor. It is not the American ideal. It is benevolent well-wishing feudalism, which desires the happiness of the people, but in such a way as to please the authorities.[324]

Little wonder that the Illinois Supreme Court later declared key provisions of the municipal charter to be illegal.[325]

By slashing wages, the Pullman company actually increased its profits during the depression that followed the Panic of 1893.[326] Employees had long been required to work 11 hour days.[327] During 1893–1894 many of the workers, after deductions for rent and other company charges, were paid less than $1 for two weeks work—

318. Fix prices
Id. at p. 25.

319. ICC refused to regulate
Id. at p. 26.

320. "Outrageous monopolies"
Id. at p. 26. The other was the Sugar Trust, which we shall see again shortly.

321. Local churches
Id. at p. 54.

322. Speakers barred
Id. at p. 64.

323. Evaded and blacklisted
Id. at pp. 71, 73, 79, and 95.

324. "Please authorities"
Id. at p. 86.

325. Illegal
Id. at p. 344.

326. Increased profits
Id. at p. 27.

327. Work 11 hours
Id. at p. 28.

some of them collecting just pennies.[328] Meanwhile, the company was rolling in money; in 1893 and 1894 the company had sufficient profits to declare dividends of 18% and 14% respectively and its managers continued to receive boomtime salaries.[329] In short, it was not a good time for a strike.

Desperate men could not afford prudence. Against the advice of union leaders, the Pullman workers struck.[330] A month later, again over the advice of their leaders, railroad workers throughout the country began a boycott of all trains that included Pullman cars.[331] Pullman was so detested that at the outset of the strike, public opinion favored the strikers.[332] In those states where the militia was called out,[333] the troops were too sympathetic to the strikers to be counted on. Defying public opinion and state officials who sought to mediate, Pullman rejected all efforts to work out a peaceful resolution of the issues.[334] As soon appeared, this was not simply mulishness but part of a plan by the railroad executives to destroy the militant American Railway union led by Eugene Debs, a union far more effective in advancing workers' claims than the more conservative craft unions associated with the American Federation of Labor.[335]

The General Managers' Association, an organization of railroad executives, formed a legal committee of leading corporate lawyers to formulate strategy and devise tactics for the railroads to follow in a coordinated fashion; for example, from the outset the railroads agreed to bypass state officials and courts in favor of working through the federal government.[336] The railroad lawyers hoped to turn the public view of the strike from one of desperate workers against a greedy employer to one of a rebellion against the govern-

328. Just pennies
Id. at p. 94.

329. Boomtime salaries
Id. at p. 100.

330. Workers struck
Id. at pp. 103, 109.

331. Boycott
Brecher, Strike!, 1972, p. 81.

332. Public opinion favored
Lindsey, The Pullman Strike, 1971, p. 125.

333. Troops sympathetic
Id. at pp. 249–251.

334. Pullman rejected
Id. at pp. 225, 231.

335. Destroy A.R.U.
Id. at p. 230.

336. Bypass state
Id. at p. 141.

ment by anarchists and aliens.[337] Their goal was to justify the use of federal troops on the ground that there was no "other resource left." Once this was done

> the strike would collapse like a punctured balloon. It is the government's duty to take this business in hand, restore law, suppress the riots, and restore to the public the service which it is now deprived of by the conspirators and lawless men.[338]

Presumably the railroad lawyers who hoped to bring the government to do their bidding did not regard themselves as "conspirators" or "lawless men."

The railroads wanted to do more than end the Pullman strike; they also wished to deter any future strikes. In discussing the prosecution of union leaders, the special U.S. Attorney in Chicago wrote the Attorney General:

> We shall be able to show that this conspiracy has extended over the entire northwest, as well as the Pacific coast, and also east through Michigan, Indiana and Ohio, and I firmly believe that the result of these trials and the punishment of the leaders will be so serious that a general strike upon any railroad will not occur again for a series of years.[339]

To do this, the railroads needed to show that anyone who seriously challenged corporate control of the economy could expect to bring down on their heads the entire organized force of society.[340] However, unionists did not underestimate the odds against them; as Debs put it:

> We have only got a number, and a limited number, of poorly paid men in our organization, and when their income ceases they are starving. We have no power of the Government behind us. We have no recognized influence in society on our side * * *.[341]

For some workers, the lesson of the strike was to

> demonstrate to the laboring men that they must get together; that no single organization can win * * * they have seen the united press against them; they have seen the united clergy against them; they have seen the entire judiciary against them; they have seen

---

337. Rebellion by anarchists
Id. at p. 142.

338. "Lawless men"
Id. at p. 144.

339. "Not occur again"
Id. at pp. 276–277.

340. Entire organized force
Brecher, Strike!, 1972, p. 94.

341. "On our side"
Ibid.

the entire office holders of this country against them——the United States Government against them * * *.[342]

Was there any basis for this seemingly extravagant statement?[343]

President Cleveland and his Attorney General Richard Olney, inspired by their success against Coxey's Army, determined to use governmental power to break the strike.[344] If they could bypass Illinois Governor Altgeld, who was still seeking some peaceful solution, they hoped to invoke martial law in Chicago.[345] Olney, who had been a railroad lawyer for more than 30 years and who still served on the board of directors of a number of railroads, needed little encouragement from the President.[346] Although the regular U.S. Attorney in Chicago was a railroad stooge who eagerly did the bidding of the General Managers Association, Olney had little faith in his ability.[347] So he appointed Edwin Walker, a longtime railroad lawyer and a member of the legal committee of the General Managers Association, to be the special U.S. Attorney in Chicago for the duration of the strike.[348] Olney told the public:

> We have been brought to the ragged edge of anarchy, and it is time to see whether the law is sufficiently strong to prevent this condition of affairs. If not, the sooner we know it the better, that it may be changed.[349]

Privately, to Walker he seemed to have even less faith in law: "the true way of dealing with the matter is by a force which is over-

---

342. "Government against them"

Ibid.

343. Extravagant

Debs held similar views: "On the other side the corporations are in perfect alliance; they have all the things that money can command, and that means a subsidized press, that they are able to control the newspapers, and that means a false or vitiated public opinion. The clergy almost steadily united in thundering their denunciation; then the courts, then the militia, then the Federal troops; everything and all things on the side of the corporation." Ibid.

344. Determined to break

Id. at p. 84; Lindsey, The Pullman Strike, 1971, p. 149.

345. Invoke martial law

Lindsey, The Pullman Strike, 1971, p. 212.

346. Olney bio

Id. at p. 148.

347. Little faith

Id. at p. 153.

348. Walker appointed

Brecher, Strike!, 1972, p. 85. Walker, in coordinating the strategy worked out by the General Managers Association, effectively took over the functions of the Department nationwide insofar as the strike was concerned. Lindsey, The Pullman Strike, 1971, p. 154.

349. "May be changed"

Id. at p. 245.

whelming."[350]

First, however, the public had to be convinced that force was justified—a job the business press did masterfully.[351] The railroads had learned early in the strike that the use of violence against strikers could produce a violent response from mobs of workers and sympathizers.[352] The railroads set out to provoke additional violence.[353] The press, in turn, provided sensationalized accounts of such violence.[354] A historian of the strike reproduced a number of drawings from Harper's Weekly, the Gilded Age's version of television footage, depicting strike violence in a manner likely to inflame public opinion; for example, one of these shows a sharply uniformed detachment of U.S. Infantry entering the Chicago stockyards surrounded by a hirsute, raggedy mob, brandishing sticks and fists, and according to the caption shouting "to hell with the United States Government."[355] Another issue contained a cartoon of Western governors who had attempted to mediate the strike dressed in clown suits under the caption "Vanguard of Anarchy."[356] These pictorial slanders were echoed in an editorial in the Nation magazine:

> a Populist or anarchist governor like Altgeld of Illinois, Lewelling of Kansas, Waite of Colorado, or Pennoyer of Oregon might allow government to be overthrown in his state, and lawlessness to run riot, and still claim there was no warrant for federal intervention. Happily, the President is armed by statute with all the power needed not only to suppress mobs, but to overcome anarchist governors.[357]

When, during the strike, the President of France was shot by a real anarchist, the business press promptly and repeatedly analogized

350. "Force overwhelming"

Wiebe, The Search for Order, 1877–1920, 1967, p. 92.

351. Masterfully

Lindsey, The Pullman Strike, 1971, p. 147.

352. Violent response

Brecher, Strike!, 1972, p. 86.

353. Provoke violence

Lindsey, The Pullman Strike, 1971, p. 215.

354. Sensationalized

Paul, Conservative Crisis and the Rule of Law: Attitudes of Bar and Bench, 1887–1895, 1960, p. 137.

355. "To hell with Government"

Lindsey, The Pullman Strike, 1971, following pp. 208, 210, 214 (drawing described in text above).

356. "Vanguard of Anarchy"

Id. at p. 315.

357. "Anarchist governors"

Id. at p. 262.

the strikers to the assassin.[358] The press was so biased that one reporter was fired after he testified before the grand jury that his first-hand account of one incident of violence had been doctored by his editors to make it appear worse than it was.[359] Not surprisingly, by the end of the strike all respectable opinion——including that of the organized bar——supported the railroads and the President.[360]

While the railroads and the business press traversed the low road, Attorney General Olney took the high road, ordering U.S. Attorneys throughout the country to employ the newest antiunion weapon——the labor injunction.[361] Beginning in Chicago, where it was issued by a federal judge who owed his appointment to George Pullman and was later indicted, this blanket injunction spread to cover most of the country.[362] The terms of the injunction were so broad that it prohibited virtually any acts by or in support of the strikers——one of the judges issuing it called it a "Gatling gun on paper" and even the New York Times was astounded at its breadth.[363] In addition to the benefits of the ordinary labor injunction, including denial of Sixth Amendment rights such as trial by jury and confrontation, this one also relieved corporations from the onus of having employed so sweeping a weapon and immediately put virtually all Pullman strikers in contempt of court.[364] Only union leaders received personal service of the injunction; others discovered they were in contempt only from reading it in the business press, seeing the injunctions posted in and around the

358. Analogized to assassin

Id. at p. 320.

359. Doctored by editors

Id. at p. 308.

360. Supported President

Id. at p. 321.

361. Labor injunction

Id. at p. 155.

362. Spread to cover most

Id. at pp. 212. For details of its issuance, see id. at p. 160. For the details about the Chicago judge, see id. at pp. 193, 360.

363. "Gatling gun"

Brecher, Strike!, 1972, p. 85. For the terms of the injunction, see Lindsey, The Pullman Strike, 1971, pp. 161–

162. The New York Times called the injunction a "veritable dragnet of legal verbiage, one of those peculiar instruments that punishes an individual for doing a certain thing, and is equally merciless if he does not do it, so it is difficult to understand how the strikers can maintain their present policy and at the same time evade its operation or escape its influence." Id. at p. 162.

364. Put in contempt

Brecher, Strike!, 1972, p. 85; Lindsey, The Pullman Strike, 1972, p. 155.

railroads, or hearing it read to them by officials seeking to disperse them.[365]

The legal justification for the injunction was two-fold; conspiracy to violate the Sherman Act and to interfere with the mail.[366] Judges had little doubt about the first; one of them wrote that a strike

> is essentially a conspiracy to extort by violence * * *. I know of no peaceful strike. I think no strike was ever heard of that was or could be successful unaccompanied by intimidation or violence * * *. The strike has become a serious evil, destructive to property, destructive to individual rights, injurious to the conspirators themselves and subversive of republican institutions * * *.[367]

However, at about the same time Olney was authorizing the use of the Sherman Act against workers, he refused to allow the U.S. Attorney in California to employ it against the railroad monopoly in that state, prompting a bitter prediction about the effect of this one-sided use of the Act on public respect for the law.[368] The interference-with-the-mails justification was embarrassed by the willingness of the strikers to allow trains carrying the mail to pass if they would first detach the Pullman cars from the train.[369] Olney got around this by convincing the courts to accept his definition of a "mail train" to include all cars usually hauled by trains that carried the mail.[370] Willingness of courts to accept this expansive definition of "mail train" contrasts markedly with their niggardly definitions of "confrontation."

To enforce the injunctions, many U.S. Marshals deputized railroad employees and local goons.[371] The marshals were ordered to arrest anyone assisting or encouraging the strike, including local

365. Service

Lindsey, The Pullman Strike, 1972, p. 163. This may have been why so many of the prosecutions of strikers for contempt had to be dismissed.

366. Conspiracy

Id. at p. 157.

367. "Republican institutions"

Id. at p. 157.

368. Refused to allow

Id. at p. 159–160. The U.S. Attorney wrote: "I do not hesitate to speak plainly when I say, that in my opinion, if the United States Government cannot protect the people of the Pacific states against these monopolies, it will require a larger standing army than the Government now possesses to uphold the power and dignity of the United States." Id. at p. 249.

369. Detach Pullman cars

Id. at p. 150.

370. "Mail train"

Id. at pp. 150–151.

371. Deputized goons

Id. at pp. 165–167.

magistrates who issued writs or otherwise interfered with the federal repression.[372] For example, when a trigger-happy trooper shot a solid citizen with no connection to the strike, a warrant for his arrest went for naught.[373] Many of the arrests made pursuant to the injunction were questionable; in Chicago, for example, of some 200 arrests, only 70 resulted in indictments——and many of these were later dismissed.[374] Nationwide, hundreds were indicted for conspiracy but most of these were later dismissed.[375]

But as Olney predicted, the strike was broken by brute force, not by legal condemnation.[376] Enforcement of the injunction escalated the level of violence.[377] However, Chicago——the hub of the strike——remained relatively orderly.[378] Despite the importunings of railroad officials, Illinois Governor Altgeld thought local officials had things well in hand and refused to ask for federal assistance.[379] However, when the U.S. Marshal in Chicago called for troops, President Cleveland overrode Altgeld and ordered out the Army.[380] The President acted pursuant to a Reconstruction statute authorizing the use of military force whenever insurrection, conspiracies, or domestic violence obstructed the course of judicial proceedings or otherwise rendered impossible the execution of federal laws by ordinary means.[381] Altgeld denied that these conditions were met and protested Cleveland's action.[382] When Cleveland then authorized the use of troops in other states, he met similar objections from local officials.[383] The Governor of Colorado wrote that federal officials had

372. Including magistrates
Brecher, Strike!, 1972, p. 87.

373. Went for naught
Lindsey, The Pullman Strike, 1971, p. 260.

374. Chicago arrests
Id. at p. 213.

375. More dismissed
Id. at pp. 274, 280.

376. Broken by force
Brecher, Strike!, 1972, p. 87.

377. Escalated violence
Lindsey, The Pullman Strike, 1971, pp. 205–207.

378. Chicago orderly
Id. at p. 172.

379. Refused assistance
Hicks, The Populist Revolt, 1961, p. 322.

380. Cleveland overrode
Wiebe, The Search for Order, 1967, p. 93; Lindsey, The Pullman Strike, 1971, p. 171.

381. By ordinary means
Id. at pp. 171–172.

382. Altgeld protested
Id. at pp. 184–185.

383. Similar objections
Id. at pp. 186, 262.

allowed the United States marshal to enlist a private army to suppress alleged state troubles, of which neither the county nor state authorities have any notice, and has called into active service United States troops without request or notice to the Governor of the State, and is waging an active war in Colorado without any declaration thereof by the United States, or notice or knowledge thereof by state authorities, and utterly in violation of law.[384]

But, as we have seen, protesting state officials were dismissed as fomenters of anarchy.

Ultimately more than 16,000 troops were used to break the strike.[385] Although nominally supposed to assist the U.S. Marshals, deployment of the troops in most areas was controlled by railroad lawyers.[386] The General in command of the soldiers cooperated eagerly, declaring that

> men must take sides either for anarchy, secret conclaves, unwritten law, mob violence, and universal chaos under the red or white flag of socialism on the one hand; or on the side of established government.[387]

With this sort of rhetoric, it is not surprising that the use of troops provoked the greatest outbreaks of violence. Of the 39 people killed, most of them lost their lives following the deployment of the Army.[388]

The Debs Case

Although the Justices of the Supreme Court might have seen from Cleveland's reliance on force a need to strengthen legal means of repression, this point was carried to the Court more directly in the Debs case. When the Pullman strike was all but broken by the military, the Government returned to court to legitimate its action.[389] A grand jury packed with folks from the boondocks who

384. "Utterly in violation"
Id. at p. 168.

385. Troops break strike
Id. at p. 239.

386. Lawyers controlled
Id. at p. 173.

387. "White flag of socialism"
Id. at p. 174. The "white flag" referred to the white ribbon worn by people to show their support for the strikers.

388. Greatest violence
Id. at p. 183; Paul, Conservative Crisis and the Rule of Law: Attitudes of Bar and Bench, 1887–1895, 1960, p. 141; Brecher, Strike!, 1972, p. 84.

389. Returned to court
Lindsey, The Pullman Strike, 1971, p. 226.

could be expected to be hostile to the union were assembled, given a hanging charge by Pullman's judge, and in less than two hours returned an indictment charging Eugene Debs and the other leaders of the union with conspiracy.[390] The evidence on which the indictment was based consisted almost entirely of telegrams among the defendants which the Government had obtained from Western Union over the company's claim of privilege.[391] Within minutes, Debs was arrested and the offices of the union were ransacked for further evidence——the Government being less concerned with the defendants' rights of privacy than Western Union.[392] When the Department of Justice conceded that the raid had been illegal, Pullman's judge ordered the return of papers seized.[393]

Almost simultaneously with the indictments, the same group of union leaders were cited for contempt of court on the same evidence relied upon by the grand jury.[394] At the contempt hearing, the defendants demanded but were denied trial by jury. Not wishing to disclose their defense to the criminal charges before a judge who had no intention of hearing a defense, the defendants introduced no evidence at the contempt hearing.[395] On the basis of the seized telegrams and testimony of railroad employees, the court sustained every one of the Government's legal claims and found the defendants all in contempt.[396] Debs was sentenced to six months in jail and promptly sought habeas corpus relief from the Supreme Court——thus arriving just as the Court was about to consider its first major confrontation case.[397]

Meanwhile, the conspiracy charges went to trial.[398] George Pullman——apparently not wishing to confront the defendants—— evaded the subpoena seeking his testimony, displaying a contempt

390. Returned indictment
Id. at pp. 277–278.

391. Claim of privilege
Id. at p. 278.

392. Ransacked offices
Brecher, Strike!, 1972, p. 89.

393. Returned
Lindsey, The Pullman Strike, 1971, p. 279.

394. Cited for contempt
Id. at p. 281.

395. No evidence
Id. at p. 288.

396. Found in contempt
Id. at p. 290.

397. Sought habeas
Id. at p. 292.

398. Conspiracy trial
Id. at p. 300.

for the legal process for which his judge graciously forgave him.[399] Faced with an adversary process, the Government's case collapsed and with the jury reportedly poised to acquit, the prosecutors sought delay and ultimately dismissed the case.[400]

All that was left of the strike were mopping-up operations. Olney managed to convince Pullman's judge that he should authorize government reimbursement to those railroads who had paid their employees to serve as strikebreakers.[401] During the strike, the House of Representatives had passed a resolution endorsing the Cleveland administration's repressive measures.[402] But later the Senate, at the urging of a Populist Senator, asked to see Department of Justice correspondence and the evidence that supported its military intervention and prosecution of union leaders.[403] But Olney skillfully engineered a cover-up that lasted through the end of the Cleveland administration.[404]

Railroads predictably praised Olney's actions: "To have suppressed a rebellion, to have practically opened a new development of the Principle of Equity * * * is glory enough for any one Attorney General."[405] Cooley, who in his role as constitutional commentator had endorsed an impoverished interpretation of the Confrontation Clause, now in his role of railroad lawyer and President of the A.B.A. saw no constitutional limitations on federal use of force, praising Cleveland and condemning Governor Altgeld.[406] Most members of the A.B.A. expressed similar hostility to Debs and his union.[407] It was left to the federal Strike Commission years later to suggest that "placing officers of the Government under the control of a combination of railroads * * * is a bad precedent, that might well lead to serious consequences."[408]

399. Graciously forgave

Id. at p. 303.

400. Dismissed case

Ibid.

401. Reimbursement

Id. at p. 169.

402. Endorsing measures

Id. at p. 326.

403. Senate asked to see

Id. at p. 330.

404. Cover-up

Id. at pp. 331–332.

405. "Glory enough"

Id. at p. 324.

406. Cooley

Id. at pp. 190–191. For Cooley's view of confrontation, see § 6350, text at notecall 237.

407. Similar hostility

Paul, Conservative Crisis and the Rule of Law: Attitudes of Bar and Bench, 1887–1895, 1960, p. 142.

408. "Bad precedent"

Lindsey, The Pullman Strike, 1971, p. 167.

Cleveland's actions did, however, earn him the hostility of Populists and union members, and apparently inspired Henry Demarest Lloyd's diatribe, "Wealth Against Commonwealth."[409] Among unionists, the strike fomented a resurgence of the old Republican "free labor" rhetoric, with Debs being compared to John Brown.[410] And, most significantly for our purposes, what railroads had seen as Olney's "glory" was denounced by unions as the "perversion of the federal judiciary."[411]

On the surface, this anti-Cleveland rhetoric appeared to have provided little benefit to the Populists in the mid-term elections of 1894.[412] While the Populists did take control of a Southern state for the first time, elsewhere the number of Populist officeholders remained the same.[413] In the South this has been attributed to the same combination of corruption and coercion employed by Democrats in 1892.[414] Indeed, in some states lynchings increased dramatically in the leadup to the election.[415] In the North, it has been hypothesized that unions and their supporters revenged themselves on Cleveland by voting Republican rather than Populist.[416] But those concerned about the rise of radicalism could take little comfort from the election results; the number of people who voted for Populist candidates increased from the election of 1892 by more than 50%.[417]

If acceptance of a strong adversary system with a robust right of confrontation requires faith in the stability of the existing sociopolitical structure (or a willingness to see it drastically changed), then 1895 was not a good year for the Supreme Court to undertake its first extensive foray into confrontational jurisprudence. It was the year that Utah became the second state to allow women to vote, that the first patent was issued for a gasoline-powered automobile engine, and Stephen Crane's realistic look at

409. "Against Commonwealth"

Hicks, The Populist Revolt, 1961, p. 322.

410. Compared to Brown

Lindsey, The Pullman Strike, 1971, p. 226.

411. "Perversion"

Id. at p. 267.

412. Elections of 1894

Hicks, The Populist Revolt, 1961, p. 338.

413. Remained the same

Id. at p. 337.

414. Employed by Democrats

Goodwyn, The Populist Moment, 1978, p. 193.

415. Lynchings increased

Id. at p. 195.

416. Voting Republican

Hicks, The Populist Revolt, 1961, p. 338.

417. More than 50%

Id. at p. 338; Wiebe, The Search for Order, 1877–1920, 1967, p. 90.

"patriotic gore", "The Red Badge of Courage", was published.[418] Even more threatening to the established interests, 1895 brought the rise of so-called "Free Silver Democrats" and a hoarding of gold that saw the nation's gold reserves sink so drastically that the government had to buy gold from the House of Morgan,[419] and, as we have seen, economic turmoil, a rebellious workforce, and an incipient agrarian revolt.

The Trilogy of 1895

Anyone supposing that the Court's confrontation analysis arose in a vacuum unaffected by the intellectual jitters of the elite need look no farther than a trilogy of cases decided that same year that many commentators, then and since, have seen as showing the Court's willingness to embrace "class justice"——cases that were to make the Court an issue in the Presidential election the following year.[420] The first of these was U.S. v. E.C. Knight Co., the government's attempt to use the Sherman Act against the Sugar Trust—— what the Act's author had called one of the "most outrageous monopolies of the day."[421] Some lawyers muttered that Attorney General Olney, who did not sympathize with the goals of the statute, had failed to introduce crucial evidence of monopolistic intent.[422] Whether or not that is true, the Court, which was about to approve the use of the Act against labor unions, wrote an opinion that seemed to gut the Act as a tool against corporations.[423] The Court's action brought an uproar from those lawyers who thought the Act provided a moderate alternative to the demands of Populists and labor unions.[424] Olney, on the other hand, read the Court's

418. "Red Badge" published

Encyclopedia of American Facts and Dates, Carruth ed. 1993, pp. 370–372.

419. Buy gold from Morgan

Id. at p. 370; Encyclopedia of American History, Morris ed. 1976, p. 315.

420. "Class justice"

Fiss, History of the Supreme Court of the United States: Troubled Beginnings of the Modern State, 1888–1910, 1993, pp. 3, 117.

421. E.C. Knight Case

1895, 15 S.Ct. 249, 156 U.S. 1, 39 L.Ed. 325. Senator Sherman's characterization of the Trust is quoted above, text at note 320.

422. Failed to introduce

Paul, Conservative Crisis and the Rule of Law: Attitudes of Bar and Bench, 1887–1895, 1960, p. 182, n. 68.

423. Seemed to gut

Mason, William Howard Taft: Chief Justice, 1965, p. 47 (describing how the future Chief Justice defended the Court's 1895 trilogy for the A.B.A.).

424. Uproar from lawyers

Paul, Conservative Crisis and the Rule of Law: Attitudes of Bar and Bench, 1887–1895, 1960, p. 182.

opinion as a vindication of his refusal to enforce the Act.[425]

The second case in the trilogy, Pollock v. Farmers' Loan & Trust Co., was the Court's only invalidation of a major piece of Congressional legislation during this era.[426] When Congress adopted a token tax on incomes as part of a tariff-reform package in 1894, it was attacked as an "entering wedge of socialism" because it exempted small income but President Cleveland allowed it to become law without his signature because a veto would have continued in effect a tariff the Democrats had pledged to remove.[427] Elite lawyers saw in the statute a key test of the power and willingness of the judiciary to protect the capitalist order from the forces of rampant democracy.[428] Accordingly, they amassed a war chest to finance a constitutional challenge.[429] To allow the case to reach the Supreme Court quickly, the Solicitor General made only a token defense that allowed the plaintiffs to evade a statute supposedly forbidding suits to restrain the collection of taxes.[430]

The rhetoric of the contestants reveals the anxieties of those who urged the Court to "stop the communistic march."[431] The debate in Congress exhibited a split in class loyalties.[432] Even the sober John Sherman of Ohio called the proposal a "low and mean form of socialism."[433] Arguments before the Court were equally apocalyptic: "one evil step will lead to another * * * until by and by we will have a revolution, then anarchy and then a tyrant to

425. Read as vindication

Id. at p. 189, n. 9.

426. Pollack case

1895, 15 S.Ct. 673, 157 U.S. 429, 39 L.Ed. 759; on reargument 1895, 15 S.Ct. 912, 158 U.S. 601, 39 L.Ed. 1108. See also, Beth, The Development of the American Constitution, 1877–1917, 1971, p. 154.

427. "Entering wedge"

Friedman, A History of American Law, 1973, p. 496.

428. Key test

Paul, Conservative Crisis and the Rule of Law: Attitudes of Bar and Bench, 1887–1895, 1960, p. 159.

429. Amassed war chest

Id. at p. 184, n. 74.

430. Allowed to evade

Id. at p. 173. The President and Olney, stung by criticism of the government's handling of the Sugar Trust Case, fired the Solicitor General. Kyvig, Explicit and Authentic Acts, 1996, pp. 196–197.

431. "Communistic march"

Beth, The Development of the American Constitution, 1877–1917, 1971, p. 158.

432. Class loyalties

Paul, Conservative Crisis and the Rule of Law: Attitudes of Bar and Bench, 1887–1895, 1960, p. 162.

433. "Mean socialism"

Fiss, History of the Supreme Court of the United States: Troubled Beginnings of the Modern State, 1888–1910, 1993, p. 81.

rule us."[434] Readers today may find this rather comical, but the fact that Wall Street lawyers could expect the Court to be moved by such arguments tells us much about how the Court would approach construction of the Confrontation Clause.[435] Hear the peroration of the lead attorney for the plaintiffs:

> This Act * * * is communistic in its purposes and tendencies, and is defended here upon principles as communistic, socialistic— what shall I call them— populistic as ever have been addressed to any political assembly in the world.[436]

Lest the reader suppose that Olney had brought in "Sockless" Jerry Simpson to defend the tax, we hasten to add that these words were aimed at James C. Carter, then one of the most respected members of the American Bar.[437] This rhetoric was even reflected in the opinions of the Justices; Justice Field called the income tax an "assault on capital" and a "stepping stone [toward] a war of the poor against the rich."[438] Even two decades later when an Amendment to overturn the Court's decision was under consideration, Justice David Brewer, Field's son-in-law and a member of the Pollock majority, called it the work of "demagogues and revolutionaries."[439]

In a decision that proved to be the Court's most controversial ruling since the Dred Scott decision, a majority of the Court held the tax unconstitutional.[440] As expected, those with Populist leanings agreed with Sylvester Pennoyer, the Governor of Oregon, who called the Court's decision a "usurpation" of power and urged the impeachment of the Justices.[441] A Populist journal fanned the flames by announcing that the Court "has declared for plutocratic

434. "Then anarchy"

Kyvig, Explicit & Authentic Acts, 1996, p. 197.

435. Court moved

For more on this rhetoric and the Court, see Beth, The Development of American Constitution, 1877–1917, 1971, p. 138; Twiss, Lawyers and the Constitution: How Laissez Faire Came to the Supreme Court, 1942, p. 114.

436. "Populistic"

Kyvig, Explicit & Authentic Acts, 1996, p. 197.

437. Carter

Ibid.

In the case devised to test the statute, Carter represented a bank sued by its shareholders to prevent it from paying the tax.

438. "War against rich"

Id. at p. 198.

439. "Revolutionaries"

Id. at p. 204.

440. Since Dred Scott

Id. at p. 199.

441. Urged impeachment

Id. at p. 199. Governor Pennoyer, as the loser in the famous case involving personal jurisdiction and due process, had his own bone to pick with the Court.

wealth" so that "people have lost confidence in the government and respect for law * * * approaching the temper of revolution."[442] Such indignation found comfort in the opinions of the dissenting Justices; Justice Henry Brown called the majority view a "national calamity" and "a surrender of the taxing power to the moneyed class" and Justice Harlan said the Court had made the Constitution "a most dangerous instrument to the rights and liberties of the people."[443] A generation later, a leading constitutional commentator called the majority opinion "bad history and bad logic."[444]

We shall see similar "bad history" when we examine the Court's confrontation decision, but the Income Tax Case is also significant because to reach the result it wanted, the majority had to overturn a century of contrary precedents.[445] Even more significantly, the decision stimulated numerous proposals between 1895 to reduce the "power of the courts, make judges subject to popular election and recall, limit judicial terms of office, give Congress power to override Court decisions, and make it easier to amend the Constitution."[446] As we shall see, such demands helped turn Populism into Progressivism—the ideology that continues to shape confrontation jurisprudence today.

A week after the Income Tax Case came down, the Court issued its last decision in the 1895 trilogy—In re Debs.[447] The importance of this case may be glimpsed in Attorney General Olney's decision to appear personally to argue the case for the government—the only other time he did this was in the Income Tax Case.[448] The defense argued that the Sherman Act was not

---

442. "Temper of revolution"

Pollack, The Populist Response to Industrial America, 1962, p. 77.

443. "Dangerous instrument"

Kyvig, Explicit & Authentic Acts, 1996, p. 198. Justice Brown described the majority opinion as "the first step toward the submergence of the liberties of the people in a sordid despotism of wealth." Glennon, Justice Henry Billings Brown: Values in Tension, 1973, 44 Colo.L.Rev. 553, 573.

444. "Bad logic"

Friedman, A History of American Law, 1973, p. 497.

445. Overturn precedents

Paul, Conservative Crisis and the Rule of Law: Attitudes of Bar and Bench, 1887–1895, 1960, p. 217.

446. "Easier to amend"

Kyvig, Explicit & Authentic Acts, 1996, p. 200.

447. Debs case

1895, 15 S.Ct. 900, 158 U.S. 564, 39 L.Ed. 1092. Paul, Conservative Crisis and the Rule of Law: Attitudes of Bar and Bench, 1887–1895, 1960, p. 219.

448. Appear personally

Lindsey, The Pullman Strike, 1971, p. 295.

intended to apply to labor unions and that the use of the contempt power to punish Debs denied him his Sixth Amendment right to trial by jury.[449]

> [N]o more tyrannous and arbitrary government can be devised than the administration of criminal law by a single judge by means of injunction and proceedings in contempt. To extend this power generally to civil cases would be absolutely destructive to liberty and intolerable to a free people.[450]

The Court disagreed, siding with the government on all points; the Court held there was no denial of the right to jury trial because

> the power of a court to make an order carries with it the equal power to punish for disobedience of that order * * *. To submit the question of disobedience to another tribunal, be it jury or another court, would operate to deprive the proceeding of half its efficiency.[451]

The Court was untroubled by the inconsistency between its broad application of the Sherman Act against Debs and the restrictive version it had used against the Sugar Trust.[452]

While the result in Debs pleased railroad executives and other capitalists, workers and Populists were critical.[453] Governor Altgeld invoked confrontation values in his response: in denying the defendant the right to the Sixth Amendment adversary system, it violated the separation of functions "the judge being legislator, court, and executioner."[454] But to understand the significance of Debs for the Supreme Court's consideration of the right of confrontation, we must view it, as have many commentators, as part of the infamous trilogy of 1895.[455]

One popular explanation of the trilogy has it simply reflecting the class biases of the judges.[456] Indeed, one writer has argued that

449. Denied Sixth right
Id. at pp. 293–294.

450. "Destructive to liberty"
Id. at p. 293.

451. "Deprive of efficiency"
Id. at p. 298 (quoting 158 U.S. at 598).

452. Inconsistency
Beth, The Development of the American Constitution, 1877–1917, p. 160.

453. Populists critical
Lindsey, The Pullman Strike, 1971, p. 298.

454. "And executioner"
Id. at p. 299.

455. Infamous trilogy
Warren, The Supreme Court in United States History, 1937, p. 699.

456. Class biases
Fiss, History of the Supreme Court of the United States: Troubled Beginnings of the Modern State, 1888–1910, 1993, p. 13 (discussing writers who take this view).

the result in Debs did not arise from any desire to favor capitalists, but rather from the fear and hatred of laboring men and unions that arises from social distance.[457] It certainly appears that Attorney General Olney's pursuit of the case was fueled by a personal animus towards Debs.[458] However, one of the purposes of the adversary system is to protect despised persons from the animus of those with power; given the attitudes of the many towards capitalists and the demands for government action against them, one might expect that the Court would be wary of whittling away Sixth Amendment rights in the belief that only the laboring classes had any use for them. But the Court's defense to charges of class bias does have implications for confrontation; this is the simple-minded distinction between "law" and "politics" that supposes that legal reasoning allows one to overcome personal prejudice.[459]

Others have explained the trilogy as the Court's response to the demand of the capitalist elite——the Court's core constituency——for protection of private property and its power and privileges from the demands of the downtrodden for regulation and amelioration of its excesses.[460] One historian has seen the change in the Court's response to economic regulation from the Granger Cases to the Sugar Trust Case as reflecting the passing of power from a generation of judges still tainted by Black Republican fear of monopoly and devotion to the Free Labor ideology of the antislavery movement to a group who came to power through their service to railroads and other capitalist power holders.[461] This theory is supported by the argument in the Income Tax Cases that the Court must act

> now or never * * *. You cannot exercise any check if you now say that Congress is untrammeled and uncontrollable * * *. I have

457. Fear and hatred

Beth, The Development of the American Constitution, 1877–1917, 1971, p. 150.

458. Animus towards Debs

Lindsey, The Pullman Strike, 1971, p. 295.

459. "Law" and "politics"

Fiss, History of the Supreme Court of the United States: Troubled Beginnings of the Modern State, 1888–1910, 1993, pp. 19–20 (explaining value of this distinction). The power of this myth can be seen in those constitutional scholars who on the one hand recognize that Presidents appoint Justices on political grounds——and even testify for or against nominees on this ground——and on the other hand struggle to explain variations in doctrine on some ground other than the changing membership of the Court.

460. Protection of property

Wiebe, The Search for Order, 1877–1920, 1967, p. 92.

461. Service to railroads

Id. at pp. 81, 92.

thought that one of the fundamental objects of all civilized government was the preservation of the rights of private property. I have thought that it was the very keystone of the arch upon which all civilized government rests, and once this is abandoned, everything was at stake and in danger.[462]

This argument resonated with those Justices who feared "the agrarian and despoiling spirit" that had brought " 'Looking Backward' [much] nearer than a dream." Under this view, Justices saw the income tax as "an attack upon accumulated property by mere force of numbers."[463]

The elevation of property rights over human rights did not augur well for the Court's attitude toward confrontation. Moreover, it was coupled with the need that the Court had created by its own nationalistic decisions; that is, having repulsed many efforts to regulate capitalism at the state level by appeal to commercial nationalism, the Court had now to augment its own power vis a vis Congress to block attempts by Populists and labor unions to capture political power at the federal level.[464] However, as the Debs case suggested, the expansion of federal judicial power was threatened by jury nullification of unpopular laws, whether judge-made or legislative. As Justice Brewer wrote:

If all the inhabitants of a State, or even a great body of them, should combine to obstruct interstate commerce or the transportation of the of the mails, prosecutions for such offenses had in such a community would be doomed in advance to failure.[465]

The spectre of jury nullification of the nationalist program in the Reconstruction South cast a long shadow over attempts to argue for a generous reading of the Sixth Amendment rights that might obstruct judicial efforts to protect property from modern-day Levellers.[466]

462. "Everything in danger"

Kyvig, Explicit & Authentic Acts, 1996, p. 197.

463. "Force of numbers"

Wiebe, The Search for Order, 1877–1920, 1967, p. 93.

464. Augment own power

Id. at p. 107.

465. "Doomed in advance"

Fiss, History of the Supreme Court of the United States: Troubled Beginnings of the Modern State, 1888–1910, 1993, p. 70.

466. Modern-day Levellers

On jury nullification in the Reconstruction South, see § 6355, text at notecall 318. On the role of the Levellers in the development of the right of confrontation, see vol. 30, § 6343, p. 272.

Judicial fear of popular resistance to capitalism creeps out in the opinion of Justice Brewer in the Debs case, where he wrote that the issue before the Court was the power of the federal government when it found itself in "the throes of rebellion or revolution."[467] But two years earlier, even before the Pullman strike and the rise of Populism, Justice Brewer had expressed these fears more explicitly in a speech to the New York State Bar Association that a historian of the Court says "provides a key to understanding * * * much of the Supreme Court's work of the early 1890s."[468] In explaining why the nation "was at the edge of revolution", Brewer said:[469]

> It is the unvarying law, that the wealth of a community will be in the hands of a few. * * * The large majority of men are unwilling to endure that long self-denial and saving which makes accumulation possible; they have not the business tact and sagacity which brings about large combinations and great financial results.[470]

Having established this 19th Century version of "The Bell Curve", Justice Brewer then denounced "the improper use of labor organizations to destroy the freedom of the laborer, and control the uses of capital."[471] To him, a strike "is coercion, force: it is the effort of the many, by the mere weight of numbers, to compel the one to do their bidding."[472] Labor-union leaders "may only open the door to lawlessness; but Berkman, the anarchist and assassin, will be the first to pass through; and thus it will be always and everywhere."[473]

Brewer expressed fear and hatred of "the black flag of anarchism, flaunting destruction to property, and therefore [the] relapse of society to barbarism" and "the red flag of socialism, inviting a redistribution of property, which, in order to secure the vaunted equality, must be repeated again and again."[474] But Brewer's fears

467. "Throes of revolution"
15 S.Ct. at 911, 158 U.S. at 597.

468. "Key to understanding"
Fiss, History of the Supreme Court of the United States: Troubled Beginnings of the Modern State, 1888–1910, 1993, p. 61.

469. "Edge of revolution"
Id. at p. 53.

470. "Tact and sagacity"
Id. at p. 54.

471. "Control capital"
Id. at p. 55.

472. "Do their bidding"
Ibid.

473. "Always and everywhere"
Ibid.

474. "Red and black flag"
Id. at p. 56.

went beyond lawlessness to those who would use lawful means such as the ballot and the adversary system:

> Who does not perceive that the mere fact of numbers is beginning to assert itself? Who does not hear the old demagogic cry, "Vox populi vox Dei" (paraphrased today, "the majority are always right"), constantly invoked to justify disregard of those guaranties which have hitherto been deemed sufficient to give protection to private property?[475]

Brewer was not, of course, speaking for the Court but he expressed the fears of those who looked to the Court for protection from the masses. The Court was responding, not only to those with a stake in preservation of the existing social order but to those who wanted an end to strikes and violence.[476] Thus the Debs case came to typify the statist bias of the Court's criminal-procedure decisions in this period—including those dealing with the right of confrontation.[477]

The Mattox Case

In this atmosphere of fear and loathing, the case of Mattox v. U.S. returned to the Supreme Court.[478] Though some writers suppose that Mattox was the Supreme Court's first encounter with a claim under the Confrontation Clause, most writers concede that it was not, but rightly assert it was the first important case.[479] Mattox involved a murder in what was then Oklahoma Indian Territory which was tried in federal District Court in Kansas.[480] In its first trip to the Supreme Court, the case was reversed because the District Court refused to allow the defense to introduce exculpatory portions of a dying declaration and refused to consider affidavits of the jurors alleging that they were apprised of a prior murder by the defendant through the remarks of the bailiff and a story in the local

---

475. "Private property"

Ibid.

476. End to violence

Beth, The Development of the American Constitution, 1877–1917, 1971, p. 222.

477. Statist bias

Id. at p. 238.

478. Mattox case

1895, 15 S.Ct. 337, 156 U.S. 237, 39 L.Ed. 409.

479. First important

Griswold, The Due Process Revolution and Confrontation, 1971, 119 U.Pa. L.Rev. 711, 713 (supposing Mattox first); Kirkpatrick, Confrontation and Hearsay: Exemptions from the Constitutional Unavailability Requirement, 1986, 70 Minn.L.Rev. 665 (gets it right); Ross, Confrontation and Residual Hearsay: A Critical Examination and a Proposal for Military Courts, 118 Mil.L.Rev. 31, 38 (ditto). For the first Supreme Court consideration, see § 6356, text at note 770.

480. In Indian Territory

The defendant was charged with having shot a black cowboy in Oklahoma City.

newspaper that had been brought into the jury room.[481] No one, and certainly not the Court, seems to have considered this violation of the blank-pad rule as raising any confrontation issue.[482]

When the case was retried, two witnesses who had testified and been subjected to cross-examination in the first trial had died so their testimony from the first trial was read to the jury from a stenographic transcript.[483] The case against the defendant was largely circumstantial and the testimony of the deceased witness was, according to the Court, the "strongest proof against the accused."[484] The defense argued that this infringed the defendant's right to "be confronted with the witnesses against him."[485] Given the many prior state cases holding that under these circumstances, past confrontation satisfied the right of confrontation, it is not surprising that the Supreme Court likewise found no violation of confrontation.[486] However, the way the Court went about this, if not surprising, is surely disappointing.[487]

First, the Court seems to think English precedents are relevant and that there is no need to explain why.[488] Second, when the Court does look at prior state cases, it intermixes cases treating the issue as solely one of the common law rules of evidence with those that consider the constitutional question with some seriousness.[489] The

481. Brought into jury room

Mattox v. U.S., 1892, 13 S.Ct. 50, 146 U.S. 140, 36 L.Ed. 917.

482. Blank-pad rule

For the modern view, see Parker v. Gladden, 1966, 87 S.Ct. 468, 385 U.S. 363, 17 L.Ed.2d 420 (finding violation of confrontation on facts similar to those in Mattox I).

483. Read from transcript

15 S.Ct. at 338, 156 U.S. at 240.

484. "Strongest proof"

Ibid.

485. "Witnesses against"

Ibid.

486. Prior state cases

See above, text at notecall 35.

487. Disappointing

Note, The True Value of the Confrontation Clause: A Study of Child Sex Abuse Trials, 1994, 82 Geo.L.J. 1605, 1632 (tracing flaws in modern confrontation jurisprudence to Mattox).

488. English precedents

15 S.Ct. at 339, 156 U.S. at 240.

489. Intermixes cases

Id. at 339, 156 U.S. at 241. Perhaps the least excusable of these is the Court's treatment of California law. The Court points out that California was one of the states that excluded former testimony offered against a criminal defendant, but that this judge-made rule was overturned by the adoption of the Field Code. The Court then says that this statute was "held to be constitutional", citing People v. Oiler, 1884, 4 P. 1066, 66 Cal. 101. This implies that it was held to have satisfied the right of confrontation. However, as the Court would have discovered had it actually read the Oiler decision, the California Constitution at this

Court relies heavily on the opinion of the Supreme Judicial Court in Massachusetts in Richards and distinguishes the earliest state confrontation decisions that are inconsistent with Richards.[490]

In the most famous paragraph in his opinion for a unanimous Court,[491] Justice Brown stated the policy of what he called the defendant's "constitutional immunity":[492]

> The primary object of the constitutional provision in question was to prevent depositions or ex parte affidavits, such as were sometimes admitted in civil cases, being used against the prisoner in lieu of a personal examination and cross-examination of the witness in which the accused has an opportunity, not only of testing the recollection and sifting the conscience of the witness, but of compelling him to stand face to face with the jury in order that they may look at him, and judge by his demeanor on the stand and the manner in which he gives his testimony whether he is worthy of belief.[493]

Justice Brown fails to support this ipse dixit with so much as a single citation of authority or the slightest shred of evidence, but this has not prevented some scholars from supposing that this passage captures what Mason had in mind when he drafted the first American confrontation clause.[494]

Since the jury did not have the benefit of demeanor evidence in Mattox, Justice Brown has to square the stated object of the right with the use of former testimony against the accused. He does this in several ways. First, he follows, without explicitly referring to, the

time had no confrontation clause; the statute was held constitutional against the claim that it exceeded the legislative authority to allow the use of depositions in criminal cases provided in the Constitution.

490. Inconsistent with Richards

Ibid. The Richards case is discussed in § 6355, text at notecall 685. The Court distinguishes the 1827 Finn case holding that confrontation bars the use of former testimony on the ground that in that case the witness was not dead but merely absent from the jurisdiction. Finn is discussed in § 6355, text at notecall 620. The Court correctly notes that the Atkins case in 1807, holding confrontation barred the use of former testimony of

a deceased witness was subsequently reversed by later Tennessee decisions. See § 6355, text at notecall 339.

491. Famous paragraph

Read, The New Confrontation–Hearsay Dilemma, 1972, 45 So.Cal.L.Rev. 1, 9.

492. "Immunity"

15 S.Ct. at 339, 156 U.S. at 242.

493. "Worthy of belief"

Id. at p. 339, 156 U.S. at 242–243.

494. Mason had in mind

Lilly, Notes on the Confrontation Clause and Ohio v. Roberts, 1984, 36 U.Fla. L.Rev. 207, 214. On Mason's drafting of the first confrontation clause, see vol. 30, § 6346, pp. 577–585.

state decisions that hold that right of confrontation is satisfied by a prior confrontation with the witness.[495]

> The substance of the constitutional protection is preserved to the prisoner in the advantage he has once had of seeing the witness face to face, and of subjecting him to the ordeal of cross-examination.[496]

This doctrinal exegesis is unsupported by authority, but Justice Brown does attempt to support it with some questionable history and with a statist policy argument.

As to the first, the opinion says:

> We are bound to interpret the Constitution in light of the law as it existed at the time it was adopted, not as reaching out for new guarantees of the rights of the citizen, but as securing to every individual such as he already possessed as a British subject——such as his ancestors had inherited and defended since the days of Magna Charta.[497]

As we have seen, the right of confrontation did not come down from "Magna Charta" and it is doubtful that it existed in England at the time the Confrontation Clause was drafted.[498] Moreover, those who demanded a Bill of Rights wanted one that protected rights that did not yet exist in England and that had been denied them during the colonial era.[499] Though Justice Brown seems to be unaware of it, his is a Federalist view of the history of the right of confrontation, but

---

495. Confrontation satisfied

See above, text at notecall 37. To say that confrontation is "satisfied" is to say that it is satisfied by past confrontation; the alternative is to admit that confrontation has not been satisfied but to find that it has been "excused" by state's inability to produce the declarant to testify despite a good faith effort to do so. Most of the prior state cases had held that former testimony was a case of confrontation excused. As we shall see, elsewhere in his opinion Justice Brown seems to suggest this as an alternate ground.

496. "Advantage once had"

15 S.Ct. at 340, 156 U.S. at 244.

497. "Since Magna Charta"

Id. at 340, 156 U.S. at 243.

498. Doubtful existed

On the Magna Charta and confrontation, see vol. 30, § 6342, pp. 209–210. On the existence of confrontation under English law, see Id., § 6343, pp. 305–310; § 6344, pp. 419–426.

499. Rights did not exist

On the demands for a Bill of Rights, see vol. 30, § 6347. As an example of the Founders' insistence on a right not recognized in England, consider the right to counsel and the right to be present during the taking of testimony——rights not recognized in England until the Nineteenth Century. Comment, An Historical Argument for the Right to Counsel During Police Interrogation, 1964, 73 Yale L.J. 1000, 1018, 1039.

the Federalists were not the persons who demanded confrontation at the time of ratification of the Constitution.[500]

Justice Brown continues, following the passage just quoted:

> Many of [the Constitution's] provisions in the nature of a Bill of Rights are subject to exceptions, recognized long before the adoption of the Constitution and not interfering at all with its spirit. Such exceptions were obviously intended to be respected.[501]

As an illustration of one such "exception", Justice Brown discussed the hearsay exception for dying declarations, pointing out such declarations are more unreliable and an even greater denial of confrontation than is former testimony.[502] What he does not do is provide any evidence that the dying-declaration exemption was recognized in American or English courts at the time of the drafting of the Bill of Rights or that the Founders intended to recognize hearsay exceptions as exceptions to the right of confrontation.[503]

When Justice Brown tries to bolster his constitutional history and interpretation with consideration of public policy, we hear the clash of arms at Homestead and the tramp of Coxey's Army.

> But general rules of law of this kind, however beneficent in their operation and valuable to the accused, must occasionally give way to considerations of public policy and the necessities of the case. To say that a criminal, after having once been convicted by the testimony of a certain witness, should go scot free simply because death has closed the mouth of that witness, would be carrying his constitutional protection to an unwarrantable extent. The law in its wisdom declares that the rights of the public shall not be wholly sacrificed in order that an incidental benefit may be preserved to the accused.[504]

500. Federalist view

See § 6355, text at notecall 704. On the Federalist view of the Bill of Rights, see vol. 30, § 6347, pp. 681–683.

501. "Intended to be respected"

15 S.Ct. at 340, 156 U.S. at 243.

502. Dying declarations

Id. at 340, 156 U.S. at 243–244. On the treatment of dying declarations by state courts, see above, text at notecall 28.

503. Recognized at time

Though he tries to give the exception ancient antecedents, Wigmore says that the leading English case was not decided until 1761. 5 Wigmore, Evidence, Chadbourne rev. 1974, § 1430, p. 275. The exception does seem to be recognized in early American evidence books. See § 6355, text at notecall 107.

504. "Incidental benefit"

15 S.Ct. at 230, 156 U.S. at 243.

These statist sentiments are seldom quoted by subsequent cases or by the commentators and they are hard to square with the Court's view that the wealthy cannot be required to support the state with a 2% tax on their income.[505]

Note that Justice Brown pays little attention to the language of the Sixth Amendment or to the other rights that surround the Confrontation Clause in that provision. Little wonder that he can consider confrontation a mere "incidental benefit" and not a crucial ingredient in an adversary system of criminal procedure.[506] If he had done so, he might have had more difficulty in deciding to place on the accused rather than state the risks of delay.[507] It was, the reader may recall, errors of the judge and the demands of the prosecutor that postponed the trial of the defendant till after the death of the crucial witnesses.[508] Had the Court considered the adjacent guarantee of a speedy trial, it might have wondered whether it was proper to deny the defendant his rights of confrontation because through no fault of his, the state's witnesses were now dead.[509]

The Mattox Court's cramped view of confrontation surfaces in a part of the opinion usually not considered by confrontation commentators.[510] After his testimony in the first trial, one of the now-deceased witnesses told others that it was too dark at the time of the crime to see the killers, that his testimony at the trial had been false and given under threats from friends of the victim, and that upon payment of a paltry bribe he was prepared to absent himself from the jurisdiction.[511] The trial court had excluded evi-

---

505. Wealthy cannot

See above, text at notecall 426.

506. Crucial ingredient

For a sketch of the holistic view of confrontation, see vol. 30, § 6341.

507. Risks of delay

Seidelson, Hearsay Exceptions and the Sixth Amendment, 1971, 40 Geo. Wash.L.Rev. 76, 90.

508. Judge and prosecutor

This is what makes the analogy to dying declarations less satisfactory; there, whether or not the accused is the one who has made the declarant unavailable, it is clearly not the state that has caused confrontation to become an im-

possibility. Compare Reynolds v. U.S., 1878, 8 Otto (98 U.S.) 145, 25 L.Ed. 244 (by procuring absence of witness, defendant forfeits right of confrontation). Reynolds is discussed in § 6356, text at notecall 747.

509. Speedy trial

See vol. 30, § 6341, p. 194.

510. Usually not

For the rare exception, see Note, Preserving the Right to Confrontation— A New Approach to Hearsay Evidence in Criminal Trials, 1965, 113 U.Pa. L.Rev. 741, 758.

511. Paltry bribe

15 S.Ct. at 340, 156 U.S. at 244–245.

dence of these statements on the ground that the prerequisites for the admission of a prior inconsistent statement had not been met, indeed, could not be met because of the death of the witness-declarant.[512] One who saw the right of confrontation as part of an adversary system might suppose that when death excuses the absence of confrontation, the defendant might be entitled to the use of the inconsistent statements as a substitute for cross-examination.[513] The Mattox Court saw no relationship between the ruling on the inconsistent statements and the defendant's right of confrontation, affirming the trial judge's exclusion on purely common-law grounds.[514]

The Court's use of precedents is more selective than might appear from the number of citations in the opinion. For example, the opinion cites with approval a trial-court opinion from 1851 in a manner that makes it appear that the lower court was addressing the confrontation question when in fact it considered the use of former testimony only on common-law grounds.[515] If trial-court opinions are authoritative, then the opinion of Chief Justice Marshall in the trial of Aaron Burr might have been more instructive.[516] At issue was the admissibility of hearsay statements of an alleged coconspirator.[517] In holding the evidence inadmissible, the Chief Justice wrote:

> The rule of evidence which rejects mere hearsay testimony, which excludes from trials of a criminal or civil nature the declarations of any other individual than of him against whom the proceeding are instituted, has been generally deemed essential to the correct administration of justice. I know not why a declaration in court should be unavailing, unless made upon oath, if a declaration out of court was to criminate others than him who made it; nor why a man should have a constitutional claim to be confronted with the witnesses against him, if mere verbal declarations, made in his absence, may be evidence against him. I know of no principle in

512. Prerequisites

Id. at 341, 156 U.S. at 245. For the modern version, see Rule 613(b).

513. Substitute for cross

See People v. Mayfield, 1972, 100 Cal. Rptr. 104, 23 Cal.App.3d 236.

514. Affirming

15 S.Ct. at 343, 156 U.S. at 250.

515. Only on common law

U.S. v. Macomb, Cir.Ct.Ill.1851, 5 McLean 286, 26 Fed.Cas. 1132, cited 15 S.Ct. at 334, 156 U.S. at 242.

516. Trial of Burr

U.S. v. Burr, Cir.Ct.Va. 1807, 25 Fed. Cas. 187.

517. Coconspirator

Id. at 193.

the preservation of which all are more concerned.[518]

Marshall, who was a member of the Virginia ratifying convention, surely has greater authority on the meaning of the Confrontation Clause than the state courts on which Justice Brown relies.[519] While Marshall might have reached the same result as the Mattox decision, it is difficult to suppose him writing an opinion that dismissed the right of confrontation as an "incidental benefit."[520]

Moreover, if judges writing in the middle of the Nineteenth Century are to be used as authorities on the intent of the Founders, Chief Justice Taney might have enlightened Justice Brown:[521]

> The colonists who established the English colonies in this country, undoubtedly brought with them the common and statute laws of England * * * so far as they were applicable to the situation and local circumstances of the colony. And among the most cherished and familiar principles of the common law was the trial by jury in civil, but still more especially in criminal cases. * * * But as the law formerly stood, the value of this right was much impaired by the mode of proceeding in criminal cases. For when a person was accused of a capital crime and his life depended on the issue of the trial, he was denied compulsory process for witnesses; and when they voluntarily appeared in his behalf, he was not permitted to examine them on oath, nor have the aid of counsel in his defense * * *. [The Chief Justice points out that these limits had been abolished in the colonies by statute prior to the Declaration of Independence.] But the memory of the abuses which had been practiced under it had not passed away. * * * It was the people of these thirteen States which formed the constitution of the United States, and engrafted on it the provision which secures the trial by jury, and abolishes the old common-law proceeding which had so often been used for the purposes of oppression.[522]

518. "All are concerned"

Ibid.

519. Greater authority

For Marshall's attitude toward confrontation at the time of the Virginia Convention, see vol. 30, § 6347, p. 745.

520. Suppose him writing

In Burr, Marshall continued, following the passage quoted in the text: "I know none, by undermining which, life, liberty and property, might be more endangered. It is therefore in-

cumbent on courts to be watchful of every inroad on a principle so truly important." 25 Fed.Cas. at 193.

521. Chief Justice Taney

U.S. v. Reid, 1851, 12 How. (53 U.S.) 361, 13 L.Ed. 1023. Note that the Chief Justice was writing in the same year as the Macomb opinion that the Court did cite.

522. "Used for oppression"

Id. at pp. 363–364.

It would be hard to find a clearer rejection of Justice Brown's view that the Bill of Rights was not intended to recognize any rights that did not come down from "Magna Charta."[523] Taney also recognizes, as Brown does not, that the Federalists were prepared to do without a Bill of Rights and it was only the clamor stirred up by their opponents that led Congress "to amend it, and to secure to a party accused of an offense against the United States, the same mode of trial" previously established by state constitutions.[524] He specifically uses the Sixth Amendment as an example of this rejection of the ancient English common law, citing its provisions for counsel, process, and confrontation.[525]

Considering these other authorities may not have changed the result in Mattox, but it would have produced an opinion that was less stingy in its interpretation of the meaning and purposes of confrontation.[526] As it was, the opinion in Mattox laid the foundation for the Wigmorean theory of confrontation that has dominated confrontation jurisprudence for much of the 20th Century.[527]

523. Did not come

Taney recognizes the source of the Bill of Rights in the state constitutions: "And the thirteen Colonies who united in the declaration of independence, as soon as they became States, placed in their respective constitutions or fundamental laws, safeguards against the restoration of proceedings which were so oppressive and odious while they remained in force. * * * And the provisions in the Constitution of the United States in this respect are substantially the same with those which had been previously adopted in the several States." Id. at 364.

524. Clamor stirred up

"But as soon as the public attention was called to the fact, that the securities for a fair and impartial jury in criminal cases had not been inserted among the cardinal principles of the new government, they hastened to amend it * * *." Ibid.

525. As an example

He also recognizes that confrontation is not an isolated right but an integral part of the adversary system of jury trial: "It was for this purpose [that is, "to secure * * * the same mode of

trial and the same mode of proceeding" established in state constitutions] that the 5th and 6th Amendments were added to the Constitution. The 6th Amendment provides that in all criminal prosecutions, the party accused shall be entitled to a trial by jury, to be confronted with the witnesses against him, to have compulsory process for the witness in his favor, and to have the aid of counsel in his defense." Id. at pp. 364–365.

526. Less stingy

Particularly given Marshall's notion that the Constitution could not have "the prolixity of a legal code" but that "only its great outlines should be marked, its important subjects designated, and the minor ingredients which compose those objects be deduced from the nature of the objects themselves." McCulloch v. Maryland, 1819, 4 Wheat. (17 U.S.) 316, 407–408, 4 L.Ed. 579.

527. Wigmorean theory

Mosteller, Remaking Confrontation Clause and Hearsay Doctrine Under the Challenge of Child Sexual Abuse Prosecutions, 1993, Ill.L.Rev. 691, 745.

The Crisis of 1896

If the fears of the elites in the 1890s were centered around the Homestead strike, Coxey's Army, and the rise of the People's Party, the Supreme Court had provided much relief with the Trilogy of 1895; it remained for Marcus Hanna to finish the job.[528] In what has been called "the political crisis of 1896", insurgents in the Democratic Party captured the Presidential nomination for William Jennings Bryan of Nebraska.[529] The Democratic platform had three planks dealing with judicial protection of capitalism; it called for packing the Supreme Court to reverse the Income Tax decision, denying life tenure to federal judges below the Supreme Court, and the abolition of "government by injunction."[530]

The election of 1896 was seen at the time as a pivotal battle in the war between capitalism and democracy.[531] Apocalyptic rhetoric abounded on both sides, though except for Bryan's "Cross of Gold Speech", most of it has been forgotten today.[532] Conservatives expressed fears of Populism: "[t]he dissatisfied, the unemployed, the tramps have joined the misguided farmers and laboring men are following blind leaders."[533] Some of their rhetoric revealed a deep fear of democracy: fusion of the Populists and Democrats made "a dangerous party in a country like ours where the elective franchise is the privilege of the ignorant and vicious as well as the enlightened and good."[534] As usual, the bogeyman of communism was trotted out:

> In the white-heat frenzy which the proletariats have worked up under the leadership of Bryan——who, as a sort of Peter the Hermit, has proved himself to be a competent leader of the commune——there is nothing which happened during the French

528. Hanna to finish

Swisher, Stephen J. Field: Craftsman of the Law, 1969, p. xvii.

529. "Crisis of 1896"

Paul, Conservative Crisis and the Rule of Law: Attitudes of Bar and Bench, 1887–1895, p. 224.

530. "Government by injunction"

Id. at p. 225.

531. Seen as pivotal

Wiebe, The Search for Order, 1877–1920, 1967, p. 100.

532. Forgotten rhetoric

Id. at pp. 96–97.

533. "Following blind"

Pollack, The Populist Response to Industrial America, 1962, p. 128.

534. "Enlightened and good"

Ibid.

Revolutions and Communes [which could not follow a Democratic victory].[535]

Theodore Roosevelt called for drastic measures: "taking ten or a dozen of [the Populist] leaders out, standing * * * them against a wall and shooting them dead."[536]

Though such comments may provide a useful backdrop to the Supreme Court's decision in Mattox, in retrospect they border on the hysterical; in fact the Populists were, at the very least, ambivalent about fusion with the Democrats.[537] The People's Party, as is common among ideological movements, had become split between grass roots organizations and leaders who could sniff the alluring aroma of power.[538] The politics of a democratic mass movement were pitted against the hierarchical demands of electoral politics.[539] As so often happens, authoritarian leaders defeated the democratic demands of the rank-and-file by stacking the Populist convention with those who favored fusion.[540] To the leaders, fusion represented no more than a conservative strategy to insure electoral success but to committed members of the Party it was a betrayal of principle.[541]

Conservatives were right about one thing; the election of 1896 was probably the last Presidential election in which masses of people were so fully engaged.[542] But Marcus Hanna, the Cleveland industrialist who served as McKinley's campaign manager, demonstrated how by careful targeting of their wealth and influence capitalists could survive the onslaught of an outraged electorate.[543] Employers, in a cruder version of the "business climate" argument that was deployed a century later, threatened workers with loss of their jobs if Cleveland won.[544] The election degenerated into a

535. "Revolutions and Communes"

Id. at p. 130.

536. "Shooting them dead"

Wiebe, The Search for Order, 1877–1920, 1967, p. 96.

537. Populists ambivalent

Pollack, The Populist Response to Industrial America, 1962, p. 100.

538. Aroma of power

Goodwyn, The Populist Moment, 1978, p. 231.

539. Movement v. politics

Id. at p. 232.

540. Stacked convention

Id. at p. 247.

541. Betrayal of principle

Pollack, The Populist Response to Industrial America, 1962, p. 100.

542. Masses engaged

Hicks, The Populist Revolt, 1961, p. 373.

543. Hanna demonstrated

Goodwyn, The Populist Moment, 1971, pp. 270–271.

544. Loss of jobs

Hicks, The Populist Revolt, 1961, p. 375.

propaganda war between adherents of the gold and silver monetary standards.[545] In this contest, the "goldbugs" had a voice in the pulpit of the most established churches and the secular support of every academic economist in the country.[546] In the South, the Bourbons who had been shouldered aside by the silverites still maintained control of the electoral machinery.[547] And everywhere McKinley had the support of the business press; for example, Harper's Weekly ran a cartoon on its cover purporting to show a Bryan Supreme Court consisting of Debs, Altgeld, Coxey, Pennoyer and other Populist leaders sitting on a bench beneath busts of the Haymarket anarchists and the assassin of President Garfield with the Constitution lying in tatters on the floor.[548]

To the delight of the wealthy, McKinley defeated Bryan by a half-million popular votes and by nearly a hundred votes in the Electoral College—and the Republicans retained control of both houses of Congress.[549] In 1897, fueled by an increase in the gold supply, the economy moved upward taking the radical edge off insurgency.[550] Shortly thereafter, the imperialist adventure distracted reformers and the patriotic propaganda that accompanied the war with Spain muted the class consciousness that had characterized the Bryan campaign.[551] Finally, the dilution of Populist principles that accompanied fusion with the Democrats doomed the People's Party as an electoral threat.[552] Even had they remained true to their principles, those principles had little appeal to the

545. War between gold and silver

Wiebe, The Search for Order, 1877–1920, 1967, p. 101.

546. Every economist

Goodwyn, The Populist Moment, 1978, pp. 266, 270.

547. Electoral machinery

Wiebe, The Search for Order, 1877–1920, p. 95.

548. Lying in tatters

Fiss, History of the Supreme Court of the United States: Troubled Beginnings of the Modern State, 1888–1910, plate following page 76.

549. Control of both houses

Encyclopedia of American History, Morris ed. 1976, p. 317; Paul, Conservative Crisis and the Rule of Law: Atti-

tudes of Bar and Bench, 1887–1895, 1960. p. 226.

550. Moved upward

Ibid.; Hicks, The Populist Revolt, 1961, pp. 388–389.

551. War muted

Id. at p. 390; Paul, Conservative Crisis and the Rule of Law: Attitudes of Bar and Bench, 1887–1895, 1960, p. 226.

552. Dilution of principles

Goodwyn, The Populist Moment, 1978, p. 216.

foreign-born working class and middle-class reformers the Populists had to attract for any but local electoral success.[553]

If the election of 1896 had merely defused, temporarily, the anxieties of elites it would have little significance for the future of confrontation but in fact it had a number of permanent consequences that were to lead to the decline in confrontation values.

> The narrowed boundaries of modern politics that date from the 1896 campaign encircle such influential areas of American life as the relationship of citizen power to corporate power, the political language legitimated to define and settle public issues within a mass society yoked to privately owned mass communications and privately financed elections, and even the style through which the reality of the American experience——the culture itself——is conveyed to each new generation in the public and private school systems of the nation. In the aggregate, these boundaries outline a clear retreat from the democratic vistas of either the eighteenth-century Jeffersonians or the nineteenth-century Populists.[554]

With the silencing of the debate over capitalism, the notion of democratic control of the economy passed into political oblivion.[555] Though it took a while for this to be understood, it meant that the Supreme Court no longer had to go out on the sort of constitutional limb it did in the Trilogy of 1895. As we shall see, with the decline of its economic constituency the Supreme Court was eventually to turn to a moral constituency.[556]

Of more immediate significance, the rise of corporate politics produced our modern political system where "democracy" is equated with "voting."[557] So defined, "democracy" was not inconsistent with the establishment of a permanent elite whose rights to deference in matters political and economic would be sanctified by science and education rather than birth.[558] This "cult of the expert", which flowered in the Progressive movement, was inconsistent with trial by jury and its ancillary right of confrontation,[559] but

553. Little appeal

Wiebe, The Search for Order, 1877–1920, 1967, p. 88.

554. "Clear retreat"

Goodwyn, The Populist Moment, 1978, p. 265.

555. Passed into oblivion

Id. at p. 269.

556. Moral constituency

See § 6359.

557. Equated with "voting"

Goodwyn, The Populist Moment, 1978, p. 265.

558. Permanent elite

Id. at p. 286.

559. "Cult of expert"

See § 6358, text at notecall 518.

it found a vocation justifying the merger movement, the rise of corporate control of the media, and the decline of public participation that followed the election of 1896.[560]

Though the Populists vanished as a political force, Populists and their ideas shaped the Progressive movement of the early 20th Century—a movement whose ideology continues to govern evidentiary thought down to the present day.[561] In 1914, Mary Ellen Lease said:

> In these later years I have seen, with gratification, that my work in the good old Populist days was not in vain. The Progressive party has adopted our platform, clause by clause, plank by plank. Note the list of reforms which we advocated which are now coming into reality. Direct election of Senators in assured. Public utilities are gradually being [regulated]. Woman suffrage is now almost a national issue.[562]

But if the Progressives picked up many Populist proposals, they did so without the democratic justifications that Mrs. Lease herself had so well expounded in her youth.[563] The Populists did not intend to construct a centralized, bureaucratic state; indeed, they hoped by destroying corporate power to restore its antithesis—small, self-governing communities of producers.[564] The Progressives, on the other hand, midwifed the movement from individualism to social control through law out of social science.[565] The results will be apparent when we examine the course of modern confrontation jurisprudence.

The Fin de Siecle Trilogy

After having decided its first confrontation cases after more than a century under the Constitution, the Supreme Court at the turn of the century rapidly issued three confrontation opinions—including its first use of the Confrontation Clause to exclude hearsay evidence.

560. Justifying mergers and decline

Goodwyn, The Populist Moment, 1978, p. 287.

561. Progressive movement

Youngdale, Populism: A Psychohistorical Perspective, 1975, p. 38.

562. "National issue"

Hicks, The Populist Revolt, 1961, p. 421.

563. Picked up proposals

Id. at p. 404.

564. Communities of producers

Wiebe, The Search for Order, 1877–1920, 1967, p. 74.

565. Social control

Hicks, The Populist Revolt, 1961, p. 405.

The first of the three cases, Robertson v. Baldwin, was a habeas-corpus proceeding brought by four seamen who had been incarcerated on the orders of a United States Commissioner in San Francisco under a statute going back to the birth of the Republic that provided this method of enforcing the obligations of sailors to their masters.[566] The issue before the Court was whether the adoption of the Thirteenth Amendment invalidated the use of the statute as a device to break the strike of mariners.[567] In holding it did not, Justice Brown invoked the rationale and holding of his opinion in Mattox without explicitly citing that decision.

> The law is perfectly well settled that the first ten amendments to the Constitution, commonly known as the Bill of Rights, were not intended to lay down any novel principles of government, but simply to embody certain guarantees and immunities which we had inherited from our English ancestors, and which had from time immemorial been subject to certain well- recognized exceptions arising from the necessities of the case. * * * Nor does the provision that an accused person shall be confronted with the witnesses against him prevent the admission of dying declarations, or the depositions of witnesses who have died since the former trial.[568]

Justice Brown, with the Federalist Anglomania that has plagued American law from the outset, failed to notice that at least two of the petitioners—like a majority of Americans since the founding of the nation—did not have "English ancestors."[569] However, the suggestion that there were only two "exceptions" to the right of confrontation was soon to bear fruit.

Two years later, in Kirby v. United States, the Court was faced with a defendant who had been convicted of receiving stolen postal property where the only evidence that property he had received had been stolen from the post office were the guilty pleas of two thieves and the conviction of a third.[570] These had been admitted under a federal statute making a judgment of conviction conclusive evidence

566. Robertson case
1897, 17 S.Ct. 326, 165 U.S. 275, 41 L.Ed. 715.

567. Break a strike
Glennon, Justice Henry Billings Brown: Values in Tension, 1973, 44 Colo. L.Rev. 553, 577.

568. "Witnesses who have died"
15 S.Ct. at 329, 165 U.S. at pp. 281–282.

569. Did not have
Two of the defendants had names suggesting Scandinavian ancestry.

570. Kirby case
1899, 19 S.Ct. 574, 174 U.S. 47, 43 L.Ed. 890.

of the theft of the property in question.[571] However, the trial judge, for reasons that do not appear in the record, instructed the jury in terms that treated the statute as creating a presumption that shifted the burden of proof to the defendant.[572] Hence, the case raised two questions regarding the adversary system established by the Sixth Amendment and related provisions in the Bill of Rights. First, whether the defendant had been denied his right to confrontation by the use of the guilty pleas against him; and, second, whether it was constitutional to shift the burden of proof on an element of the crime to the accused?[573] In an opinion by Justice Harlan, that might be seen——but was probably not intended——as an adoption of the holistic theory of the Sixth Amendment, the Court treats the two questions as one.[574]

After holding that the fact that the property was stolen was an element of the crime that the government must prove beyond a reasonable doubt, the opinion continues:

> We are of the opinion that the trial court erred in admitting in evidence the record of the convictions of Wallace, Baxter, and King, and then in its charge saying that in the absence of proof to the contrary the fact that the property was stolen from the United States was sufficiently established against Kirby by the mere production of the record showing the conviction of the principle felons. * * * Kirby was not present when Wallace and Baxter confessed their crime by pleas of guilty, nor when King was proved to be guilty by witnesses who personally testified before the jury. Nor was Kirby entitled of right to participate in the trial of the principal felons. If present at that trial he would not have been permitted to examine Wallace and Baxter upon their pleas of guilty, nor cross-examine the witnesses introduced against King, nor introduce witnesses to prove that they were not in fact guilty of the offense charged against them.[575]

Notice how this passage blends the right of confrontation and the right of compulsory process with the right to be present at trial into the adversary trial that defendant was denied on the issue the

---

571. Conclusive evidence

Id. at 574, 174 U.S. at 48 (quoting 18 Stat. 479, ch. 144).

572. Shifted burden

Id. at pp. 376, 174 U.S. at 50–53.

573. Constitutional to shift

For the modern answer, see vol. 21, § 5148.

574. Holistic theory

See vol. 30, § 6341.

575. "Nor prove not guilty"

19 S.Ct. at 576, 174 U.S. at 54.

convictions were offered to prove.[576] Note also that while the guilty pleas might have been said to be even more reliable than a dying declaration and perhaps admissible as a declaration against interest, the opinion does not even suggest that this might be another "exception" to the right of confrontation.[577]

Moreover, the opinion in Kirby, unlike that in Mattox, does not treat the right of confrontation as a mere "incidental benefit" that can be overridden by the interests of the state.

> One of the fundamental guarantees of life and liberty is found in the Sixth Amendment of the Constitution of the United States [quoting the Confrontational Clause]. Instead of confronting Kirby with witnesses to establish the vital fact that the property alleged to have been received by him had been stolen from the United States, he was confronted only with the record of another criminal prosecution, with which he had no connection and the evidence in which was not given in his presence * * *. But a fact which can be primarily established only by witnesses cannot be proved against an accused * * * except by witnesses who confront him at the trial, upon whom he can look while being tried, whom he is entitled to cross-examine, and whose testimony he may impeach in every mode authorized by the established rules governing the trial or conduct of criminal cases.[578]

At this point and with no sense that it is shifting to a different topic, the opinion turned directly to the requirement of proof beyond a reasonable doubt. The opinion suggests that the vice of the procedure provided in the statute was not merely that it shifted the burden to the defendant but that it did so by the use of unconfronted witnesses. The opinion continues:

> We cannot assent to [the procedure employed by the court below] without conceding the power of the legislature, when proscribing the effect as evidence of records and proceedings of courts, to

576. Blends right

See also, Id. at 577, 174 U.S. at 56 ("the defendant * * * was held to be presumptively or prima facie guilty * * * as soon as the government produced the records of such conviction and without making its proof whatever by witnesses confronting the accused of existence of such vital fact.") It would not be much of a stretch to read this as saying proof of the basic fact of a presumption by unconfronted testimony is unconstitutional even if the presumption were otherwise permissible.

577. Another "exception"

Of course, though the exception was recognized by this time, it did not apply to so-called "declarations against penal interest" of the sort involved in Kirby. See 2 Wigmore, Evidence, 1904, § 1476. Moreover, there was no showing that the thieves were "unavailable" as witnesses. See Evidence Rule 804.

578. "Impeach in every mode"

19 S.Ct. at 577, 174 U.S. at 55.

impair the very substance of a right long deemed so essential for the due protection of life and liberty that it is guarded against legislative and judicial action by provisions in the Constitution of the United States and in the Constitutions of most, if not of all, the states composing the union.[579]

Notice two ways in which these passages differ from Mattox. First, whereas in Mattox the focus was on the jury being able to confront the witness to assess demeanor, here the Court suggests that the defendant also has a right to confront the witness "face to face" without any suggestion that this is instrumental to the reliability of the evidence.[580] Second, unlike the Mattox opinion but recognizing the limits of that opinion, the Kirby opinion suggests that the right of confrontation includes not only the right to cross-examine but also to impeach the witness by other means.[581]

After a long passage dealing with English and American cases and writers dealing with the law of evidence regarding judicial records, Justice Harlan concludes that the "principle to be deduced from these authorities is in harmony with" his reading of the Confrontation Clause.[582] This follows Justice Brown's view in Mattox that the Founders intended confrontation rights to be compatible with the existing rules of evidence. Indeed, Justice Harlan cites not only Mattox but Cooley's treatise in support of a dictum that recognizes the admissibility of dying declarations under the Confrontation Clause.[583] But since no such exception is available here, the statute is declared unconstitutional and the conviction of the defendant is reversed.[584]

A year later, in Motes v. United States, the Court returned to the question of the admissibility of former testimony under the Confrontation Clause.[585] A group of Alabama moonshiners allegedly murdered an informer for the hated "revenooers" and were indicted under the Ku Klux Klan Act.[586] In the midst of their preliminary

579. "Composing the union"
Id. at 577, 174 U.S. at 56.

580. Mattox focus
See above, text at notecall 493.

581. Right to impeach
See above, text at notecall 514.

582. "Harmony with"
19 S.Ct. at 578, 174 U.S. at 60.

583. Cooley dictum
Id. at 579, 174 U.S. at 61.

584. Reversed
Ibid.

585. Motes case
1900, 20 S.Ct. 993, 178 U.S. 458, 44 L.Ed. 1150.

586. Ku Klux Act
Id. at 994, 178 U.S. at 460.

examination, one of their number went over to the government side, testified against his buddies, and was cross-examined by their lawyer.[587] An hour before he was scheduled to testify at trial, the turncoat escaped from protective custody through the incompetence of federal officers who had charge of him.[588] The trial court allowed the government to introduce the testimony of the absconding witness given at the preliminary hearing against the remaining defendants.[589]

On appeal, the Supreme Court was

> of the opinion that admission in evidence of Taylor's statement or deposition taken at the examining trial was in violation of the constitutional right of the defendants to be confronted by the witnesses against them. It did not appear that Taylor was absent from the trial by the suggestion, procurement, or act of the accused. On the contrary, his absence was manifestly due to the negligence of officers of the Government.[590]

The opinion by Justice Harlan treated the case as symmetrical with Reynolds;[591] that is, if the defendant could not invoke the right of confrontation when he was responsible for the absence of the witness, so the prosecution could not assert the exception recognized in Mattox when it was responsible for the absence of the declarant. This forfeiture theory made it unnecessary for the Court to decide whether absence of the witness without the fault of either party was sufficient to trigger the Mattox exception.[592] However, the Court cites and relies upon an English case in which it was held that where the absence was due to the procurement of one defendant, the prosecution could not use the preliminary hearing testimony against another defendant who bore no responsibility for the

587. Cross-examined

Id. at 997, 178 U.S. at 467, 468.

588. Incompetence

Two days prior to the trial, the officer of the Justice Department had the witness sprung from the local bastille and put up at a hotel with his family in charge of another of the prosecution's witnesses. Id. at 997, 178 U.S. at 468.

589. Allowed to introduce

Id. at 997, 178 U.S. at 470.

590. "Due to negligence"

Id. at 998, 178 U.S. at 471.

591. Reynolds

See § 6356, text at notecall 770. See also, Garcia, The Sixth Amendment in Modern Jurisprudence, 1992, pp. 73–74.

592. Sufficient to trigger

Both in Mattox and in the Robertson dictum, the Court seemed to suppose that death was the only excusing circumstance. See above, text at notecalls 504, 568.

absence of the witness.[593] Moreover, the Court quotes a passage from Cooley that suggests that only death, insanity, or physical incapacity will excuse the absence of contemporaneous cross-examination.[594]

"The Revolt Against Formalism"

In our analysis of the Supreme Court's earliest confrontation decisions, we sought to place doctrine in its sociopolitical context, to seek explanation for the Court's use of concepts in the events of the time. But judges are affected by ideas as well as events. Therefore, we need to depart from our historical chronology and retreat from the tumult of the 1890s to the quiet studies where thinkers were developing the ideas that were to shape confrontation for most of the 20th Century. These ideas require some explanation because by the end of the 20th Century, legal scholarship—including evidentiary scholarship—had returned to the very sort of formalist thinking that had been rejected a century earlier.[595]

The preeminent intellectual historian of this period uses the term "the revolt against formalism" to capture the theme that unites the men whose ideas dominated American thought for a period of fifty years—a crucial era in the development of American legal theory.[596] He selects five men as representative of, if not the dominant figures in, the intellectual life of the United States from the 1880s to the 1930s: the philosopher and educator John Dewey, the economist Thorstein Veblen, the legal scholar and judge Oliver Wendell Holmes, Jr., and the historians Charles Beard and James Harvey Robinson.[597] These thinkers developed approaches to their disciplines that have been characterized as "pragmatism, instru-

593. English case

See 20 S.Ct. at 998–999, 178 U.S. at 472–473.

594. Cooley passage

Id. at 998, 178 U.S. at 472. See also Id. at 999, 178 U.S. at 474 ("Nor (if that were material) did his disappearance occur so long prior to his being called as a witness as to justify the conclusion that he had gone out of the State and was permanently beyond the jurisdiction of the court.").

595. Return to formalism

We refer to economic analysis of law, or as it is called in its evidentiary incar-

nation "The New Evidence Scholarship."

596. Crucial era

White, Social Thought in America: The Revolt Against Formalism, 1957 ed., p. 3. On the importance of this period for evidentiary thought, see § 6358. See also, vol. 21, § 5025.

597. Five thinkers

White, Social Thought in America: The Revolt Against Formalism, 1957 ed. p. 3.

mentalism, institutionalism, economic determinism, and legal realism."[598] They "are all suspicious of approaches which are excessively formal; they all protest their anxiety to come to grips with reality, their attachment to the moving and vital in social life."[599] As we have seen "movement" and "vitality" in society might have seemed less benign to those who had a greater stake in social stability, including the members of the Court that decided Mattox.

But it would be wrong to suppose that these thinkers merely negated the qualities they abhorred; they made at least two positive contributions. The first of these Professor White calls "historicism"; that is, the attempt to explain facts in reference to earlier facts.[600] The second he calls "cultural organicism"; by this he means "the attempt to find explanations and relevant material in social sciences other than the one which is primarily under investigation."[601] The first can be illustrated by Justice Holmes' notion that since law embodies the national experience it cannot be explained deductively, summed up in the famous aphorism "the life of the law has not been logic; it has been experience."[602] The second can be illustrated by Holmes' use of anthropology in his study of common law.[603] Both historicism and cultural organicism are so common in the law today that it is hard to imagine a time when they might have been new.[604]

Of the five influential thinkers, Holmes will be most familiar to the readers of this treatise. But in an era in which some insist that

---

598. "Legal realism"

Id. at p. 6. For our purposes, it is unnecessary to enter into the debate about whether Holmes was or was not a "legal realist" because our concern is not with how that term is defined or in categorizing Holmes. For Professor White's definition, see id. at p. 8.

599. "Moving and vital"

Id. at p. 6.

600. "Historicism"

Id. at p. 12.

601. "Organicism"

Ibid.

602. "Life not logic"

Id. at p. 16. See also, Holmes, The Common Law, Howe ed. 1963, p. 5.

603. Use of anthropology

Id. at p. 13 n. 25 (citing Tylor's Primitive Culture). See also, White, Social Thought in America: The Revolt Against Formalism, 1957 ed., p. 17.

604. Common in law

Even our history of confrontation may be said to exhibit something of each. By saying that these ideas were "new", we don't mean to imply that they were unprecedented, only that they were in eclipse at the turn of the century. For example, "instrumentalism" was common in the early Republic and continued to persist even during the formalistic period of the late Nineteenth Century. For a claim that these thinkers were inspired by Hegel, see Chamberlain, Farewell to Reform, 1965 ed. p. 202.

law is, or should be, a working out of the implications of capitalist economics we can more easily see the radical implications of the opening pages of The Common Law:

> The felt necessities of the time, the prevalent moral and political theories, intuitions of public policy, avowed or unconscious, even the prejudices which judges share with their fellow men, have a good deal more to do than the syllogism in determining the rules by which men should be governed.[605]

Holmes wrote against the legal positivism of John Austin and the utilitarianism of Jeremy Bentham, thinkers who were also opposed by the other rebels against formalism.[606] Their objection, oddly enough, was that the adherents of English empiricism were not empirical enough—a charge that could easily be lodged against the practitioners of "law-and-economics" or "The New Evidence Scholarship."[607] Though Holmes never claimed that logic had nothing to do with the law or that there was anything immoral about judicial "prejudices" shaping the law, the mere hint that judges were human was too much for robe-sniffers who worshipped the "brooding omnipresence in the sky" as Wigmore did.[608]

The implications of Holmes' views for confrontation have been touched upon elsewhere but may be profitably be restated here.[609] The attempt of Holmes and his fellow thinkers to deconstruct such ideal types as logical, legal or economic "man", as well as other forms of pseudo-empiricism and a priori justifications matches the skeptical individualism at the root of the adversary system and the right of confrontation.[610] His market metaphor for "truth" mirrors

605. "More than syllogism"

Holmes, The Common Law, Howe ed. 1963, p. 5.

606. Bentham and Austin

White, Social Thought in America: The Revolt Against Formalism, 1957 ed., pp. 14, 19. On Bentham's view of confrontation, see § 6355, text at notecall 610.

607. Not empirical enough

Id. at p. 24.

608. As Wigmore did

On Wigmore, see § 6359. For an example of a passage that might have riled Wigmore, see Holmes, The Common Law, Howe ed. 1963, p. 5: "* * *

while on the one hand, there are a great many rules which are quite sufficiently accounted for by their manifest good sense, on the other, there are some which can only be understood by reference to the infancy of procedure among the German tribes, or to the social condition of Rome under the Decimvirs." Wigmore was less likely than Holmes to think that a rule originating in German procedure was per se at odds with "good sense."

609. Touched upon

See vol. 30, § 6343, p. 276.

610. Pseudo-empiricism

White, Social Thought in America: The Revolt Against Formalism, 1957 ed., p. 27.

the similar metaphor of the Leveller propagandists who popularized confrontation and embraced a "political truth" conducive to an emerging adversary system.[611] Indeed, Holmes's famous dissent in Abrams, with its embrace of "fallibalism" that so delighted the followers of John Dewey, was seen as sufficiently threatening to the tenets of Benthamism to earn him a stinging rebuke from the American Pope of that religion.[612]

Wigmore, however, overstated Holmes subversiveness. Holmes, like Wigmore, had a "scientistic" streak that was inconsistent with the more individualistic versions of confrontation.[613] His belief that science might some day develop methods for determining the value of differing ends, like those of "truth" and "efficiency" in litigation, allied him with those who hoped to substitute science for politics——a view that was not congenial to continued jury fact-finding in an adversary system.[614] Moreover, Holmes' notion that the law was merely the lawyer's way of predicting how judges would behave could easily accommodate the "managerial judge" with oodles of "discretion" who could turn procedure into the inquisitorial pathways that the Founders rejected.[615] Finally, Holmes' efforts to disconnect the law from morality left little role for the morality of confrontation, except as part of the culture that might lead judges to be more sympathetic to the adversary system than science might suggest they should be.[616] This is the side of Holmes that was given prominence by the Progressive Procedural-ists and, to a lesser extent, the Legal Realists.

John Dewey's influence on the history of confrontation was less direct, coming primarily through Progressive Proceduralists who were influenced by his thought.[617] Dewey espoused an epistemology that rejected the duality of the British empiricists between the perceiving mind and the perceived object——a duality that also

---

611. Levellers

See vol. 30, § 6343, p. 276.

612. "Fallibalism" and rebuke

White, Social Thought in America: The Revolt Against Formalism, 1957 ed., p. 178.

613. "Scientistic"

Id. at p. 208.

614. Science for politics

Id. at p. 253.

615. Law as prediction

Id. at p. 62.

616. Disconnect law

Id. at p. 65.

617. Influenced by his thought

If the tables of contents of law reviews are any indication, pragmatism seems to be coming back into vogue—— though so far as we have been able to determine, no one has yet attempted to apply it to procedure.

exists in the "naive realism" of the evidentiary writers.[618] He rejected Hume's claim that our knowledge of cause and effect was based on past experience; for him knowledge was a kind of "experience"——the response of a mind to a problem.[619] His view that perception was shaped by culture and that that culture in modern industrial societies is constantly changing is conducive to the adversary system's perceived need for cross-examination.[620]

More significant for confrontation than his epistemology was Dewey's preoccupation with "methodology"——what we lawyers would call "procedure."[621] Consider his trifurcating of liberalism:

> As a social philosophy, "liberalism" runs the gamut of which a vague temper of mind——often called "forward looking"——is one extreme, and a definite creed as to the purposes and methods of social action is another. The first is too vague to afford any steady guide to conduct; the second is so specific and fixed as to result in dogma, and thus to end in an illiberal mind. Liberalism as a method of intelligence, prior to being a method of action, as a method of experimentation based upon insight into both social desires and actual conditions, escape the dilemma. It signifies the adoption of the scientific habit of mind in application to social affairs.[622]

If "scientific procedure" could rescue liberalism, it could also serve as a substitute for the contentiousness of democratic politics; Professor White remarks Dewey's "tendency to say that if only man would agree to use scientific method in his approach to social problems, the major social and political problems of our time would automatically be solved."[623] This mirrors the beliefs of some Progressive Proceduralists——and is subject to some of the same criticisms. Randolph Bourne, one of Dewey's disciples

> thought of pragmatism as a philosophy of technique, a philosophy which tells you how to accomplish your ends once the ends have been established. * * * [so that] Dewey's disciples had become completely technique-conscious and morally blind.[624]

618. Rejected duality
Id. at p. 19.

619. Knowledge as "experience"
Id. at pp. 130, 132.

620. Shaped by culture
Id. at p. 95.

621. "Methodology"
Id. at p. 195.

622. "Scientific habit"
Id. at p. 200.

623. "Automatically solved"
Id. at p. 253.

624. "Morally blind"
Id. at p. 170.

This harsh judgement should have, but did not, warn legal Proceduralists of the dangers of a "scientific" approach to procedure; indeed, even the experience with Nazism seems to have left too many Proceduralists oblivious to the dangers of treating procedure in isolation from the substantive law it enforces. Hence, they are willing to distort confrontation and other procedural instruments to make them more efficient in producing convictions with little regard for whether those convictions are just or whether imprisonment of offenders is the best way to deal with the social problem at hand.[625]

Thorstein Veblen used anthropology to undermine classical laissez-faire economics.[626] His critique must have been particularly troubling because it provided a non-Marxist platform to attack corporate excesses.[627] As John Stuart Mill had made clear earlier, because of the partial nature of economic analysis, once anthropology examines how "economic man" actually behaves, the structure of modern economics collapses.[628] This not only raised the anxieties of turn-of-the-century elites, but it suggested the vulnerability of the sort of procedural thinking evidenced in Justice Brown's Mattox opinion to similar empirical attack; it makes little sense to focus on the reliability of hearsay evidence based on a priori assumptions about the credibility of dying persons while remaining totally oblivious to the way in which the putatively reliable evidence gets assessed by the jury.[629]

More directly relevant to confrontation and criminal procedure was Veblen's yearning for some scientific procedure for evaluating

---

625. Best way to deal

To put the point differently, confrontation and the adversary system were designed to make conviction difficult, partly to avoid resort to the criminal law as the first line of defense rather than the last resort in dealing with social problems.

626. Anthropology to undermine

Id. at p. 19.

627. Non-Marxian

Id. at p. 77.

628. Collapses

Id. at p. 25. For Mills' analysis, see id. at p. 22.

629. Gets assessed

Though scholars have sometimes attempted to assess the validity of the psychological assumptions of hearsay exceptions, only the ill-fated Chicago Jury Project has come close to examining how the jury uses evidence and it has virtually nothing to say on hearsay. As we shall see, however, modern confrontation jurisprudence has put all its eggs in the dubious hearsay basket.

goals so as to guide moral choice.[630] This was fueled by Veblen's belief that modern society was being dominated by individualistic values of the Eighteenth Century that had become embodied in the Declaration of Independence and the Constitution.[631] Indeed, Veblen went so far as to call the Constitution a "bad document" whose spirit ran counter to the Christian values of peace and good will.[632] Though he was not thinking of the right of confrontation, one could certainly see the adversary system as more like the Old Testament slaying one's enemies with the jawbone of an ass than like the New Testament values encapsulated in the Sermon on the Mount.[633]

Beard and Robinson are perhaps the most relevant of the five thinkers to the problem of confrontation because history resembles law in its need for some method for bridging the gap between historical reality and historical knowledge.[634] Beard's affinity to legal thinking of the time appears in his citations to Holmes and Roscoe Pound in his famous study of the economic origins of the Constitution.[635] Beard criticized earlier historians for treating law and politics in the abstract, divorced from their roots in the economy and the culture.[636] Beard particularly targeted Leopold von Ranke, the influential German historian whose attempt to make history more scientific might have been borrowed from Sgt. Friday——"just give us the facts, ma'am."[637] Beard thought the historian's job was to provide explanations and interpretations for

630. Evaluating goals

Id. at p. 186.

631. Embodied in the Constitution

He was particularly scornful of Jefferson's "self-evident truths." Ibid. On the impact of this concept on the right of confrontation, see vol. 30, § 6345, p. 559.

632. Christian values

Id. at p. 187.

633. New Testament values

Even in the passage from Paul cited by the Levellers in support of confrontation, Paul was relying on Roman law, not the teachings of Jesus. See vol. 30, § 6342, p. 238. But see, id. at p. 242 (passage in which Christ could be cited as supporting the right of confrontation).

634. Bridging gap

White, Social Thought in America: The Revolt Against Formalism, 1957 ed., p. 224.

635. Holmes and Pound

Id. at p. 31. Since this work of Beard's was pivotal in the development of Progressive Proceduralism, we shall take it up in more detail in the next section.

636. Divorced from roots

Id. at p. 30. This appears quite vividly in his history of the United States since the Civil War. Id. at pp. 34–38. Readers impatient of a history of the right of confrontation that is not limited to published judicial decisions can blame it on Beard.

637. Sgt. Friday approach

Id. at p. 221.

historical events.[638] He, like Ranke, wanted history to be "objective" in the sense that it was to be a scientific search for causes without any nationalistic or political special pleading.[639]

Lawyers familiar with the distinction between "fact" and "opinion" can predict about where this enterprise ran aground.[640] As the sociologist Edward A. Ross pointed out, events——even individual human actions——have myriad causes and consequences.[641] Not only must the historian determine which cause to take into account, she must also determine which facts need to be explained.[642] The law deals with this problem of selection through the substantive law as reflected through the doctrine of relevance.[643] But without anything like the substantive law to guide him, the historian must answer the question "relevant to what?"[644] Beard wrestled most of his life with the perennial problem of historical objectivity.[645] After attempting some of the same dodges lawyers have used in confronting the problem of judicial bias, late in life Beard became something of a relativist regarding the issue of historical "truth"——an approach adopted, at least subliminally, by increasing numbers of judges and lawyers over the course of the

638. Provide explanations

Id. at p. 222.

639. "Objective"

Id. at p. 221.

640. Ran aground

Indeed, Holmes' dictum about the extralegal sources that have shaped the law could, with only minor emendations, serve to explain why history will never be "scientific" in any meaningful sense.

641. Myriad consequences

Ross, Social Control, 1969 ed., p. 292. As Ross went on to say, as a result of this complexity, individuals will fix on those that have meaning to them, or that appear easiest to demonstrate, or that are closer to the event to be explained.

642. Which facts

White, Social Thought in America: The Revolt Against Formalism, 1957 ed., pp. 226–227.

643. Relevance

See vol. 22, § 5162.

644. "To what?"

White, Social Thought in America: The Revolt Against Formalism, 1957 ed., p. 98. Journalism is plagued by a similar problem; since editors have no other external criteria to determine which events of the previous day are most worthy of coverage, they tend to cover those events that they think other news media will cover——a phenomenon known, when it is noticed, as "pack journalism."

645. Beard wrestled

Id. at p. 220. Like lawyers, and like Dewey, he supposed for a time that the solution lay in historical method——that is, procedure.

next few decades.[646] Since this view is of legal truth as a sort of "political truth"——that is, whatever the jury determines after following the proper procedures is "true" so far as the law is concerned——we shall postpone spelling out its implications for the right of confrontation until we take up the modern confrontation jurisprudence.[647]

Imperialism and Immigration

Just when anxieties over Populism and labor unions seemed to be waning after the election of 1896, two other forces emerged around the turn of the century that were to have profound, though indirect, effects upon confrontation jurisprudence.[648] President McKinley had hardly taken office when a group of Anglophile young turks led by Theodore Roosevelt expressed dissatisfaction with his conservative foreign policy.[649] Anxious to emulate their English contemporaries, they were fired by a lust for imperialism.[650] In a story too familiar to require retelling here, with the help of propagandists in the business press, they turned the war with Spain from a crusade to free Cuba into an effort to acquire an empire for America.[651]

The drive for empire was supported by those capitalists who believed they had gone about as far as they could in exploiting the peoples and natural resources of the United States and needed markets, workers, and raw materials beyond our borders.[652] As Finley Peter Dunne's "Mister Dooley" put it, the policy was "hands

646. Relativist

Id. at p. 229. Beard wrote: "The assumption that any historian can be a disembodied spirit as coldly neutral to human affairs as the engineer to an automobile * * * [has] been rejected. * * * Written history that was cold, factual, and apparently undisturbed by the passions of the time served best the cause of those who did not want to be disturbed." Ibid.

647. Implications

For readers who can't wait, our position is roughly this: since factual accuracy is a chimera in litigation, it is a mistake for courts to make "reliability" the touchstone for application of the Sixth Amendment to hearsay; while reliability is a significant purpose of the adversary system and confronta-tion, fairness and efficiency are also important.

648. Anxieties waning

Mowry, The Progressive Era, 1900–1920: The Reform Persuasion, 1958, pp. 4–5.

649. Expressed dissatisfaction

Ekirch, Progressivism in America, 1974, p. 129.

650. Anxious to emulate

Id. at p. 179.

651. Propagandists

Id. at p. 187.

652. Beyond borders

Id. at p. 149.

acrost th' sea an' into somewan's pocket."[653] There was some basis for this belief as economic statistics suggested that about 10% of the gross national product was in excess of domestic needs.[654] This economic imperialism was then used to justify cartelization of the domestic economy, a movement that was opposed by the confrontation-related opposition to monopoly.[655] Moreover, as Charles Beard was soon to show, this economic imperialism tended to confirm the Marxian analysis, thus supporting the 20th Century expansion of the Socialist electorate which would ultimately produce "The Red Scare" of the 1920s—with devastating impact on civil liberties, including the right of confrontation.[656]

The Rooseveltian imperialists saw another advantage to the drive for empire; namely, that it would serve as a distraction from domestic problems.[657] As Charles Beard later wrote:

> It was fortunate for the conservative interests that the quarrel with Spain came shortly after Mr. McKinley's election, and they were able to employ that ancient political device, "a vigorous foreign policy", to divert the public mind from domestic difficulties.[658]

This Nineteenth Century version of "wagging the dog" seemed successful; even some Populists embraced the colonial enterprise.[659]

653. "Somewan's pocket"

Id. at p. 176. This was a paraphrase of a statement by Henry Cabot Lodge, who was invoking "the helping hand" of 4H fame, rather than the pickpocket.

654. 10% excess

Id. at p. 178.

655. Cartelization

Id. at p. 142. On the relationship between anti-monopoly thought and the right to confrontation, see vol. 30, § 6343, p. 287.

656. Confirm Marxian

White, Social Thought in America: The Revolt Against Formalism, 1957 ed., p. 43: "By the inexorable necessity of the present economic system, markets and safe investment opportunities must be found for surplus products and accumulated capital. All the older countries being overstocked and also forced into this new form of international rivalry, the drift is inevitably in the direction of the economically backward countries * * *." See also Chamberlain, Farewell to Reform, 1965 ed., p. 308. We assume careful readers will note that we are not suggesting that the Marxian analysis was true but only that events made people more willing to believe it was true— with the consequences described in the text.

657. Serve as distraction

Ekirch, Progressivism in America, 1974, p. 179.

658. "Divert public mind"

White, Social Thought in America: The Revolt Against Formalism, 1957 ed., p. 42.

659. Populists embraced

Ekirch, Progressivism in America, 1974, p. 183.

Imperialism flourished for more idealistic reasons.[660] One of these was a continuation of the doctrine of Manifest Destiny, expanded to carry the blessings of capitalism and democracy beyond the North American continent.[661] The fate of Native Americans and Mexicans under the earlier version did not augur well for other peoples of color within the expanded American empire.[662] Indeed, the imperialists frequently justified expansion with the use of Anglo–Saxon racism.[663] Hear William Allen White on the (no pun intended) "white man's burden":[664]

> It is the Anglo–Saxon's destiny to go forth as a world conqueror. He will take possession of the islands of the sea. He will exterminate the peoples he cannot subjugate. This is what fate holds for the chosen people. It is so written. Those who would protest will find their objections overruled. It is to be.[665]

The English, having this theory tested by the Boers, were delighted to have the Americans join them in plundering other peoples.[666] The symbiotic relationship between elites in the two countries played a part in the American intervention in World War I.[667] But in addition to the consequences of the War for the doctrine of confrontation, this Anglomania also supported the view that the right of confrontation was part of the English common law carried over by the colonists rather than, as was the case, a colonial

660. More reasons

"The expansionistic ideology * * * was a mixture of the philosophies of manifest destiny, Darwinian evolution, Anglo–Saxon racism, economic determinism, militarism and navalism, nationalism and patriotism." Id. at p. 179.

661. Carry the blessings

Id. at p. 175.

662. Peoples of color

Id. at p. 177. Here is the former Populist Senator from Kansas explaining the need to expend blood and treasure in an effort to stamp out Philippine nationalism in a war that anticipated the Vietnam War decades later: "The trouble in the Philippines has been occasioned by Aguinaldo and his associates. Americans are there of right, and they ask nothing of the natives but to be peaceable, to obey the laws and go ahead with their business; they

will not only be protected in every right, but will be aided by all the powerful influences of an advanced and aggressive civilization." At least the last adjective was justified. Id. at p. 183.

663. Anglo-Saxon racism

Id. at p. 188.

664. "White man's burden"

For the roots of this in Andrew Carnegie's Gospel of Wealth, see id. at p. 178.

665. "Chosen people"

Id. at p. 189. For less bellicose and more religious arguments, see id. at p. 179.

666. English delighted

Id. at p. 181.

667. American intervention

Id. at pp. 180–181.

response to the inquisitorial features imported into the common law by the Tudors and deployed against Americans when they rebelled against imperialism.[668]

Economic expansion, fueled at least in part by imperialism, brought material affluence to many Americans that not only dampened the impulse for radical reform of the sort demanded by the Populists, but also gave many Americans a material stake in imperialism that made it hard to resist developments in the next century.[669] First came the American incursions into the tumultuous affairs in Mexico, orchestrated by American corporations with economic interests in Mexico.[670] Then came the manipulation of a crisis in Columbia by corporate lawyers, sometimes by corrupt means, that led to the break-off of Panama and the building of the Canal.[671] This not only set the stage for relations between the United States and Latin America that have lasted to the present day, it also demonstrated the nexus between imperialism and militarism. In the next century, corporate lawyers and their clients united in a propaganda drive for expanded military forces—the beginning of what President Eisenhower was later to call the "military-industrial complex."[672] This did not go unremarked at the time; a Bryanite Congressman said "that if this Republic is in danger, it is danger not from peoples beyond the seas, but from a clique of men within this country who would tax the people until their backs break, simply that they might make profit supplying battleships, armor, and guns."[673] However, it was probably more mundane commercial colonial interests that supported U.S. entry into World War I.[674]

668. Americans rebelled

See vol. 30, §§ 6344, 6345.

669. Material stake

Weinstein, The Corporate Ideal in the Liberal State, 1900–1918, 1968, p. 253.

670. Mexico

Ekirch, Progressivism in America, 1974, pp. 240–241; Link, Woodrow Wilson and the Progressive Era, 1910–1917, 1963 ed., p. 111.

671. Panama

Mowry, The Era of Theodore Roosevelt and the Birth of Modern America, 1900–1912, pp. 151–154.

672. Drive for military

Ekirch, Progressivism in America, 1974, pp. 244–245; Chamberlain, Farewell to Reform, 1965 ed., p. x.

673. "Armor and guns"

Ekirch, Progressivism in America, 1974, p. 250.

674. Supported entry

Weinstein, The Corporate Ideal in the Liberal State, 1900–1918, 1968, p. 249.

The opposition to imperialism was led, not by former Populists, but by older Republicans whose ideological roots were in the anti-slavery, Free Labor Republicanism of the party's formative years.[675] As we have seen, it was this strain in the party, epitomized by the Radical Republicans, that favored the nationalization and expansion of civil rights.[676] Hence, their defeat meant loss of significant intellectual support for rights like confrontation. The other strand of antiimperialism grew from traditional conservatives who objected to the expansion of governmental power that imperialism entailed.[677] One of these, William Graham Sumner, argued that the lust for imperialism came from materialism and a desire for the trappings of monarchy.[678] The latter impulse, if it existed, was not congenial to the right of confrontation. Moreover, the expansion of federal power that the conservatives feared meant that any expansion of confrontation was not only a hindrance to state enforcement of traditional criminal law but more ominously a threat to "national security."[679]

At the same time that Americans began penetrating the borders of other nations, they developed a concern about immigrants from other nations penetrating ours.[680] The United States grew largely through immigration; between 1820 and 1930 over 37 million people came here in one of the largest migrations in history.[681] The first two waves of immigration, five million between 1820 and 1860 and thirteen-and-a-half million from 1860 to 1890, came largely from Western and Northern Europe.[682] The North had

---

675. Formative years

Ekirch, Progressivism in America, 1974, pp. 183–184.

676. Nationalization of rights

See § 6356, text at notecall 113.

677. Objected to expansion

Ekirch, Progressivism in America, 1974, p. 184.

678. Monarchy

Id. at p. 186.

679. "National security"

For the rise of the national security state, see vol. 26, § 5663. For the extremes of its effect on confrontation values, see id., § 5672.

680. Concern about immigrants

We do not mean to suggest that these are completely inconsistent. One of the risks of imperialism is "cosmopolitanism"——an appreciation of other cultures that, even if it does not cause one to question the worth of one's own culture, will weaken the allegiance to the culture of origin and thus the ability of culture to supplement the law as a control of conduct. See, for example, the contempt for colonials who "go native."

681. Largest migrations

Hays, the Response to Industrialism, 1885–1914, 1957, p. 95.

682. Western and Northern

Ibid.

benefited from immigration during the Civil War; during the war nearly 800,000 immigrants arrived to support the Northern war machine and more than 400,000 foreign born served in the Union Army.[683] After the war, some Southerners wanted to encourage immigration to their region to reduce their dependence on the newly freed slaves; the attempt to encourage Chinese immigration came to nothing but one Southern newspaper argued that immigration would force the Freedmen to abandon their hopes of "forty acres and a mule" when they were faced with a choice to "work or starve."[684] Immigration in the North was fostered by capitalists, primarily railroads who sent "immigration agents" and flossy publications to Europe to encourage people to come over and settle on railroad land in the West.[685]

Labor opposed immigration because immigrants depressed wages, while businessmen favored it for the same reason;[686] "[i]mmigration" wrote one prominent lawyer "would, doubtless be a blessing for us, provided we could always control it, and make it entirely subservient to our wants."[687] But the third wave of immigration—the largest, with over nineteen million between 1900 and 1930—would change the balance of public opinion.[688] Between 1900 and 1905 the rate of annual immigration doubled to over a million per year, most of them from southern and eastern Europe—Italians, Poles, Bohemians, and Russian Jews.[689] Threatening the hegemony of Anglo–Saxon Protestants, these Jewish and Catholic immigrants clustered in the cities; as early as 1900, 40% of the population of the twelve largest cities in the country were foreign born and another 20% were second-generation Americans.[690] This change in the "complexion and character" of immigra-

683. Served in Army

Encyclopedia of American History, Morris ed. 1976, pp. 275, 285.

684. "Work or starve"

Foner, Nothing But Freedom: Emancipation and its Legacy, 1983, pp. 47–48.

685. Railroad land

Josephson, The Robber Barons, 1962, p. 243.

686. Businessmen favored

Weinstein, The Corporate Ideal in the Liberal State, 1900–1918, 1968, p. 26.

687. "Make it subservient"

Foner, Nothing But Freedom: Emancipation and its Legacy, 1983, p. 47.

688. Third wave change

Hays, The Response to Industrialism, 1885–1914, 1957, p. 95.

689. Bohemians and Jews

Mowry, The Progressive Era, 1900–1920: The Reform Persuasion, 1958, p. 10. For those concerned about bias, the junior author's mother was part of this third wave.

690. Second-generation

Hays, The Response to Industrialism, 1885–1914, 1957, p. 95.

tion troubled even capitalists; August Belmont complained that "Europe gladly dumped her human refuse in our lap, and we housed, fed and clothed it."[691] This "refuse" reproduced at an astounding rate; between 1890 and 1910, the population of the United States rose nearly 40% from 60 million to 90 million.[692]

The result was a rise in the same Anglo–Saxon racism that fueled imperialism. Politicians, who had long courted the votes of immigrants, found the newer immigrants less docile and less susceptible to their blandishments.[693] For some, concern arose from the perception that these immigrants did not understand American traditions and values as readily as earlier European immigrants.[694] A president of the American Bar Association threatened immigrants that they would have to either choose to become "Americans" or go home.[695] Some leaders accused the immigrants of bringing socialism in their baggage. William Howard Taft said:

> This Bolshevism is militant and threatening in every European country. It has penetrated to this country. Because of the presence of hordes of ignorant European foreigners, not citizens * * * with little or no knowledge of our language, with no appreciation of American civilization or American institutions of civil liberty, it has taken strong hold in many of our congested centers and is the backing of a good many of the strikes from which our whole community is suffering today.[696]

Similar anti-alien sentiments could be found in other quarters.[697]

For purposes of confrontation, perhaps the most significant locus for nativism was the organized bar and the elite law schools.[698] For example, by 1916, nearly 15% of the lawyers in New

---

691. "Human refuse"

Weinstein, The Corporate Ideal in the Liberal State, 1900–1918, 1968, p. 26.

692. Rose to 90 million

Fiss, History of the Supreme Court of the United States: Troubled Beginnings of the Modern State, 1888–1910, 1993, p. 298.

693. Less docile

Wiebe, The Search for Order, 1877–1920, 1967, p. 50.

694. European immigrants

Hixson, Moorfield Storey and the Abolitionist Tradition, 1972, p. 24.

695. Or go home

Auerbach, Enmity and Amity: Law Teachers and Practitioners, 1900–1922, 1971, 5 Perspectives in American History 549, 592.

696. "Suffering today"

Cover, The Left, The Right, and The First Amendment, 1918–1928, 1981, 40 Md.L.Rev. 349, 353.

697. Other quarters

Wiebe, The Search for Order, 1877–1920, 1967, p. 54.

698. Elite law schools

Important because these attitudes were conveyed to, or approved in, students

York City were foreign born.[699] Elite lawyers and law teachers felt threatened by those who did not subscribe to their exalted view of the Anglo–Saxon race and Protestant Christianity.[700] Faculty members were careful to conceal their xenophobia, anti-urbanism, and anti-semitism under the guise of "professionalism."[701] Lawyers were not so discreet; one argued that the profession should be reserved for those who spoke "not Bohemian, not Gaelic, not Yiddish, but English."[702] Unlike Harvard, which was considering a limit on Jewish admissions, lawyers and law professors argued that higher standards would suffice to keep out Jews and radicals.[703] This was the beginning of the call, still heard today, for restricting the number of lawyers by raising educational requirements.[704] Indeed, in a few cases the organized bar tried to question the character of foreign-born applicants who had completed educational requirements and passed the bar examination.[705]

Thus immigration had the same effect on confrontation jurisprudence as imperialism; that is, by increasing Anglo–Saxon racism it made it difficult for courts to accept the notion that confrontation was largely indigenous and not an import from the English common law.[706] Worse yet, since many states and cities attempted to use the criminal law to control the foreign born population, xenophobia increased the reluctance of courts to do anything, like expansively construing confrontation, that might weaken the coercive power of the criminal law.[707] The rise in Protestant fundamen-

who would take them with them to the bench or to other law schools. This nativism was surprisingly long-lasting; when the junior author was a law student in the early 1960s, a Harvard-educated young professor thought it proper in criticizing a decision of the Nebraska Supreme Court to refer to the judges thereof as "a bunch of bohunks."

699. 15% foreign born

Auerbach, Enmity and Amity: Law Teachers and Practitioners, 1900–1922, 1971, 5 Perspectives in American History 549, 572.

700. Felt threatened

Id. at p. 578.

701. "Professionalism"

Id. at p. 579.

702. "Not Yiddish"

Id. at p. 596.

703. Jews and radicals

Id. at p. 580. On the Harvard quota, see Gal, Brandeis of Boston, 1980, p. 196.

704. Restricting number

Dos Passos, The American Lawyer, 1907, pp. 58–60.

705. Passed bar

Mitgang, The Man Who Rode the Tiger: The Life and Times of Judge Samuel Seabury, 1963, p. 101.

706. Not an import

See text at notecall 668, above.

707. Control foreign born

Wiebe, The Search for Order, 1877–1920, 1967, p. 60.

talism in response to the growth of other religions led to an increase in the imposition of sumptuary laws designed to change the lifestyles of the newer immigrants.[708] The epitome of this impulse was, of course, Prohibition——whose disastrous short-term effects on civil liberties we shall see in due course.[709]

The Turn of the Century

In 1900 most Americans were better off than they had been in the 1890s as wages rose, partly in response to the war with Spain and partly due to the optimism of investors over the possible benefits of imperialism.[710] Farm prices rose as well.[711] As one consequence of the defeat of Populism, farmers no longer thought of themselves as "the people" but merely as another interest group.[712] The Populist movement had been reduced to a drive for the development of commodity cooperatives.[713] The sense that things were looking up was enhanced by an amnesia induced by nostalgia; popular literature began its portrayal of the "Gay Nineties", an image that persists even today.[714] More hardheaded thinkers took comfort in a Pollyanna economics that argued that there was no conflict between private and public interest and that the misery produced for some by capitalism was more than outweighed by the benefits to the many.[715]

But appearances were deceptive. Though wages rose, prices rose faster so that real wages declined.[716] Moreover, the nation was in the midst of an explosion in the number of "white collar" workers; the number of clerks, salesmen, government employees, technicians, and salaried professionals rose from fewer than 800,-000 in 1870 to more than 5½ million in 1910——a far more rapid

---

708. Sumptuary law

Hays, The Response to Industrialism, 1885–1914, 1957, p. 82.

709. Prohibition

See § 6358.

710. Americans better off

Ekirch, Progressivism in America, 1954, p. 6.

711. Farm prices rose

Id. at p. 8.

712. Another interest group

O'Neill, The Progressive Years, 1975, p. 9.

713. Commodity cooperatives

Hays, The Response to Industrialism, 1885–1914, 1957, p. 62.

714. "Gay Nineties"

Chamberlain, Farewell to Reform, 1965 ed., pp. 17–19.

715. Pollyanna economics

Hays, The Response to Industrialism, 1885–1917, 1957, p. 39.

716. Real wages declined

Ekirch, Progressivism in America, 1974, p. 8.

growth than that of the traditional "middle class" of shopkeepers, doctors, and lawyers.[717] In addition to marking the return to the sort of social stratification that the Revolutionary generation had found abhorrent in England, the rise of the bureaucratized "middle class" was accompanied by a fading of the dream for independence, thus undercutting the individualism at the root of the right of confrontation.[718] Even more disturbing to this new "middle class", a Congressional committee studying industrial relations reported in 1900 that the power of corporations to crush competitors, fleece consumers, and intimidate workers was rising.[719] Whether they knew it or not, Americans were in for another 20 years of social turmoil.[720]

Not surprisingly, the turn of the century found many Americans yearning for social peace——and resentful and hostile towards Populists, Socialists, and other potential sources of conflict and confrontation.[721] Fear drove a growing desire for social control and a distrust of the pursuit of liberty.[722] As one of the leaders of the movement for "scientific management" wrote: "[t]oo great liberty results in a large number of people going wrong who would be right if they had been forced into good habits."[723] Theodore Roosevelt grasped this desire for order:

> The rich must be fair and the poor must be contented——or if not contented, at least they must be orderly. I will tell them both. No restraining of trade by the great corporations and no rioting by the toiler. Give me the power and I will make them behave.[724]

This equation of social reform with social control did not bode well for the future of confrontation.[725]

717. "White collar" growth

Hays, The Response to Industrialism, 1885–1914, 1957, p. 73.

718. Fading of dream

Id. at p. 74.

719. Power rising

Mowry, The Progressive Era, 1900–1920: The Reform Persuasion, 1958, p. 19.

720. Another 20 years

Weinstein, The Corporate Ideal in the Liberal State, 1968, p. 3.

721. Yearning for peace

Ekirch, Progressivism in America, 1974, p. 131.

722. Mistrust of liberty

Link, Woodrow Wilson and the Progressive Era, 1910–1917, 1963 ed., p. 1.

723. "Forced into habits"

Haber, Efficiency and Uplift: Scientific Management in the Progressive Era, 1890–1920, 1973 ed., p. 20.

724. "Make them behave"

Chamberlain, Farewell to Reform, 1965 ed., p. 238.

725. Reform with control

White, Social Thought in America: The Revolt Against Formalism, 1957 ed., p. 93.

Even more ominous for confrontation than the growth of the desire for control was a distrust of any but logical thinking.[726] Since feelings and intuitions are an important source of power of the jury, their denigration in the public mind did not auger well for the future of the adversary system. Dewey made the relevance of scientific logic to law explicit.

> The evangelical Protestant tradition has fostered the tendency to locate in personal feelings instead of in the control of social situations and our legal tradition has bred the habit of attaching feelings to fixed rules and injunctions instead of to social conditions and consequences of action as these are revealed to the scrutiny of intelligence.[727]

"The evangelical Protestant tradition", not "the scrutiny of intelligence" was the major source of our "feelings" toward the jury trial and the right of confrontation.[728]

The strengths and weaknesses of this drive for control can be illustrated by labor management relations at the turn of the century. An increasing number of corporate leaders sought to use the state to stabilize an economic system that had so frequently gone haywire in the Nineteenth Century, but to do this they needed the assent of government leaders if not the electorate.[729] But as the quotation from Theodore Roosevelt suggests, political leaders were looking for some way to introduce legal controls, other than government by injunction, into industrial relations.[730] At the same time, conservative union leaders, never enamored of the People's Party but now chastened by its defeat, sought to convert the unions into interest groups, shedding their image as a band of Socialist revolutionaries.[731] This desire dovetailed with the belief of a few progressive corporate leaders to use "trade unions * * * as a strong bulwark against the great wave of socialism", in the words of Louis

---

726. Logical thinking

Id. at p.167.

727. "Feelings to rules"

Id. at pp. 167–168.

728. Major source

See vol. 30, § 6343.

729. Stabilize system

Weinstein, The Corporate Ideal in the Liberal State, 1900–1918, 1968, p. 141.

730. Legal controls

Haber, Efficiency and Uplift: Scientific Management in the Progressive Era, 1890–1920, 1973 ed., p. 154.

731. Revolutionaries

O'Neill, The Progressive Years, 1975, p. 5.

D. Brandeis.[732] Corporate leaders of this stripe even went so far as to have their lawyers appear on the side of conservative unionists before the Supreme Court.[733] This opened the union leaders to attack from the more militant of their peers.[734] Conservative unionists saw this militancy through the lens of Anglo–Saxon racism and so accepted the suggestion of corporate leaders that unions needed to "Americanize" their members.[735] As we shall see, this attempt at labor-management cooperation never got off the ground; the labor-management strife of the 1890s continued unabated into the 20th Century, though the increasing use of military force to break strikes seems to have reduced the fear of anarchy and rebellion that characterized America's first encounter with labor-management confrontations.[736] However, as one historian has put it, this turmoil laid the foundations for "the bureaucratized, business-dominated, limited welfare state" that emerged in the middle of the century— along with a revived interest in the right of confrontation.[737]

The Revival of Elitism

In 1900 a former school teacher and journalist who viewed capitalists as the American nobility founded the National Civic Federation.[738] The NCF was nominally tripartite, with representatives of capital (Marcus Hanna was its first president), conservative unionism (Samuel Gompers was its first vice-president), and the public (ex-and future-Presidents Cleveland and Taft were members), and one might find a parallelism with the adversary system by envisioning the public members as jurors between labor and capital.[739] But the NCF favored cooperation and conciliation, not

732. "Strong bulwark"

Weinstein, The Corporate Ideal in the Liberal State, 1900–1918, 1968, p. 17.

733. Lawyers appear

Id. at p. 16.

734. Opened attack

Id. at p. 21.

735. "Americanize"

Id. at p. 241.

736. Use of military force

From 1877 to 1903, state or federal troops were used to quash more than 500 strikes, but this was still a minori-ty, though obviously a significant minority of the more than 30,000 strikes during this period. Lukas, Big Trouble, 1997, p. 116.

737. "Welfare state"

O'Neill, The Progressive Years, 1975, pp. v, x.

738. American nobility

Weinstein, The Corporate Ideal in the Liberal State, 1900–1918, 1968, pp. 7, 9–10.

739. Tripartite

Ekirch, Progressivism in America, 1974, p. 120.

confrontation as it sought to restore "that habitual normal sense of social solidarity which is the foundation stone of democracy."[740]

In fact, the National Civic Federation was primarily an organization of Big Business; its members were a virtual "Who's Who" of American capitalism, representing fully one third of the 367 corporations with capitalization of more than $10 million and sixteen of the 67 largest railroads.[741] Even the public members were allies of Big Business—corporate lawyers and the heads of elite private universities.[742] But the organization sought out a center between "the Socialists among labor people and the anarchists among capitalists."[743] The latter group was represented by the National Association of Manufacturers, which was relentlessly opposed to any form of government regulation and was shortly about to launch an all-out war against labor unions.[744]

The National Civic Federation expressed elite yearnings for peace and stability, which it saw as threatened primarily by the struggle between labor and capital.[745] In its early years, the NCF worked behind the scenes to mediate strikes and other labor disputes such as the Anthracite Coal Strike of 1902.[746] Later it explored the possibility of using corporate welfare as a way of supplanting labor unions.[747] Eventually, however, it became a major political force, seeking to advance legislation that would head off more radical proposals without endangering corporate interests.[748] A fair example is an NCF study of public ownership of utilities, launched in response to growing demands for municipal ownership

740. "Social solidarity"

Ibid.

741. Largest railroads

Weinstein, The Corporate Ideal in the Liberal State, 1900–1918, 1968, p. 8.

742. Elite universities

Ibid. Even the exception, Benjamin Ide Wheeler, President of the University of California, proves the rule.

743. "Anarchists"

O'Neill, The Progressive Years, 1975, pp. 55–56.

744. N.A.M.

Weinstein, The Corporate Ideal in the Liberal State. 1900–1918, 1968, p. 6.

745. Labor and capital

Id. at p. 9.

746. Coal strike

Ibid .. See also, § 6352.

747. Corporate welfare

Id. at p. 37.

748. Corporate interests

A leading historian of the N.C.F. calls it "the leading organization of politically conscious corporate leaders" prior to World War I. Id. at p. vx.

of light, power, and transit companies.[749] While avoiding taking a position on municipal ownership, the study reflected the views of utility magnates among its membership and proposed the system of private ownership with public regulation that would take the issue of utility rates out of politics and put it in the hands of commissions and courts.[750] The justification for this was "expertise", the scientific version of elitism.

On September 6, 1901, a deranged anarchist struck another blow for elitism and against confrontation when he shot President William McKinley in Buffalo, New York.[751] McKinley's death made Theodore Roosevelt the new President, thus beginning a run of three aristocratic, Ivy League educated Presidents—thereby realizing, after the long Jacksonian interlude, the Federalist ideal of a republic led by "the best and the brightest."[752] This ideal was restated by one of those "efficiency experts" who were to become its beneficiaries:

> True democracy is attained only when men are endowed with authority in proportion to their ability to use it efficiently and their willingness to promote the public good. Such men are natural leaders whom all will follow.[753]

This version of elitism appealed to many leaders of the "revolt against formalism"; John Dewey, for example, wanted to establish an "Intelligence Trust" to take control of the country away from the business trusts.[754]

Woodrow Wilson demonstrates the relationship between elitism and Anglophilia; his "ideal type" was the upper-class Englishman.[755] Supporters of Wilson shared his elitism; the not-yet-Justice Brandeis showed how it could be deployed in defense of the embattled courts, calling for the leadership of judges with the "greatest ability and intelligence" to serve as a check on the excesses of

749. NCF study

Id. at p. 24.

750. Commissions and courts

Id. at p. 25.

751. Shot McKinley

O'Neill, The Progressive Years, 1975, p. 21.

752. Aristocratic Presidents

Mowry, The Progressive Era, 1900–1920: The Reform Persuasion, 1958, p. 17.

753. "All will follow"

Haber, Efficiency and Uplift: Scientific Management in the Progressive Era, 1890–1920, 1973, p. 48.

754. "Intelligence Trust"

Id. at p. 143.

755. Upper-class Englishman

Chamberlain, Farewell to Reform, 1965 ed., p. 283.

democracy.[756] The fascistic tendencies in this are revealed in a novel by Edward Mandell House, the Rasputin of the Wilson White House, called "Phillip Dru, Administrator." The hero, at the climax of another civil war between labor and capital, sets himself up as "Administrator of the Republic" and dispenses with the Constitution to govern with the advice of a "Counsel of Twelve" expert advisers.[757] He initiates a number of reforms——expansion of the right of confrontation and the adversary system not among them.

The Caesarism implicit in this melding of elitism and expertise was apparent to some contemporaries; for example, the conservative sociologist William Graham Sumner used it as part of his libertarian attack on government.[758] But the sociologist Edward A. Ross showed how elitism could be used to undermine the individualism that supports the adversary system.

> Because it cannot dispense with a vivid consciousness of personal worth, control through ideals flourishes in the higher classes, while yet the inferior orders are under the curb of custom and authority. Always in aristocracies, nobilities, leisure classes, and military castes, the self-sense is so exaggerated that there is no leverage for control unless self be used as a fulcrum.* * *

> The humble, working, exploited people, on the other hand, have no such hypertrophied sense of personal worth as the upper class, and hence do not respond so readily to the appeal of pride. The morality they develop among themselves is, therefore, the morality of consideration, or "neighbor morality."[759]

Since confrontation does not jibe well with a "morality of consideration", one might suppose that adherents of Ross might have little fondness for it.[760] Later, however, Ross blurs the inference one might draw from this passage when he writes that "[s]ympathy with fellows and deference to the born leader are the two primitive

756. "Greatest ability"

Haber, Efficiency and Uplift: Scientific Management in the Progressive Era, 1890–1920, 1973, p. 78.

757. "Phillip Dru"

Id. at p. 105 n. 14.

758. Sumner used

Chamberlain, Farewell to Reform, 1965 ed., pp. 12–13.

759. "Neighbor morality"

Ross, Social Control, 1969 ed., p. 236.

760. Little fondness

Since many of the Progressives, perhaps including Ross, sought a path between the contending factions of labor and capital, socialism and laissez faire, it is not always possible to say where this "plague on both your houses" ideology comes out on particular issues for particular individuals. Nonetheless, we think one can validly draw inferences about the general tendencies of social thought likely to affect those with the power to affect the right of confrontation.

social facts which precede and antedate all the species of social control * * *."[761]

The one elitist during this period whose views do seem more congenial to confrontation was Walter Lippman. He saw the role of experts and elites as a mixture of the rational and the irrational.[762] The same, we shall argue, is true of the adversary system and the right of confrontation. Here we note only that Lippman's deployment of Freud had little effect on the Progressive Proceduralists and by the time it was picked up by the Legal Realists it was too late to have much effect on the future of confrontation.[763]

Darwinism and Democracy II

We have previously seen the influence of Darwinism in the latter half of the Nineteenth Century.[764] We must now return to examine how Darwinism came to be one of the major influences on thought in the Progressive era.[765] We can eliminate an apparent paradox by distinguishing two quite different uses of biology that historians have called "Social Darwinism" and "Reform Darwinism."[766]

Social Darwinism, usually exemplified by the Yale sociologist William Graham Sumner, had three major tenets: first, a monistic faith that competition was the human analog of natural selection; second, a belief in the deterministic nature of social change; and, third, a denigration of the state as an instrument for ameliorating social evils.[767] For example, Social Darwinism claimed that

> [s]trikes at best are an unnatural and unnecessary evil of the body politic. * * * They are forceful attempts to secure something unattainable through natural evolution, and they engender bitter

761. "Primitive social facts"

Id. at p. 275.

762. Mixture of irrational

Haber, Efficiency and Uplift: Scientific Management in the Progressive Era, 1890–1920, 1973, p. 92.

763. Freud

Id. at p. 93.

764. Nineteenth Century

See § 6356, text at notecall 691.

765. Progressive era

Ekirch, Progressivism in America, 1974, p. 20.

766. "Social" and "Reform"

Id. at pp. 21–22. For even finer gradations, see Russett, Darwin in America: The Intellectual Response, 1865–1912, 1976, pp. 83–120.

767. Major tenets

Ross, Social Control, 1969 ed., p. xiv. See also, Russett, Darwin in America: The Intellectual Response, 1865, 1912, 1976, pp. 98–102.

hatred and strife where from the nature of things a harmonious unit should exist.[768]

On the other hand, "the nature of things" always seemed to support the interests of capital; e.g., a business trust was "nothing but a combination of people for doing business more cheaply and largely. It is the evolution of the corporation."[769] By manipulating the concept of "natural", Social Darwinists were able to object to any governmental interference with the "natural" workings of the economy to benefit labor or the public while ignoring the role of government in the creation and maintenance of corporations.[770] Sumner himself, however, often pushed his libertarian version of Social Darwinism to its logical conclusion, heedless of its effect on business interests; for example, he opposed the protective tariff as allowing the survival of weak companies who could not compete with foreign rivals.[771]

Reform Darwinism, on the other hand, sought to understand evolution not to be ruled by it but to alter it.[772] It sought to replace the laissez faire ideology that had infected Social Darwinism with a truly scientific study of what was "natural".[773] Reform Darwinists thought society was indeterminate rather than governed by fixed rules of nature.[774] This notion of organic evolution became widely used by the post-Civil War generation in politics, science, economics, and sociology.[775] The guru of this movement was the sociologist Lester Ward whose book "Dynamic Sociology" was published in 1883; it attacked Sumner by arguing that human intelligence

768. "Harmonious unit"

See Wiebe, Businessmen and Reform: A Study of the Progressive Movement, 1962, p. 162.

769. "Evolution of corporation"

Weinstein, The Corporate Ideal in the Liberal State, 1900–1918, 1968, p. 72.

770. "Natural" workings

Wood, Constitutional Politics in the Progressive Era, 1968, p. 10.

771. Protective tariff

Chamberlain, Farewell to Reform, 1965, ed. p. 10.

772. To alter it

Ekirch, Progressivism in America, 1974, pp. 21–22.

773. Replace laissez faire

Weinstein, The Corporate Ideal in the Liberal State, 1900–1918, 1968, p. x.

774. Indeterminate

Wiebe, Businessmen and Reform: A Study of the Progressive Movement, 1962, p. viii. Of course, we now know the same thing is true of nature; that useful adaptations arise by chance and chance occurrences can bring an end to evolutionary successes——ask the dinosaurs.

775. Widely used

Ekirch, Progressivism in America, 1974, p. 21.

distinguished social evolution from natural evolution.[776] The economist Thorstein Veblen argued that social institutions actually protected the unfit; in a true state of nature the typical bloated
capitalist would find his property taken from him by the more
vigorous and forceful fighters.[777] Other Reform Darwinists used
biology to argue that human institutions, like the human body, had
vestigial features that survived long after the conditions that
brought them into existence——the institutional equivalents of pu-
bic hair.[778]

Of course, thinkers of the time did not distinguish between
Reform and Social Darwinism with the same care as subsequent
historians. For example, Teddy Roosevelt mixed the two, taking
from Social Darwinism the idea of competition and struggle as
manly and beneficial but taking from Reform Darwinism the belief
that humans could control the environment and thus shape their
own social evolution.[779] And for some purposes we need not distinguish the two; for example, the deemphasis of the supernatural in
religion——a secularization that affected Progressivism through the
Social Gospel and confrontation through its emphasis on facts
rather than feelings.[780] Lacking the supernatural sanction for the
oath, courts had to shift to cross-examination and other human
institutions to insure veracity.[781]

776. Lester Ward

Id. at p. 23; Mowry, The Era of Theodore Roosevelt and the Birth of Modern America, 1900–1912, 1962, p. 21.
See also, Russett, Darwin in America:
The Intellectual Response, 1865–1912,
1976, pp. 102–111.

777. Taken by fighters

White, Social Thought in America: The
Revolt Against Formalism, 1957 ed.,
pp. 92–93. but see, Ross, Social Control, 1969 ed., p. 208 ("in the course of
social evolution, the selective process
increasingly tends to eliminate the
men of violent appetites and passions,
and to favor the type of man who is
able to appropriate and conform to the
body of social ideas"). Veblen seems to
be right with respect to the evolution
of ideas; were it not for freedom of
speech and the coercive apparatus of
the state to protect its developers,
ideas like "The Bell Curve" would
never get off the ground since those

with cause to resent the theory could
easily overpower those favored by it.

778. Vestigial features

Id. at p. 53.

779. Teddy Roosevelt

Ekirch, Progressivism in America, 1974,
p. 133.

780. Supernatural

Weinstein, The Corporate Ideal in the
Liberal State, 1900–1918, p. 6. In
1893, long before the Scopes trial,
Clarence Darrow optimistically announced that "[t]he world has grown
tired of preachers and sermons; today
it asks for facts." Lukas, Big Trouble,
1997, p. 654.

781. Courts had to shift

As we shall see, the denial or denigration of the power of the ritualistic
aspects of confrontation was central to

As we shall see, Reform Darwinism affected confrontation and other legal doctrines indirectly through other elements of Progressive thought that it fostered. Sometimes, however, Social Darwinism was invoked more directly; for example, in a book published in 1908, Woodrow Wilson argued that

> government is not a machine, but a living thing. It falls, not under the theory of the universe but under the theory of organic life. It is accountable to Darwin, not to Newton. * * * Government is not a body of blind forces; it is a body of men. * * * Living political constitutions must be Darwinian in structure and in practice.[782]

Later, as President, Wilson argued that the Constitution should be interpreted "according to the Darwinian principle * * * that a nation is a living thing and not a machine."[783] Other Progressives used Reform Darwinism to undermine the conservative belief that the Constitution was a fixed, stable collection of concepts expounded by the Supreme Court.[784] When coupled with the belief that Holmes' common law was Darwinian this might argue that confrontation should not be construed according to the intention of the Founders but rather in accordance with contemporary needs.[785] Reform Darwinism cannot tell us what those needs are; we must find them in other features of the Progressive ideology.[786]

In 1901 the sociologist Edward Alsworth Ross published "Social Control"—whose subtitle played to middle class anxieties at the turn of the century—"A Survey of the Foundation of Or-

the Progressive attack on the adversary system.

782. "Constitutional Darwinian"

Ekirch, Progressivism in America, 1974, p. 28.

783. "Not a machine"

Wood, Constitutional Politics in the Progressive Era, 1968, p. 36.

784. Fixed, stable

Ekirch, Progressivism in America, 1974, p. 29.

785. Holmes Darwinian

White, Social Thought in America: The Revolt Against Formalism, 1957 ed., p. 17. We need not enter into the debate over how far Holmes himself was af-

fected by Darwinism of either sort. Compare id. at p. 104 (famous dictum that the Constitution did not enact Social Darwinism) with p. 119 (Holmes thought biology explained class differences).

786. Other features

As suggested by the distinction between Social and Reform Darwinism, the biological analogy can be used to support quite different views of confrontation. For example, one could view confrontation as a doctrine whose survival for so many years demonstrates its fitness for modern conditions; or one could argue that confrontation is a vestigial remnant of trial by battle ill-suited to humans who no longer drag their knuckles on the ground.

der.''[787] In the book, Ross worked out the full implications of the ideas of Lester Ward.[788] The work was to influence a whole generation of thinkers, including persons as diverse as President Theodore Roosevelt, Justice Holmes, and Dean Roscoe Pound.[789] Ross' Darwinism was both pro-and anti-individualistic and thus was largely a wash on the deeper intellectual foundations of confrontation.[790] However, what Ross had to say about law proved deeply influential in the development of confrontation jurisprudence.

Ross saw law as a primary method of social control and for intervening in the "natural" development of evolution.[791]

> In its collective manifestation sympathy fixes the legal status of the feeble and defective classes, and determines the plane of comfort they shall enjoy at public expense. * * * It throws the arm of the law about the more helpless, and intervenes actively between husband and wife, parent and child, teacher and pupil, master and servant, policeman and offender, warden and convict, employer and employee.[792]

The relentless instrumentalism of his chapter on the law seems so familiar today that it is hard to fathom how it could have been fresh a century ago.[793] His contrasting of law and public opinion as modes of social control emphasizes the logical impersonality and specificity of the law.[794]

When he turned to "justice", Ross saw it as an intellectual

---

787. Ross published

Ross, Social Control, 1969 ed . .

788. Worked out Ward

Ekirch, Progressivism in America, 1974, p. 23.

789. Holmes and Pound

Ross, Social Control, 1969 ed., p. ix.

790. On individualism

Id. at p. vii.

791. Primary method

Id. at p. lxv.

792. "Employer and employee"

Id. at p. 10.

793. Instrumental

See, especially, id. at p. 107 and following. There was, we hasten to say, nothing new about instrumentalism in law. If one wanted to distinguish between the instrumentalism of Ross and that of Justice Brown in Mattox, see above, text at notecall 504, it would be the dynamism and the centrality of that of Ross. It is one thing to say that confrontation has a purpose that can be deduced from the doctrine and another to say that purposes are not emergent properties of the concept but public-policy choices by judges.

794. Law and public opinion

Id. at p. xlv.

rather than emotional quality like "sympathy."[795] As such, justice differs from sympathy in being an acquired taste.[796] Ross traces justice to the child's discovery of the difference between "self" and "other" but it does not evolve naturally but from the law as teacher.[797] "Law itself reacts powerfully on the public, teaching it to frown on offences like malpractice or blackmail or intimidation, that it does not resent instinctively."[798]

> Law being the most progressive department of control, conduct that harms society in new ways is made crime before it has had time to become wrong or sin; and fine and imprisonment is visited upon an offence that brings, as yet, neither blame nor shame.[799]

This is rather a cry from the Darwinism that views the Sherman Act as an "unnatural" interference in the "evolution of the corporation." Moreover, Ross argued, because legal sanctions are corporal, it is capable of reaching those whose individualistic egos make them comparatively impervious to social disapprobation as a means of control.[800]

Ross' views of procedure reflect his ambivalence about individualism. In seeking to prove that justice is intellectual rather than emotional, Ross concedes that often justice is infused with elements of sympathy. Hence, we must look to situations

> that minimize or even wholly exclude natural sympathy. Let us, therefore, observe the behavior of men who are contending one with another. Any restraints that men impose upon themselves in combat and rivalry may surely be credited to something else than fellow-feeling.[801]

Ross then explores the concept of "fair play" to show that far from being based on sympathy, it is the product of egoistic self-interest.[802] He concludes that the "pure justice-motive, then crops up oftenest in dealings of equals, in such fields as war, sport, trade, business, and politics."[803] One could, though Ross does not, argue

795. Intellectual
Id. at p. 26.

796. Acquired taste
Id. at p. xxii.

797. "Self" and "other"
Id. at pp. 23, 25.

798. "Not instinctively"
Id. at p. 102.

799. "Blame nor shame"
Id. at p. 74.

800. Sanctions corporal
Id. at p. 106.

801. "Combat and rivalry"
Id. at p. 26.

802. Self-interest
Id. at pp. 27–28.

803. "Dealings with equals"
Id. at p. 27.

that procedural rules are means of imposing the rules that fair play would suggest to equals on cases in which the parties are not equal.[804] However, one suspicious of individualistic excesses, as many Progressives were, might question the fitness of rules devised between equals to situations where the parties are by hypothesis seldom equal.[805] Courts have nothing like the "mercy rule" in softball for calling off the contest when the parties are obviously mismatched.

Ross proved more appreciative of the ceremonial importance of procedure. In order to distinguish justice from vengeance, the former must be impersonal.

> Hence, developed law insists upon proceeding according to precise rules and prescribed formulas which purge punishment of its personal element. It is chiefly the absence of this protective regularity and ceremonial which distinguishes a lynching party from a court * * *.[806]

He argues that the trial should "enjoy the ceremonial backing because court procedure may be made a powerful means of intimidating both accused and onlookers."[807] He goes on to say:

> In a criminal court the impression made on the minds of actors and beholders may not be lightly sacrificed to the mere dispatch of business, to the discovering the guilt or innocence of the greatest number of accused persons in the least possible time * * *. [808]

After acknowledging the danger that ceremony can become mere formality, he concludes that the "fact remains, however, that more good form is observed in the trying of people, the fewer there will be to try."[809] For Ross, teaching is one of the instrumental purposes of procedure—a view that is largely absent from confrontation jurisprudence.

804. Not equal

Ross did, however, see the root of the "equal protection paradox"—that is, whether treating people who are not equal as equals constitutes equal protection. See id. at p. 54. Ross tried to defuse the paradox by resort to pluralism. Id. at p. 55.

805. Fitness of rules

Compare Wigmore's contemptuous rejection of the "sporting theory of justice" which rejects the notion of "fair play"

because of its origins in more primitive forms of human interaction.

806. "Lynching party"

Id. at p. 111.

807. "Intimidating accused"

Id. at p. 112.

808. "Least possible time"

Id. at p. 113.

809. "Fewer to try"

Ibid.

§ 6358. ____; The Progressive Era*

If one had to pick a date for the beginning of the Progressive Era, one promising candidate would be May 12, 1902, two days after President Theodore Roosevelt announced he was reviving the long dormant Sherman Act in a suit against J.P. Morgan's Northern Securities Company.[1] The United Mine Worker's Union struck in the anthracite coal fields of Pennsylvania after the mine operators had declined the union's offer to arbitrate their differences.[2] The union demands included a wage increase, an eight-hour day, and union recognition by management.[3] The owners response was summed up by George F. Baer: "There cannot be two masters in the management of business. God in his Infinite Wisdom has put the control of business into the hands of Christian gentlemen."[4] However, this time capitalists were not united in their response as they had been in the 1890s; led by Mark Hanna, who had been McKinley's campaign manager, the National Civic Federation called for a peaceful settlement of the strike, offering behind the scenes to mediate the conflict.[5] Moreover, despite his earlier bellicose remarks about trade unions, President Roosevelt refused to follow

1. Northern Securities suit

Encyclopedia of American Facts and Dates, 9th ed. 1993, p. 395.

2. Anthracite strike.

Wiebe, Businessmen and Reform, 1962, p. 159.

3. Union recognition

Lukas, Big Trouble, 1997, p. 320.

4. "Christian gentlemen"

Ibid.

5. Offering to mediate

Wiebe, Businessmen and Reform, 1962, p. 159 For a description of the nature and purpose of the N.C.F., see § 6357, text at notecall 738.

Cleveland's example of bringing in the military to break the strike.[6] He intervened to force a settlement.

Any hopes by the anxious middle class that the Anthracite Coal Strike marked a new, less violent stage in the development of labor-management relations were soon dashed. In strikes over the next 30 months, state and local officials reverted to the older pattern; 180 unionists were killed by police, militia, or company security forces, more than 1600 were wounded, and over 5,000 arrested.[7] Worse yet, the Anthracite Coal Strike saw a rise in class consciousness among workers that middle-class Americans thought had been wiped out by the defeat of the People's Party in 1896.[8] Big Bill Haywood would argue that "[y]ou cannot view the class struggle through the stained glass windows of a cathedral or through the eyes of capitalist made laws."[9] Even lawyers like Job Harriman, who nearly won election as mayor of Los Angeles, conceded that "[e]conomic interests wholly determined ideas of morality and law."[10] Indeed, quasi-Populist ideas even emerged around the President; his adviser Gifford Pinchot told a reporter "that economic exploitation by the privileged class was the trouble in this country" and that "control of national monopolies of production and distribution of necessities must be in the hands of the people."[11]

Rising class consciousness found support in government statistics. From 1890 to 1912, while wealth increased by 188%, wages rose only 95%, one-third of workers earned below a subsistence level so that 37% of the mothers in working class families had to work to supplement the family income and farm tenancy increased by 32%.[12] It was clear to many that only class-conscious government action could ameliorate the growing gap between the haves

---

6. Roosevelt refused

Mowry, The Progressive Era, 1900–20: The Reform Persuasion, 1958, p. 26.

7. Killed, wounded, and arrested

Mowry, The Era of Theodore Roosevelt and The Birth of Modern America, 1900–1912, 1962, p. 1.

8. Class consciousness

Adams, Age of Industrial Violence, 1910–1915, p. 9.

9. "Capitalist made laws"

Id. at p. 19.

10. "Interests determined law"

Id. at p. 23.

11. "Hands of the people"

Weinstein, The Corporate Ideal in the Liberal State, 1900–1918, 1968, p. 160.

12. Statistics supported

Weinstein, The Corporate Ideal in the Liberal State, 1900–1918, 1968, p. 211.

and have nots.[13]

But such "class legislation" was anathema to Progressives.[14] For all their desire to mediate between labor and capital, Progressives seldom tried to understand the working class.[15] Hence, even such legal reforms as limitations on the use of injunctions in labor disputes or providing jury trial for workers accused of violating labor injunctions were denounced by Progressives as "class favoritism."[16] The National Civic Federation opposed any form of what it called "class politics."[17] Instead, the Progressives wanted to believe that science and expertise could rise above narrow class interests in providing some technocratic fix to the political problems facing the nation.[18]

Given the American myth of class harmony, class consciousness came slowly to workers.[19] But the wealthy had a rich history of class consciousness.[20] As Edward Ross had argued the year before the Anthracite Strike,

> [u]nder the ascendancy of the rich and leisured, property becomes more sacred than persons, moral standards vary with pecuniary status, and it is felt that "God will think twice before He damns a person of quality." In general, the more distinct, knit together, and self-conscious the influential minority, the more likely is social control to be colored with class self-interest.[21]

Ross went on to argue that class-consciousness among the rich caused what he thought was an excess of individualism that had

13. Class-conscious action

White, Social Thought in America: The Revolt Against Formalism, 1957 ed., p. 40.

14. Anathema

Ekirch, Progressivism in America, 1974, p. 229.

15. Seldom tried to understand

Wiebe, Businessman and Reform: A Study of the Progressive Movement, 1962, p. 16.

16. "Class favoritism"

Id. at p. 197.

17. "Class politics"

Weinstein, The Corporate Ideal in the Liberal State, 1900–1918, 1968, p. 21.

18. Technocratic fix

Haber, Efficiency and Uplift: Scientific Management in the Progressive Era, 1890–1920, 1973, p. xii.

19. American myth

Adams, The Age of Industrial Violence, 1910–1915, 1966, p. 176.

20. Rich history

Mowry, The Era of Theodore Roosevelt and The Birth of Modern America, 1900–1912, 1962, p. 1.

21. "Class self-interest"

Ross, Social Control, 1969 ed., p. 86. For the significance of Ross for Progressive ideology, see § 6357, text at note-call 787.

weakened traditional instruments of social control, such as the law.[22]

The American myth of classlessness is exemplified by the Horatio Alger story , but it did not arise entirely by accident.[23] Business groups. such as the National Civic Federation tirelessly propagandized against any dissent from the myth, arguing that national progress depended upon a classless society of freely competing individuals whose merits determined their rewards.[24] They were supported by orthodox economists who undertook to demonstrate that if logically analyzed, class interests were harmonious, advancing what is today known as the "trickle-down theory"; that is, the rich are necessary to provide employment for gardeners, maids, and stockbrokers.[25] So powerful is the myth that as late as in 1991, after nearly a decade of corporate class warfare against working people, 93% of Americans in a national poll still regarded themselves as "middle-class."[26]

We need not account for the persistence of the myth but only point out its utility for the adversary system, trial by jury, and the right of confrontation.[27] If Americans were as class-conscious as some (primarily but not exclusively on the left) wish they were, it would be difficult to see why the rich would regard a jury of working-class persons as a "jury of their peers"—or vice versa.[28] If

22. Weakened control

Ibid.

23. Horatio Alger

Wiebe, Businessmen and Reform: A Study of the Progressive Movement, 1962, p. 192.

24. Merits determined

Id. at p. 180.

25. Orthodox economists

Wood, Constitutional Politics in the Progressive Era, 1968. p. 148.

26. 93% "middle-class"

Lukas, Big Trouble, 1997, p. 1. This could be a sort of "class consciousness"; that is, the respondents recognize that there are classes in our society and they wish to be identified with the one that is most acceptable to members of all classes.

27. Utility

It seems reasonable to suppose that only in a society that had some confidence in cross-class solidarity would the influential classes open themselves to the sort of attack by others presupposed by the adversary system.

28. "Jury of peers"

On the other hand, after the O.J. Simpson trial, numerous commentators pointed out that Mr. Simpson was fortunate not be tried by a jury of his peers in Brentwood inasmuch as public-opinion polls showed these were the people who more than any other group continued to believe he was guilty even after his acquittal.

people believed that the kind of trial one obtained was dependent on socio-economic status, the legitimacy of jury verdicts would be significantly undermined.[29] Finally, if one assumed that one's perceptions of society were dependent on one's status in that society, one would have to question the ability of the lawyer to cross-examine and of the jury to judge the credibility of persons of a different social class.[30] Whether or not they consciously considered it, fear of class consciousness was to drive much of the ideology of Progressivism and, through that ideology, the development of the right of confrontation.[31]

"Muckraking", P.R., and the Press

In October, 1902, McClure's magazine began publishing a series of articles on municipal corruption by Lincoln Steffens——the first in a new journalistic genre that came to be called "muckraking."[32] The term derived from an attack on this new journalism by Theodore Roosevelt.[33] Despite the derisive term, the muckrakers provided the journalistic inspiration for the Progressive movement.[34] The origins of muckraking lay in those technological changes in the late Nineteenth Century that drove newspapers and magazines toward mass circulation and an attempt to appeal to a broader audience than the ethnics and ideologues that supported a

29. Legitimacy

Indeed, in a number of recent "Trials of the Century", those who reject the acquittals have placed much emphasis on how the trials of the accused differed from the trials of ordinary people charged with crime.

30. Judge credibility

One of the arguments for the "cross-section of society" version of trial by jury seems to rest on this assumption; i.e., we need to have a cross-section to insure that someone who comprehends the social vision of the witness will be there to explain it to the jury.

31. Fear of class-consciousness

And still does. The junior author was present at a conference of evidence scholars where a paper on the history of hearsay reform suggested, inter alia, that the reforms of the Progressive era were class-biased. The vocifer-

ousness (and lack of substance) of the ensuing attack upon the paper were surprising even to one accustomed to how touchy proceduralists are about the influence of wealth on doctrine and practice in their field.

32. "Muckraking"

Mowry, The Era of Theodore Roosevelt and the Birth of Modern America, 1900–1912, 1962, p. 64.

33. Derived from attack

Roosevelt drew upon a character in Bunyan's "Pilgrim's Progress" who "could look no way but downward with the muckrake in his hands" and thus missed a proffered celestial crown. Ekirch, Progressivism in America, 1974, p. 59.

34. Journalistic inspiration

Chamberlain, Farewell to Reform, 1965 ed., p. 120.

rambunctiously diverse press in the latter half of the prior century.[35] The earliest efforts, usually attributed to Joseph Pulitzer, relied on sex, sports and mayhem——the so-called "penny press" that was ultimately to produce the kind of "yellow journalism" often associated with the jingoism that surrounded the Spanish–American War.[36] Soon demands for "purifying the press" arose from the respectable reading public.[37] The muckrakers played on the anxieties of the middle class and the growing desire to do something to ease them.[38] Thus, despite the claims that they were wallowing in the mire, muckraking journalism exuded an optimism that an aroused citizenry could do something about the evils exposed—though the muckrakers usually did not specify just what that might be.[39]

Although muckraking had roots in the abolitionist and Populist press, its immediate inspiration was Henry Demarest Lloyd's study of the Standard Oil Trust of John D. Rockefeller entitled "Wealth Against Commonwealth."[40] Examples of the genre, in addition to Steffens' expose of municipal corruption published as a book under the title "The Shame of the Cities", include Ida Tarbell's painstaking history of the Standard Oil Company, Thomas Lawson's behind-the-scenes look at the machinations of Wall Street, and David Graham Phillip's revelations concerning the corruption of the Senate by business interests.[41] What was unique about the muckrakers was their assimilation of confrontation values; instead of relying on hearsay and rumor, the muckrakers went to official records, such as the transcripts of judicial, legislative, and administrative hearings where the witnesses were under oath and subject to something

35. Technological changes

Progressivism in America, 1974, p. 60; Mowry, The Era of Theodore Roosevelt and the Birth of Modern America, 1900–1912, 1962, p. 64.

36. "Yellow journalism"

For the "Cliff Notes" version of this chapter in journalistic history, see Lukas, Big Trouble, 1997, pp. 649–659.

37. "Purifying press"

Ross, Social Control, 1969 ed., p. 137.

38. Desire to do something

Mowry, The Progressive Era, 1900–1912: The Reform Persuasion, 1958, p. 14.

39. Exuded optimism

Ekirch, Progressivism in America, 1974, pp. 58, 62.

40. "Wealth Against"

Chamberlain, Farewell to Reform , 1965, ed., p. 49.

41. Examples of genre

Hays, The Response to Industrialism, 1885–1914, 1957, p. 90.

like cross-examination.[42] Their method reflected the scientistic desire for, and faith in, "the facts."[43] Indeed, some historians have argued that the muckrakers were the model for what lawyers came to refer to as "the Brandeis brief", in which social legislation being attacked as unconstitutional was defended by showing the court the social facts that had necessitated the legislation.[44] Muckraking also appealed to the popular infatuation with private investigators in mystery novels; a less pejorative label for the muckrakers was "detective reporters."[45]

Most muckraking journalism dealt with the relations between government and business.[46] Even the judiciary was not exempt; the ideological bias of judges was characterized as "legalized corruption."[47] The muckrakers revealed the hypocrisy of most capitalists, who preached the benefits of laissez faire and the evils of government regulation while relying on the government to create their corporations and to protect them from the vicissitudes of "the market."[48] This attack on the existing order provoked a reaction.[49] Using the occasion of William Randolph Hearst's hasty, exaggerated, and careless attempt to emulate the muckrakers—an article on the symbiotic relationship between capitalists and the national legislature published as "The Treason of the Senate"—Theodore Roosevelt launched the attack that gave the genre its name.[50] However, Roosevelt's attack probably had less to do with the demise of the muckrakers than did the growing influence of advertisers on newspapers and magazines.[51]

42. Relied on records

Chamberlain, Farewell to Reform, 1965 ed., p. 54.

43. Faith in "the facts"

Id. at pp. 123, 177; Mowry, The Progressive Era, 1900–1912: The Reform Persuasion, 1958, p. 14; Lukas, Big Trouble, 1997, p. 654.

44. "Brandeis brief"

Hays, The Response to Industrialism, 1885–1914, 1957, p. 90.

45. "Detective reporters"

Lukas, Big Trouble, 1997, p. 654.

46. Government and business

Ekirch, Progressivism in America, 1974, pp. 61–62.

47. "Legalized corruption"

Chamberlain, Farewell to Reform, 1965 ed., p. 127.

48. Hypocrisy

Id. at p. 133.

49. Provoked reaction

Id. at p. 138.

50. Roosevelt attack

Id. at p. 140.

51. Advertisers

Id. at p. 141.

Another corporate response to muckraking was the development of the "public relations expert"——often a journalist who had gone over to "the other side."[52] This development was funded first by bankers who wanted to shake off their image as "economic royalists."[53] However, the "founder" of the modern public-relations profession is usually said to be John D. Rockefeller's sycophantic publicist, Ivy L. Lee, who liked to compare his boss to Henry VIII and Napoleon.[54] Lee believed that "crowds were led by symbols and phrases" and he wrote: "We know that Henry the Eighth by his obsequious deference to the forms of law was able to get the English people to believe in him so completely that he was able to do almost anything with them."[55] In their competition with lawyers for the task of corporate apologist, the public-relations people had not only an appreciation for ritual that lawyers were in the process of shedding but they were not hampered by any ethical restraints on their ability to manipulate "the facts."[56]

The development of public relations effected confrontation jurisprudence in another way.[57] Public-relations people inspired and led the government's propaganda campaign during World War I.[58] In the process, they seem to have invented the first "astroturf" organization——a purported interest group that in fact reflects

52. "Public relations"

Wiebe, Businessmen and Reform: A Study of the Progressive Movement, 1962, p. 187.

53. "Economic royalists"

Id. at pp. 188, 220–221.

54. Ivy Lee

Stauber & Rampton, Toxic Sludge is Good for You!: Lies, Damned Lies, and The Public Relations Industry, 1995, p. 19.

55. "Do almost anything"

Weinstein, The Corporate Ideal in the Liberal State, 1900–1918, 1968, p. 197.

56. Competition with lawyers

Lawyers continued to provide the ideological defense of capitalism until that task was taken from them by economists at the end of the century. The public-relations industry, particularly but not exclusively in the insurance industry, also played a leading role in undermining public confidence in the adversary system by convincing the public that "trial lawyers"——a term reserved for plaintiff's personal-injury lawyers——were deceiving credulous jurors into awarding unjustified verdicts.

57. Another way

That is, other than by generating a corrosive sentiment about the role of "facts" and "truth" in public affairs, best exemplified by the assumptions of the media that what matters is not "character" but "image."

58. Propaganda campaign

Weinstein, The Corporate Ideal in the Liberal State, 1900–1918, 1968, p. 240.

interests other than those suggested by its name.[59] The government used public relations personnel and techniques to whip up anti-German hysteria during the War and anti-radical fears afterwards that would eventually result in the "Red Scare"——a key event in the history of civil liberties, including the right of confrontation.[60]

Public relations experts probably played a lesser role than they claimed or imagined in affecting biased presentation of the news. As it had during the Nineteenth Century, the business press was flooded with anti-union stories and editorials.[61] Moreover, as Robert La Follette said in a speech to magazine publishers that did little to advance his presidential candidacy, the public was "fast coming to understand that whenever news items bear in any way upon the control of the government by business, the news is colored."[62] Even journalists acknowledged an institutional bias; as one reporter who covered the trial of leaders of the Western Federation of Miners on charges of having murdered the ex-governor of Idaho put it: "The press sends out to the world the overt acts of wage earners driven to desperation and suppresses the recital of the crimes which engender these conditions, though they may be a matter of public knowledge and judicial inquiry."[63] Indeed, when John D. Rockefeller was questioned about his role in the infamous Ludlow Massacre during a government inquiry into industrial relations, a Senator who cross-examined the millionaire was denounced in the press as "bullying" the witness and for "irresponsible and preposterous badgering"; to the press, the ideas that a capitalist should be subjected to the adversary system was "offensive and absurd."[64] But if elites were to be immune from cross-examination, they would have little interest in preserving the right of confrontation for their opponents or even for ordinary citizens.

59. "Astroturf"

Id. at p. 242.

60. Whip up hysteria

Id. at p. 247.

61. Anti-union stories

Adams, Age of Industrial Violence, 1910–1915, 1966, p. 131.

62. "News is colored"

Weinstein, The Corporate Ideal in the Liberal State, 1900–1918, 1968, p. 158.

63. "Crimes which engender"

Lukas, Big Trouble, 1997, p. 678.

64. "Offensive and absurd"

Adams, Age of Industrial Violence, 1910–1915, 1966, p. 169.

Historians have found press bias worse in small-towns, perhaps because small town editors were not confronted with ethnic and union newspapers that could question their version of the truth.[65] However, even in the urban press one can see how Progressives were driven to "the center"——the place from which certain ideas and institutions seem beyond the bounds of legitimate participation in democratic government. For example, after a group of unionists exercised their First Amendment rights, the New York Times denounced their march as "uncalled for and un-American", characterized the participants as persons who "do not understand or appreciate their privileges as citizens or denizens of the United States", and concluded that a "parade of Socialists bearing red flags and employing bands to play the 'Marseillaise' is in this country * * * profoundly asinine."[66] But when federal legislation was proposed to stamp out child labor, the Times opposed it on the ground "that it would not be right for intolerant opinion on those subjects to impose its will upon others equally entitled to their opinions."[67] On some subjects, even history was on the side of Big Business:

> The modern pressure towards organization and co-operation in business is salutary and indispensable, even irresistible * * *. A full generation of the administration of anti-trust laws has demonstrated the futility of attempting to destroy co-operation, even combination * * *.[68]

But when Charles Beard was forced out of Columbia, the Times denounced his "Economic Interpretation of the Constitution" as "a book no professor should have written, since it was grossly unscientific" and rested on ideas "borrowed from Germany."

> If this sort of teaching were allowed to go unchecked by public sentiment and the strong hands of University Trustees, we should presently find educated American youth applying the doctrine of economic determinism to everything from the Lord's Prayer to the binomial theorem.[69]

65. Small towns worse

Weinstein, The Corporate Ideal in the Liberal State, 1900–1918, 1968, p. 63.

66. "Profoundly asinine"

Lukas, Big Trouble, 1997, p. 479.

67. "Entitled to opinions"

Wood, Constitutional Politics in the Progressive Era, 1968, p. 176.

68. "Futility of attempting"

Id. at p. 296.

69. "Economic determinism"

White, Social Thought in America: The Revolt Against Formalism, 1957, ed., p. 126.

The Times apparently believed that it was necessary to destroy the Constitution, for some at least, in order to preserve it for others—not an attitude likely to encourage expansive interpretation of the Confrontation Clause.

From Billy Club to Faculty Club

In 1903, the Anthracite Coal Commission, which had been convened by the President and the House of Morgan to arbitrate the dispute issued its report.[70] In addition to settling the specific strike, the Commission tried to lay down rules to guide future disputes, in large part by declaring certain union practices, such as the boycott "cruel and cowardly" and "outside the pale of civilized war."[71] Unions were told they

> must not undertake to assume, or to interfere with the management of the business of the employer. [And furthermore] the right to remain at work where others have ceased to work, or to engage anew in work which others have abandoned, is part of the personal liberty of a citizen, that can never be surrendered, and every infringement thereof merits, and should receive the stern denouncement of the law.[72]

Other employers, rightly deciding that workingmen would never agree to this ipse dixit, launched a preemptive counterattack against unions.[73] The National Association of Manufacturers rejected the idea that labor unions had any legitimate place in American life.[74] Accordingly, businesses organized hundreds of national, state, and local antiunion organizations.[75] Thus began another 20 years of industrial warfare, suspended only briefly during World War I.[76] Employers could scarcely have seen themselves as victors, since by 1919 the number of union members reached levels it would not reach again until the New Deal.[77] Hence, the relationship between

70. Coal Commission report

Wiebe, Businessmen and Reform: A Study of the Progressive Movement, 1962, p. 160.

71. "Outside the pale"

Id. at p. 162.

72. "Stern denouncement"

Id. at pp. 161–162.

73. Counterattack

Adams, The Age of Industrial Violence, 1910–1915, 1966, p. 2.

74. Any legitimate place

Weinstein, The Corporate Ideal in the Liberal State, 1900–1918, 1968, p. 14.

75. Anti-union organizations

Wiebe, Businessmen and Reform: A Study of the Progressive Movement, 1962, p. 19.

76. Industrial warfare

Adams, The Age of Industrial Violence, 1910–1915, 1966, p. 1.

77. Union member level

Mowry, The Progressive Era, 1900–20: The Reform Persuasion, 1958, p. 29.

the government, business, and labor was the central domestic issue of the Progressive era.[78]

Law was a major instrument of employers in their war against unions.[79] The labor injunction grew even more sweeping after its sanctioning by the Debs Court.[80] In the 1911 strike of the Illinois Central Railroad, a union leader complained that the injunction entered against unionists prohibited strikers "from doing almost anything except breathing. They could not even speak to a man that was working for the Illinois Central Railroad."[81] Even the conservative union leader, and vice-president of the National Civic Federation, Samuel Gompers received a sentence of a year in jail for contempt of court.[82] Employers also sought new weapons, such as the Los Angeles ordinance that made picketing a crime.[83] Over 400 were arrested under the statute and their demands for jury trial clogged court dockets for a year.[84] The N.A.M. supported anti-union efforts by the courts and opposed any effort to increase popular influence over the government's role—measures such as the popular election of senators, the initiative and referendum, and recall of elected officials, including judges.[85]

In 1904, John Henry Wigmore published his treatise on evidence—a work that profoundly influenced confrontation jurisprudence down to the present day.[86] While Wigmore was undoubtedly heavily influenced by the same historical events as the judges he so much admired,[87] those in the academy tend to view events through

78. Central issue

Id. at p. 19.

79. Major instrument

Thought dwarfed by the use of the labor injunction, this included the use of state and federal criminal law. For a telling incident, see Adams, The Age of Industrial Violence, 1910–1915, 1966, pp. 137–138.

80. Sanctioning by Court

See § 6357, text at notecall 447.

81. "Not even speak"

Adams, The Age of Industrial Violence, 1910–1915, 1966, p. 136.

82. Year in jail

Id. at p. 34.

83. Picketing a crime

Id. at p. 5.

84. Clogged dockets

Id. at p. 6.

85. Recall of judges

Id. at p. 36.

86. Wigmore published

Twining, Theories of Evidence: Bentham & Wigmore, 1985, p. 111.

87. Wigmore influenced

For a brief sketch of some influences on Wigmore, see Graham, "There'll Always Be An England": The Instrumental Ideology of Evidence, 1987, 85 Mich.L.Rev. 1204, 1216–1217.

a different lens. Hence, we must pause to revisit trends in American higher education.

During the latter half of the Nineteenth Century, when few American colleges offered the degree, many American scholars obtained their Ph.D. from German universities.[88] Many of these expatriates studied economics or political economy as the disciplines most suited to the reform instincts of youth.[89] They found in Hegel a useful alternative to the social theory of Locke——a profound challenge to the individualism rampant in United States at the time.[90] Since the Germans are notoriously less individualistic, even those Americans who did not study philosophy came back with a greater respect for institutions and the role of government in fostering social progress.[91] For example, in 1885 at the founding convention of the American Economic Association, a "group of young rebels fresh from Germany" issued a remarkable credo that included this sentence: "We regard the state as an educational and ethical agency whose positive aid is an indispensable condition to human progress."[92]

This romantic statism, however threatening it might be to anti-state doctrines like the right of confrontation, was congenial to the Anglophilia common to elite universities and especially prevalent in their law schools. The historian Charles Beard described a "Teutonic" school "which saw in the Federal Constitution the political genius of the Germanic tribes who invaded England and whose English descendants settled America."[93] This conceit was aided by the American-trained sociologist Edward Alsworth Ross who argued that individualism and its peculiar sense of justice and social order were Teutonic in origin.[94] Hence, university-trained Progressives

88. German Ph.D.

Ekirch, Progressivism in America, 1974, p. 24.

89. Studied economics

Ekirch, Progressivism in America, 1974, p. 25.

90. Challenge to individualism

Russett, Darwin in America: The Intellectual Response, 1865–1912, 1976, p. 113. Some of them sought to blend Hegel and Darwin. Id. at p. 114.

91. Role of government

Ekirch, Progressivism in America, 1975, p. 25.

92. "State indispensable"

Mowry, The Era of Theodore Roosevelt and The Birth of Modern America, 1900–1912, 1962, p. 22.

93. "Germanic tribes"

White, Social Thought in America: The Revolt Against Formalism, 1957, ed., p. 109.

94. Teutonic in origin

Ross, Social Control, 1969 ed., pp. 16–17, 32.

admired and sought to emulate the strong administrative state their predecessors had found in Prussia.[95] As a scholar from the University of Wisconsin put it: "Bismarck did a great deal of * * * planning, and the men around him, Wagner and the other university men were brought in by him."[96]

Not until World War I did some scholars begin to worry that the Progressive emphasis on efficiency and organization would "Prussianize" the United States.[97] The association of efficiency with Germany proved particularly embarrassing to the new-fangled "efficiency experts" and other Progressives in a time when "sauerkraut" could only be sold as "victory cabbage."[98] This led to a split in the academy between those who continued to acknowledge the influence of Germany on their ideas and those who no longer wished to retain the Prussians as "honorary Englishmen."[99] But by this time German statism had merged with another trend in academic thinking—one that had a more enduring public appeal.[100]

"Scientism"—the desire to clothe one's ideas and opinions with the authority of the law of nature—did not originate with Progressive thinkers; Social Darwinism was only the most immediate in a long line of predecessors.[101] What made the Progressive scientism different was its appeal to the dynamic, explanatory science of Darwin as against the older classificatory science with its assumptions that the law of nature was static.[102] Increasingly scientistic rhetoric claimed to derive authority from the methods of the hard sciences—experiment, measurement, generalization.[103]

95. Admire administrative state

Ekirch, Progressivism in America, 1974, p. 166.

96. "University men"

Weinstein, The Corporate Ideal in The Liberal State, 1900–1918, 1968, p. 201.

97. "Prussianize"

Ekirch, Progressivism in America, 1974, p. 273.

98. Proved embarrassing

Haber, Efficiency and Uplift: Scientific Management in the Progressive Era, 1890–1920, 1973, p. 119.

99. Led to split

White, Social Thought in America: The Revolt Against Formalism, 1957 ed., p. 147.

100. Another trend

Id. at p. 159.

101. Predecessors

And successors; see, e.g., the so-called "economic analysis" of law that was popular in the 1980s.

102. Dynamic science

White, Social Thought in America: The Revolt Against Formalism, 1957 ed., p. 81.

103. Hard sciences

Haber, Efficiency and Uplift: Scientific Management in the Progressive Era,

Hence, the scientistic expert could claim his conclusions had accuracy, objectivity, and generality.[104] The new scientistic scholars claimed to apply the scientific method, not to justify the status quo, but to solve existing social problems.[105] For example, anthropology claimed to be "the reformer's science."[106] The rise of the new scientism coincided with increasing public acceptance of the concept of "social science" and the use of the adjective "scientific" as a term of approbation.[107] In all of this there was a tendency to conflate "science" with "technology."[108] And as to the latter, dissenting voices were sometimes heard.[109]

The new scientism appealed to the desire of individualist intellectuals to escape the deterministic Darwinism of the conservatives and the Hegelian determinism of the Socialists.[110] It also promised an end to messy democratic disputes over social facts and their meaning; science was touted as "the only discipline which gives any assurance that from the same set of facts men will come to approximately the same conclusions."[111] The scientistic reformer thought science would find the true political center or even transcend the traditional categories of "left" and "right":[112]

> The extreme conservative may deprecate any scrutiny of the present order; the ardent radical may be impatient of the critical and seemingly tardy processes of the investigator; but those who

1890–1920, 1973, pp. 20, 81.

104. Objectivity and generality
Id. at p. 40.

105. Solve social problems
White, Social Thought in America: The Revolt Against Formalism, 1957 ed., p. 46.

106. "Reformer's science"
Id. at p. 193.

107. "Social science"
Mowry, The Era of Theodore Roosevelt and The Birth of Modern America, 1900–1912, 1962, p. 19.

108. Conflate with "technology"
Chamberlain, Farewell to Reform, 1965 ed., p. 20.

109. Dissenting voices
"Man has mounted science, and is now run away with. I firmly believe that before many centuries more, science will be the master of man. The engines he will have invented will be beyond his strength to control. Some day science may have the existence of mankind in its power, and the human race commit suicide by blowing up the world." Russett, Darwin in America: The Intellectual Response, 1865–1912, 1976 (quoting Henry Adams).

110. Escape determinism
Mowry, The Era of Theodore Roosevelt and The Birth of Modern America, 1900–1912, 1962, p. 17.

111. "Same conclusions"
Id. at p. 18.

112. Transcend categories
Compare the slogan of the German Green Party at the end of the century: "Neither right nor left, but ahead."

have considered well the conquest which man is making of the world of nature cannot forbear the conviction that the cruder method of trial and error and the time-honored method of prejudice and partisan controversy need not longer dominate the regulation of life and society. They hope for the larger application of the scientific method to the problems of human welfare and progress.[113]

As the rhetoric of "conquest" in this passage suggests, scientistic argument also appealed to that burly "tough-mindedness" that Theodore Roosevelt exemplified.[114] It avoided any feministic appeals to "morality" or to "conscience"—two concepts that Progressive thinkers distrusted.[115] Both Veblen in economics and Robinson in history wished to repudiate the moralizing of their predecessors in favor of "scientific" study of their disciplines.[116]

The political implications of the new scientism came through clearly; its practitioners saw "the possibility of a new kind of history in which kings and warriors will give place to men of science."[117] Sociologists assumed that society follows Darwinian evolution from the simple to the complex—a neat anti-pastoral riposte to one strand of Populist thinking.[118] The practitioners of "scientific management" believed that labor-management relations followed rules that were impartial and above mere class interests.[119] These, they thought, would eventually place authority in the hands of those who followed the rules of science.[120] Workers, not surprisingly, rejected these premises.[121] Perhaps they had heard the "sci-

113. "Larger application"

White, Social Thought in America: The Revolt Against Formalism, 1957 ed., p. 55.

114. "Tough-mindedness"

Id. at p. 123.

115. Distrusted "morality"

O'Neill, The Progressive Years, 1975, p. 99.

116. Repudiate moralizing

White, Social Thought in America: The Revolt Against Formalism, 1957 ed., pp. 25, 28, 78. See also, Darwin in America: The Intellectual Response, 1865–1912, 1976, p. 129.

117. "Men of science"

White, Social Thought in America: The Revolt Against Formalism, 1957 ed., p. 15.

118. Simple to complex

Id. at p. 52.

119. Above class interests

Haber, Efficiency and Uplift: Scientific Management in the Progressive Era, 1890–1920, 1973, p. x.

120. Authority followed rules

Id. at p. 29.

121. Workers rejected

Wiebe, Businessmen and Reform: A Study of The Progressive Movement, 1962, p. 163.

entific" manager who bragged that using a phrenologist to help select employees had kept "labor agitators" out of the workplace.[122]

As we have seen, the mania for scientism inspired the muckrakers who put their faith in the "scientific method" to produce "facts, nothing but facts."[123] In the law, Holmes' ambiguity about the utility of "science" for law was atypical; others were willing to follow the half of him that called for a "scientific" evaluation of law into the schools of thought known as "sociological jurisprudence" and, later, "legal realism."[124] One potential outcome of such an evaluation might have been foreshadowed by the way in which his preoccupation with scientific management led Brandeis to shift from a concern about the distribution of wealth to an interest in its production.[125]

The new scientism passed over from the academy to public life. A number of scholars, including the sociologist Edward Ross and Roscoe Pound of "sociological jurisprudence" fame, participated in the National Civic Federation's grandiose "Survey of Social, Civic, and Economic Progress."[126] The research director of the Commission on Industrial Relations, in the wake of the Ludlow Massacre, was told by a representative of the Rockefeller interests that despite the "apprehensions excited in certain quarters both on the side of capital and on the side of labor" the Commission might "gradually convince the public both of our disinterestedness and of our strictly scientific method."[127] While some people may not have seen how "science" might reflect class bias, the Chairman of the Commission was not one of them.[128] He denounced the support of

122. Kept "agitators" out

Haber, Efficiency and Uplift: Scientific Management in The Progressive Era, 1890–1920, 1973, p. 56.

123. "Nothing but facts"

Lukas, Big Trouble, 1997, p. 654 Lincoln Steffens, one of the originators of the genre had studied in Germany. Ibid.

124. Holmes

White, Social Thought in America: The Revolt Against Formalism, 1957 ed., pp. 81, 110.

125. Brandeis

Haber, Efficiency and Uplift: Scientific Management in the Progressive Era, 1890–1920, p. 81.

126. "Economic Progress"

Weinstein, The Corporate Ideal in the Liberal State, 1900–1918, 1968, pp. 124, 127.

127. "Strictly scientific"

Id. at p. 203.

128. Reflect class bias

Haber, Efficiency and Uplift: Scientific Management in the Progressive Era, 1890–1920, 1973, p. 96.

science by Rockefeller and other foundations on the ground that it would lead to "loyalty and subserviency" to business "interests from the whole profession of scientists, social workers, and economists."[129]

Determining whether and how these general academic currents directly affected legal scholarship is difficult because of the autonomy of law-school faculties and their isolation from their colleagues in other fields; but fortunately there is little need to do more than show that legal thinking tended to parallel that of other disciplines.[130] As we shall see, trial by jury in particular and the adversary system in general provided the field on which the new and old legal ideologies faced off.[131] Because jurors tended to side with workers in the industrial battles of the Progressive era, many capitalists and politicians criticized the normal processes of the law, some preferring to resort to the use of extralegal force, whether by employing private armies or invoking martial law.[132] In response, legal scholars began to distinguish between "substance" and "procedure", arguing that while the former dealt with values and so needed to be left to the political branches, the latter was a matter of "science" that could safely be left to the "experts"; that is, judges and law professors.[133]

The political value of the "substance-procedure" dichotomy was obvious from the start; for example, it was argued that the flaws in the Sherman Act that led to its being applied to labor unions and not to capitalists were procedural, not substantive.[134] But presumably the Progressive proceduralists believed that by scientific methods they could purge procedure of the class bias that infected the judges in cases like In re Debs and Pettibone v.

129. "Loyalty and subserviency"

Weinstein, The Corporate Ideal in The Liberal State, 1900–1918, 1968, p. 205.

130. Tended to parallel

That is, for our purposes, it is sufficient to show that legal scholars were bitten by the "science" bug without deciding whether it flew in from the sociology department or from the editorial offices of the local newspaper.

131. Adversary system

See the analysis of Pound's famous St. Paul address, below, text at notecall 322.

132. Extralegal force

Lukas, Big Trouble, 1997, p. 375.

133. "Substance" and "procedure"

Haber, Efficiency and Uplift: Scientific Management in the Progressive Era, 1890–1920, 1973, p. 103.

134. Sherman Act flaws

Wiebe, Businessmen and Reform: A Study of the Progressive Movement, 1962, p. 139.

Nichols.[135] In the latter case, the Supreme Court held the fact that
the state had bypassed the proper procedure for extradition in favor
of the legalized kidnapping of labor leaders did not deprive the state
of its authority to try them.[136] For our purposes, the case is
noteworthy for demonstrating how little regard officials had for
confrontation values.[137] Justice Harlan, who wrote the court's opinion appears to have held an ex parte meeting with the lawyer for
the state at which that worthy informed him of some "facts" not
reflected in the record that were thought important to the Court's
understanding of what was at stake.[138] Meanwhile, President
Roosevelt, who had publicly blasted the defendants as "undesirable
citizens" while their case was pending, dangled a judicial opinion
for his son before Justice Harlan.[139]

In 1904, in the midst of this rising interest in procedure, John
Henry Wigmore published what was to be the most influential work
on evidence for the remainder of the century.[140] At the time, the
prior generation of lawyers were still relying on Greenleaf's treatise, which as we have seen had very little to say about the right of
confrontation.[141] Indeed, Greenleaf was actually used as an evidence
textbook in many law schools.[142] As a result of his work on the final
edition of Greenleaf's work, Wigmore developed some strong reformist impulses:

> This mass has become so voluminous and unmanageable that only
> a few judges and practitioners are able to master them and to use
> them correctly. * * * But the ten thousand details which now
> form our law of evidence represent a system dried up and gone to

135. Debs and Pettibone
See § 6357, text at notecalls 362, 390.

136. Authority to try
Lukas, Big Trouble, 1997, p. 280.

137. Confrontation values
Specifically, the blank-pad rule.

138. Ex parte meeting
Id. at p. 283.

139. "Undesirable citizens"
Id. at p. 397.

140. Most influential work
Wigmore, A Treatise on The System of
Evidence in Trials at Common Law, 4
vols., 1904. An inspection of the cases

at the turn of the millenium will reveal that courts still cite Wigmore
more than all of the other evidence
treatises even though only a handful
of states still retain the "common
law" system of evidence.

141. Still using Greenleaf
Brooks, Walter Clark, Fighting Judge,
1944, p. 41 For Greenleaf and the
right of confrontation, see § 6355,
text at notecall 783.

142. Used as textbook
Harbaugh, Lawyer's Lawyer: The Life of
John W. Davis, 1973, p. 5.

seed. They should be thoroughly pruned and reformed.[143]

Despite the bungled metaphor, Wigmore's work intended to remake the law of evidence——a task that could be frustrated by an expansive interpretation of the right of confrontation.[144]

To understand Wigmore's approach to confrontation requires that we know something about the man, but, alas, biographies of Wigmore fail to provide much insight into his intellectual preconceptions.[145] Even so, it is clear that Wigmore had only one foot in the camp of the Progressive procedural reformers; for example, he was a strong supporter of trial by jury.[146] Wigmore was an unlikely reformer. Born into the family of a wealthy San Francisco lumber dealer around the time of the Civil War, he seems to have been something of a "sissy" and a "momma's boy."[147] When he went off to the Harvard Law School, his mother insisted that the whole family move to Cambridge where she could continue to dote on her favorite child.[148] Not unexpectedly, when Wigmore chose a career and a bride against his mother's wishes, this led to a permanent rift in their relationship.[149] Wigmore and his wife remained childless, which may explain Wigmore's childlike faith in paternalistic and rational governance.[150]

Wigmore was a prodigious worker, nearly working himself into a nervous breakdown during his final year in law school.[151] He was one of the founders of the Harvard Law Review.[152] Moreover, he read or spoke a dozen languages——a fact that made him more cosmopolitan in his approach to law than the typical Harvard

143. "Pruned and reformed"

Roalfe, John Henry Wigmore, 1977, pp. 200, 204.

144. Bungled metaphor

Plants that "dry up and go to seed" are not the sort that one "prunes."

145. Biographies of Wigmore

Roalfe, John Henry Wigmore, 1977; Twining, Theories of Evidence: Bentham & Wigmore, 1985 See also, Graham, "There'll Always Be An England": The Instrumental Ideology of Evidence, 1987, 85 Mich.L.Rev. 1204.

146. Supporter of jury

Roalfe, John Henry Wigmore, 1977, p. 203.

147. "Sissy" and "momma's boy"

Id. at pp. 4, 6.

148. Move to Cambridge

Id. at p. 7.

149. Permanent rift

Id. at p. 20.

150. Faith in paternalistic

Id. at p. 76.

151. Workaholic

Id. at pp. 11, 82, 101.

152. Founders

Id. at p. 11.

Anglophile.[153] For his time, Wigmore was an advanced thinker on what today we would call "racism" and "sexism."[154] He taught for some time in Japan, where he acquired some familiarity with modern inquisitorial procedure.[155] This fueled his interest in a more "scientific" brand of evidence law.[156] His fondness for inquisitorial procedure gained strength during his military service in World War I.[157] Wigmore regarded military justice as superior to the civilian version and thought bureaucratic government better than popular government.[158] Late in life he admired the Roman Catholic Church and expressed sympathy toward fascism.[159] These attitudes explain much of Wigmore's antipathy to the right of confrontation.[160]

Wigmore shared two characteristics with leading judges and lawyers that not only shaped his own ideas about confrontation but also made them more acceptable to such judges and lawyers. The first of these was elitism. Wigmore defined "democracy "as "the progress of all under the leadership of the wisest and the best."[161] He opposed any measures to make legal education more accessible to students of modest means.[162] He blamed the degradation of the

153. Cosmopolitan

Id. at p. 106.

154. Advanced thinker

Wigmore was vociferously opposed to racist policies, particularly those aimed at the Japanese. Id. at p. 96 When students at Northwestern planned an all-male dinner, Wigmore refused to serve as master of ceremonies unless a female law student was allowed to attend. Id. at p. 67.

155. Taught in Japan

Id. at p. 17.

156. "Scientific"

Id. at p. 27.

157. Military service

While serving in Washington, Wigmore revised the provision of the Manual For Courts–Martial dealing with rules of evidence. Id. at p. 120 He loved to wear his uniform during the post-War years and insisted on being addressed as "Colonel" rather than by his academic title. Id. at pp. 124, 148 He required all students at Northwestern

to sign an oath against pacifism. Id. at p. 147.

158. Military superior

Id. at pp. 136–137 In a 1937 speech, Wigmore argued that the bureaucracy was "more efficient than the legislative branch." Id. at p. 234 He also defined "democracy" as "the progress of all under the leadership of the wisest and the best." Ibid.

159. Facism

Id. at pp. 235 (his praise of facism), 245 (favored organization of Catholics).

160. Antipathy

One might suppose that his appreciation of fascism would lead him to approve the more ritualistic features of confrontation but this does not appear to be so.

161. "Wisest and best"

Id. at p. 204.

162. Students of modest means

Id. at p. 62.

law of evidence on what he called the "hoipolloization of the bar" and consistently fought to raise standards to make it more difficult for "the hoi polloi" to become lawyers.[163] He detested the lawyer most often associated with the defense of the downtrodden— Clarence Darrow—and opposed allowing him to speak at North-western.[164]

His opposition to Darrow probably stemmed as well from Wigmore's second anti-confrontation characteristic—his opposition to radicals of any sort.[165] He hated communists to the point of wishing to deny them any First Amendment rights.[166] He supported Attorney General Mitchell Palmer's notorious "Red Scare" raids designed to round up and deport radicals.[167] He attacked Holmes' dissent in the Abrams case—now regarded as a milestone in the development of the modern law of free speech.[168] But though he thought "academic freedom" barred any criticism of his teaching, he bitterly assailed other law teachers for their supposed radicalism; e.g., Felix Frankfurter's questioning of the verdict in the Sacco–Vanzetti case and Leon Green's support of labor unions and the Roosevelt "court-packing" plan.[169] Indeed, one of his first articles as a young professor sought to show that boycotts by labor-union members were actionable torts.[170]

Anyone who doubts that his opposition to radicals carried over into his thinking on evidence should consider the episode where he insinuated himself into a controversy at Yale over a proposal to make Robert Hutchins dean of the law school; Wigmore thought Hutchin's unfitness was demonstrated by his groundbreaking work applying what Wigmore called "behaviorism of the extreme type"

163. "Hoipolloization"

Id. at pp. 204, 224.

164. Detested Darrow

Id. at pp. 86, 147.

165. Radicals of any sort

Hence, even if Wigmore had stumbled across evidence of the role of the Levellers in the development of the right of confrontation, it would have been difficult for him to recognize or acknowledge that the Sixth Amendment was fostered by the ideas of primitive communists.

166. Deny rights

Id. at p. 153.

167. "Red Scare" raids

Id. at p. 150.

168. Attacked dissent

White, Social Thought in America: The Revolt Against Formalism, 1957 ed., p. 178.

169. Frankfurter and Green

Roalfe, John Henry Wigmore, 1977, pp. 157, 163, 196.

170. Actionable torts

Id. at p. 12 See also, David, The History of The Haymarket Affair, 1963, p. 54.

to the law of evidence.[171] Wigmore compared "behaviorism in psychology" to "the free silver craze in economics" and wrote that Hutchins' "jaunty and witty but irresponsible dismissal of the recorded experiences of lawyers and judges" demonstrated "an unscientific and unsafe attitude towards the law" and threatened "to unsettle the mind of young men in these days when they are already only too much inclined to cast away" the preexisting law.[172]

Wigmore's view of confrontation set forth in his 1904 treatise was simple.[173]

> Confrontation is, in its main aspect, merely another term for the test of Cross-examination. It is the preliminary step to securing the opportunity of cross-examination and so far as it is essential, this is only because cross-examination is essential. The right of confrontation is the right to the opportunity of cross-examination.[174]

Later Wigmore expands this to show what is not the "main aspect."

> It is generally agreed that the process of confrontation has two purposes, a main and essential one, and a secondary and subordinate one. (1) The main and essential purpose of confrontation is to secure the opportunity of cross-examination. The opponent demands confrontation, not for the idle purpose of gazing upon the witness, or being gazed upon by him, but for the purpose of cross-examination, which cannot be had except by the direct and personal putting of questions and obtaining of immediate answers. * * * (2) There is, however, a secondary advantage to be obtained by the personal appearance of the witness; the judge and the jury are enabled to obtain the elusive and incommunicable evidence of a witness' deportment while testifying, and a certain subjective moral effect is produced upon the witness.[175]

Wigmore then states what he takes to be the relationship between the two aspects of "the so-called right of confrontation."

---

171. "Extreme type"

Schlegel, American Legal Realism and Empirical Social Science: From The Yale Experience, 1979, 28 Buff.L.Rev. 459, 474 n. 83.

172. "Too much inclined"

Ibid.

173. Simple

It remained substantially the same in subsequent versions of the treatise. See 5 Wigmore, Evidence, Chadbourn rev. 1974, pp. 28, 150, 153, 154, 159, 162. However, Wigmore's analysis is followed by the reviser's discussion of the post–1965 decisions of the U.S. Supreme Court. Id. at pp. 162–185.

174. "Right of cross-examination"

2 Wigmore, Evidence, 1904, p. 1695.

175. "Subjective moral effect"

Id. at pp. 1749–1750, 1751.

> The question, then, whether there is a right to be confronted with the opposing witnesses is essentially a question whether there is a right to cross-examination. If there has been a cross-examination, there has been a confrontation. * * * Nevertheless, the secondary advantage, incidentally obtained for the tribunal by the witness presence before it——demeanor-evidence——is an advantage to be insisted upon wherever it can be had. No one has doubted that it is desirable, if only it is available. But it is merely desirable. Where it cannot be obtained, it need not be required. It is no essential part of the notion of confrontation * * *.[176]

What only the most careful reader will notice is that in all of this Wigmore has been speaking of some supposed common-law "notion of confrontation"——what he calls "the so-called right of confrontation."[177] When he comes to what he entitles the "Effect of Constitutional Sanction of Confrontation", Wigmore still cannot bring himself to call it a "right" and he assumes the very point at issue; that is, that the Sixth Amendment and similar state provisions were intended to adopt the common law.[178] He supports this assumption, not by history or the language of the Bill of Rights, but by selective quotation from state-court opinions that posited a common-law origin for the right of confrontation.[179] But Wigmore makes it clear what drives his view of confrontation.

> The net result, then, under the constitutional rule, is that, so far as testimony is required under the Hearsay rule to be taken infrajudicially, it shall be taken in a certain way, namely, subject to cross-examination,——not secretly or ex parte away from the accused. The Constitution does not prescribe what kinds of testimonial statements (dying declarations, or the like) shall be given

176. "No essential part"

Id. at p. 1752.

177. "So-called right"

Ibid.

178. Adopt common law

Id. § 1397.

179. State court opinions

Id. at pp. 1755–1756, quoting from Lambeth v. State, 1852, 23 Miss. 322 (which holds, contra Wigmore, that the hearsay declarant is not a "witness against" the defendant but agreeing that constitution meant to adopt common law); Campbell v. State, 1852, II Ga. 374 (agreeing that confrontation is a common law right, but not authority for Wigmore's point because Georgia had no confrontation clause in its constitution and the court explicitly holds state not bound by Sixth Amendment); Summons v. State, 1856, 5 Ohio St. 325, 341 (similar to Lambeth, above; vigorous dissent); State v. McO'Blenis, 1857, 24 Mo. 402 (majority adopts theory espoused by Wigmore over a strong dissent that is supported by brief that invokes the sort of historical material Wigmore ignores); Jackson v. State, 1892, 51 N.W. 89, 81 Wis. 127 (constitution adopts common law as it stood at the time of ratification).

infra-judicially——this depends on the law of evidence for the time being,——but only what mode of procedure shall be followed——i.e. a cross-examining procedure——in the case of such testimony as is required by the ordinary law of evidence to be given infra-judicially.[180]

In short, the Sixth Amendment is no bar to reform of the hearsay rule and no restriction on the power of judges to abolish the right of confrontation by simply abandoning the hearsay rule.[181] This is not a reading that comports well with the history of the Sixth Amendment.[182]

How does Wigmore support his radical revision of the confrontation clauses? Not by authority; all of the passages quoted are unmarred by footnotes.[183] Instead, Wigmore seems to claim that his theory is implicit in prior authority from which he quotes excerpts.[184] These authorities are not impressive.[185] For example, in support of his claim that at common law "confrontation" meant "cross-examination" he quotes four English sources; a passage from Lord Hale discussing a statute applicable in treason cases, the arguments of counsel in a proceeding in the House of Commons, a

180. "Ordinary law of evidence"

Id. at p. 1755 Wigmore claims this theory is "represented" in the cases we have described in the previous footnote. Only one of those cases is authority for the Wigmorean view (and we have found no other cases then extant that do), so one can infer that the word "represented" was chosen because Wigmore knew his theory was all but unsupported by the caselaw. It is also worth noting that nowhere does Wigmore make reference to any of the decisions of the U.S. Supreme Court construing the Sixth Amendment.

181. No bar to reform

On Wigmore's conflicted view on hearsay reform, see Graham, "There'll Always Be An England": The Instrumental Ideology of Evidence, 1987, 85 Mich.L.Rev. 1204, 1220–1221.

182. History of Sixth

See vol. 30, §§ 6346–6347.

183. Unmarred by footnotes

There are footnotes in some of these sections but they do not purport to be authority supporting the passages quoted in the text but deal with other matters. See, e.g. 2 Wigmore, Evidence, 1904, p. 1757.

184. Implicit in authority

See note 180, above. In introducing the passages supposed to support his view of the common law right of confrontation, Wigmore is similarly evasive, claiming that his equation of confrontation and cross-examination "is demonstrated by the language" he quotes——apparently conceding that these passages do not constitute authority for his theory. Id. at p. 1750.

185. Not impressive

None of them in fact says that "confrontation" means "cross-examination" and some of them can be read as treating the two as separate or as part of a broader system of adversary procedures.

sentence from an opinion in equity, and Jeremy Bentham describing confrontation under the Roman Law system.[186] Only the last of these even uses the word "confrontation."[187] Wigmore's other "authorities" are the state cases we have previously examined.[188] As we saw, some of these do seem to equate confrontation and cross-examination but often are otherwise inconsistent with Wigmore's theory; e.g., rejecting his claim that the constitutions were intended to adopt the English common law.[189] Moreover, Wigmore himself rejects the theory espoused by some of the cases that reach the results he desires; that is, that the "witness" the defendant is entitled to confront is not the hearsay declarant but the person who testifies to the hearsay statement.[190] Finally, some of the cases Wigmore cites to support his claim that the hearsay rule controls the right of confrontation in fact only say that the confrontation clauses were not intended to repeal hearsay exceptions recognized at the time the constitution was adopted.[191]

Wigmore makes only one attempt to explain what policy is furthered by his version of the right of confrontation:

> It is well to have the sound theory fully understood and accepted, because, if the other should temporarily prevail, its overthrow and the exposure of its fallacies might be thought to involve the overthrow of the exceptions to the Hearsay rule. The revision and extension of the exceptions is gradually progressing, and it is well to appreciate fully that there is in this progress nothing inconsistent with the constitutional sanctions. So bold are nowadays the attempts to wrest the Constitution in aid of crime, and so complai-

186. Roman law

Id. at p. 1750 For more on Bentham and confrontation, see § 6355, text at notecall 610.

187. Uses "confrontation"

The equity quotation speaks of "the opportunity of confronting the witnesses and examining them publicly." 2 Wigmore, Evidence, 1904, p. 1750. This is a particularly ironic "authority" because the inquisitorial procedure in chancery was so hateful to the Founders that some states denied their courts equity powers.

188. Previously examined

See § 6356, text at notecall 102, discussing the Howser case, quoted by Wigmore at p. 1751.

189. Rejecting his claim

Indeed, Wigmore quotes (with no sense of inconsistency) the passage in Howser where the court states that there was no common-law right of confrontation. 2 Wigmore, Evidence, 1904, p. 1751.

190. "Witness" not declarant

Id. at p. 1756.

191. Not intended to repeal

See note 179, above.

sant are the Courts in listening to fantastic and unfounded objections to evidence, that the permissibility of such changes should not be left in the slightest doubt.[192]

The Founders, who themselves had invoked the right of confrontation "in aid of crime" under the Navigation Acts, would doubtless be surprised to learn that the purpose of the Sixth Amendment was to make it easier to convict defendants.[193]

Chaos and Conformity

As if to highlight the fears of Wigmore and his fellows, 1905 saw the founding of the International Workers of the World—an organization far more threatening to the comfortable classes than the unions that had been supposedly crushed or cowed in the turbulent '90s.[194] Four years later the I.W.W. launched a campaign for free speech for the working class that, like the Jehovah's Witnesses of a later day and different clause of the First Amendment, did not depend on courts and lawyers but consisted of the persistent and vociferous exercise of the right in question.[195] While this sort of "direct action" involved face-to-face confrontation between the speaker and those directly engaged in the attempt to suppress speech, the upper classes were likely to see the specter of anarchism rather than the spirit of the Sixth Amendment.[196] These fears found support when later in 1905 the former Governor of Idaho, Frank Stuenenberg, was assassinated by bomb and one of those accused of this "crime of the century" was Big Bill Haywood, one of the most prominent members of the I.W.W.[197]

Also in 1905, a New York state investigation under the leadership of future Chief Justice Charles Evan Hughes uncovered corruption in three of the nation's largest life-insurance companies.[198] Executives of these companies had used company funds to bribe politicians and investment bankers on Wall Street to secure favors for their corporations. However, unlike the "crime in the streets"

---

192. "In aid of crime"
Id. at p. 1757.

193. Founders invoked
See vol. 30, pp. 521–527.

194. Founding of I.W.W.
Encyclopedia of American Facts and Dates, 9th ed., 1993, p. 403.

195. Exercise of right
Adams, Age of Industrial Violence, 1910–1915, 1966, p. 177.

196. Specter of anarchism
Ibid.

197. Stuenenberg assassination
Lukas, Big Trouble, 1997, p. 1.

198. Uncovered corruption
Wiebe, Businessmen and Reform: A Study of the Progressive Movement, 1962, p. 47.

of the I.W.W., this "crime in the suites" produced demands for regulation, not repression.[199] This highlighted the bias in law enforcement that allowed Wigmore and his ilk to favor cutting back the confrontation rights of others without fear that they would ever see anonymous hearsay used to condemn them.[200]

While some states in the West hired out their national guard to employers to break strikes by extralegal force, most states preferred to clothe repression of the working class in the garb of legality.[201] For example, though strikes were legal under New York law, police in that state helped employers break strikes by arresting pickets for disorderly conduct.[202] A telling episode involves the socially prominent president of the Women's Trade Union League, Mary Dreir. When she was swept up with a group of pickets outside the infamous Triangle Shirtwaist Co. and a policeman was informed of her identity, he diverted her from the paddy wagon with the remark: "Why didn't you tell me you was a rich lady? I'd never arrested you in the world."[203]

Not only were Ms. Drier's poorer compatriots arrested, when they were assaulted by men assumed to be company goons, magistrates refused to issue warrants for the arrest of their attackers, one of them saying "you had no right to be picketing—you only got what was coming to you."[204] When some of the strikers sought to prove they were peaceful, another magistrate said that he did not want "bother with witnesses for the strikers." Little wonder that even lawyers denounced the magistrates as showing a "prejudiced and vindictive mind" and labor unions claimed that the office of magistrate "has thus been perverted into an instrument of persecution and oppression."[205] When the mayor of New York City expressed some sympathy with this point of view, the judges responded by issuing a sweeping injunction against the strikers.[206]

199. Regulation, not repression

Id. at p. 48.

200. Favor cutting back

At the same time, such bias could produce contempt for constitutional guarantees among ordinary people, thereby diluting support for them.

201. Hired out national guard

Lukas, Big Trouble, 1997, p. 224.

202. Disorderly conduct

Adams, Age of Industrial Violence, 1910–1915, 1966, p. 105.

203. "Never arrested you"

Ibid.

204. "Coming to you"

Id. at p. 107.

205. "Office perverted"

Id. at p. 110.

206. Sweeping injunction

Id. at p. 115.

More corrosive of confrontation than the bias of magistrates was the growing bureaucratization of American life. During the Progressive era, control of the economy seemed to shift from the swashbuckling "Robber Barons" of the prior century to "The Organization Man" of modern life.[207] As the President of the National Association of Manufacturers proclaimed:

> We are living in an age of organization, an age when but little can be accomplished except through organization; an age when organization must cope with organization; an age when organization alone can preserve your industrial freedom and mine.[208]

Bureaucratization was not only accepted, it was hailed: "Organization is the watchword of progress."[209] Progressives were preoccupied with organization——so preoccupied that few seemed to note the way in which bureaucratization threatened individuality, which was not only an assumption that underlay the right of confrontation but was also the keystone of our notions of criminal responsibility.[210]

In fact, however, bureaucratization served largely to justify and preserve the existing inequalities in American life. To some degree, "organization" meant no more than the extension of scientific management techniques from the despised blue collar workers to "white collars" who regarded themselves as superior.[211] As one of the leaders of the scientific management movement wrote: "[t]he object of modern administrative organization is to readjust the balance of responsibilities disturbed by the expansion of industrial operations, and enable central control to be restored in its essential features."[212] But while corporate leaders may have seen "the iron rule of oligarchy" at work inside their firms, they rushed to form business organizations with little regard to the power they were conferring on those who actually ran trade associations and the like.[213] Even the traditionally individualistic legal professions fell

---

207. "Robber barons"

See § 6356, text at notecall 414.

208. "Organization alone"

Wiebe, Businessmen and Reform: A Study of the Progressive Movement, 1962, p. 18.

209. "Watchword of progress"

Id. at 193.

210. Progressives preoccupied

O'Neill, The Progressive Years: America Comes of Age, 1975, p. 11.

211. Extension to "white collars"

Haber, Efficiency and Uplift: Scientific Management in the Progressive Era, 1890–1920, 1973, p. 44.

212. "Central control restored"

Id. at p. 19.

213. "Iron rule of oligarchy"

Wiebe, Businessmen and Reform: A Study of the Progressive Movement, 1962, p. 22 "The Iron Rule of Oligarchy" holds that in any organiza-

victim to this as the American Bar Association and local bar associations purported to speak for the profession in "raising standards" for entry to the profession to require lawyers for ordinary people to acquire skills more useful to those in the bureaucratic corporate law firms.[214]

Individuality threatened bureaucracy because it produced uncertainty—the enemy of planning and coordination.[215] How corporate leaders might have viewed the chaos of confrontation can be seen in their response to threats from other governmental agencies. Some corporate leaders so yearned for predictability that they were even willing to accept some measure of government regulation to achieve it.[216] Business bureaucrats were hostile to the unpredictability of democratic politics; some wanted to convert the office of the President to something like that of C.E.O. of the nation.[217] The National Civic Federation strove to control state governments without being controlled by them through the medium of uniform state laws—a device to bring stability to the first part of the space-time continuum.[218] Some corporations tried to extend their control to the personal lives of their workers by taking over some governmental functions, such a welfare.[219] Were it not for the social distance between workers and capitalists, this might have produced a system of organization similar to the idealized version of Japanese corpora-

tion, regardless how power is formally organized, it tends to flow to a few insiders with the knowledge and interest to control the organization; for example, in a military unit more power resides in the non-commissioned officers who are the only persons in a position to know both the officers and enlisted men and to have significant direct interaction with their opposite numbers in other organizations.

214. Bureaucratization of the bar

O'Neill, The Progressive Years: America Comes of Age, 1975, p. 11. The sociologist, Edward A. Ross, saw this before it was a complete reality. Ross, Social Control, 1969 ed., p. 231.

215. Uncertainty the enemy

Wiebe, Businessmen and Reform: A Study of the Progressive Movement, 1962, p. 139.

216. Accept regulation

Ibid.

217. President as C.E.O.

Id. at p. 104.

218. Uniform state laws

Weinstein, The Corporate Ideal in the Liberal State, 1900–1918, 1968, p. 31 This would ultimately lead to the homogenization of state evidentiary rules—so-called "McEvidence"—that made it easier for the Supreme Court to assess the impact of its confrontation rulings.

219. Taking over functions

Id. at pp. 18–19.

tions rampant at the end of the century.[220] But as the example of Pullman illustrates, American efforts at benign bureaucratization generally foundered.[221]

World War I hastened the pace of bureaucratization, bringing about something akin to the merger of corporate and government bureaucracies.[222] As President Wilson wrote:

> From an economical point of view, there is now very little difference between the machinery required for commercial efficiency and that required for military purposes. In both cases the whole industrial mechanism must be organized in the most effective way.[223]

How much government and corporate bureaucrats learned from each other need not detain us, but as the example of Wigmore illustrates, work in the wartime bureaucracy was the ideological training ground for the Progressives and New Dealers who were willing to trim off from the body politic individualistic excrescences such as confrontation.[224]

Traditional conservatives were not the only people opposed to the growth of bureaucracy.[225] Even among elites there was a split of opinion about the supposed efficiency of large organizations.[226] The end of the war produced something of a corporate backlash against

---

220. Japanese corporation

Consider the example of Samuel "Golden Rule" Jones, who ran a small oil-equipment manufacturing company in which workers did not punch a time clock but kept track of their own hours, and shared the firm's profits while working an eight-hour day with annual paid vacations. Mowry, The Era of Theodore Roosevelt and the Birth of Modern America, 1900–1912, 1962, p. 62.

221. Pullman

See § 6357, text at notecall 321.

222. Merger of bureaucracies

Weinstein, The Corporate Ideal in the Liberal State, 1900–1918, 1968, p. 216.

223. "Most effective way"

Id. at p. 218.

224. Ideological training ground

"The young men in Belgium, the officers' training corps, the young men being sucked into the councils at Washington and into war organizations everywhere, have among them a definite element * * *. They have absorbed the secret of scientific method as applied to political administration." White, Social Thought in America: The Revolt Against Formalism, 1957 ed., p. 169 (quoting Randolph Bourne).

225. Traditional conservatives

Wiebe, Businessmen and Reform: A Study of the Progressive Movement, 1962, p. 82.

226. Split over efficiency

Haber, Efficiency and Uplift: Scientific Management in the Progressive Era, 1890–1920, 1973, p. 45.

government bureaucracy.[227] Lacking Germanic notions of heroic and romantic conformity, many Americans continued to be too resentful of hierarchy to ever become the "good Germans" that some scientific managers demanded.[228] Nonetheless, living in a bureaucracy accustomed some Americans to having their lives controlled or threatened by persons that they never confronted face-to-face and, resentful or not, they could hardly be expected to be sympathetic to the demands of confrontation by persons accused of crime.[229] A few Progressive critics were able to see how the problems of "the intermediary" in government bureaucracies resembled the Puritan resentment of priests and other intermediaries between them and their God——an impulse that was one of the foundations of the Puritan demands for the right of confrontation.[230]

As we shall see, bureaucratization also tended to foster the "government by expert" strain in Progressive thought that would do much to undermine and subvert the balance of power within the adversary system of which the right of confrontation was a significant part.[231] One of the goals of bureaucratization is "deskilling" of workers; that is, the object is to make people who are incapable of understanding the task capable of performing it nonetheless.[232] If the judge is analogized to "the expert" who understands and the jurors to the unskilled worker who does not, it seems natural to

227. Backlash

Wiebe, Businessmen and Reform: A Study of the Progressive Movement, 1962, p. 201.

228. Romantic conformity

White, Social Thought in America: The Revolt Against Formalism, 1957 ed., p. 150.

229. Never confronted

Moreover, the corporate reliance on hearsay——rising to the level of mysticism in the case of the "C.Y.A." memo——makes it hard for people inured in that culture to see why the law should be so finicky about the use of hearsay.

230. "The intermediary"

"The modern political problem, according to William Kent, was much like the one confronting the early Protestants of how to do away with the intermediaries between themselves and their God." Kent was arguing in favor of more direct democracy: "[p]eople must get nearer the grub pile and nearer to their governmental agencies." Mowry, The Era of Theodore Roosevelt and The Birth of Modern America, 1900–1912, 1962, p. 53 On the Puritan opposition to intermediaries, see vol. 30, p. 284.

231. "Government by expert"

Weinstein, The Corporate Ideal in the Liberal State, 1900–1918, 1968, p. 218.

232. "Deskilling"

Haber, Efficiency and Uplift: Scientific Management in the Progressive Era, 1890–1920, 1973, p. 24.

shift judgments of credibility from jurors who have seen the witnesses face-to-face to judges who know what hearsay is "reliable" and what is not.[233]

Progressive Racism

The Brownsville incident of 1906 exemplifies the continuing impact of racism on the right of confrontation during the Progressive era.[234] A group of African–American soldiers of the 25th Infantry, angered at the bigoted response to their presence in the Texas town, went on a shooting spree in which one civilian was killed.[235] When none of the black soldiers would inform on their colleagues, President Roosevelt ordered them all dishonorably discharged, thus depriving the innocent as well as the guilty—including several Medal of Honor winners—of their pensions.[236] Rather than reacting with universal disapprobation to this affront to confrontation values, Americans split on sectional and partisan lines in their response to the President's action.[237]

Ironically, the Brownsville incident was both a cause and a consequence of an increasingly adversarial relationship among two African–American political ideologies.[238] In 1903 W.E.B. Du Bois had published "The Souls of Black Folk", a book that established him as one of the major opponents of George Washington Carver's gradualist vocationalism.[239] In 1905 Du Bois and other like-minded African–American leaders came together in the "Niagara Movement" to protest the increasing erosion of civil and political liberties of their people.[240] They may have been encouraged by T.R.'s false image as an opponent of racism arising from his invitation to

233. Shift judgments

As we shall see, this has been the tendency of modern confrontation doctrine.

234. Racism and confrontation

For discussion of this in earlier periods, see § 6355, text at notecall 507 and § 6356, text at notecall 274.

235. One civilian killed

Mowry, The Era of Theodore Roosevelt and the Birth of Modern America, 1900–1912, 1962, p. 212.

236. Depriving innocent

Id. at pp. 212–213.

237. Split on sectional lines

Id. at p. 213.

238. Adversarial relationship

O'Neill, The Progressive Years, 1975, p. 79.

239. Du Bois

Ibid.

240. "Niagara Movement"

Ekirch, Progressivism in America, 1974, p. 229.

Booker T. Washington to share lunch at the White House.[241] The Brownsville incident not only destroyed any illusions of Progressive support for the aspirations of African–Americans, it also led to the founding of the National Association for the Advancement of Colored People three years later and the National Urban League two years after that.[242]

Ever since the turn of the century, the already precarious position of African–Americans had suffered a rapid deterioration. The legal deprivation of political and civil rights under the so-called "Jim Crow" laws had not only consolidated racial segregation in the South but had begun to spread to the North.[243] What was left of the old "Black Republican" antislavery wing of the G.O.P. was compromised in their efforts to resist by the party's slide into racialist rhetoric to support its imperial ambitions.[244] The Progressive era also saw the rise and spread of extralegal repression of African–Americans, primarily but not exclusively through lynchings.[245] Not only had the number of lynchings risen but they became almost exclusively racist in motivation.[246] Public acceptance of these atrocities was signaled by the widespread decline in their formerly clandestine nature; some lynchings were advertised in advance and railroads ran special trains to carry men, women, and children to the ghastly spectacle.[247] It would perhaps be an understatement to say that tolerance of lynching exhibited a public ambivalence towards confrontation values.[248] The race riot in Abraham Lincoln's former hometown, Springfield, Illinois, illustrates the point; fueled by a false report that a black man had raped a

241. Invitation to lunch

Mowry, The Era of Theodore Roosevelt and the Birth of Modern America, 1900–1912, 1962, p. 165.

242. N.A.A.C.P. and Urban League

Mowry, The Progressive Era, 1900–20: The Reform Persuasion, 1958, p. 13.

243. "Jim Crow" laws

Id. at pp. 12–13.

244. Racialist rhetoric

O'Neill, The Progressive Years, 1975, p. 78. See also, § 6357, text at notecall 648.

245. Lynchings

Ekirch, Progressivism in America, 1974, p. 230.

246. Racist motivation

O'Neill, The Progressive Years, 1975, p. 78.

247. Special trains

Id. at p. 79.

248. Ambivalence

This was also signaled by the increasing glorification of the Ku Klux Klan in popular culture. Ibid. The masked assassin of the Klan takes the "faceless informer" condemned by confrontation to even higher levels.

white woman, a mob rampaged through the city, burning homes and businesses owned by African–Americans and lynching two.[249]

Racism was so prevalent in the Progressive era that most Americans took it for granted.[250] However, for modern readers it is necessary to distinguish between two kinds of "racism"; in our time the term usually means bigotry directed at people of color. While this species certainly existed at the turn of the century, it was submerged——at least among elites——by what we have called "Anglo–Saxon racism"; that is, the belief that people of English, or in some versions Germanic, antecedents constitute a "race" that is superior to other "races" such as Slavs, Italians, and Jews.[251] Adherents of this broader form of racism often invoked Darwin for scientific support, despite the fact that the theory of evolution runs counter to the notion of separate origins for "races."[252] Jack London was the cultural icon of this form of racism:

> We are a race of doers and fighters, of globe-encirclers and zone conquerors. * * * Will the Indian, the Negro, or the Mongol ever conquer the Teuton? Surely not! * * * All that the other races are not, the Anglo–Saxon, or Teuton if you please, is. All that the other races have not, the Teuton has.[253]

London's remarks show the difficulty of disentangling the two species of racism, but we may be confident that Italians, Slavs, and Jews were quite capable of rejecting the broader theory while practicing the lesser.

Racism prevailed in all sectors of society. Business groups denounced immigrants from Southern and Eastern Europe as not "from as desirable sources as in earlier times", comparing them to the "Hun, Goth, and Vandal", and despairing of democracy "in a city with a large proportion of foreign element——Bohemians, Pollacks, etc."[254] For example, the Scranton Board of Trade in 1904

---

249. Springfield riots

Ekirch, Progressivism in America, 1974, p. 230.

250. Racism prevalent

O'Neill, The Progressive Years, 1975, p. 77.

251. "Anglo–Saxon racism"

Ekirch, Progressivism in America, 1974, p. 179 See also, § 6357, text at note-call 648.

252. Invoked Darwin

Russett, Darwin in America: The Intellectual Response, 1865–1912, 1976, pp. 91–92.

253. "The Teuton has"

Id. at p. 179.

254. "Bohemians, Pollacks"

Wiebe, Businessmen and Reform: A Study of the Progressive Movement, 1962, p. 182.

described the immigrants of that year as

> the most ignorant and vicious of the European population, includ-
> ing necessarily a vast number of the criminal class: people who
> come here, not to become good citizens, but to prey upon our
> people and our industries; a class utterly without character and
> incapable of understanding or appreciating our institutions, and
> therefore a menace to our commonwealth.[255]

To corporate leaders, Anglo–Saxon racism offered an explanation
for the attraction of unions; for example, discussing the Anthracite
Coal Strike, one corporate spokesman said:

> Tens of thousands of the Anthracite miners are Poles, Hungari-
> ans, Slavs, and other foreigners who can not spell a word in
> English. * * * Many of these men are imbued with anarchistic
> and socialistic sentiments before they come to America, and they
> make excellent material for agitators to work upon.[256]

In the garment trade, it was claimed, even good Teutons "laid
meekly down before the Jewish labor power."[257]

While they had fewer occasions to exhibit it, businessmen had
similar attitudes toward African–Americans.[258] One railroad executive claimed that "the attitude of the South toward the Negro is not
one of race prejudice but of race knowledge."[259] Another business
spokesman explained:

> notoriously the Negro workman of the South is spoiled by prosper-
> ity. Advancing his wages has generally the tendency to make him
> more of an idler, since at higher wages his wants are supplied by
> fewer days of labor.[260]

A business newspaper editorialized that the "North gave the black
the ballot * * * It was the one wrong action of the war."[261]

One should not infer that racism was limited to corporate
troglodytes. We have previously seen how ambitious politicians
used Anglo–Saxon racism to justify American imperialism.[262] Theo-

---

255. "Menace to commonwealth"
Ibid.

256. "Material for agitators"
Id. at p. 191.

257. "Jewish labor power"
Ibid.

258. Similar attitudes
Id. at p. 182.

259. "Race knowledge"
Ibid.

260. "Fewer days of labor"
Ibid.

261. "One wrong action"
Ibid.

262. Justify imperialism
See, e.g., Ekirch, Progressivism in America, 1974, pp. 188–189. See also,
§ 6357, text at notecall 664.

dore Roosevelt used it to extol militarism; he told the Naval War College in 1897 that "[a]ll the great masterful races have been fighting races * * *."[263] (One assumes that this "master race" ideology played some part in the cashiering of black soldiers after the Brownsville incident.) Other politicians used racism to attack government social programs.[264] A South Dakota worthy wrote that a proposal to allow post offices to provide savings accounts for those of modest means was "gotten up for the benefit of the Poll [sic], Bohemenian [sic] and Italian, foreigners who are afraid of American institutions. [Americans] will not patronize it."[265] Even the "better sort" harbored racist notions; both Harvard and the American Bar Association wanted to bar African–Americans from their ranks.[266] As we have seen, the prominent sociologist Edward A. Ross embraced Anglo–Saxon racism.[267]

For confrontation purposes, the racism of Progressives matters most. Contrary to the impression of some that the Progressives were "liberals" on questions of race. historians have noted that the Progressives were more virulently racist than either conservatives or radicals.[268] For example, the Progressive journalist William Allen White in a book published in 1910 anticipated "Mein Kampf" by a couple of decades in praising American's "clean Aryan blood."[269] He comforted those who feared the immigrant horde with the reminder that "[w]e are separated by two oceans from the inferior races and by an instinctive race revulsion to cross breeding that marks the American wherever he is found."[270] This "instinctive revulsion", which apparently had not permeated Monticello, appeared in Southern Progressivism with its emphasis on advancing the race and class interests of the Southern elite.[271] Woodrow Wilson, a

263. "Fighting races"

Id. at p. 200.

264. Attack social programs

Wiebe, Businessmen and Reform: A Study of the Progressive Movement, 1962, pp. 97, 182.

265. "Will not patronize"

Id. at p. 97.

266. A.B.A. and Harvard

Hixon, Moorfield Storey and The Abolitionist Tradition, 1972, pp. 118, 121.

267. Ross embraced

See Ross, Social Control, 1969 ed., pp. xxv, 3.

268. More racist

Mowry, The Era of Theodore Roosevelt and the Birth of Modern America, 1900–1912, 1962, p. 93.

269. "Aryan blood"

Ibid.

270. "Instinctive revulsion"

Ibid.

271. Race and class interests

Ekirch, Progressivism in America, 1974, p. 112.

Southerner by birth who opposed civil rights for African–Americans, announced that he would "never appoint any colored man in the South because that would be a social blunder of the worst kind."[272] Moreover, the Wilson administration introduced segregation into previously integrated public services, firing black employees in the process.[273] But racist attitudes were not limited to Southern or Democratic Progressives; only a few ex-Populists protested Wilson's segregationist policies.[274] While some antislavery holdovers emulated Teddy Roosevelt in encouraging Booker T. Washington's accommodationist approach, this did not prevent the Bull Moose party from seating "lily white" Southern delegations at its 1912 Convention.[275]

As one historian wrote, by the time of the Progressives

> the pattern of racist practices and ideas seemed fully developed: the Orientals were to be totally excluded; the Negroes were to live in a segregated enclave; the Indians were to be confined to reservations as permanent wards of the nation; and all whites were expected to assimilate as rapidly as possible to a common standard.[276]

Racism infected the criminal-justice system; for example, after the assassination of ex–Governor Stuenenberg in Idaho, law enforcement went chasing after swarthy aliens as the prime suspects though those ultimately charged with the crime turned out to be all persons with fine Anglo–Saxon (or Anglicized) names.[277] The association of the accused with the dreaded "Other" did not bode well for application of the right of confrontation.[278]

Nationalism, Naturalism, and News

In the early years of Progressivism, most reform movements were state or local; only a comparative handful of persons were

272. "Social blunder"

Id. at p. 232.

273. Introduced segregation

Id. at p. 232.

274. Few protested

Link, Woodrow Wilson and The Progressive Era, 1910–1917, p. 65.

275. "Lily white" delegations

Mowry, The Progressive Era, 1900–1920: The Reform Persuasion, 1958, pp. 12–13.

276. "Common standard"

Ekirch, Progressivism in America, 1974, p. 84 (quoting Oscar Handlin).

277. Swarthy aliens

Lukas, Big Trouble, 1997, p. 59 Ironically, though the I.W.W. was castigated as an alien organization, its most prominent members all bore names suggestive of antecedants in the British Isles; e.g., "Haywood", "Jones", "Hill."

278. Association with "Other"

See also, text at notecall 255 (associating recent immigrants with criminality).

concerned with reform at the national level.[279] The early nationalizers were predominantly federal bureaucrats eager to expand their power and special interests seeking to escape diverse and more drastic state regulation.[280] For example, when states began to tighten regulation of insurance companies following the New York scandals of 1905, many insurance executives began to see some advantages in federal regulation of their industry.[281]

Arguably the earliest of the nationalizing reforms grew out of the misleadingly named "conservation movement."[282] Interest in the degradation of the natural environment predated the Progressive era; for example, Yellowstone National Park was created as early as 1872.[283] However, conservation efforts took on greater importance under Presidents Roosevelt and Taft, both of whom felt it was time to reverse the rapidly increasing privatization of the national domain.[284] Conservation, however, may have been a special case because administration of the national domain was a traditional federal function and the ultimate values of the conservation movement were congruent with the values of the new generation of corporate executives, however harmful they may have been to the financial interests of the extractive industries such as mining and lumbering that sought to further pillage the national domain.[285]

Edward Ross, whose influence we have previously discussed, was one of a triumvirate of social thinkers who advocated a "na-

---

279. Comparative handful

Wiebe, Businessmen and Reform: A Study of the Progressive Movement, 1962, p. 42.

280. Escape state regulation

Ibid.

281. Insurance executives

Id. at p. 48.

282. "Conservation"

Ekirch, Progressivism in America, 1974, p. 145. As those familiar with the struggle over federal parks today are aware, the "conservation" movement was not concerned primarily with preservation of the natural environment but with regulating the conflict-ing demands for its exploitation. Anyone who has visited Yosemite recently will have been made aware that a chain saw is not the only way to destroy a national forest.

283. Yellowstone

Mowry, The Progressive Era, 1900–20: The Reform Persuasion, 1958, p. 9.

284. Reverse privatization

Id. at p. 10. "Privatization" is of course, an anachronism but it accurately captures what was taking place even though the word was not then in use.

285. Value congruent

Ekirch, Progressivism in America, 1974, p. 145.

tionalization" of the reform impulse.[286] Ross argued that

> in order to protect ourselves against the lawlessness, the insolence, and the rapacity of overgrown private interests, we shall have to develop the state, especially on its administrative side.[287]

The growth of the regulatory state on the German model would ultimately lead, first, to an increased use of hearsay, then to a reaction in favor of confrontation values.

However, it was not Ross or Croly or other deep thinkers that triggered the turn of Progressivism toward national regulation. When the novelist Upton Sinclair delivered the manuscript for his naturalistic novel about the packing industry to the publisher who had contracted for it, the publisher found it too dangerous to publish.[288] However, after lawyers had investigated Sinclair's factual claims and found them supportable, another house published "The Jungle" in 1906.[289] Public revulsion at the novel's description of the unsanitary and unsafe working conditions in the Chicago packing houses led almost immediately to the Pure Food and Drug Act and the Packers and Stockyards Act, installing a system of federal inspection that grew and flourished down to the Reagan era.[290]

"The Jungle" not only epitomized the Progressive concern with "the facts" that led Wigmore and others to want to reform the hearsay rule, it also brought a renewed appreciation of the advantages of preemptive nationalization to many business leaders.[291] As one advocate of a system of federal incorporation of big business argued: "The only thing that works against our progress is the multiplicity of (state) laws. I say that the day has gone by when this country is simply a confederacy of States."[292] It would take time

286. Triumvirate

Ross, Social Control, 1969 ed., p. xl. The other members were Herbert Croly, whose influence will be discussed below, and Simon Nelson Patten, an exponent of the so-called "new economics."

287. "Develop the state"

Id. at p. 88.

288. Too dangerous

Chamberlain, Farewell to Reform, 1965 ed., p. 185.

289. "The Jungle"

Id. at p. 179.

290. Federal inspection

Mowry, The Progressive Era, 1900–20: The Reform Persuasion, 1958, p. 9.

291. Renewed appreciation

Wiebe, Businessmen and Reform: A Study of the Progressive Movement, 1962, p. 50.

292. "Simply a confederacy"

Ibid.

before this assumption captured the minds of most business leaders but it would eventually have a significant impact on confrontation jurisprudence by bringing business leaders into the circle of potential defendants in federal criminal prosecutions.[293]

The year 1906 presented the public with two celebrated trials, each of some significance for the history of confrontation. In the first of these, William "Big Bill" Haywood, one of the best-known leaders of the Industrial Workers of the World, and several of his colleagues in the Western Federation of Miners were acquitted of the murder of ex-Governor Stuenenberg of Idaho.[294] The prosecution exemplified the ways in which the adversary system could be compromised in political cases involving despised persons.[295] The prosecution's only significant witness was the assassin himself, an informant of dubious repute who saved his own life by claiming, at the behest of the same detective who had engineered the Molly Maguire prosecutions, that the killing had been carried out on behalf of union leaders angered by the victim's antiunion acts.[296] The prosecution had a spy in the defense camp who reported on confidential attorney-client communications.[297] Moreover, much of the prosecution was financed by the mining companies who stood to benefit from the discrediting of the union.

But perhaps the most significant incident in the trial was the remark of President Roosevelt while the case was pending that the defendants were a bunch of "undesirable citizens."[298] This seems to be one of the first cases in which the power of the press to undermine the "blank pad rule" and the presumption of innocence was demonstrated.[299] However, then as now, this was not seen as

293. Potential defendants

It is easy to endorse weakening the rights of the accused when one never expects to be accused; the use of federal criminal sanctions against "respectable" citizens reduces the sense that rights are only for the Other.

294. Steunenberg murder

See generally, Lukas, Big Trouble, 1997.

295. Political cases

The case also gives some insight into the Supreme Court's views on constitutional guarantees. See Pettibone v. Nichols, 1906, 27 S.Ct. 111, 203 U.S. 192, 51 L.Ed. 148.

296. Molly Maguire prosecution

See § 6356, text at notecall 597.

297. Prosecution spy

Lukas, Big Trouble, 1997, p. 455.

298. "Undesirable citizens"

Id. at p. 397.

299. Power of press

However, it differs from the usual case of what came to be called "trial by newspaper" in that the President did not claim to be speaking from any personal knowledge of the evidence against the accused.

implicating the right of confrontation.[300] The defense response was a statement attributed to Haywood:

> The President says I am an undesirable citizen, the inference being that as such I should be put out of the way. His influence is all powerful and his statement coming as it does on the eve of my trial for life will work me an irreparable injury and do more to prevent a fair trial than everything that has been said and done against me.[301]

Speaking out of his own mouth rather than through his lawyers', Haywood came much closer to the confrontation values implicated in the incident:

> It was while my two comrades and myself were put in cells, our hands shackled behind us, that this idol of yours in the White House wrote a letter denouncing us as "undesirable citizens." That was not the work of a great man. It was the work of a coward.[302]

Fifty years later another American President would echo Haywood in a context explicitly involving the right of confrontation; i.e., the use of anonymous accusers in the loyalty hysteria of the McCarthy era.[303]

The other "trial of the century" arising in 1906 was the prosecution of the wealthy playboy, Harry K. Thaw, for the murder of the prominent architect, Stanford White, arising out of an affair with a former chorus girl and wife of the accused, Evelyn Nesbitt Thaw.[304] The Thaw case revealed a second way in which press coverage of trial could undermine confrontation values; that is, by treating the criminal trial as a form of "entertainment", thereby trivializing the importance of evidence and confrontation.[305] More-

---

300. Not seen

See analysis of the Hearsay Rule in subsequent volumes of this Treatise.

301. "Prevent a fair trial"

Lukas, Big Trouble, 1997, p. 461.

302. "Work of a coward"

Ibid.

303. McCarthy era

See below, § 6360, text at notecall 672.

304. "Trial of the century"

Lukas, Big Trouble, 1997, p. 659.

305. "Trivializing"

One newspaper hired another wealthy playboy who had been convicted of murder but had his conviction overturned on appeal to give a "defendant's-eye" view of the proceedings. This worthy actually invoked a false analogy between formal proof and confrontation when he wrote: "No poor wretch whose life depended upon the issue of hand-to-hand encounter between Knights of old ever looked upon the tilting ground with greater dread than does the defendant." Ibid.

over, since that Thaw case and its successors, down to the trial of O.J. Simpson, involved wealthy defendants who were able to use every advantage provided by the law, including the Sixth Amendment, press coverage of these celebrity trials tends to give the public a distorted perception of the conduct of ordinary criminal trials.[306] Hence, the celebrity trial plays some part in convincing the public that the adversary system favors the guilty and frustrates punishment for crime.

Another form of entertainment that did much to undermine confrontation was the "detective story" or "crime novel."[307] The hero operates at the edges of, when not completely outside, the law—often justifying his acts by the inadequacies of officials and formal legal procedures; as one writer put it, the detective is "the silent, secret and effective Avenger of the outraged majesty of the law when everything else fails."[308] The operative word here is "secret"; the detective who operates outside the law must avoid the openness and public scrutiny that are the hallmarks of the right of confrontation. An early student of detective novels noted that the detective's "business is to deceive his victim, to gain his confidence, to learn his secret and plans and then to betray him. A sleuth's life is a lie. He is both Judas and Ananaias."[309] One of the models for the Nineteenth Century detective was Alan Pinkerton and his protege James McParland, who was involved in both the Molly Maguire prosecutions and the Steunenberg murder case.[310] In the former role, McParland made an appearance in one of the few Sherlock Holmes stories set in the United States, "The Valley of Fear."[311] The contrast between Conan Doyle's values and those of the right of confrontation can be glimpsed in the description of McParland in a defense lawyer's argument in one of the Molly Maguire trials:

306. Distorted perception

The first Thaw jury hung; the second found him not guilty by reason of insanity. His family engineered his escape from a mental hospital and flight to Canada. When he was finally returned to the U.S., not only was he not prosecuted for escape but was found to be sane and released. Encyclopedia of American Facts and Dates, 9th ed. 1993, p. 403.

307. Detective story

Lukas, Big Trouble, 1997, p. 86.

308. "Everything else fails"

Id. at p. 86.

309. "Judas and Ananais"

Id. at p. 85.

310. Models

Id. at p. 86.

311. "Valley of Fear"

Id. at p. 175.

You all dislike a spy. This man who will take you to his bosom, gain your confidence and stealthily work up your affection, your favor or your esteem, and then like a viper turn upon you and betray you, ought to be condemned by every honorable and right-thinking person.[312]

The influence of the detective novel took a more precarious turn when journalists began to analogize their work to that of the detective.[313] Little wonder then, that by the time of the O.J. Simpson trial, even persons with legal training seemed unable to distinguish between evidence introduced in open court and hearsay peddled in the press.[314]

Even more serious literary work could play a part in subverting confrontation values. For example, naturalistic crime novels that traced the causes of crime to social conditions—poverty, crowding, a culture of greed, and the like—while sometimes more sympathetic to the criminal than the detective story also tended to dilute the individualism that underlies confrontation.[315] Or consider "muckrakers", whose goal was education rather than entertainment.[316] When they turned to crime and juvenile delinquency, their realistic portrayal of the criminal-justice system also turned up facts that could be used to justify curtailment of the right of confrontation; e.g., that the murder rate in the U.S. during the early years of the century had increased at six times the rate of population increase and that murder was 30 times more frequent here than in the nations of northern Europe.[317]

Pound, Social Engineering, and Confrontation

On August 29, 1906, in the new Capitol Building in St. Paul, Minnesota, the membership of the American Bar Association gathered in the House Chamber to hear a speech by Roscoe Pound, a rising young academic from Nebraska.[318] According to Wigmore, the

312. "Like a viper"

Id. at p. 187.

313. Journalists analogize

Id. at p. 654.

314. Unable to distinguish

Readers may recall the number of pundits, including at least one evidence professor, who expressed opinions of the defendant's guilt and outrage at the jury's verdict without themselves ever having heard any of the evidence in the case.

315. Naturalistic crime novels

Chamberlain, Farewell to Reform, 1965 ed., p. 89.

316. "Muckrakers"

Id. at p. 129.

317. Murder rate

Id. at pp. 135–136.

318. Pound speech

Proceedings Honoring Roscoe Pound, 1964, 35 F.R.D. 261.

A.B.A. "was a complacent, self satisfied, genial fellowship of individual lawyers——unalive to the shortcomings of our justice, unthinking of the urgent demands of the impending future, * * * unaware of their collective duty and destiny."[319] The "complacent torpidity" of the elite lawyers was about to be disturbed by a speech Wigmore called "the spark that kindled the white flame of progress."[320] Entitled "The Causes of Popular Dissatisfaction with the Administration of Justice," the Pound speech embodies the ideology that has dominated American procedural thinking ever since—— what we have called "the Progressive Procedural Paradigm."[321]

Pound began with a catalog of ancient expressions of discontent with English law, omitting any revolutionary sentiments on this score——perhaps to avoid gratuitous offense to his conservative audience.[322] Then, in a telling remark, Pound announced that "[i]t will be assumed * * * that there is more than the normal amount of dissatisfaction with the present-day administration of justice in America."[323] The only justification for such an assumption was that

> the tendency to give the fullest scope of the common law doctrine of supremacy of law and to tie down the administration by common law liabilities and judicial review, was, until recently, very marked. Today the tendency is no less marked. Courts are distrusted, and executive boards and commissions with summary and plenary powers, freed, as far as constitutions will permit, from judicial review have become the fashion.[324]

Pound, then, promised his audience an explanation of why "courts are distrusted" in order that they could see how courts needed to be reformed to restore and enhance the common law powers of the judiciary.[325] However, despite his claims to be offering a scientific analysis, he offers no evidence to support his claims regarding the causes for public dissatisfaction——indeed, he ignores the com-

319. "Duty and destiny"

Id. at p. 248.

320. "Flame of Progress"

Id. at p. 259.

321. "Progressive Paradigm"

Vol. 21, § 5001, p. 27; id., § 5025, p. 146.

322. Ancient discontent

Pound, The Causes of Popular Dissatisfaction With the Administration of Justice, 1964, 35 F.R.D. 273. The

speech may also be found in 1906, 29 A.B.A.Rep. 395.

323. "More than normal"

Id. at p. 274.

324. "Become the fashion"

Ibid.

325. Enhance powers

Wigdor, Roscoe Pound, 1974, p. 210.

plaints of the Populists and other critics of the judiciary.[326] In short, Pound would have been more honest, though perhaps less convincing, had he entitled his speech "What I Don't Like About Our Procedural Rules."

Pound then announced that he would not be discussing criminal procedure, explaining that

> While the criminal law attracts more notice, and punishment seems to have greater interest for the lay mind that the civil remedies of prevention and compensation, the true interest of the modern community is in the civil administration of justice. Revenge and its modern outgrowth, punishment, belong to the past of legal history.[327]

Thus began the contempt for criminal procedure that characterizes American procedural scholarship down to the present day.[328] But despite Pound's disclaimer, the rest of his speech embraces values and attitudes whose impact cannot be limited to the civil side and which do much to illuminate contemporary attitudes toward confrontation.

Pound then sketched the organization of his talk, dividing it among those complaints endemic in any legal system, those peculiar to the Anglo–American common law, those peculiar to the American branch of the dyad, and those that can be attributed to American culture.[329] Pound's discussion is not as tightly compartmentalized as this but for the convenience of the reader we shall follow his organization. We pause first to note that the printed version of the speech contains footnote references to the sociologists Herbert Spencer and Edward A. Ross, but is otherwise a poor specimen of what Pound called "sociological jurisprudence."[330] Indeed, his speech looks more like the formal mode of analysis that he wished to condemn.[331]

326. Complaints of the Populists

See § 6357, text at notecall 218. Pound hated the Populists. Sayre, The Life of Roscoe Pound, 1948, p. 101.

327. "Belong to past"

Pound, The Causes of Popular Dissatisfaction With The Administration of Justice, 1964, 35 F.R.D. 273, 274.

328. Contempt for criminal

In many schools, the course in "criminal procedure" is in fact a study of constitutional law. The typical law-school graduate cannot tell the difference between an indictment and an information.

329. American culture

Id. at p. 275.

330. Footnote references

Id. at p. 277 n. 11; id. at p. 279 n. 13. On the significance of Ross, see § 6357, text at notecall 787.

331. Wished to condemn

White, Social Thought in America: The Revolt Against Formalism, 1957, ed. p. 108.

Under the first heading—causes of dissatisfaction with any legal system—Pound mentions only two that are of interest to us.[332] First, Pound states, though not in these terms, "the equal protection paradox"; that is, the conflicting desires of litigants to be recognized as unique human beings who are significantly different from others to whom the rule in question applies and—sometimes simultaneously—to be treated the same as the other unique persons from whom they differ.[333] Since Pound underestimates the degree to which the tension of these conflicting desires shapes procedure and denies that procedure has any necessary symbolic significance, we can ignore his otherwise sensible though simplistic remarks on this question.[334]

Another of Pound's causes endemic to any legal system reveals much of the Progressive attitude toward procedure; it is "the popular assumption that the administration of justice is an easy task to which anyone is competent."[335] Here Pound abandons his own expertise in biology and sociology for an analogy that, so far as we are aware, he had no special competence but which he felt would be more appealing to his audience.[336]

> Laws may be compared to the formulas of engineers. They sum up the experience of many courts with many cases and enable the magistrate to apply that experience subconsciously. So the formula enables the engineer to make use of the accumulated experience of past builders even though he could not work out a step in its evolution by himself. A layman is no more competent to construct or to apply the one formula than the other. Each requires special knowledge and special preparation.[337]

332. Two of interest

The others are: "(2) the inevitable difference in the rate of progress between the law and public opinion; * * *; (4) popular impatience of restraint." Pound, The Causes of Popular Dissatisfaction With The Administration of Justice, 1964, 35 F.R.D. 273, 275.

333. "Paradox"

Id. at pp. 275–276.

334. Shapes procedure

For example, one of the functions of the rule of relevance is to prevent a party from escaping from the relevant rule of substantive law by introducing evidence that shows some legally irrelevant difference between the defendant and the "others" to whom the rule is to apply; for example, the defendant who wants to escape criminal liability for trespass on government property by showing that the purpose of the trespass was to make a moral statement against nuclear war.

335. "Anyone competent"

Id. at p. 278.

336. More appealing

The popularity of engineering metaphors in the Progressive Era is discussed below, text at notecall 390.

337. "Special knowledge"

Ibid.

Pound departs from his announced scheme to spell out for the audience the political implications of this in the United States:

> the notion that anyone is competent to adjudicate the intricate controversies of modern community contributes to the unsatisfactory administration of justice in many parts of the United States. The older states have originally outgrown it. But it is felt in the extravagant powers of juries, lay judges of probate and legislative or judicial lawmaking against stare decisis, in most of the commonwealths of the South and the West. The public seldom realizes how much it is interested in maintaining the highest scientific standard in the administration of justice.[338]

Since the rubes in the boondocks are unlikely to criticize courts for the excessive use of persons as stupid as themselves on juries, it is clear that Pound's equation of engineering and elitism was designed to appeal to his audience rather than to accurately describe public perceptions of the courts.[339] Pound's contempt for juries not only denigrates the mode of trial the Founders guaranteed in the Sixth Amendment, it also casts doubt on their ability to gain any insights from confrontations with the witnesses against the accused.[340]

Two of the causes of dissatisfaction Pound finds peculiar to the Anglo–American legal systems are more directly relevant to confrontation.[341] The first of these is "the individualist spirit of our common law, which agrees ill with a collectivist age."[342] Confrontation clearly owes more to individualism than to statism.[343] Pound says as much.

338. "Scientific standard"

Ibid.

339. Appeal to audience

On the appeal of elitism to Progressives, see § 6357, text at notecall 764.

340. Doubts on ability

On the Progressive denigration of demeanor inferences, see vol. 30, § 6327.

341. Peculiar to Anglo–American

The others are: "(3) political jealousy, due to the strain put upon our legal system by the doctrine of the supremacy of law; (4) the lack of general ideas or legal philosophy, so characteristic of Anglo–American law, which gives us petty tinkering where comprehensive reform is needed, and (5) defects of form due to the circumstance that the bulk of our legal system is still case law." Pound, The Causes of Popular Dissatisfaction With the Administration of Justice, 1964, 35 F.R.D. 273, 279.

342. "Collectivist age"

Ibid.

343. Statism

A corporation is a "collectivist" entity but the context makes it clear that Pound is thinking of statism, not private collectives.

The chief concern of the common law is to secure and protect individual rights. * * * Such, it goes without saying, is not the popular view today. Today we look to society for protections against individuals, natural or artificial, and we resent doctrines that protect these individuals against society for fear society will oppress us.[344]

Pound regrets that American constitutions prevent us from emulating the English abandonment of individual rights.[345] Once again Pound, who imbibed his mother's hatred of Nebraska, blames this on the West, quoting Owen Wister:

> The unthinking sons of the sage brush ill tolerate anything that stands for discipline, good order and obedience; and the man who lets another command him they despise. I can think of no threat more evil for our democracy, for it is a fine thing diseased and perverted, namely, the spirit of independence gone drunk.[346]

The fear of Populism and the threat of the election of 1896 were apparently still potent in 1906.[347]

More to the point is Pound's second peculiarly Angle–American reasons for dissatisfaction with procedure: "the common law doctrine of contentious procedure, which turns litigation into a game."[348] Since confrontation is a key feature of the adversary system embodied in the Sixth Amendment, Pound's development of this point must be quoted at length:

> The sporting theory of justice, the "instinct of giving the game fair play" as Professor Wigmore has put it, is so rooted in the profession in America that most of us take it for a fundamental legal tenet. But it is probably only a survival of the days when a lawsuit was a fight between two clans in which change of venue had been taken into the forum. So far from being a fundamental fact of jurisprudence, it is peculiar to Anglo–American law; and it has been strongly curbed in modern English practice. [But] in America we take it as a matter of course that a judge should be a mere umpire, to pass upon objections and hold counsel to the rules of the game, and that parties should fight out their game in their own way without judicial interference. * * * The idea that procedure must of necessity be wholly contentious disfigures our judicial administration at every point. It leads the most conscientious

344. "Will oppress us"

Id. at pp. 280–281.

345. Emulating English

Id. at p. 281.

346. "Gone drunk"

Id. at p. 279.

347. Still potent

See § 6357, text at notecall 528.

348. "Litigation a game"

Pound, The Causes of Popular Dissatisfaction With the Administration of Justice, 1964, 35 F.R.D. 273, 279.

judge to feel that he is merely to decide the contest, as counsel present it, according to the rules of the game, not to search independently for truth and justice. It leads counsel to forget that they are officers of the court and to deal with the rules of law and procedure exactly as the professional football coach with the rules of the sport. * * * It turns witnesses, and especially expert witnesses, into partisans pure and simple. It leads to sensational cross-examinations "to affect credit" which have made the witness stand "the slaughter house of reputations." It prevents the trial court from restraining the bullying of witnesses and creates a general dislike, if not fear, of the witness function which impairs the administration of justice.[349]

If this sounds familiar, even contemporary to the reader, she will have grasped the degree to which Pound's statism and desire for "managerial judges" remain alive in our procedural ideology a century later.[350] Like modern critics, Pound offers no evidence to support his claims of abuse.[351] Moreover, his contempt for the athletic analogy is so profound and unthinking that its roots must be psychological, not scientific.[352]

Pound goes on to blame the adversary system for the "modern American race to beat the law."[353] According to him, "[i]f the law is a mere game, neither the players who take part in it nor the public who witness it can be expected to yield to its spirit when their interests are served by evading it."[354] One wonders just what sort

349. "Fear of witness function"

Id. at pp. 281–282.

350. Remains alive

See vol. 21, § 5025.

351. No evidence

Perhaps he was relying on and universalizing his own experience. Pound said that his father's office, in which he had worked, "was a nest of jury fixing." Sayre, The Life of Roscoe Pound, 1948, p. 88.

352. Psychological

Pound was too small and his eyes were too weak to allow him to participate in team sports. Hence, he became a cheerleader and what a later generation of athletes would refer to as a "jock sniffer"; that is, he liked to hang around athletes and boast of his

acquaintance with them. Id. at p. 52. In the experience of the junior author, such people pretend to a knowledge of sports that they lack and often overlook features of sports that are immediately obvious to those who have participated even casually. Moreover, admiration of the athletically talented can sometimes coexist with a feeling of superiority bordering on contempt because the athlete is not as skilled in kinds of intellectual achievement that the person supposes he or she has.

353. "Beat the law"

Pound, The Causes of Popular Dissatisfaction With The Administration of Justice, 1964, 35 F.R.D. 273, 282.

354. "Evading it"

Ibid.

of sport Pound has in mind and whether he thinks the concept of "sportsmanship" has no meaning to the players.[355] Even at the end of the century when tax lawyer's mentality has infected many sports, those who play most sports have some greater sense that they should abide by the rules than Pound gives them credit for.[356] But for Pound,

> [w]e need not wonder that one part of the community strain their oaths in the jury box and find verdicts against unpopular litigants, while another part retain lawyers by the year to advise how to evade what to them are unintelligent and unreasonable restrictions upon necessary modes of doing business.[357]

Again Pound offers no evidence to support his supposition.[358] One who did not have Pound's bias in favor of capitalists and against the adversary system might suppose that businessmen were more likely to justify their conduct in terms of a laissez-faire ideology

355. "Sportsmanship"

For example, in any sport there are acts that are either not subject to the rules or are difficult of defection yet are regarded as illegitimate by the participants. For example, in basketball "low-bridging"——moving one's body into such as position that an elevated opponent has no secure spot to land——was, in the junior author's youth not subject to a specific rule yet a person who engaged in it could expect to suffer all the sanctions available to the victim and his teammates and even condemnation by one's own teammates.

Perhaps Pound was thinking of modern economic analysis in which apparently altruistic behavior is analyzed as "self-interested." Since "low bridging" can result in injury, sometimes disabling injury, all of the players have some personal interest in preventing its occurrence. If this was what Pound had in mind, it does not defeat but it certainly weakens his point.

356. Greater sense

This is based on the junior author's unpublished study of pick-up basketball games, "The Common Law of Pauley

Pavilion." Since basketball is a game in which officials play an important role, those who play without officials have to devise rules to deal with disputes about the rule violations in the absence of officials. These rules are quite ingenious and rigorously enforced, by ostracism of the violator if necessary.

357. "Necessary modes"

Ibid. Note that despite its apparent even-handedness, this passage provides an excuse for businessmen but not for jurors.

358. Offers no evidence

Again Pound may be universalizing his own experience. He once criticized a memorial to a deceased lawyer on the ground that "we all know that as counsel to a great railroad corporation he planned, advised, and was cognizant of all manner of corruption and trickery." Sayre, The Life of Roscoe Pound, 1948, p. 88.

than by reference to the adversary system or sporting contests.[359] Moreover, a truly sociological explanation might ask whether the resemblances among laissez faire, confrontation, and football does not reflect some underlying cause common to them all rather than mutual emulation among them.[360]

When Pound turns to the causes of dissatisfaction that are uniquely American, he once again betrays the unscientific nature of his analysis.[361] In support of his claim that "waste and delay caused by archaic judicial organization and obsolete procedure" is the root of the problem, Pound compares the number of judges and the cases they dispose of in England and Wales with similar numbers for the state of Nebraska.[362] This ploy, which has remained a staple of Progressive propaganda down to the end of the century, is a fine example of what teachers of comparative law call "nit-wit comparativism"; that is, it assumes that societies and their legal cultures are sufficiently identical to make such comparisons meaningful when in fact it is the reasons for the differences that are most meaningful.[363] If someone were to compare American courts favorably to those of, say, Mexico, Pound would quickly point out the need to show that the two judicial systems are indeed comparable but his Anglophilia blinds him to the need to do the same with his own exercise in comparativism.

Pound's analysis of American legal culture ought to have alerted him to the problems of comparison but it did not. For our

---

359.　Justify by laissez faire

The very fact that Pound uses the analogy to condemn conduct would seem to make it unlikely that others would resort to the analogy to justify; it is difficult to imagine a lawyer saying, even to herself, "well, if Dennis Rodman can get away with it, so can I."

360.　Common to them

In other words, the reason that the adversary system resembles the market is that both rest upon Protestant individualism. See, e.g., vol. 30, § 6343, p. 287.

361.　Uniquely American

Pound, The Causes of Popular Dissatisfaction With The Administration of Justice, 1964, 35 F.R.D. 273, 284.

362.　Numbers for Nebraska

Id. at pp. 284–285.

363.　"Nit-wit comparativism"

To take a simple illustration, Pound fails to mention that one reason English justice seems more efficient is that many litigants were priced out of the market by the then-requirement that a litigant hire three people to gain access to the High Court—a solicitor, a barrister, and a junior. If one only has to hire a single lawyer, one is not only more likely to sue but also more willing to see the lawyer spend more time in court.

purposes, only two of the six items require mention.[364] The first of these is "the putting of our courts into politics."[365] We have previously seen similar complaints by the Federalists to the Jacksonian efforts to make courts more democratic.[366] Pound's reiteration of the point serves only as another instance of the elitism rampant in the Progressive era; we have touched on the significance of this for confrontation elsewhere.[367] The other point worth noting is "public ignorance of the real workings of the courts due to ignorant and sensational reports in the press."[368] The "average press reports distract attention from the real proceeding to petty tilts of counsel, encounters with witnesses and sensational by-incidents."[369] Thus, the press "completes the impression that the administration of justice is but a game."[370] If "encounters with witnesses" is not what the trial is really about, then confrontation is of little value.

Pound ended his speech on a hopeful note, praising the "law schools that are rivaling the achievements of Bologna and of Bourges to promote scientific study of the law."[371] Hence,

> with the passing of the doctrine that politics, too, is a mere game to be played for its own sake, we may look forward confidently to deliverance from the sporting theory of justice; we may look forward to a near future when our courts will be swift and certain agents of justice, whose decisions will be acquiesced in and respected by all.[372]

As we shall see, Pound's skills as a prophet are rivaled only by his sophistication as a proceduralist.

364. Six items

The others are: "(1) Popular lack of interest in justice, which makes jury service a bore and the vindication of right and law secondary to the trouble and expense involved; (2) the strain put upon law in that it has to day to do the work of morals also; (3) the effect of transition to a period of legislation; * * *; (5) the making the legal profession into a trade, which has superseded the relation of attorney and client by that of employer and employee; * * *." Id. at p. 289.

365. "Courts into politics"

Ibid.

366. More democratic

See § 6355, above, text at notecall 472.

367. Elitism elsewhere

See § 6357, text at notecall 738.

368. "Sensational reports"

Pound, The Causes of Popular Dissatisfaction With the Administration of Justice, 1964, 35 F.R.D. 273, 289.

369. "Distracts attention"

Id. at p. 290.

370. "But a game"

Ibid.

371. "Scientific study"

Id. at p. 291.

372. "Respected by all"

Ibid.

Before we turn to the response to Pound's speech, a word about the politics of his ideology. Pound repeatedly denied that the ideology of lawyers or their own self-interest led them to favor certain procedural rules.[373] His speech is similarly devoid of any reference to the one feature of courts that figured most prominently in public criticism of courts——their devotion to a laissez faire, procapitalist ideology.[374] We may assume, then, that Pound never saw procedure as the means of regulating the politics of litigation by carefully delimiting the power of the various participants.[375] To Pound, "[a]djective law is but an instrument" but he was remarkably reticent about what it was instrumental to.[376] His biographer traces Pound's view of procedure to two sources. The first of these was pragmatism.[377] Pound later referred to Holmes dissent in Lochner as a good example of

> the sociological movement in jurisprudence, the movement for pragmatism as a philosophy of law, the movement for the adjustment of principles and doctrines to the human condition they are to govern rather than to assumed first principles, the movement for putting the human factor in the central place and relegating logic to its true position as an instrument.[378]

As we have previously seen, pragmatism was in large part an effort to evade politics by resort to procedure.[379] We may infer that this was the reason it appealed to Pound.

But if Pound was reluctant to reveal his own ideological predilections, we may deduce them from other writings and reform efforts. Pound favored procedural reform because he, like Wigmore, wanted to increase the power of judges at the expense of lawyers, jurors, and the other branches of government.[380] Like most of his

373. Denied self-interest

Wigdor, Roscoe Pound, 1974, pp. 164, 187.

374. Devotion to laissez faire

See § 6357, text at notecall 218.

375. Delimiting power

See vol. 21, § 5026, p. 153.

376. "But an instrument"

Wigdor, Roscoe Pound, 1974, p. 159. In his St. Paul speech Pound refers to procedure as "the mere etiquette of justice." Pound, The Causes of Popular Dissatisfaction With The Adminis-

tration of Justice, 1964, 35 F.R.D. 273, 284.

377. Pragmatism

Wigdor, Roscoe Pound, 1974, pp. 183, 185.

378. "True position"

White, Social Thought in America: The Revolt Against Formalism, 1957 ed., p. 108.

379. Evade politics

See § 6357, text as notecall 621.

380. Power of judges

Wigdor, Roscoe Pound, 1974, p. 210.

followers, he seems to have believed that judges were "philosopher kings" most amenable to reason——or to put it more crassly, more likely to be influenced by what they read in the pages of the Harvard Law Review. Though this is less clear, at least at the time of the St. Paul address, Pound wanted to increase the power of judges in order that they might defeat labor unions.[381] Perhaps if he had made this clearer in his speech, it might have had a different reception.

The speech was met with hostile criticism and ringing defenses of the status quo.[382] One New York attorney described the American legal system as "the most refined and scientific" * * * ever devised by the wit of man.[383] The chairman refused to allow Pound to respond to his critics.[384] Pound's biographer argues that the fact that Pound's speech was regarded as revolutionary shows how reactionary the corporate bar had become.[385] Perhaps. But it is also possible that some of his opponents saw the possibilities of Bolshevism in Pound's elitism and statism more clearly than Pound and his supporters seem to have.

After the meeting, Wigmore and other academic "young Turks" rallied around Pound to form a group dedicated to advancing the reforms that Pound had sketched in his address.[386] This group eventually became the American Judicature Society, an organization that became something like the Vatican of Progressive Proceduralism.[387] Pound and Wigmore became close friends, especially after Pound joined Wigmore at Northwestern[388] Though Wigmore was a far from typical Progressive Proceduralist, his attitude toward the right of confrontation makes him at the very least a fellow traveler.[389]

Since Pound's analogy of lawmaking to engineering became so potent——as late as the 1960s law students were still being told they

381. Defeat labor unions

Id. at p. 219.

382. Defense of status quo

Id. at p. 126.

383. "Wit of man"

Ibid.

384. Refused to allow

Id. at p. 127.

385. Reactionary

Id. at p. 128.

386. Formed group

Id. at p. 129.

387. Judicature Society

Proceedings Honoring Roscoe Pound, 1964, 35 F.R.D. 241, 233, 264.

388. Close friends

Wigdor, Roscoe Pound, 1974, p. 133.

389. Attitude toward confrontation

See above, text at notecall 173.

should become "social engineers"——it is worth pausing to explain the power of the metaphor.[390] In the Nineteenth Century, before machine shops became bureaucratized, they provided an attractive apprenticeship for the sons of the wealthy who were ill-suited for the traditional professions yet could not soil their hands with trade——something of an American equivalent of the English navy.[391] Civil engineering in particular aspired to be a "gentlemen's profession."[392] Later in the century as corporations began to replace individual proprietorships, thus threatening the independence of the engineers, they responded to this threat with a drive to become more like the traditional professions; that is, learned and with an ethic of social service.[393] One prominent feature of this move to professionalize was the development of schools of engineering.[394] In developing engineering schools, the professional educators increasingly drew on the example of law schools.[395] Perhaps because they lacked the stabilizing influence of a long tradition of professionalism, in a few decades the engineers recapitulated and even anticipated developments that took more than a century to play themselves out in the legal profession.[396]

Among the most remarkable of these parallels between the two professions is the development of an engineering version of Langdellism.[397] As in the case of law, the engineering professors engaged

390. Pound's metaphor

See above, text at notecall 337.

391. Attractive apprenticeships

Calvert, The Mechanical Engineer in America, 1830–1910, 1967, p. 12.

392. "Gentlemen's profession"

Id. at p. 23.

393. Ethic of service

Haber, Efficiency and Uplift: Scientific Management in the Progressive Era, 1890–1920, p. 9.

394. Schools of engineering

Calvert, The Mechanical Engineer in America, 1830–1910, 1967, p. 43.

395. Example of law

"The value of a general college education as a preparation for law, medicine and theology has long been recognized. As a foundation for the

engineer's training it is quite as valuable." Id. at p. 83 (quoting the Dean of the University of Wisconsin's School of Engineering). In fact, when those words were written in 1905, the question of whether any undergraduate training should be required as a prerequisite for legal training was still contested in the legal profession.

396. Play themselves out

This will be clear to anyone who compares Calvert, The Mechanical Engineer in America, 1830–1910, 1967, with Stevens, Law School: A History of American Legal Education, 1983.

397. Langdellism

See, e.g., Calvert, The Mechanical Engineer in America, 1830–1910, 1967, p. 33: "Of two individuals engaged in the same department * * * the one who is most familiar with the principles of

in a struggle with the profession for control of professional socialization that displayed some of the same arguments as the fight between the American Bar Association and the Association of American Law Schools; e.g., that the schools were inferior to apprenticeships as a mode of training, that they did or did not open the doors of the profession to the "wrong sort"——even deploying an engineering version of the "Abraham Lincoln argument."[398] Again like the legal profession, the triumph of the schools of engineering in the "theory vs. practice" debate was aided by the growing corporatization of the profession.[399] Some engineers sought to escape the status of mere "employee" by insinuating themselves into management, thus providing aid and comfort to the "scientific management" movement.[400] Others attempted to salvage their professional dignity by a turn to elitism.[401] Hence, at the very time that Pound invoked the engineering analogy, that profession was deeply divided over its relationship to the dominant capitalist order.[402]

his business will always have an advantage over him who is expert only in the use of his tools. Further than this, of two who are equally familiar with both the science and art in question, he will have the advantage who has the most general information—the best disciplined mind—the firmest habits of mental industry, of vigilant observation of men, and things, of persevering effort, of thorough inquiry, and of systematic and accurate reasoning."

398. "Abraham Lincoln" argument

Id. at pp. 60–61 (debate over value of theory as against practice), 62–63 (struggle for control over socialization), 69 ("Lincoln argument"), 72 (struggle over apprenticeships). For those who have never encountered it before, during the struggle between lawyers and law schools over entry to the profession, lawyers argued that law schools imposed artificial standards that would bar deserving persons who lacked the required formal training from the profession—Lincoln being the best example of one

who became an outstanding lawyer with little formal training.

399. Aided by the corporatization

Id. at p. 74.

400. Insinuating themselves

Id. at pp. 14,16.

401. Elitism

Id. at pp. 220–221.

402. Deeply divided.

Id. at p. 205. See also, id. at p. 225: "It must be remembered that the financial side of engineering is always the most important, and that the sooner the young engineer recedes from the idea that simply because he is a professional man, his position is paramount, the better it will be for him. He must always be subservient to those who represent the money invested in the enterprise." A similar, albeit less blunt, version of this advice was delivered to the new associates by the managing partner of a Los Angeles law firm in the early 1960's. Anyone who can imagine the response of the

Pound was not the first person to see the rhetorical power of the contrast between society's technological successes and social failures; if he did not originate the concept, John Dewey popularized the notion of "social engineering" as the answer to the nation's problems.[403] He and his disciples saw that one way to get conservative elites to accept reform was to wrap it in the language of technological innovation, turning destructive change into "social invention."[404] The possibilities and perils could be seen in a Utopian story in a popular magazine that recounted the recollections in 1967 of a participant in

> a conspiracy of men of science, engineers, chemists, land and sea tamers and general masters of arts and of materials—a fellowship at deadly enmity with all parasites and pretenders * * * a little ruthless and unscrupulous on the side of civilization.[405]

This anticipation of "Star Trek" was a familiar genre at the turn of the century; even Jack London took a crack at it.[406]

The conceit that society could best be reformed if engineers seized power gripped the leaders of that profession; since engineering was "the science of making money for capital [whose] essentials are honesty of purpose and great care to secure accuracy of results," the engineer as "an employer and director of labor and capital" was in the best position to deal with "great social problems."[407] The metaphor appealed to those who saw the engineer as a man of "facts" rather than "opinion" who substituted "science" for "experience" (to use the language of Evidence Rule 702).[408] The engineer positioned himself as a producer of the national wealth, in contrast to the capitalist and the labor leader who were simply unproductive parasites.[409] Thus engineers converted their profes-

associates to this advice will understand the split in the engineering profession described in the text.

403. "Social engineering"

White, Social Thought in America: The Revolt Against Formalism, 1957 ed., p. 243.

404. "Social invention"

Haber, Efficiency and Uplift: Scientific Management in the Progressive Era, 1890–1920, 1973, p. 80.

405. "Ruthless and unscrupulous"

Id. at p. 46.

406. London took a crack

Id. at p. 46, note 36.

407. "Social problems"

White, Social Thought in America: The Revolt Against Formalism, 1957 ed., p. 198; Calvert, The Mechanical Engineer in America, 1830–1910, 1967, pp. 226–227.

408. "Science" for "experience"

Haber, Efficiency and Uplift: Scientific Management in the Progressive Era, 1890–1920, p. 43.

409. Simply parasites

Ibid.

411

sional ambivalence regarding capitalism into a political asset; their dissonance appealed to those who were seeking some middle way between warring social forces.[410]

This dissonance surfaces in the writings of the participants in the revolt against formalism, who seemed to confirm the claims of the engineers in the very process of repudiating them. For example, Charles Beard supported his subjectivist approach to history by claiming that "the assumption that any historian can be a disembodied spirit as coldly neutral to human affairs as the engineer to an automobile * * * [has] been challenged and rejected."[411] Thorstein Veblen contrasted the morality of engineers who actually participated in industry with that of capitalists who did not.[412] In making the captain of industry the archetype of greed and the engineer the archetype of productivity,[413] Veblen followed the engineers, though the resentments of that profession were much broader:

> Why should the merchant, the lawyer, the professor, the speculator and many others less useful in society, arrogate to themselves superior claims to power, honors and profit?[414]

The answer seemed obvious to those who saw the legal profession as parasites.

> If you please, look at the legal profession. What ground do they occupy? It is a well known fact that, they compose a very small portion of the community, and probably the most useless [but they] occupy more posts of honor and emolument than any other class.[415]

This attitude toward the profession linked with confrontation in the Sixth Amendment did not seem particularly threatening to some lawyers. For example, Felix Frankfurter, who was a double parasite according to the first quotation above, was pleased to

---

410. Dissonance appealed

Id. at pp. 15, 17.

411. "Coldly neutral"

White, Social Thought in America: The Revolt Against Formalism, 1957 ed., p. 229.

412. Actually participated

Id. at p. 82.

413. Archetype of productivity

Russett, Darwin in America: The Intellectual Response, 1865–1912, 1976, p. 164.

414. "Less useful"

Calvert, The Mechanical Engineer in America, 1830–1910, p. 39.

415. "Most useless"

Ibid.

address meetings of the Taylor Society, an association of those who desired to displace lawyers as makers of social policy.[416]

The flaws in the engineering model of politics appeared to a number of Progressive figures.[417] As Randolphe Bourne said of Dewey's use of the metaphor, "we cannot be engineers without knowing what to build."[418] A journalist who was still impressed by the engineers would later write, society cannot

> let the engineering mind (which is a non-qualitative mind) dictate to it. Engineers are notoriously careless of the master whom they work for, whether he be a red tyrant, a black tyrant, or a butter-and-egg man. They are primarily interested in means, or they would not be engineers.[419]

The career of Herbert Hoover exemplifies the problem; he succeeded as the "food dictator" after World War I because his task was clear but he failed as President when faced with the question of what to do, not how to do it.[420] But by that time the engineering metaphor had already worked its influence on American legal thought.

One illustration of that influence will suffice. Like many up-and-coming professions, engineers resented what they took to be lack of respect for their professional achievements when they appeared as expert witnesses in court.[421] When judges refused to let them dictate the outcome of cases, they justifiably blamed this on the rules under which courts operated, particularly those that served to preserve and regulate the adversary system They were particularly incensed when the hearsay rule was invoked to prevent them from reading textbooks to the jury.[422] The failure to understand the confrontation policies that support the hearsay rule doubtless had some influence on "social engineers" when they set

416. Frankfurter addressed

Haber, Efficiency and Uplift: Scientific Management in the Progressive Era, 1890–1920, 1973, p. 33.

417. Flaws

These can be glimpsed in the description of artists attributed to Stalin——"engineers of human souls."

418. "Knowing what to build"

White, Social Thought in America: The Revolt Against Formalism, 1957 ed., p. 244.

419. "Not be engineers"

Chamberlain, Farewell to Reform, 1965 ed., pp. 318–319.

420. Hoover

Haber, Efficiency and Uplift: Scientific Management in The Progressive Era, 1890–1920, p. 48.

421. Expert witnesses

Calvert, The Mechanical Engineer in America, 1830–1910, p. 155.

422. Reading textbooks

Ibid.

out to reform the rules of evidence——reforms that could only proceed if the confrontation rights of criminal defendants were devalued.[423]

At about this time the Supreme Court decided a pair of cases that suggest how it valued the Sixth Amendment. In the first of these, West v. Louisiana, the prosecution had introduced the deposition of an absent witness taken in connection with the preliminary hearing in the case.[424] The state court held that since the defendant had cross-examined the witness at the preliminary hearing, this satisfied the right of confrontation.[425] When the case reached the Supreme Court, that body held in an opinion by Justice Peckham that the Sixth Amendment did not apply to the states——a conclusion supported by earlier opinions holding that despite the intentions of the Radical Republicans, the Fourteenth Amendment did not nationalize the Bill of Rights.[426] Hence, the Court said the only real issue was whether the use of the deposition was a denial of due process of law.[427]

The Court held that it was not. Conceding that the right to use testimony given at the preliminary hearing was statutory so that its use here could not be justified by resort to the common law, the Court noted the division of the state courts on the question.[428] But, the Court reasoned, the federal Constitution does not prohibit the states from altering the common law.[429] Such alterations could hardly rise to a denial of due process where the change was but a "slight extension" of the common-law rule.[430] Despite disclaiming any intent to pass on the issue under the Sixth Amendment, Justice Peckham went on to review each of the Court's prior confrontation opinions and concluded that "there is nothing in them opposed to

423. Some influence

One influence that deserves more study than it can get here is the degree to which the drive within the engineering profession for uniform standards for tools and materials influenced the movement for uniformity in the legal system. See id. at p. 172.

424. West case

1904, 24 S.Ct. 650, 194 U.S. 258, 48 L.Ed. 965.

425. Past satisfied

Id. at p. 651, 194 U.S. at 260.

426. Did not nationalize

Id. at p. 652, 194 U.S. at 262.

427. Denial of due process

Ibid.

428. Noting division

Ibid.

429. Prohibit altering

Ibid.

430. "Slight extension"

Ibid.

our judgment in this case."[431] Apparently the Court thought that the language in Mattox about the purpose of the Confrontation Clause had been superseded by the Court's holdings that the Sixth Amendment merely incorporated the common law.[432]

Two years later in Felts v. Murphy, without so much as mentioning West, the Court specifically reiterated that the Fourteenth Amendment "did not radically change the whole theory of the relations of the state and Federal governments to each other, and of both governments to the people."[433] What is significant about Felts is that the Court went on to hold that it was not a denial of due process for the state to impose a life sentence for murder on a veteran of the Civil War who had lost his hearing in the line of duty and so "did not hear a word of the evidence that was given upon his trial" because the state court was unwilling to accommodate his deafness by allowing the evidence to be restated into his ear trumpet.[434] Apparently the court saw nothing in the Sixth Amendment of relevance despite the fact "this unfortunate man" had been virtually tried in absentia, unable to hear the evidence and to communicate with his lawyer, and unaware that he had been convicted until the clerk of the court passed him a note with this information.[435] Unlike West, this was no "slight extension" of what was permissible under the right of confrontation, particularly when that right is viewed holistically as incorporating the common-law adversary trial and the right to counsel.[436]

431. "Nothing opposed"

Id. at p. 654. 194 U.S. at 266.

432. Superseded

In Mattox, the Court had said that the purpose of the Confrontation Clause was to bar the use of "depositions" and similar unconfronted evidence. See § 6357, text at notecall 492.

433. "Did not radically change"

1906, 26 S.Ct. 366, 368, 201 U.S. 123, 50 L.Ed. 689.

434. "Did not hear a word"

Id. at p. 367, 201 U.S. at 128.

435. Passed him a note

Ibid. The facts are worse than this summary makes them appear; Justice

Peckham quotes a passage from the motion for a new trial that shows the trial judge's cavalier disregard of the defendant's plight.

436. Viewed holistically

See vol. 30, § 6341. p. 186. Since the defendant in Felts did not hear the examination of the jurors and was unable to consult with counsel on their animus, if any, toward him, one can argue that the defendant was denied not only the right to assistance of counsel and the right of confrontation but also the right to trial by an impartial jury.

In a similar case the following year, the Court—and presumably the lawyers—did not see any confrontation issue in the refusal of a federal court to appoint an interpreter to translate

Panic, Poverty, and Politics

The uneasy truce between Progressive reformers and capitalists fell apart with the Panic of 1907.[437] Though there were brief periods of upturn, the economy did not fully recover until World War I.[438] Businessmen blamed the panic on shaken investor confidence as a result of a $20 million fine levied on the Rockefeller interests for repeated violations of federal law.[439] Railroads blamed the particularly hard hit they received in the depression on government regulation.[440] Whatever its cause, the Panic brought economic issues back into prominence.[441]

For the middle class, the increasing cost of living suddenly became an issue.[442] Studies repeatedly showed that the real wages of workers had been falling even before the economic downturn.[443] During this period most of the burden of federal taxation fell on the middle and working classes.[444] Economic inequality had sharpened; on the eve of World War I, the U.S. Commission on Industrial Relations found that American workers had not received their fair share of the nation's wealth and that this inequality was a major cause of social unrest.[445] At that time 2% of the population owned 60% of the wealth, while the bottom 65% owned only 5%.[446] Even within the working class there were sharp differences; at a time when unionized miners were getting $3.50 for an eight hour day, smelters of the ore worked 12 hour days, seven days a week for less than $2.[447] Little wonder that the Commission found that between

the testimony of an accused murderer. Perovich v. U.S., 1907, 27 S.Ct. 456, 205 U.S. 86, 51 L.Ed. 722.

437. Panic of 1907

Encyclopedia of American History, Morris ed. 1976, p. 321.

438. Did not recover

Wiebe, Businessmen and Reform: A Study of the Progressive Movement, 1967, p. 70.

439. Blamed on fine

Id. at p. 72.

440. Blamed on regulation

Id. at p. 85.

441. Economic issues

Id. at p. 68.

442. Cost of living

Haber, Efficiency and Uplift: Scientific Management in the Progressive Era, 1890–1920, p. 51.

443. Real wages falling

Ekirch, Progressivism in America, 1974, p. 71.

444. Burden of taxation

Link, Woodrow Wilson and The Progressive Era, 1910–1917, p. 192.

445. Major cause

Adams, The Age of Industrial Violence, 1910–1915, p. 216.

446. Owned only 5%

Ibid.

447. Less than $2

Lukas, Big Trouble, 1997, p. 221.

a quarter and a third of the work force was not earning enough for a decent living.[448]

Hard times revived Populist rhetoric. The mayor of Cleveland thought that the "greatest movement in the world today may be characterized as the struggle of the People against Privilege."[449] Poverty was blamed on flaws in the economic structure of capitalism rather than the moral failings of the poor.[450] Attacks on the laissez-faire notions of limited government began to be heard; only a strong government, it was argued, could handle the social problems arising from the unequal distribution of wealth.[451] At the same time, some complained that the national government was in the grip of the rich.[452] Even a sober Harvard law professor dusted off the young Holmes' defense of "class legislation" to aid the impoverished.[453]

The intellectual response to economic crisis was diverse. Some of the elite took up Andrew Carnegie's "Gospel of Wealth"——an attempt to substitute philanthropy for government action to head off socialism and revolution——but insisted that such giving be made more "scientific."[454] Some, like the soon-to-be Justice Brandeis, sought refuge in the "expanding pie" argument; that is that what was needed was government action to increase wealth rather than redistributing it.[455] Any attempt to revive Darwinian defenses of inequality were embarrassed by Gustav Meyer's three-volume study of the great American fortunes, which found they were based

448. Decent living

Adams, The Age of Industrial Violence, 1910–1915, 1966, p. 216.

449. "Against Privilege"

Wiebe, Businessmen and Reform: A Study of the Progressive Movement, 1962, p. 92.

450. Economic structure

Id. at p. 71.

451. Could handle problems

White, Social Thought in America: The Revolt Against Formalism, 1957 ed., p. 56.

452. In grip of rich

Wiebe, Businessmen and Reform: A Study of the Progressive Movement, 1962, p. 96.

453. "Class legislation"

White, Social Thought in America: The Revolt Against Formalism, 1957 ed. pp. 117–118.

454. "Gospel of Wealth"

Ekirch, Progressivism in America, 1974, pp. 68–69.

455. "Expanding pie"

Haber, Efficiency and Uplift: Scientific Management in the Progressive Era, 1890–1920, 1973, p. 81.

less on individual merit and entrepreneurial skill than on inheritance, cupidity, and the ability to exploit natural and artificial monopolies.[456]

It seems likely, however, that many Progressives took their cue from Alfred Ross' analysis of economic inequality.[457] Ross argued that economic inequality was a necessary consequence of capitalist economic systems and that it drove the need for social control.[458]

> If there is any means whereby the Occidental with his private property and free enterprise can escape acute economic contrasts, he has not yet discovered it. The pristine pecuniary level gives place to the steepest inequalities in reward, possession, and inheritance. Equality before the law, political equality, religious equality,——these may delay but they cannot stop the progress of economic differentiation. But with this comes greater need of control.[459]

Failing such control "from law and morality, [society] would be ground to powder between compassion and envy, as between the upper and nether millstones."[460] Given this analysis, the outlook for rights like confrontation that restricted the needed social control was gloomy indeed. Perhaps Ross meant to assuage any such fears with his observation that economic inequality tends to deaden the sense of justice.[461]

The political response to the fears loosed by the panic was simple—forestall any Populistic tinkering with the economic system by taking it out of politics.[462] The first steps toward this were taken in 1907, but the representative of Wall Street told Congress the economic system should "be beyond the reach of politicians and without the bounds of political intrigues, ambitions or entanglements."[463] The result was the 1913 Federal Reserve Act, which

---

456. Exploit monopolies

Chamberlain, Farewell to Reform, 1965 ed., pp. 204–207.

457. Cue from Ross

See § 6357, text at notecall 789.

458. Necessary consequence

Ross, Social Control, 1964 ed., p. xxviii.

459. "Need of control"

Id. at p. 53.

460. "Millstones"

Id. at p. 12.

461. Deaden justice

Id. at p. 31.

462. Taking out of politics

Wiebe, Businessmen and Reform: A Study of The Progressive Movement, 1962 , p. 68.

463. "Entanglement"

Id. at p. 130.

shifted control over the economic system to an appointed cartel of bankers and economists.[464]

If the Federal Reserve system evinced a hostility to democracy, there were countercurrents. At about the same time the Industrial Workers of the World launched their direct-action defense of free speech for workers in the Pacific Northwest——a grassroots effort that had more to do with the rise of the modern First Amendment that some lawyers are willing to recognize.[465] But workers wanted more than talk. The Commission of Industrial Relations reported that on the eve of World War I "there exists among the workers an almost universal conviction that they, both as individuals and as a class are denied justice."[466] The Commission's final report urged a series of constitutional amendments to reinforce the Bill of Rights, including further safeguards for trial by jury——the latter often seen as synonymous with the adversary system that includes the right of confrontation.[467]

Confrontation and the Crisis in Christianity

Confrontation emerged from religious controversy in Tudor England and was carried to the colonies by Protestant dissenters.[468] So long as Protestantism was dominant in America, confrontation continued to draw support from religious thinking of judges and lawyers.[469] But a crisis had been brewing during the latter half of the Nineteenth Century that erupted in the Progressive era.[470] Sketching that crisis and its effects will add another strand to our understanding of the development of modern confrontation doctrine.

Darwinism presented the major challenge to Christian theology, primarily because it seemed to leave little room for physical proof of God's existence.[471] For those for whom outright rejection of Darwinism was not an option, the task was to find some method of

464. Shifted control

Ekirch, Progressivism in America, 1974, pp. 226–227.

465. I.W.W. and free speech

Adams, The Age of Industrial Violence, 1910–1915, 1966, p. 177.

466. "Denied justice"

Id. at p. 217.

467. Trial by jury

Ibid.

468. Emerged and was carried

See vol. 30, §§ 6342–6344.

469. Draw support

See § 6355, text at notecall 93.

470. Crisis brewing

The crisis had earlier roots; e.g., the fracturing of some Protestant denominations over the question of slavery tended to undermine the authority of the clergy on both sides of the question.

471. Leave little room

Russett, Darwin in America: The Intellectual Response, 1865–1912, 1976, p. 39.

reconciling science and religion.[472] One such effort was to situate theology in a domain of its own, whether above, below, or beside science.[473] Some clerics began to accept Darwinism because it seemed to promise the progress of humankind in the direction of perfection, thus suggesting some divine influence on the course of evolution that might serve as circumstantial evidence of the Almighty.[474] Darwinism also attracted those who saw it as a weapon to attack conservative theologians and denominations.[475] The effect of this strategy on confrontation depended on how large a part religious thought was to play in the new synthesis because the scientific defense of confrontation seemed to only support a very limited right along Wigmorean lines.[476]

But as conservatives saw at once, accommodation with Darwinism required an abandonment or drastic weakening in supernatural justifications for religion.[477] This had implications beyond the value of oaths in securing honest testimony.[478] In an era of class conflict, the demise of the "pie-in-the-sky-bye-and-bye" as an explanation for the suffering of the downtrodden opened the door for Marxism—or worse.[479] For example, clerics needed little imagination to see who were the targets of Herbert Spencer's Darwinian attack on those who go about "storing up miseries for future generations" by "fostering the good-for-nothing at the expense of the good"; for Spencer, aiding "the bad in multiplying is, in effect, the same as maliciously providing for our descendents a multitude of enemies."[480] This was not only a rather far cry from Christ's feeding the multitudes, it also undermined the one social role conservatives

472. Reconciling

Ibid. (describing several such strategies).

473. Domain of its own

Id. at p. 51. Thus the relationship between religion and science paralleled the relationship between church and state under the First Amendment.

474. Progress to perfection

Ekirch, Progressivism in America, 1974, p. 52.

475. Attack conservatives

Mowry, The Era of Theodore Roosevelt and The Birth of Modern America, 1900–1912, 1962, pp. 24, 27.

476. Wigmorean lines

See above, text at notecall 173.

477. Weakening of supernatural

Mowry, The Progressive Era, 1900–1920: The Reform Persuasion, 1958, p. 6.

478. Value of oaths

See § 6356, text at notecall 691.

479. "Pie-in-the-sky"

Mowry, The Progressive Era, 1900–1920: The Reform Persuasion, 1958, p. 6. The phrase is Joe Hill's, not Mowry's.

480. "Multitude of enemies"

Russett, Darwin in America: The Intellectual Response, 1865–1912, 1976, p. 89.

were willing to have the church play.[481] One response, that continues down to the present, is to find some evolutionary basis for the moral repugnance the clerics supposed most humans would feel at the prospect of implementing Spencer's version of laissez faire morality.[482] During the Progressive era this produced works such as "Spiritual Factors in History", which sought to collect examples where individuals and nations responded altruistically even when it endangered their immediate prospects for survival.[483]

While Protestants were still struggling with Darwinism, they faced a renewed threat from Roman Catholicism.[484] Due in large measure to patterns of immigration and comparative birth rates, the number of Catholics was growing at a more rapid rate than were Protestants.[485] Anti–Catholic organizations such as the American Protective Association would be less fearsome if this trend continued.[486] Moreover, Catholicism had a number of advantages in dealing with class conflict that made attacks on the Church less attractive to elites than they might have been in the past. Catholic priests had authority over the lowest rungs of the downtrodden and did not hesitate to use it to reduce class conflict by denouncing Socialists and Anarchists from the pulpit.[487] The Church organized

481.　Social role

See also the views of William Graham Sumner, id. at p. 99: "It would be hard to find a single instance of direct assault by positive effort upon poverty, vice, and misery which has not either failed, or, if it has not failed directly and entirely, has not entailed other evils greater than the ones which it removed."

482.　Evolutionary basis

Id. at pp. 115–116. As those who have followed the debate down to the present may be aware, it turns on what one takes to be the appropriate unit of evolution; the individual "selfish gene" may get nowhere if what contributes to the advantage of its own offspring leads to the demise of the larger unit, whether it be the entire individual or the species.

483.　"Spiritual Factors"

White, Social Thought in America: The Revolt Against Formalism, 1957 ed., p. 128.

484.　Catholicism

The threat was aided by the way in which the American Catholic hierarchy was dominated by clerics of Irish descent who favored the mystical over the intellectual elements of tradition and thus escaped the divisions in the European church over "modernism" that might have made American Catholics as divided as Protestants.

485.　More rapid rate

Ekirch, Progressivism in America, 1974, p. 52.

486.　American Protective

Lukas, Big Trouble, 1997, p. 110.

487.　Denouncing from pulpit

Id. at p. 479.

the "Militia of Christ" among workers to oppose Marxism in labor unions.[488] Finally, the Catholic Church had intellectual resources that could be marshaled in support of order that even Protestant capitalists could not lightly dismiss; for example, there were few Protestant theologians who could support natural law with the authority of Aquinas.[489]

While Protestantism grew during the Progressive era at a rate that exceeded the growth of population, Protestantism suffered from internal weaknesses that undercut the significance of the numbers.[490] With the growth of economic inequality and the rise of other professions, clergymen suffered a diminution in both income and status.[491] Moreover, the localized nature of church authority made it more difficult for Protestant ministers to ignore the impact of capitalism on members of the congregation.[492] When they attempted to justify the existing economic system, Protestant clerics heard themselves denounced as "spiritual Pinkertons" whose social function was "guarding the loot of the unrighteous rich."[493] Other critics exploited the contradictions of Calvinism to undermine the individualism that supported both capitalism and confrontation.[494] The notion that Protestantism was the basis for democracy with its denial of any need for intermediaries between the faithful and truth was being undermined by the antidemocratic strains in Progressivism, particularly the Cult of the Expert.[495] In an age that valued rationality and efficiency, few were prepared to defend these internal contradictions as illustrations of the limits of rationality in explaining the human condition.[496]

488. "Militia of Christ"

Weinstein, The Corporate Ideal in the Liberal State, 1900–1918, 1968, p. 122.

489. Support natural law

Ekirch, Progressivism in America, 1974, p. 52.

490. Protestantism grew

Ekirch, Progressivism in America, 1974, p. 52.

491. Dimunition in status

Hays, The Response to Industrialism, 1885–1914, 1957, p. 72.

492. Impact on congregation

Ibid.

493. "Guarding the loot"

Mowry, The Era of Theodore Roosevelt and the Birth of Modern America, 1900–1912, p. 25.

494. Contradictions of Calvinism

White, Social Thought in America: The Revolt Against Formalism, 1957 ed., p. 260.

495. Basis for democracy

Brooks, Walter Clark, Fighting Judge, 1944, pp. 77–78. On the attack on intermediaries and confrontation, see vol. 30, § 6343, pp. 286–288.

496. Limits of rationality

White, Social Thought in America: The Revolt Against Formalism, 1957 ed., p. 262.

Indeed, scientific explanations of religion tended to undermine its authority. Hear the Progressive guru Edward A. Ross:

> A body of religious belief * * * is a storage battery of moral emotion. It is a means of storing up for society the surplus moral energy of the ethical elite, and enabling it to do work by producing sociable emotions and modifying conduct in desirable ways.[497]

Ross went on to argue that since the religion that held together society was itself held together by beliefs rather than interests, it was at war with the ideology of capitalism.[498] Some Protestant divines had already begin to suspect that capitalism was a threat to religion.[499]

Protestantism responded to these threats in various ways, including denial.[500] For purposes of confrontation, the most significant of these involved the secularization of religion.[501] Some proposed to replace the supernatural with the mystical, arguing that the will of God worked through people, not miracles; as it would later be put, one "reads the Word of God in the faces of His people." At a less exalted level, the "New Theology" argued that since individuals were embedded in society, the only way to save souls was to save society.[502] For some this meant that religion could serve as a unifying force in a divided society, bringing together employers and workers.[503] In some versions, this came close to embracing "scientific racism" and the politics of exclusion.[504] But others sought to find a middle way between individualism and statism in a vaguely described "Christian unity."[505]

497. "Modifying conduct"

Ross, Social Control, 1964 ed., p. 212.

498. At war with capitalism

Id. at pp. 214–215.

499. Threat to religion

Hays, The Response to Industrialism, 1885–1914, 1957, p. 72.

500. Denial

Since, as Ross predicted, this response has continued down to the present, there is little need to describe Protestant denial of Darwinism, particularly since it had little impact on the development of confrontation doctrine.

501. Secularization

Wiebe, The Search for Order, 1877–1920, 1967, p. 64.

502. "New Theology"

Hays, The Response to Industrialism, 1885–1914, 1957, p. 77.

503. Employers and workers

Wiebe, The Search for Order, 1877–1920, 1967, p. 63.

504. Politics of exclusion

Ekirch, Progressivism in America, 1974, p. 54.

505. "Christian unity"

Ibid.

The most influential of these secularizing movements went by the name "The Social Gospel", though it was sometimes referred to as "Christian Socialism."[506] Influenced by American secular reformers and the English Chartists, the Social Gospel appealed to the urban middle class.[507] Though its leading figure, Walter Rauschenbusch, thought capitalism was "essential atheism",[508] the moderate versions of the Social Gospel did not want to overthrow capitalism; they merely wanted to reform its "excesses."[509] This, as we shall see, was pretty much the Progressive program.

The Panic of 1907 and the ensuing increase in poverty brought renewed attention to the so-called "settlement house" movement.[510] Anticipating the War on Poverty and the Peace Corps later in the century, settlement houses brought young, well-educated, middle-class youth into urban slums to work with the poor.[511] The first settlement house was founded in 1891 and by the time of the Panic there were more than 400 in cities across the country.[512] Settlement houses were part of a broader social-justice movement, that included adherents of the Social Gospel.[513] Together these groups made poverty a moral problem, not of the poor individuals, but of the society that created the conditions that fostered poverty.[514] Once the courts acted to alleviate the impact of poverty on the criminal justice system, this increased the social costs of confronta-

506. "Christian socialism"

Ekirch, Progressivism in America, 1974, p. 51.

507. Urban middle class

Id. at p. 50.

508. "Essential atheism"

Mowry, The Era of Theodore Roosevelt and The Birth of Modern America, 1900–1912, p. 29.

509. "Excesses"

Id. at p. 28.

There were similar movements within the Catholic Church. For example, in 1906 a Catholic priest published a book in which he argued that capitalists should not be allowed to declare a profit from their business until after each employee had been paid "a living wage." Hays, The Response to Industrialism, 1885–1914, 1957, p. 81. However, the American church as a whole was oblivious to papal decrees supporting the rights of workers and there is little evidence that this minor strain in Catholicism had significant impact beyond Social Gospel circles. Ibid.

510. "Settlement house"

Ekirch, Progressivism in America, 1974, p. 73.

511. Middle-class youth

Id. at p. 71.

512. More than 400

Id. at p. 76.

513. Broader movement

Hays, The Response to Industrialism, 1885–1914, 1957, p. 79.

514. Moral problem

Ibid.

tion.[515] But settlement houses were unique among the agencies for social justice in the leading roles they afforded women; to this day, the only settlement house most Americans can name is Hull House in Chicago and the only figure widely mentioned in history texts is Jane Adams.[516] Though settlement houses only pushed the boundaries of "women's separate sphere"——charity, teaching, and nursing were long considered appropriate activities for women——they nonetheless played a role in advancing the cause of feminism with not entirely positive effects on confrontation.[517]

Croly and the Cult of The Expert

In 1908, according to some historians, Progressives began to turn to the federal government as the agent of reform.[518] The following year, Herbert Croly published "The Promise of American Life", one of the most significant statements of the Progressive philosophy and program, in which he justified this turn.[519] Croly was a Harvard-educated journalist and disciple of John Dewey who had labored in relative obscurity for an architectural magazine.[520] His book has been described as the "best political treatise" to come out of the Progressive movement.[521] Croly, who was later to found the Progressive journal "The New Republic," became extremely influential. For example, his rhetoric frequently popped up in speeches by Theodore Roosevelt.[522]

515. Increased costs

Since the criminal-justice system is dominated by indigents who cannot afford their own lawyers and who without legal aid would either plead guilty or not be able to raise confrontation issues, the right of confrontation would be less costly when only the well-to-do few could afford it.

516. Adams and Hull House

Mowry, The Progressive Era, 1900–1920: The Reform Persuasion, 1958, p. 7.

517. Advancing feminism

As Poverty Warriors were to discover later in the century, any efforts to help the poor brought the settlement houses into conflict with local elites and inevitably plunged them into politics in ways that transgressed the boundaries of "women's work." Ekirch, Progressivism in America, 1974, p. 75.

518. Began to turn

Wiebe, Businessmen and Reform: A Study of the Progressive Movement, 1962, p. 8.

519. Justified turn

Weinstein, The Corporate Ideal in the Liberal State, 1900–1918, 1968, p. 157.

520. Relative obscurity

Id. at p. 158. See also, Haber, Efficiency and Uplift: Scientific Management in the Progressive Era, 1890–1920, 1973, p. 83.

521. "Best treatise"

Link, Woodrow Wilson and The Progressive Era, 1910–1917, 1963 ed., p. 18.

522. Roosevelt speeches

Chamberlain, Farewell to Reform, 1965 ed., p. 225.

Croly favored government intervention in the economy through programs whose effect would be to redistribute the wealth but he was anxious to divorce Progressivism from Populism.[523] His book, he wrote, was "an attempt to justify the specialized contemporary intellectual discipline against the tyranny of certain aspects of our democratic tradition."[524] Or more bluntly, Progressivism was "designed to serve as a counterpoise to the threat of working class revolution."[525] The "tyranny" of which Croly wrote was the Jeffersonian tradition that equated human freedom with a weak government.[526] He thought Hamilton had been right and his philosophy has sometimes been described as "an effort to pursue Jeffersonian ends by Hamiltonian means."[527] However, since Croly's Progressivism tended to be defined by what it was against, its program was in large measure dictated by its opponents; eventually, when the threat of "working class revolution" died with the collapse of the Soviet Union, Croly's descendants found themselves, like the armed forces, searching for a new enemy to justify their existence.[528]

For purposes of confrontation, Croly's significance lies in his elitism and opposition to the extension of democracy.[529] He argued that democracy could not realize itself without a strong state, a strong executive, and an efficient administrative apparatus; what was needed was a "constructive relation between democracy and nationality."[530] He called his construction "The New National-

523. Redistribute wealth

Ekirch, Progressivism in America, 1974, p. 158.

524. "Tyranny of tradition"

Haber, Efficiency and Uplift: Scientific Management in the Progressive Era, 1890–1920, 1973, p. 85.

525. "Threat of revolution"

Weinstein, The Corporate Ideal in The Liberal State, 1900–1918, 1968, p. xi. Later, in the inaugural issue of The New Republic, Croly wrote: "We shall be radical without being socialistic." Haber, Efficiency and Uplift: Scientific Management in the Progressive Era, 1890–1920, 1973, p. 87.

526. Weak government

O'Neill, The Progressive Years, 1975, p. 57.

527. "Hamiltonian means"

Link. Woodrow Wilson and The Progressive Era, 1910–1917, 1963 ed., p. 19.

528. Croly's descendents

In the 1960s when Progressivism had become "corporate liberalism" in the eyes of the so-called "New Left", in response The New Republic turned to what was then called "neo-conservativism".

529. Opposition to democracy

Ekrich, Progressivism in America, 1974, p. 159.

530. "Constructive relation"

Haber, Efficiency and Uplift: Scientific Management in the Progressive Era, 1890–1920, 1973, p. 85.

ism."[531] He embraced a mystical statism, arguing that if the United States was to realize its "historic mission" it would have to require citizens to think of the state before thinking of themselves.[532] To Croly, the individualism that underlies confrontation was the enemy of nationalism.[533] This brought him very close to the super-patriotism and the politics of exclusion sometimes embraced by Theodore Roosevelt.[534] However, in the short term Croly's nationalism had many enemies that delayed its implementation.

Croly was far more successful with what one historian has called his "expertism," fostering what we shall call "the cult of the expert."[535] Croly's elitism called for a government of the "best minds."[536] This meant applying the principles of "scientific management" that had been adopted by some corporations to the operation of the government.

> The parallelism is, as a matter of fact, extremely close. The successful conduct of both public and private business is becoming more and more a matter of expert administration, which demands similar methods and is confronted by the solution of similar problems.[537]

Croly should have attended to Ross' distinction between an "elite" and a "mandarinate;" the former is what the Founders had in mind while the latter seems to have been what Croly was thinking of.[538] As to them, Ross wrote:

> The mandarinate ought to include the wisest and best in society; but the false worth that attaches to purely conventional learning, and the sifting and promoting of the learned by tests that are artificial and futile, are likely to prevent it.[539]

531. "New Nationalism"

O'Neill, The Progressive Years, 1975, p. 57.

532. Think of state

Chamberlain, Farewell to Reform, 1965 ed., p. 224; Mowry, The Era of Theodore Roosevelt and The Birth of Modern America, 1900–1912, 1962, p. 145.

533. Enemy of nationalism

Ibid.

534. Super-patriotism

Ibid.

535. "Expertism"

Haber, Efficiency and Uplift: Scientific Management in the Progressive Era, 1890–1920, 1973, p. 86.

536. "Best minds"

Chamberlain, Farewell to Reform, 1965, 1965 ed., p. 225.

537. "Similar problems"

Haber, Efficiency and Uplift: Scientific Management in the Progressive Era, 1890–1920, 1973, p. 89.

538. "Elite" and "mandarinate"

Ross, Social Control, 1969 ed., p. 83.

539. "Tests artificial"

Ibid.

Other devotees of the cult of the expert mirrored Croly's confusion about the sources of expertise.

The notion that some are suited to rule and others to be ruled was hardly new, but it was the Progressives who popularized the modern version. They had

> an abiding faith in regulation, expertness, and the capacity of American government to make rational decisions provided the experts in administrative agencies could remain free from partisan political considerations.[540]

Some historians have credited the sociologist Lester Ward with first advancing this view, but it was widely held by other academics.[541] Thorstein Veblen proposed that a hierarchy of experts be established to run the economy and another prominent economist, Richard Ely, argued that democracy alone was insufficient for reform without a large dose of paternalism.[542] Perhaps the most ominous of these academic regimes of expertise—and the only one to be widely adopted—was that of Edward Ross, who wrote that

> we can only deplore the interference in penal matters of a public which, again and again, has shown itself too maudlin and womanish to uphold the stringency needed for its protection. It is likely that the problem of repressing crime without demoralizing the public can be solved only by committing the penal system into the hands of official experts checked by non-official specialists.[543]

The penal system is too close to the judicial system to expect that attitudes like this could be kept from affecting courts as well.[544]

The cult of the expert was not limited to academics.[545] Woodrow Wilson, for example, "looked to the leadership of a well-educated elite trained for government service and public adminis-

540. "Free from political"

Ekirch, Progressivism in America, 1974, p. 117.

541. Lester Ward

Russett, Darwin in America: The Intellectual Response, 1865–1912, 1976, p. 110 (Ward wanted people to choose "scientific legislators" who would rely on "true scientific sociologists and sociological inventors").

542. Dose of paternalism

Chamberlain, Farewell to Reform, 1965 ed., p. 220 (Veblen); Ekirch, Progressivism in America, 1974, p. 27 (Ely).

543. "Maudlin and womanish"

Ross, Social Control, 1969 ed., p. 111.

544. Affecting courts

Indeed, Ross uses the law as an example of a system that is governed by experts. See id., at p. 117.

545. Not limited

Even Robert LaFollette, one of the more radically democratic of the Progressives, once proposed to have a group of economists set tariffs. Chamberlain, Farewell to Reform, 1965 ed., p. 259.

tration."[546] When, during World War I, Congress created the Council of National Defense to mobilize the economy, Wilson remarked apropos of the corporate executives he appointed to it that they represented "the entrance of the nonpartisan engineer and professional man into American governmental affairs on a wider scale than ever before."[547] (One who did not keep in mind Ross' distinction between the "elite" and the "mandarinate" might suppose that this was an application of Veblen's proposal to the war effort. One of Wilson's appointees was closer to the mark when he described Wilson as having "brought business into the business of government.")[548] Wilson, of course, had come from the academy, but it should not be supposed that fondness for experts was limited to such. For example, as early as 1911 William Howard Taft called on economists and sociologists to provide scientific analyses of social problems to aid the government.[549]

Concrete efforts to answer Taft's call illustrate the possibilities and problems of government by expert. Among the more modest, and most widely emulated, was the Wisconsin Legislative Reference Bureau, which sought to replace the influence of lobbyists by providing "expert" drafting of bills for the legislature;[550] it was criticized as "interminable bill drafting [by] countless employees, experts and the like * * * [who] throw the legal profession into spasms of delight * * * while * * * fundamentals remain practically untouched."[551] One effort to examine "fundamentals" was a study of Pittsburgh by teams of economists and social workers funded by the Russell Sage Foundation in 1907; beyond embarrassing the Steel Barons, it seems to have had little effect.[552] On the other hand, in 1914 the National Civil Federation funded a massive

546. "Well-educated elite"

Ekirch, Progressivism in America, 1974, p. 168.

547. "Nonpartisan engineer"

Weinstein, The Corporate Ideal in the Liberal State, 1900–1918, 1968, p. 218. At the same time, Wilson equated business efficiency and military efficiency in a way that left no doubt that both were bureaucracies—unlike the contemporary tendency to think that only governments can be bureaucracies.

548. "Business into business"

Id. at p . 233.

549. Taft called

Adams, Age of Industrial Violence, 1910–1915, 1966, p. 30.

550. Wisconsin Bureau

Adams, Age of Industrial Violence, 190–1915, 1966, p. 205.

551. "Fundamentals untouched"

Id. at p. 210.

552. Pittsburgh study

Ekirch, Progressivism in America, 1974, p. 72.

study employing more than 400 people that was designed to counter Communist claims by proving that capitalism was good for workers; when its first reports tended to disprove this hypothesis, the effort was scuttled and the reports suppressed.[553] The Carnegie Endowment for Peace, not wanting to be labeled "radical" as the nation moved toward war, confined its experts to scholarly studies with little political impact.[554]

The Progressive desire for government by expert is, perhaps, best exemplified by the "city manager" system of municipal government, which sought to end corruption by placing many governmental functions in the hands of an administrator.[555] The system worked best with problems that were truly technical in nature— picking up garbage, for example. The system foundered when the problems were social and political.[556] A major flaw was that achievement for the city manager tended to be measured by how much costs were cut—which in turn, tended to convert technical problems into political ones.

Modern lawyers may find the Progressive faith in experts naive—at lease those lawyers capable of seeing that it is not only the other side's experts who are biased. This was tolerably clear in the Progressive era. For example, the N.Y.U. professor who denigrated the contribution of workers to the national wealth by pronouncing one corporate leader as "of more lasting service to the nation than would be 1,000,000 unskilled laborers" went on to demonstrate his scientific approach by opining that the ideas of unionists "were no better than those of the Indian Thugs, who preached robbery and murder."[557] Even those who favored government by expert often unwittingly demonstrated how easy it was for administrators to shift from philosopher kings to Fascist dictators.[558] And there were those willing to reject the claim that expert government would be superior. Elihu Root wrote that the

553. N.C.F. study

Adams, Age of Industrial Violence, 1910–1915, 1966, p . 35.

554. Carnegie endowment

Ekirch, Progressivism in America, 1974, p. 24.

555. City manager

Weinstein, The Corporate Ideal in the Liberal State, 1900–1918, 1968, p. 111.

556. System foundered

Ibid.

557. "Indian Thugs"

Adams, Age of Industrial Violence, 1910–1915, 1966, p. 167.

558. Kings to dictators

Chamberlain, Farewell to Reform, 1965 ed., pp. 291, 316.

great difficulty in the application of pure reason to practical affairs is that never in this world does the reasoner get all the premises which should affect the conclusions; so it frequently happens that the practical man who does not reason at all but who feels the effect of conditions which the reasoner overlooks, goes right while the superior intelligence of the reasoning man goes wrong.[559]

Progressives could dismiss such comments as the ravings of a man who never had a "scientific" legal education.[560] Today we can see him as arguing for a "holistic" rather than a "reductionist" approach to social problems.

But the elitism of many Progressives allowed them to blur Root's version of Ross' distinction between the "mandarin" and the "practical man." The result was antidemocratic sentiments like this:

> This vast and miscellaneous democracy of ours must be led; its giant faculties must be schooled and directed. Leadership cannot belong to the multitude; masses of men cannot be self-directed, neither can groups of communities.[561]

One of the business leaders Wilson brought into the Council of National Defense wanted to use the wartime expedient as a permanent model of government: "If we had a Government business manager with a free hand to run the business side of government * * * we should have a successful government of business."[562] Although Ross seems to have seen this, not many Progressives glimpsed how the bureaucratization of the government along corporate lines would alienate the citizenry and thus lay the groundwork for Ronald Reagan's undoing of their Jeffersonian achievements in favor of Hamiltonian ends as well as means.[563]

Historians have expressed the ambivalence at the heart of Progressive governmental theory by posing it as a

559. "Reasoning goes wrong"

Mowry, The Era of Theodore Roosevelt and The Birth of Modern America, 1900–1912, 1962, p. 43.

560. "Scientific" education

The history of American legal education involves repeated struggles between the two kinds of expertise Ross described, with lawyers characterizing law professors as mandarins and calling for a more "practical" kind of education.

561. "Cannot be self-directed"

Ekirch, Progressivism in America, 1974, pp. 224–225.

562. "Government of business"

Weinstein, The Corporate Ideal in the Liberal State, 1900–1918, 1968, p. 233.

563. Alienate citizenry

Id. at p. xiv. On Ross' prediction, see Ross, Social Control, 1969 ed., pp. 82–83.

competition between two systems of decision-making. One was based upon * * * representation and traditional ideas of grass-roots involvement in the political process; the other, growing out of the rationalization of social life made possible by scientific and technological developments, required expert analysis and worked more smoothly if decisions flowed from fewer and smaller centers outward toward the rest of society.[564]

One does not have to strain much to see how this model could be applied to the judge-jury conflict that lies at the heart of the adversary system. Be that as it may, the Progressives who favored government by experts were willing to see the growth of administrative and judicial regulation at the expense of political controls.[565]

Those who were troubled by the contradiction between expertise and democracy sought refuge in a preoccupation with method—or as lawyers would say, "procedure."[566] It also explains much of the appeal of "scientific management" to Progressive thinkers.[567] As we shall see, the Taylorites seemed to have developed a theory of democracy that did not threaten the prerogatives of the expert.[568] But in the hands of Progressives, and their contemporary descendants, procedure and method can only provide a most unsatisfactory way of pretending that political problems are reducible to problems of technique.[569]

564. "Flowed outward"

Weinstein, The Corporate Ideal in the Liberal State, 1900–1918, 1968, p. xiv.

565. Expense of political

Id. at p. 253.

566. Preoccupation with "procedure"

White, Social Thought in America: The Revolt Against Formalism, 1957 ed., pp. 194–195. To this day, many proceduralists insist that procedure is a technical matter for "managerial judges" rather than a terrain of contested values not entirely instrumental.

567. Explains appeal

"Scientific management * * * draws attention to reformers who were trying to create a program of reform without an appeal to conscience, who called for experts and elites in the name of democracy, who asked for the elevation of the college-bred to positions of influence in the interest of social harmony. * * * These reformers talked of social control, national guidance, and the end of laissez faire. * * * For this segment of progressivism, scientific management had an intrinsic appeal. It developed the notion of social control into a program of planning and placed the professional expert near the top. Its science seemed not only to rise about class interest but to bring the expert there as well." Haber, Efficiency and Uplift: Scientific Management in the Progressive Era, 1890–1920, 1973, pp. xi-xii.

568. Did not threaten

Id. at p. xi.

569. Most unsatisfactory

A good example is all of the writing about the use and abuse of forensic

The opponents of Progressive infatuation with experts saw the implications for confrontation much more clearly.[570] Indeed, one critic described the modern political problem as "much like the one confronting the early Protestants of how to do away with the intermediaries between themselves and their God."[571] This man wrote: "People must get nearer the grub pile and nearer to their Governmental agencies."[572] Another responded to Theodore Roosevelt's instrumental notion of government with this: "We would, if we had to choose, rather have bad government with democracy than good government without it."[573] His view was noninstrumental: "Democracy is a soul satisfying thing."[574] This probably comes closer to the Founders' view of confrontation than does the Progressive notion that reduces it to an instrument for producing "reliable" verdicts.[575]

The Progressive Attack on The Judiciary

In 1908, in what its semi-official historian has called "almost a replay of 1895," the Supreme Court handed down another trilogy of procapitalist opinions.[576] In Adair v. United States the Court invalidated a provision of federal law that would have outlawed anti-union "yellow dog contracts."[577] In the Employers' Liability Cases

experts that manages to discuss everything except that the issue pits corporate defendants and their scholarly allies against personal-injury lawyers and their academic adherents. See vol. 22, 5168.1 (Supp.).

570. Implications

If confrontation can be reduced to the technical problem of the "reliability" of hearsay, then the judge as the "expert" in such matters is justified in applying technical rules like the hearsay rule to decide whether or not confrontation is required.

571. "How to do away with"

Mowry, The Era of Theodore Roosevelt and the Birth of Modern America, 1900–1912, 1962, p._53 (describing position of William Kent). On how the opposition to intermediaries played into a demand for confrontation, see vol. 30, § 6343, pp. 284–288.

572. "Must get nearer"

Ibid (quoting Kent).

573. "Rather have bad"

Id. at pp. 52–53.

574. "Soul satisfying"

Id. at p. 53.

575. Founders' view

That is, the Founders preferred an adversary system as incorporated into the Sixth Amendment for reasons other than a belief that it was better at reaching "reliable" decisions than the inquisitorial system; like their rejection of monarchy in favor of a republic, instrumental arguments were dwarfed by appeals to the intrinsic merits of one over the other. See vol. 30, § 6346.

576. "Almost a replay"

Fiss, History of the Supreme Court of the United States: Troubled Beginnings of the Modern State, 1888–1910, 1993, p. 214.

577. "Yellow dog"

1908, 28 S.Ct. 277. 208 U.S. 161, 52 L.Ed. 436.

it held Congress had exceeded its authority in attempting to abolish the common-law defenses that prevented employees from recovering tort damages for work-related injuries.[578] In the Danbury Hatters Case the Court held that an employer could recover damages under the Sherman Act from a labor union that had urged a boycott of the employer's products during a labor dispute.[579] The latter case engendered controversy, not only because it stood in sharp contrast to the Court's narrow interpretations of the Sherman Act against corporations, but because the Court came dangerously close to saying that an industry-wide labor union was a per se violation of the Act.[580]

But unlike 1895, this time it was not only the Populists and Socialists who criticized the Court.[581] Reformers of all stripes chafed at judicial invalidation of social legislation; in the preceding two years more than 400 state statutes had been held unconstitutional by either state or federal courts.[582] In 1908, a federal appellate court overturned a $29 million fine levied on the Rockefeller oil interests for serial violations of the anti-rebate laws.[583] Then in 1911, in upholding Sherman Act judgments against Standard Oil and American Tobacco, the Supreme Court held that the Act only forbade "unreasonable" restraints of trade.[584] Even corporate leaders joined the attack on this decision.[585] Business leaders preferred speed, certainty, and stability over the contingencies and delay of common-law decisions, however favorable those decisions might ultimately prove to be.[586]

578. Employers' Liability Cases

Howard v. Illinois Central Rr. Co., 1908, 28 S.Ct. 141, 207 U.S. 463, 52 L.Ed. 297.

579. Danbury Hatters

Loewe v. Lawlor, 1908, 28 S.Ct. 301, 208 U.S. 274, 52 L.Ed. 488.

580. Per se violation

Hays, The Response to Industrialism, 1885–1914, 1957, p. 67.

581. Criticized Court

Fiss, History of the Supreme Court of the United States: Troubled Beginnings of the Modern State, 1888–1910, 1993, p. 215.

582. More than 400

Beth, The Development of The American Constitution, 1877–1917, 1971, p. 84.

583. Rockefeller fine

Wiebe, Businessmen and Reform: A Study of the Progressive Movement, 1962, p. 72.

584. Only "unreasonable"

Id. at p. 82.

585. Corporate leaders joined

Id. at p. 83.

586. Ultimately prove

Weinstein, The Corporate Ideal in the Liberal State, 1910–1918, 1968, p. 8 3.

As in 1895, these decisions plunged the courts back into partisan politics.[587] Radicals, not surprisingly, continued their long-held views that courts and laws were the enemy of the people.[588] But they were joined by moderate critics like the Kansas editor, William Allen White, who wrote that "the mass of federal decisions for years favored the railroads."[589] In 1912, Gustavus Myers published his "History of the Supreme Court" that purported to show class bias in the Court's decisions from the very birth of the Republic.[590] Soon even scholars at elite law schools began to point out that judicial bias aside, the constitutional guarantees that promised on paper to offer protections against an oppressive state were ignored in practice.[591] This, of course, was no news to those who had followed the Haymarket prosecutions in the previous century.[592] During an inquiry into the "Ludlow massacre" in 1914, a respected Denver judge charged that the Rockefeller interests in Colorado "owned judges on the bench as they have owned their office boys."[593] Even William Howard Taft seemed to support this, opining that in their zeal to destroy unions, mining corporations in the West had "possessed themselves of the executive and the party and seem to have gone to great lengths in reaching for the bench."[594]

We cannot understand the significance for confrontation of the Progressive attack on the courts unless we understand that the challenge facing the Supreme Court and state courts was as momentous as the slavery question 60 years earlier; namely, could Eighteenth Century constitutions provide the basis for the sort of government that Americans increasingly came to believe was neces-

587. Back into politics

See § 6357, text at notecall 530.

588. Enemy of the people

David, The History of The Haymarket Affair, 1963, p. 175.

589. "Federal decisions favored"

Chamberlain, Farewell to Reform, 1965 ed., p. 127.

590. Show class bias

Id. at p. 215.

591. Ignored in practice

Twining, Karl Llewellyn and The Realist Movement, 1973, p. 348.

592. Followed Haymarket

David, The History of the Haymarket Affair, 1963, p. 195.

593. "Owned judges"

Weinstein, The Corporate Ideal in the Liberal State, 1900–1918, 1968, p. 195.

594. "Reaching for the bench"

Mowry, The Era of Theodore Roosevelt and the Birth of Modern America, 1900–1912, 1962, p. 140.

sary for an urban, industrial nation?[595] As Roscoe Pound argued, it was not so much class bias that drove judicial decisions as the belief of judges that courts should not hinder legitimate business and their faith that technological progress required monopoly power in bureaucratically-organized corporations.[596] This was coupled with the laissez-faire values of William Graham Sumner in which property was the ultimate human right, linked as it was to freedom of contract and guaranteed by the Fourteenth and Fifth Amendments against government interference.[597] President Taft, for example, thought that property was a "preferred freedom" and dismissed the protections for those accused of crime as "mere fetish."[598] This triumph of laissez-faire constitutionalism in the 1890s embodied what came to be known as "substantive due process" and was valued much more highly than "procedural due process" of the sort that underlay rights like confrontation.[599] These constitutional values put courts on a collision course with the political demands of an increasing part of the populace.[600] Judges were slow to grasp this because like most lawyers they were so steeped in the corporate values of their youth that they could not see the extent to which even business leaders were beginning to demand a regulatory, welfare state.[601] Moreover, many judges socialized with capitalists who shared their views and who they saw as their "constituency" in the political struggles over which they presided.[602] Conservatives of this stripe had long sought to substitute the judiciary for the monarchy and the established church that they supposed provided stability in the English government.[603] To this branch of the elite,

595. Industrial nation

Wood, Constitutional Politics in the Progressive Era, 1968, p. ix.

596. Progress required monopoly

Ekirch, Progressivism in America, 1974, p. 139.

597. Ultimate human right

Chamberlain, Farewell to Reform, 1965 ed., p . 11. One can see the degree to which other rights depended on property by noting the "castle" metaphor in Fourth Amendment jurisprudence and the difficulty courts had in finding a right of privacy in a telephone booth one did not own.

598. "Mere fetish"

Mason, William Howard Taft: Chief Justice, 1965, p. 48.

599. "Substantive due process"

Wood, Constitutional Politics in the Progressive Era, 1974, p. 112.

600. Collision course

Id. at p. 113.

601. Values of youth

Weinstein, The Corporate Ideal in the Liberal State, 1900–1918, 1968, p. 55.

602. "Constituency"

Mason, William Howard Taft: Chief Justice, 1965, p. 103.

603. For monarchy and church

Mowry, The Era of Theodore Roosevelt and The Birth of Modern America, 1900–1912, 1962, p. 43.

courts were "the conservator of our institutions"——"the sheet anchor of the Republic" to which citizens could turn for justice "in times of hysteria."[604] Conservatives were horrified by Progressive proposals for recall of judges and constitutional decisions.[605] The Republican party platform in 1908 pledged to uphold "the authority and integrity of the courts."[606]

That plank in the platform was overshadowed by the increasingly radical rhetoric of the man who was still titular head of a Republican administration. In a special message to Congress earlier in 1908, Theodore Roosevelt had written:

> property has its duties no less than its rights. When the courts guarantee to the employer, as they should, the rights of the employer, and to property the rights of property, they should no less emphatically make it evident that they will exact from property and from the employer the duties which should necessarily accompany these rights; and hitherto our laws have failed in precisely this point of enforcing the performance of duty by the man of property toward the man who works for him * * *.[607]

As an example, the message cited "the abuse of injunctions in labor cases."

> The fact that the punishment for the violation of an injunction must, to make the order effective, necessarily be summary and without the intervention of a jury makes its issuance in doubtful cases a dangerous practice, and in itself furnishes a reason why the process should be surrounded with safeguards to protect individuals against being enjoined from exercising their proper rights.[608]

Though the message, Roosevelt's most radical as President, mentioned "the representatives of predatory wealth" and described his program as a "campaign against privilege,"[609] it did not go as far as some of the President's allies who said that "under the guise of an independent judiciary we have in reality an independent legislature,

604. "Times of hysteria"

Ibid.

605. Horrified by recall

Cadenhead, Theodore Roosevelt: The Paradox of Progressivism, 1974, p. 204.

606. "Integrity of courts"

Id. at p. 168.

607. "Laws have failed"

Id. at p. 325.

608. "Surrounded with safeguards"

Id. at p. 323.

609. "Against privilege"

Id. at pp. 325, 327.

or rather an independent legislature and judicial body combined."[610]

However, just two years later Roosevelt began espousing the view that courts, particularly federal courts, were obstacles to social justice.[611] In his famous speech at Osawatomie, Kansas, embracing Croly's "New Nationalism," Roosevelt told his audience:

> every special interest is entitled to justice, but not one is entitled to a vote in Congress, to a voice on the bench, or to representation in any public office. The Constitution guarantees protection to property, and we must make that promise good. But it does not give the right of suffrage to any corporation.[612]

Later the descendants of the Populists heard the ex-President say:

> I have equally small use for the man, be he a judge on the bench, or editor of a great paper, or wealthy and influential private citizen, who can see clearly enough and denounce the lawlessness of mob-violence, but whose eyes are so closed so that he is blind when the question is one of corruption in business on a gigantic scale.[613]

Though he did not mention any names, the audience could probably fill in the blanks. In his peroration he described the essence of "this New Nationalism":

> It demands of the judiciary that it shall be primarily interested in human welfare rather than in property, just as it demands that the representative body shall represent all the people rather than any one class or section of the people.[614]

Roosevelt endorsed the recall of judicial decisions and other measures that would make courts subservient to the popular branches of government.[615] By 1912 he even went so far as to attack the

610. "Judicial body combined"

Chamberlain, Farewell to Reform, 1965, ed., p. 214.

611. Obstacles to justice

Mowry, The Era of Theodore Roosevelt and The Birth of Modern America, 1900–1912, 1962, p. 271.

612. "Voice on bench"

Cadenhead, Theodore Roosevelt: The Paradox of Progressivism, 1974, p. 334.

613. "Gigantic scale"

Id. at p. 339.

614. "Rather than property"

Id. at p. 340.

615. Make courts subservient

Mowry, The Era of Theodore Roosevelt and The Birth of Modern America, 1900–1912, 1962, p. 272; Chamberlain, Farewell to Reform, 1965 ed., p. 214.

Supreme Court's decisions in the E.C. Knight and Lochner cases for creating a legal "no-man's land" where neither state nor federal governments could restrain the predatory activities of large corporations.[616]

Little wonder then that Justice Brandeis could say of judicial review of the constitutionality of legislation that "the popular protest against its exercise has never been so vehement, nor has it secured the support of so many political writers and thinkers, as in the last decade."[617] The Progressive attack on the judiciary generated reform proposals that fell into two broad categories.[618] The first was some form of electoral supervision of the judiciary; this included proposals for election of judges or for recall of appointed judges or of specific decisions of courts.[619] The second category included various proposals to modify the power of courts to declare legislation unconstitutional; e.g., to require a vote of two-thirds of the justices to strike down statutes.[620] In this category fell various proposals for "jurisdiction stripping" of the sort employed by the Radical Republicans during Reconstruction that would deny the Supreme Court the power to invalidate legislation, either particular bills or of all federal legislation.[621] The 1924 Progressive party platform would have amended the Constitution to provide that Congress could validate any legislation held unconstitutional by simply passing it a second time.[622] However, except for limits on the power of the federal courts to issue labor injunctions, most of the Progressive proposals got no farther than the proposal of one Progressive Senator to abolish all federal courts except the Su-

616. Attacked decisions

Cadenhead, Theodore Roosevelt: The Paradox of Progressivism, 1974, p. 195.

617. "Never so vehement"

Wood, Constitutional Politics in The Progressive Era, 1968, p. 303.

618. Two categories

Mowry, The Progressive Era, 1900–1920, The Reform Persuasion, 1958, p. 27.

619. Electoral supervision

Wiebe, Businessmen and Reform: A Study of the Progressive Movement, 1962, p. 7.

620. Two-thirds vote

Chamberlain, Farewell to Reform, 1965 ed., p. 321.

621. "Jurisdiction stripping"

Wood, Constitutional Politics in the Progressive Era, 1968, pp. 189–190.

622. Passing second time

Mason, William Howard Taft: Chief Justice, 1965, p. 92.

preme Court.[623]

However, this does not mean that the Progressive attacks had no effect on the course of confrontation jurisprudence, only that the effects were indirect and a long time in coming.[624] For example, with the conservatives apparently well-entrenched in the judiciary and immune from direct attack, reformers sought to construct competing power centers in administrative tribunals whose authority flowed from expertise and efficiency.[625] One feature of such tribunals was their statutory exemption from common-law rules of evidence, specifically the hearsay rule.[626] So long as administrative tribunals loomed as potential rivals to courts, those who wanted to reform evidentiary rules in judicial tribunals could exploit the rivalry by arguing that in order to compete with this "modern" form of adjudication, courts would have to abandon obsolete practices, such as confrontation and the hearsay rule.[627] We shall see later how this strategy backfired when employment of inquisitorial practices by administrative tribunals awakened courts and citizens to the virtues of an adversary system and confrontation.[628] Whether this awakening came too late has yet to be determined.

At a deeper jurisprudential level, the Progressive attack on the judiciary seems to have had one significant outcome. One student of the period has argued that the Progressives were attempting to override the class-based, antidemocratic Constitution described by Beard and others by appealing to the values of the Declaration of Independence.[629] A good example is Justice Walter Clark of the North Carolina Supreme Court who in the late Nineteenth Century became known as "the jurist of the Populists" for his radical views

623. Abolish federal courts

Id. at p . 95. The limitation on the power to issue labor injunctions did not come until the New Deal era. Mowry, The Progressive Era, 1900–1920: The Reform Persuasion, 1958, p. 27.

624. Long time

It is, of course, difficult to disentangle the effects of the attacks on courts with the effects of the Progressive alteration of legal thinking, but in our view, the latter probably were more influential than the former.

625. Competing power centers

Ekirch, Progressivism in America, 1974, p. 116.

626. Exemption from rules

2 McCormick, Evidence, Strong ed., 1992, § 352.

627. Courts abandon

1 Wigmore, Evidence, Tillers rev. 1983, § 4b.

628. Backfired

See § 6360.

629. Appeal to Declaration

Chamberlain, Farewell to Reform, 1965 ed., p. 213.

of the law.[630] A friend of all the leading Progressive politicians, in 1906 Clark gave a speech at the University of Pennsylvania, denouncing "government by judges."[631] In it he appealed to the Declaration of Independence against the Constitution, which he argued had been promulgated by the wealthy to protect their property rights over human rights.[632] As we have seen, in its appeal to the "self-evident" truths of natural law, the Declaration supported some of the same values as the Confrontation Clause.[633]

The Progressive Party platform seemed to embrace Clark's appeal to natural law, as did a number of leading Progressive intellectuals.[634] But as we have seen, capitalists seeking to be free of regulation had also appealed to the Declaration of Independence.[635] Indeed, one could hardly find a clearer statement of the natural law than the statement of a business leader just three years after Clark.

> Historically and morally the citizen and his property existed before this government and he created this government to protect himself and that which was his. He does not derive his title to his possessions from his government. His rights existed before he formed a government. The Constitution recognizes but does not create his rights.[636]

As Justice McKenna had shown, one could embrace the natural law of the corporate libertarians and still be a supporter of the rights of the accused.[637] But the variety of interests that natural law could be

630. "Jurist of Populists"

Wood, Constitutional Politics in the Progressive Era, 1968, p. 42.

631. "Government by judges"

Ibid.

632. Promulgated by wealthy

Brooks, Walter Clark, Fighting Judge, 1944, p. 195.

633. Supported same values

See vol. 30, § 6345, p. 559.

634. Embrace Clark's appeal

"We hold with Thomas Jefferson and Abraham Lincoln that the people are the masters of their Constitution, to fulfill its purposes and to safeguard it from those who, by perversion of its intent, would convert it into an instrument of injustice. In accordance with the needs of each generation the people must use their sovereign powers to establish and maintain equal opportunity and industrial justice, to secure which this Government was founded and without which no republic can endure." Cadenhead, Theodore Roosevelt: The Paradox of Progressivism, 1974, pp. 343–344. See also, White, Social Thought in America: The Revolt Against Formalism, 1957 ed., p. 278 (Walter Lippman's natural law).

635. Capitalists also appealed

See § 6356, text at notecall 445.

636. "Does not create"

Wiebe, Businessmen and Reform: A Study of The Progressive Movement, 1962, p. 203.

637. McKenna had shown

Lukas, Big Trouble, 1997, p. 286.

deployed to defend seemed to support Holmes' critique.

> The jurists who believe in natural law seem to me to be in that
> naive state of mind that accepts what has been familiar and
> accepted by them and their neighbors as something that must be
> accepted by all men everywhere.[638]

Locke had offered a similar criticism.[639] Given the growth of the
moral relativism that some scientists derived from Darwin, it is not
surprising that appeals to natural law and the Declaration of
Independence were eclipsed for the rest of the century in favor of
the Progressive values of efficiency and expertise.

The Shaking of Middle–Class Confidence

As the nation neared the end of the first decade of the 20th
Century the capitalist campaign against trade unions looked promising. Federal courts became much bolder in issuing injunctions
against strikes, even forbidding anyone from informing the public
that a strike was in progress; under such an injunction, the
publisher of a labor journal was jailed for contempt for simply
publishing an account of a strike.[640] When unionists defied injunctions, the use of military force to put down strikes became more
oppressive, particularly in the Western states; unionists were held
without judicial intervention or tried by drumhead courts, and local
editors who expressed any sympathy with the strikers were jailed
with them.[641] When the legality of such measures was questioned,
the Idaho Attorney General replied that "[a]bsurd technicalities
will not be allowed to stand in the path of justice."[642]

On another front federal and state courts continued to strike
down legislation aimed at regulating the struggle between capital
and labor.[643] For example, when Colorado passed an eight-hour law,
the state supreme court held it unconstitutional; when 72% of the
voters passed a constitutional amendment authorizing such legislation, the first statute passed pursuant to this provision was de-

---

638. "Must be accepted"

White, Social Thought in America: The
Revolt Against Formalism, 1957 ed., p.
277.

639. Similar criticism

Id. at p . 279.

640. Publishing account

Mowry, The Progressive Era, 1900–
1920: The Reform Persuasion, 1958,
p. 27.

641. Jailed with them

Lukas, Big Trouble, 1997, p. 147.

642. "Absurd technicalities"

Ibid.

643. Strike down legislation

Mowry, The Progressive Era, 1900–
1920: The Reform Persuasion, 1958,
p. 20.

clared unconstitutional on federal grounds.[644] On the federal level, despite increasing public demand, Congress refused to enact any limitations on the powers of the federal judges to intervene in labor-management disputes.[645] President Roosevelt, who threatened labor leaders with criminal prosecution, never allowed his Justice Department to indict a single corporate officer for lawbreaking.[646] And on the cultural front, best-selling novelists demonized the Populists and lionized Hamiltonian corporate aristocrats.[647]

Even if the increasing harshness of the anti-union measures failed to alert the public to the coming crisis, there remained the question: if every effort of workers to improve their position was stifled by force or held unconstitutional or illegal, where could desperate people turn for relief?[648] There were signs that the public was becoming dissatisfied with repression as the solution; for example, when a small-town editor was indicted for defaming a corporation by publishing union accounts of its misdeeds, the jury refused to convict.[649] Roosevelt, having once been duped into doing so, became increasingly reluctant to allow the military to be used as strike-breakers.[650]

Nor was all quiet on the ideological front. Charles Beard's popular histories documented the anti-union role of courts and how corporate attorneys had come to dominate the Supreme Court and write laissez faire into constitutional amendments designed to aid the newly freed slaves.[651] Moreover, the Populist bogeyman faded as the public became aware that the election of 1896 had been a struggle between large corporations and shopkeepers and farmers.[652] There was a growing fear that it was Big Business that was

644. Colorado story

Lukas, Big Trouble, 1997, p. 219.

645. Congress refused

Wiebe, Businessmen and Reform: A Study of the Progressive Movement, 1962, p. 171.

646. Never indicted

Mowry, Theodore Roosevelt and The Birth of Modern America, 1900–1912, 1962, p. 102.

647. Lionized aristocrats

Chamberlain, Farewell to Reform, 1965 ed., p. 149.

648. Where for relief

The choices seemed to be between violence and politics. Ekirch, Progressivism in America, 1974, p. 121.

649. Refused to convict

Adams, Age of Industrial Violence, 1910–1915, pp. 137–138.

650. Roosevelt reluctant

Mowry, The Progressive Era, 1900–1920, p. 27.

651. Beard's influence

White, Social Thought In America: The Revolt Against Formalism, 1957 ed., p. 36.

652. Shopkeepers and farmers

Chamberlain, Farewell to Reform, 1965

begetting Big Labor so that the increasingly self-conscious middle class came to see itself as caught in the middle of these contending forces rather than the ally of either.[653] Finally, the settlement-house movement brought middle-class women into close contact with workers and made them more sympathetic—particularly ominous when women were pressing for the right to vote.[654]

In 1910, when the passage of Halley's Comet convinced many that the end of the world was at hand, the anxious middle class had more mundane reasons for such fears.[655] First, a strike at Bethlehem Steel reprised the Homestead Strike, with a booted constabulary provoking violence and death.[656] Then New York garment workers struck, answering a call by the conservative unionist Samuel Gompers for "industrial revolution."[657] The following year, the New York Court of Appeals held that state's worker's compensation scheme unconstitutional and a violent strike broke out on the Illinois Central Railroad—in some states erupting into open warfare that had to be put down by the National Guard.[658] If the events of 1911 had starkly posed the question of alternatives for labor, an event in 1910 provided one answer.

On October 1, 1910, at 1:00 a.m., a bomb exploded in the Los Angeles Times building, setting off a fire in which 20 people lost their lives.[659] Proclaimed the first "Crime of the Century" by the virulently anti-union owner of the paper, Harrison Gray Otis, the bombing offered Otis and the Merchants and Manufacturers Association an opportunity to mount a political trial to discredit labor unions and their Socialist allies who had become a serious electoral threat to the local business elite.[660] As unionists noted at the time,

ed., p. 4.

653. Caught in the middle

Id. at p. 119; Haber, Efficiency and Uplift: Scientific Management in the Progressive Era, 1890–1920, 1973, p. 138.

654. Pressing for vote

Id. at p. 134 (increasing sympathy); Mowry, The Progressive Era, 1900–1920: The Reform Persuasion, 1958, pp. 7–8 (pressing for vote).

655. Halley's Comet

Encyclopedia of American Facts and Dates, 9th ed. 1993, p. 415.

656. Bethlehem Strike

Adams, Age of Industrial Violence, 1910–1915, 1966, p. 189.

657. "Industrial revolution"

Id. at p. 101.

658. Illinois Central

Id. at pp. 130, 133; Weinstein, The Corporate Ideal in the Liberal State, 1900–1918, 1968, p. 55 (act held unconstitutional).

659. Times bombing

Adams, Age of Industrial Violence, 1910–1915, 1966, p. 1.

660. Political trial

Id. at p. 7.

the Los Angeles authorities seemed to follow the script used in the Stuenenberg assassination case a few years earlier——lavish rewards for informers, questionable extradition of suspects from other states, and planting of spies in the defense camp to report confidential communications to prosecutors compromised by relationships with local business interests.[661] However, the Los Angeles performance was cut short when Clarence Darrow, about to be indicted for jury tampering and bribery, advised two unionists to plead guilty——pleas that effectively killed the labor movement in Los Angeles for many years.[662]

The events of 1910–1911 had consequences for confrontation both immediate and remote. The Los Angeles Times ran a series of editorials urging a revival of vigilantism——a "plain citizen's combine" for "the suppression of sedition and anarchy in the persons of the professional agitator," "a brigade * * * armed with pick handles that would drive the lawless union laborites, closed-shop murderous vermin into the sea."[663] In case anyone missed the implicit claim that the ordinary processes of the criminal law were inadequate, the Times later threatened that if those processes failed "the carcasses of some of the labor leaders who instigated disorder and dynamiting and murder might possibly be seen dangling from telegraph poles."[664] As if to underline the supposed inadequacies of the ordinary processes of the law, a Mississippi jury refused to convict the killers of three black strikebreakers brought in by the railroad during the Illinois Central strike.[665] One might also see the bold defiance of confrontation values during the Stuenenberg and Times bombing cases as evidence that the Sixth Amend-

661. Stuenenberg script

Id. at pp. 11–12, 15. The story of the Stuenenberg assassination is told with numerous digressions into the sociopolitical culture of the time in Lukas, Big Trouble, 1997. The story of the Los Angeles bombing and trial may be found in any of the biographies of Darrow, most recently Cowan, The People v. Clarence Darrow, 1993.

662. Killed labor movement

Adams, Age of Industrial Violence, 1910–1915, 1966, p. 117. The bombing had effects on the newspaper that were still operating 50 years later when the junior author came to Los Angeles. The Times was still in a re-

built facility in downtown Los Angeles that resembled a medieval fortress and the mentality within was equally antiquated. The masthead proclaimed "True Industrial Freedom" and the front page each day was graced by a crude anti-union cartoon that was the source of much jocularity outside the Times.

663. "Vermin into the sea"

Id. at p. 22.

664. "Dangling from poles"

Id. at pp. 22–23.

665. Killers of strikebreakers

Id. at p. 134.

ment was an obstacle to putting down an incipient revolution.[666] For concerned lawyers, then, these events may have given urgency to Pound's off-the-cuff criticisms of traditional criminal procedure in his St. Paul address to the American Bar Association.

Whether they saw the need to change traditional criminal procedure, ordinary citizens could certainly see the need for some alternative to the cycle of violence and repression that had characterized the previous 20 years of labor-management relations.[667] In December, 1911, Survey magazine solicited comments from middle-class and elite figures, many of whom expressed the view that the country was on the brink of civil war.[668] Older readers may have recalled the cynical statement of Republican leader during the Populist crisis that "you know you can hire half of the people of the United States to shoot down the other half if necessary, and we've got the money to hire them."[669] The Progressive response to such fears, typically, came in the form of a committee of experts to study the issues——the United States Commission on Industrial Relations.[670]

The sweeping injunction entered in the Illinois Central strike once again brought "government by injunction" into question.[671] As we have seen, by denying unionists a jury trial on charges of wrongdoing, the labor injunction was a direct assault on Sixth

666. Sixth an obstacle

Among such violations were the privatizing of the prosecution function by allowing corporate lawyers to take over from public prosecutors (thus blurring the separation of functions between accuser and prosecutor), the attempts to extradite in such a fashion that the accused would be denied counsel and an adversary hearing on the validity of the extradition, and ex parte meetings between judges and prosecutors to plan the convictions of the accused. Id. at pp. 11–12, 15; Lukas, Big Trouble, 1997, pp. 147, 149.

667. Previous 20 years

Adams, Age of Industrial Violence, 1910–1915, 1966, p. 1.

668. Brink of civil war

A labor lawyer: "The American people must awake to the fact that a bitter, merciless war divides society * * *. It is a war with all war's fury, with all its injustice, with all its crime breeding hatreds."

An efficiency expert: "Out of this situation has arisen a type of leader who thrives through the existence of acute warfare * * *. This is true in the armies of both antagonists."

A popular author: "The vital and arresting point in this affair is its disclosure of a state of internecine war in our civilization." Id. at p. 27.

669. "We've got the money"

O'Neill, The Progressive Years, 1975, p. 8.

670. Industrial Relations

Adams, Age of Industrial Violence, 1910–1915, 1966, p. 113.

671. Sweeping injunction

Id. at p. 136.

Amendment values and the unions had fought it on that ground from the start.[672] The 1908 Democratic platform had a pledge to reform this procedure.[673] Now the National Civic Federation became somewhat more receptive to the complaints of its union members and the lack of "confidence on the part of the rank and file of organized labor in our laws and courts"; "our workmen" August Belmont conceded were "imbued with the idea that our courts are used by employers for partisan purposes."[674] But the majority of the business members flatly denied that there was any "discrimination or inequality, either in the law or its administration as to labor combinations" and they denounced any limitation on labor injunctions as "class politics."[675] Even when the Commission on Industrial Relations documented the anti-labor bias of the federal judiciary, capitalists remained in denial.[676] When the Democrats came to power in 1912, again with an anti-injunction plan in the platform, the National Association of Manufacturers succeeded in blocking legislation to redeem the promise of the platform.[677]

However, the inability to agree on labor injunctions led the National Civic Federation to support worker's compensation laws in an effort to demonstrate their fairness toward legitimate union aspirations.[678] This effort took on added urgency after the Triangle Shirtwaist fire in 1911 in which 146 people, most of them young women, were killed in a sweatshop in which the fire exits had been blocked by the employer to prevent employees from taking unauthorized breaks.[679] The United States had long lagged behind other

672. Fought from start

Ekirch, Progressivism in America, 1974, p. 119. See also, § 6357, text at note-call 447.

673. Democratic pledge

Wiebe, Businessmen and Reform: A Study of the Progressive Movement, 1962, p. 172.

674. "Partisan purposes"

Weinstein, The Corporate Ideal in the Liberal State, 1900–1918, 1968, p. 28.

675. "Class politics"

Id. at p. 49. In a rhetorical move similar to the one used by those opposed to laws barring discrimination on the ground of gender or sexual orientation, capitalists argued that removing the legal disabilities that hampered the labor movement would grant

workers "special immunities and privileges before the law not enjoyed by other combinations or other classes of people." Id. at pp. 28–29.

676. Documented bias

Id. at p. 211.

677. N.A.M. succeeded

Wiebe, Businessmen and Reform: A Study of the Progressive Movement, 1962, p.173.

678. N.C.F. to support

Weinstein, The Corporate Ideal in the Liberal State, 1900–1918, 1968, p. 48.

679. Triangle Shirtwaist fire

Encyclopedia of American Facts and Dates, 9th ed.1993, p. 416. The owners were indicted for violating fire-

nations in legal protection of workers.[680] The estimates of the death toll in American industry in the years 1888–1908 reached as high as 35,000 per year and over a half-million more workers were injured; at the U.S. Steel plant in South Chicago in 1906 alone, 46 men lost their lives and 598 suffered serious injury.[681] Workers were not, of course, the only persons at risk from industry; according to the Interstate Commerce Commission in 1912 there had been more than 180,000 casualties on American railroads, including more than 10,000 deaths.[682] Hence, middle-class Americans were more receptive to efforts to end this industrial slaughter or to ameliorate its impact.

However, the public was understandably confused when business leaders came out in favor of a workers' compensation system and union leaders opposed it.[683] Business leaders, however, favored such a system because they thought it would undercut the support for unions by eliminating one of the least defensible features of the common law of master and servant.[684] Union leaders opposed the system because it would be administered by government agencies they believed would be controlled by employers.[685] In 1911 when the National Association of Manufacturers promulgated a model act, no state had an operating system of workers compensation but by 1920 every state except six in the Deep South had a system in

safety laws but acquitted. Employers were remarkably successful in avoiding criminal liability for industrial accidents because local officials were deferential to corporate lawyers. In Colorado, lawyers for mining companies were allowed to assist in the selection of coroner's juries. Not surprisingly, in 90 fatal mine accidents in one county, employers were found responsible only in one. Adams, Age of Industrial Violence, 1910–1915, 1966, p. 151.

680.　U.S. lagged behind

Ekirch, Progressivism in America, 1974, p. 88.

681.　Death toll

Weinstein, The Corporate Ideal in the Liberal State, 1900–1918, 1968, pp. 40–41. In 1903, when over 11,000 workers were injured on American railroads, there were only 172 such injuries in Austria, a striking differ-ence even when allowance is made for the differing sizes of the two railroad systems.

682.　More than 10,000 deaths

Adams, The Age of Industrial Violence, 1910–1915, 1966, p. 140.

683.　Union leaders opposed

Ekirch, Progressivism in America, 1974, p. 87; Weinstein, The Corporate Ideal in the Liberal State, 1900–1918, 1968, p. 44.

684.　Undercut support

Id. at p. 47. They also hoped it would reduce the contact between union members and personal injury lawyers and local political leaders, who workers might otherwise turn to and who might turn workers toward politics.

685.　Controlled by employers

Id. at pp. 43–44.

place.[686] The reason the N.A.M. model proved so attractive—25 states adopted it in the first three years—was that it was permissive and had relatively low payments to injured workers.[687]

The adoption of worker's compensation affected the right of confrontation in several ways. First, one of the justifications for worker's compensation was the inadequacy of the common law of torts; to the extent that confrontation could be seen as a product of the common law, the case for workers' compensation tended to undermine support for confrontation. Second, in most states disputes over compensation were remitted to an administrative tribunal that was touted as more inquisitorial than adversary—lawyers were discouraged from appearing by limiting fees. Finally, worker's compensation tribunals were typically freed from common-law rules of evidence; hence, many people became accustomed to seeing rights adjudicated on the basis of hearsay without confrontation and cross-examination.

One of the reasons employers supported worker's compensation was their belief that this would make workers less likely to return to politics, which many had abandoned after the frenzy and disappointment of 1896.[688] Since politics seems an attractive alternative to violence as a response to legal repression, this seems puzzling to those to whom it has now become unthinkable that workers might organize a class-based party on the European model.[689] However, this was not unthinkable in the early 1900s when the Republican party was still only fifty years old and the Socialists were making rapid gains, particularly in local elections.[690] Henry George and the Populists had made socialist ideas respectable in some parts of the country; in 1908 Eugene Debs got nearly a million votes in his campaign for President.[691] By 1911 even sober businessmen were concerned about the rapid growth of the Socialist Party and newspaper articles about "The Rising Tide of Social-

---

686. Had system in place

Id. at p. 611.

687. Low payments

Weibe, Businessmen and Reform: A Study of the Progressive Movement, 1962, pp. 197–198.

688. Return to politics

Weinstein, The Corporate Ideal in the Liberal State, 1900–1918, 1968, p. 47.

689. Class-based party

Id. at p. 23.

690. Socialist gains

Id. at p. 113.

691. Nearly million votes

O'Neil, The Progressive Years, 1975, p. 65; Chamberlain, Farewell to Reform 1965 ed., p. 114.

ism" became popular.[692] Moreover, despite attacks from the business press for its opposition to war, Socialists continued to gain electoral strength.[693]

In retrospect, the fear of the Socialists seems overdrawn; at the height of its success the party never received more than 10% of the vote.[694] However, it was plausible to suppose that in close elections the Socialists might hold the balance of power between the two parties and use that power to gain acceptance of some of its goals——a possibility that became more vivid when Roosevelt split the Republican party in 1912. At the very least, the rising of the Socialists made labor leaders less deferential to business leaders.[695] Worse yet, some influential figures who probably never voted Socialist were enamored of Socialist ideas, particularly after the Russian Revolution; for example, one of the gurus of Scientific Management praised the Russian Soviets as "an attempt to make the business and industrial system serve the community as a whole, and in doing so to take over the function of and entirely supplant the political system."[696] (This sort of statism also led many socialists to flirt with Taylorite ideas.)[697] Be that as it may, the Socialist Party never mounted the challenge that some hoped and many feared.[698] Popular hostility to radicals remained strong.[699] When the

692. "Rising Tide"

Weinstein, The Corporate Ideal in the Liberal State, 1900–1918, 1968, p. 120 (documenting Party gains, including electing a member of Congress); Mowry, The Era of Theodore Roosevelt and The Birth of Modern America, 1900–1912, 1962, p.66 (at time when statewide votes were still negligible, Party came to power in 18 cities and was narrowly defeated in a dozen more).

693. Continued to gain

Weinstein, The Corporate Ideal in the Liberal State, 1900–1918, 1968, pp. 137, 236.

694. Never more than 10%

Mowry, The Progressive Era, 1900–1920: The Reform Persuasion, 1958, p. 22.

695. Less deferential

Weinstein, The Corporate Ideal in the Liberal State, 1900–1918, 1968, p. 120.

696. "Supplant political"

Haber, Efficiency and Uplift: Scientific Management in the Progressive Era, 1890–1920, p. 47. Enthusiasm for and ignorance of foreign revolutions seems to have been one constant of American life.

697. Socialists flirt

Id. at p. 150.

698. Many feared

Theodore Roosevelt, with his usual understatement, proclaimed that "the growth of the socialist party in this country was far more ominous than any populist or similar movement in our past." Ekirch, Progressivism in America, 1974, p. 48.

699. Hostility strong

Id. at p. 131.

Wilson administration responded with a combination of repression and reform, the Party fell into internecine warfare and decline.[700]

Trust, Distrust, and Dowdell

Inasmuch as the rise of confrontation was linked to opposition to "monopoly", attention to the "trust" question can shed light on the subtle ideological changes in the Progressive era that undermined confrontation.[701] Though the question of monopoly as epitomized by the railroads had been around since the Civil War, permissive incorporation laws in states like New Jersey and Delaware had increased combination beyond those that had motivated the passage of the Sherman Act.[702] Six railroads now controlled 95% of the nation's trackage, each of them associated with great family fortunes.[703] By 1904, the top 4% of American corporations produced 57% of total industrial output.[704] Depression and mechanization were producing increasing concentration in holdings of agricultural land, producing tenantry and even a rural proletariat.[705]

Public response to monopoly was still sectional. In the South it was associated with colonization of Eastern capital following the Civil War, while in the West resentment at the abuses of the railroads lingered—capitalists were lumped together in public perception as "railrogues."[706] Railroads paved the way for the corruption of state and local politics that came to be associated with all large business enterprises, particularly after the publication of novels attacking this corruption.[707] Hence, during the Progressive era, the "trust question" seemed to be at the root of all social

---

700. Wilson responded

Weinstein, The Corporate Ideal in the Liberal State, 1900–1918, 1968, p. 236.

701. Linked to monopoly

See vol. 30, § 6343, p. 287.

702. Permissive laws

Chamberlain, Farewell to Reform, 1965 ed., p. 121.

703. Associated with fortunes

Id. at pp. 122–123; Adams, Age of Industrial Violence, 1910–1915, 1966, p. 128.

704. Produced 57%

Weinstein, The Corporate Ideal in the Liberal State, 1900–1918, 1968, p. 63.

705. Rural proletariat

Adams, Age of Industrial Violence, 1910–1915, 1966, p. 198.

706. "Railrogues"

Lukas, Big Trouble, 1997, pp. 19, 41.

707. Novels attacking

Chamberlain, Farewell to Reform, 1965 ed., pp. 4, 152.

problems because it symbolized the plight of the nation—"too much private economic power in too few hands."[708]

Monopoly had its defenders in the Progressive era; indeed, some of the same arguments for industrial concentration were made then as now—albeit with a Darwinian twist.[709] For example, the author of the permissive New Jersey statute that gave rise to trusts argued that trusts were an inevitable product of the workings of the market that law was powerless to prevent.[710] Most economists believed that economic concentration was good because it was more efficient, lowered prices, and made American goods more competitive.[711] One business publicist tried to cover monopoly with a conceptual fig leaf, calling price-fixing agreements and other anticompetitive devices "The New Competition."[712] Concentration was equated with progress; a leading economist wrote that "[f]ew, if any, of us, would like to see a return to the era of the small shopkeeper and industrialists."[713] In a telling remark, the Progressive guru Herbert Croly attacked Woodrow Wilson's antitrust policy as a "revival of Jeffersonian individualism."[714]

Contrary to the opinions of the economists, most Progressives did want to "return to the era of the small shopkeeper"; they were, in the denigrating phrase of the time "economic fundamentalists."[715] Much of the electoral support (as distinguished from punditry) of the Progressives came from states that had been hotbeds of Populism.[716] These Progressives were

708. "Too few hands"

Adams, Age of Industrial Violence, 1910–1915, 1966, p. 175; Weibe, Businessmen and Reform: A Study of The Progressive Movement, 1962, p. 43.

709. Darwinian twist

Russett, Darwin in America: The Intellectual Response, 1865–1912, 1976, p. 147.

710. Law powerless

Chamberlain, Farewell to Reform, 1965 ed., p. 41.

711. More competitive

Mowry, The Era of Theodore Roosevelt and The Birth of Modern America, 1900–1912, 1962, p. 53.

712. "New Competition"

Weibe, Businessmen and Reform: A Study of the Progressive Movement, 1962, p. 41.

713. "Small shopkeeper"

Mowry, The Era of Theodore Roosevelt and the Birth of Modern America, 1900–1912, 1962, p. 53.

714. "Revival of individualism"

Ekirch, Progressivism in America, 1974, p. 128.

715. "Fundamentalists"

In this they had imbibed much of the rhetoric, as distinguished from the practices, of the capitalists. Chamberlain, Farewell to Reform, 1965 ed., p. 203.

716. Hotbeds of Populism

Mowry, The Era of Theodore Roosevelt and the Birth of Modern America, 1900–1912, 1962, p. 54.

on the side of individualism as against socialism, and democracy as against plutocracy; and on the side of collectivism when necessary to curb monopoly or unfair competition as they conceived it; but not for the type of collectivism implied in [Marxism].[717]

Progressivism grew out of state and local politics in states where corruption of the political process by railroads was common and the only way to political power was to revolt against the railroad domination of government.[718] A good example is Albert Cummins, a former railroad lawyer offended by the state Republican party's pandering to corporations who ran for governor on an anti-monopoly, anti-railroad platform, and parlayed his defeat of the railroads into a Senate seat.[719] This is not to say that this brand of Progressivism was purely a matter of the heart; it could point to studies showing that concentrated industries were not more efficient—indeed, they were not even more profitable than smaller businesses.[720]

Progressive rhetoric mirrored that of the Leveller popularizers of confrontation. Woodrow Wilson adopted this rhetoric when he said:

> We must abolish everything that bears even the semblance of privilege or of any kind of artificial advantage, and put our businessmen and producers under the stimulation of a constant necessity to be efficient, economical, and enterprising, masters of competitive supremacy, better workers and merchants than any in the world.[721]

To grasp the Progressive deconstruction of the myth of laissez faire, we can turn to Robert La Follette's definition of "Special Privilege"; he argued that corporate capitalism was a creature of, rather than a natural antagonist of, government—pointing to everything from state laws that created corporations to tax subsidies and gifts

---

717. "Not for collectivism"

Chamberlain, Farewell to Reform, 1965 ed., p. 203.

718. Revolt against railroad corruption

Id. at p. 4; Hays, The Response to Industrialism, 1885–1914, 1957, p. 131.

719. Cummins example

Ekirch, Progressivism in America, 1974, p. 111.

720. Not more profitable

O'Neill, The Progressive Years, 1975, p. 34.

721. "Necessity to be efficient"

Ekirch, Progressivism in America, 1974, p. 225.

of the public domain that sustained them, and tariffs, patents, and exclusive franchises that protected them from competition.[722]

The anti-monopoly Progressives wanted to return big corporations to the Darwinian jungle from which they claimed to have emerged by breaking them up into competing firms.[723] Noting that the Sherman Act had been used by the government only 18 times in its first eleven years——and never against a large corporation or trust——they wanted to show that law was not powerless to prevent combination.[724] Moreover, to supplant the "race-to-the-bottom" that was corrupting state franchising of corporations, many Progressives favored a federal incorporation law for corporations engaged in interstate commerce.[725] In short, what they sought was a Jacksonian political economy with an emphasis on individualism that was more compatible with the ideology of confrontation than the increasing bureaucratization of American life.[726]

However, these anti-monopoly Progressives did not prevail in either the ideological or the political battle; Theodore Roosevelt split from other Progressives on this issue and led his faction to victory.[727] Roosevelt's reputation as a "trust-buster" is largely the creation of his corporate enemies.[728] Roosevelt, despite his self-image as a man of the people, surrounded himself with Eastern intellectuals and capitalists who had little interest in restoring the Jacksonian economy.[729] Roosevelt did not want to break up large corporations because he saw this as a return to the predatory capitalism of the Gilded Age; returning corporations to the jungle would simply mean a sharpening of claws that he thought were now

722. "Special Privilege"

Chamberlain, Farewell to Reform, 1965 ed., p. 133.

723. Breaking up

Mowry, The Progressive Era, 1900–1920: The Reform Persuasion, 1958, p. 21.

724. Never against corporation

Cadenhead, Theodore Roosevelt: The Paradox of Progressivism, 1974, p. 78.

725. Federal incorporation

Mowry, The Progressive Era, 1900–1920: The Reform Persuasion, 1958, p. 21.

726. Jacksonian political economy

Weinstein, The Corporate Ideal in the Liberal State, 1900–1918, 1968, p. 6.

727. Roosevelt split

Mowry, The Era of Theodore Roosevelt and the Birth of Modern America, 1900–1912, 1962, p. 55.

728. "Trust-buster"

Cadenhead, Theodore Roosevelt: The Paradox of Progressivism, 1974, p. 80.

729. Intellectuals and capitalists

Mowry, The Era of Theodore Roosevelt and The Birth of Modern America, 1900–1912, 1962, p. 55.

vestigal.[730] Instead of the jungle——if we may pursue the Darwinian metaphor to the end——Roosevelt wanted to put corporations into a zoo, what was often called a system of "regulated monopoly."[731] Roosevelt saw corporations as a new instrument of social control, a sort of nongovernmental "state" that existed in economic rather than geographical space and whose bureaucratic structure could be brought into some sort of pseudo-federal relationship with the states and federal government.[732] Hence, it was neither paradox nor mere political opportunism that led Roosevelt to attack Taft's antitrust policy, particularly the proposed break-up of the United States Steel Company.[733]

The contrast between Roosevelt and the anti-monopoly Progressives comes through vividly in his famous (or infamous) Osawatomie "New Nationalism" speech in 1910. Standing on ground where Populism had sprouted, Roosevelt first agreed that government on all levels "must be freed from the sinister influence or control of special interests."[734] But Roosevelt went on to argue that corruption was not the consequence of corporate size but rather of the unregulated use of corporate funds for political ends; hence, the remedy was to bar such political activity on the part of corporations.[735] Then, echoing his mentor Ross, Roosevelt proclaimed that the "effort at prohibiting all combination has substantially failed."[736] He continued:

> The way out lies, not in attempting to prevent such combinations, but in completely controlling them in the interest of the public

730. Did not want to break up

Ekirch, Progressivism in America, 1974, p. 141.

731. "Regulated monopoly"

Id. at p. 143.

732. Pseudo-federal

Weinstein, The Corporate Ideal in the Liberal State, 1900–1918, 1968, p. 149.

733. U.S. Steel

Ibid. Ekirch, Progressivism in America, 1974, p. 162.

734. "Special interests"

Cadenhead, Theodore Roosevelt: The Paradox of Progressivism, 1974, p. 334.

735. Bar activity

"There can be no effective control of corporations while their political activity remains. * * * It is necessary that laws should be passed to prohibit the use of corporate funds directly or indirectly for political purposes; it is still more necessary that such laws should be thoroughly enforced. Corporate expenditures for political purposes * * * have supplied one of the principle sources of corruption in our political affairs." Id. at p. 335.

736. "Substantially failed"

Id. at p. 336. See also, Ross, Social Control, 1969 ed., p. 123.

welfare. * * * It is my personal belief that the same kind and
degree of control and supervision which should be exercised over
public-service corporations should be extended to combinations
which control the necessaries of life, such as meat, oil, and coal, or
which deal in them on an important scale.[737]

Roosevelt was probably unaware that what he was proposing was
something like a revival of the common-law control of the economy,
except that prices would be fixed not by justices of the peace, but by
a tribunal of experts like the Interstate Commerce Commission or
state utility regulators. After proposals on labor and taxation of
wealth that made this speech one of the most radical he ever
delivered,[738] Roosevelt ended with a twist on Darwinian determinism:

> Those who oppose all reform will do well to remember that ruin in
> its worst form is inevitable if our national life brings us nothing
> better than swollen fortunes for the few and the triumph in both
> politics and business of a sordid and selfish materialism.[739]

Roosevelt did not regain the Presidency, but the Wilson administration went some way down the path of "regulated monopoly."[740]

Given that the right of confrontation is a sort of regulation of
the government's monopoly of force, "regulated monopoly" is not
inherently antithetical to confrontation values. But it is difficult to
devalue competition in the market without casting doubt on its
legitimacy in the courtroom. Moreover, by giving expertise a special
place in regulation of monopoly, one tends to move the adversary
system away from the jury and the lawyers and toward the judge.
Finally, when bureaucracy and the sacrifices of individuality it
entails become a way of life in the economic world, it is difficult to
expect jurors to have much sympathy for someone who wants to
assert his individual version of truth against the truth certified by
government bureaucrats.

Confrontation encountered bureaucracy in Dowdell v. United
States, a case that came to the Supreme Court under a statutory
extension of the Court's jurisdiction apparently designed to accom-

---

737. "Necessaries of life"

Cadenhead, Theodore Roosevelt: The
Paradox of Progressivism, 1974, p.
336.

738. Most radical ever

Id. at pp. 195, 338–339.

739. "Sordid and selfish"

Id. at p. 341.

740. Wilson administration

Link, Woodrow Wilson and The Progressive Era, 1910–1917, 1963 ed., p. 76.

modate colonialism within the Constitution.[741] The defendants were police officers charged with embezzlement. When the record proved inadequate, the Supreme Court of the Philippine Islands, rejecting the suggestion of the Attorney General that the case be sent back for a new trial, patched the record with affidavits from the trial judge, court clerk, and court reporter.[742] The defendants claimed the use of the affidavits violated the Sixth Amendment and a statutory extension of that provision under the so-called "Philippine Bill of Rights."[743]

Though the statutory provision said "the accused shall enjoy the right * * * to meet the witnesses face to face", Justice Day writing for a majority of the Court held that it was "substantially similar" to the Sixth Amendment Confrontation Clause.[744] Invoking the authority of Wigmore for the first time, the Court said that the right of confrontation

> tends to secure the accused in the right to be tried, so far as acts provable by witnesses are concerned, by only such witnesses as meet him face to face at trial, who give their testimony in his presence, and give to the accused an opportunity of cross-examination. It was intended to prevent the conviction of the accused upon depositions or ex parte affidavits, and particularly to preserve the right of the accused to test the recollection of the witness in the exercise of the right of cross-examination.[745]

But this Wigmorean right of confrontation "has always had certain well recognized exceptions."[746] As examples, the court repeats those recognized in Mattox—former testimony (but only of "deceased witnesses") and dying declarations. But the Dowdell Court goes on to add a third—"[d]ocumentary evidence to establish collateral facts, admissible under the common law."[747] The Court cites Cooley

---

741. Dowdell case

1911, 31 S.Ct. 590, 221 U.S. 325, 55 L.Ed. 753. The statute gave the Court the power of review only of judgments involving "the Constitution, or any statute, treaty, title, right or privilege of the United States." Id at 591, 221 U.S. at 327.

742. Patched record

Id. at 591, 221 U.S. at 327–328.

743. "Philippine Bill of Rights"

Id. at 592, 221 U.S. at 329. This allowed the Court to pass over the question of whether the defendants, who were ap-parently members of the occupying U.S. Army rather than Pilipinos, had Sixth Amendment rights in a colonial court.

744. "Substantially similar"

Id. at 592, 221 U.S. at 329–330.

745. "Right of cross-examination"

Id. at 592, 221 U.S. at 330.

746. "Always had exceptions"

Ibid.

747. "Under common law"

Id. at 592, 221 U.S. at 330.

for this proposition and does not expand upon the meaning of "collateral facts."[748] Apparently this is a dictum, though one might read what follows as intended as an application of this third exception.[749]

However, the Court seems to hold, not that an exception applies, but that this is a case that is beyond the scope of the Sixth Amendment.

> In the present case, the judge, clerk of the court, and the official reporter were not witnesses against the accused within the meaning of this provision of the statute. They were not asked to testify to facts concerning their guilt or innocence,——they were simply required to certify, in accordance with a practice approved by the Supreme Court of the Philippine Islands, as to certain facts regarding the course of trial * * *. The taking of such certification involved no inquiry into the guilt or innocence of the accused * * *.[750]

Just in case anyone missed it the first time, Justice Day repeated that in the method used to supplement the record "there is no production of testimony against the accused, within the meaning of this provision as to meeting witnesses face to face."[751] This is the first time, so far as we are aware, in which the Court, in deciding a confrontation question, actually consulted the language of the Sixth Amendment.[752] However, before we applaud this resort to the text, we must point out that the Court claimed it was talking, not about the Sixth Amendment, but about the confrontation provision in the Philippine Bill of Rights; that provision, as careful readers will have noted, does not limit the right to "witnesses against" the accused.[753] Nonetheless, Dowdell is a promising turn in the Court's

---

748. Cites Cooley

Ibid. On Cooley's views of confrontation, see § 6356, text at notecall 237.

749. Read as an application

That is, one could say that a fact is "collateral" if it does not concern the "guilt or innocence" of the accused.

750. "No inquiry into guilt"

Id. at 592, 221 U.S. at 331.

751. "Within the meaning"

Id. at 596, 221 U.S. at 331.

752. Consulted language

If one supposes, as the Court's earlier opinions do, that the Amendment was only intended to incorporate the common law, then the precise language used to do this matters little; if, on the other hand, one thinks the Founders had something else in mind, the language matters.

State courts had placed more emphasis on the language, some exploiting the same language the Dowdell Court relied upon. See § 6357, text following notecall 1.

753. Does not limit.

See the language quoted above, text at notecall 744.

confrontation jurisprudence.[754] Alas, as we shall see, the Court failed to follow up on its Dowdell analysis.

The Dowdell opinion missed an opportunity for a holistic analysis of the right of confrontation.[755] The defendants apparently raised the additional claim that they had a right to be present during the appellate court's consideration of the affidavits. Given that the Court had previously suggested that the defendant's right to be present at trial arose, at least in part, from the right of confrontation, one might have supposed that the Court's holding that the affiants were not "witnesses against" the accused would have pointed the way to the proper response to this question; that is, given that the defendants had no right to confront the witnesses, does the adversary system encapsulated in the Sixth Amendment nonetheless give them a right to be present to assist counsel in challenging the affidavits on appeal?[756]

The Dowdell court abandoned confrontation analysis and the Sixth Amendment and leaped to "due process" to dispose of this objection. Distinguishing prior authority that the Court describes as holding "that the due process of law required the accused to be present at every stage of the trial", the Court relied on another earlier holding "that due process of law did not require the accused to be present in an appellate court, where he was represented by counsel and where the only function of the court is to determine whether there is error in the record to the prejudice of the accused."[757] The Court's opinion adds that though the Philippine Supreme Court has the power to modify sentences, "the record before us does not show that any additional testimony was taken

754. Promising turn

By focusing on which hearsay declarants amount to "witnesses against" the accused, the Court could have avoided the equation of confrontation with the hearsay rule that was to embarass the Court's confrontation jurisprudence for the balance of the century.

755. Holistic analysis

See vol. 30, § 6341.

756. Assist counsel

The Court could have reached the same result by pointing out that at trial the defendant has to be present to help counsel with the witnesses because decisions have to be made almost imme-diately; the appellate process, on the other hand, gives counsel an opportunity to go over the affidavits with the client and take whatever steps are necessary to meet them before filing a brief responding to the factual assertions being made. Moreover, since the questions are technical and there is no jury, counsel has less need of lay assistance in formulating a reply.

757. "Prejudice of accused"

Dowdell v. U.S., 1911, 31 S.Ct. 590, 592, 221 U.S. 325, 331, 55 L.Ed. 753, citing Schwab v. Berggren, 1872, 12 S.Ct. 525, 143 U.S. 442, 36 L.Ed. 218.

against the accused * * * bearing upon their guilt or innocence of the crime charged."[758] This suggests that, without explicitly saying so, the Court was allowing confrontation considerations to drive its due-process analysis since identical grounds were used in deciding the confrontation issue. While due-process analysis may give the Court more flexibility than would a holistic analysis, it leaves the Court open to the charge that "due process" is subjective and arbitrary.

Taylorism and The Efficiency Craze

In 1911 a group of efficiency experts and sympathizers founded "The Taylor Society" to spread the word about scientific management.[759] Three years later, an "Efficiency Exposition" with Taylor as the featured speaker drew nearly 70,000 people during its run in New York.[760] The Taylor group spawned other groups ranging from "The National Society For the Promotion of Efficiency" to President Taft's "Efficiency and Economy Commission."[761] The "efficiency craze", originally fostered by business groups, soon saw other groups try to cash in on or coopt the phrase——even churches, schools, and feminists.[762] When the craze died out with the collapse of Progressivism, the Taylor Society remained to provide a safe-house for reformers awaiting the New Deal.[763]

As is often the case with fad words, "efficiency" was widely used in the Progressive era but it was seldom defined.[764] In its association with "social engineering", "social efficiency" was an offshoot of the cult of the expert.[765] Thorstein Veblen showed that

---

758. "Of crime charged"

31 S.Ct. at 592, 221 U.S. at 331–332.

759. "Taylor Society" founded

Haber, Efficiency and Uplift: Scientific Management in the Progressive Era, 1890–1920, 1973, p. 31.

760. Nearly 70,000 people

Id. at p. 61.

761. "Efficiency Commission"

Adams, Age of Industrial Violence, 1910–1915, pp. 27, 31. The workings of the Taft Commission are described in Haber, Efficiency and Uplift: Scientific Management in the Progressive Era, 1890–1920, 1973, p. 113.

762. Cash in or coopt

Id. at pp. 52, 61–63. Perhaps the only enduring monument to feminist participation were the courses in "Home Economics" offered in Midwestern high schools in the 1950s.

763. Safe-house for New Deal

Id. at p. 167.

764. Seldom defined

O'Neill, The Progressive Years, 1975, p. 97.

765. Cult of expert

Weinstein, The Corporate Ideal in the Liberal State, 1900–1918, 1968, p. xiv. See also, above, text beginning at notecall 518.

at its deepest level, "efficiency" was linked with the American fondness for instrumentalism as a seeming measure of the fitness of persons and institutions.[766] As such, it was associated in the Progressive lexicon with "bigness" and "success."[767] When Progressives spoke, as they often did, of the "inefficiency" of government, it was a polite way of referring to "corruption."[768] The leading student of the subject found that "efficiency" was used in at least four different ways.[769] Exploration of these will help us to understand the appeal of the concept.

At its most technical, "efficiency" meant the ratio between the energy put into a machine and the work put out.[770] Probably only scientists and engineers used it in this sense, but it was the technical meaning that gave the word its metaphorical appeal. In the Victorian age and after, social commentators had used both Newtonian physics and Darwinian biology as models for social theorizing; for example, it was common for historians to speak of social "forces" or the "growth" of institutions and ideas.[771] Thermodynamics offered an attractive alternative to the determinism of the older models because it was associated with machines, man-made contrivances rather than intractable natural processes.[772] Since few people grasped the Second Law, no one saw that entropy was inconsistent with the notion of Progress.[773]

A second meaning of "efficiency" was "commercial efficien-

766. Measure of fitness

White, Social Thought in America: The Revolt Against Formalism, 1957 ed., p. 85.

767. "Bigness" and "success"

Hofstadter, The Age of Reform: From Bryan to F.D.R., 1956, p. 242. This association remains today; when people speak of "economies of scale", they almost always mean "scaling up"——it is never supposed that smaller might be cheaper.

768. "Corruption"

Ekirch, Progressivism in America, 1974, p. 29.

769. Used four ways

Haber, Efficiency and Uplift: Scientific Management in the Progressive Era, 1890–1920, 1973, pp. ix–x.

770. Energy ratio

Id. at p. ix.

771. Physics and biology

Russett, Darwin in America: The Intellectual Response, 1865–1912, 1976, pp. 18, 74, 130–131.

772. Thermodynamics

Id. at pp. 133–134.

773. Entropy and Progress

We speak metaphorically——and a bad metaphor at that. Since the Second Law only applies to closed systems and scientists have still not decided if the universe is a closed system, it seems a stretch to suppose that social systems are closed. N.Y. Public Library, Science Desk Reference, 1995, pp. 283–284.

cy"——that is, profitability.[774] This was the way the word was used in scientific management from which it emerged and by capitalists in defending monopoly.[775] As we saw, Veblen thought engineers were devotees of efficiency while the capitalists who employed them were still greedy, inefficient predators.[776] Businessmen turned this argument on its head, arguing that it was competition that was inefficient.[777] Since some firms were doomed to fail at extravagant social cost and competition led to overproduction and waste, it was argued that a regulated monopoly would be more efficient.[778]

As Veblen's use suggests, "efficiency" was also seen as a personal attribute——an amalgam of character and social conscience.[779] It was in this sense that Benjamin Franklin was hailed as "The Father of Efficiency"; Poor Richard had cautioned: "[l]ose no time; be always employed in something useful; cut off all unnecessary action."[780] Similarly, Theodore Roosevelt wrote in 1910: "[t]he citizen is not a good citizen unless he is an efficient citizen."[781] Roosevelt praised Lincoln as "an efficient leader of the forward movement" and George Washington as "the efficient leader of the radicalism of the time."[782] Jefferson, on the other hand, failed to measure up to Roosevelt's standard of efficiency. It was in this sense, as well as in the sense of "profitability", that "efficiency" proved to be a useful stick to beat labor unions.[783] Business

---

774. Profitability

Haber, Efficiency and Uplift: Scientific Management in the Progressive Era, 1890–1920, 1973, p. x.

775. Defending monopoly

Ekirch, Progressivism in America, 1974, p. 143.

776. Greedy, inefficient predators

Russett, Darwin in America: The Intellectual Response, 1865–1912, 1976, pp. 163–164.

777. Competition inefficient

Ekirch, Progressivism in America, 1974, p. 152.

778. Regulated monopoly

Weinstein, The Corporate Ideal in the Liberal State, 1900–1918, 1968, p. 252.

779. "Efficiency" as character

Haber, Efficiency and Uplift: Scientific Management in the Progressive Era,

1890–1920, 1973, p. ix. See also, id. at p. 58 (used in this sense by author of book entitled "The Man Who Sneered at Santa Claus")

780. "Unneccesary action"

Id. at p. 57.

781. "Efficient citizen"

Ekirch, Progressivism in America, 1974, p. 137.

782. "Efficient leader"

Ibid.

783. Beat labor unions

Haber, Efficiency and Uplift: Scientific Management in The Progressive Era, 1890–1920, 1973, p. 71.

leaders constantly linked "efficiency" to "responsiblity" as moral imperatives.[784]

Precisely because the concept was so empty, "efficiency" attracted adherents outside the corporations that fostered it, including some of the leading figures in Progressive thought——Croly, Lippman, and Brandeis.[785] The latter signifies the most for the impact of "efficiency" on confrontation; Brandeis was no apologist for bigness——he argued that the failure of many railroads proved that monopoly was inefficient.[786] In a ratemaking proceeding in which he represented a group of Eastern shippers, Brandeis argued that if the railroad were made more efficient, pointing out a number of ways that this might be done, there would be no need for rate hikes.[787] Brandeis popularized "scientific management"——indeed, he has been credited with giving it that name.[788]

Many of the enthusiasts for "efficiency" were naive about scientific management; Walter Lippman thought the Taylorites were "humanizing" the corporate workplace.[789] Bosses had no such illusions, defending "piece work" as "scientific management" because it linked wages to productivity.[790] Workers hated scientific management because it sought to eliminate creativity, play, and even joy from the workplace.[791] Unions fought scientific manage-

784. Moral imperatives

Weinstein, The Corporate Ideal in the Liberal State, 1900–1918, 1968, p. xi.

785. Leading figures

Haber, Efficiency and Uplift: Scientific Management in The Progressive Era, 1890–1920, 1973, p.75.

786. Monopoly inefficient

Todd, Justice on Trial: The Case of Louis D. Brandeis, 1964, p. 62.

787. Might be done

Kolko, Railroads and Regulation, 1877–1916, 1965, p. 196; Wiebe, Businessmen and Reform: A Study of the Progressive Movement, 1962, p. 87; Haber, Efficiency and Uplift: Scientific Management in the Progressive Era, 1890–1920, 1973, p. 53.

788. Giving it name

Id. at p. 55.

789. "Humanizing" workplace

Id. at p. 94.

790. Linked to productivity

Weibe, Businessmen and Reform: A Study of the Progressive Movement, 1962, p. 162. Hence, at the same time that they were arguing that competition was "inefficient" for them, capitalists were encouraging competition among workers.

791. Eliminate play

Haber, Efficiency and Uplift: Scientific Management in the Progressive Era, 1890–1920, p. 23. People who have never worked in a factory, as the junior author once did, may be surprised to find these elements in the workplace but workers, like authors of law review articles and treatises, find elements of creativity even in what are for the most part highly routinized activities.

ment because employers used it to "sweat" workers, treating them like machines even before economists had coined the phrase "human capital."[792] A scholarly study, "Scientific Management" by Robert Hoxie, attacked the concept of "efficiency" as both economically and socially irresponsible.[793] Since even popular novelists were capable of debunking the efficiency craze, it is difficult to see why so many educated professionals could not see through it.[794]

Historians find a number of ideological and psychological features to explain the appeal of "efficiency." For one, it provided a route to reform that did not require stirring the masses into dangerous revolt.[795] As the leading student of the movement wrote:

> [e]fficiency provided a standpoint from which progressives who had declared their allegiance to democracy could resist the leveling tendencies of the principle of equality. They could advance reform and at the same time provide a safeguard to the "college bred."[796]

Given that Levellers popularized the idea of confrontation, this anti-democratic impulse seems unlikely to foster Sixth Amendment values. This can be seen in the writing of Woodrow Wilson, who fearful of the inefficiency of democracy advocated a science of "public administration" to justify the hegemony of the "college bred."[797]

> The progressives who greeted efficiency with enthusiasm were often those who proposed to let the people rule through a program in which the bulk of the people, most of the time, ruled hardly at all.[798]

792. "Sweat" workers

Ekirch, Progressivism in America, 1974, p. 119. The workers, at least in the era before electronic surveillance, found ways to resist. For example, since managers used the productivity of the fastest workers to set piece rates, systems of barter-cum-coercion arose in which the fastest workers put their product into the bins of their slower shopmates in return for a portion of their wage or other favors that amounted to a socializing of output.

793. Irresponsible

Adams, Age of Industrial Violence, 1910–1915, 1966, p. 223.

794. Novelists

Chamberlain, Farewell to Reform, 1965 ed., p. 196.

795. Stirring masses

Ekirch, Progressivism in America, 1974, p. 27.

796. "College bred"

Haber, Efficiency and Uplift: Scientific Management in the Progressive Era, 1890–1920, 1973, p. 116.

797. Woodrow Wilson

Ekirch, Progressivism in America, 1974, p. 224.

798. "Hardly at all"

Haber, Efficiency and Uplift: Scientific Management in the Progressive Era, 1890–1920, 1973, p. xii.

This could be seen in the New York Constitutional Convention of 1915 in which Progressives sought to increase the power of the executive branch while increasing limitations on democracy.[799]

But Progressives did not use "efficiency" only as a cover for personal interest or class bias; they saw it as a solution to industrial strife.[800]

> Men like Theodore Roosevelt found the alternative to social disorder in the concept and practice of efficiency, the systematic use of resources——human, natural, and financial——to produce the most possible material goods for the entire nation with the least energy. Competition and group struggle for power produced not efficiency but waste, waste of natural resources, of human lives, of human energy used for selfish ends rather than for the public interest. The social problem could be solved not by quarreling over pieces of the pie but by "baking a bigger pie," by more efficient and greater production so that there would be more to go around. Such leaders conceived of a whole society moving toward a common purpose under the guidance of efficiency, of the ideals of science and technology.[801]

One can see how such people would see the adversary system of competition and confrontation as a waste of time, particularly when Thorstein Veblen argued that it was the superior "efficiency" of the German government (with its inquisitorial system of justice) that allowed Germany to surpass England (that still claimed to have an adversary system).[802]

Finally, "efficiency" appealed to Progressives as a way of driving values and morality out of politics, of achieving reform without appealing to the "conscience" of the nation or its elite.[803] But despite it "scientistic" claims, the concept of "efficiency" was, as we have seen, both technical and moral.[804] For example, capital-

799. New York Convention

Id. at pp. 115–116.

800. Solution to strife

O'Neill, The Progressive Years, 1975, p. 98.

801. "Guidance of efficiency"

Hays, The Response to Industrialism, 1885–1914, 1957, pp. 88–89.

802. "Efficiency" of German

White, Social Thought in America: The Revolt Against Formalism, 1957 ed., p. 155.

803. Without "conscience"

O'Neil, The Progressive Years, 1975, p. 99.

804. Technical and moral

Haber, Efficiency and Uplift: Scientific Management in the Progressive Era, 1890–1920, 1973, p. 55.

ists were "good" if they grew rich through increased efficiency but "bad" if they relied on predatory practices.[805] But one person's "predatory practices" were another's "efficiency." Hence, the Progressive effort to conceal their values produced, at best, a corrosive and ill-defined moral relativism.[806] Thus, when Theodore Roosevelt praised the Japanese and Germans for their "military efficiency", he advanced, however slightly, the emulation of enemies that did so much to corrode humanitarian standards and limitations of warfare later in the century.[807]

As the example of Brandeis suggests, lawyers were not immune from the efficiency craze.[808] The President of the American Bar Association urged the members to strive to make legislatures more efficient.[809] Brandeis chimed in that courts too must be made "efficient instruments of justice."[810] President Taft gave meaning to this when he argued that judicial administration would have to improve if courts were to be effective protectors of private property.[811] Later, as Chief Justice, Taft testified before the Senate Judiciary Committee that federal courts had to be made more efficient, prompting the criticism that he was seeking a judiciary modeled on the Prussian Army.[812] Bar associations were praised for working "to promote the efficiency of the judiciary."[813] The craze

805. Relied on predatory

Hofstadter, The Age of Reform: From Bryan to F.D.R., 1956, p. 248.

806. Moral relativism

Wiebe, Businessmen and Reform: A Study of The Progressive Movement, 1962, p. 208.

807. "Military efficiency"

Ekirch, Progressivism in America, 1974, p. 246; Cadenhead, Theodore Roosevelt: The Paradox of Progressivism, 1974, p. 149.

808. Lawyers not immune

Progressive lawyers embraced efficiency for reasons similar to those of their non-professional brethren. "Efficiency appealed to [Thurman] Arnold because it offered an ideological defense against the politics of social conflict. It justified the rule of the competent. While it permitted a slight expansion of the elite, it did not endanger the social system that assured an unequal distribution of power, property, and deference." Ayer, In Quest of Efficiency: The Ideological Journey of Thurman Arnold in the Interwar Period, 1971, 23 Stan.L.Rev. 1049, 1052.

809. Legislatures more efficient

Hixson, Moorfield Storey and The Abolitionist Tradition, 1972, p. 29.

810. "Efficient instruments"

Todd, Justice on Trial: The Case of Louis D. Brandeis, 1964, p. 159.

811. Protectors of property

Mason, William Howard Taft: Chief Justice, 1965, p. 13.

812. Prussian judiciary

Id. at pp. 99, 104.

813. "Promote efficiency"

Strong, Landmarks of a Lawyer's Lifetime, 1914, pp. 169–170.

even penetrated the sanctuary of legal academia where one of the most prominent theologians proclaimed efficiency, equality of opportunity, and individual responsibility as the three cardinal virtues.[814]

While no one seems to have made the connection explicit, the implications of the efficiency mania for the right of confrontation could be deduced from its applications to other areas of the law. Law, according to John Dewey, was no more than "a method for employing force economically, efficiently, so as to get results with the least waste."[815] The problem with this sort of cost-benefit analysis is that to harried (or simple-minded) judges, the costs of providing confrontation are immediate and obvious while the benefits are remote and uncertain——and not easily quantifiable; how does one compare saving one innocent person from wrongful conviction with 1,000 hours of apparently pointless cross-examination? To the scientifically-minded, one could resolve the problem of "dwarfing of soft variables" like wrongful convictions by ignoring them; as one law teacher said, "the efficiency expert cannot allow himself the luxury of the softer emotions."[816] This genteel sadomasochism retains its appeal to the sophomoric.[817]

The impact of Progressive proceduralism on legal thought has been well documented.[818] Scholars wrote articles attacking the "inefficiency of the American jury" and proclaiming the need to increase the power of judges over jurors.[819] This, of course, required judges of the right sort; hence "efficiency" in judicial administration consisted of removing judges from politics so that governors could appoint only those approved by elite bar associations.[820] One

---

814. Three cardinal virtues

Twining, Karl Llewellyn and The Realist Movement, 1973, p. 126.

815. "Least waste"

Haber, Efficiency and Uplift: Scientific Management in the Progressive Era, 1890–1920, 1973, p. 19.

816. "Softer emotions"

Auerbach, Enmity and Amity: Law Teachers and Practitioners, 1900–1922, 1971, 5 Perspectives in American History 549, 567 n. 54.

817. Sophomoric

Taking positions that offend common sense or common decency is frequently praised in the law schools of today as "counter-intuitive" and therefore "tough-minded" or "penetrating."

818. Well documented

Graham, Book Review: The Persistence of Progressive Proceduralism, 1983, 61 Texas L.Rev. 929, 940.

819. Power of judges

Thayer, Observations on the Law of Evidence, 1915, 13 Mich.L.Rev. 355, 361.

820. Approved by bar

Strong, Landmarks of a Lawyer's Lifetime, 1914, p. 170.

of the gurus of the judicial administration movement believed that "divided authority does not make for efficiency", thus disparaging the separation of functions that is one of the hallmarks of the adversary system.[821] And lest they be accused of overindulgence of the "softer emotions", evidence scholars, decrying "the hardship suffered by the state through our extravagant protection of the accused", favored the abolition of the privilege against self-incrimination.[822] In short, "efficiency" required the replacement of the adversary system incorporated in the Fifth and Sixth Amendments with the inquisitorial system that the Founders had rejected.[823]

What the Founders intended was the subject of a book published the same year the Taylor Society organized. Charles Chamberlayne's treatise on "The Modern Law of Evidence" was one of the most remarkable works of Progressive evidentiary scholarship, not the least because it demonstrates the views of evidence and confrontation that were suppressed by the long domination of Wigmore's work.[824] Early in the first volume, Chamberlayne acknowledges, as Wigmore does not, that the Founders did not intend to further efficiency. Speaking of judges who valued vindication of constitutional rights over claims of efficiency, Chamberlayne writes:

821. "Divided authority"

Vanderbilt, Changing Law: A Biography of Arthur T. Vanderbilt, 1977, p. 23.

822. "Extravagant protection"

Thayer, Observations on The Law of Evidence, 1915, 13 Mich.L.Rev. 355, 359.

823. Inquisitorial system

One of the first of the "managerial judges" came very close to equating quantity with quality in assuming that if the courts were more efficient, this automatically meant that the quality of justice would be improved. This is the jurisprudential equivalent of those Progressives who believed that if you "increased the size of the pie" everybody would get a bigger piece rather than the powerful simply taking a bigger slice.

824. Domination of Wigmore

It is clear that Chamberlayne was aware of Wigmore's views because he acknowledges his work in the Preface. 1

Chamberlayne, The Modern Law of Evidence, 1911, p. xi.

Writers have attempted to account for Chamberlayne's lack of influence. See, e.g., Twining, Theories of Evidence: Bentham and Wigmore, 1985, p. 8. Ironically, Chamberlayne may have been undone by the very Progressive values he so eagerly embraced. As the American editor of two English treatises, Chamberlayne might seem as qualified as Wigmore to pontificate upon the law, but Wigmore as an academic was a certified "expert" whereas Chamberlayne had only his experience to vouch for him. Nor did it help that Chamberlayne's attempts to theorize were sometimes incoherent. Wigmore may have been wrong but he always went wrong with clarity.

in preferring the interests of the individual to those of society courts are occupying precisely the attitude which the men who founded the American commonwealth occupied to the government of the Tudors and Stuarts. * * * Justice, conventionalized by laws of political and religious oppression, as matters then stood, was precisely what these men did not want. Confessedly guilty, their hope of escape lay in obstructing the efforts of government to get at the truth. Truth was nothing which could assist them. * * * Insistence upon strictest legal proof, clinging to what a sympathetic jury might regard as the "rights of Englishmen" and properly resent when invaded; such was the reliance in sixteenth and seventeenth century England alike of the Dissenter, the Roundhead, or the Poacher.[825]

Chamberlayne concedes that the Founders rejected the instrumentalism and efficiency so beloved by Progressives, thus valuing means over ends, but he returns to the Federalist lament—a democratic society no longer has Dissenters in the dock so all the benefits go to the Poacher.[826]

When he deals with confrontation, Chamberlayne rejects Wigmore's view that it is a right of cross-examination—indeed, he only alludes to the right of confrontation in his discussion of cross-examination.[827] Instead, Chamberlayne writes that:

[p]rominent among rights with which the substantive law has endowed a litigant is that of confrontation;—the privilege of meeting the witnesses against him face to face. In other words, the object to be secured is that the witness should give his evidence in

---

825. "Roundhead or Poacher"

1 Chamberlayne, Modern Law of Evidence, 1911, § 326, pp. 425–426.

826. Benefits to Poacher

"When democracy in America assumed the functions and responsibilities of government, the limitations which, in a position of rebellion against authority, it had sought to impose upon the right of the state to punish its offenders, returned to plague it. Involved as these limitations were claimed to be with the most sacred and fundamental rights of the citizen, democracy has long clung to them and, without greater consideration, as of something once and for all been settled, has extended rather than checked their scope and application. Changes in social conditions or in the character and objects of those who are in opposition to the decrees of society are not, in all quarters, fully noticed. The result is the general breakdown in the effectiveness of criminal procedure to deal with crime, general lawlessness and popular contempt for the work of courts." Id. at pp. 426–427. For a similar argument by the Federalist opponents of the Bill of Rights, see vol. 30, § 6347, p. 692.

827. Only alludes

1 Chamberlayne, The Modern Law of Evidence, 1911, § 378, p. 505, text at notecall 12.

the presence of the adverse party.[828]

Indeed, according to Chamberlayne the right is so fundamental that it even arises as a matter of natural law in civil cases.[829] However, like Wigmore, Chamberlayne wants to deny that the right is absolute because in his view it is also antithetical to the admission of hearsay evidence.[830]

Chamberlayne falls back on "lawyer's history"——that is, the history recorded by judicial opinions, even if that history has little support in the historical record.[831] Drawing on the Nineteenth Century state opinions that we have discussed, Chamberlayne argues that the confrontation clauses were not intended to change the rules of evidence.[832] However, unlike Wigmore, Chamberlayne comes close to a holistic reading.

> The founders of the original constitutions justly deemed any procedure in opposition to this rule as being contrary to law. They were apprehensive of the future, and sought to limit the power of the executive in this particular, for much the same reason that they forbade unreasonable searches or attached a sacramental value to the "trial by jury."[833]

But Chamberlayne rejects the so-called "purist approach" under which only those exceptions to the hearsay rule known to the founders will pass muster; according to him, any hearsay exception is automatically an exception to the right of confrontation.[834]

828. "In the presence"

Id., § 458, pp. 586–587.

829. Civil cases

Id. at p. 588.

830. Antithetical to hearsay

That is, the declarant does not "give his evidence in the presence of the" defendant.

831. "Lawyer's history"

Since the earliest confrontation cases did not adopt Chamberlayne's view, he has to depend on opinions of judges who had no personal knowledge of the Founders' intent and who cite no evidence to support their plausible, but largely incorrect, historical suppositions.

832. Not intended to change

"No attempt was made to alter the then existing state of the law of evidence by [the confrontation clauses]. The object was rather to emphasize and enforce certain rights regarded as already existing and having a recognized place in the entire system of jurisprudence which it was not intended to disturb." Ibid.

833. "Sacramental value"

Id., § 460, pp. 593–594. For more on the "holistic approach" to confrontation, See Gutman, Academic Determinism: The Division of The Bill of Rights, 1981, 54 So.Cal.L.Rev. 295, 331–355.

834. Any hearsay exception

Id., § 459. The "purist approach" is discussed in Larkin, The Right of Con-

In reaching this result, Chamberlayne rejects the Mattox opinion's view that the evil against which the Sixth Amendment was aimed at was trial by deposition as used in the inquisitorial vice-admiralty courts.[835]

> There was, however, a very real mischief, as to which they were properly sensitive and which they earnestly desired to eliminate by law, as being unjust and contrary to the rights of Englishmen. They felt that in the conflict between the liberties of the people and the perogative of the crown, the latter had found no instrument of oppression more serviceable than secret tribunals——like the courts of star chamber or high commission.[836]

Chamberlayne does not trouble to explain why a right of confrontation could not have been exercised in a secret tribunal as well as a public one.[837] Hence, it is not surprising that he goes on to suggest that the Founders did not intended that confrontation be any limitation on "the ordinary and regular course of administering justice by the legally constituted tribunals."[838] Hence, confrontation does not bar the use of hearsay. This is efficiency with a vengeance——and questionable history to boot.[839]

The Bull Moose Bellows

The election of 1912 was one of the most significant in American history.[840] The split of the Republican Party produced the "Progressive Party" with its Bull Moose emblem, one of the most

frontation: What Next?, 1969, 1 Tex. Tech.L.Rev. 67, 68.

835. Rejects Mattox

See § 6357, text at notecall 478.

836. "Like star chamber"

1 Chamberlayne, The Modern Law of Evidence, 1911, § 460, p. 594.

837. Does not explain

Indeed, the presence of rights to public trial along with the right to confrontation in the Sixth Amendment and similar state provisions suggests otherwise.

838. "Ordinary and regular"

Ibid.

839. Questionable history

Though the prerogative courts, such as Star Chamber, created antipathy for the inquisitorial mode of procedure with its trial by dossier, there is little evidence that secrecy was the major or only objection, or that anyone thought the confrontation clauses would bar secret trials, or even that Star Chamber was the most immediate abuse in the minds of the Founders. See vol. 30. §§ 6343–6347.

840. Election of 1912

Ekirch, Progressivism in America, 1974, p. 154. Since we are concerned with Progressive ideas rather than the issues and personalities, readers will have to look elsewhere for these, except as they help explain the ideology. See generally, O'Neill, The Progressive Years, 1975, p. 58 and following.

successful third parties since the emergence of the Republican Party itself.[841] For the first time since the Civil War there was no avowedly pro-corporate party contesting for the Presidency and the Progressive Party platform was the most radical ever to capture so many votes.[842] Some of the Progressive planks, such as the recall of judicial decisions, had implications for confrontation but it was the ideology underlying the proposals that was to have the greatest impact on the future of confrontation jurisprudence.[843] Although Theodore Roosevelt lost, his ideas prevailed over the vestigal Jeffersonianism of Woodrow Wilson's Democratic Party.[844] By 1912, then, the revolt against formalism had swept the field and the Progressive ideology was complete——and it was this replacement for Darwinian laissez faire that would dominate American legal and political thought down to the era of Ronald Reagan.[845]

Understanding the Progressive ideology may be aided by a sense of who the Progressives were.[846] Though it has often been

841. Republican split

Cadenhead, Theodore Roosevelt: The Paradox of Progressivism, 1974, pp. 187–197.

842. Progressive platform

Ekirch, Progressivism in America, 1974, p. 165; Weinstein, The Corporate Ideal in the Liberal State, 1900–1918, 1968, p. 166 (no pro-corporate party).

843. Progressive planks

Ekirch, Progressivism in America, 1974, p. 165; Cadenhead, Theodore Roosevelt: The Paradox of Progressivism, 1974, pp. 207, 343. One does not have to go as far as some historians in finding links between proposals for recall of judicial decisions and greater willingness of courts to uphold social welfare legislation to accept the notion that the popularity of recall provided a marker for public dissatisfaction with the direction of constitutional law and that this dissatisfaction played some part in the attempt of some members of the Supreme Court to find a moral constituency to replace or supplement the Court's economic constituency. Wiebe, Businessmen and Reform: A Study of the Progressive Movement,

1962, p. 173 (suggesting that demands for recall led Court to uphold protective labor legislation for women).

844. Ideas prevailed

Id. at p. 127; Ekirch, Progressivism in America, 1974, p. 165.

845. Dominate thought

Weinstein, The Corporate Ideal in the Liberal State, 1900–1918, 1968, pp. x-xi (but not, of course, seeing the revival of laissez faire under Reagan); White, Social Thought in America: The Revolt Against Formalism, 1957 ed. pp. 107, 147.

There does not seem to be any conventional name for this ideology, though for a time in the 1960s it was reviled as "corporate liberalism." We shall refer to it as "the Progressive ideology" despite the fact that it was held by many people who did not regard themselves as "Progressives."

846. Who Progressives

Since we are interested in ideas rather than programs or political success, we need not enter into the debate among historians as to who was doing what

noted that the Progressive ideas appealed more to the "middle class" than to other classes, that is unhelpful for reasons other than the vagueness of the term.[847] Progressives can be divided into three not completely distinct categories. The most ideologically influential group consisted of urban professionals, supposedly suffering from status anxiety and thus attracted to Progressive elitism; lawyers and urban newspaper editors led this group.[848] The second sort of Progressive was the rural influential who was repelled by the Populists but shared their concern about the inability of capitalism to rationalize the agricultural economy; this group was typified by William Allen White and was more likely to be led by Republican politicians.[849] The third group were businessmen, split between the former "Goo-goos" and "Mugwumps" and the reform capitalists of the sort who made up the National Civic Federation; this group gave the Progressive movement much of its clout but probably contributed least to its ideas—at least if one can judge by the rapidity with which this group bailed out when the implications of those ideas were made clear by The New Deal.[850]

We have seen the events that shaped the Progressives and the ideologies from which they could draw, particularly Darwinism and pragmatism.[851] But Progressives defined themselves in relation to other political movements of the time, laissez faire conservatism on the right and various kinds of radicalism on the left. Of the latter, the two most formidable adversaries were the Socialists and the Neo–Populists.[852] Since programatically Progressives were closer to

to whom; e.g., was Progressivism simply a case of businessmen turning the reform impulse to their own benefit. See Mowry, The Progressive Era, 1900–1920: The Reform Persuasion, 1958, pp. 29–36.

847. "Middle class"

Ross, Social Control, 1969 ed., p. xl.

848. Lawyers and editors

Hofstadter, The Age of Reform: From Bryan to F.D.R., 1956, 135; Ekirch, Progressivism in America, 1974, pp. 94–95; Mowry, The Era of Theodore Roosevelt and The Birth of Modern America, 1900–1912, 1962, pp. 89–96; Mowry, The Progressive Era, 1900–20: The Reform Persuasion, 1958, pp. 6, 6, 26.

849. Rural Progressives

Wiebe, Businessmen and Reform: A Study of the Progressive Movement, 1962, p. 69; Chamberlain, Farewell to Reform, 1965 ed., p. 195.

850. New Deal

Wiebe, Businessmen and Reform: A Study of the Progressive Movement, 1962, pp. 124, 196.

851. Darwinism and pragmatism

Ekirch, Progressivism in America, 1974, pp. 19–23; Russett, Darwin in America: The Intellectual Response, 1865–1912, 1976, p. 208.

852. Two most formidable

Weinstein, The Corporate Ideal in the Liberal State, 1900–1918, 1968, p. 5.

the left than the right, some assessment of their relationship with radicals will assist in understanding their thinking.

Historians differ among themselves on the relationship between Progressivism and Populism; though all seem to agree Progressivism was rooted in Populism they cannot agree on how deep those roots ran.[853] Though Theodore Roosevelt had denounced Populism during the Crisis of '96, he later advocated a number of Populist reforms; indeed, those still professing Populism were chagrined to find many of their reforms achieved by those who denounced their ideology.[854] It has been argued that the Progressives differed from the Populists less in terms of ideology than in terms of constituency, leadership and scope; that is, the Populists were mass-based, sectional, and rural where the Progressives were a national, elite-driven movement.[855] To the extent that this is so, it explains the Progressive ambivalence toward democracy and its related institutions, such as trial by jury and confrontation.

Conservatives claimed the Progressives were leading the country down the road to socialism.[856] Herbert Croly was labeled a "Socialist", the National Association of Manufacturers attacked Progressive academics for fostering subversive "isms" and the Child Labor Amendment to the Constitution was denounced as "Bolshevism."[857] Given the statism of the Progressives, such attacks were not completely unwarranted; a number of academics, particularly the historian James Robinson, had been influenced by Marxist ideas.[858] Moreover, if not yet social-democratic, the Social-

---

853. Historians differ

Ekirch, Progressivism in America, 1974, p. 35; Mowry, The Progressive Era, 1900–20: The Reform Persuasion, 1958, pp. 5, 29; Wiebe, Businessmen and Reform: A Study of the Progressive Movement, 1962, p. 211.

854. Those who denounced

Cadenhead, Theodore Roosevelt: The Paradox of Progressivism, 1974, p. 137; O'Neill, The Progressive Years, 1975, p. 9.

855. Differed

Mowry, The Progressive Era, 1900–20: The Reform Persuasion, 1958, p. 5.

856. Down the road

Ekirch, Progressivism in America, 1974, p. 12.

857. "Bolshevism"

Id. at p. 160; Wiebe, Businessmen and Reform: A Study of the Progressive Movement, 1962, p. 186; Wood, Constitutional Politics in the Progressive Era, 1968, p. 215. This sort of invective had been a part of the political rhetoric of the nation almost since Marx first was heard of. See § 6356, text at notecall 223.

858. Marxist ideas

White, Social Thought in America: The Revolt Against Formalism, 1958 ed., pp. 111, 120.

ists were becoming more conservative during the Progressive era.[859] However, Socialism enjoyed its greatest successes at the municipal level where its ideology was easiest to square with the American fondness for individualism.[860] In addition, if we look at the leading figures in Progressive thought, they shared little with the Marxists except opposition to laissez faire capitalism; most of them claimed allegiance to the more optimistic forms of indigenous radicalism.[861]

Progressives were probably less attracted by the appeal of Socialist ideas and more afraid of the impact of those ideas on voters. Businessmen were anxious over the spread of socialist ideas for practical rather than ideological reasons.[862] Shortly before the election of 1912 a Harvard historian wrote that

> a large minority of the American people, which is likely soon to be a majority, feels dissatisfied and resentful and is bound to make things different. Unless that movement is checked, within sixteen years there will be a Socialist President of the United States.[863]

The way to avoid that, he continued, was for one of the two major parties to "take over the reasonable part of the Socialist programme" as he thought the Progressives had done.[864] Theodore Roosevelt had earlier expressed a similar thought in a way that made it more appealing to those who liked to see themselves as "centrists."

859. More conservative

Ekirch, Progressivism in America, 1974, p. 41.

860. Municipal level

Id. at p. 97. That is, since municipalities had been providing water and sewage services almost from the beginning, no one supposed America was on "the road to serfdom" if they added electricity and bus services, even if the city administration was in the hands of Marxists.

861. Indigenous radicalism

Mowry, The Era of Theodore Roosevelt and the Birth of Modern America, 1900–1912, p. 45. Edward Ross was a Populist sympathizer turned Progressive, Ross, Social Control, 1969 ed., p. xxxvii, Charles Beard claimed to be a "Madisonian", White, Social Thought in America: The Revolt Against Formalism, 1958 ed., p. 121, "Golden

Rule" Jones was a philosophical anarchist (which did not prevent him from becoming the Progressive mayor of Toledo), Tager, The Intellectual as Urban Reformer: Brand Whitlock and The Progressive Movement, 1968, p. 52, Brand Whitlock seems to have drawn his inspiration from the Radical Republicans, id. at p. 10, and Robert LaFollette was an unreconstructed Granger, Chamberlain, Farewell to Reform, 1965 ed., p. 247.

862. Businessmen anxious

Weinstein, The Corporate Ideal in the Liberal State, 1900–1918, 1968, p. 135.

863. "Socialist President"

Id. at p. 170.

864. "Reasonable part"

Ibid.

It seems to me [Roosevelt wrote] that our attitude should be one of correcting the evils and thereby showing that, whereas the Populists, Socialists, and others really do not correct the evils at all, or else only do so at the expense of producing others in aggravated form, on the contrary we Republicans hold the just balance and set ourselves as resolutely against improper corporate influence on the one hand as against demagogy and mob rule on the other.[865]

In a more aphoristic, or philosophical, mood Roosevelt said after his defeat in 1912 that "[t]he growth in the complexity of community life means the partial substitution of collectivism for individualism, not to destroy, but to save individualism."[866] Or as Herbert Croly put it more bluntly, Progressivism was "designed to serve as a counterpoise to the threat of working class revolution."[867]

Historians have seen further evidence for this mediating vision of Progressivism in the actions of Progressives. Roosevelt sometimes justified his acts as President by pointing out that if too much for businessmen, they were a long way from what "radicals" were calling for.[868] The California Progressives attacked both the conservative corporate machine that had dominated state politics for years and the radical labor left.[869] Other organizations were not so even-handed; the National Civic Federation spent more time campaigning against the spread of socialism than against corporate depredation.[870] The problem with the "centrist" position seems not to have been fully appreciated at the time. When Wilson came to power, the Populists and Socialists had nowhere else to turn so Wilson turned on them.[871] He joined businessmen in attacking their lack of patriotism in refusing to support the war.[872] Later he used

---

865. "Hold the just balance"

Cadenhead, Theodore Roosevelt: The Paradox of Progressivism, 1974, p. 64.

866. "Save individualism"

Ekirch, Progressivism in America, 1974, p. 229.

867. "Threat of revolution"

Weinstein, The Corporate Ideal in the Liberal State, 1900–1918, p. xi.

868. Long way from "radicals"

Cadenhead, Theodore Roosevelt: The Paradox of Progressivism, 1974, p. 123.

869. Attacked both

Weinstein, The Corporate Ideal in the Liberal State, 1900–1918, 1968, p. 78.

870. Against socialism

Id. at p. 123.

871. Turned on them

Ekirch, Progressivism in America, 1974, p. 223.

872. Attacking patriotism

Weinstein, The Corporate Ideal in the Liberal State, 1900–1918, 1968, p. 136.

the Espionage Act to suppress recalcitrant radicals—apparently not appreciating that with no leftist "Mutts" it would be hard to play "Jeff" in dealing with conservative opponents.[873]

But Progressivism was more than simply a mediating strategy or a set of transient programs; at a deeper level it had, if not a consistent ideology, at least a set of interlocking values.[874] We have previously examined the Progressive infatuation with scientism, elitism, and expertism, their turn toward nationalism and opposition to class conciousness while clinging to a scientific racism that embraced Anglophilia and Tuetonism, and their penchant for social engineering and anxieties about the bureaucratization it produced.[875] It remains only to discuss the Progressive attitude toward change; for it was the ill-formed notion of "progress" that held together the other discrepant Progressive values and distinguished them—at least in their own eyes—from traditional conservatives and radical leftists.[876]

Edward Ross, as he so often did, spoke for Progressives when ten years before there was a Progressive Party he wrote:

> In social arrangements the prime desiderata have always been order and progress. If one must come first, it is the former, for there can be no progress without order. But their rivalry lies in the fact that order can be somewhat impaired for the sake of quicker progress, or progress can be somewhat checked for the sake of better order. Which will be favored in such interference depends on how they are esteemed. For obvious reasons order was prized before progress was, and until modern times enjoyed far greater consideration. But the visible triumphs of physical science

873. Espionage Act to suppress

Id. at p. 237.

For those unfamiliar with police interrogation techniques, "Mutt" is the heavy who threatens the suspect both physically and with exaggerated accusations whereupon "Jeff" enters as the voice of reason who can protect the suspect from "Mutt" if he can only reciprocate Jeff's reasonableness by avoiding exaggerated claims of innocence.

874. Progressive values

For a somewhat different statement of these values, see Wiebe, Businessmen and Reform: A Study of The Progressive Movement, 1962, p. 9.

875. Previously examined

See above, text at notecalls 15 (opposition to class conciousness), 93 (Anglophilia and Teutonism), 101 (scientism), 202 (bureaucratization), 234 (racism), 279 (nationalism), 390 (social engineering), 535 (expertism).

876. Ill-formed notion

An interesting illustration of how twisted the concept would become was Theodore Roosevelt's attempt to convince an anticolonial audience that English colonialism represented the "progress" of Western civilization. Cadenhead, Theodore Roosevelt: The Paradox of Progressivism, 1974, p. 178.

in these latter days have implanted the idea that progress is vastly beneficial and must be provided for.[877]

"Beneficient", indeed. This was the era in which we had a "new history", a "new economics", a "new jurisprudence", a "New Freedom", and eventually, a "New Deal."[878] This legacy of the Progressive era remains inscribed on every box of soap powder.

For many Progressives, conservatism favored control over progress, a preference that was linked to the Puritan distrust of the instinctual as against the rational in human experience.[879] For such Progressives, progress was written into the laws of nature as described by Darwin.[880] They explained social problems with Veblen's concept of "cultural lag."[881] In the political realm, the difference between these Progressives and conservatives was symbolized by the differing spirits of the Declaration of Independence and the Constitution.[882] For such Progressives, one imagines that the supposed common law source of the right of confrontation would be sufficient condemnation.

Other Progressives, perhaps the majority, were uncomfortable with the notion that progress was inevitable as this smacked too much of the laissez-faire conservatism they opposed; they believed that change was "progress" only if humans could control it for beneficial purposes.[883] However, this was problematic because according to Ross, it was the institutions of social control that

877. "Vastly beneficient"

Ross, Social Control, 1969 ed. 195.

878. "New, new, new"

White, Social Thought in America: The Revolt Against Formalism, 1957 ed., p. 47 (referring to an "age of news").

879. Puritan distrust

Ross, Social Control, 1969 ed., p. 190.

880. Described by Darwin

Haber, Efficiency and Uplift: Scientific Management in the Progressive Era, 1890–1920, 1973, p. 11. See, e.g., Thorstein Veblen: "The law of natural selection, as applied to human institutions, gives the axiom: 'whatever is, is wrong.'" Russett, Darwin in America: The Intellectual Response, 1865–1912, 1976, p. 155.

881. "Cultural lag"

Id. at p. 154. See also, id. at p. 155: "History records more frequent and more spectacular instances of triumph of imbecile institutions over life and culture than of peoples who have by force of instinctive insight saved themselves alive out of a desperately precarious institutional situation, such, for instance, as now faces the peoples of Christendom." (quoting Veblen).

882. Declaration and Constitution

Chamberlain, Farewell to Reform, 1965 ed., p. 213.

883. Humans control

White, From Sociological Jurisprudence to Realism: Jurisprudence and Social Change in Early Twentieth Century America, 1972, 58 Va.L.Rev. 999, 1003.

suffered the most from cultural lag——they changed too slowly to be charged with managing change.[884] This may explain the Progressive preoccupation with institutions and methods of government—— "procedure" in the language of the law. For Progressives, the solution to the problem of cultural lag in governmental institutions was to cleanse them of all values except efficiency and expertise, to substitute impartial administration for the political clash of partisan interests and values.[885] In other words, the way to control change was with a government that could mediate between those who favored and those who opposed it.[886] These Progressives were not so much opposed to traditions such as confrontation as they were immersed in a sort of "presentism" that asked whether or not the tradition was useful in resolving some current conflict.[887]

In a sense, the Progressive ideology was the Progressive psyche inscribed in politics. The middle class thinkers who shaped the movement were neither as complacent as the rich nor as desperate as the poor; unwilling to take sides in the class war, they wanted a government that would protect noncombatants rather than intervene on one side or the other.[888] In order to do this, it was essential that the noncombatants be seen as having no interest on one side or the other but rather having only interests that transcend politics.[889] Anyone who has seen a contemporary law-school class with its "on-the-one-hand, on-the-other-hand" treatment of contested

884. Changed too slowly

"We can now lay down the law that all institutions having to do with control change reluctantly, change slowly, change tardily, and change within sooner than without." Ross, Social Control, 1969 ed., p. 192.

885. Substitute for clash

White, From Sociological Jurisprudence to Realism: Jurisprudence and Social Change in Early Twentieth Century America, 1972, 58 Va.L.Rev. 999, 1003.

886. Mediate between

Cadenhead, Theodore Roosevelt: The Paradox of Progressivism, 1974, p. 66.

887. "Presentism"

White, Social Thought in America : The Revolt Against Formalism, 1957 ed., pp. 50, 52.

888. Protect non-combatants

To paraphrase a historian of the period, they wanted a government that was "capitalistic in function and socialistic in purpose." Mowry, The Era of Theodore Roosevelt and the Birth of Modern America, 1900–1912, 1962, p. 293.

889. Transcend politics

This may be why the resemblance between Progressive reforms in the United States and those urged by labor or social democratic parties in Europe tends to be ignored; those parties are class-based so their reforms could hardly claim to "neutral policy-making." Ekirch, Progressivism in America, 1974, pp. 10–11, 14.

values has seen the legacy of Progressivism. This is why Pound's "Sociological Jurisprudence" can be seen as the legal analog of political Progressivism.[890] It allows one to denounce a precedent as "outmoded" without questioning its values or those of the judges who decided it; it is enough that it does not serve the instrumental needs of the moment.[891]

Since the Progressive ideology had no serious rivals as an alternative to laissez-faire conservatism until at least the 1960s and remains strong in the law schools even today,[892] it is worth examining how its mediating role was implemented at the outset. The reigning myth is that Progressivism was a crusade against business plutocracy by ordinary Americans led by a group of public-spirited men.[893] Certainly this is how the Bull Moose Party sought to portray itself in its first platform.[894] President Wilson invoked this image when he announced in a message to Congress in 1914 that "the antagonism between business and government is over."[895] There were enough instances in which capitalists did not get what they wanted to lend credence to the myth; e.g., the I.C.C. denial of a railroad rate increase and the Pujo Committee's investigation of the "Money Trust" that revealed the influence of bankers and the corruption of the stock markets.[896] But as we have seen, Roosevelt's image as a "trust buster" was completely at odds with his own predilections for "regulated monopoly."[897]

890. Legal analog

White, From Sociological Jurisprudence to Realism: Jurisprudence and Social Change in Early Twentieth Century America, 1972, 58 Va.L.Rev. 999.

891. Denounce as "outmoded"

Haber, Efficiency and Uplift: Scientific Management in the Progressive Era, 1890–1920, p. 79. For example, in the junior author's law school days, the teachers of Constitutional Law tended to denounce the cases of so-called "substantive due process", not for employing monstrous values, but for employing values—period.

892. No rivals

Weinstein, The Corporate Ideal in the Liberal State, 1900–1918, 1968, p. 254.

893. Progressive myth

Wiebe, Businessmen and Reform: A Study of the Progressive Movement, 1962, p. 206.

894. First platform

Cadenhead, Theodore Roosevelt: The Paradox of Progressivism, 1974, p. 344.

895. "Antagonism is over"

Ekirch, Progressivism in America, 1974, p. 234.

896. Instances

Wiebe, Businessmen and Reform: A Study of the Progressive Movement, 1962, pp. 28, 141.

897. "Trust buster"

Mowry, The Progressive Era, 1900–20: The Reform Persuasion, 1958, p. 22.

Fifty years later the Progressive myth bred a countermyth; namely, that Progressivism was a device by which the dominant economic interests in the country used the federal government to head off threats to their power emerging in the states.[898] The role of Big Business in shaping Progressivism still divides historians.[899] On the other hand, few dispute that labor union leaders were peripheral players, at best, in the Progressive movement.[900] But the activist business community was split between Eastern and Midwestern capitalists.[901] Some influential capitalists favored regulated monopoly.[902] They apparently had enough clout that Brandeis was able to sell much of Roosevelt's program to Wilson after the election of 1912.[903] It seems fair to say that the business community altered Progressivism more than it was altered by Progressivism.[904]

This is illustrated by the issue that relates most closely to the confrontation values; namely, the relationship between business, labor, and government.[905] One of the major pro-labor statutes of the Progressive era was the Clayton Act—what one union leader called "Labor's Magna Carta," a characterization that was more historically apt than politically prophetic.[906] The Clayton Act gave unions a limited immunity from the antitrust, took some tentative steps to legalize strikes, picketing, and boycotts in the narrow area where federal law was controlling, and provided for jury trial for contempt proceedings growing out of labor injunctions.[907] However,

898. Head off threats

Wiebe, Businessmen and Reform: A Study of the Progressive Movement, 1962, p. 6.

899. Divides historians

Mowry, The Progressive Era, 1900–20: The Reform Persuasion, 1958, pp. 32–33.

900. Labor peripheral

Wiebe, Businessmen and Reform: A Study of the Progressive Movement, 1962, p. 158.

901. Business split

Id. at p. 154.

902. Favored regulated

Ekirch, Progressivism in America, 1974, p. 166 (one business publication observed that the Progressive Party "does not believe in the destruction of big corporations, but it believes in controlling them").

903. Sell to Wilson

Id. at p. 176.

904. More than it was

Wiebe, Businessmen and Reform: A Study of the Progressive Era, 1962, p. 217.

905. Relationship

Weinstein, The Corporate Ideal in the Liberal State, 1900–1918, 1968, p. 169.

906. "Labor's Magna Carta"

Mowry, The Progressive Era, 1900–20: The Reform Persuasion, 1958, p. 28.

907. Provided jury trial

Ibid.

like the original Magna Carta, the Clayton Act could be seen as returning to the status quo—in this case to the status prior to the Supreme Court's anti-labor rulings in the 1890s.[908]

The Clayton Act seems like rather small potatoes compared to the infestation into political discourse of pro-business Progressive values such as efficiency and elitism.[909] The epitome of this was the notion that government was just another business; one capitalist referred to the President and the state governors as the "board of directors" of that "great economic corporation known as the United States of America."[910] Similar characterizations appeared in the writing of many Progressive reformers.[911] This looks more like the "government of constitutionally mitigated absolutism" favored by those who took the Prussian state as their model than like the one to which the Founders attached the Confrontation Clause.[912]

One explanation for the Progressive "tilt" in favor of business and against working people is that the Progressives both feared and admired big corporations whereas fear alone governed their attitude toward labor unions.[913] They associated unions with class consciousness, aliens, Marxism, anarchism, and revolution.[914] Hence, they could oppose collectivism from below while accepting it when imposed from above.[915] Capitalism had an anti-union credo that resonated with the individualism and Americanism of the middle-class reformers.[916] One element of that credo that was

908. Return to status quo

This may explain why even the Democrats were willing to advocate such reforms. Ekirch, Progressivism in America, 1974, p. 235.

909. Efficiency and elitism

See above, text at notecalls 535, 759.

910. "Great corporation"

Weibe, Businessmen and Reform: A Study of the Progressive Movement, 1962. p. 196.

911. Writing of many

Haber, Efficiency and Uplift: Scientific Management in the Progressive Era, 1890–1920, 1973, p. 107.

912. "Mitigated absolutism"

White, Social Thought in America: The Revolt Against Formalism, 1957 ed., p. 156.

913. Progressive "tilt"

Mowry, The Era of Theodore Roosevelt and The Birth of Modern America, 1900–1912, 1962, p. 102.

914. Unions and class

Id. at p. 101.

915. Imposed from above

Id. at p. 100.

916. Credo that resonated

Weibe, Businessmen and Reform: A Study of the Progressive Movement, 1962, p. 162.

accepted eventually by both Wilson and Roosevelt was the futility of attempting to stop business consolidation.[917] Roosevelt asked voters to distinguish between "good" and "bad" corporations.[918] While Wilson originally favored some dispersion of private economic power, he soon came around to Roosevelt's position of "regulated monopoly."[919] As we shall see, the Great War had much to do with this conversion.[920]

Once one accepted the distinction between "good" and "bad" capitalism, a bias against unions followed easily. Benevolent (or regulated) capitalism would render unions unnecessary.[921] Unlike corporations that had lawyers to cover their anti-union tactics with the cloak of legality, the most common weapons of labor unions were regarded as unethical if not illegal;[922] "most progressives felt that the closed shop violated individual rights, the boycott the canons of decency, and violence during strikes the elementary principles of social order."[923] Progressives seldom noted that "bad unions" were in part a product of the existing legal order that made even peaceful forms of organizing potentially indictable offenses whereas the criminal law was seldom used against corporate practices of doubtful legality.[924] Perhaps the ultimate expression of

917. Futility element

Weinstein, The Corporate Ideal in the Liberal State, 1900–1918, 1968, pp. 71 (Roosevelt: "any effort to prevent combination will * * * only be useless"), 162 (Wilson: "business is no doubt best conducted upon a great scale * * *. Money and men must be massed in order to do the things that must be done for the support and facilitation of modern life").

918. "Good" and "bad"

Id. at p. 67.

919. Wilson came around

Mowry, The Progressive Era, 1900–1920: The Reform Persuasion, 1958, p. 24.

920. Great war

Ekirch, Progressivism in America, 1974, p. 271.

921. Render unnecessary

Weibe, Businessmen and Reform: A Study of the Progressive Movement, 1962, p. 166.

922. "If not illegal"

"There is nothing ethical about the labor movement. It is coercion from start to finish. In every aspect it is a driver and not a leader. It is simply a war movement, and must be judged by the analogues of belligerence and not by industrial principles." Mowry, The Era of Theodore Roosevelt and the Birth of Modern America, 1900–1912, 1962, p. 100 (quoting Southern progressive leader).

923. "Violated social order"

Weibe, Businessmen and Reform: A Study of the Progressive Movement, 1962, p. 157.

924. Seldom used

Mowry, The Era of Theodore Roosevelt and the Birth of Modern America, 1900–1912, 1962, p. 100.

Progressive anti-union animus was Croly's opinion that the Constitution made a labor party on the European model antithetical to American political values.[925] Finally, one should note that for those Progressives who were middle managers, labor unions threatened to increase the power of workers and thus erode the limited powers they were alloted in the corporate bureaucracy.[926]

Progressivism began to alter the relationship between Big Business and politics in ways that would have long term repercussions for the right of confrontation. For much of the Nineteenth Century, business influence or control of American politics had been largely informal, based on personal, social, and professional relationships rather than by participation by businessmen, as such, in politics.[927] For example, the House of Morgan was able to exploit such ties to make the federal government often almost an agent of Eastern capitalism.[928] These methods continued into the Progressive era; for example, President Taft had five corporation lawyers in his cabinet, despite the political costs of this.[929] However, beginning with the Populist uprising, the effectiveness of such methods increasingly seemed insufficient, especially to Midwestern businessmen and bankers—many of whom had no college ties, let alone the Ivy League associations that gave Eastern capitalists access to the Ivy League Presidents.[930]

Accordingly, in 1908 the National Association of Manufacturers, which had long been a trade association for non-Eastern business interests, was converted into a probusiness pressure group.[931] The N.A.M. wished to continue the longstanding commit-

---

925. Labor party antithetical

Id. at p. 101.

926. Erode limited powers

Haber, Efficiency and Uplift: Scientific Management in the Progressive Era, 1890–1920, 1973, p. 33.

927. Largely informal

Weinstein, The Corporate Ideal in the Liberal State, 1900–1918, 1968, p. 3.

928. Almost an agent

Cadenhead, Theodore Roosevelt: The Paradox of Progressivism, 1974, p. 76. This relationship is exemplified by J.P. Morgan's suggestion to President Roosevelt, at the time of the filing of the Northern Securities anti-trust case, that Roosevelt should send the Attorney–General to meet with one of

Morgan's lawyers so that "[i]f we have done anything wrong * * * they can fix it up." Id. at p. 79.

929. Five corporation lawyers

Mowry, The Era of Theodore Roosevelt and The Birth of Modern America, 1900–1912, 1962, p. 237.

930. No college ties

A study of leading businessmen in 1900 found that 84% of them had no formal education beyond high school. Russet, Darwin in America: The Intellectual Response, 1865–1912, 1976, p. 94.

931. Pressure group

Wiebe, Businessmen and Reform: A Study of the Progressive Movement, 1962, pp. 108–109.

ment of its constituents to the Republican Party.[932] However, the N.A.M.'s naivete about politics often led to their being outmaneuvered by professional politicians.[933] While to the Progressives, this might have demonstrated how even politics had become the realm of experts, for the N.A.M. this meant that more businessmen should run for public office.[934] After all, if the government was just another corporation, who better to run it than those with experience running corporations?

The N.A.M.'s "hard line" approach to politics, particularly with respect to labor, brought it into conflict with some Eastern capitalists, particularly those in the National Civic Federation who wanted to find a less "confrontational" approach to politics.[935] It was typical of the N.C.F. approach that businessmen, faced with the prospect that the Progressive Party might revive Populism under the leadership of Robert LaFollette of Wisconsin, intervened to help throw the nomination to Theodore Roosevelt, whose support for regulated monopoly seemed more promising than the N.A.M. approach.[936] While there had always been some businessmen in the Democratic party, particularly in the South, the willingness of some capitalists to abandon what the N.A.M. called "our party"——the G.O.P.——even if this meant the election of a Democrat, tended to erode the possibility that had arisen with the Bryan candidacy in 1896 for two class-based parties.[937] When Wilson, largely under the influence of pro-business Democrats, adopted parts of the Progressive business program, this tended to weaken the notion, spawned in 1895, that the election of Democrats spelled trouble for businessmen. Though the New Deal seemed a reprise of '96 for some businessmen,[938] the Progressive era tended to foster the image of politicians as "technicians of consent", fueled by ambition rather than ideology. Ultimately, this led businessmen to look on politics

---

932. Longstanding commitment
Id. at p. 117.

933. N.A.M. naivete
Id. at p. 114.

934. Businessmen should run
Id. at p. 116.

935. Conflict with N.C.F.
Weinstein, The Corporate Ideal in the Liberal State, 1900–1918, 1968, pp. 4–5.

936. Throw nomination
Id. at p. 154.

937. "Our party"
Weibe, Businessmen and Reform: A Study of the Progressive Movement, 1962, p. 119.

938. New Deal reprise
Id. at p. 223.

as an investment rather than a crusade.[939] The resulting lessening of confrontation as a political value is symbolized by the prevalence of "bipartisanship" as a political virtue after the middle of the 20th Century.[940]

The Diaz Aura

In 1912, the Supreme Court reprised the Dowdell decision in another case from the Philippine Islands, Diaz v. United States.[941] The case involved a conviction of murder arising out of an altercation between two Pilipinos. The defendant had been charged with assault and battery and convicted of that charge prior to the death of the victim. At the trial on the murder charge, the defendant raised a defense of double jeopardy and introduced the record of the trial for assault and battery and of the preliminary investigation in the criminal case. However, the defense objected to the prosecution use of these records to prove guilt on the murder charge.[942]

Writing for a unanimous Court, Justice Van Devanter noted that the objection was "that the accused was deprived of the right, secured to him by § 5 of the Philippine civil government act * * * 'to meet the witnesses face to face * * *.' "[943] Though the opinion does not, as the Dowdell opinion did, explicitly state that this provision was substantially the same as the Sixth Amendment, the Court relies on cases under the state and federal rights of confrontation.[944] The Court disposed of the objection on the ground that by offering the evidence himself, without any limitation on the purposes for which it was admitted, the defendant waived his right of

---

939. Politics as investment

This was particularly true at the municipal level, where Progressive reforms had given money an electoral advantage over grass-roots organizing and where many issues had been removed from electoral politics and made more subject to influence by businessmen. Weinstein, The Corporate Ideal in the Liberal State, 1900–1918, 1968, pp. 109, 112.

940. "Bipartisanship"

Ironically, in view of the Pound–Wigmore critique of the "sporting theory of justice", the effect was to convert politics into a game——or to use the current rhetoric, a "horse race"——a spectator sport in which citizens are mere bystanders as candidates struggle to become "frontrunners" in the polls rather than to advance a coherent program.

941. Diaz case

1912, 32 S.Ct. 250, 223 U.S. 442, 56 L.Ed. 500. The Dowdell case is discussed above, text at notecall 741.

942. Objected to prosecution use

32 S.Ct. at 250–251, 223 U.S. at 444–445.

943. "Meet the witnesses"

Id. at p. 251, 223 U.S. at 251.

944. Relies on cases

Id. at 252–253, 223 U.S. at 452–453.

confrontation.[945] The opinion comes as close as the Court had so far come to explicitly equating the hearsay rule and the right of confrontation. "True," Justice Van Devanter wrote, "the testimony could not have been admitted without the consent of the accused, first, because it was within the hearsay rule, and, second, because the accused was entitled to meet the witnesses face to face."[946]

After disposing of the hearsay claim with a string citation to cases involving evidence admitted without objection, the opinion continues:

> And of the fact that it came from witnesses who were not present at the trial, it is to be observed that the right of confrontation secured by the Philippine civil government act is in the nature of a privilege extended to the accused, rather than a restriction upon him. * * * That this is so is a necessary conclusion from the adjudged cases relating to the like right secured by the Constitutions of the several states and the Constitution of the United States.[947]

The opinion then reviews a number of state cases that support the conclusion that the right can be waived, quoting extensively from an opinion by Cooley.[948]

Unfortunately, Justice Van Devanter blurred the distinction between "waiver" and "forfeiture" or "estoppel" when he attempted to gild the lily with a quotation from the Court's Reynolds decision.[949] In that opinion, the Court did not even use the word "waiver." It merely said the

> Constitution does not guarantee an accused person against the legitimate consequences of his own wrongful acts. It grants him the privilege of being confronted with the witnesses against him; but if he voluntarily keeps the witnesses away, he cannot insist on his privilege. If, therefore, when absent by his procurement, their evidence is supplied in some lawful way, he is no condition to assert that his constitutional rights have been violated.[950]

Reynolds, it is submitted, is a case of "forfeiture" or "estoppel"; that is, the denial of the right of confrontation is justified by the

945. Waived his right
Id. at 252, 223 U.S. at 451–452.

946. "Within hearsay rule"
Ibid.

947. "Like right secured"
Ibid.

948. Quoting extensively
Id. at p. 252, 223 U.S. at 451–452.

949. Reynolds decision
See § 6356, text at notecall 747.

950. "No condition to assert"
Quoted 32 S.Ct. at 253, 223 U.S. at 452–453.

defendant's own wrongful act that prevented confrontation.[951] The conduct in Diaz, on the other hand, involved a "waiver"; that is, a voluntary relinquishment of his Sixth Amendment right to exclude hearsay.[952]

As in Dowdell, Diaz also raised an issue of the defendant's right to be present during the taking of testimony.[953] The defendant had twice absented himself from trial, but in both instances he sent the court a message consenting that the trial proceed in his absence. On appeal, he then argued that the right to be present was not waivable—a claim the Court rejected at great length.[954] However, what is significant is that in listing the various bases for the right to be present at trial, the Court nowhere mentions the right of confrontation nor the fact that in Dowdell it had said that the right of confrontation meant that testimony could only be heard from "such witnesses * * * who give their testimony in his presence."[955] Instead, the Court based the Constitutional right to be present on the Sixth Amendment right to counsel, as embodied in the Philippine law.[956] This is less an error than an illustration of the holistic nature of the Sixth Amendment; that is, the various rights in combination entail a number of requirements that are not

951. "Forfeiture" or "estoppel"

Though at some deep level the concepts are similar, the conditions that call for their application differ; e.g., it is normally supposed that in order to "waive" a right, the accused must be aware of this right, whereas the right can be forfeited when the accused kills a witness even though he is unaware of the right. Similarly, "estoppel" usually involves an element of reliance by the adversary but this is not required for waiver.

952. Voluntary relinquishment

See vol. 21, § 5033, p. 162. This does not seem to be the case where the defendant is forced to surrender one right in order to vindicate another, see Simmons v. U.S., 1968, 88 S.Ct. 967, 390 U.S. 377, 19 L.Ed.2d 1247 (discussed in Vol. 21, § 5056, p. 289), because the Court seems to suggest that the result would have been different had the defendant introduced the former testimony only to support his claim of double jeopardy rather than "without

qualification or restriction" as was done here. 32 S.Ct. at 251, 223 U.S. at 445.

953. Right to be present

Id. at 253, 223 U.S. at 453–454.

954. Court rejected

Id. at 253–255, 223 U.S. at 452–459.

955. "Testimony in presence"

See above, text at notecall 745. The Dowdell Court's basing of the right on due process rather than confrontation is, perhaps, explicable on the ground that in that case the defendant claimed a right to be present in an appellate court when affadavits were received. See above, text at notecall 755. In Diaz, on the other hand, the defendant was absent during the cross-examination and cross-examination of witnesses.

956. Right to counsel

32 S.Ct. at 253, 223 U.S. at 454.

explicitly stated in the language of the Amendment but which are implicit in the adversary system it was intended to preserve.

§ 6359. ____; Warfare State to Welfare State*

The election campaign of 1912 triggered another round of labor unrest. On January 27, 1913, a strike broke out in the silk mills in Paterson, New Jersey.[1] The authorities borrowed the tactics used in the New York garment workers' strike of 1910, using police as strikebreakers to beat and arrest hundreds of unionists.[2] When the IWW moved its free speech-campaign in to aid the strikers, this upped the ante, both sides claiming the strike had become a "war."[3] As in war, even the judiciary was drawn into the fray; on the one side, hundreds of strikers were found guilty and sentenced to jail in drumhead trials without juries and on the other side, police who killed a striker were set free by a grand jury that refused to indict.[4] Later that same year, the refusal of the Rockefeller

§ 6359

*This is a long section; the listing below of the notecalls at which particular subjects are discussed may assist the reader in search of a specific topic.

1. **Paterson strike**

Adams, Age of Industrial Violence, 1910–1915, 1966, p. 77.

2. **Beat and arrest**

Id. at pp. 81, 89.

3. **Strike a "war"**

Id. at p. 75.

4. **Refused to indict**

Id. at pp. 84, 89. The convictions of the strikers were, with a single exception, all reversed on appeal.

interests to abide by Colorado labor laws provoked a strike in the Colorado coal mines in which "war" was more than a metaphor as a private army was deployed to put down the strike.[5] Meanwhile, a revolution broke out in Mexico that became the first test of the Roosevelt Corollary to the Monroe doctrine when President Wilson used diplomacy and troops to protect the interests of U.S. corporations doing business in Mexico.[6]

The abuses of the judiciary in Paterson were highlighted when, that same year, Charles Beard published his "Economic Interpretation of the Constitution."[7] Beard's work was only one of many works that laid out the Progressive philosophy but it attracted the most attention from judges and lawyers.[8] Beard's book applied a moderate, Americanized version of Marx's economic determinism.[9] Beard attacked the heroic version of the Founders as agents of the public interest in a stronger national government, arguing instead the Founders all had economic interests furthered by the government they created.[10] Beard's indictment was far milder than Profes-

---

5. Colorado coal strike

Weinstein, The Corporate Ideal in the Liberal State, 1900–1918, 1968, pp. 191–192.

6. Protect interests

Link, Woodrow Wilson and The Progressive Era, 1910–1917, 1963 ed., pp. 107, 111. The "Roosevelt Corollary" added to the Monroe Doctrine's inhibition on European intervention in Latin American affairs the right of the United States to intervene to insure that those nations "act with decency in industrial and political matters." Cadenhead, Theodore Roosevelt: The Paradox of Progressivism, 1974, p. 94.

7. "Economic interpretation"

White, Social Thought in America: The Revolt Against Formalism, 1957 ed., p. 31.

8. One of many

Chamberlain, Farewell to Reform, 1965 ed., pp. 199–200.

9. Economic determinism

White, Social Thought in America: The Revolt Against Formalism, 1957, ed., p. 111.

10. Interests furthered

Id. at p. 113. Here is how Beard himself summed up his thesis: "The movement for the Constitution * * * was organized and carried through principally by four groups of personality interests which had been adversely affected under the Articles of Confederation: money, securities, manufacturers, trade and shipping."

"No popular vote was taken directly or indirectly on the proposition to call the Convention which drafted the Constitution.

"The propertyless masses under the prevailing suffrage qualifications were excluded at the outset from participation (through representatives) in the work of framing the Constitution.

"The Constitution was essentially an economic document based upon the concept that the fundamental private rights of property are anterior to government and morally beyond the reach of popular majorities.

"The Constitution was ratified by a vote of probably not more than one-sixth of adult males.

sor J. Allen Smith's 1907 book, "The Spirit of American Government", which undertook to show that "government, so far as it is instituted for the security of property, is in reality instituted for the defense of the rich against the poor."[11] But Smith was quoting Adam Smith, not Marx, and he was not writing in the aftermath of a Presidential campaign in which the national judiciary was a major issue.[12] As Vernon Parrington later wrote, Beard and Smith undertook to state

> the democratic case against the Constitution as it was formulated by the liberalism [of the time], and they go far to explain the temper of the Progressive movement in its labors to democratize the instrument through the direct primary, the initiative, the referendum, the recall and the like.[13]

If Justice Holmes is to be believed, the other members of the Supreme Court were outraged by Beard's book.[14]

But the judiciary took a more direct hit during the campaign of 1912. That year a federal circuit judge who had been detailed for duty on the Commerce Court was impeached for having business dealings with litigants before his court and trading favors with railroad interests.[15] Judicial ethics had been under attack for some time; a Progressive judge in North Carolina criticized federal judges for accepting passes and the use of private cars from railroads, hinting that the use (or abuse) of receiverships to aid the railroads was due in part to these petty bribes.[16] Judicial ethics were a

---

"In the ratification, it became manifest that the line of cleavage for and against the Constitution was between substantial personality interests on the one hand and the small farming and debtor interests on the other.

"The Constitution was not created by 'the whole people' as the jurists have said; neither was it created by 'the States' as Southern nullifiers long contended; but it was the work of a consolidated group whose interests knew no state boundaries and were truly national in their scope." Quoted in Chamberlain, Farewell to Reform, 1965 ed., p. 213.

11. "Defense of the rich"

Id. at pp. 208–209, 211.

12. Judiciary major issue

See § 6358, text at notecall 840. Nor did Smith rely on legal writers such as

Holmes, Pound, and Goodnow to support his argument. White, Social Thought in America: The Revolt Against Formalism, 1957 ed., p. 31.

13. "Labors to democratize"

Id. at p. 114.

14. Supreme Court outraged

Ibid.

15. Trading favors

Harbaugh, Lawyer's Lawyer: The Life of John W. Davis, 1973, p. 83; Kolko, Railroads and Regulation, 1877–1916, 1965, p. 201.

16. Petty bribes

Brooks, Walter Clark, Fighting Judge, 1944, pp. 90, 93.

problem for the Progressive Proceduralists who wished to shift power from juries to judges and remove judges from the electoral process; if judges were going to behave like other politicians, it was difficult to justify removing them from politics and increasing their power over juries.[17]

This may account for the criticism directed at Learned Hand, then a federal district court judge, when he ran for the New York Court of Appeals on the Progressive ticket without resigning from the bench.[18] President Taft put this down to Hand's being "a wild Roosevelt man and a Progressive."[19] However, Taft was not the best person to criticize Hand; while Chief Justice he was an active participant in Republican politics.[20] Moreover, it was later revealed that as Chief Justice he got $10,000 per year from the Carnegie steel interests, an annuity that his wife was to continue to receive after his death.[21] Justice Brandeis, whose ethics had been attacked during his confirmation hearings had to be more circumspect; he paid Professor Felix Frankfurter of Harvard more than $250,000 for his services as Brandeis's secret agent for political affairs.[22]

But establishment lawyers were slow to perceive the connection between judicial ethics and the legitimacy of courts. When a New York judge was attacked for awarding receiverships to his old law firm and paying them excessive fees, lawyers from Wall Street leaped to his defense.[23] However, this may be a peculiarity of the New York legal culture where judgeships were purchased like fancy foreign cars; in the 1930's the going rate was $25–50 thousand, depending on the prestige of the judgeship and purse of the would-

---

17. Increasing power

See § 6358, text at notecall 233.

18. Hand criticized

Note, The Politics of Appointment Process: An Analysis of Why Learned Hand was Never Appointed to The Supreme Court, 1973, 25 Stanford L. Rev. 251, 267. President Taft wrote that a "man who is on the bench should consider himself cloistered from politics." Mason, William Howard Taft: Chief Justice, 1965, p. 182.

19. "Wild and Progressive"

Id. at p. 171.

20. Active participant

Id. at p. 279.

21. After his death

Id. at p. 274.

22. Brandeis secret agent

Levy & Murphy, Preserving The Progressive Spirit In A Conservative Time: The Joint Reform Efforts of Justice Brandeis and Professor Frankfurter, 1916–1933, 1980, 78 Mich. L.Rev. 1252, 1262.

23. Leaped to defense

Harbaugh, Lawyer's Lawyer: The Life of John W. Davis, 1973, pp. 301, 306.

be judge.[24] One such was the infamous Judge Crater, who disappeared mysteriously, leaving behind a divorcee-mistress and a surprised wife.[25] When federal judge Martin Manton was removed from the Second Circuit after his conviction for taking bribes to write favorable opinions, one of the lawyers who was found to have paid him off was a pillar of the Wall Street bar.[26]

But the ethical behavior of judges compares favorably with that of the leading capitalists of the time.[27] By the early years of the 20th Century, businessmen had corrupted the governments of all but five of the states as well as those of most major cities.[28] One Progressive reformer argued that the dependence of the apostles of laissez faire on government favor meant that to

> keep, extend, and renew these privileges, they must have their lawyers, and their newspapers to mislead and debauch the public mind; they must go into politics, organize and control the machines of both parties, bribe councilmen and legislators and jurors, and even have judges on the bench, subservient to their will, so that the laws of the state and the grants of the municipality might be construed in their favor* * *.[29]

The so-called "Pinchot–Ballinger" controversy of 1908 revealed that the Morgan–Guggenheim interests were involved in fraudulent claims on the public domain.[30] However, they were not alone in using corrupt means to obtain title to government lands and favors.[31]

24. Going rate for judgeships

Mitgang, The Man Who Rode The Tiger: The Life and Times of Judge Samuel Seabury, 1963, pp. 159–161.

25. Judge Crater

Id. at pp. 167–168.

26. Pillar of the bar

Harbaugh, Lawyer's Lawyer: The Life of John W. Davis, 1973, pp. 313–314. Since the statute of limitations had run, the lawyer could not be prosecuted; he was disbarred, instead. The lawyer was Louis Levy, a founder of the Columbia Law Review and partner in Chadbourne, Stenchfield & Levy.

27. Leading capitalists

For example, in 1907 Standard Oil was subject to nearly a thousand indictments in various jurisdictions. Mowry, The Era of Theodore Roosevelt and

The Birth of Modern America, 1900–1912, 1962, p. 83.

28. Corrupted all

Id. at p. 67; Ekirch, Progressivism in America, 1974, p. 108; Weinstein, The Corporate Ideal in The Liberal State, 1900–1918, 1968, p. 94.

29. Construed in favor

Chamberlain, Farewell to Reform, 1965 ed., p. 115.

30. Fraudulent claims

Mowry, The Era of Theodore Roosevelt and The Birth of Modern America, 1900–1912, 1962, p. 253.

31. Not alone

Lukas, Big Trouble, 1997, p. 625.

But for purposes of confrontation, more significant than such blatant illegalities was the resort to extralegal means to preserve private power. For example, rather than go through the process of extradition of those accused of the bombing of the Los Angeles Times, the Merchants and Manufacturers Association used private detectives to remove them by force to Los Angeles.[32] These activities frequently required the cooperation of government officials to give them a patina of legitimacy.[33] As in the case of the Pullman strike, when military force was brought in, ostensibly to quell labor violence, employers were allowed to use the troops to break the strike, by such means as rounding up unionists and their sympathizers, holding them without trial, deporting them from the state, and imprisoning publishers of local newspapers to prevent news of these depredations from getting out to the community.[34] In some cases, military and civilian authorities simply ignored writs of habeas corpus issued by state judges.[35] As one journalist put it, " * * * defiance or evasion of the law, social selfishness, and a denial of the fundamental rights of man were everywhere to be detected."[36]

The epitome of these excesses was "detected" by the investigation of the United States Commission on Industrial Relations into the infamous 1914 "Ludlow Massacre."[37] By means legal and extralegal, the Rockefeller interests had erected a semifeudal empire in Southern Colorado that was reminiscent of Pullman, Illinois, in power if not amenities.[38] Mineworkers were housed in hovels, paid in scrip in defiance of state law, and had schools, churches, and even their reading materials controlled by Rockefeller minions.[39] When the miners struck in protest, they were evicted

32. Remove by force

Weinstein, The Corporate Ideal in the Liberal State, 1900–1918, 1968, p. 175.

33. Patina of legitimacy

For example, without the cooperation of local officials, these irregular extraditions would be prosecutable as kidnapping. Lukas, Big Trouble, 1997, p. 144.

34. Imprisoning publishers

Id. at pp. 104, 147, 231.

35. Ignored writs

Id. at p. 226.

36. "Denial of rights"

Chamberlain, Farewell to Reform, 1965 ed.,. p. 130.

37. "Ludlow Massacre"

Adams, Age of Industrial Violence, 1910–1915, 1966, p. 146.

38. Reminiscent of Pullman

Id. at p. 148. On Pullman, see § 6357, text at notecall 314.

39. Reading controlled

Adams, Age of Industrial Violence, 1910–1915, 1966, pp. 148–149. Among the books banned "to protect our peo-

from their "homes" and set up a tent city that soon came under assault, first by a private army of thugs, then by the National Guard called out at the behest of and controlled by company officials.[40] The rabble-rousing matron known as "Mother Jones" was held for weeks without trial and deported from the area in what a law professor at the University of Colorado called "one of the greatest outrages upon civilized American jurisprudence [ever] perpetrated."[41]

Having seen what happened to other unionists when troops were called out, the miners at Ludlow were not about to be herded into concentration camps.[42] When the military attempted to enter the tent city, the unionists opened fire and a pitched battle ensued.[43] Caught in the cross-fire and an ensuing conflagration, families of the strikers suffered the fate of combatants; along with other casualties, two women and eleven children were killed.[44] Regardless of how responsibility for this, and other atrocities alleged, is apportioned, one cannot escape the inference that this sort of anarchy had more to do with popular attitudes toward the legal system than many of the "causes of popular dissatisfaction" listed by Roscoe Pound.[45]

The Ludlow massacre produced one of the most widely-followed confrontations of the Progressive era when John D. Rockefeller, Jr. appeared before the Commission on Industrial Relations.[46] In his first appearance, Rockefeller denied any knowledge of conditions in Colorado and any responsibility for the steps taken to break the

ple from erroneous ideas" were Darwin's "Origin of the Species" and "The Rubaiyat of Omar Khayyam." The company was less careful about infection by microbes than it was of contagious ideas; the year prior to the strike 151 people contracted typhoid from unsafe drinking water supplied by the company.

40. Controlled by company

Id. at pp. 152–153.

41. "Outrages"

Id. at pp. 155–156. Because the company controlled the local judiciary, no writ of habeas corpus could be obtained, id. at pp. 151, 155, but it is doubtful that the military would have honored it because the commander told newsmen Mother Jones "was a person who was

dangerous to the peace of the community [who] civil authorities were not capable of handling * * *."

42. Concentration camps

Lukas, Big Trouble, 1997, p. 104.

43. Pitched battle

Adams, Age of Industrial Violence, 1910–1915, 1966, p. 157.

44. Eleven children

Id. at pp. 158–159.

45. "Popular dissatisfaction"

See § 6358, text at notecall 318.

46. Confrontations of era

Adams, The Age of Industrial Violence, 1910–1915, 1966, p. 161.

strike, but expressed contrition and a desire to improve conditions among his employees——he was so impressive that even unionists were impressed.[47] However, when Rockefeller returned a second time, Commission investigators had subpoenaed letters and memos from company files showing that Rockefeller had lied in his first appearance.[48] His "pitiless cross-examination" at hands of Commission Chairman Frank Walsh brought criticism from the business press——"bullying" and "badgering" were among the milder epithets——that probably did nothing to enhance judicial appreciation of the right of confrontation.[49]

The Ludlow Massacre provided the counterpoint to another event of the same year——passage of the Clayton Act with its proclamation that "the labor of a human being is not a commodity."[50] But if the Act failed to provide labor with the complete exemption from the Sherman Act they hoped for, it did give most businessmen what they desired——a forum of experts to enforce the antitrust laws, who, it was hoped, would create standards that if not more favorable to business than those created by the courts would at least be more certain.[51] The Act started out as an effort by the National Civic Federation to revise the Sherman Act; when Congress suggested the NCF draft a bill embodying its proposal, they produced a measure that was a compromise between President Taft's antitrust views and those of the House of Morgan.[52] When Brandeis won Wilson over to this version of Roosevelt's "regulated monopoly", passage was assured.[53] When businessmen used the war as a cover to capture the fledgling Federal Trade Commission created by the Act,[54] seeds were planted that bore bitter fruit when

---

47. Unionists impressed

Id. at pp. 162–163.

48. Rockefeller lied

Id. at pp. 166–168.

49. Enhance appreciation

Id. at p. 169; Weinstein, The Corporate Ideal in the Liberal State, 1900–1918, 1968, p. 207 ("pitiless cross").

50. "Not a commodity"

Foner, The Story of American Freedom, 1999, p. 144.

51. More certain

Ekirch, Progressivism in America, 1974, p. 235; Weinstein, The Corporate Ideal

in the Liberal State, 1900–1918, 1968, p. 79.

52. Compromise of views

Id. at pp. 72, 77–78.

53. "Regulated monopoly"

Id. at p. 62.

54. Captured Commission

Wiebe, Businessmen and Reform; A Study of the Progressive Movement, 1962, pp. 138, 147.

the Truman administration sought to use the administrative process for repressive purposes during the Cold War—the abuses of which ultimately produced a revival of interest in the right of confrontation.[55]

Competition, Cooperation, and Confrontation

Along with the Ludlow Massacre and the Clayton Act, 1914 brought war in Europe.[56] These three events could well symbolize the Progressive ambivalence toward conflict and cooperation; Ludlow exemplified the worst aspects of the industrial conflict that many Progressives detested and the Clayton Act showed how such conflict might be ameliorated by government action.[57] The initial response to World War I may also evidence the nation's preference for peace and the dangers of competition for empire—though the cynic might well detect some desire for lucre since selling arms to both sides could bring more profits than joining one side or the other.[58] Profits were a concern because 1914 also saw a brief depression that produced a clamor for the end of Progressive reforms.[59] But the need for further reforms was documented by Brandeis's "Other People's Money"—a popular explanation of the exposes of the Pujo Committee.[60]

But one need not be a cynic to suggest that more widely read than Brandeis's book—and certainly more influential in shaping public attitudes toward the right of confrontation—was Sir Arthur Conan Doyle's "The Valley of Fear", published the same year.[61] The novel is unusual in that nearly half of it is set in the United States and that half is marked by the absence of Sherlock Holmes—except as the implicit auditor of the tale told by the man Holmes has just proved to be a killer. The hero is a Pinkerton man

55. Revival of interest

See below, § 6360 at notecall 915.

56. Brought war

Encyclopedia of American Facts and Dates, 9th ed. 1993, p. 424.

57. Conflict ameliorated

A less dramatic exemplar of the virtues of cooperation, also from 1914, was the decision of Henry Ford to pay his workers $5 for an eight-hour day, at least partly so they could afford to buy the cars they were making. Wiebe, Businessmen and Reform: A Study of The Progressive Movement, 1962, p. 167 (Ford was denounced by other capitalists for "demoralizing" workers).

58. War and profits

Id. at p. 145.

59. End of reforms

Id. at p. 143.

60. "Other People's Money"

Chamberlain, Farewell to Reform, 1965 ed., pp. 232–233.

61. "Valley of Fear"

Doyle, Valley of Fear, 1994 ed., p. 4.

(loosely modeled after James McParlan, the celebrated American detective) who killed the man sent to assassinate him for his role in breaking an organization that bears some resemblance to the Molly Maguires.[62] The novel fits nicely into upper-class paranoia regarding Irish immigrants, labor unions, and Marxism; the villain spouts Marxist jargon, the unions have corrupted and thus control local politics, and their victims are local reformers and small, "model employers" who demand nothing of their employees but "efficiency."[63] The hero repeats the real Pinkertons' excuse for their failure to warn people they knew had been marked for murder by the Molly Maguires.[64]

Anyone who accepted Doyle's picture of Nineteenth Century American society would find it hard to resist Roscoe Pound's attack on the adversary system.[65] The hero repeatedly tells us, as his tale illustrates, that the regular system of criminal justice is inadequate to deal with industrial unrest.[66] Hence, it is necessary to resort to private armed force, private police, and spies and informers—— Doyle's Pinkerton at his moment of triumph delivers a quite unrealistic, though quite effective, speech on behalf of the role of informers.[67] The adversary system fails because witnesses are frightened or corrupt and jurors are incapable or unwilling to determine the truth; indeed, cross-examination appears only as a device by which corrupt lawyers confuse or intimidate honest witnesses.[68] Confrontation values are embraced by criminals——and the hero when he is passing himself off as a criminal.[69] Any comfort

62. Resemblance to Molly Maguire

Id. at p. 282. On the Molly Maguires, see § 6356, text at notecall 597. On McParlan's fame, see Kenny, Making Sense of The Molly Maguires, 1998, pp. 155–156.

63. Nothing but "efficiency"

Doyle, The Valley of Fear, 1994 ed., pp. 194 (unions corruptly control local government), 211 (villain and Socialist jargon), 291 (model employers).

64. Failure to warn

Id. at p. 312. See also, Kenny, Making Sense of the Molly Maguires, 1998, p. 200 (McParlan's failure to warn).

65. Pound's attack

See § 6358, text at notecall 318.

66. System inadequate

Doyle, The Valley of Fear, 1994 ed., pp. 188, 216.

67. Behalf of informers

Id. at pp. 210 (private force), 313 (defense of informers).

68. Confuse or intimidate

Id. at p. 254 ("Cross-examined by the clever attorney who had been engaged by [the villain], they were even more nebulous in their evidence [about the identity of criminals who assaulted a newspaper editor])."

69. Values embraced

Id. at p. 203:

"So, said he with a furious glance at [the hero], 'you got here first, did you?

readers might take from historical distance is shattered when at the end of the story the hero is destroyed by an international criminal conspiracy supposed to be still operative and linked to American unionists.[70]

But the Progressive attitude toward confrontation and competition stemmed from deeper currents than popular culture and detective fiction. Perhaps at the bottom one would find an enduring paradox of Progressivism; namely, the desire for social change that did not alter the status quo.[71] An early historian of the movement argued that Progressives were split between two "schools", one typified by Brandeis, the other by Croly:

> The one school cherished the competitive system with its individual values and feared the powerful state; the other welcomed concentrated power whether in industry or politics, looked to a paternalistic state staffed by an educated elite for leadership, and deprecated individualism.[72]

At least with respect to confrontation, bureaucratic paternalism seemed to prevail over competitive individualism, perhaps because the corporate status quo was less threatened by the former than the latter.[73] One of the leading spokesmen for Progressive capitalism told his fellows:

> Cooperation in business is taking and should take the place of ruthless competition. [If] this new order of things is better for

I've a word to say to you, [addressing the villain], about this man.'

'Then say it here and now before my face,' cried [the hero].

'I'll say it at my own time, in my own way.'

'Tut! Tut!' said [the villain] 'This will never do.' * * * [proceeding to require the complainant to express his grievance against the hero]."

70. International conspiracy

Id. at p. 319.

71. Did not alter

Chamberlain, Farewell to Reform, 1965 ed., pp. 222–223.

72. "Deprecated individualism"

Mowry, The Era of Theodore Roosevelt and The Birth of Modern America, 1900–1912, 1962, p. 57.

73. Less threatened

It was unionists, not capitalists, who had the most to fear from the criminal law, which was seldom used to enforce business regulation; indeed, one of the functions of the Clayton Act was to provide an alternative to criminal sanctions to enforce the antitrust laws. Even the respectable "middle class" Progressives had little to fear from the prosecutor. However, as we shall see, the growth of sumptuary laws, symbolized by Prohibition, was to increase middle-class interest in criminal justice.

capital and better for the consumer, then in order to succeed permanently it must demonstrate that it is better for the laborer.[74]

Woodrow Wilson thought the demise of competitive individualism, at least in the corporate world, was inevitable: "I dare say we shall never return to the old order of individual competition, and that the organization of business upon a great scale of cooperation is, up to a certain point, itself normal and inevitable."[75] "Cooperation" was linked with "efficiency" in the Progressive corporate lexicon; the latter aimed to provide a "scientific" basis for big business while the former was supposed to provide a moral justification.[76]

However, insofar as labor was concerned, Progressives could not decide whether the word was "cooperation" or "cooptation."[77] One wing of the movement wanted to strengthen the labor movement to the point where it was at least "competitive" with capitalism at the negotiating table; such folk ran the danger of being mistaken for disciples of William Graham Summer, who argued that "[i]ndustrial warfare is in fact an incident of liberty * * * a sign of vigor in society. It contains the promise of a sound solution."[78] The other wing of Progressivism wanted to appeal to the paternalism of capitalists rather than to socialize the competitiveness of workers into unions; such folk, including Theodore Roosevelt, adopted Veblen's distinction between "business" ("bad") and "industry" ("good" capitalism).[79] An example of the latter would be Henry Ford, who gave his workers an unprecedented $5 wage and a limited workweek.[80] Exactly how these two strands of Progressive thought would have played themselves out will never be known for, as we shall see, war brought a sort of government coerced "cooperation" between labor and capital designed to make

74. "Better for laborer"

Weinstein, The Corporate Ideal in the Liberal State, 1900–1918, 1968, p. 45.

75. "Normal and inevitable"

Id. at p. 163.

76. Moral justification

Haber, Efficiency and Uplift: Scientific Management in the Progressive Era, 1890–1920, 1973, p. 72.

77. Or "cooptation"

Weinstein, The Corporate Ideal in the Liberal State, 1900–1918, 1968, p. 202.

78. "Sign of vigor"

Chamberlain, Farewell to Reform, 1965 ed., p. 14.

79. "Business" and "industry"

Id. at p. 218.

80. Henry Ford

Wiebe, Businessmen and Reform: A Study of The Progressive Movement, 1962, p. 167.

the war effort more "efficient" rather than to provide a "sound solution."[81]

The adversary system, including the right of confrontation, can be seen as a similar system of "coerced cooperation." It exhibits the same tension between "cooperation" and "cooptation" that characterized Progressive thought. At the one extreme, an "adversary" system can resemble Sumner's "industrial warfare" with the judge's role limited to that of a kind of "jurisprudential Red Cross." At the other extreme, the individualism of the parties can be so submerged in bureaucratic control that the "cooperation" resembles that of a chain gang, the appearance of cooperation without the substance. Insofar as criminal justice is concerned, Progressive proceduralists resemble their secular counterparts in dividing between those who believe justice is better served by strengthening the hand of the weaker party (usually, but not inevitably the defendant) and those who think that justice depends upon the paternalism of the state, as represented by the judge and the prosecutor.

However, at least during the Progressive era, the tide was running against anything that smacked of competitive individualism; when Herbert Hoover analogized his version of "rugged individualism" to a "rule-bound track meet", the Pounds of the time thought more of the Ludlow Massacre than the Oklahoma land rush.[82] Attempts, whether in court or in the industrial sphere, to alter the rules to favor the less powerful were apt to be seen not as a strengthening of competition or making for a more meaningful "cooperation" but rather as exhibiting a preference for "socialism" over "individualism."[83] Since Thorstein Veblen did much to discredit the economic notion of "competition" by contrasting the economist's idealized version with that of the real world, Progressives were probably receptive to his debunking of competitors in the legal world.[84]

81. War and cooperation

Weinstein, The Corporate Ideal in the Liberal State, 1900–1918, 1968, pp. 230, 232.

82. Oklahoma land rush

Chamberlain, Farewell to Reform, 1965 ed., p. 23.

83. Preference for "socialism"

White, Social Thought in America: The Revolt Against Formalism, 1957 ed., p.

54. Exactly why "cooperation" was seen as antithetical to "competition" is not easy to see; after all, one form of "cooperation" seems to be part of the reigning constitutional doctrine of "liberty contract."

84. Discredit economic notion

Id. at p. 37.

The lawyer is exclusively occupied with the details of predatory fraud, either in achieving or checkmating chicane, and success in the profession is therefore accepted as marking a large endowment of that barbarian astuteness which has always commanded men's respect and fear.[85]

However, Progressive attacks on competition were not limited to lawyers and capitalists—indeed, in some ways the Progressive era anticipates a similar development in the 1960's. Competitiveness was associated, as in the Veblen quote above, with a sort of primitive masculinity and the entry of women into the political world was seen as the prelude to a new reign of cooperation.[86] Similarly, grades in the classroom were attacked as inducing an unhealthy competitiveness among students.[87]

As in the 1960's, even lawyers got caught up in the silliness of supposed novelty. "Golden Rule" Jones, the anarchist-Progressive mayor of Toledo, thought that competitive legal and economic institutions fomented social belligerence and looked forward to the day when the primacy of "love" would lead to the abolition of courts.[88] However, most lawyers did not want to abolish courts but to make them less adversarial. Moorfield Storey, past-President of the A.B.A., in his Storrs lecture urged the revival of Tudor inquisitorial institutions like the justice of the peace and the preliminary hearing.[89] John Dos Passos, the father of the novelist, thought adversarial excesses led lawyers to the brink of crime.[90] In arguing that lawyers went too far in aiding their clients to evade the law, Dos Passos did not limit himself to litigators—using as examples of such excesses the Northern Securities case and the New Jersey corporation law.[91] And, unlike other Progressive reformers, Dos

85. "Respect and fear"

Id. at p. 60.

86. Entry of women

Haber, Efficiency and Uplift: Scientific Management in the Progressive Era, 1890–1920, 1973, pp. 126–127.

87. Grades unhealthy

White, Social Thought in America: The Revolt Against Formalism, 1957 ed., p. 97.

88. "Love" and courts

Tager, The Intellectual as Urban Reformer: Brand Whitlock and The Progressive Movement, 1968, p. 62.

89. Revival of inquisitorial

Hixson, Moorfield Storey and The Abolitionist Tradition, 1972, p. 177.

90. Brink of crime

Dos Passo, The American Lawyer, 1907, p. 10.

91. Examples of excesses

Id. at pp. 77, 79.

Passos placed the blame on Langdellian legal education: "[l]awyers are made to be mere instruments for their clients, without any attention being paid to their duties to the state."[92] For him, the lawyer's "primary duty is to the State."[93]

Few lawyers went as far as Dos Passos in opposing adversariness. Brandeis, for example, was too much the traditionalist and realist to suppose the clash of force could be banned from the courtroom.[94] Other lawyers blamed the excess of adversariness, not on the elite law schools, but on the entry into the profession of non-Anglo–Saxons like Brandeis who did not appreciate the English instinct for fairness that was essential to make the system work.[95] Indeed, the then-Dean of the West Virginia Law School, in a kind of "reverse Darwinism", argued for raising standards for admission to law schools on the ground that a "man of gentlemanly instincts and cultural background often finds himself handicapped in competition with persons of inferior character and greater aggressiveness."[96]

For confrontation, it is as an argument for procedural reform rather than academic eugenics that the deprecation of competition is most significant. One of Roscoe Pound's allies, not content with the analogy to the fox hunt or the boxing ring, claimed that the "average lawyer feels that if much of the form and many of the formulas of practice are dispensed with, he will be disarmed of his weapons of war."[97] Indeed, so strong had the dogma of adversary excess become, that when the first major empirical study of American criminal justice—The National Commission on Law Observance and Enforcement, popularly known as the "Wickersham Commission" after its chairman—could find no evidence to support "the sporting theory of justice", indeed, discovering an excess of "cooperation" among supposed adversaries that in the words of the researchers "seems almost too efficient" in producing uncontested guilty pleas, the Chairman of the Commission ordered this conclu-

---

92. "Duties to state"

Id. at p. 50.

93. "Primary duty"

Id. at p. 127.

94. Too much realist

Chamberlain, Farewell to Reform, 1965 ed., p. 233.

95. Did not appreciate

Todd, Justice on Trial: The Case of Louis D. Brandeis, 1964, p. 87.

96. "Handicapped in competition"

Ayer, In Quest of Efficiency: The Ideological Journey of Thurman Arnold in the Interwar Period, 1972, 23 Stan. L.Rev. 1049, 1063.

97. "Weapons of war"

Wigdor, Roscoe Pound, 1974, p. 148.

sion deleted because it was "at variance with the conclusions which were reached in other [non-empirical] reports."[98] This sort of "cooperation" in suppressing contradictory evidence is——need it be said?——not conducive to development of a robust right of confrontation.[99]

Colleges, Consumers, and Civil Liberties

Though the year 1915 saw 852 Americans killed when an overloaded excursion steamer capsized in Lake Michigan, it is best remembered for the sinking of the Lusitania in which 128 Americans of somewhat higher social status lost their lives.[100] The Lusitania, together with the discovery of a German spy ring in New York, forced President Wilson to weaken his pacifist stance with consequences for confrontation we shall see later. The same year, the Child Labor Act was passed, the Supreme Court decided the Grandfather Clause cases, Georgia rechartered the Ku Klux Klan, the trustees of the University of Pennsylvania fired an economics teacher for his socialist beliefs, Margaret Sanger was jailed for dispensing birth-control information, the millionth Model T rolled off the assembly line, and the motion picture "Birth of a Nation" opened.[101] The relevance of these events to the right of confrontation requires some explanation.

As evidenced by the publication of Dewey's "Democracy and Education" the following year, education was an important, if sometimes overlooked, battleground for Progressive values.[102] One of the motivations for the Child Labor Act was to get children out of factories and into classrooms.[103] Schools were important because many Progressives believed that part of the solution for the influx of alien persons and ideas was to get the former into schools where they could be inculcated in American values and turned from

98. "At variance"

Schlegel, Ameican Legal Realism and Empirical Social Science: From The Yale Experience, 1979, 28 Buff.L.Rev. 459, 503–505.

99. Not conducive

Dean Charles E. Clark of Yale, one of the researchers and a prominent proceduralist, was said to be "slightly bitter" about this deletion. Id. at p. 505.

100. Lusitania sinking

Encyclopedia of American History, Morris ed.1976, pp. 328, 359.

101. Motion picture opened

The Encyclopedia of American Facts and Dates, 9th ed.1993, pp. 426–430.

102. Progressive values

Chamberlain, Farewell to Reform, 1965 ed., p. 230.

103. Child Labor Act

Wood, Constitutional Politics in the Progressive Era, 1968, p. 41.

anarchism to patriotism.[104] Enrollment in high schools and colleges doubled during the Progressive era, much of this in the South where the rise of segregation removed one objection to public schools.[105] It has been estimated that one new high school was built for each day of the years 1900–1920, setting the stage for a rapid increase in college enrollment in the 1920's.[106]

Given the ideological role assigned to education, it is to be expected that among the outside influences penetrating the academy would be business instrumentalism.[107] President McKinley had complained of "the influence of professors in some of our institutions of learning, who teach science contained in books, and not practical business."[108] A disciple of Taylor, hired by the Carnegie Foundation for the Advancement of Teaching, proposed a series of proposals to make teachers "more efficient producers" with standards to measure their achievement.[109] The rise of "educational administration" and the founding of the American Association of Universities led to increasing bureacratization, standardization, and uniformity in higher education.[110] Not that colleges and universities did not need improvement—boring teachers led both Jack London and Frank Norris to drop out of the University of California after one semester, pioneers not only in literature but in the "educational consumerism" that would eventually become as serious a threat to higher education as political meddling.[111]

104. Turned to patriotism

O'Neill, The Progressive Years, 1975, p. 10.

105. Enrollment doubled

Ekirch, Progressivism in America, 1974, p. 82.

106. Increase in college

Mowry, The Progressive Era, 1900–1920: The Reform Persuasion, 1958, p. 11.

107. Business instrumentalism

That is, that schools should train students to be workers and bureaucrats, not citizens or thinkers. Ekirch, Progressivism in America, 1974, p. 82.

108. "Not practical business"

Chamberlain, Farewell to Reform, 1965 ed., p. 16.

109. "Efficient producers"

Haber, Efficiency and Uplift: Scientific Management in the Progressive Era, 1890–1920, 1973, p. 65. The sorts of standards envisaged will be familiar to those who have ever looked closely at the U.S. News and World Report's method of ranking law schools at the end of the century.

110. Uniformity in education

O'Neill, The Progressive Years, 1975, pp. 99–101.

111. "Educational consumerism"

Chamberlain, Farewell to Reform, 1965 ed., p. 189.

An apt illustration of Progressive values is the so-called "Wisconsin Idea", in which university professors provided the "expertise" and even drafted bills for reformers in that state.[112] One enthusiast proclaimed that "in Wisconsin, wealth is sanctified by commonwealth and the people of the state willingly let University professors write their laws and administer their departments."[113] For example, the exemplary Progressive, John Rogers Commons, working for the University's Legislative Reference Bureau, drafted a utility-regulation statute along lines favored by utility magnates and the National Civic Federation.[114] While some Progressives carried the "Wisconsin Idea" to other states, others were critical of the "Idea"——at least as it was implemented.[115]

Given the political role of Progressive education, it was inevitable that those with the most to lose from politics would intervene to protect their interests.[116] Hence, the businessmen in the National Civic Federation who had Scott Nearing fired from his teaching position because he espoused socialism could defend their actions both on the grounds that his ideology was neither "practical business" nor Americanism.[117] Nor was the act unprecedented; the guru of many Progressives, the sociologist Edward A. Ross had been fired from Stanford in 1900 for his political beliefs and ended up, not surprisingly, at the University of Wisconsin.[118] Firing professors for their beliefs may have itself taught the students a significant civics lesson; that is, the value of civil liberties to Progressives——a matter to which we now turn.

112. "Wisconsin Idea"

Ekirch, Progressivism in America, 1974, p. 110.

113. "Professors write laws"

Haber, Efficiency and Uplift: Scientific Management in the Progressive Era, 1890–1920, 106. Authors expounding upon procedural rules written by law professors are not unbiased regarding the wisdom of this.

114. Commons and regulation

Weinstein, The Corporate Ideal in the Liberal State, 1900–1918, 1968, p. 25.

115. As implemented

Id. at p. 200 ("interminable bill-drafting, by countless employees, experts, and the like, 'of scientific training'——the very thought of which should throw the legal profession into spasms of delight, and the proletariat into hopeless despair"); Chamberlain, Farewell to Reform, 1965 ed., p. 73 ("Idea" carried into other states).

116. Protect interests

Since virtually every early American educational institution was church affiliated; the notion of "academic freedom" was not a longstanding tradition.

117. Nearing fired

Weinstein, The Corporate Ideal in the Liberal State, 1900–1918, 1968, p. 129.

118. Ross precedent

Ross, Social Control, 1969 ed., p. xv.

In considering the Progressive attitude toward individual rights, and in criticizing judicial interpretations of the confrontation clause, we must recall that the Bill of Rights had not then assumed the importance it would late in the century; compare the hoopla surrounding the 200th anniversary of the first ten amendments with the nearly unmarked passage of their centenary in 1891.[119] The First Amendment provides an apt illustration; it has been said that "no genuinely effective, legally enforceable right to freedom of speech" existed in the Progressive Era.[120] Indeed, when Zecharaiah Chafee of Harvard wrote "Freedom of Speech", which was published in 1920, he all but invented free-speech jurisprudence.[121] As we have seen, the I.W.W. played a role in development of the speech clause of the First Amendment analogous to that played by Jehovah's Witnesses for the religion clause; there were more free-speech cases between 1900 and 1915 than in the previous century—most of them hostile to the right.[122] As we shall see, Wold War I did much to end judicial complacency about the First Amendment.

This is where Margaret Sanger comes in. The Progressive Era was accompanied by a transformation in the arts, loosely described as "modernist", and the growth of Bohemian romanticism in the largest cities.[123] Artists were welcome even in Progressive circles where the I.W.W. was anathema. When what one historian has called "the lyrical left" was crossed with the movement for women's suffrage, the result was a kind of radical feminism that in conjunction with consumerism would eventually produce that symbol of 1920's decadence—the "flapper." This sort of feminism, according to one of its acolytes, had two "dominating ideas: the emancipating of woman both as a human being and a sex-being."[124] The massive entrance of women into the work force in World War I posed a radical challenge to traditional mores that was made even

119. Unremarked centenary

Foner, The Story of American Freedom, 1998, p. 163.

120. "No enforceable right"

Ibid.

121. Invented jurisprudence

Ibid.

122. Most hostile

Id. at p. 164. Most of these were state-court decisions, in part because of the limited scope given the First Amendment at that time.

123. Bohemian romanticism

Id. at p. 166.

124. "Sex-being"

Ibid.

more threatening when the flamboyant anarchist orator Emma Goldman began distributing information on contraceptives at her lectures on women's rights.[125] Margaret Sanger was single-mindedly devoted to the cause of contraception; when threatened with a 45-year sentence under the federal anti-obscenity Comstock Act, she fled to England until the indictment was dismissed.[126] When she returned in 1915, she began distributing contraceptive devices to poor Jewish and Italian women; her second prosecution for obscenity, for which she served a month in jail, raised free-speech issues among people who did not care a whit for what happened to the Wobblies.[127]

But this was all in the future when Progressive attitudes toward civil liberties were being formulated. At the turn of the century, the traditional civil-rights lexicon was tainted by its association with Darwinian laissez faire; hence, even when such issues were raised, it was usually in the name of "democracy", not "rights" or "freedom."[128] But many Progressives were more concerned with creating new rights than vindicating those found in the Bill of Rights; as in the alternative constitutions proposed by some unionists, these novel rights tended to be more collective than individual——the right to organize and strike, for example.[129] Progressives were more concerned with economic than with governmental restraints on citizens; when Wilson hit a Jeffersonian note in describing his "New Freedom", Theodore Roosevelt replied with contempt that Wilson's conception of freedom "has not one particle of foundation in the facts of the present day" but constituted a program for "the enslavement of the people by great corporations who can only be held in check by the extension of governmental power."[130]

But the debate between Wilson and Roosevelt was more apparent than real; Wilson himself said that "freedom today is something

---

125. Goldman distributed

Id. at p. 167. Goldman is best remembered today as the source of a popular t-shirt quotation in the 1960s that still pops up on campuses to this day: "If I can't dance, I don't want to join your revolution." She was deported and lived out her days, presumably not dancing, in the Soviet Union——as it then was.

126. Fled to England

Id. at pp. 167–168.

127. Raised free speech issues

Id. at p. 168.

128. Lexicon tainted

Id. at p. 140.

129. Right to strike

Id. at p. 164.

130. "Enslavement by corporations"

Id. at p. 160.

more than being let alone. The program of a government of freedom must in these days be positive, not negative merely."[131] In fact, many Progressives were under the influence of the British philosopher T.H.Green, who had argued in 1880 that " 'freedom' was a positive concept; that is it did not mean simply freedom from government restraint but rather empowerment through collective action that can only be realized through government."[132] As Randolph Bourne put it, "[f]reedom means a democratic cooperation in determining the ideals and purposes and industrial and social institutions of a country."[133] Or as another Progressive put it, Progressivism "looks to state action as the only * * * practicable means now in sight, of giving to individuals, all individuals, not merely an economically strong class, real freedom."[134]

Progressives of this stripe were on to something that, had it been applied to the Sixth Amendment, might have had a significant impact on the right of confrontation.[135] One historian of the concept has spoken of the "tension between freedom as the power to participate in public affairs and freedom as a collection of individual rights requiring protection against governmental interference."[136] Later he describes the dichotomy of individual rights which are "simultaneously democratic and a negation of democracy—democratic in the sense that they can be claimed by anyone; undemocratic in that they need to be protected against abuses of power, including the power of people themselves."[137] A Progressive could hardly have put it better, but one of them did. John Commons "believed that conflicts of interest made for progress, but he also stressed the mutual dependence of the contending forces and the

131. "Not negative merely"

Id. at p. 159.

132. Freedom as empowerment

Id. at p. 153.

133. "Democratic cooperation"

Ibid.

134. "Real freedom"

Ibid.

135. On to something

In the terminology of Wesley Hohfeld of Yale, confrontation is less a "right" than a "power"; whereas a "right" means someone else is under a "duty", a "power" places the other under a "liability"; that is, the possibility that its exercise will alter the relationship between the parties by imposing a duty that did not exist prior to its exercise—in the case of confrontation, the duty to produce a witness. See Corbin, Legal Analysis and Terminology, 1919, 29 Yale L.J. 163.

136. "Governmental interference"

Foner, The Story of American Freedom, 1998, p. 7.

137. "People themselves"

Id. at p. 25.

need to impose some order upon them."[138]

Like Commons, we can see the Sixth Amendment in general and the Confrontation Clause in particular as avoiding the dichotomization suggested by some analysts and recognizing the mutual interdependence of the prosecutor and the accused and the tribunal, whether judge alone or judge and jury.[139] The "right" of confrontation is more than simply a protection of the defendant from the use of unconfronted hearsay.[140] It empowers the defendant to require the prosecution to produce declarants for cross-examination that will allow the defendant to test the basis of their statements, not merely for his own benefit but for the benefit of the tribunal. It empowers judge (and jury) by freeing them of the difficult task of evaluating the evidence they have called for (as would be the case under an inquisitorial system) and frees them from control by appellate courts because of their presumed access to demeanor and other evidence not available to the reviewing court. Hence, it would be a mistake to think that the "right of confrontation" was of the same sort as the right to work children in coal mines——or the right to wear a jacket with rude expressions about the draft.

Whatever their attitudes toward the Sixth Amendment, Progressives in their quest for a "positive" notion of freedom may have played an unwitting role in undermining public respect for the traditional "rights." One of the new, positive freedoms Progressives advocated was the right of a job, including the right to a "living wage"——even a right to an "American standard of living."[141] Enter Henry Ford. He not only provided one standard for a "living wage" with his $5 minimum for all employees, but also raised the level of an "American standard of living" by holding out the promise of an automobile affordable to every family. Ford was, it seems, on the cutting edge as American corporations shifted emphasis from the production of capital goods to consumer goods.[142]

138. "Need to impose order"

Haber, Efficiency and Uplift: Scientific Management in the Progressive Era, 1890–1920, 1973, p. 145.

139. Interdependence

We suspect that there is a kind of conceptual interdependence at work as well——that is, the dichotomy is in some sense a false one. But it would take us far beyond our skills and the needs of the reader to explore this.

140. Confrontation is more

See vol. 30, § 6341, p. 186.

141. "American standard"

Foner, The Story of American Freedom, 1998, p. 144.

142. Shift to consumer

Id. at p. 147.

This shift did much to create the advertising industry, whose task was to convince Americans they had "wants" their ancestors never heard of.[143] Much as advertisers later in the century seized on 60s symbols and feminist rhetoric to sell soft drinks and cigarettes, Progressive era ad writers coopted and cheapened the political rhetoric of the time.[144] One adman claimed that "every free-born American has a right to name his own necessities."[145] The effort to move freedom from the political arena to the marketplace resonated not only with Progressive rhetoric but also with conservative laissez faire ideology; the right to buy whatever one wants could be portrayed as the ultimate "liberty of contract." Not only did this conflation of democracy with consumerism replace the traditional values of thrift and self denial with an ethos of personal fulfillment through acquisition of goods, it also made American ideology "materialist" in a way Marx could not have imagined.[146] One indicia of the success of the advertisers in the shift from political to marketplace democracy is that by the early 1920s fewer ballots were being placed in the box.[147] Not long afterwards, one newspaper could say that the "American citizen's first importance to his country is no longer that of a citizen but that of a consumer."[148]

For purposes of confrontation, the importance of consumerism was less that its use of "rights" to sell soap cheapened the concept but that it infantalized the public. Most of us realize that one indicia of adulthood is that we no longer cry when our material wants are not instantly gratified. Democratic politics and adversary

143. Had "wants"

Ibid.

144. Coopted and cheapened

See id. at pp. 149–150. This led to statutes forbidding the use of some national icons, particularly the flag, in advertising—prohibitions long overlooked by those concerned with "desecration" of the flag and now, if one can judge from contemporary advertising, deemed invalidated by the flag-burning cases.

145. "Right to name his own"

Id. at p. 147.

146. Made ideology "materialist"

Id. at p. 148. If anything, this conflation of democracy with consumerism is even stronger at the end of the century; both Americans and Soviet citizens associated "communism" in the Soviet Union with the absence of consumer goods and democracy with abundance. This is ironic, indeed, for those raised in the 1950s when "materialistic" was joined with "Godless" in popular condemnations of communism.

147. Fewer ballots

Id. at p. 151.

148. "Not citizen but consumer"

Ibid.

factfinding are not about giving everybody what they want but about reconciling inconsistent interests in ways that satisfy no one but make an equitable distribution of a limited number of possibilities. Compared to the right to "whatever you want" promised by the culture of abundance, the right to confrontation may seem like a pale imitation of a right, except when resentment at the inability to hurt others who one wishes to blame for some calamity leads one to exaggerate the value of the right to the defendant and overlook the necessarily limited benefits it provides to individual members of the public.

Progressive resentment of the rights of others reached its pinnacle with respect to the ultimate Other—African Americans, or "Negroes" as they were called. The Progressive Era was the worst period for American Blacks since the Civil War.[149] Despite massive white opposition after the collapse of Reconstruction, the liberated slaves had disproved the racist claims of their former masters in following the accomodationist strategy of Booker T. Washington and making massive gains in literacy, economic self-sufficiency, and (contra Washington) assertiveness.[150] When the ex-slaves did not lapse into dependency through racial inadequacy as predicted, Southern whites resorted to governmental and private repression to induce the desired subservience.[151] Reenter the Ku Klux Klan. Lynching was linked to law as the Black Codes suppressed during Reconstruction rose again as Jim Crow laws.[152] Sanctified by the President and the Supreme Court, a system of apartheid that would provide the model for South Africa was installed across the American South.[153]

One key to this was the massive legal disenfranchisement of those African–Americans not sufficiently deterred from voting by force and economic sanctions.[154] Beginning in Mississippi, in response to the Populist threat of an alliance between poor Whites and Blacks, and concluding in Georgia in 1908, every state in the

149. Worst period for Blacks

Bickel & Schmidt, History of The Supreme Court of the United States: The Judiciary and Responsible Government, 1910–1921, 1984, p. 726.

150. Assertiveness

Id. at p. 741.

151. Subservience

Id. at p. 741.

152. Jim Crow laws

Id. at p. 760.

153. Apartheid installed

Id. at pp. 729, 748.

154. Massive disenfranchisement

Id. at p. 919.

Old Confederacy raised legal bars to Black voting.[155] The Supreme Court's refusal to do anything to enforce the Fifteenth Amendment was so striking that a writer in the Harvard Law Review could devote an article to the question of whether the amendment was now "void."[156] When, through a remarkable confluence of contingencies, a case testing the so-called "grandfather clause" reached the Supreme Court, even the White Court had to strike down a disenfranchising device that had been called "a fraud upon the Constitution of the United States."[157] However, the Court's decision had little effect and a few years later the Court upheld a substitute device, the "white primary."[158]

An even more hideous instrument of repression was the system of peonage that had been erected to replace slavery as a support for the plantation economy of the South following the Thirteenth Amendment.[159] The Southern criminal "justice" system, through a byzantine combination of newly created status crimes and the threat of being worked to death on the chain gang under lease to their former masters, was used to coerce black defendants to plead guilty and agree to "work off" their sentences under conditions that resembled slavery in all but name.[160] Indeed, by the Progressive era many investigations, including one by the Justice Department, had shown that peonage was in many respects far worse than slavery.[161] When a case raising the issue finally reached the Supreme Court, the Court commendably found it violated the Thirteenth Amendment despite impressive contrary arguments, some of

155. Every state

Foner, The Story of American Freedom, 1998, p. 154.

156. "Void"

Machen, Is The Fifteenth Amendment Void?, 1910, 23 Harv.L.Rev. 169. See also, Bickel & Schmidt, History of The Supreme Court of the United States; The Judiciary and Responsible Government, 1910–1921, 1984, pp. 908, 911.

157. "Fraud upon Constitution"

Id. at pp. 923, 927. See also, Guinn v. U.S., 1915, 35 S.Ct. 926, 238 U.S. 347, 59 L.Ed. 1340.

158. "White primary"

Newberry v. U.S., 1921, 41 S.Ct. 469, 256 U.S. 232, 65 L.Ed. 913, See also Bickel & Schmidt, History of The Su-

preme Court of the United States: The Judiciary and Responsible Government, 1910–1921, 1984, p. 969.

159. Peonage system

See § 6356, text at notecall 754.

160. Resembled slavery

Bickel & Schmidt, History of The Supreme Court of the United States: The Judiciary and Responsible Government, 1910–1921, 1984, p. 850.

161. Worse than slavery

Id. at p. 151.

them made in dissent by Justice Holmes.[162] However, the times were such that Justice Hughes felt compelled to begin his opinion with a preposterous disclaimer that the case had nothing to do with race.[163] Worse yet, the careful language of the opinion was easily evaded by new legislation and the peonage system survived down to World War II.[164]

In other respects, the Court contributed to "the heyday of Jim Crow" by following the path it had laid down in Plessy v. Ferguson.[165] Perhaps the most striking abandonment of the abolitionist legacy was the Court's upholding of a Kentucky statute that required a religious college founded to "promote the cause of Christ" to cease educating black and white students in the same classroom and permitting their teaching in separate classrooms only if they were 25 miles apart.[166] Even the Court's one decision resisting Jim Crow, the overturning of another Kentucky statute requiring residential segregation, can be explained in terms of white property rights and laissez faire constitutionalism.[167]

Unlike some of its decisions dealing with social and economic regulation, the Supreme Court's civil-rights decisions were consistent with Progressive values. Part of the Progressive notion of "cooperation" over "conflict" involved sectional reconciliation after the Civil War and the "bloody shirt" politics that followed it; hence, the rights of Freedmen under the Reconstruction amendments were sacrificed to North–South harmony and Republican political ambitions.[168] Moreover, even judges and lawyers who were in no sense "Progressive" could be influenced by Darwinian racism and

---

162. Made by Justice Holmes

Id. at p. 866.

163. Nothing to do with race

"We at once dismiss from consideration the fact that plaintiff in error is a black man," Bailey v. Alabama, 1911, 31 S.Ct. 145, 147, 219 U.S. 219, 231, 55 L.Ed. 191.

164. System survived

Bickel & Schmidt, History of The Supreme Court of the United States: The Judiciary and Responsible Government, 1910–1921, 1984, pp. 872, 903–905.

165. Laid down in Plessy

Id. at p. 727.

166. 25 miles apart

Id. at pp. 729–730. See Berea College v. Kentucky, 1908, 29 S.Ct. 33, 211 U.S. 45, 53 L.Ed. 81.

167. White property rights

Buchanan v. Warley, 1917, 38 S.Ct. 16, 245 U.S. 60, 62 L.Ed. 149. See Bickel & Schmidt, History of The Supreme Court of the United States: The Judiciary and Responsible Government, 1910–1921, 1984, p. 811.

168. Political ambitions

Id. at p. 987.

the rhetoric of imperialism to devalue the claims of people of color.[169] President Wilson and Chief Justice White attended private screenings of the racist movie that glorified the Ku Klux Klan, "Birth of A Nation", the editors of the Harvard Law Review applauded Jim Crow decisions, and Harvard alumni groups barred their black classmates from social functions.[170] Little wonder that Justice Holmes could exhibit his "legal realism" by expressing doubt that the Supreme Court had the power to overcome Southern intransigence to enforce the Fifteenth Amendment.[171] Even Progressive consumerism played its part; the massive migration of African–Americans during the Progressive era was explained as a search for economic betterment, not a flight from apartheid and enslavement.[172]

Brandeis, Democracy, and "The Other"

In an ironic embrace of the Progressive value of "cooperation", in 1916 the two wings of the business community that had split over the election of 1912 came together to form the National Industrial Conference Board; its first project was a renewed attack on labor unions invoking icons of "efficiency" and "scientific management."[173] The Presidential election of that year turned on a snub and fewer than 4,000 votes in California, raising for a moment the spectre of 1876.[174] Woodrow Wilson won reelection on the slogan "he kept us out of war" despite a program of militarism that included the Council of National Defense—the first step in what would become "the military-industrial complex."[175]

The Supreme Court came into politics in 1916 in two ways. First, Charles Evans Hughes left the Court to accept the Republi-

169. Devalue claims

Id. at pp. 737, 918.

170. Harvard alumni barred

Id. at pp. 755, 742, 962. Until he disavowed this, the Chief Justice's attendance was used as an endorsement by the producers of the movie.

171. Court had power

Id. at pp. 923–925.

172. Not a flight

Id. at p. 742. For the way the migrants viewed it, see Foner, The Story of American Freedom, 1998, p. (one migrant from Florida to Chicago said he

was "looking for a free state to live in"; collecting similar evidence).

173. N.I.C.B. attack on unions

Wiebe, Businessmen and Reform: A Study of the Progressive Movement, 1962, p. 32.

174. Spectre of 1876

Encyclopedia of American Facts and Dates, 9th ed.1993, p. 430. On the election of 1876, see § 6356, text at notecall 727.

175. "Military-industrial"

Encyclopedia of American History, Morris ed.1976, pp. 328–330.

can nomination for the Presidency, dispelling any vestige of the myth that judges are apolitical monks.[176] Paradoxically, though Hughes may have cost himself the election by his disrespect for the Progressive Governor of California, Hiram Johnson, he himself embraced Progressive values in defense of the Supreme Court:

> I like to think of the courts as in the truest sense the expert agents of democracy——expressing deliberate judgements under conditions essential to stability, and therefore in their proper action the necessary instrumentalities of progress.[177]

This succinct statement of the Progressive belief in the possibility of progress without change apparently appealed to the voters as much as it appealed to logic.

The Court's other appearance in politics was more tumultuous; for those who looked to the Court to protect them both from "progress" and The Other, the appointment of Louis Dembitz Bradeis must have been doubly shocking for not only was he a Progressive confidant of the President, he was also only a step above a Negro in the hierarchy of scientific racism.[178] We have elsewhere described the anti-semitism, subtle and crude, that figured in the fight so there is little need to soil these pages again.[179] However it is worth noting that even subtle anti-semitism must have seemed more ominous in light of the lynching that same year of Leo Frank.[180] Frank, who suffered from the dual disability of being a Jew and a Yankee, had been convicted of the rape-murder of a young white girl in Georgia in 1913. Because of mob domination of the trial that brought the case to the Supreme Court in an early episode in the application of the Due Process Clause to state criminal trials, Frank's conviction was a national scandal.[181] The

176. Apolitical monks

Bickel & Schmidt, History of the Supreme Court of the United States: The Judiciary and Responsible Government, 1910–1921, 1984, p. 393.

177. "Expert agents of progress"

Id. at p. 402.

178. Brandeis nomination

Id. at p. 367.

179. Anti-semitism described

See § 6356, text at notecall 374; § 6352, text at notecall 234. For a detailed study of the nomination struggle that illustrates the pervasiveness of anti-

semitism, see Todd, Justice on Trial: The Case of Louis D. Brandeis, 1964.

180. Lynching of Leo Frank

Encyclopedia of American Facts and Dates, 9th ed.1993, p. 427.

181. National scandal

See Frank v. Mangum, 1915, 35 S.Ct. 582, 237 U.S. 309, 59 L.Ed. 969.

The Frank case touches upon the right of confrontation. Because the trial was held in a mob-dominated courtroom, the trial judge told counsel for defendant, out of defendant's presence, that he feared for their lives and those of

governor of Georgia, believing Frank probably innocent (as have most outside students then and since), commuted his death sentence to life imprisonment. In a perverse illustration of "popular dissatisfaction with the administration of justice", a Georgia mob dragged Frank out of jail and lynched him, then for good measure ran the governor out of the state.[182]

Except for ex-President, and future Brandeis colleague, Taft—who in characteristic fashion branded the nominee a "socialist," most of those who took the high road in opposing the Brandeis nomination did so in revealing institutional terms.[183] The New York Times wrote:

> The Supreme Court by its very nature must be a conservative body; it is the conservator of our institutions, it protects the people against the errors of their legislative servants, it is the defender of the Constitution itself. To place on the Supreme Bench judges who hold a different view of the Court, to supplant conservatism by radicalism, would be to undo the work of John Marshall and strip the Constitution of its defenses.[184]

the defendant, and asked that they and their client absent themselves from the courtroom during the receipt of the verdict and the polling of the jury. Id. at 584–585, 235 U.S. at 315–316.

The defense argued that this violated the right of the defendant under the Fourteenth Amendment to be present at trial. Under the Sixth Amendment the right of presence is, in part, governed by the Confrontation Clause. Defense counsel apparently recognized this because in their brief before the Supreme Court they cited Dowdell and Diaz (See § 6358, text at notecalls 741, 941.). 235 U.S. at 319.

The Court's opinion goes off on the point that the Fourteenth Amendment does not require state courts to follow the Sixth Amendment. In considering the opinion of the Georgia court, the majority opinion says: "the State declares, in effect, as it reasonably may declare, that the right of the accused to be present at the reception of the verdict is but an incident of the right of trial by jury; and since the

State may, without infringing on the Fourteenth Amendment, abolish trial by jury" so it may allow reception of the verdict in the defendant's absence. Id at 593, 235 U.S. at 343. This passage demonstrates how under a holistic view of the Sixth Amendment one may reach the same result by different paths.

182. Ran governor out of state

Bickel & Schmidt, History of the Supreme Court of the United States: The Judiciary and Responsible Government, 1910–1921, 1984, pp. 362–363.

183. Except for Taft

"He is a muckraker, an emotionalist for his own purposes, a socialist, prompted by jealousy, a hypocrite, a man who has certain high ideals in his imagination, but who is utterly unscrupulous in method in reaching them, a man of infinite cunning, of great tenacity and purpose, and, in my judgment, of much power for evil." Id. at p. 377.

184. "Strip the Constitution"

Id. at p. 376.

The view that Brandeis was a "radical" was an error of his supporters as well as his opponents; only Senator Borah correctly foresaw the role Brandeis would play in the development of the administrative state.[185]

For our purposes, the most interesting feature of the Brandeis nomination struggle was the employment of confrontation values by his opponents. For example, among the adjectives used to describe the nominee were "active, adroit", a "man of unbounded audacity", and a "man, I should say, of duplicity, double-dealing; a man who works under cover."[186] Apparently these virtues, while valued in a Pinkerton informant of the sort lionized by Conan Doyle, have no place on the Supreme Court—a paragon of institutional openness.[187] Given the penchant of prominent businessmen for backdoor dealings with their supposed political enemies and secret anti-democratic yearnings of some Progressive politicians, a Freudian analyst might see elements of projection at work here.[188]

Both the Brandeis nomination and narrow margin of the Presidential election brought into sharper focus Progressive ambivalence about "democracy."[189] It is easy to suppose that the Progressives favored increasing democracy because a number of their reforms pointed in that direction, from woman's suffrage to so-called "direct democracy"—the initiative, referendum, and recall.[190] Direct democracy was, in subtle ways, linked to confrontation values; for example, the recall was a device for making officials accountable for their actions by having to "face" the voters much as confrontation attempts to foster witness accountability by bringing the witness "face to face" with the accused in the presence of the jury.[191] However, some of the democratic reforms of the Pro-

---

185. Role Brandeis would play

Id. at pp. 378, 387, 389.

186. "Under cover"

Id. at p. 385.

187. Pinkerton informant

See above, text at notecall 61.

188. Projection at work

For the backdoor dealings of the House of Morgan and others, see Wiebe, Businessmen and Reform: A Study of the Progressive Movement, 1962, pp. 45–47, 74, 99, 106–107, 110, 150. Even President Taft was two-faced; when

asked publicly by reporters he said he had no comment, then shared the diatribe quoted above in a letter to a reporter-friend.

189. "Democracy"

On the significance of this word in the Progressive lexicon, see above, text at notecall 128.

190. Referendum and recall

Ekirch, Progressivism in America, 1974, p. 114.

191. "Face" the voters

Hofstadter, The Age of Reform: From Bryan to F.D.R., 1956, p. 259.

gressives in fact originated with the Populists; e.g., the direct election of Senators.[192]

The Brandeis nomination raised fears similar to those raised by the recall of judicial decisions—one of the more controversial planks in the 1912 Progressive Party platform.[193] Theodore Roosevelt's endorsement of recall of judicial decisions was limited to state courts.[194] While some Progressives thought of recall as a way of democratizing the Constitution, Roosevelt seems to have been influenced by a decision of the New York Court of Appeals striking down that state's first workers' compensation statute.[195] Roosevelt thought such decisions played into the hands of socialists and saw recall as a method of defusing calls for more radical reforms.[196] If voters did not recall the decision, this tended to weaken claims that judicial review was undemocratic; if they recalled the decision, this created less constitutional instability than the enactment of an amendment—even one as narrowly tailored as the Income Tax Amendment.

Opponents of recall of judicial decisions feared that this would give labor unions a direct influence on the judiciary—a fear hardly weakened when the New York Court of Appeals upheld a second workers' compensation scheme after Progressives mounted an electoral challenge to some of the sitting judges.[197] The appointment of Brandeis, which was also seen as giving unions a voice on the bench, heightened business fears by suggesting that capitalists could not rely solely on the Supreme Court to protect their interests—not that their fears needed any reinforcement; it is widely supposed that Roosevelt's support of recall of judicial decisions cost him business support in 1912.[198] Similarly, it was fear of the labor

192. Originated with Populists

Mowry, The Progressive Era, 1900–20: The Reform Persuasion, 1958, p. 17.

193. Progressive plank

O'Neill, The Progressive Years, 1975, p. 60.

194. Limited to state courts

Ekirch, Progressivism in America, 1974, p. 163.

195. Roosevelt influenced

Bickel & Schmidt, History of the Supreme Court of the United States: The Judiciary and Responsible Government, 1910–1921, 1984, p. 14; White, Social Thought in America: The Re-

volt Against Formalism, 1957 ed., p. 114.

196. Defusing radical reform

Weinstein, The Corporate Ideal in the Liberal State, 1900–1918, 1968, p.1968.

197. Labor influence

Wiebe, Businessmen and Reform: A Study of the Progressive Movement, 1962, p. 173.

198. Cost business support

Weinstein, The Corporate Ideal in the Liberal State, 1900–1918, 1968, p. 167. Of course, one did not have to

vote that made the narrow margin of the Presidential election of 1916 of such concern.[199] Even if the unions could not elect a labor ticket to office, they could, at least in theory, hold the balance of power in close elections, throwing their support to the candidate that promised the greatest support for the union program.[200] When Southern leaders faced a similar danger from black voters, they responded by disenfranchising them——a tactic that seemed more difficult to accomplish with union voters, though capitalists did use other Southern tactics, such as intimidation and electoral fraud to offset union power at the ballot box.[201]

But Progressive rhetoric about democracy and capitalist fears for their judicial veto obscure a more complex reality. We have previously seen the strong strand of elitism in Progressive thought.[202] Hence, we should not suppose that when corporate lawyers and conservative politicians hurled Hamiltonian jibes about the democratic electorate as a "mob", that their targets must have held the opposite view.[203] Indeed, one can find similar opinions expressed in the writings of the Progressive guru, Edward Ross.[204] Similarly, William Howard Taft, who at least by a generous definition of the term was a "Progressive" President, vetoed the resolution admitting Arizona to the union because its constitution provided for recall of judicial decisions.[205] Moreover, after his defeat in 1912, Taft retreated to Yale from whence he castigated all proposals

---

favor big business to have reservations about the influence of the electorate; for example, on who had seen the corruption of judicial elections by urban political machines would have other reasons for not wanting judicial decisions placed on the ballot. See, e.g., Strong, Landmarks of a Lawyer's Lifetime, 1914, pp. 106, 145–146.

199. Fear of labor vote

Weibe, Businessmen and Reform: A Study of the Progressive Movement, 1962, p. 171.

200. Throwing support

We say "in theory" because it is our impression that there are not many examples in American political history where this tactic has worked for groups, as distinguished from individuals.

201. Intimidation and fraud

O'Neill, The Progressive Years, 1975, p. 63.

202. Elitism

See § 6357, text at notecall 738.

203. Hamiltonian jibes

Mowry, The Era of Theodore Roosevelt and The Birth of Modern America, 1900–1912, 1962, pp. 40–41.

204. Expressed in Ross

Ross, Social Control, 1969 ed., pp. 72, 83–84, 100.

205. Vetoed Arizona

Mowry, The Era of Theodore Roosevelt and the Birth of Modern America, 1900–1912, 1962, pp. 264–265.

for further democratization of American life.[206] However, a better illustration of Progressive ambivalence was Walter Lippman, who acquired much of his fame writing for the Progressive publication "The New Republic", yet who later became one of the primary proponents of a new aristocracy and continuously bemoaned democracy on the ground that it turned "statesmen" into "lackeys."[207]

In fact, only radical Progressives——mainly those with Populist roots——were unqualified supporters of "democracy."[208] For many, "the people" were limited to those like them——"the thinking members of society", the "better citizens" with "natural and patent superiority" that qualified them to lead.[209] Progressives agreed that "democracy" in the sense of "universal suffrage" was a threat to civilization.[210] Instead of the property qualifications of the Founders, they favored more scientific restrictions on the vote, such as literacy tests. This, when coupled with racist assumptions, does much to explain the Progressive acquiescence in the disenfranchisement of black citizens.[211] What "the people" needed was not more democracy but "parental guardianship" under the "sustaining and guiding hand of the state."[212] In short, what the Progressives wanted was "a regulated democracy" analogous to the "regulated monopoly"; as one of them put it, it was "the work of the state to think for the people and plan for the people——to teach them how to do, what to do, and to sustain them in the doing."[213] This is a rather far cry from the traditional notions of self-government but it does much to explain the Progressive Proceduralists' view of the jury and their denigration of confrontation.[214] Be that as it may, it

206. Castigated proposals

Wood, Constitutional Politics in the Progressive Era, 1968, pp. 156–157.

207. Into "lackeys"

White, Social Thought in America: The Revolt Against Formalism, 1957 ed., pp. 248, 264.

208. Unqualified supporters

Chamberlain, Farewell to Reform, 1965 ed., p. 211.

209. "Natural superiority"

Wiebe, Businessmen and Reform: A Study of the Progressive Movement, 1962, p. 181.

210. "Universal suffrage" a threat

Kolko, Railroads and Regulation, 1877–1916, 1965, p.12.

211. Acquiescence

Foner, The Story of American Freedom, 1998, p. 154.

212. "Parental guardianship"

Weinstein, The Corporate Ideal in the Liberal State, 1900–1918, 1968, p. 155.

213. "Think for the people"

Ibid.

214. View of jury

Businessmen opposed jury trials in injunction cases because this would

was the inability of the Progressives to come out with a convincing way to institutionalize a "regulated democracy" that cost them business support for their proposals for direct democracy.[215] For the business wing of Progressivism, democratic majorities were a greater threat to individual liberties (as defined by laissez faire jurisprudence) than monarchy; for other Progressives, direct democracy was a way around corrupt political machines and judicially entrenched minorities.[216] Their inability to agree upon some democratic means for channeling working class dissent no doubt played its part in the illegal and extralegal repression of those dissenters that was about to unfold.

The Progressive War

In 1917, the Progressive thinker John Dewey published "Creative Intelligence" and Congress declared war on the Central Powers.[217] Though participation of the United States lasted only a year and a half, that participation had significant impact on Progressive proceduralism, civil liberties, and the right of confrontation.[218] The changes the war brought were both ideological and institutional as the nation passed through "a cycle of hope, hatred, and disillusionment."[219] At the outset of the war, the Wilson administration faced two interrelated problems: first, how to regiment a free market economy for war, and; second, how to create support (or neutralize opposition) among workers, farmers, and political dissidents.[220]

Opposition to the war was strongest in the rural South and Midwest.[221] Indeed, in August, 1917, in a former hotbed of populism

place justice in the hands of the "mob." Wiebe, Businessmen and Reform: A Study of the Progressive Movement, 1962, p. 197. Those who cannot discriminate between the means by which Leo Frank met his end and the means by which verdicts are reached are poor sources of procedural wisdom.

215. Cost business support

Id. at p. 181.

216. Corrupt minorities

Mason, William Howard Taft: Chief Justice, 1965, p. 42; Ekirch, Progressivism in America, 1974, p. 114; O'Neill, The Progressive Years, 1975, p. 12.

217. Declared war

Encyclopedia of American Facts and Dates, Ninth ed.1993, p. 434; White,

Social Thought in America: The Revolt Against Formalism, 1957 ed., p. 135.

218. Significant impact

Foner, The Story of American Freedom, 1998, p. 179.

219. "Hope, disillusionment"

May, The End of American Innocence, 1964 ed., p. 355.

220. Two problems

Weinstein, The Corporate Ideal in the Liberal State, 1900–1918, 1968, p. 216.

221. Opposition strongest

Id. at pp. 234–235.

in Oklahoma, nearly a thousand farmers engaged in armed rebellion against the draft in what came to be known as the "Green Corn Rebellion."[222] Socialists opposed the war, partly because of the party's Germanic roots, partly because the internationalist wing of the party saw the war as a case of workers dying for capitalism, and partly because they feared that a strengthened military would be used against unions and other domestic dissenters.[223] Despite the administration's efforts to bring unions aboard, labor support for the war was lukewarm.[224] Echoing the Socialists, some unionists argued that since capitalists were profiting from the war, the government should confiscate wealth as well as bodies to fight it.[225]

Prior to American entry, most Progressive leaders (including the President) opposed the war.[226] Some of them foresaw that the growth of militarism would lead to the kind of political "Caesarism" that had brought on the disastrous Grant presidency.[227] Still others opposed the war out of a kind of provincial nationalism that argued that the nation had enough problems at home without going to the rescue of the decadent aristocracies of Europe.[228] Robert LaFollette, the Wisconsin Progressive, exemplified this outlook when he predicted, correctly as it turned out, that war would "set progress back a generation."[229] Finally, there were the pacifist Progressives whose economic determinism led them to see wars as "necessarily evil because bankers with money to lend, munition-makers with sordid profits to earn, and industrialists with markets to win were the chief promoters and beneficiaries of war."[230] Even

222. "Green Corn Rebellion"

Id. at p. 234; Woodward, Home-grown Radicals, N.Y.Rev.Bks., April 5, 1979, p. 5.

223. Socialists opposed

Ekirch, Progressivism in America, 1974, p. 219.

224. Labor lukewarm

Weinstein, The Corporate Ideal in the Liberal State, 1900–1918, 1968, p. 246.

225. Confiscate wealth

Link, Woodrow Wilson and the Progressive Era, 1910–1917, 1963 ed., p. 193.

226. Most Progressives opposed

Id. at p. 181.

227. "Caesarism"

Id. at p. 182.

228. Problems at home

Id. at p. 180.

229. "Set progress back"

Chamberlain, Farewell to Reform, 1965 ed., p. 260.

230. "Chief promoters"

Link, Woodrow Wilson and The Progressive Era, 1910–1917, 1963 ed., p. 180. In debate, Senator George Norris said "[w]e are going into war upon the command of gold." Lauchtenburg, The Perils of Prosperity, 1914–1932, 1958 p. 30.

Henry Ford took this position, rounding up some prominent Progressives to endorse or even board his "Peace Ship", a pathetic attempt to mediate an end to the war.[231]

Though prior to the war the National Association of Manufacturers had opposed military spending, largely on budgetary grounds, the Progressive capitalists associated with the National Civic Federation saw the war as an opportunity to ease the depression—and incidentally increase their profits.[232] This seemed low risk, particularly to those who recalled that they, or their ancestors, had bought their way out of military service and made their fortunes on the Civil War.[233] A particularly foresighted businessman might have predicted that the government's use of business methods, such as combination, press agentry, and scientific management, would tend to validate them.[234] Be that as it may, despite the brevity of the war it did forge one of the first trusses in the military-industrial complex when iron and steel manufacturers found an enduring source of profit in government shipbuilding.[235]

Once Wilson opted for war, the Progressives discovered embedded in their own ideology ample reasons to follow him. John Dewey argued for "the social possibilities of war", a sort of manipulation of crisis in which war could serve as a demonstration of how the economy could be used for public ends rather than private profit.[236] He appealed to the centrist inclinations of Progressives in urging them to find a middle way between "the Tolstoian, to whom all force is violence and all violence is evil, and that glorification of

---

231. Ford "Peace Ship"

May, The End of Innocence, 1964 ed., p. 376; Leuchtenburg, The Perils of Prosperity, 1914–1932, 1958, p. 13 ("Do you want to know the cause of war? It is capitalism, greed, the dirty hunger for dollars. Take away the capitalist and you sweep war from the earth."; quoting Ford). Similar claims were made by the Nye Committee in 1934–1935. Link, Woodrow Wilson and The Progressive Era, 1910–1917, 1963 ed., p. 278.

232. Increase profits

Wiebe, Businessmen and Reform: A Study of the Progressive Movement, 1962, p. 145 (profits); Ekirch, Progressivism in America, 1974, p. 202 (N.A.M. opposition).

233. Civil war

Lukas, Big Trouble, 1997, p. 20.

234. Tend to validate

Haber, Efficiency and Uplift: Scientific Management in the Progressive Era, 1890–1920, 1973, pp. 19, 39.

235. Shipbuilding

Ekirch, Progressivism in America, 1974, p. 196.

236. "Social possibilities"

Leuchtenburg, The Perils of Prosperity, 1914–1932, 1958, p. 41; Foner, The Story of American Freedom, 1998, p. 169.

force which is so easy when war arouses turbulent emotion."[237] While Dewey had emotional reasons for his own choice, including his growing hostility to German ideology, he preferred to rely on Progressive values:

> The objection to violence is not that it involves the use of force, but that it is a waste of force; that it uses force idly or destructively. And what is called law may always, I suggest, be looked at as describing a method for employing force economically, efficiently, so as to get results with the least waste.

> No ends are accomplished without the use of force. It is consequently no presumption against a measure, political, international, jural, economic that it involves the use of force. Squeamishness about force is the mark not of idealistic but of moonstruck morals. But antecedent and abstract principles can not be assigned to justify the use of force. The criterion of value lies in the relative efficiency and economy of the expenditure of force as a means to an end.[238]

One could hardly find a better example of hard-headed Progressive instrumentalism.[239] Indeed, "the war to end all wars" is, in an ironic sense, the ultimate instrumental argument——one in which the means swallow the end. Or is it the other way around?

Dewey illustrated one of the "social possibilities" of war by using it as an occasion to attack libertarian laissez-faire constitutionalism. Like the question of war

> the question of the limits of individual power, or liberties, or rights is finally a question of the most efficient use of means for ends. That at a certain period liberty should have been set up as something antecedently sacred per se is natural enough. * * * But it is as an efficiency factor that its value must be assessed.[240]

237. "Turbulent emotion"

White, Social Thought in America: The Revolt Against Formalism, 1958 ed., pp. 162–163.

238. "Means to an end"

Id. At p. 163. On Dewey's emotional involvement in war, see May, The End of American Innocence, 1964 ed. pp. 372, 374.

239. Hard-headed

A number of Dewey's disciples, and many other Progressives, found it hard to follow, or swallow, Dewey's reasoning. The fact that so many "impartial experts" on both sides of the Atlantic were bitten with the war bug should have, but apparently did not, provide a cautionary tale for this element of the Progressive ideology. Id. at pp. 362, 364.

240. "Must be assessed"

Id. at p. 373.

Though Dewey may not have anticipated this, the government was shortly to illustrate the "inefficiency" of constitutional rights.

Dewey's "hard-headed" pragmatism purported to be at some distance from Theodore Roosevelt's macho posturing, but other Progressive heroes were not above romantic moralizing.[241]

> In this snug, over-safe corner of the world we need [war], that we may realize our comfortable routine is no eternal necessity of things, but merely a little space of calm in the midst of the tempestuous untamed streaming of the world in order that we may be ready for danger. We need it in this time of individualist negations, with its literature of French and American humor, revolting at discipline, loving fleshpots, and denying that anything is worthy of reverence——in order that we may remember all that buffoons forget. * * * For high and dangerous action teaches us to believe as right beyond dispute things for which our doubting minds are slow to find words of proof.[242]

Holmes at least had some experience with combat, something not true of all the Progressives who shared his vision of war as a means of purifying society of its decadent elements.[243]

Among the Progressives who gagged on Dewey's Orwellian argument that war, if not peace, is the means to peace were those who thought that "progress" meant that civilized nations had outgrown the need for war.[244] Many of these people, like the Wilson administration itself, had endorsed various peace organizations; there was growing support for international law and for some means of judicial resolution of disputes——a desire that was to culminate in the League of Nations.[245] Few of these people seem to have noticed the domestic implications of the Wilsonian argument for war; if the absence of adequate judicial institutions to resolve disputes justifies war, then does not the inadequacy of our own legal system to eliminate those who dispute American values justify the use of vigilante violence to silence them with greater efficiency?

241. Macho posturing

Ekirch, Progressivism in America, 1974, p. 200.

242. "Words of proof"

White, Social Thought in America: The Revolt Against Formalism, 1957 ed., pp. 173–174.

243. Means of purifying

May, The End of American Innocence, 1964 ed., pp. 365, 376. The railings of these cultural conservatives will seem eerily familiar to those who have seen Stalin and Hitler's responses to modern art.

244. "Progress" meant outgrown

Ekirch, Progressivism in America, 1974, pp. 213, 219.

245. Judicial resolution

Id. at pp. 212–214.

Pound, of course, had used the inadequacies of the legal system to explain, not to justify, extralegal use of force—a distinction too subtle to be observed in the hysteria of war.

But it was statism, not vigilantism, that led many Progressives to applaud the U.S. entrance into the war.[246] The massive concentration of federal power over the economy far exceeded the wildest peacetime dreams of the Progressives; at one point, Bernard Baruch was granted near dictatorial powers.[247] Not only were these economic controls approved by businessmen, they were all upheld by the Supreme Court.[248] War, it was said, created the opportunity for and the demand for governmental powers not needed at other times.[249] Or as Randolph Bourne would later put it: "War is the health of the state."[250]

But despite Baruch's self-promoted prominence, the real architect of the Warfare State was a corporation lawyer, Elihu Root, who served as Wilson's Secretary of War.[251] Root, more than any other figure, saw the need to overcome the longtime American aversion to a large, standing Army; his own Progressivism may have seen that the absence of a common military experience contributed to many of the elements of American culture that Progressives found offensive.[252] Root pushed the expansion of the National Guard as a means to "the creation of the military spirit among the youth of the country, to the education and training of that military spirit."[253] As the original bureaucracy, the Army could serve not only as a boot

246. Progressives applaud

Id. at p. 270.

247. Dictatorial powers

Leuchtenburg, The Perils of Prosperity, 1914–1932, p. 39.

248. Upheld by Supreme Court

Id. at pp. 41–42; Ekirch, Progressivism in America, 1974, p. 271; Beth, The Development of the American Constitution, 1877–1917, 1971, p. 162. For a listing of the major Supreme Court decisions, see Encyclopedia of American History, Morris ed.1976, pp. 674–675.

249. Powers not needed

Beth, The Development of The American Constitution, 1877–1917, 1971, p. 165.

250. "Health of state"

Foner, The Story of American Freedom, 1998, p. 168.

251. Root architect

Ekirch, Progressivism in America, 1974, p. 204.

252. Aversion to standing army

Id. at p. 204.

253. "Military spirit"

Id. at p. 207.

camp for the modern industrial Army, it also provided a way to reconcile the dichotomy of cooperation and conflict that so bedeviled Progressive thought——albeit, and somewhat ominously, at the expense of The Other.[254] Moreover, "war" was to provide an alternative metaphor to competitive sports in describing domestic cooperation; think, for example, of the "War on Poverty" and "The War on Drugs." Like the right of confrontation, the Army combined rationality with emotion; as one recruit put it: "There is a fine restraint in military ceremony that enables the purest product of New England self-repression to *feel*——without awkwardness or self-consciousness."[255] Even Progressives less interested in bureaucratic discipline and ritual might still agree with Dewey that "conscription has brought home to countries which have in the past been the home of the individualistic tradition the supremacy of public need over private possession."[256] However, perhaps because they had little experience with modern militarism, few Progressives foresaw that while war might foster communal loyalty among the troops, it also fostered a contempt for civilian values and authority that would play a far from positive role in the post-War world.[257]

With most of the Progressives enlisted in the war effort, dissent was left to radicals and traditional conservatives.[258] The administration met dissent with a combination of repression and persuasion. The latter effort was headed by the newly created Committee on Public Information——the "information" being pro-war propaganda.[259] Whatever its effect on the war effort, the CPI subsidized the development of the "public relations" industry; some of the leaders in the profession of public relations got their start or made their fame with the CPI.[260] Over the balance of the century, public relations——or political propaganda, if you will——

254. Reconcile dichotomy

Ibid.

255. "Without awkwardness"

May, The End of American Innocence, 1964 ed., p. 366.

256. "Supremacy of public"

Ekirch, Progressivism in America, 1974, p. 268.

257. Contempt for civilian

May, The End of American Innocence, 1964 ed., p. 378.

258. Left to radicals

Ekirch, Progressivism in America, 1974, p. 271.

259. Public Information

It was also known as the "Creel Committee" after its chairman, George Creel. Leuchtenburg, The Perils of Prosperity, 1914–1932, p. 44.

260. PR industry

Foner, The Story of American Freedom, 1998, p. 169.

was to provide part of the solution to the Progressive's problem with democracy.[261]

The CPI exploited Progressive rhetoric and symbols like "democracy" and "freedom."[262] This propaganda, along with the speeches of politicians, created utopian expectations for the post-War world that produced some of the disillusionment that characterized the "return of normalcy."[263] Soldiers who endured gas and shell in the name of lofty ideals discovered the ambiguity of these abstractions when employers turned them against unions during the 1920's.[264]

The negative side of the CPI emerged in its anti-German agitation.[265] Atrocity stories had been used before to demonize The Other, but despite pious disclaimers from the President, the CPI raised hatemongering to new levels of sophistication.[266] For those who wanted subtlety, the CPI published works by conservative literary critics who blamed the incursion of German values for everything from modern music to the decline of Puritan values; for those who thrived on the flamboyant, there were erotically laden tales of maidens ravished by the "unspeakable Hun", who also bayoneted babies or fed them poisoned candy.[267] The effect on Americans of German descent has often been noted; speaking German or possessing beer steins from the Old Country was treated as evidence of disloyalty—for the duration of the war "sauer-

261. Solution

Reasonable people could disagree about whether the "problem" is "solved" because people believe political propaganda or because people who fear democracy believe public relations is effective.

262. Progressive symbols

For some samples, see id. at p. 170. It is difficult to exaggerate, or even to parody, the CPI's work; e.g., the war was "a Crusade not merely to re-win the tomb of Christ, but to bring back to earth the rule of right, the peace goodwill to men and gentleness he taught." Leuchtenberg, The Perils of Prosperity, 1914–32, 1958, p. 46.

263. Produced disillusionment

The CPI published pamphlets asserting that "our interest in justice and democracy begins at home" and predict-

ing the postwar world would be an "industrial democracy" with a "universal eight-hour day." Foner, The Story of American Freedom, 1998, p. 170.

264. Turned against unions

Id. at p. 179.

265. Anti-German agitation

Weinstein, The Corporate Ideal in the Liberal State, 1900–1918, 1968, p. 247.

266. New levels

Lukas, Big Trouble, 1997, p. 653.

267. Poisoned candy

May, The End of American Innocence, 1964 ed., pp. 377, 387–388, 390.

kraut" became "liberty cabbage."[268] However, the CPI's aptly named "black propaganda" rebounded most cruelly on African–Americans who enlisted in the war under the banner of freedom only to return to a nation where expressions of that freedom were met with the redirected fury at The Other by lynch mobs.[269]

Propaganda, like much of the war effort, was a private-public collaboration that went far beyond the reprinting of atrocity stories by the newspapers.[270] The CPI created the earliest "astroturf" organizations——ostensibly "grassroots" groups supposedly representing some segment of society that are actually created and funded by outsiders——to drum up labor support for the war.[271] But there were plenty of genuine organizations with their own reasons for whipping up or exploiting wartime hysteria; e.g., the Republican party.[272] The American Bar Association adopted a resolution that equated opposition to the war with pro-German sympathies.[273] As we shall see, private organizations had an even more important role to play on the other side of the government's campaign against dissent——repression.

On June 15, 1917, Congress adopted the Espionage Act, which made it a crime to aid the enemy, obstruct recruiting, or to cause insubordination, disloyalty, or refusal of duty in the armed services.[274] The Act also authorized the Postmaster General to exclude from the mails any newspaper, periodical, or other material

268. "Victory cabbage"

Id. at pp. 387–388; Leuctenburg, The Perils of Prosperity, 1914–31, 1958, p. 44.

269. Lynch mobs

Foner, The Story of American Freedom, 1998, p. 172.

270. Went far beyond

For example, Red Cross leaders spread stories that German–American women were joining some chapters so they could put glass shards into bandages. Leuchtenburg, The Perils of Prosperity, 1914–32, 1958, p. 44.

271. "Astroturf" labor group

Weinstein, The Corporate Ideal in the Liberal State, 1900–1918, 1968, p. 240.

272. Republican party

Link, Woodrow Wilson and The Progressive Era, 1910–1917, 1963 ed., p. 179.

273. Opposition pro-German

Auerbach, Enmity and Amity: Law Teachers and Practitioners, 1900–1922, 1971, 5 Perspectives in American History, 549, 582.

274. Espionage Act

Encyclopedia of American History, Morris ed.1976, pp. 330–331.

thought to be treasonable or seditious.[275] Acting under the latter provision, Postmaster General Burleson first barred from the mails his hometown newspaper, which had revealed that he had evicted tenant farmers from his land and replaced them with convict labor.[276] He then turned to other publications, including "The Appeal to Reason", a Populist paper that had over a half-million mail subscribers.[277] However, the government held off prosecutions under the Act until after the elections in the fall of 1917, an election in which the Socialist Party made substantial gains in local elections——presumably because of its antiwar position.[278] The following year, the Act was amended by the Sedition Act, which criminalized any false statements interfering with the prosecution of the war, any urging of the curtailment of necessary war materials, the use of "disloyal, profane, scurrilous, or abusive language" about the flag, Constitution, or military and naval forces, or advocating, teaching, defending, or suggesting the doing of any such acts.[279] This was the statute upheld in the famous Abrams case, whose dissents can be seen as the beginning of free speech jurisprudence.[280]

Meanwhile, practitioners of free speech, not spies and saboteurs, were the major targets of the government's orgy of repression. There were more than 2000 prosecutions under the two statutes, only about half of them successful.[281] Among the victims were Eugene Debs, the future Socialist candidate for President, and the leaders of the Green Corn Rebellion.[282] However, the principal targets were members of the I.W.W., whose campaign to carry free speech into the workplace had enraged employers who were now

275. Exclude from mails

Ibid.; Foner, The Story of American Freedom, 1998, p. 177.

276. Convict labor

Weinstein, The Corporate Ideal in the Liberal State, 1900–1918, 1968, pp. 237–238.

277. "Appeal to Reason"

Id. at p. 238.

278. Socialist gains

Id. at pp. 236, 238.

279. Sedition Act

Encyclopedia of American History, Morris ed.1976, p. 332. The Act also au-

thorized the deportation of alien anarchists, a key tool in the "Red Scare" and the impetus for the Sacco–Vanzetti case. Foner, The Story of American Freedom, 1998, p. 177.

280. Abrams case

Abrams v. U.S., 1919, 40 S.Ct. 17, 250 U.S. 616, 63 L.Ed. 1173.

281. Half successful

Foner, The Story of American Freedom, 1998, p. 177.

282. Debs and Green Corn

Ibid.; Renshaw, The Wobblies, 1968, p. 173.

eager to see their anti-union efforts disguised as resistance to sedition.[283] In 1917–1918 alone, more than 100 "Wobblies" were convicted in federal prosecutions, including the leader of the Green Corn rebellion, who was sentenced to fifteen years in prison.[284] But the I.W.W. was also the target of prosecutions under similar state statutes.[285] In Kansas, 34 I.W.W. members were arrested during a strike in the oil fields, held for nearly two years in a local jail where they were beaten by jailers and served fetid meals, before being sent to the federal penitentiary for terms from one to nine years.[286] Under similar conditions in California, five of the 46 Wobblies being held for state charges died in jail before their cases came to trial.[287]

The most celebrated of the I.W.W. trials was the prosecution of Tom Mooney, an I.W.W. labor organizer from San Francisco. During a 1916 pro-war parade promoted by local businessmen to forge a link between patriotism and anti-union sentiment, someone threw a bomb that killed ten people.[288] The local business press immediately exploited the tragedy, calling for the authorities to "rid our city of these vermin"——"base and mean political and journalistic demagogues [who] seized control of and used to their own greedy ends labor organizations."[289] In this atmosphere, Moody was convicted despite the shoddy character of the prosecution's witnesses and press photographs that disproved their testimony.[290] When the witnesses later recanted, the Attorney General filed a petition with the state Supreme Court consenting to a reversal of Money's conviction, but the Court declined to do so on procedural grounds.[291]

283. Resistance to sedition
Id. at p. 85.

284. Sentenced to fifteen years
Id. at pp. 3, 173.

285. State statutes
Id. at p. 142.

286. Kansas case
Id. at p. 190.

287. Died in jail
Ibid.

288. Killed ten people
Cray, "It Was Lies, All Lies", Cal.Lawyer, Sept. 1983, p. 42, 43.

289. "Own greedy ends"
Ibid.

290. Disproved testimony
Id. at p. 44. Among the witnesses were a drug addict, a prostitute, an exconvict seeking favors from the prosecution, and a woman who claimed she witnessed the crime in her "astral presence."

291. Court declined
Id. at p. 45.

However, in 1918 President Wilson appointed a Mediation Commission to look into the conviction. The Commission's general counsel, Professor Felix Frankfurter of Harvard, wrote a scathing indictment of California justice, saying that the "feeling of disquietude aroused by the case must be heeded, for, if unchecked, it impairs the faith that our democracy protects the lowliest and even the unworthy against false accusations."[292] Protection against "false accusation" is, or course, one of the functions of the right of confrontation.[293] The Commission's report and a federal investigation whose wiretaps of the District Attorney's office revealed that he had conspired with business leaders and a member of the State Supreme Court to uphold the Mooney conviction got Mooney a commutation of his death sentence but not before he served 20 years in prison, despite another condemnation of the fairness of his trial in 1931 by the Wickersham Commission.[294] Even a condemnation by the U.S. Supreme Court did not move the state judiciary and it took a gubernatorial pardon to release Mooney from what by then all but the most doctrinaire conceded was an unjust conviction.[295] For all the harm it did to Mooney, his case did serve to keep alive the memory of wartime repression and its perversion of the criminal justice system until a time when the Supreme Court was ready to do something to enforce constitutional rights designed to prevent such abuses.[296]

As in the case of propaganda, governmental repression of dissent was linked with private suppression, only a small part of which has been documented by historians.[297] For example, on

292. "Even the unworthy"

Ibid.

293. Confrontation

Confrontation figured in the Mooney case through the "blank pad rule"; one of the grounds for the Wickersham Commission's condemnation was the contamination of the jury by prejudicial publicity. Ibid.

294. Wickersham Commission

Ibid.

295. Unjust conviction

Ibid. See Mooney v. Holohan, 1935, 55 S.Ct. 340, 294 U.S. 103, 79 L.Ed. 791; In re Mooney, 1937, 73 P.2d 554, 10 Cal.2d 1.

296. Keep alive memory

The case also demonstrated that the First Amendment alone did not suffice to bar political prosecutions. The Founders knew this but it can easily be overlooked in the modern reductionist analysis of the Bill of Rights. See vol. 30, § 6341, p. 194.

297. Small part

Much private repression would come in the form of a threat, explicit or implicit, to report the would-be dissident to those responsible for official repression. For other forms, see Leuchtenburg, The Perils of Prosperity, 1914–32, 1958, p. 44.

August 1, 1917, Frank Little, an I.W.W. organizer who was leading a strike against the Anaconda Copper Company in Butte, Montana, but who was also an outspoken opponent of the war, was dragged from his bed, tied behind a speeding car and dragged several miles, and hung from a railroad trestle with a sign pinned to his chest reading "First and last warning."[298] Police claimed the lynching was the work of a deranged drug addict and no serious efforts were made to find the true perpetrators. A month earlier, the Bisbee, Arizona, Loyalty League rounded up 1200 strikers, I.W.W. organizers, and sympathizers at gun point, "tried" them before a kangaroo court, then herded them on a cattle train and dumped them in the middle of the New Mexico desert without food or water. After 36 hours, they were "rescued", many of them beaten, and held in a federal stockade for three months without any charges being brought against them. A federal grand jury later indicted 23 leaders of the Loyalty League but none was ever convicted.[299]

While the victims of the "Bisbee Deportation" fit the Progressive vision of The Other, some victims of private repression did not. Even before the War began, a mob in Baltimore broke up a meeting of the American League Against Militarism that had gathered to hear an address from David Starr Jordan, the President of Stanford.[300] In October of 1917, Columbia University fired several faculty members because of their opposition to the War.[301] The President of the University told the American Bankers Association that "you might just as well put poison in the food of every American [soldier] as permit [antiwar Senator Robert LaFollette] to talk as he does."[302] As a result, the historian Charles Beard, himself a supporter of the War, resigned his professorship at Columbia saying:

> I have merely held that teachers should not be expelled without a full and fair hearing by their peers, surrounded by all of the safeguards of judicial process. Professors in Columbia University have been subjected to humiliating doctrinal inquisitions by the trustees, they have been expelled without notice or hearing, and

298. "Last warning"

Id. at p. 45; Renshaw, The Wobblies, 1968, p. 162–163.

299. None convicted

Id. at p. 187.

300. Jordan address

May, The End of American Innocence, 1964 ed., p. 385.

301. Columbia fired

White, Social Thought in America: The Revolt Against Formalism, 1957 ed., p. 179.

302. "Talk as he does"

Leuchtenburg, The Perils of Prosperity, 1914-32, p. 45.

their appointment and promotion depend upon securing, in advance, the favor of certain trustees.[303]

An "inquisition" may have been just what some members of the legal profession thought was needed. A future Harvard law professor, then in the Department of Justice, prepared a plan that would have turned much of the nation into a police state.[304] When the University of Michigan fired a professor for his antiwar views, the action was applauded in the pages of the Pennsylvania Law Review.[305]

The brief wartime repression had a number of repercussions beyond dealing a major, and perhaps fatal, blow to the indigenous democratic left and laying the groundwork for the "Red Scare."[306] As Walter Weyl said, it "diverted America's rich and generous impulses from the quest for social justice and burned them out in a hunt for German witches."[307] For purposes of confrontation, two long term consequences are important. First, the combination of public and private repression would, during the Cold War, be formalized into the Truman Loyalty system in which the nexus between employment and government contracts would be developed into a mechanism to stifle dissent by means that were difficult to reach by existing First Amendment doctrine; hence, the Supreme Court was forced to use procedural grounds, including the confrontation right, to curb abuses.[308] Second, by targeting respectable

303. "Doctrinal inquisitions"

White, Social Thought in America: The Revolt Against Formalism, 1957 ed., p. 179.

304. Police state

Harbaugh, Lawyer's Lawyer: The Life of John W. Davis, 1973, p. 127.

305. Action applauded

Aerbach, Enmity and Amity: Law Teachers and Practitioners, 1900–1922, 1971, 5 Perspectives in American History 549, 583 n. 103.

306. Blow to left

Weinstein, The Corporate Ideal in the Liberal State, 1900–1918, 1968, p. 238.

307. "Hunt for witches"

Chamberlain, Farewell to Reform, 1965 ed., p. 302.

308. Curb abuses

For those who never knew, or have forgotten, employment in defense-related industries (which was broadly defined) required a "security clearance." Hence, by denying dissidents such clearance on the grounds that they were potential spies, the government could have them fired by "private" actors. Since the private action was beyond the First Amendment and the government's action was an exercise of the War Power, those who invoked the First Amendment got nowhere. A similar function was performed by the Attorney General's list of subversive organizations or the designation of one as a "Communist" by some legislative committee; the government supplied "the facts", but the employer provided the sanction.

Anglo–Saxon folk, repression weakened the association between race, ethnicity, and The Other and returned the nation to the situation at the time of the Founders, where The Other was defined by ideology and religion as much as by ancestry.[309] This not only meant that upperclass Americans could, like the Founders, see themselves as targets of repression, but, defining The Other by ideas rather than ethnicity also made the connection between criminal procedure and the First Amendment much clearer.

Consequences of War

When World War I ended, not in the triumph of Progressive ideals, but in the sordid marketplace of colonialism, ambition, and retribution, some people said that the War killed Progressivism.[310] As the historians tell it, the story is more complex but all of the strands of this complexity need not be unraveled here.[311] Suffice it to say that after the War, the moral certainty of the Progressives and their belief in the inevitability of progress diminished great-ly——except in the advertising for consumer products.[312] During the war, the reformist values of Progressivism, such as they were, gave way to naked statism.[313] The backlash left reformers powerless before the post-War resurgence of business and conservative liber-tarianism.[314] Not that there was much left of the reforming im-pulse; the experience during the War shattered the Progressive faith in direct democracy, regulated monopoly, and enlightened business leadership.[315] The War——and its aftermath——exposed the shallowness of Progressive analysis and the plasticity of their values.[316] The problem with Progressive ideals were not that they

309. By ancestry

The link between race and The Other was weakened further, but by no means broken, by civil rights laws and changing public opinion in the latter part of the century. Hence, today "fundamentalist" or "Islamic" is the usual adjective for the terroristic Oth-er.

310. Killed Progressivism

May, The End of American Innocence, 1964 ed., p. 394.

311. Need not be unravelled

We only wish to say enough so that the reader can see the parallels between political Progressivism, which died, and Progressive Proceduralism, which Elvis-like lives on.

312. Belief in progress

Id. at pp. 333, 354, 361.

313. Naked statism

Ekirch, Progressivism in America, 1974, p. 260.

314. Resurgence of laissez faire

Foner, The Story of American Freedom, 1998, p. 180.

315. Shattered faith

Wiebe, Businessmen and Reform: A Study of the Progressive Movement, 1962, p. 10.

316. Exposed plasticity

Weinstein, The Corporate Ideal in the Liberal State, 1900–1918, 1968, p. 214.

were idealistic but that they were superficial and vague; when others could see that war was a poor instrument for achieving Progressive ideals, the Progressives replied with clever and glib rationalizations that concealed a yielding of values to technique.[317] What the Progressives did accomplish during the War was to destroy indigenous ideological alternatives to laissez-faire conservatism.[318] What was left of Progressivism was a commitment to anti-ideological reformism of the sort that triumphed briefly during the New Deal.[319] In the meantime, Progressives after the War were like Federalists after Jefferson; a vestigal set of political attitudes that could only survive in arenas free of democratic control like the law schools and the courts.[320]

The post-War sociopolitical landscape featured few changes of immediate relevance to confrontation. With the collapse of the Hapsburgs and Hohenzollern monarchies, historical aristocracy retreated to comic operas and ceased to be a realistic threat to democracy, thus opening the door to a new aristocracy of wealth sanctified not by Divine Right but by the scientistic testing of experts.[321] Reform politics turned from economic reform to Prohibition, immigration restriction, and eugenics.[322] With the prop of wartime federal support removed, unions were decimated by a new anti-labor campaign.[323] Meanwhile, experience during the War, when increased wages were linked to increases in profits seemed to demonstrate the wisdom of the "business unionism" of Samuel Gompers.[324] Whereas the war had highlighted the conflict between the worker's role as a wage-earner and his role as a citizen, business unionism tended to substitute "consumer" for "citizen" in

317. War a poor instrument

Ekirch, Progressivism in America, 1974, p. 269.

318. Killed off alternatives

May, The End of American Innocence, 1964 ed., p. 394.

319. Briefly during New Deal

The decline of New Deal "liberals" at the end of the century thus replicates the experience of their anti-ideological predecessors.

320. Only in law schools

On the survival of Progressivism in the field of procedure, see vol. 21, § 5005.

321. New aristocracy

May, The End of American Innocence, 1964 ed., p. 371.

322. Turned to eugenics

Ekirch, Progressivism in America, 1974, p. 270.

323. Unions decimated

Foner, The Story of American Freedom, 1998, p. 179.

324. "Business unionism"

Weinstein, The Corporate Ideal in the Liberal State, 1900–1918, 1968, p. 226.

the schizophrenia of the movement.[325] Finally, as previously mentioned, the war increased the number of businessmen who saw the government less as a natural ally and more as a source of support and plunder.[326]

Meanwhile, back at the academy, the War had cast a pall over Germanic scholarship and scientism and dampened the efficiency craze.[327] Indeed, the war seems to have radicalized the Taylorites, leading many to question the institutions they served and the amorality of their techniques—moves that made them less appealing models for academics who had just undergone the purge of pacifists and other dissidents.[328] As we shall see, the War had weakened traditional morality as an instrument of social control, a development that spawned a new wave of sumptuary laws and a new academic interest in social science.[329] These two trends were eventually to meet in the Wickersham Commission, whose exposes of police and prosecutorial abuses did much to spark renewed interest in constitutional criminal procedure.[330] At the same time, the decline of traditional morality opened new avenues for social reform for those like Roscoe Pound, who traced the flaws in American law to Puritanism with its emphasis on man as a free moral agent that made contract the basis for all social relations.[331] Finally, the war deepened the academic ambivalence about the use of force; whereas before it had sufficed to condemn unionists, anarchists, and revolutionaries because they used force, now it was necessary to distinguish between "good" and "bad" uses of force.[332]

325. "Consumer" for "citizen"

This conflict was overlooked by Progressives who thought that Big Business would combine with Big Labor to mulct the public.

326. Source of plunder

Weinstein, The Corporate Ideal in the Liberal State, 1900–1918, 1968, p. 251.

327. Dampened craze

White, Social Thought in America: The Revolt Against Formalism, 1957 ed., p. 152; Haber, Efficiency and Uplift: Scientific Management in The Progressive Era, 1890–1920, 1973, p. 74.

328. Radicalized Taylorites

Id. at pp. 132–133.

329. Interest in social science

White, From Sociological Jurisprudence to Realism: Jurisprudence and Social Change in Early Twentieth Century America, 1972, 58 Va.L.Rev. 999, 1013–1015.

330. Wickersham Commission

See below, text at notecall 783.

331. Flaws to Puritanism

Wigdor, Roscoe Pound, 1974, p. 180.

332. Uses of force

White, Social Thought in America: The Revolt Against Formalism, 1957 ed., p. 165.

Procedure was a handy tool for legitimating government use of force, whether in war or in domestic law enforcement.

The effect of the war on confrontation values is difficult to gauge. For example, the frenzy of Anglo–Saxon racism unleashed by the war might have redounded to the benefit of confrontation with those who believed the Sixth Amendment to be a product of the superior race.[333] However, that supposition would cut little ice with members of the degraded ethnic groups, such as the Irish or Italians. Moreover, given the association of the adversary system with trial by combat, one might expect that the glorification of militarism might increase the appeal of adversary doctrines like confrontation.[334] However, the end of the war brought a revulsion against militarism, not because World War I was more bloody than the Civil War but because new methods of depicting it, such as newsreels and newspaper photographs made the horror more vivid.[335]

Woodrow Wilson put confrontation values into play with consequences that are difficult to discern. Having appointed probably the first dedicated Christian pacifist to ever hold the office of Secretary of State, Wilson took office desiring to apply the structures of private morality to public affairs.[336]

> We are at the beginning of an age in which it will be insisted upon that the same standards of conduct and responsibility for wrong shall be observed among nations and their governments that are observed among the individual citizens of civilized states.[337]

Though courts are loathe to admit it, confrontation is an application of private morality to public affairs; that is, the notion that it is wrong to say things behind a person's back that one would not say to her face. In his famous Fourteen Points, Wilson embraced a similar value of openness as his first point:

333. Superior race

On the other hand, closer acquaintance with English customs and traditions may well have convinced even dedicated Anglophiles that some of them were unfit in America. Friedman, A History of American Law, 1973, p. 573.

334. Glorification

See, e.g., the macho posturing of Theodore Roosevelt quoted in Ekirch, Progressivism in America, 1974, p. 200.

335. More vivid

People who recall Matthew Brady's photos of Civil War carnage are less likely to recall that they were not published in newspapers of the time.

336. Morality to public affairs

May, The End of American Innocence, 1964 ed., pp. 356, 358.

337. "Civilized states"

Id. at p. 385.

1. Open covenants of peace, openly arrived at, after which there shall be no private international understandings of any kind but diplomacy shall proceed always frankly and in the public view.[338]

That the criterion of openness should be one of the first to go, after having been attacked as naive or worse, seems likely to have had some impact on how Americans thought about confrontation. But what?

If Wilson's failure was taken as indicating the folly of attempting to insert morality into public affairs, then defenders of the right of confrontation are left with the instrumental justification employed by courts then and since; i.e., confrontation is a device for insuring the reliability of evidence through adversary cross-examination.[339] But World War I did much to discredit instrumentalism. As Randolph Bourne explained:

> One has a sense of having come to a sudden, short stop at the end of an intellectual era. To those of us who have taken Dewey's philosophy almost as our American religion, it never occurred that values could be subordinated to technique. We were instrumentalists, but we had our private utopias so clearly before our minds that the means always fell into its place as the contributory.[340]

Similarly, to the Progressive Proceduralists, the values of confrontation were subordinated to the technique of cross-examination and to the goal of enforcing the substantive criminal law.

War undermined confrontation values in another way. The model of combat, like the model of the adversary system, brings the combatants "face to face" so they can see who they are killing or being killed by and so each assumes comparable risks. The low moral status of assassins or bomb throwers (like those that produced the Haymarket Affair and the conviction of Tom Mooney) stems, at least in part, from the fact that they do not "confront" their adversaries and thus do not face equal risks from the encounter. This "knight in shining armor" view of combat had probably been strained by the invention of the cross-bow, but it was still sufficiently alive at the time of the Revolution to elicit English complaints that the colonists "fought like Indians", that is, from

338. "Frankly in public view"

Wilson, Selected Addresses, 1918, p. 247 (speech to Congress of January 8, 1918).

339. Reliability of evidence

See generally, 4 Mueller & Kirkpatrick, Federal Evidence, 2d ed.1994, § 394.

340. "Subordinated to technique"

Chamberlain, Farewell to Reform, 1965 ed., p. 300.

behind trees and rocks, rather than standing in rows in highly visible uniforms to exchange slaughter in the traditional European fashion. But by the time of World War I, technology had rendered this version of warfare obsolete; whether in tanks, submarines, or using Big Berthas to fire shells of poisonous gas at an unseen enemy, the strategy of modern warfare was to kill as many of the enemy with the least risk to your own troops as possible. That we tend to think of World War I in terms of "the Red Baron" and aircraft duels rather than of submarines and poison gas is precisely because aerial combat was simultaneously both novel and anachronistic.[341] If there was no longer any nobility in dying, why should there be any honor in facing cross-examination?

Armistice, Reaction, and The Red Scare

On November 11, 1918, the Progressive's war to "make the world safe for democracy" ended——and with it, the Progressive movement for reform.[342] A few days earlier, the Republicans had recaptured control of Congress.[343] But the demise of Progressivism was foreshadowed earlier in 1918 when, emblematic of the Social Darwinism reinvigorated by the War, the Supreme Court held that the children of the poor could be conscripted for military service and their younger brothers and sisters enlisted for work in Southern cotton mills.[344]

The failure to end child labor symbolized Progressive futility because it was a cause with broad popular support, combining as it did both the Progressive desire to limit the hegemony of the market and the conservative desire to foster what in recent times have been called "family values."[345] Since the turn of the century, most industrialized states had enacted statutes limiting child labor but these laws were weakened by the same "race to the bottom" that

341. Anachronistic

Even today movies that glorify fighter pilots try to invoke the old myth by allowing the audience to see both the hero and his adversary in the dogfight, to see what the combatants do not.

342. War ended

Encyclopedia of American History, Morris ed.1976, p. 372.

343. Recaptured control

Id. at p. 373.

344. Southern cotton mills

Arver v. U.S., 1918, 38 S.Ct. 159, 245 U.S. 366, 62 L.Ed. 349 (conscription); Hammer v. Dagenhart, 1918, 38 S.Ct. 529, 247 U.S. 251, 62 L.Ed. 1101 (child labor).

345. Family values

Ekirch, Progressivism in America, 1974, pp. 79–80.

characterized state regulation of corporations.[346] Hence, when Congress passed the Keating–Owens bill in 1916, which banned goods made with child labor from interstate commerce, it was met with nearly universal approval.[347] The opposition came from the National Civic Federation, which claimed that the evils of child labor had been exaggerated by "socialist writers", and Southern mill owners, who stood to lose 60% of their work force if the new statute was effective.[348]

The mill owners promptly devised a collusive suit to challenge the statute, but both government lawyers and the lower courts chose to pass over any technical problems with the suit in order to get it to the Supreme Court.[349] To assist in the defense of the statute, the government enlisted the aid of some of the leading legal Progressives, including Roscoe Pound and William Draper Lewis, the Dean of the University of Pennsylvania Law School and later Director of the American Law Institute.[350] Despite the array of legal talent and an impressive legal argument, the Supreme Court declared the statute unconstitutional by a vote of 5–4.[351] The majority held that although Congress had the power to bar the lottery tickets, oleomargarine, and fornicators from interstate commerce, it lacked the power to bar the products of child labor.[352] The decision was widely criticized in the press, though at the time few seemed to note how in the name of states rights the Supreme Court had sanctified a system in which states would surrender their right to

346. "Race to the bottom"

Mowry, The Progressive Era, 1900–20: The Reform Persuasion, 1958, p. 12; Wood, Constitutional Politics in the Progressive Era, 1968, pp. 6, 9.

347. Met with approval

Bickel & Schmidt, History of the Supreme Court of The United States: The Judiciary and Responsible Government, 1984, p. 448.

348. Lose 60% of work force

Wood, Constitutional Politics in the Progressive Era, 1968, p. 8; Weinstein, The Corporate Ideal in the Liberal State, 1900–1918, 1968, pp. 27–28.

349. Technical problems

Bickel & Schmidt, History of the Supreme Court of The United States, The Judiciary and Responsible Gov-

ernment, 1910–1921, 1984, pp. 449–450; Wood, Constitutional Politics in the Progressive Era, 1968, pp. 92–94.

350. Aid of Progressives

Id. at p. 29; Bickel & Schmidt, History of the Supreme Court of The United States: The Judiciary and Responsible Government, 1910–1921, 1984, p. 448.

351. Unconstitutional

Hammer v. Dagenhart, 1918, 38 S.Ct. 529, 247 U.S. 251, 62 L.Ed. 1101.

352. Lacked power

Bickel & Schmidt, The History of The Supreme Court of the United States: The Judicary and Responsible Government, 1910–1921, 1984, p. 451.

govern in order to attract corporate employers.[353]

The Court's Child Labor decision put the Court back into politics, briefly reviving the Populist–Progressive critique of judicial power and triggering a search for ways to evade or overturn the ruling.[354] The public furor may have played a part in William Howard Taft's resolve to put the Court beyond politics and above criticism, a desire that led to his efforts as Chief Justice to squelch dissent on the Court.[355] The decision had a parallel sequel when, in a remarkable instance of the collapse of the adversary system, both sides in the subsequent Child Labor Tax cases were represented by lawyers who thought the tax was unconstitutional——as the Court then held.[356]

In 1919, the Treaty of Versaille was completed, the debate on American membership in the League of Nations began, and Wilsonian idealism collapsed.[357] The same year saw the ratification of the Eighteenth Amendment, the passage of the Volstead Act, the publication of John Reed's "Ten Days That Shook The World", and the formation of the Communist Labor Party——all significant events in the development of the right of confrontation.[358] Those who wanted a "return to normalcy" got it with a vengeance, beginning with bloody race riots in Chicago.[359]

The first post-War year brought a period of renewed labor unrest——in the opinion of some historians, the most massive wave of strikes in history.[360] The strikes were triggered by a "silent wage cut"——rapid inflation following the repeal of wartime price con-

353. Widely criticized

Id. at pp. 454–455.

354. Reviving critique

Wood, Constitutional Politics in the Progressive Era, 1968, p. 184.

355. Squelch dissent

Id. at pp. 259, 286.

356. Both sides represented

Id. at pp. 238–239, 274. The losing government lawyer wrote a letter to Taft praising the Court's decision, claiming that if the Court had accepted his argument, "our form of government would have sustained serious injury." Id. at p. 274. If this is the standard, it is little wonder that such lawyers could have accused Brandeis of an excessive adversariness.

357. Idealism collapsed

Encyclopedia of American History, Morris ed., 1976, p. 375.

358. Significant events

Encyclopedia of American Facts and Dates, Ninth ed.1993, pp. 442, 444.

359. Race riots

Foner, The Story of American Freedom, 1998, p. 174.

360. Massive wave

Id. at p. 175.

trols.[361] By 1920, prices had doubled from pre-War levels.[362] But union militance fed on more than just economic hardship; inspired by the Government's propaganda, workers now sought to democratize the workplace.[363] These noneconomic demands brought more resistance because they required action more radical than raising wages. For example, transportation unions, which had grown dramatically when the railroads were being run by the government, proposed that they be nationalized——a proposal that was denounced as an attempt to "sovietize" industry.[364]

Rank-and-file radicalism threatened the position of Samuel Gompers and those who had embraced his brand of "business unionism."[365] Such leaders tried, in vain, to prevent the great steel strike of 1919 in which 365,000 mostly foreign-born workers walked out seeking some measure of the utopia promised by the press agents of the C.P.I.[366] Instead they got more of that "old time repression"; the company planted Pinkerton informers to stir up ethnic strife and hired thugs who clubbed strikers and locked them up in jails without any charges being filed, while local officials banned union meetings.[367] Similarly, in the coal mines a one-day strike in protest of the imprisonment of Tom Mooney escalated into a full-blown strike that brought federal intervention.[368] Attorney General Palmer, using powers created by the Sedition Act and other wartime statutes, obtained a federal injunction and in these and other strikes arrested and deported union leaders as "Reds."[369]

However, two other strikes raised unprecedented issues and raised the anxiety of well-to-do Americans far more than other reprises of earlier labor unrest. The first of these began in Seattle when 35,000 shipyard workers struck for higher wages and shorter

361. "Silent wage cuts"

Brecher, Strike!, 1972, p. 104.

362. Prices doubled

Id. at p. 128.

363. Sought to democratize

Id. at pp. 128, 131; Foner, The Story of American Freedom, 1998, p. 176.

364. "Sovietize" railroads

Leuchtenburg, The Perils of Prosperity, 1914–32, 1958, p. 70.

365. Threatened Gompers

Brecher, Strike!, 1972, p. 101.

366. Steel strike

Id. at p. 118; Foner, The Story of American Freedom, 1998, p. 156.

367. Banned union meetings

Brecher, Strike!, 1972, pp. 123–124.

368. Federal intervention

Id. at pp. 130, 134. Leuchtenburg, The Perils of Prosperity, 1914–32, 1958, p. 76.

369. Deported leaders

Brecher, Strike!, 1972, pp. 124, 130.

workdays.[370] The Seattle Labor Council, under the influence of an admirer of the Russian Revolution, turned the walkout into a general strike that shut down all business and governmental activity in the city for five days.[371] Though the strike was described even by the Army officer sent to break it as "peaceful", the business press characterized it as an "attempted revolution."[372] The strike was ended under the threat of military force and the refusal of conservative union leaders to support it.[373]

Even more frightening was the Boston Police strike later that year.[374] Tired of low wages, miserable working conditions, and a dictatorial police commissioner, the policemen voted to affiliate with the American Federation of Labor——as policemen in other cities had done without incident. When 19 policemen were fired, the rest walked out and within a day violence and lawlessness broke out on the streets of the city; two men were killed, a few stores were looted, and winos rolled dice on the Boston Common.[375] Though rather small potatoes in comparison with labor warfare of the era and urban riots later in the century, the newspapers were soon depicting it as the Storming of The Winter Palace.[376] When Gompers convinced the strikers to return to work and seek arbitration of their grievances, the city announced that all the strikers were fired and permanent replacements were being hired.[377] Governor Calvin Coolidge, who up to this point had done nothing, then uttered the lines that made him famous: "There is no right to strike against the public safety by anybody, anywhere, anytime."[378] The strike etched indelibly in the minds of the frightened middle-class a link between labor unions, radicalism, and threats to the public safety.[379]

---

370. Shipyard workers

Id. at p. 106.

371. General strike

Leuchtenburg, The Perils of Prosperity, 1914–32, 1958, p. 71.

372. "Attempted revolution"

Brecher, Strike!, 1972, p.111.

373. Refusal to support

Id. at p. 113.

374. Boston Police Strike

Id. at p. 116.

375. Rolled dice on Common

Leuchtenburg, The Perils of Prosperity, 1914–32, 1958, p. 73.

376. The Winter Palace

E.g., The Wall Street Journal: "Lenin and Trotsky are on their way!" Brecher, Strike!, 1972, p. 116.

377. Replacements hired

Leuchtenburg, The Perils of Prosperity, 1914–32, 1958, p. 74.

378. "No right to strike"

Ibid.

379. Threats to safety

Brecher, Strike!, 1972, p. 116; Haber, Efficiency and Uplift: Scientific Management During the Progressive Era, 1890–1920, 1973, p. 136.

Back on the other coast, the citizens of Centralia, Washington, demonstrated the possibilities and perils of public-private cooperation in repression of radicals. Timber owners enlisted the American Legion and local officials to drive members of the I.W.W., who were organizing workers, out of town.[380] After Legion members entered the I.W.W. headquarters and beat the Wobblies with pipes and rubber hoses with no effort to prevent or punish them by local police, the Wobblies armed themselves.[381] On Armistice Day, 1919, the Legion marched on the Wobblies again, firing broke out and one Legion member was killed.[382] In retaliation the mob seized Wesley Everett, an I.W.W. leader who was dressed in his Army uniform in celebration of the day, dragged him behind a car to jail; later that night the mob removed Everett from the jail, castrated him, hung him from a bridge and riddled his body with bullets.[383] No effort was made to find or punish those responsible for the lynching of Everett, but eleven Wobblies were convicted of murder after a trial that was a travesty of Sixth Amendment values.[384]

After Centralia, the events that make up the "Red Scare" of 1919–1920 look civilized by comparison.[385] As we have seen, ever since the emergence of Marxism in the middle of the Nineteenth Century, American conservatives saw Communists behind every effort at social or political reform.[386] Just prior to the War, Progressives such as Herbert Croly had been attacked as socialists in drag.[387] The Russian Revolution changed little except for the rheto-

380. Drive out of town

Renshaw, The Wobblies, 1968, p. 164.

381. Armed themselves

Ibid.

382. Member killed

Ibid.

383. Riddled with bullets

Id. at p. 164.

384. Trial a travesty

The judge who presided had delivered the funeral oration for the dead Legion member, after deciding a fair trial could not be had in the local community it was held in the most hostile venue in that area, employers hired American Legion members in uniform to pack the courtroom, defense witnesses were indicted for perjury after giving their testimony, and employers pressured the jurors to convict. Despite this, the jury acquitted one person and found the others guilty only of second degree murder but the judge refused to accept the verdict and sent the jury out until they convicted all defendants of first degree murder, then sentenced them to 25–40 years in prison. Id. at pp. 165–166.

385. Red Scare

Leuchtenburg, The Perils of Prosperity, 1914–32, 1958, pp. 77–78.

386. Communists behind

See § 6356, text at notecall 223.

387. Socialists in drag

Ekirch, Progressivism in America, 1974, pp. 160.

ric; efforts to stamp out child labor were now "Bolshevism" and nationalization of railroads was now called an effort to "sovietize" the economy.[388] The post-War formation of the Communist International and attempted revolutions in several of the defeated nations gave claims of Communist influence a new credibility.[389]

Employers and corporate lawyers seized the opportunity provided by the resurgence of union activity after the war to redirect wartime super-patriotism toward the domestic left.[390] The Seattle General Strike was used to raise the spectre of Bolshevism.[391] William Howard Taft, who two years earlier had praised the "end of absolutism in Russia" as "the first great triumph of this war", now claimed that the result of the war had "been to weaken the supremacy of lawful authority."

> * * * Bolshevism is militant and threatening in every European country. It has penetrated this country. Because of the presence of hordes of ignorant European foreigners, not citizens * * * with little or no knowledge of our language, with no appreciation of American civilization or American institutions of civil liberty, it has taken strong hold in many of our congested centers and is the backing of a good many of the strikes from which our whole community is suffering today.[392]

However, when a Senate committee was convened to investigate Bolshevism, it discovered that domestic Socialists and indigenous radicals were some of the most vociferous critics of the Soviet experiment and spent most of its time studying events in Russia, even allowing John Reed to vent his enthusiasms for Lenin.[393]

However, a rash of bombings in 1919 seemed to confirm Taft's opinion (though the available evidence suggests that they were the work of anarchists or deranged persons, not agents of the Comin-

388. "Bolshevism" and "sovietize"

Wood, Constitutional Politics in the Progressive Era, 1968, p. 215; Leuchtenburg, The Perils of Prosperity, 1914–32, 1958, p. 70.

389. New credibility

Id. at pp. 67, 69.

390. Toward domestic left

Aeurbach, Enmity and Amity: Law Teachers and Practitioners, 1900–1922, 1971, 5 Perspectives in American History 549, 584.

391. Seattle raised spectre

Haber, Efficiency and Uplift: Scientific Management in The Progressive Era, 1890–1920, 1973, p. 135.

392. "Backing many strikes"

Cover, The Left, The Right, and The First Amendment: 1918–1928, 1981, 40 Md.L.Rev. 349, 353.

393. Reed to vent

Haber, Efficiency and Uplift: Scientific Management in the Progressive Era, 1890–1920, 1973, p. 135.

tern).[394] But ever since Haymarket and the assassination of McKinley, the business press had indiscriminately associated terrorism with all forms of radicalism, not just those radicals who embraced "propaganda by deed."[395] Hence, Congress gave Attorney General Palmer $500,000 to form an anti-radical bureau and he appointed a clerk in the Department, J. Edgar Hoover, to head it.[396] As we have seen, Palmer and Hoover had been using their new money and old powers against unionists, but an attempted bombing of Palmer's own home unleashed the so-called "Palmer raids."[397]

Acting under authority that a court would later determine properly belonged to immigration officials in the Department of Labor, Hoover, with the aid of local police and company informers, arrested several hundred members of the Union of Russian Workers on November 7, 1919.[398] Though none of these were charged with any crime, 249 of them were deported to Russia on a ship the business press dubbed "The Red Ark."[399] Just in case the public needed any reminder of the inadequacy of the criminal-justice system to deal with extraordinary threats to middle-class values, those deported included Emma Goldman, the anarchist proponent of birth control, and her sometime lover, Alexander Berkman, who had served fourteen years in prison for attempting to assassinate Henry Clay Frick, the commander of company forces during the Homestead battles of 1892.[400] The "Red Scare" was now in full swing.[401]

The manifestations of hysteria in 1919 will sound familiar to

394. Rash of bombings

Leuchtenburg, The Perils of Prosperity, 1914–32, 1958, pp. 71–72, 80.

395. Terrorism with radicalism

Id. at p. 71. "Propaganda by deed" was what some anarchists called assassinations and bombings. See Woodcock, Anarchism, 1962, pp. 328–329.

396. Hoover to head

Leuchtenberg, The Perils of Prosperity, 1914–32, 1958, p. 77.

397. "Palmer Raids"

Id. at p. 77.

398. Arrested several hundred

Irons, "Fighting Fair": Zechariah Chafee, Jr., The Department of Justice, and "The Trial At The Harvard Club," 1981, 94 Harv.L.Rev. 1205, 1218.

399. "Red Ark"

Id. at p. 1219.

400. Goldman and Berkman

Ibid. On Goldman, see above, text at notecall 125. On Berkman, see Berkman, Prison Memoirs of An Anarchist, 1970 ed., pp. 1–36. Berkman's memoir was originally published in 1912.

401. Full swing

See generally, Murray, Red Scare: A Study of National Hysteria, 1919–1920, 1955.

readers who can recall the McCarthyite reprise.[402] In New York, school teachers were fired during a campaign to decide "Who's Red and Who's True Blue." An Indiana jury required only two minutes of deliberation to acquit the murderer of a man who had shouted "To hell with the United States." Southern political leaders asked for federal troops to quell a Communist-led uprising of Negroes they feared was about to take place. A Southern Senator wanted to deport all radicals to a penal colony in Guam. General Leonard Wood, Army Chief of Staff, went Palmer one better by urging that Bolshevists be deported "in ships of stone with sails of lead, with the wrath of God for a breeze and with Hell for their first port." Not to be outdone in the theology of hate, the popular preacher Billy Sunday, proposed his own plan for dealing with radicals: "stand them up before a firing squad and save space on our ships."

The Red Scare reached its peak on the night of January 2–3, 1920, when Hoover's minions arrested nearly 5,000 radicals in cities across the country.[403] This time, however, Progressives associated with the National Popular Government League and the Department of Labor, began to see that "American institutions of civil liberty" were threatened as much by Hoover and Palmer as they were by Taft's "hordes of ignorant European foreigners."[404] With the assistance of two Harvard law professors, Zechariah Chafee, Jr., and Felix Frankfurter, they conducted an investigation of, began a law suit challenging, and issued a report condemning the Palmer Raids:

> Under the guise of a campaign for the suppression of radical activities, the office of the Attorney General * * * has committed continual illegal acts. Wholesale arrests of both aliens and citizens have been made without warrant or any process of law; men and women have been jailed and held incommunicado without access to friends or counsel; homes have been entered without search warrant and property seized and removed; other property has been wantonly destroyed; workingmen and workingwomen suspected of radical views have been shamefully abused and maltreated. Agents of the Department of Justice have been introduced into

402. Manifestations of hysteria

All the examples in this paragraph are taken from Leuchtenburg, The Perils of Prosperity, 1914–32, 1958, p. 66.

403. Arrested nearly 5,000

Irons, "Fighting Fair": Zechariah Chafee, Jr., The Department of Justice, and "The Trial At The Harvard Club", 1981, 94 Harv.L.Rev. 1205, 1219.

404. Threatened by Hoover

Id. at 1223.

radical organizations for the purpose of informing upon their members or inciting them to activities * * *.[405]

This intriguing blend of property and confrontation values succeeded in convincing a Progressive federal-court judge to issue an opinion validating the accusations and freeing many of the arrestees.[406] Opposition to his policies inspired Hoover to adopt a tactic that was to become the hallmark of his regime over the next fifty years; a massive investigation of his opponents seeking some hearsay he could use to intimidate or discredit them.[407]

The rallying of respectable opinion against its excesses ended the Red Scare almost as rapidly as it had begun. When the New York legislature, acting at the behest of a committee that prefigured the Senate Internal Security Committee by 30 years, expelled five members of the democratic and completely legal Socialist Party from the Assembly, even the Chicago Tribune and soon-to-be President Warren Harding denounced the act.[408] A Committee of the Association of the Bar of the City of New York, headed by Charles Evans Hughes, past governor, Republican Presidential candidate, and future Chief Justice of the Supreme Court, undertook the legal defense of the Socialists.[409] President-elect Harding later summed-up the sentiments of many Americans about the Red Scare: "[t]oo much has been said about Bolshevism in America."

Since despite the attacks upon him at the time as "disloyal" and "pro-German', Chief Justice Hughes later recalled his role in opposing the Red Scare with some pride, it seems reasonable to suppose that the events of 1919–1920 played a significant role in the rising interest among lawyers in the implementation, or lack thereof, of the Bill of Rights.[410] However, Hoover engineered a remarkable sequel that cast doubt on any notion that respectable Progressives were immune from the excesses of the nascent machinery of repression they had done so much to create.

405. "Purpose of informing"

Id. at p. 1224.

406. Freeing arrestees

Id. at 1226 (describing Coyler v. Skeffington, D.C.Mass.1920, 265 Fed.17).

407. Use to discredit

Id. at 1222. On Hoover's abuses, see vol. 26, § 5663, pp. 532–533.

408. Tribune and Harding

Leuchtenburg, The Perils of Prosperity, 1914–1932, 1958, p. 79.

409. Hughes undertook defense

Ibid.

410. Recalled with pride

The Autobiographical Notes of Charles Evans Hughes, Danielski & Tulchin eds. 1973, p. 195.

Acting on information secretly provided to them by Hoover and with the assistance of Harvard graduates in the Department of Justice, a cadre of conservative Wall Street lawyers, including the man who had led the opposition to the Brandeis nomination, engineered an inquisition into the political beliefs and the anti-Red Scare activities of Professors Chafee and Frankfurter before the Harvard Board of Overseers.[411] In the infamous "Trial at the Harvard Club" before a committee that included federal judge Augustus Hand and the evidence scholar John Wigmore, Chafee's detractors could produce only evidence that Chafee had committed a number of minor factual errors, which he readily admitted and had already taken steps to correct, in an article he had written attacking the Palmer Raids.[412] After Chafee testified he had little sympathy with radical beliefs and was motivated largely by devotion to civil liberties, he was acquitted by a vote of 5–4, with Judge Cardozo of the New York Court of Appeals casting the deciding vote.[413] The charges against Frankfurter petered out, to be revived after his attack on the conduct of the Sacco–Vanzetti trial.[414]

Though in the long term the Red Scare may have revived interest in confrontation values, its short term effects were mixed. It may have been the final nail in the coffin of Progressivism, displaying as it did the dangers of the Progressive statism and the shallowness of their defenses against it.[415] More importantly, Progressive centrism produced a "plague-on-both-your-houses" denunciation of political enthusiasm; both the bombings and the Red Scare that ensued could be attributed to excesses of rhetoric over reason.[416] For some, the Jazz Age, with its hedonism and consumerism, replaced politics as the center of interest.[417] For others, social

---

411. Board of Overseers

Irons, "Fighting Fair": Zechariah Chafee, Jr., The Department of Justice, and The "Trial at The Harvard Club", 1981, 94 Harv.L.Rev. 1205, 1228–1230.

412. Minor errors

Id. at pp. 1231–1233. Wigmore's membership on the committee appears in Wigdor, Roscoe Pound, 1974, p. 238.

413. Cardozo deciding vote

Irons, "Fighting Fair": Zechariah Chafee, Jr., The Department of Justice, and The "Trial at The Harvard Club", 1981, 94 Harv.L.Rev. 1205, 1233–1234.

414. Frankfurter

Sayre, The Life of Roscoe Pound, 1948, p. 220.

415. Coffin of Progressivism

Leuchtenburg, The Perils of Prosperity, 1914–32, 1958, p. 8.

416. Excesses of rhetoric

Id. at p. 81.

417. Replaced politics

Id. at p. 83.

science, amoral procedure, and a cynical realism were the answer.[418]

Prohibition and the Nationalization of Morals

The Red Scare revealed the ugly side of federal law enforcement just as increasing numbers of middle-class citizens became subject to it. The expansion of federal criminal jurisdiction arguably began with the Income Tax and the Pure Food and Drug Act.[419] The latter, at least, showed the propensity of federal law enforcement agencies to expand their powers far beyond the evils that supposedly brought federal intervention; e.g., the long campaign to declare Coca–Cola "misbranded" because it had caffeine but no "coca" in it.[420] But it took the federal move into sumptuary crimes to reveal that repression was not reserved for The Other.

The Mann Act of 1911 arose from public hysteria over "white slavery" fueled by lurid, semi-pornographic accounts of innocent young women debauched into a life of prostitution by urbanized foreigners and drugs.[421] This hysteria, which some historians have thought rivaled the Red Scare in its intensity, was aided by the extreme versions of Anglo–Saxon racism that emerged during the war years and by the backlash against militant feminism and its calls for the sexual emancipation of women.[422] The Mann Act, particularly during the years of hysteria, was enforced with uncom-

418. Cynical realism

Progressives in the academy had reason to fear the Red Scare; colleges and universities had long been attacked for nurturing, if not indoctrinating, Marxism. Wiebe, Businessmen and Reform: A Study of the Progressive Movement, 1962, p. 186. Moreover, the charges had some basis in fact; there were academics who openly espoused Marxist analysis, if not its politics. White, Social Thought in America: The Revolt Against Formalism, 1957 ed., pp. 120–121. However, the purge of campus pacifists during the war may have provided some innoculation against the Red Scare.

419. Pure Food and Drug

Foner, The Story of American Freedom, 1998, p. 152.

420. Coca-Cola misbranded

Bickel & Schmidt, History of The Supreme Court of the United States: The Judiciary and Responsible Government, 1910–21, 1984, p. 422.

421. Young women debauched

Friedman, Crime and Punishment in American History, 1993, p. 326; May, The End of American Innocence, 1964 ed., p. 343. This genre of erotic fantasy remains a staple of pulp magazines and other pornographic fare down to fairly recent times and has long historical antecedents in locales as far flung as Turkish harems and Catholic monastaries.

422. Racism and feminism

Id. at pp. 347–348, 390–391.

mon vigor resulting in sentences that were severe by the standards of the time.[423]

Prosecutors, aided by generous Supreme Court interpretations, rapidly used the "White Slavery Act" to expand their powers. The first, but less surprising, extension was to criminalize the conduct of the supposed "victims"—not surprising inasmuch as "loose women" were an implicit target of the reformers.[424] The extension of the statute to amateur males is more difficult to explain.[425] Caminnetti v. United States was the political prosecution of the son of a Democratic political leader in San Francisco brought by a Republican prosecutor that led to a minor scandal when the incoming Attorney General James McReynolds tried to delay the prosecution for review.[426] Caminetti and a friend supposedly violated the Mann Act by driving their girl friends from Sacramento to Reno, Nevada for a weekend of skiing and sex—a common itinerary then as now.[427] A majority of the Supreme Court, refusing to look at the legislative history, held that the statute required neither coercion nor a profit motive.[428]

The Caminetti decision soon spawned a number of similar federal prosecutions; among the most startling were the travelling stock broker who took his common-law wife along on some of his peregrinations and the theatrical agent who booked a woman to work as a chorus girl in a low-class burlesque house in another state.[429] State lawmakers joined in the war on illicit sex; the City of

423. Severe sentences

The number of prosecutions under the Act escalated rapidly during the early years—years that coincide with the hysteria. Statistics may be found in Bickel & Schmidt, History of the Supreme Court of The United States: The Judiciary and Responsible Government, 1910–1921, 1984, pp. 423–424.

424. "Loose women"

Id. at p. 424.

425. Amateur males

Racism probably played a role. Caminetti does not sound like an Anglo–Saxon name and Jack Johnson, the first black heavyweight champion, was prosecuted under the Act for sending $75 to his white inamorata to travel from Pittsburgh to join him in Chicago. Friedman, Crime and Punishment in American History, 1992, p. 328.

426. Tried to delay

Bickel & Schmidt, History of the Supreme Court of the United States: The Judiciary and Responsible Government, 1910–1921, 1984, p. 425.

427. Skiing and sex

Friedman, Crime and Punishment in American History, 1993, p. 327.

428. Neither coercion nor profit

Caminetti v. U.S., 1917, 37 S.Ct. 192, 242 U.S. 470, 61 L.Ed. 442.

429. Stockbroker and burlesque

Friedman, Crime and Punishment in American History, 1993, p. 327.

San Diego, home to a major naval base and a large army of street walkers made it a crime to fornicate in a hotel or apartment.[430] Some of these statutes demonstrated little sympathy with confrontation values; for example, a Michigan statute allowed the use of reputation evidence to prove that an establishment was a house of prostitution.[431] Commentators on Caminetti and its progeny noted how the decision gave expanded opportunities for blackmail; fear of political blackmail apparently explains why no one in Congress was willing to amend the Mann Act to limit its scope.[432]

The Harrison Narcotic Act of 1914 was likewise rooted in fear of The Other.[433] Here, however, the Supreme Court gave the Act a narrow construction, seemingly out of concern that it might lead to federal prosecution of members of the then-still loosely regulated medical profession.[434] Federal criminal jurisdiction got another boost with the enactment of the Dyer Act in 1919, the Supreme Court holding that Congress had the power to criminalize the interstate transportation of stolen motor vehicles despite its lack of power to bar interstate transportation of goods made with child labor.[435]

But these earlier statutes all paled before the Grand Experiment; Prohibition marked the greatest increase in federal criminal jurisdiction in the first half of the century—and the one with the greatest impact on confrontation jurisprudence.[436] It had long roots; the temperance movement was one of the most durable and popular reform movements in the Nineteenth Century.[437] By 1912, half of the citizenry lived under some form of Prohibition and a much greater number had encountered the politics of Prohibition.[438]

430. Fornicate in hotel
Id. at p. 330–331.

431. Use of reputation
Id. at p. 330.

432. Blackmail
Bickel & Schmidt, History of The Supreme Court of the United States: The Judiciary and Responsible Government, 1910–1921, 1984, pp. 429, 433.

433. Harrison Narcotic Act
Friedman, Crime and Punishment in American History, 1984, p. 356.

434. Narrow construction
Bickel & Schmidt, History of The Supreme Court of The United States: The Judiciary and Responsible Government, 1910–1921, 1984, p. 435.

435. Dyer Act
Friedman, Crime and Punishment in American History, 1984, p. 265.

436. Greatest impact
Ibid.

437. Durable and popular
Kyvig, Explicit and Authentic Acts, 1996, p. 218.

438. Politics of Prohibition
Id. at p. 219; Wiebe, The Search for Order, 1877–1920, 1967, p. 56.

Starting in 1876, virtually every session of Congress saw the introduction of some constitutional amendment aimed at alcohol.[439] Prohibition had, however, to overcome more than the desire of people for intoxicants; though it was possible to distinguish the two, Prohibition involved the largest expropriation of private property since the passage of the Thirteenth Amendment.[440] It might not have succeeded had it not been for World War I, which centralized authority over the economy, provided a national security justification, and demonized Germans—who brewed and drank much of the nation's beer.[441]

But if we are to recapture the enthusiasm for Prohibition and the varied responses to it, we must understand that—like the abortion debate today—the anti-alcohol crusade and its allied sumptuary laws were surrogates for deeper divisions in society.[442] Prohibition was, in large measure, a conservative reaction to the revolution in morals that was taking place in the Progressive era and after.[443] This was a time when "Puritan"—a word having deep associations with the right of confrontation—became a term of opprobrium.[444] Freudianism stood traditional morality on its head, turning "repression" of sexual instincts into a symptom of disease rather than an indicia of self-discipline.[445] At the same time, a rising standard of living increased the number of people who had both the time and money to afford dissolute behavior.[446] The rise of spectator sports provided an arena for the public display of unrepressed violence—Congress banned the importation of fight films.[447] The "dance craze" of the pre-War years had mingled

439. Constitutional amendment

Kyvig, Explicit and Authentic Acts, 1996, p. 220.

440. Expropriation of property

Id. at p. 226; Bickel & Schmidt, History of The Supreme Court of The United States: The Judiciary and Responsible Government, 1910–1921, 1984, p. 541.

441. Demonized Germans

Id. at p. 531.

442. Like abortion debate

Like the "coathanger abortion" when medical abortions were illegal, Prohibition gave rise to "do-it-yourself" clandestine substitutes that were often fatal. Leuchtenburg, The Perils of Prosperity, 1914–32, 1958, p. 215.

443. Revolution in morals

Id. at p. 158.

444. "Puritan" opprobrium

May, The End of American Innocence, 1964 ed., p. 340.

445. Freudian "repression"

Leuchtenburg, The Perils of Prosperity, 1914–32, 1958, pp. 164–165.

446. Afford dissolute behavior

Id. at p. 178.

447. Banned films

Id. at p. 195; Bickel & Schmidt, History of The Supreme Court of The United States: The Judiciary and Responsible Government, 1910–1921, 1984, p. 439.

music, youth, alcohol, and sex in a way that is always frightening to the older generation.[448] "Ragtime", "jazz", and "race music" combined the volatile youth movement with The Other.[449] While Prohibition was linked with Anglo–Saxon racism in that its presumed targets were Germans and Irish, alcohol and skin color had always been both associated with the absence of repression of basic urges.[450] Progressivism contributed a final ingredient; the state as "moral agent."[451] As William Graham Sumner observed: "there are two chief things with which government has to deal. They are the property of men and the honor of women. these it has to defend against crime."[452] Moreover, for some Progressives, drink was the vice of the rich and the ruin of the poor.[453] Toss in the anti-urban bias of rural Progressives, and the appeal of Prohibition becomes almost irresistible.[454]

Prohibition has often been related to the rise of feminism, but the relation has a duality that must be kept in mind.[455] The temperance movement provided a politics in which "women's sphere" overlapped public affairs and certainly provided some support for those who wanted to think that the Nineteenth Amendment would bring a new moral force into political life.[456] But like the abortion debate in modern life, women were on both sides and those who favored Prohibition were as much afraid of "the flapper"

448. "Dance craze"

May, The End of American Innocence, 1964 ed., p. 338.

449. "Jazz" and The Other

Id. at pp. 337–338. As late as 1964, a past-President of the American Bar Association argued to a snickering audience at the U.C.L.A. Law School that the fondness of one of the Justices of the Supreme Court for jazz was evidence that Brown v. Board of Education was meant to foster miscegenation.

450. Prohibition and racism

Leuchtenburg, The Perils of Prosperity, 1914–32, 1958, p. 213.

451. State as "moral agent"

Foner, The Story of American Freedom, 1998, p. 152.

452. "Honor of women"

Bickel & Schmidt, History of The Supreme Court of the United States: The Judiciary and Responsible Government, 1910–1921, 1984, p. 12.

453. Ruin of poor

Hofstadter, The Age of Reform: From Bryan to F.D.R., 1956, p. 288.

454. Anti-urban bias

Leuchtenburg, The Perils of Prosperity, 1914–32, 1958, p. 214.

455. Prohibition and feminism

Kyvig, Explicit and Authentic Acts, 1996, p. 226.

456. New moral force

Furnas, The Americans: A Social History of the United States, 1587–1914, 1969, pp. 914–916.

as they were the saloon.[457] After all, the new sex craze in literature, movies, and advertising threatened traditional domesticity as much as did The Demon Rum.[458] Anthony Comstock, with his attempt to censor "September Morning" and Theodore Drieser, appealed to the same instincts that supported Prohibition and other sumptuary laws.[459] Finally, morality, including sexual morality, had long been thought to be the domain of women and preachers; now that many women had been degraded by feminism, immigration, or modern culture, law (read "men") would have to take over.[460]

Prohibition took effect on January 29, 1920; the federal Volstead Act was imitated in many states.[461] As many had predicted, Prohibition had limited effects on consumption of alcohol; demands for stricter enforcement and tougher laws soon followed.[462] But the fact that many people were drinking does not mean that many people did not also feel the weight of the law; the number of prosecutions, in the states and federal courts for which there are statistics, is staggering.[463] Given the demands for enforcement and the signs of its futility, it is understandable that enforcers were not overly nice in their enforcement techniques; this soon provoked some public outrage.[464] Finally, given the extravagant profits, it was

457. "Flapper"

May, The End of American Innocence, 1964 ed., p. 339. The association of feminism and "flappers" with birth control played into racist fears that the dominant Anglo–Saxons were committing "race suicide" by limiting their families while the "inferior races" were breeding like muskrats—with frightening electoral consequences. Id. at p. 342.

458. Sex in advertising

Leuchtenburg, The Perils of Prosperity, 1914–32, 1958, p. 167. For evidence that the use of sex to sell is not as modern as is often supposed, see Yalom, A History of The Beast, 1997, p. 184.

459. Comstock censor

May, The End of American Innocence, 1964 ed., p. 345.

460. Law take over

Id. at p. 340.

461. Imitated in states

Friedman, Crime and Punishment in American History, 1993, p. 339. For the constitutional arguments against Prohibition that the Supreme Court rejected, see Bickel & Schmidt, History of the Supreme Court of the United States: The Judiciary and Responsible Government, 1910–1921, p. 544.

462. Tougher law

Leuchtenburg, The Perils of Prosperity, 1914–32, 1958, p. 215; Friedman, Crime and Punishment in American History, 1993, p. 339.

463. Statistics staggering

Id. at p. 340.

464. Public outrage

Leuchtenberg, The Perils of Prosperity, 1914–32, 1958, p. 214.

to be expected that men——not all of them "gangsters"——would enter into a business that relied on the corruption of local officials and the discipline of the machine gun rather than the market.[465] In time, Prohibition would trigger renewed public interest in the relationship between the police and constitutional rights, including confrontation.

Sacco-Vanzetti and Legal Science

The year 1920 included a number of events with less momentous impact on the right of confrontation than Prohibition. Warren Harding, campaigning for a "return to normalcy", received nearly two votes for every one cast for the Democratic candidate for President; Eugene Debs collected nearly a million votes as the Socialist candidate, though he had to campaign from jail.[466] "Normalcy" probably did not include ratification of the Nineteenth Amendment, the climax to the changes in the legal status of women during the Progressive years; more "normal" was the "Mattewan War", in which a dispute between local officials and private detectives working for mine owners ended up in a shootout between them and a pitched battle between miners and state troops called out to suppress the strike in which upwards of 20 people were killed.[467]

1920 was also the year of the "Black Sox scandal", in which eight members of the American League champions of 1919 were indicted for taking bribes to throw the World Series to the Cincinatti Reds (who despite the Red Scare held on to the name they quickly shed during the later McCarthy hysteria).[468] The scandal even besmirched the jury system, when the jurors, after quickly acquitting the players, hoisted them to their shoulders and marched around the courtroom to the cheers of the spectators. The scandal also illustrated how employers, using the employment relation,

465. Corruption of officials

Id. at p. 216. In 1929, the Illinois Crime Survey noted "the fact that liquor prohibition has introduced the most difficult problems of law enforcement in the field of organized crime. The enormous revenues derived from bootlegging have purchased protection for all forms of criminal activities and have demoralized law enforcing agencies." Friedman, Crime and Punishment in American History, 1993, p. 340.

466. Million votes from jail

Encyclopedia of American History, Morris ed.1976, p. 391.

467. "Normalcy" and "Mattewan"

Brecher, Strike!, 1972, p. 136; Foner, The Story of American Freedom, 1998, pp. 155–158, 172.

468. "Black Sox"

Encyclopedia of American Facts and Dates, Ninth ed.1993, p. 445.

could achieve social control beyond the powers of law; despite the acquittal, the players were barred from baseball for life.[469]

On April 15, 1920, robbers shot and killed two men carrying the payroll for a shoe factory in South Braintree, Massachusetts, leading to the conviction the following year of two Italian anarchists, Nicola Sacco and Bartolmeo Vanzetti, in a trial whose conduct and verdict became the subject of international dispute.[470] Until they were executed in 1927, Sacco and Vanzetti kept the question of the fairness of the American criminal justice system in the public eye during a time when more Americans than ever before were being brought into criminal courts for sumptuary crimes.[471] The trial and ensuing campaign to reverse the verdict reminded anyone who needed reminding that political trials do not require political crimes; despite the fact that the defendants were not on trial for their beliefs, those beliefs were put on trial in what some regarded as a prosecutorial attempt to sway the jury.[472]

The Sacco–Vanzetti case also left an indelible mark on one who before long would have the power to do something about such abuses; as enraged as he was by the execution, Professor Felix Frankfurter may well have been even more outraged had he known that the Attorney–General of Massachusetts had his phone bugged

469. Barred for life

Ibid. In a less celebrated example of the same method, the New York State Commissioner of Education ruled that school teachers could be fired for Communist activity. Id. at p. 447. The employment nexus was clearer in the case of baseball, where the newly-installed Commissioner was a federal judge with the colorful name of Kennesaw Mountain Landis.

470. International dispute

Id. at p. 444. Leuchtenburg, The Perils of Prosperity, 1914–32, 1958, pp. 81–83.

471. Question of fairness

The literature is voluminous. A good, brief summary can be found in Parrish, Felix Frankfurter and His Times: The Reform Years, 1982, pp. 176–196.

472. Prosecutorial attempt

Anyone who reads the transcript of the trial, as the writer of this footnote has, will find things more complex. The defendants' alibis included much evidence of political activity and they sought to explain their attempts to evade capture and their inconsistent stories to the police on the grounds of the fear of The Red Scare, which was then in full sway——a few days before their arrest a fellow Italian anarchist had fell (or been pushed) to his death while in custody. While the prosecutor certainly exploited the opportunities thus opened up to parade anarchism and radicalism in horrific garb before the jury in violation of our current standards for prosecutorial rhethoric, a glance at some of Clarence Darrow's trials suggests that our predecessors may have been less squeamish about the use of inflammatory argument.

while he was involved in the effort to save the two men.[473] Professor Frankfurter had already been attacked for his legal and political efforts on behalf of despised defendants; in addition to the opprobrium heaped on him for his opposition to the Red Scare, his condemnation of the Bisbee Deportation led no less a figure than Teddy Roosevelt to accuse him of "excusing men precisely like the Bolsheviki in Russia, who are murderers and encouragers of murder, who are traitors to their allies, to democracy and to civilization."[474] For his role in the Sacco–Vanzetti defense, Frankfurter was attacked by conservatives renewing their effort to get him fired, called "an expert in attempting to save murderous anarchists from the gallows" by the Chief Justice of the United States, and subjected to an intemperate critique——rife with Anglo–Saxon racism——from Dean Wigmore.[475] Despite Wigmore's expertise and the assistance he received from the trial judge, Wigmore's temper betrayed him and he was easily skewered in rebuttal by Frankfurter.[476]

But in 1920, Frankfurter was involved in a scholarly project of even greater significance for confrontation——the Cleveland Crime Survey.[477] The notion that law should be "scientific" probably goes back to the days when the word was applied to any knowledge that was not based on revelation or faith. In its modern meaning, Langdell was the most influential of those who wanted a "scientific law."[478] In Langdell's hands, "science" served to give academic respectability to vocational instruction in the newly Germanized

473. Frankfurter bugged

Parrish, Felix Frankfurter and His Times: The Reform Years, 1982, pp. 176, 192.

474. "Excusing Bolsheviki"

Baker, Felix Frankfurter, 1969, p. 73. Roosevelt went on to excuse the Bisbee perpetrators with the same argument Pound had made in his St. Paul speech: "[w]hen no efficient means are employed to guard honest, upright and well-behaved citizens from the brutal kind of lawlessness, it is inevitable that these citizens shall try to protect themselves." In other words, since legal repression is inadequate to the task of defeating labor unions, vigilantism is justified. Needless to say, Roosevelt did not excuse violence by workers on similar grounds.

475. Frankfurter attacked

Id. at pp. 177, 186–187.

476. Easily skewered

Apparently Wigmore had relied on hearsay accounts of the trial or his reading of the transcript was uncharacteristically careless. Id. at p. 187; Baker, Felix Frankfurter, 1969, p. 125. Even his admirers do not regard it as Wigmore's finest hour. Roalfe, John Henry Wigmore, 1977, p. 151.

477. Cleveland Crime Survey

Baker, Felix Frankfurter, 1969, p. 118.

478. "Scientific law"

Twining, Karl Llewellyn and The Realist Movement, 1973, p. 11.

university.[479] He tried to compare legal education to the training of scientists:

> We have * * * constantly inculcated the idea that the library is the proper workshop of professors and students alike; that it is to us all that the laboratories of the university are to chemists and physicists, all that the museum of natural history is to zoologists, all that the botanical garden is to the botanists.[480]

Despite the catholicity of this passage, Langdell was most influenced by Darwinian biology; the judicial opinions in his casebook were like the specimens that Darwin brought back on the Beagle and the task of the student was to properly label and categorize each specimen so it could be arranged in its proper place in the evolution of the common law.[481]

Langdell's achievements, alas, were more propagandistic than scientific. Since there are many kinds of "science", scholars could seize any one that seemed appropriate to gave their ideas a cachet. Corbin used science to justify his thinly disguised Social Darwinism.[482] When his detractors argued that his political ideology was infecting his teaching and scholarship, Felix Frankfurter defended himself by invoking the value-free neutrality of science.[483] Even Michael and Adler, in an analysis of the law of evidence that was as arid as anything the scholastics ever attempted, were able to find a scientific analogy for their work.[484] During the Progressive era, Einstein's theory of "relativity" was invoked to justify all sorts of juvenile iconoclasm and moral relativism—an ideology that had nothing in common save a Latin root with Einstein's thought.[485]

A transitional figure in the move from analogy to action was the former botanist, Roscoe Pound. Pound used science as a political analogy. In his youth, Pound thought that conservative judges of the time were treating law as a form of geometry, in which all

479. Give respectability

Id. at p. 13.

480. "To the botanist"

Id. at p. 12.

481. Categorize and label

Id. at p. 138.

482. Corbin

Id. at p. 33.

483. Frankfurter defended

Baker, Felix Frankfurter, 1969, p. 97.

484. Micheal and Adler

Mueller, Crime, Law, and The Scholars, 1969, p. 107.

485. "Relativity" and relativism

Russett, Darwin in America: The Intellectual Response, 1865–1912, 1976, p. 214; Verdun–Jones, Cook, Oliphant and Yntema: The Scientific Wing of American Legal Realism, 1979, 5 Dalhousie L.J. 3, 6.

the rules could be worked out by logic from a set of axioms and postulates.[486] Relying on his botanical training, Pound evolved an organicist approach to law that he thought was flexible enough to adapt the common law to modern needs and thus defeat the demands of the Populists for a more democratic judiciary.[487] Later he used relativity to support his version of moral relativism.[488] But Pound appreciated the fact that analogies were not enough, perhaps because of the way the analogy was flung back in his face after his controversial St. Paul address.[489] In any event, he urged that judges should be given scientific advisers to help them understand modern life and that scholars should engage in sociological research so that appellate courts could have facts they needed to adapt the law but that were not reflected in the typical appellate record.[490]

Pound inspired what has been called the "scientific wing" of Legal Realism. The leaders of this group were, like Pound, all legal academics who had begun their careers in other disciplines.[491] One of these, Walter Wheeler Cook, in 1919 began emphasizing the need for empirical research to support the instrumental pretensions of the new "policy" approach to the common law: "the worth or value of a given rule of law can be determined only by finding out how it works, that is, by ascertaining so far as it can be done, whether it promotes or retards the attainment of desired ends."[492] Cook, who was a disciple of John Dewey, thought even legal values would yield to scientific inquiry but for other Realists, "justice" was a "non-testable truth"——a matter of faith or revelation but not of science.[493] This stance probably owed as much to the Progressive desire to be above politics after the Red Scare as it did to the ideas of Einstein or Dewey.[494]

486. Law as geometry

Wigdor, Roscoe Pound, 1974, p. 214.

487. Defeat Populists

Id. at pp. 24, 216–217.

488. Moral relativism

Sayre, The Life of Roscoe Pound, 1948, p. 175.

489. Flung in his face

Widgor, Roscoe Pound, 1974, p. 126 (critic of Pound: "[the common law is] the most refined and scientific system ever devised by the wit of man").

490. Advisers and research

Id. at p. 142.

491. Other disciplines

Verdun–Jones, Cook, Oliphant, and Yntema: The Scientific Wing of American Legal Realism, 1979, 5 Dalhousie L.J. 3.

492. Promotes or retards

Twining, Karl Llewellyn and The Realist Movement, 1973, pp. 38–39.

493. "Non-testable truth"

Id. at p. 185.

494. Dewey

Verdun–Jones, Cook, Oliphant, and Yntema: The Scientific Wing of American Legal Realism (Part II), 1979, 5 Dalhousie L.J. 249, 250.

But the scientific wing of Legal Realism did launch a boomlet of enthusiasm for applying scientific methods to law. Some, if not most, of the work consisted of applying the findings of real scientists to legal rules; for example, the Hutchins–Slesinger articles in which what was then known about psychology was applied to the rules of evidence.[495] However, a few legal scholars attempted to do scientific work of their own——a form of legal scholarship that continues down to the present day with more modest goals and still modest numbers of participants.[496] Rather quickly most of the experimental Legal Realists found that truly scientific methods were generally unsuited to deal with the complex social phenomenon with which legal rules are concerned.[497] Only a few hardy souls persisted, in the face of some ridicule, in the attempt to prove otherwise.[498] For the most part, the effort to apply scientific methods to law has been judged a "failure"——its only legacy an analogy that has been exploited in recent times by the practitioners of "law-and-economics" to justify their sometimes insightful and sometimes ludicrous efforts to justify the status quo.[499]

The reason for this failure are many. Legal scholars, like the lawyers they once were, are tempted to utilize social science as a tool of argument, not of inquiry.[500] The structure of legal publishing plays a role; law reviews are not peer-reviewed scientific journals and there are few other publishers of the kind of monographs that are the outlet for much social-science research.[501] But a central role in the failure of "legal science" was the nearly total disregard of

495. Applied to evidence

See, e.g., Hutchins & Slesinger, Some Observations on The Law of Evidence: Family Relations, 1929, 13 Minn. L.Rev. 675.

496. Continues to present

See any issue of The Law & Society Review.

497. Methods unsuited

Verdun–Jones, Cook, Oliphant, and Yntema: The Scientific Wing of American Legal Realism, 1979, 5 Dalhousie L.J. 3, 18.

498. Few persisted

Id. at p. 20; American Legal Realism and Empirical Social Science: From The Yale Experience, 1979, 28 Buff.L.Rev. 459, 463.

499. Judged "failure"

Id. at p. 581.

500. Argument, not inquiry

Id. at pp. 540–541.

501. Few outlets

Mueller, Crime, Law and The Scholars, 1969, p. 120. The junior author has personal knowledge of this, having once been part of a team of scholars that conducted a broad study of the preliminary hearing in this country and England that had to be broken up into a series of law-review articles because the sponsor was unable to find a publisher who would produce it as a book.

any sort of social, economic, or political theory in the work of the Legal Realists.[502] This is understandable, given the recent collapse of the Progressive belief "that American society rested on a set of common values" and the long preference for improvisation as a response to change.[503] But the Realist acceptance of the extreme inductivism touted by some practitioners of science did more than open the door for the moral nihilism of business that permeates legal education today; it also overlooked a truth that some legal scholars did appreciate: namely, "science cannot come into existence in a given field until a theory or an analysis has been constructed."[504] The result was that the Legal Realists seem to have substituted one form of mysticism ("policy") for another ("the common law"),[505]

The Cleveland Crime Survey typifies an exception to this gloomy picture of "legal science" in the interwar years. It was the first in a line of similar studies that culminated with the Wickersham Commission's study of federal law enforcement a decade later.[506] In May of 1920, the chief judge of the Cleveland Municipal Court was charged with conspiring in the murder of his favorite bootlegger. Though the principal witness against him was his own mistress, the judge decided to bribe a witness to obtain his acquittal. When the scandal broke, the Cleveland Foundation hired Raymond Moley, a future member of Franklin Roosevelt's "Brain Trust" but then a professor of political science at Western Reserve University, to organize a thorough study of the Cleveland criminal-justice system looking toward its reform. Moley brought in Roscoe Pound as director of the study and Pound named Felix Frankfurter as his codirector.[507]

502. Disregard of theory

Verdun–Jones, Cook, Oliphant, and Yntema: The Scientific Wing of American Legal Realism, 1979, 5 Dalhousie L.J. 3, 42.

503. Collapse of "values"

White, From Sociological Jurisprudence to Realism: Jurisprudence and Social Change in Early Twentieth Century America, 1972, 58 Va.L.Rev. 999, 1024; Hurst, Law and Social Progress in United States History, 1960, p. 31.

504. "Science cannot come"

Mueller, Crime, Law and The Scholars, 1969, p. 107.

505. "Policy" mysticism

Verdun–Jones, Cook, Oliphant, and Yntema: The Scientific Wing of American Legal Realism (Part II), 1979, 5 Dalhousie L.J. 249, 275.

506. Similar studies

Mueller, Crime, Law and The Scholars, 1969, p. 96.

507. Pound named Frankfurter

Wigdor, Roscoe Pound, 1974, pp. 242–243.

Unlike The American Law Institute, which thought that "scientific legal work" meant a continuation of the codification wars of the previous century in a formalist manner,[508] Pound and Frankfurter brought in a number of experts in various disciplines to do what might be generously described as "sociology" but could be more accurately called "descriptive empirical analysis."[509] In addition to exposing archaic police methods, sloppy judicial administration, political influence, and simple incompetence, the final report proposed a number of changes to meet these deficiencies; improved police work, reorganization of the prosecutor's office, streamlined judicial administration, and improvements in legal education.;[510] Though they did not explicitly deal with the adversary system, the Cleveland study and its successors did suggest that cutting constitutional corners in the investigation and punishment of crime, far from making the system more "efficient", was costly not only in public confidence but in the integrity of convictions and the swiftness and certainty of punishment.[511] Moreover, these studies fostered an academic interest in the criminal-justice system that would eventually produce law-school courses in criminal procedure and the casebooks necessary to teach them.[512] Academic study and criticism played a significant role in the Supreme Court's attempt to revive the adversary system after World War II.

Valentino, Harding, and Legal Realism

In 1921, the Harding era began with a short but severe recession.[513] In a premonitory demonstration of the future needs of "the Ohio Gang", the President issued Christmas presents to

---

508. Unlike A.L.I.

A.L.I., History of The American Law Institute, 1945, pp. 3, 5; Friedman, A History of American Law, 1973, p. 354.

509. "Descriptive empirical"

For an illustrative specimen of this genre that demonstrates we do not use the term to demean, see Graham & Letwin, The Preliminary Hearing in Los Angeles: Some Field Findings and Legal–Policy Observations, 1971, 18 U.C.L.A.L.Rev. 635.

510. Legal education

Parrish, Felix Frankfurter and His Times: The Reform Years, 1982, p. 173.

511. Cutting corners costly

Id. at p. 174; Schlegel, American Legal Realism and Empirical Social Science: From The Yale Experience, 1979, 28 Buff.L.Rev. 459, 503–504.

512. Produce casebooks

Mueller, Crime, Law and The Scholars, 1969, p. 114.

513. Severe recession

Encyclopedia of American History, Morris ed.1976, p. 352.

Eugene Debs and 23 others convicted under the Espionage Act of 1917.[514] By commuting their sentences rather than pardoning them, Harding offered something to both sides in the debate over the Supreme Court's Schenck–Abrams decisions, which had upheld the Act while suggesting some First Amendment limitations on its scope.[515] Under Harding, the conservative ideology that had been partially eclipsed by Progressivism reasserted itself——a resurgence symbolized by the appointment of William Howard Taft as Chief Justice.[516] The President's aphorism summed up his goal: "We want less government in business and more business in government."[517] As Teapot Dome would soon make clear, this meant that government existed to subsidize business, not to "provide for the general welfare."[518]

Ironically, in the same year that the census showed for the first time that urban-dwelling Americans outnumbered farmers, in Progressivism's last gasp, Congress enacted several pieces of legislation designed to protect farmers.[519] However, most middle-class Americans were tired of demands for activism, self-sacrifice, and disciplined efficiency.[520] As the acerbic H.L. Mencken put it, "[i]f I am convinced of anything, it is that Doing Good is in bad taste."[521] While other members of the intellectual elite uttered similar sentiments, the mass of those with the wherewithal to do so, moved from citizenship to consumerism.[522] Margaret Sanger founded the

514. Christmas presents

Encyclopedia of American Facts and Dates, 9th ed.1993, p. 450.

515. Suggesting limits

Schenck v. U.S., 1919, 39 S.Ct. 247, 249 U.S. 47, 63 L.Ed. 470; Abrams v. U.S., 1919, 40 S.Ct. 17, 250 U.S. 616, 63 L.Ed. 1173. The dissent in the latter case was a watershed in the creation of modern civil liberties and opened the door to implementation of the other provisions of the Bill of Rights, including the Sixth Amendment and its Confrontation Clause.

516. Symbolized by Taft

Wood, Constitutional Politics in The Progressive Era, 1968, pp. 255, 259.

517. "Less and more"

Id. at p. 256.

518. Subsidize business

Leuchtenburg, The Perils of Prosperity, 1914–32, 1958, p. 181.

519. Protect farmers

Encyclopedia of American History, Morris ed.1976, pp. 392–393; Encyclopedia of American Facts and Dates, Ninth ed.1993, p. 448.

520. Americans tired

Leuchtenburg, The Perils of Prosperity, 1914–32, 1958, p. 84.

521. "Good in bad taste"

Id. at p. 150.

522. Moved to consumerism

"The great problems of the world—social, political, economic and theological—do not concern me in the slightest. If all Armenians were to be killed

American Birth Control League and the book that would become Rudolph Valentino's "The Sheik" was published in 1921[523]; sex was clearly no longer solely for procreation when ravishment became entertainment. So much for "white slavery", the justification for the Mann Act and other sumptuary laws.[524]

While some features of the nation's return to the excesses of the "Gilded Age" may have horrified traditional conservatives, the remnants of Progressivism found their culture of reform was replaced by one of disillusionment.[525] For some of those who autopsied the corpse of the movement, it was not that their ideology had failed "the people" but that people had failed to live up to the ideology.[526] Typical of this response was Walter Lippman's "Public Opinion", published the following year.[527] Agreeing with the adman who proclaimed that the "great bulk of people are stupid", Lippman argued that the idea of "the people" as a rational collective entity enshrined in the preamble to the Constitution was a myth.[528] The techniques of modern public relations had reduced politics to the "manufacture of consent." With the rise of the Ku Klux Klan and Naziism, Lippman became convinced that it was Freud, not Marx or Adam Smith, who provided the key to understanding modern political-economy. Attitudes like this undermined confrontation and the adversary system along with traditional notions of

tomorrow and if half of Russia were to starve to death the day after, it would not matter to me in the least. What concerns me alone is myself, and the interests of a few close friends.", wrote a leading drama critic. Another commentator thought that relief of starving children "was one of the least engaging ways in which money could be spent." Id at pp. 150–151. Foner, The Story of American Freedom, 1998, pp. 147–148, 151.

523. Sanger and "The Sheik"

Encyclopedia of American Facts and Dates, 9th ed.1993, pp. 449–451.

524. "White slavery"

That women might enjoy cinematic ravishment by Valentino was not inconsistent with Sanger, at least in the sense that these women were choosing their ravisher——not submitting to some swarthy stranger out of fear. On the other hand, the notion that women might choose any kind of sexual activity was antithetical to the notions of female purity that underlay traditional morality and the Mann Act.

525. "Gilded Age" disillusionment

Leuchtenburg, The Perils of Prosperity, 1914–32, 1958, pp. 140, 145. The "Gilded Age" refers to the period of capitalist excess from the end of the Civil War to the rise of Populism.

526. People had failed

Id. at p. 125.

527. "Public opinion"

Ibid.

528. "People" a myth

Foner, The Story of American Freedom, 1998, p. 181.

democracy.[529]

The legal embodiment of the culture of disillusionment is sometimes called "Legal Realism." Some writers draw distinctions between Legal Realism, which they associate with the New Deal, and Sociological Jurisprudence, which is supposed to be the legal manifestation of Progressivism.[530] For one of these writers, Legal Realism is Progressive legal ideology, shorn of its moral values and respect for legal rules.[531] Other writers reject this dichotomization, finding the roots of legal realism in earlier thinkers who wrestled with the problem of the unification of American law.[532] Since we believe that at least in the field of procedure and evidence the Progressive ideology remains alive, we think that the former view, at the very least, overstates the discontinuity of legal thought following the death of political Progressivism, in part because of an overreliance on Roscoe Pound as a representative of Progressive legal thought.[533] Perhaps, the problem rests on the difficulty of defining "Legal Realism."[534] To us, Legal Realism is more an attitude than an ideology.

One of the leaders of Legal Realism wrote that "[s]ince law is a means of social control, it ought to be studied as such."[535] This, as we have seen, states the view of Edward A. Ross, one of the intellectual leaders of legal Progressivism.[536] Similarly, the Johns Hopkins Institute for Study of Law, an institution that is indisputably Legal Realist in orientation, claimed its founding ideology was comprised of three ideas: "scientific method", "social engineering", and the "community of scholars."[537] As we have seen, the first two

---

529. Freud, not Marx

Haber, Efficiency and Uplift: Scientific Management in the Progressive Era, 1890–1920, 1973, p. 93.

530. Realism and Progressivism

White, From Sociological Jurisprudence to Realism: Jurisprudence and Social Change in Early Twentieth Century America, 1972, 58 Va.L.Rev. 999.

531. Shorn of moral values

Id. at p. 1020.

532. Earlier thinkers

Twining, Karl Llewellyn and The Realist Movement, 1973, pp. 7, 20 (John Chipman Grey); White, Social Thought in America: The Revolt Against Formalism, 1957, pp. 3, 8 (Holmes).

533. Reliance on Pound

Wigdor, Roscoe Pound, 1974, pp. 255, 262, 264 (Pound and Realism, attacks as "Marxist").

534. Difficulty in defining

Twining, Karl Llewellyn and The Realist Movement, 1973, pp. 73–74.

535. "Law is social control"

Id. at p. 50.

536. Ross

See above, § 6357. text at notecall 787.

537. "Community of scholars"

Twining, Karl Llewellyn and The Realist Movement, 1973, p. 60.

of these figured prominently in Progressive legal thought.[538] Karl Llewellyn, a Realist not inclined to grant Roscoe Pound great influence, was willing to credit Pound with providing the idea that law was a form of "social engineering."[539] Llewellyn, like many Progressives, wanted law to be ethically neutral and politically pure; "Realism in law" he wrote "is * * * as ethically neutral as the science of mechanics or the art of bridge-building."[540] When he claimed that the procedural problems revealed by the Sacco–Vanzetti case were "technical" ones that "only technicians are equipped to handle", Llewellyn exhibits the same "Cult of the Expert" we have seen in Progressive thought.[541] Since even one who seeks to distinguish between Realism and Progressivism concedes that Progressive values persisted after Progressivism had disappeared from politics, we need not belabor the point.[542]

Because of the dominance of the "Columbia school" of evidence writers at the end of the century, we find it significant that Columbia and Yale were early centers of Legal Realism.[543] Given the Realist view of the lawyer as "conformist", one would expect those who follow that tradition to write books for lawyers that do not challenge the Progressive notion that law should be apolitical.[544] While some Realists tried to use social science as a substitute for political ideology as a basis for criticism, insofar as evidence was concerned, this dabbling in social science did little to conceal the underlying Progressive ideology.[545] Some Realists did depart from Progressivism in recognizing a role for ritual and emotion in procedure; Hessel Yntema wrote that the judicial process was "an emotive experience in which principles and logic play a secondary

538. Figured prominently

See § 6358, above, text at notecalls 70, 318.

539. "Social engineering"

Id. at p. 23.

540. "Bridge-building"

Id. at p. 188.

541. "Only technicians"

Id. at p. 347. See, on The Cult of the Expert, § 6358, above, text at notecall 518.

542. Values persisted

White, From Sociological Jurisprudence to Realism: Jurisprudence and Social Change in Early Twentieth Century America, 1972, 58 Va.L.Rev. 999, 1013.

543. Columbia and Yale

Twining, Karl Llewellyn and The Realist Movement, 1973, p. 26.

544. "Conformist"

Id. at p. 143.

545. Dabbling in social science

Schlegel, American Legal Realism and Empirical Social Science: From The Yale Experience, 1979, 28 Buff.L.Rev. 459, 480–481.

role."[546] However, for most Progressive proceduralists, emotion was something to be purged——to the detriment of rituals such as confrontation.[547]

The difference between the attitude of Realists and those of their predecessors can be gauged in two passages dealing with how laissez-faire judges served the interests of the dominant social interests.[548] Wrote Brooks Adams:

> I should not suppose that any man could calmly turn over pages of recent volumes of the reports to the Supreme Court of the United States and not rise from the perusal convinced that the rich and the poor, the strong and the weak, do not receive a common measure of justice before the judgement seat.[549]

For Adams, this followed from the need of capitalists to control the judiciary in order to retain their political power.[550] The Realists, like the other disillusioned Progressives, preferred a less explicitly politically explanation, such as this one.

> It is the great disservice of the classical conception of law that it hides from judicial eyes the ethical character of every judicial question, and thus serves to perpetuate class prejudice and uncritical moral assumptions which could not survive the sunlight of ethical controversy.[551]

Under this view, injustice is a psychological rather than a political problem.[552] But many Realists would reject even this passage for its suggestion that ethics had anything to do with law. Ignorance of ethics makes Legal Realism as unrealistic as the jurisprudence it

546. "Emotive experience"

White, From Sociological Jurisprudence to Realism: Jurisprudence and Social Change in Early Twentieth Century America, 1972, 58 Va.L.Rev. 999, 1016.

547. Emotion purged

Id. at pp. 1013–1015.

548. Dominant interests

Adams, The Theory of Social Revolutions, 1913, p. 37.

549. "Do not receive justice"

Id. at p. 107.

550. Retain power

Id. at p. 47. Adams, interestingly, recognized the role of separation of functions——one of the purposes of the Confrontation Clause——in safeguarding rights: "unless the judge can be separated from the sovereign, and be strictly limited in the performance of his function by a recognized code of procedure, the public, as against the dominant class, has, in substance, no civil rights." Id. at p. 37.

551. "Sunlight of controversy"

Harbaugh, Lawyer's Lawyer: The Life of John w. Davis, 1973, p. 412.

552. Psychological

This was the burden of one of the best-known works of Legal Realism, Jerome Frank's "Law and The Modern Mind."

sought to replace. A good example is Karl Llewellyn's analysis of the Sacco–Vanzetti trial, which founders on his unwillingness to distinguish between trial by jury and a lynch mob.[553] The denial of moral values in law left Legal Realists helpless in the face of immoral legal systems like those of Nazi Germany and this led to its demise.[554] However, the Progressivism that Legal Realists wanted to deny lived on in procedural scholarship.

Wartime sumptuary laws closed Storyville, the famous New Orleans "red light" district, but Prohibition brought speakeasies as a new venue for the development of jazz.[555] Because of its association with alcohol and African–Americans, no one noticed that jazz provided a better metaphor for the adversary system than the factory. European classical music was essentially bureaucratic with the talent of the musicians subordinated to the control of the composer or the conductor. Jazz, like the adversary system, was a fluid mixture of cooperation and control; the composition exerted no more control over the musicians than the pleadings over the lawyers while the function of the leader of a jazz band, like that of the judge, was to determine what and when, not how——the latter flowed from the beat of the drum and the need for the musicians to cooperate to reach an outcome fixed only within broad limits but not necessarily the one intended by anyone when the performance began. But the need for cooperation in jazz does not stifle competition——in its purest form there are "cutting contests" in which each musician, in turn, tried to outdo his or her fellows. As in confronta-

553. Llewellyn's analysis

"American law is not exhausted with paper rules on books. It extends to what goes on, to what officials do about disputes, about suspects, about criminals with influence, about trial and pardon——and the third degree. The American Constitution is not limited to a venerable document prepared a century and a a half ago, with nineteen passages on paper added since; the American Constitution is the actual framework of our government as we are governed. * * * when the rules on the books do not square with the third degree of biased judge, when the paper Constitution says freedom of speech and assembly, but the governing officials deport or break up meetings * * * I see no clarity to be gained by denying that bigotry, intolerance, ma- nipulation and even corruption of the police and judicial machinery to protect men dear to those in power and to attack or frame their enemies——or their victims——I see no clarity to be gained by denying that these are an established American tradition." Twining, Karl Llewellyn and The Realist Movement, 1973, pp. 348–349.

554. Led to its demise

White, From Sociological Jurisprudence to Realism: Jurisprudence and Social Change in Early Twentieth Century America, 1972, 58 Va.L.Rev. 999, 1026.

555. Development of jazz

May, The End of American Innocence, 1964 ed., p. 337.

571

tion, jazz required the participants be in each other's presence though not literally "face to face."

However, another cultural development of the time was antithetical to both jazz and confrontation. Confrontation was, in part, a response to the capacity of writing to separate the unity of time and space in the presentation of testimony. Now new technologies—the telephone, motion pictures, and radio—provided new ways in which the testimony of the witness might be presented to the judge, jury, and defendant without the presence of the witness at the time and place scheduled for trial.[556] Like the new technologies at the end of the century, exaggerated claims were made for motion pictures; e.g., that they would soon replace books, at least in education.[557] However, unlike later technologies, it was some time before courts were invited to substitute telephonic or cinematic testimony for the sort envisaged by the Confrontation Clause. But though movies did not often appear in court, the ability of the film to "recreate" a past reality for the audience must have made the law's attempts to bring back the past through witnesses and documents seem much inferior if not antiquated. Thus movies could undermine confidence in confrontation without being offered as a replacement for it.

Business Triumphant and Teapot Dome

The year 1922 brought the first radio play-by-play of a World Series game, the first use of the term "robot", and the first unravelling of what would become the "Teapot Dome Scandal."[558] As Louis Armstrong arrived in Chicago to join King Oliver's Creole Jazz Band, Attorney General Harry Daugherty got a sweeping injunction from a judge in that city, had union leaders led off in handcuffs, and broke a railroad strike.[559] The Attorney General, who was about to be driven from office as a crook, told reporters, "[s]o long and to the extent that I can speak for the government * * * I will use the power of the government to prevent the labor unions of the country from destroying the open shop."[560]

556. New technologies
Id. at pp. 334–335.

557. Replace books
Id. at p. 335.

558. "Teapot Dome"
Encyclopedia of American Facts and Dates, 9th ed.1993, pp. 450–452.

559. Broke railroad strike
Leuchtenberg, The Perils of Prosperity, 1914–32, 1958, p. 99.

560. "Destroying open shop"
Ibid.

The administration's alliance with business came as no surprise to surprise William Allen White, who had written of the convention that nominated Harding: "I have never seen a convention—and I have watched most of them since McKinley's first nomination—completely dominated by sinister predatory economic forces as was this."[561] But Harding was primarily a politician interested in popularity; his successor Calvin Coolidge was a dedicated ideologue who wanted to run a "businessman's government" and turn the Republican party into the party of Big Business.[562] He appointed as head of the Federal Trade Commission a man who had denounced the F.T.C. as "an instrument of oppression and disturbance and injury" and "a publicity bureau to spread socialist propaganda."[563] He promptly turned the agency into a "help to business" by reducing competition. As the Wall Street Journal wrote of the Coolidge administration, "[n]ever before, here or anywhere else, has a government so completely fused with business."[564]

The Harding–Coolidge era was one of corporate mergers and massive concentration of economic power.[565] Power over the economy was matched by power in other spheres; municipal reform during the Progressive era had increased the power of businessmen over local government.[566] Thanks in part to the growth of the public relations industry, judges and politicians who took positions contrary to those of the corporados found themselves excoriated by the press.[567] Business control over higher education, including the power to fire teachers with a real or supposed antibusiness bias, flourished.[568] Businessmen were thought to be experts in management; Calvin Coolidge said "[b]rains are wealth and wealth is the chief end of man."[569] As experts, businessmen were privileged over

561. "Predatory economic forces"
Id. at p. 86.

562. "Businessman's government"
Id. at p. 96.

563. "Spread socialistic"
Id. at p. 190.

564. "Completely fused"
Id. at p. 103.

565. Massive concentration
Id. at pp. 191–193.

566. Local government
Vanderbilt, Changing Law: A Biography of Aurthur T. Vanderbilt, 1977, p. 98.

567. Excoriated by press
Mitgang, The Man Who Rode The Tiger: The Life and Times of Judge Samuel Seabury, 1963, p. 70.

568. Fire teachers
Brooks, Walter Clark, Fighting Judge, 1944, pp. 104, 116; Wigdor, Roscoe Pound, 1974, p. 111.

569. "Chief end of man"
Leuchtenburg, The Perils of Prosperity, 1914–32, 1958, p. 188.

citizens, consumers, and workers in projects for law reform then being run by the American Law Institute and the Commissioners on Uniform State Laws.[570]

Partly as a result of corporate power, partly as a result of the decline of the traditional professions, businessmen enjoyed a status in the 1920s that was unrivaled by any of the traditional high-status professions.[571] But unlike the previous highpoint of business influence in the Gilded Age, the Coolidge businessman was a political bureaucrat, not an individualistic buccaneer.[572] A voluminous literature on bureaucratic theology was published and everyone from farmers to federal judges was encouraged to be more "business-like."[573] Coolidge, with his usual astuteness, grasped the religiosity afoot: "[t]he man who builds a factory builds a temple, the man who works there worships there."[574] Not to be outdone, the advertising baron, Bruce Barton, wrote a bestseller in which Jesus Christ was revealed as the consumate bureaucrat; "He picked twelve men from the bottom ranks of business and forged them into an organization that conquered the world."[575] To Barton, the Christian parables were "the most powerful advertisements of all time."[576] With even the Lord against them, it is not surprising that many prominent Progressives went over to business.[577] The ex-muckraker Lincoln Steffens proclaimed that "Big business in America is producing what the Socialists held up as their goal; food, shelter and clothing for all."[578] Walter Lippman now found capital-

570. Privileged in projects

Twining, Karl Llewellyn and The Realist Movement, 1973, p. 291.

571. Status unrivaled

Brooks, Walter Clark, Fighting Judge, 1944, p. 116; Leuchtenburg, The Perils of Prosperity, 1914–32, 1958, p. 188.

572. Not an individualist

Id at p. 199; Hofstadter, The Age of Reform: From Bryan to F.D.R., 1956, pp. 10, 217.

573. More "business-like"

Id. at pp. 125, 241.

574. "Worships there"

Leuchtenburg, The Perils of Prosperity, 1914–32, 1958, p. 188.

575. "Organization conquered"

Id. at p. 189. In addition to being blasphemous, Barton is historically inac-

curate; Christianity as a bureaucracy did not emerge for several centuries. But then accuracy has never been the hallmark of the advertising man.

576. "Powerful advertisements"

Ibid. Apparently Barton saw Christ as a sort of travelling salesman for the Deity, quoting his words that "I must be about my Father's business."

577. Progressives went over

Id. at p. 126.

578. "Clothing for all"

Id. at p. 202. Steffens's understanding of Socialism is on a par with Barton's understanding of Christianity.

ism "more novel, more daring, and in general more revolutionary than the theories of the progressives."[579] With the desertion of the Eastern elite, indigenous radicalism survived only on the Great Plains.[580]

Only the most doctrinaire adherent of the autonomy of the legal system will suppose that lawyers and judges could resist the allure of bureaucratic values espoused by the business elite.[581] Chief Justice Taft was a leader in the movement to bring "business principles" into the administration of justice.[582] One enthusiast for this movement contrasted courts "with the high degree of efficiency in the administration of most large business corporations."[583] An apostate later described the judicial administration movement as

> based on the unexamined assumption that courts are business institutions which are engaged in some sort of production (presumably the production of justice measured in statistical terms by the production of convictions). A comparison with the U.S. Steel Corporation is invoked. Speed and efficiency are the tests resorted to.[584]

In what may have been the high-water mark of the interwar period, judges in New Jersey were ordered to turn in weekly time cards.[585] Roscoe Pound even thought that the law of contracts and property

579. "More revolutionary"

Ibid.

580. Radicalism survived

Id. at p. 128.

581. Lawyers and judges

Auerbach & Bardach, "Born to an Era of Insecurity": Career Patterns of Law Review Editors, 1918–1941, 1977, 17 Am.J.L.Hist. 3, 4.

582. "Business principles"

Mason, William Howard Taft: Chief Justice, 1975, p. 62. Taft's colleague, Brandeis, was enamored of "scientific management", even using it against its corporate sponsors. Todd, Justice on Trial: The Case of Louis D. Brandeis, 1964, p. 63.

583. "High efficiency"

Vanderbilt, Changing Law: A Biography of Aurthur T. Vanderbilt, 1977, p. 175. During his enthusiastic period,

Thurman Arnold wrote: "It has been said that if a business organization were conducted with as little study of efficient methods as our judicial system, it would be bankrupt in a year." Ayer, In Quest of Efficiency: The Ideological Journey of Thurman Arnold in the Interwar Period, 1972, 23 Stan. L.Rev. 1049, 1060.

584. "Speed and efficiency"

Id. at p. 1070. By the time he wrote this, Arnold had switched to drama as a more appropriate analogy for judicial procedure. Id. at p. 1071.

585. Turn in time cards

Vanderbilt, Changing Law: A Biography of Arthur T. Vanderbilt, 1977, p. 176.

should be molded to suit business interests.[586] After the Depression, the example of U.S. Steel had less appeal substantively, but the language of the businesslike law movement so permeated procedural scholarship that most modern scholars are unaware of its source and thus accept its values without testing the validity of the analogy. "Production of convictions" is not a value that the Confrontation Clause was designed to foster.

The so-called "Teapot Dome Scandals" were the first drops of rain on this triumphal parade of capitalism. Except for the fact that they all involved members of Harding's "Ohio Gang" of cronies, Teapot Dome was in fact a series of otherwise unrelated crimes.[587] In 1921, shortly after taking office, Harding transferred authority over the naval oil reserves on the public domain in Teapot Dome, Wyoming and Elk Hills, California from the Navy to the Department of Interior. The Secretary of the Interior, Albert Fall, after receiving $100,000 in a black bag from Edward Doheny's son, entered into a secret lease of the Elk Hills reserve to Doheny's oil company. In return for a similar lease of Teapot Dome, Fall's son-in-law received $233,000 in government bonds and Fall received another $85,000 in cash and a herd of blooded cattle from the Sinclair Oil Company.[588]

Meanwhile, over at the Veteran's Bureau, bandages, bedding, and drugs needed by disabled veterans were being sold off to businessmen at a fraction of what they had cost the government in return for kickbacks to the head of the Bureau. Other business-government frauds were perpetrated in the purchase of land for and the construction of hospitals for veterans.[589] Similarly, the Alien Property Custodian took $50,000 in bonds and in return sold off confiscated German chemical patents for much less than they were worth. These bonds were then deposited in a bank account controlled by the Attorney General.[590]

586. Suit business interests

Wigdor, Roscoe Pound, 1974, p. 95 (property and contracts "are primarily questions of business and business usage so far as not foreclosed by any established course of decision, ought to be resolved in a liberal spirit, to promote the interests of business.")

587. Series of crimes

Our description is based on Encyclopedia of American History, Morris ed. 1976, pp. 383–384 and Leuchtenburg, The Perils of Prosperity, 1914–32, 1958, pp. 92–94, primarily the latter. We have reorganized these accounts to make them more accessible to the reader.

588. Oil scandal

Id. at p. 93.

589. Veterans Bureau

Id. at pp. 92–93.

590. Alien Property bonds

Id. at p. 94.

Attorney General Daugherty and Jesse Smith, a person described in the euphemism of the time as his "housekeeper and confidant", had rented a house on K Street, which they then used to provide sex and alcohol to the President and other influentials.[591] Smith also took bribes from bootleggers in return for immunity from prosecution and pardons for those already convicted, presumably with the knowledge and acquiescence of the Attorney General.

The scandal began to unravel when business rivals, the American Legion, and others complained to members of Congress.[592] When word got out, Jesse Smith and the legal adviser to the Veterans Bureau both committed suicide.[593] President Harding escaped inquiry into his role, if any, in the scandal when he died on August 2, 1923.[594] When called before a Senate investigating committee in 1924, Attorney General Daugherty refused to submit to cross-examination, apparently on grounds of executive privilege.[595] The unravelling scandal presented problems for the incoming Coolidge administration. In the first place, prosecution of businessmen for crimes was all but unheard of at the time.[596] In the second place, the business press, instead of denouncing the scandal, attacked those who had brought it to light.[597]

The results of the Teapot Dome trials did nothing to improve the public perception of trial by jury and the adversary system.[598] Sinclair and Doheny were acquitted, the jury apparently accepting their claim that the bribes were in fact "loans" (though Sinclair was sentenced to nine months in jail for contempt of court). Fall, on the other hand, was convicted of bribery for his receipt of the "loans" and sentenced to a year in prison.[599] Similarly, the head of the Veterans Bureau was convicted of fraud, conspiracy, and brib-

591. **Sex and alcohol**

Id. at pp. 91–92.

592. **Complained to Congress**

Id. at pp. 92–93; Encyclopedia of American Facts and Dates, 9th ed.1993, p. 452.

593. **Suicide**

Leuchtenburg, The Perils of Prosperity, 1914–32, 1958, pp. 92, 93.

594. **Harding died**

Id. at p. 92.

595. **Refused to submit**

Id. at p. 94.

596. **Prosecution unheard of**

Friedman, Crime and Punishment in American History, 1993, p. 290.

597. **Brought it to light**

Leuchtenburg, The Perils of Prosperity, 1914–32, 1958, p. 94.

598. **Results of trials**

Encyclopedia of American History, Morris ed.1976, p. 384.

599. **Year in prison**

Fall was the first cabinet officer to ever receive a prison sentence. Leuchtenburg, The Perils of Prosperity, 1914–32, 1958, p. 93.

ery and sentenced to two years in Leavenworth and the Alien Property Custodian got an 18 month sentence for conspiring to defraud the government.[600] Attorney General Daugherty, after being belatedly forced from office by the President, was acquitted of all charges.[601] Despite the fact that no businessmen were convicted, Teapot Dome may have played some small part in renewing the interest of the upper classes in the adversary system just as it was coming under attack from the Progressive proceduralists.

The Ku Klux Klan, The Other, and Confrontation

In 1922, a popular history of the Constitution became one of the first books to suggest a non-common law origin for the right of confrontation.[602] Norton's "The Constitution of the United States: Its Sources and Its Application" claimed that the Confrontation Clause was "framed against the odious practice which had prevailed in England of taking depositions * * * of witnesses and reading them in court."[603] Norton cites Sir Walter Raleigh and Saint Paul, not English judges, as the "sources" of the right.[604] He suggests that there are, however, exceptions such as dying declarations and former testimony.[605]

The following year, 1923, brought the first electric shaver, Bix Biederbecke and the Wolverine Orchestra, and the death of President Harding.[606] It was also the year that the Ku Klux Klan, which had been revived in 1915, reached its peak——an estimated five million members.[607] The Klan controlled politics in a number of states.[608] In Indiana, it took over the Republican party and installed a Klan hack as governor.[609] In Oregon the Klan worked through the

600. Defraud government

Id. at pp. 93, 94.

601. Forced from office

Id. at p. 94.

602. One of the first to suggest

Norton, The Constitution of the United States: Its Sources and Its Application, 1922, p. 219.

603. "Odious practice"

Ibid.

604. Raleigh and Saint Paul

See vol. 30, § 6342, pp. 238, 258.

605. Exceptions

Id. at p. 220.

606. Biederbecke and Harding

Encyclopedia of American Facts and Dates, 9th ed.1993, pp. 454–455; Encyclopedia of American History, Morris ed.1976, p. 393.

607. Five million KKK

Ibid. See also, Leuchtenburg, The Perils of Prosperity, 1914–32, 1958, p. 211.

608. Controlled politics

Encyclopedia of American History, Morris ed.1976, p. 393.

609. Indiana

Leuchtenburg, The Perils of Prosperity, 1914–32, 1958, p. 210.

Democratic party to control the governor and was the moving force behind a statute outlawing parochial schools, later declared unconstitutional by the Supreme Court.[610]

The rise of the Klan was linked to a political fundamentalism that wanted to wipe out the increasing heterogeneity in American society.[611] As one of the more respectable leaders of this movement put it: "We Americans have got to * * * hang our Irish agitators and shoot our hyphenates and bring up our children with reverence for English history and in awe of English literature."[612] The Klan limited membership to "native-born, white, Gentile" Americans—but in Klan lexicon the latter term excluded Catholics as well as Jews.[613] But the revived Klan did not limit its fury to the ethnic and religious Other; it was also anti-urban, anti-sex, and anti-booze.[614] One of its political slogans was "Back to the Constitution."[615] It was strongest in the Northern states, in rural areas, and among workers in business unions that were fighting the I.W.W. and its more radical unionism.[616]

In the South, the Klan's terror was primarily aimed at blacks, many of who had become more militant in response to wartime propaganda and military service; in two typical incidents, a bell-hop in Texas had "KKK" branded on his forehead and a woman in Alabama was flogged to death. But the Klan also targeted Catholics; a Klansman who murdered a priest was acquitted by an Alabama jury. In Naperville, Illinois, the Klan burned a Catholic church to the ground. Moreover, in both parts of the country the Klan used extralegal force against violators of its perverted morality; bootleggers, divorcees, and foreign-born men who married or dated native-born women were objects of Klan violence.[617]

The Klan boom collapsed almost as quickly as it had risen. In 1923, Northern newspapers began to publish exposes of Klan vio-

610. Oregon

Ibid.

611. Fundamentalism

Id. at p. 205.

612. "Awe of English"

Id. at p. 206.

613. "Gentile" Americans

Id. at p. 209.

614. Anti-sex and anti-booze

The Fear of Conspiracy: Images of Un–American Subversion From The Revo-

lution To The Present, Davis ed.1971, p. 210.

615. "Back to Constitution"

Leuchtenburg, The Perils of Prosperity, 1914–32, 1958, p. 205.

616. Strongest

Id. at p. 209.

617. Klan violence

Id. at p. 211.

lence and corruption.[618] The hideous reign of terror in rural Southern communities reminded older folks of the atrocities put down by Reconstruction. Indeed, in Oklahoma the governor invoked martial law to suppress Klan violence.[619] Probably more effective in discrediting the Klan was the corruption and hypocrisy of its leaders, many of whom had become wealthy off the Klan.[620] They used the Klan to advance their own political and economic interests; for example, dynamiting the home of a mayor who was a political opponent or beating African–Americans to force them to sell property for less than its market value.[621] David Stephenson, who ran the Klan in the Midwest, typified the moral hypocrisy; a sexual sadist, he was undone when a 28–year-old state secretary he had forced to submit to his desires took poison.[622] Convicted of second-degree murder and sentenced to life in prison, Stephenson expected to be pardoned by the governor of Indiana, a Klan crony. When the pardon failed to materialize, Stephenson revenged himself by opening a "little black box" to provide evidence that led to the conviction of other Klan politicians, including a member of Congress and the mayor of Indianapolis.[623]

The Klan declined rapidly; by 1930 it was estimated that it had less than 10,000 members—most of them in the South.[624] However, at its peak the Klan may have played a role in the Supreme Court's first hesitant steps in enforcing the Sixth Amendment.[625] In Moore v. Dempsey, in an opinion by Justice Holmes, the Court opened the door to federal habeas corpus relief for black defendants convicted in mob-dominated trials following a race riot in Arkansas.[626] Holmes, for one, could recall the federal military interven-

---

618. Publish exposes

Encyclopedia of American History, Morris ed.1976, p. 393.

619. Martial law

Encyclopedia of American Facts and Dates, 9th ed.1993, p. 454.

620. Corruption and hyprocrisy

Leuchtenburg, The Perils of Prosperity, 1914–1932, 1958, p. 212.

621. Force to sell

Id. at p. 211.

622. Took poison

Id. at p. 212.

623. "Little black box"

Ibid.

624. Less than 10,000

Encyclopedia of American History, Morris ed.1976, p. 393.

625. First steps

Bickel & Schmidt, History of the Supreme Court of the United States: The Judiciary and Responsible Government, 1910–1921, 1984, p. 986.

626. Moore case

1923, 43 S.Ct. 265, 261 U.S. 86, 67 L.Ed. 543. The Court's opinion sets forth facts that graphically illustrate the de-

tion to prevent similar evils during Reconstruction.[627] Perhaps it was hoped that the mere threat of federal judicial intervention would suffice to encourage states to forego the most egregious violations of constitutional rights.

Political Progressivism had its farewell tour in 1924, the same year that saw the operetta "Rose Marie", with its ludicrous faux "Indian Love Call", and heard Gershwin's "Rhapsody in Blue."[628] In the Presidential election of that year, Robert LaFollette polled nearly five million votes, took Wisconsin's electoral votes, and finished ahead of the Democratic nominee in ten states.[629] The Ku Klux Klan supported Coolidge, who attacked LaFollette as a "Bolshevik"; the issue, he proclaimed, was "whether America will allow itself to be degraded into a communistic or socialistic state or whether it will remain American."[630] Few seem to have foreseen that if "Progressivism was communist", some folks might suppose that "the Communists are Progressives"—as many seem to have done after 1929.[631]

With the Populist–Progressives largely done in, the urban-Eastern Progressives, who had long since lapsed into jingoism,

termination of rural Southern communities to keep African–Americans in peonage and the depth of their paranoia about any resistance. The defendants had gathered at a church to consider how to improve their condition under the aegis of an organization called "The Progressive Farmers' and Household Union of America." The killings occurred when they were attacked by a mob that had been told they were planning an "insurrection" by banding together "for the killing of white people." The hearsay used to prove those charges were obtained by the use of torture and they were convicted following a 45 minute trial in which the defense put on no evidence and the jury deliberated for five minutes. Id. at 261 U.S. at 86–89.

627. Similar evils

See § 6356, text at notecall 318.

628. "Rose Marie", "Rhapsody"

Encyclopedia of American Facts and Dates, 9th ed.1993, pp. 456, 458.

629. LaFollette finished ahead

Encyclopedia of American History, Morris ed.1976, p. 395. The states he did best in were all hotbeds of Populist Progressivism; California, Idaho, Minnesota, Nevada, Montana, North Dakota, Oregon, South Dakota, Washington, and Wyoming. Chamberlain, Farewell to Reform, 1965 ed., p. 262.

630. "Bolshevik", "communistic"

Ibid.; Leuchtenburg, The Perils of Prosperity, 1914–32, 1958, p. 134.

631. After 1929

With the Wall Street lawyer John W. Davis as the lackluster Democratic candidate, and with LaFollette given no chance, only 50% of those eligible to vote in 1924 actually went to the polls. Encyclopedia of American Facts and Dates, 9th ed.1993, p. 456.

enjoyed something of a vindication in 1924 with the passage of the National Origins Act.[632] When Congress rushed through an emergency act to restrict immigration in 1921, the bill had been opposed by traditional conservatives like Charles Evans Hughes and by business interests looking for cheap labor.[633] But by 1924, "scientific racism" was in its prime as a political force and Anglo–Saxon America was under siege.[634] "On the one side," shouted a supporter of the statute, "is beer, bolshevism, unassimilating settlements and perhaps many flags——on the other side is constitutional government; one flag, stars and stripes * * *."[635] The bill, passed with scant opposition, forbade all immigration from the Orient and restricted European immigration by imposing numerical quotas supposedly proportional to the numbers from each nation already in this country.[636] African–Americans were, of course, ignored in these ethnic computations and in deference to the desire of California growers for cheap farm workers——"braceros" they were called later——no restrictions were imposed on immigration from Central and South America.[637]

Jingoism was, however, not inconsistent with imperialism. Contrary to the myth of "isolationist" America stemming from the rejection of the League of Nations, the United States was engaged in military interventions throughout the hemisphere during the Harding–Coolidge era.[638] Indeed, by 1924 the United States controlled the economies of ten Latin–American states.[639]

Against this historical background, the Supreme Court decided Delaney v. United States, a prosecution for violation of the Volstead Act against a number of defendants with non-Anglo–Saxon

632. Lapsed into jingoism

Leuchtenburg, The Perils of Prosperity, 1914–32, 1958, p. 122.

633. Opposed in 1921

Id. at p. 207. President Wilson had successfully vetoed two earlier efforts to restrict immigration.

634. Anglo-Saxon under siege

Id. at p. 207; May, The End of American Innocence, 1964 ed., p. 349.

635. "One flag, stars and stripes"

Leuchtenburg, The Perils of Prosperity, 1914–32, 1958, p. 208.

636. Imposing quotas

Ibid.

637. Deference to growers

Foner, The Story of American Freedom, 1998, p. 189.

638. Interventions in hemisphere

Leuchtenburg, The Perils of Prosperity, 1914–32, 1958, p. 107.

639. Controlled ten

Ibid.

names.[640] In an opinion by Justice McKenna, the Court brushed off their confrontation claim in an enigmatic paragraph.

> It is contended that hearsay evidence was received against petitioner, and this is erected into a charge of the deprivation of his constitutional right to be confronted with the witnesses against him. Hearsay evidence can have that effect and its admission against objection constitute error.[641]

Having thus paid homage to Diaz, the opinion then asserts that the defendant had failed to preserve the error except for the statement of a now-deceased coconspirator.[642] As to that, the Court holds that it was admissible under the coconspirators exception to the hearsay rule and so, the opinion seems to assume, the right of confrontation is satisfied.[643] But just to be sure, Justice McKenna smears a gob of discretion over the trial court's ruling.[644] Since the opinion was unanimous, Mr. Justice Brandeis, who had taught evidence as a lecturer at Harvard, must have found this result compatible with his Progressive ideology.[645]

Science, Scopes, and Salinger

1925 brought "The Great Gatsby", "An American Tragedy", and 40,000 members of the Ku Klux Klan to parade through Washington D.C.[646] That same year, four other men, though not in their robes, went up to the Capitol and returned with the so-called "Judges' Bill."[647] Drafted by several members of the Supreme Court and pushed by Chief Justice Taft, the new legislation drastically restricted appeals to the Court under a writ of error, essential-

---

640. Non-Anglo Saxon

1924, 44 S.Ct. 206, 263 U.S. 586, 587, 68 L.Ed. 462.

641. "Have that effect"

44 S.Ct. at 207, 263 U.S. at 590.

642. Homage to Diaz

The Diaz case is discussed in § 6358, above, text at notecall 941.

643. Assume satisfied

The opinion cites three precedents to support its ruling, all of them dealing with the hearsay exception, not the right of confrontation: American Fur Co. v. U.S., 1829, 2 Pet. (27 U.S.) 358, 7 L.Ed. 450; Nudd v. Burrows, 1875, 1 Otto (91 U.S.) 426, 23 L.Ed. 286; Wi-

borg v. U.S., 1894, 16 S.Ct. 1127, 163 U.S. 632, 41 L.Ed. 289.

644. Gob of discretion

44 S.Ct. at 207–208, 263 U.S. at 590.

645. Brandeis

Bickel & Schmidt, History of the Supreme Court of the United States: The Judiciary and Responsible Government, 1910–1921, 1984, p. 372.

646. "Tragedy" and the Klan

Encyclopedia of American Facts and Dates, 9th ed.1993, p. 460.

647. "Judges' Bill"

Encyclopedia of American History, Morris ed.1976, p. 396.

ly giving the Court discretionary control of its own docket through the granting of writs of certiorari.

The same year saw two trials that said much about the state of civil liberties in the third decade of the Twentieth Century. In the first of these, Colonel William "Billy" Mitchell, a champion of air war was cashiered by a court martial that convicted him of "conduct prejudicial to good order and military discipline."[648] Mitchell's "crime" was criticizing his military superiors for negligence bordering on treason in their strategic planning for the next war.[649] Mitchell was vindicated by history; his success was an important step down the road to the Warfare State.[650]

The Scopes "Monkey Trial" was more than a clash between the religious version of political fundamentalism and secular modernism—though it was that, too.[651] The 1920s marked the highpoint of the school of psychology known as "behaviorism."[652] As expounded by its founder and chief propagandist, John Watson, behaviorism argued that humans were nothing but machines responding to stimuli. Behaviorism was congruent with the literary realism of Drieser and others in which individuals were depicted as trapped by social forces they could not control.[653] For some Progressives, behaviorism was appealing because it seemed to support the argument that the solution to problematic social behavior was to alter the society that engendered it. But as expounded by Watson in the 1925 edition of his book, "Behaviorism" entailed a punitive penology and bureaucratic child rearing: to Watson, affection was harmful to the development of the psyche and he advised parents facing a crying child "[n]ever to hug and kiss them, never let them sit on your lap."[654] To some, the appeal of behaviorism was that it

648.   "Prejudicial to good order"

Ibid.

649.   Negligence in planning

His exact words were "incompetency, criminal negligence, and almost treasonable administration of national defense." Encyclopedia of American Facts and Dates, 9th ed.1993, p. 460.

650.   Warfare State

Mitchell's case might also serve as an illustration of how the First Amendment can be bypassed by using the employment relation rather than the criminal law to suppress dissent.

651.   Scopes "Monkey Trial"

Id. at p. 461.

652.   Highpoint of "behaviorism"

Leuchtenburg, The Perils of Prosperity, 1914–32, 1958, p. 162.

653.   Trapped by social forces

Hays, The Response to Industrialism, 1885–1914, p. 91; May, The End of American Innocence, 1964 ed., pp. 185–192.

654.   "Never kiss them"

Leuchtenburg, The Perils of Prosperity, 1914–32, 1958, p. 163. Watson wanted

was counterintuitive and thus rational rather than emotional, but for others it undermined the notions of free will and personal responsibility that formed the foundation of the criminal law and confrontation.[655]

In heaping scorn on religion, Watson typified the arrogance of modern scientists toward those who sought other explanations for things that science could not explain.[656] As one philosopher said, science had become "superstition in another guise."[657] Thus it was ironic that in the same year that Watson published the most influential version of his book, Florida required daily Bible readings in all public schools and some states banned the teaching of evolution.[658] William Jennings Bryan, the former Secretary of State and Populist Presidential candidate, who led the anti-evolutionist cause was more than a Biblical literalist; he was also Jacksonian in his rejection of the cult of expertise and the aristocracy of the learned.[659] The anti-evolution campaign was not only anti-Darwinian; it was also anti-elite, anti-modern, and anti-urban.[660]

Though we now know that the prosecution of John Scopes for violation of the Tennessee anti-evolution statute was less a battle of free thought against the forces of darkness and more an entertainment concocted by the town fathers to draw tourists, the examination of Williams Jennings Bryan by Clarance Darrow may be one of the best-known courtroom confrontations of modern times.[661]

rigid scheduling of activities of the infant; e.g., feeding when "science" said the child should be hungry rather than when it acted hungry. If the experience of the junior author's mother is typical, Watsonian child-rearing placed strains on and between parents as well as hardship on the infant. The now much-reviled books of Dr. Benjamin Spock were a rejection (or overreaction) to the regimentation of the behaviorists.

655. Undermined free will

May, The End of American Innocence, 1965 ed. pp. 175–177.

656. Scorn on religion

Leuchtenburg, The Perils of Prosperity, 1914–32, 1958, p. 221.

657. "Superstition"

Ibid.

658. Required Bible readings

Encyclopedia of American Facts and Dates, 9th ed.1993, p. 461.

659. Jacksonian

Leuchtenburg, The Perils of Prosperity, 1914–32, 1958, p. 218.

660. Anti-modern, anti-urban

Id. at p. 219. This was the period in which farmers became a minority and began to lose political power. Throughout the 1920's, federal legislation to ease the ravages that unbridled capitalism was inflicting on the family farm were regularly defeated. Id. at p. 102.

661. Best known

Primarily through the play, and later a movie, "Inherit The Wind."

Though often characterized as "cross-examination"——and it certainly partook of that——Bryan was not in fact testifying on the merits; rather, he was called to the stand by Darrow to lay the foundation for expert testimony that the Bible could not be literally true——a hearing under Rule 104 in modern evidentiary parlance.[662] If the Darrow–Bryan confrontation embodied all the contending forces of society, as some historians have argued, it certainly also exemplified the tension between the ritualistic and rationalistic sides of confrontation.[663] Thus, when Darrow emerged victorious from his conflict with Bryan, it was not only a triumph of those who would despoil the environment over those who knew from first-hand experience how dependent humans were on uncontrollable forces of nature; it was also a triumph of Wigmore over Lilburne.[664] Those who cheered for Darrow for having put the Yahoos in their place were often the same people who wanted to substitute the judge for the jury and inquisitorial science for the adversary system.

The following year, the marines landed in Nicaragua to put down a rebellion against the Chamorro regime by dissident forces under Colonel Augusto Sandino and the United States declined to be bound by judgments of the World Court. Closer to home, Tunney fought Dempsey, Ferdinand "Jelly Roll" Morton began his classic recordings with the Red Hot Peppers, the Book-of-the-Month Club was founded, and Henry Ford confounded other capitalists by initiating a 40–hour work week in his factories.[665] All of these forces "prejudicial to good order and military discipline" were in play when the Supreme Court decided Salinger v. United States, adhering to its prior interpretations of the Confrontation Clause.[666]

Salinger was a mail-fraud prosecution. In a sense, everything in Justice Van Devanter's opinion about the right of confrontation is dicta, because the issue was not the admissibility of evidence but rather whether the Court had jurisdiction over the case under a

---

662. Hearing under Rule 104

Allen, Bryan and Darrow at Dayton, 1967 ed., pp. 100–158.

663. Contending forces

Leuchtenburg, The Perils of Prosperity, 1914–32, 1958, p. 221.

664. Triumph

Id. at p. 222. On Wigmore, see § 6358, text at note 173; on Lilburne, see vol. 30, § 6343, p. 310.

665. Ford and events of 1926

Encyclopedia of American Facts and Dates, 9th ed.1993, pp. 462–465.

666. Salinger case

1926, 47 S.Ct. 173, 272 U.S. 542, 71 L.Ed. 398.

writ of error. This turned on whether the case raised a substantial constitutional question; in his third justification for review the defendant claimed that:

> [o]n the trial hearsay evidence was admitted over the accused's objection that its admission would be in derogation of his right under that amendment to be confronted with the witnesses against him.[667]

Justice Van Devanter wrote that the "evidence which is characterized as hearsay" consists of "letters, bank deposit slips and book entries."[668]

For most of this evidence, the Court was able to avoid decision, either because it was not admitted against Salinger or he had been acquitted on the counts as to which it had been admitted or because any error would have been "negligible." As to the rest, they

> were received on the theory, not that they were admissible in themselves, but that Salinger's acts and conduct, shown by other evidence, had brought him into such relation to them as to make them admissible in connection with that evidence.[669]

As an example, the Court mentions a letter to which Salinger had written an answer; this would be admissible, to use the modern jargon, to show "its effect on" Salinger (or perhaps under the completeness doctrine to show the meaning of Salinger's letter). It is also possible, though the Court does not say this, that some of the writings were "legally operative conduct" as the means by which the fraud was committed. In any event, the Court concludes the writings were "more than hearsay" and did not have "merely a hearsay status."[670]

Having concluded the evidence was not hearsay, the Court might have then simply applied Diaz in reverse, stating that if the evidence is not hearsay it does not raise any confrontation issue—or as we would put it, if the writing is not being used testimonially, then its author is not a "witness against" the defendant. However, as it had done in Delaney, the Court seems to be reluctant to equate the right of confrontation with the hearsay rule even though in Salinger this can be defended under the language of the Sixth Amendment.

667. "Derogation of right"

Id. at 174; 272 U.S. at 545.

668. "Deposit slips, book entries"

Id. at p. 174, 272 U.S. at p. 547.

669. "Into such relation"

Id. at 174–175, 272 U.S. at p. 547.

670. "Merely hearsay status"

Id. at 175, 272 U.S. at 547–548.

The Court's treatment of the relationship between nonhearsay writings and the right of confrontation must be quoted in full:

> The right of confrontation did not originate with the provision in the Sixth Amendment, but was a common law right having recognized exceptions. The purpose of that provision, this court has often said, is to continue and preserve that right, not to broaden it or disturb the exceptions. [The opinion here cites Mattox, Robertson, Kirby, and Dowdell.] The present contention attributes to the right a much broader scope than it had at common law, and could not be sustained without departing from the construction put on the constitutional provision in the cases just cited.[671]

Hence, this part of the opinion concludes, "the question in respect of confrontation is not of any substance."[672]

The Salinger opinion is formalism of the worst kind, though apparently consistent with the Taft Court's cautious, conservative approach to civil liberties.[673] Even though there were apparently both conceptual and policy grounds for holding the right of confrontation does not apply to writings that are instruments of the charged crime, the Court was not willing to depart from the questionable history of its prior opinions even at the expense of an opinion that does little to clarify the law and opens the Court to charges of inferior craftsmanship.

The Kallikaks, The Crash, and Confrontation

In the same year that Babe Ruth hit 60 home runs and Lindbergh flew alone across the Atlantic, the Supreme Court pitted the individual against the state in opinions that face in opposite directions.[674] In Whitney v. California the court took another small step toward holding that the states were limited by the federal Bill of Rights in suppressing individual political opinions; but in Buck v. Bell the Court gave a boost to the power of the states to suppress the individual's genes.[675]

---

671. "Cases just cited"

Id. at 175, 272 U.S. at 548.

672. "Not of any substance"

Ibid.

673. Cautious, conservative

Wood, Constitutional Politics in the Progressive Era, 1968, p. 259.

674. Lindburg and Ruth

Encyclopedia of American Facts and Dates, 9th ed.1993, pp. 464, 465.

675. Suppress genes

Whitney v. California, 1927, 47 S.Ct. 641, 274 U.S. 357, 71 L.Ed. 1095; Buck v. Bell, 1927, 47 S.Ct. 584, 274 U.S. 200, 71 L.Ed. 1000. Prior to Buck v. Bell, only a handful of states authorized compulsory sterilization; in the ten years following the decision, it was authorized in half of the states—though in some states judges continued to refuse to authorize this form of punishment. Gaylord, The Sterilizaton

Ever since Mendel's discovery of the "laws of inheritance", scientists had sought to find similar forces at work in human society; the discovery of two families, the Jukes in the Nineteenth Century and the Kallikaks in the 20th, that seemed to breed feeble-minded and antisocial offspring, stirred some physicians to propose sterilization to rid society of further propagation of the deficient Other.[676] The conflation of "science" with paranoia provided an explanation of the "dangerous classes"——tramps, poor farmers, slum dwellers, unskilled laborers, Negroes, and immigrants.[677] In the face of declining birth rates among the Anglo–Saxon elite, compulsory sterilization was, according to the Virginia Supreme Court of Appeals, necessary to advance the interests of society "by mitigating race degeneracy and raising the average standard of intelligence of the people of the State."[678] It was probably no coincidence that in Indiana, a state dominated by the Ku Klux Klan, more than 300 convicts were sterilized before the state Supreme Court struck down the statute authorizing sterilizations on the ground that the prisoners were given no opportunity to confront the "experts" who provided the supposed justification for the operation.[679] After Buck v. Bell, the state legislature cured this procedural defect and reenacted the statute.[680]

The eugenics movement interbred scientism, statism, and Progressivism so by its own tenets we should not have been surprised that it produced such a grotesque jurisprudential offspring as Buck v. Bell.[681] Carrie Bell had apparently been incarcer-

---

of Carrie Buck, Sept.-Oct.1978, Case and Comment 18, 20.

676. Rid of deficient Other

Id. at p. 18; Friedman, Crime and Punishment in American History, 1993, p. 335.

677. "Negroes and immigrants"

Id. at p. 338 (collecting additional quotations showing relationship between eugenics movement and scientific racism).

678. "Race degeneracy"

Buck v. Bell, 1925, 130 S.E. 516, 143 Va. 310.

679. Indiana struck down

Friedman, Crime and Punishment in American History, 1993, 336, 337.

680. Reenacted

Id. at p. 337.

681. Grotesque offspring

Holmes argued that since the state could require military service, it "would be strange if it not could call upon those who already sap the strength of the state for these lesser sacrifices * * * in order to prevent our being swamped with incompetence." 47 S.Ct. at 585, 274 U.S. at 207. It is even more "strange" that a jurist who once wrote that "even a dog distinguishes between being stumbled over and being kicked" could not himself distinguish between state action likely to produce death and state action intended to accomplish "lesser sacrifices."

ated as an incorrigible juvenile after she had a child out of wedlock who, the state claimed was of "defective mentality." Hence, it was asserted, "by the laws of heredity, [Carrie, who allegedly had a "feeble-minded" mother] is the probable potential parent of socially inadequate offspring" and unless sterilized, she would have to be locked up for 30 years "during which time she will be a charge upon the state."[682] In fact, Justice Holmes' infamous dictum that "three generations of imbeciles are enough" was false; Carrie's daughter was described by her teachers as "very bright" and Carrie herself led a productive life following her release.[683] But Buck v. Bell was as much a perversion of the adversary system as it was of science; like the Child Labor case, it was a contrived "test case" in which Carrie's lawyer raised no challenge to the scientific basis of the statute, called no witnesses, and filed a two-page brief in the Supreme Court.[684] Since there were no amicus curiae briefs, the Court was as a practical matter affirming the statute in the same sort of ex parte proceeding the Confrontation Clause was designed to prevent.[685] Though Buck v. Bell involved a civil proceeding, it was regularly applied to penological sterilization.[686]

While 1928 was an election year, Coolidge wisely did "not choose to run" after his veto of farm relief legislation and approval of a subsidy to the shipbuilding industry set up a potential rural-urban split in the electorate.[687] Though in 1910 54% of the American population lived in areas defined by the census as "rural", in

682. "Charge upon the state"

Gaylord, The Sterilization of Carrie Buck, Sept.-Oct.1978, Case and Comment 18.

683. Led productive life

Id. at pp. 24 (even by state's own intelligence tests, Carrie did not qualify as "feeble minded"), 26 (five years later she married widower and was respected by his children and the community; lived on her own following death of husband.)

684. Two-page brief

Id. at p. 24.

685. Ex parte proceeding

Not that any of this would have made much different to Holmes, who wrote Harold Laski that he got "pleasure

from establishing the constitutionality of a law permitting the sterilization of imbeciles." Id. at 26. Justice Butler, the only dissenter, wrote no opinion but was apparently acting from Catholic religious scruples; the Church had condemned eugenics long before Hitler made it unpopular. For an account of the case that is far more detailed and devastating, see Leuchtenburg, The Supreme Court Reborn, 1995, pp. 3–25.

686. Penological sterilization

Friedman, Crime and Punishment in American History, 1993, p. 337.

687. Rural-urban split

Encyclopedia of American History, Morris ed.1976, p. 397.

the intervening period that number had dropped by 10%.[688] The new urbanite majority showed an arrogant contempt for all things rural, exemplified by the response to the Scopes trial and the sale of books like Sinclair Lewis' "Main Street" in which rural communities were depicted as narrow, conformist, and mean.[689] Had the ruralists been so inclined, they might have used the same three adjectives to describe the business bureaucracies that were the urban equivalents of the village, perhaps even citing Holmes' opinion in Buck v. Bell as an exemplar.[690] Instead, they invoked a Biblical image of cities as centers of debauchery and degeneracy, mingling racism and moralism in resentful reaction against the citified Other, whether Al Capone or Al Smith.[691]

The shift from rural to urban meant more for the right of confrontation than a shift from Babbitt to The Man in the Grey Flannel Suit. In rural communities, even if there was no one on the jury who knew the accused and the witnesses against him, jurors were likely to know someone "just like them." In small towns, homes of the rich and the poor were not segregated from those of the middle class; people of all strata of society confronted each other in church, school, and in business.[692] Moreover, before the

688. Dropped by 10%

Leuchtenburg, The Perils of Prosperity, 1914–32, 1958, p. 225. The census defined anyone who did not live in an incorporated area with a population of more than 2,500 as "rural."

689. Narrow and mean

Id. at pp. 225–226.

690. Urban equivalents

In the countryside, place is one, though only one, of the means by which one defines oneself; moreover, the other institutional and physical indicia of self-identification are often coequal with the place——the small town Catholic does not have to identify her parish because in the community "Catholic" means "St. Mary's."

In larger communities, place is a less important component of self-identification and the place of work takes on some of the functions of the rural community. When the junior author went from a town of 1800 to the Uni-

versity of Michigan, he was well aware of the provincialism, the pressures to conform, and the intrusive invasions of privacy that constituted "neighborliness" in Morenci, Michigan, but he was nonetheless amused to hear the countryside criticized in these terms by frat boy sophisticates from Detroit who slept in barracks-like houses, wore the uniform of the day (then khaki pants, charcoal-gray sweaters, and pink neckties), and conformed to a creed of macho crudeness that none of them would ever have individually espoused——even in the city.

691. Resentful reaction

Id. at pp. 225–226 (collection of anti-urban diatribes).

692. Confronted each other

The ambivalence of Americans about rural life is typified by Greenfield Village in Dearborn, Michigan, in which the form but not the substance of Nineteenth Century rural life has been re-

rise of the automobile, victim and accused were as likely to confront each other outside of court as they were within——social pressures thus reinforced the legal pressures against careless accusation. Urbanization, and the mobility and social stratification that accompanied it, increased the likelihood that the only place one would encounter The Other was in court. To the city-dwelling bureaucrat, a sweatshop seamstress and the local coal miner charged with assaulting her might just well have been from another country (as they often were) so far as his ability to understand their words, values, and motives for acting and speaking. As a result, much more pressure was placed upon confrontation in court than it could realistically bear, especially if it could only be evaluated in rationalistic and instrumental fashion.

Though wages rose slightly during the Harding–Coolidge prosperity and prices were relatively stable, the incomes of the upper classes rose at an unprecedented rate——creating an income disparity that would not be approached again until the end of the century.[693] The 36,000 wealthiest families had a combined income exceeding that of the 12,000,000 Americans who earned less than $1500 per year; 71% of American families earned less than the $2500 per year then thought to be the minimum for a decent living. Americans received a vivid reminder of these facts in the bloody Gastonia, North Carolina textile strike, in which the local Chamber of Commerce boasted that children were only allowed to work eleven hours a day in the mills where their fathers earned $18 and their mothers $9 for a 70 hour workweek.[694]

Nonetheless, the political and social dominance of Big Business was so strong that the Democrats selected a Republican, John Raskob, to run their campaign.[695] Raskob, who proudly proclaimed himself a "capitalist" though he was really something of an industrial bureaucrat, was supposed to represent business expertise; indeed, his name was so magic that when he suggested that business looked good for his company, General Motors, the words sent the stock market into another frenzy of speculation.[696] The

---

constructed, for the reverence of urbanites who never knew the real thing, using the wealth of a man who went into the automobile business because he hated the farm. Id. at p. 229.

693. Income disparity
Id. at p. 193.

694. Gastonia
Id. at p. 194.

695. Democrats selected
Id. at pp. 233–234.

696. Business expertise
Id at p. 233; Galbraith, The Great Crash: 1929, 1988, pp. 13.

Republicans, not to be outdone, nominated Herbert Hoover, who as both an engineer and a capitalist, had a double claim to expertise.[697] "The sole function of government," Mr. Hoover proclaimed, "is to bring about a condition of affairs favorable to the beneficial development of private enterprise."[698] This was only one of many statements Mr. Hoover would make over the next few years that would discredit not only business expertise but also his philosophy of "rugged individualism"——and thereby open the door to the statism of the New Deal.[699]

Although Big Business threatened workers with loss of their jobs if the Democrats won, that seems to have had less influence on the outcome of the election than the fact that the Democratic nominee was not only an urban politician but one who eagerly associated himself with New York, favored the repeal of Prohibition and——certainly not the least——was a practicing Roman Catholic.[700] So strong was the fear (or appeal) of The Other that, despite the fact that the party platforms were virtually identical and the Republican candidate dull, the proportion of the electorate that turned out for this apparently inconsequential election rose from one-half of the voters in 1924 to two-thirds in 1928.[701] Despite the fact that Smith attracted many of the first-time voters, he was nonetheless swamped in both the popular and electoral vote——even five states of the "Solid South" went Republican for the first time since Reconstruction.[702]

1928 looked like a good year to be elected as the tribune of capitalism; despite its unequal distribution, wealth was being produced at an unprecedented rate.[703] In retrospect, however, there

697. Double claim

Leuchtenburg, The Perils of Prosperity, 1914–32, 1958, pp. 232–233.

698. "Sole function"

Schlesinger, Hoover Makes a Comeback, N.Y.Rev.Bks. March 8, 1979, pp. 10, 14.

699. "Rugged individualism"

Encyclopedia of American History, Morris ed.1976, p. 398.

700. Practicing Catholic

Leuchtenburg, The Perils of Prosperity, 1914–32, 1958, pp. 234–235.

701. Rose to two-thirds

Id. at p. 235.

702. "Solid South"

Encyclopedia of American History, Morris ed.1976, p. 398.

703. Unprecedented rate

For a collection of impressive statistics on the growth of real wealth, see Galbraith, The Great Crash: 1929, 1988, p. 2. The noneconomist may be pardoned for wondering just how much of this "new" wealth was produced at the expense of nonrenewable natural resources and the production of externalities that would have to be paid for by future generations.

were a number of disturbing indicators; there was a rapid rise in the stock market fueled by a rapid rise in trading on margin——the Wall Street equivalent of borrowing money to play the ponies.[704] Of course, in 1928, economists rejected the analogy; one of them explained that gambling was a zero-sum game where one person's loss was another person's gain, whereas in the stock market one can profit by selling at a profit to a third person who can profit by selling it to a fourth.[705] As we shall see, however, both the rise and fall of the stock market were accompanied by an increase in the number of stupid statements by economists. An analogy that economists might have accepted had they understood it was the rise and collapse of the Florida land boom——another pyramid scheme that collapsed when the supply of suckers ended.[706] The Florida land boom not only exposed the "get-rich-quick" mentality that undermined traditional values of reward and work, it also demonstrated for many Americans the dangers of a "faceless" commerce——a sense that might have enhanced their appreciation of confrontation.[707]

Before the "Great Engineer" could be inaugurated as the 31st President, seven members of the "Bugs" Moran gang were executed by members of a rival gang——some of them dressed as policemen——in what became known as the "St. Valentine's Day Massacre."[708] Symbolizing the rise of organized crime in the wake of Prohibition, the Massacre seems to have stimulated the President to appoint the National Commission on Law Observance and Law Enforcement, better known after its chairman as "the Wickersham Commission."[709] But the enforcement of morality continued unabated; the same year Margaret Sanger and a physician were arrested at the instigation of the Daughters of the American Revolution for operating a birth control clinic in New York City and in Boston

---

704. Play the ponies

Id. at pp. 15, 17, 18, 21.

705. Selling to fourth

Id. at pp. 22–23. This resembled a pyramid scheme, such as a chain letter, in which the profit depends on the purchaser's ability to find another person to sell to.

706. Florida land boom

Id. at p. 3.

707. "Faceless" commerce

Until well past midcentury, "Florida land" stood alongside the "Brooklyn Bridge" as comedic symbols of the stupidity of relying on the representations of strangers.

708. "St. Valentine's Massacre"

Encyclopedia of American Facts and Dates, 9th ed.1993, p. 471.

709. "Wickersham Commission"

Id. at p. 476.

performance of Eugene O'Neil's Pulitzer Prize-winning play, "Strange Interlude", was banned by the censors.[710]

In another strange interlude, though the other leading economic indicators had turned downward in 1927, the stock market continued its upward trend fueled by a renewed wave of speculation following the Republican victory.[711] However, shortly after Inauguration Day the market fell and the Federal Reserve Board began signalling its concern about the wave of speculation. However, defying the Board, the head of the New York Federal Reserve Board announced plans to continue to loan to speculators, saying "we have an obligation which is paramount to any Federal Reserve warning * * * to avert any crisis in the money market."[712] Encouraged by this statement, the market rose and others joined the attack on "the Fed." An economics professor from Princeton accused the Board of being motivated by Populist impulses.[713] Another expert bluntly announced that if "buying and selling stocks is wrong the government should close the Stock Exchange. If not, the Federal Reserve should mind its own business."[714] When the President himself tried "jawboning" Richard Whitney of the New York Stock Exchange into doing something to curb speculation, he was ignored.[715]

Of the various concerns about the boom, two are relevant to the right of confrontation. One was the changed nature of mergers during the 1920's. Whereas the early wave of mergers had been designed to reduce competition by combining competitors, the later one was designed to increase centralization of what had previously been local quasi-monopolies.[716] The assumption was that the folks

710. Sanger and O'Neil

Id. at pp. 471, 472.

711. Speculation following victory

Encyclopedia of American History, Morris ed. 1976, p. 751.

712. "Avert any crisis"

Galbraith, The Great Crash: 1929, 1988, p. 37.

713. Populist impulses

Professor Walsh accused the Federal Reserve Board of a bias "founded upon a clash of interests and a moral and intellectual antipathy between the wealthy, cultured, and conservative settlements on the seacoast and the poverty stricken, illiterate, and radical pioneer communities of the interior." Id. at p. 39.

714. "Mind its own business"

Ibid. Professor Galbraith thinks the contempt for the Fed was justified by its incompetence; even President Hoover evaluated the men appointed by his Republican predecessors as "mediocrities." Id. at pp. 27–28.

715. President ignored

Id. at p. 41.

716. Increase centralization

Id. at p. 44.

in New York were more capable of running the business than the boys in the boondocks——an attitude similar to that which led many Progressive proceduralists to favor judicial control of the jury.[717]

The second source of concern was the rapid increase in the formation of investment trusts, which made it possible to increase the stocks in circulation without increasing the corporate assets on which they were supposedly based.[718] Increasing the instruments of speculation was justified on Progressive grounds; if an investment trust owned shares in many corporations it supposedly benefited from the "combined efficiency of their presidents, officers and boards of directors."[719] This, it was said, "mobilizes to a large extent the successful business intellect of the country."[720] This was necessary because "[i]nvesting is a science."[721] Some of the trusts tried to "out-expert" their competitors by hiring academic economists to promote their stock.[722] Soon most of the leading figures in economics departments across the country were consulting for Wall Street; one trust had economists from Yale, Stanford, and the University of Michigan in its stable.[723] Progressives could only be thrilled as the stock of experts rose along with those on the market.

During the summer of 1929, the market continued its meteoric rise amid another frenzy of speculation, especially in investment trusts.[724] The market was the dominant story during those months, dominating not only the press but also the popular culture.[725] It was a glorious time for businessmen and economists who liked to see their names in the paper.[726] John J. Raskob apparently had

717. Similar attitude

Id. at pp. 44–45.

718. Without increasing assets

Id. at p. 47.

719. "Combined efficiency"

Id. at p. 55.

720. "Successful intellect"

Id. at p. 56.

721. "Investing a science"

Ibid.

722. Hiring economists

Id. at p. 55.

723. Three in stable

Ibid.

724. Especially trusts

Id. at pp. 48–50, 66–67.

725. Dominating culture

Id. at p. 74.

726. Name in paper

Another economics professor marveled at the change from the days of the "Robber Barons": "The common folks believe in their leaders. We no longer look upon the captains of industry as magnified crooks. Have we not heard their voices over the radio? Are we not familiar with their thoughts, ambitions, and ideals as they have expressed them to us almost as a man talks to a friend?" The professor's belief that he was as one with the Gasto-

suffered no loss in repute from his failures as Al Smith's campaign manager; he appeared in the Ladies Home Journal with a plan to make $80,000 dollars by investing only $15 per month under the modest title "Everybody Ought to Be Rich."[727] Bernard Baruch opined that "the economic condition of the world seems to be on the verge of a great forward movement."[728] The Harvard Economic Society, a group of professors of economics, happily predicted that "a severe depression like that of 1920–1921 is outside the range of probability."[729] Professor Lawrence of Princeton offered a procedural justification for optimism:

> the consensus of judgement of the millions whose valuations function on that admirable market, the Stock Exchange, is that stocks are not at present over-valued. * * * Where is that group of men with the all-embracing wisdom which will entitle them to veto the judgement of this intelligent multitude?[730]

Professor Lawrence seems not to have contemplated how by thus praising the multitude he was diminishing his own expertise and raising the status of the jury. Perhaps he intuited that the market, like the jury, can also function as a scapegoat when things go awry——as they were very soon to do.

The beginning of the end came with a market decline on September 3, 1929.[731] Two days later the economic guru, Roger Babson, told the annual National Business Congress: "[s]ooner or later a crash is coming, and it may be terrific." Using the Florida land boom as an analogy, he concluded that "factories will be shut down * * * men will be thrown out of work * * * the vicious circle will be in full swing and the result will be a serious business depression."[732] As was the case with earlier skeptics, Babson brought the assembled power of conventional wisdom down on his head; he was widely ridiculed in the business press.[733] Less than

---

nia strikers is far from the most surreal fantasy that was voiced in the summer of 1929. Id. at p. 170.

727. "Ought To Be Rich"

Id. at p. 52.

728. "Great forward movement"

Id. at p. 70.

729. "Outside of probability"

Id. at p. 71. This was perversely correct——the Panic of 1929 was far worse than that of 1920–1921.

730. "Intelligent multitude"

Id. at p. 70.

731. Beginning of end

Id. at p. 84.

732. "Serious depression"

Id. at pp. 84–85.

733. Ridiculed

Id. at pp. 72, 84–89.

three weeks later, on October 24, the Panic was on; five days later the stock market suffered the most devastating day in its history.[734]

As the market spiraled downward, the "experts" remained positive. President Hoover proclaimed that "[t]he fundamental business of the country * * * is on a sound and prosperous basis."[735] Since his "rugged individualism" did not permit more, the President held ritual meetings with the leading capitalists, each of them producing rosy rhetoric but little action.[736] Hoover's Secretary of Commerce echoed the President's prognosis— "the fundamental soundness of [the] great mass of economic activities."[737] An economics professor expected "to see the stock market a good deal higher than it is today within a few months." According to him, the Crash was a mere "shaking out of the lunatic fringe."[738] It is not clear whether this category included John D. Rockefeller, who issued a statement that "my son and I have for some days been purchasing sound common stocks."[739] That "sound" must have been the stocks hitting the bottom. Nonetheless, similar "sounds" were heard from every corner of respectable opinion until they were eventually drowned out by the jeers and angry voices of the populace.[740]

In fairness, we must point out that the Panic of 1929 was unlike any prior economic crash; earlier panics were discrete events——they happened and were over, they did not go on and on for month after month.[741] Hence, when the Harvard Economic Society continued issuing monthly predictions of an upturn in the apparent hope that sooner or later they would be right, the "lessons of history" were on their side.[742] But fairness was not foremost

---

734. Most devastating day
Id. at pp. 98,111.

735. "Sound and prosperous"
Id. at p. 106.

736. Ritual meetings
The economist J.K. Galbraith credits President Hoover as being a "pioneer" of the "no-business meeting"——a proceeding in which people are assembled to have a meeting rather than to accomplish any task. Id. at pp. 138–141.

737. "Fundamental soundness"
Id. at p. 118.

738. "Lunatic fringe"
Id. at pp. 94, 97.

739. "Sound common stocks"
Id. at p. 119.

740. Similar "sounds"
For a collection of Pollyanna statements, many of them featuring the adjective "sound", see id. at pp. 106, 121.

741. Month after month
Id. at p. 108.

742. Harvard Economic Society
Id. at pp. 144–145.

in the minds of those who saw their savings wiped out or their jobs gone. As the Crash turned into a full Depression, the experts began to turn defensive. The President of the National Association of Manufacturers blamed the crash on the American people; if "they did not * * * practice the habits of thrift and conservation, or if they gamble away their savings in the stock market or elsewhere, is our economic system, or government, or industry to blame?"[743] The editors of Fortune magazine rejected the concept of the "social responsibility" of investors on the ground that the introduction of moral factors would interfere with the workings of the "free market."[744] Echoing Fortune, one prominent capitalist said: "I've never thought of paying men on the basis of what they need. I pay for efficiency. Personally, I attend to all those other things, social welfare stuff, in my church work."[745] This was not news to most workers, but the economic facts of life remained obscure to J.P. Morgan, who responded to the levelling tendencies then being voiced with if "you destroy the leisure class, you destroy civilization. By the leisure class, I mean the families who employ one servant—twenty five or thirty million families."[746] (Census figures at the time showed there could not be more than two million such families.) But perhaps the highpoint of business "expertise" was the statement of the Chairman of the Republican National Committee:

> Persons high in Republican circles are beginning to believe that there is some concerted effort on foot to utilize the stock market as a method of discrediting the Administration. Every time an Administration official gives out an optimistic statement about business conditions, the market immediately drops.[747]

By this time the Administration needed no help from the stock market; through "rugged individualism" it was quite capable of discrediting itself without help from others.

Early in 1930 the stock market seemed to rally, then began a steady drop until it hit rock bottom in 1932.[748] By then, the Panic

---

743. "Industry to blame"

Leuchtenburg, Franklin Roosevelt and The New Deal, 1932–1940, 1963, p. 21.

744. Fortune rejected

Manchester, The Glory and The Dream, 1974, 25.

745. "My church work"

Id. at p. 38.

746. "Leisure class"

Id. at p. 44.

747. "Immediately drops"

Galbraith, The Great Crash: 1929, 1988, p. 143.

748. Began a steady drop

Id. at p. 141.

of 1929 had become the worldwide Great Depression that lasted until World War II.[749] As hunger, fear, and disillusionment spread across the land, the Great Engineer went into denial; "[n]obody is actually starving," he told reporters, "[t]he hoboes, for example are better fed than they have ever been. One hobo in New York got ten meals in one day."[750] For this version of the "welfare Cadillac", Hoover was jeered; even Fortune magazine called him a liar.[751] Soon the President could not go out in public without enduring catcalls and shouts of "Hang Hoover"; crowds of mounted police were required to protect him from crowds carrying signs blaming him for the deaths of the Bonus Marchers—"Down with Hoover, Slayer of Veterans!" read one and another added "Billions for Bankers, Bullets for Vets."[752] Given the President's popular association with the engineering profession, their reputation went down with his; outside of the law schools, the Progressive enthusiasm for "social engineering" was all but dead—at least by that name.[753]

Economic expertise was also hard hit by the Crash and the Depression. No one wanted to hear their explanations for the Crash; unlike the President they were more often ignored rather than jeered.[754] The Harvard Economic Society disbanded.[755] Elsewhere economists stopped making predictions about the real world and turned to writing about events in an imaginary world of monomaniacal profit maximizers with free and perfect information whose achievements could be compared unfavorably with the imperfections of an economy operated by human beings.[756]

But it was the expertise of businessmen that was hardest hit by economic downturn; since they had claimed credit for the boom, the public readily assumed that they must be responsible for the bust.[757] The credibility of bankers fell even faster than the stock

749. Great Depression

Id. at p. 168.

750. "Ten meals in one day"

Manchester, The Glory and The Dream, 1974, p. 41.

751. Even Fortune jeered

Ibid.

752. "Bullets for Vets"

Id. at p. 52; Leuchtenburg, Franklin D. Roosevelt and The New Deal, 1932–1940, 1963, p. 16.

753. "Social engineering"

Haber, Efficiency and Uplift: Scientific Management in the Progressive Era, 1890–1920, 1973, p. 156.

754. Economists ignored

Galbraith, The Great Crash: 1929, 1988, p. 146.

755. Society disbanded

Ibid.

756. Predictions about real world

Id. at p. 144.

757. Responsible for bust

Leuchtenburg, Franklin D. Roosevelt and The New Deal, 1932–1940, 1963,

market; despite the myth of financiers leaping to their deaths from skyscrapers, their past arrogance made bankers the targets of hate rather than pity.[758] Andrew Mellon, once proclaimed as "the greatest Secretary of the Treasury since Alexander Hamilton", now heard schoolchildren singing:

> Mellon pulled the whistle,
>
> Hoover rang the bell,
>
> Wall Street gave the signal,
>
> And the country went to hell.[759]

No longer was the American businessman "the most influential person in the nation."[760]

But it was more than bad predictions and the conceit that they had "discovered the philosopher's stone which would transmute the uncertainties of the capitalist system into permanent prosperity" that ended the mystique of Big Business.[761] The Pecora investigation by Congress in 1932 produced evidence of cupidity and corruption on Wall Street beyond the Populists' dreams.[762] During 1929 alone, more than 100 stocks on the New York Exchange were shown to have been subject to manipulation by insiders.[763] Like investors, many embezzlers were "caught short" when the market collapsed; no longer able to conceal their crimes with fresh speculations they had to confess their guilt.[764] In addition, it was disclosed that newsmen were being paid to issue rosy reports even when the market was falling.[765]

As is common in a society imbued with individualism, rugged or not, Americans prefer to personalize institutional failings. Ivar Kreuger, had been featured on the cover of Time Magazine during the early weeks of the downturn and a story in the Saturday

---

p. 19.

758. Targets of hate

Galbraith, The Great Crash: 1929, 1988, pp. 113, 115. The suicide myth is demolished in id. at pp. 128–130.

759. "Country went to hell"

Manchester, The Glory and The Dream, 1974, p. 43.

760. "Most influential person"

Ibid.

761. "Permanent prosperity"

Ibid.

762. Pecora investigation

Leuchtenburg, Franklin D. Roosevelt and The New Deal, 1932–1940, 1963, p. 20; Galbraith, The Great Crash: 1929, 1988, p. 156.

763. Manipulation

Id. at p. 79.

764. Embezzlers

Id. at pp. 132, 134.

765. Newsmen paid

Id. at p. 73.

Evening Post compared him to the President: "Krueger, like Hoover, is an engineer. He has consistently applied engineer precision to the welding of his farflung industry. Kreuger rules through pure reason."[766] Well, not entirely. When Krueger put a bullet through his brain, it was discovered that he was a swindler who had deceived bankers and forged $100,000,000 in bonds.[767] Similarly, another Time cover boy, the utilities tycoon Samuel Insull, who had once proclaimed that "[t]he best guarantee of efficiency is a long line [of jobseekers] at the factory gate", was discovered to have been running a genteel version of the Ponzi scam.[768] Then there was the blowhard head of National City Bank——the man who had defied the Federal Reserve Board in the early stages of the downturn; he was indicted for tax evasion, acquitted in what the Attorney General regarded as a blow against the jury system, but later lost a civil suit to recover the taxes evaded.[769] Even Alfred Landon, the future Republican Presidential candidate, characterized capitalists as "racketeers."[770]

But the true poster-boy for Nefarious Capitalism was Richard Whitney, for five years during the Crash the president of the New York Stock Exchange.[771] Apparently the sort of well-bred nincompoop newsmen like to celebrate as "patrician", Whitney parlayed his money and his connections into "Doctorate of Commercial Science" from N.Y.U. and the Board of Overseers Visitors' Committee for the Harvard Department of Economics.[772] Supercilious and intimidating, when summoned before Congress he blamed the Depression on the government and suggested recovery would be hastened if the pay for civil servants and the pension benefits of war veterans were cut.[773] He went about the country giving

766. "Pure reason"

Id. at p. 93.

767. Forged $100,000

Leuchtenburg, Franklin D. Roosevelt and the New Deal, 1932–1940, 1963, p. 20.

768. Insull and Ponzi

Manchester, The Glory and The Dream, 1974, pp. 44, 67.

769. Taxes evaded

Galbraith, The Great Crash: 1929, 1988, pp. 150–154.

770. "Racketeers"

Manchester, The Glory and The Dream, 1974, p. 76.

771. Whitney

Galbraith, The Great Crash: 1920, 1988, p. 165.

772. "Patrician"

Manchester, The Glory and The Dream, 1974, pp. 145–146.

773. Pay and pension cuts

Galbraith, The Great Crash: 1920, 1988, p. 157.

speeches on "Business Honesty", telling a St. Louis audience that one of the needs "of a great market is that brokers must be honest and financially responsible."[774] Whitney was neither. When he mismanaged his brokerage firm into insolvency, he first stole to cover his losses, the tried to cover his losses with loans from shady characters and incredibly stupid investments.[775] When caught, he tried to bluff his way through but was indicted for embezzlement and went off to Sing Sing prison on a 5–10 year sentence.[776]

The Depression was not caused by the dishonesty or stupidity of a handful of men. But the perception that it was had several consequences for the right of confrontation. By discrediting the then-reigning forms of economic "expertise", it revived the respectability of "common sense" of the sort thought to be embodied in the jury.[777] By revealing the "two-faced" behavior of the paragons of capitalist virtue, it revived the skepticism of "things as they appear to be" that underlies the adversary system.[778] The boom was built on faith in the good intentions of anonymous others; the Depression suspicion of intermediaries like stockbrokers and newsmen paralleled the suspicion of declarants that is one of the sources of the right of confrontation.[779] Finally, with the criminal prosecution of the well-bred, it weakened the illusion that the criminal courts were reserved for The Other, reviving an interest in values other than efficiency, including those that support the adversary system and confrontation.[780]

774. "Brokers must be honest"

Id. at p. 163.

775. Stupid investments

Id. at pp. 160–163. Whitney not only stole from the New York Yacht Club, he also filched the securities of widows and orphans. Manchester, The Glory and The Dream, 1974, p. 146.

776. Off to Sing Sing

Id. at p. 147.

777. "Discrediting expertise"

Leuchtenburg, Franklin Roosevelt and The New Deal, 1932–1940, 1963, p. 22.

778. "Two-faced"

Whitney's hypocrisies were matched by those of others; several pillars of Wall Street, including J.P. Morgan, were made aware of Whitney's misdeeds, but did nothing because that was the "gentlemanly" thing to do. Manchester, The Glory and The Dream, 1974, p. 147. Ironically, this secret refusal to become informers reflects one of the values that supports confrontation.

779. Suspicion of intermediaries

Galbraith, The Great Crash: 1929, 1988, p. 170.

780. Interest in values

The fact that Whitney was one of the few miscreants to be found guilty may have led the enemies of Wall Street to hope for a more stringent criminal procedure, but they had more to fear from that than the wealthy and less power to bring it about.

Wickersham, Dillinger, and Revolution

In 1930, as the nation plunged into Depression, President Hoover proposed and Congress funded public works projects to stem the tide of unemployment.[781] Elsewhere, Charles Evans Hughes, who would preside over one of the most remarkable jurisprudential reversals in our history, was named Chief Justice, illiteracy among the populace from which jurors were selected fell to less than 5%, vocational education became increasingly popular, Sinclair Lewis became the first American to win the Nobel Prize for literature, and the Babbits in the Customs Office seized James Joyce's "Ulysses" as "obscene."[782]

In 1931 the Wickersham Commission published its report on law enforcement.[783] For politicians, its most important findings concerned Prohibition; the Commission recommended federalization of enforcement and revision but not repeal of Prohibition.[784] The Commission also recommended increasing the professionalism of local police, perhaps inspired by J. Edgar Hoover's propaganda blitz that was giving the F.B.I. its largely unwarranted reputation.[785] In true Progressive fashion, the Commission wanted cities to "take the police out of politics"—a step whose consequences were exemplified later in the century by the Los Angeles Police Department.[786] However, for purposes of confrontation, the most significant findings of the Commission concerned lawlessness in law enforcement—including levels of brutality that the comfortable classes found shocking.[787] These abuses were eventually to lead to a "federalization" of law enforcement by the Supreme Court far beyond anything the Commission had envisioned.[788]

781. Public works projects

Encyclopedia of American History, Morris ed.1976, p. 399.

782. "Ulysses" as "obscene"

Encyclopedia of American Facts and Dates, 9th ed.1993, pp. 474–476.

783. Wickersham report

Id. at p. 476. The Report consisted of 14 volumes and more than a million and a half words. Sayre, The Life of Roscoe Pound, 1948, pp. 252–253.

784. Revision not repeal

Encyclopedia of American History, Morris ed.1976, pp. 399–400.

785. F.B.I. reputation

Manchester, The Glory and The Dream, 1974, p. 95.

786. "Out of politics"

Friedman, Crime and Punishment in American History, 1993, p. 360.

787. Levels of brutality

Id. at pp. 361–362.

788. Eventually led to

The immediate results of the recommendations were nil. Encyclopedia of American Facts and Dates, 9th ed. 1993, p. 476.

For modern readers, the Wickersham Commission's claim that "law-and-order" was the nation's number-one problem may seem strikingly obtuse for a year in which financial panic, bank failures, massive unemployment, and mortgage foreclosures that were swamping rural courts—and the Gershwins' "Of Thee I Sing" lampooned politics in terms unusually cynical even for musical comedy.[789] But 1931 was also the year in which Al Capone was convicted of tax evasion and "Legs" Diamond, who had just been acquitted of kidnapping, was assassinated—many thought by associates of the victim.[790] "Dick Tracy" offered an explanation that Roscoe Pound would understand: "Big gangsters were running wild but going to court and getting off scot-free. I thought: why not have a guy who doesn't take the gangsters to court but shoots 'em?"[791]

But lawlessness in the early 1930's was not confined to urban police and gangsters. Farmers reacted violently to the loss of their land triggered by the rapid drop in farm prices and a commodities glut.[792] In supposedly conservative Iowa, where farmers were being paid 2¢ for a quart of milk that was being sold in Sioux City for 8¢, they blocked all the highways into the city with spiked logs and telephone poles and (with advance warning from sympathetic telephone operators) disarmed sheriff's posses sent to arrest them.[793] Along the blockaded roads, the embattled farmers sang:

> Let's call a farmers' holiday
>
> A holiday let's hold;
>
> We'll eat our wheat and ham and eggs
>
> And let them eat their gold.[794]

As if this mocking of the "holidays" that stock markets and banks were taking to save themselves were not enough, the farmers revolt

789. Lampooned politics

Id. at pp. 476, 478; Leuchtenburg, Franklin D. Roosevelt and The New Deal, 1932–1940, p. 1963, p. 27; Manchester, The Glory and The Dream, 1974, p. 27.

790. Capone and "Legs Diamond"

Encyclopedia of American Facts and Dates, 9th ed.1993, p. 477.

791. "Doesn't take to court"

Manchester, The Glory and The Dream, 1974, p. 95 (quoting Chester Gould, creator of the comic strip; until the

days of the Warren Court, the strip itself was seldom this explicit though its message was clear enough).

792. Farmers violent

Leuchtenburg, Franklin D. Roosevelt and The New Deal, 1932–1940, 1963, p. 23.

793. Disarmed posses

Id. at p. 24; Manchester, The Glory and The Dream, 1974, p. 58.

794. "Eat their gold"

Id. at p. 59.

sparked similar acts of "self-help" by workers and consumers—taking groceries from stores, coal from mines, gas and electricity from pipes and wires, and in one memorable incident dismantling a four-story building brick by brick.[795] When miners began to work closed mines to sell the coal themselves, juries refused to convict them.[796]

But perhaps the most frightening to those who remembered the Populist era was the violent resistance to judicial foreclosures of farmland. Foreclosures took place on a massive scale—in Mississippi it was estimated that one-quarter of the farmland in the state was auctioned-off in a single day.[797] Courts were mobbed, judges and lawyers were killed and threatened by lynchings, and auctioneers were forced to accept miniscule bids on foreclosed farms.[798] In some states foreclosures were brought to a halt by violence or by officials fearful of triggering it.[799]

Even more frightening than the acts of the farmers and workers was the rhetoric used to justify them. The blockaded highway in Iowa was known as "Bunker Hill" and the images of Concord and the Boston Tea Party were invoked.[800] An Oklahoma rancher muttered "[w]e've got to have a revolution here like they had in Russia."[801] The reactionary racist governor of Mississippi, Theodore Bilbo, conceded "I'm getting a little pink myself."[802] Even the sober President of the American Farm Bureau predicted that "[u]nless something is done for the American farmer, we'll have revolution in the countryside in less than twelve months."[803]

795. Similar "self-help"

Leuchtenburg, Franklin Roosevelt and The New Deal, 1932–1940, 1963, pp. 24–25.

796. Refused to convict

Id. at p. 25.

797. One-quarter in a day

Id. at p. 23.

798. Miniscule bids

Id. at pp. 24, 51; Manchester, The Glory and The Dream, 1974, pp. 59–50.

799. Halt by officials

Leuchtenburg, Franklin D. Roosevelt and The New Deal, 1932–1940, 1963, pp. 25–26.

800. Boston Tea Party

Manchester, The Glory and The Dream, 1974, pp. 58–59.

801. "Like in Russia"

Id. at p. 58.

802. "Pink myself"

Id. at p. 24.

803. "Less than twelve"

Manchester, The Glory and The Dream, 1974, p. 60.

When the nation's revolutionary past mingled with the outlaw tradition, it could threaten even traditional law enforcement. As the wave of Prohibition induced violence reached its peak and ex-bootleggers turned to bank robbery, these thugs were glamorized as Robin Hoods.[804] Speaking of then-Public Enemy Number One, John Dillinger, an Indianapolis man said: "Dillinger does not rob poor people. He robs those who became rich by robbing poor people. I am for Johnnie."[805] Such statements suggest why movie censors were almost as anxious to remove glamorous portrayals of criminals from the screen as they were to prevent moviegoers from catching a whiff of sex.[806]

To later commentators, the talk of revolution seems overblown. In fact, the response of American farmers and workers to the Depression seems almost docile when compared with the actions of their European counterparts.[807] But reasonable or not, their correspondence suggests that in the aftermath of the Crash and with their prestige about as low as it would get during the century, the possibility of revolution seemed all too real to American politicians and business leaders.[808] Hence, any tendency that may have existed to look on the constitutional rights of criminal defendants more kindly when stockbrokers were in the dock must have been offset if not overpowered by the fear that the criminal law might prove inadequate to protect person and property against gangsters and revolutionists.

The Bonus Marchers and The "Brain" "Trust"

The year 1932, when Amelia Earhart crossed the Atlantic and the leaders of Cold War America crossed into puberty, was one of the worst years in American history, economically speaking.[809] Industrial production was at half the 1929 levels, businesses lost more than $5 billion, fifteen million men were unemployed and those who had jobs were receiving less than half of what they had

804. Robin Hoods

Id. at p. 94.

805. "I'm for Johnnie"

Ibid.

806. Whiff of sex

Id. at pp. 66, 120.

807. Almost docile

Leuchtenburg, Franklin D. Roosevelt and The New Deal, 1932–1940, 1963, pp. 26–27.

808. Seemed real

Id. at p. 25 n. 22 (collecting expressions of such fear).

809. One of worst years

Manchester, The Glory and The Dream, 1974, p. 60 (listing ages in 1932 of those who came to power in the 50s and 60s); Encyclopedia of American Facts and Dates, 9th ed.1993, pp. 479, 481.

earned in 1929.[810] President Hoover and most of his cabinet took voluntary pay cuts, but this gesture meant little, given the endemic cynicism that was symbolized by the award of the Pulitzer prize for drama (the first time it had ever been awarded to a musical) to "Of Thee I Sing"——a show that treated the Supreme Court with contempt.[811]

It was a year of continued disorder. In the South, lynching was on the rise.[812] In Dearborn, Michigan, when three thousand hungry men and women demonstrated outside the gates of the Ford Motor Company plant, police fired on them, killing four and wounding hundreds. The business press placed the blame on "Red agitators" and the company threatened its remaining workers with loss of their jobs if President Hoover was not reelected.[813] However, when the child of Charles Lindbergh and his wealthy wife was kidnapped from their mansion, Congress promptly made kidnapping a federal crime and gave the F.B.I. the power to displace local police in investigations of the crime.[814]

But the most politically significant episode of violence in 1932 was the government's attack on the Bonus Expeditionary Force—— the "Bonus Marchers."[815] In 1931 organized military veterans had sought, first loans, then payments on benefits that Congress had promised in 1924; the loan proposal was enacted over Hoover's veto but the demand for payment in cash languished.[816] In imitation of Coxey's Army a generation earlier, impoverished veterans and their families descended on Washington; eventually some 17,000 people

810. Receiving less than half

Id. at p. 480; Manchester, The Glory and The Dream, 1974, p. 28.

811. Treated with contempt

Leuchtenburg, Franklin D. Roosevelt and The New Deal, 1932–1940, 1963, p. 27.

812. Lynching on rise

Id. at p. 186.

813. "Dearborn massacre"

Manchester, The Glory and The Dream, 1974, pp. 10–11, 52.

814. Lindbergh law

Friedman, Crime and Punishment in American History, 1993, p. 266. Ironi-

cally, Congress, which felt itself powerless to overcome the Supreme Court's invalidation of federal child-labor legislation, thought creation of a presumption was all it took to give the F.B.I. power to protect the children of the rich.

815. "Bonus Marchers"

Encyclopedia of American Facts and Dates, 9th ed.1993, p. 480. The official name and its acronym, "B.E.F.", were derived from the title given the American military contingent in World War I——the "Allied Expeditionary Force" or "A.E.F."

816. Demand for cash

Encyclopedia of American History, Morris ed.1776, p. 401.

were camped out on the edge of the city or took refuge in shacks and unused public buildings.[817] While they had the sympathy of the nation and the local police, the White House and local merchants were hostile; the sight of so many poor people was having a "depressing effect on business" in establishments accustomed to dealing with practitioners of conspicuous consumption.[818]

The heat of summer and the inaction of Congress took their toll; the dwindling B.E.F. might have passed little noticed from the historical stage had not the President decided to dispel his "do-nothing" image with a bold strike. The military had already drafted plans to put the Bonus Marchers into concentration camps, but cooler heads suggested that ordinary law enforcement, which had sufficed to defeat Coxey's Army, be used instead. But men who had faced the German Army were not about to be dispersed by club-swinging policemen; when the vets hurled bricks, the police fired on them, killing four. Claiming that the resisting vets were "entirely of the Communist element", the President sent in the troops. Sword-wielding cavalry under Major George Patton, bayonet-brandishing infantry, a detachment of machine guns, tanks, and chemical-warfare units marched on the vets—and on a much larger group of curiosity-seeking tourists and homeward bound civil servants. Tear gas dispersed the crowd and the troops descended on the B.E.F. encampment and burned it to the ground.[819]

The commander of the victorious troops, General Douglas MacArthur, ungallantly described the foe as a "mob * * * animated by the essence of revolution."[820] The business press, led by the New York Times, echoed these accusations; one editorialist proclaimed that the "people * * * have had enough of holdups by the undeserving."[821] In his euphoria, the President told the nation that the

817. Unused buildings

Leuchtenburg, Franklin D. Roosevelt and The New Deal, 1932–1940, 1963, pp. 13–14 (placing number at more than 20,000).

818. "Depressing effect"

Manchester, The Glory and The Dream, 1974, pp. 3–4.

819. Burned to ground

The description in this paragraph is a distillation of longer accounts in id. at pp. 12–16; Leuchtenburg, Franklin D. Roosevelt and The New Deal, 1932–

1940, 1963, pp. 14–15. Since the estimates are too varied and, in any event irrelevant for our purposes, we take no position on the number of casualties, though it is generally agreed that there were fatalities and injuries.

820. "Essence of revolution"

Id. at p. 15.

821. "Hold-ups by undeserving"

Manchester, The Glory and The Dream, 1974, p. 17.

Bonus Marchers were "not veterans", but "Communists and persons with criminal records."[822] MacArthur had announced that "less than half of them ever served under the American flag."[823] Unhappily for the President and the General, the eager bureaucrats at the fledgling Veterans Administration had conducted a thorough survey of the marchers and found that 94% of them had Army or Navy records, 67% had served overseas, and 20% had suffered disabling wounds.[824] Worse yet, MacArthur's claim that his men had used no violence and were not responsible for firing the encampment could be seen as lies by anyone with the price of admission to a theatre where newsreels of the event were shown.[825] In addition to discrediting Hoover and the military, the Bonus March fiasco encouraged officials thereafter to rely more on the ordinary processes of the criminal law——an inclination that led to increasing militarization of police departments.

The attack on the B.E.F. cleared the streets of Washington but it did not drive the homeless away. When the lame-duck Congress returned that fall, they were greeted by 2500 men, women, and children on the steps of the Capitol chanting "Feed the hungry, tax the rich!"[826] People in towns and villages across the country also met the unemployed face-to-face as a cadre of more than 2 million wandered about the country seeking work and food.[827] Income inequality in the country had reached levels that would not be seen again till the end of the century; in 1929 the top one-tenth of 1 percent earned as much as the bottom 42%.[828] The Depression did not improve things. At General Motors, the top 20 executives made

822. "Criminal records"

Ibid.

823. "Less than half"

Ibid. A federal judge embroidered this hearsay and passed it on in an inflammatory charge to the local grand jury. Ibid.

824. Suffered wounds

Ibid.

825. Newsreels shown

Leuchtenburg, Franklin D. Roosevelt and The New Deal, 1932–1940, 1963, p. 16.

826. "Tax the rich"

Manchester, The Glory and The Dream, 1974, p. 54. This group was dealt with, not too kindly, by the local police and they emerged from their "detention camp" singing the words of the Communist anthem, "The Internationale." Id. at pp. 54–55.

827. Wandered seeking work

Id. at p. 19. Though very few of these were probably remnants of the Bonus Army, they were commonly called "hoboes"——a name first used for Civil War veterans who were "homeward bound."

828. As much as bottom 42%

Foner, The Story of American Freedom, 1998, p. 199.

over $200,000 per year while the average worker got by on $1,000.[829] U.S. Steel, with profits in excess of $32 million, paid its workers an average of $369 each year.[830] To add insult to injury, the captains of industry were urging workers to pay taxes, complaining about their own, and paying none.[831]

When economic collapse brought Hitler to power in 1932, some Americans began clamoring for a dictatorship here.[832] Barron's business magazine wrote that "a mild species of dictatorship will help us over the roughest spots in the road ahead"; however, they nominated no one for the role of "genial and light-hearted dictator."[833] Walter Lippman wanted to grant all power to the President: "the danger" he said "is not that we shall lose our liberties, but that we shall not be able to act with the necessary speed and comprehensiveness."[834] A Republican Senator chimed in "[i]f this country ever needed a Mussolini, it needs one now."[835] What he got was a dictatorship of the professoriat.

When the party conventions met to nominate candidates for the Presidential elections that fall, they seemed more concerned with Prohibition than with unemployment.[836] The Democratic candidate, Franklin Roosevelt, realized that the party's platform would not do the trick and having often turned to academics for advice while governor of New York, he decided to seek advice from the professors again.[837] Roosevelt's law partner recruited Raymond Moley, a professor from Barnard College; Moley, in turn, brought aboard two Columbia professors—Rexford G. Tugwell, an expert on agriculture, and Adolphe Berle, Jr., who had recently co-authored a study of modern corporations.[838] A newspaper columnist

829. General Motors

Id. at p. 154.

830. U.S. Steel

Id. at p. 157.

831. Paying none

Id. at pp. 44–45.

832. Hitler

Leuchtenburg, Franklin D. Roosevelt and The New Deal, 1932–1940, 1963, p. 137.

833. "Genial dictator"

Id. at p. 30.

834. "Not lose liberties"

Manchester, The Glory and The Dream, 1974, p. 58.

835. "Needed a Mussolini"

Ibid.

836. Concerned with Prohibition

Leuchtenburg, Franklin D. Roosevelt and The New Deal, 1932–1940, 1963, p. 9.

837. Advice from professors

Id. at p. 32.

838. Tugwell and Berle

Ibid.

called the group "the brains trust" and the name, sans the "s" caught on.[839] The original Brain Trust, except for Moley, returned to academia after the election but they turned out to be only an advance guard.[840]

Though the Democratic platform was, given the crisis, a rather conservative document, the speeches the Brain Trust prepared for Roosevelt were tinged with radicalism and appeals for the "forgotten man at the bottom of the economic pyramid."[841] In the heady atmosphere of California, he even spoke "of distributing wealth and products more equitably", though his hearers would have been justified in thinking this would be tried "only as a last resort."[842] Hoover's campaign showed none of the hubris of 1928, but the candidate presciently observed:

> This campaign is more than a contest between two men. It is more than a contest between two parties. It is a contest between two philosophies of government * * *. They are proposing changes and so-called new deals which would destroy the very foundations of our American system.[843]

Despite Hoover's prediction that "the grass will grow in the streets of a hundred cities, a thousand towns", the voters went for the wreckers by a landslide.[844] Roosevelt's brand of economic nationalism carried every state save those in the Northeast where Federalism had had its last gasp.[845]

Meanwhile, the Supreme Court opened another chunk in the "foundations of our American system." Like the earlier cases where the Supreme Court had been invited to intervene in a state criminal trial, Powell v. Alabama—the so-called "First Scottsboro

839. Name caught on

Manchester, The Glory and The Dream, 1974, p. 49.

840. Returned to academia

Leuchtenburg, Franklin D. Roosevelt and The New Deal, 1932–1940, p. 33.

841. "Economic pyramid"

Encyclopedia of American History, Morris ed.1976, p. 402.

842. "Only as a last resort"

Ibid.

843. "Destroy foundations"

Schlesinger, Hoover Makes a Comeback, N.Y.Rev.Bks., Mar. 8, 1979, pp. 10, 12. For a collection of Hoover's trium-

phalist remarks in 1928 that came back to haunt him four years later, see Leuchtenburg, Franklin D. Roosevelt and The New Deal, 1932–1940, 1963, pp. 16–17.

844. Landslide

Id. at p. 17. It was the worst defeat up to that time for a united Republican party. For the grisly statistics, see Encyclopedia of American History, Morris ed.1976, p. 402.

845. Federalism last gasp

Manchester, The Glory and The Dream, 1974, p. 54.

Case"——was a Southern trial that sought to avoid the demands of a mob by means of a judicial lynching. The victims were a group of African–American youngsters, who had joined the army of the footloose roaming the country at that time till they were taken off a train in rural Alabama on the say-so of some whites they had bested in a fistfight, tried with only military force between them and the mob, and on the word of two young women of easy virtue (one of whom later recanted her testimony) found guilty of rape and sentenced to death.[846]

Eschewing any intent to do so, the Supreme Court, in an opinion by Justice Sutherland took the first step toward making the Sixth Amendment binding upon the states.[847] Seizing upon the trial judge's lackadasical appointment of the entire local bar to defend the accused, the Court found this a denial of due process. After determining that "due process" includes both "notice and a hearing"——two elements, it should be noted, that are specifically found in the Sixth Amendment——the opinion continues:

> The right to be heard would be, in many cases, of little avail if it did not comprehend the right to be heard by counsel. Even the intelligent and educated layman has small and sometimes no skill in the science of law. If charged with crime, he is incapable, generally, of determining for himself whether the indictment is good or bad. He is unfamiliar with the rules of evidence. Left without the aid of counsel he may be put on trial without proper charge, and convicted upon incompetent evidence, or evidence irrelevant to the issue or otherwise inadmissible.[848]

Though it would be many years before the promise of this passage would be vindicated,[849] it does (admittedly under the goad of the Court's Fourteenth Amendment rationale) partake of a holistic view of the Sixth Amendment's adversary system. The presence of

---

846. "Scottsboro Case"

Id. at pp. 21–22. For a full account of the case from which some of the facts above are taken, see Carter, Scottsboro: A Tragedy of the American South, 1969.

847. Opinion by Sutherland

Powell v. Alabama, 1932, 53 S.Ct. 55, 287 U.S. 45, 77 L.Ed. 158. In view of what was to happen later, it deserves noting that the Communist Party had made the case a world-wide scandal; indeed, the lawyer who finally defended the accused said at the time that if it had not been for the Communist Party, they would have been executed before he arrived on the scene. Liebowitz, The Defender: The Life and Career of Samuel Leibowitz, 1893–1933, 1981, p. 200.

848. "Evidence irrelevant"

53 S.Ct. at 64, 287 U.S. at 69.

849. Before vindicated

The development is traced in Whitebread, Criminal Procedure, 1980, p. 516.

counsel is essential to exercise of other rights, but it is also true that in the absence of any right to notice and to confront witnesses, the role that counsel could play would be diminished to the point of insignificance.

On another front, the Depression had a devastating impact on the legal profession; it was particularly hard on recent graduates from elite law schools who came from despised ethnic groups and saw the professional ladder to upward mobility withdrawn.[850] But after the election, inspired by the Brain Trust, Roosevelt sought to add to his administration

> fifteen or twenty youthful Abraham Lincolns from Manhattan and the Bronx * * *. They must be liberal from belief and not by lip service. They must have an inherent contempt for the John W. Davises of the world. They must know what life in a tenement means.[851]

Young lawyers, not all meeting this job description, flocked to Washington.[852] Many of them were sent down from Harvard by Felix Frankfurter, a Presidential confidant whom another member of the President's entourage called "the most influential single individual in the United States" and William Randolph Hearst dubbed Roosevelt's "Iago."[853] Namecalling aside, many college students began to fill up the pipeline, turning away from careers in business and seeking classes that "would point them toward the Brain Trust."[854]

Thus the Cult of the Expert, seemingly dealt a deadly blow by the Crash and Depression, simply packed up and moved from the boardroom and the economics department over to the law school. While few professors would openly confess to dreaming of garnering the President's ear when Frankfurter moved on to the Supreme

---

850. Ladder withdrawn

Aerbach & Bardach, "Born to An Era of Insecurity": Career Patterns of Law Review Editors, 1918–1941, 1973, 17 Am.J.Leg.Hist. 3.

851. "Life in a tenement"

Id. at p. 19.

852. Flocked to Washington

Historians had asserted this on anecdotal evidence, but a study of the editors of the law reviews at Harvard, Yale, and Columbia offers more substantial evidence. In the period from 1918–1929, 81% went into private practice, whereas by 1941 fully half of the Depression era editors had taken government jobs; indeed, in one year, 1933, as many took government jobs as had done so in the prior 14 years. Id. at 7–13.

853. Roosevelt's "Iago"

Leuchtenburg, Franklin D. Roosevelt and The New Deal, 1932–1940, 1963, p. 64.

854. "Point toward Brain Trust"

Ibid.

Court, all could aspire to the brilliance of the crowd assembled at the Department of Agriculture where Rexford Tugwell was the assistant secretary and Jerome Frank was general counsel: Adlai Stevenson from Chicago, Thurman Arnold and Abe Fortas from Yale, and Nathan Witt, John Abt, Lee Pressman, and Alger Hiss from Harvard.[855] Great things were expected from this group, particularly Hiss who was a Frankfurter protege and former law clerk for Justice Holmes.[856]

The worship of expertise did not become any less democratic or hostile to the values of the Sixth Amendment when it shifted from businessmen to elite lawyers.[857] Democratic politicians had a point when they called the New Dealers a "Phi Beta Kappa Tammany Hall" and opined that "Thomas Jefferson would not speak to these people."[858] Jefferson, or course, came long before Langdell had turned professional training down narrow vocational lines. While a few law schools and law professors tried seriously to turn students into experts in public policy of the sort the New Dealers thought they were, law-school graduates took mostly arrogance and naivete with them to Washington.[859] This is a deadly combination as Frank's crew discovered; when they tried to stand up for poor tenant farmers and sharecroppers against the Bourbon racist elite, they were unceremoniously sacked.[860] While on balance the increasing number of young lawyers who turned on government service was probably good for them and for the country, its effects on legal education and confrontation values is less positive. The would-be Frankfurters dashing off to consult with some governmental bureau increased the subtle anti-intellectualism that Langdell's voca-

---

855. Hiss from Harvard

Id. at pp. 75–76. Readers can presumably identify all but the lesser members of the Harvard group; they, like Hiss, were to be caught up in the Second Red Scare after World War II.

856. Particularly Hiss

Manchester, The Glory and The Dream, 1974, p. 84.

857. Hostile to Sixth

See § 6358, text at notecall 518.

858. "Would not speak"

Leuchtenburg, Franklin D. Roosevelt and The New Deal, 1932–1940, 1963, p. 253.

859. Took naivete

For some readers the fact that so many of them flirted with Stalinism long after the nature of the Soviet government had been exposed and many serious Marxists had denounced the Communist Party will illustrate this point.

860. Sacked

Id. at p. 139.

tionalism had bequeathed the law schools; with so many colleagues off in the Real World of government or business, those with a scholarly bent were irresistibly drawn to topics of immediate use to the profession and away from theoretical and speculative work that might have eventually informed the lawyer's desire to dominate.[861] More to the point, flattering young lawyers with the conceit that their degree made them fit to govern fostered an identification with judges and a contempt for the jury that played a significant role in the continuing diminution of the role of the jury and the accompanying distortion of the adversary system, including the right of confrontation.[862]

Confrontation and New Deal Values

In 1933, Roosevelt and the Brain Trust came to power, launching the greatest change in American government since the Civil War and Reconstruction.[863] Since many of the New Deal innovations were ephemeral or their effects on confrontation were not felt until much later, we can skip over the alphabet soup of programs of the first 100 days.[864] But we must say a word about New Deal values. That Roosevelt was more a pragmatic tinkerer than a political philosopher is one of those historical truisms that can easily mislead.

We agree that the New Deal lacked a coherent philosophy; it was a melange of ideas drawn from ideologies we have previously described—Populism, Progressivism, Pragmatism and the like.[865]

861. Anti-intellectualism

Id. at p. 341. The point is not that scholars should not be active in the world; the danger is that scholarship becomes equated with activism so that any idea that cannot be used to change the world is devalued.

862. Distortion of adversary

Moreover, there is a tendency for activists turned law teacher to want to refight the battles of their youth so that their students, like the Army, are always prepared to fight the last war. Auerbach & Bardach, "Born to An Era of Insecurity": Career Patterns of Law Review Editors, 1918–1941, 1973, 17 Am.J.Leg.Hist. 3, 23–24.

863. Greatest since Reconstruction

Leuchtenburg, Franklin D. Roosevelt and The New Deal, 1932–1940, 1963, p. xii.

864. Until much later

In 1934, few liberals were prepared to think of the rapid expansion of administrative tribunals, such as the Securities & Exchange Commission, as instruments of despotism. Galbraith, The Great Crash: 1929, 1988, p. 166. It was only when these agencies were involved in the Second Red Scare that these potentialities were grasped.

865. Pragmatism and the like

Leuchtenburg, Franklin D. Roosevelt and The New Deal, 1932–1940, 1963, p. 33.

This absence of a coherent ideology made many of the New Deal institutions vulnerable to the revival of laissez faire capitalism at the end of the century.[866] But the absence of a coherent ideology does not mean that the New Dealers lacked values, however reluctant the Legal Realist contingent might have been to admit this.[867]

Despite F.D.R.'s campaign rhetoric against "economic royalists", even the most innovative New Deal measures rested on capitalist values or deferred to the sensibilities of Big Businessmen.[868] The most influential New Dealers rejected the Brandeis–Wilson version of Progressivism that sought to restore an economy of hearty yeoman and small shopkeepers. William O. Douglas, who would become the head of the Securities & Exchange Commission, described the statute that created it as "Nineteenth Century legislation."[869] Without invoking his cousin Teddy's notion of "regulated monopoly", Franklin Roosevelt favored cartelization of the economy.[870]

Though the administration did not grant businessmen the exemption from the antitrust laws they thought was necessary to restore order to chaotic competition, several New Deal projects allowed anticompetitive action under government supervision.[871] When small businessmen complained that one of these, the National Recovery Administration, favored Big Business, the NRA administrator, Hugh Johnson, named Clarence Darrow to head an inquiry into the operation of the agency. When the Darrow panel reported that large corporations dominated the NRA and used it to squeeze out smaller competitors, defeat union organizing, and mulct con-

---

866. Vulnerable

An ideology provides an alternative to consequences as the measure of the worth of an activity; hence, criticisms of the New Deal from both the right and the left tended to focus on its failures to meet some ideological ideal rather than its failures to bring the nation out of economic doldrums. However when the New Deal claimed credit for post-War prosperity, they, like the capitalists who claimed credit for pre-Crash boom, were discredited when the economy headed down again.

867. Had values

We are here concerned only with those values of most immediate effect on confrontation; others will be taken up as their impact appears.

868. Deferred to Businessmen

Leuchtenburg, Franklin D. Roosevelt and The New Deal, 1932–1940, 1963, p. 165.

869. "Nineteenth Century"

Id. at pp. 34, 60.

870. Cartelization

Id. at p. 248.

871. Anti-competitive action

Id. at p. 56.

sumers, Johnson had the gall to invoke that epitome of regulated competition, the adversary system; "Bloody old Jeffries," he snarled, "never conducted any hearing to equal those [of the Darrow panel] for cavalier disposal of cases."[872]

This outburst did not typify New Deal thinking; for the most part, they rejected individualism in favor of bureaucracy.[873] The President used military metaphors; the country must act "as a trained and loyal army willing to sacrifice for the good of a common discipline."[874] In lectures in 1934 at the University of Virginia Law School, Attorney General Cummings expressed the New Deal's collectivist jurisprudence in which "greater concern is shown for [a person's] rights in terms of the social organism than for his rights in terms of law."[875] For Cummings "so far as individual liberty goes, it may be achieved better by seeing ourselves more as parts of the social whole and of the social whole than as free men."[876] Linking his legal philosophy to the President's call for sacrifice, the Attorney General said "[i]f in the process, freedom seems to be abridged individually, it is ultimately increased by being enlarged collectively. The individual gives up his lesser for a larger freedom."[877] Cummings did not specify the "whole" that was to receive the donated rights or of what the "larger freedom" would include.[878] Was this a plea for the individual workers to merge their right to freely contract into a union rather than with the employer or were capitalists to surrender their property rights in the corporation so that it could be turned into an industrial democracy with workers and shareholders voting on how to divide the profits and

872. "Bloody Old Jeffries"

Id. at p. 67.

873. Rejected individualism

Foner, The Story of American Freedom, 1998, p. 197.

874. "Willing to sacrifice"

Leuchtenburg, Franklin D. Roosevelt and The New Deal, 1932–1940, 1963, p. 41. This was part of a plea to Congress to give the President powers over civilians like those Lincoln had exercised as Commander-in-Chief of the military.

875. "Rights in terms of law"

Cummings, Liberty Under Law and Administration, 1934, p. 104.

876. "Parts of whole"

Id. at p. 41.

877. "Lesser for larger"

Id. at p. 20.

878. "Larger" would include

One could, for example, cite the adversary system as an example of surrendering the freedom to resolve disputes by extrajudicial combat in return for a ritualized judical version of combat in which the combatants gain as part of the larger community when their dispute is resolved in ways less disruptive of society than the blood feud.

losses? For some New Dealers, as for Stalin, "collectivism" was simply a fancy word for old-fashioned statism——a view that became more popular when the nation entered a real rather than a metaphorical war.[879]

One version of collectivist jurisprudence had deeper historical roots than seems to have been recognized by some; this is what has been called "the social conditions of freedom."[880] In 1941, a popular writer of the time claimed that "economic security has at last been recognized as a political condition of personal freedom."[881] But this recognition goes at least as far back as the Founders, who assumed that a republic required a relatively equal distribution of wealth.[882] John Dewey grasped this when he argued that freedom "signifies liberation from material insecurity."[883] But whereas the Founders responded to the danger of economic dependency by denying the vote to those who lacked a minimum level of personal wealth, the New Dealers wanted to free wage earners of their dependence on employers.[884] This required seeing liberty as protection by rather than protection from the government.[885] A 1935 survey of the beneficiaries of such a policy by Fortune magazine found that 90% of them believed that the government should guarantee that "every man who wants to work has a job."[886] Those who favored redistributive action by the government did not have to resort to foreign ideologies like Marxism; they could rely on the rhetoric the Radical Republicans used to justify confiscation of Southern property for the benefit of the Freedman.[887] Unionists emphasized the analogy

879. New Dealer's statism

A good example is Frankfurter's opinion in the Flag Salute Cases, in which the Jehovah's Witnesses were to surrender a small portion of their First Amendment rights in order to maintain the flag as a symbol of national unity that was necessary if the larger part of their First Amendment freedoms were to be defended against foreign tyranny supposed to be more harmful to religion than the local school board. Baker, Felix Frankfurter, 1969, p. 245.

880. "Social conditions"

Foner, The Story of American Freedom, 1998, p. 196.

881. "Condition of freedom"

Ibid.

882. Distribution of wealth

See vol.30, § 6346, p. 616.

883. "Material insecurity"

Foner, The Story of American Freedom, 1998, p. 198.

884. Free from dependence

Id. at p. 199.

885. Protection by, not from

Id. at p. 198.

886. "Has a job"

Ibid.

887. Justify confiscation

See § 6356, text at notecall 176.

by references to their jobs as "wage slavery."[888] And in the New Deal era they revived Joe Hill's union anthem (to the tune of "The Battle Hymn of the Republic"):

> It is we who plowed the prairies, built the cities where they trade,
>
> Dug the mines and built the workshops, endless miles of railroad laid,
>
> Now we stand outcast and starving mid the wonders we have made
>
> But the union makes us strong!
>
> Solidarity forever! * * *[889]

While this may not have been what Cummings had in mind, the President invoked even earlier revolutionary symbolism in a crusade against "economic royalists" and called for a "democracy of opportunity for all people."[890]

Modern thought has added to the Founders' insight. To start with the idea most distant from confrontation, modern economists have argued that in the absence of a comparative equality of wealth, increased productivity requires a great deal of spending on luxury goods.[891] The New Deal's redistributive schemes were based on an "underconsumption" theory of the causes of the Depression.[892] But as Brandeis foresaw, economic inequality reduces politics to a struggle between the "haves" and the "have-nots" and, since the "have-nots" have the votes, the "haves" must resort to anti-democratic institutions such as the Federal Reserve Board and the Supreme Court.[893] But too frequent resort to such anti-democratic institutions tends to delegitimize the government.[894] This

888. "Wage slavery"

Foner, The Story of American Freedom, 1998, pp. 60, 202–203 (photo of strikers with poster "Wage Slavery is Un–American"), p. 420 (index with more than 15 entries for this phrase).

889. "Solidarity forever"

Manchester, The Glory and The Dream, 1974, p. 135.

890. "For all people"

Leuchtenburg, Franklin D. Roosevelt and The New Deal, 1932–1940, 1963, p. 204.

891. Luxury goods

Galbraith, The Great Crash: 1929, 1988, p. 177.

892. "Underconsumption"

Foner, The Story of American Freedom, 1998, p. 199.

893. Resort to anti-democratic

Baker, Felix Frankfurter, 1969, p. 17.

894. Delegitimize

The classic example is the use of the Supreme Court to resolve the political conflict over slavery. However, as we have seen, this was also true of the use of the courts to protect corporations. See § 6359, text at notecall 576.

places great stress on those organs of government most closely allied to coercion and force——the courts, the police, and the military.[895] For courts——and the right of confrontation——the problem is not limited to the increasingly rare insurrection. Rather, since the "haves" fear, justifiably but excessively, that the "have-nots" are out to get them and their goods, they will insist that the criminal justice system be not simply punitive but that it also be preventative.[896] The result is an increasing resort to the criminal law for punishment of inchoate crimes, for the creation of new crimes, and for severity of punishment that raises the costs of unjust convictions.

The New Deal, probably intentionally, relieved some of the stress on the criminal-justice system that might have arisen from demands for social control arising from the Crash and the Depression by resorting to administrative tribunals rather than courts.[897] While administrative sanctions could function preventively, they did so without the same constitutional restraints as the courts. To the extent that administrative tribunals were effective, this might have discredited courts and the constitutional guarantees that seemed to make them incapable of similar expedition. Moreover, while the President's equation of "the right to work" and "the right to live" with "the right to vote" may have been intended to elevate the former, it had the potential to degrade the latter.[898] A hungry person asked to choose between a right to a job and the right to confront witnesses would have to have a highly sophisticated understanding of his or her long-term interests to pick the right of confrontation. Hence, of Roosevelt's famous "Four Freedoms,"

895. Great stress

One of the consequences of the Norris–LaGuardia Act of 1932 was to get federal courts out of the business of suppressing labor disputes. Encyclopedia of American History, Morris ed.1976, p. 769.

896. Preventative

One of the consequences of the growth of consumerism was to increase the range of crime victims beyond the upper classes. In the past, it was only the rich who were likely to have property that was both transportable, disposable, and worth stealing. Stealing carriages seems never to have become the kind of problem that auto theft quickly became. In the Twentieth Century demands for "law-and-order" came from a broader segment of society than in the Nineteenth.

897. Resorting to administrative

This was probably more from lack of trust of the courts than from any desire not to put them on the firing line against those who opposed the goals of the SEC or the NLRB.

898. "Right to vote"

Foner, The Story of American Freedom, 1998, p. 204.

there was a complex tension between "freedom from want" and "freedom from fear."

The Depression hit bottom in 1934——and it was not a good year for confrontation jurisprudence either.[899] The failure of the New Deal to have any appreciable effect on the economy fed the rise of various strains of indigenous radicalism.[900] In the South, Huey Long of Louisiana, who had come to power on a vaguely Populist program, now tried to go national with a redistributive program he called "Share Our Wealth."[901] In Royal Oak, Michigan, a Roman Catholic priest, Charles Coughlin, combined Catholic social doctrine, a gift for invective, and hatred of the English and Anglophiles into a series of popular radio sermons that were picked up by CBS and garnered an audience of millions until his increasingly anti-semitic attack on the New Deal led the church to pull the plug.[902] And in Long Beach, California, Dr. Francis Townsend, a dentist, came up with a plan that entailed paying senior citizens $200 per month on condition that they spend it all.[903] The wide following these programs attracted led some opponents to compare them with Hitler's; for a time it appeared that "fascist" would rival "communist" as a term of political opprobrium——but the true fascists had a defender in William Randolph Hearst and the threat receded.[904]

Meanwhile, in part because of the influence of the real Commu-

899. Hit bottom

Leuchtenburg, Franklin D. Roosevelt and The New Deal, 1932–1940, 1963, p. 118.

900. Indigenous radicalism

This included revivals of Progressivism and Populism, but these were generally allied with the New Deal and thus escaped the contempt heaped on those who proposed more radical programs. Id. at p. 195.

901. "Share Our Wealth"

Id. at pp. 96–100. Long posed the most serious threat to the New Deal because he had a solid record of Populist accomplishments in his home state and because he was more politically astute; but he had a streak of megalomania and a contempt for democratic

processes that made him the enemies that eventually did him in. Manchester, The Glory and The Dream, 1974, pp. 111–117.

902. Father Coughlin

Id. at pp. 108–111; Leuchtenburg, Franklin Roosevelt and The New Deal, 1932–1940, 1963, pp. 100–103.

903. Townsend plan

Id. at pp. 103–106. The plan was endorsed by the Republican candidate for Governor of California to defeat the even more radical candidacy of the novelist Upton Sinclair. Manchester, The Glory and The Dream, 1974, p. 101.

904. True fascists

Id. at p. 111.

nists, the labor movement began to show a new militancy.[905] The unions were aided in obtaining public support by the continued arrogance of some employers; for example, in the Pennsylvania coalfields, the coal owners routinely paid the $100 fine imposed for using child labor, then deducted the amount from the wages of their youthful employees.[906] We can understand why "coal bootlegging" became a major industry and why juries refused to convict miners accused of working closed mines.[907]

In the year 1934 there were nearly 1900 strikes, most of them for union recognition.[908] The employers, being unable to count on federal courts and the Army, began a rapid buildup in the armaments of their private police and local law enforcement.[909] On their side, unions began to organize the unemployed who often joined their employed fellows in strikes.[910] The strikes of 1934 included some of the most violent in an already violent history.[911] However, since the federal courts played an insignificant role in these strikes, there is little need to recite the bloody details.[912]

As if Big Business did not have enough problems, it was also accused of fomenting World War I.[913] In the March, 1934 issue of Fortune magazine an article charged that Allied industrialists had prolonged the war by secretly selling armaments to the Kaiser; according to the magazine, munitions manufacturers followed two axioms: "(a) prolong war, (b) disturb peace."[914] Congress launched

905. New militancy

Foner, The Story of American Freedom, 1998, p. 199; Brecher, Strike!, 1972, p. 145.

906. Deducted from wages

Manchester, The Glory and The Dream, 1974, pp. 131–132 (collecting similar abuses).

907. "Coal bootlegging"

Brecher, Strike!, 1972, p. 147. In 1934, it was estimated that nearly 5 million tons of coal were produced by these bootleg operations.

908. Nearly 1900 strikes

Manchester, The Glory and The Dream, 1974, p. 133.

909. Buildup in armaments

Ibid.

910. Organized unemployed

Brecher, Strike!, 1972, pp. 145, 158.

911. Most violent in history

Manchester, The Glory and The Dream, 1974, p. 131; Leuchtenburg, The Glory and The Dream, 1974, p. 131; Leuchtenburg, Franklin D. Roosevelt and The New Deal, 1932–1940, 1963, pp. 111–114.

912. Bloody details

These can be found, complete with photographs, in Brecher, Strike!, 1972, pp. 158–177.

913. Fomenting World War I

Encyclopedia of American History, Morris ed.1976, p. 411.

914. "Disturb peace"

Leuchtenburg, Franklin Roosevelt and The New Deal, 1932–1940, 1963, p. 217.

an investigation under Senator Gerald Nye of North Dakota that turned up some startling evidence to support the charges, including a "smoking gun" letter from one business executive denouncing the efforts of the State Department to mediate a dispute between Peru and Chile as "pernicious" on the ground that it "put the brake on armament orders from Peru."[915] Summing up the role that American capitalists such as J.P. Morgan had played in convincing Wilson to enter the war, Nye told audiences across the land: "We didn't win a thing we set out for in the last war. We merely succeeded, with tremendous loss of life, to make secure the loans of private bankers to the Allies."[916] Though the Nye Committee's revelations delayed slightly the entry of the United States into World War II, they did little to permanently delegitimize the Warfare State or the popularity of military metaphors.[917]

It was amidst all this tumult that the Hughes Court decided Snyder v. Massachusetts, the only case during the New Deal era to consider the meaning and scope of the Confrontation Clause.[918] Snyder was a murder prosecution arising from a gas station robbery. When the prosecution wanted to take the jury to view the scene of the crime, the trial judge, for reasons that do not appear in the Court's opinion, refused to allow the defendant to accompany them.[919] During the view, the prosecutor made assertions about changes in the locale since the murder that defense counsel, who was unfamiliar with the area, could not contradict.[920] The trial judge charged the jury that under state law, the jury view was "evidence" to be considered in determining the guilt of the defendant.[921] The Court found this not to be a denial of Due Process, over the dissent of Justice Roberts, joined by Brandeis, Sutherland, and Butler.

915. "Brake on orders"

Ibid.

916. "Secure the loans"

Manchester, The Glory and The Dream, 1974, p. 126.

917. Military metaphors

The argument of Nye illustrates a fallacy that was often used at the height of the Second Red Scare in opposition to civil liberties, including confrontation; namely, if some proposal is supported by a despised person or someone with nefarious motives, it must therefore be a bad idea.

918. Snyder case

1934, 54 S.Ct. 330, 291 U.S. 97, 78 L.Ed. 674.

919. Refused to allow

Id. at 331, 291 U.S. at 102–103.

920. Could not contradict

Id. at 331–332, 291 U.S. at 103–105.

921. Was "evidence"

Id. at 332, 291 U.S. at 104.

Justice Cardozo's opinion for the majority illustrates how a reductionist analysis of the Sixth Amendment can slice it so thin that the light shines through. One can, however, reassemble the pieces into something like a holistic analysis. At the outset, he writes:

> the privilege to confront one's accusers and cross-examine them face to face is assured to a defendant by the Sixth Amendment in prosecutions in the federal courts * * * and in prosecutions in the state courts is assured very often by the constitutions of the states. For present purposes we assume that the privilege is reinforced by the Fourteenth Amendment, though this has not been squarely held.[922]

Later Cardozo makes the interrelationship of the various clauses of the Sixth Amendment even clearer.

> A defendant in a criminal case must be present at trial when evidence is offered, for the opportunity must be his to advise with his counsel * * * and cross-examine his accusers.[923]

Cardozo also predicts boldly (but as we shall see, erroneously):

> If the defendant in a federal court were to be denied the opportunity to be confronted with the "witness against him", the denial of the privilege would not be overlooked as immaterial because the evidence thus procured was persuasive of the defendant's guilt.[924]

---

922. "Not squarely held"

Id. at 332, 291 U.S. at 106. The dissent, by comparison, paraphrases the Sixth Amendment, points out that some state constitutions "[o]ut of an excess of caution" add a right "to appear and defend in person", but goes on to say that regardless of "phraseology" all of the provision have one overriding goal "—a fair hearing." We would have said "preservation of the adversary system." But more emphatically than the majority, the dissent concludes "the courts have uniformly and invariably held that the Sixth Amendment * * * and the analogous declarations of right of the state constitutions * * * secure to the accused the privilege of presence at every stage of his trial." Id. at 341, 291 U.S. at 130.

923. "Advise and cross-examine"

Id. at 335, 291 U.S. at 114. The dissent takes issue with the proposition "that the prisoner's privilege of presence is for no other purpose than to safeguard his opportunity to cross-examine the adverse witnesses. * * * the privilege goes deeper than the mere opportunity to cross-examine, and secures his right to be present at every stage of the trial." Id. at 342, 291 U.S. at 131. The opinion argues that "the right is fundamental and assures him who stands in jeopardy that he may in person, see, hear, and know all that is placed before the tribunal having power by its finding to deprive him of liberty or life." Id at 342, 291 U.S. at 132.

924. "Persuasive of guilt"

Id. at 336, 291 U.S. at 116. The dissent thinks this principle should be applied to Snyder's case. After disputing the majority's claim that the error was harmless, the dissent continues: "Nor ought this court to convert the inquiry

Given all this, one might suppose with the dissenters that since the defendant was denied the right to "advise with his counsel" about the prosecutor's statements at the view, that he was denied his "privilege."

But, Cardozo tells us, we must make a number of important cuts into this rhetoric. First, since this is a state prosecution, and states are not bound by the Sixth Amendment, they can do whatever they like unless "in so doing [the state] offends some principle so rooted in the tradition and conscious of our people as to be ranked as fundamental."[925] He then lists some acts that would not offend this standard, including abolition of trial by jury and the privilege against self-incrimination.[926] Since the state can thus abolish the adversary system, one almost has to agree with the proposition that whatever right the defendant may have as an aspect of due process under the Fourteenth Amendment is limited to cases where "where his presence has a relation, reasonably substantial, to the fulness of his opportunity to defend against the charge."[927] This instrumental analysis does, however, seem a bit inconsistent with his apparently noninstrumental approach to the federal right.

But, says Cardozo, our "confusion" results from our failure "to mark the distinction between requirements in respect of presence that have their source in the common law, and requirements that have their source, either expressly or by implication, in the federal constitution."[928] If one distinction is not enough to clarify our "confusion", Cardozo offers another.

from one as to the denial of the right into one as to the prejudice suffered by the denial. * * * The very substance of the defendant's right is to be present. By hypothesis it is unfair to exclude him. * * * Procedural due process has to do with the manner of the trial; dictates that in the conduct of judicial inquiry certain fundamental rules of fairness be observed; forbids the disregard of those rules, and is not satisfied, though the result is just, if the hearing was unfair." Id. at 343–344, 291 U.S. at 136–137.

925. "Ranked as fundamental"

Id. at 332, U.S. at 105.

926. Self-incrimination

Id. at 332, 291 U.S. at 105.

927. "Fulness of opportunity"

Id. at 332, 291 U.S. at 105–106. The dissent, by contrast, takes a position

that would later be called "incorporation", though this is concealed by an excess of negatives: "It cannot successfully be contended that as the Sixth Amendment has no application to trials in state courts, and the Fourteenth Amendment does not draw to itself and embody the provisions of state constitutions * * * the due process secured by the Fourteenth Amendment does not embrace a right secured by those instruments." Justice Roberts relies on a long quotation from Powell v. Alabama to support this claim. Id. at 342, 291 U.S. at 133–134.

928. "Source in common law"

Id. at 333, 291 U.S. at 107. Since the defendant was not arguing he had

Confusion will result again if the privilege of presence be identified with the privilege of confrontation, which is limited to stages of the trial where there are witnesses to be questioned. * * * "It was intended to prevent the conviction of the accused upon depositions and ex parte affidavits, and particularly to preserve the right of the accused to test the recollection of the witness in the exercise of the right of cross-examination." * * * Nor has the privilege of confrontation at any time been without recognized exceptions, as for instance dying declarations or documentary evidence. * * * The exceptions are not even static, but may be enlarged from time to time if there is no material departure from the reason of the general rule.[929]

If the right to be present is not to be measured by the right of confrontation, the reader may well be confused about the reason for this string of apparent dicta.[930]

The majority opinion now draws a number of distinctions among the various kinds of jury view. If the view is "a bare inspection * * * where nothing is said by anyone to direct the attention of the jury to one feature or another", the defendant has no right to be present.[931] Why not? Because if he has any doubt as to whether the bailiffs took the jury to the wrong place or that the scene remains unchanged, he can always test this by putting the bailiffs on the stand and cross-examining them. Cardozo does not attempt to justify this shifting of the burden of proof to the defendant, except to say that "the chance is so remote that it dwindles to the vanishing point."[932] Nor does he tell us how an incarcerated defendant can advise with his counsel to determine what questions to ask the bailiff about changes to the scene if he has not been to the scene since the crime.[933] Instead, Cardozo says

some common law right to be present, apparently this is an anticipatory jab at the dissent, whose cases Cardozo will later argue were common law, not constitutional decisions. Id. at 336 n. *, 291 U.S. at 117 n. *.

929. "May be enlarged"
Id. at 333, 291 U.S. at 107.

930. Not to be measured
In fact, Cardozo later relies on confrontation cases to support his claim that the view is not a "trial" at which "evidence" is presented and therefore defendant need not be present.

931. "Bare inspection"
Id. at 333, 291 U.S. at 108.

932. "Vanishing point"
Id. at 333, 291 U.S. at p. 108.

933. Questions to ask
Nor does he explain how the bailiffs would know whether what they and the jurors saw on the view was there at the time of the crime. Suppose, for example, that a tire display rack had been installed blocking the sightline of one of the defense witnesses. The bail-

that since the defendant admits he was at the gas station when his codefendant killed the attendant, it makes no difference whether the view was proper.[934]

The opinion then turns to the case where in addition to the "bare inspection", the prosecutor is allowed to make hearsay statements about the scene.[935] The difference, Cardozo writes, "is one of degree, and nothing more."[936] Since such statements "have been a traditional accompaniment of a view for about two centuries, if not longer", Fourteenth Amendment due process "has not displaced the procedure of the ages."[937] He then takes a long excursion through English cases, the earliest being a civil case in 1747, supposed to show that this was the "procedure of the ages" for the Founders. But he does not attempt to show that the Founders were aware of these cases or that the procedure had been adopted in the colonies. Instead, he argues that the defendant would gain nothing by being present because he can inspect the transcript of the view to see if the prosecutor has failed to point out "anything material."[938] Unfortunately, in most cases there is no stenographic transcript available at trial and even if there were, the defendant would have no way of knowing when the prosecutor told the jurors to "look at that" whether he was pointing at anything "material."

iffs would not know it was not there at the time and the only way the defendant could know of this change is if the bailiffs were asked to list everything they saw during the view.

934. Makes no difference

According to Cardozo, since the defense admitted every element of felony murder except the intent of the codefendants, the only issue was one as to which the view added nothing. Id. at , 291 U.S. at p. 109. The dissent disagrees, pointing out that the layout of the gas station "were vital factors in corroboration or contradiction" of the conflicting testimony regarding the defendant's "abandonment of the common plan before the shot was fired." Id. at 338, 291 U.S. at 123.

935. Hearsay statements

Cardozo disguises this by describing the prosecutor's statements as simply pointing out features and asking the

jurors to observe them. Id. at 334, 291 U.S. at 110. The dissent, on the other hand, says that "what he said closely approached argument." Without access to the complete record, it is not clear why the dissent says this; the portion they quote in the footnote does not seem to support this claim. Id. at 339, 291 U.S. at 124.

936. "One of degree"

Id. at 334, 291 U.S. at 110.

937. "Procedure of ages"

Id. at 334, 291 U.S. at 111.

938. "Anything material"

Id. at 335, 291 U.S. at 112.

Sensing the weakness of the instrumental argument, Cardozo leaps deftly to a conceptual argument.

> We may assume that the knowledge derived from an inspection of the scene may be characterized as evidence. Even if this be so, a view is not a "trial" nor any part of a trial in sense in which a trial was understood at common law.[939]

Once again he resorts to the law of England, "the land where these maxims had their genesis and from which they were carried to our shores" to prove that "the proceeding known as a trial was thought of as something very different from the proceeding known as a view."[940] According to him, the defendant only has a right to "be present at trial when evidence is offered."[941] Hence, even though the jurors were told that the view and the accompanying hearsay was "evidence", since the evidence was not offered at "trial", defendant's right was not violated. Amidst this formal conceptualism Cardozo has the chutzpah to say that "[a] fertile source of perversion in constitutional theory is the tyranny of labels."[942]

As his last line of defense, Cardozo retreats from the Sixth Amendment to the Fourteenth Amendment, which "has not said in so many words" that "the accused must be present every second or minute or even hour of the trial."[943] Unlike the Sixth Amendment, the Fourteenth only "requires that the proceedings be fair, but fairness is a relative, not an absolute concept."[944] Hence, the defendant must only be provided with a trial that is not "flagrantly unjust."[945] Since even under the Sixth Amendment the defendant can be absent "for a few moments while formal documents are marked in evidence", it would not violate Due Process to bar the defendant from a view.[946]

Finally, Cardozo concedes that the proceedings below are subject to "a word of criticism."[947] This "word", unlike the hundreds

939. "Not a trial"
Id. at 335, 291 U.S. at 113.

940. "Something very different"
Id. at 335, 291 U.S. at 114.

941. "When evidence offered"
Id. at 335, U.S. at 114.

942. "Tyranny of labels"
Id. at 335, U.S. at 114.

943. "Every hour"
Id. at 336, 291 U.S. at 116.

944. "Not absolute"
Id. at 336, 291 U.S. at 116.

945. "Flagrantly unjust"
Id. at 336, 291 U.S. at 115.

946. "For a few moments"
Id. at 336, 291 U.S. at 117.

947. "Word of criticism"
Id. at 337, 291 U.S. at 118.

before it, is the only one aimed at the case of Snyder rather than the hypothetical cases the majority opinion has been discussing to this point; that is, the case where the trial judge, in the absence of the defendant, tells the jury that the scene has changed since the time of the crime. The judge, of course, was not under oath, presumably had no personal knowledge of the state of the scene at the time of the robbery, and under the separation of functions built into the Sixth Amendment's adversary system could not testify to that fact even were he otherwise qualified.[948] This makes no difference, Cardozo tells us, because the error was harmless——citing cases of jury misconduct.[949] Moreover "there is another answer more convincing"; since later at trial when the prosecutor offered in evidence a diagram of the scene and repeated the judge's statement about the changes to the scene, by not objecting at that point, "defendant and his counsel gave assent by acquiescence."[950]

Had Cardozo engaged in a holistic view of the Sixth Amendment rather than the salami-slicing of his majority opinion, he might have wondered whether the Fifth Amendment did not have some part to play; how can the defendant question the statements of the judge and prosecutor about the state of the scene at the time of the crime without the self-incriminating statement that he was there at the time?[951] Or what about the Fourth and Eighth Amendments; since the only reason that defendant could be kept from the jury view was because he had been "seized" and not granted bail, isn't it a denial of equal protection to prevent his being present when a well-heeled defendant could be there? Finally, in a 25-page opinion that cites scores of authorities, Cardozo never asks what interest the state has in excluding the defendant from the view.[952]

948. Could not testify

Compare Evidence Rule 605.

949. Harmless

Id. at 337, 291 U.S. at 118.

950. "Assent by acquiescence"

Id. at 337, 291 U.S. at 118.

951. Self-incriminating

That is, Cardozo supposes that when the judge repeats at trial the concession his counsel had made in his absence at the view, the defendant must protest that this was not so, implying he was there at the time of crime so he knows that the changed feature was then in existence. One assumes that Cardozo would dismiss this as harmless also since the defendant had conceded he was there at the time of the crime in his own testimony.

952. State interest

It cannot be either the expense or the danger that defendant might escape or be rescued, since earlier in the opinion Cardozo says "the record makes it clear that upon request he would have been allowed to go there afterwards in company with his counsel." Id. at 333, 291 U.S. at 108–109.

This is a particularly telling point, given that at the time it was deciding Snyder the Court was busily striking down state regulations that had far more weighty support than anything that can be conjured up to justify conducting a jury view in the absence of the defendant.

Unless, that is, one is to take this pseudo-Poundian justification as a kind of policy:

> justice, though due to the accused, is due to the accuser also. The concept of fairness must not be strained till it is narrowed to a filament. We are to keep the balance true. * * * There is a danger that the criminal law will be brought into contempt * * * if gossamer possibilities of prejudice to a defendant are to nullify a sentence pronounced by a court of competent jurisdiction in obedience to local law, and set the guilty free.[953]

No one could quarrel with these eloquent statements in the abstract, but like most of the Court's opinion, they have little to do with the case at hand.[954] No one is suggesting that defendant is to go free if he is in fact guilty and Cardozo never explains how allowing the defendant to be present at the view would be unfair to the accuser, whether the word be taken to mean the State or the "witnesses against" the accused.[955]

§ 6360. ____; The Rights Revolution*

In 1935, a Jewish clarinetist from Chicago provided a more bureaucratic model for the musical combination of individualism and collectivism; Benny Goodman's "swing" music distressed par-

953. "Set the guilty free"

Id. at 338, 291 U.S. at 122.

954. Case at hand

Cardozo says the court was acting "in obedience to local law", but no one was claiming that Massachusetts law required that the defendant be excluded, only that it did not mandate his presence.

955. Never explains

While it is possible that some of the failings of the majority opinion cannot be completely taxed to Cardozo but may be the product of the need to add an argument in order to get the fifth vote needed for the majority, this language so resembles some of Cardozo's equally fatuous but more infamous

dismissals of constitutional rights that it is hard to shift the blame elsewhere. See, e.g., People v. Defore, 1926, 150 N.E. 585, 587, 242 N.Y. 13, 21 ("criminal is to go free because the constable has blundered" in response to claim of exclusion of evidence that was the product of an illegal search).

§ 6360

* This is a long section; the list below may help in locating discussion of particular topics. The number is the notecall where the discussion begins.

ents and launched "jitterbugging."[1] Not that conservatives needed further reminders that the country was in trouble; the off-year elections had increased Democratic majorities in Congress, inaugurating what came to be called "The Second New Deal."[2] But the first one was already too much for a federal judiciary, staffed as it was largely with business lawyers appointed by Coolidge and Hoover.[3]

By the end of the first thousand days of the Roosevelt administration, the lower federal courts had issued more than 1600 injunctions against government action responding to the economic crisis.[4] The tide seemed to have turned during the prior year when the Supreme Court upheld state statutes providing for a moratorium on foreclosure of mortgages and fixing milk prices.[5] In the first of these, Chief Justice Hughes said that while an emergency, such as

1. "Jitterbugging"

Manchester, The Glory and The Dream, 1974, p. 119. Unlike earlier jazzbands, misleadingly lumped together under the label "Dixieland," swing bands were larger and more European—that is, the "leader" took on more of the attributes of an employer-conductor and the performances relied less on improvisation and more on formal arrangements that were themselves becoming more like original compositions. Swing bands were also more bureaucratic in being more specialized; e.g., the distinction between "lead" players and other members of "the section." Despite this, swing was an appropriate metaphor for the adversary system in the way in which it combined cooperation and competition. In short, like the courts and business, popular music was becoming more bureaucratized.

2. "Second New Deal"

Encyclopedia of American History, Morris ed. 1976, p. 413.

3. Business lawyers

Manchester, The Glory and The Dream, 1974, p. 136.

4. More than 1600

Ibid.

5. Fixing milk prices

Leuchtenburg, Franklin D. Roosevelt and The New Deal, 1932–1940, 1963, pp. 143–144.

the Depression, "does not create power [it] may furnish the occasion for the exercise of power"; in the second, Justice Roberts declared that "[n]either property rights or contract rights are absolute"—a position consistent with that of the majority in Snyder.[6] These decisions, Justice McReynolds wrote a friend, mean "the end of the Constitution as you and I regarded it."[7]

McReynolds may have been too hasty. The Supreme Court, which in the prior 140 years had invalidated some 60 statutes, suddenly within the span of a year declared eleven statutes unconstitutional.[8] The most notorious of these, Schecter Poultry Corp. v. United States (popularly known as "The Sick Chicken Case"), invalidated the National Industrial Recovery Act which, among many other things gave workers the right to join unions and bargain collectively.[9] Many people viewed these cases as marking an attempted judicial counter-revolution; even some conservatives were appalled.[10] Herbert Hoover opined that "[s]omething should be done to give back to states the power they thought they already had."[11]

The President was furious. At a press conference he called the Schecter opinion "more important than any decision probably since the Dred Scott case."[12] He accused the five-member majority of having relegated the nation "to the horse-and-buggy definition of

6. Consistent with Snyder

Home Building & Loan Association v. Blaisdell, 1934, 54 S.Ct. 231, 290 U.S. 398, 78 L.Ed. 413; Nebbia v. New York, 1934, 54 S.Ct. 505, 291 U.S. 502, 78 L.Ed. 940; In 1935, in a case reminiscent of Marbury v. Madison, another 5–4 majority held that the New Deal repudiation of the gold clauses in government bonds was unconstitutional but found procedural grounds to deny the bondholders relief. Perry v. U.S., 1935, 55 S.Ct. 432, 294 U.S. 330, 79 L.Ed. 912.

7. "End of the Constitution"

Leuchtenburg, Franklin D. Roosevelt and The New Deal, 1932–1940, 1963, p. 144.

8. Eleven unconstitutional

Manchester, The Glory and The Dream, 1974, p. 137.

9. "Sick Chicken Case"

1935, 55 S.Ct. 837, 295 U.S. 495, 79 L.Ed. 1570; Leuchtenburg, Franklin D. Roosevelt and The New Deal, 1932–1940, 1963, p. 145; Encyclopedia of American History, Morris ed. 1976, pp. 407, 676.

10. Conservatives appalled

Leuchtenberg, Franklin D. Roosevelt and The New Deal, 1932–1940, 1963, p. 143; Manchester, The Glory and The Dream, 1974, p. 138.

11. "Thought they had"

Ibid.

12. "Dred Scott case"

Leuchtenburg, Franklin D. Roosevelt and The New Deal, 1932–1940, 1963, p. 145; Manchester, The Glory and The Dream, 1974, p. 136.

interstate commerce."[13] Privately, the Attorney General told the President that "they mean to destroy us. We will have to find a way to get rid of the present membership of the Supreme Court."[14] Perhaps the President thought the "way" he chose would meet with popular approval because of the vilification of the Court that followed the decisions of 1935; the "nine old men" was among the least vituperative of these.[15] Writing of the Chief Justice, Time magazine said "the pure white flame of liberalism has burned out in Hughes, to a sultry ash of conservatism."[16] Had the President followed the suggestion of some Democrats and sought an amendment to the Constitution, the subsequent history of the nation and of the Confrontation Clause might have been much different.[17]

If the President took any comfort from the abuse heaped upon the Supreme Court, it was probably short-lived. With the beginning of the Second New Deal, the invective and innuendo directed at Roosevelt and his programs reached levels that did not recede much for the rest of his term.[18] Herbert Hoover, like the majority of the Supreme Court, thought the New Deal endangered "fundamental American liberties."[19] A Republican legislator saw in the Securities & Exchange Act a plot "to Russianize everything."[20] In part, such opinions were examples of a conservative backlash orchestrated by lawyers.[21] A committee under Senator Hugo Black unmasked the lengths to which some opponents of the New Deal were willing to go to defeat regulation—including forgery, destruction of evidence, and bribery.[22]

13. "Horse-and-buggy"

Ibid.

14. "Way to get rid of"

Id. at p. 137.

15. "Nine old men"

Id. at p. 135.

16. "Ash of conservatism"

Ibid.

17. Sought amendment

Id. at p. 138.

18. Invective and innuendo

Rather than sully these pages with quotations, we will simply say that much of this was anti-Semitic or reflected on the President's physical disability. Id. at p. 165.

19. "Fundamental liberties"-

Foner, The Story of American Freedom, 1998, p. 205.

20. "Russianize everything"

Manchester, The Glory and The Dream, 1974, p. 164.

21. Orchestrated by lawyers

The Fear of Conspiracy: Un–American Subversion From The Revolution to The President, Davis ed. 1971, p. 270.

22. Black unmasked

Leuchtenburg, Franklin D. Roosevelt and The New Deal, 1932–1940, 1963, p. 156.

However, much of the resurrection of laissez faire was due less to political machinations and more to the revival of previously demoralized voices, now recovered from the shock of the Crash and the fear of revolution—and encouraged by the leadership of the Supreme Court majority.[23] Editorials in the business press began to exonerate business leaders of any responsibility for the Depression and even to endorse child labor as a way to build character.[24] Among the more ludicrous bits of anti-administration propaganda was the suicide of "Daddy Warbucks," the plutocratic godfather of the comic strip character "Little Orphan Annie," who could not stand to live in a society governed by Roosevelt.[25] Among the more substantial came from former Democratic presidential candidate Al Smith:

> It is all right with me if they want to disguise themselves as Norman Thomas or Karl Marx, or Lenin, or any of the rest of that bunch but what I won't stand for is allowing them to march under the banner of Jefferson, Jackson, and Cleveland.[26]

Mr. Smith might have been surprised to learn how many real Communists were marching under that banner.

The Year 1935 saw the inauguration of the so-called "Popular Front"—Stalin's campaign to get Communists in western countries to ally themselves with anyone who would move those nations to oppose Hitler.[27] The years 1935–1939 were the high point of communism in the United States.[28] Though the number of people actually enrolled in the Communist Party probably never exceeded 100,000—far less than such now-forgotten parties as the Greenback and Prohibition parties in their prime—the figure is misleading.[29] People flowed in and out of the party like guests at a "hot-pillow" motel, revolted by the authoritarianism of the Party leadership or

---

23. Encouraged by Court

Not all of the backlash was conservative; the unanimity of the Court in Schecter was due to a revival of Brandeisian notions about the virtues of the deconcentration of institutions—and not only on the Court. Id. at p. 148.

24. Endorse child labor

Manchester, The Glory and The Dream, 1974, p. 164.

25. "Daddy Warbucks" suicide

Id. at p. 166.

26. "March under the banner"

Leuchtenburg, Franklin D. Roosevelt and The New Deal, 1932–1940, 1963, p. 178.

27. "Popular Front"

Id. at p. 282.

28. High point of communism

Klehr, The Party's Over, N.Y.Rev.Bks., Nov. 18, 1982, p. 55.

29. Figure misleading

Foner, The Story of American Freedom, 1998, p. 211.

by the latest Soviet atrocity.[30] More significantly, the influence of the Party was greater than the number of its members might suggest.

During the Popular Front, Communists for the first time began to have some influence in the indigenous left; ironically, more so than among other American Marxists.[31] It has been estimated that Communists occupied leadership roles in more than one-third of the unions that made up the Congress of Industrial Organizations.[32] Moreover the Party had a following—"fellow travelers" they were later to be called—among New Deal intellectuals, though it is probably only in the N.L.R.B. that they had any influence on policy.[33] One of the great ironies—or mysteries—of American history is how a party that was so authoritarian and doctrinaire could appeal to so many people as a vehicle for advancing American values that owed more to Thomas Paine than Karl Marx.[34] Part of the answer may be that during the time of the Popular Front the Party was, as Smith charged, marching under the flag of traditional American values.[35] But at the time when the administration was tinkering and their opponents were into "blame-the-victim" denial, the Communists provided answers that could be seen as reviving the faith of the Founders in "the people."[36] Popular Front culture dovetailed with Rooseveltian rhetoric in celebrating "the common man." And for people of color, the Communist Party was probably the only largely white organization that placed as much emphasis

30. Latest Soviet atrocity

During the Second Red Scare many of those under attack attributed their disillusionment to the Hitler–Stalin pact; but as we shall see, there were several other occasions for exodus. Ibid.

31. Other Marxists

On the anti-Communist role of the Trotskyites and other Marxist groups, see Schrecker, No Ivory Tower: McCarthyism and the Universities, 1986, p. 73.

32. One-third of CIO

Leuchtenburg, Franklin D. Roosevelt and The New Deal, 1932–1940, 1963, p. 282.

33. Only in N.L.R.B.

Ibid.

34. Paine than Marx

Foner, The Story of American Freedom, 1998, p. 211. For an attempt to explain the appeal of Communism to academics, see Schrecker, No Ivory Tower: McCarthyism and the Universities, 1986, pp. 29–31.

35. Traditional values

Indeed, the Party went so far as to claim the mantle of "the traditions of Jefferson, Paine, Jackson, and Lincoln." Foner, The Story of American Freedom, 1998, p. 213.

36. "The people"

Id. at p. 212; Manchester, The Glory and The Dream, 1974, p. 86.

on resisting racism; those who attacked the defense of the Scotts-boro case as "Communist-led" probably did more to aid Party recruiting than they did to discourage the defense.[37] Be that as it may, the Communist Party's brief alliance with the New Deal and its defense of workers and minorities probably did as much as its attacks on capitalism or its spying for the Soviet Union to bring about The Second Red Scare—and the flowering of the right of confrontation.

It is sometimes assumed that organized, official anticommun-ism ended with the demise of the first Red Scare, only to re-arise in a far more virulent form—"McCarthyism"—after World War II.[38] We reject the title, and with it the implication that those who joined the Communist Party during the Popular Front era did so without realizing the risks involved. Indeed, in April, 1935, after the owner of a chain of drugstores complained that students at the University of Chicago were being indoctrinated by their teachers, the Illinois legislature began an investigation of "subversive Com-munistic teachings and ideas" at the University.[39] Despite testimo-ny linking the accused professors with the ideas of such "Commu-nists" as Justice Brandeis and Senator William Borah, the majority of the committee ultimately concluded that the charges were un-founded.[40] In 1935, Joseph McCarthy was still a law student at Marquette University. As we shall see, The Second Red Scare differed from the first not in the personalities involved, but in their ability to use institutional mechanisms that the New Deal itself had done much to foster.

Sit-ins, Sit-downs, and Subversives

But in 1936, one of the major instruments of the Second Red Scare was aimed at employers, not Reds. Senator Robert LaFollette, Jr.'s Senate subcommittee exposed the methods used by employers to fight unionization, including a large network of spies, informers, and private police forces.[41] For example, General Motors had four-teen detective agencies under contract during the years 1934–1936

---

37. Scottsboro defense

Foner, The Story of American Freedom, 1998, p. 214.

38. "McCarthyism"

Fariello, Red Scare, 1997, pp. 27–28.

39. "Subversive teachings"

Schrecker, No Ivory Tower: McCarthy-ism and the Universities, 1986, p. 72.

40. Charges unfounded

Ibid.

41. Private police

Foner, The Story of American Freedom, 1998, p. 215.

at a cost of over $1 million.[42] In addition, in Flint, Michigan, the local police force was like an arm of the corporation, which had provided the funds to make the city the 11th largest purchaser of tear gas in the nation.[43] However, details about the company's use of spies and informers are lost because General Motors destroyed all of its records when the congressional investigation began.[44] Not surprisingly, a GM employee told the committee that workers there "had no liberties at all."[45] In its final report, the committee found the use of official and unofficial violence against workers in California made that state seem "more like a fascist European dictatorship than part of the United States."[46] It is telling that with all the available models from American history, the committee felt obliged to employ an alien simile.

In that same year, the Marxist journal "Science and Society" began publishing, a teacher was fired for Communist beliefs, and the Daughters of the American Revolution were in the midst of a campaign, that eventually enlisted some 19 states, to require loyalty oaths of public school teachers.[47] It was also the year that the F.B.I. began an extensive investigation of the leadership of the Communist Party.[48] Much later an agency official was to admit that the Party was more effective in gaining increasing appropriations for the F.B.I. than it was in subverting American institutions.[49] So it might seem; from 1939 to 1943 the F.B.I. grew from 851 to 4,600 agents.[50] Despite all this manpower, the F.B.I. relied primarily on informers to gather information about Communists.[51] Given the traditional hostility to informers that shaped the right of confronta-

42. Cost over $1 million

Fine, Sit–Down: The General Motors Strike of 1936–1937, 1969, p. 38.

43. Purchaser of tear gas

Id. at p. 108.

44. Destroyed all records

Id. at p. 39.

45. "No liberties at all"

Foner, The Story of American Freedom, 1998, p. 215.

46. California "fascist"

Ibid.

47. Loyalty oaths

Schrecker, No Ivory Tower: McCarthyism and the Universities, 1986, pp. 51,

63; Encyclopedia of American Facts and Dates, 9th ed. 1993, p. 491.

48. Began investigation

Belknap, Cold War Political Justice: The Smith Act, The Communist Party, and American Civil Liberties, 1977, p. 35.

49. Increasing appropriations

Id. at p . 175.

50. Grew to 4,600

Id. at p. 36.

51. Relied on informers

Ibid.

tion, it was to be expected that some would protest; Senator George Norris told his colleagues that the "methods of the Federal Bureau of Investigation are wrong and, if continued, mean the destruction of human liberty in the United States."[52] Portentously, 1936 was also the year in which the motion picture "The Informer" received an Academy Award.[53]

Other groups did not fare as well under the Roosevelt administration as the F.B.I. Many New Deal programs fostered discrimination against women and African–Americans; imbued with the policy of a "family wage," women were denied jobs to make them available to the traditional "head of the family" and Jim Crow reigned in many programs in the South.[54] Worse yet, the New Deal's housing programs actually worsened racial segregation in all parts of the nation.[55] In 1936, when students in the nation's schools were still using racist textbooks and "Gone With the Wind" sold a million copies in the first six months after publication, Southern Democrats defeated an anti-lynching bill with a filibuster.[56] The N.A.A.C.P. denounced the President for failing to throw his influence behind the measure and no other civil rights legislation even came close to passage during Roosevelt's term of office.[57]

Nonetheless, the Roosevelt years did see a discernable rise in the tolerance of ethnic pluralism for white Americans beyond the

52. "Destruction of liberty"

Schlesinger, Hoover Makes A Comeback, N.Y.Rev.Bks., Mar. 8, 1879, pp. 10, 14.

53. Academy Award

Encyclopedia of American Facts and Dates, 9th ed. 1993, p. 494.

54. Jim Crow reigned

Foner, The Story of American Freedom, 1998, p. 207.

55. Worsened segregation

Id. at p. 210.

56. Filibuster

Encyclopedia of American Facts and Dates, 9th ed., 1993, p . 492; Leuchtenburg, Franklin D. Roosevelt and The New Deal, 1932–1940.

"Although he was in a state of slavery, the Negro of plantation days was usually happy. He was fond of the compa-ny of others and liked to sing, dance, crack jokes, and laugh; he admired bright colors and was proud to wear a red or yellow bandana. He wanted to be praised, and he was loyal to a kind master or overseer. He was never in a hurry, and was always ready to let things go until tomorrow. Most of the planters learned that not the whip, but loyalty, based upon pride, kindness, and rewards brought the best returns." Manchester, The Glory and The Dream, 1974, p. 65 (quoting Marshall, American History, 1930, one of the most widely used textbooks of the era).

57. No other civil rights

Leuchtenburg, Franklin D. Roosevelt and The New Deal, 1932–1940, 1963, p. 186.

Anglo–Saxon norm.[58] In large part this was the result of assimilation and the embrace of American nationalism among the previously hyphenated groups.[59] One ironworker, perhaps recalling the C.I.O. slogan that "Unionism is Americanism," complained to the Secretary of Labor that "I'm in the U.S.A. but the Mesabi Range isn't Americanized yet."[60] The New Deal played some role, however; for example, Jewish lawyers were probably more prominent in the New Deal agencies than in most other public or private organizations. In addition, the percentage of Roosevelt's judicial appointments that went to Catholics showed a ten-fold increase over those of his predecessors; this is significant because Catholicism was often a surrogate for ethnicity.[61] We should not, however, overestimate the change; those anxious for careers in Hollywood still found it prudent to Anglicize names suggestive of Jewish or Eastern European ancestry until well into the 1960s.[62]

Meanwhile, the Supreme Court continued its rampage of invalidation through state and federal legislation aimed at restructuring the economy.[63] The President repeated his cousin's claim earlier in the century that the Court seemed to have created a constitutional "no-man's-land" where neither state nor federal governments had the power to act to end or alleviate the Depression.[64] However, for the moment the President bided his time till after the election.

The election of 1936 was one of the most bitterly contested in history.[65] More than 80% of the business press opposed the Democratic ticket and employers warned employees that if Roosevelt were reelected they would lose their jobs.[66] For his part, the

---

58. Rise in pluralism

Foner, The Story of American Freedom, 1998, p. 210.

59. Assimilation

Ibid.

60. "Isn't Americanized"

Id. at p. 211.

61. Catholics

Leuchtenburg, Franklin D. Roosevelt and The New Deal, 1932–1940, 1963, p. 184.

62. Anglicize names

Manchester, The Glory and The Dream, 1974, p. 198.

63. Continued rampage

Leuchtenburg, Franklin D. Roosevelt and The New Deal, 1932–1940, 1963, p. 231.

64. "No-man's-land"

Ibid.

65. Bitterly contested

Perhaps because the Republicans knew from the start they had no chance to win and used the airwaves to vent their spleen rather than appeal for support. Id. at pp. 178–179.

66. Lose their jobs

Manchester, The Glory and The Dream, 1974, pp. 142–143.

President stepped up his anti-capitalist rhetoric.[67] In accepting the Democratic nomination, Roosevelt attacked "economic royalists who have created a new despotism and wrapped it in the robes of legal sanction"—language that was calculatedly ambiguous as to its target; some may have taken it as aimed at the Supreme Court.[68] Roosevelt was not above wrapping himself in other robes; he told an audience in Syracuse that the "true conservative seeks to protect the system of private property and free enterprise by correcting such injustices and inequalities as arise from it."[69] When the votes were counted, the "true conservative" swept to the most lopsided victory since Monroe's in 1820, capturing the electoral votes of every state save Maine and Vermont.[70] In addition the Democrats received overwhelming majorities in both houses of Congress.[71]

The election year also brought an increase of student activism, much of it aimed at campus administrators seeking to suppress radical and pacifist thought on campuses.[72] Some campuses saw demonstrations of the sort that anticipated the 1960s; indeed, the firing of a pacifist teacher at C.C.N.Y. produced what one historian claims was the first "sit-in."[73] If so, it was eclipsed at the end of the year by a more celebrated "sit-down."

On December 30, 1936, workers at the General Motors Fisher Body plant in Flint, Michigan, who had tired of following the advice of union leaders to wait for management to meet its obligations under the Wagner Act, called a spontaneous strike.[74] But instead of "walking out," they decided to try a tactic first used by rubber workers in Akron, Ohio; they sat down at their machines and

---

67. Anti-capitalist rhetoric

Id. at pp. 141, 143–144.

68. "Robes of legal sanction"

Encyclopedia of American History, Morris ed. 1976, p. 419.

69. "True conservative"

Id. at p. 420.

70. Maine and Vermont

Ibid. The Communist candidate received 80,000 votes, more than 100,000 less than the Socialist Norman Thomas did. Ironically, the Schecters, the victors in the "Sick Chicken Case" claimed that they had voted for

Roosevelt. Manchester, The Glory and The Dream, 1974, p. 144.

71. Majorities in Congress

Ibid.

72. Radical and pacifist thought

Schrecker, No Ivory Tower: McCarthyism and the Universities, 1986, p. 64.

73. First "sit-in"

Id. at p. 66.

74. Spontaneous strike

The background of the strike, much condensed in the text, may be found in Brecher, Strike!, 1972, pp. 188–194.

refused to work or leave the plant.[75] To end the occupation of the plant, the company sought an injunction in state court, federal courts now being unavailable because of the Norris–LaGuardia Act and a state prosecutor having advised that the "sit-down" did not constitute a crime under state law.[76]

When the injunction issued, the union showed that the judge owned over $200,000 in General Motors stock, thus disqualifying him under state law.[77] The judge retired, muttering that accusations of bias were "Communist talk"; the local bar association leaped to his defense.[78] The state prosecutor then had 300 "John Doe warrants" issued, planning to arrest strike leaders for criminal syndicalism, but before his plan could be put into action, it was revealed that he, too, owned General Motors stock.[79] Meanwhile, the tactic spread to other General Motors plants.[80] The business unionists at the A.F.L. denounced the "sit-down" and conservatives saw it as a revolutionary attack on private property.[81] However, John L. Lewis, head of the C.I.O., went on the radio to support the strikers.[82]

The strikers already had substantial support in the local community.[83] When the local police tried to enter the plant to evict the strikers, they were repulsed with the aid of a mob outside the plant in what became locally famous as "The Battle of Running Bulls."[84] The company, unwilling to see further violence, tried to sway public opinion with the support of local elites.[85] In view of the later attacks that were made upon Communist teachers for politicizing the class room, the most striking feature of the company's campaign was the action of the local school board in prohibiting

75. Akron tactic

Id. at p. 180–181; Leuchtenburg, Franklin D. Roosevelt and The New Deal, 1932–1940, 1963, p.239.

76. Not a crime

Fine, Sit–Down: The General Motors Strike of 1936–1937, 1969, p. 131.

77. Owned stock

Id. at pp. 193–194.

78. Leaped to defense

Id. at p. 194.

79. He, too, owned stock

Id. at p. 240.

80. Spread to other plants

Manchester, The Glory and The Dream, 1974, p. 154.

81. Attack on property

Id. at p. 155.

82. Went on radio

Ibid.

83. Support in community

Brecher, Strike!, 1972, pp. 197–198.

84. "Running Bulls"

Id. at p. 199–200.

85. Local elites

Id. at p. 199.

children from wearing pins supporting the strike and requiring them to write papers stating what was wrong with the strike.[86]

The company then obtained another injunction against the strikers.[87] However, the then-Governor of Michigan and future Supreme Court Justice Frank Murphy not only refused to allow the National Guard to be used to enforce the injunction but also warned the company against attempting to starve out the strikers by using force to prevent food from being thrown to them.[88] Despite the claim of the local judge that he had authority to order the National Guard into action, General Motors, seeing that the other automakers, far from showing solidarity, were busily carving up GM's share of the market, decided to capitulate and recognize the union.[89] Except for Ford, other automobile companies quickly followed suit.[90]

The Flint strike, while in the short run it may have discredited the courts and the legal system, was probably beneficial in the long term. For the first time in a major industrial dispute, state and federal officials refused to allow the use of force to end a strike.[91] By making injunctions futile, this forced employers to rely on the institutions provided for by the Wagner Act to deal with labor disputes.[92] Removing courts from the highly politicized field of strikebreaking was a significant step toward restoring the neutrality presupposed by the adversary system.[93] Just as the division of authority with the jury under the Sixth Amendment tends to limit the judge's responsibility for the conviction, so does sharing responsibility for labor disputes with the N.L.R.B. tend to avoid the kinds

---

86. Write papers

Fine, Sit–Down: The General Motors Strike of 1936–1937, 1969, p. 227.

87. Another injunction

Brecher, Strike!, 1972, p. 200.

88. Murphy refused

Manchester, The Glory and The Dream, 1974, p. 156.

89. Capitulate

Ibid. The aftermath of the strike is not as tidy as the text may imply; there was a long struggle over just what the company had agreed to and what union members were willing to accept. Brecher, Strike!, 1972, pp. 202–206.

90. Followed suit

Leuchtenburg, Franklin D. Roosevelt and The New Deal, 1932–1940, 1963, p. 240.

91. Refused to use force

There were isolated exceptions to this generalization. Id. at pp. 241–242.

92. Forced to rely

A federal statute barring interstate transportation of strikebreakers also helped. Id. at p. 242.

93. Restoring neutrality

See § 6357, text at notecall 314.

of political attacks that government by injunction engendered.[94]

"The Switch in Time"

The Moscow "show trials" of 1937 brought the inquisitorial system of justice before the American public in the worst possible light; Stalin's use of the judicial process to condemn his rivals to death for supposedly serving as agents for Western governments also led some Americans to turn against Communism.[95] Meanwhile, as the sit-down strikes in the automobile industry wound down, the C.I.O. turned to a long planned campaign against the steel companies.[96] Management's often-violent response to pickets and union organizers made 1937 the high water mark for such bloody confrontations.[97] The climax was the "Memorial Day Massacre" in which a police attack on a holiday protest march outside the Republic Steel plant in South Chicago left ten dead and 90 wounded.[98] The violence was blamed on communist agitators but efforts to suppress a newsreel that graphically depicted the police brutality backfired; public opinion turned against the companies, forcing them to do business with the unions.[99]

The crash of the dirigible Hindenberg that same year was also caught on film but it was hardly more spectacular than the crash of laissez-faire constitutionalism.[100] To understand the latter, we must return briefly to the Supreme Court's triumphal march through New Deal legislation in 1936 to look more closely at three of the decisions invalidating state and federal legislation.[101] In U.S. v.

94. Avoid attacks

As the criticisms of President Roosevelt for not intervening to end the sit-down strikes suggests, political attacks would not be reduced by appointing judges who were more sympathetic to unions. Leuchtenburg, Franklin D. Roosevelt and The New Deal, 1932–1940, 1963, p. 243.

95. "Show trials"

Foner, The Story of American Freedom, 1998, p. 212.

96. C.I.O. turned to steel

Leuchtenburg, Franklin D. Roosevelt and The New Deal, 1932–1940, 1963, p. 239.

97. High-water mark

Manchester, The Glory and The Dream, 1974, p. 161.

98. "Memorial Day Massacre"

Id. at pp. 159–160.

99. Public opinion turned

Id. at pp. 160–161; Brecher, Strike!, 1972, p. 214.

100. Hindenburg crash

Encyclopedia of American Facts and Dates, 9th ed. 1993, p. 496.

101. Triumphal march

Leuchtenburg, The Supreme Court Reborn, 1995, p. 168.

Butler, the Court by a vote of 6–3 struck down a processing tax imposed by the Agricultural Adjustment Act.[102] Not content with a declaration of unconstitutionality, Justice Roberts' opinion for the majority went on to castigate the statute—and by implication, the legislators who had voted for it—as an illegitimate "expropriation of money from one group for the benefit of another."[103]

Congress reacted with outrage at this imputation of socialistic motives.[104] A Southern Senator denounced the opinion as "a political stump speech" and a state governor accused the Supreme Court of becoming a "political body."[105] If so, it was not a very astute one; farmers were not only among the worst victims of the Depression but also the group with the longest set of grievances with the Supreme Court and a significant history of mobilizing against the Court.[106] However, these criticisms illustrate a double bind for its adversaries that was to serve the Court well in the coming crisis. To criticize the Court for engaging in "politics" suggests that it could and should be above politics, thus honoring by the criticism that very myth which supports judicial power.[107] On the other hand to say that the Court is properly a political body but its politics are wrong deprives the attack of much of its moral edge and sinks the critic into the mire of the appropriate procedure for legitimizing judicial politics—an issue with less appeal to the public and one on which the Court is far less vulnerable.[108]

The Court could not afford to lose the farm bloc—in Iowa the majority justices were hung in effigy—because it had already alien-

102. Struck down AAA

Id. at p. 170. The Butler decision is found at 1936, 56 S.Ct. 312, 297 U.S. 1, 80 L.Ed. 477.

103. "Expropriation"

Id. at 317, 297 U.S. at 61.

104. Outrage

It did not help that the decision was followed by a sharp drop in farm prices. Leuchtenburg, Franklin D. Roosevelt and The New Deal, 1932–1940, 1963, p. 171.

105. "Political body"

Ibid.

106. Farmers and Court

See above, § 6356, text at notecall 254; § 6357, text at notecall 218.

107. The very myth

Moreover, for those who do not accept the criticism, the critic will be seen as sullying the Court by dragging it into politics.

108. Less vulnerable

That is, even as a political body, the Court is controlled by procedures more rigid than those that limit Congress; moreover, at a time when much of Congress was from rotten boroughs or elected through all-white primaries, the argument that elections are a superior method of legitimating power fell flat.

ated labor.[109] The Court's choice of workers to pick on demonstrated little political acumen; railroad workers not only suffered in the Depression but they had also suffered more than most from industrial injuries—in 1934, 526 railroad workers were killed in the line of duty and some 17,000 men were injured.[110] Moreover, railroad workers were not swarthy Others confined to some urban ghetto; they worked on right of ways beside the farmer's fields and in switchyards and on sidings in villages and hamlets across the land.[111] Justice Roberts' opinion for the majority striking down the Railroad Retirement Act was not only unusually obtuse about the conditions faced by workingmen, it also anticipated his Butler epithet; "a naked appropriation of private property."[112] It "denies due process of law by taking the property of one and bestowing it upon another."[113]

The business press reacted with glee to "the worst setback the New Dealers have received," very few editors noticing that there were losers besides those in the administration; only Business Week was troubled by the possibility that Roberts's opinion endangered programs such as Social Security and the Wagner Act that some business leaders favored.[114] On the other hand, Roberts's opinion was scorched in an editorial in the Progressive magazine, The New Republic, by Professors Felix Frankfurter and Henry Hart of Harvard.[115] In addition to trotting out such examples of judicial overreaching as Dred Scott, the Income Tax, and Child Labor cases and wondering "how many more such decisions * * * can be absorbed without destroying the very Constitution the odd man in the Court

109. Burned in effigy

Leuchtenburg, Franklin D. Roosevelt and The New Deal, 1932–1940, 1963, p. 171.

110. Killed and injured

Leuchtenburg, The Supreme Court Reborn, 1995, pp. 27, 29.

111. Villages and hamlets

Moreover, consumer debt, such as it was in those days, was owed to local merchants, not some bank in Dover, Delaware. In the small town where the junior author was raised, many people would not patronize chain stores because during the Depression it had been the local grocers who had sold food on credit to people who were

unable to pay because they had lost their jobs.

112. "Naked appropriation"

Railroad Retirement Board v. Alton Railroad Co., 1935, 55 S.Ct. 758, 762, 295 U.S. 330, 348, 79 L.Ed. 1468.

113. "Bestowing it upon another"

Id. at 762, 295 U.S. at 350.

114. Endangered Social Security

Leuchtenburg, The Supreme Court Reborn, 1995, pp. 50–51.

115. Frankfurter and Hart

The editorial was unsigned but regular readers of the magazine could easily deduce authorship.

thinks he is preserving," the professors attacked Roberts more directly, accusing him of making "debaters points that evoke cheers from the Bar Association gallery," of "intellectual frivolity," and writing "the most persuasive brief of our times in favor of government ownership of railroads."[116] Worse yet, the decision moved Attorney General Cummings to put his minions to seeking some method for getting the New Deal around the Court.[117]

Finally, on the last day of the term, in a lawsuit financed by New York hotels that wanted to work their chambermaids twelve hours a day, seven days a week, the Court struck down the minimum-wage law on the ground that it violated the worker's "liberty of contract."[118] This time the most scathing commentary came from the dissenters who accused the majority of enforcing its "own personal economic predilections" instead of the Constitution.[119] Justice Stone was moved to find "grim irony in speaking of freedom of contract of those who, because of economic necessities, give their service for less than is needful to keep body and soul together."[120] A Republican newspaper in upstate New York found another irony; that the "law that would jail any laundryman for having an underfed horse [cannot] jail him for having an underfed girl employee."[121] In addition to employers in low-wage industries, the Court's opinion was applauded by radical feminists who found it demeaning to poor women to have their wages regulated by a paternalistic state.[122]

Each blow the Supreme Court struck at New Deal efforts provoked a new outburst of anti-Court sentiment.[123] For example, after the railroad-pension case, which one leader called a "bitter

116. "Government ownership"

Id. at pp. 45–46.

117. Seeking some method

Id. at p. 51.

118. "Liberty of contract"

The nominal plaintiff was the owner of a laundry who had paid the minimum wage, but then forced the women to kick back a portion of their wages to him; because this was a criminal violation, the action was habeas corpus. Id. at p. 166. Morehead v. New York ex rel Tipaldo, 1936, 56 S.Ct. 918, 298 U.S. 587, 80 L.Ed. 1347.

119. "Personal predilections"

Id. at 933, 298 U.S. at 633.

120. "To keep body and soul"

Id. at 932, 298 U.S. at 632.

121. "Underfed girl"

Leuchtenburg, The Supreme Court Reborn, 1995, p. 168.

122. Radical feminists

Ibid.

123. Anti-Court sentiment

Id. at p. 96.

disappointment," the President received a note from a man in Texas with capital ideas:

> I Had an idea they would turn Down that Railroad Pension. I told you that Rich Men always Run to the Supreme Court to Beat Our Laws. * * * The Supreme Court is a Public Nuisance.[124]

As the decisions escalated, so did the anti-Court rhetoric, shifting from criticisms of individual decisions and the Court's ideological bias to the very idea of judicial review.[125] In a speech on the Senate floor in 1936, Senator George Norris accused the Supreme Court of supposing it was a "continuous constitutional convention."

> Nowhere in that great document is there a syllable, a word, or a sentence giving to any court the right to declare an act of Congress unconstitutional. The members of the Supreme Court are not elected by anybody. They are responsible to nobody. Yet they hold dominion over everybody.[126]

A Congressman from Maryland told a reporter that the power of judicial review had been usurped by John Marshall and "today every jackanapes judge brushes aside legislative enactments as whim or prejudice may suggest."[127] An assault on judicial review could potentially have a devastating effect on the future enforcement of the right of confrontation.[128]

For many Americans, the Tipaldo case was the proverbial "last straw."[129] As Secretary of the Interior Ickes wrote:

> The sacred right of liberty of contract again—the right of an immature child or a helpless woman to drive a bargain with a great corporation. If this decision does not outrage the moral sense

124. "Public Nuisance"

Id. at p. 89.

125. Rhetoric escalated

Id. at p. 91.

126. "Dominion over everybody"

Id. at p. 103.

127. "Jackanapes judge"

Id. at p. 49. The thought was expanded for the readers of a newspaper for black workers:

"The power in very truth was never delegated to the Supreme Court by the Constitution. It was usurped.

* * * It is a ridiculous procedure, to say the least, that a group of tottering old men should be permitted to nullify the will of the people where expressed in Congressional acts that are unpopular with the social philosophy of erstwhile corporation lawyers." Id. at p. 50.

128. Effect on confrontation

And perhaps on other civil rights as well, depending exactly how sweeping a restriction was imposed on the Court's power.

129. "Last straw"

Id. at p. 104.

of the country, then nothing will.[130]

It did. Not only did it ignite the drive of the New Dealers to do something, it also undercut conservative opponents who had invoked the high ground of federalism and opposition to centralization; how could they argue that the problems of labor should be left to the states when the Supreme Court had held that states could do nothing either?[131] Now as we have seen, public condemnation of the Court was nothing new—but never before had it been led by a President with such a partisan majority in Congress.[132] However, had public-opinion polling assumed the importance it has today, the New Dealers might have proceeded with more caution; a Gallup poll showed that despite widespread disapproval of the Court, there was little support for proposals to limit judicial review.[133]

Ideas for altering the Court were everywhere; the years 1935–1937 saw more anti-Court legislation introduced than in any comparable period in history.[134] Senator Norris proposed a constitutional amendment requiring a seven-vote super-majority to invalidate congressional legislation.[135] Some of the ideas revived schemes that had been used during Reconstruction; e.g., attaching jurisdiction-stripping clauses to measures the Court had invalidated, then readopting them.[136] An attorney from Arizona wanted to avoid the "seizure of this government by special interests" by increasing "the membership of the Supreme Court to fifteen" and appointing to the Court "men who place human rights above the rights of predatory wealth."[137] The President suggested a democratic method; a consti-

130. "Nothing will"

Id. at p. 105.

131. States could do nothing

Ibid.

132. Partisan majority

The partisan majority was, however, misleading; many members of the President's party were far more conservative than the typical midwestern Republican, much less Progressive Republicans like Norris and LaFollette. Moreover, the Southern conservatives looked on the Supreme Court as the protector of white supremacy.

133. Limited support

Asked "would you favor limiting the power of the Supreme Court to declare acts of Congress unconstitution-al?," 53% said "no": only 31% said "yes." Id. at p. 94.

134. More anti-Court legislation

Id. at p. 102.

135. Norris super-majority

Id. at p. 103.

136. Jurisdiction-stripping

Id. at p. 49.

137. "Above predatory wealth"

Id. at 97 (collecting other similar suggestions). The author of the language quoted in the text suggested Felix Frankfurter and Floyd Olson, the Governor of Minnesota, as two men who satisfied this criterion. Olson, however, died before the President

tutional amendment that would allow Congress to override the Supreme Court declaration of unconstitutionality by reenacting the invalid legislation, so long as a Congressional election intervened between the Court's decision and the Congressional override—an election that Roosevelt thought would provide something like a referendum on the Court's decision.[138]

The President eventually decided that proposals requiring a constitutional amendment were too risky; by concentrating their money and effort in a number of small, but conservative, states, the "malefactors of great wealth" could defeat the amendment.[139] Jurisdiction-stripping schemes were abandoned after Alexander Holtzoff, an attorney in the Justice Department (who was later the coauthor of the precursor to this Treatise), submitted two memoranda detailing the objections to this method.[140] In the President's mind, this left only the option he had once pronounced "distasteful"—"packing the Supreme Court."[141]

When Roosevelt submitted his plan to Congress on February 5, 1937, it generated as much controversy across the nation as anything since Wilson's proposal that the United States join the League of Nations.[142] In addition to a number of procedural changes that served to disguise the proposal as one to improve the efficiency of the federal judicial system, the heart of the plan was legislation that would allow the President to appoint additional justices, up to a maximum of six, for every justice over 70 who refused to retire.[143]

---

had an opportunity to follow up on this suggestion.

138. Like a referendum

Id. at p. 95.

139. Could defeat amendment

Leuchtenburg, Franklin D. Roosevelt and The New Deal, 1932–1940, 1963, p. 232. At the time, inaction by thirteen states was sufficient to prevent amendment of the Constitution.

140. Holtzoff objections

Leuchtenburg, The Supreme Court Reborn, 1995, p. 93.

141. "Packing the Court"

Id. at p. 95.

142. Since the League

Id. at p. 134.

143. Refused to retire

Id. at p. 134. The proposal would also have added 50 judges to the lower federal courts, provided direct appeal to the Supreme Court from decisions involving constitutional questions, forbade injunctions against federal legislation without government attorneys having been heard, and allowed the assignment of district-court judges to assist congested courts. Encyclopedia of American History, Morris ed. 1976, p. 420.

Although Anglophiles thought the President was moved by Asquith's threat to pack the House of Lords, the President reportedly was bemused by an indigenous precedent.[144] In preparing to write a history of the Justice Department, Attorney General Cummings (or an aide) found in the files of a predecessor a similar proposal, though designed for a different purpose, prepared for President Wilson in 1913.[145] The memorandum noted that although members of the Supreme Court could retire with a pension at 70, some justices "have remained upon the bench long beyond the time that they are able to adequately discharge their duties, and in consequence the administration of justice has suffered."[146] Not only was this language written during the administration of a Southern-bred President that some still thought a martyr, but its author was James McReynolds—now one of the infamous "Four Horsemen" who had formed a solid bloc against New Deal legislation.[147]

In the brief, but brutal, fight over the court-packing plan, the Justices and the country got a good look at the Court's core constituency: the anti-Roosevelt and often anti-Semitic Liberty League, the nativist Daughters of the American Revolution, big business organizations like the U.S. Chamber of Commerce and the National Association of Manufacturers, small-town Babbitts associated with the Constitutional Government Committee and the Kiwanis Club, beer-swilling jingoists down at the American Legion, and Southerners who saw the Court as a bastion of white supremacy.[148] Whatever their motives, these people and others with no axe to grind had principled objections to Roosevelt's proposal.[149] Even those opposed to everything the Court then stood for were concerned about setting a precedent that might be exploited by a

144. Asquith's threat

Leuchtenburg, Franklin D. Roosevelt and The New Deal, 1932–1940, 1963, p. 232.

145. Found in the files

Manchester, The Glory and The Dream, 1974, p. 151; Leuchtenburg, The Supreme Court Reborn, 1995, p. 120.

146. "Justice has suffered"

Ibid.

147. Author McReynolds

Ibid.; Manchester, The Glory and The Dream, 1974, p. 151; Leuchtenburg,

Franklin D. Roosevelt and The New Deal, 1932–1940, 1963, p. 232.

148. White supremacy

Leuchtenburg, The Supreme Court Reborn, 1995, p. 137, 139; Manchester, The Glory and The Dream, 1974, p. 151.

149. Principled objections

Leuchtenburg, The Supreme Court Reborn, 1995, pp. 137–140.

reactionary President.[150] A few were concerned with crippling a body that might in the future protect civil liberties other than the right to work children in coalmines.[151] But what probably swung the balance for the Court was its role in the secular religion of American nationalism, the myth of neutrality and the be-robed ritual that surrounded it.[152] The legal profession, the keepers of the flame, rallied to the cause.[153] Charles E. Clark of Yale was the only law dean to testify in defense of Roosevelt's plan; many other prominent legal academics either supported the Court or remained silent.[154]

Some writers have thought that confrontation values such as openness played a role in the struggle.[155] Some people thought it

150. Setting a precedent

Leuchtenburg, Franklin D. Roosevelt and The New Deal, 1932–1940, 1963, p. 235.

151. Protect civil liberties

Ibid.; Leuchtenburg, The Supreme Court Reborn, 1995, p. 139.

152. Myth of neutrality

Id. at p. 138; Manchester, The Glory and The Dream, 1974, p. 150.

153. Rallied to cause

Leuchtenburg, The Supreme Court Reborn, 1995, p. 141.

154. Supported or remained silent

Schick, Learned Hand's Court, 1970, p. 9. Among the prominent no-shows was Felix Frankfurter. A biographer infers that his silence meant he, too, opposed the plan. Baker, Felix Frankfurter, 1969, pp. 181–183. William O. Douglas, with his usual generosity toward his foes, claims that Frankfurter said nothing because he expected to be appointed to one of the vacancies and did not want to harm his chances for confirmation. Douglas, Go East, Young Man, 1979, p. 327.

155. Confrontation values

Roosevelt might have expected these values to be employed. Earlier, in the run-up to one of the cases in which

the Supreme Court rebuffed him, the President had sought to fire the Chairman of the Federal Trade Commission, William E. Humphrey, who when last we met him was turning the F.T.C. into an ally of business rather than "a publicity bureau to spread socialist propaganda." Leuchtenburg, The Supreme Court Reborn, 1995, p. 54.

After receiving his pink slip, Humphrey wrote the President a letter that is a virtual thesaurus of the words used to describe those who offend the confrontation values. According to him, his adversaries "are character assassins. They stab only in the back and in the dark. This same collection of political hypocrites tried twice to defeat my confirmation * * *. These insurgents are too cowardly and dishonest to accept the verdict of an open and honorable fight, and now to accomplish their purpose, they come with slanderous and polluted lips and spew their putrid filth upon you under a pledge of secrecy."

If the reference to "the verdict" does not suffice to show the source of the values, Humphrey also wrote: "I must presume that the charges made were given to you under seal of secrecy and that you feel honor bound to regard them as such. I cannot think of any other reason for your refusal to give

was hypocritical—"two-faced"—for Roosevelt to disguise a political ruse as a principled program to improve the efficiency of the judiciary.[156] Many legislators thought that the secrecy that surrounded the hatching of the plan was an effort to avoid an adversary confrontation with members of Congress who would bear the brunt of defending the plan, thus depriving the President of ideas that might have made the plan more acceptable.[157] Roosevelt was accused of "deviousness" and a "lack of candor" that "verged on deceit."[158] Particularly poignant in terms of the rhetoric that would be employed later to characterize the events of December 7, 1941, it was said the President "gave the impression of sneaking up on the Nine Old Men"; to use the words that John Randolph had applied to Martin Van Buren, Roosevelt "rowed to his object with muffled oars."[159] Indeed, even Attorney General Cummings was uncomfortable, telling a confidant, "I feel too much like a conspirator."[160]

As an example of what might have been avoided had the President been less conspiratorial and shared his plan with some friendly adversaries, consider his ill-advised attempt to equate age with inefficiency.[161] In his message accompanying the plan, Roosevelt (ironically, in the name of "frank discussion") addressed the "question of aged or infirm judges."[162] In expostulating on this theme, the President said the aged "are often unable to perceive their own infirmities."[163] He continued: "[a] lower mental or physical vigor leads man to avoid an examination of complicated and changed conditions."[164] While the message did attempt to qualify this stereotypical coupling of ideological conservatism with senility, the "geezer" faction in Congress and the press had great fun in

me an opportunity to meet these charges. These certain insurgents are cowards. They will not fight like men." Id. at p. 62.

156. Disguise ruse

Leuchtenburg, Franklin D. Roosevelt and The New Deal, 1932–1940, 1963, p. 233.

157. Made more acceptable

Id. at pp. 233–234.

158. "Verged on deceit"

Manchester, The Glory and The Dream, 1974, p. 150.

159. "Muffled oars"

Ibid.

160. "Like a conspirator"

Id. at p. 151.

161. Age with inefficiency

Leuchtenburg, Franklin Roosevelt and The New Deal, 1932–1940, 1963, p. 233.

162. "Aged or infirm judges"

Leuchtenburg, The Supreme Court Reborn, 1995, p. 133.

163. "Unable to perceive"

Id. at p. 134.

164. "Changed conditions"

Ibid.

attacking the generalizations and ignoring the qualifications, pointing, for example, to the President's firmest supporter on the Court, the then-eighty-year-old Louis Brandeis.[165]

If the Supreme Court as a body was politically inept, it was headed by a man who was Roosevelt's equal at political wheeling and dealing, having also been the Governor of New York and a presidential candidate. Chief Justice Charles Evans Hughes was not about to let the Court be manhandled on his watch; he prepared a point-by-point rebuttal of Roosevelt's spurious justifications, then persuaded both Brandeis and Van Devanter to endorse his conclusions.[166] Hughes then delivered the letter to Senator Burton K. Wheeler, the lapsed Progressive who was leading the fight against court packing, on the eve of the opening of Senate hearings on the plan.[167] When Wheeler read the letter to the Senate Judiciary Committee, "[y]ou could have heard a pin drop in the caucus room," he later recalled.[168]

Then on March 29, 1937, "White Monday," the Court dropped a bombshell rather than a pin; it upheld by a 5–4 vote a revised version of a New Deal statute it had struck down on "Black Monday" two years earlier.[169] Even more surprising, in what one Congressman called "the Greatest Constitutional Somersault in History," the Court, again 5–4, upheld a Washington wages-and-hours statute virtually identical to the New York statute it had invalidated less than a year before in Tipaldo.[170] Two weeks later the Court upheld the National Labor Relations Act and on May 24 it validated Social Security.[171] Liberty of contract was dead; the

---

165. "Geezer" faction attacking

Id. at p. 138; Leuchtenburg, Franklin D. Roosevelt and The New Deal, 1932–1940, 1963, p. 233.

166. Endorse his conclusions

Manchester, The Glory and the Dream, 1974, p. 152.

167. Gave to Wheeler

Ibid. For a different version of how the letter came to be written, see Leuchtenburg, Franklin D. Roosevelt and The New Deal, 1932–1940, 1963, p. 237 (claiming the letter was in response to inquiry from Wheeler).

168. "Heard pin drop"

Manchester, The Glory and The Dream, 1974, p. 152; Leuchtenburg, The Supreme Court Reborn, 1995, pp. 140–141.

169. "White Monday"

Id. at p. 178.

170. "Greatest Somersault"

Id. at p. 176. West Coast Hotel Co. v. Parrish, 1937, 57 S.Ct. 578, 300 U.S. 379, 81 L.Ed. 703.

171. Validated Social Security

Id. at pp. 142. The cases are NRLB v. Jones & Laughlin Steel Corp., 1937, 57 S.Ct. 615, 301 U.S. 1, 81 L.Ed. 893,

Court would not strike down state or federal socioeconomic regulations for a long time.[172]

Since Justice Roberts was the swing vote, he received most of the attention over what Thomas Reed Powell, a constitutional law professor at Harvard, called "the switch in time that saved nine."[173] As one New Dealer put it, "Owen Roberts * * * had amended the Constitution of the United States by nodding his head instead of shaking it. The lives of millions were changed by this nod."[174] Those who want to save the myth of judicial autonomy like to point out that Roberts had voted to reverse Tipaldo before Roosevelt had even announced his court-packing plan.[175] But this seems beside the point; the President had made it clear for some time that he was going to do something and it was clear that the majority of the country wanted something done and had given the Democrats the votes to do it.[176] As one critic explained the Court's behavior, it had been baptized "in the waters of public opinion."[177] Professor Felix Frankfurter, soon to benefit from "the switch," worried about its effect on his ability to instill respect for the Court in his law students.[178] But later he conceded that perhaps FDR was following the wisdom of his cousin Teddy, who once said "I may not know much about law, but I do know one can put the fear of God into judges."[179] Without entering into the always murky question of

and Chas C. Steward Machine Co. v. Davis, 1937, 57 S.Ct. 883, 301 U.S. 548, 81 L.Ed. 1279.

172. For a long time

Id. at p. 216.

173. "Switch in time"

Id. at p. 177; Fiss, History of the Supreme Court of the United States: Troubled Beginnings of the Modern State, 1888–1910, 1993, p. 8 (attributes to Powell).

174. "Changed by nod"

Leuchtenburg, The Supreme Court Reborn, 1995, p. 176. For other comments, see id. at p. 177.

175. Before announced

Ibid.

176. Votes to do it

Manchester, The Glory and The Dream, 1974, pp. 150–151.

177. "Waters of public opinion"

Leuchtenburg, The Supreme Court Reborn, 1995, p. 143 (collecting other comments).

178. Instill respect

"What kind of respect do you think one can instill in law students for the process of the Court when things like this can happen?" Id. at p. 176. One answer might be: "a more realistic respect that does not assume that the Court can do no wrong."

179. "Fear of God into judges"

Bickel & Schmidt, History of the Supreme Court of the United States: The Judiciary and Responsible Government, 1910–21, 1984, p. 24.

causation, one can say that the court-packing plan provided the occasion for some members of the Court, and not only Justice Roberts, to think about the consequences of their rulings for the Court and the country.[180]

Whatever its cause, "the switch" did in fact "save nine."[181] When Justice Van Devanter announced that he was retiring, the court-packing plan was dead.[182] Within the next two-and-a-half years, President Roosevelt was able to appoint his own majority to the Court.[183] We need not follow all the political machinations and face-saving maneuvers that accompanied the burial of Roosevelt's scheme.[184] But a word about the consequences may be in order.

Historians concern themselves with the political consequences; that Roosevelt squandered the fruits of his electoral victory in the battle with the Court, divided the Democratic Party, and alienated "middle class" voters.[185] Moreover, it has been argued that by foregoing the less certain and more time consuming alternative of constitutional amendment, Roosevelt left the institutional changes of the New Deal vulnerable to subsequent political changes, whether in Congress or the Court.[186] However, we are concerned with

180. Think about consequences

Leuchtenburg, The Supreme Court Reborn, 1995, p. 177 (collecting speculation about causation).

181. "Save nine"

Manchester, The Glory and The Dream, 1974, pp. 152–153.

182. Plan dead

Leuchtenburg, Franklin D. Roosevelt and The New Deal, 1932–1940, 1963, p. 237; Leuchtenburg, The Supreme Court Reborn, 1995, p. 143.

183. Appoint own majority

Id. at p. 154; Leuchtenburg, Franklin D. Roosevelt and The New Deal, 1932–1940, 1963, p. 238.

184. Political machinations

Id. at p. 238; Leuchtenburg, The Supreme Court Reborn, 1995, pp. 142–149.

185. Alienated "middle class"

Id. at pp. 157–159. We do note one consequence historians have not—the vindication of the Court. To the extent that the New Deal measures held unconstitutional were sought to be justified by the need to get the economy moving again, the majority of the Court were empirically correct; once the New Deal got its way constitutionally, it did no better with the economy than it had when the Court was restraining it. This is not to say that the New Deal measures were not justified on other grounds or that the Court was right in its earlier invalidations.

186. Subsequent changes

Kyvig, Explicit and Authentic Acts, 1996, pp. 314, 481. For a detailed look at the amendments proposed and the debate over whether or not to seek amendments, see id. at pp. 296–306.

only one of these structural changes—the increase in the power of the federal government.[187] When these powers were brought to bear on radical dissenters during the Second Red Scare, they opened the door to the reinvigoration of the Confrontation Clause. Moreover, though the Court ceased to monitor federal socioeconomic regulations, a similar "hands-off" attitude did not apply to the states; this probably made it easier for the Court to begin its interventions into the state criminal justice systems to enforce the rights of the accused.[188]

But for the purposes of confrontation, the most momentous consequence of the "switch in time" was a change in the Court's conception of its "constituency."[189] In the jargon of political science, the "constituency" of an institution refers to the group or groups outside the institution whose interests it serves and to which the institution looks to for ideas, values, and for political support against its enemies.[190] From the end of the Civil War down to 1937, the Supreme Court's constituency consisted largely, if not exclusively, of the business community and the elite law firms and law schools that served the business community.[191] With the decline of the Fourteenth Amendment as a protection of private property, the Court's ability to serve that community declined.[192] It may also be the case that the behavior of the Court's constituency during the New Deal made that constituency less attractive to the Court.[193] If the Court proved unable to protect the business community in its

187. Increase in power

Leuchtenburg, The Supreme Court Reborn, 1995, p. 213.

188. Not to states

Id. at p. 225 (statistics on Court's invalidation of state legislation after 1937).

189. "Constituency"

No claim is made that, to the extent this was a conscious process, the Court thought about it in these terms.

190. Against its enemies

Alas, it has been so long since we studied political science that we are at a loss to say where we learned this useful concept or even if it is still part of the lingo. The reader may, however, be sure that the term is much richer than the one-sentence squib above makes it seem.

191. Business community

We do not assert or imply that service to its constituency was the only cause of the behavior of the Court or its members, then or now. However, among the many determinants of judicial behavior, the change in constituency strikes us as most salient in discussing the Court's behavior after 1937.

192. As protection of property

Id. at p. 225.

193. Less attractive

Joe Tipaldo was hardly a poster-boy for benevolent capitalism, id. at p. 166, but seeing the uses to which he was prepared to put "liberty of contract" may have allowed judges to glimpse the reality behind more genteel versions of "wage slavery."

hour of greatest need, the same might be said of the ability of the business community to support the Court.[194] Moreover, the Court might well think that the business community asked too much of the Court when it continued to ask the Court to strike down legislation that seemed to have the support of an overwhelming majority of the voters.[195] Finally, at the subconstitutional level, the Court's need and ability to serve business interests through its development of a "federal common law" was drastically reduced with the Court's later decision in Erie Railroad v. Tomkins.[196]

If the reader has followed us so far, then perhaps she will understand what we mean when we say that during the period of after World War II, the Court sought, with varying degrees of success to construct a "moral constituency" to replace the "constituency of interest" it had served prior to 1937.[197] The Court's rulings began to favor the less advantaged members of society— what in Roman Catholic theology would be called a "preferential option for the poor."[198] In the 1930s this meant that the Court only had to stop using the Due Process Clause to protect the wealthy and allow the other branches to adopt redistributive policies; but by the 1960s the Court began to act affirmatively to protect those persons and interests disfavored by the market economy.[199] For example, in Gideon v. Wainwright, the Court held that states were obligated to provide "the assistance of counsel" mentioned in the

194. Ability to support

The fact that the Court, which for more than a century had viewed the wealthy as the minority most in need of protection from electoral majorities, now felt compelled to abandon that minority provides a cautionary tale for those who would chastise the Court for not being more willing to go to the mat for far weaker constituencies in later years.

195. Asked too much

This is the jurisprudential equivalent of a common marital dispute: "if you love me, how can you refuse?" against "if you love me, how can you ask?"

196. Erie decision

1938, 58 S.Ct. 817, 304 U.S. 64, 82 L.Ed. 1188.

197. "Moral constituency"

We do not claim this is an original insight. It is made, albeit without employing the concept of "constituency," in Leuchtenburg, The Supreme Court Reborn, 1995, p. 235.

198. Favor less advantaged

Id. at p. 154.

199. Disfavored by market

A good, though certainly not the only, example is segregation in housing. From the point of view of property owners, realtors, and developers, refusing to sell to nonwhites in white neighborhoods could be market-justified, even if the market was not the only or predominant reason for racial discrimination in housing.

Sixth Amendment to those who could not afford to pay a lawyer's fee.[200]

In seeking a moral constituency, the Court sought to appeal not to self-interest but to self-image; not "do this because someday you may need to have it done for you" but "do this because this is the kind of person you are and it will make the kind of nation we want to become."[201] Trying to force, cajole, or prod Americans to live up to their professed ideals in the face of a consumerist culture whose message was "you can have it all" was to prove as difficult, if not more difficult, than trying to protect a wealthy minority who feared the use of the ballot box to expropriate their property.[202] In large part this was because self-interest is, or can be made to appear, certain; ideals and values are vague and contested.[203] But even though the Court was to fail in its effort to develop a moral constituency, it deserves credit for sparking a dialogue on American values of the sort probably not seen since the battle over ratification of the Constitution.[204]

Now the customary caveats. First, we do not mean to claim that judges prior to 1937 were immoral or amoral.[205] During the Antebellum era—and for some years thereafter—the United States was economically, culturally, and to a lesser extent politically, an

200. Gideon case

1963, 83 S.Ct. 792, 372 U.S. 335, 9 L.Ed.2d 799.

201. "Want to become"

This, so far as we can tell, has not been the predominant rhetoric in civil-liberties adjudication or teaching. In keeping with the individualist ethos, the focus is on the individual who is the recipient of the rights and not the collective that grants them.

202. "Have it all"

This was in fact a slogan used in a television commercial during the "Me Decade" but it is the underlying premise of many advertisements that are less revealing. It is a tribute to the power of advertising that we can no longer recall the product being sold so the reader will have to take our word for it.

203. Contested

Even people who agree that slavery was evil and eradicating its vestiges is good can still disagree about what this means in a specific controversy; e.g., law-school admissions.

204. Debate about values

We do not claim that the Court's earlier decisions did not spark debates about values that were even more vociferous than those in the post-World War II era; e.g., the controversy over slavery. Rather, the later debates were far more comprehensive in terms of the values involved.

205. Amoral

"Thou shalt not steal" is a moral precept; but we suppose that even those who view redistributive government policies as theft by ballot would agree that it is not the only value that can be found in the Constitution.

English colony.[206] Judges could well suppose that the development of a national economy was necessary if the nation was going to survive and obtain the economic independence needed to work out the promise of its founding documents.[207] In the latter half of the Nineteenth Century, the struggle for economic independence merged with the drive to industrialize what had been an agricultural society.[208] As the earlier example of England and the later example of Soviet Russia suggest, forcing farmers off their land and into factories necessarily requires hardship, if not brutality.[209] One could certainly argue that prolonging the process was no favor to those who had to pass through the wringer of industrialization and might have well put the goal in jeopardy—and failure meant that the brutality and suffering would have been for naught.[210]

Second, we do not claim that 1937 marked some sort of jurisprudential epiphany. Individual judges, and sometimes the Court itself, had attempted to give meaning to the moral and political values of the Bill of Rights in earlier times.[211] Moreover, in the remaining pages of this section we will show how events after "the switch in time" moved the Court in the direction it was to take under Earl Warren.[212] But we do claim that the direction that the Court embarked upon in 1937 provided an opportunity as well as the need to build support from those segments of society that the Court had previously ignored—when it was not warring upon

206. English colony

See § 6355, text at notecall 357.

207. Necessary to survive

This is similar to the argument made for denial of civil liberties during war or other national dangers.

208. Drive to industrialize

See § 6356.

209. Brutality

The fact that in one case the brutality was the part of a deliberate government policy and in the other two was the product of market forces does not alter the nature of the suffering. Demonstrations against enclosures in England and farm-mortgage foreclosures in the United States and against forced collectivization in Stalin's Russia differ in many ways but they are alike in that in each case agriculturalists were seeking to preserve a way of life inconsistent with massive industrialization.

210. For naught

We do not suggest that these arguments were advanced or that we would agree with them; our only point is that there were moral arguments to support the Court's constitutional jurisprudence prior to 1937.

211. Earlier time

Leuchtenburg, The Supreme Court Reborn, 1995, p. 230.

212. After World War II

For statistics demonstrating the change, see id. at p. 235.

them.[213] Whether the Justices saw it this way or not, if the Court was to rise above the interests of caste and class, it would have to develop a constituency capable of doing the same thing.[214]

Finally, we do not claim that the quest for moral constituency was the only thing or even the predominant task the Court set for itself during the post-War years. With the national government now assuming much of the burden the Court had carried under Swift v. Tyson, the Court still had a docket full of cases that resembled those of the state courts—cases requiring interpretation of statutes, filling the gaps they left, and other subconstitutional tasks. Our only claim is that the desire to create a moral constituency does much to explain the rise of confrontation jurisprudence after nearly two centuries of desuetude.

The aftermath of "the Constitutional Revolution of 1937" produced a significant political confrontation.[215] When Justice Van Devanter retired, President Roosevelt, in attempt to flummox expected conservative opposition to liberalization of the Court, appointed Senator Hugo Black of Alabama to the vacant seat.[216] The opposition to Black invoked confrontation values, particularly the separation of functions; Black was said to lack judicial temperament because he was "a prosecutor and not a judge."[217] This opinion was based on Black's reputation during congressional investigations; even his admirers conceded that in his interrogations he "was relentless as a terrier pursuing a rat."[218] A political scientist later summed up the complaints against Black's inquisitorial practices this way: "Senator Black in 1936 was the kind of

213. Direction embarked upon

Kyvig, Explicit and Authentic Acts, 1996, p. 290.

214. Develop a constituency

We take it that this is one of the subtexts of the allusions to the events of 1937 in opinions dissenting from the Court's opinions during the Warren Court's expansion of protections for criminal defendants.

215. "Revolution of 1937"

Leuchtenburg, The Supreme Court Reborn, 1995, p. 213.

216. Appointed Black

Id. at p. 184. On the theory that knowledge of their own colleagues makes it unnecessary, the Senate customarily approves the nomination of one of its number without conducting a hearing into the nominee's fitness. Roosevelt apparently assumed that once the first olive was out of the bottle, the rest would follow more easily. Since Black's appointment would give the New Deal a 6–3 majority on the Court, resistance to increasing that number would be less fervid.

217. "Not a judge"

Id. at p. 185.

218. "Relentless as a terrier"

Ibid. (quoting William O. Douglas).

legislator Justice Black had no use for twenty years later."[219] As this quotation implies, Black brought the fervor of a convert to the Court's attempt to limit the excesses of the Second Red Scare.

The NAACP and the Socialist Party had a different objection to the Black nomination; his presumed lack of commitment, if not opposition, to the civil rights of African–Americans based upon his membership in the Ku Klux Klan and his conduct as a Senator regarding anti-lynching legislation and the Scottsboro case.[220] The nominee, pursuant to the practice that then obtained, did not appear before the Senate Judiciary Committee to confront these charges, his supporters minimized them, and he was easily confirmed.[221] However, less than a month later, a series of articles by an investigative reporter for a Pittsburgh newspaper described evidence of Black's relationship with the KKK that was far more serious than his detractors had claimed, including a suggestion that Black was still a member.[222]

The public reaction to these charges, though probably fueled as much by resentment of Black's liberalism as by opposition to racism or the Klan, called for some response.[223] Perhaps because it was thought inconsistent with his role as a member of the Court, Black chose to refute the charges in a venue where he could not be subject to cross-examination.[224] In a radio address of eleven minutes carried by all three networks to the largest audience for any speech by an American during the decade, Black made his defense.[225] Although historians have found the defense unconvincing and the newspapers of the time even less so, public-opinion polls showed that 56% of their respondents rejected the demand, made most vociferously by Catholics, that Black should resign from the

219. "Had no use for"

Ibid.

220. Scottsboro case

Id. at p. 188.

221. Easily confirmed

Id. at p. 190.

222. Still a member

Id. at pp. 191–192.

223. Called for response

Id. at pp. 192–195.

224. Not subject to cross

The alternative explanation is that Black, knowing full well the way such questioning could be abused, was reluctant to face confrontation. This was the construction put on his dodging of reporters' questions—though not as starkly as it has been put here. Id. at p. 196.

225. Made his defense

Id. at pp. 196–197. Black's address outdrew any of FDR's speeches; only the abdication of Edward VIII drew more listeners.

Court.[226]

Next to the more dramatic events of 1937, two cases that mark the Court's stance regarding civil liberties at the time of "the switch in time" seem pale by comparison.[227] In De Jonge v. Oregon, the Court reversed the conviction under the state's criminal-syndicalism law of a Communist candidate for mayor for organizing a protest against antiunion police brutality.[228] In the process, the Court incorporated the First Amendment "right of peaceable assembly" into the Due Process Clause of the Fourteenth Amendment.[229] However, when the argument was made that the double-jeopardy protections of the Fifth Amendment should be similarly incorporated, the Court drew the line in Palko v. Connecticut.[230]

A cynic might say that the difference between the two cases is that as members of "the chattering class" the Court thought that infringements on speech were more important than the practice of retrying criminal defendants when the state's own agents erred in the conduct of the first trial.[231] However, Justice Cardozo has to disguise the point in the kind of airy eloquence that moves the

226. Respondents rejected

Id. at p. 199. Some of the criticisms of historians have an air of anachronism about them; e.g., Black's use of the "some-of-my-best-friends-are" defense may have been less hackneyed in 1937 than it was later to become because in those days it was not common for WASPs to have Catholic, Jewish, or African–American friends as Black claimed he did. However, the other criticisms of Black's addresses are of the sort that Black would probably have corrected had he expected to be cross-examined; e.g., failure to say why he had remained silent when the accusations were first made and failed to disavow the activities of the Klan during the time that he was a member. Id. at p. 197.

227. Mark Court's stance

Id. at pp. 249–250.

228. De Jonge

1937, 57 S.Ct. 255, 299 U.S. 353, 81 L.Ed. 278.

229. Incorporated

Id. at 260, 299 U.S. at 364.

230. Palko case

1937, 58 S.Ct. 149, 302 U.S. 319, 82 L.Ed. 288.

231. Agents erred

The grounds the state relied upon for retrying the defendant were that the trial judge erred in the admission of evidence and instructions to the jury. He had been found guilty of second-degree murder but upon retrial was found guilty of first degree murder. Id. at 149–150, 302 U.S. at 320–322.

Those who think the parody in the text is wide of the mark should compare what Cardozo says about the insignificance of the rights of the accused with this panegyric to free speech: "neither liberty nor justice would exist if [it] were sacrificed. * * * one may say that it is the matrix, the indispensable condition, of nearly every other form of freedom." Id. at 152, 302 U.S. at 327.

feather-headed.[232] In a reprise of his Snyder opinion, Cardozo restates all of the provisions of the Bill of Rights that the Court had held that states could abolish without offending due process, but this time suggesting that abolition of the privilege against self-incrimination might be a good idea.[233] The right to trial by jury and other features of the adversary system found in the Sixth Amendment deserve no protection according to Cardozo because "they are not of the very essence of a scheme of ordered liberty."[234] It would be "narrow and provincial," he says, to suppose "that a fair and enlightened system would be impossible without them."[235] It was apparent that the Court had a long way to go before it would take the adversary system seriously.[236]

The New Deal, Ideology, and Un–Americanism

In 1938, the economy was still going nowhere.[237] Going back to Teddy Roosevelt for answers, the administration turned Thurman Arnold loose on a new round of "trust-busting."[238] Acts like this make one wonder whether the New Deal was truly "pragmatic" or whether it was just floundering.[239] If "pragmatic" suggests a scientific experimentalism in which ideas were tried out, their results

---

232. Airy eloquence

E.g., that after Connecticut was allowed retrial at the instance of the state for errors of the state judiciary (a practice forbidden by the Fifth Amendment and similar constitutional provisions in every other state): "There is here no seismic innovation. The edifice of justice stands, its symmetry, to many, greater than before." Id. at 153, 302 U.S. at 328.

233. Good idea

Id. at 152, 302 U.S. at 325–326. Cardozo also borrows from Snyder his "tyranny of labels" argument and the claim that the state should have equal rights to those afforded the accused. Id. at 153, 302 U.S. at 328.

234. "Very essence"

Id. at 152, 302 U.S. at 325.

235. "Narrow and provincial"

Id. at 152, 302 U.S. at 325.

236. Take seriously

The Founders knew they were being "narrow and provincial" in rejecting the inquisitorial system, but having had some experience with the civil law in admiralty, they had a different view than Cardozo as to whether it was a "fair and enlightened system."

237. Going nowhere

The stock market was down by 50 points from the prior August and the Republicans made gains in the off-year elections. But on the bright side, the number of golfers was up. Encyclopedia of American Facts and Dates, Ninth ed. 1993, pp. 498, 499, 501. See also, Leuchtenburg, Franklin D. Roosevelt and The New Deal, 1932–1940, 1963, p. 263.

238. "Trust-busting"

Id. at p. 259.

239. "Pragmatic" or floundering

Id. at p. 344.

measured, and generalizations to support future action developed, the New Deal does not qualify.[240] Apparently for the New Dealers, "pragmatic" meant nothing more than "non-ideological," absence of method posing as method.[241] At first it seems paradoxical to describe the New Deal as "non-ideological" because the campaigns of 1932 and 1936 were probably more partisan than any since the Bryan crusade of 1896.[242] Rather than the traditional "Republicrat Party," two different factions of the business community that had contested the prior presidential elections, the New Deal seemed to promise a return to a truly adversarial politics.[243] Instead, wittingly or not, the New Deal was a forerunner of modern image politics in which the two wings of the business party compete less with programs than with personalities, where the "sound bite" and the "30 second spot" replace the Lincoln–Douglas debates.[244] If the adversariness of politics is a sham, it is easier to believe that the adversary system in court is also largely a pretense.

In large part, the New Deal was less interested in restoring the two-party system than it was in restoring the economy—this, after all, is what had been promised the voters. Yet with the ideological left suspect and the modern state just being built, all they had to work with were.business ideas and institutions; whether this was what they had intended or not, the New Deal ended up being "the savior of capitalism."[245] "Saving capitalism" required a drastic expansion of the coercive power of the state to enable it to match, regulate, and boost the power of Big Business.[246] Having created the expectation that the federal government would not only move the economy out of this Depression but also take steps to prevent or dampen future economic cycles, the government had to be expanded to monitor and regulate the major elements of one of the

240. Does not qualify

Ibid.

241. "Non-ideological"

Ibid.

242. Since Bryan

Id. at p. 326.

243. Truly adversarial

Since our concern is solely with its effects on confrontation, we need not enter the debate as to whether it is possible or desirable to have parties that are programmatically and ideologically opposites.

244. Replace Lincoln–Douglas

If they were to return today, Lincoln and Douglas would be making their pitch to potential campaign contributors, not to the voters.

245. "Savior of capitalism"

Id. at p. 336.

246. Expansion of coercive power

Id. at p. 633.

world's largest economies.[247] Like the Progressives, the New Deal wanted to govern the economy through experts, not through a democratizing of economic structures; "there is almost nothing, however fantastic, that (given competent organization) a team of engineers, scientists, and administrators cannot do today," wrote one New Dealer.[248]

"Nothing," that is, except develop an ideological defense of reform.[249] The New Deal rhetoric encouraged impulses to group activity, whether one calls these "collectivist," "communitarian," or "social"; but without an ideology to support them, these impulses were left rudderless and easily moved by others who did have an explanatory ideology.[250] A group of social scientists who had studied Muncie, Indiana in 1925 at the height of the Ku Klux Klan influence in that state, returned in 1935 to reassess the community after the battering of the Depression and four years of New Deal rhetoric. They found the people still uttering the same laissez-faire pieties as ten years earlier.[251] Somewhere between "The Lone Ranger" riding the airwaves in America and the lockstep industrial armies marching across Stalinist art, there may have been some other vision of social reform but the New Deal never found it.[252]

Worse yet, the New Dealers managed to pervert the ideals of the Founders with consumerism.[253] Whereas the Founders had thought that a relatively equal distribution of income was essential for a democratically governed republic, the New Deal rejected the notions that "social justice" or a "healthier national life" were

---

247. Created expectation

Id. at p. 335. "Laissez-faire is dead and the modern state has become responsible for the modern economy * * * the task of insuring the continuity of the standard of life for its people." Foner, The Story of American Freedom, 1998, p. 201. (quoting Walter Lippman).

248. "Nothing cannot do"

Leuchtenburg, Franklin D. Roosevelt and The New Deal, 1932–1940, 1963, p. 342.

249. Ideological defense

Id. at p. 273.

250. Left rudderless

Id. at p. 340.

251. Same laissez faire pieties

Id. at p. 273.

252. Other vision

This is ironic because Americans were notorious as a nation of "joiners" and there was no shortage of indigenous, non-capitalist ideas to work with; e.g., the Radical Republicans or the Populists.

253. Consumerism

See, e.g., the Lippman quotation in note 247, above, in which the function of the state is not as an instrument for self-government but a device to obtain a higher standard of living.

relevant.[254] According to Adolph Berle, all the New Deal needed was "the hard-boiled student to work out the simple equation that unless the national income was pretty widely diffused there were not enough customers to keep the plants going."[255] With moral considerations out of the equation, all that was left was "tough-mindedness."[256] The New Deal culture was heavily populated with amoral "tough guys"—Cagney, Bogart, the "Gas House Gang," the "Dead End Kids," and the heroes of Dashiell Hammett.[257] This association of masculinity with lack of moral concern was a mixed blessing for the adversary system and confrontation.[258]

Their own lack of ideology did not make the New Deal unconcerned with other people's thoughts; 1937 was the year in which the House Un–American Activities Committee was created.[259] Apparently many of its supporters thought of the committee as antifascist as well, but the committee devoted the overwhelming portion of its work to communists.[260] From the beginning, H.U.A.C. developed the pattern that was to make it famous during the Second Red Scare; allowing witnesses to make unsubstantiated charges without giving the accused any chance to reply.[261] In its first few days of hearings, witnesses claimed that 640 organizations, 483 newspapers, and 280 labor unions were advancing communism.[262] Although few thought much of the inclusion of elements of the Popular Front as "communistic," calling Roman Catholic organizations, the Boy Scouts, and the Campfire Girls by that name opened the committee to ridicule.[263] When one witness pointed out

254. "Social justice"

Id. at p. 338.

255. "Not enough customers"

Ibid.

256. "Tough-mindedness"

Ibid. As many have suggested, this was partly an overreaction to Teddy Roosevelt and Woodrow Wilson, both of whom larded their politics with simple-minded morality.

257. "Tough guys"

Ibid. As we shall see, not all of them proved to be so tough when faced with hostile cross-examination by Congressional inquisitors during the Second Red Scare.

258. Mixed blessing

As we have previously seen, the adversary system and confrontation have individualist roots, but they also depend heavily on moral principles and ethical restraint. Ignoring the moral basis of confrontation leaves only the inadequate instrumental rationale.

259. H.U.A.C. created

Id. at p. 280.

260. Devoted to communists

Ibid.

261. Without chance to reply

Ibid.

262. Advancing communism

Ibid.

263. Ridicule

Foner, The Story of American Freedom, 1998, p. 217.

that Shirley Temple had lent her name to some Popular Front groups, Secretary of the Interior Ickes laughed at "a burly Congressman leading a posse comitatus in a raid upon Shirley Temple's nursery to collect her dolls as evidence of her implication in a Red Plot."[264] However, the committee would soon cease to be a laughing matter.

One might say that 1939 was a "worldly" year. New York and San Francisco opened competing "World's Fairs."[265] Hitler marched into Czechoslovakia and the pro-Nazi American ambassador to England, Joseph Kennedy, urged that the Slavic peoples be written off.[266] Joseph Stalin did something like that when he entered into a Non–Aggression pact with Hitler, who promptly invaded Poland without a declaration of war—what would be called a "sneak attack" when the Japanese did it two years later.[267] France and England did declare it and World War II began.[268] In the misnamed "Neutrality Act of 1939," Congress lifted a ban on the export of armaments.[269] The boomlet in the arms industry produced an upturn in the economy—the first proof of the validity of an economic theory known as "military Keynesianism."[270]

264. "Dolls as evidence"

Leuchtenburg, Franklin D. Roosevelt and The New Deal, 1932–1940, 1963, p. 280.

265. "World's Fairs"

Encyclopedia of American Facts and Dates, Ninth ed. 1993, p. 503.

266. Slavics be written off

Leuchtenburg, Franklin D. Roosevelt and The New Deal, 1932–1940, 1963, pp. 287–288. The failure of the Western powers to resist Hitler, usually characterized as "appeasement" was one of those "lessons of history" that was to be invoked to justify wars for the rest of the Century. As these lines were being written supporters of war in the Balkans were repeating this argument.

267. Invaded Poland

Manchester, The Glory and The Dream, 1974, p. 201; Encyclopedia of American Facts and Dates, Ninth ed. 1993, p. 564.

268. World War II began

Ibid.

269. "Neutrality Act"

There was nothing "neutral" about the purpose of the Act; it was designed to aid the Allies. Leuchtenburg, Franklin D. Roosevelt and The New Deal, 1932–1940, 1963, p. 295. However, it did have some provisions insisted upon by those who opposed war, usually called "isolationists" by those who favored U.S. entrance into the War.

270. "Military Keynesianism"

Encyclopedia of American Facts and Dates, Ninth ed. 1993, p. 503. John Maynard Keynes was an English economist who argued that the way to relieve economic depression was by what came to be known as "pump-priming"; that is, entrance of the Government into the economy to purchase goods or services. Though Keynes had in mind government public-works projects, such as building roads and

Meanwhile, in another world entirely, Orson Welles proved the power of the new electronic media (television having been invented several years earlier).[271] On October 30, 1939, Welles' Mercury Theatre on CBS broadcast a dramatization of H.G. Wells' "War of the Worlds."[272] Though it was announced several times that it was a dramatization, the program was presented with all the features of a news broadcast, including remotes from locations where the Martians were supposedly landing and comments from fictional government officials and experts.[273] The show produced a brief nationwide panic.[274] A later academic study estimated that nearly two million listeners had believed the show to be a true news broadcast despite the improbability of the "news" presented.[275] Welles had inadvertently demonstrated both the power and the limitations of electronic confrontation, though as the response to the television program "The X–Files" sixty years later suggests, the lesson was lost on many people.[276]

Welles' fake drew on the reality that CBS had, during the Munich crisis earlier in the year began the practice of live radio coverage of events in Europe.[277] After a CBS broadcast of a Nazi

schools, these proved to be unpopular voters who did not want tax dollars used for this purpose. However, if this could be justified for "national defense," only diehard "isolationists" or pacifists could protest.

271. Television invented

The first television broadcast was in 1927, starring Herbert Hoover. Encyclopedia of American Facts and Dates, Ninth ed. 1993, p. 467.

272. "War of the Worlds"

Manchester, The Glory and The Dream, 1974, p. 190.

273. Fictional experts

Id. at p. 191.

274. National panic

It was later discovered that while Welles's show only had about 4% of the audience, the vast majority of the audience was listening to a variety show featuring the ventriloquist's dummy, "Charlie McCarthy," but picked up Welles's show when turning

around the dial during commercials, thus missing the warnings about the fictional nature of the news broadcast. Id. at p. 192.

275. Improbability of news

Id. at p. 194. For long extracts from the script of the show, see id. at pp. 192–194.

276. "X–Files"

For those who will read this after the show has been forgotten, the premise of the program is that the government is an elaborate conspiracy to conceal evidence of alien invasions by flying saucers and the reality of paranormal psychological powers. A small, but significant number of people believed that the show was loosely based on fact. The program employs just enough instances of real governmental abuses to make the fictional ones seem plausible.

277. Began live coverage

Id. at p. 179.

rally at Nuremberg, a trade paper said of Hitler: "[a] dynamic, spellbinding speaker, the broadcast was most impressive when he worked up the thousands of Nazis in attendance to frenzied cheers, 'Heil Hitlers' and 'Seig Heils' * * *."[278] Those who could understand German found Hitler's ranting less impressive and the sound of his voice made the words more chilling than they appeared in print.[279] Thus, while the broadcast's immediacy gave it some of the impact of live confrontation, it also showed how that immediacy could be manipulated.

Hitler's broadcast came at a time when fascism was on the rise in America.[280] Hitler's emphasis on the need for discipline and family values appealed to American fundamentalists who believed that the Depression was divine punishment for the hedonism of the 1920s.[281] But Hitler also appealed to people who claimed to know better. Nicholas Murray Butler, the President of Columbia University, proclaimed that fascist regimes produced "men of far greater intelligence, far stronger character, and far more courage than the system of elections" that prevailed in America.[282] William Randolph Hearst told readers of his newspapers that whenever "you hear a prominent American called a 'Fascist', you can usually make up your mind that the man is simply a loyal citizen who stands up for Americanism."[283]

While "fascism" might have been thrown around a bit too loosely, it did not have quite the same effect on those who were defining "Un–Americanism" as did the word "communist."[284] The F.B.I. reopened its surveillance of radicals that Attorney General Stone had ordered closed during the prior decade.[285] College administrators at some of the nation's most prestigious universities

278. "Spellbinding speaker"
Id. at p. 180.

279. More chilling
Id. at p. 181.

280. Fascism on the rise
Leuchtenburg, Franklin D. Roosevelt and The New Deal, 1932–1940, 1963, pp. 276–277.

281. Punishment for hedonism
Id. at p. 343.

282. "Far more courage"
Manchester, The Glory and The Dream, 1974, p. 57.

283. "Stands up for Americanism"
Id. at p. 111.

284. Not quite same
For an example of Felix Frankfurter's loose use of the epithet, see Parrish, Felix Frankfurter and His Times, 1982, p. 251.

285. Stone had closed
Caute, The Great Fear, 1978, p. 111.

banned the Communist candidate for President from speaking on their campuses.[286] The anti-Communists got a boost when the Communist Party endorsed the Hitler–Stalin pact, providing the excuse that many would later give for leaving the Party or turning informer for the F.B.I.[287]

War and Repression

In 1940, "Native Son" and "For Whom The Bell Tolls" were published, "Grapes of Wrath" won the Pulitzer Prize, and "Gone With the Wind" won the Academy Award.[288] But over where most Americans thought of as "far away," Hitler was setting in motion events that would turn Americans more to conformity than to diversity.[289] The Armies of the Third Reich swept to the English Channel and prepared to invade what to some American elites was still "The Mother Country."[290] In what was then seen as a vindication of "Billy" Mitchell, the English turned back the Germans in an aerial campaign that came to be known as "The Battle of Britain."[291] On the economic front, the effect of the draft caused a drop in unemployment but unions were urged to restrain their wage demands to assist in the war effort.[292] The Supreme Court did its part by holding that the First Amendment did not bar jingoistic school boards from forcing the children of Jehovah's Witnesses to violate their religious scruples by participating in a salute to the Flag.[293]

286. Banned from speaking

Schrecker, No Ivory Tower: McCarthyism and the Universities, 1986, p. 89 (the colleges included Harvard, Dartmouth, Cornell, Vassar, N.Y.U., and Princeton).

287. Endorsed pact

Manchester, The Glory and the Dream, 1974, p. 201; Klehr, The Party's Over, N.Y. Rev. Bks., Nov. 18, 1982, p.55.

288. "GWTW" Academy Award

Encyclopedia of American Facts and Dates, Ninth ed. 1993, pp. 506, 508.

289. Hitler set in motion

Encyclopedia of American History, Morris ed. 1976, pp. 430–431 (summarizing events in Europe).

290. Swept to Channel

Leuchtenburg, Franklin D. Roosevelt and The New Deal, 1932–1940, 1963, p. 299.

291. "Battle of Britain"

Encyclopedia of American History, Morris ed. 1976, p. 432. As is usual in wartime, the reality was more complex than Allied propaganda tried to make it appear.

292. Restrain demands

Encyclopedia of American Facts and Dates, Ninth ed. 1993, p. 507. This had something to do with the defection of some unionists to the Republicans.

293. Salute to flag

Minersville School District v. Gobitis, 1940, 60 S.Ct. 1010, 310 U.S. 586, 84 L.Ed. 1375.

Coerced patriotism seemed necessary because President Roosevelt's moves to help the British split the country.[294] Former Progressives formed organizations to support the President, such as the committee to Defend America by Aiding the Allies headed by William Allen White.[295] In response, those opposed to intervention in the war formed the America First Committee, whose best known spokesman was the Nazi sympathizer, Charles Lindbergh, but which also numbered among its supporters pacifists, respectable businessmen, and ethnic groups with reason to fear the outbreak of war.[296] For purposes of confrontation, we should note that at a visceral level, many of those who opposed the war were opposed to both the English and the American Anglophiles who had cultivated the manners and attitudes of the English aristocracy.[297] That the attack on the English came from groups that included Nazi sympathizers and anti-Semites could easily confirm the rightness of their attitudes in the minds of the Anglophiles—thus strengthening the view that confrontation was a product of English common law.

The presidential election of 1940 was remarkable in several ways.[298] Roosevelt shattered the precedent set by Washington and followed by every president since of retiring after two terms—a step that led to a constitutional amendment giving the two-term limit the force of law.[299] The Republicans shattered precedent as well by nominating as their candidate, Wendell Wilkie—the man who did as much as anyone to make the term "liberal Republican" less an

294. Split country

Leuchtenburg, Franklin D. Roosevelt and The New Deal, 1932–1940, 1963, pp. 310–311.

295. Headed by White

Id. at p. 310.

296. Fear outbreak

Id. at p. 311–312. If one recalled the fate of German–Americans during World War I, one did not have to be a Nazi sympathizer to oppose another war against Germany.

297. Opposed to Anglophiles

Manchester, The Glory and The Dream, 1974, pp. 174–175. This was later to provide a leitmotif in the Second Red Scare.

298. Election remarkable

For those familiar with the conduct of elections at the end of the century, perhaps most remarkable was the willingness of newspapers to honor an understanding between the parties that if the Democrats did not mention Wilkie's mistress, the Republicans would not reveal that Henry Wallace, the Democratic vice-presidential candidate believed in spiritualism. Douglas, Go East, Young Man, 1974, p. 339.

299. Two-term limit

Or as it was called at the time, the "third term issue." Leuchtenburg, Franklin D. Roosevelt and the New Deal, 1932–1940, 1963, p. 316; Kyvig, Explicit & Authentic Acts, 1996, pp. 325–336 (describing adoption of Twenty–Second Amendment).

oxymoron.[300] Though ridiculed by Democrats as a "barefoot Wall Street lawyer," Wilkie was more sympathetic to the New Deal goals than many in the President's own party.[301] Wilkie was supported by such union leaders as John L. Lewis and Harry Bridges—the latter having just escaped being deported as a Communist and soon to play a small role in the revival of the Confrontation Clause.[302] Nonetheless, Roosevelt easily won reelection, though not by the margins he had enjoyed in his two previous campaigns.[303]

While some were preparing for the War on Hitler, others were laying the groundwork for the Second Red Scare. In 1940, Congress adopted the Alien Registration Act, better known in later years as "The Smith Act."[304] The statute required all aliens to register with the government; given the ominous resemblance to the Nazi registration of Jews and with memories of the massive deportation of aliens during the First Red Scare, it was to be expected that registrants would be fearful.[305] More significant for our purposes was the way the Smith Act, in defiance of the increasing Supreme Court protection of First Amendment rights, made it a crime for anyone to advocate or to belong to an organization that advocated the overthrow of the government.[306] When the Act had first been proposed, it had been opposed by much of the business press, by publishers, academics, and the American Civil Liberties Union and went down to defeat.[307] However, after the Nazi–Soviet pact, opposition evaporated and a coalition of the Daughters of the American

300. "Liberal Republican"

Manchester, The Glory and The Dream, 1974, pp. 225–226.

301. "Barefoot Lawyer"

Leuchtenberg, Franklin D. Roosevelt and The New Deal, 1932–1940, 1963, pp. 310–311. The isolationist Gerald Nye attributed Wilkie's nomination to a sinister conspiracy—a reminder that conspiracy theories are never out of season. Id. at p. 322.

302. Lewis and Bridges

Id. at p. 320.

303. Not by margins

Id. at p. 321.

304. "Smith Act"

Encyclopedia of American History, Morris ed. 1976, p. 432.

305. Registrants fearful

Nonetheless, eventually more than 5 million registered. American Encyclopedia of Facts and Dates, Ninth ed. 1993, p. 508.

306. Advocate overthrow

Foner, The Story of American Freedom, 1998, p. 217. The Supreme Court decisions are collected in Encyclopedia of American History, Morris ed. 1976, p. 677.

307. First opposed

Belknap, Cold War Political Justice: The Smith Act, The Community Party, and American Civil Liberties, 1977, p. 18.

Revolution, the American Legion, and the U.S. Chamber of Commerce succeeded in pushing the Act through.[308] However, the Justice Department did not wait for the Smith Act; in 1940 it prosecuted the Communist newspaper, "The Daily Worker," publishers of Communist books, and a travel agency specializing in tours of the Soviet Union for failure to register as agents of a foreign government.[309]

The adoption of the federal statute encouraged a number of states to adopt "Little Smith Acts."[310] In 1940 alone, more than 350 members of the Communist Party were arrested in 13 states under such provisions.[311] Meanwhile, in California, a legislative committee led by an apostate Communist held a series of hearings into the Red Menace that anticipated the H.U.A.C. hearings of the Second Red Scare—lawyers evicted from the hearing room, witnesses prosecuted for contempt for refusal to answer questions, and the like.[312] The only substantive result of the hearings was a statute barring the Communist Party from the ballot—which the state Supreme Court promptly struck down as unconstitutional.[313]

Meanwhile, the Board of Regents of the University of California pioneered the use of the employment relation as a means of suppressing despised ideologies, adopting a resolution proclaiming

> that the Communist Party * * * gives its first loyalty to a foreign political movement and, perhaps, to a foreign government; that by taking advantage of the idealism and inexperience of youth, and by exploiting the distress of underprivileged groups, it breeds suspicion and discord, and thus divides the democratic forces upon which the welfare of our country depends. * * * therefore * * * membership in the Communist Party is incompatible with membership in the faculty of a State University.[314]

308. Coalition succeeded
Id. at pp. 18, 22.

309. Failure to register
Caute, The Great Fear, 1978, p. 25.

310. "Little Smith Acts"
Foner, The Story of American Freedom, 1998, p. 217.

311. More than 350 arrested
Belknap, Cold War Political Justice: The Smith Act, The Communist Party, and American Civil Liberties, 1977, p. 24.

312. Lawyers evicted
Barrett, The Tenney Committee, 1951, p. 8.

313. Court struck down
Id. at pp. 9–10.

314. "Incompatible"
Schrecker, No Ivory Tower: McCarthyism and the Universities" 1986, p. 75.

Notice the assumption that membership in the Party confers Svengali-like powers on teachers who are otherwise unable to convince students to avoid the passive voice or to observe the distinction between "that" and "which."[315] This assumption was later to be taken up by respectable organizations that should have known better.

However, statutes and resolutions were not required to foster a repressive attitude toward free speech. The City College of New York rescinded an invitation to the English philosopher Bertrand Russell to teach at C.C.N.Y. after he was attacked by religious groups, as much for his eccentric attitudes towards sexual morality as for his radical political beliefs.[316] However, the appointment of Russell triggered a legislative investigation into "subversive activities" in the state's schools and colleges.[317] Seeing the handwriting on the wall, a number of C.I.O. unions adopted anti-Communist resolutions that would come back to haunt them during the Second Red Scare.[318]

"The Good War"

Joe Dimaggio's 56–game hitting streak is probably the only prominent historical event of 1941 that did not have ramifications for the right of confrontation.[319] On January 6, in his State of the Union address, the President first enunciated the famous "Four Freedoms"—the first indication that the Second World War, like the First, was going to be cast as an ideological struggle.[320] The Four Freedoms, as immortalized on a Norman Rockwell poster distributed by the Office of War Information, were freedom of speech, freedom of worship, freedom from want, and freedom from fear.[321] A Republican member of Congress introduced a joint resolu-

---

315. Svengali-like

Very few teachers who were fired for their beliefs were ever shown to have expressed those beliefs in the classroom, let alone convinced anyone to adopt them.

316. Bertrand Russell

Schrecker, No Ivory Tower: McCarthyism and the Universities 1986, p. 76.

317. "Subversive activities"

Ibid.

318. Adopted resolutions

Id. at p. 74.

319. Hitting streak

American Encyclopedia of Facts and Dates, Ninth ed. 1993, p. 513; Manchester, The Glory and The Dream, 1974, p. 247.

320. Four freedoms

Encyclopedia of American History, Morris ed. 1976, p. 434.

321. Rockwell poster

The poster is reproduced in Foner, The Story of American Freedom, 1998, p. 226 and in Kennedy, Freedom From Fear, 1999, opposite page 652. It could

tion to adopt a Fifth Freedom, without which, she said, the other four "are meaningless"—that is, "Freedom of Private Enterprise."[322]

Two of the President's Four Freedoms were part of the First Amendment, which at the time the Supreme Court was giving increasing meaning.[323] "Freedom from Fear" was vague enough to connote anything; most commentators saw it as a right to personal security, a right which the sophisticated might have seen as including the Sixth Amendment rights such as confrontation.[324] "Freedom from Want" got the most attention, not all of it favorable. The President explained that "[t]here can be no real freedom for the common man without enlightened social policies."[325] Even Fortune magazine agreed that the government must establish a minimum standard of living by taking "unequivocal responsibility for maintaining employment."[326] Congress, on the other hand, thought this was all New Deal propaganda, so in 1943 it cut off virtually all funding from the Office of War Information for domestic propaganda.[327] Hence, there would be no more O.W.I. pamphlets like the one proclaiming that the government must assume "responsibility for the solution of economic problems."[328]

But Congress could not prevent the President from projecting an American ideology abroad, from whence it would be reflected back later to cast Americans in a light unfamiliar to most of them.[329] On August 14, the President and Prime Minster Churchill proclaimed "The Atlantic Charter."[330] Along with some Wilsonian principles such as national self-determination, it also endorsed the

still be found on the walls of barbershops and gas stations in the Midwest during the junior author's adolescence.

322. "Private Enterprise"

Foner, The Story of American Freedom, 1998, p. 230.

323. Increasing meaning

The Flag Salute Case was to have a short life.

324. "Freedom from Fear"

Id. at p. 223.

325. "Social policies"

Id. at p. 225.

326. "Maintaining employment"

Ibid.

327. Congress cut off

Id. at p. 229

328. "Economic problems"

Id. at p. 227.

329. Light unfamiliar

That is, when Stalinist governments used American failures to live up to our ideals to draw attention away from their failures to live up to theirs.

330. "Atlantic Charter"

Encyclopedia of American History, Morris ed. 1976, p. 436.

right of peoples to select their own leaders, to regain lands taken by force, to free trade and equal access to raw materials, to disarm aggressors, to freedom of the seas, and freedom from fear and want.[331] In this context, the freedom from want and fear more easily appear to be collective rights; but that is not how the Four Freedoms were seen. They were generally taken to be individual rights.[332] Even as such they had serious limitations. For example, there is no "Freedom from Invidious Discrimination."[333] More significant for the right of confrontation, the Four Freedoms all concern what might be called "the morality of ends" as distinguished from "the morality of means."[334] But by the end of the War it would be means, not ends, that would raise moral unease.[335]

Meanwhile, others offered alternative justifications for the War. In October, an interventionist group of the Eastern elite, calling itself the "Fight for Freedom Committee," tried to revive the World War I ploy of casting the war as one between democracy and totalitarianism.[336] They sponsored a "Fight for Freedom" rally in Madison Square Garden, whose posters enlisted Disney characters as "The Spirit of '76."[337] But perhaps the most prescient of the apologists for war was publisher Henry Luce, whose "The American Century" was published in 1941.[338] Luce correctly foresaw that the end of the war would find the United States the dominant power, both militarily and economically. Fusing consumerism and nationalism, Luce wanted to use postwar power to promote Ameri-

331. Fear and want

Manchester, The Glory and The Dream, 1974, p. 234. The reason no one ever quotes the "Charter" is that it was not a signed document as its name implies, but merely an agreement between the two heads of state as to the war aims they wished to project to the world. Ibid.

332. Individual rights

Foner, The Story of American Freedom, 1998, p. 227.

333. "From Discrimination"

The reason for the absence of this—and the other two of the four freedoms, religion and speech—may reflect Churchill's understanding that these were inconsistent with the English colonial system.

334. "Morality of means"

"Democracy" and "confrontation" fall within the latter, as does "free speech" in some of its rationalia.

335. Raise moral unease

E.g., the tactic of making war on noncombatants.

336. Revive World War I

Foner, The Story of American Freedom, 1998, p. 221.

337. Disney characters

Id. at p. 222.

338. "The American Century"

Id. at p. 232.

can values—"the abundant life" and "the free enterprise system."[339]

At the time this high-minded rhetoric was being loosed, nine million Americans were still unemployed.[340] In the South, those Anglo–Saxon "good old boys" revived their dreams of military glory by conducting some thirteen lynchings.[341] "Negro leaders," as they were then called, concerned that the Army and Navy only accepted Blacks in segregated and menial units and the Marines and Air Force would not accept them at all, called on President Roosevelt.[342] The President gave them his usual blarney and left it to an aide to announce two weeks later that there would be no change.[343] A. Phillip Randolph, head of the Brotherhood of Sleeping Car Porters, was outraged. In the face of opposition or lukewarm support from other organizations, Randolph called for a protest march on Washington.[344] When the idea fired so much enthusiasm in the Black community that it looked like Randolph's call for 100,000 might be met, Roosevelt was forced to take the issue seriously.[345]

After trying through several intermediaries to get Randolph to call off the march "for the good of the country," the President agreed to meet with Randolph two weeks before the scheduled date.[346] Once again Roosevelt trotted out his considerable charm and powers of persuasion, but Randolph was unmoved.[347] Finally, the President capitulated, giving Randolph what he had told him was impossible: an executive order barring discrimination on grounds of race, religion, or ethnicity in government employment and among defense contractors.[348] Executive Order 8802 also created a Fair Employment Practices Commission to monitor compli-

339. "Free enterprise system"

Ibid.

340. Still unemployed

Manchester, The Glory and The Dream, 1974, p. 239.

341. Lynchings

Foner, The Story of American Freedom, 1998, pp. 241–242.

342. Called on Roosevelt

Manchester, The Glory and The Dream, 1974, p. 242; Kennedy, Freedom From Fear, 1999, p. 765.

343. No change

Id. at p. 766.

344. Called for march

Ibid.

345. Forced to take seriously

Id. at p. 767.

346. Agreed to meet

Ibid.

347. Unmoved

Ibid.

348. Order barring

Ibid.

ance, whose weak powers were nonetheless of more than symbolic importance.[349] Though the March on Washington was called off, a precedent had been set.[350]

Throughout 1941 there was a steady rise in interventionist sentiment.[351] That sentiment was strongest in the South, with its tradition of romantic militarism and Bourbon Anglophilia, and among the WASP elite; the latter were ready for an immediate declaration of war.[352] War sentiment was boosted by a collection of Anglophile verse, "The White Cliffs of Dover," which quickly became a best seller and was later the source of a popular song.[353] One wonders if all these people would have been so enthusiastic could they have foreseen the way in which the War would transform American society—generally to their detriment.[354]

Amidst this flowering of sentiment, Congress moved slowly to create the sinews of the Warfare State. The President asked for and was granted near dictatorial powers over the civilian economy.[355] Slowly the administration assembled the bureaucracy to exercise those powers, including restraints on wages and prices.[356] Hoping to beat the anticipated wage freeze, unions called some 4,000 strikes

349. F.E.P.C.

Manchester, The Glory and The Dream, 1974, p. 242; Kennedy, Freedom From Fear, 1999, p. 244; Foner, The Story of American Freedom, 1998, pp. 242.

350. Precedent set

Prior to Randolph's second visit, Black leaders had always come as supplicants rather than as significant political adversaries; indeed much of the opposition to Randolph's march was from those who appreciated the consequence of their constituents adopting an "uppity" political approach. Kennedy, Freedom From Fear, 1999, p. 766. Perceiving The Other as a legitimate adversary was a necessary ingredient for a workable adversary system and right of confrontation.

351. Rise in sentiment

Manchester, The Glory and The Dream, 1974, p. 228.

352. Immediate declaration

Ibid.

353. "White Cliffs of Dover"

Id. at p. 218. In an apt illustration of the relationship between reason and ritual, the poem seems treacly and the song maudlin to those who hear them now and are unable to appreciate the responsive chord they struck in those who first heard them when the outcome of the war was uncertain and the fate of civilization seemed linked to the fate of England.

354. Transform society

Foner, The Story of American Freedom, 1998, p. 219.

355. Dictatorial powers

Manchester, The Glory and The Dream, 1974, pp. 230–231.

356. Wages and prices

Encyclopedia of American Facts and Dates, 9th ed. 1993, p. 509.

during 1941.[357] Congress, for its part, created the Special Senate Committee to Investigate the National Defense Program, known after its chairman as "The Truman Committee."[358] The committee exposed profiteering and mismanagement in the construction of army camps, abuses of cost-plus contracts, and the delivery of substandard material—including a ship with faulty plating that split in two and sank.[359] The Truman Committee is estimated to have saved the taxpayers $15 billion but it saved defense contractors from the loss of reputation, at least among civilians, which had tarred capitalism after prior wars.[360]

In June of 1941, Hitler made the napoleonic mistake of invading the Soviet Union.[361] This not only brought a flood of confrontation values to the editorial pages of American newspapers, but also flip-flopped the American Communist Party from pacifism to interventionism.[362] Stalin's joining of the Allies ended overt anti-Communist government activity for the duration; indeed, the only such action of note between 1940 and 1946 was the 1941 prosecution of a band of Trotskyites under the Smith Act.[363] However, as would become clear in the Second Red Scare, the F.B.I. devoted far more of its time during the War to pursuit of Reds than to saboteurs or organized crime.

War finally came on December 7, 1941—"the day that will live in infamy."[364] The Japanese attack on Pearl Harbor was called "a

357. 4,000 strikes

Id. at p. 511.

358. "Truman Committee"

Kennedy, Freedom from Fear, 1999, p. 791.

359. Split in two

Ibid.

360. Tarred capitalism

Ibid. Until the return of their sons and daughters and plays like Arthur Miller's "All My Sons," many Americans had a positive impression of the armaments rolling off assembly lines—largely as a result of movies and other government propaganda. For example, the airplane featured in many of the thinly disguised Air Force propaganda pictures that can still be seen on American Movie Classics—the B-17 "Flying Fortress"—was anything but. Its crews were slaughtered until the

Air Force gave up the pretense and provided fighter planes to protect them. Id. at p. 609. Similarly, contrary to the heroic movies, almost as many airmen lost their lives in aircraft accidents as were killed in combat. Id. at p. 606.

361. Invading Soviet Union

Encyclopedia of American Dates and Facts, 9th ed. 1993, p. 508.

362. Flip-flopped

Klehr, The Party's Over, N.Y. Rev. Bks., Nov. 19, 1982, p. 55.

363. Trotskyites

Caute, The Great Fear, 1978, p. 25.

364. "Live in infamy"

The quotation is from President Roosevelt's message to Congress requesting a declaration of war.

sneak attack" and the battle cry for many Americans was "Remember Pearl Harbor!"[365] If one looks at the many synonyms for "sneak" in a thesaurus, one will understand why it can be said that the attack on Pearl Harbor probably provoked one of the broadest outbreaks of confrontation values in recent times.[366] The Japanese not only did not inform Americans of "the nature and cause" of their attack through a prior declaration of war, but they had pretended to engage in negotiations with the American government looking to a resolution of their differences even as their armada was making its way toward Oahu.[367] When the hapless Japanese envoys belatedly delivered a message breaking off the talks that was supposed to have been delivered simultaneously with the outbreak of hostilities, they had to endure a tirade from Secretary of State Cordell Hull that used every bit of diplomatic invective short of the actual word to condemn them as "two-faced."[368]

In fact, the events of December 7 supported confrontation values in another way; i.e., by discrediting the notion of the efficiency of the executive bureaucracy. American military leaders knew from the study of prior Japanese wars that they did not share the confrontation values of Americans.[369] Several days before the attack, the armed forces had been put on alert because of the apparent breakdown of negotiations.[370] Though few expected the attack to come in Hawaii, in fact local commanders had numerous clues in the hours and days preceding the attack that it was

365. "Remember Pearl Harbor!"

Encyclopedia of American Dates and Facts, 9th ed. 1993, p. 507; Encyclopedia of American History, Morris ed. 1976, p. 437; Manchester, The Glory and The Dream, 1974, pp. 257.

366. Confrontation values

Roosevelt's own departures from confrontation values, such as his deviousness regarding the court-packing plan, came back to haunt him over Pearl Harbor. Some noninterventionists claimed that wanting to go to war in Europe but being denied by Hitler's refusal to attack American vessels in the Atlantic, Roosevelt had deliberately sought a "back door to war" through the Pacific. Kennedy, Freedom From Fear, 1999, p. 524. There is little to support this implausible claim, except Roosevelt's character.

367. Pretended negotiations

Id. at pp. 514–515. The negotiations were real enough, but the two sides were too far apart to settle their differences. Hence, it was easy for Americans to suppose that either the Japanese or Roosevelt or both had been insincere.

368. Condemn as two-faced

Manchester, The Glory and The Dream, 1974, p. 256.

369. Did not share

The Russo–Japanese War had been begun with a similar surprise attack.

370. Put on alert

Id. at p. 253.

coming—but all these were ignored.[371] In the most dramatic example, on December 7, after reading a deciphered Japanese code message, General George C. Marshall understood that war was imminent and dispatched an immediate warning to all military commanders.[372] Because of radio static, the one destined for Hawaii was sent by Western Union and arrived only twenty minutes before the first wave of Japanese planes. The delivery boy was caught in the attack so the message did not reach its intended recipients until hours after the attack.[373] In an even more incredible blunder, "Dugout Doug" MacArthur—the hero of the attack on the Bonus Marchers—learned of the Japanese attack on Pearl Harbor ten hours before he was attacked in the Philippines, yet did nothing to disperse or protect his airplanes, which were gathered together in nice targets for the Japanese aviators.[374]

Oh—and in 1941 we celebrated the 150th anniversary of the Bill of Rights.[375]

Bataan, Sleepy Lagoon, and Manzanar

Early in 1942, the news from the front was mostly bad. MacArthur fled the Philippines for Australia and the American and Filipino forces on the Bataan Peninsula and Corregidor surrendered not long afterwards.[376] Then the Japanese advance across the Pacific was halted at the Battles of the Coral Sea and Midway, the first naval battles in which vessels of the opposing forces did not fire on each other.[377] This "nonconfrontational" brand of warfare tended to undermine the military metaphor for the adversary

371. All ignored

The whole story is detailed exhaustively in the almost minute-by-minute account of the attack in Prange, At Dawn We Slept, 1981.

372. Immediate warning

Kennedy, Freedom From Fear, 1999, p. 519.

373. Hours after attack

Id. at pp. 519–520.

374. Nice targets

Id. at p. 527. General MacArthur's earning of this sobriquet is described id. at p. 529. No one expected generals to ride with their troops like Custer;

what made many in the military despise MacArthur was his penchant for staging little tableaux for newsreel cameras that made him appear to be closer to the action than he was.

375. Celebrated anniversary

Foner, The Story of American Freedom, 1998, p. 217.

376. Surrendered

Encyclopedia of American History, Morris ed., 1976, p. 438.

377. Did not fire

Id. at p. 439; Kennedy, Freedom From Fear, 1999, p. 542 (battle carried out entirely by carrier-borne aircraft).

system and to dilute the morality of real battle.[378] Meanwhile at the end of the year, the United States finally entered the European war, through the bombing of Germany and the campaign against Rommel in North Africa.[379]

The fall of Corregidor was followed by the "Bataan Death March," a grisly 80–mile trek through the jungle in which prisoners were denied water, beaten, and bayoneted; 600 Americans and 10,000 Filipinos died.[380] This was the first indication that, contrary to the mechanistic imagery of warfare created by the Battle of Midway, the war in the Pacific would be the most brutal combat that American forces engaged in since the Indian wars.[381] The parallels are striking; racist rhetoric, the use of gruesome weapons (flame-throwers instead of knives and tomahawks), and grisly rituals on enemy dead (cutting open cheeks to pry out gold teeth in place of scalping)—and this was just on the American side.[382]

The Pacific war was brutal because, despite the Four Freedoms rhetoric, it was fought on both sides as a race war—a "war without mercy" in the phrase of one historian.[383] The Japanese, priding themselves on their racial purity and military valor, despised the polyglot American troops who had so little self-respect that they would surrender rather than die.[384] Japanese troops were fed a steady diet of horror stories about what the Americans did to captives—creating a fear that bolstered the ideological reasons for refusing to surrender.[385] The refusal of Japanese troops to surrender even when there were no instrumental reasons for continued

---

378. Dilute morality

During the battle of Manila Bay in the Spanish American War, when American sailors cheered the sight of a Spanish vessel sinking, Admiral Dewey chided them: "Don't cheer, boys—brave men are dying over there." During World War II, Admiral Halsey erected huge billboards urging his men to "Kill Japs!" Manchester, The Glory and The Dream, 1974, p. 269.

379. North Africa

Encyclopedia of American History, Morris ed. 1976, p. 443.

380. "Bataan Death March"

Kennedy, Freedom From Fear, 1999, p. 530.

381. Since Indian wars

Manchester, The Glory and The Dream, 1974, p. 269. The suppression of the Pilipino independence movement certainly runs a close second.

382. American side

Ibid.

383. "War without mercy"

Kennedy, Freedom From Fear, 1999, p. 810.

384. Polyglot Americans

Ibid.

385. Bolstered ideological

Id. at pp. 811–812

resistance purportedly justified the use of weapons like flame-throwers.

American propaganda fueled a racism that had little need for it. Movies shown to American troops dehumanized the Japanese, portraying them as military automatons.[386] Whereas the war in Europe was not blamed on the Germans or the Italians but on their "bad leaders," the Pacific war was attributed to the supposed racial characteristics of the Japanese people.[387] Once they became known, the horrors of the Bataan Death March were used to inspire troops before battle, an inspiration that led to atrocities of the sort not to be seen again till the Viet Nam War.[388] Civilians were fed similar kinds of propaganda by Hollywood, though somewhat restrained by the Hays Office.[389]

Meanwhile, back on the home front, while things were going badly for the troops, civilian morale was being bolstered with cheerful lies.[390] Not that it needed much bolstering; save for rationing and the need to adjust to "War Time," it was in many ways a "Good War" for civilians.[391] Massive unemployment suddenly turned into labor shortages that led to the importation of workers from Mexico under a revived "bracero" program.[392] So much were Americans concerned with making money that cities on the East Coast refused to abide by blackout regulations for fear of hurting the tourist trade, thus outlining coastal shipping for easier targeting by German submarines.[393] In the off-year elections in 1942, Republicans made massive gains that produced the most conserva-

---

386. Military automatons

Id. at p. 811.

387. Racial characteristics

Foner, The Story of American Freedom, 1998, p. 200

388. Led to atrocities

Manchester, The Glory and The Dream, 1974, p. 269; Kennedy, Freedom From Fear, 1999, pp. 812–813.

389. Civilians fed

For example, a 1942 film supposedly depicting General Doolittle's attempted air raid on Tokyo had a scene in which captured airmen were tortured by the Japanese. Id. at p. 811. Nothing like this ever happened. Id. at p. 535.

390. Cheerful lies

Manchester, The Glory and The Dream, 1974, p. 270 (collecting some of these).

391. "War Time"

"War Time" was a year-round version of Daylight Saving Time. Encyclopedia of American Facts and Dates, 9th ed. 1993, p. 517.

392. Labor shortages and braceros

Kennedy, Freedom From Fear, 1999, p. 777.

393. German submarines

Id. at p. 566.

tive Congress in years.[394] By the end of 1943, Congress had dismantled many of the key New Deal programs—aided in large part by the public perception that with the return of prosperity, they were no longer needed.[395]

On the confrontation front, Roosevelt had called off prosecution of the Communist Party under the Smith Act because he feared the adverse effect of such prosecutions on the war effort.[396] However, for similar reasons he pushed prosecution of American Nazis under the Smith Act.[397] The result was a political trial of a sort not heretofore seen in American jurisprudence. Though he tried to be fair, the judge was constantly assailed by both the defendants and their lawyers.[398] When he died, the trial had to first be postponed, then later dismissed under the speedy trial guarantees of the Sixth Amendment.[399] Later, during the Foley Square trial of the leaders of the Communist Party, defendants and their lawyers were accused of adopting the same "scorched earth" tactic as the Nazis.[400]

1942 was also the year of the infamous "Sleepy Lagoon" trials in Los Angeles.[401] After an attempt to crash a party, a brawl broke out among groups of mostly Mexican–American youths in which one man was stabbed to death.[402] An "expert" from the Los Angeles Sheriff's office told the grand jury that because of their descent from Mayans, who practiced ritual murder, Mexicans were "biologically" predisposed to violence.[403] The grand jury indicted 22 young men for conspiracy. The trial was held in the midst of the sort of racial hysteria that Los Angeles newspapers were getting good at; "zoot-suit gangsters" and "pachuco killers" were the terms rou-

394. Conservative Congress

Id. at p. 782.

395. No longer needed

Id. at p. 783.

396. Called off prosecution

Belknap, Cold War Political Justice: The Smith Act, The Communist Party, and American Civil Liberties, 1977, p. 37.

397. Nazis under Smith

Id. at p. 40.

398. Constantly assailed

Ibid.

399. Dismissed under speedy trial

Ibid.

400. Adopting same

Id. at p. 69.

401. "Sleepy Lagoon"

Friedman, Crime and Punishment in American History, 1993, p. 382.

402. Stabbed to death

People v. Zammora, 1944, 152 P.2d 180, 66 Cal.App.2d 166.

403. "Biologically" predisposed

Friedman, Crime and Punishment in American History, 1993, p. 382.

tinely used to describe the defendants.[404] They were convicted despite evidence so weak that the Court of Appeals found it insufficient to support a verdict.[405] Meanwhile, the Los Angeles County District Attorney told the Tenney Committee, California's "little H.U.A.C.," that the defense of the case was "communistic."[406] The committee later published a report repeating this canard—and neglecting to note that the conviction had been reversed on appeal.[407]

Originally there had been no call for the removal of Japanese–Americans from the Pacific Coast.[408] Unlike Hawaii, where they were a substantial portion of the population, there were only about 125,000 Americans of Japanese descent in California and smaller numbers in the other Pacific states.[409] The majority of those in California were American citizens—and the rest probably would have been had this not been blocked by racist naturalization laws.[410] Initially, then, officials on the Pacific Coast followed the same strategy they used in Hawaii and with Germans and Italians elsewhere; i.e., dealing with suspected disloyalty on a case-by-case basis where evidence justified action.[411]

Hearsay put an end to this; rumors of actual or impending Japanese attacks on the mainland soon begat hysteria over suspected saboteurs among the Japanese–Americans.[412] (In fact, except for two aerial incendiary attacks that fizzled and did not figure in the rumors, and two widely separate shellings, there was never any

404. "Pachuco killers"

Ibid.

405. Insufficient to support

People v. Zammora, 1944, 152 P.2d 180, 66 Cal.App.2d 166.

406. "Communistic"

Barrett, The Tenney Committee, 1951, p. 93.

407. Neglecting to note

Id. at p. 96.

408. No call for removal

Kennedy, Freedom From Fear, 1999, p. 749 (the man who would later be the most vociferous military proponent of removal then called the idea "damn nonsense").

409. Smaller numbers

Id. at pp. 748–749; Manchester, The Glory and The Dream, 1974, p. 297 (less than 1% of the California population were Japanese–American).

410. Naturalization law

The "Nisei," or second-generation, were American by birth; but their parents, the "Issei," were ineligible for citizenship by virtue of the exclusion of Orientals from the Immigration Act of 1924. Ibid.

411. Evidence justified

Ibid.; Kennedy, Freedom From Fear, 1999, p. 749.

412. Begat hysteria

Id. at p. 750.

Japanese contact with the mainland.)[413] California newspapers, some of which were later to profit from the Japanese removal, whipped the hysteria into a frenzy directed against Japanese–Americans, calling for boycotts of both Japanese businesses and customers.[414] Insurance companies cancelled insurance and dairies ceased delivering milk to Japanese–American homes.[415] Nearly 10,-000 Japanese–Americans fled the coast, only to meet with similar responses further inland.[416]

Since contemporary California politicians prefer to focus on the federal government when discussing this episode, it deserves emphasis that California's liberal Governor Cuthbert Olson and its liberal Attorney General Earl Warren did not wait for the federal government to act on their requests to "do something" about the supposed Japanese–American threat.[417] They fired Japanese–Americans from state jobs, revoked their professional licenses and business permits, and froze their assets in banks throughout the state.[418] They were supported in this by the state's business elite—some of who were business rivals of the Japanese–Americans.[419] For example, the Japanese–Americans not only produced half of the state's fruits and vegetables but they were a constant embarrassment to the state's agricultural establishment because they showed it was economically possible to grow produce on other than factory farms requiring massive infusions of federal water.[420] A leader of the Grower–Shipper Vegetable Association candidly admitted that his organizations wanted to "get rid of the Japs for selfish rea-

413. Two shellings

Id. at pp. 746, 750 n. 5. The shellings damaged the pump house on an oil field near Santa Barbara and the backstop of a baseball field near Ft. Stevens in Oregon; both of these took place after the removal order had been signed.

414. Boycotts

Id. at p. 750; Manchester, The Glory and The Dream, 1974, p. 298.

415. Ceased delivering milk

Ibid.

416. Similar responses

Ibid.; Kennedy, Freedom From Fear, 1999, p. 753.

417. "Do something"

None of the organizations traditionally concerned with civil liberties or discrimination against minorities covered themselves with glory during this period. Foner, The Story of American Freedom, 1998, p. 241.

418. Froze assets

Manchester, The Glory and The Dream, 1974, p. 297.

419. Business rivals

E.g., other commercial fishermen.

420. Grow produce

Id. at p. 299.

sons."[421]

However, it is doubtful that greedy Central Valley businessmen would have been able to accomplish their goals without the assistance of the "hard-headed" Progressive hero, Walter Lippman.[422] In one of his columns, Lippman wrote: "It is a fact that the Japanese have been reconnoitering the Pacific Coast for a considerable period of time, testing and feeling out American defenses."[423] This was sheer fabrication.[424] Lippman followed it up with another: "The Pacific Coast is officially a combat zone: some part of it may at any moment be a battlefield. Nobody's constitutional rights include the right to reside or do business on a battlefield."[425] Lippman was soon joined by coarser voices. "The Japanese in California should be under armed guard to the last man and woman right now, and to hell with habeas corpus until the danger is over."[426]

The opposition to such sentiments was surprising both in its weakness and its source.[427] J. Edgar Hoover opposed removal and repeatedly deflated the factual assertions of the paranoids.[428] Two young lawyers fought hard against removal and for some time propped up Attorney General Biddle against the claims of the military.[429] Milton Eisenhower resigned rather than preside over what even Roosevelt conceded were "concentration camps."[430] And after the removal was underway, the only significant politician to publicly oppose it was the conservative Republican Senator, Robert

---

421. "Selfish reasons"

Kennedy, Freedom From Fear, 1999, p. 751.

422. "Hard-headed" hero

The cause was also aided by a report on the Pearl Harbor attack prepared by Justice Roberts, which asserted without any documentation that the Japanese forces had been aided by Japanese–American spies. Ibid.

423. "Testing defenses"

Manchester, The Glory and The Dream, 1974, p. 299.

424. Fabrication

Kennedy, Freedom From Fear, 1999, p. 751.

425. "Business on battlefield"

Ibid.; Manchester, The Glory and The Dream, 1974, p. 299.

426. "Hell with habeas corpus"

Kennedy, Freedom From Fear, 1999, p. 751 (quoting Westbrook Pegler).

427. Surprising source

Manchester, The Glory and The Dream, 1974, p. 297.

428. Hoover

Ibid.

429. Young lawyers

Kennedy, Freedom From Fear, 1999, p. 752.

430. Milton Eisenhower

Id. at p. 754; Manchester, The Glory and The Dream, 1974, p. 300 ("concentration camps").

Taft of Ohio.[431] It would be difficult to find a better illustration of the dangers of the amoral instrumentalism of the Progressives.[432]

Attorney General Biddle, who seems to have had sole custody of the Cabinet's constitutional conscience, eventually crumbled in the face of the military.[433] On February 19, 1942, President Roosevelt signed Executive Order 9066, directing the War Department to "prescribe military areas * * * from which any and all persons may be excluded."[434] The military moved quickly, first barring any further voluntary exodus from the prescribed area, then rounding up men, women, and children and trucking them off to temporary camps in barns and stables, from whence they would eventually be removed to permanent camps in some of the most desolate parts of the West.[435] Reading descriptions of the removal in later years, writers noted the eerie resemblance to the manner in which the Nazis had rousted out the Jews for Auschwitz.[436] The bureaucratic mind functions alike in quite different cultures.[437]

Given only 48 hours to dispose of what they could not carry, the Japanese–Americans lost millions of dollars in real and personal property.[438] Their loss was someone else's gain, but since many of the key transactions were through "straw men," only those with access to privileged attorney-client records could name the number of prominent Californians who took advantage of this "forced sale."[439] Worst yet, the Japanese–Americans were kept prisoners for

431. Robert Taft

Foner, The Story of American Freedom, 1998, p. 241.

432. Dangers of instrumentalism

That is, once one concedes that consequences are the test of policy, then one is totally at the mercy of those who claim to be able to say what those consequences will be.

433. Biddle crumbled

Kennedy, Freedom From Fear, 1999, p. 752. In fairness to Biddle, it should be pointed out that he had only recently joined the Cabinet and was later to demonstrate far more character than shown in this initial foray.

434. "May be excluded"

Id. at p. 753.

435. Most desolate parts

Id. at pp. 753–754.

436. Rousted out Jews

Manchester, The Glory and The Dream, 1974, p. 300.

437. Bureaucratic mind

As these lines were being written, similar descriptions were being published of the Serbian removal of Albanians from Kosovo.

438. Millions lost

Ibid.; Kennedy, Freedom From Fear, 1999, (estimating loss at $400 million).

439. "Forced sale"

This, rather than stupidity, explains why every account of the episode we have seen provides some discussion of the financial losses of the Japanese–Americans but none of them mentions who might have been the beneficiaries of the government's policy.

years without trial in what the A.C.L.U. would call "the worst single wholesale violation of civil rights of American citizens in our history."[440] To add insult to injury, when the inmates of the camps reacted violently to attempts by the military to further violate their rights by planting spies and informers in their midst, this was cited by newspapers as evidence of their "disloyalty."[441]

The following year, in Hirabayashi v. U.S., the Supreme Court unanimously upheld the validity of military curfew on Japanese–Americans, with Justice Murphy's concurrence noting that the actions ran "to the very brink of constitutional power."[442] Hence, in preparing the subsequent case of Korematsu v. U.S., which raised the validity of exclusion, the Justice Department was concerned that its factual basis be complete.[443] In its preparation, lawyers for the government discovered that the military's final report on the removal repeated the same baseless charges that had been used to justify removal in the first place and added some new falsehoods.[444] Anxious to avoid misleading the Court, the lawyers added a footnote to their brief disclaiming any reliance on the false information in the report.[445] When the War Department learned of this footnote, they brought pressure to bear to have it removed, once again the Department of Justice caved in, and the Supreme Court decided the case in ignorance of the lies it had been told to justify the government's action.[446] Even so, this time Justices Roberts, Murphy, and Jackson dissented.

Beyond the injustice done to Japanese–Americans, their removal starkly revealed the flaw in the amoral instrumental justifica-

440. "Worst single violation"

Manchester, The Glory and The Dream, 1974, pp. 300–301.

441. "Disloyalty"

Id. at p. 301; Kennedy, Freedom From Fear, 1999, p. 754.

442. "To very brink"

1943, 63 S.Ct. 1375, 1390, 320 U.S. 81, 111, 87 L.Ed. 1774.

443. Korematsu

1944, 65 S.Ct. 193, 323 U.S. 214, 89 L.Ed. 194.

444. New falsehoods

Kennedy, Freedom From Fear, 1999, p. 757.

445. Disclaiming reliance

Id. at p. 758 (quoting disclaimer). The disclaimer asked the Court to rely on the report only for the description of how the removal was carried out, not for the facts purporting to justify it—pointing out that since the latter clashed with facts known to the Justice Department, it was the inappropriate subject of judicial notice.

446. Decided in ignorance

Ibid.

tions that had become popular in legal circles since the Progressive era. Moreover, it seems likely that some lingering institutional shame at the role it played had some influence on the Supreme Court's renewed interest in the "morality of means" during the post-War era, an interest that aided the revival of the Confrontation Clause. Indeed, the fact that the Court itself may have been misled by the unconfronted hearsay in the government's brief was about as dramatic an example as one could wish of the dangers of relying on government-sponsored hearsay.

Years later, an inmate of one of the camps who had been a boy at the time was asked about his education in the government's schools. He responded: "One of our basic subjects was American history. They talked about freedom all the time."[447]

Pluralism, "One World," and Zoot Suits

. In 1941, as the "island hopping" campaign began in the Pacific, Congress ended the total exclusion of Orientals by the Immigration Act of 1924 by creating a small immigration quota for the Chinese, our nominal ally in the Pacific war.[448] On the other side of the globe, the North African campaign concluded and Allied troops invaded first Sicily, then Italy itself—an act that led to the surrender of the Italian government after the deposition of Mussolini.[449] On the home front, the revolutionary musical comedy by Rogers and Hammerstein, "Oklahoma," opened on Broadway, zoot suits came into fashion, and more than 1,000—mostly children— died as a result of an epidemic of infantile paralysis.[450]

In his State of the Union message, the nation's best known polio victim called for "a second Bill of Rights * * * an economic bill of rights that would guarantee every citizen a job, a living wage, decent housing, adequate medical care, education," and "protection from the economic fears of old age, sickness, accident, and unemployment."[451] The speech followed the blueprint for a peacetime

447. "Talked about freedom"

Foner, The Story of American Freedom, 1998, p. 241.

448. Quota for Chinese

Encyclopedia of American History, Morris ed. 1976, p. 440; Foner, The Story of American Freedom, 1998, p. 240.

449. Deposition of Mussolini

. Encyclopedia of American History, Morris ed. 1976, p. 446.

450. Polio epidemic

Encyclopedia of American Facts and Dates, 9th ed. 1993, pp. 518–520.

451. "Fears of old age"

Kennedy, Freedom From Fear, 1999, p. 784.

economy developed by the National Resources Planning Board.[452] In endorsing the Board's conclusions, Roosevelt said that "[w]e have come to a clear realization of the fact that true individual freedom cannot exist without economic security and independence."[453] But, as one of his biographers observed, the President's words "fell with a dull thud into the half-empty chambers of the United States Congress."[454]

Meanwhile, the existing Bill of Rights got an injection of pluralism when the Supreme Court reversed itself to hold that compulsory flag salute rituals imposed on Jehovah's Witnesses violated the First Amendment.[455] Pluralism got an even greater boost from the publication of Wendell Wilkie's "One World."[456] A perhaps-unintended rebuttal of Henry Luce's "American Century," the defeated presidential candidate's tract sold more than a million copies in two months.[457] In contrast to Luce's "McFreedom," Wilkie warned that unless the United States was to become another imperialist power, it would have to respect the right of other peoples to be "free in their own way."[458] In contradiction of Luce's materialism, Wilkie wanted to justify American power in terms of its constitutional ideals, not its economic system.[459] But to do that, Wilkie argued, we would have to eliminate "our imperialisms at home," particularly the "mocking paradox" of racism.[460] "If we want to talk about freedom," Wilkie wrote, "we must mean freedom for everyone inside our frontiers."[461]

Pluralism made some progress during the war years. In part, this was the product of one of the great internal migrations in our

452. National Resources Planning

Foner, The Story of American Freedom, 1998, p. 233.

453. "Without economic security"

Id. at p. 234.

454. "Fell with dull thud"

Kennedy, Freedom From Fear, 1999, p. 784.

455. Violated first

West Virginia Board of Education v. Barnette, 1943, 63 S.Ct. 1178, 319 U.S. 624, 87 L.Ed. 1628. See Wright, My Favorite Opinion—The Second Flag-Salute Case, 1996, 74 Texas L.Rev. 1297.

456. "One World"

Encyclopedia of American Facts and Dates, 9th ed. 1993, p. 518.

457. More than a million

Ibid.

458. "In their own way"

Foner, The Story of American Freedom, 1998, p. 245.

459. Economic system

Id. at p. 232.

460. "Mocking paradox"

Id. at p. 246.

461. "Freedom for everyone"

Ibid.

history. Fifteen million men and several hundred thousand women left home for military training camps, at least three-quarters of them to encounter The Other on foreign shores.[462] Another fifteen million persons changed their county of residence during the war.[463] While the heartland suffered a loss of population, the population of the Pacific Coast states grew by a third; California alone increased its population by 72% between 1940 and 1950.[464] By its end, one in every five Americans had joined the great wartime migration.[465] This was a remarkable change in a country where, only a few decades earlier, the vast majority of its people had never been more than 100 miles from home.[466]

A second cause for the progress of pluralism was the government's attempt to portray racism as an Axis ideology.[467] Secretary of State Cordell Hull pompously proclaimed that "[w]e have always believed—and we believe today, that all peoples, without distinction of race, color, or religion, who are prepared and willing to accept the responsibilities of liberty are entitled to its enjoyment."[468] The Office of War Information even got Hollywood to enlist in this Orwellian rewriting of history.[469] Movies about the war regularly portrayed platoons, even foxholes, of statistically implausible ethnic diversity.[470] Indeed, one such movie had a Black soldier in the mix—at a time when the Army was entirely Jim Crow.[471] Such

462. Foreign shores

Kennedy, Freedom From Fear, 1999, p. 747.

463. Changed county

More than half of these moved to another state. Id. at pp. 747–748.

464. Increased by 72%

Id. at p. 248.

465. One in five

Id. at p. 247.

466. Never more than 100

We must also recall that for many of these people, life revolved around ethnic enclaves in both the city and the country. War undermined these ghettos in small, but subtle, ways. For example, rationing forced people to patronize merchants of different ethnicity because small ethnic grocers, for example, might not have sufficient

sales of a particular commodity to justify an allocation.

467. Axis ideology

Foner, The Story of American Freedom, 1998, p. 237.

468. "Are entitled"

Id. at p. 238.

469. Hollywood

Id. at p. 239.

470. Implausible diversity

Kennedy, Freedom From Fear, 1999, p. 761. An unscientific sampling by the junior author suggests that "Jewish boys from Brooklyn" were overrepresented and "poor white trash" from across the South were underrepresented.

471. Entirely Jim Crow

Foner, The Story of American Freedom, 1998, p. 239.

gaffes aside, pluralism did begin to work for white ethnics; Anglo–Saxon racism all but disappeared, save in a few hothouses of reaction such as the Daughters of the American Revolution and some law schools.[472] Even more significantly for the right of confrontation, the war saw a substantial decline in elitism and class deference—perhaps fueled by the prominence of the well-to-do on both sides of the debate and usual genteel draft-dodging by the upper crust that accompanies every American war.[473]

Unscientific racism continued to fester. In Los Angeles in 1943, soldiers and sailors on leave and on alcohol encountered Mexican and Mexican–American youth out flaunting the garb that wartime prosperity enabled them to buy.[474] When a fight broke out, police sent to break it up joined the mob of club-swinging military in an assault on the Hispanic youths in what came to be known as the "Zoot Suit riots."[475] Though the riots were probably triggered by equal parts of racism and resentment at civilian prosperity, the Tenney Committee blamed them on Communist agitators.[476]

At the outset of the War, most African–Americans were still where they had been left after the collapse of reconstruction and the rise of Jim Crow.[477] As we have previously noted, the military services that would admit Blacks were as racially segregated as any Southern town.[478] Hence, the South Carolina legislature could suppose that it did the war effort no harm when it resolved that in taking on the Axis "we are fighting for white supremacy."[479] The experience of the Benny Goodman orchestra, which was later to produce one of the most successful pieces of pluralist propaganda,

---

472. Anglo-Saxon racism

Id. at p. 239.

473. Decline in deference

Manchester, The Glory and The Dream, 1974, p. 291.

474. Flaunting garb

One wonders if the soldiers and sailors would have reacted differently had the Hispanic youth been dressed in serapes and straw hats. Resentment may have been as much at their attempt to represent themselves as Americans as at their representation of civilian affluence. Foner, The Story of American Freedom, 1998, p. 240.

475. "Zoot Suit riots"

Id. at p. 243.

476. Communist agitators

Barrett, The Tenney Committee, 1951, p. 95.

477. Rise of Jim Crow

Kennedy, Freedom From Fear, 1999, p. 764.

478. Military segregated

Manchester, The Glory and The Dream, 1974, p. 242.

479. "For white supremacy"

Id. at p. 243.

nicely symbolizes the plight of American Blacks.[480] Goodman made no secret that "swing" was an appropriation of an African–American idiom and his band was one of the first to break the color line.[481] Yet, despite their immense popularity with fans, the Black members of Goodman's ensemble had to endure Jim Crow in their tours of the South and were not allowed to appear with the band in some Northern ballrooms.[482] The plight of African–Americans was meticulously documented in Gunnar Myrdal's "An American Dilemma," which was published the following year.[483]

African-Americans joined the wartime migration. It was estimated that more than a million went north during the War.[484] But they traveled in other directions, too; in 1943, 10,000 Blacks a month moved into Los Angeles.[485] Because the C.I.O. was one of the more racially integrated American institutions, labor unions came to assume increasing importance in African–American communities.[486] But, despite labor shortages, corporate employers refused to hire Blacks. The President of North American Aviation announced: "[w]e will not employ Negroes. It is against company policy."[487] A

480. Pluralist propaganda

The Benny Goodman Quartet, consisting of Goodman, who was Jewish, pianist Teddy Wilson and vibraharpist Lionel Hampton, who were presented as Black Protestants, and drummer Gene Krupa, depicted as a Slavic Catholic, were regularly deployed in Cold War propaganda as symbols of American pluralism.

481. Break color line

Id. at p. 244. Goodman's band regularly featured the arrangements and compositions of the Black bandleader Fletcher Henderson. Hence, it was a source of some amusement in the 1960s when young Black militants "discovered" that white musicians had "stolen" jazz from Blacks. Whether Henderson and other Black progenitors were adequately compensated for their contributions is, of course, another matter.

482. Not allowed to appear

Ibid. In one of those ironies that fill the history of American racism, the singer Billy Holliday (who cut some early records with Goodman before either of them were famous, who occasionally

appeared with his band, and who did as much as any person to influence Goodman's instrumental style) was required to darken her skin when she appeared in Black venues. Ibid.

483. "American Dilemma"

Foner, The Story of American Freedom, 1998, p. 246.

484. More than a million

Manchester, The Glory and The Dream, 1974, p. 243.

485. Los Angeles

Kennedy, Freedom From Fear, 1999, p. 768.

486. Union's importance

Foner, The Story of American Freedom, 1998, p. 244.

487. "Against policy"

Kennedy, Freedom From Fear, 1999, p. 765.

Kansas City steel mill proclaimed: "We have had not had a Negro worker in twenty-five years, and we do not plan to start now."[488] This recalcitrance led the President to strengthen the F.E.P.C. and to urge the N.L.R.B. to decertify segregated unions.[489] By war's end, the number of African–American government employees had tripled.[490]

The mixture of the races in Detroit was explosive.[491] Black migrants from the Deep South and "hillbillies" from the Border States poured into a community that already had a mature and increasingly self-confident Black community and a white community still split along ethnic lines.[492] In 1943, white workers at a plant manufacturing aircraft engines went on a "hate strike" to protest the upgrading of Black workers into skilled jobs.[493] On June 20, 1943, more than 100,000 people sought refuge from the summer heat in a modest waterfront park, Belle Isle.[494] Rumor soon escalated some scuffles between Black and White teenagers into a story that three Blacks had been killed. Blacks began attacking Whites on streetcars and a race riot erupted. By the time troops succeeded in quelling the violence, twenty-five Blacks and nine Whites were dead.[495] Similar, if less deadly, racial strife erupted in other cities and in military camps.[496]

J. Edgar Hoover told the President that "a good proportion of unrest as regards race relationship results from communist activities."[497] Others were not so sure. The military services began nibbling around the edges of segregation.[498] The following year,

488. "Do not plan to start"

Ibid.

489. Decertify

Id. at p. 775.

490. Tripled

Ibid.

491. Detroit

See generally, Kempton, The Lost Tycoons, N.Y. Rev. Bks., May 20, 1999, p. 68.

492. Ethnic lines

Kennedy, Freedom From Fear, 1999, p. 770.

493. "Hate strike"

Foner, The Story of American Freedom, 1998, p. 243.

494. Belle Isle

Kennedy, Freedom From Fear, 1999, p. 770.

495. Dead

Ibid.

496. Military camps

Id. at pp. 770–771.

497. "Communist activities"

Manchester, The Glory and The Dream, 1974, p. 243.

498. Nibbling

Kennedy, Freedom From Fear, 1999, p. 773.

more than 320 men—202 of them Black—were killed in an explosion at Port Chicago, California that was blamed on the Navy's use of inexperienced and segregated Black sailors to rush the packing of a shipload of ammunition. When fifty of the survivors refused to return to work under such unsafe conditions, they were court-martialed and sentenced to fifteen years at hard labor and dishonorable discharges.[499] The resulting furor moved the Navy to take steps towards integration. By the end of 1945, the Navy became the first branch to end segregation.[500] For purposes of confrontation, the most significant result of the war was the increasing militancy of Black organizations; Thurgood Marshall and the N.A.A.C.P. led the attack on the Navy after Port Chicago.[501] A Black newspaper launched the "Double V" campaign—"victory over our enemies at home and victory over our enemies on the battlefields abroad."[502] Inspired by the success of the abortive March on Washington, Blacks flocked to civil rights organizations; the N.A.A.C.P. alone grew ten-fold to half a million members.[503] Blacks carefully exploited the government's projection of racism onto the Axis; pickets outside a segregated Washington restaurant carried signs reading "Are you for Hitler's Way or the American Way?" and "We Die Together, Let's Eat Together."[504] Thus was the stage set for the postwar attack on Jim Crow.

Economy and Ideology

In 1944, island hopping continued in the Pacific; MacArthur staged a dramatic return to the Philippines.[505] In Europe, following the invasion of Normandy in June, the Allies swept forward quickly toward war's end till they were temporarily repulsed in the "Battle of the Bulge"—Hitler's last gasp as it turned out.[506] As the war wound down, the Japanese launched "kamikaze" suicide missions against Allied ships and troops while the Germans began firing

499. Dishonorable discharges

Id. at pp. 773–774.

500. Navy first branch

Id. at p. 774.

501. Led attack

Ibid.

502. "Enemies at home"

Id. at p. 768.

503. Ten-fold

Ibid.

504. "Let's Eat Together"

Ibid.

505. MacArthur return

Encyclopedia of American History, Morris ed. 1974, pp. 441–442.

506. Last gasp

Id. at p. 447.

rockets on London.[507] These two extremes epitomized the two kinds of threat that would dominate American military thinking at the end of the century.

On the home front, the infantile jingle "Mairzy Doats" and the smutty historical novel "Forever Amber" blazed the trail for postwar popular culture.[508] To the great disgust of elitists, Congress unanimously passed the so-called "G.I. Bill of Rights" that not only provided for reemployment of returning soldiers and sailors and the pensions and disability payments typical of earlier wars but also promised to support those veterans who wanted to enhance their skills through college or vocational training.[509] The President of the University of Chicago groused that "colleges and universities will find themselves converted into educational hobo jungles."[510] He added: "[e]ducation is not a device for coping with mass unemployment."[511]

1944 was also an election year. President Roosevelt, in his last great display of contempt for confrontation values, concealed from the voters just how ill he was.[512] The Democrats decided to dump the leftish and mercurial Henry Wallace from the ticket and replace him with Harry S Truman.[513] That and the reluctance of voters to "shift horses in the middle of the stream" sufficed to defeat the Republican nominee, Thomas Dewey, Governor of New York and his running mate, Senator John Bricker of Ohio.[514] The popular vote was, however, the narrowest of FDR's four campaigns.[515] The Democrats retained control of the Senate and added to their majority in the House.[516] For the first time in many years, the Communist

507. Firing rockets

Encyclopedia of American Facts and Dates, 9th 3d. 1993, pp. 522, 524.

508. "Forever Amber"

Id. at p. 522.

509. "G.I. Bill"

Kennedy, Freedom From Fear, 1999, p. 786.

510. "Hobo jungles"

Id. at p. 787

511. "Mass unemployment"

Ibid.

512. Concealed how ill

Id. at p. 798.

513. Dump Wallace

Manchester, The Glory and The Dream, 1974, p. 319.

514. Republican nominees

Dewey was from the interventionist, or as it used to be called, the "liberal" wing of the party. Id. at p. 318.

515. Popular vote

Encyclopedia of American Facts and Dates, 9th ed. 1993, p. 525.

516. Added to majority

Ibid.

Party was not on the ballot; it had been reconstituted as the "Communist Political Association," a sort of ideological American Legion.[517] That same year, membership in the Party/Association peaked at 100,000—many of them paid F.B.I. informants.[518]

In 1940, Republican Senator Henry Cabot Lodge told General H.H. Arnold that "[i]t is the general feeling of Congress, and as far as I can gather, among public opinion throughout the country, to provide all of the money necessary for the National Defense, so all you have to do is ask for it."[519] Ask they did. Military spending increased by more than 1,000% from 1940 to 1941.[520] By 1942, the government was pumping more than $300 million every day into the economy.[521] This was military Keynesianism with vengeance.

The statistics told the tale. The gross national product went from $91 billion in 1939 to $215 billion in 1945—an unprecedented increase.[522] And this does not include the value of the confiscated property of the Japanese and a black market economy estimated at more than $1 billion in 1944.[523] Corporate profits rose from $6.4 billion in 1940 to more than $11 billion in 1945.[524] Military spending favored large corporations.[525] Moreover, industrial concentration was advanced when, after the war, the government disposed of more than $17 billion worth of productive facilities to a handful of corporations at bargain basement prices.[526]

Because of the wage freeze, workers did not do quite as well. Weekly earnings rose 65% over the war years, most of this due to overtime.[527] Even so, real wages rose by 27% from 1940 to 1945—obviously some workers did very well, especially if they compared

---

517. "Political Association"

Id. at p. 525.

518. Membership peaked

Fariello, Red Scare, 1995, p. 201.

519. "Ask for it"

Kennedy, Freedom From Fear, 1999, p. 476.

520. More than 1000%

Ibid.

521. $300 million per day

Manchester, The Glory and The Dream, 1974, p. 289.

522. Unprecedented increase

Id. at p. 290.

523. Black-market economy

Id. at p. 302; Encyclopedia of American Facts and Dates, 9th ed. 1993, p. 523.

524. Corporate profits

Kennedy, Freedom From Fear, 1999, p. 622.

525. Favored large

Ibid.

526. Bargain basement prices

Ibid.

527. Earnings

Id. at p. 641.

their wartime earnings and savings with the Depression years.[528] The rise in overall prosperity is captured by the number of Americans filing tax returns. Only 4 million Americans filed in 1940 but by the end of the war this number had increased ten-fold to more than 42.6 million.[529] While a significant proportion of this increase is due to the lowering of the personal exemption from $1500 to $624 in the Revenue Act of 1942, this still remains a remarkable increase in the number of Americans with an interest in government fiscal policy.[530]

The significance of this for criminal procedure, including the right of confrontation, is conditional but straightforward. If the wartime prosperity could be made permanent, this would mean that almost all Americans would have a personal stake in the status quo. If labor-management conflict could be turned into peaceful channels through the N.L.R.B. (and union membership had risen from ten to fifteen million during the war), one of the major causes of prewar social disorder could be avoided.[531] This process would be aided if unions could be convinced, or coerced, into abandoning their sociopolitical agenda for a purely economic one.[532] The rise of business prestige during the war years would certainly further this goal.[533] Business was already putting a consumerist spin on the war effort; one advertisement claimed we were fighting "to hasten the day when you * * * can once more walk into any store in the land and buy anything you want."[534] One need not go so far as to say that "you are what you buy" to see that if material needs were primary, then they depended on employment. This presented the possibility that the employment relation could be substituted for the criminal law as a method of social control.[535] One of the

528. Real wages

Ibid.

529. Tax returns

Id. at p. 624.

530. Lowering exemption

Ibid.

531. Union membership

Id. at p. 642.

532. Sociopolitical agenda

This was by no means assured. Even Samuel Gompers, thought of as the founder of "business unionism" once said: "[w]hat does labor want? We want more schoolhouses and less jails, more books and less arsenals, more learning and less vice, more leisure and less greed, more justice and less revenge." Raskin, On the Virtual Picket Line, The Nation, May 31, 1999, pp. 28, 30.

533. Business prestige

Kennedy, Freedom From Fear, 1999, p. 623.

534. "Anything you want"

Foner, The Story of American Freedom, 1998, p. 230

535. Substituted for criminal law

This does not require anything as crude or coercive as the drug testing of em-

achievements of the Second Red Scare would show the power of the employment relationship as a tool for social conformity.[536] If the criminal law need no longer be the first line of defense against revolution nor the major system for disciplining the working class to middle class morals, its efforts could be directed against those whose behavior was all but universally seen as deviant.[537] This still left a lot of work for the adversary system but it also left room to further many other goals in addition to social control.[538]

The major challenge to an expanded role for the adversary system and the right of confrontation was the "hard right" in American politics, which reemerged in 1944.[539] The same year also saw the publication of F.A. Hayek's "The Road to Serfdom," which by the end of the century would be something like a bible of libertarian anarchism.[540] Hayek was an Austrian economist who had settled in England and was bright enough to notice the similarity of bureaucracies everywhere.[541] Hayek, like most economists, was given to uncomplicated views of the world.[542] He repopularized the laissez-faire definition of "liberty"; that is, "freedom

ployees that became common at the end of the century. But this practice demonstrates how employers, who are not bound by the Bill of Rights, are much more "efficient" agents of conformity than the state. Moreover, the monitoring of the behavior of employees even in rather mild bureaucracies is far more intense than anything that could be achieved by the most rigorous police state. Hiring one employee to eavesdrop on others is much cheaper than paying policemen to do the same thing.

536. Show the power

See below, text at notecall 787.

537. Seen as deviant

As the inspection of criminal dockets discloses, we are a long way from such a world. But at least one of the reasons that courts are still handling sumptuary offenses like drug abuse is that judges cut constitutional corners to make the criminal sanction less expensive and more prevalent than the Founders probably intended. And, of course, the fact that so many of those in the drug trade are people for whom there is no decent employment in the legal economy.

538. Other goals

E.g., popular monitoring of the criminal-justice system.

539. "Hard right" reemerged

Manchester, The Glory and The Dream, 1974, p. 318.

540. "Road to Serfdom"

Foner, The Story of American Freedom, 1998, p. 235.

541. Bureaucracies

This could be seen in the Second Red Scare, though that is not where most of Hayek's disciples were looking.

542. Uncomplicated view

If Hayek had ever lived in Michigan or been a member of the Roman Catholic faith, he might have had less faith in the distinction between private and public bureaucracies that seems crucial to his disciples.

from coercion."[543] Once one accepts this, his major thesis follows: "government planning leads to dictatorship"—the road referred to in his title.[544] Hayek, unlike some of his devotees, saw, though he did not say, that "capitalism" means, "if no one needs you, you die."[545] Hence, he was willing to allow for a limited welfare state to prevent the market's "race to the bottom" of wages and to provide for those no longer needed by employers.[546] Tellingly, however, this portion of Hayek's book was removed when it was condensed for Americans by The Reader's Digest.[547]

Hiroshima, Harry Bridges, and the Morality of Means

The year 1945 is best known for the end of World War II, in Europe on May 9 and on August 14 in the Pacific.[548] It was also the year that President Roosevelt met Churchill and Stalin in Yalta and, in the view of his enemies, gave away the fruits of victory.[549] For persons of this view, then, 1945 also marked the beginning of The Cold War.[550] President Roosevelt died on April 12, leaving an ill-prepared Harry Truman to lead the nation through the aftermath of war.[551] Some indication of what was to come can be glimpsed by the fate of the Full Employment Act—a statute intended to civilianize the lessons of military Keynesianism.[552] Introduced in 1945 with the backing of virtually every element of the old New Deal coalition, the act was gutted by a conservative Congress and passed the following year without the guarantee that gave the bill its name.[553]

543. "Freedom from coercion"

Ibid.

544. "Planning leads to dictatorship"

Ibid.

545. "You die"

We have been unable to lay our hands on the source of this quotation, but the reader may be sure that someone once said it.

546. Limited welfare state

Id. at p. 236.

547. Condensed out

Ibid.

548. End of war

Encyclopedia of American History, Morris ed. 1976, pp. 443, 449.

549. Yalta

Encyclopedia of American Facts and Dates, 9th ed. 1993, p. 528.

550. Beginning of Cold War

Kennedy, Freedom From Fear, 1999, p. 807.

551. Death of Roosevelt

Manchester, The Glory and The Dream, 1974, pp. 349–362.

552. Full Employment Act

Foner, The Story of American Freedom, 1998, p. 234.

553. Passed without guarantee

Id. at p. 235.

In 1945 the Federal Communications Commission made its first allocation of television channels, signifying the medium that was to bring Americans face to face with the image of The Other while distancing them from their neighbors.[554] In an early instance of the politics of imagery, the Communist Political Association voted to disband.[555] Meanwhile, the "Kilroy" craze came and went; G.I.s in Europe began chalking and writing the phrase "Kilroy was here" on walls, buildings, and billboards—in some instances with a crude cartoon of a stick figure climbing a fence.[556] The practice spread like wildfire around the world and, while various pundits tried to explain its meaning, ceased as suddenly as it began. No one seems to have thought that "Kilroy" might be a metaphor for the anonymous informant who would soon become the ubiquitous symbol of dread.

But for the Confrontation Clause, the most portentous events of 1945 were the dropping of the atomic bombs on Hiroshima and Nagasaki.[557] We need not enter into the contentious question of whether there is a factual basis for the instrumental justifications advanced for nuclear warfare because we are concerned with the morality of instrumental justifications generally, not with their specific application to the events of 1945.[558]

In 1940, while the United States was still technically neutral, President Roosevelt called on the belligerents to refrain from "bombardment from the air of civilian populations or of unfortified cities."[559] The President thus invoked a tenet of warfare, admittedly often honored in the breach, that went back to the time that the Church had attempted to Christianize warfare; namely, the distinction between combatants and noncombatants.[560] While not apparently part of international law, the principle could be seen at work in various international regulations of war; for example, the Gene-

554. First television channels

Encyclopedia of American Facts and Dates, 9th ed. 1993, p. 528.

555. Voted to disband

Id. at p. 529.

556. "Kilroy was here"

Id. at p. 527.

557. Dropping of atomic bombs

Rhodes, The Making of the Atomic Bomb, 1986, pp. 708–711, 749–750.

558. Not specific applications

For an account of the latest resurgence of the conflict, see Linenthal & Engelhardt, History Wars, 1996.

559. "Unfortified cities"

Kennedy, Freedom From Fear, 1999, p. 426.

560. Noncombatants

Chadwick, A History of Christianity, 1995, p. 256.

va Convention on the treatment of prisoners of war and of hospitals and medical personnel on the field of battle.[561]

What Roosevelt and his audience did not know was that the military mind had already crossed the divide. In his 1921 book, "The Command of the Air," the Italian strategist Giulio Douhet had linked air power with the concept of "total war."[562] Modern warfare, in Douhet's view, was not a clash of combatants but of entire nations. He lumped together as legitimate targets "the woman loading shells in a factory, the farmer growing wheat, the scientist experimenting in his laboratory" as well as "the soldier carrying his gun."[563] Civilians, Douhet noted, were untrained and easier to break than soldiers. "How could a country go on living and working oppressed by the nightmare of imminent destruction and death?"[564]

Douhet's book was required reading in American military schools. But American strategists such as Billy Mitchell rejected the concept of total war in favor of what came to be called "precision bombing"—today called "surgical strikes"—on economic targets.[565] A 1926 training manual admitted that air power provided "a method of imposing will by terrorizing the whole population."[566] By 1930 this had shifted to balancing the military value of attacks "on civilian populations in the back areas of the hostile country" against "the effect of public opinion."[567] In 1941, an Air Corps battle plan provided that "as German morale begins to crack," it might be "highly profitable to deliver a large-scale, all-out attack on the civil population of Berlin."[568] Notice that in all this rampant instrumentalism, there is no consideration of the morality of bombing helpless women and children.

By the time American aviators arrived in Europe, the British had already discovered that "precision bombing" was not only all but physically impossible but that attempts at precision were costly

---

561. **Geneva Convention**

Craig, The War Against War, N.Y. Rev. Bks., June 24, 1999 pp. 40, 42.

562. **"Total war"**

Kennedy, Freedom From Fear, 1999, p. 602.

563. **Carrying his gun**

Ibid.

564. **"Destruction and death"**

Ibid.

565. **"Precision bombing"**

Id. at p. 603.

566. **"Terrorizing population"**

Ibid.

567. **"Public opinion"**

Ibid.

568. **"Highly profitable"**

Ibid.

in planes and men.[569] Under the euphemism of "area bombing," in 1942 they began to use bombing to "destroy the morale of the enemy civil population and in particular the industrial workers."[570] When the Americans arrived later that year, they rejected the concept of "area bombing" because of the effect they feared it would have on American public opinion.[571] The Americans pushed ahead with "precision bombing" on the grounds that it was "in accordance with American principles using methods for which our planes were designed."[572] They, like the British, discovered it could not be done without unacceptable costs.[573]

In 1944, the worst fears of the American aerial strategists were realized when a British pacifist condemned "area bombing" in a religious journal.[574] This sparked an intense flurry of commentary in the United States, where some Americans were already upset over the bombing of Monte Cassino, a religious and historical landmark in Italy.[575] However, the furor soon blew over.

Later in 1944, the British proposed "Operation Thunderclap," a saturation bombing campaign aimed at killing 275,000 civilians in Berlin in an effort to break German morale.[576] Some Americans were astounded; one senior officer described it as another of the English "baby killing schemes."[577] Such a raid, it was objected, "would be a blot on the history of the Air forces and of the U.S. * * * It gives full rein to the baser elements of our people."[578] But

569. Impossible and costly

Id. at p. 604

570. "Industrial workers"

Ibid.

571. Rejected "area bombing"

Ibid.

572. "American principles"

Ibid.

573. Unacceptable costs

Id. at pp. 605–606.

574. Pacifist condemned

Id. at p. 704.

575. Monte Cassino

Id. at pp. 704–705. The Monte Cassino flap may have been what led to the elimination of Kyoto, a city with shrines sacred to the Japanese, from the list of potential targets for atom bombing. Rhodes, The Making of the Atomic Bomb, 1986, p. 641.

576. "Thunderclap"

Kennedy, Freedom From Fear, 1999, p. 743.

577. "Baby killing schemes"

Ibid. General Spaatz told Eisenhower that the British were attempting "to have the U.S. tarred with the moral bombing aftermath which we feel will be terrific." Id. at p. 744.

578. "Baser elements"

Id. at p. 743.

General Eisenhower provided the instrumental response to such moral reservations: "I am always prepared to take part in anything that gives real promise to ending the war quickly."[579]

On February 3, 1945, a saturation bombing of Berlin killed 25,000 civilians.[580] Ten days later, an incendiary attack on Dresden ignited a firestorm that killed 35,000 people by flame and suffocation—an event memorialized in "Slaughterhouse–Five" by Kurt Vonnegut, who was a prisoner of war in Dresden at the time of the attack.[581] American newspapers embraced Eisenhower's instrumentalism; one paper editorialized that "Allied air bosses have made the long-awaited decision to adopt deliberate terror bombing of the German population centers as a ruthless expedient to hasten Hitler's doom."[582] No one had the bad grace to invoke an analogy to Lidice.[583]

The lessons of Dresden were immediately transferred to the Pacific. General Curtis LeMay arrived in Guam to take charge with Douhet's philosophy unvarnished: "I'll tell you what war is about," he said; "You've got to kill people, and when you have killed enough, they stop fighting."[584] The firebombing of Japanese cities began. In one raid on Tokyo that generated a worse firestorm than Dresden, nearly 90,000 people were killed, some boiled to death in canals where they had sought refuge from the heat.[585] In all, 900,000 Japanese were killed and more than a million injured in similar "firebombings."[586]

Hence, by the time the decision was made to use atomic weapons on Japan, the United States had long since crossed the

579. "Ending war quickly"

Id. at p. 744.

580. Berlin

Ibid.

581. Dresden

Ibid.

582. "Ruthless expedient"

Ibid.

583. Lidice

The reference is to an incident during the Nazi occupation of Czechoslovakia when, after the assassination of a Nazi commander, presumably by Czech partisans, the Germans rounded up the population of a village near the site of the assassination and killed them. No doubt the Germans could have justified this as a method to break the morale of the Czech resistance. It was featured prominently in war propaganda. See Conot, Justice at Nuremberg, 1983, p. 265.

584. "Got to kill"

Id. at p. 845.

585. Tokyo fire raids

Id. at p. 847.

586. 900,000 killed

Ibid.

moral boundary into total war.[587] Hiroshima demonstrated the departures from pre-war ideals but it did not create them. If Americans felt any moral anguish at the time, it is not a conspicuous part of the historical record.[588] Even those who did protest, like the Socialist Norman Thomas, used instrumental reasoning: "[w]e shall pay for this in a horrible hatred of millions of people which goes deeper and farther than we think."[589] Ironically, an elaborate Air Force study of Germany and Germans after the war failed to find much empirical support for the factual assumptions of the instrumental argument.[590] While Hiroshima undoubtedly triggered the end of the war in the Pacific, it did not do this by breaking the morale of the civilian population but by demonstrating to the leaders of the Japanese government that morale was irrelevant.[591]

As Americans were later to discover, it was difficult to limit the concept of "total war" to the Air Force; its use in Viet Nam by ground troops provoked some courts-martial and some debates over the morality of war.[592] However, for the purposes of the right of confrontation it is sufficient to suggest that moral unease over our embrace of total war played a subconscious reinforcement for the horrors of the Holocaust in triggering a brief post-war concern among academic lawyers about the relationship between morality and law.[593]

Meanwhile, elsewhere in 1945, the Supreme Court approached the morality of means and the right of confrontation from a somewhat oblique angle.[594] Harry Bridges was an Australian national who had lived in the United States for a quarter of a century

587. Long since crossed

Id. at p. 845. This may explain the surprisingly little debate over their use once the bombs had been built. See Rhodes, The Making of the Atomic Bomb, 1986, pp. 624–651.

588. Not part of the record

Once other nations had the bomb, this generated significant discussion in religious circles and elsewhere about the morality of nuclear warfare, but that was a far different question. The Oxford Illustrated History of Christianity, McManners ed. 1990, p. 613–616.

589. "Hatred of millions"

Manchester, The Glory and The Dream, 1974, p. 208.

590. Empirical support

Kennedy, Freedom From Fear, 1999, p. 744.

591. Morale irrelevant

Id. at pp. 850–851.

592. Use in Viet Nam

Manchester, The Glory and The Dream, 1974, pp. 1175–1178.

593. Morality and law

White, From Sociological Jurisprudence to Realism: Jurisprudence and Social Change in Early Twentieth Century America, 1972, 58 Va.L.Rev. 999, 1026.

594. Oblique angle

Bridges v. Wixon, 65 S.Ct. 1443, 326 U.S. 135, 89 L.Ed. 2103.

and during that time had become one of the most powerful labor leaders on the Pacific Coast.[595] In that role, he gathered an impressive list of enemies, including the Navy (Bridges had warned the Navy of the danger that would later produce the Port Chicago catastrophe.).[596] These enemies carried out a systematic attempt to get rid of him.[597]

In both 1934 and 1935, attempts to deport him came to nothing because the I.N.S. could find no evidence that he had been a Communist at the time of his entry in 1920, a requirement of the statute in existence at the time.[598] Nonetheless, the I.N.S. tried again in 1938, but after an administrative trial before a hearing officer, Dean Landis of the Harvard Law School, he was found to have been clear of Communist taint.[599] Congress then tried to get rid of Bridges by a special immigration bill until the Attorney General pointed out that the Constitution forbids bills of attainder.[600] Hence, Congress passed an amendment to the immigration statute in the Alien Registration Act that was clearly aimed at Bridges.[601] As one of the sponsors said, this "bill changes the law so that the Department of Justice should now have little trouble in deporting Harry Bridges and all others of similar ilk."[602]

595. Bridges

Id. at 1495, 326 U.S. at 137. For an account of Bridges' role in the 1934 general strike, see Brecher, Strike!, 1972, pp. 150–158.

596. Warned of catastrophe

Kennedy, Freedom From Fear, 1999, p. 774.

597. Enemies

The objection to Bridges, insofar as the junior author could glean during his work in labor law in the early 1960s, was that, unlike the leaders of longshoreman's unions on the East Coast, he was not associated with the Mob and thus was unwilling to sell out union membership in the kind of sweetheart deals shipping companies were accustomed to making in the East.

598. 1934 and 1935 attempts

Id. at 1454, 326 U.S. at 158 (Murphy, J., concurring).

599. Landis hearing

Id. at 1445, 326 U.S. at 138.

600. Attainder

Ibid.

601. Amended

Id. at 1445, 326 U.S. at 138. The author of the bill said: "[i]t is my joy to announce that this bill will do, in a perfectly legal and constitutional manner, what the bill specifically aimed at the deportation of Harry Bridges seeks to accomplish." Id. at 1454, 326 U.S. at 158–159 (Murphy, J., concurring).

602. "Similar ilk"

Id. at 1454, 326 U.S. at 159 (Murphy, J., concurring).

The Department had more than a "little trouble." Despite wire taps and repeated searches without warrants of Bridges' home by government agents, the evidence produced at the deportation hearing was found insufficient by the majority of the Supreme Court to uphold the deportation order.[603] The one bit of evidence that did support the order was a prior statement by a witness at the hearing which the hearing officer admitted as substantive evidence, relying partly on Wigmore and partly on a provision in the statute that, according to the dissenters, allowed him to ignore "technical rules of evidence."[604] Deportation was not regarded as a "criminal prosecution" so the Confrontation Clause did not directly apply.[605] But the majority said, the hearsay

> certainly would not be admissible in any criminal case as substantive evidence. * * * So to hold would allow men to be convicted on the unsworn testimony of witnesses—a practice which runs counter to the notions of fairness on which our legal system is founded. * * * Though deportation is not technically a criminal proceeding, it visits great hardship on the individual and deprives him of the right to stay and live and work in this land of freedom. That deportation is a penalty—at times a most serious one—cannot be doubted. Meticulous care must be exercised lest the procedure by which he is deprived of that liberty not meet the essential standards of fairness.[606]

Hence, it was error correctable by habeas corpus for the government to rely on this evidence to support the order of deportation.[607]

The dissenters, Chief Justice Stone and Justices Frankfurter and Roberts, treated the case as simply another question of judicial review of the work of administrative tribunals, found the evidence sufficient to meet the low standards applied in cases of business

603. Insufficient

Id. at 1450, 326 U.S. at 149. The description of the illegal gathering of evidence is in Justice Murphy's concurring opinion. Id. at 1454, 326 U.S. at 157.

604. Wigmore and statute

The prior statements, which the witness denied making, were in a stenographic recording of his interrogation by I.N.S. agents. Id. at 1451, 326 U.S. at 150–151. The basis of the admission of the statement appears in Chief Justice Stone's dissenting opinion. Id. at 1462–1463, 326 U.S. at 176–177.

605. Did not apply

The Court's failure to mention the Sixth Amendment, even by way of analogy, may have been due to the decision of the majority to avoid the many constitutional questions raised by Bridges. Id. 1453–1454, 326 U.S. at 156–157.

606. "Standards of fairness"

Id. at 1452, U.S. 153–154.

607. Habeas corpus

Id. at 1453, 326 U.S. at 156.

regulation, and criticized the majority for imposing "technical rules of evidence" on administrative tribunals contrary to the intent of Congress.[608] The inability of the dissenters to distinguish administrative prosecution of political dissent from a trademark dispute did not augur well for victims of administrative tribunals in the upcoming Red Scare.

Two events, little noticed in 1945, later assumed totemic significance during the Red Scare. In Suchow, China, a headstrong 27–year-old Baptist fundamentalist working as a spy violated his orders to treat Communist officers with "diplomacy," got into a shouting match, and was shot by Communist troops.[609] Less than a month later, Igor Gouzenko, a code clerk at the Soviet embassy in Ottawa, Canada, sought asylum and to show his good faith brought with him an armful of cables disclosing Soviet spying in the United States and Canada, including the names of two spies who had worked on the atomic bomb and passed along secrets to the Soviets.[610]

Nuremberg, Instrumentalism, and Communism

In 1945, the United Nations began operation and wartime idealism took a beating.[611] It began with demobilization riots among the troops in Europe. Newspapers were horrified that soldiers should take seriously the promises of peace.[612] However, investigation disclosed the troops had legitimate grievances; they were surviving on a diet of C-rations while officers were eating caviar and swilling champagne.[613] At least confrontation values were not

608. "Technical rules"

Id. at 1463 n.3, 326 U.S. at 177 n. 3.

609. Shot by Communist troops

Manchester, The Glory and The Dream, 1974, p. 393. The officer gave his name to one of the most paranoid of the antiradical movements of the time, The John Birch Society, which among other things posted billboards around the country calling for the impeachment of Chief Justice Earl Warren.

610. Gouzenko

Id. at p. 493. The trail would ultimately lead to the Rosenbergs, who were con-

victed of espionage and executed after a controversial trial at the height of the Red Scare.

611. United Nations

Encyclopedia of American History, Morris ed. 1976, p. 463.

612. Promises of peace

Manchester, The Glory and The Dream, 1974, p. 409.

613. Caviar and champagne

Id. at p. 406.

dead; the rioting troops denounced their commanders as "cowards" who were unwilling to confront the bearers of their grievances.[614]

Similar pent-up grievances burst forth on the home front. Workers had, by and large, honored the no-strike pledge made by union leaders before Pearl Harbor.[615] By working 48 hours a week, workers had been able to nearly double their wages during the war.[616] However, Congress had ended rationing and price controls despite predictions of inflation that proved to be correct.[617] Angered at this silent pay cut, workers sought a 40–hour week and wage hikes. In the first year after the end of the war, more than five million men were on strike at one time or another.[618] Angered, President Truman sought and received from Congress the power to draft strikers into the Army.[619]

The end of the war also saw a revival of student radicalism, which campus administrators paternalistically sought to limit, requiring student organizations to provide lists of their members— lists that were potent tools for the perpetrators of the Second Red Scare.[620] Perhaps more squeamish about academic freedom, deans and hiring committees treated radical political beliefs as a symptom of immaturity or psychological instability and screened faculty applicants on those grounds.[621]

1946 was also the year of Winston Churchill's well-known "Iron Curtain" speech, which for some marked the beginning of the Cold War.[622] In the midterm elections, the Republicans gained control of both houses of Congress.[623] Joseph McCarthy used a

614. Unwilling to confront

Id. at p. 408.

615. No-strike pledge

Id. at p. 400.

616. Double wages

Id. at p. 397.

617. Inflation

Id. at p. 398.

618. Five million on strike

Id. at p. 400.

619. Draft strikers

Id. at pp. 401–403.

620. Paternalistically limit

Schrecker, No Ivory Tower: McCarthyism and the Universities, 1986, p. 84. As one dean presciently announced:

"We should protect students from the harm it will do them in the future if they have joined a Communist League." Id. at p. 88.

621. Psychological instability

Id. at pp. 88–89.

622. "Iron Curtain" speech

Encyclopedia of American History, Morris. ed. 1976, p. 464.

623. Republicans gained

Encyclopedia of American Facts and Dates, 9th ed. 1993, p. 557.

phony war record to secure election to the Senate and a group of conservative Republican businessmen bankrolled Richard Nixon's election to the House over a New Deal Democrat.[624] Congress took the first step in the use of the employment relationship to control dissent without running afoul of the First Amendment when, in the McCarran Rider to the State Department appropriation, it gave the Secretary of State "absolute discretion" to fire employees.[625] And, in a foretaste of the sort of reasoning that was soon to dominate American culture, Senator William Langer of North Dakota denounced the war crimes trial of Axis leaders as a Communist plot.[626]

The Nuremberg trials had several implications for the right of confrontation. The tribunal employed a hybrid procedure; basically the Anglo–American adversary system with inquisitorial features such as the use of hearsay, principally dossiers of interrogations, grafted on.[627] When the defense objected to the discriminatory application of the inquisitorial procedures, the judges had to resort to sidestepping the issue.[628] However, the trials disclosed that confrontation values were not confined to those trained in Anglo–American procedure; when the prosecution proposed to try an ailing German industrialist in absentia, it was a French judge who objected to this proposal.[629] However, the value of cross-examination as an adversary tool was brought into question when Justice Jackson, functioning as a prosecutor, botched the cross-examination of Hermann Goering, whether through ineptitude or lack of preparation, thus allowing Goering to project himself as a sympathetic figure.[630] In the aftermath of the trials, some criticism of the tribunal focused on its procedures.[631]

624. McCarthy and Nixon

Manchester, The Glory and The Dream, 1974, pp. 394, 395. McCarthy campaigned as "Tailgunner Joe"; in fact, he never flew anything but a desk.

625. "Absolute discretion"

Caute, The Great Fear, 1978, p. 26.

626. Communist plot

"It is the Communists' avowed purpose to destroy the western world, which is based on property rights. It was intended to try the accused as aggressors, convict them of having started the war, and then confiscate their property." Conot, Justice at Nuremberg, 1983, p. 517.

627. Hybrid procedure

Id. at pp. 86, 324.

628. Sidestepping

Id. at p. 148.

629. French judge objected

Id. at p. 77.

630. Botched cross-examination

Id. at p. 338.

631. Criticism of procedures

Id. at p. 354.

A more excusable failing of the tribunal was its rejection of the prosecution's attempt to construct a theory of collective guilt.[632] This was important because the defendants adopted a schizophrenic strategy; on the one hand, they insisted on the individualization of guilt, yet on the other hand, they sought to excuse their behavior by resorting to group loyalties and the morality of role.[633] In opposition to the prosecution, the defense argued that conspiracy was a concept unknown to international law.[634] Ironically, the judge who took the leading role in rejecting collective guilt was the American, Francis Biddle.[635] One may wonder whether his objections may not have rested, at least in part, on a subconscious appreciation of the implications of collective guilt for his own responsibility for the American use of concentration camps. But perhaps the most significant impact of the Nuremberg trials was the way in which they forced Americans to confront what a later writer was to call "the banality of evil."[636] Judges, lawyers, and members of the press were struck when brought face-to-face with the masterminds of the Nazi regime to discover that they were not the raving psychotics sometimes portrayed in Allied propaganda but among "the best and the brightest" of the German elite.[637] As one writer put it:

> [w]hat had taken place in this culture of lunacy was not that ordinary human sensibilities had disappeared, or that the denizens had been unable to distinguish right and wrong, or moral and immoral actions, but that Hitler had convinced them that commonly accepted ethics and morality were Judeo–Christian inventions to be superseded by doctrines based on utilitarianism and necessity.[638]

632. Collective guilt

Id. at p. 345.

633. Schizophrenic strategy

"In Germany, as in all other states, the punishment of groups and organizations is not known at all, only the punishment of individuals is known." Id. at p. 456 (quoting counsel for the defense).

"It is tragic to have to realize that the best I had to give as a soldier, obedience and loyalty, was exploited for the purposes, which could not be recognized at the time, and that I did not see that there is a limit set even on a soldier's performance of his duty." Id. at p. 475 (quoting defendant Keitel's testimony).

634. Conspiracy unknown

Id. at p. 482.

635. Biddle

Id. at p. 484–485.

636. "Banality of evil"

The phrase is Hannah Arendt's, in her book, "Eichmann in Jerusalem."

637. "Best and brightest"

Conot, Justice at Nuremberg, 1983, p. 102.

638. "Utilitarianism, necessity"

Id. at p. 512.

Listening to genocide justified as a logical instrument for the solution of "the Jewish problem" would be enough to jar even the most dedicated instrumentalist into awareness of the need for a morality of means to at least supplement, if not replace, the amoral consequentialism that had dominated American legal thought since the Progressive era.[639]

Some of the criticisms of the fairness of the war crimes trial also had implications for American procedure.[640] For example, the prosecution had developed overwhelming evidence that the leading German industrialists not only profited from slave labor but also provided the gas and the ovens used at Auschwitz, yet most of the executives of these companies (some of which can be seen advertising on television today) were either found not guilty or were sentenced to time served awaiting trial.[641] Similarly, whereas only a handful of the perpetrators of the Holocaust were executed (none of them low-level military officers), the Tokyo War Crimes Trials resulted in the execution of 720 Japanese.[642] The race war in the Pacific seems to have ended with racialized justice.

Truman Institutionalizes the Red Scare

In 1947, George Kennan published his famous "X" article outlining the notion of "containment" of the Soviet empire, the President embraced Kennan's thesis in what came to be known as the "Truman Doctrine," and the National Security Council codified it in a policy paper known as "NSC–68."[643] In addition to institutionalizing "military Keynesianism," NSC–68 set up the Cold War for American citizens and policymakers as a contest between "slavery" and "freedom."[644] Among the consequences of this dichotomi-

---

639. Genocide justified

Id. at pp. 257–273.

640. Criticisms of fairness

The prosecution had tried, with limited success, to prevent the defense from proving that the Allies had engaged in conduct similar to that for which the defendants were charged with crimes. Id. at p. 325.

641. Time served

Id. at p. 517. An American accused the judges of bias but it seems to have been the same kind of bias one finds when corporate executives are charged

with murder for putting dangerous products on the market.

642. Execution of 720

Encyclopedia of American History, Morris ed. 1976, p. 462 (comparing statistics from both tribunals).

643. "NSC–68"

Manchester, The Glory and The Dream, 1974, p. 437.

644. "Slavery" and "freedom"

Foner, The Story of American Freedom, 1998, p. 253. The author, Paul Nitze, would later become a leading figure in

zation is that it allowed for no gradations; you were either for "freedom" or against it.[645] In addition to requiring some ludicrous characterizations (fascist Spain and racist South Africa were part of "the free world"), it led to equally rigid and ludicrous classifications of "American" and "Un–American."[646]

Ironically, 1947 was the year "The Freedom Train," a collection of many of the nation's sacred documents such as the Mayflower Compact, the Declaration of Independence, and the Gettysburg Address, began its national tour.[647] More than three-and-a-half-million Americans actually boarded the train and many more participated in civic celebrations that accompanied its appearance in local communities.[648] In a rare indication of attitudes changed by the war, the organizers refused to schedule the train into any community in which local officials insisted on racial segregation of visitors.[649]

Two weeks after proclaiming the "Truman Doctrine," the President, in what he frankly conceded was an attempt to steal the thunder of the House Un–American Activities Committee and to position himself and his party as sufficiently anti-Red for the 1948 elections, issued Executive Order 9835—one of the founding documents of the Second Red Scare.[650] Aimed at "disloyal" civil servants, E.O. 9835 provided for the discharge of any government

the revival of the Cold War under President Reagan.

645. No gradations

As on observer noted, the dichotomization produced a "kind of upside-down Russian veto" in domestic politics; that is, if the Soviets favored public housing or universal medical care, Americans had to oppose these. Id. at p. 262.

For a remarkably accurate prediction of what the Truman doctrine would entail for American foreign policy, see the quotation from Walter Lippman in id. at p. 254.

646. "Free world"

Ibid.

647. "Freedom Train"

Id. at p. 249. To defuse the claim that it was government propaganda—the idea for the train emanated from the Justice Department—management of the train was turned over to a committee of businessmen. Ibid. The committee excluded documents suggested by the National Archives that were deemed too "liberal," including the Reconstruction amendments to the Constitution and Roosevelt's "Four Freedoms." Id. at p. 250.

648. Boarded train

Ibid. The junior author was among them.

649. No racial segregation

Ibid.

650. E.O. 9835

Id. at p. 255; Caute, The Great Fear, 1978, p. 27 (includes complete account of genesis of order); Manchester, The Glory and The Dream, 1974, p. 494.

employee who was a member of or in "sympathetic association" with a subversive organization.[651] This was the beginning of the infamous "guilt by association"; for example, a foreign service officer who was a staunch anti-Communist was fired because of an affair with the leftist writer Lillian Hellman.[652]

The standards for dismissal became broader when President Eisenhower issued Executive Order 10450, which shifted the focus of the inquiry from whether the employee was "disloyal" to whether he was a "security risk"; the employee was to be suspended immediately without pay for "any behavior, activities, or associations which tend to show that the individual is not reliable or trustworthy."[653] Under E.O. 10450, any deviation from the accepted norms would do; "drunkenness, drug addiction, participation in unusual [read "homosexual"] sexual practices, membership in a nudist colony, unsanitary habits, a reputation for lying."[654] As a result of the Eisenhower order, those who had previously passed muster under the Truman standards had to undergo another inquisition into their personal habits and beliefs.[655] The dragnet inquiries undertaken under this standard by loyalty boards and the F.B.I. are shocking under any sort of First Amendment standard.[656]

More troubling than the vague substantive standards were the procedures established to govern the loyalty boards that would

651. "Sympathetic association"
Id. at p. 495.

652. "Guilt by association"
Caute, The Great Fear, 1978, p. 274; Fariello, Red Scare, 1995, p. 165 (Hellman).

653. E.O. 10450
Id. at p. 40 (quoting order).

654. "Reputation for lying"
Manchester, The Glory and The Dream, 1974, p. 671; Foner, The Story of American Freedom, 1998, p. 256 (homosexuals).

655. Another inquisition
Caute, The Great Fear, 1978, p. 273.

656. Dragnet inquiries
Id. at p. 281 (who did you vote for, did you favor the United Nations, have you provided religious training for you children, do you believe in government ownership of utilities, do you favor redistribution of wealth, how would you define "reactionary," do workers get a fair deal under the capitalist system?).

Id. at pp. 392–393 (do you think members of Community Party are guilty of treason, what newspapers do you read and what book clubs do you belong to, does your wife have liberal political viewpoints, have you read books by Howard Fast, Theodore Dreiser or Lion [sic] Feuchtwanger, what do you think of the Truman Doctrine and the Italian situation?).

See also, id. at pp. 396–397; Manchester, The Glory and The Dream, 1974, p. 495 (collecting accusations from those who were lucky enough to get such).

enforce them.[657] The Truman order first required only that the evidence provide "reasonable grounds" to believe that the employee was disloyal.[658] However, by a later executive order, E.O. 1024, it was sufficient if the evidence raised a "reasonable doubt" as to the person's loyalty.[659] A later Eisenhower order made it grounds for dismissal if the employee exercised any provision of the Bill of Rights in response to official inquiry—a provision aimed at so-called "Fifth Amendment Communists," though it was broad enough to cover anyone who claimed the First Amendment barred inquiry into his beliefs or who demanded to confront the witnesses against him.[660]

Under E.O. 9335 and its successors, the employee was supposed to be provided notice of the charges against him "if security considerations permit."[661] They seldom did. Similarly, though witnesses were supposed to confront the employee, the F.B.I. almost always claimed the informer or other government privilege to prevent confrontation with informers.[662] Attorney General Brownell later claimed that during his administration he had attempted to get the courts to clarify the constitutionality of such practices and other government officers were into denial on these procedural protections.[663] Since all of the accused and their lawyers claimed confrontation was usually denied, a scholarly study sampled cases and found that in only 6% of the cases were employees confronted by their accusers.[664]

657. Procedures

Bad as they were, at least civilian personnel had some procedural protections; civilian employees of the military had none. Caute, The Great Fear, 1978, p. 294.

658. "Reasonable grounds"

Fariello, Red Scare, 1995, p. 40.

659. "Reasonable doubt"

Ibid.

660. "Fifth Amendment"

Ibid.

661. "Security considerations"

Manchester, The Glory and The Dream, 1974, p. 495.

662. Prevent confrontation

Ibid.

663. Brownell claimed

Fariello, Red Scare, 1995, p. 110; Caute, The Great Fear, 1978, p. 277 (Harry Truman claims confrontation and notice of charges supplied).

664. Only 6%

Fariello, Red Scare, 1995, p. 36 (employees usually denied notice of charges and confrontation of witnesses); Caute, The Great Fear, 1978, p. 277 (only 6%).

The victims well understood what they were being denied. Here is how a union representative who attempted to aid government employees put it:

> I soon found out what the process was about; these were kangaroo courts. No cross-examination of witnesses—in fact no witnesses. Not only no witnesses but also no evidence. And because of that the cases became extremely difficult. The prevailing rule was guilt by association. If you ever had the courage to speak out on an issue like segregation, you were a marked man. The members of the boards would read from documents which would state, "T–17 stated that so-and-so belonged to such-and-such an organization," or "T–17 stated that an employee's brother was a member of the Communist Party, * * *" This was unadulterated, raw stuff that the F.B.I. turned over to the loyalty boards. They had no way of knowing whether it was any good or not.[665]

Other victims made similar statements.[666] In those rare cases where the boards did order confrontation, the cases against the accused collapsed—sometimes quite dramatically.[667]

As an example of the horror cases that began to surface, consider that of Abraham Chasanow, who had worked in the Navy Hydrographic Office for 23 years. He was suspended without pay when someone accused him of being a security risk. Two months later, a loyalty board examined the evidence and found it to be worthless, but the Assistant Secretary of the Navy fired him anyway. He was living on loans from his wife's relatives when reporter Anthony Lewis revealed his plight.[668] The Navy reexamined the charges and discovered that some anti-Semitic coworkers had accused the conservative Chasanow of left-wing associations, charges that they had no evidence to corroborate.[669] Chasanow was reinstated. Not all falsely accused were so lucky.[670] As a result of

---

665. "Good or not"

Fariello, Red Scare, 1995, pp. 142–143.

666. Similar statements

"The way the system worked in those days, you were given charges but you were not told who made them. You were not permitted to confront the accuser, and you were not permitted to answer him directly. You couldn't refer to files or anything." Id. at op. 166 (quoting John Melby, foreign service officer fired for association with Lillian Hellman).

667. Quite dramatically

Caute, The Great Fear, 1978, pp. 278–279 (collecting accounts of such cases).

668. Lewis revealed

Manchester, The Glory and The Dream, 1974, p. 671.

669. Anti-semitic charges

Caute, The Great Fear, 1978, p. 278.

670. Not so lucky

Fariello, Red Scare, 1995, p. 129 (bootblack accused of donating $10 to the Scottsboro Defense Fund—at a time

such cases, writers and judges began to denounce the use of "faceless informers."[671]

Under the loyalty programs, employees were subject to multiple jeopardy; a loyalty inquiry could be reopened any time additional adverse information was received or the governing standards were changed.[672] This was burdensome because though some agencies initially provided counsel to the accused, this was ordered stopped; legal costs of defending an accusation of disloyalty were

when he had not yet been born—took 70 F.B.I. interviews to clear).

A case that figured prominently in raising opposition to the Red Scare was that of Dorothy Bailey, a 41-year old exemplary employee of the U.S. Employment Service—an obvious target for Soviet spies. After a 14-year career in which her only known political activity was as President of the local chapter of the United Public Workers of America, she was hauled before a loyalty board and found to have associated with Communists. She denied these charges, no witnesses were called to substantiate them, and the only "evidence" was the hearsay statements of persons whose identity was not even known to the members of the board. Manchester, The Glory and The Dream, 1974, pp. 496–497; Caute, The Great Fear, 1978, pp. 276–277.

On appeal, represented by Thurman Arnold, all of her claims were rejected, over vigorous dissent. The majority opinion gives a sense of the attitudes of judges during the Second Red Scare: "[w]e cannot ignore the world situation in which not merely two ideologies but two potentially adverse forces presently exist * * *. Infiltration of government service is now a recognized technique for overthrow of government. We do not think that individual rights guaranteed by the Constitution necessarily mean that a government dedicated to those rights cannot preserve itself in the world as it is." Bailey v. Richardson, C.A.D.C.,

1950, 182 F.2d 46, 64–65. The decision was affirmed by an equally divided Court in Bailey v. Richardson, 1951, 71 S.Ct. 669, 341 U.S. 918, 95 L.Ed. 1352. See also, Murphy, The Constitution in Crisis Times, 1918–1969, 1972, p. 300.

671. "Faceless informers"

"A hearing at which these faceless informers are allowed to present their whispered rumors and yet escape the test and torture of cross-examination is not a hearing in the Anglo–American sense. We should have done with this practice." Caute, The Great Fear, 1978, p. 279 (quoting William O. Douglas).

"Experience in actual security cases shows that, when it can be exposed or challenged, the so-called information supplied by casual informers rarely results in an adverse decision * * *. On the other hand, the anonymity given to such informers is an open invitation to scandalmongers, crackpots, and personal enemies. Ibid. (quoting American Jewish Congress).

"Is this system of secret informers, whisperers and talebearers of such vital importance to the public welfare that it must be preserved at the cost of denying to the citizen even a modicum of the protection traditionally associated with due process?" (Id. at pp. 398–399, quoting federal judge ordering Coast Guard to allow confrontation).

672. Multiple jeopardy

Id. at pp. 273, 286.

substantial.[673] One study found that in 16% of a sample of cases, the attorney for the accused either received no compensation or accepted a fee that was less than the out-of-pocket costs of the defense.[674] Nor was simply walking away from a job an option; the loyalty agencies informed prospective civilian employers that the employee was considered disloyal.[675] The exact number of employees involved in loyalty inquiries was a political football and estimates vary.[676] But by any guess, the number of Americans touched by this phase of the Second Red Scare was substantial—far more than the numbers in more publicized events such as the Hollywood Blacklist.[677]

While Truman's loyalty boards were pursuing imaginary enemies, corporations were going after real ones; during the War, union membership had risen to an all-time high of nearly one-third of the civilian work force and, as we have seen, those unions were increasingly militant.[678] Hence, business groups and individual companies launched a campaign to destroy unions or at least force them to retreat to "business unionism."[679] In the 80th Congress more than 60 bills attacking labor unions were introduced.[680] Out of these emerged the Labor–Management Relations Act of 1947, popularly known as the "Taft–Hartley Act."[681]

673. Legal costs

Id. at p. 290.

674. Less than costs

Id. at p. 291.

675. Informed employers

Ibid.

676. Estimates vary

Id. at pp. 274–275 (estimating 2700 fired and 12,000 quit from 1947–1956); Farillo, Red Scare, 1995, p. 131 (6,000–9,000 fired, 8,000 forced to resign, seven committed suicide, three imprisoned); Manchester, The Glory and The Dream, 1974, p. 498 (1947–52: F.B.I. screened more than 3 million, subjected 10,000 to full field investigations, charges filed against more than 9,000; not a single spy found). See also, id. at p. 671 (Eisenhower administration claims 1,500 left government

service in the first four months under E.O. 10450).

677. Number touched

Id. at p. 494 (F.B.I. undertook loyalty investigations of 2 million government employees from cabinet members to mailmen, plus investigations of a half-million applicants for government jobs each year).

678. Unions militant

Kennedy, Freedom From Fear, 1999, p. 642.

679. "Business unionism"

Caute, The Great Fear, 1978, pp. 347, 349.

680. Bills attacking unions

Id. at p. 355.

681. "Taft–Hartley"

Fariello, Red Scare, 1995, p. 18.

The portions of Taft–Hartley of concern to us here rested on the assumption that legitimate labor unions had been infiltrated by Communists—a false premise since many of the C.I.O. unions had been built largely by Communist organizers.[682] To prevent such "infiltration," Taft–Hartley required all union officials to file annual affidavits swearing that they were not members of the Communist Party; if any official failed to comply, the union lost all rights under federal law to organize and bargain collectively.[683] Signing the affidavits opened union officials to perjury prosecutions if the government could produce witnesses who would testify to membership in the Party; indeed, by wheeling out its informants again, the government finally got rid of Harry Bridges—temporarily, as it turned out.[684] The Supreme Court held that the loyalty-oath provisions of Taft–Hartley were constitutional.[685]

Taft-Hartley, though it never turned up any spies or revolutionaries, did create schisms in the labor movement between conservatives, often Gomperites or Roman Catholics, and radicals, frequently Jewish or East European ethnics.[686] Losers in union elections or unions competing to organize often claimed that their adversaries were Communists.[687] The C.I.O. expelled unions representing more than a million workers on grounds there were "Communist-dominated."[688] General Electric Co., long known for its antiunion stance, was able to use the leverage provided by Taft–Hartley to substitute a company union for the more militant union that had originally organized its workers.[689] In some cases, existing unions were destroyed and workers were left unorganized.[690] It is

682. Built by Communist

Id. at pp. 375–376.

683. Lost all rights

Foner, The Story of American Freedom, 1998, p. 257.

684. Got rid of Bridges

Caute, The Great Fear, 1978, pp. 237–238. On Bridges subsequent career, see Fariello, Red Scare, 1995, pp. 58–63.

685. Constitutional

American Communications Assn., C.I.O. v. Douds, 1950, 70 S.Ct. 674, 339 U.S. 382, 94 L.Ed. 925.

686. Schisms

Caute, The Great Fear, 1978, pp. 376–377. It also separated American labor

unions from the international labor unions, particularly after the A.F.L. took C.I.A. money to undermine indigenous labor unions in other countries.

687. Claimed Communists

Id. at pp. 354, 394.

688. Expelled unions

Foner, The Story of American Freedom, 1998, p. 257.

689. Company union

Caute, The Great Fear, 1976, pp. 376–391.

690. Left unorganized

Aronowitz, White Shirt, Blue Collar, The Nation, June 14, 1999, pp. 54, 56 (social workers' union).

estimated that over 200,000 persons were required to file affidavits under Taft–Hartley, that roughly two dozen were convicted of filing false affidavits, though all but seven of these were overturned on appeal.[691]

One of the latter was Clinton Jencks, of "Jencks Act" fame.[692] Jencks was an organizer for the International Mine, Mill, and Smelter Workers Union—an offshoot of Big Bill Haywood's Western Federation of Miners and the I.W.W.[693] After the war, Jencks was sent from Colorado to New Mexico to organize a force of largely Mexican–American miners, a campaign that is the subject of the motion picture, "Salt of the Earth." After a series of grand-jury inquiries netted nothing, the government trotted out two paid informants—one of them the infamous Harvey Matusow, who later recanted his testimony—and Jencks was convicted of perjury after an all-white jury deliberated only twenty minutes over a case that, save for the testimony of the informers, was large circumstantial. On appeal, the Supreme Court, employing confrontation values but without explicitly referring to the right of confrontation, held that it was an error for the trial judge to deny the defense access to the statements that the informants had given to the F.B.I. on the basis of an ex parte examination on the government's claim of privilege.[694] The government dismissed the prosecution rather than reveal the informers' statements. But the F.B.I. was not finished; for ten years, armed with a picture and story that appeared in Time magazine after the reversal of his conviction, agents followed Jencks from job to job, pressuring employers to fire him, and when he applied for and received a Woodrow Wilson Fellowship for graduate study, had him summoned before H.U.A.C. Jencks eventually got his degree and spent more than 20 years as an economics professor at San Diego State in California.[695]

691. Overturned on appeal

Fariello, Red Scare, 1995, p. 380.

692. "Jencks Act"

18 U.S.C.A. § 3500. The purpose of the statute was to restrict the scope of the Supreme Court's decision, described at notecall 694, below. See vol. 2, § 436.

693. Jencks story

The account in this paragraph is condensed from Jencks' account in Fariello, Red Scare, 1995, pp. 380–390.

694. Supreme Court

Jencks v. U.S., 1957, 77 S.Ct. 1007, 353 U.S. 657, 1 L.Ed.2d 1103.

695. Economics professor

Fariello, Red Scare, 1995, p. 390.

One other institution of the Second Red Scare was established in 1947—the so-called "Attorney General's List."[696] The President authorized the Justice Department to compile a list of organizations considered to be "totalitarian, Fascist, Communist, or subversive, or as having adopted a policy of approving the commission of acts of force or violence to deny others their constitutional rights."[697] Given these broad standards, the Department had no trouble coming up with a list of 90 organizations in 1947; 32 more were added in 1948, including the Consumer's Union, publishers of the magazine "Consumer Reports."[698] The Tenney Committee in California published a similar list that was twice as long—and included the American Civil Liberties Union.[699]

The Justice Department provided no procedure for listed organizations to challenge their listing or even to know the basis for their selection.[700] When the Supreme Court finally held that organizations had a constitutional right to challenge their listing, Attorney General Brownell issued a sketchy set of procedures for post-listing challenge.[701] Courts held that the list was unadulterated hearsay and refused to allow its use as evidence.[702] But the loyalty boards used evidence of membership in one of the listed organizations as prima facie evidence of disloyalty.[703] And private employers used it for similar purposes.

It is somewhat ironic that at about the time that the former head of the Justice Department was defeating an effort to apply notions of collective guilt to Nazi organizations, the Department

696. "Attorney General's List"

Manchester, The Glory and The Dream, 1974, p. 494.

697. "Force to deny rights"

Caute, The Great Fear, 1978, p. 269.

698. "Consumer Reports"

Manchester, The Glory and The Dream, 1974, p. 494; Fariello, Red Scare, 1995, p. 130 (Consumer's Union). Since the Consumer's Union was primarily engaged in the testing of consumer products for safety and durability, one assumes the listing reflects the organization's support of universal medical care—what the A.M.A. was then demonizing as "socialized medicine." Caute, The Great Fear, 1978, p. 403

699. Tenney Committee list

Fariello, Red Scare, 1995, p. 280.

700. Procedure to challenge

Manchester, The Glory and The Dream, 1974, p. 495.

701. Post-listing challenge

Caute, The Great Fear, 1978, p. 170. Joint Anti–Fascist Refugee Committee v. McGrath, 1951, 71 S.Ct. 624, 341 U.S. 123, 95 L.Ed. 817.

702. Use as evidence

Caute, The Great Fear, 1978, p. 169

703. Loyalty boards used

Fariello, Red Scare, 1995, p. 142.

was imputing collective guilt to members of "subversive" organizations.[704] The most significant effect of the Attorney General's List was not so much its use as the way it gave official sanction to the notion that the Communist Party and affiliated organizations were not legitimate political or social organizations entitled to protection under the First Amendment, but criminal, if not treasonous, conspiracies.[705] So effective was this ideological jump that liberals who opposed the Second Red Scare almost always phrased their opposition in terms of the harm it did to "innocent" victims—thus deflecting attention from just what it was that the "guilty" were guilty of.[706]

Courts, Chambers, and "Reducators"

In 1948, much that was traditional in American life seemed to vanish: following up on Jackie Robinson's breaking the color line in baseball, the military services abolished Jim Crow, and the Supreme Court held racially restrictive covenants in deeds to be unenforceable; the Berlin airlift and the Marshall Plan signaled the end of isolationism; Dr. Alfred Kinsey revealed what Americans had been doing in bed—and if they did not believe him, they could rush out and buy a Polaroid camera to take pictures of themselves doing it.[707]

It was also an unusual election year. The Democratic Party fragmented, its left wing going off into the Progressive Party of Henry Wallace and its conservative Southern segregationists enlisting in the State's Rights (or "Dixiecrat") Party of Strom Thurmond.[708] Harry Truman, calling for a "Fair Deal" and attacking the "do-nothing 80th Congress," not only defeated the Republican candidate, Thomas Dewey, but also enabled the Democrats to

---

704. Collective guilt

See above, text at notecall 635.

705. Criminal conspiracies

Fariello, Red Scare, 1995, p. 74.

706. "Innocent" victims

Schrecker, No Ivory Tower: McCarthyism and the Universities, 1986, p. 370.

707. Traditional vanish

Manchester, The Glory and The Dream, 1974, pp. 442 (Berlin airlift), 461 (fragmentation of Democrats), 477 (Kinsey Report); Encyclopedia of American History, Morris ed. 1976, pp. 515 (ending segregation in military), 516 (election); Encyclopedia of American Facts and Dates, 9th ed. 1993, pp. 535 (Jackie Robinson), 538 (Marshall Plan), 539 (Polaroid cameras go on sale); Shelley v. Kraemer, 1948, 68 S.Ct. 836, 334 U.S. 1, 92 L.Ed. 1161.

708. Democrats fragment

Manchester, The Glory and The Dream, 1974, p. 461.

recapture Congress.[709]

Federal courts came into the Second Red Scare in a big way in 1948. Proceeding on Attorney General Clark's philosophy that "[t]hose who do not believe in the ideology of the United States shall not be allowed to stay in the United States," the Justice Department indicted twelve members of the national board of the American Communist Party under the Smith Act for "conspiracy to advocate" the overthrow of the government.[710] The ensuing "Foley Square Trial" lasted more than nine months (making it the longest trial up to that point in American history) with what some critics characterized as a biased judge and jury.[711] Instead of relying on an indigenous tradition of revolutionary radicalism, the defendants tried to pass themselves off as Fabian socialists and the increasingly bitter altercations between them and their lawyers and the trial judge alienated the jury and much of the public.[712] The defendants were convicted and sentenced to five years in prison and the defense counsel were cited for contempt and five of them went to prison.[713]

When a majority of the Supreme Court affirmed the convictions, the Justice Department immediately arrested and indicted the so-called "second line leadership" of the Party under the membership clause of the Smith Act, which carried a higher penalty than the advocacy provision.[714] This prosecution in New York was followed by a series of regional show trials throughout the United States; the U.S. Attorney in Los Angeles candidly told the press

709. Recapture Congress

Id. at p. 340. The Fair Deal, which never went very far, "focused on the creation and equitable distribution of abundance, which now loomed as an attainable reality." Id. at p. 473.

710. "Conspiracy to advocate"

Fariello, Red Scare, 1995, pp. 84 (Clark quotation), 201 (charges): Caute, The Great Fear, 1978, p. 187 (defendants).

711. Biased judge and jury

Id. at pp. 187, 188–189.

712. Alienated public and jury

Id. at pp. 192, 198.

713. Five went to prison

Id. at pp. 192, 193. Four of the defendants fled to avoid prison. Id. at p. 205. The contempt convictions of their lawyers were affirmed by a divided Supreme Court in the notorious case of Sacher v. U.S., 1952, 72 S.Ct. 451, 343 U.S. 1, 96 L.Ed. 717. One of the cited lawyers, George Crockett, went on to a brilliant career as a civil-rights lawyer and as a distinguished trial judge in Detroit.

714. Under membership cause

Fariello, Red Scare, 1995, p. 202; Caute, The Great Fear, 1978, p. 195. The convictions were affirmed in Dennis v. U.S., 1951, 71 S.Ct. 857, 341 U.S. 494, 95 L.Ed. 1137.

that the trial there was "the first move in a program to destroy the Communist Party in the West."[715] The goal was manifested in Pittsburgh, where the local business press and the steel companies sought to use the prosecutions to weaken or destroy powerful trade unions.[716] In all, some 145 leaders of the Communist Party were prosecuted under the Smith Act and 108 were convicted; at least 20 were also convicted under state versions of the Smith Act.[717] These numbers are nearly miniscule compared to the number sanctioned under other instruments of the Second Red Scare; for example, the I.N.S. deported more than a thousand people, some of them Americans who had to be first stripped of their citizenship.[718] But the conduct of the courts had symbolic importance far beyond the numbers.

Neither state nor federal judges covered themselves with glory during the Second Red Scare.[719] Much of this is explainable by the facts that the Vinson Supreme Court, some of whose members owed their appointments more to their friendship with the President than to their legal acumen, was not up to the challenge, that the Justice Department exercised its role in the appointment and elevation of federal judges to reward judges who went along with the campaign to destroy the Communist Party, and those judges who did rule in favor of defendants were abused in the press in ways that foreshadowed what would happen during the later efforts to dismantle Jim Crow.[720] However, the Second Red Scare also demonstrated that without the constituency that had supported them earlier in campaigns against labor unions and Populists, courts were not as immune to popular opinion as some academics like to suppose.[721]

715. "Destroy Communist Party"

Caute, The Great Fear, 1978, pp. 197 (New York trial); 200 (California, Baltimore, Honolulu, Seattle), 202 (Detroit, Philadelphia, Cleveland); Fariello, Red Scare, 1995, 213 (quotation).

716. Pittsburgh

Id. at p. 216.

717. 20 under state

Fariello, Red Scare, 1995, p. 203.

718. Stripped of citizenship

Ibid.

719. Glory

Foner, The Story of American Freedom, 1998, p. 256.

720. Judges abused

Caute, The Great Fear, 1978, p. 143. On the Vinson Court, see id. at pp. 144–145; Murphy, The Constitution in Crisis Times, 1918–1969, 1972, pp. 263–266. On the Justice Department's role in getting rabid anti-Communists appointed and advanced, see Caute, the Great Fear, 1978, pp. 142–143.

721. Popular opinion

Probably few judges consciously considered the rewards and punishments

The open bias of many federal judges was so palpable that higher courts sometimes had to intervene to preserve the image of unbiased adjudication.[722] Some of the worst offenses were, however, not discovered until much later; e.g., that Irving Kauffman, the trial judge in the Rosenberg case, regularly had ex parte meetings with the prosecutors—in one case to receive advice on sentencing.[723] State judges similarly went over the line; one in Pennsylvania thought it no ground for disqualification in the prosecution for conspiracy to overthrow the government of the state that he was a founding member of "Americans Battling Communism."[724]

The evidence in Smith Act prosecutions raised serious questions.[725] The typical Smith Act trial devoted many hours to readings from the works of Marx, Engels, and Lenin—and any other leftist books that were found in the possession of the defendant.[726] The live witnesses were mostly government informers, some of whom later turned out to be spectacular perjurers.[727] Some of the circumstantial evidence offered was ludicrous; e.g. a political cartoon critical of the Korean War that appeared in a magazine found in the defendant's home.[728] Ironically, accused Communists fared better in civil actions against their accusers than they did when they

---

that popular opinion might impose; rather, they too easily accepted the factual and ideological premises that drove popular opinion; e.g., that Communism was an alien conspiracy to undermine the nation's security rather than an ideology as deserving of protection under the First Amendment as Jehovah's Witnesses or the National Association of Manufacturers.

722. Bias of judges

Caute, The Great Fear, 1978, pp. 140–141.

723. Ex parte meetings

Fariello, Red Scare, 1995, p. 185.

724. "Americans Battling"

Caute, The Great Fear, 1978, p. 141; Fariello, Red Scare, 1995, p. 204.

725. Evidence

The one rule that did serve as a serious restraint was the two-witness rule for treason prosecutions, which forced the government to convict the atom-bomb spies under special espionage statutes. Id. at p. 184.

726. Reading from books

The junior author can attest to this from painful personal experience; in connection with a law-review note (never published) on the Scales case, he read all the transcripts of Smith Act trials available in the University of Michigan Law Library, acquiring great sympathy for the juries who had to listen to hours of this. For documentation of the point, see id. at pp. 221, 228.

727. Perjurers

Id. at p. 211.

728. Political cartoons

Id. at p. 208.

were criminal defendants.[729]

The year 1948 also produced the most famous confrontation of the Second Red Scare—tellingly, it was not a courtroom confrontation.[730] Whittaker Chambers, a former editor of Time Magazine, appeared before the House Un–American Activities Committee to testify to a Soviet spy ring operating in pre-War Washington, naming 37 people as members of that ring—including many of the would-be "brain trusters" surrounding Jerome Frank in the Agriculture Department during the New Deal.[731] All but one of these disappeared into obscurity without ever having been proved to be involved with espionage.[732] The exception, Alger Hiss, was an attractive target for H.U.A.C.—a bona fide member of the New Deal establishment who had graduated from Harvard Law School, clerked for Justice Holmes, worked in a number of government jobs, and played a significant role in the development of the United Nations and other internationalist groups inimical to American isolationists.[733]

Hiss demanded to appear before H.U.A.C. to deny the charges and his Ivy League demeanor both charmed and intimidated the committee—except for Richard Nixon, whose resentments toward the "Eastern establishment" would later become well known.[734] Nixon asked for and got a face-to-face confrontation between Hiss and his accuser.[735] Faced with Chambers in a private session of the

729. Civil actions

Caute, The Great Fear, 1978, p. 555. However, these were generally tried after the Second Red Scare had subsided.

730. Famous confrontation

Encyclopedia of American History, Morris ed. 1976, p. 516.

731. Spy ring

Chambers's testimony was supported by Elizabeth Bentley, the mistress of a leading Soviet espionage agent in the United States. Manchester, The Glory and The Dream, 1974, p. 502. On Miss Bentley's subsequent career as a professional witness, see Caute, The Great Fear, 1978, pp. 33, 56–57, 91, 108–109, 139, 152, 240, 287–289, 315–316, 571.

732. Disappeared into obscurity

One of them was convicted of perjury in a highly disputed trial and murdered in prison by anti-Communist thugs. Fariello, Red Scare, 1995, pp. 140–141; Caute, The Great Fear, 1978, pp. 287–289. For the fate of the others, see Manchester, The Glory and The Dream, 1974, pp. 502–503.

733. Hiss biography

Id. at p. 503; Caute, The Great Fear, 1978, pp. 58–59.

734. Except Nixon

Manchester, The Glory and The Dream, 1974, pp. 504–505.

735. Confrontation

This was an inquisitorial confrontation, in which the accuser identifies the accuser. See vol. 30, § 6342, p. 199. The

committee, Hiss began to waver and in a later public confrontation with his accuser, Hiss' façade of innocence shattered completely.[736] Attempting to carry out the bluff, Hiss demanded that Chambers repeat his charges outside the shield of Congressional immunity; Chambers did so—and upped the ante, producing the famous "pumpkin papers," microfilms of papers that Hiss had supposedly delivered to the Soviets through Chambers.[737]

Hiss was indicted for perjury in his denials before H.U.A.C.[738] In the trial before a judge who was accused of bias in Hiss's favor and in which Hiss was able to produce an impressive stable of character witnesses—including two members of the Supreme Court, the future Secretary of State John Foster Dulles, a past and future Democratic presidential nominee (John Davis and Adlai Stevenson), the jury deadlocked 8–4 for conviction.[739] At his retrial, during the height of the Second Red Scare, Hiss was convicted and sentenced to prison.[740] For many members of the American elite, the Hiss case became the Sacco–Vanzetti trial of the Second Red Scare—a litmus test of liberalism and a warning that the abuses of inquisitorial procedures were not reserved for obscure government clerks but could be directed even against those with a listing in Who's Who.[741]

The Hiss success emboldened Congressional inquisitors; Congressmen flocked to join H.U.A.C. in record numbers, and when they could not be accommodated, they turned other Congressional

witness Chambers was not cross-examined by Hiss, though there was some interchange between them and the committee members asked questions of both. Id. at pp. 505–506.

736. Façade shattered

Ibid.

737. "Pumpkin papers"

Id. at pp. 507–508. None of the information contained in the papers would have been of any value to the Soviet Union. Id. at p. 508.

738. Perjury

The charges involved Hiss's denial of meetings with Chambers of and passing him the "Pumpkin Papers"; the statute of limitations had run on the espionage charges. Caute, The Great Fear, 1978, p. 60.

739. Deadlocked for conviction

Manchester, The Glory and The Dream, 1974, p. 509; Caute, The Great Fear, 1978, pp. 60–61. The list of Hiss' character witnesses is at Manchester, The Glory and The Dream, 1974, p. 503. The Supreme Court Justices who testified were Frankfurter and Reed. Fariello, Red Scare, 1995, p. 151.

740. Hiss convicted

Manchester, The Glory and The Dream, 1974, p. 510; Caute, The Great Fear, 1978, p. 61.

741. Litmus test

Ibid. Hiss's listing in Who's Who is reproduced in Manchester, The Glory and The Dream, 1974, p. 503. For Hiss's later account of his trial and conviction, see Fariello, Red Scare, 1995, p. 146–152.

committees into anti-Communist inquisitions.[742] The political advantages of the legislative inquisition have been summed up by one scholar as follows:

> as congressmen constitutionally immune from lawsuits, they could make accusations without having to worry about being sued for libel. In addition, since legislative investigations were not judicial proceedings, these politicians could use witnesses whose testimony did not have to stand up in court. Best of all, committee hearings created headlines. American politics had never offered a more dramatic spectacle than the confrontation between the investigators and their witnesses * * *.[743]

However, these Congressional "confrontations" bore little relationship to the sort preserved in the Sixth Amendment.

The major difference was the absence of the separation of functions found in the Sixth Amendment; committee members determined what evidence to seek, whether or not it was admissible, and what it proved—thus combining in the committee functions that under the Sixth Amendment are divided among counsel, court and jury.[744] This combination of functions allowed the committee to intimidate witnesses who did not perform as desired.[745] Moreover, the accused was discouraged from retaining counsel and when counsel did appear, they were disparaged, intimidated, and denied any role in the proceedings.[746] Bar groups, including the American Bar Association, tried to carve out a role for attorneys in Congressional investigations, primarily by providing for cross-examination of accusers.[747] Committee members had little interest in seeing their own role in the investigations diminished by granting powers to counsel for the "accused."

742. Record numbers

Caute, The Great Fear, 1978, p. 90 (in 1953, 185 of 221 Republican members of the House sought a H.U.A.C. assignment). Congress had authorized 285 investigations between 1789 and 1925; it authorized 225 between 1950 and 1952. There were four anti-Communist investigations in the 79th Congress, twenty-two in the 80th, twenty-four in the 81st, thirty-four in the 82nd and an all-time high of fifty-one in the 83rd. Id. at p. 85.

743. "Dramatic spectacle"

Schrecker, No Ivory Tower: McCarthyism and the Universities, 1986, p. 7.

744. Combining functions

Murphy, The Constitution in Crisis Times, 1918–1969, 1972, pp. 293–294.

745. Intimidation of witnesses

Caute, The Great Fear, 1978, p. 99.

746. Denied role

Id. at pp. 97–98.

747. Cross-examination

Id. at p. 98.

Congressional inquisitions served several functions during the Second Red Scare, beyond publicizing their members and legitimating the notion that the national security was being endangered by "the International Communist Conspiracy." First, witnesses who denied the accusations of the inquisitors could be indicted for perjury.[748] As Senator McCarthy explained:

> It is hard to get them for their criminal activities in connection with espionage, but a way has been found. We are getting them for perjury and putting some of the worst of them away. * * * [E]very witness who comes here is put under oath and his testimony is gone over with a fine tooth comb, and if we cannot convict some of them for their disloyal activities, perhaps we can convict some of them for perjury.[749]

Second, those who refused to cooperate with the committee could be cited for contempt of Congress.[750] Third, those who invoked the privilege against self-incrimination were labeled "Fifth Amendment Communists" and turned over to employers and neighbors for punishment.[751] Finally, for those who were willing to cooperate with the committee and "name names," the hearings were a "degradation ceremony" in which, by accepting the anti-Communist view of the world and renouncing their past, people could be re-integrated into the world, purged of leftist impulses.[752]

As we shall see, the Supreme Court's confrontation with the inquisitorial system in Congressional investigations and loyalty boards produced a renewed appreciation of Sixth Amendment values. And, ironically, it was in opposition to the inquisitorial proce-

---

748. For perjury

Id. at pp. 317, 358; Fariello, Red Scare, 1995, p. 130. For a case study in how expensive and protracted these could be, see the account of the prosecutions of Owen Lattimore, an Asian scholar accused of being one of those who "lost China" to the Communists. Caute, The Great Fear, 1978, pp. 317–321.

749. "Fine tooth comb"

Barth, Government by Investigation, 1955, p. 83.

750. Contempt of Congress

Caute, The Great Fear, 1978, p. 96. From 1945–1971 there were 187 contempt citations approved by Congress, 174 from H.U.A.C. alone; 142 of these failed in court. Id. at pp. 96–97.

751. "Amendment Communists"

Murphy, The Constitution in Crisis Times, 1918–1969, 1972, p. 294.

752. "Degradation ceremony"

Navasky, Naming Names, 1980, p. 322. As the controversy over the Academy Award for Lifetime Achievement in 1999 to Elia Kazan, a cooperative witness, demonstrated, the ceremony did not always have the desired effect.

dures of H.U.A.C. that the so-called "New Left" of the 1960s got its start.[753]

As we have previously seen, attacks on academics for "red-leanings" began in the Nineteenth Century, increased during the first Red Scare, and continued intermittently thereafter down to the Second Red Scare.[754] But the association of some prominent academics with the Progressive presidential campaign of Henry Wallace spurred a vigorous attack on so-called "Reducators."[755] In high schools in New York and Los Angeles, there is some evidence that attacks were initiated by Catholics eager to discredit the public schools in order to strengthen their claims for public aid to parochial schools.[756] However, for the most part, the attacks probably manifested the perennial fear of parents that their children are being taught to disagree with them.[757] And more to the point, Communists did have many adherents among teachers at all levels.[758]

It has been estimated that nearly twenty percent of the witnesses in Congressional hearings were professors or graduate students.[759] More than 1200 college and university professors were investigated by federal, state, or internal university investigators and 330 were either fired or resigned under pressure.[760] However, in not a single case was it ever shown that the accused Communist had attempted to proselytize in class—in most cases, the investigators did not even try to show this.[761]

753. "New Left" start

Fariello, Red Scare, 1995, p. 521.

754. Attacks on academics

Schrecker, No Ivory Tower: McCarthyism and the Universities, 1986, pp. 15, 19–23, 63–83; Caute, The Great Fear, 1978, p. 404.

755. Wallace and "Reducators"

Id. at pp. 403, 407.

756. Aid to parochial

Id. at pp. 431, 437; Fariello, Red Scare, 1995, p. 424.

757. Taught to disagree

Anyone who doubts the constancy of this fear has not been playing close attention to local school-board politics.

758. Many adherents

Caute, The Great Fear, 1978, p. 406.

759. Professors and students

Schrecker, No Ivory Tower: McCarthyism and the Universities, 1986, p. 10.

760. Fired or resigned

Id. at p. 426.

761. Did not even try

Id. at p. 419; Fariello, Red Scare, 1995, 42–44, 99.

Though there were stirrings elsewhere, the Second Red Scare took off in academia in 1948 at the University of Washington, where a conservative president and a Red-hunting legislative committee led the attack on leftist professors.[762] It then spread to schools in the Midwest such as Ohio State and the University of Michigan.[763] Those who suppose that the attack was directed at "football factories" with modest academic pretensions should note that M.I.T. was one of the early victims and even Harvard eventually came under attack.[764]

College and campus administrators, when they did not initiate the Red Scare, did little to resist it.[765] A group of prominent anti-Communist academics developed a rationale for excluding those with Communist beliefs or sympathies from the teaching profession and many of the leading academic organizations soon embraced the Orwellian notion than academic freedom imposed a duty of informing and self-accusation inconsistent with the Fifth Amendment, but which provided a handy excuse to surrender to demands to fire "Fifth Amendment Communists."[766] The American Association of University Professors, which claims to be a hybrid trade union and academic A.C.L.U., has been severely criticized for the role it played in furthering the Second Red Scare on campuses.[767]

However, it is difficult to see what the A.A.U.P. could have done without more backbone in its membership.[768] The same desire for a simplifying global theory that makes some scholars take up Marxism, enabled others to accept the anti-Communist view of the world.[769] Even Zechariah Chafee, Jr., who had played such a heroic

---

762. Washington

Caute, The Great Fear, 1978, pp. 408–410. The Washington president was later hired by the University of California Board of Regents to fulfill a similar role at U.C.L.A.

763. Ohio State and Michigan

Schrecker, No Ivory Tower: McCarthyism and the Universities, 1986, p. 207, 219.

764. M.I.T. and Harvard

Id. at pp. 410–411.

765. Little to resist

Id. at p. 405.

766. Fire "Fifth Amendment"

Id. at pp. 105, 186–188.

767. A.A.U.P. criticized

Id. at pp. 93–94, 314–315, 334.

768. More backbone

Id. at p. 179.

769. Global theory

Nor was "the world is a complicated place"—"there is something to be said for everything"—"on the one hand, on the other hand" world view one from which it was easy to launch a dogmatic defense of academic freedom.

role in the First Red Scare, succumbed to the Second with little fanfare.[770] After the Chandler Davis case at the University of Michigan showed the price and futility of resistance, professorial opposition to the Second Red Scare, such as it was, limited itself to procedural demands to protect the innocent.[771] Few were prepared to stand up for the First Amendment rights of the guilty. Anecdotal evidence, as well as one empirical survey, suggests that fear was the dominant response of the professoriate to the attack on academic freedom.[772]

Though it is easy for scholars to exaggerate the significance of the Second Red Scare in academia, it does seem likely that the preoccupation of faculty members with procedural matters in academic disciplinary hearings had something to do with the revival of interest in criminal procedure during those years.[773] Though law schools had fewer victims of the Red Scare than other academic units, those that did occur were high-profile cases that were much-talked about in the comparatively small legal-academic community; e.g., the Countryman affair at Yale or the Lubell twins at Harvard.[774]

770. Chafee succumbed

Id. at p. 184.

771. Procedural demands

Id. at pp. 181–182. Chandler Davis, a Communist mathematician at the University of Michigan, was one of the few academic witnesses before H.U.A.C. to defend himself from the committee on the ground that his ideology was none of their business. The inability of his supposed colleagues to understand this elemental First Amendment position makes for painful reading. Id. at pp. 3, 219, 233. For the rest of the story, see Fariello, Red Scare, 1995, pp. 434–440.

772. Fear of the professoriate

Caute, The Great Fear, 1978, p. 429; Schrecker, No Ivory Tower: McCarthyism and the Universities, 1978, p. 309.

773. Revival of interest

In at least one case, the connection is patent. Compare id. at pp. 184–185 with Griswold, The Due Process Revo-

lution and Confrontation, 1971, 119 U.Pa.L.Rev. 711.

774. Countryman and Lubell twins

Countryman was a bankruptcy expert and active civil libertarian who had come to Yale from the University of Washington Law School; in 1954 his promotion to tenure was held up during a controversy over his criticisms of the Second Red Scare at Washington. Countryman resigned but later returned to academic life at New Mexico and Harvard. Schrecker, No Ivory Tower: McCarthyism and the Universities, 1978, pp. 252–253.

Jonathon and David Lubell were second-year law students who pleaded the Fifth Amendment when asked about their radical activities as undergraduates at Cornell; the Harvard Law School revoked their scholarships and their fellow students kicked them off the Law Review and the school newspaper. Id. at pp. 200–201.

The Warfare State and the Employment Nexus

In 1949, in his State of the Union message, President Truman outlined his "Fair Deal"—the high-water mark of the Welfare State; later that year the founding of the North Atlantic Treaty Organization institutionalized the Warfare State that would endure for the rest of the century.[775] Meanwhile, a journalist and a lawyer launched the first serious opposition to The Second Red Scare and the former chairman of the House Un–American Activities Committee went to prison on a fraud conviction.[776] But while J. Parnell Thomas mingled behind bars with victims of H.U.A.C., the Second Red Scare rolled on unabated, fueled by two developments in 1948.[777]

The first of these was the victory of Mao's Communist forces and the flight of Chiang Kai-shek's Nationalist forces to Taiwan.[778] Given the myth of American omnipotence fueled by atomic weaponry, the search was on for those who had "lost China" to Commu-

775. Fair Deal and N.A.T.O.

Encyclopedia of American History, Morris ed. 1976, p. 471. The President called for repeal of the Taft–Hartley Act, a minimum wage of 75¢ per hour, expansion of Social Security to all workers, federal aid to education, public housing and slum clearance, and broad civil rights legislation. Encyclopedia of American Facts and Dates, 9th ed. 1993, p. 542.

776. Fraud conviction

Caute, The Great Fear, 1978, p. 91. The book, "Washington Witch Hunt," by a reporter for The New York Herald–Tribune contained a recital of some of the worst abuses of the loyalty program. Manchester, The Glory and The Dream, 1974, p. 496.

O'Brian, Loyalty Tests and Guilt by Association, 1948, 61 Harv.L.Rev. 592 was a revised version of a speech given by John Lord O'Brian to the New York State Bar Association. The author posed his talk as a cost-benefit analysis of the Truman loyalty program, pointing out how it had stretched the already strained doctrine of conspiracy to encompass

"guilt by association." Id. at pp. 597–605. He also showed the violations of confrontation arising from the F.B.I.'s use of unadulterated hearsay in compiling the reports and the practices of denying the accused access to the names of these faceless informants. Id. at pp. 606–609. He then pointed out that because of the employment nexus, the finding of disloyalty was the functional equivalent of a criminal conviction. Id. at pp. 607–608. Finally, reminding his audience of the role that the bar had played in resisting the First Red Scare and how assiduously it had fought for procedural reforms in New Deal administrative agencies when property rights were at issue, he called on the bar to take a role in resisting the excesses of the Second Red Scare. Id. at pp. 593, 610–611.

777. Mingled with victims

Fariello, Red Scare, 1995, p. 263.

778. Flight to Taiwan

Encyclopedia of American History, Morris ed. 1976, p. 473; Manchester, The Glory and The Dream, 1974, p. 487.

nism; as Congressman John F. Kennedy said: "[t]his is the tragic story of China, whose freedom we once fought to preserve. What our young men saved, our diplomats and President have frittered away."[779] Since the impeachment of the President was then unthinkable, the wrath of Congress fell upon foreign-service officers and academic experts on China who had been rash enough to predict the fall of Chiang.[780]

After Joe McCarthy delivered his infamous Wheeling speech, claiming that there were 205 known Communists working in the State Department with the knowing approval of Secretary of State Dean Acheson, Congressional inquisitors, and later the State Department itself, began a search for the 205 "traitors"; of some twenty-two State Department experts on China, only two remained in 1954.[781] The search for scapegoats extended to academic experts on the Far East, symbolized by Owen Lattimore, and by institutions such as the Voice of America, whose relationship to the "fall of China" seems obscure.[782]

In 1949, the Soviet Union detonated its first atomic explosion, and cryptologists working on what would be called "the VENONA decrypts" when they were finally revealed in 1995, discovered a Soviet espionage ring headed by Julius Rosenberg that had provided the Russians with information about the design of the first American atomic weapons.[783] Even before the Rosenbergs were arrested, H.U.A.C. claimed that the American nuclear laboratories were riddled with spies and set out to prove this.[784] So powerful was the fear unleashed by the espionage hysteria that even lawyers like Abe Fortas, who had represented other victims of the Second Red Scare, were unwilling to represent physicists targeted by Congressional inquisitors.[785] By the middle of the following decade, nearly one thousand scientists had been accused of disloyalty; not surpris-

779. "Frittered away"

Id. at p. 491.

780. Wrath of Congress

Caute, The Great Fear, 1978, p. 303.

781. Only two remained

Fariello, Red Scare, 1995, pp. 145–145.

782. Lattimore and V.O.A.

Caute, The Great Fear, 1978, pp. 317, 321.

783. Design of atomic weapons

Fariello, Red Scare, 1995, pp. 175, 177–178.

784. H.U.A.C. and spies

Caute, The Great Fear, 1978, p. 446; Schrecker, No Ivory Tower: McCarthyism and the Universities, 1986, pp. 141–142.

785. Fortas unwilling

Id. at p. 143.

ingly, a survey of graduate students in physics found that they wished to avoid working for the government if at all possible.[786]

The case of scientists exemplifies what we have called "the employment nexus"; that is, the method by which dissent can be suppressed without violating the First Amendment by using the need for employment to coerce conformity.[787] The employment nexus generally involved two different institutions functioning in tandem; the "fact-finding" body, which determined that the person was deserving of sanctions but did not itself sanction, and the sanctioning body, typically the employer, which undertook no independent fact-finding and thus was immune from charges of defamation.[788] Without too much oversimplification, these dual bodies can be classified in the following pairs; government-government; government-private; and private-private.[789]

The government-government pairing was involved in the case of most of the atomic scientists; that is, one organ of government, whether Congressional inquisitors or an administrative loyalty board, would determine that the person was unfit for employment, and the employing agency then fired or refused to employ the individual.[790] This employment nexus was significantly broadened by the development of the concept of a "security risk"—that is, someone who was not necessarily ideologically predisposed to disloyalty but whom for other reasons might be inclined to endanger the national security.[791] The concept was at the heart of "the security clearance"—the certification by appropriate authority that one was not a "security risk."[792] The paradigm case is Robert Oppenheimer, the physicist most responsible for the success of the American atomic bomb program, whose security clearance was

786. Avoid government

Caute, The Great Fear, 1978, p. 461.

787. "Employment nexus"

Id. at p. 456.

788. Two different

This distinction was often blurred in cases of state and local employees. Id. at p. 339.

789. Private-private

As in the case of the American Legion and defense contractors, one must not expect too much of the distinction between "public" and "private."

790. Fired

Again, our concern here is less with the organization chart—whether the loyalty board was part of or independent of the agency—but whether the persons who investigated were not the same as those who had the power to hire or fire.

791. "Security risk"

Id. at p. 273.

792. "Security clearance"

Id. at p. 364.

withdrawn because his youthful association with persons supposed to be Communists and his opposition to the development of the hydrogen bomb were said to cast doubt on his character and judgment—thus making him a security risk.[793] With the growth of the Warfare State and the extension of the requirement of a security clearance for those working in the weapons industry, the program passed into a "government-private" form of the employment nexus.[794]

However, the purer form of the public-private employment nexus is exemplified by the case of the "Fifth Amendment Communists" in academia that we have previously discussed.[795] As one student of the topic described it, the process "took place in two stages":

> First, the objectionable groups and individuals were identified—during a committee hearing, for example, or an F.B.I. investigation; then they were punished, usually by being fired. The bifurcated nature of the process diffused responsibility and made it easier for each participant to dissociate his or her action from the larger whole.[796]

Though it was probably not the model, the process resembles that of the Spanish Inquisition, in which the inquisitorial church courts determined that the person was a heretic, then turned him or her over to the "secular arm" for punishment—thus evading the religious inhibitions on the shedding of blood.[797]

That the public-private employment nexus was no scholarly construct is shown by the advice of Roy Cohn to the McCarthy Senate Subcommittee on Investigations in June of 1954:

> The way to get results, sir, is to hold our hearings, get these people in public sessions, have them fired from defense plants. * * * The employers have adopted an arrangement that they will not act against these people unless and until we hold these hearings * * *[798]

793. Oppenheimer

Id. at pp. 473–479; Fariello, Red Scare, 1995, p. 176–177.

794. Government-private

Nearly four-million employees fell within the Industrial Personnel Security Program. Caute, The Great Fear, 1978, p. 364.

795. "Fifth Amendment"

Id. at p. 414.

796. "Dissociate from whole"

Schrecker, No Ivory Tower: McCarthyism and the Universities, 1986, p. 9.

797. "Secular arm"

Kamen, The Spanish Inquisition, 1997, pp. 202–203.

798. "Employers adopted"

Caute, The Great Fear, 1978, p. 360.

As the case of "The Hollywood Ten" illustrates, the public-private employment nexus was not limited to "defense plants."[799] It eventually extended to all forms of employment, with F.B.I. agents visiting employers to let them know they had a "subversive" employee.[800] Eventually, some employers either had F.B.I. agents detailed to their employment offices or hired F.B.I. agents to check out their employees—thus crossing over to the private-private form of the employment nexus.[801]

The usual case of the private-private employment nexus, however, involved freelance blacklisters or private groups of vigilantes.[802] The American Legion was among the most prominent of the latter and their best-known success was the Hollywood blacklist.[803] The American Legion claimed that such stars as Judy Holliday, Charlie Chaplin, John Garfield, and Burt Lancaster were "Communist collaborators," and urged its members to boycott their movies.[804] Fearful of the economic impact, the film industry developed a list of unemployable persons that eventually numbered some 350 actors, writers, and technicians—including several future Academy Award winners.[805]

Because of its dependence on advertisers who were susceptible to boycotts, the nascent television industry was even more susceptible to the private-private nexus.[806] By exploiting his connection with the American Legion, a grocer in Syracuse, New York became a virtual one-man blacklister for the industry.[807] He was aided and abetted by a group of private vigilantes who published a booklet

---

799. "Hollywood Ten"

Id. at pp. 491–498.

800. Visiting employers

Fariello, Red Scare, 1995, p. 389.

801. Or hired ex-F.B.I. agents

Id. at pp. 378–379. Many academic institutions during this period had an on-campus F.B.I. agent to do security checks and cooperate with university police in keeping an eye on campus radicals. Caute, The Great Fear, 1978, pp. 427–428.

802. Vigilantes

Id. at pp. 502–504.

803. Hollywood blacklist

Id. at pp. 504–506.

804. "Communist collaborators"

Fariello, Red Scare, 1995, p. 260.

805. Academy Award winners

Id. at pp. 260–261. The blacklist, it is now known, was not as effective as the vigilantes would have liked; a number of those on the list managed to work under assumed names. Id. at p. 264.

806. Television

Caute, The Great Fear, 1978, p. 523.

807. Grocer in Syracuse

Fariello, Red Scare, 1995, p. 324 n. 3.

called "Red Channels" listing more than 150 prominent television personalities, including such luminaries as Leonard Bernstein, Harry Belafonte, Abe Burrows, Gypsy Rose Lee, and Judy Holliday.[808] The problem with the private-private nexus was that private parties were not immune from libel actions; their inability to defend their accusations or insinuations in court discredited some and destroyed others.[809]

For those in positions of power, the employment nexus faded with the end of the Second Red Scare.[810] But for the more obscure victims, there was no relief; the academic blacklist remained in effect for many years.[811] And the security-clearance system remains in effect to this day. For purposes of the right of confrontation, what the employment nexus did was to provide an alternative means of suppressing dissent. This means that courts could expand the adversary protections of criminal defendants without leaving society powerless against revolutionary ideologies.

Korea, Corruption, and Informers

In 1950, the United States entered the Korean War under the auspices of the United Nations and swept the length of the peninsula, only to be forced back when Chinese armies entered the War.[812] Early that same year, the President decided to proceed with the building of thermonuclear weapons (the "hydrogen bomb," as it was popularly called) and a group of scientists, not yet having the example of Oppenheimer before them, attempted to revive the morality of means from the obscurity cast over it by Hiroshima.[813]

808. "Red Channels"

Caute, The Great Fear, 1978, p. 1978, pp. 521–523; Fariello, Red Scare, 1995, p. 321.

809. Discredited and destroyed

Id. at p. 324 n. 3; Caute, The Great Fear, 1978, p. 533–535.

810. Faded

For example, the Ford Motor Company was the first to break the television blacklist when it sponsored a concert conducted by Leonard Bernstein. Fariello, Red Scare, 1995, p. 325.

811. Academic blacklist

None of those fired for refusing to cooperate with Congressional inquiries

ever got a respectable academic position again. Schrecker, No Ivory Tower: McCarthyism and the Universities, 1986, pp. 104, 266.

812. Korean War

Encyclopedia of American History, Morris ed. 1976, pp. 477–478; Manchester, The Power and The Glory, 1974, pp. 530, 532, 546.

813. "Hydrogen bomb"

Id. at p. 572 (statement of 12 senior physicists: "We believe that no nation has the right to use such a bomb, no matter how righteous its cause. The bomb is no longer a weapon of war but a means of extermination of whole populations. Its use would be a betray-

Also in 1950, "McCarthyism," properly so-called, was launched when the Senator from Wisconsin made his famous speech at Wheeling, West Virginia, Alger Hiss was convicted, and J. Edgar Hoover announced there were still 50,000 Communists in the United States and over a half-million "fellow travelers."[814] The collapse of the liberal Democratic opposition allowed the passage of the McCarran Act and P.L. 733 and the Supreme Court upheld the constitutionality of the anti-Communist oath requirement of the Taft–Hartley Act.[815]

The appearance of another kind of Congressional investigation in 1950—the Kefauver investigation of organized crime—brought another sort of informer onto television screens across America, highlighting the national ambivalence about the role of informers in law enforcement and the Second Red Scare.[816] Given the variety of activities during the Second Red Scare that earned the actors the title of "informer," it may be helpful to begin our discussion with some distinctions not always observed that make the question appear more complicated than is sometimes supposed.[817]

al of all standards of morality and of Christian civilization itself."),

814. "Fellow travelers"

Encyclopedia of American Facts and Dates, 9th ed. 1993, p. 546; Manchester, The Glory and The Dream, pp. 520–530.

815. Oath requirement

American Communications Assn., C.I.O. v. Douds, 1950, 70 S.Ct. 674, 339 U.S. 382, 94 L.Ed. 925.

P.L. 733 allowed the suspension from employment of anyone accused of being a "security risk" without any due process protections. Fariello, Red Scare, 1995, p. 128.

The McCarran Act (also known as "The Internal Security Act" of 1950) after finding a Communist conspiracy to establish a "totalitarian dictatorship in the countries throughout the world," authorized construction of concentration camps for use in national emergencies, and established the Subversive Activities Control Board, with power to determine which organizations were "Communist-action,"

"Communist-front," or "Communist-infiltrated," to require such organizations to register, disclose membership lists and sources of funding, and to mark any literature they distributed as disseminated by "a Communist Organization," and barred issuance of or renewal of passports for members of such organizations. Id. at pp. 17–18; Caute, The Great Fear, 1978, p. 36.

816. Kefauver investigation

Manchester, The Glory and The Dream, 1974, pp. 600–601. The American public, which tuned to the hearings in greater numbers than for the previous World Series, got a lesson in the value of demeanor evidence; when Frank Costello refused to allow the television cameras to focus on his face, they were pointed instead at his hands—hands that most thought highly revealing of his state of mind as he testified. Ibid.

817. Variety of "informer"

See the descriptions of various informers in Caute, The Great Fear, 1978, pp. 547–550.

The first category, and the one that seems to fuel the greatest popular antipathy and is the most difficult to reconcile with confrontation values, is the person who enters into a relationship with another person with the secret intent to betray that person. The second category is the person who enters into a relationship in good faith and, during that relationship, forms the secret intent to betray the other person. Finally, we have the person who has no relationship with the other person or whose relationship with that person has ended before the intent to betray originates.[818] When we add to these three categories such considerations as the nature of the relationship, the nature of the betrayal, and the motives of the betrayer, it would seem that the subject does not lend itself to the easy moralizing one sometimes finds in discussions of anti-Communist informers.[819]

With the rapid expansion of the F.B.I. and its budget during the Red Scare, the use of informers multiplied.[820] One knowledgeable F.B.I. official has said that after the Communist Party leadership went underground, there were party cells where all the members were F.B.I. agents and by the early 1960s, half of the membership of the Communist Party in Chicago were paid F.B.I. informers.[821] Some of these informers were being paid more than the F.B.I. agents who were supervising them.[822] For example, Harvey Matusow testified that in 1952 he was paid $10,000, or more than $40,000 in 1965 dollars; when Matusow was testifying regularly for the government, he was housed in a 26–room mansion that had formerly been the residence of the German ambassador.[823] As late as 1966–1976, the F.B.I. still had 5,145 paid po-

818. Ended before

Although the record is not complete enough to have confidence in it, many, if not most, of the celebrated informers, e.g., Elia Kazan, fall into this category.

819. Easy moralizing

It is noteworthy that one seldom finds this in those who actually faced the choice, irrespective of how they resolved it. See e.g., Fariello, Red Scare, 1995, pp. 260–337. Compare the discussions in the business press in 1999 about the controversy over the award of a Lifetime Achievement Award to Elia Kazan.

820. Expansion of F.B.I.

The statistics are collected in Caute, The Great Fear, 1978, p. 112 (number of agents increased from 411 in 1939 to 4,602 in 1952; budget went from $7 million in 1940 to $53 million in 1950).

821. Half paid informers

Fariello, Red Scare, 1995, p. 92.

822. Paid more

Ibid.

823. German ambassador

Id. at p. 100, n. 10.

litical informants in the Chicago area alone.[824]

At the other extreme were those who informed for ideological, personal, or business reasons. Future president Ronald Reagan was an F.B.I. informant during his days as an official of the Screen Actors Guild in Hollywood, as was Walt Disney.[825] In academia, prominent informers included Harvard professors Granville Hicks and Daniel Boorstin, who would later become the Librarian of Congress.[826] In the publishing world, Henry Holt and Bennett Cerf were informers.[827] Perhaps most disturbing was the revelation that the noted civil-libertarian Morris Ernst and other lawyers for the A.C.L.U. were informers, turning over privileged information to the F.B.I. and volunteering to undertake the defense of the Rosenbergs if this would aid the Bureau.[828] Each of these informers differed from the others in the nature of their activities and their moral culpability, if any, for betraying others.

For purposes of the right of confrontation, the most disturbing type of informer is the perjurer—particularly when the perjury is carried off in proceedings where they confront the accuser.[829] Most of these perjurers were paid informers, some of whom have figured prominently in discussions of the Second Red Scare: Manning Johnson, the informer used by the government to get Harry Bridges.[830] George Hewitt, who led the purge at the University of Washington; when the State of Washington sought to extradite him to stand trial for perjury, New York officials, reputedly under pressure from the F.B.I. and the McCarthyites, refused to render him up.[831] Paul Crouch, whose lies cost the Hearst publications a $5,000 libel judgment when they reprinted his accusations against a

824. Still had 5,145

Id. at p. 526.

825. Reagan and Disney

Id. at p. 257 nn. 7, 9.

826. Hicks and Boorstin

Schrecker, No Ivory Tower: McCarthyism and the Universities, 1986, p. 194.

827. Holt and Cerf

Schrecker, No Ivory Tower: McCarthyism and the Universities, 1986, p. 139, n. 1.

828. A.C.L.U. lawyers

Id. at p. 133.

829. Where confronted

See, e.g. U.S. v. Flynn,, D.C.N.Y.1955, 130 F.Supp. 412 (reviewing lies of Harvey Matusow, rejecting claim he was suborned by prosecutors, but granting motion to set aside verdict.)

830. Manning Johnson

Navasky, Naming Names, 1980, pp. 14–15.

831. George Hewitt

Id. at pp. 38–39; Schrecker, No Ivory Tower: McCarthyism and the Universities, 1986, p. 96.

labor leader.[832]

But the Prince of Perjurers was Harvey Matusow.[833] After seven years in the Communist Party, he lived high on the hog for four years as a government informant, testifying in 25 trials and deportation proceedings and naming more than 180 people as Communists in testimony at the Second Smith Act trial in New York and before H.U.A.C., Senator McCarthy's committee, other state and federal legislative committees, and the Subversive Activities Control Board.[834] However, Matusow began to recant much of this testimony, as we saw in the Jencks case.[835] Some of his lies seem, at least in retrospect, to border on the preposterous; e.g., that the Communists had infiltrated the Boy Scouts of America.[836]

Matusow, despite F.B.I. efforts to prevent this, published a book called "False Witness" in which he recounted his perjury and, worse yet, claimed that he had been suborned by Roy Cohn, the prosecutor of the Rosenbergs and now counsel to the McCarthy committee.[837] After the government summoned all those connected with the publishing of the book before the grand jury to see if they could uncover Communist influence, it was decided to prosecute Matusow for perjury.[838] However, since prosecuting him for the cases in which he conceded he perjured himself might open those convictions to question, he was charged with lying when he claimed that Cohn had suborned his perjury.[839] After Matusow's conviction, his prosecutor went into practice with Roy Cohn.[840]

If those who testified in open court could get away with perjury, this raised serious problems for those faceless informers whose accusations were never tested by cross-examination. As a

---

832. Paul Crouch

Caute, The Great Fear, 1978, p. 132; Navasky, Naming Names, 1980, p. 14; Fariello, Red Scare, 1995, p. 98 n. 2.

833. Harvey Matusow

Navasky, Naming Names, 1980, pp. 40–41 and n. .

834. Career as informer

Id. at p. 40; Caute, The Great Fear, 1978, pp. 133–138; Fariello, Red Scare, 1995, pp. 97–108.

835. Jencks

Id. at p. 103. See above, text at notecall 694.

836. Infiltrated Boy Scouts

Id. at p. 102

837. Suborned by Cohn

Id. at pp. 352–353; Navasky, Naming Names, 1980, p. 40.

838. Prosecute for perjury

Fariello, Red Scare, p. 353.

839. Claimed suborned

Navasky, Naming Names, 1980, p. 40; Fariello, Red Scare, 1995, p. 354.

840. Practice with Cohn

Navasky, Naming Names, 1980, pp. 40–41.

lawyer who represented many people before the Truman Loyalty boards said:

> I spent ten years of my life trying to knock out Hoover's position on [the use of informers]. He would not put up the names of his informants except when they agreed, and generally they didn't agree. So you knew what was said but you didn't know who the hell said it.[841]

In some of the cases it was revealed that personal or professional rivalry fueled the accusations.[842] And given the flimsy basis on which politicians were hurling around accusations of subversion, it would not be surprising that private persons would be equally reckless; when Pete Seeger of The Weavers could be accused of Communistic leanings for songs that celebrated the American Revolution, it was easy for informers to assume that anyone who possessed a book in which the names "Marx" or "Lenin" appeared was reading "Communistic literature."[843]

Given the portrayal of informers in the Judeo–Christian tradition and in the popular culture, some resisted informing by quoting Forster: "[i]f I had to choose between betraying my country and betraying my friend, I hope I should have the guts to betray my country."[844] Some did, though, at a cost; Elizabeth Gurley Flynn,

---

841. "Who the hell said it"

Fariello, Red Scare, 1995, p. 238 (quoting Joseph Rauh).

842. Professional rivalry

Schrecker, No Ivory Tower: McCarthyism and the Universities, 1986, p. 165.

843. "Communistic literature"

Fariello, Red Scare, 1995, p. 138. When Pete Seeger and Lee Hays appeared before H.U.A.C., they were questioned about a "subversive song"—"Wasn't That a Time," which was later the title theme of a movie about The Weavers. The song begins:

"Our fathers bled at Valley Forge,

The snow was red with blood,

Our faith cried out at Valley Forge,

Our faith was brotherhood,

Wasn't that a time?

Wasn't that a time?

A time to try the soul of man

Wasn't that a terrible time?"

Id. at p. 374.

In an ironic tie with confrontation, Seeger also sang a Leveller song that includes these lines:

"You poor take courage

You rich take care,

This earth was made a common treasury

For everyone to share."

Id. at p. 366. This song, "The World Turned Upside Down," was probably not known to the congressional inquisitors though it was what was played by the band when the British army surrendered at Yorktown. For the relationship between the Levellers and confrontation, see vol. 30, § 6343, p. 272.

844. "Guts to betray"

Navasky, Naming Names, 1980, pp. x-xi. For more on attitudes towards informers, see vol. 26A, § 5702.

who made no secret of her own Communist beliefs, spent 60 days in jail for contempt when she responded to a request to name others with a refusal "to degrade or debase myself by becoming an informer."[845] Or as one of the Hollywood resisters explained, the punishment for refusing to become an informer would eventually be over, but for "those who talked it's never over. Their whole lives they carry the pain of having informed * * * not out of principle [but] out of self-preservation."[846]

But as the differing responses to the Watergate informer, "Deep Throat," or to Naderite "Whistle-blowers" demonstrate, the perception of informers is not as clear-cut as some suppose.[847] Indeed, some of those who became informers did so out of a belief that the Communist Party was "criminal" in nature.[848] Assistant Attorney General Warren Olney played on this ambiguity when he justified the government's use of informers on instrumental grounds and decried "the unprecedented barrage of abuse" against the Department of Justice for its use of informers.[849] Other members of the Department suggested that the Communists were behind the attack on informers.[850]

Those who had become informers leaped to the defense of informing; one of these suggested that those who attacked him had adopted the ethics of the Mafia.[851] A number of books, movies, and television programs undertook to defend the role of the anti-Communist informer; none of them were artistically or commercially successful save the best known of this genre, Elia Kazan and Budd Schulberg's movie, "On the Waterfront."[852] Hence, few were

845. "Degrade or debase"

Navasky, Naming Names, 1980, p. 36.

846. "Carry pain"

Fariello, Red Scare, 1995, p. 330.

847. "Deep Throat"

Navasky, Naming Names, 1980, p. xiv.

848. "Criminal" in nature

Edward Dmytryk, one of the "Hollywood Ten" who later recanted, reasoned that since the Communists called those who testified against them "informers" and "informers" were only used against criminals, by using the epithet, the Communists were admitting they were criminals. Caute, The Great Fear, 1978, p. 512.

849. "Barrage of abuse"

Id. at p. 132.

850. Communists behind

Ibid.

851. Ethics of Mafia

Fariello, Red Scare, 1995, p. 303 (Edward Dmytryk).

852. "On the Waterfront"

Navasky, Naming Names, 1980, p. 16–17, 41. Ironically, "On the Waterfront" was not explicitly about anti-Communist informing. Id. at pp. 209–210.

surprised when a 1954 academic study found that 73% of the public would inform on friends or neighbors suspected of being Communists.[853] When Harvey Matusow tried to tell newspapers, including The New York Times, about his perjury, none of them would touch the story.[854]

However, as the Red Scare subsided, a more balanced view of informers seems to have emerged. Partly this was the result of the attempts by famous informers to justify their actions with varying degrees of success.[855] Partly it was the result of the reemergence of traditional views of informers in popular culture; Arthur Miller's two plays, "A View From the Bridge" and "The Crucible" exemplify this trend.[856] Then Harvey Matusow began to justify his informing on the grounds that the secrecy of the Communist Party was inconsistent with the American value of openness.[857] By the 1990s, even Eisenhower's Attorney General, Herbert Brownell, was claiming to have tried to limit the government's use of anonymous informants.[858]

Stalemate, "The Silent Generation," and Stein

The year 1951 saw stalemate in Korea, the mutiny of General MacArthur, his firing by President Truman, and the majority of Americans cheering MacArthur's pretended anti-bureaucratic and anti-authoritarian stance.[859] Also, the Supreme Court affirmed the convictions in the Foley Square Trial and the leadership of the Communist Party went underground.[860] By now, the official anti-Communist culture was in place; Hollywood, perhaps in response to criticism of its wartime propaganda films praising the Soviets, had

853. 73% would inform

Fariello, Red Scare, 1995, p. 41.

854. None would touch

Id. at p. 106.

855. Informers justify

Navasky, Naming Names, 1980, pp. 222–278.

856. "The Crucible"

Id. at pp. 211–212, 214–215.

857. Value of openness

Fariello, Red Scare, 1995, p. 99.

858. Tried to limit

Id. at p. 110.

859. Cheering anti-bureaucratic

Manchester, The Glory and The Dream, 1974, pp. 555, 561, 562–563. MacArthur's rebellion against the Army hierarchy and the President in his desire to carry the war into China, even if this would require the use of nuclear weapons, resonated with the outlaw mentality of Spillane's hero, Mike Hammer.

860. Went underground

Dennis v. U.S., 1951, 71 S.Ct. 857, 341 U.S. 494, 95 L.Ed. 1137; Fariello, Red Scare, 1995, p. 238.

already ground out more than 50 money-losing anti-Communist films; the Cincinnati Reds had changed their name, and Mickey Spillane was sexualizing the violently anti-intellectual vigilante tradition that Roscoe Pound had viewed as a challenge to criminal procedure.[861] When comic books began to out-Spillane Spillane in denigrating the morality of means, even the semi-literate had been prepared for the violent resistance to desegregation that was only a few years away.[862]

Meanwhile, elders began to project their own fears on the young, creating a "silent generation" of "organization men" who abandoned individualism and competition as they flocked to business schools, eager to emulate "The Man in the Grey Flannel Suit."[863] Few of those whose idealism was exhausted were able to see that their children might have simply been responding prudently to corporate attacks on dissent, H.U.A.C. investigations of campus radicalism, the presence of F.B.I. agents on campus, or the ban on "controversial speakers."[864]

861. Sexualizing vigilante

Manchester, The Glory and The Dream, 1974, pp. 566 (anti-Communist culture), 567 (Reds change name), 567–568 (Spillane); Fariello, Red Scare, 1995, p. 259 (50 movies), 273 (émigré novelist Ayn Rand attacks wartime movie made at request of government, "Mission to Moscow," as Communist propaganda because it showed smiling Russian children).

In those relatively innocent times, one had to be either fairly sophisticated or a devotee of the genre to see Spillane's work as sexual sado-masochism. In his aptly named breakthrough novel, "I, the Jury" in 1947, the climactic (no pun intended) scene involves the description of the whipping of a nude woman that could have been copied from any of the sorts of sado-masochistic pornography then-extant—a scene that was featured with ever-increasing explicitness on subsequent paperbacks.

862. Comic books

Id. at pp. 568–569. Manchester's description of the sado-masochism need not be repeated here but it should be not-

ed that no one could escape its sexual content for long because it was featured prominently in a book by a psychologist attacking the comics industry. See Wertheimer, Seduction of the Innocent, 1957.

863. "Silent generation"

Id. at pp. 576 (naming), 578 (decline of individualism and "The Organization Man"), 579 (growth of business majors and "The Man in the Grey Flannel Suit"); Foner, The Story of American Freedom, 1998, p. 270; Halberstam, The Fifties, 1993, pp. 520–536.

864. Controversial speakers

Schrecker, No Ivory Tower: McCarthyism and the Universities, 1986, p. 194 (H.U.A.C. investigation of higher education); Fariello, Red Scare, 1995 p. 422 (F.B.I. and H.U.A.C. agents installed on college campuses).

The ban on controversial speakers, Schrecker, No Ivory Tower: McCarthyism and the Universities, 1986, p. 90, had an episode involving confrontation values. When one of the victims

In 1952, the G.O.P., encouraged by the response to MacArthur but sensitive to his political vulnerabilities, went for another "man on horseback"; when the Democrats nominated a New Deal intellectual (or "egghead" as he was soon dubbed), the stage was set for one of the most vicious election campaigns in years.[865] Perhaps the only good sign for confrontation was when Eisenhower went before television cameras during the convention struggle against the Taft forces to plead for "openness" and "fair play."[866]

When the Republicans came to power in 1953, Stalin died, an armistice was reached in Korea, and the military began to search for a new enemy in Viet Nam.[867] Though the President promulgated a more sweeping loyalty program with E.O. 10450, this was not enough for the party's conservative, anti-internationalist wing; H.U.A.C. went after the churches, Senator Bricker sought a constitutional amendment to limit presidential power, and McCarthy went after the President himself.[868]

In retrospect, it is easy to see this as the beginning of the end for the Second Red Scare. Edward R. Murrow, on the popular CBS television program "See It Now," showed the abuses of the loyalty program with an expose of the Radulovich case.[869] Hubert Hum-

---

of the purge at the University of Washington was invited to speak at U.C.L.A., the administration consented to this with the proviso that one of those who had favored his dismissal be allowed to present that side from the same platform; even so, the event was closed to undergraduates. Id. at p. 92.

865. Vicious campaigns

Manchester, The Glory and The Dream, 1974, pp. 607, 612, 625–626. One political pundit explained that if Stevenson were elected, "the eggheads will come back into power and off again we will go on the scenic railway of muddled economics, Socialism, Communism, crookedness and psychopathic instability." Id. at p. 626. One detects a whiff of resentment of the expert as exemplified by the Brain Trust. This is even clearer in the way Republicans exploited Stevenson's appearance as a character witness for Alger Hiss, his former colleague in the Agriculture

Department during the New Deal. Id. at pp. 612–613.

866. "Fair play"

Id. at p. 617. This was also the election that illustrated the power of the televised pseudo-confrontation when the Republican vice presidential candidate, Richard Nixon, went before the American people to justify a so-called "slush" fund created for him by anti-Communist Los Angeles businessmen. Id. at p. 629.

867. Viet Nam

Id. at pp. 660, 663, 687.

868. Goes after President

Id. at pp. 671, 668, 655, 672.

869. Radulovich

Radulovich was a senior at the University of Michigan who had been declared a security risk and dismissed from the Air Force Reserve on the basis of a

phrey introduced a farcical, and patently unconstitutional, bill to criminalize Communism—and it passed by overwhelming margins in both houses of Congress.[870] Voices began to be heard in opposition to the procedures of the Red-hunters.[871] For purposes of confrontation, the most significant of these was the President's "Code of Abilene" speech; at a Washington dinner in November of 1953, Eisenhower said:

> I was raised in a little town of which most of you have never heard. But in the West it is a famous place. It is called Abilene, Kansas. We had as our Marshal for a long time a man called Wild Bill Hickock. * * * Now that little town has a code, and I was raised as a boy to prize that code. It was: meet anyone face to face with whom you disagree. You could not sneak up on him from behind, or do any damage to him without suffering the penalty of an outraged citizenry. * * * In this country, if someone dislikes you or accuses you, he must come up in front. He cannot hide behind the shadow. He cannot assassinate you or your character from behind.[872]

Even more significantly for the right of confrontation, Eisenhower appointed Earl Warren as Chief Justice.[873]

statement from an anonymous informer that the loyalty board had refused to reveal. Another secret informer told Murrow that the statement accused Radulovich of association with suspicious persons—his father and his sister. Their crime consisted of reading Serbian-language newspapers published at Yugoslavia. Id. at p. 670. See also Caute, The Great Fear, 1978, p. 300.

870. Humphrey farce

The bill would have destroyed the McCarran Act by allowing the privilege against self-incrimination to be asserted in response to its registration requirements. Manchester, The Glory and The Dream, 1974, p. 670.

871. Opposition

"Where a man is accused of a crime * * * our Constitution and laws protect him so far as possible with the strength of objective and impartial procedure; a court independent of the State, a jury trial, definite charges, no hearsay, an open public proceeding, the presumption of innocence. He is treated thus because so much is at stake—his livelihood, his freedom, his good name. All these considerations are present in the loyalty cases." Murphy, The Constitution in Crisis Times, 1918–1969, 1972, p. 257 (quoting former Attorney General Francis Biddle).

It was about this time that one began to hear the defensive phrase, "I don't approve of McCarthy's methods, but * * *." Manchester, The Glory and the Dream, 1974, p. 569.

872. "From behind"

Pollitt, The Right of Confrontation: Its History and Modern Dress, 1959, 8 J.Pub.L. 380; Caute, The Great Fear, 1978, p. 277.

873. Appointed Warren

Id. at p. 146; Murphy, The Constitution in Crisis Times, 1918–1969, 1972, pp. 310–311.

Meanwhile, earlier in 1953, the Supreme Court, still in the grip of the Vinson Court's statism in criminal procedure, made a passing swipe at the right of confrontation.[874] Stein v. New York was, for the most part, simply another in a long line of cases in which the Supreme Court had attempted to deal with the problem of coerced confessions.[875] However, one of the non-confessing defendants raised what would today be seen as a "Bruton problem"; that is, "that the federal rights were infringed because he was unable to cross-examine witnesses, i.e., the confessors."[876] The defendant relied upon a dictum in Snyder that the majority opinion was able to show did not mean what defendant claimed it did.[877] That done, the majority concluded:

> [b]asically, [defendant's] objection to the introduction of these confessions is that as to him they are hearsay. The hearsay-evidence rule, with all its subtleties, anomalies, and ramifications, will not be read into the Fourteenth Amendment.[878]

As Justice Black's dissent makes clear, Stein is another chapter in the Court's internal debate over the "incorporation" of the Bill of Rights into the Fourteenth Amendment.[879]

The Decline of Communism and the Rise of Confrontation

In 1954, the doctrine of massive "retaliation" was announced, the C.I.A. overthrew the democratically-elected government of Guatemala, and the Democrats recaptured control of Congress.[880] Also, Robert Oppenheimer had his security clearance withdrawn, Congress enacted the Communist Control Act, and Attorney General Brownell, in a nationwide television address, announced plans to destroy the Communist Party.[881] But the Red Scare fell apart with

874. Statism in criminal procedure

Id. at p. 303

875. Coerced confessions

Id. at p. 205.

876. "The confessors"

Stein v. New York, 1953, 73 S.Ct. 1077, 1098, 346 U.S. 156, 195, 97 L.Ed. 1522.

877. Snyder dictum

Ibid.

878. "Will not be read"

73 S.Ct. at 1098, 346 U.S. at 196.

879. "Incorporation" debate

Murphy, The Constitution in Crisis Times, 1918–1969, 1972, pp. 264–267.

880. Democrats recaptured control

Encyclopedia of American History, Morris ed. 1976, pp. 483, 522; Halberstam, The Fifties, 1993, p. 375.

881. Plans to destroy

Brownell called members of the Party "scheming and devious men and women dedicated to the destruction of our government and our way of life." Fariello, Red Scare, 1995, p. 111. On the Oppenheimer case, see Manchester,

the unraveling of the Cohn–Schine affair, the televised Army–
McCarthy hearings in which the Senator demanded and got the
right to cross-examination he had denied his victims and used it to
destroy his image; Republicans turned on "Tailgunner Joe," he was
censured by the Senate, and soon lost all influence.[882] Meanwhile,
invoking Cold War propaganda needs, Thurgood Marshall convinced the Supreme Court to take its most dramatic step towards a
moral constituency by overruling Plessy v. Ferguson in Brown v.
Board of Education.[883]

In 1955, James Dean, an early hero of the youth rebellion that
was to come, died in an auto accident and the Davey Crockett boom
revived a superficial interest in frontier values of the sort celebrated in the "Code of Abilene."[884] In this year of the Dixon-Yates
scandal, President Eisenhower eased Cold War tensions and invoked confrontation values with his "Open Skies" proposal for
mutual aerial surveillance of missile sites.[885] Meanwhile, African-
Americans made clear that they did not intend to rely on courts

The Glory and the Dream, 1974, pp.
695–699; Halberstam, The Fifties,
1993, p. 330. The President also
claimed that during his administration, 2,000 "security risks" had been
fired and another 4,000 had resigned
rather than face loyalty boards.

The Communist Control Act, a revision
of the Humphrey farce, set down fourteen indicia of Communist Party
membership, stripped the Party of
"all rights, privileges and immunities
of legal bodies," denied unions found
to be "Communist infiltrated" access
to the N.L.R.B. and federal courts,
and barred Communists from holding
union offices. Caute, The Great Fear,
1978, pp. 50, 358; Fariello, Red Scare,
1995, p. 19.

882. Lost all influence

Cohn was counsel to Senator McCarthy's committee and G. David Schine
was his playboy sidekick; when Schine
was drafted, Cohn tried to pull strings
to get him cushy assignments; when
the Army was not sufficiently compliant, Cohn engineered an attack on the
Army that led to hearings into the
treatment of the Army by McCarthy

and vice versa. American Encyclopedia
of Facts and Dates, 9th 3d. 1993, pp.
564, 566; Manchester, The Glory and
the Dream, 1974, pp. 705–716.

George Bender, a conservative Ohio congressman, said that "McCarthyism
has become a synonym for witch-hunt-
ing, star-chamber methods, and the
denial of civil liberties which have distinguished our country in its historic
growth." Id. at p. 717.

883. Brown v. Board of Education

1954, 74 S.Ct. 686, 347 U.S. 483, 98
L.Ed. 873. Manchester, The Glory and
the Dream, 1974, p. 734; Halberstam,
The Fifties, 1993, p. 411; Foner, The
Story of American Freedom, 1998, pp.
258–259.

884. Davey Crockett

American Encyclopedia of Facts and
Dates, 9th 3d. 1993, pp. 567, 571; Halberstam, The Fifties, 1993, pp. 480–
481 (influence of Dean).

885. "Open Skies"

Encyclopedia of American History, Morris ed. 1976, pp. 486. 522.

alone to obtain their rights, confronting the power of white segregationists with the moral force of the Montgomery bus boycott.[886] But the murder of Emmett Till in Mississippi showed the lengths to which some Southerners would go to maintain Jim Crow and how all-white juries could once again be a bar to implementation of a national policy of racial equality.[887] Meanwhile, the Red Scare began to parody itself with the publication of an Army pamphlet on "How To Spot a Communist" that suggested that Reds were predisposed to discuss civil rights, racial and religious discrimination, the immigration laws, anti-subversive legislation, and curbs on unions and peace; they also used words such as "chauvinism," "bookburning," "colonialism," "demagogy," "witch hunt," "reactionary," "Progressive," and "exploitation."[888]

In 1956, Americans were "all shook up"; the last surviving member of the Union Army died, Ringling Brothers, Barnum & Bailey circus gave its last performance under "the Big Top," Grace Metalious's "Peyton Place" proved how awful small towns were by selling millions of copies of hot, sweaty sex to women as well as to men, and her readers shook their heads as their children made Elvis "The Pelvis" Presley the hottest-selling record artist in years.[889] Abroad, the Suez crisis and the Hungarian revolt gave both sides in the Cold War a chance to flex their muscles and made a liar out of the "Voice of America."[890] Every major Southern

---

886. Montgomery bus boycott

Id. at p. 523; Manchester, The Glory and the Dream, 1974, p. 740; Halberstam, The Fifties, 1993, p. 539.

887. Murder of Emmett Till

Manchester, The Glory and the Dream, 1974, p. 738; Halberstam, The Fifties, 1993, p. 431.

888. "How To Spot a Communist"

Caute, The Great Fear, 1978, p. 296. The pamphlet was subject to such ridicule that it was quickly withdrawn. The Army seems to have had some strange views of ideology; one intelligence officer testified before Truman's Commission on Employee Loyalty that a "liberal is only a hop, skip, and a jump from a Communist. A Communist starts as a liberal." Fariello, Red Scare, 1995, p. 128. This was sane, however, compared to the civilian blacklister who described Arthur Miller's prize-winning "Death of a Salesman" as a "Communist-dominated play." Caute, The Great Fear, 1978, p. 536.

889. "All shook up"

Encyclopedia of American Facts and Dates, 9th ed. 1993, pp. 570 (last union soldier), 572 (Elvis "All Shook Up"), 575 (last show in circus tent); Halberstam, The Fifties, 1993, p. 457 (Elvis), 577 ("Peyton Place").

890. Liar out of "Voice"

Encyclopedia of American History, Morris ed. 1976, p. 487. The V.O.A. had broadcast behind the Iron Curtain to encourage revolt among the Soviet satellite regimes; when the Soviet Army crushed the revolt in Hungary, the United States did nothing to pre-

politician signed the so called "Southern Manifesto," in which they promised "massive resistance" to efforts to desegregate schools and other public facilities.[891] Despite the fact that his party's platform pledged support for the Brown decision that he himself did not share, President Eisenhower was reelected in a landslide but the Democrats retained control of Congress.[892] This was also the year that the first law-review treatment of the right of confrontation, inspired by the excesses of the Red Scare, appeared.[893]

Despite the "Impeach Earl Warren" billboards that were popping up across the land, the Supreme Court in 1957 decided two cases that put a crimp in whatever hopes some might have had for a revival of the Second Red Scare.[894] It was also the year of the first videotaped television program, the revolutionary musical "West Side Story," and the small, beeping object called "Sputnik" circled the earth to launch the "space race" between the two supposed superpowers.[895] America's other "race" problem continued; Congress adopted the first Civil Rights Act since Reconstruction and the President, reluctantly, had to call out federal troops to enforce court-ordered integration of Little Rock Central High School after the Governor of Arkansas, Orville Faubus, called out the National Guard to prevent black students from attending the school.[896] Elsewhere, J. Edgar Hoover was embarrassed when a state policeman uncovered a meeting of Mafia leaders in Appalachian New York, a group that the F.B.I., despite the Kefauver investigations,

vent this. The crushing of the revolt did, however, lead to the last massive exodus from the American Communist Party.

891. "Massive resistance"

Encyclopedia of American History, Morris ed. 1976, pp. 521, 679.

892. Retained control

Id. at p. 523.

893. First law review

Mulvaney, Government Secrecy and the Right of Confrontation, 1956, 31 Notre Dame L. 602.

894. Crimp in Red Scare

Watkins v. U.S., 1957, 77 S.Ct. 1173, 354 U.S. 178, 1 L.Ed.2d 1273 (reversing conviction for contempt of H.U.A.C. on grounds that questions asked were not pertinent to Committee's charge); Yates v. U.S., 1957, 77 S.Ct. 1064, 354 U.S. 298, 1 L.Ed.2d 1356 (holding that the Smith Act did not forbid abstract advocacy of revolution apart from any incitement of acts directed to that end). Manchester, The Glory and the Dream, 1974, pp. 739–740 ("Impeach Warren" billboards).

895. "Space race"

Encyclopedia of American Facts and Dates, 9th ed. 1993, pp. 576, 577, 578; Halberstam, The Fifties, 1993, p. 607 ("space race").

896. Little Rock

Encyclopedia of American History, Morris ed. 1976, p. 524; Halberstam, The Fifties, 1993, p. 607.

claimed did not exist.[897] Little wonder that some Americans began to share the concerns about private power expressed by Hans Morgenthau and C. Wright Mills.[898]

In 1958, the major crises were abroad—in Lebanon, Taiwan, and Berlin—and Vice President Nixon cemented his chances for the 1960 Presidential nomination when he was attacked by anti-U.S. mobs while on a tour of South America.[899] It was also the year that N.A.S.A. was established, Soviet-American relations seemed improved when Van Cliburn won the Tchaikovsky piano competition in Moscow, and the Adams-Goldfine "vicuna coat" scandal helped the Democrats make big gains in the off-year Congressional elections.[900] And, thanks to the Second Red Scare and Soviet repression in Hungary, membership in the Communist Party was estimated at less than 3,000.[901] Little wonder, with both parties seeming to embrace the warfare-welfare state, that some unlucky pundits began to speak of "the end of ideology."[902]

It was also a time in which scholars and others began to compute the social, political, and cultural costs of the Second Red Scare.[903] For our purposes it is enough to note how deeply the Second Red Scare permeated government—federal, state, and local.[904] We have previously discussed the actions and institutions of the federal government, but 39 states had "little Smith Acts" under which at least 20 people were imprisoned.[905] States also had local versions of H.U.A.C. and local police departments had "Red Squads" whose activities have been little studied.[906] It is known

897. Appalachian meeting

Fariello, Red Scare, 1995, p. 93.

898. Morgenthau and Mills

Foner, The Story of American Freedom, 1998, p. 289; Halberstam, The Fifties, 1993, p. 527.

899. Attacked by mobs

Encyclopedia of American History, Morris ed. 1976, pp. 488–489.

900. Gains in elections

Id. at p. 525; Encyclopedia of American Facts and Dates, 9th ed. 1993, pp. 580–582.

901. Less than 3,000

Fariello, Red Scare, 1995, p. 203.

902. "End of ideology"

Foner, The Story of American Freedom, 1998, p. 288.

903. Costs of Red Scare

Navasky, Naming Names, 1980, p. 333.

904. State and local

Some of these seem ludicrous today; e.g., a seditious conspiracy to overthrow the government of Pennsylvania. Fariello, Red Scare, 1995, p. 205.

905. 20 imprisoned

Id. at p. 203.

906. "Red squads"

Caute, The Great Fear, 1978, p. 121; Schrecker, No Ivory Tower: McCar-

that in some states these anti-Communist organs were deployed against the emerging civil rights movement.[907] Although many states had loyalty oaths for government employees, the best-studied of these is California, where the loyalty oath controversy deprived the University of California of some of its best scholars, produced purges of "Reds" there and elsewhere, and for a time had a legislative committee screening applicants for faculty positions at state colleges.[908]

In addition to direct sanctions imposed by courts and employers, suspected Communists were subjected to a variety of collateral sanctions for their political beliefs, such as the harassment by the F.B.I. we have previously mentioned.[909] The costs of defending against criminal and administrative charges were high, but when friends and colleagues contributed to a "defense fund," they, too, were harassed.[910] In addition to deportation, Communists were denied veterans benefits, welfare payments, unemployment compensation, and passports; "Communist front" organizations were denied tax exempt status, had their insurance coverage taken away, and were denied the use of public facilities for meetings.[911]

thyism and the Universities, 1986, p. 86. The fate of the Red Squad of the Los Angeles Police Department is telling. For years, it had served as something of an arm of the Merchants and Manufacturers Associations, providing employers with intelligence about union organizing. Then, in the late 1960s, it was turned loose on dissenters and student activists—a project whose excesses led to a scandal and calls for investigation and reform. As a result, the Red Squad was supposedly disbanded. A few years later it resurfaced with a new designation as the "Organized Crime Unit," but apparently still functioning much as it always had.

907. Against civil rights

Fariello, Red Scare, 1995, p. 480.

908. Screening applicants

Schrecker, No Ivory Tower: McCarthyism and the Universities, 1986, pp. 116–124, 279. The California controversy is also described in Caute, The

Great Fear, 1978, p. 422; Fariello, Red Scare, 1995, p. 422; Manchester, The Glory and the Dream, 1974, p. 498. One of the faculty members who refused to take the oath later returned and became the president of the University.

909. Harassed by F.B.I.

Fariello, Red Scare, 1995, pp. 85, 181.

910. "Defense funds"

Caute, The Great Fear, 1978, p. 178; Schrecker, No Ivory Tower: McCarthyism and the Universities, 1986, p. 186. In addition, lawyers who defended those accused of subversive beliefs were attacked. Navasky, Naming Names, 1980, p. 37.

911. Use of facilities

Caute, The Great Fear, 1978, pp. 161 (use of facilities), 173 (insurance), 180 (tax exempt status), 187 (veterans benefits, welfare, unemployment benefits), 224 (deportation), 245 (passports).

Not all the collateral sanctions were governmental; private persons did their part, from physical attacks, such as the infamous Peekskill riots, to petty acts such as denying Communists admission to Broadway plays.[912] Communists were expelled from scholarly organizations, denied housing, barred from advertising in major newspapers; sometimes these sanctions spilled over to others—as when books and movies critical of those involved in the Second Red Scare were suppressed or foreign scholars and artists were excluded from the country.[913] Typical of the lengths to which the public and private Red-hunters were willing to go was the incident in 1965 in which a decorated veteran of World War II was denied burial in Arlington National Cemetery because he had served a five-year sentence under the Smith Act.[914]

But in 1958, the tide was turning; even legal scholars began to wonder why there was not a right to confrontation in loyalty-board hearings—a question that would come before the Supreme Court the following year.[915]

In 1959, the American Football League was founded, the Los Angeles Dodgers became the first West Coast baseball team to win the World Series, and Alaska and Hawaii became the 49th and 50th states—and the first non-contiguous states.[916] In politics, the Landrum–Griffin Act further restricted the power of labor unions, the Cuban Revolution led to a break of diplomatic relations when the U.S. objected to Cuba's links with the Soviet bloc, and Richard Nixon and Nikita Kruschev exchanged visits to each other's countries—marking a further "thaw" in the Cold War.[917]

During Mr. Nixon's visit to the American National Exhibition in Moscow, he and Premier Kruschev engaged in their famous

---

912. Peekskill and Broadway

Id. at pp. 163–164 (physical attacks, Peekskill), 535 (Broadway); Fariello, Red Scare, 1995, pp. 74–75 (Peekskill).

913. Books and movies suppressed

Id. at pp. 138, 139, 184; Schrecker, No Ivory Tower: McCarthyism and the Universities, 1986, p. 200.

914. Denied burial

Fariello, Red Scare, 1995, p. 545.

915. Confrontation in hearings

Krasnowiecki, Confrontation By Witnesses in Government Employee Security Proceedings, 1958, 33 Notre Dame Law. 180. This is one of the few articles to take issue with Wigmore's history of the right of confrontation. See id. at p. 203.

916. Non-contiguous states

Encyclopedia of American Facts and Dates, 9th ed. 1993, pp. 585, 586, 590, 591.

917. Nixon-Kruschev visits

Id. at p. 584; Encyclopedia of American History, Morris ed. 1978, pp. 489–490, 526.

"kitchen debate," in which Mr. Nixon conflated consumerism with freedom, arguing that what made the United States superior to Russia was not its democratic government but its "extraordinarily high standard of living" with "prosperity for all in a classless society."[918] Certainly the nation had achieved remarkable economic growth; the gross national product had doubled since World War II and while it was ludicrous to call the United States a "classless society," economic inequality was about as low as it would get during the 20th Century.[919]

Mr. Nixon did not originate the substitution of consumerism for democracy as the hallmark of the nation; government and business propagandists had long made capitalism the national creed—the American system of "free enterprise" was the usual slogan.[920] As one "public service" advertisement proclaimed: "[w]ithout a free exchange of goods, you cannot have a free people."[921] In 1958, a public opinion poll found that 82% of those surveyed agreed that "our freedom depends on free enterprise."[922] Few seem to have noticed how many nations in "the Free World" had free markets and repressive governments or that even the "free press" in this country did not dare to reveal the link between cigarette smoking and cancer.[923]

But scholars were already beginning to notice how the link between consumerism, conformity, and corporate bureaucracy that had been so powerful in eliminating leftist radicalism was beginning to generate a backlash; the titles of the books in which these findings were popularized were indicative of the concern—"The Lonely Crowd," "The Organization Man," and "The Hidden Persuaders."[924] The first open opposition to capitalist conformity began in the popular culture and the arts; James Dean was the "Rebel Without A Cause" and the "Beats" or "Beatniks," like Elvis Presley, looked to African-American culture to find oppositional

918. "Classless society"

Foner, The Story of American Freedom, 1998, p. 271.

919. GNP doubled

Id. at p. 264.

920. "Free enterprise" slogan

Id. at p. 262.

921. "Cannot have free people"

Id. at p. 263

922. "Depends on free enterprise"

Ibid.

923. Dare to reveal

Only Reader's Digest, which at the time did not carry any advertising, dared publish the story. Halberstam, The Fifties, 1993, p. 504.

924. "Hidden Persuaders"

Foner, The Story of American Freedom, 1998, p. 270.

values.[925] The establishment culture still clung to the unrealistic "Ozzie and Harriet" view of the American family; the anti-feminist thrust of this vision would produce a more militant feminism in the next decade.[926] The desperation of some defenders of the genteel tradition is symbolized by the action of Postmaster General Arthur Summerfield in banning "Lady Chatterley's Lover" from the mails on the grounds that "[a]ny literary merit the book may have is far outweighed by the pornographic and smutty passages and words, so that the work, taken as a whole, in an obscene and smutty work"—this at a time when "Peyton Place," "Playboy" magazine, and the sadomasochistic novels of Mickey Spillane were all circulated much more widely than D. H. Lawrence's novel.[927]

Meanwhile, in a work that was even less widely read, Professor Robert McKay of N.Y.U. was speculating about how the Supreme Court was likely to resolve the issues in the upcoming case of Greene v. McElroy.[928] Professor McKay was one of the first scholars to suggest a holistic version of the Sixth Amendment, albeit a more limited one than ours.[929] Even more significantly, in a work that would not be published until after the Supreme Court's decision, Professor Daniel Pollitt demonstrated the shallowness of Wigmore's history of the Confrontation Clause.[930]

Greene v. McElroy was a case of an engineer who lost his means of livelihood when his security clearance was cancelled and he could no longer work in the defense industry.[931] He was accused

---

925. "Beatniks"

Halberstam, The Fifties, 1993, p. 301. "Beatniks" were also "hipsters" after the modern jazz phrase, and this became "hippies" in the 1960s.

926. "Ozzie and Harriet"

Id. at pp. 508, 587; Foner, The Story of American Freedom, 1998, p. 266.

927. "Pornographic and smutty"

Encyclopedia of American Facts and Dates, 9th ed. 1993, p. 598.

928. McKay speculating

McKay, The Right to Confrontation, 1959 Wash.U.L.Q. 122.

929. More limited one

He connects the right of confrontation with the right to a public trial, the right of compulsory process, and the right to counsel, but does not mention the connections to the First and Fifth Amendments. Id. at p. 125.

930. Wigmore's history

Pollitt, The Right of Confrontation: Its History and Modern Dress, 1959, 8 J.Pub.L. 381. The article deserves a wider audiences; we owe much to it, though we do not agree with all of its conclusions.

931. Greene case

1959, 79 S.Ct. 1400, 360 U.S. 474, 3 L.Ed.2d 1377.

of being a security risk because he "associated with Communists," "visited officials of the Russian embassy," and attended a dinner for the "Southern Conference for Human Welfare"—an organization said to be a "Communist front" by H.U.A.C.[932] At his initial hearing, Greene was able to refute the charges, which all involved events that took place in 1943-1947; the Communists with whom he associated were all friends of his first wife (who he had subsequently divorced because of their ideological incompatibility), his visits to the Russian embassy were attempts to sell his company's products to a nation that was then allied with the United States, and he had attended the dinner with his first wife and a number of other Washington luminaries were also present—including two Justices of the Supreme Court.[933] Though the loyalty board was obviously relying upon the statements of faceless informers never disclosed to Greene, it apparently discounted these statements because his security clearance was restored.[934]

However, when Eisenhower took office and imposed more stringent standards, Greene's clearance was once more in jeopardy.[935] The second loyalty-board hearing clearly used faceless informers; the Chairman stated this at the outset of the hearing.[936] Though the second hearing was largely a rehash of the charges at the first, it became apparent from the questioning of Greene that the board was impressed by the accusations of anonymous informers who claimed that the defendant shared his first wife's political views as shown by his failure to prevent her from violating "Ozzie and Harriet" standards of appropriate feminine conduct.[937] The board affirmed the denial of Greene's security clearance, the district court granted summary judgment for the government in

932. "Communist front"

Id. at 1404, 360 U.S. at 478.

933. Including Supreme Court

Id. at 1404, 1407, n. 14, 360 U.S. at 478–479, 485 n. 14.

934. Clearance restored

Id. at 1405, 360 U.S. at 479–480.

935. Once more in jeopardy

Id. at 1405, 360 U.S. at 480–481.

936. Chairman stated

"The transcript to be made of this hearing will not include all material in the file of this case, in that it will not include reports of investigations conducted by the Federal Bureau of Investigation or other investigative agencies which are confidential. Neither will it contain information concerning the identity of confidential informants or information which reveals the source of confidential information." Id. at 1408, 350 U.S. at 486.

937. Appropriate feminine conduct

Id. at 1409 n. 16, 360 U.S. at 487 n. 16.

Greene's civil suit, and the Court of Appeals affirmed on the ground that Greene's claim was "nonjusticiable."[938]

The Supreme Court had previously managed to duck the question of whether there was a due-process right of confrontation in hearings before loyalty boards.[939] Any hope that the Court was now going to decide the question was shattered at the outset of Chief Justice Warren's opinion for the Court:

> The issue, as we see it, is whether the Department of Defense has been authorized to create an industrial security clearance program under which affected persons may lose their jobs and may be restrained in following their chosen professions on the basis of fact determinations concerning their fitness for clearance made in proceedings in which they are denied the traditional procedural safeguards of confrontation and cross-examination.[940]

The Chief Justice then sketched the history of the security clearance procedures.[941]

The majority opinion then provides some "background" for the issue about to be decided.

> Certain principles have remained relatively immutable in our jurisprudence. One of these is that where governmental action seriously injures an individual, and the reasonableness of the action depends on fact findings, the evidence used to prove the Government's case must be disclosed to the individual so that he has an opportunity to show that it is untrue. While this is important in the case of documentary evidence, it is even more important where the evidence consists of the testimony of individuals whose memory might be faulty or who, in fact, might be perjurers or persons motivated by malice, vindictiveness, intolerance, prejudice, or jealousy. We have formalized these protections in the requirement of confrontation and cross-examination. They have ancient roots. [The opinion here drops a footnote reference to the Biblical story of Paul's appearance before Festus.[942]] They find expression in the Sixth Amendment which provides that in all criminal cases the accused shall enjoy the right "to be confronted

938. "Non-justiciable"

Id. at 1410–1411, 360 U.S. at 490–491.

939. Managed to duck

Pollitt, The Right of Confrontation: Its History and Modern Dress, 1959, 8 J.Pub.L. 381, 406–408; Rauh, Nonconfrontation in Security Cases: The Greene Decision, 1959, 45 Va.L.Rev. 1175, 1177–1179.

940. "Traditional safeguards"

Id. at 1412, 360 U.S. at 493.

941. "Sketched history"

Id. at 1412–1413, 360 U.S. at 494–496.

942. Paul footnote

Id. at 1413, n. 25, 360 U.S. at 496 n. 25.

with the witnesses against him." This Court has been zealous to protect these rights from erosion.[943]

The Chief Justice then cites some criminal cases in which only the incurably optimistic would find the posited zeal.[944] If the reader will reexamine the rights the Chief Justice thinks "find expression in the Sixth Amendment," she will note a couple of anomalies. First, the broad statement of the defendant's right to disclosure of the government's evidence finds little support in the court's prior opinions, unless Jencks is to be taken as such a case. Second, it requires some sophistication to find a right of access to documentary evidence in a constitutional provision that seems to be limited to "witnesses against" the defendant. Perhaps the Court blurs the distinction because in the case of depositions or affidavits the distinction becomes quite illusory.

Apparently unaware that he has stated a right much broader than the one Wigmore recognizes, the Chief Justice then quotes Wigmore on the value of cross-examination.[945] The Court's opinion then continues:

> Little need be added to this incisive summary statement except to point out that under the present clearance procedures not only is the testimony of absent witnesses allowed to stand without the probing questions of the person under attack which often uncovers inconsistencies, lapses of recollection, and bias, but, in addition, even the members of the clearance boards do not see the informants or know their identities, but normally rely on an investigator's summary report of what the informant said without even examining the investigator personally.[946]

Notice that in this passage hearsay declarants are treated as "absent witnesses" rather than sources of documentary evidence.

After all this dicta, the Court turns to the issue it originally stated and unsurprisingly finds no authority for the existing security clearance program.[947] But in so doing, the opinion comes very close to expressing itself on an issue it claims not to be deciding.

> Thus, even in the absence of specific delegation, we have no difficulty in finding, as we do, that the Department of Defense has

943. "Zealous to protect"
Id. at 1413, 360 U.S. at 496–497.

944. Cites cases
Id. at 1413–1414, 360 U.S. at 497.

945. Cites Wigmore
Ibid.

946. "Without even examining"
Id at. 1414–1415, 360 U.S. at 497–499.

947. No authority
Id at. 1415–1418, 360 U.S. at 499–506.

been authorized to fashion and apply an industrial clearance program which affords affected persons the safeguards of confrontation and cross-examination. But this case does not present that situation. We deal here with substantial restraints on employment opportunities of numerous persons imposed in a manner which is in conflict with our long-accepted notions of fair procedures. Before we are asked to judge whether, in the context of security clearance cases, a person may be deprived of the right to follow his chosen profession without full hearings where accusers may be confronted, it must be made clear that the President or Congress * * * specifically has decided that the imposed procedures are necessary and warranted and has authorized their use.[948]

Little wonder that Justices Frankfurter, Harlan, and Whittaker concurred only in the Court's judgment, with the intimation that the Chief Justice's opinion had expressed a view on the constitutionality of the challenged procedures.[949] Justice Clark dissented on the grounds that governmental privilege sufficed to justify the action of the loyalty boards, and in any event, the procedure used was authorized by Congress.[950]

The Court's decision had several significant consequences. First, a lawyer with substantial experience in defending loyalty cases published an article concluding that a majority of the Court now "believe that there is a constitutional right of confrontation and cross-examination in hearings"—not only under the industrial security program but in other loyalty hearings as well.[951] Congress seems to have agreed, though before it could act, President Eisenhower issued an executive order providing for confrontation in security-clearance proceedings.[952] Finally, the Greene case convinced some scholars of the inadequacy of Wigmore's narrow view of confrontation; "faceless informers," not merely cross-examination began to be seen as part of the policy of the Sixth Amendment.[953]

948. "Authorized their use"

Id at. 1419, 360 U.S. at 506–507.

949. Concurred only

Id at. 1420, 360 U.S. at 508.

950. Clark dissent

Id at. 1421–1428, 360 U.S. at 510–524. Justice Harlan also concurred especially to accuse Clark of misstating the majority's holding. Id. at 360 U.S. at 509–510.

951. "There is a right"

Rauh, Nonconfrontation in Security Cases: The Greene Decision, 1959, 45 Va.L.Rev. 1175, 1185.

952. Eisenhower order

Id. at 1185–1187; Murphy, The Constitution in Crisis Times, 1918–1969, 1972, pp. 347–348.

953. Part of policy

Schwartz, Commentary on the Constitution of the United States, 1963, p. 123.

The Supreme Court was to retreat from the boldness of its Greene dicta the following year, in holding that there was no due-process right of confrontation in investigative hearings before the Commission on Civil Rights.[954] Nonetheless, it seems reasonable to suppose that the Court's consideration of due-process rights of confrontation played a significant role in the Court's decision to give the Sixth Amendment's Confrontation a somewhat bolder reading than in the past—a matter to which we now turn.

§ 6361. Modern Confrontation Decisions—An Uncertain Pointer

Like the 1890s, when the Supreme Court first gave the right of confrontation a narrow construction, the 1960s were turbulent times.[1] The civil-rights movement, in its quest for an all-encompassing freedom, and the antiwar movement orchestrated by the "New Left" produced physical confrontations that could lead to violence; indeed, even as the Supreme Court was considering its first confrontation decision in 30 years, some 25,000 young people were descending on Washington for a protest at the Pentagon.[2] Abroad, the U2 incident, the Bay of Pigs, and the Cuban missile crisis had brought the nation to the to the brink of nuclear war.[3] At home, "the Pill," the sexual revolution, and the rise of feminism were threatening the 1950s nuclear family.[4] Finally, assassinations and urban riots triggered by the failures of the civil-rights movement in the North and West led to demands for "law-and-order" that ultimately put Richard Nixon in the White House and allowed him to reconstitute the Court.[5] Why, then, did the Supreme Court

---

954. No due process right

Hannah v. Larche, 1960, 80 S.Ct. 1502, 363 U.S. 420, 4 L.Ed.2d 1307. The dissenting opinion of Justices Black and Douglas has a useful compendium of confrontation quotations. Id at. 1546–1553 363 U.S. at 493–508.

§ 6361

1. Turbulent times

On the 1890s, see § 6357.

2. Protest at Pentagon

Foner, The Story of American Freedom, 1998, pp. 291, 292. On the civil-rights movement, see id. at p. 292; Viorst, Fire in the Streets, 1979, pp. 91, 125, 197. On the antiwar movement, see id.

at p. 421; Gitlin, The Sixties: Years of Hope, Days of Rage, 1987, pp. 242–340.

3. Brink of nuclear war

Encyclopedia of American History, Morris ed. 1976, pp. 491 (U2), 492 (Bay of Pigs), 495 (Cuban missile crisis).

4. Nuclear family

Foner, The Story of American Freedom, 1998, p. 294.

5. Assassinations and riots

Encyclopedia of American History, Morris ed. 1976, pp. 529 (Kennedy assassination), 531 (Watts riots), 531 (King

pick this time to revive the Confrontation Clause of the Sixth Amendment?

The Second Red Scare had destroyed the revolutionary left and showed that the state had weapons more pervasive and less expensive than the criminal law to suppress dissent.[6] Labor unions had been subjected to increasing administrative controls and had traded their ambitious social agendas for consumerism and business unionism.[7] Finally, the "New Left" had jettisoned the traditional rhetoric of rebellion for what was, or soon degenerated into, an ideological version of consumerism.[8]

The generation that was in power in the 1960s had lived through wars, both hot and cold, that had been justified by the traditional values found in the Bill of Rights.[9] Yet those wars also found the government emulating its adversaries in ways that were inconsistent with those values.[10] For example, while Americans liked to think their government was characterized by democratic openness, the Viet Nam War was entered into and carried out by stealth and deception that did not comport with the traditional view of democracy.[11] And the My Lai massacre was soon to suggest

---

assassination and ensuing riots), 533 (campus demonstrations and riots at Democratic convention in Chicago); Manchester, The Glory and the Dream, 1974, pp. 1004–1008 (John Kennedy), 1070 (Robert Kennedy), 1128 (Martin Luther King), 1131–1134 (Chicago).

6. Suppress dissent

See § 6360. And as events at Kent State and Jackson State showed, Americans were willing to shoot their children if necessary to preserve order. Encyclopedia of American History, Morris ed. 1976, p. 502; Manchester, The Glory and the Dream, 1974, pp. 1212–1216.

7. Business unionism

Foner, The Story of American Freedom, 1998, p. 292.

8. "New Left"

Id. at pp. 287, 293, 303. For a somewhat more favorable account by a partici-

pant, see Gitlin, The Sixties: Years of Hope, Days of Rage, 1987.

9. Wars justified

See § 6359, text at notecall 217; § 6360, text at notecall 319.

10. Emulated adversaries

See § 6359, text at notecall 217; § 6360, text at notecall 545. This was particularly true of the Cold War; during the very time that the Soviet Union was being denounced as a police state that eavesdropped on its citizens, set informers among them, and used the criminal law to suppress dissent, our government was doing much the same thing as part of the Second Red Scare. See § 6360, text at notecall 643.

11. Viet Nam deception

Foner, The Story of American Freedom, 1998, p. 292; Manchester, The Glory and the Dream, 1974, pp. 1016–1019 (Tonkin Gulf resolution and deception of public).

that American forces were not committed to the rules of war or to any other restraints on their power.[12]

The Court's search for a moral constituency to replace the support of Big Business had been derailed by the Vinson Court during the Second Red Scare but it was now free to resume that search.[13] Capitalism had shown that it was quite capable of taking care of itself politically, undoing much of the New Deal with little assistance from the Court.[14] Indeed, such enemies as capitalism had left seemed to be at the state level and corporations were soon to turn to Congress, not the Court, to free them from new rules of tort and contract that threatened traditional ways of doing business.[15]

We should also recognize the tendency to hold fast to traditional values in times of rapid change.[16] The Bill of Rights is a compendium of such values and those values were being invoked even by those who sought change; e.g., the civil rights movement.[17] Indeed, in the year Pointer v. Texas was decided, a group of student supporters of voting rights for African–Americans held a sit-in at the site of the Liberty Bell in Philadelphia, which, in American iconography, was also the home of the Constitution.[18]

Among those traditional values is the Court's perception of its own role as an antimajoritarian force——a group whose heroism

12. My Lai massacre

Id. at pp. 1175–1178.

13. Resume search

Foner, The Story of American Freedom, 1998, p. 301. On the Court's switch, see § 6460, text at notecall 95.

14. Taking care of itself

Since the end of the Second New Deal, both major parties have been pro-business and corporations provide money to both parties as well as cabinet members for each. The days when the National Association of Manufacturers could refer to the Republicans as "our party" are long gone. See § 6359, text at notecall 561.

15. Turn to Congress

See Vol. 23, § 5285 (Supp.).

16. Times of rapid change

This, of course, was precisely what the Court probably thought it was doing in 1895 and in 1933. The point is that it is easy, because of the striking difference in doctrine, to overlook the degree to which the Warren court was much like its predecessors. See Fiss, History of the Supreme Court of the United States: Troubled Beginnings of the Modern State, 1888–1910, 1993, p. 10.,

17. Those who sought change

Foner, The Story of American Freedom, 1998, pp. 278–279 (describing Martin Luther King's invocation of the American tradition). Even the "New Left" owed much more to an indigenous revolutionary tradition than some of its members were prepared to admit. Id. at pp. 288–289.

18. Sit-in at Liberty Bell

Id. at p. 274.

consisted in standing fast for traditional values in the face of popular demands for some "quick fix."[19] If the Court did not already know this, it was soon to learn that there is no more thankless task than undertaking to be the custodian of the nation's conscience.[20]

Ironically, just at the time when some legal scholars were beginning to question the autonomy of legal thought, the Court was becoming more autonomous——or isolated——than in any time in its history. The days when John Marshall could dine with Aaron Burr and his lawyer at the same time he was presiding over Burr's criminal trial or when Stephen Field could consult with the Robber Barons about cases pending before the Court were over; as the cases of William O. Douglas, Abe Fortas, and Clement Haynsworth (whose conduct was far less egregious) demonstrated, the demands of judicial ethics no longer allowed Justices of the Supreme Court to associate with potential litigants or to dabble in politics.[21] Members of the Court now spent more time with their clerks than they did hobnobbing with capitalists or politicians. Moreover, criticism and analysis of the Court's work was increasingly detached from popular fora such as newspapers and political speeches and began to repose in the law reviews and other legal writings.[22]

Unlike the 1890s, when the Civil War was still fresh in many minds, by the 1960s, with the Red Scare just behind us, it was no longer possible to see the national government as a fragile institution that could not survive the Bill of Rights. Indeed, the national government was now so powerful that it was not just traditional conservatives who could see it as a threat to civil liberties. Nor was it possible to view the states as the virtuous defender of the rights of all its citizens; if that dream did not die with the Wickersham

---

19. Antimajoritarian role

Indeed, the criticisms of the Warren Court bear a close resemblance to the criticisms New Dealers made of the Hughes Court. Id. at p. 304.

20. Custodian of conscience

Id. at p. 280.

21. Dabble in politics

Encyclopedia of American History, Morris ed. 1976, pp. 533, 535 (Fortas, Douglas, Haynsworth cases); Cummings & McFarland, Federal Justice, 1937, p. 62 (Marshall dines with Burr); Magrath, Morrison R. Waite,

The Triumph of Character, 1963, pp. 200–221 (Field and Robber Barons); Manchester, The Glory and the Dream, 1974, pp. 1138–1139 (Fortas), 1164 (Haynsworth, Carswell).

22. Law reviews

Law reviews had, of course, been around for over 80 years, but they could not have had as much influence when very few members of the Court had attended law school; Justice Jackson was the last member of the Court who did not graduate from law school.

Commission's revelations of corruption and abuse of local law enforcement, Little Rock surely did it in. Indeed, the civil-rights movement was now looking to the national government as "the custodian of liberty."[23]

In this connection, it is well to remind ourselves of the connection between an increasingly mobile population and the desire for standardization. Just as an American expects to find a McDonald's or a Holiday Inn in every part of the nation, so they expect to find a system of law enforcement that will protect them as they were protected at home.[24] The reaction of people in other parts of the country to the Emmett Till case strongly suggests that people were unwilling to tolerate differential standards of justice.[25] This standardization of justice was important to tourists and to corporations that liked to ship their executives from one part of the country to another.

The 1960s were also a time of the revival of idealism.[26] From the Ghandian nonviolence of the first sit-ins to the statist platitudes of "Camelot" to the Peace Corps to "The Great Society," Americans embraced ideals that had been submerged in the 1950s.[27] Eventually, as was the case with the Progressives and the New Dealers, the Warfare State would overwhelm the Welfare State but, while it lasted, this idealism played a part in the revival of confrontation.[28]

23. "Custodian of liberty"

Foner, The Story of American Freedom, 1998, p. 279. On the power of the government, recall President Eisenhower's farewell address warning people of the "military-industrial complex." Encyclopedia of American History, Morris ed., p. 527.

24. McDonald's and Holiday Inn

Halberstam, The Fifties, 1993, pp. 161 (McDonald's), 173 (Holiday Inn).

25. Emmett Till

Id. at pp. 431–440. Till was the 14-year-old from Chicago who, while visiting his mother's family in rural Mississippi, refused to conform to local customs regarding conduct toward white women, was murdered, and his killers acquitted by a jury that only deliberated long enough to consume a soft drink.

26. Revival of idealism

Foner, The Story of American Freedom, 1998, p. 275.

27. Embraced ideals

Encyclopedia of American History, Morris ed. 1976, pp. 492 (the Peace Corps), 527 (JFK inaugural; "ask not what your country can do for you— ask what you can do for your country"), 529 (War on Poverty), 530 ("Great Society"). On the "Great Society" programs, see Manchester, The Glory and the Dream, 1974, pp. 1042–1044.

28. Warfare overwhelms Welfare

Foner, The Story of American Freedom, 1998, pp. 284–287.

The Other was now less fearsome than in 1895. The culture and politics of the 1960s destroyed the WASP ascendancy and took a big bite out of Anglo–Saxon racism. As African–Americans became prominent and admired in sports and music, other groups only slightly less despised advanced as well. When a Catholic could be elected President and Barry Goldwater could run for the office without anyone remarking on his Jewish ancestry, the nation had moved some distance from the bigotry invoked in opposition to Brandeis's appointment to the Supreme Court.[29] Symbolic of the decline, or perhaps the exportation, of The Other was the Hart–Celler Act which abolished the national-origins-quota system of the Immigration Act of 1924.[30] By 1976, a public opinion poll found that 85% of those asked agreed that "the United States was meant to be * * * a country made up of many races, religions, and nationalities."[31]

Nor was the ethnic Other the only kind that was becoming more familiar and less threatening. The youth rebellion of the 1960s brought the political and ideological dissenter into many American homes——or the home next door.[32] Dress, musical taste, sexual attitudes, and drug use revealed the tensions that were concealed in the "Ozzie and Harriet" family of the 1950s.[33] Then, just as men were learning to accommodate to love beads and coed dormitories, feminism brought dissent right into the bosom of the traditional male-dominated family. The notion that "the personal is political" was frightening to those who thought home was a place where one went to escape politics.[34]

29. Moved from bigotry

Manchester, The Glory and the Dream, 1974, pp. 881, 1026. Actually, one person did comment on Goldwater; Harry Golden, the editor and publisher of "The Carolina Israelite" said: "I always knew the first Jewish president would be an Episcopalian."

30. Abolished national origins

Foner, The Story of American Freedom, 1998, pp. 280–281.

31. "Country of many races"

Id. at p. 281. We are not claiming that racism and bigotry vanished in the 1960s, only that their influence was less pervasive and less respectable.

32. Youth rebellion

Id. at pp. 292–294.

33. Concealed in "Ozzie"

Halberstam, The Fifties, 1993, pp. 508–520 (offstage tensions in Nelson family).

34. "Personal is political"

Foner, The Story of American Freedom, 1998, p. 299. As one feminist wrote: "[t]here is no private domain of a person's life that is not political and there is no political issue that is not ultimately personal." Ibid.

There was also an element of judicial self-confidence—or hubris—involved in the revival of confrontation. The Supreme Court had just finished setting out the doctrinal framework for one of the most massive bits of social engineering in American history—the dismantling of Jim Crow. Now it was left to the Congress and to the Executive to carry the weight of further elaboration and implementation.[35] Judges who had undertaken what the Union Army could not accomplish during Reconstruction were not likely to shrink from reforming state criminal-justice systems.[36]

Finally, ignorance and inertia must have played a significant part in the Court's embrace of confrontation. The Court had already embarked on the process of "incorporation" of other provisions of the Bill of Rights into the Due Process Clause of the Fourteenth Amendment; in the years just prior to Pointer, the courts had held states to be bound by the Fourth and Fifth Amendments and invoked the Sixth Amendment's right to counsel provision to require states to provide lawyers for indigents.[37] Adding the right of confrontation was simply another step in this process and one that must have seemed to be "small potatoes" compared to other cases that made up the Warren Court's "rights revolution."[38] Given the amount and depth of the scholarly writing on confrontation and the poor quality of the prior confrontation caselaw, the Court could not have foreseen the problems it was creating for itself and its successors.[39]

35. Implementation

Id. at p. 277. Moreover, the Court had just undertaken to change the rural "rotten borough" system that had denied suburban voters a voice in the legislatures of the Northern states. Baker v. Carr, 1962, 82 S.Ct. 691, 369 U.S. 186, 7 L.Ed.2d 663.

36. Union army could not

See § 6356, text at notecall 176.

37. "Incorporation"

Mapp v. Ohio, 1961, 81 S.Ct. 1684, 367 U.S. 643, 6 L.Ed.2d 1081 (Fourth Amendment); Gideon v. Wainwright, 1963, 83 S.Ct. 792, 372 U.S. 335, 9 L.Ed.2d 799 (right to counsel); Malloy v. Hogan, 1964, 84 S.Ct. 1489, 378 U.S. 1, 12 L.Ed.2d 653 (Fifth Amendment).

On the process of incorporation, see generally, Murphy, The Constitution in Crisis Times, 1918–1969, 1972, pp. 191–192, 205–209, 264–267, 268–269, 303–304, 378–380.

38. "Rights revolution"

Foner, The Story of American Freedom, 1998, pp. 299–304.

39. Scholarly writing

For discussion of the Supreme Court's prior confrontation jurisprudence, see § 6356, text at notecalls 748 (Burr), 756 (Reid), 764 (Walsh v. Rogers), 770 (Reynolds); § 6357, text at notecalls 478 (Mattox), 566 (Robertson, Kirby, Motes); § 6358, text at notecalls 424 (West), 433 (Felts), 741 (Dowdell), 941 (Diaz); § 6359, text at notecalls 640 (Delaney), 666 (Salinger), 918 (Sny-

Pointer v. Texas was the first Sixth Amendment confrontation case to reach the Supreme Court in more than 30 years.[40] It offered the Court an opportunity to take a holistic view of the Sixth Amendment, because, as originally presented to the Court, it raised the question whether the Sixth Amendment gave a criminal defendant the right to counsel at a preliminary hearing. This question was linked to confrontation because the testimony of a witness at the preliminary hearing was later introduced in evidence against the defendant at the trial on the merits.[41] However, the Court decided to pass over the right-to-counsel question because

> the arguments * * * make it clear that petitioner's objection is based not so much on the fact that he had no lawyer when [the declarant] made his statement at the preliminary hearing, as on the fact that the use of the transcript at the trial denied petitioner any opportunity to have the benefit of counsel's cross-examination of the principal witness against him.[42]

Notice how this passage first assumes that a hearsay declarant is a "witness against" the defendant within the meaning of the Sixth

der); § 6360, text at notecalls 594 (Bridges), 931 (Greene v. McElroy).

For the prior treatise writers that have touched on confrontation, see § 6355, text at notecalls 563 (Kent), 610 (Bentham), 704 (Story), 783 (Greenleaf); § 6356, text at notecalls 13 (Appleton), 237 (Cooley); § 6358, text at notecalls 140 (Wigmore), 824 (Chamberlayne). See also, Dumbauld, The Bill of Rights (And What It Means Today), 1957, pp. 12, 15, 18, 22, 30, 33 (potted history of confrontation).

The only scholarly articles available in 1965 were: Donnelly, The Role of Rules of Evidence, 1953, 13 U.Chi. Conf.Ser. 39, 46 (suggesting confrontation is more than cross-examination; part of symposium on Freedom and the Law); Krasnowiecki, Confrontation By Witnesses In Government Employee Security Proceedings, 1958, 33 Notre Dame Law. 180 (shows inadequacy of Wigmore's history); McKay, The Right of Confrontation, 1959, Wash.U.L.Q. 122 (brief anticipation of Greene; suggests holistic analysis);

Mulvaney, Government Secrecy and the Right of Confrontation, 1956, 31 Notre Dame Law. 602 (Wigmorean analysis); Pollitt, The Right of Confrontation: Its History and Modern Dress, 1959, 8 J.Pub.L. 381 (best article at the time and well-worth reading today).

40. Pointer case

1965, 85 S.Ct. 1065, 380 U.S. 400, 13 L.Ed.2d 923. The last case in which the Court had considered the application of the Sixth Amendment to the states was the Snyder case in 1934. See § 6353, text at notecall 918. In the interim the Court had considered the application of due-process confrontation to federal administrative agencies during the Second Red Scare. See § 6354, text at notecalls 594, 931.

41. Originally counsel case

Id. at 1066–1067, 380 U.S. at 401–404.

42. "Benefit of cross-examination"

Id. at 1067, 380 U.S. at 403.

Amendment, then hints that this is only so if the declarant is "the principal witness" against the accused.[43]

Justice Black, for the majority of the Court, spends most of his time on the incorporation question; he holds that the "Sixth Amendment's right of an accused to confront the witnesses against him is * * * a fundamental right and is made obligatory on the States by the Fourteenth Amendment."[44] He brushes off the West case on the grounds that it is made obsolete by the Court's subsequent incorporation decisions.[45] The majority and the concurring opinions were so concerned with the incorporation question that the application of the right of confrontation gets comparatively short shrift.[46]

Justice Black never considers the question of why a hearsay declarant is "a witness against" the defendant; the point is simply assumed—"the Sixth Amendment's guarantee of confrontation and cross-examination was unquestionably denied petitioner in this case."[47] Earlier the opinion suggests that confrontation is more than simply a right of cross-examination; "the right of cross-examination is included in the right of an accused in a criminal case to confront the witnesses against him."[48] Now, however, the opinion turns Wigmorean: "a major reason underlying the constitutional right of confrontation rule is to give a defendant charged with crime an opportunity to cross-examine the witnesses against him."[49] Similar statements appear in the discussion of incorporation.[50]

Assuming with the Court that a hearsay declarant is a "witness against" the defendant, what does it take to satisfy his right; that is, what does it mean to "confront" a witness?[51] Justice Black

43. "Principal witness"

Ibid. Earlier this person was described as the state's "chief witness." Id. at 1066, 380 U.S. at 401.

44. "Fundamental right"

Id. at 1068, 380 U.S. at 403.

45. Brushes off West

Id. at 1069, 380 U.S. at 406. The West case is discussed in § 6352, text at notecall 424.

46. Concurring opinions

Id. at 1070–1074, 380 U.S. at 409–414.

47. "Unquestionably denied"

Id. at 1069, 380 U.S. at 406.

48. "Included in right"

Id. at 1068, 380 U.S. at 404.

49. "Major reason"

Id. at 1069, 380 U.S. at 406–407.

50. Similar statements

Id. at 1068, 380 U.S. at 404–406.

51. Mean to "confront"

This question is related to the question just discussed but is not identical with it; even if confrontation is equated with cross-examination, this still leaves the question of what one means by "cross-examination." For example, must the questioning take place be-

says that

> [t]he case before us would be quite a different one had [the declarant's] statement been taken at a full-fledged hearing at which petitioner had been represented by counsel who had been given a complete and adequate opportunity to cross-examine.[52]

Though the opinion justifies this conclusion by the Court's prior decisions, those cases do not suggest that confrontation is "satisfied" by past cross-examination as Justice Black assumes; rather they hold that confrontation is "excused" because of the absence of the declarant through no fault of the state or because confrontation has been "forfeited" by the accused's procurement of the absence of the witnesses.[53] To make Pointer square with the earlier cases, one must assume that the fact that the witness has moved to another state is insufficient to "excuse" the absence of present cross-examination.[54]

What does it mean for the declarant's statement to be taken at a "full-fledged hearing"?[55] Justice Black suggests that this does not mean an adversary proceeding of the sort defined by the Sixth Amendment; apparently even an inquisitorial proceeding like the English preliminary hearing will do if defendant has counsel and counsel has an opportunity to cross-examine.[56] However, in one of

fore the tribunal that will decide guilt—what we call "present confrontation"—or will "past confrontation" suffice?

52. "Adequate opportunity"

Id. at 1069–1070, 380 U.S. at 407.

53. "Excused" and "forfeited"

See, e.g. the Mattox case, discussed in § 6357, text at notecall 478, which involved the former testimony of a deceased witness and the Reynolds case, discussed in § 6356, text at notecall 720, in which former testimony was admitted because the defendant had procured the absence of the witness.

54. Moved to another state

Id. at 1066–1067, 380 U.S. at 401. In other words, Mattox required not only that the state show that the past cross-examination was adequate but also show some good reason for deny-

ing the defendant the right of present cross-examination; that is, past confrontation does not "satisfy" the Sixth Amendment unless present confrontation is excused. Black mentions that Mattox involved a "deceased witness" Id. at 1069, 380 U.S. at 407.

55. "Full-fledged"

This was to become important because there are a number of ways in which a preliminary hearing differs from a trial even if the defendant has counsel; for example, often counsel will not know enough about the case to conduct a searching cross-examination. Of course, this could be handled as a question of the adequacy of the opportunity for cross-examination.

56. "Inquisitorial"

See vol. 30, § 6342, p. 229.

the cases cited to support the incorporation of the right of confrontation, the Court had taken a more holistic view.

> A person's right to reasonable notice of a charge against him, and an opportunity to be heard in his defense——a right to his day in court——are basic in our system of jurisprudence; and these rights include as a minimum, a right to examine the witnesses against him, to offer testimony and to be represented by counsel.[57]

Suppose that the testimony of the declarant is taken at a secret proceeding in which the defendant has no prior notice of the charges at the proceeding; is this a "full-fledged" hearing?[58] In a related case, the Supreme Court held that the Sixth Amendment's separation of functions is applicable to the states through the Fourteenth Amendment.[59] Does this mean that if the judge at the preliminary does not think the prosecutor is doing a good job and takes over the examination of the witness that the hearing is not "full-fledged"?[60]

However, it turns out that past cross-examination is not the only way in which confrontation can be satisfied; Justice Black acknowledges prior dicta in which the "court has recognized the admissibility against an accused of dying declarations."[61] He adds that "[t]here are other analogous situations which might not fall within the scope of the constitutional rule requiring confrontation of witnesses."[62] One can justify the case of dying declaration as a case of "forfeiture" of confrontation; that is, since it is the defendant, not the state, who has made the witness unavailable for cross-examination at trial, he is estopped to complain.[63] But this still

---

57. "Day in court"

Id. at 1068, 380 U.S. at 405 (quoting in re Oliver, 1948, 68 S.Ct. 499, 507, 333 U.S. 257, 273, 92 L.Ed. 682).

58. Secret proceeding

The main holding in Oliver was that a witness could not be held in contempt of court at a secret hearing. Hence, the question is whether a secret hearing is "full-fledged" if it would violate the Sixth Amendment right to a public trial if it were an adjudication of guilt.

59. Separation of functions

In re Murchison, 1955, 75 S.Ct. 623, 349 U.S. 133, 99 L.Ed. 942.

60. Takes over examination

At the inquisitorial English preliminary examination, which was one of the targets of the English movement for a right of confrontation, the justice of the peace mixed both investigatory and adjudicative functions. See vol. 30, § 6342, p. 230.

61. "Dying declarations"

Id. at 1069, 380 U.S. at 407.

62. "Analogous situations"

Id. at 1070. 380 U.S. at 407.

63. Estopped to complain

However, most of the state cases admitting dying declarations have done so on the theory that the declarant is not a "witness against" the accused. See § 6355, text at notecall 820.

leaves the question of how the use of hearsay in "analogous situations" can be justified——a question that the Court was to wrestle with for the rest of the century.[64]

If the Court did not see the problem, student writers did.[65] Since the Court held that a hearsay declarant became a "witness against" the defendant when his statement was to be used at trial, when can hearsay be admitted without violating the defendant's right of confrontation?[66] Some students picked up the ploy used by some 19th-century state courts; the right of confrontation is a common-law right so all of the common-law exceptions satisfy the state and federal confrontation clauses.[67] The problem with this approach is that it is not clear what exceptions were recognized at common law either in 1789 or when the various states adopted their own confrontation clauses; hence, either the court will have to honor every hearsay exception the state court chooses to recognize as a matter of state common law or it must impose a more stringent federal standard on the states.[68]

Some student writers tried to apply what they took to be the policy of the Confrontation Clause to each of the hearsay exceptions——an approach that raises at least two problems; how does one determine the policy of the Confrontation Clause and how can that policy be squared with the language of the Clause?[69] Some

64. For rest of century

See §§ 6363–6375, below.

65. Student writers

By and large, the scholars did not weigh in until later so their views of Pointer are affected by subsequent developments. Those who jumped right in sometimes missed significant features of the early cases. See Graham, The Right of Confrontation and the Hearsay Rule: Sir Walter Raleigh Loses Another One, 1972, 8 Crim.L.Bull. 99 (a condensation of an earlier treatment in the Alaska Law Journal). We shall take up their views in due course. See Murphy, The Constitution in Crisis Times, 1918–1969, 1972, p. 383 (treating as incorporation case).

66. When hearsay admitted

Note, Preserving the Right to Confrontation——A New Approach to Hearsay Evidence in Criminal Trials, 1965, 113 U.Pa.L.Rev. 741, 743; Note, Criminal Law——Sixth Amendment Right to Confrontation——Obligatory in State Proceedings, 1966, 6 Washburn L.J. 171, 174.

67. All satisfy

Note, The Use of Prior Recorded Testimony and the Right of Confrontation, 1968, 54 Iowa L.Rev. 360, 363–364. On the state courts' use of this ploy, see § 6355, text at notecall 820; § 6357, text at notecall 1.

68. Stringent standard

Note, Right of Confrontation Applies to States, 1965, 19 U. Miami L.Rev. 500, 505.

69. Policy squared

Note, Preserving the Right to Confrontation——A New Approach to Hearsay Evidence in Criminal Trials, 1965, 113 U.Pa.L.Rev. 741, 746–766; Note, Confrontation, Cross–Examination and The Right to Prepare a Defense, 1968, 56 Geo.L.J. 939, 941–951.

students found Wigmore's solution attractive, but others showed that Wigmore's theory was too narrow because it did not consider confrontation in relation to the right of counsel and the rest of the adversary system.[70]

Perhaps the most provocative student piece tried to narrow the Confrontation Clause by use of its own language, arguing that a hearsay declarant was only a "witness against" the accused if her statement proved the prosecution's case.[71] This student was among the first to grasp the holistic approach to the Sixth Amendment, showing how confrontation as part of the adversary system was related to the blank-pad rule, trial by newspaper, and the right of compulsory process.[72] This approach helps to differentiate the hearsay rule from the right of confrontation because the latter is concerned with more than merely the reliability of evidence used to prove guilt.[73]

The federal cases interpreting Pointer were a mixed bag.[74] Some saw it as adopting the Wigmorean scheme.[75] Hence, if the statement was inadmissible hearsay, it also violated the right of confrontation.[76] Taking Pointer at face value, courts held that confrontation barred the use of depositions unless the defendant had an adequate opportunity to cross-examine the declarant.[77] Only much later did the lower courts relate the holding in Pointer to the language of the Sixth Amendment.[78]

70. Wigmore's theory

Note, Constitutional Law—Due Process—Accused's Right to Confront the Witnesses Against Him is Obligatory on States, 1966, 30 Alb.L.J. 151, 152 (Wigmore theory); Note, The Use of Prior Recorded Testimony and The Right of Confrontation, 1968, 54 Iowa L.Rev. 360, 365 (attacks Wigmore).

71. Statement proved

Note, Confrontation, Cross–Examination, and the Right to Prepare a Defense, 1968, 56 Geo.L.J. 939, 957.

72. And compulsory process

Id. at 958–959, 966–972.

73. More than reliability

Id. at p. 940.

74. Mixed bag

Because many of these cases were rendered obsolete by subsequent developments, we offer only a sampling. Cases that advance the analysis of confrontation will be taken up when we address that task in the next volume in this Treatise.

75. Adopts Wigmore

U.S. v. Amaya, C.A.5th, 1976, 533 F.2d 188, 190.

76. Inadmissible violated

U.S. v. Ragano, C.A.5th, 1973, 476 F.2d 410, 415.

77. Depositions

U.S. v. Provencio, C.A.9th, 554 F.2d 361; Phillips v. Wyrick, C.A.8th, 1977, 558 F.2d 489.

78. Relate to language

Mattes v. Gagnon, C.A. 7th, 1983, 700 F.2d 1096, 1101 (who is "witness against").

§ 6362. ___; Douglas, Bruton, and The "Blank Pad Rule"

On the same day that it decided Pointer, the Supreme Court faced another case that suggested the pitfalls of reductionist analysis of the Sixth Amendment and the Confrontation Clause.[1] In Douglas v. Alabama the defendant was charged with assault with intent to murder.[2] An accomplice who had previously been convicted and who was represented by the same lawyer as Douglas was called to testify, but invoked his privilege against self-incrimination because his own case was still pending on appeal and he did not want to harm himself in the event of a retrial.[3] The trial judge held that the accomplice could not assert the privilege but he still refused to answer, despite threats of contempt.[4] Claiming to be refreshing the accomplice's recollection, the prosecutor then took the accomplice's confession and went through it sentence by sentence, reading a line and asking the recalcitrant accomplice, "did you say that?" or "did you make that statement?"[5] Included in the accomplice's statements was an accusation that Douglas was the triggerman in the assault.[6]

One can see that this is an abuse of the adversary system but if one singles out any one of the provisions in the Bill of Rights that the Founders intended as indicia of that system, none seems individually adequate.[7] One could argue that this is a violation of

§ 6362

1. Reductionist

That is, analysis that tries to explain a ruling by reference to a single provision in the Sixth Amendment rather than seeing the Amendment and related provisions in the Bill of Rights as a way of describing an adversary rather than an inquisitorial system of justice. See vol. 30, § 6347, text at notecall 314 (Founders intended Sixth this way).

2. Douglas case

1965, 85 S.Ct. 1074, 380 U.S. 415, 13 L.Ed.2d 934.

3. Did not want to harm

Id. at 1075, 380 U.S. at 416.

4. Refused to answer

Id. at 1075, 380 U.S. at 416. The trial court thought that the conviction erased the accomplice's right to claim the privilege.

5. "Did you make?"

Id. at 1075, 380 U.S. at 416–417. Since the confession was in writing, the justification for this mode of procedure is unclear. Worse yet, the prosecution was allowed to call three officers to authenticate the confession, though it was never admitted in evidence.

6. Triggerman

Id. at 1076 n.3, 380 U.S. at 417 n. 3.

7. None adequate

However, by combining them, one can develop a more satisfactory response.

the privilege against self-incrimination, but it is not clear that the defendant is entitled to complain on behalf of the accomplice.[8] It could also be claimed that this was a violation of defendant's right to counsel because counsel was hampered in his defense of Douglas by his duties to the accomplice.[9] It could be also said that defendant was denied his right to an impartial jury because the jurors were aware of both the accomplice's inadmissible confession and that it had previously been found sufficient to convict him by another jury.[10]

The Supreme Court, in an opinion by Justice Brennan, reversed on the ground that "petitioner's inability to cross-examine [the accomplice] as to the alleged confession plainly denied him the right of cross-examination secured by the Confrontation Clause."[11] It may be "plain" to Justice Brennan but it is far from obvious.[12] The opinion goes on to explain that since the prosecutor "was not a witness, the inference from his reading that [the accomplice] made the statement could not be tested by cross-examination."[13] True enough. If we can analyze the prosecutor's questions as hearsay, then he is a "witness against" the defendant under Pointer.[14] The difficulty with this is that the jury is usually instructed that the statements of counsel are not "evidence"; if that was done in this case, then there is a confrontation problem only if Bruton applies.[15]

8. Entitled to complain

See U.S. v. White, 1944, 64 S.Ct. 1248, 322 U.S. 694, 88 L.Ed. 1542.

9. Duties to accomplice

Cf. Holloway v. Arkansas, 1978, 98 S.Ct. 1173, 435 U.S. 475, 55 L.Ed.2d 426.

10. Impartial jury

Parker v. Gladden, 1966, 87 S.Ct. 468, 385 U.S. 363, 17 L.Ed.2d 420.

11. "Denied cross-examination"

Id. at 1077, 380 U.S. at 419.

12. Far from obvious

Since the codefendant was also represented by the same lawyer that represented the defendant, it could be argued that the defendant procured the unavailability of the witness and could not, therefore, complain about the absence of cross-examination. Compare Reynolds, § 6350, text at notecall 770.

However, the state apparently did not make this argument. Id. at 1077, 380 U.S. at 420.

13. "Not a witness"

Id. at 1077, 3809 U.S. at 419.

14. "Witness against"

"Although the [prosecutor's] reading of [the accomplice's] alleged statement and [the accomplice's] refusal to answer were not technically testimony, the [prosecutor's] reading may have been the equivalent in the jury's mind of testimony that [the accomplice] in fact made the statement * * *" Id. at 1077, 380 U.S. at 419.

15. Bruton applies

See text at notecall 31, below. But see People v. Murillo, 1987, 236 Cal.Rptr. 362, 191 Cal.App.3d 328 (prosecutor's description in closing argument of demeanor of victim during testimony of

What about the accomplice? The Court tells us that he "could not be cross-examined on a statement imputed to but not admitted by him."[16] One would suppose defense counsel could simply reverse the prosecutor's ploy, asking the accomplice about each incriminating statement: "that was a lie, wasn't it?"[17] The Court simply repeats that "effective confrontation of [the accomplice] was possible only if [he] affirmed the statement as his."[18]

The Court goes on to point out that cross-examination of the police officers who later testified that the accomplice did confess did not satisfy Pointer because they were not the hearsay declarants.[19] As the opinion states, "since their evidence tended to show only that [the accomplice] made the confession, cross-examination of them as to its genuineness could not substitute for cross-examination of [the accomplice] to test the truth of the statement itself."[20] Moreover, by cross-examining the officers about the confession, defense counsel would only strengthen the false inference that it was evidence in the case.[21]

While we can agree with the Court's conclusion, it is not completely satisfying.[22] Cross-examination was designed to deal with evidence that is legitimately before the jury.[23] If one sees this as an abuse by the prosecution of the adversary system, cross-examination is a less than adequate response.[24] Suppose that the

others a violation of Sixth Amendment).

16. "Imputed but not admitted"

Id. at 1077, 380 U.S. at 419.

17. "That was a lie"

However, this raised ethical problems because the jury might suppose the counsel knows the statements are false by virtue of his representation of the accomplice.

18. "Only if affirmed"

Id. at 1077, 380 U.S. at 420.

19. Not declarants

Id. at 1077, 380 U.S. at 419–420.

20. "Test the truth"

Id. at 1077, 380 U.S. at 420.

21. Strengthen inference

The Court makes a similar point about the direct examination of the officers. Id. at 1077, 380 U.S. at 419.

22. Not satisfying

But see Garcia, The Sixth Amendment in Modern American Jurisprudence, 1992, p. 76 (apparently satisfied).

23. Designed to deal

All of the praise heaped on cross-examination by the writers and the courts center on its ability to reveal weaknesses in testimony; none suggests it as a tool to redress prosecutorial misconduct.

24. Less than adequate

Indeed, by cross-examining the witness in Douglas, the defense may end up legitimizing the prosecution's misconduct, particularly if the witness does not persist in his refusal to answer.

bailiff were to tell the jury that the accused had a criminal record "as long as your arm"; is cross-examination of the bailiff a sufficient response?[25] Or suppose that members of the jury have not revealed that they are well-acquainted with a major prosecution witness; is cross-examination likely to address those matters known to the jurors that they may think makes the witness credible?[26] What we wish to suggest is that Douglas is a case on the dividing line between the kind of confrontation question at issue in Pointer——the right of the defendant to test by cross-examination and other means evidence that is legitimately before the jury——and those cases involving the "blank pad rule"——the right of the defendant to be tried on evidence that is part of the record and subject to all the safeguards of the adversary system, not just confrontation and cross examination.[27] As the Court said in one of the leading cases on the "blank pad rule," the "requirement that the jury's verdict 'must be based upon the evidence developed at trial' goes to the fundamental integrity of all that is embraced in the constitutional concept of trial by jury."[28] The Court went on to explain this holistic vision of trial by jury.

> In the constitutional sense, trial by jury in a criminal case necessarily implies at the very least that the "evidence developed" against a defendant shall come from the witness stand in a public courtroom where there is full judicial protection of the defendant's right of confrontation, of cross-examination, and of counsel. [29]

In that case the Court held that cross-examination was not an adequate cure for violations of the "blank pad rule."[30] Douglas, unlike some of the "blank pad" cases, was only a slight departure——the witness was on the witness stand in a public courtroom but the evidence did not come from him directly but through the

---

25. Bailiff

Compare Parker v. Gladden, 1966 87 S.Ct. 468, 385 U.S. 363, 17 L.Ed.2d 420 (treating as a violation and right to impartial jury).

26. Acquainted with witness

Compare Turner v. Louisiana, 1965, 85 S.Ct. 546, 379 U.S. 466, 13 L.Ed.2d 424 (holding cross-examination inadequate).

27. "Blank pad rule"

See vol. 21, § 5102.

28. "Concept of trial by jury"

Turner v. Louisiana, 1965, 85 S.Ct. 546, 549, 379 U.S. 466, 472, 13 L.Ed.2d 424.

29. "From witness stand"

Id. at 550, 379 U.S. at 472–473.

30. Not adequate cure

Id. at 550, 379 U.S. at 473.

prosecutor's ventriloquism in putting his out-of-court statements before the jury as if they had come from the witness.

This reading of Douglas is confirmed by the way the Court dealt with Douglas three years later in Bruton v. U.S.[31] In that case, Bruton and a codefendant were jointly tried for a postal robbery.[32] The codefendant did not testify but the prosecution was allowed to introduce his confession to postal inspectors in which he named Bruton as a participant in the crime.[33] The jury was instructed that the confession was not admissible against Bruton.[34] Both defendants were convicted but the codefendant's conviction was set aside on the ground that his confessions were improperly admitted and on retrial he was acquitted.[35] This does not seem right and the Solicitor General conceded error.[36]

But the Court rejected the confession of error and went on to hold that, because of the substantial risk that the jury, despite instructions to the contrary, looked to the incriminating extrajudicial statements in determining petitioner's guilt, admission of [the co-defendant's] confession in this joint trial violated petitioner's right of cross-examination secured by the Confrontation Clause of the Sixth Amendment.[37]

As in Douglas, the problem seems different from the one the Court addressed in Pointer——the admission of hearsay evidence against the defendant. The Court concedes as much. After a brief description of the holding of Pointer, the majority opinion by Justice Brennan, the author of the Douglas opinion describes Douglas as an application of Pointer "in circumstances analogous to those in the present case."[38] After describing Douglas, the opinion continues:

> The risk of prejudice in petitioner's case was even more serious than in Douglas. * * * Here [the codefendant's] confessions were in fact testified to and were therefore actually in evidence. That

31. Bruton case

1968, 88 S.Ct. 1620, 391 U.S. 123, 20 L.Ed.2d 476.

32. Postal robbery

Id. at 1621, 391 U.S. at 124.

33. Named Bruton

Ibid.

34. Jury Instructed

Id. at 1622 n.2, 391 U.S. at 125 n. 2.

35. Acquitted on retrial

Id. at 1621 n. 1, 391 U.S. at 124 n. 1.

36. Solicitor General conceded

Id. at p. 1622, 391 U.S. at 125.

37. "Violated right of cross"

Id. at 1622, 391 U.S. at 126.

38. "Circumstances analogous"

Id. at 1623, 391 U.S. at 126.

testimony was legitimately evidence against [the co-defendant] and to that extent properly before the jury during its deliberations. Even greater, then, was the likelihood that the jury would believe [the co-defendant] made the statements and that they were true—not just the self-incriminating portions but those implicating petitioner as well. Plainly the introduction of the confession added substantial, perhaps even critical, weight to the Government's case in a form not subject to cross-examination, since [co-defendant] did not take the stand. Petitioner was thus denied his constitutional right of confrontation.[39]

The opinion goes on to explain why a limiting instruction is not adequate to protect the accused from the threatened breach of the "blank pad rule."[40] Since Bruton is considered at other places, it requires no further analysis here.[41]

The point here is that Douglas and Bruton are cases stemming from the "blank pad rule"—a rule not explicitly mentioned in the Sixth Amendment but one that emerges from the adversary system the Amendment is designed to preserve.[42] In Bruton and Douglas the Court fixed on the Confrontation Clause but one could just as well pick out other provisions of the Sixth Amendment that are implicated as well.[43] Since we are concerned with confrontation as a limitation on this the use of hearsay, the "blank pad rule" and the cases developing it will not be discussed here.[44] But it is worth

39. "Did not take the stand"

Id. at 1623, 391 U.S. at 127–128.

40. Instruction not adequate

Id. at 1623–1628, 391 U.S. at 128–136.

41. Bruton considered

See vol. 1A, § 224; vol. 21, § 5064.

42. Emerges from adversary system

See text at notes 28–29, above.

43. Equally implicated

For example, one could claim that the absence of cross-examination denied defendant the assistance of counsel since cross-examining witnesses is one of the functions of counsel.

44. Not discussed here

Douglas has not played a prominent role in subsequent confrontation jurispru-
dence: Vogel v. Percy, C.A. 7th, 1982, 691 F.2d 843 (cross-examination adequate despite witness's claim not to remember statement); Tolbert v. Jago, C.A.6th, 1979, 607 F.2d 753 (similar to Douglas except witness claimed lack of memory of prior statement; no violation, apparently because court thinks defendant threatened witness to produce lack of memory); Rado v. Connecticut, C.A.2d, 1979, 607 F.2d 572 (similar to Douglas but statement not crucial, had indicia of reliability, and witness apparently amenable to cross); U.S. v. Fleming, C.A.7th, 1974, 504 F.2d 1045 (witness refused to answer questions about his guilty plea to charged crime; not harmful to remaining defendants so Douglas not applicable); Cota v. Eyman, C.A.9th, 1972, 453 F.2d 691 (prosecutor related expected testimony in opening statement but witness refused to answer

noting that "the blank pad rule" and other features of the adversary system may be relevant when dealing with hearsay; e.g., when a statement is admitted on the ground that it is not "hearsay" because it is not offered for the truth of the matter asserted.[45]

§ 6363. _____; Barber, Mancusi, and Confrontation Excused

In 1968, the Supreme Court took its first serious look at the question of what circumstances, if any, would excuse the absence of confrontation.[1] Barber. v. Page was an Oklahoma prosecution for armed robbery in which the "principal evidence" against the accused was the reading of the transcript of the preliminary-hearing testimony of an accomplice who was now serving a sentence in a federal prison in Texas some 225 miles away.[2] At the preliminary hearing, defendant's attorney had represented both defendant and the accomplice but had withdrawn as the accomplice's attorney when he decided to testify against defendant.[3] Defendant's attorney did not cross-examine the accomplice, apparently for ethical reasons.[4]

The Supreme Court, in an opinion by Justice Marshall, began with a quotation from Mattox explaining that the purpose of the Confrontation Clause was to "prevent the use of depositions * * * being used against the prisoner" in place of contemporaneous confrontation and cross-examination.[5] However, Mattox also recog-

not the same "flagrant impropriety" as Douglas).

Four Justices of the Supreme Court have opined that Douglas "is no longer good law" in making cross-examination essential. New Mexico v. Earnest, 1986, 106 S.Ct. 2734, 477 U.S. 648, 91 L.Ed.2d 539.

45. Not for truth

Tennessee v. Street, 1985, 105 S.Ct. 2078, 471 U.S. 409, 85 L.Ed.2d 425 (no violation of confrontation); Lee v. McCaughtry, C.A.7th, 1990, 892 F.2d 1318 (no Bruton problem).

§ 6363

1. First serious look

From almost its first opinion, the Supreme Court had assumed that the right of confrontation could be ex-

cused by the unavailability of the witness, but it had seldom devoted much attention to the question. See, e.g., Reynolds, discussed in § 6356, text at notecall 770.

2. Barber case

1968, 88 S.Ct. 1318, 390 U.S. 719, 20 L.Ed.2d 255

3. Testify against defendant

Id. at 1319, 390 U.S. at 720.

4. Ethical reasons

Id. at 1319, 1321 n. 1, 390 U.S. at 720, 722 n. 1.

5. "Prevent depositions"

Id. at 1320, 390 U.S. at 721. Mattox is discussed in § 6351, text at notecall 478.

nized "an exception to the confrontation requirement where a witness is unavailable and has given testimony at a previous judicial proceeding against the same defendant. [and] was subject to cross-examination by that defendant."[6] Justice Marshall cites Wigmore for the policy basis of the "exception":

> This exception has been explained as arising from necessity and justified on the ground that the right of cross-examination initially provides substantial compliance with the purposes behind the confrontation requirement.[7]

Since the Confrontation Clause has no "exceptions" and in order to avoid confusion with other circumstances that have been held to allow the use of unconfronted hearsay, we shall refer to what the Court calls an "exception" to a case in which "confrontation is excused."[8]

In terms of the first of the two requirements for "confrontation excused"——past cross-examination——the Court's opinion assumes that requirement is met if the defendant was given an opportunity to cross-examine but waived it, though doubting that the facts support such a waiver in Barber's case.[9] Turning to the second requirement——unavailability of the witness at trial——Justice Marshall admits that prior state and federal cases have held that mere absence from the jurisdiction suffices.[10] But, the opinion argues, those cases have been undermined if not rendered obsolete by modern developments allowing witnesses to be brought across state lines to testify.[11] Hence, a more stringent standard of "unavailability," is now required: "a witness is not 'unavailable' for purposes of the [Mattox] exception to the confrontation requirement unless the prosecutorial authorities have made a good-faith effort to obtain his presence at trial." Since the Oklahoma prosecutors had done nothing, this standard was not met.[12]

6. "Exception to confrontation"

Id. at 1320, 390 U.S. at 722.

7. "Substantial compliance"

Ibid.

8. "Confrontation excused"

For the origins of this analysis, see Graham, The Right of Confrontation and the Hearsay Rule: Sir Walter Raleigh Loses Another One, 1972, 8 Crim. L.Bull. 99, 107–108.

9. Doubting facts support

Id. at 1320–1321, 390 U.S. at 722. It is here that the opinion suggests the counsel felt constrained by ethics from cross-examining the accomplice, whom he had represented until just before the accomplice took the stand.

10. Mere absence suffices

Id. at 1321, 390 U.S. at 722.

11. Modern developments

Id. at 1321, 390 U.S. at 723–724.

12. "Good-faith effort"

Id. at 1322, 390 U.S. at 724–725.

Being unable to claim that confrontation was "excused," the state then claimed that the defendant had "waived" his right to confront the accomplice by failing to cross-examine him at the preliminary hearing.[13] The Court responds by holding that the waiver of the right of confrontation must meet the standard of Johnson v. Zerbst——"an intentional relinquishment or abandonment of a known right or privilege."[14] This standard was not met because Barber could not have known at the time of the preliminary hearing that the accomplice would be unavailable at trial.[15] Justice Marshall then tacks a mystifying coda on the end of the opinion that has to be quoted in full to be appreciated:

> Moreover, we would reach the same result on the facts of this case had petitioner's counsel actually cross-examined [the accomplice] at the preliminary hearing * * *. The right of confrontation is basically a trial right. It includes both the opportunity to cross-examine and the occasion for the jury to weigh the demeanor of the witness. A preliminary hearing is ordinarily a much less searching exploration into the merits of a case than a trial, simply because its function is the more limited one of determining whether probable cause exists to hold the accused for trial. While there may be some justification for holding that the opportunity for cross-examination of testimony at a preliminary hearing satisfies the demands of the confrontation clause where the witness is shown to be actually unavailable, this is not, as we have pointed out, such a case.[16]

Since the defendant would not have "waived" the right of confrontation if he had cross-examined at the preliminary hearing, the "moreover" at the beginning of the passage makes no sense.[17] If the passage is meant to suggest that past confrontation at a preliminary hearing does not meet the first requirement for "con-

13. Defendant "waived"

The Court, as we read it, distinguishes between the "waiver" of the right at the preliminary examination, which makes past confrontation satisfy the first element of "confrontation excused," see text at notecall 9, above, and the "waiver" for purposes of the trial on the merits, which does away with any need to "excuse" the absence of confrontation.

14. "Known right or privilege"

Id. at 1322, 390 U.S. at 725.

15. Could not have known

Ibid.

16. "Not such a case"

Id. at 1322, 390 U.S. at 725–726

17. Makes no sense

The "moreover" suggests that this is a further reason for rejecting the waiver argument made in the immediately preceding paragraph.

frontation excused," it is inconsistent with the last sentence.[18] To say that this passage is "unclear" is a bit of an understatement.

To complete this chapter of "confrontation excused," we may look four years ahead to Mancusi v. Stubbs.[19] The facts are complicated. The defendant sought habeas corpus from a New York conviction claiming that a Tennessee conviction used to punish him as a second offender was constitutionally invalid for violating his right of confrontation.[20] The Tennessee conviction was for murder and it had been tried twice.[21] At the first trial, the victim's husband testified to his personal knowledge of the killing and was cross-examined.[22] After a federal court set aside the conviction for the inadequacy of counsel, the state opted to retry defendant.[23]

However, by the time of the retrial, the victim's husband had returned to his native Sweden and had taken up permanent residence there.[24] The state made no effort to return him for the retrial and the court of appeals held it had, therefore, not satisfied the Barber standard for the second element of "confrontation excused."[25] The Supreme Court reversed, rejecting the defendant's claim that the state could have availed itself of a federal statute to compel the witness to return.[26] Justice Rehnquist, writing for the majority, stated that "so far as this record shows" the state "was powerless to compel his attendance at the second trial, either through its own process or through established procedures depend-

18. Inconsistent with last

That is, the last sentence says that if the second element of "confrontation excused" is satisfied, then past cross-examination would satisfy the first.

19. Mancusi case

1972, 92 S.Ct. 2308, 408 U.S. 204, 33 L.Ed.2d 293.

20. Tennessee invalid

Id. at 2309, 408 U.S. at 205.

21. Tried twice

Id. at 2310–2311, 408 U.S. at 207–209.

22. Testified to killing

Id. at 2311, 408 U.S. at 208.

23. Opted to retry

Id. at 2311, 408 U.S. at 209. The Court rejected the defendant's claim that the

inadequacy of his counsel made the cross-examination at the first trial inadequate to satisfy the first element of "confrontation excused" by suggesting that since the habeas court used the wrong standard for determining the inadequacy of counsel, its findings were not alone sufficient to demonstrate the inadequacy of cross-examination and defendant had failed to produce sufficient other evidence of inadequacy below. Id at pp. 2313–2314, 408 U.S. at 214–215.

24. Returned to Sweden

Id. at 2311, 408 U.S. at 209.

25. Not satisfied Barber

Id. at 2311, 408 U.S. at 209.

26. Federal statute

Id. at 2311, 408 U.S. at 211–212.

ing on the voluntary assistance of another government."[27] Hence, the showing of "unavailability was sufficiently stronger here than in Barber" to satisfy the requirements of the Sixth Amendment.[28] Implicit in this holding is the rejection of any interpretation of the Barber "good-faith effort" that would require the state to attempt non-compulsory means of making the witness available; e.g., offering to pay his expenses if he would voluntarily return.[29]

After Barber, the Court's analysis of the Confrontation Clause seems to have produced the following structure. First, a hearsay declarant is a "witness against" the defendant—at least if her testimony provides crucial evidence of guilt.[30] Second, confrontation is satisfied only by present cross-examination; that is, the cross-examination and the testimony are contemporaneous with the trial on the merits.[31] Third, past cross-examination will suffice if it was adequate and confrontation is "excused" by the unavailability of the declarant.[32] Fourth, the standards for finding the "unavailability" of the declarant are high; the state must make a "good-faith effort" to use available means to compel the witness to attend.[33] Finally, the standard for "waiver" of the right of confrontation is the stringent Johnson v. Zerbst test.[34]

If the Court were to maintain this mode of analysis, the Confrontation Clause would prove to be a rather severe limitation on the use of hearsay against criminal defendants.[35] One could

27. Powerless to compel

Id. at 2311, 408 U.S. at 212.

28. "Sufficiently stronger"

Id. at 2311, 408 U.S. at 212–213.

29. Pay expenses

Since this is what prosecutors do when they want the witness to testify, it is difficult to see why the same method should not be required under Barber.

30. Structure

Compare, Note, Constitutional Law—Witnesses—The Confrontation Clause of the Sixth Amendment Requires State Authorities to Make a Good-Faith Effort to Produce Out of State Witnesses at Trial, 1969, 47 Tex. L.Rev. 331.

31. "Witness against"

This is the implicit holding of Pointer. See § 6361. In each of the other cases,

the Court's opinion notes that the hearsay supplied an important part of the prosecution's case.

32. Satisfied only by present

This is implicit in other opinions and may be what the Court is saying in the passage quoted above at notecall 15.

33. "Good-faith effort"

This is stated in both Barber and Mancusi.

34. Johnson v. Zerbst test

See text at notecall 14 above.

35. Severe limitations

Note, Preserving the Right to Confrontation—A New Approach to Hearsay Evidence in Criminal Trials, 1965, 113 U.Pa.L.Rev. 741.

square large parts of this analysis with the history of the Confrontation Clause and the intent of the Founders—but not with emerging demands for "law-and-order."[36] As we shall see, for the most part, the latter would prevail over the former. About the only consistent pattern one can discern in the Supreme Court's confrontation jurisprudence for the balance of the century was that in almost every decision the Court was obliged to reverse or retreat from something it had said in a previous opinion. The result was to create a smorgasbord of authority from which state and lower federal courts could pick and choose cases to reach almost any decision they desired.

§ 6364.   ____; Green: Present Cross and Past Statements

Five years after Pointer, the scholars had begun to respond to the Supreme Court's modern confrontation jurisprudence.[1] Professor Larkin demonstrated the inadequacy of the Wigmorean approach, both historically and theoretically.[2] He suggested that the Founders had intended to require confrontation except where it was impossible.[3] He described a "purist" approach in which hearsay would be admissible under the Sixth Amendment only where it would have been admissible in 1789.[4] He saw a trend in some state-court decisions to resurrect the view that the Confrontation Clause was not designed to make criminal prosecutions "convenient" for the state.[5] Other writers showed that confrontation involved more than hearsay; e.g., that it required the appointment of interpreters for non-English-speaking defendants.[6] One author argued that the right of confrontation was the basis of the Jencks decision and, as such, could be used to support a right to discover evidence needed for cross-examination.[7]

36. Intent of Founders

See vol. 30, § 6348.

§ 6364

1. Scholars respond

The responses of student writers are noted in connection with the cases they have addressed.

2. Inadequacy of Wigmore

Larkin, The Right of Confrontation: What Next?, 1969, 1 Tex.Tech.L.Rev. 67.

3. Except where impossible

Id. at p. 80.

4. "Purist" approach

Id. at p. 68.

5. Not make "convenient"

Id. at p. 82.

6. Interpreters

Morris, The Sixth Amendment's Right of Confrontation and the Non–English Speaking Accused, 1967, 41 Fla.B.J. 475.

7. Right to discover

Semerjian, The Right of Confrontation, 1969, 55 A.B.A.J. 152.

In California v. Green, the Supreme Court returned to the question of what was required to satisfy the right of confrontation.[8] To understand the Court's opinion, it will be helpful to distinguish three situations.[9] In the first, the hearsay statement was uttered at some time in the past and was then subjected to confrontation and cross-examination; this "past statement/past cross" can be described as "past confrontation."[10] Second, the statement was made during the present trial and was subject to confrontation and cross-examination; so-called "present confrontation" or "contemporaneous cross-examination."[11] The California Supreme Court had interpreted the Supreme Court's decisions as holding that only "contemporaneous cross-examination" satisfied the requirements of the Sixth Amendment.[12] Finally, we have the situation where the statement was made in the past and not then subject to cross-examination, but the defendant appears at trial and is subject to cross-examination; this "past statement/present cross" situation was at issue in Green.[13]

In Green, a 16–year-old who had been caught selling marijuana, while in custody and under pressure from police officers, named Green as his supplier.[14] At Green's preliminary-hearing, the seller

8. Green case

1970, 90 S.Ct. 1930, 399 U.S. 149, 26 L.Ed.2d, 489.

9. Three situations

There is a fourth; past statement and no cross-examination. This situation was involved in Green but the Court chose not to pass on it. See below, text at notecall 41. No one claims that confrontation is "satisfied" when un-cross-examined hearsay is introduced, though it may be admissible on other grounds. In this context, "cross-examination" means "constitutionally adequate cross-examination."

10. "Past confrontation"

This was the situation in Mancusi, § 6363, above.

11. "Contemporaneous"

Everyone agrees that this satisfies the Confrontation Clause.

12. California interpreted

People v. Johnson, 1968, 68 Cal.Rptr. 599, 68 Cal.2d 646, 441 P.2d 111.

13. "Past statement/present cross"

Apparently the only prior case involving this situation was Bridges v. Wixon, 1945, 65 S.Ct. 1443, 326 U.S. 135, 89 L.Ed. 2103. However, that case was not decided on Sixth Amendment grounds because it was not a criminal prosecution. See § 6360, text at notecall 594.

14. Named Green

Id. at 1931, 399 U.S. at 151. The majority opinion does not describe the circumstances under which the statement was elicited, but Justice Brennan's dissenting opinion does; the seller testified that the police told him they knew that Green was his supplier and that unless the seller implicated Green "they would see that I was put out of circulation for a

once again identified Green as his supplier, though the details of his story differed from the one given to the police, and he was cross-examined by counsel for Green.[15] However, at trial the seller became evasive, claiming an LSD-induced lack of memory.[16] The prosecution was allowed to introduce the seller's preliminary-hearing testimony and his statements to the police as prior inconsistent statements under a provision of the California Evidence Code that made such statements admissible as substantive evidence, not simply to impeach the witness.[17] Since these prior statements were virtually the only evidence against Green, the California Supreme Court reversed, holding that, since the statements had not been subject to contemporaneous cross-examination, they did not satisfy the defendant's right of confrontation.[18]

The majority opinion by Justice White shows that some members of the Supreme Court were concerned about the implications of the Confrontation Clause for reform of the hearsay rule by the then-pending Proposed Federal Rules of Evidence.[19] After summarizing, the traditional views of the use of prior inconsistent statements and the proposals of the reformers, Justice White says that

> the issue before us is * * whether a defendant's right "to be confronted with the witnesses against him is necessarily inconsistent with a State's decision to change its hearsay rules * * *." While it may readily be conceded that the hearsay rules and the Confrontation Clause are generally designed to protect similar values, it is quite a different thing to suggest that the overlap is complete and that the Confrontation Clause is nothing more or less than a codification of the rules of hearsay and their exceptions as they existed historically at common, law.[20]

long time * * *." Id. at 1952 n. 2, 399 U.S. at 190 n. 2.

15. Cross-examined

Id. at 1931, 399 U.S. at 151 ("extensive cross-examination").

16. Claimed lack of memory

Id. at 1931–1932, 399 U.S. at 151–152.

17. Substantive evidence

Id. at 1932, 399 U.S. at 152.

18. Did not satisfy

People v. Green, 1969, 75 Cal.Rptr. 782, 70 Cal.2d 654, 451 P.2d 422.

19. Implications for reform

Id. at 1933, 1940 n. 18, 499 U.S. at 134–135, 168 n. 18. Justice White may have been particularly influenced by Comment, Confrontation and the Hearsay Rule, 1966, 75 Yale L.J. 1434. See id. at 1934 n. 8, 399 U.S. at 156 n. 8.

20. "Confrontation codification"

Id. at 1933–1934, 399 U.S. at 155.

The rejection of the "congruence" between hearsay and confrontation—what we call "fusion"—would become one of the more quoted passages from the Court's opinion.[21]

Justice White, having conceded that some hearsay reforms may raise confrontation problems, then turns to the "lawyer's history" of the Confrontation Clause.[22] He assumes that the Founders were concerned with ancient English grievances, stating

> that the particular vice which gave impetus to the confrontation claim was the practice of trying defendants on "evidence" which consisted solely of ex parte affidavits or depositions secured by the examining magistrates, thus denying the defendant the opportunity to challenge his accuser in a face-to-face encounter in front of the trier of fact.[23]

21. "Congruence" quoted

"Our decisions have never established such a congruence; indeed, we have more than once found a violation of confrontation values even though the statements in issue were admitted under an arguably recognized hearsay exception. * * * The converse is equally true: merely because evidence is admitted in violation of a long-established hearsay rule does not lead to the automatic conclusion that confrontation rights have been denied." Id. at 1934, 399 U.S. at 155–156.

Barker v. Morris, C.A.9th, 1985, 761 F.2d 1396, 1400 (videotaped deposition inadmissible under state law; no violation of confrontation); Payne v. Janasz, C.A.6th, 1983, 711 F.2d 1305, 1314 (evidence tag used to authenticate pistols; hearsay but no confrontation violation); DeBenedictis v. Wainwright, C.A.11th, 1982, 674 F.2d 841 (legally operative conduct); U.S. v. Fielding, C.A.9th, 1980, 630 F.2d 1357, 1366 (admissible under co-conspirators exception; confrontation violated); U.S. v. Blakey, C.A.7th, 1979, 607 F.2d 779, 787 (questionable present sense impression; no violation); Rado v. Connecticut, C.A.2d, 1979, 607 F.2d 572, 578 n. 4 (makes no difference whether admissible under state law); U.S. v. Nick, C.A.9th, 1199, 1202 (even though admissible under

exception, may still violate); U.S. v. Eaglin, C.A.9th, 1977, 571 F.2d 1069, 1079 (inadmissible under co-conspirators exception; no violation); U.S. v. Lynch, C.A.D.C., 1974, 499 F.2d 1011, 1024 (preliminary hearing testimony of witness not shown to be unavailable; no need to determine if violates confrontation); Favre v. Henderson, C.A.5th, 1972, 464 F.2d 359, 363 (fact that statements are inadmissible hearsay does not establish violation); Phillips v. Neil, C.A.6th, 1971, 452 F.2d 337, 345 (admissible under business records exception; violation found).

22. "Lawyer's history"

That is, history found in legal texts. See the Preface to this volume.

23. "Face-to-face encounter"

Id. at 1934, 499 U.S. at 156. The passage continues: "[p]rosecuting attorneys 'would frequently allege matters which the prisoner denied and called upon them to prove. The proof was usually given by reading depositions, confessions of accomplices, letters, and the like; and this occasioned frequent demands by the prisoner to have his 'accusers,' i.e. the witnesses brought before him face to face * * *.'" The internal quotation in this passage is from an English legal

Though an advance over Mattox, Justice White's history is woefully inadequate, particularly in supposing that the right of confrontation was derived from English law.[24]

The White opinion then considers the Court's prior confrontation jurisprudence.

> Our own decisions seem to have recognized at an early date that it is this literal right to "confront" the witness at the time of trial which forms the core of the values furthered by the Confrontation Clause.[25]

After the ritual quotation from Mattox, the White opinion continues:[26]

> Viewed historically, then, there is good reason to conclude that the Confrontation Clause is not violated by admitting a declarant's out-of-court statements, as long as the declarant is testifying as a witness and is subject to full and effective cross-examination.[27]

In other words, "past statement/present cross" satisfies the right of confrontation.[28]

The majority opinion then turns to "the purposes of confrontation."

> Confrontation: (1) insures that the witness will give his statements under oath——thus impressing him with the seriousness of the matter and guarding against the lie by the possibility of a penalty for perjury; (2) forces the witness to submit to cross-examination, the "greatest legal engine ever invented for the

historian whose documentation of these claims is thin. In any event, it provides no proof that the Founders were moved by these practices in adopting the Sixth Amendment.

24. "Woefully inadequate"

For example, Justice White invokes the hoary myth of Sir Walter Raleigh, id. at 1934 n. 10, 399 U.S. at 157 n. 10, but makes no mention of the abuses of the vice-admiralty courts even though——or perhaps, because——they more closely resemble the situation in Green and had already been shown to be a more likely cause of the Confrontation Clause than Raleigh. See Pollitt, The Right of Confrontation: Its History and Modern Dress, 1959, 8 J.Pub.L. 381, 396–398.

25. "Core of values"

Id. at 1934–1935, 399 U.S. at 157.

26. Ritual quotation

Id. at 1935, 399 U.S. at 158.

27. "Full and effective cross"

Id. at 1935, 399 U.S. at 158.

28. "Past/present" satisfies

Note that this statement has broader implications than prior inconsistent statements; it would allow the prosecution to use depositions and affidavits——the very form of evidence Mattox says the Sixth Amendment was aimed at——so long as the prosecution brought in the declarants and tendered them for cross.

discovery of truth' "; (3) permits the jury that is to decide the defendant's fate to observe the demeanor of the witness in making his statement thus aiding the jury in assessing his credibility.[29]

Justice White then argues that only demeanor evidence is affected by "past statement/present cross" and he thinks this is insignificant.[30]

The opinion then addresses the issue posed: "the California Supreme Court's view that belated cross-examination can never serve as a constitutionally adequate substitute for cross-examination contemporaneous with the original statement."[31]

> * * * neither evidence nor reason convinces us that contemporaneous cross-examination before the ultimate trier of fact is so much more effective than subsequent examination that it must be made the touchstone of the Confrontation Clause.[32]

Justice White reviews the Court's prior decisions at length and finds that none of them support the view that contemporaneous cross-examination is required.[33]

The majority's conclusion is emphatic:

> the Confrontation Clause does not require excluding from evidence the prior statements of a witness who concedes making the statement and who may be asked to defend or otherwise explain the inconsistency between his prior and his present versions of the events in question, thus opening himself to full cross-examination at trial as to both stories.[34]

This sounds, as some lower courts have held, that Green validates the hearsay exception for prior inconsistent statements.[35]

Having disposed of the issue of whether confrontation is satisfied by present cross-examination of a past statement, Justice White seeks to bolster that conclusion by opining that the past confrontation of the accomplice would also meet the requirements for "confrontation excused." In explaining why the accomplice's testimony at a preliminary hearing was admissible even if there

---

29. "Aiding the jury"
Id. at 1935, 399 U.S. at 158.

30. Insignificant
Id. at 1936, 399 U.S. at 160.

31. "Adequate substitute"
Id. at 1935, 399 U.S. at 159.

32. "Made touchstone"
Id. at 1936, 399 U.S. at 161.

33. None support
Id. at 1936–1938, 399 U.S. at 161–164.

34. "Both stories"
Id. at 1938, 399 U.S. at 164.

35. Validates prior statements
See, e.g., Vidal v. Sullivan, C.A.2d, 1988, 863 F.2d 2, 4.

had been no effective confrontation at trial, the opinion states that the

> statement at the preliminary hearing had already been given under circumstances closely approximating those that surround the typical trial. [The declarant] was under oath; [Green] was represented by counsel—the same counsel in fact who later represented him at trial; [he] had every opportunity to cross-examine [declarant] as to his statement; and the proceedings were conducted before a judicial tribunal, equipped to provide a judicial record of the hearings.[36]

This seems to be something of a retreat from what was said about preliminary hearings in Barber.[37] Be that as it may, Justice White's rosy view of the preliminary hearing is not borne out by empirical studies.[38]

Having concluded that Green has no cause for complaint because confrontation is both "satisfied" and hypothetically "excused," the majority opinion turns to one last issue.[39] This was the issue of whether the accomplice's claimed lack of memory about his confession to the police impaired the defendant's ability to cross-examine him about that statement.[40] The Court decided to remand that question to the California courts for decision.[41]

As useful, if less authoritative, than the majority opinion is the concurring opinion of Justice Harlan.[42] He was unhappy with the Court's embrace of the Wigmorean equation that "confronta-

36. "Judicial record"

Id. at 1938, 399 U.S. at 165.

37. Said in Barber

In fact, Justice White quotes only the latter portion of Justice Marshall's statement about preliminary hearings in Barber, paraphrasing his critical remarks. Id. at 1939, 399 U.S. at 166. For the full remark, see § 6363, text at notecall 16.

38. Empirical studies

Graham & Letwin, The Preliminary Hearing in Los Angeles: Some Field Findings and Legal–Policy Observations, 1971, 18 U.C.L.A.L.Rev. 635.

39. "Satisfied" and "excused"

Justice White argues that since the seller's testimony at the preliminary hearing could have been admitted against Green had the seller been unavailable, it follows a fortiori that confrontation is "satisfied" where he is available and this prior testimony is used. Id. at 1939–1940, 399 U.S. at 166–168.

40. Impaired ability

Id. at 1940, 399 U.S. at 168.

41. Remanded

Id. at 1941, 399 U.S. at 170.

42. Concurring opinion

If published, the opinion would have been one of the best law-review articles written on the Confrontation Clause up to that time.

tion=cross-examination."[43] However, he endorses the Wigmorean view of history:

> the Confrontation Clause comes to us on faded parchment. History seems to give us very little insight into the intended scope of the Sixth Amendment Confrontation Clause.[44]

However, Harlan is prepared to draw some conclusions from history.

> Such scant evidence as can be culled from the usual sources suggests that the Framers understood "confrontation" to be something less than a right to exclude hearsay, and the common-law significance of the term is so ambiguous as not to warrant the assumption that Framers were announcing a principle whose meaning was so well understood that this Court should be constrained to accept those dicta in the common law that equated confrontation with cross-examination.[45]

The error here is in supposing that the Founders thought they were adopting the English common law and that hearsay was such an important evidentiary concept at the time that the Founders would have thought about it at all.[46]

Justice Harlan then turns, commendably, to the language of the Sixth Amendment.[47] He notes that the Clause can be read either as Wigmore wanted to read it——as a right to confront the witnesses the prosecution chooses to call——or as the Court read it in Pointer——so that every hearsay declarant is a "witness against" the defendant.[48] Harlan comes tantalizingly close to a holistic view:

> the Confrontation Clause was apparently included without debate along with the rest of the Sixth Amendment package of rights—— to notice, counsel, and compulsory process——all incidents of the adversarial proceeding before a jury as evolved during the 17th and 18th centuries.[49]

43. Unhappy with equation

Id. at 1942, 399 U.S. at 172.

44. "Faded parchment"

Id. at 1943, 399 U.S. at 173–174.

45. "Equated confrontation"

Id. at 1943, 399 U.S. at 174–175.

46. Thought about it at all

See vol. 30, § 6346, pp. 647–649. In fairness to Justice Harlan, it should be pointed out that much of the material about the adoption of the Sixth Amendment was not readily available in 1970.

47. Language of Sixth

Id. at 1944, 399 U.S. at 175.

48. Every hearsay declarant

Id. at 1944, 399 U.S. at 174.

49. "Adversarial proceeding"

Id. at 1944, 399 U.S. at 176.

However, he does not mention the hated inquisitorial procedures or refer to the other related provisions in the Bill of Rights so he sees the Sixth Amendment as designed "merely to constitutionalize the right to a defense" rather than as an attempt to preserve an adversary system of criminal justice.[50]

Having surveyed the history he was able to find, Justice Harlan reaches a conclusion that comports with his position on the old incorporation debate.[51]

> From the scant information available it may tentatively be concluded that the Confrontation Clause was meant to constitutionalize a barrier against flagrant abuses, trials by anonymous accusers, and absentee witnesses. That the Clause was intended to ordain common law rules of evidence with constitutional sanction is doubtful, notwithstanding English decisions that equate confrontation and hearsay. Rather, having established a broad principle, it is far more likely that the Framers anticipated it would be supplemented, as a matter of judge-made law, by prevailing rules of evidence.[52]

This is fine as far as it goes but misses the point made earlier in Harlan's opinion.[53] That is, the Founders did not so much enshrine a "principle" as they safeguarded a democratic system of criminal justice.[54]

Justice Harlan then turns to a review of the Supreme Court's early confrontation jurisprudence to support his view that "availability underlies the confrontation right."[55] However, after all of its labor, the Harlan concurrence produces a mouse:

> the early holdings and dicta can, I think, only be harmonized by viewing the confrontation guarantee as being confined to an availability rule, one that requires the production of a witness when he is available to testify.[56]

This conclusion then allows Justice Harlan to refight the incorporation battle under the guise of interpreting the right of confronta-

---

50. "Right to defense"
Id. at 1944, 399 U.S. at 176.

51. Incorporation debate
See § 6361, text at notecall 46.

52. "Prevailing rules"
Id. at 1946, 399 U.S. at 179.

53. Earlier in opinion
See text at notecall 49, above.

54. System of criminal justice
See vol. 30, § 6348, p. 780.

55. "Availability underlies"
Id. at 1946, 399 U.S. at 179.

56. "When available"
Id. at 1948, 399 U.S. at 182.

tion.[57] In the course of this, he makes a number of sensible points that might well be used to construct a somewhat more robust version of the Confrontation Clause than he is prepared to acknowledge.[58]

Had Justice Harlan taken a broader view of history and a more holistic view of the Confrontation Clause, he might have seen some parallels between Green and John Hancock.[59] As in the hated vice-admiralty courts, the case against Green rested almost entirely on statements first elicited from an informer in private, then incorporated in a "deposition" before a magistrate, and finally presented to the ultimate trier of fact, not viva voce, but from the records of the inquisitorial magistrate.[60] In terms of the confrontation values, defendant was convicted on the basis of the statements of an "accuser" who was unwilling to avow and therefore take responsibility for his accusation at trial.[61] The reason that the Court—and many readers as well—might recoil from the analogy is because we view Green's "smuggling" of marijuana as the English viewed Hancock's smuggling of untaxed goods.[62]

What was the "need" to construe the Confrontation Clause to enable the state to punish Green?[63] If, as the police officers told the accomplice, they knew that Green was a dope dealer, eventually they could have gotten sufficient evidence to convict him using the normal methods of narcotics enforcement.[64] Green was not like a murderer who, if not caught this time, will escape punishment forever.[65] However the use of wiretaps, surveillance, undercover

---

57. Refight incorporation

Id. at 1948–1950, 399 U.S. at 184–186.

58. Robust version

Id. at 1950 n. 20, 399 U.S. at 186 n. 20 (would not allow conviction resting solely on unconfronted evidence to stand; arguments, cautionary instructions on dangers of unconfronted evidence); id. at 1951 n. 22, 399 U.S. at 189 n. 22.

59. Green and Hancock

See vol. 30, § 6345, pp. 514–522.

60. Not viva voce

See the dissenting opinion of Justice Brennan, id. at 1951, 1952, 399 U.S. at 189–191.

61. Confrontation values

See vol. 30B.

62. View as English viewed

See § 6358, text at notecall 824.

63. Need to construe

Id. at 1939 n. 16, 399 U.S. at 167 n. 16 ("the only necessity is the State's 'need' to introduce evidence").

64. Eventually enough

Either that or they would have driven him out of business since narcotics sellers cannot endure surveillance.

65. Escape forever

Unlike crimes of violence, punishment for sumptuary crime usually only covers one of a series of continuing violations. The real problem for the police in the enforcement of sumptuary laws is that if enough people want the for-

agents, and informants more willing than the one used against Green is expensive; it is much cheaper to rely on reluctant hearsay declarants.[66] But the Sixth Amendment was not designed to make criminal prosecutions cheap and efficient; it was designed to make them fair.[67] Cheapening criminal justice makes it the weapon of first rather than last resort for politicians looking for a "quick fix" for some current social problems.[68]

But the Court in 1970 was unlikely to see parallels between Green's case and Prohibition.[69] This was a time of rebellious youth culture, "reefer madness," and a President elected and a Court reconstituted to meet demands for "law and order."[70] One assumes that the Justices of the Supreme Court did not even consider the

bidden substance, another seller will appear to meet their needs once this one is removed.

66. Much cheaper

This is true only because ordinary defendants cannot afford to conduct the searching kind of cross-examination that Green presupposes. If every criminal defendant could afford O. J. Simpson's lawyers, the "quick-and-dirty" preliminary hearings that allow the criminal-justice system in Los Angeles to flourish would soon become quite expensive. Id. at p. 1955, 399 U.S. at 136–137 (Brennan, J., dissenting).

67. Not designed to make cheap

This is why in order to accommodate the public demand for a criminal remedy for every social ill, those who operate the system have to resort to overcharging, plea-bargaining, and other methods of avoiding a full adversary trial—methods unknown to the Founders.

68. "Quick fix"

A skimming of the California Penal Code is like walking through a museum of past hysteria; only the historically sophisticated can imagine why some conduct was criminalized. Selling cigarettes to minors or spraying graffiti on public buildings is reprehensible but surely criminal conviction is not the best or only way to show public disapproval. Only now that the prison system is absorbing more of the state budget than higher education are politicians seriously considering other solutions for social problems.

69. And Prohibition

That is, that it did not make much difference whether Green was convicted or not; people who wanted drugs would find them. Moreover, the attempt to make sure that every bootlegger was punished was not only doomed to failure but was likely to lead to evils worse than that supposed to be cured.

70. "Law and order"

Foner, The Story of American Freedom, 1998, p. 304. The year that Green was decided was also the year of the Carswell–Haynsworth failed appointments, massive antiwar demonstrations in Washington and elsewhere, the trials of "The Chicago Seven" (for disrupting the 1968 Democratic convention), and "The Harrisburg Seven" (for supposedly plotting to kidnap Henry Kissinger), the Kent State shootings, and the Scranton Commission on Campus Unrest. Encyclopedia of American

possibility that after polishing up the footnotes on the opinions in Green's case, their clerks would go sneaking off to meet their own suppliers.[71] It is only now, with the virtual decriminalization of marijuana possession and use in most urban areas, that one can put Green's case in perspective.[72] This is not to say that confrontation jurisprudence should be driven by considerations of the substantive law but only that when courts are tempted to trim constitutional rights to meet some supposed threat to public order that they take into account the uncertain capabilities of the criminal sanction, as well as the role of the Court in times of hysteria.[73]

Even taken on their own terms, the Green opinions were less successful than their authors had hoped.[74] After the Court construed the Sixth Amendment to allow the substantive use of prior inconsistent statements, Congress intervened to limit this proposed reform.[75] In less than a year, Justice Harlan repudiated the position he had laboriously constructed in his concurrence.[76] And Chief Justice Burger's call to "let a hundred flowers bloom" produced such a poisoned garden of experimentation in the lower courts that the Supreme Court was eventually required to "ramrod" them back into some conformity with federal standards of confrontation.[77]

Facts and Dates, 9th ed. 1993, pp. 771–675.

71. Own suppliers

We hasten to add we have no personal knowledge of any such event——but, given the widespread use of marijuana among the children of the elite at the time, it is a highly plausible scenario.

72. Perspective

There is no "free lunch" in the criminal justice system; every change has costs. However, one indicium that the Green majority's belief that it was necessary to allow testimony from preliminary hearings to keep the system working may have been erroneous is the fact that, a couple of decades later, the California Constitution was amended at the behest of prosecutors so that witnesses no longer had to be called at preliminary hearings; a finding of probable cause could be made on the basis of hearsay provided by police officers. No one supposes that such hearsay would then be admissible at trial.

73. Times of hysteria

If any judges are still alive from the days in which courts were regularly cutting corners on the Fourth Amendment and the hearsay rule in order to convict bookmakers, one wonders what they think now that, in most parts of the country, the state is the biggest bookie around.

74. Less successful

Note, Constitutional Law——The Confrontation Test for Hearsay Exceptions: An Uncertain Standard, 1971, 59 Calif. L.Rev. 580, 590 (case means that if the declarant is available for cross-examination, need not show unavailability to introduce prior hearsay statements).

75. Limit proposed reform

See F.R.Ev. 801(d)(1)(A).

76. Harlan repudiated

See § 6365, text at notecall 28.

77. "Ramrod"

Id. at 1942, 399 U.S. at 171–172.

Though the lower courts paid lip service to the notion that there was no "congruence" between hearsay and confrontation, their behavior suggested they did not really believe it.[78] Some read the Court as holding that prior inconsistent statements satisfied the right of confrontation.[79] Others took the Court up on its invitation to admit hearsay if the declarant was present and testified.[80] Others followed the branch of Green holding that past confrontation met the requirements of the Sixth Amendment.[81] There were a number of rulings dealing with the kind of evidence Mattox identified as the target of the Confrontation Clause—affidavits and depositions.[82]

However, it is difficult to say what other courts might have made of Green because very quickly the Supreme Court had to throw "that son-of-a-bitch Alex Evans" into the constitutional fray.[83]

78. Did not believe

Ring v. Erickson, C.A. 8th, 1992, 983 F.2d 818 (where statement does not meet requirements of hearsay exception, cannot be "reliable"); U.S. v. Drew, C.A.8th, 1990, 894 F.2d 965, 968 (requirements of hearsay exceptions "are coterminous with the constitutional requirements of the confrontation clause"); Collins v. Francis, C.A.11th, 1984, 728 F.2d 1322, 1336 (despite Green "rare" that satisfaction of hearsay rule does not satisfy confrontation); U.S. v. King, C.A.7th, 1980, 613 F.2d 670 (similar); U.S. v. Carlson, C.A.8th, 1976, 547 F.2d 1346, 1356 ("propensity" of courts to equate two; collects cases); Stewart v. Cowan, C.A.6th, 1976, 528 F.2d 79, 88 (since protect same values, should reach similar results); U.S. v. Puco, C.A.2d, 1973, 476 F.2d 1099, 1102 (similar).

79. Prior statements satisfied

Vidal v. Sullivan, C.A.2d, 1988, 863 F.2d 2.

80. Declarant present

Jones v. Dugger, C.A.11th, 1989, 888 F.2d 1340, 1343; Collins v. Francis, C.A.11th, 1984, 728 F.2d 1322, 1336.

81. Past confrontation

Phillips v. Wyrick, C.A.8th, 1977, 558 F.2d 489, 494–495 (even though no record of testimony at preliminary examination); United States v. Ricketson, C.A.7th, 1974, 498 F.2d 367, 374 (deposition).

82. Affidavits and depositions

U.S. v. Sines, C.A.9th, 1985, 761 F.2d 1434, 1441–1442 (videotaped deposition of witness taken without defendant's presence satisfies Green); U.S. v. Stone, C.A.5th, 1979, 604 F.2d 922, 926 (ex part affidavit violates Green); U.S. v. King, C.A.9th, 1976, 552 F.2d 833, 839 (videotaped deposition satisfies); U.S. v. Singleton, C.A.2d, 1972, 460 F.2d 1148, 1152 (deposition satisfies).

83. "Alex Evans"

See § 6365, below, text at notecall 8.

§ 6365. ___; Dutton v. Evans and Chaos

Dutton v. Evans was originally taken and argued along with California v. Green because it completed the set of potential hearsay-confrontation problems the Court wished to address; i.e., it involved a prior statement that had never been subjected to confrontation, either present or past.[1] However, because the Court was split and shorthanded, the case was put over so that the newly appointed Justice Blackmun could participate.[2] Alas, even with a full complement, the Court was unable to resolve the confrontation question, splitting 4–1–4.[3]

Evans, along with two other men, was charged with the murder of three Georgia police officers.[4] One of the accomplices was given immunity and became the "principal prosecution witness" against Evans.[5] Among the nineteen other witnesses called by the prosecution, the one who raised the confrontation question had been a fellow prisoner with Evans's other accomplice in a federal prison in Atlanta.[6] He testified that after Evans's accomplice returned from his arraignment on the state murder charge, the witness asked him: "How did you make out in court?".[7] According to the witness, the accomplice replied: "[i]f it hadn't been for that dirty son-of-a-bitch Alex Evans, we wouldn't be in this now."[8]

Had the Court not been committed to the notion that every hearsay declarant is a "witness against" the defendant, it might have asked whether Evans's accomplice fit within the language of the Sixth Amendment that defines those the accused is entitled to confront.[9] Instead, the Court, in attempting to follow the path laid

---

§ 6365

1. Argued with Green

California v. Green, 1970, 90 S.Ct. 1930, 1942 n. 2, 399 U.S. 149, 172 n. 2, 26 L.Ed.2d 489.

2. Case put over

Dutton v. Evans, 1970, 91 S.Ct. 210, 213, 400 U.S. 74, 77–78, 27 L.Ed.2d 213.

3. Split 4–1–4

The Chief Justice and Justices White and Blackmun joined an opinion by Justice Stewart. Justices Black, Douglas, and Brennan joined Justice Marshall's dissenting opinion. Justice Harlan concurred in the result only.

4. Murder of police officers

Id. at 213, 400 U.S. at 76.

5. "Principal witness"

Id. at 213, 400 U.S. at 76.

6. Fellow prisoner

Id. at 214, 400 U.s. at 77.

7. "How did you make out?"

Id. at 214, 400 U.S. at 77–78.

8. "Wouldn't be in this"

Ibid.

9. "Witness against"

That is, one would read "witness against" as something like the word

out in its prior decisions went off in four different directions.[10]

In an opinion for four members of the Court, Justice Stewart first reprised Green, pointing out that simply because Georgia had a peculiar version of the coconspirators exception, its use to admit the accomplice's statement did not mean that Evans's right of confrontation was violated.[11] After reviewing the Court's prior decisions, the Stewart opinion finds it

> apparent that the Sixth Amendment's Confrontation Clause and the evidentiary hearsay rule stem from the same roots. But this Court has never equated the two, and we decline to do so now.[12]

Whatever one can see in this principle, it does not do much to decide the case before the Court.[13]

Justice Stewart then distinguishes the Court's prior cases, but given what he just said, the simple route is not open to him.[14] Hence, he has to go the long way around the barn:

> This case does not involve evidence in any sense "crucial" or "devastating," as did all of the cases just discussed. It does not involve the use, or misuse of a confession made in the coercive atmosphere of official interrogation, as did Douglas [and] Bruton * * *. It does not involve any suggestion of prosecutorial misconduct or even negligence, as did Pointer, Douglas, and Barber. It

---

"accusers" that was used in the state confrontation clauses that were the model for the Sixth Amendment. See vol. 30, § 6347, pp. 760–764. The hearsay statement in Dutton is some ways removed from an "accusation" and it is doubtful that either Evans or his accomplice thought the latter had made himself a "witness against" Evans with the stray remark.

10. Four different

In Marks v. U.S., 1977, 97 S.Ct. 990, 993, 430 U.S. 188, 193, 51 L.Ed.2d 260, Justice Powell wrote for the majority that when "a fragmented Court decides a case and no single rationale explaining the result enjoys the assent of five Justices, 'the holding may be viewed as that position taken by those Members who concurred in the judgments * * *.' " By that rule, the Blackmun–Burger "harmless error" opinion

would be the holding. But as we shall see, that is not what happened.

11. Peculiar hearsay

Id. at 215–217, 400 U.S. at 29–81. Under the Georgia rule, a statement could qualify for the exception even though the conspiracy had been frustrated by the arrest of the conspirators and even thought it was not "in furtherance" of the conspiracy. Compare Evidence Rule 801(d)(2)(E).

12. "Equated the two"

Id. at 218, 400 U.S. at 86.

13. Does not do much

In any event, the Court would eventually do just what Stewart says it has never done. See § 6367, below.

14. Simple route

That is, that none of the prior cases involves totally unconfronted hearsay.

does not involve the use by the prosecution of a paper transcript, as did Pointer * * * and Barber. It does not involve a joint trial, as did Bruton * * *. And it certainly does not involve the wholesale denial of cross-examination * * *.[15]

Amazingly, some lower courts later attempted to use this negative definition as a test for the admissibility of evidence under Dutton.[16]

Turning then to what was involved in the case, the Stewart opinion says:

Evans was not deprived of any right of confrontation on the issue of whether [the accomplice] actually made the statement related by [the witness]. Neither a hearsay nor a confrontation question would have arisen had [the] testimony been used to prove merely that the statement had been made.[17]

This is correct neither with respect to hearsay nor confrontation, but since the Court is right about this case, we can pass over the dicta about the hypothetical case.[18]

Turning to the statement attributed to the accomplice, Justice Stewart continues:

the jury was being invited to infer that [the declarant] had implicitly identified Evans as the perpetrator of the murder when he blamed Evans for his predicament. But we conclude there was no denial of the right to confrontation as to this question of identity. First, the statement contained no express assertion about past fact, and consequently it carried on its face a warning to the jury against giving the statement undue weight. Second, [the

---

15. "Wholesale denial"

Id. at 219, 400 U.S. at 87.

16. Use as test

U.S. v. Huber, C.A.9th, 1985, 772 F.2d 585, 588 (means unconfronted hearsay admissibility if not "crucial" or "devastating"); U.S. v. Fielding, C.A.9th, 1980, 630 F.2d 1357, 1368 ("crucial" or "devastating" statements violate confrontation); Stewart v. Cowan, C.A.6th, 1976, 528 F.2d 79, 85 (Barber only applies if evidence was "crucial" or "devastating"). But see, U.S. v. West, C.A.4th, 1978, 574 F.2d 1131, 1138 (rule of Dutton not limited to evidence "crucial" or "devastating").

17. "Statement had been made"

Id. at 219, 400 U.S. at 88.

18. Hypothetical case

The opinion is wrong, or at least incomplete, because in order to be admissible merely to show that the statement was made, there must be some showing that the mere making of the statement is relevant, without regard to its truth or falsity. If it is relevant, the court must then balance its probative worth for the nonhearsay purpose against the danger that the jury will use it for the truth of the matter. As this Rule 403 balancing suggests, if there is a danger that the instruction cannot limit the evidence to the nonhearsay purpose, then we have a Bruton problem. See § 6362.

declarant's] personal knowledge of the identity and role of the other participants in the triple murder is abundantly established by [the immunized accomplice's] testimony and by [the declarant's] prior conviction. * * * Third, the possibility that [declarant's] statement was founded on faulty recollection is remote in the extreme. Fourth, the circumstances under which [declarant] made the statement were such as to give reason to suppose [he] did not misrepresent Evans' involvement in the crime. These circumstances go beyond a showing that [the declarant] had no apparent reason to lie to [the witness]. His statement was spontaneous and it was against his penal interest to make it. These are indicia of reliability which have been widely determinative of whether a statement may be placed before the jury though there is no confrontation of the declarant.[19]

Lower courts attempted to construct a confrontation "test" out of this analysis.[20]

The Stewart opinion then makes a subtle, but crucial, shift in the direction of confrontation jurisprudence; he writes:

[t]he decisions of this Court make it clear that the mission of the Confrontation Clause is to advance a practical concern for the

---

19. "Indicia of reliability"

Id. at 219–220, 400 U.S. at 88–89.

20. Construct "test"

Williams v. Melton, C.A.11th, 1984, 733 F.2d 1492, 1496, 1497–1498 (four Dutton factors provide indicia of reliability that is an alternate test to one laid down in Roberts); U.S. v. Ordonez, C.A.9th, 1983, 722 F.2d 530, 535 (failure to satisfy Dutton indicia; business records, violate); U.S. v. Foster, C.A.9th, 1983, 711 F.2d 871, 881 (need not satisfy all four Dutton criteria to make coconspirator hearsay admissible); Mattes v. Gagnon, C.A.7th, 1983, 700 F.2d 1096, 1103 (applying Dutton to bar former testimony of unavailable witness); U.S. v. Vadino, C.A.11th, 680 F.2d 1329, 1334 (perfunctory application to coconspirator hearsay); Davis v. Franzen, C.A.7th, 1982, 671 F.2d 1056, 1058 (paraphrasing Dutton to approve coconspirator hearsay); U.S. v. Brown, C.A.6th, 1982, 667 F.2d 566 (sloppy application of Dutton to avoid Bruton problem); U.S. v. Perez,

C.A.9th, 1981, 658 F.2d 654, 661 (applying Dutton rather than Roberts to coconspirator hearsay; rigorous application of criteria); U.S. ex rel Haywood v. Wolff, C.A.7th, 1981, 658 F.2d 455, 463 (applying Dutton rather than Roberts to testimony from preliminary hearing); U.S. v. King, C.A.7th, 1980, 613 F.2d 670, 674 (applying four criteria to business records); U.S. v. Carlson, C.A.8th, 1976, 547 F.2d 1346, 1357 (Dutton test applies to all unconfronted hearsay; approving use of grand jury testimony); U.S. v. Kelley, C.A.8th, 1975, 526 F.2d 615, 621 (Dutton applies to all recognized hearsay exceptions); U.S. v. Snow, C.A.9th, 1975, 521 F.2d 730, 734–735 (careful application of Dutton factors to coconspirator hearsay); U.S. v. Menichino, C.A.5th, 1974, 497 F.2d 935, 943 (need not apply factors where statements neither "crucial" nor "devastating"); U.S. v. Burke, C.A.5th, 495 F.2d 1226, 1233 (similar); U.S. v. Puco, C.A.2d, 1973, 476 F.2d 1099, 1103 (finds Dutton puzzling but applies carefully to coconspirator statements).

accuracy of the truth determining process in criminal trials by assuring that "the trier of fact [has] a satisfactory basis for evaluating the truth of the prior statement."[21]

If we look carefully we can see here the beginning of the trend in which confrontation ceases to be a right of the defendant to a fair procedure——what we have called "the morality of means"——and becomes the interest of the state in the reliability of outcomes in criminal trials——the morality of ends.[22] If the concern is "reliability" of the evidence rather than defendant's right to an adversarial procedure, then we could do as well with inquisitorial procedures so long as they are more "reliable" than the one the Founders placed in the Sixth Amendment.[23] In case anyone is in any doubt that Justice Stewart is more concerned with the legitimacy of courts than he is with the autonomy of criminal defendants, he ends his opinion by quoting Justice Cardozo's peroration in the Snyder case.[24]

Chief Justice Burger and Justice Blackmun, while joining in Justice Stewart's opinion, also joined in a concurring opinion that justifies the result on grounds of harmless error.[25]

Justice Harlan, in a remarkable opinion, concurs only in the result.[26] He thinks the four dissenters have refuted arguments of both the Stewart and Blackmun opinions, but he refuses to join the dissent because it maintains the Pointer position that unconfronted hearsay does not satisfy the Confrontation Clause.[27] In a remarka-

---

21. "Satisfactory basis"

Id. at 220, 400 U.S. at 89.

22. "Morality of ends"

This is not to say that the defendant does not have an interest in the reliability of factfinding. But his view of what that might entail is not the same as that of the state. The Confrontation Clause was not designed to guarantee either the defendant or the state their versions of a "reliable" outcome but to insure that the defendant would have the means to place his version before the jury and the public.

23. Do with inquisitorial

To understand the shift that Stewart is making, we can compare it to the argument that the defendant has no right to a jury trial in cases in which the Supreme Court thinks that a

judge trial would produce a more reliable verdict.

24. Quoting Cardozo

"There is danger that the criminal law will be brought into contempt * * * if gossamer possibilities of prejudice to a defendant are to nullify a sentence * * * and set the guilty free." Id. at 220, 400 U.S. at 89–90. For discussion of the Snyder opinion, see § 6359, text at notecall 998, above.

25. Harmless error

Id. at 220–222, 400 U.S. at 90–93.

26. Concurs in result

Id. at 222, 400 U.S. at 93.

27. Refuses to join

Id. at 222, 400 U.S. at 94–94.

ble about-face, he abandons the position he took in Green a few months earlier and now adopts the position of Wigmore; that is, the Confrontation Clause only gives the defendant the right to be present and to cross-examine those witnesses the prosecution chooses to produce within the limits established by the state hearsay rules.[28] He adopts the position he said in Green made the right of confrontation "meaningless" because he sees the Confrontation Clause as "a threat to much of the existing law of evidence and to future developments in that field."[29] He now thinks that "the historical understanding of the clause furnishes no solid guide to adjudication."[30] His shift requires him to realign the cases he had lined up to support his position in Green——a task he handles with his usual skill.[31]

The opinion of Mr. Justice Marshall for the four dissenters hues to the Pointer–Douglas line of cases, reading them to make unconfronted hearsay inadmissible.[32] Since much of the opinion is taken up with refutation of the Stewart and Blackmun opinions, it breaks no new ground, though it does suggest that the threat of the Pointer view to the existing rules of evidence is overstated, using language that might be read as sensing the possibilities of manipulating the meaning of "witness against" to salvage some of the existing rules.[33]

28. Adopts Wigmore

Id. at 222–223, 400 U.S. at 94–96.

29. "Future developments"

Id. at 222, 400 U.S. at 94.

In Green, Justice Harlan wrote: "Wigmore's reading would have the practical consequence of rendering meaningless what was assuredly in some sense meant to be an enduring guarantee. It is inconceivable that if the Framers intended to constitutionalize a rule of hearsay they would have licensed the judiciary to read it out of existence by creating new and unlimited exceptions." California v. Green, 1970, 90 S.Ct. 1930, 1946, 399 U.S. 149, 179, 26 L.Ed.2d 489.

30. "No solid guide"

Id. at 223, 400 U.S. at 95.

31. Realign cases

Id. at 223–224, 400 U.S. at 97–99.

32. Inadmissible

"The teaching of this line if cases seems clear: Absent the opportunity for cross-examination, testimony about the incriminating and implicating statement allegedly made by [the accomplice] was constitutionally inadmissible in the trial of Evans." Id. at 226–227, 400 U.S. at 103.

33. "Witness against"

"Constitutionalization of 'all common-law hearsay rules and their exceptions * * *' would seem to be a prospect more frightening than real. Much of the complexity afflicting hearsay rules comes from the definition of hearsay as an out-of-court statement presented for the truth of the matter stated——a definition nowhere adopted by this Court for confrontation purposes. Rather, the decisions, while looking to the availability of a declarant * * *, recognize that 'cross-examination is

Very few courts were willing to see that the Stewart opinion was not binding authority.[34] Amazingly, Dutton became and remains one of the most frequently cited Supreme Court opinions and lower courts continued to rely upon it even after the Supreme Court announced a global theory of confrontation that seemingly rendered Dutton obsolete.[35] Dutton was often cited for the proposition that the coconspirators exception to the hearsay rule satisfies the requirements of confrontation.[36] It was also used, along with Green, as the authority for the lack of congruence between confrontation and the hearsay rule.[37] The lower courts quickly grasped the

included in the right of an accused in a criminal case to confront the witnesses against him' * * * and that admission in the absence of cross-examination of certain types of suspect and highly damaging statements is one of the 'threats to a fair trial' against which 'the Confrontation Clause was directed' * * *." Id. at 228 n. 7, 400 U.S. at 165 n. 7. In other words only those who make "suspect and highly damaging statements" are "witnesses against" the defendants.

34. Not binding

For a rare example, see Horton v. Zant, C.A.11th, 1991, 941 F.2d 1449, 1464 n. 32 (invalidating use of Georgia coconspirator exception supposed to have been approved in Dutton).

35. Continued to rely

U.S. v. Huber, C.A.9th, 1985, 772 F.2d 585, 588 (Dutton dispenses with the unavailability requirement of Ohio v. Roberts); U.S. v. Barlow, C.A.6th, 1982, 693 F.2d 954, 964 (allows use of unconfronted grand-jury testimony); U.S. v. Washington, C.A.5th, 1982, 688 F.2d 953, 959 (allows use of business records without showing of unavailability of declarant); Flewallen v. Faulkner, C.A.7th, 1982, 677 F.2d 610, 613 (where court thinks cross-examination would be useless, can admit hearsay statements of available declarants).

36. Coconspirator does not violate

U.S. v. Shepherd, C.A.10th, 1984, 739 F.2d 510, 514 (if not "devastating"); U.S. v. Brown, C.A.6th, 1982, 667 F.2d 566, 568; U.S. v. Cella, C.A.9th, 1977, 568 F.2d 1266, 1287; Grieco v. Meachum, C.A.1st, 1976, 533 F.2d 713, 716; Park v. Huff, C.A. 5th, 1975, 506 F.2d 849, 857; U.S. v. De Lazo, C.A.3d, 1974, 497 F.2d 1168, 1170 n. 4; U.S. v. D'Amato, C.A.2d, 1974, 493 F.2d 359, 365; U.S. v. Puco, C.A.2d, 1973, 476 F.2d 1099, 1105 n. 11; Ottomano v. U.S., C.A.1st, 1972, 468 F.2d 269, 273; U.S. v. Clayton, C.A.1st, 1971, 450 F.2d 16, 20.

Student writers have taken the same view: Note, Preliminary Hearing and The Right to Confrontation: Disheroon v. State, 1975, 10 Tulsa L.J. 663, 664; Note, Constitutional Law—The Right of Confrontation—Georgia's Co–Conspirator Exception to the Hearsay Rule Upheld, 1971, 22 Mercer L.Rev. 791; Note, Criminal Procedure—State Hearsay Exception For Co-conspirator's Statement Held Not to Violate Sixth Amendment Confrontation Clause, 1971, 40 N.C.L.Rev. 788.

Contra: Horton v. Zant, C.A.11th, 1991, 941 F.2d 1449, 1464; U.S. v. Snow, C.A.9th, 1975, 521 F.2d 730, 734 n. 2.

37. Lack of congruence

U.S. v. Doerr, C.A.7th, 1989, 886 F.2d 944, 957; U.S. v. Guinan, C.A.7th,

way the Stewart opinion had shifted the basis of confrontation from cross-examination to reliability.[38] Some courts thought this meant the Supreme Court had adopted the Wigmorean theory of confrontation spelled out in Harlan's opinion.[39] However, most courts read Dutton as admitting all hearsay so long as it had "indicia of reliability."[40] However, there were varying opinions on exactly what this meant.[41]

Dutton attracted a good deal of attention from student writers.[42] Some thought the decision was inconsistent with Barber and that it undermined Douglas.[43] It was suggested that the Stewart

1988, 836 F.2d 350, 358; U.S. v. Boulahanis, C.A.7th, 1982, 677 F.2d 586, 589; Davis v. Franzen, C.A.7th, 1982, 671 F.2d 1056, 1058; Phillips v. Neil, C.A.6th, 1971, 452 F.2d 337, 345; U.S. v. Cerone, C.A.7th, 1971, 452 F.2d 274, 283.

38. Shift to reliability

U.S. v. Nick, C.A.9th, 1979, 604 F.2d 1199, 1203; U.S. v. King, C.A.9th, 1976, 552 F.2d 833, 839.

39. Adopts Wigmorean

U.S. v. Boulahanis, C.A.7th, 1982, 677 F.2d 586, 589; Davis v. Franzen, C.A.7th, 1982, 671 F.2d 1056, 1058; U.S. v. Green, C.A.8th, 1979, 600 F.2d 154, 158.

40. "Indicia of reliability"

U.S. v. Fielding, C.A.9th, 1980, 630 F.2d 1357, 1368 (declaration of co-conspirator lacks); Lacoste v. Blackburn, C.A.5th, 1979, 592 F.2d 1321, 1325 (need not apply where not "crucial or devastating"); U.S. v. West, C.A.4th, 1978, 574 F.2d 1131, 1136 (grand jury testimony has); U.S. v. Eaglin, C.A.9th, 1977, 571 F.2d 1069, 1080 (statement in custodial interrogation has); U.S. v. Carlson, C.A.8th, 1976, 547 F.2d 1346, 1357 (grand-jury testimony, assumes does not); Stewart v. Cowan, C.A. 6th, 1976, 528 F.2d 79, 88 (statements of anonymous informants lack); U.S. v. Kelley, C.A.8th, 1975, 526 F.2d 615, 620 (coconspirator statement has); McLaughlin v. Vin-

zant, C.A.1st, 1975, 522 F.2d 448, 450 (excited utterance has); U.S. v. Puco, C.A.2d, 1973, 476 F.2d 1099, 1104 (co-conspirator statement has).

41. Varying opinions

Adamson v. Ricketts, C.A.9th, 1985, 758 F.2d 441, 446 (declarant without personal knowledge; lacks); Williams v. Melton, C.A.11th, 1984, 733 F.2d 1492, 1496 (other evidence that defendant is guilty satisfies); U.S. v. Bienvenue, C.A.1st, 1980, 632 F.2d 910, 914 (declining to decide whether availability of declarant to testify means statement lacks indicia); U.S. v. Blakey, C.A.7th, 1979, 607 F.2d 779, 786 (tape recording of contemporaneous statement and circumstantial evidence of truth satisfies); U.S. v. Eaglin, C.A.9th, 1977, 571 F.2d 1069, 1081 (satisfies four factors used by Dutton Court).

42. Student writers

Generally scholars seem to have regarded Dutton as a "sport," affording it far less prominence than it has in student writings. See § 6366, text at notecall 42.

43. Inconsistent and undermined

Note, Constitutional Law—The Confrontation Test for Hearsay Exceptions: An Uncertain Standard, 1971, 59 Calif.L.Rev. 580, 590; Note, Constitutional Law—The Right to Confron-

opinion's use of the "crucial or devastating" criterion actually made it a disguised holding of harmless error akin to the Burger–Blackmun concurrence.[44] The Court was criticized for not differentiating between "witnesses" and hearsay "declarants."[45] One writer wondered if the Court meant to say that if the out-of-court statement was "reliable," then the defendant could be barred from calling and cross-examining the declarant.[46] Others endorsed the switch from cross-examination to reliability, but pointed out the irony of the Court's rationale since the co-conspirators exception is not based upon reliability but upon an agency theory.[47]

Other student authors were critical of the Court's reliance on the Wigmorean theory, seeing this as an abandonment by the Court of any efforts to use confrontation as a limit on the use of hearsay.[48] One writer saw the change as emblematic of the desire of the Nixon–Thurmond judges to play to the "law-and-order" constituency, claiming this made the Burger Court every bit as political as the Warren Court.[49] It was also thought that Dutton superseded the Supreme Court's prior cases, creating a presumption of constitutionality for hearsay admitted pursuant to an exception.[50]

The later student articles looked at the way state and federal courts had applied Dutton, generally agreeing that the lower courts were confused about just what the Supreme Court had intended.[51]

tation—Admissibility of Hearsay, 1971, 22 Case West.Res.L.Rev. 575, 579.

44. Disguised harmless error

Second Circuit Review, 1972–73 Term, 1974, Brooklyn L.Rev. 825, 1233.

45. "Witnesses" and "declarants"

Note, Constitutional Law—The Right of Confrontation—Admissibility of Hearsay, 1971, 22 Case West.Res. L.Rev. 575, 576.

46. Defendant barred

Id. at 577.

47. Reliability

Second Circuit Review, 1972–1973 Term, 1974, 40 Brooklyn L.Rev. 825, 1235, 1236. But see, Note, A Perspective on The Decisional Demise of The Right of Confrontation, 1973, 7 Suff. U.L.Rev. 443 (attacking use of harmless-error doctrine on ground it as-

sumes that reliability is the core of confrontation).

48. Abandonment

Id. at 579; Note, Hearsay and The Confrontation Guaranty, 1978, 38 La. L.Rev. 858, 862.

49. Burger Court political

Note, The Burger Court and The Confrontation Clause: A Return to The Fair Trial Rule, 1973, 7 John Marsh. J.Prac. & Proc. 136, 167.

50. Presumption

Note, Interplay of The Confrontation Clause and The Hearsay Rule, 1975, 29 Ark.L.Rev. 375, 377, 381, 382.

51. Courts confused

Id. at 378; Note, Evidence—Constitutional Law—Criminal Procedure— Defendant's Right of Confrontation is

In one state the courts were reported to be relying on Dutton to routinely admit evidence of testimony given at preliminary hearings.[52] On the other hand, one state court was applying Dutton to evidence used at sentencing and another thought business records were inadmissible without a showing that the maker was unavailable as a witness.[53] Both state and federal courts were criticized for holding that the Sixth Amendment did not bar the use of unconfronted testimony before a grand jury.[54] Perhaps the most extreme was the state holding said to reason that since cross-examination was no longer the key, it was possible to dispense with the physical presence of the defendant and allow witnesses to testify by the closed-circuit television—an issue the Supreme Court would address later in the century.[55]

§ 6366. ____; Chambers and The Holistic Sixth

Despite the criticisms of its handling of the relationship between the right of confrontation and the hearsay rule, the Supreme Court did not return to the issue for ten years after Dutton.[1] However, there were two cases during the dormant decade with implications for the Court's confrontation jurisprudence.

Not Denied by Admission of Out-of-Court Declarations of His Co–Conspirator, 1975, 44 U.Cinci.L.Rev. 622, 624, 628; Note, Criminal Procedure: The Confrontation Clause, Short Circuited, 1976, 44 U.M.K.C.L.Rev. 517.

52. Routinely admit

Note, Preliminary Hearing and The Right to Confrontation: Disheroon v. State, 1975, 10 Tulsa L.J. 663, 666.

53. Sentencing, business records

Note, Confrontation Clause—The State is Constitutionally Prohibited From Admitting Documentary Hearsay Into Evidence at Punishment Phase Proceedings Unless The Evidence Bears Substantial Indicia of Reliability, 1979, 7 Am.J.Crim.L. 413; Note, Hearsay and The Confrontation Guaranty, 1978, 38 La.L.Rev. 858.

54. Grand jury

Note, Constitutional Law—Confrontation Clause—Admission At Trial of

Slain Informant's Prior Grand Jury Testimony Against Defendants Does Not Violate Confrontation Clause Despite Lack of Cross–Examination, 1978, 31 Vand.L.Rev. 682; Note, United States v. Carlson: Eighth Circuit Implies Waiver of Accused's Express Confrontation Right, 1977, 22 So. Dak.L.Rev. 447.

55. Closed-circuit television

Note, Criminal Procedure: The Confrontation Clause, Short Circuited, 1976, 44 U.M.K.C.L.Rev. 517.

§ 6366

1. Criticisms

See, e.g., Note, Constitutional Law—Confrontation Clause—Admission at Trial of Slain Informant's Prior Grand Jury Testimony Against Defendants Does Not Violate Confrontation Clause Despite Lack of Cross–Examination, 1978, 31 Vand.L.Rev. 682, 692 (Court's decisions have rendered Confrontation Clause meaningless).

The first of these, Mancusi v. Stubbs, we have previously analyzed in our discussion of the standard for "unavailability" needed to excuse the absence of confrontation.[2] However, as Justice Rehnquist explained in Mancusi, "confrontation excused" requires more than a showing of the declarant's unavailability.[3] He wrote: "Before it can be said that [the defendant's] constitutional right to confront witnesses was not infringed, however, the adequacy of [declarant's] examination at the first trial must be taken into consideration."[4] Now that we have examined Dutton, we are prepared to consider that question.[5]

Citing both Green and Dutton, Justice Rehnquist continued:

> The focus of the Court's concern has been to insure that there "are indicia of reliability which have been widely viewed as determinative of whether a statement may be placed before the jury though there is no confrontation of the declarant" * * * and to "afford the trier of fact a satisfactory basis for evaluating the truth of the prior statement."[6]

This sounds as if the Court wishes to ground the new "reliability" focus in the Court's prior opinions making cross-examination the core of the right of confrontation.[7] This seems clear when the next line says:

> It is clear from these statements, and from numerous prior decisions of this Court, that even though the witness be unavailable his prior testimony must bear some of these "indicia of reliability" referred to in Dutton.[8]

2. Previously discussed

See § 6363, above, text at notecall 19.

3. Requires more

The Court in Barber did not have to deal with this problem because it had already found that the declarant was not unavailable so that having failed on the first element of "confrontation excused" it was not necessary to decide whether testimony at the preliminary hearing met the second—though the Court did express an opinion on this.

4. "Taken into consideration"

Mancusi v. Stubbs, 1972, 92 S.Ct. 2308, 2313, 408 U.S. 204, 213, 33 L.Ed.2d 293.

5. Examined Dutton

See § 6365, above.

6. "Satisfactory basis"

Id. at 2313, 408 U.S. at 213.

7. Cross-examination core

See §§ 6361–6363, above.

8. "Referred to in Dutton"

Ibid.

This rewrites history; what the Court's prior decisions have held is that "confrontation excused" requires past cross-examination, not a judicial determination that his testimony on direct was "reliable."[9]

Turning to the "indicia or reliability," the Rehnquist opinion states:

> The 1953 Tennessee proceeding [in which the absent declarant made the statements at issue] was a trial of a serious felony on the merits, conducted in a court of record before a jury rather than before a magistrate. [Defendant] was represented by counsel who could and did effectively cross-examine witnesses.[10]

In other words, the reason past confrontation suffices for "confrontation excused" is that it provides an indicium of reliability.[11] This opens the door to the possibility that confrontation can be excused, despite the absence of past confrontation, if the hearsay of an unavailable declarant can be shown to have other indicia of reliability.[12]

The defendant argued that the past confrontation was inadequate because his conviction at that trial had been set aside on habeas corpus for ineffective assistance of counsel, but the Court rejects that claim.[13] The opinion concludes:

> Since there was adequate opportunity to cross-examine [declarant] at the first trial and counsel for [defendant] availed himself of that opportunity, the transcript of [declarant's] testimony in the first trial bore sufficient "indicia of reliability" and afforded "the trier of fact a satisfactory basis for evaluating the truth of the prior statement." * * * [The declarant] * * * could have been and was found by the trial court to be unavailable at the time of the second

9. Not "reliable"

The opinion smudges this by describing Mattox, the leading case on "confrontation excused" as holding past confrontation adequate "in appropriate cases." Ibid.

10. "Effectively cross-examine"

Id. at 2313, 408 U.S. at 213–214.

11. Provides indicium

Does this mean that the defendant can defeat the invocation of "confrontation excused" by showing that, despite the opportunity for cross-examination, the prior testimony was "unreliable"? Or does past confrontation create a conclusive presumption of "reliability"? If the latter is so, then it suggests that cross-examination is, for some purposes, still the core of confrontation.

12. Other indicia

For example, in the case of a business record by a dead declarant.

13. Court rejects

Id. at 2323–2314, 408 U.S. at 214–216.

trial.[14]

Hence, confrontation was "excused" and defendant's rights under the Sixth Amendment were not violated.[15]

The Court's second Confrontation Clause case during the dormant decade—Chambers v. Mississippi—involved a murder prosecution with a complicated procedural history.[16] A police officer was shot while attempting to make an arrest in the face of a hostile crowd. Thinking that Chambers was the killer, officers shot him and left him for dead while they took their fallen comrade to the hospital. No attempt was made to search the defendant for evidence of guilt or to secure the crime scene.[17]

When it was discovered that defendant was alive, he was arrested and charged with the officer's murder. In preparing for trial, defendant's lawyer obtained a written confession to the killing of the officer from another member of the crowd. However, at his preliminary hearing, the confessor repudiated the confession, testified to his own innocence, and was discharged.[18]

At his trial, defendant produced substantial evidence of his own innocence.[19] He also called the confessor to the stand, after introducing other evidence of his guilt, and laid the foundation for the admission of his written confession.[20] However, on cross-examination, the confessor once again repudiated the confession and claimed innocence. When the defendant asked that the confessor be declared a hostile witness so that he could be cross-examined by the defense without violating the state's "voucher rule," the trial court refused.[21] The trial court also sustained the state's hearsay objections to testimony that the confessor had made three other incriminating admissions.[22]

---

14. "Found to be unavailable"
Id. 2314–2315, 408 U.S. at 216.

15. Not violated
Id. at 2315, 4087 U.S. at 216.

16. Chambers case
1973, 93 S.Ct. 1038, 410 U.S. 284, 35 L.Ed.2d 297.

17. Secure crime scene
Id. at 1041, 410 U.S. at 285–286.

18. Repudiated and discharged
Id. at 1042, 410 U.S. at 287–288.

19. Evidence of innocence
Id. at 1042, 410 U.S. at 288–289.

20. Laid foundation for admission
Id. at 1043–1044, 410 U.S. at 291.

21. Court refused
Id. at 1044, 410 U.S. at 291–292.

22. Three other admissions
Id. at 1044–1045, 410 U.S. at 292–293.

As Justice Powell summed it up,

> [t]his was Chambers' predicament. As a consequence of the combination of Mississippi's "party witness" or "voucher rule" and its hearsay rule, he was unable to cross-examine [the confessor] or present witnesses in his own behalf who would have discredited [the confessor's] repudiation and demonstrated his complicity. * * * Chambers' defense was far less persuasive than it might have been had he been given an opportunity to subject [the confessor's] statements to cross-examination or had the other confessions been admitted.[23]

Submitted to a reductionist analysis, this looks like two problems: first, a denial of confrontation in refusing to allow cross-examination; second, a denial of compulsory process in the refusal to allow the witnesses to testify to the hearsay.[24]

This was not the way the majority of the Court saw it. Justice Powell begins this way:

> The right of an accused in a criminal trial to due process is, in essence, the right to a fair opportunity to defend against the State's accusations. The rights to confront and cross-examine witnesses and to call witnesses in one's own behalf have long been recognized as essential to due process.[25]

He then quotes from In re Oliver, one of the Court's leading holistic analyses of the Bill of Rights.[26] Having brought the rights together, Justice Powell now separates them.

Turning to the trial court's refusal to allow defendant to cross-examine the confessor, Justice Powell says that defendant "was denied an opportunity to subject [the confessor's] damning repudia-

---

23. "Had been admitted"

Id at 1045, 410 U.S. at 294.

24. Compulsory process

The Court had already held that the Compulsory Process Clause gave the defendant more than a right to a subpoena; it had been applied to give the defendant the right to introduce evidence—even over a state evidentiary rule barring the evidence. Washington v. Texas, 1967, 87 S.Ct. 1920, 388 U.S. 14, 18 L.Ed.2d 1019.

25. "Essential to due process"

Id. at 1045, 410 U.S. at 294.

26. Leading holistic analyses

"A person's right to reasonable notice of a charge against him, and an opportunity to be heard in his defense—a right to his day in court—are basic in our system of jurisprudence; and these rights include as a minimum, a right to examine the witnesses against him, to offer testimony, and to be represented by counsel." In re Oliver, 1948, 68 S.Ct. 499, 333 U.S. 257, 92 L.Ed. 682, quoted id. at 1045, 410 U.S. at 294. See also, § 6354, text at notecall 931.

tion and alibi to cross-examination."[27] This is important because

> [t]he right of cross-examination is more than a desirable rule of
> trial procedure. It is implicit in the constitutional right of confron-
> tation and helps assure the "accuracy of the truth-determining
> process."[28]

Recognizing that the right to confront the witnesses is not absolute,
Justice Powell nonetheless thinks that "its denial or significant
diminution calls into question the ultimate 'integrity of the fact-
finding process' and requires that the competing interest be closely
examined."[29]

Subjecting Mississippi's "voucher" rule to such an examination, the majority concludes that it is an outmoded rule, abandoned
by most jurisdictions and not sufficient to justify curtailing the
defendant's right to cross-examination.[30] This is confirmed in Justice Powell's eyes by the fact that, in arguments before the Court,
the state did not claim that the rationale of the voucher rule
sufficed to override the constitutional rights of the defendant.[31]
Instead, it argued that since defendant had called the witness to the
stand himself, the witness could not be a witness "against" the
defendant within the meaning of the Confrontation Clause.[32] Justice Powell rejects this conceptual argument.

> The availability of the right to confront and to cross-examine
> those who give damaging testimony against the accused has never
> been held to depend on whether the witness was initially put on
> the stand by the accused or by the State. We reject the notion that
> a right of such substance to the criminal process may be governed
> by that technicality or by any narrow and unrealistic definition of
> the word "against."[33]

Notice that in none of this is there anything about the "reliability"
of the evidence that defendant wishes to introduce. It is the
"criminal process" that is important.

27. "Damning repudiation"
Id. at 1045, 410 U.S. at 295.

28. "Helps assure 'accuracy'"
Id. at 1046, 410 U.S. at 295.

29. "Closely examined"
Ibid.

30. Not sufficient to justify
Id. at 1046–1047, 410 U.S. at 295–298.

31. Did not claim sufficed
Id. at 1047, 410 U.S. at 297.

32. Not "witness against"
Ibid.

33. "Unrealistic definition"
Id. at 1047, 410 U.S. at 297–298.

This changes when the majority turns to the question of the exclusion of the defendant's proffered hearsay. The opinion notes that the statement might fall within the hearsay exception for declarations against interest, which, like most hearsay exceptions, is based on a notion that the statements covered have greater "reliability" than most hearsay.[34] Though Mississippi recognizes this exception, it limits it, as did the common law, to declarations against pecuniary interest.[35] Brushing this aside, Justice Powell observes that the

> hearsay statements involved in this case were originally made and subsequently offered at trial under circumstances that provide considerable assurances of their reliability.[36]

Turning Green on its head, the majority opinion notes that since the confessor was present in court, the state could have tested him by cross-examination.[37] Justice Powell concludes that

> [f]ew rights are more fundamental than that of the accused to present witnesses in his own defense. [citing cases construing the Compulsory Process Clause] * * * In these circumstances, where constitutional rights directly affecting the ascertainment of guilt are implicated, the hearsay rule may not be applied mechanistically to defeat the ends of justice.[38]

At this point a purely reductionist analysis might have ended it; it has been shown the rights of confrontation and compulsory process have been violated.

However, rather than relying on the separate violations, the majority opinion combines them.

> We conclude that the exclusion of this critical evidence, coupled with the State's refusal to permit [defendant] to cross-examine [the confessor], denied him a trial in accord with the traditional and fundamental standards of due process.[39]

In short, applied holistically the Sixth Amendment carries more weight than when applied reductively.[40] Although Justice Powell

---

34. Greater "reliability"
Id. at 1047–1048, 410 U.S. at 298–299.

35. "Against pecuniary"
Id. at 1048, 410 U.S. at 299.

36. "Considerable assurances"
Id. at 1048, 410 U.S. at 300.

37. State could have tested
Id. at 1049, 410 U.S. at 301.

38. "Not applied mechanistically"
Id. at 1049, 410 U.S. at 301–302.

39. "Traditional standards"
Id. at 1049, 410 U.S. at 302.

40. Carries more weight
For example, considered alone, the confrontation clause seems less persuasive; given the number of times that the confessor had repudiated his con-

was explicit in denying any intent to enunciate any "new principles of constitutional law," those unaccustomed to holistic analysis have insisted that Chambers does in fact establish a new right apart from those explicitly mentioned in the Sixth Amendment or in the Court's opinion.[41]

Though neither Mancusi nor Chambers had much of an impact on the lower courts, the decade of the 1970s saw the scholars turn in larger numbers to the Confrontation Clause and the Supreme Court's caselaw.[42] However, the scholars had surprisingly little to say about confrontation policy.[43] The Solicitor General bragged in a public lecture that the government's brief in Green had alerted the Court to the danger to reform of constitutionalizing the hearsay rule.[44] Other scholars also thought that it would be a mistake to equate the hearsay rule with the right of confrontation.[45] However, the Solicitor General went on to tell his audience that he was prepared to accept an inquisitorial procedure that allowed trial by dossier.[46]

fession and asserted his innocence— and his obvious motives for continuing to do so—what are the chances that cross-examination would shake anything out of him that would be helpful to Chambers? However, once his other confessions are before the jury and he must repudiate these as well, the questioning on cross-examination is likely to be more productive.

41. "New principles"

Id. at 1049, 410 U.S. at 303.

Imwinkelreid, The Constitutional Right to Present Defense Evidence, 1973, 62 Mil.L.Re. 225; Note, Chambers v. Mississippi: Due Process and The Rules of Evidence, 1974, 35 U.Pitt.L.Rev. 725; Note, The Constitutional Right to Present Defense Evidence, 1973, 62 Mil.L.Rev. 225.

42. Much impact

See, e.g. Lee v. McCaughtry, C.A.7th, 1991, 933 F.2d 536 (Chambers does not give defendant right to introduce uncorroborated declaration against interest); U.S. v. Rivera, C.A.4th, 1988, 859 F.2d 1204, 1207 (depositions of alien witnesses deported by govern-

ment are admissible under Mancusi); U.S. v. King, C.A.9th, 1976, 552 F.2d 833, 839 (Mancusi makes depositions taken abroad admissible if they satisfy Dutton reliability test).

43. Confrontation policy

That is, beyond the policies enunciated in Supreme Court opinions; e.g. cross-examination v. "reliability" as the core value.

44. Brief alerted Court

Griswold, The Due Process Revolution and Confrontation, 1971, 119 U.Pa. L.Rev. 711, 721 (text of the Owen J. Roberts Memorial Lecture; for Justice Roberts' indirect impact on the right of confrontation, see § 6360, text at notecall 95).

45. Mistake to equate

Read, The New Confrontation–Hearsay Dilemma, 1972, 45 So.Calif.L.Rev. 1, 2.

46. Trial by dossier

Griswold, The Due Process Revolution and Confrontation, 1971, 119 U.Pa.

The scholars also had little to say about the manner in which the Court had chosen to interpret the Confrontation Clause.[47] The Solicitor General was confident that "experience with the Sixth Amendment has taught us that it does not mean what it says"— hardly a profound or reassuring opinion, coming as it does from one who was responsible for helping the Court interpret the Amendment.[48] At the other extreme, one writer argued that the Green– Dutton cases had all but abolished the right of confrontation.[49] On a historical note, critics noted sardonically the resemblance between the peroration of Justice Stewart's opinion in Dutton and the justifications of Raleigh's judges for denying him confrontation with his accusers.[50] However, most of the law-review articles were more concerned with interpretation of the Court's opinions than they were with the Court's interpretation of the Confrontation Clause; e.g., what effect does the opinion in Dutton have on the unavailability requirement laid down in Barber?[51]

Some writers explained the Court's caselaw in terms of judicial politics; that is, since the Burger Court was constituted to satisfy the demands of the public for more "law-and-order," it was to be expected that it would attempt to restrict decisions of the Warren Court that empowered criminal defendants and their lawyers.[52] For others, it was the personal views of the Justices about confronta-

L.Rev. 711, 726. He approves of U.S. v. Lloyd, C.A.9th, 1970, 431 F.2d 160, a draft prosecution in which the government's entire case consisted of the introduction of the defendant's Selective Service file—and the trial judge refused to allow the defense to subpoena the declarants; held, affirmed.

47. Chosen to interpret

That is, few asked how the holdings of the cases could be reconciled with the language of the Sixth Amendment.

48. "Does not mean"

Griswold, The Due Process Revolution and Confrontation, 1971, 119 U.Pa. L.Rev. 711, 728.

49. Abolished right

Davenport, The Confrontation Clause and The Co–Conspirator Exception in Criminal Prosecutions: A Functional Analysis, 1972, 85 Harv.L.Rev. 1378, 1381.

50. Raleigh's judges

Garland & Snow, The Co–Conspirators Exception to the Hearsay Rule: Procedural Implementation and Confrontation Clause Requirements, 1972, 63 J.Crim.L., Crim. & P.S. 1, 20. To see what Raleigh's judges said, see vol. 30, § 6342, p. 264. For Justice Stewart's justifications, see § 6365.

51. Dutton-Barber

Phillips, The Confrontation Clause and the Scope of the Unavailability Requirement, 1973, 6 U.Mich.J.L.Ref. 327, 328; Younger, Confrontation and Hearsay: A Look Backward, A Peek Forward, 1973, 1 Hofstra L.Rev. 32.

52. "Law-and-Order" Court

Seidelson, Hearsay Exceptions and the Sixth Amendment, 1971, 40 Geo. Wash.L.Rev. 76, 84.

tion that were more important than simplistic political categories; one writer tried to decipher the positions of the individual justices from the way they had voted or written in the cases decided by the Court.[53]

Most of the articles did what scholars do best—criticize.[54] Justice Stewart's opinion in Dutton took most of the abuse; one writer even thought it created too much hardship for prosecutors.[55] Other worried about its meaning for the coconspirator exception in jurisdictions that did not have such an idiosyncratic version.[56] Another writer pondered the relationship between "indicia of reliability" and statements not "crucial or devastating."[57] However, the most serious criticism, made explicit in some but implicit in most of the law review articles, was that the Supreme Court's confrontation jurisprudence lacked coherence and that the lower courts were too confused to develop a satisfactory reconciliation of the Court's cases.[58]

When it came to dishing out praise, the writers tended to single out Justice Harlan's opinions, which were more scholarly than most; unhappily, the writers could not agree on whether it was his Green or his Dutton concurrence that had got it right.[59] Some

53. Positions of Justices

Read, The New Confrontation Hearsay Dilemma, 1972, 45 So.Calif.L.Rev. 1, 24–40.

54. Criticize

For a particularly critical treatment, see Graham, The Confrontation Clause, The Hearsay Rule, and The Forgetful Witness, 1978, 56 Texas L.Rev. 151, 183.

55. Stewart abuse

Id. at 187 (too tough on government); Natali, Green, Dutton, and Chambers: Three Cases in Search of a Theory, 1975, 7 Rutgers–Camden L.J. 43, 51.

56. Co-conspirators

Davenport, The Confrontation Clause and The Co–Conspirator Exception in Criminal Prosecutions: A Functional Analysis, 1972, 85 Harv.L.Rev. 1378, 1382; Garland & Snow, The Co–Conspirator's Exception to the Hearsay Rule: Procedural Implementation and Confrontation Clause Requirements, 1972, 63 J.Crim.L., Crim. & P.S. 1, 15.

57. "Indicia" and "crucial"

Davenport, The Confrontation Clause and The Co–Conspirator Exception in Criminal Prosecutions: A Functional Analysis, 1972, 85 Harv.L.Rev. 1378, 1380 p. 11.

58. Lacked coherence

Natali, Green, Dutton and Chambers: Three Cases in Search of a Theory, 1973, 7 Rutgers–Camden L.J. 43, 46, 54.

59. Harlan's opinions

Graham, The Confrontation Clause, The Hearsay Rule, and the Forgetful Witness, 1978, Texas L.Rev. 151, 189 (Dutton); Younger, Hearsay and Confrontation, or What Every Criminal Defense Lawyer Should Have in Mind When He Objects to the Prosecutor's Offer of Hearsay, 1976, 11 Nat.J.Crim. Def. 65, 77 (Dutton); Younger, Con-

writers approved the shift from cross-examination to "reliability" as the core of confrontation.[60] However, others criticized the change.[61]

It was one thing to criticize the Court for lacking a coherent theory of confrontation; it was much more difficult to construct one of your own.[62] One author suggested a number of theories of confrontation, based on the views apparently espoused in Supreme Court opinions: "the federalist approach" (Stewart in Dutton); "the constitutional purist approach" (Brennan's dissent in Green): "the availability approach" (Harlan in Dutton); "the due process-cross-examining approach" (Harlan in Green); "the McCormick exception approach" (a variation of Wigmore); "the traditionalist approach" (the majority opinion in Green), the one favored by the author.[63] Another writer proposed what is less a theory of confrontation than a codification of it—a scheme so complex it has to be read to be believed.[64] Remarkably, one author developed a theory of

frontation and Hearsay: A Look Backward, A Peek Forward, 1973, 1 Hofstra L.Rev. 32, 38 (Green); Baker, The Right to Confrontation, the Hearsay Rules and Due Process—A Proposal for Determining When Hearsay May Be Used in Criminal Trials, 1974, 6 Conn.L.Rev. 529, 536 (Green).

60. Approved "reliability"

Davenport, The Confrontation Clause and The Co–Conspirator Exception in Criminal Prosecutions: A Functional Analysis, 1972, 85 Harv.L.Rev. 1378, 1379.

61. Criticize change

Younger, Confrontation and Hearsay: A Look Backward, A Peek Forward, 1973, 1 Hofstra L.Rev. 32, 41.

62. One of your own

For an early effort that is less a theory than a method for analyzing issues that arise in interpreting the Confrontation Clause, see Graham, The Right of Confrontation and the Hearsay Rule; Sir Walter Raleigh Loses Another One, 1972, 8 Crim.L.Bull. 99.

63. Favored by author

Read, The New Confrontation–Hearsay Dilemma, 1972, 45 So.Calif.L.Rev. 1, 41–48.

64. Has to be read

"Irrespective of hearsay definitions of particular exceptions, the confrontation clause requires as a prerequisite to the admission of any out-of-court-declaration the presence in court of the declarant accompanied by effective cross-examination, unless substantial guarantees of trustworthiness are present which satisfy the trial court that the defendant's confrontation rights are fully compensated; provided, however, that no statements taken in police custody or under other circumstances which indicate one party's 'control' of the declarant may be admitted for the truth of the matter unless the proponent of the evidence can demonstrate by the preponderance of the evidence that the declarant fully and voluntarily gave the statement. Testimony by the declarant that his declaration was false or involuntary creates a rebuttable presumption that it was. Clear and convincing evidence is necessary to over-

confrontation that bears a striking resemblance to the one the Supreme Court would adopt—eventually and briefly.[65] Of course, those favoring one theory also criticized its rivals.[66]

Not all these articles on confrontation dealt with its impact on hearsay.[67] The individual articles are more valuable than this synopsis will make them appear, but for historical purposes this summary will suffice.[68] One of the consequences of the Supreme Court's zigzag course over the right of confrontation is that scholarly articles on confrontation have a shelf life only slightly better than a loaf of bread.

§ 6367. ____; Roberts, Rules and Order

As the dormant decade drew to a close, the need for the Supreme Court to revisit confrontation doctrine became more apparent.[1] Scholars had revealed issues that existing caselaw seemed inadequate to handle.[2] Moreover, the existing doctrine seemed to

come such rebuttable presumption. Moreover, the party against whom the evidence is offered is entitled to a jury instruction that the absence of the declarant may, standing alone, or taken with other circumstances in the case be reason for the jury to reject the statement as being unreliable. Absence as used herein means that the declarant is (1) dead, (2) physically or mentally incapacitated, (3) claiming the privilege against self-incrimination, or (4) persisting in a refusal to testify after ordered to do so. In no event may such statement be admitted until there is prima facie evidence which would support a conviction of each and every defendant against whom it is offered." Natali, Green, Dutton and Chambers: Three Cases in Search of a Theory, 1975, 7 Rutgers–Camden L.J. 43, 62–63.

65. Striking resemblance

Baker, The Right to Confrontation, The Hearsay Rules and Due Process—A Proposal for Determining When Hearsay May Be Used in Criminal Trials, 1974, 6 Conn.L.Rev. 529, 544–549 (state must make a good-faith effort to produce declarant; if unavailable, state should have to prove the hearsay

is trustworthy; presumption of trustworthiness for statements that fall within hearsay exception).

66. Criticized rivals

Natali, Green, Dutton and Chambers: Three Cases in Search of a Theory, 1975, 7 Rutgers–Camden L.J. 43, 58, 61 (critical of Baker, Graham).

67. Not all hearsay

See, e.g., Carlson, Argument to the Jury and the Constitutional Right of Confrontation, 1973, 9 Crim.L.Bull. 293. See also the articles in footnote 41, above.

68. Summary will suffice

We will consider the articles in more detail in connection with our analysis of confrontation the next doctrine in the next volume in the Treatise.

§ 6367

1. Need apparent

See the writings discussed in § 6366.

2. Inadequate

See, e.g., Imwinkelreid, The Constitutionality of Introducing Evaluative Laboratory Reports Against Criminal Defendants, 1979, 30 Hast.L.J.621.

threaten long-established confrontation pieties.[3] The Supreme Court's commitment to Pointer was being questioned; one article on the "future of confrontation" came close to suggesting that it had none.[4] Finally, two members of the Court with very different opinions on the right of confrontation urged their colleagues to revisit the issue because the lower courts were "struggling with the problem of admissibility of hearsay evidence not falling within one of the traditional exceptions to inadmissibility."[5]

Hence, it was with great anticipation that Ohio v. Roberts came before the Supreme Court.[6] The defendant was charged with forgery and possession of stolen credit cards.[7] At his preliminary hearing, the defense called the daughter of the victims to testify; she denied that she had given her parents' check and credit cards to the defendant without telling him they were stolen.[8] At trial, the daughter failed to appear despite subpoenas served at the home of her parents; her mother testified that she had left home after the preliminary hearing, bound for Tucson, Arizona, but her present whereabouts were unknown.[9]

The trial court admitted the daughter's testimony from the preliminary hearing and the defendant was convicted.[10] On appeal, the Ohio courts both held that admission of the daughter's hearsay

3. Threaten pieties

Jaffee, The Constitution and Proof by Dead of Unconfrontable Declarants, 1979, 33 Ark.L.Rev. 227, 267 (arguing that dying declarations, one of the oldest "exceptions" to the right of confrontation, are now inadmissible under the Court's modern confrontation jurisprudence).

4. Had none

Westen, The Future of Confrontation, 1979, 77 Mich.L.Rev. 1185, 1187 (favoring Harlan position in Green). This reading may be colored by an earlier article, Westen, Confrontation and Compulsory Process: A Unified Theory of Evidence for Criminal Cases, 1978, 91 Harv.L.Rev. 567.

5. "Struggling with problems"

McKethan v. U.S., 1978, 99 S.Ct. 333, 335, 439 U.S. 936, 938, 58 L.Ed.2d 333 (Marshall and Stewart, J.J., dissenting from denial of certiorari in case in which trial court had admitted unconfronted grand-jury testimony under "wild card" exception to hearsay rule).

6. Roberts case

1980, 100 S.Ct. 2531, 448 U.S. 56, 65 L.Ed.2d 597. See also, Note, Constitutional Law: Sixth Amendment, Right of Confrontation, Unavailable Witness, 1979, 12 Akron L.Rev. 572 (discussing Ohio opinions in Roberts).

7. Forgery and credit cards

Id. at 2535, 448 U.S. at 58.

8. Telling stolen

Ibid.

9. Whereabouts unknown

Id. at 2535–2536, 448 U.S. at 59–60.

10. Admitted and convicted

Id. at 2536, 448 U.S. at 60.

violated the defendant's right of confrontation, but they could not agree on which branch of the doctrine of "confrontation excused" the prosecution had failed to prove.[11]

Justice Blackmun began the long-awaited opinion by quoting the Confrontation Clause, then noting:

> If one were to read this language literally, it would require, on objection, the exclusion of any statement made by a declarant not present at trial. * * * But, if thus applied, the Clause would abrogate virtually every hearsay exception, a result long rejected as unintended and too extreme.[12]

What, then, was "intended"?

Not for Justice Blackmun the "faded parchment" approach to the history of the Confrontation Clause.[13] He says that "[t]he historical evidence leaves little doubt, however, that the clause was intended to exclude some hearsay."[14] He adds that the congruent policies of hearsay and confrontation point in the same direction.[15] He solves the problem of "how much hearsay" the clause was designed to exclude by converting the supposed "right" of confrontation into a "preference" for confrontation.[16]

> The Court has emphasized that the Confrontation Clause reflects a preference for face-to-face confrontation at trial, and that "a primary interest secured by [the provision] is the right of cross-examination".[17]

In a long footnote, he justifies what might otherwise look like a retreat from the Dutton shift to "reliability" by explaining that cross-examination is instrumental to "reliability."[18] He does not

---

11. Could not agree

The Court of Appeals found the showing of "unavailability" inadequate; the Supreme Court held that the past confrontation was not sufficient to satisfy the second element. Id. at 2536, 448 U.S. at 60–61.

12. Unintended and too extreme

Id. at 2537, 448 U.S. at 63.

13. "Faded parchment"

See § 6364, text at notecall 44.

14. "Intended to exclude"

Id. at 2537, 448 U.S. at 63.

15. Same direction

Ibid.

16. "Preference"

This shift is credited in Westen, The Future of Confrontation, 1979, 77 Mich.L.Rev. 1185, 1189, to Justice Harlan's opinion in Green.

17. "Interest secured"

Id at 2537, 448 U.S. at 63.

18. Instrumental to "reliability"

Id. at 2537 n. 6, 448 U.S. at 63 n. 6.

trouble to explain what interests "reliability" serves, perhaps supposing that this is obvious.[19]

After quoting Mattox on the glory of confrontation, Blackmun turns to those "competing interests [that] if 'closely examined' * * * may warrant dispensing with confrontation at trial."[20] He bows to the "law-and-order" lobby that brought him to the bench:

> every jurisdiction has a strong interest in effective law enforcement, and in the development and precise formulation of the rules of evidence applicable in criminal proceedings.[21]

Anyone familiar with how statists "balance" the interests of powerholders against the powerless can see where this is headed.[22]

Blackmun then responds to the charges that the Court's confrontation jurisprudence is "incoherent."[23]

> This Court, in a series of cases, has sought to accommodate these competing interests. True to the common-law tradition, the process has been gradual, building on past decisions, drawing on new experience, and responding to changing conditions. The Court has not sought to map out a theory of the Confrontation Clause that would determine the "validity of all * * * hearsay 'exceptions.'" * * * But a general approach to the problem is discernable.[24]

Anyone who has read the Court's prior confrontation decisions would have a difficult task seeing how they fit Justice Blackmun's

---

19. Interests serves

Nor does he tell us who holds this interest. In order to know what moral values are being served, we must trace the instrumental argument to its roots in moral values, but this is seldom done.

20. "May warrant dispensing"

Id. at 2538, 448 U.S. at 64.

Ironically, the Mattox passage reveals the adversary interests of the participants that are missing from the Court's wizened version. Confrontation, according to Mattox, requires "a personal examination and cross-examination of the witness, in which the accused has an opportunity, not only of testing the recollection and sifting the conscience of the witness, but of compelling him to stand face to face

with the jury in order that they may look upon him, and judge by his demeanor upon the stand and the manner in which he gives his testimony whether he is worthy of belief."

21. "Effective law enforcement"

Id. at 2538, 448 U.S. at 64.

22. Statists balance

To the statists, the interests of the individual will always appear puny when compared with whatever banner government officials are parading under as tribunes of "the people."

23. Incoherent

See § 6366, text at notecall 58.

24. "Discernable"

Id. at 2358, 44 U.S. at 64–65.

utopian vision of the common-law tradition.[25]

Having just eschewed the task, the Court's opinion begins to "map out a theory of the Confrontation Clause."[26]

> The Confrontation Clause operates in two separate ways to restrict the range of admissible hearsay. First, in conformance with the Framers' preference for face-to-face accusation, the Sixth Amendment establishes a rule of necessity. In the usual case (including cases where prior cross-examination has occurred), the prosecution must either produce or demonstrate the unavailability of the declarant whose statement it wishes to use against the declarant.[27]

For those who wonder what the "unusual" case might be, Justice Blackmun drops a footnote explaining that a "demonstration of unavailability * * * is not always required," citing Dutton and describing it as a case in which "the Court found the utility of trial confrontation so remote that it did not require the prosecution to produce a seemingly available witness."[28] Of course, "the Court" did no such thing, but this footnote was to give the Stewart opinion the vitality it needed to survive as an alternative to Roberts.[29]

Turning to the second "way" in which confrontation "restricts" the use of hearsay, Justice Blackmun writes:

> [t]he second aspect operates once a witness is shown to be unavailable. Reflecting its underlying purpose to augment accuracy in the fact-finding process by ensuring the defendant an effective means to test adverse evidence, the Clause countenances only hearsay marked with such trustworthiness that "there is no material departure from the reason of the general rule."[30]

25. Fit vision

Few of the Court's cases before Roberts thought that confrontation was a rule of preference, like the opinion or best-evidence rules, nor did they suppose they were "balancing" the interests of the individual against the state; they supposed that those interests had been balanced by the Founders when they incorporated the Sixth Amendment in the Bill of Rights.

26. "Map out theory"

Justice Blackmun does not elucidate the difference between a "theory" and a "general approach" but what he presents is what the writers had in mind when they criticized the Court for failing to develop a "theory."

27. "Use against declarant"

Id. at 2538, 448 U.S. at 65.

28. "Utility so remote"

Id. at 2538 n. 7, 448 U.S. at 65 n.7.

29. Vitality to survive

See § 6365, text at notecall 34. "The Court" did nothing in Dutton because it could not muster a majority for any of the four positions embraced.

30. "Reason of general rule"

Id. at 2539, 448 U.S. at 65.

After a long quotation from Mancusi's endorsement of the "reliability" theory of hearsay, the opinion continues.[31]

> The Court has applied this "indicia of reliability" requirement principally by concluding that certain hearsay exceptions rest on such solid foundations that admission of virtually any evidence within them comports with the "substance of the constitutional protection." * * * This reflects the truism that "hearsay rules and the Confrontation Clause are generally designed to protect similar values" * * * and "stem from the same roots." * * * It also responds to the need for certainty in the workaday world of conducting criminal trials.[32]

In its attempt to rewrite history by giving his theory the sanction of Mattox and other pre-Pointer cases, the Blackmun opinion is a breathtaking tour de force.[33] However, it makes no attempt to anchor its theory in either the language of the Sixth Amendment or its history.[34]

The Blackmun opinion then states what has been generally been taken to be the "Roberts' test" for the admissibility of hearsay over a confrontation objection.[35]

> In sum, when a hearsay declarant is not present for cross-examination at trial, the Confrontation Clause normally requires a showing that he is unavailable. Even then, his statement is admissible only if it bears adequate "indicia of reliability." Reliability can be inferred without more in cases where the evidence falls within a firmly rooted hearsay exception. In other cases, the evidence must be excluded, at least absent a showing of particularized guarantees of trustworthiness.[36]

In short, confrontation is only "satisfied" by contemporaneous cross-examination; it is "excused" by unavailability of the declarant

31. Mancusi "reliability"

Id. at 2539, 448 U.S. at 65–66. For discussion of Mancusi, see § 6360.

32. "World of criminal trials"

Id. at 2539, 448 U.S. at 66.

33. Tour de force

For one thing, most of the pre-Pointer cases dealt with the right of confrontation in the highly formal style of the time and in a quite cursory fashion.

34. History or language

For example, if Justice Blackmun had been aware that the Founders saw confrontation as one of the defining features of trial by jury, he would have to explain why one is a "right" and the other is a "preference."

35. "Roberts' test"

See below, text at notecall 53.

36. "Particularized guarantees"

Id. at 2539, 448 U.S. at 66.

on a showing of a "firmly rooted" hearsay exception or "particularized guarantees of trustworthiness."[37]

At the end of his "test," Justice Blackmun drops a highly amusing footnote in which he analyzes the scholarly efforts to develop a "theory" or "test" of confrontation.[38] The scholars are lined up according to Blackmun's assessment of whether their favored "approach" would benefit the defendant, the prosecution, or are indeterminate in their partisanship.[39] What is so droll about the footnote, besides the consternation it generated in the authors who did or did not make the cut, is that Blackmun also identifies a group of scholars who "have generally agreed with the Court's present approach" but these scholars are exempt from categorization in term of partisanship.[40] If Justice Blackmun had been required to categorize them by determining whether the Supreme Court's past decisions favored the prosecution or the defense, these scholars would have to be thrown in with the "pro-prosecution" group.[41]

When it comes to applying its "test," Justice Blackmun's opinion seems rather casual in its use of the "approach" just enunciated. First it applies the test "bassackwards"; that is, it begins with the second prong of the test for "confrontation excused," ostensibly because it was on this second "prong" that the Ohio Supreme Court had reversed Roberts' conviction.[42] Second, and more significantly, it does not ask whether the hearsay statements of the daughter fall within the "former testimony" exception, whether that exception is "firmly rooted," or whether the statements have "particularized guarantees of trustworthiness."[43]

37. "Satisfied" and "excused"

Notice that under the Roberts formula, there is no room for Dutton. Confrontation was not "satisfied" because the witness was absent and it was not "excused" because he was not "unavailable."

38. Scholarly efforts

Id. at 2539 n. 9, 448 U.S. at 66 n. 9.

39. Indeterminate

The author whose suggested theory most resembles the one adopted in Roberts, see § 6366, text at notecall 65, is placed in the "indeterminate" category along with the junior author and one of his students.

40. Exempt from categorization

Id. at 2539 n. 9, 448 U.S. at 66 n. 9.

41. "Pro-prosecution" group

Of the score of hearsay-confrontation decisions prior to Roberts, less than a half-dozen could be said to be "in favor of the defense."

42. Second prong first

Id. at 2540, 448 U.S. at 66–67.

43. "Firmly rooted"

One inclined to be generous could read the Court's reliance on Green as an implicit holding that the former-testimony exception is firmly rooted and satisfied by the facts of Roberts.

Instead, it holds the testimony was properly admitted because dicta in Green stated that the preliminary-hearing testimony of an absent witness was admissible over a confrontation objection.[44] Thus it was that the downfall of the "Roberts test" was foreshadowed in the very case in which it was established.[45]

Leaving a couple of questions about the first element of the test unresolved, Justice Blackmun now turns to the first prong.[46] He begins by reaffirming the Barber standard for "unavailability" of an absent witness.[47] As Blackmun restates it, the standard is "whether the witness is unavailable despite good-faith efforts undertaken prior to trial to locate and present that witness."[48] However, the application of that standard is much less rigorous than in Barber.[49] The only steps the prosecution took to obtain the presence of the declarant was to serve subpoenas at an address at which they knew she no longer resided; this, according to the Court, and over the objections of the dissent, was a "good faith" effort.[50] Because the parents of the declarant, who were apparently estranged from the daughter, did not know where she was, the majority of the Court thought the prosecution was excused from the steps routinely undertaken by prosecutors and civil-process servers who want to find a witness; e.g., inquiring of known acquaintances, checking licensing records, credit agencies, and F.B.I. files.[51] If, as the Court's opinion says, the Sixth Amendment contains a "prefer-

44. Said was admissible

Id. at 2540–2541, 348 U.S. at 66–70.

45. Downfall of Roberts

See below, §§ 6368–6377.

46. Unresolved

E.g., whether an opportunity to cross-examine satisfied Green—a question that seems irrelevant to the formula the Court says is being applied. It. at 2541, 448 U.S. at 70.

Instead, the Court devotes a couple of pages to refuting the claim that because the witness was technically under direct examination at the preliminary hearing, Green was not satisfied. Id. at 2541–2542, 448 U.S. at 70–73.

47. Reaffirming Barber

Id. at 2543, 448 U.S. at 74. Barber is discussed in § 6363, above.

48. "Locate and present"

Ibid.

49. Less rigorous

Barber held that the mere fact that the witness was beyond state lines did not satisfy the state's burden when there were other methods available—admittedly onerous—that might have produced the witness for trial.

50. "Good faith effort"

Id at 2543, 448 U.S. at 75.

51. Routinely taken

Or at least this was what was "routine" when the junior author was a civil litigator and a prosecutor in the 1960s and early 1970s.

ence" for confrontation of witnesses, Roberts suggests that preference is not a strong one.

Although some judges dismissed the Roberts formula as "dicta,"[52] most lower courts embraced the "Roberts test."[53] As always, application of the test raised issues not foreseen; e.g., must the "firmly rooted exception" be one that was actually applied or can the prosecution import an exception from elsewhere to satisfy confrontation?[54] Roberts was read to say that if the statement was not within any hearsay exception, it was presumptively unreliable.[55] Despite the Dutton footnote, courts held that coconspirator hearsay must satisfy the test.[56] So doing, one court held that the Georgia version of the exception involved in Dutton was not "firmly rooted."[57] However, courts divided on applying Roberts to hearsay exceptions that do not themselves require "unavailability"; e.g., the business-records exception.[58]

52. Dicta

Williams v. Melton, C.A.11th, 1984, 733 F.2d 1492, 1495.

53. "Roberts test"

U.S. v. Doerr, C.A.7th, 1989, 886 F.2d 944, 957 (employing court's variant of the original); Martinez v. Sullivan, C.A.10th, 1989, 881 F.2d 921, 928; U.S. v. Chapman, C.A.11th, 1989, 866 F.2d 1326, 1330; Smith v. Fairman, C.A.7th, 1988, 862 F.2d 630, 635; Marshall v. Young, C.A.7th, 1987, 833 F.2d 709, 716; Fuson v. Jago, C.A.6th, 1985, 773 F.2d 55, 59; U.S. v. Huber, C.A.9th, 1985, 772 F.2d 585, 588; U.S. v. Cruz, C.A.11th, 1985, 765 F.2d 1020, 1024; U.S. v. Monaco, C.A.9th, 1984, 735 F.2d 1173, 1175 (truncated version); U.S. v. Licavoli, C.A.6th, 1984, 725 F.2d 1040, 1049; U.S. v. Ordonez, C.A.9th, 1983, 722 F.2d 530, 535; Hutchins v. Wainwright, C.A.11th, 715 F.2d 512, 516; Haggins v. Warden, C.A.6th, 1983, 715 F.2d 1050, 1055; Payne v. Janasz, C.A.6th, 1983, 711 F.2d 1305, 1314; U.S. v. Foster, C.A.9th, 1983, 711 F.2d 871, 881; U.S. v. Barlow, C.A.6th, 1982, 693 F.2d 954, 963; U.S. ex rel. Haywood v. Wolff, C.A.7th, 1981, 658 F.2d 455, 460; Holt v. Wyrick, C.A.8th, 1981, 649 F.2d 543, 548.

54. Import from elsewhere

Terrovona v. Kincheloe, C.A.9th, 1988, 852 F.2d 424, 427 (assumes must satisfy local law); Fuson v. Jago, C.A.6th, 773 F.2d 55, 61 (assuming does not satisfy Roberts if not within local version of exception even though it would qualify under exceptions that are firmly rooted elsewhere).

55. Presumptively unreliable

U.S. v. Flannigan, C.A.7th, 1989, 884 F.2d 945 (assumes); U.S. v. McKinney, C.A.9th, 1985, 707 F.2d 381, 384.

56. Must satisfy

U.S. v. Ordonez, C.A.9th, 1984, 737 F.2d 793; U.S. v. McKinney, C.A.9th, 1983, 707 F.2d 381, 383; U.S. v. Perez, C.A.9th, 658 F.2d 654, 658.

57. Georgia version

Horton v. Zant, C.A.11th, 1991, 941 F.2d 1449, 1464.

58. Business records

U.S. v. Johnson, C.A.10th, 1993, 971 F.2d 562, 572 (not required); U.S. v. Franks, C.A.8th, 1991, 939 F.2d 600, 603 (implies not); U.S. v. Ray, C.A.9th, 1990, 920 F.2d 562, 566 (im-

Much of the caselaw was devoted to determining just which hearsay exceptions were "firmly rooted."[59] Courts quickly found the most commonly used hearsay exceptions had firm roots, without regard to whether the exception was itself premised on "reliability" or not: adoptive admissions,[60] vicarious admissions,[61] and statements of coconspirators qualified.[62] Among the exceptions in Rule 803, those found to be "firmly rooted" included excited utterances,[63] the state-of-mind exception,[64] and business records;[65] courts disagreed about the exception for statements for medical diagnosis—not surprising since no one had heard of this exception prior to the Federal Rules of Evidence.[66] The major Rule 804 exceptions were "firmly rooted"—declarations against interest,[67]

plies not); U.S. v. Ordonez, C.A.9th, 737 F.2d 793, 802 (required); U.S. v. Chappell, C.A.7th, 1983, 698 F.2d 308, 312 (required); U.S. v. Washington, C.A.5th, 1982, 688 F.2d 953, 959 (required except under Dutton proviso).

59. "Firmly rooted"

The cases cited are illustrative only; the question will be more comprehensively addressed in connection with the analysis of each hearsay exception in the ensuing volumes.

60. Adoptive admission

Marshall v. Young, C.A.7th, 1987, 833 F.2d 709, 716 (collecting cases); Berrisford v. Wood, C.A.8th, 1987, 826 F.2d 747, 751.

61. Vicarious admissions

U.S. v. Chappell, C.A.7th, 1983, 698 F.2d 308, 312.

62. Coconspirators

U.S. v. Drew, C.A.8th, 1990, 894 F.2d 965, 968.

63. Excited utterances

Martinez v. McCaughtry, C.A.7th, 1991, 951 F.2d 130, 134; Cole v. Tansy, C.A.10th, 1991, 926 F.2d 955, 958; Webb v. Lane, C.A.7th, 1991, 922 F.2d 390, 393; Martinez v. Sullivan, C.A.10th, 1989, 881 F.2d 921, 928; Stidum v. Trickey, C.A.8th, 1989, 881 F.2d 582; Smith v. Fairman, C.A.7th,

1988, 862 F.2d 630, 636; Berrisford v. Wood, C.A.8th, 1987, 826 F.2d 747, 750; U.S. v. Moore, C.A.7th, 1986, 791 F.2d 566, 574 (collects cases); Haggins v. Warden, C.A.6th, 1983, 715 F.2d 1050, 1055.

64. State of mind

Terrovona v. Kincheloe, C.A.9th, 1988, 852 F.2d 424, 427 (Alcalde statement).

65. Business records

U.S. v. Johnson, C.A.10th, 1992, 971 F.2d 562, 573; U.S. v. Franks, C.A.8th, 1991, 939 F.2d 600, 603; U.S. v. Ray, C.A.9th, 1990, 920 F.2d 562, 566; U.S. v. Miller, C.A.9th, 1987, 830 F.2d 1073, 1077.

66. Medical diagnosis

Dana v. Department of Corrections, C.A.8th, 1992, 958 F.2d 237, 239 (firmly rooted); U.S. v. George, C.A.9th, 1992, 960 F.2d 97, 99 (same); Gregory v. North Carolina, C.A.4th, 1990, 900 F.2d 705 (assumes not).

67. Declarations against interest

U.S. v. One Star, C.A.8th, 1992, 979 F.2d 1319, 1323; Jennings v. Maynard, C.A. 10th, 1991, 946 F.2d 1502, 1505; U.S. v. York, C.A.7th, 1991, 933 F.2d 1343, 1363; U.S. v. Garcia, C.A.7th, 1990, 897 F.2d 1413, 1421; U.S. v. Seeley, C.A.1st, 1989, 892 F.2d 1, 2;

dying declarations,[68] and former testimony.[69]

Among matters not "firmly rooted," the "wild card" exceptions are most prominent.[70] Given the way in which former testimony was handled in Roberts, it was to be expected that the lower courts would have problems with it.[71] Some courts have held the former testimony exception is not "firmly rooted" when applied to matters not within the traditional exception; e.g., preliminary hearing testimony where defendant was not present or represented by counsel or former testimony from a case in which defendant was not a party.[72] Similarly, courts have found that strained applications of the declarations against interest exception do not satisfy Roberts; e.g. the "he and I did it" confession of an accomplice.[73] In addition, other stray forms of hearsay have been held not to meet the Roberts test. [74]One of the issues that lower courts tended to pass over was the meaning of "firmly rooted"; does it mean that the exception is long standing or that it has been widely adopted?[75]

Berrisford v. Wood, C.A.8th, 1987, 826 F.2d 747, 751.

68. Dying declarations

Webb v. Lane, C.A.7th, 1991, 922 F.2d 390, 393.

69. Former testimony

U.S. v. Zannino, C.A.1st, 1990, 895 F.2d 1, 5. Most courts, however, have followed the lead of the Roberts opinion in validating the use of former testimony outside the Roberts' formula. See, e.g., U.S. v. Licavoli, C.A.6th, 1984, 725 F.2d 1040, 1049.

70. "Wild card" not

Mitchell v. Hoke, C.A.2d, 1991, 930 F.2d 1, 2 (by implication); Hopkinson v. Shillinger, C.A.10th, 1989, 866 F.2d 1185, 1200.

71. Problems

Most courts have followed Roberts in adjudicating the admissibility of former testimony outside the Roberts formula. See, e.g., U.S. ex rel. Bell v. Director of Department of Corrections, C.A.7th, 1988, 847 F.2d 399; James v. Wainwright, C.A.11th, 1982, 680 F.2d 102; Holt v. Wyrick, C.A.8th, 1981, 649 F.2d 543, 549.

72. Not a party

U.S. v. Zannino, C.A.1st, 1990, 895 F.2d 1, 6 (not a party); Barker v. Morris, C.A.9th, 1985, 761 F.2d 1396, 1400 (videotaped testimony at preliminary hearing not meeting former testimony exception).

73. "He and I did it"

U.S. v. Innamorati, C.A.1st, 1993, 996 F.2d 456, 475; U.S. v. Flores, C.A.5th, 1993, 985 F.2d 770, 775; U.S. v. Vernor, C.A.5th, 1990, 902 F.2d 1182, 1187.

74. Stray forms

Ring v. Erickson, C.A.8th, 1992, 983 F.2d 818, 821 (state kiddy hearsay statute only recently adopted not firmly rooted).

75. Long or wide

For example, the state statutes allowing the use of child hearsay are of recent vintage but have been widely adopted. Ibid. On the other hand, the "res gestae" exception has been around for years, but is now only in force in a handful of states. See Haggins v. Warden, C.A.6th, 1983, 715 F.2d 1050, 1056–1057.

Courts have had little difficulty with the meaning of the "unavailability" branch of the Roberts test, perhaps because it is generally assumed to be the same as the standards provided in the hearsay rules.[76] The same cannot be said for "particularized guarantees of trustworthiness"; courts have been all over the road on what factors go into this element.[77] Some have thought that other evidence of the defendant's guilt suffices,[78] yet proof of defendant's other crimes does not.[79] Testimony by an expert has been relied upon by one court.[80] Another said that "trustworthiness" refers only to the question of the sincerity of the utterance, not to personal knowledge, recollection, or ambiguity.[81] One court even thought the standard was variable, depending on how "crucial" the statement was to the prosecution's case.[82] Courts have divided over the question of whether the standard for "wild card" hearsay is to be equated with "particularized guarantees of trustworthiness."[83]

Courts have found "particularized guarantees" for the preliminary-hearing testimony of a dead witness not cross-examined by defendant who was a fugitive at the time,[84] for a declaration against interest that does not shift the blame or suggest an intent for revenge,[85] an autopsy report,[86] an informant-accomplice who com-

76. "Unavailability"

Steele v. Taylor, C.A.6th, 1982, 684 F.2d 1193, 1201, n. 8 (rejecting "waiver" analysis of some cases, but holding that where the defendant procures the absence of the witness, witness is unavailable for purposes of Roberts analysis).

77. "Particularized"

This was probably because the Roberts opinion did not apply the concept; once the Supreme Court developed the concept in subsequent cases, the lower courts had a better idea of what was involved.

78. Proof of guilt

Berrisford v. Wood, C.A.8th, 1987, 826 F.2d 747, 750.

79. Other crimes

Gregory v. North Carolina, C.A.4th, 1990, 900 F.2d 705, 708 (evidence of subsequent child abuse cannot corroborate claim of earlier abuse).

80. Expert testimony

Myatt v. Hannigan, C.A.10th, 1990, 910 F.2d 680, 685.

81. Only sincerity

McCafferty v. Leapley, C.A.8th, 1991, 944 F.2d 445, 452.

82. Variable

U.S. v. Mokol, C.A.7th, 1991, 939 F.2d 436, 440.

83. "Wild card" standard

Id. at 439 (no); U.S. v. Doerr, C.A.7th, 1989, 886 F.2d 944, 958 (yes); U.S. v. Guinan, C.A.7th, 1988, 836 F.2d 350, 358 (yes).

84. Fugitive

Barker v. Morris, C.A.9th, 1985, 761 F.2d 1396, 1401.

85. Blame or revenge

U.S. v. Vernor, C.A.5th, 1990, 902 F.2d 1182, 1188.

mitted suicide after incriminating the defendant,[87] an accusation of sexual abuse by a child deemed too young to invent such tales,[88] and where the child had no motive to lie, was not led by interviewers, and employed childish diction.[89]

On the other hand, no "guarantees of trustworthiness" were found where former testimony could not be cross-examined,[90] where witnesses were inconsistent on the substance of what was said,[91] in a codefendant's confession,[92] in statements by an incoherent senior citizen given to fantasizing,[93] and in the case of an accusation of crime by an unknown person.[94] Other cases leave one wondering whether this is what the Roberts majority had in mind.[95]

It is clear that unlike other portions of the Roberts test, there is a rival for "particularized guarantees of trustworthiness." Noting that the "indicia of reliability" language was derived from Dutton, some courts have reasoned that it retains validity as a test for the admission of the testimony of available witnesses.[96] Courts have held, following Dutton, that to satisfy "indicia of reliability," there must be some evidence that the hearsay statement was made.[97] It

86. Autopsy report

Manocchio v. Moran, C.A.1st, 1990, 919 F.2d 770, 777.

87. Informant suicide

U.S. v. Ellis, C.A.4th, 1991, 951 F.2d 580, 583.

88. Too young to invent

Dana v. Department of Corrections, C.A.8th, 1992, 958 F.2d 237, 239.

89. Childish diction

U.S. v. George, C.A.9th, 1992, 960 F.2d 97, 100.

90. Could not be cross

U.S. v. Monaco, C.A.9th, 1984, 735 F.2d 1173.

91. Witnesses inconsistent

U.S. v. Cruz, C.A.11th, 1985, 765 F.2d 1020, 1024–1025.

92. Confession

Fuson v. Jago, C.A.6th, 1985, 773 F.2d 55.

93. Senior citizen

Sherley v. Seabold, C.A.6th, 1991, 929 F.2d 272, 275.

94. Unknown person

U.S. v. Dean, C.A.9th, 1992, 980 F.2d 1286, 1288.

95. Had in mind

Government of Virgin Islands v. Joseph, C.A.3d, 1992, 964 F.2d 1380, 1388 (must show more than absence of motive to lie, must show a motive for telling truth).

96. Dutton retains validity

U.S. v. Chapman, C.A.11th, 1989, 866 F.2d 1326, 1330; Hopkinson v. Shillinger, C.A.10th, 1989, 866 F.2d 1185, 1202; U.S. v. Ordonez, C.A.9th, 1984, 737 F.2d 793, 802–803.

97. Proof made

U.S. v. Garcia, C.A.7th, 1990, 897 F.2d 1413, 1421; Hopkinson v. Shillinger, C.A.10th, 1989, 866 F.2d 1185, 1201.

has also been said that after Roberts, such "indicia" must be found in the abstract, not on the facts as in Dutton.[98] Courts have found the Dutton standard satisfied by depositions and by the cross-examination of others in former testimony.[99]

As in the case of other judicial decisions, Roberts has generated its share of discrepant readings.[100] However, we need not attempt to reconcile these because the Roberts standards would prove even less enduring than the Warren Court interpretations, though the law reviews generally approved Roberts.[101]

§ 6368. ___; Street, Inadi, and Lee

Given that the Court had just undertaken to map out an "approach" for dealing with confrontation questions, one might have supposed that the "Me Decade" would be as uneventful as the one that preceded it while the Court waited and watched for the "common-law tradition" to work its magic on the plan laid out in Roberts.[1] Instead, the 1980s saw more significant confrontation decisions than in any comparable period in the Court's history.[2]

The first post-Roberts case, Tennessee v. Street, was a murder prosecution involving two perpetrators.[3] The defendant confessed to the crime, but at trial the defendant claimed that he was innocent

98. In abstract

U.S. v. Sines, C.A.9th, 1985, 761 F.2d 1434, 1442.

99. Former testimony

U.S. v. Zannino, C.A.1st, 1990, 895 F.2d 1, 6 (cross by others); Reardon v. Manson, C.A.2d, 1986, 806 F.2d 39, 43 (lab reports); U.S. v. Terrazas–Montano, C.A.8th, 1984, 747 F.2d 467, 469 (depositions).

100. Discrepant readings

U.S. v. Hans, C.A.6th, 1982, 684 F.2d 343, 346 (Roberts only requires unavailability if the hearsay rule employed requires this).

101. Reviews approved

Note, Constitutional Law—Right of Confrontation—Admission of Evidence of Unavailable Declarant's Preliminary Hearing Testimony Does Not Violate a Defendant's Right of Confrontation Guarantees by the Sixth Amendment when the Testimony was Subject to Questioning Equivalent to Significant Cross–Examination, 1980, 59 U.Det.J.Urb.L. 127; Note, Balancing the Right to Confrontation with the Admission Into Evidence of Preliminary Hearing Testimony, 1980, 10 Cap.U.L.Rev. 365.

§ 6368

1. "Me Decade uneventful"

See § 6367.

2. In any comparable period

Compare §§ 6362–6367 with §§ 6368–6370.

3. Street case

1985, 105 S.Ct. 2078, 471 U.S. 409, 85 L.Ed.2d 425.

and that his confession was coerced.[4] According to him, the police interrogator read him the confession of his alleged accomplice and "directed him to say the same thing."[5] The interrogator took the stand and denied doing any such thing.[6]

In order to "corroborate" the interrogator's denial, the prosecution was allowed to introduce into evidence the confession of the accomplice—which was far more incriminating to the defendant than his own.[7] However, the confession of the accomplice did not have certain details about the killing that were reflected in defendant's confession.[8] In his closing argument, the prosecutor made much of these discrepancies in rebutting the claimed coercion.[9] The trial court gave the jury a somewhat cursory limiting instruction:

> "The Court has allowed an alleged confession of or statement by [defendant's accomplice] to be read by a witness. I instruct you that such can be considered by you for rebutable [sic] purposes only, and you are not to consider the truthfulness of the statement in any way whatsoever."[10]

The Tennessee Court of Appeals found this to be a violation of the defendant's right of confrontation.[11]

In reversing, Chief Justice Burger's opinion for the Court notes that all of the Court's hearsay-confrontation cases dealt with the substantive use of evidence.[12]

> In this case, by contrast, the prosecutor did not introduce [the] out-of-court confession to prove the truth of [the confessor's] assertions. Thus, * * * [the] confession was not hearsay under traditional rules of evidence.[13]

4. Confession coerced

Id. at 2080, 471 U.S. at 411.

5. "Say same thing"

Ibid.

6. Denied doing.

Ibid.

7. Far more incriminating

Id. at 2080, 471 U.S. at 411–412.

8. More details

Ibid.

9. Prosecutor made much

Id. at 2081, 471 U.S. at 412.

10. "In any way whatsoever"

Ibid. A juror could well have understood this to mean that the statement must be assumed to be true since the jury was not "to consider the truthfulness of the statement."

11. Found violation

Id. at 2018, 471 U.S. at 412–413.

12. Dealt with substantive use

Id. at 2081, 471 U.S. at 413.

13. "Not hearsay"

Ibid.

So much for the Green Court's attempt to insist that confrontation and hearsay should not be equated.[14]

After explaining why the prosecution needed to use the confession—and conceding that it was not particularly compelling evidence of lack of coercion—Chief Justice Burger continued:[15]

> The nonhearsay aspect of [the] confession—not to prove what happened at the murder scene but to prove what happened when respondent confessed—raises no Confrontation Clause concerns. The Clause's fundamental role in protecting the right of cross-examination * * * was satisfied by [the interrogator's] presence on the stand.[16]

In short, when his confession is used this way, the accomplice was not a "witness against" the accused.[17] The Chief Justice comes close to saying this: "[i]n short, the State's rebuttal witness against respondent was not [the confessor] but [the interrogator]."[18]

However, because the jury could have used the confession for hearsay purposes, the case presents a Bruton problem.[19] The opinion concedes as much but attempts to distinguish Bruton. First, unlike the Bruton case, the confession of the accomplice was needed as evidence against the defendant; the Court even manages to turn the Confrontation Clause on its head as an argument for admitting evidence against the defendant.[20] Second, unlike Bruton, there were no alternatives; if the prosecution was going to use the evidence to rebut the coercion claim, it had to use the confession with its

14. Should not be equated

See § 6364.

15. Not compelling

Id. at 2081 n. 5, 471 U.S. at 414 n. 5.

16. "Presence on the stand"

Id. at 2081–2082, 471 U.S. at 414.

17. Not "witness against"

That is, even if the accomplice intended to "accuse" the defendant of the crime—which seems doubtful—the prosecution did not use it as an accusation.

18. "Rebuttal witness against"

Id. at 2082, 471 U.S. at 414.

19. Bruton problem

See § 6362.

20. Turn on its head

The Court says that without the defendant's confession, the jury would have been "impeded" and "handicapped" in evaluating the truth of defendant's testimony—"a result * * * at odds with the Confrontation Clause's very mission—to advance the 'accuracy of the truth-determining process in criminal trials." Id. at 2082, 471 U.S. at 415. Notice how this passage, where the Court is not concerned with cross-examination, sounds much more as if confrontation is an aspect of trial by jury. Otherwise, it would seem odd for defendant to have a "right" that can be used to harm him.

incriminating possibilities.[21] Third, well, actually there is an alternative, but the Court does not like it. The interrogator could have simply testified to the differences between the defendant's confession and that of the accomplice without introducing the whole confession—a procedure that resembles the redaction remedy in Bruton.[22] Chief Justice Burger's rather lame response is that this is an option, but not one that is constitutionally required.[23]

Finally, making explicit what was implicit in his holding that the non-hearsay use of statements is not within the scope of the Confrontation Clause, the Chief Justice rejects the attempt to apply Roberts to the case; the State was not required to call the accomplice to the stand to prove his unavailability.[24] In the unlikely event that cross-examination of the accomplice would have been helpful to defendant in rebutting the non-hearsay use of the confession, he could call the accomplice himself.[25]

Street can be seen as another step down the road that the Court once said it would never take; that is, the constitutionalization of the hearsay rule.[26] As such, it was consistent with Roberts.[27] However, it does represent a significant departure from Bruton, not merely in its application to the facts, but doctrinally; contra Bruton, we are now told that the "assumption that jurors are able to follow the court's instructions" fully applies when rights guaranteed by the Confrontation Clause are at issue.[28]

The Court's next case, U.S. v. Inadi, represents a remarkable turnabout.[29] Inadi was a prosecution for conspiring to manufacture

21. Had to use

Id. at 2082, 471 U.S. at 2082.

22. Resembles redaction

Id. at 2082–2083, 471 U.S. at 416. For discussion of redaction, see vol. 21, § 5064, pp. 321–322.

23. Constitutionally required

Id. at 2082–2083, 471 U.S. at 416. The logic seems circular; the reason for considering alternatives is to decide what the constitution requires.

24. Not required to call

Id. at 2083, 471 U.S. at 416.

25. Call himself

Ibid. Shifting the burden to the defendant to call the witnesses for cross-examination became popular in this period. See discussion of Inadi at note 56, below.

26. Constitutionalization

See §§ 6364, 6365.

27. Consistent with Roberts

See § 6367.

28. "Assumption applies"

Id. at 2082 N. 6, 471 U.S. at 415 n. 6.

29. Inadi case

1986, 106 S.Ct. 1121, 475 U.S. 387, 89 L.Ed.2d 390.

and distribute drugs in which the "linchpin" of the government's case was a set of wiretapped conversations among the coconspirators.[30] The fact that the evidence was in the form of tape-recording deserves emphasis because tapes are the modern counterpart of affidavits and depositions; that is, they are a means of bringing the declarant's exact words before the jury without the use of a witness.[31]

At trial, the court held that the tapes were admissible under the coconspirators exemption from the hearsay rule, but when defendant objected on confrontation grounds, the court conditioned its ruling on the government's calling one of the conspirators to establish unavailability under the first prong of Roberts.[32] The prosecution subpoenaed the witness, but he failed to appear at trial, allegedly because of "car trouble."[33] The trial judge retracted his earlier ruling, admitted the tapes, and the defendant was convicted.[34] The court of appeals reversed, holding that Roberts applied and that the failure to prove that the witness was unavailable violated defendant's right of confrontation.[35]

Notice how this case might have been disposed of by relying on Street. Since, as we all learned in criminal law, "conspiracy is a contract to commit a crime" and many of the acts of the conspiracy are words, use of those words to prove the crime is not hearsay; in the jargon of the classroom, the words are "legally operative conduct"—sometimes called "verbal acts."[36] Indeed, the coconspira-

---

30. "Linchpin"

The Supreme Court's opinion is thin on the facts of the case; the importance of the evidence is laid out in U.S. v. Inadi, C.A.3rd, 1984, 748 F.2d 812, 815 ("linchpin").

31. Without witness

This is significant for at least two reasons. First, one of the objections to lack of confrontation was that it put an "intermediary" between the trier and the accuser—the witness who relates the hearsay. See vol. 30, § 6343, pp. 284–288. Second, Mattox claimed that one of the motivations for the Confrontation Clause was to do away with the inquisitorial trial and its use of affidavits and depositions. See § 6357, text at notecall 478.

32. Conditioned on calling

Id. at 1124, 475 U.S. at 390.

33. "Car trouble"

Ibid. The Court of Appeals has a somewhat more sordid tale to tell, suggesting that the prosecutors were being something less than forthright in accounting for his absence. U.S. v. Inadi, C.A.3d, 1984, 748 F.2d 812, 819–820.

34. Convicted

Id. at 1124, 475 U.S. at 391.

35. Violated right

Ibid.

36. "Verbal acts"

See 2 Graham, Handbook of Federal Evidence, 4th ed. 1996, p. 208.

tors exception apparently developed out of a misunderstanding of this elemental point; no one claims that declarations among thieves are particularly reliable.[37] Of course, not every utterance relevant to prove a conspiracy fits within this nonhearsay analysis and, even of that which does, there is the danger that the jury will use it for a hearsay purpose.[38] But this is where Street comes in; we can deal with these problematic statements under Bruton.[39] The Court's opinion comes close to recognizing that it might have reversed by using Street.[40] The only problem with that approach is that it would not require the Court to dismantle Roberts—which seems to be what it wanted to do.

Justice Powell begins his opinion for the Court by noting that the court of appeals relied on Roberts in requiring the prosecution to prove unavailability as a prerequisite for the use of the tapes.[41]

> Roberts, however, does not stand for such a wholesale revision of the law of evidence, nor does it support such a broad interpretation of the Confrontation Clause. Roberts itself disclaimed any intention of proposing a general answer to the many difficult questions arising out of the relationship between the Confrontation Clause and hearsay.[42]

After milking Justice Blackmun's self-effacing statements in Roberts for about all they are worth, Justice Powell continues:[43]

> * * * Roberts should not be read as an abstract answer to all questions not presented in that case, but rather as a resolution of

37. No one claims "reliable"

Id. at 1131–1132, 475 U.S. at 405–407 (Marshall, J., dissenting)

38. Use for hearsay purpose

Some coconspirator hearsay comes in to show its effect on the other members of the conspiracy and the statements of each member can come in against them as admissions—as was done in Inadi. U.S. v. Inadi, C.A.3d, 1984, 748 F.2d 812, 815.

39. Under Bruton

See above, text at notecall 19.

40. Recognizing

"In addition to the reasons mentioned in the text why an unavailability rule would be of little value, many co-conspirator statements are not introduced to prove the truth of the matter as-

serted and thus do not come within the traditional definition of hearsay * * * Thus, some of the out-of-court statements in this case presumably could be admitted without implicating the Confrontation Clause." Id. at 1128 n. 12, 475 U.S. at 399 note 12. The footnote goes on to show that some of the evidence in the case came in "as background for the conspiracy or to explain the significance of certain events."

41. Relied on Roberts

Id. at 1125, 475 U.S. at 392.

42. "Roberts disclaimed"

Ibid.

43. Milking statements

Id. at 1125, 475 U.S. at 392.

the issue the Court said it was examining: "the constitutional propriety of the introduction of evidence of the preliminary hearing testimony of a witness not produced at the defendant's subsequent state criminal trial.[44]

In other words, the language that most lower courts have thought established a "test" for judging the admissibility of hearsay over a confrontation objection is nothing but dicta.[45]

What, then, was the holding in Roberts?

The Confrontation Clause analysis in Roberts focuses on those factors that come into play when the prosecution seeks to admit testimony from a prior judicial proceeding in place of live testimony at trial.[46]

Given that most of the cases that the Roberts opinion drew on for the policy of the Confrontation Clause were in fact cases involving former testimony, Justice Powell is able to read them as narrowly as he wants to read Roberts to support his claim.[47] He concludes that

Roberts cannot fairly be read to stand for the radical proposition that no out-of-court statement can be introduced by the government without a showing that the declarant is unavailable.[48]

Despite his trashing of Roberts, this last sentence can be read, together with an earlier disclaimer that the issue of reliability of the hearsay is not before the Court, as saying that it is only the first prong of Roberts that has been demolished.[49] This seems to be the way the dissenters read the majority opinion.[50]

Having shown that Roberts did not establish an unavailability requirement for coconspirator hearsay, Justice Powell turns to the question of whether the Court should now impose such a requirement. He begins by pointing out that former testimony is a pale imitation of live testimony with contemporaneous cross-examina-

---

44. "Not abstract answer"

Id. at 1125, 475 U.S. at 392–393.

45. Nothing but dicta

For the reading of Roberts by the lower courts, see § 6367. Justice Powell carefully avoids quoting the language in Roberts that led those courts to conclude that Roberts was not limited to former testimony.

46. "In place of live testimony"

Id. at 1125, 475 U.S. at 393.

47. Read narrowly

Id. at 1125–1126, 475 U.S. at 393–395.

48. "Radical proposition"

Id. at 1126, 475 U.S. at 394.

49. Only first prong demolished

Id. at 1124 n. 3, 475 U.S. at 391 n. 3.

50. Dissenters read

Id. at 1129 n.1, 475 U.S. at 401 n. 1.

tion, twisting the words of one of the writers into a suggestion that, in this context, the Confrontation Clause is sort of a constitutional "best evidence rule."[51] But, Justice Powell wants to argue, coconspirator statements are different.

> Because they are made while the conspiracy is in progress, such statements provide evidence of the conspiracy's context that cannot be replicated, even if the declarant testifies to the same matters in court. When the government—as here—offers the statement of one drug dealer to another in furtherance of an illegal conspiracy, the statement will often derive its significance from the circumstances in which it was made. Conspirators are likely to speak differently when talking to each other in furtherance of their illegal aims than when testifying on the witness stand. Even when the declarant takes the stand, his in court testimony will seldom reproduce a significant portion of the evidentiary values of his statements during the course of the conspiracy.[52]

Notice several things about this passage. First, the opinion assumes that what was important about the statement is not the information conveyed but the way in which it is uttered. This sounds very much as if the statement is not hearsay because it is not offered for the information conveyed. Second, to the extent that the declarant cannot produce the extra-informational content of the communication through testimony, the same thing is true of some third party who testifies about the contents of a coconspirator confab. Hence, it sounds as if Justice Powell is thinking of taped statements, not testimony about the contents of the statements.[53]

51. "Best evidence rule"

Id. at 1126, 475 U.S. at 394–395. The passage cited from Graham, The Right of Confrontation and the Hearsay Rule: Sir Walter Raleigh Loses Another One, 1972, 8 Crim.L.Bull. 99, 143 is not arguing that the Confrontation Clause is a rule of "preference" like the best-evidence rule. Rather, it is dealing with the case where confrontation has been excused and supposes a case in which the prosecution could prove the hearsay either by a transcript or by calling a witness to testify to what was said in the prior hearing, as was done in Green, and asks, must the prosecutor prove the testimony by a transcript? That is a much different question than the one Justice Powell

is addressing—namely, what does it take to "satisfy" the defendant's right of confrontation?

52. "Seldom produce"

Id. at 1126, 475 U.S. at 395.

53. Taped statements

"[C]oconspirator statements derive much of their value from the fact that they were made in a context very different from trial, and therefore are usually irreplaceable as substantive evidence." Id. 1126, 475 U.S. at 395–396. To the extent that this is true, it is true whether or not the prosecution calls the declarant to repeat his statement or some third person to relate what she heard. It is only the taped

After explaining why the declarant is a particularly bad source of testimony about coconspirator statements, Justice Powell then turns to a sort of "cost-benefit analysis" of an unavailability requirement.[54] First, the unavailability rule will exclude no evidence because the prosecution will produce available declarants or prove their unavailability and in either event the statements will be admissible.[55] Second, if the defendant really thinks cross-examination will do him any good, he can subpoena the declarant himself.[56] Finally, "an unavailability rule" places a significant practical burden on the prosecution.[57] Finally, Justice Powell tosses in Dutton to support his conclusion that the Confrontation Clause does not impose an unavailability requirement except in cases of former testimony.[58]

Justice Marshall, joined by Justice Brennan dissented, not only from the Court's reading of Roberts, but also from its refusal to impose limits on the use of unreliable coconspirator statements and for shifting the burden of producing declarants from the prosecution to the defense.[59] The two dissenting Justices were, however, about to give the wheel another spin.

Just a few weeks after being left for dead, Roberts seemed to come back to life in Lee v. Illinois.[60] Lee was a double-murder case with two perpetrators, both of whom confessed.[61] However, the confession of the codefendant was more harmful than defendant's

---

statement that is "irreplaceable" by testimony. As between the declarant and some third person relating what was said, what the declarant has over the third person is that he knows what was meant by ambiguous statements; normally the third person who relates the statements of co-conspirators is no less likely to be biased than the declarant since he is likely to be a police informer or a turncoat conspirator.

54. "Cost benefit"

This is presumably the passage the dissent has in mind when it accuses the majority of "subordinating" the values of the Sixth Amendment to "prosecutorial efficiency." Id. at 1129, 475 U.S. at 401.

55. In either event admissible

Id. at 1127, 475 U.S. at 396.

56. Subpoena himself

Id. at 1127, 475 U.S. at 397.

57. Burden on prosecution

Id. at 1128, 475 U.S. at 399.

58. Tosses in Dutton

Id. at 1129, 475 U.S. at 400.

59. Shifting burden

Id. at 1129–1134, 475 U.S. at 401–411.

60. Lee case

1986, 106 S.Ct. 2056, 476 U.S. 530, 90 L.Ed.2d 514.

61. Both confessed

Id. at 2058–2059, 476 U.S. at 532–535.

was because it was the only evidence of premeditation.[62] At a joint trial before a judge sitting without a jury, both confessions were admitted and, in explaining his decision to find the defendant guilty of murder, the judge explicitly relied on the contents of the code-fendant's confession.[63] The Illinois court affirmed in reliance on Bruton, but the state seems to have conceded this was an error because Bruton did not involve the substantive use of the confession.[64]

In the Supreme Court, the state argued that the confession of the codefendant satisfied the Roberts test.[65] The state seems to have assumed that Roberts was still good law after Inadi, an assumption that neither the majority nor the dissent appears to question.[66] However, the majority opinion, by Justice Brennan, avoids a head-on collision with Inadi, stating

> [w]e need not address the question of the [co-defendant's] availability, for we hold that [his] statement, as the confession of an accomplice was presumptively unreliable and that it did not bear sufficient "indicia of reliability" to overcome that presumption.[67]

Now, if in fact the majority were following Roberts, the first question would be whether or not the confession fell within a "firmly rooted" hearsay exception; only if it did not would the confession be presumed to be unreliable and the search for "indicia of reliability" be required.[68]

But the Brennan opinion does not follow the Roberts analysis.[69] Instead, he goes back to Pointer, collects some "golden oldies" from

62. More harmful

Id. at 2059, 476 U.S. at 535.

63. Relied on contents

Id. at 2060–2061, 476 U.S. at 538. The majority notes that the prosecution "invited" the trial court to this impropriety, but since no claim was made regarding this "misconduct," the Court passes over it. Id. at 2060 n.3, 476 U.S. at 537 n.3.

64. Conceded error

Id. at 2061, 476 U.S. at 539. In any event, the majority says that "this is not strictly speaking a Bruton case because we are not here concerned with the effectiveness of a limiting instruction in preventing spillover prejudice to a defendant when his co-defendant's confession is admitted

against the codefendant in a joint trial." Id. at 2063, 476 U.S. at 542.

65. Satisfied Roberts

Id. at 2061, 476 U.S. at 539.

66. Neither seems to question

Indeed, Justice Blackmun in dissent applies Roberts' analysis. See below, text at notecall 85.

67. "Need not address"

Id. at 2061, 476 U.S. at 539.

68. Search for "indicia"

See § 6367, above.

69. Does not follow

Compare the dissent, Id. at 2066–2070, 476 U.S. at 549–557.

the Confrontation Hall of Fame, and attempts to revive a broader view of the Confrontation Clause more in keeping with the Founders' holistic vision.[70]

> On one level, the right to confront and cross-examine adverse witnesses contributes to the establishment of a system of criminal justice in which the perception as well as the reality of fairness prevails. To foster such a system, the Constitution provides certain safeguards to promote to the greatest possible degree society's interest in having the accused and accuser engage in an open and even contest in a public trial. The Confrontation Clause advances these goals by ensuring that convictions will not be based on the charges of unseen and unknown—and hence unchallengeable— individuals.[71]

If Justice Brennan had linked confrontation to trial by jury, as the Founders did, Lee would have raised the question of whether and how confrontation can apply to the sort of trial the Founders never imagined—a joint trial before a bored judge by overworked lawyers in a mass-production urban-criminal-justice system.[72]

Perhaps sensing the unreality of this rhetoric, Justice Brennan returns to the narrow, instrumental version of confrontation through this telling transition: "But the confrontation guarantee serves not only symbolic goals."[73] If the most avid defender of the Bill of Rights on the Court sees party autonomy, the separation of functions, and a participatory system of criminal justice as only "symbolic goals," it is difficult to be too critical of others on the Court who are even more willing to grease the slide to an increasingly inquisitorial system.[74]

70. "Golden oldies"

That is, cases in which the Confrontation Clause was applied more expansively. Id. at 2061–2062, 476 U.S. at 539–540.

71. "Unseen, unchallengeable"

Id. at 2062, 476 U.S. at 540.

72. Mass production

This seems to be the only explanation for the willingness of a lawyer to allow his client to go to a joint trial before a judge, knowing that the codefendant's confession would be highly damaging to his client.

Notice that removing the jury removes some of the features of the adversary system as the Founders saw it; e.g., there is no separation of functions— the judge who is going to decide the case will see unconfronted hearsay in her role as adjudicator of admissibility. In many urban courts, the trial judges routinely have access to the prosecutor's file, with the defendant's record, police reports, and other unconfronted evidence.

73. "Symbolic goals"

Id. at 2062, 476 U.S. at 540.

74. Inquisitorial system

Of course, one never knows how much of the majority opinion represents Brennan's views and how much repre-

After a ritual genuflection before Green, Justice Brennan proceeds to line up the cases in support of the proposition

> that [the] truthfinding functions of the Confrontation Clause is uniquely threatened when the accomplice's confession is sought to be introduced against a criminal defendant without the benefit of cross-examination.[75]

Douglas, Bruton, and the Harlan concurrence in Green are enlisted in this campaign.[76]

Finally, Justice Brennan turns to Roberts to see if the confession "bears sufficient 'indicia of reliability' to rebut the presumption of unreliability that attaches to codefendants' confessions * * *."[77] Of course, the Roberts "indicia" inquiry only comes after a determination that the statement does not fall within a "firmly rooted" hearsay exception; here the state apparently argued that the confession was a declaration against interest.[78] The majority opinion disposes of this argument in a footnote:

> [w]e reject [the state's] categorization of the hearsay involved in this case as a simple "declaration against penal interest." That concert defines too large a class for meaningful Confrontation analysis. We decide this case as involving a confession by an accomplice which incriminates a criminal defendant.[79]

So much for the pretense that Roberts is still good law.[80]

---

sents the need to hold together a somewhat disparate majority. In addition to Brennan, the majority included White, Marshall, Stevens, and O'Connor.

75. "Uniquely threatened"

Id. at 1062, 476 U.S. at 541.

76. Enlisted in support

Id. at 2062–2063, 476 U.S. at 541–542. Bruton and Douglas are described in § 6357, above, and the Harlan concurrence in § 6358.

77. "Presumption that attaches"

Id. at 2063, 476 U.S. at 543.

78. Declaration against interest

This would have raised some interesting questions about the meaning of "firmly rooted." Is the exception "firmly rooted" when, though it has existed for more than a century, it has only been widely applied to declarations against penal interest in the last few decades? Is it "firmly rooted" when the authorities are badly divided on the question at issue here—the "he and I did it" declaration offered against "he"? See Williamson v. U.S., 1994, 114 S.Ct. 2431, 512 U.S. 594, 129 L.Ed.2d 476.

79. "Too large a class"

Id. at 2064 n. 5, 476 U.S. at 544 n. 5.

80. Robert still good

One cannot infer that the majority thought it was following Roberts from its use of the "indicia or reliability" test because that concept originated in Dutton, a case that the majority has earlier said was relevant authority. Id. at 2063, 476 U.S. at 542.

Turning to the "indicia" inquiry, since the presumption is against the state, all the majority has to do is shoot down the arguments tossed up by the state; that the circumstances surrounding the confession show the accomplice told the truth, that the interlocking of the two confessions confirms reliability, and that the failure of the defense to cross-examine the accomplice at a suppression hearing shows they believed it was truthful.[81] The majority opinion disposes of each of these without adding much to our understanding of the meaning of "indicia of reliability."[82]

Finding no "indicia of reliability," the majority concludes

> that on the record before us, there is no occasion to depart from the time honored teaching that a codefendant's confession inculpating the accused is inherently unreliable, and that convictions supported by such evidence violate the constitutional right of confrontation.[83]

The Court then remands the case to the Illinois courts for a determination of whether or not the error was "harmless."[84]

Ironically, Justice Blackmun's dissent applying Roberts is joined by three of those who had just demolished Roberts in Inadi.[85] Justice Blackmun argues that the accomplice is "unavailable" because of his ability to assert the privilege against self-incrimination, that the state need not provide inducements for him to waive or grant him immunity to establish "unavailability," that his statement was a declaration against interest—a "firmly rooted" exception—and that, in any event, the confession bore sufficient "indicia of reliability" to justify admission.[86] But for a single vote, the Blackmun opinion would have resolved a number of important confrontation issues not addressed by the majority opinion.[87]

81. Shoot down arguments

Id. at 2064–2065, 476 U.S. at 544–546.

82. Adding to understanding

However, the Court's rejection of the argument that opportunity to cross-examine at a suppression hearing rebutted the presumption of unreliability may have ramifications for the interpretation of Green. Id. at 2065 n. 6, 476 U.S. at 546 n. 6.

83. "Convictions violate"

Id. at 2065, 476 U.S. at 546.

84. Remands

Id. at 2065, 476 U.S. at 547.

85. Those who demolished

That is, the Chief Justice and Justices Rehnquist and Powell.

86. Sufficient indicia

Id. at 2066–2070, 476 U.S. at 547–557.

87. Important issues

E.g., the issues raised in footnote 78, above. See id. at 2068 n. 4, 2068–2069, 474 U.S. at 552–553 n. 4, 552–554.

As we have previously indicated, most lower courts did not read Inadi as overruling Roberts.[88] Some have extended the notion that "unavailability" is not required for co-conspirator hearsay to other hearsay exceptions that did not traditionally require unavailability.[89] One court has thought the decision applied even when the coconspirator's statements were admitted under some other exceptions.[90] Lee has been given an even narrower reading.[91]

§ 6369. ____; Bourjaily, Owens, and Fusion

The Roberts "approach" seemed to revive in Bourjaily v. United States, a prosecution for possession of and conspiracy to distribute cocaine.[1] At trial the government introduced evidence of a conversation between the defendant's source and a government agent who was their supplier.[2] However, from the Court's opinion it is unclear whether the evidence was or was not a tape recording as in Inadi—a clear indication that this made no difference to the majority.[3] The Court of Appeals affirmed defendant's conviction, finding no confrontation violation in the use of the hearsay.[4]

After disposing of the evidentiary issues raised, Chief Justice Rehnquist turned to the holding of the Court of Appeals that "the requirements of admission under [the Evidence Rules] are identical to the requirements of the Confrontation Clause."[5] After repeating

88. Read as overruling

See § 6367.

89. Other exceptions

Manocchio v. Moran, C.A.1st, 1990, 919 F.2d 770, 774–775 (business records, autopsy report); Martinez v. Sullivan, C.A.10th, 1989, 881 F.2d 921, 929 (reading Inadi as limited to co-conspirators exemption, requiring unavailability for excited utterance).

90. Admitted under other

U.S. v. Patterson, C.A.9th, 1987, 819 F.2d 1495, 1504 (co-conspirator's statement not in furtherance of conspiracy but admitted as a declaration against interest; Inadi applies).

91. Lee reading

U.S. v. Flores, C.A.5th, 985 F.2d 770, 776 n. 13 (Lee means exception for declarations against interest cannot be "firmly rooted"); U.S. v. Guinan,

C.A.7th, 1988, 836 F.2d 350, 358 n. 14 (Lee does not require higher standard for indicia of reliability for non-accomplice hearsay).

§ 6369

1. Bourjaily case

1987, 107 S.Ct. 2775, 483 U.S. 171, 97 L.Ed.2d 144.

2. Government supplier

Id. 2778, 483 U.S. at 173–174.

3. Inadi tape recording

See § 6368.

4. No violation

Id. at 2778, 483 U.S. at 174.

5. "Requirements identical"

Id. at 2782, 483 U.S. at 192.

the claim in Roberts that literal application of the Confrontation Clause was both "unintended and too extreme," the opinion restates the "preference" theory of confrontation as a balancing exercise:[6]

> * * * we have attempted to harmonize the goal of the Clause—placing limits on the kind of evidence that may be received against a defendant—with a societal interest in accurate fact-finding, which may require consideration of out-of-court statements.[7]

Notice how accurate factfinding, which only a few opinions ago was the purpose of confrontation, now has become its enemy.[8]

Having placed confrontation at odds with truth as it will be found in hearsay, the opinion continues.

> To accommodate these competing interests, the Court has, as a general matter only, required the prosecution to demonstrate both the unavailability of the declarant and the "indicia of reliability" surrounding the out-of-court declaration.[9]

Having thus revived Roberts, at least for the moment, Justice Rehnquist says that in Inadi

> we held that the first of these two generalized inquiries, unavailability, was not required when the hearsay statement is the out-of-court declaration of a co-conspirator. Today, we conclude that the second inquiry, independent indicia of reliability, is also not mandated by the Constitution.[10]

Thus having demolished Roberts in order to avoid its first prong, the Court now revives it to escape the second.[11] Here the Chief Justice foreshadows the way in which the lower courts began to view the Court's confrontation jurisprudence—not as articulating a doctrinal structure but as providing a smorgasbord of doctrine from which one can select according to one's tastes and needs of the

---

6. "Too extreme"
Ibid.

7. "Societal interest"
Ibid.

8. Now its enemy
Recall that in the earlier cases confrontation and cross-examination were so instrumental to reliability that the latter could be substituted for them; now somehow reliability is a value that can trump confrontation.

9. "Indicia surrounding"
Ibid.

10. "Also not mandated"
Ibid.

11. Escape the second
But in the process he seems to show that Inadi destroyed the first prong only with respect to the coconspirators exception.

moment.[12]

To be sure, the Rehnquist opinion is quick to point out that Roberts only provided "a general approach," not a test.[13] But without pausing to explain why the "approach" should be followed here when it was trashed in Inadi, the Chief Justice quickly concludes that

> [w]e think that the co-conspirator exception to the hearsay rule is firmly enough rooted in our jurisprudence that, under this Court's holding in Roberts, a court need not independently inquire into the reliability of such statements.[14]

Having changed what Inadi thought was only "dicta" in Roberts to a "holding," the Chief Justice parenthetically invokes Dutton to explain that a "reliability inquiry [is] required where [the] evidentiary rule deviates from the common-law."[15]

Apparently the Chief Justice reads "firmly rooted" as largely a question of historical antiquity.[16]

> The admissibility of co-conspirators' statements was first established in this Court over a century and a half ago * * * and the Court has repeatedly reaffirmed the exception as accepted practice. * * * We think that these cases demonstrate that co-conspirators' statements * * * have a long tradition of being outside the compass of the general hearsay rule.[17]

This is significant because in his dissent, Justice Blackmun—the creator of the "firmly rooted" concept—argues that "firmly rooted" means that "through experience in its use, the exception has proved to promote the 'accuracy of the factfinding process'".[18]

12. Smorgasbord

This does not seem much like "the common law method" that was romanticized in Roberts. See § 6367.

13. Only "general approach"

Id. at 2782, 483 U.S. at 182.

14. "Need not inquire"

Id. at 2782, 483 U.S. at 183.

15. "Deviates from common law"

Ibid. This raises the perplexing question of just what constitutes "the common law"; think of the business-records exception, which is almost entirely a creature of statute—and differing statutes at that.

16. Historical antiquity

An alternative, or supplement, would be to ask how widely the exception has been adopted. After the codification of the rules of evidence in the last few decades, the most discrepant rules are likely to be the most ancient; consider the "voucher rule" the Court faced in Chambers. See § 6366.

17. "Long tradition"

Id. at 2783, 483 U.S. at 183.

18. "Proved to promote"

Id. at 2791, 483 U.S. at 200.

The Chief Justice has another illuminating exchange with the dissent over the meaning of "firmly rooted." The dissent charges that the exception that the Court has now approved is not the one that is "firmly rooted" because, in another portion of its opinion, the majority has held that under Evidence Rule 104 the preliminary facts of the exception no longer must be proved by evidence other than coconspirator declarations.[19] The Chief Justice replies in a footnote.

> We reject any suggestion that by abolishing the bootstrapping rule, the Federal Rules of Evidence have changed the co-conspirator hearsay exception such that it is no longer "firmly rooted" in our legal tradition. The bootstrapping rule relates only to the method of proof that the exception has been satisfied. It does not change any element of the co-conspirator exception, which has remained substantively unchanged since its adoption in this country.[20]

This is clear enough; it is only through a change in one of its elements that a hearsay exception ceases to be "firmly rooted."[21] This is amusing because in one of the cases the Chief Justice has creatively read to uphold the constitutionality of the coconspirator exception, the coconspirator in question was dead—i.e., unavailable; hence, whatever "roots" may be found in Delaney, they do not seem to run to the exception the Supreme Court has approved in Inadi.[22]

However, the meaning of "firmly rooted" would soon appear less momentous because the year after reviving Roberts, the Supreme Court abandoned it again in U.S. v. Owens.[23] Owens was charged with assault to commit murder in connection with a brutal assault on a prison counselor.[24] During a first interview with the

19. Not the same

Id. at 2791–2792, 483 U.S. at 200–201.

20. "Not change any element"

Id. at 2783 n. 5, 483 U.S. at 184 n. 4.

21. Ceases to be firmly rooted

Notice that this does not seem to differentiate among the various ways in which an element might be altered—abolished completely or modified to either weaken or strengthen the element. For example, the declaration-against-interest exception has been altered to include penal interest as well as pecuniary interest—and social interest as well in a few states.

22. Delaney

For the Chief Justice's treatment of Delaney, see id. at 2783, 483 U.S. at 183. Compare Delaney v. U.S., 1924, 44 S.Ct. 206, 207, 263 U.S. 586, 590, 68 L.Ed. 462, discussed in § 6353, text at notecall 640.

23. Owens case

1988, 108 S.Ct. 838, 484 U.S. 554, 98 L.Ed.2d 951.

24. Brutal assault

Id. at 841, 484 U.S. at 556.

F.B.I., the victim was unable to identify his attacker—ostensibly as the result of injuries suffered in the attack.[25] However, in a second interview, the victim not only identified defendant as his attacker, but picked him out from a photo spread.[26]

At the time of trial, the victim's memory was once again "severely impaired"; he could no longer recall seeing his attacker, though he could recall identifying the defendant in his second F.B.I. interview.[27] The trial court admitted this prior identification under the hearsay exemption in Evidence Rule 801(d)(1)(C).[28] A divided court of appeals found this a violation of the right of confrontation.[29]

Now, if the Roberts analysis were followed, the Court would first have to ask if the lack of memory made the victim "unavailable" within the meaning of Barber.[30] If so, the Court would then ask whether the exception for prior identification is "firmly rooted."[31] If not, then the prosecution would have to show particularized guarantees of trustworthiness.[32] However, the Court does not follow Roberts.[33] Instead, Justice Scalia approaches the issue from a most oblique angle.

25. Unable to identify
Ibid.

26. Photo spread
Ibid.

27. Recall identifying
Ibid.

28. Court admitted
Ibid.

29. Found violation
Id. at 841, 484 U.S. at 556–557.

30. Made "unavailable"
This would require some showing that the lack of memory was likely to persist so that a continuance would not be a reasonable method of making the witness available.

31. "Firmly rooted"
This is debatable; it seems to have emerged as a separate exception only comparatively recently.

32. "Particularized"
This also seems questionable, given the vacillations in the witness's ability to recall and the suggestion during cross-examination that he may also have identified someone else as his assailant.

33. Does not follow
Nor does the Court consider developing the notion expressed in Reynolds, § 6356, text at notecall 770, that the defendant is estopped to object to lack of confrontation if he has made the declarant unavailable. This requires the Court to find, or assume, that the defendant is guilty before he has been convicted, but this is just what the Court permits in Inadi.

He begins by going back to Mattox to revive the notion that the right of confrontation secures "an adequate opportunity to cross-examine adverse witnesses."[34] He then jumps to Green, not for its holding but for the issue the Court did not decide.[35] He then detours through two cases that do not involve the use of hearsay but rather involved limitations on the cross-examination of witnesses who appear and confront the defendant.[36] He then expresses the view that a quotation from one of these cases answers the question in Owens: "the Confrontation Clause guarantees only an opportunity for effective cross-examination, not cross-examination that is effective in whatever way, and to whatever extent, the defense might wish."[37]

Justice Scalia then characterizes one of the prior cases where an expert expressed an opinion but claimed not to know the basis for that opinion as a case "when a witness testifies to his current belief but is unable to recollect the basis for that belief."[38] He sees no difference between that case and one in which "the witness's past belief is introduced and he is unable to recollect the basis for that belief."[39] The key here is the sleight-of-hand by which a present statement of opinion is equated with a past statement of fact under the muddy description that they are both "beliefs."[40]

After a long discussion of the possibilities for cross-examination in his hypothetical case about "beliefs," Justice Scalia returns to the present case.[41] He seems mystified by the notion that the majority of the court of appeals had expressed; that is, that the

34. "Adequate opportunity"
Id. at 841, 484 U.S. at 557.

35. Did not decide
Id. at 841–842, 484 U.S. at 557–558.

36. Limits on cross
Id. at 842, 484 U.S. at 558.

37. "Defense might wish"
Id. at 842, 484 U.S. at 559 (quoting Delaware v. Fensterer, 1985, 106 S.Ct. 292, 296, 474 U.S. 15, 22, 88 L.Ed.2d 15).

38. "Basis for belief"
Ibid.

39. "Past belief introduced"
Ibid.

40. Sleight-of-hand

One assumes that Justice Scalia understands why the law of evidence distinguishes between statements of past fact and statements of present opinion. The expert who testifies "I have this opinion but I don't know why" looks foolish. The ordinary witness who says "I forget why I said that" only exhibits ordinary human frailty—though in fact the claimed lack of memory may simply be an excuse for not taking responsibility for the statement.

41. Hypothetical cross
Id. at 842–843, 484 U.S. at 559–560.

Confrontation Clause requires "indicia of reliability" or "particularized guarantees of trustworthiness" when hearsay is introduced that does not fall within a "firmly rooted" hearsay exception.[42] For him, and the rest of the majority, Owens is governed by Green:

> We do not think such an inquiry is called for when a hearsay declarant is present at trial and subject to unrestricted cross-examination. In that situation, as the Court recognized in Green, the traditional protections of the oath, cross-examination and opportunity for the jury to observe the witness's demeanor satisfy the constitutional requirements.[43]

The Court seems to forget not only Roberts, but also that in Green the declarant was testifying in a preliminary hearing and that the Court had emphasized the difference between former testimony and other forms of hearsay in Inadi.[44]

An extravagant opinion deserves an extravagant holding—and this one gets one:

> We do not think that a constitutional line drawn by the Confrontation Clause falls between a forgetful witness's live testimony that he once believed this defendant to be the perpetrator of the crime, and the introduction of the witness's earlier statement to that effect.[45]

In other words, all the person who wishes to wound without taking responsibility for his words need do is say "I forgot."[46]

§ 6370. ____; The Child Abuse Cases; Coy, Wright, and White

Child abuse—whether sexual or physical—has long presented problems of both policy and proof.[1] However, in the middle of the

---

42. Need for indicia

Id. at 483, 484 U.S. at 560.

43. "Satisfy requirements"

Ibid.

44. Emphasis on former testimony

See § 6368.

45. "Earlier statement"

Id. at 843, 484 U.S. at 560.

46. "I forgot"

Compare, The White House Transcripts, Gold ed. 1976, p. 171:

"Haldeman: You can say you have forgotten, can't you?

Dean: Sure, but you are chancing a very high risk for a perjury situation

The President: But you can say I don't remember. You can say I don't recall. I can't give any answer to that that I can recall."

§ 6370

1. Problems of proof

The major policy problem is the appropriate role of criminal punishment in attempting to alleviate child abuse. That courts have been concerned about the evidentiary problem for some time may be seen in the excep-

1980s, this cause was paradoxically taken up by feminists, who put the problem on scholarly agendas and brought it to the attention of the press.[2] The press, perhaps overreacting to past practices of ignoring—even covering up—child sexual abuse, began to publicize a few notorious (and atypical) cases, producing a fear bordering on hysteria.[3] Responding to this "mini" version of The Red Scare, legislators adopted a number of statutory innovations to deal with the problem—including a number that altered the law of evidence to make it easier to prove sexual abuse of children.[4] Courts were caught up in the crusade to "do something" about the problem, responding with expansive interpretations of existing rules to ease the burden of the prosecution.[5]

The first case arising out of this frenzy of reform to reach the Supreme Court—Coy v. Iowa—did not involve the confrontation-hearsay question, but it did have implications for that question.[6]

tion for crimes against family members in the spousal and other family privileges. See vol. 25, § 5593.

2. Feminists

The paradox is that, while Feminist activism in this area can be seen as an attack on the patriarchal abuses of the family, it can also be seen as a retreat to "women's sphere"—the care and nurturing of children.

3. Hysteria

Readers who did not live through this period will find it hard to believe that even smiling at a passing child was enough to earn a scowl from parents. Several high-school athletic associations, in response to complaints about coaches patting football players on the behind when sending them into the game adopted, policies forbidding coaches from touching athletes—a ludicrous rule that could only have been seen as workable by someone who had never coached or been coached.

Like most of the media's "sixty-second hates," this one collapsed rather quickly, its demise hastened by several notorious cases of prosecutorial and journalistic misconduct symbolized by the McMartin case in Los Angeles.

4. Statutory innovations

See, e.g., Note, The Testimony of Child Victims in Sex Abuse Prosecutions: Two Legislative Innovations, 1985, 98 Harv.L.Rev. 806; Note, Sexually Abused Children: The Best Kept Legal Secret, 1986, 3 N.Y.L.S. Hum.Rts. Ann. 441.

5. Expansive

One of these was applying the statements for medical-diagnosis exception to children who were too young to be within the rationale of the rule: another was stretching the excited-utterance exception to statements long after the "excitement" could reasonably have been supposed to persist. These developments will be discussed in our analysis of those exceptions in subsequent volumes.

For one indicium of legal concern, see the concurring and dissenting opinions in Coy, cited at notes 28, 29, below.

6. Coy case

1988, 108 S.Ct. 2798, 487 U.S. 1012, 101 L.Ed.2d 857.

The Coy case is discussed also in vol. 2, § 415, and vol. 27, § 6101.

Coy was charged with molesting two 13–year-old neighbor girls who were spending the night in a backyard tent.[7] Pursuant to an Iowa child abuse reform statute, the trial court, rather than allow the witnesses to testify by closed-circuit television, elected to use a large screen placed between the defendant and the witness stand to protect the victims from defendant's gaze as they testified.[8] The Iowa courts rejected defendant's claim that this violated his right of confrontation.[9]

Justice Scalia, writing for the majority, begins his opinion with a dollop of history.[10] Though some of his historical references, which are scattered through the rest of the opinion, are designed to support his doctrinal arguments, they are far more significant as one of the few efforts in the history of the Court's jurisprudence to suggest values for the Confrontation Clause that go beyond the instrumental-statist values of the Progressive proceduralists.[11] And showing some "progress" from his opinion in Owens, Justice Scalia is here able to distinguish between the confrontation-hearsay problem and the problem of limits on cross-examination.[12]

Justice Scalia's opinion is also unique in looking to the language of the Sixth Amendment as a starting point for analysis.[13] "We have never doubted * * * that the Confrontation Clause guarantees the defendant a face-to-face meeting with the witnesses appearing before the trier of fact," he writes.[14] He pulls up dicta from the Court's prior opinions to support that claim.[15]

Not content to rely on the text of the Amendment and the Court's prior cases, Justice Scalia invokes values.

> The Sixth Amendment's guarantee of face-to-face encounter between witnesses and accused serves ends related both to appearances and to reality. This opinion is embellished with references to and quotations from antiquity in part to convey that there is

7. Night in tent

Id. at 2799, 487 U.S. at 1014.

8. Large screen

Ibid.

9. Rejected claims

Id. at 2799–2800, 487 U.S. at 1015.

10. Dollop of history

Id. at 2800, 487 U.S. at 1015.

11. Values of Progressives

See § 6358, text at notecall 840.

12. Distinguish

Id. at 2800, 487 U.S. at 1015. For his previous problems with the distinction, see § 6369.

13. Looking to language

Id. at 2800, 487 U.S. at 1016.

14. "Never doubted"

Id. at 2801, 487 U.S. at 1016.

15. Pulls dicta

Ibid.

something deep in human nature that regards face-to-face confrontation between accused and accuser as "essential to a fair trial in a criminal prosecution."[16]

After a long quotation from President Eisenhower's Code of Abilene speech, the opinion continues.[17]

> The phrase still persists, "Look me in the eye and say that." Given these human feelings of what is necessary for fairness, the right of confrontation "contributes to the establishment of a system of criminal justice in which the perception as well as the reality of fairness prevails."[18]

Like Justice Brennan in the passage from Lee he has just quoted, Justice Scalia seems to suppose that these confrontation values are simply "perceptions" or "appearances" rather than qualities that can be instantiated in procedure to give it moral value of its own rather than simply being instrumental to some other values.[19]

Perhaps uncomfortable with this excursion into the morality of means, Justice Scalia quickly turns to the more familiar instrumental form of justification.

> The perception that confrontation is essential to fairness has persisted over the centuries because there is much truth to it. A witness "may feel quite differently when he has to repeat his story looking at the man whom he will harm greatly by distorting or mistaking the facts. He can now understand what sort of human being that man is."[20]

In other words, it is not sufficient that a procedure is moral—"fair" as lawyers say—it must also lead to more "reliable fact-finding" and thereby legitimate the courts and the state.[21]

After further analysis of how physical confrontation, like cross-examination, can ensure "the integrity of the fact-finding process," Justice Scalia concludes with irony.

> The State can hardly gainsay the profound effect upon a witness of standing in the presence of the person the witness accuses since it

---

16. "Deep in human nature"

Id. at 2801, 487 U.S. at 1017.

17. Code of Abilene

Id. at 2801, 487 U.S. at 1017–1018. For more on the Eisenhower speech, see § 6354, text at notecall 880.

18. "Look me in the eye"

Id. at 2801–2802, 487 U.S. at 1018.

19. Instrumental

For more on the differences between instrumental and noninstrumental arguments, see vol. 23, § 5422.1 (Supp.).

20. "Sort of human being"

Id. at 2802, 487 U.S. at 1019.

21. Legitimate state

Instrumental arguments often conceal their ultimate values.

is the very phenomenon it relies upon to establish the potential "trauma" that allegedly justified the extraordinary procedure in the present case. That face-to-face presence may, unfortunately, upset the truthful rape victim or abused child: but by the same token it may confound and undo the false accuser, or reveal the child coached by a malevolent adult. It is a truism that constitutional protections have costs.[22]

One could only wish the last sentence could be taken into account when the "costs" are borne by the taxpayers rather than by the witnesses.[23]

After all this, Justice Scalia has little difficulty concluding that "the right to confrontation was in fact violated in this case."[24] In responding to the prosecution argument that the need to protect the victims of child abuse must be "balanced" against the rights of the defendant, Justice Scalia first suggests that the "literal right" of confrontation requires more to offset it than the implied right to exclude unreliable hearsay, but then decides the question should be left for "another day."[25] However, perhaps responding to the concurring opinion of Justices O'Connor and Kennedy, he draws an analogy to Roberts in suggesting that such balancing must be done on a case-by-case basis rather than in the abstract.[26] The majority then remands to the state courts for a determination of "harmless error."[27]

The concurring opinion of O'Connor and White puts the majority opinion in the context of the child-abuse-reform movement, but agrees with the majority opinion that the finding of necessity must be case-specific.[28] The dissent, by Justice Blackmun with the Chief Justice, would adopt the Wigmorean view of physical confrontation as a mere incident of contemporaneous cross-examination that can

22. "Have costs"

Id. at 2802, 487 U.S. at 1020.

23. Borne by witnesses

The dissenters in Inadi accused the majority of being more concerned with the costs to the state of producing unavailable witnesses than they were of the right of confrontation. See § 6368.

24. "Right violated"

Id. at 2802–2803, 487 U.S. at 1020.

25. "Another day"

Id. at 2803, 487 U.S. at 1021.

26. Case-by-case

Ibid. This is what the Court did in Maryland v. Craig, 1990, 110 S.Ct. 3157, 497 U.S. 836, 111 L.Ed.2d 666.

27. "Harmless error"

Id. at 2803, 487 U.S. at 1021–1022.

28. Must be case-specific

Id. at 2804–2805, 487 U.S. at 1022–1025.

therefore be balanced away without a case-specific finding of necessity.[29]

Unlike the child molesting in Coy, the Court's next case involved a "baby raper."[30] The defendant in Idaho v. Wright was accused of assisting her paramour in the rape of her two daughters, aged 2-1/2 and 5-1/2 at the time of the crime.[31] The younger child was found incompetent to testify but statements she made to a treating physician were admitted in evidence under the state version of the "wild card" exception.[32] On appeal from defendant's conviction, the Idaho Supreme Court held that admission of the child's hearsay violated the defendant's right of confrontation.[33]

Justice O'Connor's opinion for five members of the Court begins with a ritual recitation of cliches from prior opinions; e.g. even though a literal interpretation of the Confrontation Clause would exclude all hearsay, that was "unintended and too extreme."[34] Despite the Court's all-but-total fusion of the hearsay rule and the Sixth Amendment, Justice O'Connor can still write that "we have also been careful not to equate the Confrontation Clause's prohibitions with the general rule prohibiting the admission of hearsay statements."[35] Turning to the case that did the most to accomplish fusion, the opinion treats Roberts as still good law—easy enough to do when one describes Inadi as a case that "applied" Roberts rather than demolishing it.[36]

Turning to the application of Roberts to this case, Justice O'Connor begins by stating that "we assume without deciding that, to the extent the unavailability requirement applies in this case, the younger daughter was an unavailable witness within the mean-

---

29. Adopt Wigmorean

Id. at 2805–2810, 487 U.S. at 1025–1034.

30. "Baby raper"

One of the frustrating features of child-abuse cases is the variety of conduct it covers, both in physical abuse and sexual abuse. While the public does not distinguish among the cases, prosecutors and investigators do—grading them on a spectrum that runs from "baby rapers" at one extreme to "Grandpa cases" at the other.

31. Wright case

1990, 110 S.Ct. 3139, 497 U.S. 805, 111 L.Ed.2d 638.

32. Under "wild card"

Id. at 3143–3145, 497 U.S. at 808–812.

33. Held violated

Id. at 3145, 497 U.S. at 812–813.

34. "Too extreme"

Id. at 3145, 497 U.S. at 813–814.

35. "Careful not to equate"

Id. at 3146, 497 U.S. at 814.

36. Inadi "applied" Roberts

Id. at 3146, 497 U.S. at 815.

ing of the Confrontation Clause."[37] She then states that the Idaho "wild card" exception is not "firmly rooted."[38] In explaining why not, she adopts the Blackmun interpretation from Lee; because "wild card" hearsay is ad hoc and episodic, it cannot amass the kind of specific "experience" with reliability needed to make an exception "firmly rooted."[39] Though she adds that a finding that "wild card" exceptions were firmly rooted would lead to fusion, she says nothing about either the antiquity or the pervasiveness of the exception—two elements relied upon in earlier definitions of "firmly rooted."[40]

This leaves only the claim that the hearsay in this case had "particularized guarantees of trustworthiness" sufficient to make it admissible despite the lack of confrontation. The Idaho court, in rejecting this claim, had relied upon a number of "procedural safeguards" it had derived from the writings of legal scholars and child-abuse-reform advocates and statutes.[41] Justice O'Connor writes that although

> we agree with the court below * * * we reject the apparently dispositive weight placed by that court on the lack of procedural safeguards at the interview. * * * Although the procedural guidelines propounded by the court may well enhance the reliability of out-of-court statements of children regarding sexual abuse, we decline to read into the Confrontation Clause a preconceived and artificial litmus test for the procedural propriety of professional interviews in which children make hearsay statements against a defendant.[42]

The reason for this reluctance is the "wide variety of circumstances" in which such statements are made.[43]

Also disagreeing with the Idaho court, the majority rejects the claim that "particularized guarantees of trustworthiness" may be

---

37. "Assume unavailable"

Id. at 3145, 497 U.S. at 816.

38. Not "firmly rooted"

Id. at 3147, 497 U.S. at 817.

39. Amass "experience"

Id. at 3147–3148, 497 U.S. at 817.

40. Lead to fusion

"[W]ere we to agree that the admission of hearsay under the residual exception automatically passed Confrontation Clause scrutiny, virtually every codified hearsay exception would assume constitutional stature, a step this Court has repeatedly declined to take." Id. at 3148, 497 U.S. at 817–818.

41. Derived from scholars

State v. Wright, 1989, 775 P.2d 1224, 1227–1231, 116 Idaho 382.

42. "Artificial litmus test"

Id. at 3148, 497 U.S. at 819.

43. "Wide variety"

Id. at 3148, 497 U.S. at 818.

found in other evidence of the defendant's guilt—what is loosely referred to as "corroboration."[44] Instead, "the relevant circumstances include only those that surround the making of the statement and that render the declarant particularly worthy of belief."[45] The reason for this limitation is the purpose of the "particularized guarantees" tests as part of confrontation doctrine; that is, to determine "if the declarant's truthfulness is so clear from the surrounding circumstances that the test of cross-examination would be of marginal utility * * *."[46] Or, as she puts it after repeating the limits being imposed, the evidence must be shown to be "so trustworthy that the adversarial testing would add little to its reliability."[47] Perhaps reacting to the dissent, the majority opinion goes on to point out that there are alternatives to use of other evidence of guilt as "corroboration" of unconfronted hearsay.

> The state and federal courts have identified a number of factors that we think properly relate to whether hearsay statements by a child witness in a child abuse cases are reliable. * * * [W]e think the factors identified also apply to whether such statements bear "particularized guarantees of trustworthiness." These factors are, of course, not exclusive, and courts have considerable leeway in their consideration of appropriate factors. We therefore decline to endorse a mechanical test determining "particularized guarantees of trustworthiness" under the Clause.[48]

Justice O'Connor repeats that "the unifying principle is that these factors relate to whether the child declarant was particularly likely to be telling the truth when the statement was made."[49]

After explaining away cases like Dutton and Lee that seem to allow other evidence of guilt to serve as indicia of reliability and rejecting a per se rule that would apply to children found incompetent to testify, the majority turn to the facts of this case.[50] Looking at the facts relied upon by the trial court, the majority finds that only two of them related to the new test; i.e., first whether the child

---

44. "Corroboration"

Id. at 3153, 497 U.S. at 828 (Kennedy, J., dissenting).

45. "Worthy of belief"

Id. at 3148, 497 U.S. at 819.

46. "Marginal utility"

Id. at 3149, 497 U.S. at 820.

47. "Adversary add little"

Id. at 3149, 497 U.S. at 821.

48. "Decline mechnical test"

Id at 3150, 497 U.S. at 822.

49. "Telling the truth"

Ibid.

50. Dutton and Lee

Id. at 3150–3151, 497 U.S. at 823–824.

had a motive to fabricate, and second, whether a child of such tender years would be expected to be able to fabricate such a story.[51] However, these are sufficiently offset by the leading questions used to elicit the statements so that the presumption of unreliability was not rebutted.[52]

Four members of the Court dissented in an opinion by Justice Kennedy that argues for allowing other evidence of guilt to "corroborate" the questioned hearsay statements and, applying such evidence, finds the state had met its burden to rebut the presumption of unreliability.[53]

The final case in the Court's child abuse trilogy—White v. Illinois—involved a crime that resembled Coy more than Wright. A friend of the victim's mother entered her home late at night and sexually assaulted a four-year-old girl.[54] The victim made hearsay statements describing the crime and identifying its perpetrator to her babysitter, her mother, a police officer and a doctor and nurse at the emergency room to which she was taken.[55] Although the victim did not testify at trial, apparently because of forensic fright, she was never found to be unavailable.[56] Her statements were introduced under the state's common-law exception for excited utterances and a statute making statements for purposes of medical diagnosis and treatment admissible.[57] Defendant was convicted and the Illinois Appellate Court rejected a Roberts-based confrontation objection on the ground that Inadi had superseded Roberts.[58]

Chief Justice Rehnquist began his opinion with a "preliminary matter" which we shall pass over for the moment.[59] Turning to

51. Only two related

Id. at 3152, 497 U.S. at 826. The Idaho Supreme Court added "the spontaneity of the statement and the demeanor of the witness," factors the majority also seems to approve, though not quite as explicitly as the other two.

52. Leading questions

Ibid.

53. Dissenting opinion

The opinion was joined by the Chief Justice and Justices White and Blackmun. Id. at 3153, 497 U.S. at 827.

54. Entered home at night

1992, 112 S.Ct. 736, 739, 502 U.S. 346, 349, 116 L.Ed.2d 848.

55. Victim statements

Id. at 739, 502 U.S. at 349–350.

56. Never found unavailable

Id. at 739, 502 U.S. at 350.

57. Under exceptions

Id. at 740, 502 U.S. at 350–351.

58. Inadi superseded

Ibid.

59. "Preliminary matter"

Id. at 740, 502 U.S. at 352.

Roberts, the Chief Justice announced that the first prong had been eliminated by Inadi.[60] After that decision

> Roberts stands for the proposition that unavailability analysis is a necessary part of the Confrontation Clause inquiry only when the challenged out-of-court statements were made in the course of a prior judicial proceeding. * * * These observations, although expressed in the context of evaluating co-conspirator statements, apply with full force to the case at hand.[61]

What about the second prong of Roberts?

The Rehnquist opinion begins by arguing that excited utterances and medical diagnosis exceptions are like coconspirator statements in being better than in-court testimony about the same events.[62] But he does not seem to rely on this argument to satisfy the second prong, going on to write that "where proffered hearsay has sufficient guarantees of reliability to come within a firmly rooted exception to the hearsay rule, the Confrontation Clause is satisfied."[63] However, his discussion of the second prong of Roberts is relegated to a footnote.

> There can be no doubt that the two exceptions we consider in this case are "firmly rooted." The exceptions for spontaneous declarations is at least two centuries old * * * and * * * is currently recognized under the [Evidence Rules] and in nearly four-fifths of the states. * * * The exception for statements made for purposes of medical diagnosis or treatment is similarly recognized in the [Evidence Rules] and is equally widely accepted among the states.[64]

Notice two things about this use of the "firmly rooted" test.[65] First, a pervasiveness element has been added to the antiquity element in

60. First prong eliminated

Id. at 741, 502 U.S. at 353–354.

61. "Case at hand"

Id. at 742, 502 U.S. at 355.

62. Better than in-court

Id. at 742–743, 502 U.S. at 355–356. To argue that what one says about the cause of the injury the moment after one has hit one's thumb with a hammer is more likely to be truthful than what one says later in court under oath sounds ludicrous, even if the evidence is better than nothing when the witness is unavailable.

63. "Satisfied"

Id. at 743, 502 U.S. at 356.

64. "Widely accepted"

Id. at 742, n. 8, 502 U.S. at 355 n. 8.

65. Two things

There is a third. Nothing is said about the "experience" that Justice O'Connor relied upon in Wright, see text at notecall 39 above. Probably because this is at odds with the Court's employment of the pervasiveness criterion to uphold an exception for which there is little "experience."

prior opinions and is apparently sufficient to make an exception firmly rooted despite lack of antiquity; the medical-diagnosis exception may be widely adopted but it was virtually unheard of prior to the Federal Rules of Evidence.[66] Second, the "elements" test for how much an exception must change to lose the benefits of antiquity, which was enunciated in Bourjaily, is here abandoned; the excited-utterance exception did not develop out of the much different doctrine of "res gestae" until the middle of this century.[67]

Finally, the Chief Justice rebuffs an effort to use Coy and its successor case to construct a "necessity" argument akin to the unavailability requirement already rejected.[68]

> [Defendant's] reliance is misplaced. Coy and Craig involved only the question of what in-court procedures are constitutionally required to guarantee a defendant's confrontation right once a witness is testifying. Such a question is quite separate from that of what requirements the Confrontation Clause imposes as a predicate for the introduction of out-of-court declarations.[69]

Obviously, the Court sees the hazards of holistic analysis and swerves to avoid them.

Now to that "preliminary matter." In an amicus brief, the Justice Department advanced a historical argument for further limiting the right of confrontation that is best glimpsed through the concurring opinion of Justice Thomas, joined by Justice Scalia.[70] Justice Thomas begins with an appropriate textual analysis:

> in recent cases in this area, the Court has assumed that all hearsay declarants are "witnesses against" a defendant within the meaning of the Confrontation Clause * * * an assumption that is neither warranted nor supported by the history or text of the Confrontation Clause.[71]

With this we can heartily agree.[72]

Turning to history, Justice Thomas goes well beyond Justice Harlan's "faded parchment," stating flatly that "[t]here is virtually

---

66. Unheard of

See discussion of Evidence Rule 803(4) in subsequent volume.

67. Out of "res gestae"

See Morgan, Res Gestae, 1937, 12 Wash. L.Rev. 91.

68. Construct "necessity"

Id. at 743, 502 U.S. at 357–358.

69. "Quite separate"

Id. at 743–744, 502 U.S. at 358.

70. Justice amicus brief

Id. at 740, 502 U.S. at 352.

71. "History or text"

Id. at 744, 502 U.S. at 359.

72. Agree

See vol. 30, §§ 6342–6348.

no evidence of what the drafters of the Confrontation Clause intended it to mean."[73] At the very least, this is an exaggeration.[74] And it is tolerably clear that the concurring judges do not believe it.[75] After explaining the reasons for rejecting the Wigmorean theory of confrontation, Justice Thomas continues.[76]

> Relevant historical sources and our own earlier decisions, nonetheless, suggest that a narrower reading of the Clause than the one given to it since 1980 may well be correct.[77]

Having rejected Wigmore's theory of confrontation, the concurring opinion now embraces his history—a "lawyer's history" that claims that the right was developed in England and brought over on the Mayflower.[78] We need no further critique of the Justice Department's use of history.

According to Justice Thomas, the "lesson" of this "lawyer's history," as seen by the Justice Department, is

> that the Confrontation Clause should apply only to those persons who provide in-court testimony or the functional equivalent, such as affidavits, depositions, or confessions that are made in contemplation of legal proceedings.[79]

There is something to be said for this, both textually and historically, but Justice Thomas points out some problems in its implementation and proposes a somewhat narrower formulation:[80]

> The federal constitutional right of confrontation extends to any witness who actually testifies at trial, but the Confrontation Clause is implicated by extrajudicial statements only insofar as they are contained in formalized testimonial materials, such as affidavits, depositions, prior testimony, or confessions.[81]

Justice Thomas then goes on to suggest how the Court's pre-Roberts cases can be squared with this analysis and invites the

---

73. "Virtually no evidence"
Id. at 744, 502 U.S. at 359.

74. Exaggeration
See vol. 30, §§ 6346–6347.

75. Don't agree
See Justice Scalia's opinion in Coy, text at notecall 10, above, which has many historical references that are used to support a meaning supposedly shared by the Founders.

76. Rejecting Wigmore
Id. at 744–745, 502 U.S. at 360.

77. "Narrower may be correct"
Id. at 745, 502 U.S. at 361.

78. Brought over on Mayflower
Id. at 745–746, 502 U.S. at 361–362.

79. "Made in contemplation"
Id. at 747, 502 U.S. at 364.

80. Points out problems
Ibid.

81. "Or confessions"
Id. at 747, 502 U.S. at 365.

Court to adopt some version of the Justice Department's proposal in a subsequent case.[82]

What does the majority make of this? The Chief Justice summarizes the Justice Department's proposal, without its questionable history, then says:

> Such a narrow reading of the Confrontation Clause, which would virtually eliminate its role in restricting the admission of hearsay testimony, is foreclosed by our prior cases. [summarizing them] We think the argument presented by the Government comes too late in the day to warrant reexamination of this approach.[83]

There is something to be said for this—but we shall not say it.

In his concurring opinion, Justice Thomas complains that "[t]he Court has never explored the historical evidence on this point."[84] If it ever does, we hope that it will find these volumes of some use.

§ 6371.   ____; Back to the Future

Readers of earlier sections will note that after 1965 we have little to say about the impact of politics, culture, and ideology on the Supreme Court's confrontation jurisprudence. Our major reason for this is that historians, whom we have relied on elsewhere, are just beginning to turn to writing the history of these years.[1] It is impossible to write with detachment about events that you have experienced, however remote and vicarious that experience may have been; the temptation to refight old battles or to settle scores with one's real or imaginary adversaries is too strong.[2] It is not that we do not have opinions about, say, the significance for those values that support the right of confrontation of the impeachment of President Clinton or of the movie industry's use of an anonymous

---

82. Adopt in subsequent case
Id. at 747–748, 502 U.S. at 366.

83. "Too late in day"
Id. at 741, 502 U.S. at 353.

84. "Never explored"
Id. at 746, 502 U.S. at 362.

§ 6371

1. Just beginning
Indeed, the only historian we have found who is willing to come close to covering the entire period in ways relevant to our discussion is Foner, The Story of American Freedom, 1998. We do not agree with all of Professor Foner's interpretations nor should our exclusive citations to his work lead the reader to suppose that he agrees with us.

2. Too strong
Or so it seems to us.

panel to rate movies for sex and violence.[3] But we have resisted, so far as we are able, the temptation to confuse history and punditry.

Nonetheless, those who will write the history of the Confrontation Clause during this period may find it useful to know how those who lived through it and were inevitably biased by it may view the time in which they lived. In addition, lawyers and judges who will make the history of the right of confrontation may derive some benefit from speculation about how we got where we are and where we are likely to go from here. Hence, we sketch a "first draft" of the history of confrontation since 1965.

The Warren Court's "rights revolution" emerged from an era of liberal triumphalism. At the dawn of the Second Red Scare, a commentator wrote that "liberalism is not only the dominant but even the sole intellectual tradition. For it is plain that nowadays there are no conservative or reactionary ideas in general circulation."[4] Those who may have held that view were probably not worried about the possibility that the lack of adversariness might lead lawyers and judges to misunderstand the unique set of circumstances that made it seem plausible for the Supreme Court to create a constituency of values to replace the constituency of interests that had served the Court well for nearly a century. But values, even the values that supported the adversary system, are more ambiguous than interests and can be—and were—contested. All that laissez faire demanded of the Supreme Court is that—in the words of Nancy Reagan—it "just say 'no.'" Constructing a set of values that would appeal to most Americans was a far more daunting task.

In 1960, Barry Goldwater, a senator from Arizona, published "The Conscience of a Conservative"—a tract that became for the Young Americans for Freedom what the Port Huron Statement was to the Students for a Democratic Society.[5] The YAF provided the shock troops for Goldwater's presidential campaign in 1964, and its attack on the centrism so favored by the business press.[6] Despite

---

3. Anonymous panel

See Wallace, MPAA's Dozen Judge Movies for Millions, Los Angeles Times, Sunday, July 18, 1999, p. A1.

4. "No conservative ideas"

Foner, The Story of American Freedom, 1998, p. 308.

5. Goldwater and YAF

Id. at p. 312. The young conservatives shared another weakness of their left-wing counterparts—their preference for foreign thinkers, such as Ayn Rand and Frederick Hayek.

6. Goldwater campaign

Id. at p. 307. See also, id. p. 313 (famous remark that "extremism in defense of liberty is no vice").

his drubbing at the polls, Goldwater's campaign was the spark that re-ignited and re-invented American conservatism.

In 1968, the clash between the Warfare and the Welfare State divided the heirs of the New Deal.[7] Meanwhile, the so-called "New Left" fractured along the line between the political "Movement" and "Counterculture," both of which succeeded in offending large numbers of voters. As the "Summer of Love" and Woodstock gave way to Altamont and hard drugs, even previously tolerant parents began to worry about the directions that this consumerist wing of the youth movement was taking their children. Meanwhile, the political wing of the New Left began to realize that much of their supposed following was moved by "sex, and drugs, and rock-and-roll" rather than their ideology and became increasingly strident. Those frustrated by the discovery that politics did not bring the sort of instant gratification promised by advertisers and drugs passed over from Ghandian nonviolent resistance to acts of violence that discredited those who remained behind on the other side of the line.[8]

The revolt of the "Silent Americans" returned the presidency to the Republicans in the person of Richard Nixon. Despite his role in the Second Red Scare and his "law-and-order" rhetoric, Nixon was not the sort of conservative his adversaries supposed.[9] After a life in politics, he was more a politician than an ideologue, but it was easy to mistake his resentments for a philosophy. But, coming from California, a state built from the ground up with federal assistance, Nixon was not the antistatist that some conservatives desired and some on the left feared.[10]

In 1972, the New Deal had its last gasp in the Democratic candidacy of George McGovern—a campaign that failed partly from its own ineptness, partly from the resentment of professionals in the Democratic Party who feared the loss of power from McGover-

---

7. Divided heirs

Id. at p. 305.

8. Discredited

In one of the judgments we question, Professor Foner thinks the collapse of left-wing idealism played some role in the "Me Decade" that followed. Ibid.

9. Not sort of conservative

Id. at p. 304.

10. Federal largesse

Consider just this partial listing. The federal government destroyed the land title of the Californios to make the land available for Anglos, subsidized the railroads that brought settlers west and allowed goods to go east, provided the water that turned what was largely desert into a major agricultural area, and built the defense industry that swelled the state's population.

nite reforms of the Party, partly from the nearly universal ridicule from the business press, and only slightly, if at all, from the "dirty tricks" practiced by elements of the Nixon reelection campaign. However, those campaign excesses and other misdeeds in the Nixon administration, usually lumped together under the heading "Watergate", led to Nixon's resignation as he was about to be impeached.[11]

Although it was widely predicted at the time that the Watergate revelations would deal conservatives a serious setback, it now seems more likely that the impeachment and resignation of Nixon actually set the stage for a resurgence of conservatism. It did this by discrediting the so-called "liberal Republicans," some of whom had joined Democrats in the presidential impeachment or who had been to eager to take advantage of the opportunities afforded by the temporary discrediting of the conservatives. Moreover, the association of Republicans with campus chapters of the YAF led many who would have previously been recruits for the liberal wing of the party to become Democrats instead.[12]

In the midst of the political turmoil, the postwar economic boom finally ended and the economy entered "stagflation"—the combination of stagnant productivity with inflation—that was to last for most of the rest of the century.[13] This, together with the perception that the nation had become militarily as well as politically weak because of the unwillingness of the Carter administration to use sufficient force to free American hostages in Iran and elsewhere, brought Ronald Reagan to the White House.[14]

The "Reagan Revolution" revealed certain contradictions in the conservative movement. While the Reaganauts engineered one of the greatest shifts in wealth since the administration of Franklin Roosevelt, they also increased the national debt to unprecedented levels—although Democrats in Congress certainly can share some of the credit or blame for both.[15] Perhaps most significantly, the Reagan administration followed up the destruction of liberals in the Republican Party by destroying those among the Democrats—by

11. Watergate

See volume 26, § 5661, pp. 423–567. The senior author, having been counsel to the President in the Watergate Tapes Litigation, took no part in the formulation of this and the following paragraph.

12. YAF and "liberal Republicans"

Id. at p. 312.

13. "Stagflation"

Id. at p. 316.

14. Carter and Reagan

Id. at pp. 316–317.

15. Wealth and debt.

Id. at p. 322, 324.

the end of the century, few politicians were willing to admit they were "liberals."[16] Moreover, President Reagan was able to fill the federal bench with conservatives—many of them young members of The Federalist Society, who like the "midnight judges" of the original Federalists, could be expected to remain in office long after Reagan left it.

There does not seem to be any reason why conservatives should be ideologically opposed to confrontation. Reagan came to power on an anti-statist platform and individualist rhetoric.[17] In the confrontation between the power of the state and the freedom of the individual, the criminal justice system is, as they say, "where the rubber meets the road." However, because Reagan himself was less ideological than he seemed, his administration brought into prominence the many varieties of "conservatism" and the conflicts among them.[18]

Because of its association with the economic policies of the Reagan administration, the best-known conservative ideology is the libertarian school associated with the economist Milton Friedman.[19] The libertarians were the most antistatist of the conservatives, being willing to "privatize" almost every government function with the possible exception of the criminal justice system.[20] Because of its ideological roots in and resemblance to the market, the adversary system would seem to be appealing to libertarians as an "invisible land" of justice. Moreover, the libertarians were willing to tolerate cultural pluralism and a degree of ethical relativism. Even those who claimed to be non-racists were willing to tolerate bigotry in others.[21] Moreover, given their embrace of the morality of the marketplace, particularly the maxim of the advertisers that desire is good and must not be thwarted, they would seem not to be bothered by the fact that confrontation made it difficult to enforce sumptuary laws.[22]

16. Willing to admit "liberals"

Id. at p. 324.

17. Anti-statist

Id. at pp. 308, 322, 327.

18. Varieties of conservatism

Id. at p. 320.

19. Milton Friedman

Id. at p. 309.

20. Privatize

Ibid.

21. Tolerate bigotry

Id. at p. 315.

22. Sumptuary laws

Libertarians have generally been sympathetic to the notion of decriminalizing drug use.

This feature of the libertarian ideology put them at odds with other branches of conservatism. The oldest group, the so-called "new conservatives," and the newest group, the "neoconservatives" were opposed to ethical relativism and the morality of the market.[23] Barry Goldwater had early identified liberals with materialism and argued that conservatism was based upon values that were spiritual—derived from "the nature of man, and from the truths that God had revealed."[24] Like the Marxists, new conservatives thought one of the roles of the government was to remake humans, arguing that with the increasing secularization of the culture, it was up to government not to make humans free, but make them good.[25] Hence, they opposed welfare on the ground that it induced a state of dependency in people that was "bad."[26]

The "new" and "neo" conservative raised a challenge to both libertarians and liberals; namely, was it possible to have a society of autonomous individuals without some common moral values to hold them together?[27] This was a concern that some liberals shared, particularly with the rise of "identity politics"—what one critic called the "rebellion of particularisms."[28] In terms of confrontation, we can put the question this way: how is it possible to appeal to the Founders in support of the right of confrontation to people who regard Adams, Jefferson, and Hamilton as "a bunch of dead white guys?"

A sophisticated conservative who believed in traditional values might argue that the way to inculcate the values of the Founders is not by lecturing or advertising but by making sure that those values are instantiated in the practice as well as in the philosophy of the adversary system. If the jury trial and the right of confrontation can teach lessons about taking responsibility for one's utterances as well as one's acts and dramatize the need to restrain the state, then we should have more jury trials and less bureaucratic dispositions of criminal cases. On the other hand, this may well be outweighed for such a conservative by the way in which the adversary system and right of confrontation interferes with the

---

23. Opposed ethical relativism

Id. at p. 309.

24. "God had revealed"

Id. at p. 313.

25. Make them good

Id. at p. 313.

26. Welfare dependency

Id. at p. 312.

27. Common moral values

Id. at p. 310.

28. "Particularisms"

Id. at p. 320–321, 328.

prosecution of sumptuary laws, which frequently depend upon the use of anonymous informers for their enforcement.

The branch of conservatism that seems most opposed to confrontation is what has loosely been called "religious conservativism."[29] Since these people are drawn from religions that rely more on the Old Testament than the New, they are not likely to be as impressed with Paul's endorsement of confrontation. They support the free market but only to a point—the point where materialism tends to overcome spiritualism. The purpose of individual freedom is to permit one to lead a moral life and when that freedom is abused, the state must step in.[30] As he so often did, Ronald Reagan could reduce this to a sound-bite: "We're not set free so we can become slaves of sin."[31] Religious conservatives are opposed to pornography, abortion, feminism, and anything that threatens the patriarchal family. Since "the Warren Court" is their enemy, the association of the revival of confrontation with that Court is not likely to count in its favor.[32]

Finally, though it is not clear that this constitutes a separate branch, are those who may be called "pragmatic conservatives."[33] They are prepared to accept big government as a fact of life if that is what it takes to get elected.[34] These conservatives tend to be those who came of age during the Cold War and were realistic enough to realize that "the market" and private entities are unlikely to provide the means to wage hot or cold wars against the enemies of capitalism. Moreover, a cynic might say that they need big government as a common enemy to unite the diverse elements of the conservative coalition, which might otherwise fall apart over their different versions of domestic policy.[35]

Moreover, the pragmatist may understand that ideology matters only to a handful of the people who really control politics today—corporations and wealthy individuals.[36] Corporate attitudes

29. "Religious conservativism"
Id. at p. 317.

30. Must step in
Id. at p. 318.

31. "Slaves of sin"
Id. at p. 323.

32. "Warren Court"
Id. at p. 317.

33. "Pragmatic conservatives"
Id. at p. 310.

34. Fact of Life
Id. at p. 310.

35. Fall apart
Professor Foner argues that something like this followed the collapse of the Soviet Union.

36. Corporations and wealthy
Id. at p. 310.

toward the adversary system are driven more by their experience with civil justice than with criminal justice; they have no realistic expectation that they will be defendants in need of protection of the right of confrontation nor are they likely to think that a repressive criminal justice system is in their best interests—particularly when it leads to increased taxes.

The corporate alliance with conservatism is likely to last only so long as it suits corporate interests. The rise of right-wing violence in the 1990s may tilt corporations away from the more extreme versions of conservatism, particularly those versions that threaten the image that corporations want to project in the market-place.[37] However much corporate executives may rail against feminism and "political correctness" and endorse the resurgence of Anglo–Saxon racism among some conservatives, they are unlikely to openly endorse candidates or ideologies that may offend large numbers of the people they wish to make customers.[38]

Having said all this, we must confess that we have seen little evidence that ideology has had much impact on Supreme Court confrontation jurisprudence over the last thirty years. True, there may have been some judges who were driven by a dislike for doctrines associated with the Warren Court but that attitude does not take one very far in answering specific questions. Once the Warren Court's decisions are overruled or limited, the Confrontation Clause remains in the Constitution and must be addressed. Moreover, even had the Warren Court remained in power it seems unlikely that it would have been able to sustain the version of the Confrontation Clause it had hardly started to develop when it was repudiated by Green.

Moreover, if the various conservative lawyers and scholars known to the junior author are typical, they are likely to be as much in thrall to the Progressive ideology as their liberal adversaries. To the extent that conservatives have focused on the New Deal as the root of all evil, they may overlook how much the doctrines

37. Right-wing violence

E.g., the bombing of abortion clinics, the murder of physicians, the shootouts at Waco and elsewhere, and the bombing of the courthouse in Oklahoma City. Id. at p. 322.

38. Resurgence of racism

Id. at pp. 314, 329–330. Advertisers may agree with the authors of The Bell

Curve that many people are genetically inferior but they are unlikely to reveal that view in their advertising. We need not enter into the debate into how much certain debates contain coded references to race.

that have shaped confrontation are the product of an ideology they probably never heard of. So far as we are aware, there is no conservative theory or philosophy of procedure that can be invoked against the Progressive one. Conservative as well as liberal proceduralists are equally likely to accept the notion that Progressive values are not values at all, but simply the only rational way to think about procedure.

Moreover, because they are as marginal in academia as radical leftists, conservatives have as much to fear from one of the worst surviving relics of Progressivism and the Second Red Scare—that is, the notion that one cannot talk about values in the classroom or in scholarship without violating canons of neutrality—and this is particularly true if one is teaching or writing in an area that one's colleagues or tenure committees are likely to think of as technical. It may be acceptable to discuss values in legal philosophy or even constitutional law, but do it in procedure and one is likely to be seen as importing one's own "politics" into a discussion where it has no place.

Yet the adversary system and confrontation do contain values. Feminists may be right or wrong when they identify adversariness with the male propensity for aggressiveness, but they are surely right that there are some values there. Unless those values can be elucidated and defended in ways that appeal to a broad range of Americans, the future of confrontation is not very promising, irrespective of the ideologies of the judges who will interpret it.

§§ 6372–6374 are reserved for supplementary material.

†